sH

D0801600

THE WISDOM OF THE NOVEL

GARLAND REFERENCE LIBRARY
OF THE HUMANITIES
(VOL. 459)

THE WISDOM OF THE NOVEL
A Dictionary of Quotations

David Powell

GARLAND PUBLISHING, INC. • NEW YORK & LONDON
1985

Library of Congress Cataloging in Publication Data

Powell, David, 1934–
    The wisdom of the novel.

    (Garland reference library of the humanities ;
vol. 459)
    Bibliography: p.
    Includes index.
    1. Quotations, English. 2. Novelists, American—
Quotations. 3. Novelists, English—Quotations.
4. American fiction—Miscellanea. 5. English fiction—
Miscellanea. I. Title. II. Series: Garland reference
library of the humanities ; v. 459.
PN6083.P58   1985   828'.02   83-49080
ISBN 0-8240-9017-9 (alk. paper)

Printed on acid-free, 250-year-life paper
Manufactured in the United States of America

For M. D. P.
M. R. P.
A. N. P.
M. A. G.
C. E. C.

"None are wise but they who determine to be wiser."
Samuel Richardson, *Sir Charles Grandison*

CONTENTS

PREFACE

The Wisdom of the Novel draws its quotations from all of the major British and American novels, and hundreds of the lesser ones, from 1470 through 1900.

All of the quotation dictionaries before the present one omit, except for a few pages, references from even the greatest novelists. Samuel Richardson, one of the most quotable (but unquoted) novelists in history, does not occupy a single line in *The Oxford Dictionary of Quotations* and does not have so much as one page devoted to him in Bartlett's *Familiar Quotations*, Bergen Evans' *Dictionary of Quotations, Peter's Quotations*, or any other similar volume. Though he is infinitely quotable about infinite matters, Herman Melville is treated as if he were an author of finite things. Jane Austen is given scant attention, and Dickens is credited with only eccentricities.

Herein, things are set right so that the dearth of novel quotations ends. Richardson makes wise but simple pronouncements on subjects as diverse as libertinism and liberty, Melville finally has his timeless day, Jane Austen regales us beside the harpsichord, Dickens takes us through unfamiliar corners of the great room of humanity, and three hundred other novelists, major and minor, tease us into a fascinated concern with the minds and the mores of the past.

The quotations are universal, down-to-earth, and practical rather than pedantic or esoteric. Every subject of first or of middling importance appears. Then, too, for the casual reader, subjects of no importance at all (such as quadrille, warming-pans, cosmetics, the *h*umblebee) are here.

Arrangement of the subjects is alphabetical; under each subject heading the quotations are ordered alphabetically according to author and book title; within a particular book, the ordering is chronological. A keyword index appears at the end of the volume.

Punctuation has been simplified to modern usage. Also, given the surprising fact that British authors occasionally use American variants and American authors occasionally use British variants, spelling has been Americanized.

David Powell
Western New Mexico University

LIST OF SUBJECT HEADINGS

abandonment
absence
abuse
accident
accountability
accusation
achievement
acknowledgment
acquaintance
action
adaptability
admiration
advantage
adventure
adversity
advice
advocacy
affectation
affection
affliction
affluence
affront
age and youth
aggression
agitation
agreeableness
alienation
ambition
ambivalence
amusement
angel
anger
animal life
antipathy
anxiety
apathy
apology
appearance
appetite
approbation
architecture
argumentation
aristocracy
art
aspiration
association

asylum
atheism
atonement
attempt
attraction
audience
authority
authorship
avarice
avoidance
awe
awkwardness
balance
bargain
baseness
beauty
beginning
belief
benevolence
betrayal
birth
blushing
bluster
body
books
brevity
brotherhood
bullying
burden
bureaucracy
calamity
calmness
cannibalism
capacity
capitalism
cause
cause and effect
caution
celibacy
censure
ceremony
chance
change
character
characteristic(s)
charity

charm
chastity
cheating
childhood
choice
Christianity
circumstance
citizenship
civility
civilization
clarity
class
cleanliness
clergy
cleverness
climax
colonization
comfort
command
commerce
commitment
commonality
commonplaceness
common sense
communication
community
company
comparison/contrast
compassion
compensation
competition
complaint
completeness
compliments
composure
compromise
compulsion
concealment
conceit
concentration
conception
concession
condescension
condition
confession
confidence

conflict
conjecture
conquest
conscience
conscientiousness
consecration
consequence
conservatism
consistency
consolation
contemplation
contempt
contentment
contest
contract
contradiction
control
convenience
conventionality
conversation
conviction
coquetry
correction
corruption
cost
counterpart
courage
courtesy
courtship
covetousness
cowardice
coxcombry
coyness
craftiness
creation
credit
credulity
crime
critic/criticism
cruelty
culture
cunning
curiosity
curse
cynicism
dance/dancing

danger
daring
death
deceit
decision
deduction
defect
defense
delay
deliberation
delicacy
deliverance
delusion
demagoguery
demand
democracy
demon
denial
denunciation
departure
dependence
depravity
deprivation
derision
description
desertion
design
desire
despair
despotism
destination
destiny
destruction
determination
development
deviation
devil
devotion
difference
difficulty
dignity
digression
dining
direction
disappointment
discard
discomfiture
discomfort
discord

discourse
discretion
disgrace
disobedience
disposition
distinction
distress
diversion
diversity
divineness
doctrine
domesticity
dominance
doubt
dream
dress
drink
duel
dullness
duty
earnestness
economics
education
effectiveness
effort
egotism
emotions
encouragement
endurance
energy
enjoyment
ennui
entertainment
enthusiasm
envy
equality
error
escape
essentials
esteem
eternality
etiquette
evasion
eventuality
exaggeration
example
excellence
exception
excess

exchange
excitation
excuse
execution
exile
expectation
experience
explanation
exploration
expression
extermination
extremes
extrovertedness
eyes
fact
failure
fainting
faith
fallacy
falsehood
fame
familiarity
family
fanaticism
fashion
fatness
fault
favor
fear
ferocity
feudalism
fickleness
fiction
fidelity
fighting
fire
firmness
fitness
flattery
foibles
fool
forbearance
force
foresight
forgetfulness
forgiveness
form and function
fortune
frankness

fraud
freedom
friendship
frivolity
gain
gallantry
gambling
generosity
genius
gentility
ghosts
gift
giving and receiving
glory
gluttony
God
good and evil
good-heartedness
goodness
government
grace
grandeur/grandness
gratitude
gravity
greatness
grief
group psychology
growth
guidance
guilt
habit
handsomeness
happiness
harm
hate
health
heart
heaven/earth/hell
heritage
heroism
hideousness
history
holiness
home
honesty
honor
hope
horseback
hospitality

humankind	innocence	love	nation
human nature	inquiry	luck	naturalness
humbleness	inquisition	luxury	nature
humor	insanity	machinery	necessity
hunger	insatiability	magic	neighbor
hunting	insight	male/female	nerves
hypocrisy	inspiration	marriage	news
iconoclasm	instinct	martyrdom	nicety
idea	institution	matching	night
ideal	instruction	materialism	nobility
identity	integrity	meaning	non-conformity
idleness	intellect	means	nonsense
ignorance	intensity	measure	nostalgia
illegitimacy	interdependence	media	novelty
illusion	interest	medicine	nudity
illustration	interpretation	meditation	obedience
illustriousness	involvement	melancholia	obligation
imagination	isolation	memory	obscurity
imitation	jealousy	mercy/"mercy	obsession
immobility	*joie de vivre*	killing"	obstacle
immorality	joking	merit	obstinacy
immortality	joy and sorrow	message	occupancy
impartiality	judgment	microcosm	occupation
impenetrableness	justice	middle class	ocean
impertinence	justification	military service	omission
importance	kind	mind	omniscience
imposition	kindness	miracle	opinion
impossibility	kissing	misanthropy	opportunity
imposture	knighthood	mischief	opposition
impression	knowledge and	miserliness	oppression
imprisonment	learning	misery	optimism
improvement	labor	misfortune	oratory
impudence	language	mist	order
impulse	laughter	mob	ordinariness
incident	law	moderation	origin
inconsistency	leading and following	modesty	originality
independence	leisure	money	ostentation
indifference	levity	mood	pain
indignation	liberalism	morality	painting
individuality	libertinism	motherhood	panic
indulgence	life/living	motion	parable
industry	light	motivation	parasites
inevitability	like	murder	pardon
infatuation	limitation	music	parting
inferiority	listening	mystery	passion
influence	literature	mysticism	past-present-future
ingenuity	logic	name	pastime
injustice	loneliness	narcotics	patience
innateness	loss	narration	patriotism

pause
peace
pedigree
perception
perfection
performance
persecution
perseverance
personalness
perspective
persuasion
perversity
petition
philanthropy
philosophy
physique
piety
pity
place
pleasantness
pleasure
pliability
plot
poetry
politeness
politics
popularity
population
possession
possibility
posterity
poverty
power
practicality
praise
prayer
preachment
prediction
preference
prejudice
preparation
prevention
pride
principle
priorities
prisoners
privilege
probability
process

profession
profit
progress
progression
prohibition
promise
proof
prophecy
propriety
prospect
prosperity
prostitution
prostration
protection
proverbs
prudence
psychology
public
punishment
purification
purity
purpose
pursuit
pushiness
quackery
querulousness
questions
rain
raising
rape
rarity
rascality
reaction
reading
reality
reason
rebuke
receptiveness
reconciliation
refinement
reflection
reform
refuge
regard
regeneration
regret
rejoicing
relief
religion

remedy
remorse
renunciation
reparation
repentance
repercussion
repetition
representation
reprimand
reputation
rescue
resentment
reserve
resignation
resistance
resolution
resource
respect
responsibility
restraint
retaliation
retribution
revelation
revolt
reward
ridicule
right and wrong
risk
romance
routine
royalty
ruination
rule
rumor
sacrifice
sadness
saints
sanity
sarcasm
satire
savagery
scandal
scheme
science
scriptures
seasons
secrecy
security
seduction

self
self-command
self-consciousness
self-deception
self-denial
self-destruction
self-displeasure
self-esteem
self-examination
self-exposure
self-improvement
self-indulgence
self-infliction
selfishness
self-knowledge
self-love
self-preservation
self-reproach
self-respect
self-support
sense(s)
sensibility
sentiment
separation
serenity
seriousness
servant
sexuality
shadow and
  substance
shallowness
shame
sign
significance
silence
silliness
similarity
simplicity
sincerity
singularity
slander
slavery
sleep
smoking
society
soldiery
solidity
solitude
song

LIST OF SUBJECT HEADINGS

THE WISDOM OF THE NOVEL

ABANDONMENT: *see also* DESERTION

There is a forsaking which still sits at the same board and lies on the same couch with the forsaken soul, withering it the more by unloving proximity.
Eliot, *Middlemarch*, Book VIII, LXXIV

He had left the door wide open, and he was driven to conclude that, owing to this negligence, some unfortunate creature had seized this opportunity to get rid of her child forever [by leaving it with him]. More than one hermit had received a present of this kind.
Reade, *The Cloister and the Hearth*, XCIV

ABSENCE

It is generous, nay, it is but just, to take the part of those who are absent, if not flagrantly culpable.
Richardson, *Sir Charles Grandison*, Two, IV

ABUSE

His ill nature dwells nowhere but in his tongue, and the very people whom he so industriously endeavors to abuse, he would do anything in his power to serve.
Fielding, S., *David Simple*, I

So great is his love of abuse that when no one else is talked of, to give him an opportunity of displaying his favorite talent, he falls to abusing himself.
Ibid.

ACCIDENT

We do not suffer by *accident*.
Austen, *Pride and Prejudice*, Volume II, II

I always like a little accident early; it makes us safe for the rest of the day.
Howells, *A Modern Instance*, XL

Lucky accidents are anticipated only by fools.
Meredith, *Lord Ormont*, XXX

ACCOUNTABILITY

Going home must be like going to render an account.
Conrad, *Lord Jim*, XXI

Cursed be that mortal interindebtedness which will not do away with ledgers. I would be free as air; and I'm down in the whole world's books.
Melville, *Moby Dick*, CVIII

There is blood on the garments of many a man who sits fearfully at home, and thinks that because he does nothing he will be free of guilt when the great account is called.
Mitchell, S.W., *Hugh Wynne*, X

ACCUSATION: *see also* COMPLAINT

[An accusation of] insolence—the tyrant's ready plea.
Hildreth, *Slave*, Volume I, VI

All accusations claim attention from justice.
Parsons, *The Mysterious Warning*, IV

Better a finger off, as aye wagging.
Scott, *Redgauntlet*, II

All well-doing stands so in the middle betwixt his two contrary evils that it is a ready matter to cast a slanderous shade upon the most approved virtues.
Sidney, *Arcadia*, IV

ACHIEVEMENT: *see also* SUCCESS

A man may reasonably hope to accomplish his end, when he proposes nothing but his own good.
Brown, C.B., *Ormond*, 93

Human reason, fortitude, and perseverance, are adequate to the accomplishment of anything upon the earth.
Dacre, *Passion*, Letter XLI

1

ACHIEVEMENT (*continued*)

What are the material obstacles that man never subdued?　　Godwin, *Caleb Williams*, II

How easy and how hopeless to teach fine things! Of erections, how few are domed like St. Peter's! Of creatures, how few vast as the whale!　　Melville, *Moby Dick*, LXVIII

Nothing is achieved before it be throughly attempted, and lying still, doth never go forward.　　Sir Philip Sidney, *Arcadia*, II

ACKNOWLEDGMENT: *see also* CONFESSION, FAULT, GUILT, etc.

When the inferior creature acknowledges her fault, she is already rising in the scale.　　Meredith, *Ordeal of Richard Feverel*, I

Next to being without fault is the acknowledgment of a fault; since no amendment can be expected where an error is defended.　　Richardson, *Clarissa Harlowe*, I

ACQUAINTANCE

Seven years would be insufficient to make some people acquainted with each other, and seven days are more than enough for others.　　Austen, *Sense and Sensibility*, XII

ACTION, ACTIVITY, CREATIVITY: *see also* ART; LEISURE; MOTION

There is nothing like employment, active, indispensable employment, for relieving sorrow.　　Austen, *Mansfield Park*, Volume III, XV

Human beings must have action; and they will make it if they cannot find it.　　Bronte, C., *Jane Eyre*, XII

No sooner have you got settled in a pleasant resting-place, than a voice calls out to you to rise and move on, for the hour of repose is expired.　　Bronte, C., *Ibid.*, XXIII

To save the mind from preying inwardly upon itself, it must be encouraged to some outward pursuit. There is no other way to elude apathy, or escape discontent; none other to guard the temper from that quarrel with itself which ultimately ends in quarreling with all mankind.　　Burney, *Camilla*, I, I

An active man, devoted heart and soul to his profession, is not a man who can learn the happy knack of being idle at a moment's notice.　　Collins, *Heart and Science*, I

Conceding for a moment that there is any analogy between a bee and a man in a shirt and pantaloons, and that it is settled that the man is to learn from the bee, the question remains, What is he to learn? To imitate? Or to avoid? When your friends the bees worry themselves to that highly fluttered extent about their sovereign, and become perfectly distracted touching the slightest monarchical movement, are we men to learn the greatness of Tuft-hunting, or the littleness of the Court Circular? They work: but don't you think they overdo it?　　Dickens, *Our Mutual Friend*, Book I, VIII

All passion becomes strength when it has an outlet from the narrow limits of our personal lot in the labor of our right arm, the cunning of our right hand, or the still, creative activity of our thought.　　Eliot, *Adam Bede*, XIX

Philosophers tell you that the great work of the steam engine is to create leisure for mankind. Do not believe them: it only creates a vacuum for eager thought to rush in.　　*Ibid.*, LII

I have never had to feel things. I have had to *do* them, to make myself felt.　　James, H., *The American*, III

He that has much to do will do something wrong.　　Johnson, *Rasselas*, 105

To do, is to act; so all doers are actors.　　Melville, *Confidence-Man*, VI

The French are the lads for painting action.　　Melville, *Moby Dick*, LVI

Living faces, if they're to show the soul, which is the star on the peak of beauty, must lend themselves to commotion. Meredith, *Amazing Marriage*, XXX

Action energizes men's brains, generates grander capacities, provokes greatness of soul between enemies, and is the guarantee of positive conquest for the benefit of our species. To doubt that is to doubt of good being to be had for the seeking.
Meredith, *The Tragic Comedians*, III

Deeds are the only evidences of intentions. Richardson, *Clarissa Harlowe*, I

How art produces art! *Ibid.*, II

It seems to superficial observers that all Americans are born busy. It is not so. They are born with a fear of not being busy. Warner, *A Little Journey*, I

ADAPTABILITY, ACCOMMODATION

By being a willow, and not an oak, he came to rise high in the church.
Anonymous, *Private Letters*, 116

What is spent one way must be saved another. Bellamy, *Looking Backward*, X

If one expedient loses its virtue, another must be devised.
Bronte, C., *Jane Eyre*, XXIV

All our lives long, every day and every hour, we are engaged in the process of accommodating our changed and unchanged selves to changed and unchanged surroundings; living, in fact, in nothing else than this process of accommodation; when we fail in it a little we are stupid, when we fail flagrantly we are mad, when we suspend it temporarily we sleep, when we give up the attempt altogether we die.
Butler, *The Way of All Flesh*, LXIX

The world is a lively place enough, in which we must accommodate ourselves to circumstances, sail with the stream as glibly as we can, be content to take froth for substance, the surface for the depth, the counterfeit for the real coin. I wonder no philosopher has ever established that our globe itself is hollow. It should be, if Nature is consistent in her works. Dickens, *Barnaby Rudge*, XII

Heaven suits the back to the burden. Dickens, *Nicholas Nickleby*, XVIII

It is impossible to say what will suit eccentric persons.
Eliot, *Middlemarch*, Book VI, LVIII

He was simply a man whose desires had been stronger than his theoretic beliefs, and who had gradually explained the gratification of his desires into satisfactory agreement with those beliefs. *Ibid.*, LXI

When a workman knows the use of his tools, he can make a door as well as a window.
Eliot, *Mill on the Floss*, Book I, III

If we only look far enough off for the consequence of our actions, we can always find some point in the combination of results by which those actions can be justified; by adopting the point of view of a Providence who arranges results, or of a philosopher who traces them, we shall find it possible to obtain perfect complacency in choosing to do what is most agreeable to us in the present moment. Eliot, *Ibid.*, Book V, III

A burden becomes lightest when it is well borne. Fielding, H., *Tom Jones*, 47

We are not to judge the feelings of others by what we might feel in their place. However dark the habitation of the mole to our eyes, yet the animal itself finds the apartment sufficiently lightsome. Goldsmith, *The Vicar of Wakefield*, 26

We seem to want the oldest and simplest human clothing where the clothing of the earth is so primitive. Hardy, *Return of the Native*, Book I, I

You mustn't pretend that practically the human affections don't reconcile themselves to any situation that the human sentiments condemn. Howells, *Silas Lapham*, XX

ADAPTABILITY, ACCOMMODATION (*continued*)

Everyone fancies the laws which fill his pockets to be God's laws.

Kingsley, *Alton Locke*, X

Little spirits will always accommodate themselves to the subject they would work upon: will fawn upon a sturdy-tempered person: will insult the meek.

Richardson, *Clarissa Harlowe*, I

Many accept the but half-worthy for fear a still worse should offer.

Ibid., II

We might dispense with the sweet in the coffee, could we escape from the bitter of life.

Simms, *The Scout*, XXXIII

We can't all be sound: we've got to be the way we're made.

Twain, *Tom Sawyer Abroad*, II

ADMIRATION

Beloved by the wise, she dies if she is not likewise the admiration of fools.

Anonymous, *The Wanderer*, I

That mixture of spite and over-fed merriment which passes for humor with the vulgar. In their fun they have much resemblance to a turkey-cock. It has a cruel beak, and a silly iteration of ugly sounds; it spreads its tail in self-glorification, but shows you the wrong side of that ornament—liking admiration, but knowing not what is admirable.

Eliot, *Felix Holt*, XII

He who engages your admiration today will probably attract your contempt tomorrow.

Fielding, H., *Tom Jones*, 267

Self-admiration, from the smallest beginnings soon spreadeth and enlargeth itself till it reacheth the clouds; and the elated imagination can nourish a thousand gay pleasant ideas in its extended branches.   Fielding, S., *Countess of Dellwyn*, I

Remarkable parts more frequently attract admiration than procure esteem.

Mackenzie, *The Man of the World*, I

The language of admiration is not always that of compliment.

Radcliffe, *Romance of the Forest*, 374

ADVANTAGE

Where a man does his best with only moderate powers, he will have the advantage over negligent superiority.   Austen, *Emma*, XIII

Adam and Eve had many advantages, but the principal one was, that they escaped teething.   Twain, *Pudd'nhead Wilson*, IV

ADVENTURE: *see also* ROMANCE

Romance had singled Jim for its own.   Conrad, *Lord Jim*, XXIX

In the pursuit of adventures, men are ordinarily governed by their habits or deluded by their wishes.   Cooper, *The Prairie*, II

There's romance enough at home without going half a mile for it.

Dickens, *Pickwick Papers*, XXI

Adventures are to the adventurous.   Disraeli, *Coningsby*, Book III, I

Adventures are life.   Meredith, *Harry Richmond*, XI

ADVERSITY: *see also* AFFLICTION, CALAMITY, MISERY, MISFORTUNE, etc.

Adversity, if a man is set down to it by degrees, is more supportable with equanimity by most people than any great prosperity arrived at in a single lifetime.

Butler, *The Way of All Flesh*, V

Great minds only can bear adversity. Dacre, *The Libertine*, XXII

Men love not the remembrance of their crimes; firm friendships can be never founded on the basis of guilt; hence the wicked have no sympathy for each other in the hour of adversity. *Ibid.*, XXX

Abused prosperity is oftentimes made the very means of our greatest adversity.
Defoe, *Robinson Crusoe*, 36

What availeth high dignity in time of adversity? It neither helpeth the sorrow of the heart, nor removes the body's misery. Deloney, *Thomas of Reading*, 250

One who can heroically endure adversity will bear prosperity with equal greatness of soul. Fielding, H., *Amelia*, II

People in difficulty and distress, or in any manner at odds with the world, can endure a vast amount of harsh treatment, and perhaps be the stronger for it; whereas, they give way at once before the simplest expression of what they perceive to be genuine sympathy.
Hawthorne, *House of the Seven Gables*, III

Who never heard the voice of reproof, or felt the keen blast of the wintry wind, is usually a slave to himself, and a tyrant to his vassals; while he that, by adversity, has been taught that he is no more than his fellows, treats his dependents with gentleness, and becomes a blessing to all. Helme, *St. Margaret's Cave*, Volume I, XI

All are not born to buffet with adversity. *Ibid.*, Volume IV, VII

Lapham stood in the isolation to which adversity so often seems to bring men.
Howells, *Silas Lapham*, XXV

Never was a nature more perfectly fortunate. It was not a restless, apprehensive, ambitious spirit, running a race with the tyranny of fate, but a temper so unsuspicious as to put Adversity off her guard, dodging and evading her with the easy, natural motion of a wind-shifted flower. James, H., *The Europeans*, IV

He knows himself, and all that's in him, who knows adversity.
Melville, *Mardi*, CLXXX

The likelihood of great calamities occurring seldom obtrudes upon the minds of ignorant men; for the things which wise people know, anticipate, and guard against, the ignorant can only become acquainted with by meeting them face to face. And even when experience has taught them, the lesson only serves for that day. Melville, *Redburn*, XIX

Adversity teaches one to play sword and target with etiquette and retinue better than any crowned king in Europe. Meredith, *Harry Richmond*, XXI

People in adversity (which is the state of trial of every good quality) should endeavor to preserve laudable customs, that, if sunshine return, they may not be losers by their trial.
Richardson, *Clarissa Harlowe*, I

Adversity is your shining-time. *Ibid.*, II

Adversity is like the period of the former and of the latter rain-cold, comfortless, unfriendly to man and to animal; yet from that season have their birth the flower and the fruit, the date, the rose, and the pomegranate. Scott, *The Talisman*, XIV

ADVICE, COUNSEL

Nothing is more common than to find people most swayed by that advice which squares most with their own inclination. Annesley, *Memoirs*, II

With a delicate mind, advice is control, and persuasion compulsion.
Anonymous, *The Fruitless Repentance*, I

In vacant moments people will find that advice comes with double force. We meet with it unexpectedly, and when we have most leisure to reflect upon it.
Anonymous, *The Ladies Advocate*, 298

I love to advise, when I am sure the heart of the person advised is on my side.
Brooke, *Emily Montague*, II

Counsel cannot call back an oath.
Burney, *Cecilia*, I

Take the advice of a man who has been a fool in his time.
Conrad, *Outcast of the Islands*, Part III, IV

I called a council in my thoughts.
Defoe, *Robinson Crusoe*, 53

Said Mr. Micawber, "At present, and until something turns up (which I am, I may say, hourly expecting), I have nothing to bestow but advice! Still my advice is so far worth taking that—in short, that I have never taken it myself."
Dickens, *David Copperfield*, XII

It doth not become green heads to advise grey hairs.
Fielding, H., *Joseph Andrews*, 267

Good counsel rejected returns to enrich the giver's bosom.
Goldsmith, *The Vicar of Wakefield*, 157

Nothing so easy as to give advice and consolation; nothing more difficult than to recall the oppressed mind to relish such arguments.   Kimber, *Juvenile Adventures*, II

Good advice is what everybody cannot, and many will not, give.   Lennox, *Sophia*, I

He that cannot follow good counsel never can get commodity.
Lyly, *Euphues and His England*, 230

The wit's abus'd that will no counsel take.
Sidney, *Arcadia*, II

Advice improperly administered generally acts in diametrical opposition to the purpose for which it is supposed to be given.   Smollett, *Ferdinand, Count Fathom*, XI

Who does not know how useless advice is?   Thackeray, *Henry Esmond*, Book III, II

ADVOCACY

How dangerous an advocate a lady is when she applies eloquence to an ill purpose.
Fielding, H., *Tom Jones*, 700

His sword is his advocate.
Lyttleton, *The Court Secret*, 11

Never a cause or a person so bad as to want advocates.
Richardson, *Clarissa Harlowe*, II

If an advocate has nothing to say for his client, what hope of carrying a cause?
Ibid., III

He must be a silly fellow who has not something to say for himself, when every cause has its black and its white side.
Ibid.

Power and riches never want advocates.
Richardson, *Pamela*, 56

AFFECTATION

Affectation of fine breeding is destructive to morals.
Brown, W.H., *The Power of Sympathy*, 89

A heartless man begging for sympathy is, of all kinds of affectation, the most contemptible.
Caruthers, *The Kentuckian*, Volume I, XVIII

The most dangerous of all affectations is that of being unaffected.
Ibid.

Ignorance I can bear without emotion, but the affectation of learning gives me a fit of the spleen.
Mackenzie, *Julia De Roubigné*, 28

Beware of that affectation of speaking technically, by which ignorance is often disguised and knowledge disgraced.　　　　　　　　　　Mackenzie, *The Man of the World*, I

Can affected ignorance be ever graceful, or a proof of true delicacy?
　　　　　　　　　　Richardson, *Sir Charles Grandison*, One, I

AFFECTION: *see also* LOVE

Natural affection only, of all the sentiments, has permanent power over me.
　　　　　　　　　　Bronte, C., *Jane Eyre*, XXXII

Man cannot long live with any companion, without bestowing upon it his affection.
　　　　　　　　　　Caruthers, *Cavaliers*, Volume II, III

The affection of a parent for his child is never permitted to die.
　　　　　　　　　　Cooper, *Last of the Mohicans*, XI

Men of the sea place their affections, often, on the fabric in which they dwell.
　　　　　　　　　　Cooper, *The Water-Witch*, XVI

If there is anything real in this world, it is those amazingly fine feelings and those natural obligations which must subsist between father and son.
　　　　　　　　　　Dickens, *Barnaby Rudge*, XII

We hear the world wonder at monsters of ingratitude. It often looks for monsters of affection, as though they were things.　　　　　　　　*Ibid.*, LXXIX

The affections may not be so easily wounded as the passions, but their hurts are deeper, and more lasting.　　　　　　　　　　*Ibid.*, LXXXI

Mature affection, homage, devotion, does not easily express itself. Its voice is low. It is modest and retiring, it lies in ambush, waiting and waiting. Such is the mature fruit. Sometimes a life glides away, and finds it still ripening in the shade.
　　　　　　　　　　Dickens, *David Copperfield*, XLI

If I could be less affectionate and sensitive, I should have a better digestion and an iron set of nerves.　　　　　　　　　　Dickens, *Great Expectations*, XI

When a tender affection has been storing itself in us through many of our years, the idea that we could accept any exchange for it seems to be a cheapening of our lives.
　　　　　　　　　　Eliot, *Middlemarch*, Book VI, LVII

We can set a watch over our affections and our constancy as we can over other treasures.
　　　　　　　　　　Ibid.

You have been to my affections what light, what color is to my eyes, what music is to the inward ear; you have raised a dim unrest into a vivid consciousness.
　　　　　　　　　　Eliot, *Mill on the Floss*, Book VII, III

The highest form of affection is based on full sincerity on both sides.
　　　　　　　　　　Hardy, *Jude*, Part Five, I

When a real and strong affection has come to an end, it is not well to mock the sacred past with any show of those commonplace civilities that belong to ordinary intercourse.
　　　　　　　　　　Hawthorne, *Blithedale*, XVI

Affection can make any sacrifice.　　　　　　　　Marryat, *Peter Simple*, V

Thou art tied to me by cords woven of my heart-strings.　　Melville, *Moby Dick*, CXXV

Affection sharpens the wits, and often it has made an innocent person more than a match for the wily.　　　　　　　Reade, *The Cloister and the Hearth*, XII

Affection rules us all.　　　　　　　　　　　　*Ibid.*, XLVIII

His affections are as fickle as the moon.　　　　Scott, *Kenilworth*, VII

Affection may now and then withstand very severe storms of rigor, but not a long polar frost of downright indifference.　　　　　　　Scott, *Waverley*, LIV

AFFECTION (*continued*)

Affection mustn't stand in the way of business. Simms, *Woodcraft*, XLIII

The affection of young ladies is of as rapid growth as Jack's beanstalk, and reaches up to the sky in a night. Thackeray, *Vanity Fair*, IV

AFFLICTION: *see also* ADVERSITY, etc.

The mind of man is never so much set upon heavenly things as when visited by affliction; prayers and penitence are her daughters, and her offspring contrition and tears. Anonymous, *Adventures of a Jesuit*, II

Affliction enlarges the heart, and extends the affection.
Caruthers, *The Kentuckian*, Volume I, VII

The greatest spirits, when overwhelmed by their afflictions, are subject to the greatest dejections. Defoe, *Moll Flanders*, 328

The world payeth ever that which it promiseth, which is nothing else but continual trouble and vexation of the mind. Deloney, *Thomas of Reading*, 271

Deep affliction has but strengthened and refined my best affections.
Dickens, *Oliver Twist*, XIV

I hold with Christ that afflictions are not sent by God in wrath as penalties for sin.
Gaskell, *Cousin Phillis*, IV

The angels of affliction spread their toils alike for the virtuous and the wicked, for the mighty and the mean. Johnson, *Rasselas*, 144

Affliction is the best monitor to teach a callous heart the duties of humanity.
Kelly, I., *The Abbey of St. Asaph*, III

They who have never known prosperity can hardly be said to be unhappy; it is from the remembrance of joys that we have lost that the arrows of affliction are pointed.
Mackenzie, *Julia De Roubigné*, 16

It is from the indulgence of sorrow that we first know a respite from affliction.
Ibid., 177

Affliction tempers the proud. Reade, *Griffith Gaunt*, XXX

There is a wholesome stir in strife itself, which, like the thunderstorm in the sluggish atmosphere, imparts a renewed energy, and a better condition of health and exercise, to the attributes and agents of the moral man. Simms, *The Partisan*, Volume II, I

Before an affliction is digested, consolation ever comes too soon; after it is digested, it comes too late. Sterne, *Tristram Shandy*, III

AFFLUENCE: *see also* MONEY, POVERTY, WEALTH, etc.

In the greatest affluence, savage men are miserable.
Amory, *The Life of John Buncle*, I

Grandeur and pomp change people's nature; they don't think the same in affluence as they do in indigence. Anonymous, *Genuine Memoirs of Maria Brown*, II

AFFRONT

If it be an affront to call a man a villain, it can be no less to shew him you suppose him one.
Fielding, H., *Jonathan Wild*, 162

AGE AND YOUTH

Thirty seems the end of all things to five-and-twenty. Alcott, *Little Women*, XLIII

A man is more than one being in his life. If the last persists, why not the first? If there be a hereafter for his age, why not for his youth?   Atherton, *Los Cerritos*, Part II, XVI

No young people's evenings are merry, when those they look up to are at home.
Austen, *Mansfield Park*, Volume Two, III

The last born has as good a right to the pleasures of youth, as the first.
Austen, *Pride and Prejudice*, Volume II, VI

A young man of eighteen is not in general so earnestly bent on being busy as to resist the solicitations of his friends to do nothing.
Austen, *Sense and Sensibility*, Volume I, XIX

What is so headstrong as youth? What so blind as inexperience?
Bronte, C., *Jane Eyre*, XXII

Boys are inconstant from vanity and affectation, old men from decay of passion.
Brooke, *History of Emily Montague*, I

How hard it is to convince youth, that sees all the world of the future before it, and covers that future with golden palaces, of the inequalities of life!
Bulwer, *The Caxtons*, Book VII, I

The old see afar; they stand on the height of experience, as a warder on the crown of a tower.   Bulwer, *Harold*, Book IV, V

Timidity solicits that mercy which pride is most gratified to grant; the blushes of juvenile shame atone for the deficiencies that cause them.   Burney, *Camilla*, One, II

Facility, that dangerous, yet venial, because natural, fault of youth.   *Ibid.*, Two, IV

The loss of youth is the same to everybody, and age is equally unwelcome to the ugly and the handsome.   *Ibid.*

Those who regard the first sorrows of early youth as too trifling for compassion do not enough consider that it is the suffering, not its abstract cause, which demands human commiseration.   *Ibid.*, Three, V

After four-and-twenty a man is seldom taken by surprise; at least, not till he is past forty: and then, the fear of being too late sometimes renovates the eagerness of the first youth.   *Ibid.*, *Camilla*, Three, VI

In the fervor of a strong attachment, youth is as open-eyed, as observant, and as prophetic as age, with all its concomitants of practice, time, and suspicion.   *Ibid.*

How true it is, yet how inconsistent, that while we all desire to live long, we have all a horror of being old.   Burney, *Cecilia*, I

Autumn is mellower, and what we lose in flowers, we more than gain in fruits.
Butler, *The Way of All Flesh*, VI

In old age we live under the shadow of Death, which, like a sword of Damocles, may descend at any moment, but we have so long found life to be an affair of being rather frightened than hurt that we have become like the people who live under Vesuvius, and chance it without much misgiving.   *Ibid.*

It is the young and fair who are the truly old and truly experienced, inasmuch as it is they who alone have a living memory to guide them.   *Ibid.*, XXXIII

When we say that we are getting old, we should say rather that we are getting new or young, and are suffering from inexperience; trying to do things which we have never done before, and failing worse and worse, till in the end we are landed in the utter impotence of death.   *Ibid.*

A traveler who has all but gained the last height of the great mist-covered mountain looks back over the painful crags he has mastered to where a light is shining on the first easy slope. That light is ever visible, for it is youth.   Churchill, *Richard Carvel*, II

Youth is soon raised.   Cleland, *Memoirs of a Woman of Pleasure*, 27

Youth is insolent; it is its right—its necessity; it has got to assert itself, and all assertion in this world of doubts is a defiance, is an insolence.　　　　Conrad, *Lord Jim*, XXIII

Youth, with its grand blindness, asks but the heart.
　　　　　　　　　　　　　　　Cooke, *Virginia Comedians*, Volume II, XXIII

Youth commonly loves life.　　　　　　　　Cooper, *Last of the Mohicans*, XXVI

Youth sleeps, ay, and dreams too; but age is awake and watchful.
　　　　　　　　　　　　　　　　　　　　　Cooper, *The Prairie*, III

Young women rarely understand their power; older ones too often overrate what they have.　　　　　　　　　　　　　　Crawford, *A Rose of Yesterday*, X

The voice of consolation is always sweet, but doubly sweet when coming from buoyant youth to age.　　　　　　　　　　　　　　　　Dacre, *Zofloya*, XII

As young maids are fickle, so are old women jealous: the one a grief too common, the other a torment intolerable.　　　　　　Deloney, *Jack of Newbury*, 320

There is a ruin of youth which is not like age.　　　Dickens, *Bleak House*, LX

Dombey was about eight-and-forty years of age. Son about eight-and-forty minutes.
　　　　　　　　　　　　　　　　　Dickens, *Dombey and Son*, I

Age, especially when it strives to be self-reliant and cheerful, finds much consideration among the poor.　　　　　　　　　　Dickens, *Hard Times*, Book II, VI

We are too apt to believe that the character of a boy is easily read. 'Tis a mystery the most profound. Mark what blunders parents constantly make as to the nature of their own offspring, bred too under their eyes, and displaying every hour their characteristics.
　　　　　　　　　　　　　　　　　Disraeli, *Coningsby*, Book I, III

Almost everything that is great has been done by youth.　　　*Ibid.*, Book III, I

Youth is a blunder; manhood a struggle; old age a regret.　　　　　　　*Ibid.*

Genius, when young, is divine.　　　　　　　　　　　　　　　　　　*Ibid.*

The history of heroes is the history of youth.　　　　　　　　　　　　*Ibid.*

Eloquent youth is generally prone to believe in the resistless power of its appeals.
　　　　　　　　　　　　　　　　　　　　　　Ibid., Book VIII, IV

We live in an age when to be young and to be indifferent can be no longer synonymous. We must prepare for the coming hour. The claims of the future are represented by suffering millions; and the Youth of a Nation are the trustees of Posterity.
　　　　　　　　　　　　　　　　　Disraeli, *Sybil*, Book VI, XIII

Until a man comes to the autumn of his days he can scarce say what hath been ill-luck and what hath been good.　　　　　　　Doyle, *Micah Clarke*, XXIV

Young souls, in pleasant delirium, are as unsympathetic as butterflies sipping nectar; they are isolated from all appeals by a barrier of dreams.　　Eliot, *Adam Bede*, IX

If youth is the season of hope, it is often so only in the sense that our elders are hopeful about us; for no age is so apt as youth to think its emotions, partings, and resolves are the last of their kind. Each crisis seems final, simply because it is new. We are told that the oldest inhabitants in Peru do not cease to be agitated by the earthquakes, but they probably see beyond each shock, and reflect that there are plenty more to come.
　　　　　　　　　　　　　　　　　Eliot, *Middlemarch*, Book VI, LV

A boy's sheepishness is by no means a sign of overmastering reverence; and while you are making encouraging advances to him under the idea that he is overwhelmed by a sense of your age and wisdom, ten to one he is thinking you extremely queer. The only consolation I can suggest to you is, that the Greek boys probably thought the same of Aristotle.　　　　　　　　　　　Eliot, *Mill on the Floss*, Book I, IX

Things look dim to old folks: they'd need have some young eyes about 'em, to let 'em know the world's the same as it used to be.   Eliot, *Silas Marner*, Conclusion

Youth can enjoy the benefit of the experience of age, and that at a time of life when such experience will be of more service to a man than when he hath lived long enough to acquire it of himself.   Fielding, H., *Amelia*, I

Margaret was at an age when any apprehension, not absolutely based on a knowledge of facts, is easily banished for a time by a bright sunny day, or some happy outward circumstance.   Gaskell, *North and South*, II

Five-and-twenty is the first judicious period; all before is romantic and superficial.
          Gibbes, *Mr. Francis Clive*, I

Pessimism is the affectation of youth, the reality of age.
          Glasgow, *The Descendant*, Book III, V

Youth is the season of benevolence.   Godwin, *St. Leon*, 375

The transplanting of old people is like the transplanting of old trees; a twelvemonth usually sees them wither and die away.   Hardy, *An Indiscretion*, Part I, III

The renown of youth is lost in the stupor of old age.   Harley, *Priory of St. Bernard*, I

Man's own youth is the world's youth; at least, he feels as if it were, and imagines that the earth's granite substance is something not yet hardened, and which he can mould into whatever shape he likes.   Hawthorne, *House of the Seven Gables*, XII

Our first youth is of no value; for we are never conscious of it, until after it is gone.
          Ibid., XIV

Externally, the jollity of aged men has much in common with the mirth of children; the intellect, any more than a deep sense of humor, has little to do with the matter; it is, with both, a gleam that plays upon the surface, and imparts a sunny and cheery aspect alike to the green branch, and gray, mouldering trunk. In one case, however, it is real sunshine; in the other, it more resembles the phosphorescent glow of decaying wood.
          Hawthorne, *The Scarlet Letter*, Introductory

Youth is a busy season.   Holcroft, *Hugh Trevor*, III

Men are but grown-up boys.   Howells, *Silas Lapham*, XXV

In America, Newman reflected, lads of twenty-five and thirty have old heads and young hearts, or at least young morals; here [in Europe] they have young heads and very aged hearts, morals the most grizzled and wrinkled.   James, H., *The American*, VII

It's our peculiar good luck that we don't see the limits of our minds. We're young, compared with what we may one day be. That belongs to youth; it's perhaps the best part of it.   James, H., *Roderick Hudson*, V

They say that old people find themselves at last face to face with a solid blank wall and stand thumping against it in vain. It resounds, it seems to have something beyond it, but it won't move. That's only a reason for living with open doors as long as we can.   *Ibid.*

Ardor is the natural effect of virtue animated by youth.   Johnson, *Rasselas*, 39

Youth is the time of gladness.   *Ibid.*, 74

The colors of life in youth and age appear different, as the face of nature in spring and winter.   *Ibid.*, 101

Age looks with anger on the temerity of youth, and youth with contempt on the scrupulosity of age.   *Ibid.*

The son is eager to enjoy the world before the father is willing to forsake it, and there is hardly room at once for two generations. The daughter begins to bloom before the mother can be content to fade, and neither can forbear to wish for the absence of the other.   *Ibid.*, 112

When the desultory levity of youth has, with age, settled into regularity, it is soon succeeded by pride ashamed to yield, or obstinacy delighting to contend.   *Ibid.*, 113

Placing a confidence is the surest way of attaching a young mind.　　Lee, *The Recess*, I

Hoary hairs, ambassadors of experience.　　Lyly, *Euphues*, 94

Old men are not unlike unto old trees, whose barks seemeth to be sound when their bodies are rotten.　　Lyly, *Euphues and His England*, 231

Old age is but a mask; let us not call the mask the face.
　　MacDonald, *The Seaboard Parish*, I

Nothing like preserving in manhood the fraternal familiarities of youth. It proves the heart a rosy boy to the last.　　Melville, *Confidence-Man*, XXIX

All of us, in our very bodies, outlive our own selves.　　Melville, *Mardi*, CLXXXV

Old age is always wakeful; as if, the longer linked with life, the less man has to do with aught that looks like death.　　Melville, *Moby Dick*, XXIX

Youth is no philosopher.　　Melville, *Pierre*, Book III, III

Talk not of the bitterness of middle-age and after life; a boy can feel all that, and much more, when upon his young soul the mildew has fallen; and the fruit, which with others is only blasted after ripeness, with him is nipped in the first blossom and bud.
　　Melville, *Redburn*, II

A *boy* means a green-hand, a landsman on his first voyage. And never mind if he is old enough to be a grandfather, he is still called a *boy*; and boy's work is put upon him.
　　Ibid., XII

If youth be giddy, old age is staid; even as young saplings, in the litheness of their limbs, toss to their roots in the fresh morning air; but, stiff and unyielding with age, mossy trunks never bend.　　Melville, *White Jacket*, LIV

A man's beginning his prime at fifty, or there never was much man in him.
　　Meredith, *Beauchamp's Career*, XI

Saltwater keeps a man's youth in pickle.　　Meredith, *Harry Richmond*, IX

In youth, there is nothing like a pent-up secret of the heart for accumulating powers of speech.　　*Ibid.*, X

At twenty forty is charming; at forty twenty.　　*Ibid.*, XXII

At the period when the young savage grows into higher influences, the faculty of worship is foremost in him.　　Meredith, *Ordeal of Richard Feverel*, XV

A swimmer and a cricketer is nowhere to be scorned in youth's republic.　　*Ibid.*

Every act, every fostered inclination, almost every thought, in the blossoming season of youth, bears its seed for the future. The living tree now requires incessant watchfulness.
　　Ibid.

That boys will be boys is a palliation which is frequently an incentive.　　*Ibid.*, XX

The beardless crew know that they have not a chance of pay: but what of that when the rosy prospect of thwarting their elders is in view?　　*Ibid.*, XXX

The world is the golden apple. Thirst for it is common during youth.
　　Meredith, *The Tragic Comedians*, I

It was the fashion to respect old age for what it had, if not for what it could do.
　　Payson, *Golden Dreams*, I

Old age opens the fountains of tears.　　Porter, *Scottish Chiefs*, VI

The happy benevolence of our feelings when we are young prompts us to believe that everybody is good, and excites our wonder why everybody is not happy.
　　Radcliffe, *Castles of Athlin and Dunbayne*, 6

The weakness of humanity is never willingly perceived by young minds.
Radcliffe, *A Sicilian Romance*, I

There is one time of life for imagination and fancy to work in: then, when riper years and experience direct the fire to glow rather than to flame out, something between both might perhaps be produced that would not displease a judicious eye.
Richardson, *Clarissa Harlowe*, I

Time enough for obscenity when ye grow old, and can only talk.   *Ibid.*, II

Young men's frolics old men feel.   *Ibid.*

In youth, middle age, or dotage, females take us all in.   *Ibid.*

Youth is a good subject for a physician to work upon.   *Ibid.*, IV

When the old die it is well; they have had their time. It is when the young die that the bells weep drops of blood.   Schreiner, *Story of an African Farm*, Part II, XII

An old man is easily brought to speak of olden times.
Scott, *Fair Maid of Perth*, XXIX

She is at the most dangerous period for maidens as well as mares, being barely in her fifteenth year.   Scott, *Ivanhoe*, XL

In the April of your age, you should be like April.   Sidney, *Arcadia*, III

Youth and discretion are with respect to each other as two parallel lines, which, though infinitely produced, remain still equidistant, and will never coincide.
Smollett, *Peregrine Pickle*, 110

To claim the advantage of superior age is to give sure offense.
Stevenson, *Prince Otto*, Book II, VI

Mischief is the fun of youth.   Thackeray, *Catherine*, Chapter the Last

'Tis an error, surely, to talk of the simplicity of youth. No persons are more hypocritical, and have a more affected behavior to one another, than the young.
Thackeray, *Henry Esmond*, Book I, IX

The weakness of age is the penalty paid by the folly of youth.
Trollope, *He Knew He Was Right*, XLVI

In youth, as at the opera, everything seems possible.   Warner, *A Little Journey*, VII

Youth! There is absolutely nothing in the world but youth!
Wilde, *Picture of Dorian Gray*, II

To get back one's youth, one has merely to repeat one's follies.   *Ibid.*, III

The secret of remaining young is never to have an emotion that is unbecoming.
Ibid., VII

Youth smiles without any reason. It is one of its chiefest charms.   *Ibid.*, XIV

To get back my youth I would do anything in the world, except take exercise, get up early, or be respectable.   *Ibid.*, XIX

Life has revealed to youth her latest wonder.   *Ibid.*

The tragedy of old age is not that one is old, but that one is young.   *Ibid.*

What was youth at best? A green, an unripe time, a time of shallow moods, and sickly thoughts.   *Ibid.*, XX

AGGRESSION: *see also* CONFLICT, WAR, etc.

Aggressors lay themselves open to severe reprisals.
Richardson, *Sir Charles Grandison*, Two, IV

AGITATION: *see also* EMOTION

Strong mental agitation and disturbance was no novelty to him, even before his late sufferings. It never is, to obstinate and sullen natures; for they struggle hard to be such.
Dickens, *Dombey and Son*, LIX

Miss Bolo rose from the table considerably agitated, and went straight home, in a flood of tears and a sedan-chair.
Dickens, *Pickwick Papers*, XXXV

AGREEABLENESS; DISAGREEABLENESS

I never in my life saw a man more intent on being agreeable than Mr. Elton. It is downright labor to him where ladies are concerned. With men he can be rational and unaffected, but when he has ladies to please, every feature works.
Austen, *Emma*, XIII

There is hardly any personal defect which an agreeable manner might not gradually reconcile one to.
Austen, *Persuasion*, V

An agreeable manner may set off handsome features, but can never alter plain ones.
Ibid.

To be born with a most agreeable way as a natural heritage is to be a social millionaire.
Burnett, *Through One Administration*, XV

Bentley Drummle was so sulky a fellow that he even took up a book as if its writer had done him an injury.
Dickens, *Great Expectations*, XXV

Nothing disagreeable should ever be looked at.
Dickens, *Little Dorrit*, Book II, V

An agreeable person is one who agrees with me.
Disraeli, *Lothair*

ALIENATION

It is one of the chief earthly incommodities of some species of misfortune, or of a great crime, that it makes the actor in the one, or the sufferer of the other, an alien in the world, by interposing a wholly unsympathetic medium betwixt himself and those whom he yearns to meet.
Hawthorne, *The Marble Faun*, XI

Where in this strange universe is not one a stranger?
Melville, *Confidence-Man*, XXXVI

The mass of mankind, are they not necessarily strangers to each individual man?
Ibid., XLII

AMBITION: *see also* ASPIRATION, SUCCESS, etc.

The Temple of Ambition is an edifice of counterfeited splendor.
Anonymous, *The Birmingham Counterfeit*, I

The most aspiring ambition and the most abject meanness are generally found in the same bosom.
Ibid.

With an ambitious man, all means are good that tend to accomplish his designs.
Ibid.

Ambition hath its ardor as well as love.
Anonymous, *Memoirs of the Court of H—*, 13

There is a bad and criminal ambition and a good and commendable one.
Arbuthnot, *Miss Jenny Cameron*, 196

Be not too ambitious, else wilt thou die of thy victories. And do not love the polar star, lest thou set fire to it and fall to ashes.
Atherton, *Doomswoman*, II

Ambition is the looting of hell in chase of biting flames swirling above a desert of ashes.
Ibid., XIX

Ambition, that accursed root that poisons the world.

Brackenridge, *Modern Chivalry*, Part II, Volume I

Take a lesson from the fowls of heaven, and the brutes of the field. It is not the elevation of place, but the conveniency of accommodation that governs them. Ambition is an accursed germ of evil in the human mind. *Ibid.*

Can ambition come in competition with tenderness?   Brooke, *Emily Montague*, II

A youthful mind is seldom totally free from ambition; to curb that is the first step to contentment, since to diminish expectation is to increase enjoyment.

Burney, *Evelina*, 15–16

All generous spirits are ambitious.   Dickens, *Bleak House*, LX

Indefinite visions of ambition are weak against the ease of doing what is habitual or beguilingly agreeable; and we all know the difficulty of carrying out a resolve when we secretly long that it may turn out to be unnecessary. In such states of mind the most incredulous person has a private leaning towards miracle.

Eliot, *Middlemarch*, Book VI, LX

Ambition scarce ever produces any evil but when it reigns in cruel and savage bosoms; and avarice seldom flourishes at all but in the basest and poorest soil.

Fielding, H., *Amelia*, I

The great are deceived if they imagine they have appropriated ambition and vanity to themselves. These noble qualities flourish as notably in a country church and churchyard as in the drawing-room or in the closet. Schemes have indeed been laid in the vestry which would hardly disgrace the conclave. Here is a ministry, and here is an opposition. Here are plots and circumventions, parties and factions, equal to those which are to be found in courts.   Fielding, H., *Tom Jones*, 128

Like a conjurer's wand, ambition had so confined his mind that he could no more give his thoughts liberty to range than if he had been under the power of enchantment.

Fielding, S., *The Countess of Dellwyn*, I

Every pursuit of the human mind is of a restless nature, and partakes of that most turbulent of all passions, ambition itself. *Ibid.*

Every pursuit, the end of which is human applause, is ambition. *Ibid.*

Although I spoke lightly of ambition and said that easy happiness was worth most, I could defend ambition very well, and in the only pleasant way: on the broad ground of the loveliness of any dream about future triumphs. In looking back there is a pleasure in contemplating a time when some attractive thing of the future appeared possible, even though it never came to pass.   Hardy, *An Indiscretion*, Part I, II

Ambition is a talisman more powerful than witchcraft.

Hawthorne, *House of the Seven Gables*, XVIII

The world owes all its onward impulse to men ill at ease. The happy man inevitably confines himself within ancient limits. *Ibid.*, XX

Ambition, baneful ambition, hath ruined angels, and lost them heaven.

Kelly, *The Abbey of St. Asaph*, III

Ambition is purely earthly, and not angelical. It is false, that any angels fell by reason of ambition. Angels never fall; and never feel ambition.   Melville, *Pierre*, Book III, III

In life you mustn't wait for the prize of the race till you touch the goal.

Meredith, *Harry Richmond*, XXXIX

Whenever was an ambitious mind satisfied by acquisition?

Richardson, *Clarissa Harlowe*, I

Ambition is temptation which could disturb the bliss of heaven itself.

Scott, *Ivanhoe*, XXIV

AMBITION (*continued*)

Women are but the toys which amuse our lighter hours—ambition is the serious business of life. *Ibid.*, XXXVI

Ambition, like love, can abide no lingering and ever urgeth on his own successes; hating nothing but what may stop them. Sidney, *Arcadia*, II

Ambitious emulation is the soldier's principle.
Simms, *The Partisan*, Volume II, XVIII

"It's a good thing to excel." "I'm not so sure of that. A man who can kill more salmon than anybody else can rarely do anything else." Trollope, *Phineas Finn*, XV

If I were ambitious, I should not for so many years have been a prey to all the hell of conscientious scruples. Walpole, *The Castle of Otranto*, 68

The slippery paths of ambitious greatness. Young, *The Adventures of Emmera*, II

AMBIVALENCE, PARADOX: *see also* COMPARISON/CONTRAST; CONTRADICTION, etc.

A man may be a saint, yet there are circumstances under which a saint may be forgiven for recollecting that he is a man. Aldrich, *Prudence Palfrey*, XV

Ione has but one vice—she is chaste. Bulwer, *Pompeii*, Book I, IV

Let a king and a beggar converse freely together, and it is the beggar's fault if he does not say something which makes the king lift his hat to him.
Bulwer, *What Will He Do With It?*, Book III, XVIII

No wind so cutting as that which sets in the quarter from which the sun rises.
Ibid., Book X, V

No practice is entirely vicious which has not been extinguished among the comeliest, most vigorous, and most cultivated races of mankind in spite of centuries of endeavor to extirpate it. If a vice in spite of such efforts can still hold its own among the most polished nations, it must be founded on some immutable truth or fact in human nature, and must have some compensatory advantage which we cannot afford altogether to dispense with. Butler, *The Way of All Flesh*, LII

The book rang with the courage alike of conviction and of an entire absence of conviction; it appeared to be the work of men who had a rule-of-thumb way of steering between iconoclasm on the one hand and credulity on the other; who cut Gordian knots as a matter of course when it suited their convenience; who shrank from no conclusion in theory, nor from any want of logic in practice. *Ibid.*, LXXXV

The dual life—that outward existence which conforms, the inward life which questions.
Chopin, *The Awakening*, VII

She was fond of her children in an uneven, impulsive way. She would sometimes gather them passionately to her heart; she would sometimes forget them. *Ibid.*

No man who has had any real experience of life can have failed to observe how amazingly close, in critical situations, the grotesque and the terrible, the comic and the serious, contrive to tread on each other's heels. At such times, the last thing we ought properly to think of comes into our heads, or the least consistent event that could possibly be expected to happen does actually occur. Collins, *A Rogue's Life*, VIII

I never saw a man, in all my experience, whom I should be so sorry to have for an enemy. Is this because I like him, or because I am afraid of him?
Collins, *Woman in White*, Part I, Second Epoch

He was imprisoned within the very freedom of his power. Conrad, *Lord Jim*, XXIX

Like seeks unlike. Cooke, *The Virginia Comedians*, Volume II, XIII

The fairest snow is the easiest discolored. Dacre, *Passions*, Letter XXII

From rough outsides, serene and gentle influences often proceed.

Dickens, *Bleak House*, VIII

What's the use of living cheap when you have got no money? You might as well live dear.

Ibid., XX

Peachy-cheeked charmers with the skeleton throats.

Ibid., LVIII

While the grass grows, the steed starves.

Dickens, *The Mystery of Edwin Drood*, XVII

There are really no miseries except natural miseries: conventional misfortunes are mere illusions.

Disraeli, *Coningsby*, Book IX, III

The existence of insignificant people has very important consequences in the world. It can be shown to affect the price of bread and the rate of wages, to call forth many evil tempers from the selfish and many heroisms from the sympathetic, and, in other ways, to play no small part in the tragedy of life.

Eliot, *Adam Bede*, V

Human experience is usually paradoxical.

Eliot, *Daniel Deronda*, LXIX

Your dunce who can't do his sums always has a taste for the infinite.

Eliot, *Felix Holt*, X

We hear with the more keenness what we wish others not to hear.

Eliot, *Middlemarch*, Book IV, XLII

What we call the "just possible" is sometimes true and the thing we find it easier to believe is grossly false.

Ibid., Book VIII, LXXIII

A long, deep sob of that mysterious, wondrous happiness that is one with pain.

Eliot, *Mill on the Floss*, Book VII, V

The impetuosity of passion unrequited is bearable, even if it stings and anathematizes—there is a triumph in the humiliation, and a tenderness in the strife.

Hardy, *Far From the Madding Crowd*, XX

The heaven being spread with this pallid screen and the earth with the darkest vegetation, their meeting-line at the horizon was clearly marked. In such contrast the heath wore the appearance of an installment of night which had taken up its place before its astronomical hour was come: darkness had to a great extent arrived hereon, while day stood distinct in the sky.

Hardy, *Return of the Native*, Book I, I

The pole suggests the tropic.

Hawthorne, *Blithedale Romance*, II

With only an inconsiderable change, the gladdest objects and existences become the saddest.

Hawthorne, *The Marble Faun*, XXV

No man for any considerable period can wear one face to himself and another to the multitude, without finally getting bewildered as to which may be the true.

Hawthorne, *The Scarlet Letter*, XX

Grief seems more like ashes than like fire; but as grief has been love once, so it may become love again.

Holmes, *Elsie Venner*, XXXI

The house of mourning is decorously darkened to the world, but within itself it is also the house of laughing.

Howells, *Silas Lapham*, XXIV

The effects of innocence and guilt often bear so near a resemblance as to be mistaken for each other.

Johnstone, *The Reverie*, I

Pepper though it be hot in the mouth is cold in the maw.

Lyly, *Euphues*, 127

Nothing so fast knit as glass, yet once broken, it can never be joined.

Lyly, *Euphues and His England*, 324–325

Nothing fuller of metal than steel, yet overheated it will never be hardened.

Ibid.

Friendship is ye best pearl, but by disdain thrown into vinegar, it bursteth rather in pieces, than it will bow to any softness.

Ibid.

Straight trees have crooked roots, smooth baits sharp hooks. *Ibid.*, 327

Talk the more it is seasoned with fine phrases, the less it savoreth of true meaning.
Ibid.

The brightest lights appear in darkest sky, and beauteous colors paint the poisonous insect. McCarthy, *The Fair Moralist*, 21

I am pleased to believe that beauty is at bottom incompatible with ill, and therefore am so eccentric as to have confidence in the latent benignity of that beautiful creature, the rattlesnake, whose lithe neck and burnished maze of tawny gold, as he sleekly curls aloft in the sun, who on the prairie can behold without wonder?
Melville, *Confidence-Man*, XXXVI

No fury so ferocious, as not to have some amiable side. Melville, *Mardi*, XIII

All victories are not triumphs, nor all who conquer, heroes. *Ibid.*, XLII

Final, last thoughts you mortals have none. *Ibid.*, CXX

A victory turned to no wise and enduring account is no victory at all. Some victories revert to the vanquished. *Ibid.*, CLXI

To enjoy bodily warmth, some small part of you must be cold, for there is no quality in this world that is not what it is merely by contrast. Nothing exists in itself.
Melville, *Moby Dick*, XI

A sleeping apartment should never be furnished with a fire, which is one of the luxurious discomforts of the rich. For the height of this sort of deliciousness is to have nothing but the blanket between you and your snugness and the cold of the outer air. Then there you lie like the one warm spark in the heart of an arctic crystal. *Ibid.*

No man can ever feel his own identity aright except his eyes be closed; as if darkness were indeed the proper element of our essences, though light be more congenial to our clayey part. *Ibid.*

The ship must fly all hospitality; one touch of land, though it but graze the keel, would make her shudder through and through. *Ibid.*, XXIII

While his one live leg made lively echoes along the deck, every stroke of his dead limb sounded like a coffin-tap. On life and death this old man walked. *Ibid.*, LI

Oh, man! admire and model thyself after the whale! Do thou, too, remain warm among ice. Do thou, too, live in this world without being of it. Be cool at the equator; keep thy blood fluid at the Pole. Like the great dome of St. Peter's, and like the great whale, retain, O man! in all seasons a temperature of thine own. *Ibid.*, LXVIII

Doubts of all things earthly, and intuitions of some things heavenly; this combination makes neither believer nor infidel, but makes a man who regards them both with equal eye. *Ibid.*, LXXXV

That is hard which should be soft, and that is soft which should be hard. *Ibid.*, CVIII

A smile is the chosen vehicle of all ambiguities. Melville, *Pierre*, Book IV, V

Sometimes a lie is heavenly, and truth infernal. *Ibid.*, Book V, II

It is not for man to follow the trail of truth too far, since by so doing he entirely loses the directing compass of his mind. *Ibid.*, Book IX, I

As the more immense the Virtue, so should be the more immense our approbation; likewise the more immense the Sin, the more infinite our pity. In some sort, Sin hath its sacredness, not less than holiness. And great Sin calls forth more magnanimity than small Virtue. *Ibid.*, Book X, II

Though the world worship Mediocrity and CommonPlace, yet hath it fire and sword for all contemporary Grandeur; though it swears that it fiercely assails all Hypocrisy, yet hath it not always an ear for Earnestness. *Ibid.*, Book XVIII, II

With the soul of an Atheist, he wrote down the godliest things.   *Ibid.*, Book XXV, III

Surrounded as we are by the wants and woes of our fellowmen, and yet given to follow our own pleasures, regardless of their pains, are we not like people sitting up with a corpse, and making merry in the house of the dead?   Melville, *Redburn*, XXXVII

Oh! he who has never been afar, let him once go from home, to know what home is.
Melville, *Redburn*, LX

The scene of suffering is a scene of joy when the suffering is past; and the silent reminiscence of hardships departed, is sweeter than the presence of delight.   *Ibid.*

Dark-eyed Renée was not beauty but attraction; she touched the double chords within us which are we know not whether harmony or discord, but a divine discord if an uncertified harmony, memorable beyond plain sweetness or majesty. There are touches of bliss in anguish that superhumanize bliss, touches of mystery in simplicity, of the eternal in the variable. These two chords of poignant antiphony she struck throughout the range of the hearts of men, and strangely intervolved them in vibrating unison.
Meredith, *Beauchamp's Career*, XXXIV

This is to be a story of a battle, at least one murder, and several sudden deaths. For that reason it begins with a pink tea and among the mingled odors of many delicate perfumes and the hale, frank smell of Caroline Testout roses.
Norris, *Moran of the Lady Letty*, I

Grief is ever an inmate with joy.   Richardson, *Clarissa Harlowe*, II

Though grief and joy will not show themselves at the same window at one time, yet they have the whole house in common between them.   *Ibid.*

There may be consent in struggle; there may be yielding in resistance.   *Ibid.*

In all human affairs, the convenient and inconvenient, the good and the bad, are so mingled, that there is no having the one without the other.   *Ibid.*

I do not expect a direct consent but a yielding reluctance.   *Ibid.*

Heroes have their fits of fear; cowards their brave moments; and virtuous women their moment critical.   *Ibid.*

We must not expect that our roses will grow without thorns: but then they are useful and instructive thorns.   *Ibid.*, IV

The deeper the griefs, the greater the joys, when restored to health and favor.   *Ibid.*

Joy is not absolutely inconsistent with melancholy.   *Ibid.*

One who can count up all her woe is in a way to be happy.   *Ibid.*

Is it not strange, that love borders so much upon hate?   Richardson, *Pamela*, 49

I am either nearer my happiness, or my misery, than ever I was.   *Ibid.*, 221

Fears of the brave and follies of the wise.   Scott, *Quentin Durward*, XXVII

There are many things ower bad for blessing, and ower gude for banning, like Rob Roy.
Scott, *Rob Roy*, XXXIX

Joy and sorrow in excess will produce tears.   Shebbeare, *Lydia*, II

To examine the causes of life, we must first have recourse to death.
Shelley, *Frankenstein*, IV

The snake [in Eden] was as bold and subtle as he was ugly. The boldness and subtleness reconciled the woman to the beast; and once reconciled, to behold without loathing, she soon discovered a beauty in his very ugliness.   Simms, *The Scout*, XXXII

If not handsome, be hideous, if you wish to succeed with women: the more hideous (wit and audacity not being wanting) the more likely to be successful.   *Ibid.*

It is through the weakness of the man that we know his proper strength.
Simms, *Woodcraft*, LXVI

By my soul, I have gained a loss!   Smollett, *Roderick Random*, 313

It may be that our present faculties have among them a rudimentary one, like the germs of wings in the chrysalis, by which the spiritual world becomes sometimes an object of perception; there may be natures in which the walls of the material are so fine and translucent that the spiritual is seen through them as through a glass darkly.

        Stowe, *Orr's Island*, VII

Sometimes it is hard to say where honest pride ends and hypocrisy begins.

        Thackeray, *Philip*, IV

There are human beings who are dual in character;—in whose breasts not only is evil always fighting against good,—but to whom evil is sometimes horribly, hideously evil, but is sometimes also not hideous at all.   Trollope, *The Eustace Diamonds*, XVIII

I live in that detestable no-man's land, between respectability and solvency, which has none of the pleasure of either.   *Ibid.*, LXII

There is a limit beyond which good time ends, and being shamefully late at once begins.

        Trollope, *Phineas Finn*, LIII

The way of paradoxes is the way of truth.   Wilde, *The Picture of Dorian Gray*, III

To test reality we must see it on the tight rope. When the verities become acrobats, we can judge them.   *Ibid.*

There was animalism in the soul, and the body had its moments of spirituality. The sense could refine, and the intellect could degrade. Who could say where the fleshly impulse ceased, or the physical impulse began?   *Ibid.*, IV

The knowledge of one generation is the ignorance of the next.

        Wright, *A Few Days in Athens*, XVI

Such another victory, and I am undone!   Young, *The Adventures of Emmera*, I

AMUSEMENT: *see also* DIVERSION

Nothing is entertaining for two minutes together.   Burney, *Cecilia*, I

A masquerade is a pleasure of too loose and disorderly a kind for the recreation of a sober mind.   Fielding, H., *Amelia*, II

The playhouse is as much the house of the Devil as the church is the house of God.

        Graves, *The Spiritual Quixote*, II

Happiness is not the product of any particular place, or way of life. Much less is it to be found in a state of absolute inactivity: some employment is necessary, to divert the mind from preying upon itself.   *Ibid.*, III

You seem to hold that if a thing amuses you for the moment, that is all you need ask for it.

        James, H., *The American*, V

I don't care for the great questions. I care for pleasure—for amusement.

        James, H., *The Europeans*, VIII

It is better to have amused oneself for awhile and have done with it.

        James, H., *Washington Square*, XII

ANGEL

Her beautiful hair dropping over me—like an angel's wing.

        Dickens, *David Copperfield*, VIII

All angel is not'ing more dan de shark well goberned.   Melville, *Moby Dick*, LXIV

Our world cannot brand an angel.   Meredith, *One of Our Conquerors*, II

People who act like angels ought to have angels to deal with.

Richardson, *Clarissa Harlowe*, I

The devil's plagues arise from angels.

Ibid., III

The devil cannot stop what an angel bids.

Ibid.

There are angels as well as devils in the flesh.

Ibid.

Angelic opinions are at a discount in this age.

Tourgée, *Pactolus Prime*, I

I fear no bad angel and have offended no good one.

Walpole, *The Castle of Otranto*, 30

ANGER, RAGE

Angry people are not always wise.

Austen, *Pride and Prejudice*, Volume III, III

Rage must either progress or decline.

Brown, C., *Arthur Mervyn*, II

Anger is the food of anger.

Ibid.

White men are quick in anger and slow in gratitude.

Conrad, *Almayer's Folly*, VIII

The satisfaction of my animosity is as acceptable to me as money.

Dickens, *Little Dorrit*, Book II, XXX

There are answers which, in turning away wrath, only send it to the other room.

Eliot, *Middlemarch*, Book III, XXIX

Anger and jealousy can no more bear to lose sight of their objects than love.

Eliot, *Mill on the Floss*, Book I, X

If Tom's friends must have confessed his temper to have been a little too easily ruffled, his enemies must at the same time have confessed that it as soon subsided; nor did it at all resemble the sea, whose swelling is more violent and dangerous after a storm is over than while the storm subsists.

Fielding, H., *Tom Jones*, 592

Anger, when removed, often gives new life to affection.

Ibid., 837

Men over-violent in their dispositions are, for the most part, as changeable in them.

Ibid., 861

Warmth of temper too often carries man out of his proper sphere, and renders him wretched, by a retrospection of his former conduct.

Harley, *Priory of St. Bernard*, I

No wise thing was ever done in rage.

Keenan, *The Money-Makers*, XXIV

Anger against a man of straw is a whit less wise than anger against a man of flesh.
Madness, to be mad with anything.

Melville, *Confidence-Man*, XXX

What is said in heat, that thing unsays itself.

Melville, *Moby Dick*, XXXVI

There are men from whom warm words are small indignity.

Ibid.

The rage of a youth to prove himself in the right of an argument.

Meredith, *Harry Richmond*, XXII

Excellent and sane is the outburst of wrath to men, when it stops short of slaughter. For who that locks wrath up to eat it solitary can say that it is consumed?

Meredith, *Ordeal of Richard Feverel*, XXXVII

Keep your anger for those who fear it.

Mozeen, *Young Scarron*, 112

Anger seems to have some fine buoyant quality, which makes it rise and come uppermost in an agitated mind.

Reade, *Griffith Gaunt*, III

Well said the ancients that anger is a short madness. When we reflect in cold blood on the things we have said in hot, how impossible they seem! how out of character with our real selves! And this is one of the recognized symptoms of mania.

Ibid., XX

When some folks find their anger has made them considerable, they will always be angry or seeking occasions for anger.

Richardson, *Clarissa Harlowe*, II

ANGER, RAGE (*continued*)

There are some who have wisdom in their anger. *Ibid.*

Keep anger alive, lest it sink into compassion. *Ibid.*

Angry people should never write while their passion holds. *Ibid.*, III

Anger unpolishes the most polite. *Ibid.*

Angry men make to themselves beds of nettles. *Ibid.*, IV

We think there wants fire where we find no sparkles, at least of fury.
Sidney, *Arcadia*, III

One of the great conditions of anger and hatred is, that you must tell and believe lies against the hated object in order to be consistent. Thackeray, *Vanity Fair*, XVIII

When angry, count four; when very angry, swear. Twain, *Pudd'nhead Wilson*, X

ANIMAL AND INSECT LIFE; ATAVISM

Among beasts there are none who do not owe their accommodations to their own exertions. Brown, C.B., *Alcuin*, III

Beware of him as has no use for horses. Churchill, *Richard Carvel*, IV

Most animals are easily awed by the appearance of intrepidity, while they are invited to pursue by marks of fear and apprehension. Day, *Sandford and Merton*, 267

The monkey is a very extraordinary animal which closely resembles a man in his shape and appearance. *Ibid.*, 268

There are unknown worlds of knowledge in brutes; and whenever you mark a horse, or a dog, with a peculiarly mild, calm, deep-seated eye, be sure he is an Aristotle or a Kant, tranquilly speculating upon the mysteries in man. Melville, *Redburn*, XL

No philosophers so thoroughly comprehend us as dogs and horses. *Ibid.*

What is a horse but a species of four-footed dumb man, in a leathern overall, who happens to live upon oats, and toils for his masters, half-requited or abused, like the biped hewers of wood and drawers of water? *Ibid.*

There is a touch of divinity even in brutes, and a special halo about a horse, that should forever exempt him from indignities. As for those majestic, magisterial truck-horses of the docks, I would as soon think of striking a judge on the bench, as to lay violent hand upon their holy hides. *Ibid.*

The immortal atavism of man. Moore, *Evelyn Innes*, XIX

Nothing can be more obvious than that all animals were created solely and exclusively for the use of man. Peacock, *Headlong Hall*, II

All animals in creation are more or less in a state of hostility with each other.
Richardson, *Clarissa Harlowe*, II

Ye are worse than brute beasts in your actions, and will you imitate them in their very dumbness? Scott, *Ivanhoe*, XXI

ANTIPATHY: *see also* FRIENDSHIP

It is not seldom the case in this conventional world of ours—watery or otherwise—that a person placed in command over his fellowmen finds one of them to be very significantly his superior in general pride of manhood, straightway against that man he conceives an unconquerable dislike and bitterness; and if he have a chance he will pull down and pulverize that subaltern's tower, and make a little heap of dust of it.
Melville, *Moby Dick*, LIV

The born preacher we feel instinctively to be our foe. He may do some good to the wretches that have been struck down; [but] he rouses deadly antagonism in the strong.
Meredith, *Ordeal of Richard Feverel*, X

ANXIETY: *see also* AGITATION; DISTRESS; EMOTION; etc.

On her beauty there has fallen a heavier shade than Time of his unassisted self can cast, all-potent as he is—the shadow of anxiety and sorrow; and the daily struggle of a poor existence.
Dickens, *Dombey and Son*, XXXIII

So great a torment is anxiety to the human mind, that we always endeavor to relieve ourselves from it by guesses, however doubtful or uncertain; on all which occasions, dislike and hatred are the surest guides to lead our suspicion to its object.
Fielding, H., *Amelia*, I

All bodily racks and torments are nothing compared with certain states of the human mind.
Godwin, *St. Leon*, 56

People often do the idlest acts of their lifetime in their heaviest and most anxious moments.
Hawthorne, *The Marble Faun*, XXIII

The state of a mind oppressed with a sudden calamity is like that of the fabulous inhabitants of the new-created earth, who, when the first night came upon them, supposed that day would never return.
Johnson, *Rasselas*, 134

APATHY: *see also* INVOLVEMENT; SENSIBILITY; etc.

Apathy is a vice more hateful than all the errors of sensibility.
Radcliffe, *The Mysteries of Udolpho*, I

APOLOGY

The dinner in its turn was highly admired; and Mr. Collins begged to know to which of his fair cousins the excellence of its cookery was owing. But here he was set right by Mrs. Bennet, who assured him with some asperity that they were very well able to keep a good cook, and that her daughters had nothing to do in the kitchen. He begged pardon for having displeased her. In a softened tone she declared herself not at all offended; but he continued to apologize for about a quarter of an hour.
Austen, *Pride and Prejudice*, Volume I, XIII

I detest an apology. If a man respects me, he will not give himself occasion for apology.
Howe, *The Story of a Country Town*, XXX

An offense cannot be wiped out by an apology. If it could, we would substitute apologies for hangings.
Ibid.

Never apologize to me; I should regard it as evidence that you had wronged me.
Ibid.

What signifies owning a fault without mending it?
Richardson, *Clarissa Harlowe*, I

Sorry for the detection, not for the fault.
Ibid.

Miss Morris's idea of an apology is a repetition of her offense with increased rudeness.
Trollope, *The Eustace Diamonds*, XXIX

APPEARANCE; APPEARANCE VS. REALITY: *see also* HYPOCRISY; TRUTH; etc.

In vain does the unjust aspirer hope to cover his infamy with ill-got titles and the glare of pomp. The base groundwork is visible through all the tinselled outside.
Annesley, *Memoirs*, I

The generality of human actions, like a great deal of our current coin, is counterfeit.
Anonymous, *The Birmingham Counterfeit*, I

The many think no man a hero but a soldier. Let us weigh these sons of triumph in the balance of reason and equity, and we shall find them mere counterfeits, and pretenders to the pompous titles that have been lavished upon them.   *Ibid.*

A partial affection hides faults, and creates beauties.
Anonymous, *The History of Betty Barnes*, II

There are people who starve themselves at home, to make their acquaintance stare whenever they go abroad.   Anonymous, *Memoirs of a Coquet*, 93

The worst game should be played with the best face.   Beckford, *Vathek*, 197

Graces and agreeablenesses are found oftener in the mind than in the countenance.
Brooke, *Emily Montague*, III

We owe to ourselves a detestation of folly, and, to the world, the appearance of it.
Brown, W.H., *The Power of Sympathy*, 91

It is not the hood which makes the monk.   Brunt, *A Voyage to Cacklogallinia*, 162

What if my gold be wrapped up in ore? None throws away the apple for the core.
Bunyan, *Pilgrim's Progress*, 169

Let us be grateful to the mirror for revealing to us our appearance only.
Butler, *Erewhon*, III

The deception of dress is as silly and inconsistent as that of a merchant who would attempt to pass a bale of dowlass under the false package of cambric wrappers, whilst a principal part of the contents was left staringly open, in contradiction to the fraud.
Cleland, *Memoirs of a Coxcomb*, 199

What the eye does not see, the heart does not rue.   Collyer, *Felicia to Charlotte*, II

Men expect one to take into account their fine linen.   Conrad, *Lord Jim*, VIII

Systems may have a very fair appearance on paper and as theories, they are execrable in practice.   Cooper, *The Redskins*, IX

A man shows his parts in nothing more than in the choice of his clothes and equipage.
Coventry, *Pompey the Little*, 25-26

Every man that beholds a man in the face knows not what he hath in his purse.
Deloney, *The Gentle Craft*, 113

All things are not as they seem.   Deloney, *Jack of Newbury*, 318

You don't carry in your countenance a letter of recommendation.
Dickens, *Barnaby Rudge*, II

Seeming may be false or true.   Dickens, *The Mystery of Edwin Drood*, XXIII

Mr. Squeers had but one eye, and the popular prejudice runs in favor of two.
Dickens, *Nicholas Nickleby*, IV

Whisper nothings that sound like something.   Disraeli, *Sybil*, Book IV, XII

A face like an underwriter in a tempest.   Doyle, *Micah Clarke*, XXXV

Nature never makes a ferret in the shape of a mastiff. You'll never persuade me that I can't tell what men are by their outsides. If I don't like a man's looks, depend upon it I shall never like *him*.   Eliot, *Adam Bede*, V

Appearances have very little to do with happiness.
Eliot, *Middlemarch*, Book VII, LXIV

Nothing is so good as it seems beforehand.   Eliot, *Silas Marner*, XVIII

If you wear but the appearance of a gentleman among the French, they never suspect you are not one.   Fielding, H., *Amelia*, I

A good face is a letter of recommendation. O Nature, Nature! Why art thou so dishonest as ever to send men with these false recommendations into the world? *Ibid.*, II

The doctor had one positive recommendation—this was a great appearance of religion.
Fielding, *Tom Jones*, 27

It is not enough that your designs, nay that your actions, are intrinsically good; you must take care they shall appear so. *Ibid.*, 97

A good countenance is a letter of recommendation. *Ibid.*, 377

I can jest without joy, and laugh without lust. Gascoigne, *Master F. J.*, 23

To give out appearances which bear a strong resemblance to vice is next to the actual commission of it. Gentleman, *A Trip to the Moon*, II

The most promising appearances may end in the foulest disgrace.
Godwin, *Caleb Williams*, II

Superior finery ever seems to confer superior breeding.
Goldsmith, *The Vicar of Wakefield*, 41

There is far more of the picturesque, more truth to native and characteristic tendencies, and vastly greater suggestiveness, in the back view of a residence, whether in town or country, than in its front. Hawthorne, *The Blithedale Romance*, XVII

She would rather have perished than have looked dressed in her Sunday best.
James, H., *The Spoils of Poynton*, I

There is no truth to be given to appearances. Kimber, *David Ranger*, I

What is person in a man? Lennox, *Henrietta*, I

Do we not commonly see that in painted pots is hidden the deadliest poison? that in the greenest grass is the greatest serpent? in the clearest water the ugliest toad?
Lyly, *Euphues*, 110

Be careful not always to impute knowledge to the appearance of acuteness, or give credit to opinions according to the confidence with which they are urged.
Mackenzie, *The Man of the World*, I

Worthiness and good taches and good deeds are not only in arrayment, but manhood and worship are hid within man's person, and many a worshipful knight is not known unto all people, and therefore worship and hardiness are not in arrayment.
Malory, *Le Morte D'Arthur*, One, II

Charity is one thing, and truth is another. Looks are one thing, and facts are another.
Melville, *Confidence-Man*, III

Negro minstrels are apt to overdo the ebony; exemplifying the old saying, not more just than charitable, that "the devil is never so black as he is painted." *Ibid.*, VI

When any creature is by its make inimical to other creatures, nature in effect labels that creature, much as an apothecary does a poison. So that whoever is destroyed by a rattlesnake, or other harmful agent, it is his own fault. He should have respected the label. *Ibid.*, XXXVI

Things visible are but conceits of the eye: things imaginative, conceits of the fancy. If duped by one, we are equally duped by the other. Melville, *Mardi*, XCIII

Appearances all the world over are deceptive. Little men are sometimes very potent, and rags sometimes cover very extensive pretensions. Melville, *Typee*, XXIV

We must not depend too much on the smooth, well-timed speeches of a man of fashion.
Moore, *Grasville Abbey*, I

No artificial resources can give brilliancy to the eyes, or health and vivacity to the figure; acquired bloom can never deceive. Parsons, *Castle of Wolfenbach*, I

Candor and good nature will give beauty to the most indifferent faces, whilst envy and malice will render the most beautiful persons truly contemptible. *Ibid.*, II

I used to think the world would grow old along with me, but I believe it's younger than ever. But it's no such thing—it's only paint and varnish; the older it grows, the thicker they lay it on. Wash that off, and what is there but a withered, wrinkled old hag?
Payson, *Golden Dreams*, I

A silly soul, to neglect to cultivate the opinions of individuals, when the whole world is governed by appearance!
Richardson, *Clarissa Harlowe*, III

Always mistrust most when appearances look fairest.
Richardson, *Pamela*, 208

Turn the best side of the garment outward.
Richardson, *Sir Charles Grandison*, Two, IV

The sun, like a noble hart, began to show his greatest countenance in his lowest estate.
Sidney, *Arcadia*, I

In French, grandeur is more in the word and less in the thing.
Sterne, *A Sentimental Journey*, 53

Have people an honest right to keep up appearances?
Thackeray, *Philip*, IV

Even mourning might be made becoming if no expense be spared.
Trollope, *Ayala's Angel*, V

His hair is lank and of a dull pale reddish hue. His face is nearly of the same color as his hair, though perhaps a little redder: it is not unlike beef—beef, however, one would say, of a bad quality.
Trollope, *Barchester Towers*, IV

She well knew the great architectural secret of decorating her constructions and never descended to construct a decoration.
Ibid., IX

Your behavior is above your seeming.
Walpole, *The Castle of Otranto*, 30

It is only shallow people who do not judge by appearances. The true mystery of the world is the visible, not the invisible.
Wilde, *The Picture of Dorian Gray*, II

There is hardly a single person in the House of Commons worth painting, though many of them would be the better for a little whitewashing.
Ibid., VI

APPETITE: *see also* DESIRE

Appetite furnishes the best sauce.
Melville, *Typee*, VII

A young sinner's amusements will resemble those of a confirmed debauchee. The satiated, and the insatiate, appetite alike appeal to extremes.
Meredith, *Ordeal of Richard Feverel*, XX

Mankind has some instinctive disgust for the victims of their appetites. We pity any other functional derangement than that.
Ibid., XXIX

The overloaded appetite loathes even the honeycomb.
Scott, *The Talisman*, XXII

How finely some people can hang up quarrels—or pop them into a drawer—as they do their work, when dinner is announced, and take them out again at a convenient season!
Thackeray, *Lovel the Widower*, IV

The wild desire to live, most terrible of all men's appetites.
Wilde, *The Picture of Dorian Gray*, XVI

APPROBATION, APPRECIATON: *see also* ENCOURAGEMENT

High appreciation and intimate acquaintance are generally in inverse ratios.
Evans, *St. Elmo*, XV

There is no pleasure more congenial to the human heart than the approbation and affection of our fellows.
Godwin, *St. Leon*, 282

Encouragement and approbation make people show talents they never suspected to have.
Richardson, *Clarissa Harlowe*, I

They take upon them to approve of your actions, by which is implied a right to disapprove if they think fit. *Ibid.*, II

I never approve or disapprove. It is an absurd attitude to take towards life.
Wilde, *The Picture of Dorian Gray*, VI

ARCHITECTURE: *see also* ART; FORM AND FUNCTION; etc.

"We didn't find that London come up to its likeness in the red bills at the shop doors; which I meantersay," added Joe, in an explanatory manner, "as it is there drawd too architectooralooral." Dickens, *Great Expectations*, XXVII

Sculpture is a kind of architecture. Stevenson, *The Wrecker*, III

ARGUMENTATION: *see also* EXPRESSION; PREACHMENT; etc.

There are only a certain number of arguments in any brain, and after they have been reiterated a sufficient number of times they pall.
Atherton, *Senator North*, Book III, XIX

Arguments are too much like disputes. Austen, *Pride and Prejudice*, Volume I, X

A thought suggested is sometimes more than an argument.
Brackenridge, *Modern Chivalry*, Part II, Volume I

In an argument, value more the judgment of selection than the labor of collecting.
Ibid.

Force is to be resisted by force, or eluded by flight: but he that argues, whatever be his motives, should be encountered with argument. Brown, C.B., *Alcuin*, III

Argeyment is a gift of Natur. If Natur has gifted a man with powers of argeyment, a man has a right to make the best of 'em, and has not a right to stand on false delicacy, and deny that he is so gifted; for that is a turning of his back on Natur, a flouting of her, a slighting of her precious caskets, and a proving of oneself to be a swine that isn't worth her scattering pearls before. Dickens, *Barnaby Rudge*, I

"Not to put too fine a point upon it—" —a favorite apology for plain-speaking with Mr. Snagsby, which he always offers with a sort of argumentative frankness.
Dickens, *Bleak House*, XI

Abuse is not argument. Disraeli, *Sybil*, Book III, II

One hears very sensible things said on opposite sides. Eliot, *Middlemarch*, Book I, III

Arguments are never wanting, when a man has no constancy of mind.
Ibid., Book II, XVII

When you get me a good man made out of arguments, I will get you a good dinner with reading you the cookery-book. *Ibid.*

Arguments among men are like bones among dogs; serve to set them together by the ears. Ergo, an argument is called a bone of contention.
Fielding, H., *Jonathan Wild*, 114

In all disputes, especially about trifles, that party who is most convinced they are right shall always surrender the victory. Fielding, H., *Joseph Andrews*, 273

The persons who maintain the worst side in any contest are the warmest. *Ibid.*, 274

If he could not get the better of him by his arguments, he would put him out of countenance by his impudence. Fielding, S., *David Simple*, II

He ran through all the arguments he could think of, to prove that pleasure is pleasure, and that it is better to be pleased than displeased. He talked of Epicurus's saying, "Pleasure is the chief good," from which he very wisely concluded that vice is the greatest pleasure. *Ibid.*

Argument is powerless against bias or prejudice. Hardy, *Pair of Blue Eyes*, X

ARGUMENTATION (*continued*)

Of all things in the world contention was most sweet to her.

James, H., *The Bostonians*, II

No argument like matter of fact is.

Kimber, *David Ranger*, I

To persuade or dissuade, you must interest the head or the heart.

Lawrence, *Guy Livingstone*, VII

Never think that any narrative, which is not confuted by its own absurdity, is without one argument at least on its side.

Lennox, *The Female Quixote*, II

Do we never take up the wrong side of an argument, merely to enliven the conversation?

Marishall, *Miss Clarinda Cathcart*, II

We think so well of our own arguments that we very seldom are so happy as to convince one another. A pretty common case in all vehement debatings.

Richardson, *Clarissa Harlowe*, I

Poor arguments will do when brought in favor of what we like.

Ibid., II

Like stones, hard arguments knock down a pertinacious opponent.

Ibid., IV

People who cannot answer will rave.

Ibid.

The *argumentum ad hominem*, the last to which a polite man has recourse, may be justified by circumstances, but seldom or never the *argumentum ad faeminam*.

Scott, *Redgauntlet*, Letter XII

Jests are no arguments.

Ibid., XIV

The Scotch are more remarkable for their exercise of their intellectual powers, than for the keenness of their feelings; they are, therefore, more moved by logic than by rhetoric, and more attracted by acute and argumentative reasoning on doctrinal points, than influenced by the enthusiastic appeals to the heart and to the passions.

Scott, *Rob Roy*, XX

It is so easy to follow a line of argument, and so difficult to grasp the facts that underlie it!

Shaw, *Cashel Byron's Profession*, IV

Heatedness in debate is in proportion to the want of true knowledge.

Sterne, *Tristram Shandy*, IV

How finely we argue upon mistaken facts!

Ibid.

Argument is a great emboldener.

Stevenson, *Treasure Island*, IV

It is only the intellectually lost who ever argue.

Wilde, *The Picture of Dorian Gray*, I

ARISTOCRACY: *see also* GOVERNMENT, etc.

"What do you call it, when Lords break off door-knockers and beat policemen, and play at coaches with other people's money, and all that sort of thing?" "Aristocratic?" "Ah! aristocratic; something very aristocratic about him, isn't there?"

Dickens, *Nicholas Nickleby*, XV

The superiority of the animal man is an essential quality of aristocracy.

Disraeli, *Sybil*, Book II, XI

The old gentleman pronounced these aristocratic names with the greatest gusto. Whenever he met a great man he grovelled before him, and my-lorded him as only a freeborn Briton can do. He fell down prostrate and basked in him as a Neapolitan beggar does in the sun.

Thackeray, *Vanity Fair*, XIII

ART; ARTIST; ARTISTRY: *see also* AUTHORSHIP; CREATION; EXPRESSION; NATURE

An artist must be man, woman, and demigod.

Adams, *Esther*, IV

"Love of an art presupposes a certain degree of talent."—May Heaven forgive me for that lie, he thought.   Atherton, *The Californians*, Book I, XVI

Nature is above all art.   Brackenridge, *Modern Chivalry*, Part II, Volume II

The artist's faculty of making the most of present pleasure.   Bronte, C., *Villette*, VII

The artist must possess the courageous soul that dares and defies.
Chopin, *The Awakening*, XXXIX

There may be plenty that is painful in real life; but for that very reason, we don't want it in books.   Collins, *Armadale*, Book V, III

Art has its trials as well as its triumphs. It is powerless to assert itself against the sordid interests of everyday life.   Collins, *The Black Robe*, Book I, IV

The greatest book ever written, the finest picture ever painted, appeals in vain to minds preoccupied by selfish and secret cares.   *Ibid.*

In the affairs of art, as in other matters, important discoveries are sometimes made, and great events occasionally accomplished, by very ignoble agencies.
Collins, *Hide-and-Seek*, Book II, V

What has art to do with truth? Is not truth the imagination's deadly enemy? If the two meet, they must fight to the death.   Crawford, *A Rose of Yesterday*, XIII

An honest man is one of the few great works that can be seen for nothing.
Dickens, *Martin Chuzzlewit*, XII

She'll vish there wos more [from you in your letter], and that's the great art o' letter writin'.   Dickens, *Pickwick Papers*, XXXIII

Among the heirs of Art, as at the division of the promised land, each has to win his portion by hard fighting: the bestowal is after the manner of prophecy, and is a title without possession.   Eliot, *Daniel Deronda*, Book III, XXIII

There is a great deal in the feeling for art which must be acquired.
Eliot, *Middlemarch*, Book II, XXI

Art is an old language with a great many artificial affected styles.   *Ibid.*

Perfect art always obscures the difficulties it overcomes.
Gaskell, *Wives and Daughters*—concluding remarks, not by author, who had died.

"Don't you think that, even today, really good work will sooner or later be recognized?" "Later, rather than sooner."   Gissing, *New Grub Street*, III

What true votary of art would not purchase unrivalled excellence, even at a sacrifice?
Hawthorne, *The Marble Faun*, IV

The customs of artist life bestow such liberty upon the female sex, which is elsewhere restricted within so much narrower limits.   *Ibid.*, VI

She ceased to aim at original achievement in consequence of the very gifts which fitted her to [copy] the works of the old masters.   *Ibid.*

Sculptors are, of necessity, the greatest plagiarists in the world.   *Ibid.*, XIV

If anywise interested in art, a man must be difficult to please who cannot find fit companionship among a crowd of persons, whose ideas and pursuits all tend towards the general purpose of enlarging the world's stock of beautiful productions.   *Ibid.*, XV

Success in art is apt to become partly an affair of intrigue.   *Ibid.*

Artists are lifted by the ideality of their pursuits a little way off the earth, and are therefore able to catch the evanescent fragrance that floats in the atmosphere of life above the heads of the ordinary crowd.   *Ibid.*, XVII

A picture, however admirable the painter's art, and wonderful his power, requires of the spectator a surrender of himself; in due proportion with the miracle which has been wrought.   *Ibid.*, XXXVII

He could hardly be reckoned a consummate artist, because there was something dearer
to him than his art. *Ibid.*, XLVI

Art is "Give 'em what they know, and when you've done it once do it again."
Kipling, *The Light That Failed*, IV

We cannot all be romantic about landscapes. Nature has worshippers enough not to
grudge a few to Art. Lawrence, *Guy Livingstone*, XXXII

The great art of fencing is knowing nothing about it. Marryat, *Peter Simple*, XX

Omnipotent is art. Melville, *Moby Dick*, VI

Art is her soul's husband. Meredith, *Vittoria*, XLV

When man ceased to capture women, man invented art whereby he might win them.
Moore, *Evelyn Innes*, VI

Women, having no necessity for art, have not been artists. *Ibid.*

All art is convention of one kind or another, and each demands its own interpretation.
Ibid., XVI

Painting is only dreaming. Moore, *Muslin*, I

Ancient sculpture is the true school of modesty. Peacock, *Crotchet Castle*, VII

We painters are no match for boors. We are glass, they are stones. We can't stand the
worry of little minds; and it is not for the good of mankind we should be exposed to it. It
is hard enough to design and paint a masterpiece, without having gnats and flies
stinging us to death in the bargain. Reade, *The Cloister and the Hearth*, IX

The attribute of all true art, the highest and the lowest, is that it says more than it says,
and takes you away from itself. It is a little door that opens into an infinite hall where
you may find what you please. Schreiner, *The Story of an African Farm*, Part II, II

Beauty of external form, the other half of art. *Ibid.*, Part II, II

Hath not Art the means of completing Nature's imperfect concoctions in her attempts to
form the precious metals, even as by art we can perfect those other operations, of
incubation, distillation, fermentation, and similar processes of an ordinary description,
by which we extract life itself out of a senseless egg, summon purity and vitality out of
muddy dregs, or call into vivacity the inert substance of a sluggish liquid?
Scott, *Kenilworth*, XVIII

Photography is not an art. It is a process. Shaw, *An Unsocial Socialist*, XII

The limit to human art has not yet been found. Simms, *The Scout*, XXVII

The eyes of the artist are turned in. He lives for a frame of mind.
Stevenson, *The Wrecker*, IV

To an artist, let his art be everything—above wife and children, above money, above
health, above even character. Trollope, *Ayala's Angel*, IV

Every portrait that is painted with feeling is a portrait of the artist, not of the sitter.
Wilde, *The Picture of Dorian Gray*, I

There is nothing that art cannot express. *Ibid.*

An artist should create beautiful things, but should put nothing of his own life into
them. We live in an age when men treat art as if it were meant to be a form of
autobiography. *Ibid.*

Art should be unconscious, ideal, and remote. *Ibid.*, IX

It is a mistake to think that the passion one feels in creation is ever really shown in the
work one creates. Art is always more abstract than we fancy. Form and color tell us of
form and color—that is all. *Ibid.*

Art conceals the artist far more completely than it ever reveals him. *Ibid.*

There is something fatal about a portrait. It has a life of its own. *Ibid.*

Art is a malady. *Ibid.*, XVII

His work was that curious mixture of bad painting and good intentions that always entitles a man to be called a representative British artist. *Ibid.*, XIX

If a man treats life artistically, his brain is his heart. *Ibid.*

Art has a soul, but man has not. *Ibid.*

Life has been your art. You have set yourself to music. Your days are your sonnets.
Ibid.

ASPIRATION: *see also* AMBITION

The hand is only the rudest type of the universal necessity that pervades us to take hold. The body is furnished with two; the mind, the heart, the spirit—who shall number the invisible, the countless hands of these? Allen, J. L., *The Choir Invisible*, VI

It is no imperfection in a dove to want the strength of an eagle.
Anonymous, *The Birmingham Counterfeit*, II

All of us make an occasional attempt to realize a dream.
Atherton, *Senator North*, Book II, VII

There is nothing makes a man so ridiculous as to attempt what is above his sphere.
Brackenridge, *Modern Chivalry*, Part I, Volume I

He that looks for a star puts out his candles.
Bulwer, *What Will He Do With It?*, Book VIII, III

The prettiest are always further. Carroll, *Through the Looking Glass*, V

When waters engulf us we reach for a star. Dreiser, *Sister Carrie*, XXVII

Man has not yet comprehended the dreamer any more than he has the ideal. For him the laws and morals of the world are unduly severe. Ever hearkening to the sound of beauty, straining for the flash of its distant wings, he watches to follow, wearying his feet in travelling. *Ibid.*, XLVII

What we strive to gratify, though we may call it a distant hope, is an immediate desire: the future estate for which men drudge up city alleys exists already in their imagination and love. Eliot, *Middlemarch*, Book IV, XLII

Ardent souls, ready to construct their coming lives, are apt to commit themselves to the fulfillment of their own visions. *Ibid.*, Book VI, LV

Life never seems so clear and easy as when the heart is beating faster at the sight of some generous self-risking deed. We feel no doubt then what is the highest prize the soul can win; we almost believe in our power to attain it. Eliot, *Romola*, Book III, LV

There is nothing that human imagination can figure brilliant and enviable that human genius and skill do not aspire to realize. Godwin, *St. Leon*, 1

The man who has many gratifications is apt to wander in imagination from daily and familiar joys, and confidently to reach after things yet untried. *Ibid.*, 262-263

So wholesome is effort! So miraculous the strength that we do not know of!
Hawthorne, *House of the Seven Gables*, III

A man of thought, fancy, and sensibility may, at any time, be a man of affairs if he will only choose to give himself the trouble. Hawthorne, *The Scarlet Letter*, Introductory

Fishes have the water assigned to them, yet beasts can swim by nature and men by art. He that can swim needs not despair to fly; to swim is to fly in a grosser fluid, and to fly is to swim in a subtler. Johnson, *Rasselas*, 32

ASPIRATION (*continued*)

Nothing will ever be attempted, if all possible objections must be first overcome.
Ibid., 34

Fire cannot be forced downward. Lyly, *Euphues*, 99

He that desireth riches must stretch the string that will not reach, and practice all kinds of getting. Lyly, *Euphues and His England*, 338

He that attempts the impossible will often achieve the extremely difficult.
Mackenzie, *The Man of the World*, I

If eagles gaze at the sun, may not men at the gods? Melville, *Mardi*, CXXXV

To scale great heights, we must come out of lowermost depths. *Ibid.*, CLXXX

The way to heaven is through hell. *Ibid.*

Life only becomes wrong when it ceases to aspire. Moore, *Evelyn Innes*, XXV

Architas made a wooden dove to fly, by which proportion I see no reason that the veriest block in the world should despair of nothing. Nashe, *The Unfortunate Traveller*, 44

We should not aim at all we have power to do. Richardson, *Clarissa Harlowe*, I

Who shoots at the mid-day sun, though he be sure he shall never hit the mark, yet as sure he is he shall shoot higher than who aims but at a bush. Sidney, *Arcadia*, II

Would ye shoot at the moon with a handgun? Stevenson, *The Black Arrow*, Book I, II

ASSOCIATION

There are people from whom we secretly shrink, whom we would personally avoid, though reason confesses that they are good people: there are others with faults of temper, etc., evident enough, beside whom we live content, as if the air about them did us good.
Bronte, C., *Villette*, XVII

The tie that binds the happy may be dear; but that which links the unfortunate is tenderness unutterable. Mackenzie, *Julia De Roubigné*, 109–110

There is no tax so heavy on a little man as an acquaintance with a great one.
Mackenzie, *The Man of the World*, I

It is not for the lamb to live with the wolf. Nashe, *The Unfortunate Traveller*, 39

Though you have kept company with a wolf, you have not learnt to howl of him.
Richardson, *Clarissa Harlowe*, II

Keep good men company, and you shall be of their number. *Ibid.*

Love me, love my dog. *Ibid.*

An honest heart is not always to be trusted with itself in bad company.
Richardson, *Pamela*, 153

Beauty and the Beast is a frequent alliance. Simms, *The Scout*, XXXII

ASYLUM

A nunnery, that comfortable asylum for old maids, woe-begone widows, and lovelorn damsels. Anonymous, *The Modern Fine Gentleman*, II

ATHEISM: *see also* RELIGION, etc.

I will drink no wine with an atheist. I should expect the devil to make a third in such company; for, since he knows you are his, he may be impatient to have his due.
Fielding, H., *Jonathan Wild*, 246

ATONEMENT: *see* REPENTANCE

ATTEMPT: *see also* AMBITION; ASPIRATION; etc.

Shall we never make an attempt, because we do not always succeed?
August, *Horrid Mysteries*, I

Few things are impossible to diligence and skill. Johnson, *Rasselas*, 61

ATTRACTION; ATTRACTIVENESS: *see also* BEAUTY

Warmth and tenderness of heart, with an affectionate, open manner, will beat all the clearness of head in the world, for attraction. Austen, *Emma*, XXXI

It's always a mystery what people see in each other. Howells, *Silas Lapham*, XII

Inlanders all, they come from lanes and alleys, streets and avenues—north, east, south, and west. Yet here they all unite. Tell me, does the magnetic virtue of the needles of the compasses of all those ships attract them thither? Melville, *Moby Dick*, I

Were Niagara but a cataract of sand, would you travel your thousand miles to see it?
Ibid.

The qualities which are the most attractive before dinner sometimes become the least so in the evening. Trollope, *Phineas Finn*, LXXII

AUDIENCE

As thoughts are frozen and utterance benumbed unless the speaker stand in some true relation with his audience, it may be pardonable to imagine that a friend, a kind and apprehensive, though not the closest friend, is listening to our talk; and then, a native reserve being thawed by this genial consciousness, we may prate of the circumstances that lie around us, and even of ourselves, but still keep the inmost Me behind its veil.
Hawthorne, *The Scarlet Letter*, Introductory

Was there ever an audience anywhere, though there wasn't a pair of eyes in it brighter than pickled oysters, that didn't think it was distinguished for intelligence?
Holmes, *Elsie Venner*, III

AUTHORITY: *see also* LAW

There is something elevating in the possession of authority, however it may be abused.
Cooper, *The Prairie*, XXXI

Authority is a [mere] phrase. Disraeli, *Coningsby*, Book I, I

Turn me a prey to the wild beasts, so I be never again the victim of man dressed in the gore-dripping robes of authority. Godwin, *Caleb Williams*, III

A dictionary is nothing without an authority. Peacock, *Gryll Grange*, XXIX

Lingering reason still strives at authority even in the head of the insane man.
Simms, *The Partisan*, Volume II, X

To be vested with enormous authority is a fine thing; but to have the onlooking world consent to it is a finer. Twain, *A Connecticut Yankee*, VIII

AUTHORSHIP: *see also* ART; EXPRESSION; FICTION; NARRATIVE; POETRY; etc.

The ideas of authorship and poverty are so immediately connected, that after a man has once read Locke, and understood him, they are ever after looked upon as a part of the same complex idea of mixed modes. Anonymous, *The Adventures of an Author*, I

Though it frequently happens among the brethren of the quill that many are starved into writing, it will be found upon examination that full as many are starved out of it.
Ibid.

33

I would not have it believed, that every man who may accidentally be seen writing in public, in a shabby coat, a dirty shirt, and a fluxed periwig, is absolutely and bona fide an author by profession. *Ibid.*

Hackney attorneys clerks, news collectors, and penny-post men are very frequently mistaken for men of letters, for no other reason than because they write in public, and look like pickpockets. *Ibid.*

The poverty of writers is a greater stigma upon the public than it is upon themselves. *Ibid.*

The whole tribe of scribblers are the most unnecessary animals in the whole commonwealth. Anonymous, *The Adventures of Oxymel Classic*, II

Talk about literary merit to a bookseller, and he will think you distracted. Anonymous, *The Egg*, 27

Authors are as jealous of their prerogative as kings, and can no more bear a rival in the empire of wit than a monarch could in his dominions. Anonymous, *The Ladies Advocate*, 61

Were I king, I would hinder all females from scribbling any books. Anonymous, *The Temple-beau*, 121

Novelists should never allow themselves to weary of the study of real life. Bronte, C., *The Professor*, XIX

The pen is a pacifier. It checks the mind's career; it circumscribes her wanderings. It traces out, and compels us to adhere to one path. Brown, C.B., *Arthur Mervyn*, II

It is not study alone that produces a writer; it is intensity. Bulwer, *The Caxtons*, Book III, V

It is one thing to write and another to publish. *Ibid.*, Book IV, III

Authors in all ages address themselves to what interests their readers; the same things do not interest a vast community which interested half a score of monks or bookworms. *Ibid.*, Book VII, I

I wish only for such readers as give themselves heart and soul up to me. Bulwer, *The Pilgrims of the Rhine*, II

A lady should never degrade herself by being put on a level with writers, and such sort of people. Burney, *Cecilia*, I

The assailants of the quill have their honor as much at heart as the assailants of the sword. *Ibid.*, III

His *Meditations upon the Epistle and Character of St. Jude* was so exhaustive that no one who bought it need ever meditate upon the subject again—indeed it exhausted all who had anything to do with it. Butler, *The Way of All Flesh*, XXVII

Editors are like the people who bought and sold in the book of Revelation; there is not one but has the mark of the beast upon him. *Ibid.*, LXXXI

Writing for reviews or newspapers is bad training for one who may aspire to write works of more permanent interest. *Ibid.*

What opinion can any sane man form about his own work? *Ibid.*, LXXXVI

I wonder whether the gentlemen who make a business and living out of writing books ever find their own selves getting in the way of their subjects like me? Collins, *The Moonstone*, First Period, II

Chroniclers are privileged to enter where they list, to come and go through keyholes, to ride upon the wind, to overcome, in their soarings up and down, all obstacles of distance, time, and place. Dickens, *Barnaby Rudge*, IX

An author passes in review at the tribunal of criticism, as a pickpocket stands a scrutiny from the constituents of the civil power.   Donaldson, *Sir Bartholomew Sapskull*, II

It becomes an author generally to divide a book, as it does a butcher to joint his meat, for such assistance is of great help to both the reader and the carver.
Fielding, H., *Joseph Andrews*, 75

Pity an author who is present at the murder of his works.   *Ibid.*, 221

The excellence of the mental entertainment consists less in the subject than in the author's skill in well dressing it up.   Fielding, H., *Tom Jones*, 2-3

No author ought to write anything besides dictionaries and spelling-books who hath not the privilege to be admitted behind the scenes of the great theatre of Nature.   *Ibid.*, 267

An author will write the better for having some knowledge of the subject on which he writes.   *Ibid.*, 648

To write—is not that the joy and the privilege of one who has an urgent message for the world?   Gissing, *New Grub Street*, VIII

Corrected into illegibility.   *Ibid.*, IX

He kept as much as possible to dialogue; the space is filled so much more quickly, and at a pinch one can make people talk about the paltriest incidents of life.   *Ibid.*

Whatever a man writes for effect is wrong and bad.   *Ibid.*, X

The regular resource of people who don't go enough into the world to live a novel is to write one.   Hardy, *A Pair of Blue Eyes*, XII

It is only those who half know a thing that write about it.   *Ibid.*, XIII

It is a heavy annoyance to a writer, who endeavors to represent nature, its various attitudes and circumstances, in a reasonably correct outline and true coloring, that so much of the mean and ludicrous should be hopelessly mixed up with the purest pathos which life anywhere supplies to him.   Hawthorne, *The House of the Seven Gables*, II

There is infinite pathos in unsuccessful authorship. The book that perishes unread is the deaf mute of literature. The great asylum of Oblivion is full of such, making inaudible signs to each other in leaky garrets and unattainable dusty upper shelves.
Holmes, *The Guardian Angel*, XXIV

Who would be at the pains of writing, if it were not for the hope of making his name immortal?   Johnstone, *The Pilgrim*, I

Judicious writers consult the humor of the times.   Kidgell, *The Card*, I

Authorship is a mania, to conquer which no reasons are sufficiently strong. As easily persuade not to love as not to write.   Lewis, *The Monk*, 157

The fight of all fights is to write.   Melville, *Mardi*, CLXXX

It is necessary that authors should be poor: first, because overeating spoils wit and conceit; and secondly, because none but poor dogs will ever be at the pains of writing at such a rate.   Ridley, *James Lovegrove*, II

The novelist cannot do always as he would with his own creations.
Simms, *Vasconselos*, XXXI

The novelist may create, but he cannot control. It is upon this very condition that he is permitted to create.   *Ibid.*

Writers had need look before them, to keep up the spirit and connection of what they have in mind.   Sterne, *Tristram Shandy*, II

The life of a writer is not so much a state of composition, as a state of warfare.   *Ibid.*, V

Let biographers, novelists, and the rest of us groan as we may under the burdens which we so often feel too heavy for our shoulders; we must either bear them up like men, or own ourselves too weak for the work we have undertaken.
Trollope, *Barchester Towers*, XX

AUTHORSHIP (*continued*)

There is no way of writing well and also of writing easily. *Ibid.*

Is it not singular how some men continue to obtain the reputation of popular authorship without adding a word to the literature of their country worthy of note?
Trollope, *The Way We Live Now*, I

The one most essential obstacle to the chance of success was probably Lady Carbury's conviction that her end was to be obtained not by producing good books, but by inducing certain people to say that her books were good. *Ibid.*, II

She warn't particular, she could write about anything you choose to give her to write about, just so it was sadful. Twain, *Huckleberry Finn*, XVII

If I'd a knowed what a trouble it was to make a book I wouldn't a tackled it and ain't agoing to no more. *Ibid.*, Last Chapter

There are three infallible ways of pleasing an author, and the three form a rising scale of compliment: 1, to tell him you have read one of his books; 2, to tell him you have read all of his books; 3, to ask him to let you read the manuscript of his forthcoming book. No. 1 admits you to his respect; No. 2 admits you to his admiration; No. 3 carries you clear into his heart. Twain, *Pudd'nhead Wilson*, XI

Poets know how useful passion is for publication. A broken heart will run to many editions. Wilde, *The Picture of Dorian Gray*, I

AVARICE: *see also* SELFISHNESS

Ambition in the worst of princes never did half the mischief to mankind as the avarice of private men. Anonymous, *The Lady's Drawing Room*, 195

Ancient lovers had only dragons to combat; ours have the worse monsters of avarice and ambition. Brooke, *Emily Montague*, IV

Avarice, with all its black attendants, is confessedly a crime of old age, and seldom arrives at maturity till accompanied with grey hairs. Collyer, *Felicia to Charlotte*, I

The busy devil that drew me in had too fast hold of me to let me go back; but as poverty brought me in, so avarice kept me in. Defoe, *Moll Flanders*, 208

Avarice is an uniform and tractable vice. Johnson, *Rasselas*, 146

Avarice is rarely the vice of youth. Lee, *The Recess*, I

Avarice and envy are two passions that are not to be satisfied the one by giving, the other by the envied person's continuing to deserve and excel.
Richardson, *Clarissa Harlowe*, I

AVOIDANCE

It is singular how long a time often passes before words embody things; and with what security two persons, who choose to avoid a certain subject, may approach its very verge, and retire without disturbing it. Hawthorne, *The Scarlet Letter*, XX

AWE; WONDER

There's wonders in the deep. Dickens, *Dombey and Son*, XLIX

Like the wonder a man feels at the added power he finds in himself for an art which he had laid aside for a space. Eliot, *Adam Bede*, LI

One cannot find tongue upon the threshold of the holy of holies.
Gissing, *A Life's Morning*, III

Until a person has thought out the stars and their interspaces, he has hardly learnt that there are things much more terrible than monsters of shape, namely, monsters of magnitude without known shape. Such monsters are the voids and waste places of the sky. Hardy, *Two on a Tower*, IV

There is a size at which dignity begins; further on there is a size at which grandeur begins; further on there is a size at which solemnity begins; further on, a size at which awfulness begins; further on, a size at which ghastliness begins. That size faintly approaches the size of the stellar universe. *Ibid.*

The vastness of the field of astronomy reduces every terrestrial thing to atomic dimensions. *Ibid.*, XXXIV

Let us cease wondering, and become wonder-workers. Judd, *Margaret*, Volume III

With marvels we are glutted, till we hold them no marvels at all.
Melville, *Mardi*, CLXXV

Ahab's been used to deeper wonders than the waves; fixed his fiery lance in mightier, stranger foes than whales. Melville, *Moby Dick*, XVI

Wonderfullest things are ever the unmentionable; deep memories yield no epitaphs; this six-inch chapter is the stoneless grave of Bulkington. *Ibid.*, XXIII

Terrors of the terrible! *Ibid.*

Alone, in such remotest waters, that though you sailed a thousand miles, and passed a thousand shores, you would not come to any chiselled hearthstone, or aught hospitable beneath that part of the sun; in such latitudes and longitudes, pursuing too such a calling as he does, the whaleman is wrapped by influences all tending to make his fancy pregnant with many a mighty birth. *Ibid.*, XLI

Whalemen are far more familiar with the wonders of the deep than any other class of seaman. Melville, *Redburn*, XXI

With the awe of one who has looked at heavenly things. Sheldon, *In His Steps*, XXXI

It was wonderful to find America, but it would have been more wonderful to miss it.
Twain, *Pudd'nhead Wilson*, Conclusion

AWKWARDNESS

What you take for the White Whale's malice is only his awkwardness.
Melville, *Moby Dick*, C

BALANCE: *see also* AMBIVALENCE; EQUALITY; etc.

With scrupulous exactness the good and bad are ever balanced. Burney, *Cecilia*, III

There is throughout this world a levelling principle, at war with pre-eminence, and destructive of perfection. *Ibid.*

We cannot calculate on any corresponding advance in man's intellectual or physical powers which shall be a set-off against the far greater development which seems in store for the machines. Some people may say that man's moral influence will suffice to rule them; but I cannot think it will ever be safe to repose much trust in the moral sense of any machine. Butler, *Erewhon*, XXIII

Some good and some bad goes to all callings. Dickens, *David Copperfield*, XXX

If man would help some of us a little more, God would forgive us all the sooner perhaps.
Dickens, *Dombey and Son*, XXXIII

A sense of ineffable joy, attainable at will, and equal in intensity and duration to, let us say, an attack of sciatica, would go far to equalize the sorrowful, onesided conditions under which we live. DuMaurier, *Peter Ibbetson*, Part Second

When a man turns a blessing from his door, it falls to them as take it in.
Eliot, *Silas Marner*, XIX

The equity of Providence has balanced peculiar sufferings with peculiar enjoyments.
Johnson, *Rasselas*, 20

Every vice is balanced by an opposite virtue.   Johnstone, *The Pilgrim*, II

There is no more dangerous error than this, of thinking that vice and virtue can be so far reconciled as to inhabit the same breast; or, that it is possible to compound for the obstinate, habitual transgression of one duty by the occasional performance of another.
Johnstone, *The Reverie*, I

Be merry but with modesty, be sober but not too solemn, be valiant but not too venturous.
Lyly, *Euphues*, 97

Let thy attire be comely, but not costly.   *Ibid.*

Amongst men, he that hath not a good wit, lightly hath a good iron memory, and he that hath neither of both, hath some bones to carry burthens.
Nashe, *The Unfortunate Traveller*, 45

Blind men have better noses than other men: the bull's horns serve him as well as hands to fight withal.   *Ibid.*

Consent on one side adds sometimes to obligation on the other.
Richardson, *Clarissa Harlowe*, II

Every nation have their refinements and grossnesses, in which they take the lead, and lose it of one another by turns.   Sterne, *A Sentimental Journey*, 67

There is a balance of good and bad everywhere; and nothing but the knowing it is so can emancipate one-half of the world from the prepossession which it holds against the other.   *Ibid.*

BARGAIN

When men drive a bargain, they strive to get the sunny side of it; it matters not one straw whether it is with man or Heaven they are bargaining.
Reade, *The Cloister and the Hearth*, XXXV

BASENESS: *see also* GOOD AND EVIL; GUILT; INNOCENCE; etc.

Who is so base as the debtor who thinks himself free?   Eliot, *Romola*, Book II, XL

BEAUTY; FAIRNESS; PLAINNESS; UGLINESS

I know of nothing useful in life except what is beautiful or creates beauty.
Adams, *Esther*, IV

Aurora, in the shape of a cherry-cheeked lass.
Anonymous, *The Adventures of Jack Wander*, 31

It is almost impossible to withstand two enemies at once, such as wine within and beauty without.   Anonymous, *The Adventures of Oxymel Classic*, I

A person who admires beauty must be inconstant, for he will admire it wherever he meets with it; consequently, his mistress can only share that admiration with others.
Anonymous, *Fatal Friendship*, I

The beauty of holiness.   Anonymous, *The Fruitless Repentance*, I

If dress is not beauty, it is frequently much more than beauty.
Anonymous, *Genuine Memoirs of Maria Brown*, II

The love of beauty is the loss of reason.
Anonymous, *The History of Tom Jones in His Married State*, 214

Beauty is apt to depend too much on itself.   Anonymous, *The Lady's Drawing Room*, 2

True beauty is seated in the mind. *Ibid.*, 139

Beauties may be allowed to call in the assistance of affection—but ugliness and affection will never go down. Anonymous, *Memoirs of a Coquet*, 70

Even in silence, beauty is eloquent beyond the power of words.
Anonymous, *Memoirs of the Court of H—*, 54

Superior beauty claims superior respect.
Anonymous, *Memoirs of an Oxford Scholar*, 75

There is a powerful charm in mourning beauty, which holds the generous heart almost entirely at its disposal. Anonymous, *The Wanderer*, I

All women are beautiful when they are young.
Atherton, *The Californians*, Book I, XVIII

If girls could only be made to understand that youth is always beautiful, they would be even prettier than they are. *Ibid.*

There is a beauty in every family. Austen, *Mansfield Park*, Volume Two, XI

To look *almost* pretty is an acquisition of higher delight to a girl who has been looking plain the first fifteen years of her life than a beauty from her cradle can ever receive.
Austen, *Northanger Abbey*, I

The worst of Bath was, the number of its plain women. There certainly were a dreadful multitude of ugly women in Bath; and as for the men! they were infinitely worse. Such scarecrows as the streets were full of! It was evident how little the women were used to the sight of anything tolerable, by the effect which a man of decent appearance produced.
Austen, *Persuasion*, XV

"When a woman has five grown up daughters, she ought to give over thinking of her own beauty." "In such cases, a woman has not often much beauty to think of."
Austen, *Pride and Prejudice*, Volume I, I

A woman never looks better than on horseback. Austen, *The Watsons*, II

Beauty is that quality which, next to money, is generally the most attractive to the worst kinds of men. Bronte, A., *The Tenant of Wildfell Hall*, XVI

There is no excellent beauty, no accomplished grace, no reliable refinement, without strength as excellent, as complete, as trustworthy. Bronte, C., *Villette*, XXVII

As well might you look for good fruit and blossom on a rootless and sapless tree as for charms that will endure in a feeble and relaxed nature. *Ibid.*

For a little while the blooming semblance of beauty may flourish round weakness; but it cannot bear a blast; it soon fades, even in severest sunshine. *Ibid.*

If beauty is given for the purpose of pleasing, she who pleases most is the most beautiful.
Brooke, *Emily Montague*, II

There is, in general, nothing so insipid, so uninteresting, as a beauty. *Ibid.*

There is an invisible charm, a nameless grace which depends not on beauty, and which strikes the heart in a moment. *Ibid.*

Of all those undescribable things which influence the mind, and which are most apt to persuade, none is so powerful an orator, so feelingly eloquent, as beauty.
Brown, W.H., *The Power of Sympathy*, 17

How amiable is that beauty which has its foundation in goodness! *Ibid.*

Does not beauty constrain our admiration? Bulwer, *Pompeii*, Book IV, III

In life, as in art, the beautiful moves in curves.
Bulwer, *What Will He Do With It?*, Book VII, XXI

We can neither get beauty when we haven't it; nor keep it when we have it.
Burney, *Camilla*, Two, IV

Glasses are the ruin of all beauty; no complexion can stand them.   Burney, *Cecilia*, I

Before objects of beauty, enthusiasm is simply the consequence of not being blind.
Burney, *Evelina*, 74

The magnetic power of beauty irresistibly draws and attracts whatever has soul and sympathy.   *Ibid.*, 100

Can anyone paint the living, breathing soul of a very young and beautiful female? No! If a man had the genius to do so, the very enthusiasm which always attends it would throw him into very unpainter-like raptures at the sight of such a one.
Caruthers, *The Kentuckian in New-York*, Volume I, V

Beauty unadorned is adorned the most.   Chesnutt, *The House Behind the Cedars*, XV

Why is beauty given us, unless it be like sunlight to bless and gladden the world?
Child, *Philothea*, II

Beauty is given to remind us that the soul should be kept as fair and perfect in its proportions as the temple in which it dwells.   *Ibid.*

The woman who first gives life, light, and form to our shadowy conceptions of beauty, fills a void in our spiritual nature that has remained unknown to us till she appeared.
Collins, *Woman in White*, Part I, First Epoch

The mystery which underlies the beauty of women is never raised above the reach of all expression until it has claimed kindred with the deeper mystery in our own souls.
Ibid.

Nothing in nature is there required to make a woman handsome but eyes.
Coventry, *Pompey the Little*, 37

I have the money and want the beauty; but as times go now, the first will do, so I have the better of my neighbors.   Defoe, *Moll Flanders*, 15

Guard against the mischiefs which attend an early knowledge of your own beauty.
Ibid., 18

If a young woman once thinks herself handsome, she never doubts the truth of any man that tells her he is in love with her.   *Ibid.*

Beauty's a portion, and good humor with it is a double portion.   *Ibid.*, 39

Cheerfulness and content are great beautifiers, and are famous preservers of youthful looks.   Dickens, *Barnaby Rudge*, Chapter the Last

Alas! How few of Nature's faces are left alone to gladden us with their beauty!
Dickens, *Oliver Twist*, XXIV

All beauty is sexless in the eyes of the artist at his work.   DuMaurier, *Trilby*, II

There are various orders of beauty, causing men to make fools of themselves in various styles, from the desperate to the sheepish; but there is one order of beauty which seems made to turn the heads not only of men, but of all intelligent mammals, even of women. It is a beauty like that of kittens, or very small downy ducks making gentle rippling noises with their soft bills, or babies just beginning to toddle and to engage in conscious mischief—a beauty with which you can never be angry, but that you feel ready to crush for inability to comprehend the state of mind into which it throws you.
Eliot, *Adam Bede*, VII

Human feeling is like the mighty rivers that bless the earth: it does not wait for beauty—it flows with resistless force and brings beauty with it.   *Ibid.*, XVII

All honor and reverence to the divine beauty of form! Let us cultivate it to the utmost in men, women, and children—in our gardens and in our houses. But let us love that other beauty too, which lies in no secret of proportion, but in the secret of deep human sympathy.   *Ibid.*

The beauty of a lovely woman is like music. *Ibid.*, XXXIII

That kind of beauty which seems to be thrown into relief by poor dress.
Eliot, *Middlemarch*, Book I, I

Plainness has its peculiar temptations and vices quite as much as beauty.
Ibid., Book I, XII

She didn't see why women were to be told with a simper that they were beautiful, any more than old men were to be told that they were venerable.
Eliot, *Mill on the Floss*, Book VI, II

Much beauty will go a long way with the judge and the jury. Fielding, H., *Amelia*, I

The vast power of exquisite beauty, which nothing almost can add to or diminish.
Ibid.

To withdraw admiration from exquisite beauty, or to feel no delight in gazing at it, is as impossible as to feel no warmth from the most scorching rays of the sun. *Ibid.*

She was so far from regretting want of beauty, that she never mentioned that perfection without contempt. Fielding, H., *Tom Jones*, 4

If thou hast seen things of beauty without knowing what beauty is, thou hast no eyes; if without feeling its power, thou hast no heart. *Ibid.*, 109

Smallpox, frequently the grave of beauty. Fielding, S., *Ophelia*, I

Fine girls are spoiled by foolish mothers, who are continually trumpeting beauty in their ears without taking any care of their principles and dispositions.
Gentleman, *A Trip to the Moon*, II

The beauty of false appearances. *Ibid.*

Beauty is like lightning, lovely but destructive. Haggard, *She*, XIII

Perhaps to a woman it is almost as dreadful to think of losing beauty as of losing reputation. Hardy, *A Pair of Blue Eyes*, XXVIII

It is a woman's duty to be as beautiful as she can. *Ibid.*

A sensible woman would rather lose her wits than her beauty. *Ibid.*

There never was a woman that stept handsomer in her shoes than Zenobia did.
Hawthorne, *The Blithedale Romance*, XXVII

Descriptions of beauty are never satisfactory. Hawthorne, *Fanshawe*, I

The beauty and glory of a great picture are confined within itself.
Hawthorne, *The Marble Faun*, VI

It is a woeful thing, a sad necessity, that any Christian soul should pass from earth without once seeing an antique painted window, with the bright Italian sunshine glowing through it. *Ibid.*, XXXIII

Her beauty shone out and made a halo of the misfortune and ignominy in which she was enveloped. Hawthorne, *The Scarlet Letter*, II

No man or woman can appropriate beauty without paying for it.
Holmes, *Elsie Venner*, VIII

How terrible is the one fact of beauty! . . . Paint Beauty with her foot upon a skull and a dragon coiled around her. Holmes, *A Mortal Antipathy*, XX

Really beautiful things can't go out. Howells, *Silas Lapham*, III

I should hate the day when a daughter of mine was married for her beauty. *Ibid.*, IX

She had once heard an enthusiastic musician, out of patience with a gifted bungler, declare that a fine voice is really an obstacle to singing properly; and it occurred to her that it might perhaps be equally true that a beautiful face is an obstacle to the acquisition of charming manners. James, H., *The American*, III

41

The most beautiful girl in the world can give but what she has.   *Ibid.*

We know a good many pretty girls, but magnificent women are not so common.   *Ibid.*

The power of beauty, when aided by compassion, is irresistible.   Johnstone, *Arsaces*, II

Beauty comes from Love.   Judd, *Margaret*, Volume II

Beauty is musical, music is beautiful.   *Ibid.*, Volume III

Beauty is Truth's usher, whereby it is introduced to the heart.   *Ibid.*

No truth is received till it puts on a beautiful aspect.   *Ibid.*

There is a beauty in the simplicity of nature which the most accomplished works of art can but faintly imitate.   Lawrence, *Common Sense*, II

If you would be embraced in the waning of your bravery, be not squeamish in the waxing of your beauty.   Lyly, *Euphues*, 111

Were all equal in beauty, there would be no beauty, for beauty is only by comparison.
Marryat, *Mr. Midshipman Easy*, XXXVI

In many natural objects, whiteness refiningly enhances beauty, as if imparting some special virtue of its own, as in marbles, japonicas, and pearls.
Melville, *Moby Dick*, XLII

Beauty made the first Queen.   Melville, *Pierre*, Book II, II

Where a beautiful woman is, there is all Asia and her Bazaars.   *Ibid.*, Book II, IV

With a wild exclamation of delight, she disengaged from her person the ample robe of tappa which was knotted over her shoulder, and spreading it out like a sail, stood erect with upraised arms in the head of the canoe. We American sailors pride ourselves upon our straight clean spars, but a prettier little mast than Fayaway made was never shipped aboard of any craft.   Melville, *Typee*, XVIII

People may say what they will about the taste evinced by our fashionable ladies in dress. Their jewels, their feathers, their silks, and their furbelows would have sunk into utter insignificance beside the exquisite simplicity of attire adopted by the nymphs of the vale on this festive occasion. I should like to have seen a gallery of coronation beauties, at Westminster Abbey, confronted for a moment by this band of Island girls; their stiffness, formality, and affectation contrasted with the artless vivacity and unconcealed natural graces of these savage maidens. It would be the Venus de' Medici placed beside a milliner's doll.   *Ibid.*, XXII

A fine head of hair is the pride and joy of every [Typee] woman's heart.   *Ibid.*, XXXI

Ugly is only halfway to a thing.   Meredith, *Amazing Marriage*, XIII

Jenny Denham: an amazingly pretty girl: beautiful thick brown hair, real hazel eyes, and walks like a yacht before the wind.   Meredith, *Beauchamp's Career*, XXIX

On which does the eye linger longest—which draws the heart? A radiant landscape, where the tall ripe wheat flashes between shadow and shine in the stately march of summer, or the peep into dewy woodland on to dark water?   *Ibid.*, XXXIV

The purer the beauty, the more it will be out of the world.   Meredith, *The Egoist*, VII

It is never too late for beauty to awaken love.
Meredith, *Ordeal of Richard Feverel*, XVI

Beauty does not speak bad grammar.   *Ibid.*, XXVI

There is a power in their troubled beauty women learn the use of, and what wonder? They have seen it kindle Ilium to flames so often!   *Ibid.*, XXXI

Beauty is for the hero.   *Ibid.*, XXXII

It is the dull, commonplace, man into whose slow brain Beauty drops like a celestial light, and burns lastingly. The poet, for instance, is a connoisseur of Beauty: to the artist she is a model.   *Ibid.*

Malice is the barb of beauty.   Meredith, *Sandra Belloni*, XLIII

Beauty and stupidity could not exist in the same face, stupidity being the ugliest thing on earth.   Moore, *Evelyn Innes*, VIII

He contended that two-thirds of human beauty were the illumination of matter by the intelligence, and but one-third proportion and delicacy of line.   *Ibid.*

True beauty lies only in the unattainable.   Moore, *Muslin*, XXI

Even to the most vulgar souls, there is something attractive in beauty.
                                                    Parsons, *The Mysterious Warning*, II

Beauty cannot co-exist with baldness; but it may and does co-exist with deceit.
                                                        Peacock, *Gryll Grange*, XXIX

Strange that things beautiful should be terrible and deadly.
                                            Reade, *The Cloister and the Hearth*, XX

Comeliness, having not so much to lose as beauty had, would hold, when that would evaporate or fly off.   Richardson, *Clarissa Harlowe*, I

Nothing can be either sweet or pretty that is not modest, that is not virtuous.   *Ibid.*

What need has the prettiest foot in the world of ornament?   *Ibid.*

Her features are all harmony, and made for one another.   *Ibid.*, II

Nothing can be lovely in a man's eye with which he is thoroughly displeased.   *Ibid.*

Ugliness made familiar to us will be beauty all the world over.   *Ibid.*, III

Everything is pretty that is young.   Richardson, *Pamela*, 47

There are sometimes beautiful colors in a weed.   *Ibid.*, 234

Give me the beauty that grows upon us every time we see it; that leaves room for something to be found out to its advantage.
                                            Richardson, *Sir Charles Grandison*, One, I

Beauty is an accidental and transient good.   *Ibid.*, Two, IV

Beauty is God's wine, with which he recompenses the souls that love him; he makes them drunk.   Schreiner, *The Story of an African Farm*, Part II, XIV

She was a queen, and therefore beautiful.   Sidney, *Arcadia*, I

Beasts only cannot discern beauty, and let them be in the roll of beasts that do not honor it.
                                                                                    Ibid.

It is the right nature of beauty to work unwitting effects of wonder.   *Ibid.*, III

Beauty is the crown of the feminine greatness.   *Ibid.*

As colors should be as good as nothing if there were no eyes to behold them, so is beauty nothing without the eye of love behold it.   *Ibid.*, III

Beauty maintains a glorious elasticity in its own ecstasies of hope, provided you do not crush it with a doubt of its own purity.   Simms, *Vasconselos*, XXIV

Beauty which, whether sleeping or awake, shot forth familiar graces.
                                                        Smollett, *Roderick Random*, 463

All old women were beauties once.   Thackeray, *Vanity Fair*, X

It is quite edifying to hear women speculate upon the worthlessness and the duration of beauty.   *Ibid.*, XII

The tastes of men and women about beauty are never the same.
                                                            Trollope, *Phineas Finn*, LIV

Is there a beauty in the knowledge of evil, a beauty that shines out in the face of a person whose inward life is transformed by some terrible experience? Is the pathos in the eyes of the Beatrice Cenci from her guilt or her innocence?

Twain and Warner, *The Gilded Age*, Volume I, XVIII

Beauty ends where an intellectual expression begins.

Wilde, *The Picture of Dorian Gray*, I

Beauty is a form of genius—is higher, indeed, than genius, as it needs no explanation. It is of the great facts of the world, like sunlight, or springtime, or the reflection in dark waters of that silver shell we call the moon. It cannot be questioned. It has its divine right of sovereignty. It makes princes of those who have it. *Ibid.*, II

Most American women behave as if they were beautiful. It is the secret of their charm.
Ibid.

Dandyism is an attempt to assert the absolute modernity of beauty. *Ibid.*, XI

There were moments when he looked on evil simply as a mode through which he could realize his conception of the beautiful. *Ibid.*

"I never tilt against beauty." "That is your error. You value beauty far too much."
Ibid., XVII

It is better to be beautiful than to be good. But it is better to be good than to be ugly.
Ibid.

"Ugliness is one of the seven deadly sins?" "Ugliness is one of the seven deadly virtues."
Ibid.

BEGINNING

All things are best at the beginning. Anonymous, *The Temple-beau*, 135

Every life has its natural burden: it is therefore a blessing for mortals if they can lay all the weight of future days on the beginning of their career, in order to exempt thereby the evening of their journey from the pressure of sorrow. August, *Horrid Mysteries*, I

Our beginning shows what our end will be. Bunyan, *Pilgrim's Progress*, 202

The contrast of beginning and end is almost always melancholy.
Burney, *Camilla*, Two, III

The beginning of things, of a world especially, is necessarily vague, tangled, chaotic, and exceedingly disturbing. Chopin, *The Awakening*, VI

This scene of my life may be said to have begun in theft, and ended in luxury; a sad setting-out, and a worse coming home. Defoe, *Captain Singleton*, 157

The foundation of my new life was not the superstructure. Defoe, *Colonel Jack*, 157

In all failures, the beginning is certainly the half of the whole.
Eliot, *Middlemarch*, Book III, XXXI

Our beginnings are lost in clouds; we live in darkness all our days, and perish without an end. Melville, *Mardi*, CLXXXV

The most apprehensive beginnings make the happiest conclusions.
Richardson, *Clarissa Harlowe*, I

Good beginnings are necessary to good progresses, and happy conclusions.
Richardson, *Sir Charles Grandison*, One, I

Lives that have noble commencements have often no better endings.
Thackeray, *Henry Esmond*, Book I

BELIEF: *see also* CREDULITY [INCREDULITY]; FAITH; RELIGION; etc.

I don't believe or disbelieve anything I don't understand.
Atherton, Senator North, Book I, XXII

Both of these men were loyal to their sect, but larger. Like vines planted in a garden, they covered the walls, overtopped them, and climbed into the neighboring trees, bearing as much fruit in the great common highway as in the garden. Such men are sometimes called unbelievers, because they believe so much more than others.
Beecher, Norwood, LVI

It is as easy to believe that all things always were, as that they began to be.
Brackenridge, Modern Chivalry, Part II, Volume II

Whatever, in Truth, makes a man's heart warmer, and his soul purer, is a belief not a knowledge.   Bulwer, <i>The Caxtons</i>, Book III, IV

Proof is a handcuff—belief is a wing.   *Ibid.*

Proof is a low, vulgar, levelling, rascally Jacobin—Belief is a loyal, generous, chivalrous gentleman.   *Ibid.*

Nothing is more flattering to the pride and the hopes of man than the belief in a future state.   Bulwer, <i>Pompeii</i>, Book Three, IV

Mosquitoes are thought by some to keep the air pure.   Cable, <i>The Grandissimes</i>, II

One *can't* believe impossible things.   Carroll, <i>Through the Looking Glass</i>, V

Sometimes I've believed as many as six impossible things before breakfast.   *Ibid.*

That maudlin substitute for belief which consists in a patronage of fantastic theories.
Disraeli, Coningsby, Book III, II

The most obstinate beliefs that mortals entertain about themselves are such as they have no evidence for beyond a constant, spontaneous pulsing of their self-satisfaction.
Eliot, Daniel Deronda, Book III, XXIII

It is not generous to believe the worst of a man.   Eliot, <i>Middlemarch</i>, Book III, XXV

Human beliefs, like all other natural growths, elude the barriers of a system.
Eliot, Silas Marner, XVII

It is impossible a man should steadfastly believe the Scriptures without obeying them.
Fielding, Joseph Andrews, 141

You've got to believe in a thing before you can put any heart in it.
Howells, Silas Lapham, XI

They commonly are soonest believed that are best beloved.   Lyly, <i>Euphues</i>, 127

Let not them that speak fairest be believed soonest.
Lyly, Euphues and His England, 391–392

As particular food begets particular dreams, so particular experiences or books particular feelings or beliefs.   Melville, <i>Confidence-Man</i>, XLI

In some universe-old truths, all mankind are disbelievers.   Melville, <i>Mardi</i>, XCVII

While we fight over creeds, ten thousand fingers point to where vital good may be done.
Ibid., CLXXV

We split upon hairs; but stripped, mere words and phrases cast aside, the great bulk of us are orthodox. None who think, dissent from the grand belief.   *Ibid.*

Look not too long in the face of the fire, O man! Never dream with thy hand on the helm! Turn not thy back to the compass; accept the first hint of the hitching tiller; believe not the artificial fire, when its redness makes all things look ghastly.
Melville, Moby Dick, XCVI

Let faith oust fact; let fancy oust memory; I look deep down and do believe.
Ibid., CXIV

Creeds will not die not fighting. Meredith, *Beauchamp's Career*, XXIX

They that made of his creed a strait-jacket for humanity. *Ibid.*

There is always a moment when the religionist doubts, and there is also a moment when the atheist says, "Who knows, perhaps." Moore, *Evelyn Innes*, XXVI

When I'm bad I believe. When I'm good I doubt. *Ibid.*, XXXIII

Think is not synonymous with believe. Peacock, *Nightmare Abbey*, VIII

Doctrine should govern practice. Richardson, *Clarissa Harlowe*, IV

Elderly skeptics generally regard their unbelief as a misfortune.
Stowe, *Orr's Island*, XXIV

All true believers shall break their eggs at the convenient end.
Swift, *Gulliver's Travels*, "Lilliput"

He had a way of believing people, especially when such belief was opposed to his own interests, and had none of that self-confidence which makes a man think that if opportunity be allowed him he can win a woman in spite of herself.
Trollope, *The Way We Live Now*, XIV

BENEVOLENCE

Benevolence is the duty of one who aspires to wisdom.
Bulwer, *Pompeii*, Book IV, VII

Objects are never wanting for the exercise of benevolence. Burney, *Cecilia*, I

I cried to find so much goodness in the world, when I thought there was so little. *Ibid.*

To despise riches may be philosophic, but to dispense them worthily must surely be more beneficial to mankind. Burney, *Evelina*, 116

He that gives to the poor lends to the Lord. Defoe, *Roxana*, 25

A hard thing, that we should judge a man to be wicked because he's charitable, and vicious because he's kind. *Ibid.*, 30

In this stupid world most people never consider that a thing is good to be done unless it is done by their own set. Eliot, *Middlemarch*, Book V, XLIV

Love or benevolence may be the reigning passion in a beggar as well as in a prince; and wherever it is, its energies will be the same. Fielding, *Amelia*, I

The only certain as well as laudable way of setting ourselves above another man: by becoming his benefactor. *Ibid.*

Where ambition, avarice, pride, or any other passion governs the man and keeps his benevolence down, the miseries of all other men affect him no more than they would a stock or a stone. And thus the man and his statue have often the same degree of feeling or compassion. *Ibid.*, II

When Alexander had with fire and sword overrun a whole empire, and destroyed the lives of millions of innocent people, we are told as an example of his benevolence, that he did not cut the throat of an old woman, and ravish her daughters whom he had before undone. Fielding, H., *Jonathan Wild*, 11

It is wonderful and delightful to think how long a good man's beneficence may be potent, even after his death. Hawthorne, *The Marble Faun*, XXXIV

The benevolence, the good nature, the humanity of a slaveholder, avail as little as the benevolence of the bandit, who generously clothes the stripped and naked traveler in a garment plundered from his own portmanteau. Hildreth, *Slave*, Volume II, II

Benevolence, like religion, awes even those it cannot win.   Lee, *The Recess*, III

The truly beneficent mind looks upon every child of sorrow as their relation, and entitled to their assistance.   Parsons, *Castle of Wolfenbach*, II

The unfortunate have claims upon the hearts of those whom God has blessed with affluence.   *Ibid.*

A man in whom the organ of benevolence is not developed cannot be benevolent: he in whom it is so, cannot be otherwise.   Peacock, *Headlong Hall*, V

One act of beneficence—one act of real usefulness—is worth all the abstract sentiment in the world.   Radcliffe, *The Mysteries of Udolpho*, I

How many ways there are to overcome persons who may be naturally beneficent!   Richardson, *Sir Charles Grandison*, Two, V

To a benevolent soul, the odds is worth the throw; and though it be against him at the present, he may win it in the future.   Wright, *A Few Days in Athens*, XI

BETRAYAL

We often admire the folly of the dupe, when we should transfer our whole surprise to the astonishing guilt of the betrayer.   Fielding, H., *Amelia*, II

Man is false to himself, and betrays his own succors ten times where nature does it once.   Sterne, *A Sentimental Journey*, 81

BIRTH; REBIRTH

Nature has provided in the distress and inconvenience of the maternal function a sufficient check upon its abuses, just as she has in regard to all the other natural functions.   Bellamy, *Equality*, XXXVIII

I have know'd that sweetest and best of women ever since afore her First, which Mr. Harris who was dreadful timid went and stopped his ears in a empty dog-kennel, and never took his hands away or come out once till he was showed the baby, wen bein' took with fits, the doctor collared him and laid him on his back upon the airy stones, and she was told to ease her mind, his owls was organs. And I have know'd her when he has hurt her feelin' art by sayin' of his ninth that it was one to [sic] many, if not two, while that dear innocent was cooin' in his face, which thrive it did though bandy.   Dickens, *Martin Chuzzlewit*, XLIX

It is a pleasant thing to reflect upon, and furnishes a complete answer to those who contend for the gradual degeneration of the human species, that every baby born into the world is a finer one than the last.   Dickens, *Nicholas Nickleby*, XXXVI

In this workhouse was born [Oliver Twist,] the item of mortality whose name is prefixed to the head of this chapter.   Dickens, *Oliver Twist*, I

Oliver cried lustily. If he could have known that he was an orphan, left to the tender mercies of churchwardens and overseers, perhaps he would have cried the louder.   *Ibid.*

Born old.   Eliot, *Felix Holt*, I

"If it's true that we breed faster than the Lord provides for us, we maun drown the poor folks' weans like kittlings." "Na, na! Ye're a' out, neighbor—I see now the utility of church censures."   Galt, *Ayrshire Legatees*, V

Man's desire of earthly experience draws him to rebirth, and he is born into a form that fits his nature as a glove a hand; the soul of a warrior passes into the robust form of a warrior; the soul of a poet into the sensitive body of a poet.   Moore, *Evelyn Innes*, XXIII

I wish either my father or my mother, or indeed both of them, as they were in duty both equally bound to it, had minded what they were about when they begot me.   Sterne, *Tristram Shandy*, I

BIRTH; REBIRTH (*continued*)

My Tristram's misfortunes began nine months before ever he came into the world.
Ibid.

BLUSHING

Do females ever blush at those things by themselves at which they have so charming a knack of blushing in company?   Richardson, *Clarissa Harlowe*, II

Where there are freedoms in public, every modest eye will sink under the shameless effrontery, and every modest face will be covered with blushes for those who cannot blush.   *Ibid.*

BLUSTER

It is a dangerous thing to see anything in the sphere of a vain blusterer, before the vain blusterer sees it himself.   Dickens, *Hard Times*, Book III, IX

BODY: *see also* MIND

Mind rules the world. But what rules the mind? The body.
Collins, *Woman in White*, Part II, Third Epoch

The body is but a passive machine, calculated for the reception and influence of those amazing faculties which are annexed to human nature.
Gentleman, *A Trip to the Moon*, II

A state of physical well-being can create a kind of joy, in spite of the profoundest anxiety of mind.   Hawthorne, *Blithedale Romance*, XXIV

Our souls belong to our bodies, not our bodies to our souls.   Melville, *Mardi*, CLV

Our bodies are our betters.   *Ibid.*

These eyes are windows, and this body of mine is the house.   Melville, *Moby Dick*, II

Like most men who have little to say, he was an orator in print, but that was a poor medium for him—his body without his fire.   Meredith, *Beauchamp's Career*, XIV

Domandun est corpus; the body must be tamed.
Reade, *The Cloister and the Hearth*, XCIII

What a poor, passive machine is the body when the mind is disordered!
Richardson, *Clarissa Harlowe*, I

BOOKS: *see also* AUTHORSHIP; LITERATURE; READING; etc.

"What books have you read?" "History, divinity, belles-letters." "What is the characteristic of history?" "Fiction." "Of Novels?" "Truth." "Of metaphysics?" "Imagination." "Of natural philosophy?" "Doubt." "What is the best lesson in moral philosophy?" "To expect no gratitude."   Brackenridge, *Modern Chivalry*, Part II, Volume I

Nothing furnishes a room like books.   Howells, *Silas Lapham*, IX

You can't put a more popular thing than self-sacrifice into a novel.   *Ibid.*, XIV

If our hearts was only right, we shouldn't want any books.
Judd, *Margaret*, Volume I, XIV

You books must know your places.   Melville, *Moby Dick*, XCIX

Every age makes its own guidebooks, and the old ones are used for waste paper. But there is only one Holy Guide-Book that will never lead you astray, if you but follow it aright; and some noble monuments that remain, though the pyramids crumble.
Melville, *Redburn*, XXXI

48

Books are not the same things when you are living among people. I cannot tell why, but they are dead. On the farm they would have been living beings to me.

Schreiner, *Story of an African Farm*, Part II, XI

BREVITY

The extreme study of brevity arises frequently from too much sensibility to public opinion; too great a fear of wearying the reader.

Brackenridge, *Modern Chivalry*, Part II, Volume IV

Give good news in as few words as possible.

Simms, *The Scout*, XXXIII

BROTHERHOOD: *see also* FRIENDSHIP; LOVE; etc.

The solidarity of the race and the brotherhood of man are ties as real and as vital as physical fraternity.

Bellamy, *Looking Backward*, XII

The idea of the vital unity of the family of mankind, the reality of human brotherhood.

Ibid., XXVI

The men who learn endurance are they who call the whole world brother.

Dickens, *Barnaby Rudge*, LXXIX

BULLYING

That most contemptible of all human beings, a social bully, usually *does* nothing, when matters come to a crisis. Even when he fights, he fights bunglingly, and innocently.

Cooper, *Satanstoe*, Volume II, II

A man who was the Bully of humanity.

Dickens, *Hard Times*, Book I, IV

BURDEN

A bill at three months sits easier on a man than one at sixty days; and a bill at six months is almost as little of a burden as no bill at all.

Trollope, *He Knew He Was Right*, L

The heart when it is burdened, though it may have ample strength to bear the burden, loses its buoyancy and doubts its own power.

Ibid., LIII

BUREAUCRACY: *see also* GOVERNMENT

Whenever there is a great national establishment, employing large numbers of officials, the public must be reconciled to support many incompetent men; for such is the favoritism and nepotism always prevailing in the purlieus of these establishments, that some incompetent persons are always admitted, to the exclusion of many of the worthy.

Melville, *White Jacket*, XXVII

CALAMITY: *see also* ADVERSITY; MISERY; etc.

Every calamity severs a string from the heart, until one scene of sorrow on the back of another matures us for eternity.

Brown, W.H., *The Power of Sympathy*, 85

Calamity may be classed in two great divisions: 1st, the afflictions, which no prudence can avert; 2d, the misfortunes, which men take all possible pains to bring upon themselves.

Bulwer, *What Will He Do with It?*, Book VII, X

Calamities can, and do occur, to bring back an army to a sense of its true nature and its dependence on Providence.

Cooper, *Satanstoe*, Volume II, XIV

What quarrel, what harshness, what unbelief in each other can subsist in the presence of a great calamity, when all the artificial vesture of our life is gone, and we are all one with each other in primitive mortal needs?

Eliot, *Mill on the Floss*, Book VII, V

CALAMITY (*continued*)

Most men have a natural indifference, if not an absolutely hostile feeling, towards those whom disease, or weakness, or calamity of any kind, causes to falter and faint amid the rude jostle of our selfish existence. Hawthorne, *Blithedale Romance*, VI

Nothing gives a sadder sense of decay, than the loss or suspension of the power to deal with unaccustomed things and to keep up with the swiftness of the passing moment.
Hawthorne, *House of the Seven Gables*, XI

There's no new trouble under the sun. Howells, *Silas Lapham*, XVIII

What revolution and hubbub does not that little instrument, the needle, avert from us! Alas, that in calamity, women cannot stitch!
Meredith, *Ordeal of Richard Feverel*, XXXIX

People in calamity have little weight in anything, or with anybody.
Richardson, *Clarissa Harlowe*, III

Calamity, rightly supported, is a blessing.
Richardson, *Sir Charles Grandison*, Two, V

CALMNESS

It is the nature of that happiness which we derive from our affections to be calm; its immense influence upon our outward life is not known till it is troubled or withdrawn.
Bulwer, *Harold*, Book X, X

CANNIBALISM

Who is not a cannibal? Melville, *Moby Dick*, LXV

CAPACITY; INCAPACITY: *see also* IMPOSSIBILITY

There are three things that none of the young men of the present generation can do. They can't sit over their wine; they can't play at whist; and they can't pay a lady a compliment. Collins, *Woman in White*, Part I, First Epoch

For some moments he could not flee no more than a little finger can commit a revolution from a hand. Crane, *The Red Badge of Courage*, V

A pretty face may presume much; a willful nature may carry all things.
Wright, *A Few Days in Athens*, XII

CAPITALISM: *see also* CIVILIZATION; GOVERNMENT; etc.

Buying and selling is essentially antisocial in all its tendencies.
Bellamy, *Looking Backward*, IX

CAUSE: *see* PURPOSE

CAUSE AND EFFECT: *see also* DESTINY; CIRCUMSTANCE; CONSEQUENCE

It is not the barometer which has a great effect on the weather; rather the weather has a great effect on it. Anonymous, *Adventures of Sylvia Hughes*, 48

When the cause ceases, the effect ought likewise to cease.
Anonymous, *Peregrinations of Jeremiah Grant*, 151

Only the few look at causes, and trace them to their effects.
Arthur, *Ten Nights in a Bar-Room*, Night the Fifth

The great American public loves a show, and when the show is not to its taste it has no hesitation in making its displeasure known. Atherton, *Senator North*, Book I, XV

The law of cause and effect does not hide in the realm of the unexpected when intelligent beings go looking for it.
Ibid., Book II, XXI

Those who see quickly will resolve quickly and act quickly.
Austen, *Mansfield Park*, Volume One, VI

Conduct, the result of good principles.
Ibid., Volume One, IX

She grew clean as she grew smart.
Austen, *Northanger Abbey*, I

My courage always rises with every attempt to intimidate me.
Austen, *Pride and Prejudice*, Volume II, VIII

Her mind was so busily engaged, that she did not always know when she was silent.
Ibid., Volume III, XI

Nothing in this world can be truly said to be more wonderful than anything else.
Bellamy, *Looking Backward*, III

Wretched men, because they will not learn to be helpers of one another, are doomed to be beggars of one another from the least to the greatest.
Ibid., XXVIII

The cause is often won, with judgment, and silence like the game of chess. All depends upon the move.
Brackenridge, *Modern Chivalry*, Part II, Volume I

The stars of the heavens are not at marked distances. There is a concealed regularity, order and proportion in all that affects. The mind remains cold where there is nothing that surprises and comes unexpectedly upon it.
Ibid.

It is so extremely difficult to engage attention to anything serious, that one must enliven with something singular in order to be read.
Ibid., Part II, Volume II

Mutual wants produce reciprocal accommodation.
Ibid.

Good fences preserve good neighborhoods.
Ibid., Part II, Volume IV

If people were always kind and obedient to those who are cruel and unjust, the wicked people would have it all their own way.
Bronte, *Jane Eyre*, VI

Unheard-of combinations of circumstances demand unheard-of rules.
Ibid., XIV

The vague sense of insecurity which accompanies a conviction of ignorance.
Ibid.

To participate in the mirth of a buffoon is to render yourself equally ridiculous.
Brown, W.H., *The Power of Sympathy*, 91

The world will not examine the causes that give birth to our actions.
Ibid., 166

When we seek for diversion in any place, and there is nothing to be found that we wish, it is certainly time to depart.
Ibid., 172

"Nothing venture, nothing have." "Nothing have, nothing venture."
Bulwer, *Caxtons*, Book IV, IV

Whatever is worth having must be bought; therefore, he who cannot buy has nothing worth having.
Ibid., Book IV, V

Most of our best and wisest men have lived in capitals.
Ibid., Book VII, IX

In the ferment of great events the dregs rise.
Bulwer, *Leila*, Book IV, V

Many a criminal is made by pondering over the fate of some predecessor in guilt. There is a fascination in the dark and forbidden, which, strange to say, is only lost in fiction. No man is more inclined to murder his nephews, or stifle his wife, after reading *Richard the Third* or *Othello*.
Bulwer, *My Novel*, Book VI, XVII

A little fire burns up a great deal of corn.
Bulwer, *What Will He Do with It?*, Book VIII, I

Saying and doing are as diverse as are the soul and the body.
Bunyan, *Pilgrim's Progress*, 82

Hearing is but as the sowing of the seed; talking is not sufficient to prove that fruit is indeed in the heart and life.
Ibid.

We are almost all of a nature so pitifully plastic, that we act from circumstances and are fashioned by situation.
Burney, *Camilla*, Three, VI

Results have nothing to do with the moral guilt or blamelessness of him who brings them about; they depend solely upon the thing done, whatever it may happen to be. The moral guilt or blamelessness in like manner has nothing to do with the result.
Butler, *The Way of All Flesh*, V

Well-to-do parents seldom eat many sour grapes; the danger to the children lies in the parents eating too many sweet ones.
Ibid., VI

It is involved in the very essence of things that rich men who die old shall have been mean.
Ibid., XIX

Men can no more cure their own souls than they can cure their own bodies, or manage their own law affairs.
Ibid., LII

Dwellers in swamps cannot be mountaineers.
Cable, *The Grandissimes*, XXVI

There was no "One, two, three, and away!" but they began running when they liked, and left off when they liked, so that it was not easy to know when the race was over. However, when they had been running half an hour or so, and were quite dry again, the Dodo suddenly called out "The race is over!" and they all crowded round it, panting, and asking "But who has won?" . . . At last the Dodo said, "*Everybody* has won, and *all* must have prizes."
Carroll, *Alice in Wonderland*, III

Now, here, you see, it takes all the running *you* can do, to keep in the same place. If you want to get somewhere else, you must run at least twice as fast as that!
Carroll, *Through the Looking Glass*, II

Slight sufferings make us captious; great ones, humane and benevolent.
Caruthers, *Kentuckian in New-York*, Volume I, VII

The way to become rich is to make money, not to save it.
Chopin, *The Awakening*, XVIII

The rash way is sometimes the best way.
Collins, *Moonstone*, Third Narrative, Chapter VI

A letter which has nothing of the slightest importance in it is not always an easy letter to answer.
Ibid., Third Narrative, Chapter VIII

Evil report, with time and chance to help it, travels patiently, and travels far.
Ibid., Third Narrative, Chapter IX

Men of his sensitive organization are fortunately quick in feeling the effect of remedial measures.
Ibid., Fourth Narrative, June 21

Manifest no distrust, or you may invite the danger you appear to apprehend.
Cooper, *Last of the Mohicans*, II

There is a drug in every word he utters.
Cooper, *The Prairie*, XII

What's the good of having a title unless you make it work?
Crane, *Active Service*, XXIX

It is the innocent old scandalmongers, poor placid-minded well-protected hens, who are often the most harmful. The vicious gabblers defeat themselves very often.
Crane, *The O'Ruddy*, XXI

Men do not abandon their habits, or their prejudices, without some strong inducement.
Dacre, *The Libertine*, II

Vice can never take root where the soil is ungenial.
Dacre, *The Passions*, Letter XC

When the mind is dissatisfied, whether upon grounds just or unjust, it ever views objects through an exaggerated medium. Dacre, *Zofloya*, XVI

A song is as necessary to sailors as the drum and fife to a soldier. They can't pull in time, or pull with a will, without it. Dana, *Two Years Before the Mast*, XXIX

What we are at twenty depends upon what we were at fifteen; what we are at fifteen, upon what we were at ten. Day, *The History of Sandford and Merton*, 248

Few people are so perfect as not to err sometimes; and if you are convinced of your errors, you will be more cautious how you give way to them a second time. *Ibid.*, 337

It is always safest travelling after a highway robbery. Defoe, *Moll Flanders*, 191

Roving stones gather no moss, nor milestones. Dickens, *Barnaby Rudge*, III

There's no simile for his lungs. Talking, laughing, or snoring, they make the beams of the house shake. Dickens, *Bleak House*, IX

The character of people may be changed by the circumstances surrounding them. *Ibid.*, XIII

The man was necessary. If we make such men necessary by our faults and follies, or by our want of worldly knowledge, or by our misfortunes, we must not revenge ourselves upon them. *Ibid.*, XV

Has the difficulty grown easier because of so many failures? *Ibid.*, XXXVII

Said Mr. Micawber, "Annual income twenty pounds, annual expenditure nineteen nineteen six, result happiness. Annual income twenty pounds, annual expenditure twenty pounds ought and six, result misery. The blossom is blighted, the leaf is withered, the God of day goes down upon the dreary scene and—and in short you are forever floored. As I am!" Dickens, *David Copperfield*, XII

A man who labors under the pressure of pecuniary embarrassments is, with the generality of people, at a disadvantage. *Ibid.*, XXXIX

I have never believed it possible that any natural or improved ability can claim immunity from the companionship of the steady, plain, hardworking qualities, and hope to gain its end. *Ibid.*, XLII

No varnish can hide the grain of the wood; and the more varnish you put on, the more the grain will express itself. Dickens, *Great Expectations*, XXII

Nothing that a Noodle does can awaken surprise or indignation; the proceedings of a Noodle can only inspire contempt. Dickens, *Hard Times*, Book, III, IX

Words never influence the course of the cards, or the course of the dice. Dickens, *Little Dorrit*, Book II, XXVIII

"What's the reason," said Mr. Squeers; "what's the reason of rheumatics? What do they mean? What do people have 'em for—eh?" Mrs. Sliderskew didn't know, but suggested that it was possibly because they couldn't help it. Dickens, *Nicholas Nickleby*, LVII

There are chords in the human heart. Dickens, *The Old Curiosity Shop*, LV

Hunger and recent ill-usage are great assistants if you want to cry. Dickens, *Oliver Twist*, II

"Oliver Twist has asked for more [to eat]!" "That boy will be hung. I never was more convinced of anything in my life, than I am that that boy will come to be hung." *Ibid.*

Orange-peel will be my death, or I'll be content to eat my own head! *Ibid.*, XIV

Happily acquainted with his own merit and importance, Mr. Podsnap settled that whatever he put beind him he put out of existence. Dickens, *Our Mutual Friend*, Book I, XI

If there is one thing more than another that makes a girl look ugly, it is stooping. Dickens, *Pickwick Papers*, IV

"Whatever is is right" would be as final an aphorism as it is lazy, did it not include the troublesome consequence, that nothing that ever was, was wrong.

Dickens, *A Tale of Two Cities*, Book II, II

A nod or a wink will speak volumes.   Disraeli, *Coningsby*, Book II, VI

There is nothing more interesting than to trace predisposition.   *Ibid.*, Book IX, I

A density of population implies a severer struggle for existence, and a consequent repulsion of elements brought into too close contact.   Disraeli, *Sybil*, Book II, V

In great cities men are brought together by the desire of gain. They are not in a state of co-operation, but of isolation, as to the making of fortunes; and for all the rest they are careless of neighbors.   *Ibid.*

The Crusades had their origin in a great impulse, and in a certain sense, led to great results.   *Ibid.*, Book II, XI

The police ought to put machines down, and then everybody would be comfortable.

Ibid., Book II, XIV

Little things affect little minds.   *Ibid.*, Book III, II

Great things spring from casualties.   *Ibid.*, Book V, III

It generally happens that where a mere physical impulse urges the people to insurrection, though it is often an influence of slow growth and movement, the effects are more violent and sometimes more obstinate than when they move under the blended authority of moral and physical necessity, and mix up together the rights and the wants of Man.

Disraeli, *Sybil*, Book VI, VI

A majority is always the best repartee.   Disraeli, *Tancred*

Base minds put into action what bad hearts dictate.

Donaldson, *Sir Bartholomew Sapskull*, II

Transplantation is not always successful in the matter of flowers or maidens.

Dreiser, *Sister Carrie*, VI

It is good to be a soldier and a detrimental; you touch the hearts of women and charm them—old and young, high or low. They take the sticking of your tongue in the cheek for the wearing of your heart on the sleeve.   DuMaurier, *Trilby*, IV

The kinship of human passion, the sameness of mortal scenery, inevitably fill fact with burlesque and parody. Error and folly have had their hecatombs of martyrs.

Eliot, *Daniel Deronda*, Book VI, XLI

Men collectively can only be made to embrace principles, and to act on them, by the slow stupendous teaching of the world's events. Men will go on planting potatoes, and nothing else but potatoes, till a potato-disease comes and forces them to find out the advantage of a varied crop.   Eliot, *Felix Holt*, Address to Working Men

When young ardor is set brooding over the conception of a prompt deed, the deed itself seems to start forth with independent life, mastering ideal obstacles.

Eliot, *Middlemarch*, Book IV, XXXVII

It's rather a strong check to one's self-complacency to find how much of one's right doing depends on not being in want of money. A man will not be tempted to say the Lord's Prayer backward to please the devil, if he doesn't want the devil's services.

Ibid., Book VII, LXIII

There is the terrible Nemesis following on some errors, that it is always possible for those who like it to interpret them into a crime: there is no proof in favor of the man outside his own consciousness and assertion.   *Ibid.*, Book VIII, LXXII

There are episodes in most men's lives in which their highest qualities can only cast a deterring shadow over the objects that fill their inward vision.

Ibid., Book VIII, LXXIII

The presence of a noble nature, generous in its wishes, ardent in its charity, changes the lights for us.   *Ibid.*, Book VIII, LXXVI

Amidst the conditions of an imperfect social state, great feelings will often take the aspect of error, and great faith the aspect of illusion.   *Ibid.*, Book VIII, Finale

If boys and men are to be welded together in the glow of transient feeling, they must be made of metal that will mix, else they inevitably fall asunder when the heat dies out.
                                                                          Eliot, *Mill on the Floss*, Book II, VI

It's right to be prepared for all things, and if trouble's sent, to remember as it isn't sent without a cause.   *Ibid.*, Book III, III

We get a deal o' useless things about us, only because we've got the money to spend.
                                                                                                                  Ibid.

Fly-fishers fail in preparing their bait so as to make it alluring in the right quarter, for want of a due acquaintance with the subjectivity of fishes.   *Ibid.*, Book III, VII

Feeble limbs easily resign themselves to be tethered, and when we are subdued by sickness it seems possible to us to fulfill pledges which the old vigor comes back and breaks.   *Ibid.*, Book III, IX

There is something sustaining in the very agitation that accompanies the first shocks of trouble, just as an acute pain is often a stimulus, and produces an excitement which is transient strength.   *Ibid.*, Book IV, II

Every strong feeling makes to itself a conscience of its own—has its own piety.
                                                                              Eliot, *Romola*, Book II, XXXIV

An ass may bray a good while before he shakes the stars down.   *Ibid.*, Book III, L

If there is an angel who records the sorrows of men as well as their sins, he knows how many and deep are the sorrows that spring from false ideas for which no man is culpable.   Eliot, *Silas Marner*, I

When events turn out so much better for a man than he has had reason to dread, is it not a proof that his conduct has been less foolish and blameworthy than it might otherwise have appeared?   *Ibid.*, XIII

The burden becomes light by being well borne.   Fielding, H., *Amelia*, I

A mind once violently hurt grows callous to any future impressions of grief and is never capable of feeling the same pangs a second time.   *Ibid.*, II

We reason from our heads, but act from our hearts.   *Ibid.*

Our hero executed the greatest exploits with the utmost ease imaginable, by means of those transcendent qualities which nature had indulged him with, a bold heart, a thundering voice, and a steady countenance.   Fielding, H., *Jonathan Wild*, 72

Men are apt to draw comforting conclusions from malign events.   *Ibid.*, 124

To adopt the fruits of sin is to give countenance to it.   Fielding, H., *Tom Jones*, 42

The father hath eaten sour grapes, and the children's teeth are set on edge.   *Ibid.*, 43

Small things affect light minds.   *Ibid.*, 118

To be sure it is natural for us to wish our enemies dead, that the wars may be at an end, and our taxes be lowered.   *Ibid.*, 316

Tobacco smoke chokes me!   Gaskell, *North and South*, XVII

"Why do people find the subject of love so interesting?" "Because there is so little love in real life. Why do poor people care only for stories about the rich? The same principle."
                                                                              Gissing, *New Grub Street*, XXVI

Petty causes may produce great mischiefs.   Godwin, *Caleb Williams*, I

The unknown is generally taken to be terrible, not as the proverb would infer, from the inherent superstition of man, but because it so often *is* terrible.   Haggard, *She*, III

He who would tamper with the vast and secret forces that animate the world may well fall a victim to them.   *Ibid.*

A harp can give out but a certain quantity of sound, however heavily it is smitten.
                                                                    Ibid., XXVI

The external reality of heavenly things is but little felt.   Hale, *Liberia*, II

Material causes and emotional effects are not to be arranged in regular equation.
                                        Hardy, *Far From the Madding Crowd*, XVII

Men thin away to insignificance and oblivion quite as often by not making the most of good spirits when they have them as by lacking good spirits when they are indispensable.
                                                                    Ibid., XXII

A useless declaration, like a rare china teacup with a hole in it, has its ornamental value in enlarging a collection.   Hardy, *Hand of Ethelberta*, XX

She held that defilement of mind often arose from ignorance of eye.   *Ibid.*, XXV

Harsh feelings produce harsh usage, and this by reaction quenches the sentiments that gave it birth.   Hardy, *Return of the Native*, Book V, VI

Human beings, in their generous endeavor to construct a hypothesis that shall not degrade a First Cause, have always hesitated to conceive a dominant power of lower moral quality than their own; and, even while they sit down and weep by the waters of Babylon, invent excuses for the oppression which prompts their tears.
                                                              Ibid., Book VI, I

Take it gentle. 'Tis knack, not strength, that does it.   Hardy, *Tess*, XVII

There is a singular effect oftentimes when, out of the midst of engrossing thought and deep absorption, we suddenly look up, and catch a glimpse of external objects.
                                              Hawthorne, *The Marble Faun*, XXXV

This final despair, and sense of shortcoming, must always be the reward and punishment of those who try to grapple with a great or beautiful idea. It only proves that you have been able to imagine things too high for mortal faculties to execute.   *Ibid.*, XLI

We do not always see the event of our actions, or the results of the accidents which cross them.   Hill, *Mr. George Edwards*, 91

A man is master in his own house generally through the exercise of a certain degree of brutality.   Howells, *A Modern Instance*, V

I never was one to feel good because another man felt bad.
                                                      Howells, *Silas Lapham*, XVIII

He had looked out all the pictures to which an asterisk was affixed in those formidable pages of fine print in his Bädeker; his attention had been strained and his eyes dazzled, and he had sat down with an aesthetic headache.   James, H., *The American*, I

The causes of good and evil are so various and uncertain, so often entangled with each other, so diversified by various relations, and so much subject to accidents which cannot be foreseen, that he who would fix his condition upon incontestable reasons of preference must live and die inquiring and deliberating.   Johnson, *Rasselas*, 73

Perpetual levity must end in ignorance, and intemperance, though it may fire the spirits for an hour, will make life short or miserable.   *Ibid.*, 75

To know anything, we must know its effects.   *Ibid.*, 117

The present state of things is the consequence of the former.   *Ibid.*, 117

The Pyramid is a monument of the insufficiency of human enjoyments.   *Ibid.*, 124

Man cannot so far know the connection of causes and events as that he may venture to do wrong in order to do right.   *Ibid.*, 129

Dissonance and disorder are sympathetic and reciprocal.

Judd, *Margaret*, Volume II, III

Aversion reproduces aversion, and selfishness is answered by selfishness. *Ibid.*

The more haste, the worse speed. Kidgell, *The Card*, I

When we know the worst of our situation, we are more able to support it.

Kimber, *Maria*, I

Dear is bought the honey that is licked off the thorn. Kingsley, *Hereward the Wake*, I

I am no theologian; but I doubt if, in the elaborate divinity of fourteen epistles, the apostle of the Gentiles ever went so straight to his hearer's heart as in that farewell charge, when the elders of Ephesus gathered round him on the sea sand, "Sorrowing most of all for the words that he spake, that they should see his face no more."

Lawrence, *Guy Livingstone*, VII

Mistrust no man without cause, neither be thou credulous without proof, be not light to follow every man's opinion, nor obstinate to stand in thine own conceit.

Lyly, *Euphues*, 97

The sun doth harden the dirt and melt the wax. *Ibid.*, 98

He that loppeth the vine causeth it to spread fairer. *Ibid.*, 117

He that casteth water on the fire in the smith's forge, maketh it to flame fiercer. *Ibid.*

He that payeth another man's debt seeketh his own decay.

Lyly, *Euphues and His England*, 229

Farming weans man from his sorrows. Melville, *Israel Potter*, III

The calmer the sea, the more the barnacles grow. Melville, *Mardi*, XXVI

Will a longing bring the thing desired? *Ibid.*, LXXVIII

Doth dread divert its object? *Ibid.*

Does he abstain, who is not incited? *Ibid.*, CXLIII

The only way to civilize a people is to form in them habits of industry.

Melville, *Omoo*, XLIX

The most impressive, sudden, and overwhelming event, as well as the minutest, is but the product of an infinite series of infinitely involved and untraceable foregoing occurrences. Melville, *Pierre*, Book IV, I

Every effect is but the cause of another and a subsequent one. *Ibid.*, Book XIX, I

Whenever, in intervals of mild benevolence, or yielding to mere politic dictates, kings and commodores relax the yoke of servitude, they should see to it well that the concession seem not too sudden or unqualified; for, in the commoner's estimate, that might argue feebleness or fear. Melville, *White Jacket*, LIV

A family passion for land, that survives a generation, is as effective as genius in producing the object it conceives. Meredith, *Beauchamp's Career*, II

Intellectual differences do not cause wounds, except when very unintellectual sentiments are behind them. *Ibid.*, XXII

They who provoke huge battles, and gain but lame victories over themselves, insensibly harden to the habit of distilling sour thoughts from their mischances and from most occurrences. So does the world they combat win on them. *Ibid.*, XLII

There is no calculating the effect of a few little words at a wrong season.

Meredith, *Diana of the Crossways*, XLII

There's no such thing as accident. There's a cause for every disaster: too much cargo, want of foresight, want of pluck. Meredith, *Harry Richmond*, IX

In youth, it is love, or lust, makes the world mad: in age, prejudice. Superstition holds a province; pride an empire. Meredith, *Ordeal of Richard Feverel*, VII

A light heart in a fat body ravishes not only the world but the philosopher.

Meredith, *Sandra Belloni*, IX

It is by denial of the sexual instinct that we become religious.

Moore, *Evelyn Innes*, XXXV

'Tis the mode of conferring favors that either obliges or wounds a feeling heart.

Parsons, *Castle of Wolfenbach*, I

We must not be too nice in our search after the motives of our best actions, but be content to judge of them by their effects.   Parsons, *The Mysterious Warning*, I

Time and accident develop the darkest schemes.   *Ibid.*

Let us not harass ourselves by stating possible evils, and then, to avoid them, fly to those which are certain.   Radcliffe, *The Romance of the Forest*, 402

We arrive at causes by noting coincidences; yet, now and then, coincidences are deceitful.

Reade, *The Cloister and the Hearth*, XXII

Sloth and greed are ill mated. Lovers of money must sweat or steal.   *Ibid.*, XLII

Earthly trouble turns the heart heavenwards.   Reade, *Griffith Gaunt*, XLII

The fond mother ever made a hardened child.   Richardson, *Clarissa Harlowe*, I

All my wisdom now, by a strange fatality, likely to become foolishness!   *Ibid.*

Great consequences, like great folks, are generally attended, and even made great, by small causes and little incidents.   *Ibid.*, II

I only point the lightning, and teach it where to dart without the thunder.   *Ibid.*

Sometimes, to make us fear, and, even, for a short space, to hate, is productive of the contrary extreme.   *Ibid.*

The thunder slept till I awakened it.   *Ibid.*

A head to contrive, a heart to execute.   *Ibid.*

Why should one make a long harvest for a little corn?   *Ibid.*

He that eats the king's goose shall be choked with his feathers.   *Ibid.*

A high price paid is but submission to be cheated.   *Ibid.*, III

We are apt to attribute to the devil everything that happens that we would not have happen.   *Ibid.*

I tried by gentleness and love to soften marble.   *Ibid.*

One extreme produces another.   *Ibid.*

A bad heart, and a bad cause, are confounding things.   *Ibid.*

What friends does prosperity make! What enemies adversity!   *Ibid.*, IV

Bold men will turn shadows into substance in their own favor.

Richardson, *Sir Charles Grandison*, One, I

When we labor like brutes, do our hearts become like theirs, till to eat and have rest becomes all our ambition?   Schreiner, *Undine*, XV

Light meals, light slumbers.   Scott, *The Bride of Lammermoor*, IX

Men may use the assistance of pagans and infidels in their need, and there is reason to think that one cause of their being permitted to remain on earth is that they might minister to the convenience of true Christians.   Scott, *The Talisman*, VIII

There are few bosoms in which a series of successful iniquity does not create arrogance and security.   Shebbeare, *The History . . . Sumatrans*, I

That eternal causes should bring forth chanceable effects is as sensible as that the sun should be the author of darkness.
Sidney, *Arcadia*, III

The body craves food only that the mind may think.
Simms, *The Partisan*, Volume II, X

The cold sneer is, of all other modes, the most effectual in influencing the mind which does not receive its laws from well-grounded principles.
Simms, *The Scout*, XXXI

How many good purposes have been parried by a sneer!
Ibid.

As fear is often caught by contagion, so is courage communicated among the individuals of an army.
Smollett, *Ferdinand, Count Fathom*, XVIII

If you should be sentenced to the pillory, your fortune is made.
Smollett, *Humphry Clinker*, XIII

The hatred of vice is always a progress towards virtue.
Thackeray, *Vanity Fair*, XIX

There is nothing like a little journey together to make people understand each other.
Trollope, *Ayala's Angel*, XLVI

"Fine feathers make fine birds." "Feathers ever so fine don't make well-bred birds."
Ibid., XLIX

I have always observed that when people are interrupted in the performance of some egregious stupidity their feelings are hurt.
Ibid., LVII

If anything can rescue a man from the slough of luxury and idleness combined, it is a cradle filled annually.
Ibid., LXIV

Nothing fatigues the body so much as weariness of spirit.
Trollope, *Barchester Towers*, XLIV

Day after day, and almost every day, one meets censure which is felt to be unjust;—but the general result of all this injustice is increased efficiency.
Trollope, *The Eustace Diamonds*, XLIX

It is not mere industry that will produce good work, nor yet skill, nor even genius. The heart of the artist must be thrust with all its gushing tides into the performance.
Trollope, *The Last Chronicles of Barset*, Volume II, XXII

Expediency is the dangerous wind by which so many of us have wrecked our little boats.
Trollope, *The Three Clerks*, XXIX

Arrogance will produce submission.
Trollope, *The Way We Live Now*, LIV

A burnt child loves the fire.
Wilde, *The Picture of Dorian Gray*, XVII

CAUTION

He that hath been bitten by a serpent is afraid of a rope.
Bulwer, *What Will He Do with It?*, Book VIII, III

The English intellect is always cautious in the wrong place.
Collins, *Woman in White*, Part II, Third Epoch

Caution against sin, even to the innocent, can never be unwholesome.
Fielding, H., *Amelia*, II

Timorous thieves, by extreme caution, often subject themselves to discoveries, which those of a bolder kind escape.
Fielding, H., *Tom Jones*, 383

It is rare to meet with a man who has lived much in the world who has not persuaded himself that caution is always the result of wisdom.
Jenner, *The Placid Man*, I

Precaution is the brave man's clean conscience.
Meredith, *The Amazing Marriage*, XIV

CAUTION (*continued*)

Always be careful of back doors.　　　　　　Richardson, *Clarissa Harlowe*, II

Excessive caution shall often overreach itself.　　Webster, *The Banker and the Bear*, III

CELIBACY: *see* MARRIAGE

CENSURE; CENSORSHIP: *see also* AUTHORSHIP; POETRY; READING

So little excuse do the slightest errors sometimes find, while greater shall pass uncensured by the world, and reflect no obloquy on the person guilty of them.
　　　　　　　　Annesley, *Memoirs of an Unfortunate Young Nobleman*, I

Ivanhoe: DANGEROUS READING FOR CHRISTIAN YOUTH. TOUCH NOT THE UNCLEAN THING.　　　　　　　　Holmes, *The Guardian Angel*, XXXIII

All men are censors who have lungs.　　　　　　Melville, *Mardi*, CLXII

Should we not be particularly careful to keep clear of the faults we censure?
　　　　　　　　　　　　　　Richardson, *Clarissa Harlowe*, I

Many who have escaped censure have not merited applause.　　　　　*Ibid.*

It is difficult for persons of cheerful dispositions so to behave as to avoid censure.
　　　　　　　　　　　　　　　　　　　　　　Ibid., III

Censure from those who are always finding fault is regarded so much as a matter of course that it ceases to be objectionable.　　Trollope, *The Way We Live Now*, I

The man who will not endure censure has to take care that he does not deserve it.
　　　　　　　　　　　　　　Trollope, *Dr. Wortle's School*, VIII

There is no such thing as being poisoned by a book. Art has no influence upon action. It annihilates the desire to act. It is superbly sterile. The books that the world calls immoral are books that show the world its own shame.
　　　　　　　　　　Wilde, *The Picture of Dorian Gray*, XIX

CEREMONY

Almost all unnecessary ceremony is displeasing to a man of sense. The finest expression on this head is in the *Arcadia* of Sir Philip Sidney: "There was ceremony without being ceremonious."　　　　　Brackenridge, *Modern Chivalry*, Part II, Volume IV

There are certain polite forms and ceremonies which must be observed in civilized life, or mankind relapse into their original barbarism.
　　　　　　　　　　Dickens, *Nicholas Nickleby*, XXXVI

All civilized nations appear to accept it as an axiom that ceremony is the touchstone of morals.　　　　　　　　　　　　Haggard, *She*, VI

Where there's much feeling there's little ceremony. Where there's little love, there is no ceremony at all.　　　　　Hardy, *Hand of Ethelberta*, XXII

CHANCE: *see also* DESTINY; FORTUNE; GAMBLING; LUCK; etc.

The best-laid schemes often owe their success more to chance than human wisdom.
　　　　　　　　　　　　　Anonymous, *The Wanderer*, I

Do the events of human life really follow a pre-delineated trait, or does chance sometimes produce oddly united circumstances?　　August, *Horrid Mysteries*, III

So little can be certainly known that it is better not to try to know more than is in everybody's mouth, and to leave the rest to chance.
　　　　　　　　　　　Butler, *The Way of All Flesh*, LXXII

Chance, whose ally is Time that cannot be hurried, and whose enemy is Death, that will not wait.
Conrad, *Lord Jim*, XXXIV

In the most insensible or childish minds, there is some train of reflection which art can seldom lead, or skill assist, but which will reveal itself, as great truths have done, by chance, and when the discoverer has the plainest end in view.
Dickens, *The Old Curiosity Shop*, LV

The smiles of chance.
Eliot, *Middlemarch*, Book VII, LXIII

I don't see that there's any money-getting without chance; if a man gets it in a profession, it's pretty sure to come by chance.
Ibid.

Things don't happen because they're bad or good, else all eggs would be addled or none at all, and at the most it is but six to the dozen. There's good chances and bad chances, and nobody's luck is pulled only by one string.
Eliot, *Felix Holt*, I

Favorable Chance is the god of all men who follow their own devices instead of obeying a law they believe in.
Eliot, *Silas Marner*, IX

When the most exquisite cunning fails, chance often hits the mark, and that by means the least expected.
Fielding, H., *Joseph Andrews*, 144

Many useful hints are obtained by chance.
Johnson, *Rasselas*, 28

Chance had brought them face to face, and mysterious instincts as ungovernable as the winds of heaven were at work knitting their lives together.
Morris, *McTeague*, VI

Do not submit to chance what you are already sure of.
Richardson, *Clarissa Harlowe*, IV

That blind deity, Chance, is often a powerful friend.
Scott, S., *A Description of Millenium Hall*, 128

Nothing is the work of chance. Nothing is the consequence of free-will.
Scott, W., *Redgauntlet*, IX

Chance could never make all things of nothing.
Sidney, *Arcadia*, III

CHANGE AND CHANGELESSNESS; TRANSFORMATION

In spite of the laughing at them, the world would never get on without reformers.
Alcott, *Little Women*, XXIX

If man could only moult—his mind once a year its errors, his heart once a year its useless passions.
Allen, J.L., *Kentucky Cardinal*, VIII

If change be not from outward circumstances, it must be from within.
Austen, *Persuasion*, XXIII

People alter so much that there is something new to be observed in them forever.
Austen, *Pride and Prejudice*, Volume I, IX

Even love cannot completely alter the course of life in a moment.
Bates, *Puritans*, XI

The effect of change in surroundings is like that of lapse of time in making the part seem remote.
Bellamy, *Looking Backward*, XX

The change of a dynasty in a petty kingdom of the old world often cost more lives than did the revolution which set the feet of the human race at last in the right way.
Ibid., XXVI

Unimpressionable natures are not so soon softened, nor are natural antipathies so readily eradicated.
Bronte, C., *Jane Eyre*, XXI

I was getting inured to the harness of school, and lapsing from the passionate pain of change to the palsy of custom.
Bronte, C., *Villette*, XXI

My love for Linton is like the foliage in the woods: time will change it, I'm well aware, as winter changes the trees. My love for Heathcliff resembles the eternal rocks beneath—a source of little visible delight, but necessary. I *am* Heathcliff! He's always in my mind— not as a pleasure, any more than I am always a pleasure to myself, but as my own being.
Bronte, E., *Wuthering Heights*, IX

The love of change merely as change is not in nature.   Brooke, *Emily Montague*, I

Life is dependent on a thousand contingencies, not to be computed or foreseen.
Brown, C.B., *Arthur Mervyn*, I

Change is precious for its own sake.   Brown, C.B., *Edgar Huntley*, 83

Embryo minds, like embryo bodies, pass through a number of strange metamorphoses before they adopt their final shape.   Butler, *The Way of All Flesh*, LIII

Too sudden a jump from bad fortune to good is just as dangerous as one from good to bad.
Ibid., LXXVIII

Today we love what tomorrow we hate.   Collins, *The Moonstone*, First Period, II

What a change is that from the triumph of victory to the sudden approach of death!
Cooper, *Satanstoe*, II, XIV

If you are sensible of your faults, that is a very great step towards amending them.
Day, *The History of Sandford and Merton*, 337

It was nothing at all unusual for Mr. Micawber to sob violently at the beginning of one of these Saturday night conversations, and sing about Jack's delight being his lovely Nan, towards the end of it. I have known him come home to supper with a flood of tears, and a declaration that nothing was now left but a jail; and go to bed making a calculation of the expense of putting bow-windows to the house, "in case anything turned up," which was his favorite expression.   Dickens, *David Copperfield*, XI

The changes of a fevered room are slow and fluctuating; but the changes of the fevered world are rapid and irrevocable.   Dickens, *Little Dorrit*, Book II, XXXIII

Change begets change. Nothing propagates so fast.
Dickens, *Martin Chuzzlewit*, XVIII

Shakespeare turned familiar things into constellations which should enlighten the world for ages.   Dickens, *Nicholas Nickleby*, XLVIII

Such are the changes which a few years bring about, and so do things pass away, like a tale that is told.   Dickens, *The Old Curiosity Shop*, Last Chapter

Time and accident change everything.   Disraeli, *Sybil*, Book V, XI

The age of chivalry is past. Bores have succeeded to dragons.
Disraeli, *The Young Duke*, Book II, V

A great experience transforms. We must ever be more or less than our old selves.
Eggleston, *Roxy*, LIX

The natur o' things doesn't change, though it seems as if one's own life was nothing but change.   Eliot, *Adam Bede*, XI

It's well we should feel as life's a reckoning we can't make twice over; there's no real making amends in this world, any more nor you can mend a wrong subtraction by doing your addition right.   *Ibid.*, XVIII

No story is the same to us after a lapse of time—or rather, we who read it are no longer the same interpreters.   *Ibid.*, LIV

All changes are painful when people have been happy.
Eliot, *Daniel Deronda*, Book II, XVI

A man might see good arguments for changing once, and not see them for changing again.   Eliot, *Middlemarch*, Book II, XVII

We have no right to come forward and urge wider changes for good, until we have tried to alter the evils which lie under our own hands. *Ibid.*, Book IV, XXXIX

Like the waves of the ocean, human affairs are merely in a state of ebb and flow.
Godwin, *St. Leon*, 338

The great inviolate place [Egdon Heath] had an ancient permanence which the sea cannot claim. Who can say of a particular sea that it is old? Distilled by the sun, kneaded by the moon, it is renewed in a year, in a day, or in an hour.
Hardy, *Return of the Native*, Book I, I

Faces change so much from hour to hour, that the same set of features has often no keeping with itself; to an eye, at least, which looks at expression more than outline.
Hawthorne, *The Marble Faun*, II

I seemed to feel a new man inside my old skin, and I longed for a new world.
James, *The American*, II

The eye is hurt by what it is not accustomed to see. Jenner, *The Placid Man*, II

A man used to vicissitudes is not easily dejected. Johnson, *Rasselas*, 58

Our minds, like our bodies, are in continual flux; something is hourly lost, and something acquired. *Ibid.*, 134

Such is the state of life, that none are happy but by the anticipation of change; the change itself is nothing. *Ibid.*, 179

A good part of the Old World on its passage to the New World was lost overboard. Our ancestors were very considerably cleansed by the darling waters of the Atlantic.
Judd, *Margaret*, Volume II, IV

Great reforms must be gradual. *Ibid.*, Volume III

It is easier to tear down than to build up. *Ibid.*

Easier to remove an error than supply a truth. *Ibid.*

Custom changes the very nature of things, and what was honorable a thousand years ago may probably be looked upon as infamous now. Lennox, *The Female Quixote*, II

No change can make the virtuous man despised, except by knaves and fools.
McCarthy, *The Fair Moralist*, 16

A Phoebus Apollo turned fasting friar. Meredith, *The Egoist*, II

What revolutions may occur in a short space of time to overthrow the best formed plans for happiness! Parsons, *The Mysterious Warning*, II

Writing an earnest letter seldom leaves the mind *in statu quo.*
Reade, *The Cloister and the Hearth*, LXXXIII

Nobody ever thought of turning a sword into a sponge.
Richardson, *Clarissa Harlowe*, I

When things are at worst they will mend. *Ibid.*, II

The increase of manners from barbarity to good breeding is as imperceptible as the hand of a clock. Shebbeare, *The Marriage Act*, I

Man's yesterday may ne'er be like his morrow;/ Nought may endure but mutability!
Shelley, M., *Frankenstein*, X

That restless love of change, which forms so legitimate a portion of our original nature.
Simms, *The Partisan*, Volume II, I

Our misdeeds do not change us. Stevenson, *Prince Otto*, Book III, II

Last week I saw a woman flayed, and you will hardly believe how much it altered her person for the worse. Swift, *A Tale of a Tub*, Section IX

In former times great objects were attained by great work. We get on now with a lighter step, and quicker: ridicule is found to be more convincing than argument, imaginary agonies touch more than true sorrows, and monthly novels convince, when learned quartos fail to do so. If the world is to be set right, the work will be done by shilling numbers.   Trollope, *The Warden*, XVI

There are some that never know how to change.   Twain, *Joan of Arc*, Book II, XXVI

The hog is an uninteresting beast. His way of life is monotonous and restricted; he has but one ambition, which in nearly all cases is satisfied. There is no individuality about him; no interesting variation from the normal to attract our studious attention. But when, by a swift and highly ingenious metamorphosis, he ceases to be Hog, and becomes Provisions, he assumes a national importance; his fluctuations become fascinating, romantic.   Webster, *The Banker and the Bear*, VI

The world is changed because you are made of ivory and gold. The curves of your lips rewrite history.   Wilde, *The Picture of Dorian Gray*, XX

CHARACTER

First of all things in the world a man must be a man—with all the grace and vigor and, if possible, all the beauty of the body. Then he must be a gentleman—with all the grace, the vigor, the good taste of the mind. And then with both of these—no matter what his creed, his dogmas, his superstitions, his religion—with both of these he must try to live a beautiful life of the spirit.   Allen, J.L., *The Choir Invisible*, XIII

The strong impregnable man, the man whom no vice tempts, no weakness assails, who is loyal without effort,—such a man lacks breadth and magnetism and the power to read the human heart and sympathize with both its noble impulses and its terrible weaknesses.   Atherton, *Doomswoman*, XXIV

"He is just what a young man ought to be—sensible, good humored, lively; and I never saw such happy manners—so much ease, with such perfect good breeding!" "He is also handsome, which a young man ought likewise to be, if he possibly can. His character is thereby complete."   Austen, *Pride and Prejudice*, Volume I, IV

Affectation of candor is common enough—one meets it everywhere. But to be candid without ostentation or design—to take the good of everybody's character and make it still better, and say nothing of the bad—belongs to you alone.   *Ibid.*

Implacable resentment is a shade in a character.   *Ibid.*, Volume I, XI

There is in every disposition a tendency to some particular evil, a natural defect, which not even the best education can overcome.   *Ibid.*

It is hard to fix character by conduct.   Brooke, *Emily Montague*, III

No author ever drew a character, consistent to human nature, but what he was forced to ascribe to it many inconsistencies.   Bulwer, *What Will He Do with It?*, Book IV, XIV

To judge human character rightly, a man may sometimes have very small experience, provided he has a very large heart.   *Ibid.*, Book V, IV

Where anything of a person's character is doubtful, the ties of society and the laws of humanity claim a favorable interpretation.   Burney, *Evelina*, 202

Your genuine rogue is a man of elastic temperament, not easily compressible under any pressure of disaster.   Collins, *A Rogue's Life*, IV

Steadiness of character belongs only to the woman of experience, how is it to be acquired in a state of isolation from society?   Dacre, *Passions*, Letter LI

She was a good plain sample of a nature that is ever, in the mass, better, truer, higher, nobler, quicker to feel, and much more constant to retain, all tenderness and pity, self-denial and devotion, than the nature of men.   Dickens, *Dombey and Son*, III

There is no influence at the same time so powerful and so singular as that of individual character. It arises as often from the weakness of the character as from its strength.
Disraeli, *Coningsby*, Book II, I

He would not argue, he would not talk freely. In his manner was something of the dogmatist. What he could not correct, he would ignore. There was a tendency in him to walk away from the impossible thing.
Dreiser, *Sister Carrie*, IX

Adam had a devout mind, though he was perhaps impatient of devout words, and his tenderness lay very close to his reverence, so that the one could hardly be stirred without the other.
Eliot, *Adam Bede*, XXXVIII

Character is not cut in marble—it is not something solid and unalterable. It is something living and changing, and may become diseased as our bodies do.
Eliot, *Middlemarch*, Book VIII, LXXII

There's folks as things 'ull allays go awk'ard with; empty sacks 'ull never stand upright.
Eliot, *Mill on the Floss*, Book I, VIII

[A person's] history is a thing hardly to be predicted even from the completest knowledge of characteristics. For the tragedy of our lives is not created entirely from within.
Ibid., Book VI, VI

That inexorable law of human souls, that we prepare ourselves for sudden deeds by the reiterated choice of good or evil which gradually determines character.
Eliot, *Romola*, Book II, XXIII

It is a more useful capacity to be able to foretell the actions of men, in any circumstance, from their characters, than to judge of their characters from their actions.
Fielding, H., *Tom Jones*, 76

What sort of a character is that which must be supported by witnesses?
Godwin, *Caleb Williams*, I

Many women can sit gracefully; some can stand gracefully; and a few can assume a series of graceful positions. But natural movement is the result and expression of the whole being, and cannot be well and nobly performed, unless responsive to something in the character.
Hawthorne, *Blithedale Romance*, XVIII

Character must go for something.
Howells, *Silas Lapham*, XXIII

"You're so many-sided." "If one's two-sided it's enough." "You're the most charming of polygons!"
James, H., *Portrait of a Lady*, XV

There are some characters of such a cast as to elude all penetration; but as they can only be the result of a union between a very good head and a very bad heart, they are not very common in the world.
Jenner, *The Placid Man*, I

When you find me a virtuous jockey, I will find you a benevolent wise man.
Melville, *Confidence-Man*, III

Let nature, to the perplexity of the naturalists, produce her duck-billed beavers as she may, lesser authors, some may hold, have no business to be perplexing readers with duck-billed characters. Always, they should represent human nature not in obscurity, but transparency, which, indeed, is the practice with most novelists, and is, perhaps, in some cases, some way felt to be a kind of honor rendered by them to their kind.
Ibid., XIV

For much the same reason that there is but one planet to one orbit, so can there be but one original character to one work of invention. Two would conflict to chaos.
Ibid., XLIV

The history of the patriarch Jacob is interesting not less from the unselfish devotion which we are bound to ascribe to him, than from the deep worldly wisdom and polished Italian tact, gleaming under an air of Arcadian unaffectedness. The diplomatist and the shepherd are blended; a union not without warrant; the apostolic serpent and dove. A tanned Machiavelli in tents.
Melville, *Israel Potter*, VIII

Having carefully weighed the world, Franklin could act any part in it. Jack of all trades, master of each and mastered by none—the type and genius of his land. Franklin was everything but a poet.
Ibid.

Much of a man's character will be found betokened in his backbone.
Melville, *Moby Dick*, LXXX

The wild beast in him was not the less deadly because it did not roar, and the devil in him not the less active because he resolved to do nothing.
Meredith, *Ordeal of Richard Feverel*, XXXVII

The introduction of a passion into a character does not add to it any more than a gust of wind does to a landscape.
Moore, *A Mummer's Wife*, XXVII

She was dignified without haughtiness, religious without bigotry, though decisive and firm. She possessed penetration to discover what was just, resolution to adhere to it, and temper to practice it with gentleness and grace.
Radcliffe, *The Italian*, III

What has a man's face to do with his character? Can a man of good character help having a disagreeable face?
Radcliffe, *The Mysteries of Udolpho*, I

Wherever she goes, she confers a favor; whomever she leaves, she fills with regret.
Richardson, *Clarissa Harlowe*, I

A person willing to think favorably of him would hope that a brave, a learned, and a diligent man cannot be naturally a bad man.
Ibid.

Characters extremely good or extremely bad are seldom justly given. Favor for a person will exalt the one, as disfavor will sink the other.
Ibid.

The man's head is better than his heart.
Ibid.

I love a virtuous character, as much in man, as in woman.
Ibid.

Character biases and runs away with all mankind.
Ibid., III

The stillest water is the deepest, while the bubbling only betrays shallowness.
Ibid., IV

She never stirred out, but somebody was the better for it.
Ibid.

Born to undo, or to be undone.
Richardson, *Pamela*, 48

The gentleman has never been controlled: the lady has never been contradicted.
Ibid., 471

Never judge of character by report.
Richardson, *Sir Charles Grandison*, Two, III

You cannot always separate bad qualities from good in the same person.
Ibid., Three, VI

What is the boasted character of most of those who are called heroes, to the unostentatious merit of a truly good man?
Ibid., Three, VII

It is a cruel thing they do, who fasten on a man too high a character.
Schreiner, *Undine*, XI

If you wish to ruin a man's character, if you wish to have your revenge on an enemy, if you wish to blight a man's life because you have done him an injury, be sparing with your words.
Ibid.

The care of our virtue we owe to ourselves; the preservation of our characters is due to the world.
Scott, *A Description of Millenium Hall*, 94

Doing justice to all mankind is the most amiable character amongst men.
Shebbeare, *Lydia*, II

She be no bee, yet full of honey is.
Sidney, *Arcadia*, I

Firmness of character usually implies a large share of cheerfulness and elsasticity.
Simms, *The Scout*, XXXII

If a man's character is to be abused, there's nobody like a relation to do the business.
Thackeray, *Vanity Fair*, XIX

Do all men who wear big diamond breastpins flourish their knives at table, and use bad grammar, and cheat?   Twain and Warner, *The Gilded Age*, Volume I, XV

CHARACTERISTICS: *see also* TYPE

I combine the opposite characteristics of a man of sentiment and a man of business.
Collins, *Woman in White*, Part II, Third Epoch

This was your true mediaeval. Proud, amorous, vindictive, generous, foolish, cunning, impulsive, unprincipled; and ignorant as dirt.
Reade, *The Cloister and the Hearth*, LXIV

CHARITY: *see also* BENEVOLENCE

The rector was not vindictive—and some philanthropists have been so. He was not intolerant—and there is a rumor that some zealous theologians have not been altogether free from that blemish. Although he would probably have declined to give his body to be burned in any public cause, and was far from bestowing all his goods to feed the poor, he had that charity which has sometimes been lacking to very illustrious virtue—he was tender to other men's failings, and unwilling to impute evil.   Eliot, *Adam Bede*, V

Charitable people never know vinegar from wine till they have swallowed it and got the colic.   Eliot, *Middlemarch*, Book I, VI

An ardent charity was at work setting the virtuous mind to make a neighbor unhappy for her good.   *Ibid.*, Book VIII, LXXIV

There is no command more express, no duty more frequently enjoined, than charity.
Fielding, H., *Joseph Andrews*, 141-142

Whoever is void of charity is no Christian.   *Ibid.*, 142

Though he never gave a farthing, he had always the word charity in his mouth.
Ibid., 143

Charity is a generous disposition to relieve the distressed.   *Ibid.*, 233

Captain Blifil, with great learning, proved that the word *charity* in Scripture nowhere means beneficence or generosity.   Fielding, H., *Tom Jones*, 55

Those come nearer to the Scripture meaning of *charity* who understand by it candor, or the forming of a benevolent opinion of our brethren, and passing a favorable judgment on their actions.   *Ibid.*

Nothing less than a persuasion of universal depravity can lock up the charity of a good man.   *Ibid.*, 57

Charity doth not adopt the vices of its objects.   *Ibid.*, 782

Charity never fears infection, in attending upon the sick.   Johnstone, *The Pilgrim*, II

To be the subject of alms-giving is trying, and to feel in duty bound to appear cheerfully grateful under the trial must be still more so.   Melville, *Confidence-Man*, III

To heaven with charity!   *Ibid.*

Charity, like poetry, should be cultivated, if only for its being graceful.   *Ibid.*, XXVIII

The innocent heart will be a charitable one.
Richardson, *Sir Charles Grandison*, Two, IV

Charity may be given with the left hand so privily that the right hand does not know it, and yet the left hand may regret to feel that it has no immediate reward.
Trollope, *The Warden*, XIII

CHARM

A charm must be accompanied by a strong wish on the part of the charmer that it may succeed.
Bulwer, The Caxtons, Book II, V

His great charm was attentiveness.
Dreiser, Sister Carrie, X

Experience had not yet taken away that freshness of the spirit which is the charm of the body.
Ibid., XV

Decisive action is seen by appreciative minds to be frequently objectless, and sometimes fatal; but decision, however suicidal, has more charm for a woman than the most unequivocal Fabian success.
Hardy, A Pair of Blue Eyes, XII

I find him charming. He atones for being occasionally somewhat overdressed by being always absolutely over-educated.
Wilde, The Picture of Dorian Gray, XV

CHASTITY: *see also* VIRTUE

Was once lost always lost really true of chastity?
Hardy, Tess, XV

CHEATING: *see also* HONESTY

We don't cheat in America, but you can, if you choose.
Alcott, Little Women, XII

CHILDHOOD; CHILDREN: *see also* AGE AND YOUTH; FAMILY

After being unusually good, children are apt to turn short round and refresh themselves [by acting like Sancho].
Alcott, Old-Fashioned Girl, V

Children can feel, but they cannot analyze their feelings; and if the analysis is partially effected in thought, they know not how to express the result of the process in words.
Bronte, C., Jane Eyre, III

No sight so sad as that of a naughty child.
Ibid., IV

The Catechism was written too exclusively from the parental point of view.
Butler, The Way of All Flesh, VII

Why could not children be born into the world grown up?
Ibid., XX

Soldiers are like children—but for that matter, what men are not?
Cooke, Surry of Eagle's-Nest, LV

Emperors, kings, presidents and statesmen are all overgrown children.
Ibid.

Shakespeare said that the man who has no music in his soul should not be trusted; and far less trust the man who does not find, in the gay prattle of children, a music sweeter than the harp of Aeolus.
Cooke, Virginia Comedians, Volume II, XXXIV

To neglect children is to murder them.
Defoe, Moll Flanders, 176–177

In the little world in which children have their existence, whosoever brings them up, there is nothing so finely perceived and so finely felt as injustice.
Dickens, Great Expectations, VIII

These bitter sorrows of childhood!
Eliot, Mill on the Floss, Book I, V

We could never have loved the earth so well if we had had no childhood in it.
Ibid.

Surely if we could recall that early bitterness, and the dim guesses, the strangely perspectiveless conception of life that gave the bitterness its intensity, we should not pooh-pooh the griefs of our children.
Ibid., Book I, VII

Childhood has no forebodings; but then, it is soothed by the memories of outlived sorrow.
Ibid., Book I, IX

There is no sense of ease like the ease we felt in those scenes where we were born.
Ibid., Book II, I

When children are doing nothing, they are doing mischief.
Fielding, H., *Tom Jones*, 691

The old rigmarole of childhood.
Gaskell, *Wives and Daughters*, I

The gift of sudden insight is sometimes vouchsafed to children.
Hardy, *Jude the Obscure*, Part I, IV

Of the various sentimental fallacies entertained by adult humanity in regard to childhood, none are more ingeniously inaccurate and gratuitously idiotic than a comfortable belief in its profound ignorance of the events in which it daily moves, and the motives and characters of the people who surround it. Harte, *Cressy*, XIII

Children have always a sympathy in the agitations of those connected with them.
Hawthorne, *Scarlet Letter*, XXI

To play with a child you must be childish. James, H., *Confidence*, XXIX

What is the child's first sense of death? Judd, *Margaret*, Volume I, V

Boyhood is a natural state of rascality. Melville, *Confidence-Man*, XXII

Childhood is to youth what manhood is to age. Melville, *Mardi*, CL

It was the devious-cruising Rachel, that in her retracing search after her missing children, only found another orphan. Melville, *Moby Dick*, Epilogue

Children of the poor have happy mothers. Meredith, *Amazing Marriage*, XXXII

Eight children is not a number to stop at. Nine if you like, but not eight. No one thinks of stopping at eight. Meredith, *Ordeal of Richard Feverel*, XXII

"Children cry, but don't die, for their lumps of sugar. When they grow older, they—"
"Simply have a stronger appreciation of the sugar, and make a greater noise to obtain it." *Ibid.*, XXVII

It is cruel to compliment children, since they mistake flattery for truth.
Radcliffe, *The Mysteries of Udolpho*, I

When little, children make their parents fools; when great, mad.
Richardson, *Clarissa Harlowe*, II

The easy pardon perverse children meet with is the reason so many follow their example. *Ibid.*, IV

The child so much a woman, what must the woman be? *Ibid.*

If the world was all children I could like it.
Schreiner, *Story of an African Farm*, Part II, XI

Children must first by fear be induced to know that which after when they do know, they are most glad of. Sidney, *Arcadia*, III

The temperaments of children are often as oddly unsuited to parents as if capricious fairies had been filling cradles with changelings Stowe, *Orr's Island*, XX

[Adolescence:] the period when the boy wishes he were dead, and everybody else wishes so too. *Ibid.*

The wretched, half-fledged, half-conscious, anomalous creature [the adolescent boy] has all the desires of the man, and none of the rights; has a double and triple share of nervous edge and intensity in every part of his nature, and no definitely perceived objects on which to bestow it—and all sorts of unreasonable moods and phases are the result. *Ibid.*

One of the most common signs of this period [of adolescence], in some natures, is the love of contradiction and opposition,—a blind desire to go contrary to everything that is commonly received among the older people. *Ibid.*

If people would but leave children to themselves, small harm would accrue.
Thackeray, *Vanity Fair*, V

CHILDHOOD; CHILDREN (*continued*)

Ugly children must be minded as well as pretty ones.

Trollope, *The Way We Live Now*, LXXX

That golden treasure denied them by Nature, a child.

Twain, *Pudd'nhead Wilson*, XIX

CHOICE: *see also* COMPARISON/CONTRAST; DECISION; etc.

"Tragedy may be your choice, but it will certainly appear that comedy chooses *you*."

Austen, *Mansfield Park*, Volume One, XIV

Their religion was of a simple, semi-pagan kind, but there was no heresy in it,—if heresy properly means choice.　　　Eliot, *Mill on the Floss*, Book IV, I

How easy a choice poverty and honesty, rather than plenty and wickedness.

Richardson, *Pamela*, 28

I'd as lief give forty shillings as be hanged.　　　Smollett, *Sir Launcelot Greaves*, 181

When a man is hemmed in by two indecorums, and must commit one of them, let him choose which he will, the world will blame him.　　　Sterne, *Tristram Shandy*, VIII

Better be killed than frightened to death.

Surtees, *Mr. Facey Romford's Hounds*, XXXII

CHRISTIANITY: *see also* GOD; PHILOSOPHY; RELIGION; etc.

You ought certainly to forgive them as a Christian, but never to admit them in your sight, or allow their names to be mentioned in your hearing.

Austen, *Pride and Prejudice*, Volume III, XV

The Nazarene [not Christ here] was one of those hardy, vigorous, and enthusiastic men, by whom God in all times has worked the revolutions of earth, and those, above all, in the establishment and in the reformation of His own religion—men who were formed to convert, because formed to endure.　　　Bulwer, *Pompeii*, Book One, VIII

Sorrow and sympathy! Oh, what Pagan emotions to expect from a Christian English-woman anchored firmly on her faith!　　　Collins, *Moonstone*, Second Period, Chapter III

The true Christian faith believes in Man as well as in God.

Collins, *The New Magdalen*, XVII

If there can be a Christian without humanity and charity, a devil may be a saint.

Collyer, *Felicia to Charlotte*, II

As for Bob and the mates, I never heard any more of them. The former most probably continued a "*kickee*," until years and experience enabled him to turn the tables on humanity, when, as is usually the case with Christians, he would be very likely to take up the business of a "kicker" with so much the greater zeal, on account of his early sufferings.　　　Cooper, *The Monikins*, Conclusion

Humility and penitence are the seals of Christianity.　　　Cooper, *The Pioneers*, XXVIII

It is premature to think of introducing Christianity on this frontier. Christianity is essentially a civilized religion, and can only be of use among civilized beings.

Cooper, *Satanstoe*, Volume II, XV

The Christian religion, though not exclusively, is, emphatically speaking, the religion of the poor.　　　Day, *The History of Sandford and Merton*, 241

The precepts of the Christian religion are founded upon the most perfect knowledge of the human heart, as they furnish a continual barrier against the most destructive passions, and the most subversive of human happiness.　　　*Ibid.*, 245

A Turk turns his face, after washing it well, to the East, when he says his prayers; these good people, [the Christians,] after giving their faces such a rub against the World as to take the smiles off, turn with no less regularity, to the darkest side of Heaven. Between the Mussulman and the Pharisee, commend me to the first!

Dickens, *Oliver Twist*, XLVI

Muscular Christianity.   Disraeli, *Endymion*

Christianity teaches us to love our neighbor as ourself; modern society acknowledges no neighbor.   Disraeli, *Sybil*, Book II, V

There is no calamity so great that a Christian philosopher may not reasonably laugh at it.   Fielding, H., *Amelia*, I

A true Christian can never be disappointed if he doth not receive his reward in this world; the laborer might as well complain that he is not paid his hire in the middle of the day.   *Ibid.*, II

What matters where a man's treasure is whose heart is in the Scriptures?

Fielding, H., *Joseph Andrews*, 140

If we judge according to the sentiments of some critics, and of some Christians, no author will be saved in this world, and no man in the next.

Fielding, H., *Tom Jones*, 491

Christian faith is a grand cathedral, with divinely pictured windows.

Hawthorne, *The Marble Faun*, XXXIII

Alas Christianity! What does it avail,—thy concern for the poor,—thy tenderness for the oppressed, thy system of fraternal love and affection!   Hildreth, *Slave*, Volume I, XIX

They [the preachers of Isms] would convert us from Christ to John Wesley or John Calvin.   Judd, *Margaret*, Volume III

To each man alive one particular precept of the Christian code is harder to realize and practice than all the rest put together.   Lawrence, *Guy Livingstone*, XXX

As a soldier out of honor is quick in taking affront, so a Christian out of religion is quick, sometimes perhaps a little too much so, in spying heresy.

Melville, *Confidence-Man*, XXII

In this matter of christening ships of war, Christian nations are but too apt to be daredevils. Witness the following, British names all: The Conqueror, the Defiance, the Revenge, the Spitfire, the Dreadnaught, the Thunderer, and the Tremendous.

Melville, *Mardi*, XXVIII

We talk of the Turks, and abhor the cannibals; but may not some of *them* go to heaven before some of *us*?   Melville, *Redburn*, LVIII

We may have civilized bodies and yet barbarous souls. We are blind to the real sights of this world; deaf to its voice; and dead to its death. And not till we know, that one grief outweighs ten thousand joys will we become what Christianity is striving to make us.

Ibid.

Heaven help the "Isles of the Sea"!—The sympathy which Christendom feels for them has, alas! in too many instances proved their bane.   Melville, *Typee*, XXVI

Have not errors and abuses crept into the most sacred places, and may there not be unworthy or incapable missionaries abroad, as well as ecclesiastics of a similar character at home?   *Ibid.*

Christians are not born in hermitages.   Meredith, *Ordeal of Richard Feverel*, IV

Extremes bring ruin to the best Christian societies.   Mitchell, *Hugh Wynne*, X

The true Celt is still a pagan—Christianity has been superimposed.

Moore, *Evelyn Innes*, XXVI

"The loaves and fishes are typical of a mixed diet; and the practice of the Church in all ages shows—" "That it never loses sight of the loaves and fishes."

Peacock, *Headlong Hall*, II

CHRISTIANITY (*continued*)

This was a century in which the fine arts and the higher mechanical arts were not separated by any distinct boundary, nor were those who practiced them; and it was an age in which artists sought and loved one another. Should this last statement stagger a painter or writer of our day, let me remind him that even Christians loved one another at first starting.   Reade, *The Cloister and the Hearth*, I

Them that havena dipped their hands in any little difficulty should be very mindful of the case of them that have. And that is the good Christianity.
Stevenson, *Kidnapped*, XVIII

Christianity is emphatically the religion of humanity. Earth and man are its themes.
Tourgee, *Murvale Eastman*, XI

Civilization is not necessarily progress. Christianity is not necessarily righteousness.
Ibid., XLII

As to an open enemy, the Christian's path is clear. We are but soldiers under orders. What business have we to be truce-making on our own account? The war is not ours, but God's!   Ward, *Robert Elsmere*, Book II, XII

To re-conceive the Christ is the special task of our age, though in some sort and degree it has been the ever-recurring task of Europe since the beginning.
Ibid., Book V, XL

CIRCUMSTANCE: *see also* CAUSE AND EFFECT; DESTINY; etc.

The only art of living is to confine our wishes within the limits of our circumstances.
Anonymous, *The Fruitless Repentance*, I

Helpless women should be forgiven much that they do, in their desperate battle with Circumstance.   Atherton, *Senator North*, Book II, XXIV

When plans for the future are futile, live in the present and be careful to make no mistake. It is the only philosophy for those who are not in the favor of Circumstance.
Ibid., Book III, XII

There are some circumstances which even women cannot control.
Austen, *The Watsons*, II

Our virtues and our vices depend too much on our circumstances.
Cleland, *Memoirs of a Woman of Pleasure*, 71

Through all the ways of our unintelligible world the trivial and the terrible walk hand in hand together. The irony of circumstances holds no mortal catastrophe in respect.
Collins, *Woman in White*, Part II, Third Epoch

The Duke of Wellington has ever been the votary of circumstances. He cares little for causes. He watches events rather than seeks to produce them. It is a characteristic of the military mind.   Disraeli, *Coningsby*, Book I, VII

It always remains true that if we had been greater, circumstance would have been less strong against us.   Eliot, *Middlemarch*, Book VI, LVIII

Unwonted circumstances may make us all rather unlike ourselves: there are conditions under which the most majestic person is obliged to sneeze, and our emotions are liable to be acted on in the same incongruous manner.   *Ibid.*, Book VI, LXII

Extraordinary circumstances often bring along with them extraordinary strength.
Godwin, *St. Leon*, 117

One favorable circumstance is often sufficient to remove the most disadvantageous opinion.   Johnstone, *The Reverie*, I

Poetry, love, and such-like are the drugs earth has to offer to high natures, as she offers to low ones debauchery.   Meredith, *Ordeal of Richard Feverel*, XVI

How do different circumstances either sanctify or condemn the same action!
Richardson, *Clarissa Harlowe*, I

The hint of least moment is often pregnant with events of the greatest.   *Ibid.*, II

Occasion calls not out every man equally.
Richardson, *Sir Charles Grandison*, One, II

By unlikeliest means greatest matters may come to conclusion.   Sidney, *Arcadia*, IV

I am governed by circumstances—I cannot govern them.
Sterne, *A Sentimental Journey*, 83

CITIZENSHIP

The vote of the citizen takes place of the sword of the adventurer. This is at the bottom of all order and subordination. A vote given wrong, or withheld, may occasion ultimately a convulsion in the commonwealth.
Brackenridge, *Modern Chivalry*, Part II, Volume II

You can paint a man dying for his country, but you can't express on canvas a man fulfilling the duties of a good citizen.   Howells, *Silas Lapham*, XIV

CIVILITY; ETIQUETTE: *see also* GOOD MANNERS; COURTESY; etc.

Civility should take leave: where nothing is due to love, something is due to good manners.   Anonymous, *Memoirs of an Oxford Scholar*, 38

Though civility is due to other people, there is also civility due to oneself.
Brooke, *Emily Montague*, I

To the utter consternation of the company, he took off his wig to wipe his head, which occasioned such universal horror, that all who were near the door escaped into other apartments, while those who were too much enclosed for flight with one accord turned away their heads.   Burney, *Cecilia*, II

Her civility is too formal to be comfortable, and too mechanical to be flattering.
Burney, *Evelina*, 262

True politeness banishes all restraint and embarrassment.   *Ibid.*, 273

Perhaps the best civility is to mind our own business.
Dickens, *The Mystery of Edwin Drood*, VIII

Ceremony keeps fools at a distance; sensible people easily dispense with it in favor of one another.   Jenner, *The Placid Man*, II

I am naturally civil when I am civilly used.   Smollett, *Peregrine Pickle*, 413

CIVILIZATION; CITY *VS.* COUNTRY

Washington more than any other city in the world swarms with simple-minded exhibitions of human nature; men and women curiously out of place, whom it would be cruel to ridicule and ridiculous to weep over.   Adams, *Democracy*, V

Civilization makes us believe that conventions are the only comfortable conditions in the world, certainly indispensable.   Atherton, *Senator North*, Book II, III

The worst of civilization is, it either produces discontented savages or goes too far and turns the whole body into brain.   *Ibid.*, Book II, X

What else does civilization mean if those of us that have its highest advantages are not wiser and more fastidious than the mob?   *Ibid.*, Book III, VI

When I am in the country, I never wish to leave it; and when I am in town it is pretty much the same. They have each their advantages, and I can be equally happy in either.
Austen, *Pride and Prejudice*, Volume I, IX

Those Chinamen knew what they were about when they refused to let in our Western civilization.
Bellamy, *Looking Backward*, II

In our modern system of civilization, celebrity is the lever that will move anything.
Collins, *Moonstone*, Fifth Narrative

Men too much practiced in the interests of life, constantly overreach themselves when brought in contact with the simple and intelligent and the experience of every day proves that, as there is no fame permanent which is not founded on virtue, so there is no policy secure which is not bottomed on the good of the whole.
Cooper, *The Bravo*, XXIV

Civilization is arbitrary, meaning one thing in France, another thing at Leaphigh, and still a third in Dorsetshire.
Cooper, *The Monikins*, Conclusion

There is no such stimulant of humanity as a good moneyed stake in its advancement.
Ibid.

Civilization is just as much a means of providence as religion itself; and it is clearly intended that one should be built on the other.
Cooper, *Satanstoe*, Volume II, XV

Civilization and Progress are not the same thing. We have too much progress and too little civilization.
Crawford, *A Rose of Yesterday*, XIII

Progress is omnivorous, eager after new things, seeking above all to save trouble and get money. Civilization is eclectic, slow, painstaking, wise, willing to buy good at the price it is worth.
Ibid.

Civilization has no time for ceremony.
Disraeli, *Coningsby*, Book III, IV

Villagers never swarm: a whisper is unknown among them, and they seem almost as incapable of an undertone as a cow or a stag.
Eliot, *Adam Bede*, II

A town "familiar with forgotten years."
Eliot, *Mill on the Floss*, Book I, XII

That civilization which has its basis in despotism is more worthless and hateful than the state of savages running wild in the woods.
Godwin, *St. Leon*, 320

When she plodded on in the shade of the hedge, silently thinking, she had the hard, half-apathetic expression of one who deems anything possible at the hands of Time and Chance except, perhaps, fair play. The first phase was the work of Nature, the second probably of civilization.
Hardy, *Mayor of Casterbridge*, I

The love of social superiority, the very impulse of the human heart, which is the mainspring of civilization and the chief source of all human improvement, is able, when suffered to work on, uncontrolled by other more generous emotions, to corrupt man's whole nature, and to drive him to acts the most horrid and detestable.
Hildreth, *Slave*, Volume I, XIX

All civilization comes through literature now.
Howells, *Silas Lapham*, IX

I doubt if the theater is a factor in civilization among us. I dare say it doesn't deprave a great deal, but from what I've seen of it I should say that it was intellectually degrading.
Ibid.

Our manners and customs go for more in life than our qualities.
Ibid., XXVII

It is very rare in country life, where high days and holidays are few, that any occasion of general interest proves to be less than great.
Jewett, *The Country of the Pointed Firs*, XVIII

What separates the enlightened man from the savage? Is civilization a thing distinct, or is it an advanced stage of barbarism?
Melville, *Israel Potter*, XIX

Thrice happy are they who, inhabiting some yet undiscovered island in the midst of the ocean, have never been brought into contaminating contact with the white man.
Melville, *Typee*, II

A high degree of refinement does not seem to subdue our wicked propensities so much after all; and were civilization itself to be estimated by some of its results, it would seem perhaps better for what we call the barbarous part of the world to remain unchanged.

Ibid., III

When the inhabitants of some sequestered island first descry the "big canoe" of the European rolling through the blue waters towards their shores, they rush down to the beach in crowds, and with open arms stand ready to embrace the strangers. Fatal embrace!

Ibid., IV

How often is the term "savages" incorrectly applied! None really deserving of it were ever yet discovered by voyagers or by travellers. They have discovered heathens and barbarians, whom by horrible cruelties they have exasperated into savages.

Ibid.

The Polynesian savage, surrounded by all the luxurious provisions of nature, enjoys an infinitely happier, though certainly a less intellectual existence than the self-complacent European. The voluptuous Indian, with every desire supplied, whom Providence has bountifully provided with all the sources of pure and natural enjoyment, and from whom are removed so many of the ills and pains of life—what has he to desire at the hands of Civilization?

Ibid., XVII

For every advantage she imparts, Civilization holds a hundred evils in reserve.

Ibid.

There were none of those thousand sources of irritation that the ingenuity of civilized man has created to mar his own felicity.

Ibid.

In this secluded abode of happiness there were no cross old women, no cruel step-dames, no withered spinsters, no lovesick maidens, no sour old bachelors, no inattentive husbands, no melancholy young men, no blubbering youngsters, and no squalling brats.

Ibid.

Let the savages be civilized, but civilize them with benefits, and not with evils; and let heathenism be destroyed, but not by destroying the heathen.

Ibid., XXVI

Among the islands of Polynesia, no sooner are the images overturned, the temples demolished, and the idolaters converted into nominal Christians, than disease, vice, and premature death make their appearance.

Ibid.

The abominations of Paganism have given way to the pure rites of the Christian worship,—the ignorant savage has been supplanted by the refined European! Look at Honolulu, the metropolis of the Sandwich Islands!—A community of disinterested merchants, and devoted self-exiled heralds of the Cross, located on the very spot that twenty years ago was defiled by the presence of idolatry. What a subject for an eloquent Bible-meeting orator! Nor has such an opportunity for a display of missionary rhetoric been allowed to pass by unimproved!—But when these philanthropists send us such glowing accounts of one half of their labors, why does their modesty restrain them from publishing the other half of the good they have wrought?—Not until I visited Honolulu was I aware of the fact that the small remnant of the natives had been civilized into draught horses, and evangelized into beasts of burden.

Ibid.

In every case where Civilization has in any way been introduced among those whom we call savages, she has scattered her vices, and withheld her blessings.

Ibid., XXVI

Civilization does not engross all the virtues of humanity: she has not even her full share of them.

Ibid., XXVII

If truth and justice, and the better principles of our nature, cannot exist unless enforced by the statute-book, how are we to account for the social condition of the Typees?

Ibid.

After passing a few weeks in this valley of the Marquesas, I formed a higher estimate of human nature than I had ever before entertained.

Ibid.

A safe percentage on savings is the basis of civilization.

Meredith, *Beauchamp's Career*, XXVI

The good law will come with a better civilization; but before society can be civilized it has to be de-barbarized.

Meredith, *Diana*, XVIII

A woman who has mastered sauces sits on the apex of civilization.
Meredith, *Ordeal of Richard Feverel*, XXXVIII

A perfectly civilized state is just respect for property: a state in which no man takes wrongfully what belongs to another.　　　　Peacock, *Crotchet Castle*, III

How are we to look for love in great cities?　　Radcliffe, *The Mysteries of Udolpho*, I

When it is mere enlightened selfishness, Civilization is better than barbarism only in its methods. It *seems* worse, no doubt, to kill with a club than with an obstructed answer, or by the restriction of opportunity; but it is the same thing to the man who dies.
Tourgee, *Murvale Eastman*, XLII

Civilized society is never very ready to believe anything to the detriment of those who are both rich and fascinating.　　　　Wilde, *The Picture of Dorian Gray*, XI

Anybody can be good in the country.　　　　　　　　　　　　*Ibid.*, XIX

There are only two ways by which man can reach civilization. One is by being cultured, the other by being corrupt.　　　　　　　　　　　　　　*Ibid.*

Country people have no opportunity of being either cultured or corrupt, so they stagnate.
Ibid.

Great cities, those receptacles of misery, those graves of humanity.
Young, *The Adventures of Emmera*, II

CLARITY

That sense of mental empire which belongs to us all in moments of exceptional clearness.
Eliot, *Romola*, Book II, XXXVIII

Clear as a London fog.　　　　　Hawthorne, *The Marble Faun*, Conclusion

CLASS: *see also* CIVILIZATION; SOCIETY

The only power that has no class sympathy is the sovereign.
Disraeli, *Coningsby*, Book VII, II

CLEANLINESS

Mrs. Joe was a very clean housekeeper, but had an exquisite art of making her cleanliness more uncomfortable and unacceptable than dirt itself. Cleanliness is next to Godliness, and some people do the same by their religion.　　　Dickens, *Great Expectations*, IV

CLERGY: *see also* PROFESSION; RELIGION; etc.

It will be everywhere found that as the clergy are, or are not, what they ought to be, so are the rest of the nation.　　　　Austen, *Mansfield Park*, Volume One, IX

A sensible man cannot be in the habit of teaching others their duty every week, cannot go to church twice every Sunday and preach good sermons, without being the better for it himself.　　　　　　　　　　　　*Ibid.*, Volume One, XI

A clergyman has nothing to do but to be slovenly and selfish—read the newspaper, watch the weather, and quarrel with his wife.　　　　　　　　　　*Ibid.*

One great reason why clergymen's households are generally unhappy is because the clergyman is so much at home or close about the house.
Butler, *The Way of All Flesh*, XXIV

The clergyman is expected to be a kind of human Sunday.　　　*Ibid.*, XXVI

If we look to our clergymen to be more than men, we shall probably teach ourselves to think that they are less, and can hardly hope to raise the character of the pastor by denying to him the right to entertain the aspirations of a man.

Trollope, *Barchester Towers*, I

There is no infallible head for a church on earth.

Ibid., XXI

CLEVERNESS: *see also* GENIUS; INTELLECT

A clever fellow knows how to use the brains of other people.

Gissing, *New Grub Street*, XII

Cleverness is an attribute of the selecter missionary lieutenants of Satan.

Meredith, *Diana*, I

He was not clever enough to have enemies.   Wilde, *The Picture of Dorian Gray*, XIX

CLIMAX

There should be climax in all things.   Young, *The Adventures of Emmera*, II

COLONIZATION: *see also* CIVILIZATION; GOVERNMENT; SOCIETY

The founders of a new colony, whatever Utopia of human virtue and happiness they might originally project, have invariably recognized it among their earliest practical necessities to allot a portion of the virgin soil as a cemetery, and another portion as the site of a prison.   Hawthorne, *The Scarlet Letter*, I

COMFORT; RELIEF; SECURITY

A ride of two hundred and odd miles in severe weather, is one of the best softeners of a hard bed that ingenuity can devise.   Dickens, *Nicholas Nickleby*, VIII

Sighs are some present ease to the pensive mind.   Gascoigne, *Master F. J.*, 41

In verse principally a man may best contrive his way of comfort in himself.   *Ibid.*, 42

Blessed be the man that first invented warming pans!

Graves, *The Spiritual Quixote*, I

The house had that pleasant aspect of life, which is like the cheery expression of comfortable activity, in the human countenance.

Hawthorne, *The House of the Seven Gables*, XIII

Only sound institutions can indulge in comforts.   Locke, *A Paper City*, XIX

The secure and comfortable have to pay in occasional panics for the serenity they enjoy.

Meredith, *Beauchamp's Career*, XVIII

One who goes on doggedly enduring, doggedly doing his best, must subsist on comfort of a kind that is likely to be black comfort.   Meredith, *Sandra Belloni*, LV

COMMAND; COMMANDMENT; ENTREATY

Think not, is my eleventh commandment; and sleep when you can, is my twelfth.

Melville, *Moby Dick*, XXIX

This man has very ready knees.   Richardson, *Clarissa Harlowe*, I

I command thee to be convinced.   *Ibid.*, II

COMMERCE: *see also* BUSINESS; MONEY; TRADE

The bank is the heart of the business system. From it and to it, in endless flux and reflux the life blood goes.   Bellamy, *Looking Backward*, XXVIII

COMMERCE (*continued*)

Very odd and very curious, the mental process is, in men of business.
Dickens, *Bleak House*, VI

Here's the rule for bargains: Do other men, for they would do you. That's the true business precept. All others are counterfeits.   Dickens, *Martin Chuzzlewit*, XI

When one is in a difficulty or at a loss, one never knows in what direction a way out may chance to open. It is a business principle of mine not to close up any direction, but to keep an eye on every direction that may present itself.
Dickens, *The Mystery of Edwin Drood*, XXI

The business of our modern world is to open heart and stretch out arms to numbers. In numbers we have our sinews; they are our iron and gold. Scatter them not; teach them the secret of cohesion.   Meredith, *Beauchamp's Career*, LIV

Ilka man maun speak sae as to be understood—that is, when he speaks about business.
Scott, *St. Ronan's Well*, X

If you force a sale on a dull market, I don't care what the property is, you are going to make a poor business of it.   Twain, *Connecticut Yankee*, XXXIV

A banker has to be a sort of commercial father confessor to all his customers.
Webster, *The Banker and the Bear*, I

A run on a bank is like a slit in a man's vein; it does no particular harm if it can be stopped in time, but the stopping of it is imperative, and it will not stop itself.
Ibid., XVII

COMMITMENT: *see also* INVOLVEMENT

The moth that would not be burned must keep out of the flame.
Anonymous, *Memoirs of an Oxford Scholar*, 33–34

The art of sitting gracefully on a fence has never been brought to greater perfection than at the Erewhonian Colleges of Unreason.   Butler, *Erewhon*, XXII

Our charge is great, and therefore our care ought not to be small.
Deloney, *Thomas of Reading*, 234

You bid me unravel a web, and will not suffer me to touch it with one of my fingers.
Godwin, *St. Leon*, 320

He which toucheth the nettle tenderly is soonest stung.   Lyly, *Euphues*, 121

Since all human affairs are subject to organic disorder, since they are created in and sustained by a sort of half-disciplined chaos, he who in great things seeks success must never wait for smooth water, which never was and never will be, but, with what straggling method he can, dash with all his derangements at his object, leaving the rest to Fortune.   Melville, *Israel Potter*, XVIII

Better is it to perish in that howling infinite, than be ingloriously dashed upon the lee, even if that were safety!   Melville, *Moby Dick*, XXIII

All visible objects are but as pasteboard masks. But in each event—in the living act, the undoubted deed—there, some unknown but still reasoning thing puts forth the mouldings of its features from behind the unreasoning mask. If man will strike, strike through the mask! How can the prisoner reach outside except by thrusting through the wall?   *Ibid.*, XXXVI

Never will I give my hand where my heart does not accompany it.
Radcliffe, *The Castles of Athlin and Dunbayne*, 191–192

Words are wind; but deeds are mind.   Richardson, *Clarissa Harlowe*, III

Life is discontent. Hope, which is one of our chief sources of enjoyment, is discontent, since it seeks that which it has not. Content is a sluggard, and should be a slave—a thing to eat and sleep, and perhaps to dream of eating and sleeping, but not a thing to live. Discontent is the life of enterprise, of achievement, of glory—ay, even of affection. Without discontent—a serious and unsleeping discontent—life would be a stagnant stream as untroubled as the back water of the swamps of Edistoh, and as full of the vilest reptiles. Simms, *Yemassee*, XXX

Hardly do we guess aright at the things that are upon the earth, and with labor do we find the things that are before us. Sterne, *Tristram Shandy*, II

COMMONALITY: *see also* SOCIETY; UNITY

No bond unites congenial hearts more firmly than that of a common great aim. August, *Horrid Mysteries*, IV

Human events are conjoined by links imperceptible to keenest eyes. Brown, C.B., *Ormond*, 215

In New York the sea was already full of whales. A common fish must needs disappear wholly from view—remain unseen. Dreiser, *Sister Carrie*, XXX

Even while we are talking and meditating about the earth's orbit and the solar system, what we feel and adjust our movements to is the stable earth and the changing day. Eliot, *Middlemarch*, Book V, LIII

COMMONPLACENESS

Commonplace, that ogre whose girth increases from year to year, and who sits remorseless in the dwellings of the united. Atherton, *Senator North*, Book I, XIX

It is remarkable how things do go on and on and on. They become a habit, then a commonplace. It is because they are so mixed up with the other details of life. Nothing stands out long by itself. Atherton, *Senator North*, Book II, XII

All that can be expected from human weakness, even in working after the most perfect model, is barely to arrive at mediocrity; and were the model less perfect, or the duties less severe, there is the greatest reason to think that even that mediocrity would never be attained. Day, *The History of Sandford and Merton*, 246

Let us always have men ready to give the loving pains of a life to the faithful in representing of commonplace things—men who see beauty in these commonplace things, and delight in showing how kindly the light of heaven falls on them. Eliot, *Adam Bede*, XVII

Because I utter commonplace words, you must not suppose I think only commonplace thoughts. Hardy, *A Pair of Blue Eyes*, XIX

Persons who have wandered, or been expelled, out of the common track of things, even were it for a better system, desire nothing so much as to be led back. Hawthorne, *The House of the Seven Gables*, IX

No commonplace is ever effectually got rid of, except by essentially emptying oneself of it into a book; for once trapped in a book, then the book can be put into the fire, and all will be well. Melville, *Pierre*, Book XVIII, I

Life on any shore is a dull affair. Stowe, *Orr's Island*, VIII

COMMON SENSE: *see also* GENIUS; INTELLECT; JUDGMENT; SENSE

It is more useful to go through life with common sense than with all the taste in the world. Anonymous, *Memoirs of a Coquet*, 185

If you meet each development of every question in the most natural and reasonable manner—presupposing that you possess that highest attribute of civilization, common sense—no question will ever resolve itself into a problem. And difficulties usually disappear as the range of vision contracts. Atherton, *Senator North*, Book I, X

COMMON SENSE (*continued*)

Common sense I take to be a judgment upon common subjects; and that degree of it which falls to the share of the bulk of mankind.
Brackenridge, *Modern Chivalry*, Part II, Volume II

A want of discrimination is a want of common sense. *Ibid.*

Common sense: sense in common things. *Ibid.*, Part II, Volume IV

Good sense will shew you the power of self-conquest, and point out its means.
Burney, *Camilla*, Three, V

There is nothing more likely to succeed with an audience than a good history of witchcraft, or something so very marvelous, as to do violence to common sense, before we give it our faith. Cooper, *Satanstoe*, Volume II, IV

Common Sense—an excellent man—a good deal wrinkled—dreadfully practical—change for a ten-pound note in every pocket—ruled account-book in his hand—say, upon the whole, resembling a tax-gatherer. Dickens, *Bleak House*, XXXVII

Common sense is a sturdy despot that, for the most part, has its own way.
Melville, *Mardi*, CLXXV

In almost everything, we act but upon probabilities; and one exception out of a thousand ought never to determine us. Richardson, *Sir Charles Grandison*, Three, VII

Common sense accords with philosophy and religion more frequently than pedants or zealots are apt to admit. Scott, *The Heart of Midlothian*, LI

Common sense will get the better in all cases, when a man will but give it fair play.
Scott, *Redgauntlet*, Letter VIII

Most people die of a sort of creeping common sense, and discover when it is too late that the only things one never regrets are one's mistakes.
Wilde, *The Picture of Dorian Gray*, III

COMMUNICATION

The liberty of communication cannot be mine till it has lost all its value.
Austen, *Pride and Prejudice*, Volume II, XVII

Why have we the power of speech, but to communicate our thoughts?
Godwin, *Caleb Williams*, II

If nobody was suffered to speak till he had something to say, what pains everybody would take to know something! Jenner, *The Placid Man*, I

They who know how to speak are the only people who know how to hold their tongues.
Ibid.

COMMUNITY: *see also* SOCIETY

There is no community in England; there is aggregation, but aggregation under circumstances which make it rather a dissociating, than an uniting, principle.
Disraeli, *Sybil*, Book II, V

It is a community of purpose that constitutes society; without that, men may be drawn into contiguity, but they still continue virtually isolated. *Ibid.*

COMPANY: *see also* SOCIETY; etc.

Company is always cheerful. Austen, *Northanger Abbey*, XV

"My idea of good company is the company of clever, well-informed people who have a great deal of conversation." "You are mistaken, that is not good company, that is the best." Austen, *Persuasion*, XVI

No single thing is so important to every man as to have for neighbors intelligent, companionable persons.
                                            Bellamy, *Looking Backward*, XXI

If the company of fools irritates, the society of clever men leaves its own peculiar pain also.
                                            Bronte, C., *Shirley*, XII

Books are companionable creatures.   Collins, *The Black Robe*, Book I, I

There are times when a man must act as though life were equally sweet in any company.
                                            Conrad, *Lord Jim*, V

A man may, from various motives, decline to give his company, but perhaps not even a sage would be gratified that nobody missed him.   Eliot, *Middlemarch*, Book III, XXXI

Horses, a sort of animals which, as they dirty no sheets, are thought in inns to pay better for their beds than their riders, and are therefore considered as the more desirable company.
                                            Fielding, H., *Tom Jones*, 365

Good heads and good hearts generally go together, but they are not inseparable companions.
                                            Fielding, S., *David Simple*, I

Good company upon the road is the shortest cut.
                                            Goldsmith, *The Vicar of Wakefield*, 95-96

Good company upon the road makes always the shortest cut.
                                            Jenner, *The Placid Man*, II

People who like any society better than none are, in general, those who know least how to enjoy it.
                                            Ibid.

Much company, much knavery.   Nashe, *The Unfortunate Traveller*, 34

Like little souls will find another out, and mingle, as well as like great ones.
                                            Richardson, *Clarissa Harlowe*, I

Keeping witty company sharpeneth the apprehension.   Scott, *Ivanhoe*, XL

People of fortune choose their company.   Shebbeare, *Lydia*, IV

A companionable man will put up with many inconveniences for the sake of enjoying agreeable society. The wine cannot be bad where the company is agreeable.
                                            Smollett, *Humphry Clinker*, 128

Good society can never go wrong.   Thackeray, *Vanity Fair*, XIII

COMPARISON/CONTRAST; COUNTERPART; COUNTERPOINT: *see also* AMBIVALENCE; DIFFERENCE

Life is full of the saddest and the strongest contrasts.
                                            Ainsworth, *Tower of London*, Book Two, XXV

The humblest painter of real life, if he could have his desire, would select a picturesque background for his figures; but events have an inexorable fashion of choosing their own landscape.
                                            Aldrich, *Stillwater*, V

Is not the one-eyed man who is king among the blind the most fortunate of monarchs? Your little talent in a provincial village looms a great deal taller than your mighty genius in a city.
                                            Ibid., VIII

There is no light without its shade, no good without its inconvenience.
                                            Anonymous, *The Adventures of a Jesuit*, II

Every object is best viewed by contrast. Comparison is a touchstone of truth.
                                            Anonymous, *The Egg*, 110

"I dare say you will find him very agreeable." "Heaven forbid!—*That* would be the greatest misfortune of all!—To find a man agreeable whom one is determined to hate!—Do not wish me such an evil."   Austen, *Pride and Prejudice*, Volume I, XVIII

"How much I shall have to tell!" "And how much I shall have to conceal."
Ibid., Volume II, XV

There certainly was some great mismanagement in the education of those two young men. One has got all the goodness, and the other all the appearance of it.
Ibid., Volume II, XVII

The man who surrenders himself to the arms of a superannuated female, for the sake of a fortune, acts a part not less unworthy and disgraceful, than the prostitute who does the same for half a crown.   Brackenridge, *Modern Chivalry*, Part I, Volume II

The man that covets good will more than money, and the praise of benevolence more than that of private gain has some soul in him; and, other things equal, is to be trusted before him of a contracted spirit, and self-love, in all his actions.
Ibid., Part II, Volume I

Why is it, that a public body is more apt to take offense than an individual? Because everyone becomes of consequence in proportion as he is careful of the honor of the whole.
Ibid.

It is better to bear an individual mischief than a public inconvenience.   *Ibid.*

Little things recall us to earth: the clock struck in the hall; I turned from moon and stars.   Bronte, C., *Jane Eyre*, XII

The gulf that separates man from insects is not wider than that which severs the polluted from the chaste among women.   Brown, C.B., *Wieland*, 132

It is the general brilliancy of the atmosphere which prevents your noticing the size of any particular star.   Bulwer, *The Caxtons*, Book VII, I

Winter is an excellent invigorator, but we all love summer better.   *Ibid.*

The bitter must come before the sweet, and that will make the sweet the sweeter.
Bunyan, *Pilgrim's Progress*, 190

Without the contrast of vice, virtue unloved may be lovely; without the experience of misery, happiness is simply a dull privation of evil.   Burney, *Cecilia*, III

Nothing sets off a compliment so much as a long face.   *Ibid.*

You must not judge by the work, but by the work in connection with the surroundings.
Butler, *The Way of All Flesh*, I

"There's nothing like eating hay when you're faint," the King remarked to her, as he munched away. "I should think throwing cold water over you would be better," Alice suggested: "—or some sal-volatile." "I didn't say there was nothing *better*," the King replied. "I said there was nothing *like* it." Which Alice did not venture to deny.
Carroll, *Through the Looking Glass*, VII

At the end of the reckoning one is no cleverer than the next man—and no more brave.
Conrad, *Lord Jim*, XIII

There is something haunting in the light of the moon; it has all the dispassionateness of a disembodied soul, and something of its inconceivable mystery.   *Ibid.*, XXIV

There are comparisons that should never be made, on account of circumstances that overrule all common efforts.   Cooper, *Satanstoe*, Volume I, IX

The most expert swordsman with his tongue, and the deadest shot at a shingle, are commonly as innocent as lambs of the shedding of blood on the ground.
Ibid., Volume II, II

An Indian *does* seem to have a nose much like that of a hound. Yet a compass would carry a man through the woods with more certainty than any signs on the bark of trees, or looks at the sun.   *Ibid.*, Volume II, VII

A wounded man cannot excite one-half the interest he otherwise might, when there is a chance that others may be slain every minute. *Ibid.*, Volume II, XII

There are two sorts of great worlds; the great vulgar world, which includes all but the very best in taste, principles, and manners, whether it be in a capital or a country; and the great *respectable* world, which, infinitely less numerous, contains the judicious, the instructed, the intelligent, and, on some questions, the good. *Ibid.*, Volume II, XV

Heirs are usually more abundant than estates. Cooper, *Two Admirals*, I

Nine seamen in ten prefer a respectable gale to a flat calm. *Ibid.*, XVII

Second thoughts are always the best. Crane, *The O'Ruddy*, XXIII

It is always best to dodge. A good dodger seldom gets into trouble in this world, and lives to a green old age, while the noble patriot and others of his kind lie in dungeons. *Ibid.*, XXV

A man is better sitting than standing; better lying than sitting; better dead than lying down. Crawford, *Mr. Isaacs*, II

There are moments in human existence, when no evil appears commensurate to that which we at present suffer. Dacre, *Passions*, Conclusion

When people are angry and passionate, one does not so much mind what they say. But when they speak with kindness it seems to pierce to the very heart. Day, *The History of Sandford and Merton*, 337

We never see the true side of our condition, till it is illustrated to us by its contraries; nor know how to value what we enjoy, but by the want of it. Defoe, *Robinson Crusoe*, 129

Many a gentleman lives well upon a soft head, who would find a heart of the same quality a very great drawback. Dickens, *Barnaby Rudge*, XLV

Never fear, good people of an anxious turn of mind, that Art will consign Nature to oblivion. Set anywhere, side by side, the work of God and the work of man; and the former, even though it be a troop of Hands of very small account, will gain in dignity from the comparison. Dickens, *Hard Times*, Book I, XI

Dear reader! It rests with you and me, whether, in our two fields of action, similar things shall be or not. Let them be! We shall sit with lighter bosoms on the hearth, to see the ashes of our fires turn gray and cold. *Ibid.*, Book III, IX

She stood for some moments gazing at the sisters, with affection beaming in one eye, and calculation shining out of the other. Dickens, *Martin Chuzzlewit*, VIII

There are shades in all good pictures, but there are lights too, if we choose to contemplate them. Dickens, *Nicholas Nickleby*, VI

Yolk of egg does not match any waistcoat but a yellow waistcoat, demmit. *Ibid.*, XVII

He's enough to break his mother's heart, is this boy. I wish I had never brought him up. He'd be sharper than a serpent's tooth, if he wasn't as dull as ditch water. Dickens, *Our Mutual Friend*, Book III, X

It is a touching thing to hear the mind reverting to the ordinary occupations and pursuits of health, when the body lies before you weak and helpless; but when those occupations are of a character the most strongly opposed to anything we associate with grave or solemn ideas, the impression produced is infinitely more powerful. Dickens, *Pickwick Papers*, III

All men whom mighty genius has raised to a proud eminence in the world have usually some little weakness which appears the more conspicuous from the contrast it presents to their general character. *Ibid.*, XIII

In England, when a new character appears in our circles, the first question always is, "Who is he?" In France it is, "What is he?" In England, "How much a year?" In France, "What has he done?" Disraeli, *Coningsby*, Book V, VII

Life has become so swift, that all may see now that of which they once could only read.
Ibid., Book VI, II

I prefer fame to life; and yet, the consciousness of heroic deeds to the most widespread celebrity.
Ibid., Book VII, II

A man may speak very well in the House of Commons, and fail very completely in the House of Lords. There are two distinct styles requisite.
Disraeli, *The Young Duke*, Book V, VI

See the difference between the impression a man makes on you when you walk by his side in familiar talk, or look at him in his home, and the figure he makes when seen from a lofty historical level, or even in the eyes of a critical neighbor who thinks of him as an embodied system or opinion rather than as a man.
Eliot, *Adam Bede*, V

Perhaps there is no time in a summer's day more cheering than when the warmth of the sun is just beginning to triumph over the freshness of the morning—when there is just a lingering hint of early coolness to keep off languor under the delicious influence of warmth.
Ibid., XIX

Fancy what a game at chess would be if all the chessmen had passions and intellects, more or less small and cunning: if you were not only uncertain about your adversary's men, but a little uncertain also about your own; if your knight could shuffle himself on to a new square by the sly; if your bishop, in disgust at your castling, could wheedle your pawns out of the places; and if your pawns, hating you because they are pawns, could make away from their appointed posts that you might get checkmate on a sudden. You might be the longest-headed of deductive reasoners, and yet you might be beaten by your own pawns. You would be especially likely to be beaten, if you depended arrogantly on your mathematical imagination, and regarded your passionate pieces with contempt.
Eliot, *Felix Holt*, XXIX

To discern between the evils that energy can remove and the evils that patience must bear, makes the difference between manliness and childishness, between good sense and folly.
Ibid., Address to Working Men

One always believes one's own town to be more stupid than any other.
Eliot, *Middlemarch*, Book II, XVI

There's ways o' doing things worse than speaking out plain.
Eliot, *Mill on the Floss*, Book I, XII

It is astonishing what a different result one gets by changing the metaphor!
Ibid., Book II, I

What demonstrates the beauty and excellence of anything but its reverse? Thus the beauty of day, and that of summer, is set off by the horrors of night and winter.
Fielding, H., *Tom Jones*, 161

All the pleasures of life are heightened by sometimes experiencing their contrary.
Fielding, S., *David Simple*, II

The difference between a man who has a real understanding and one who has a little low cunning is just as great as that between a man who sees clearly and one who is purblind.
Ibid.

A contrast in nature is said to afford the mind of man much entertainment.
Fielding, S., *The History of The Countess of Dellwyn*, I

A headstone without an epitaph is no better than a body without the breath of life in't.
Galt, *Annals of the Parish*, V

Man in London is not quite so good a creature as he is out of it.
Galt, *Ayrshire Legatees*, VII

It is better to pick a bone under a hedge than to rot in a gaol.
Graves, *The Spiritual Quixote*, I

He began to see that the town life was a book of humanity infinitely more palpitating, varied, and compendious than the gown life.   Hardy, *Jude the Obscure*, Part Two, VI

Attack is more piquant than concord.   Hardy, *A Pair of Blue Eyes*, XV

Men have oftener suffered from the mockery of a place too smiling for their reason than from the oppression of surroundings oversadly tinged.
                                    Hardy, *The Return of the Native*, Book I, I

A man, no less than a landscape, who awakens an interest under uncertain lights and touches of unfathomable shade, may cut but a poor figure in a garish noontide shine.
                            Hardy, *The Romantic Adventures of a Milkmaid*, XVII

A stale article, if you dip it in a good, warm, sunny smile, will go off better than a fresh one that you've scowled upon.   Hawthorne, *The House of the Seven Gables*, IV

A forced smile is uglier than a frown.   Hawthorne, *The Marble Faun*, V

The number of those who have done anything worth recollecting bears a small proportion to those who would wish to forget everything they ever did in their lives.
                                                            Jenner, *The Placid Man*, I

We differ from ourselves, just as we differ from each other.   Johnson, *Rasselas*, 109

A fire is detestable enough at all times, but most detestable by day.
                                            Kingsley, *Hereward the Wake*, XXVI

Fire maketh the gold to shine and the straw to smother.   Lyly, *Euphues*, 98

It is better to be raw than rotten.   Melville, *Confidence-Man*, XXX

Herein lies the difference between the Altantic and Pacific:—that once with the Tropics, the bold sailor who has a mind to quit his ship round Cape Horn, waits not for port. He regards that ocean as one mighty harbor.   Melville, *Mardi*, I

The little Pilot fish darted hither and thither; keeping up a mighty fidgeting, like men of small minds in a state of nervous agitation.   *Ibid.*, XVIII

A flowery landscape, you must come out of, to behold.   *Ibid.*, LXIV

All objects look well through an arch.   *Ibid.*, LXVII

Generally your tumbledown old homesteads yield the most entertainment; their very dilapidation betokening their having seen good service in hospitality; whereas, spruce-looking, finical portals, have a phiz full of meaning; for niggards are oftentimes neat.
                                                                    Ibid., XCIV

Better sleep with a sober cannibal than a drunken Christian.
                                            Melville, *Moby Dick*, III

How I spurned that turnpike earth!—that common highway all over dented with the marks of slavish heels and hoofs; and turned me to admire the magnanimity of the sea which will permit no records.   *Ibid.*, XIII

It's better to sail with a moody good captain than a laughing bad one.   *Ibid.*, XVI

The port would fain give succour; the port is pitiful; in the port is safety, comfort, hearthstone, supper, warm blankets, friends, all that's kind to our mortalities. But in that gale, the port, the land, is that ship's direst jeopardy.   *Ibid.*, XXIII

There is a Catskill eagle in some souls that can alike dive down into the blackest gorges, and soar out of them again and become invisible in the sunny spaces. And even if he forever flies within the gorge, that gorge is in the mountains; so that even in his lowest swoop the mountain eagle is still higher than other birds upon the plain, even though they soar.   *Ibid.*, XCVI

The landlubber at sea is the veriest wretch the watery world over.
                                                    Melville, *Omoo*, XIV

Faith and philosophy are air, but events are brass. Amidst his gray philosophizings, Life breaks upon a man like a morning.   Melville, *Pierre*, Book XXI, II

Contrasts produce quaint ideas in excited spirits.

Meredith, *Beauchamp's Career*, XXI

Comparisons come of a secret leaning that is sure to play rogue under its mien of honest dealer.

Ibid., XXIV

Stones are easier to move than the English.

Ibid., XLII

She was a lady of incisive features bound in stale parchment.

Meredith, *Diana of the Crossways*, XIV

Between the ascetic rocks and the sensual whirlpools.

Ibid., XXXVII

A dainty rogue in porcelain.

Meredith, *The Egoist*, V

He told me that he thought one's country was like one's wife: you were born in the first, and married to the second, and had to learn all about them afterwards, ay, and make the best of them.

Meredith, *Harry Richmond*, III

When Nature turns artist, and produces contrast of color on a fair face, where is the sage, or what the oracle, shall match the depth of its lightest look?

Meredith, *Ordeal of Richard Feverel*, XVIII

There is no consolation in shining by comparison with a lower standard.

Ibid., XXI

Alas, that grey, so spirit-touching in Art, should be so wintry in reality!

Meredith, *The Tragic Comedians*, IV

When one has been expecting something to happen, and has been preparing one's courage, one's temper, one's fortitude, in anticipatory rehearsals—when one has placed oneself in the attitude of a martyr, and prepared to meet with fiery trials—it is mortifying when one finds all the necessities of the case disappear, and the mildest calm replace that tragical anticipation: the quiet falls blank upon the excited fancy.

Oliphant, *The Doctor's Family*, II

When safe, life and liberty are little thought for; for they are matters of course. Endangered, they are rated at their real value.

Reade, *The Cloister and the Hearth*, XXIII

Shades and lights are equally necessary in a fine picture.

Richardson, *Clarissa Harlowe*, II

Peevish affirmatives are so much like intentional negatives.

Ibid., II

Preaching and practicing require quite different talents.

Ibid., III

When united in the same person, preaching and practicing make a man a saint; as wit and judgment going together constitute a genius.

Ibid.

Meek men abroad are not always meek men at home.

Ibid., IV

No one is so high as to be above being humbled; so low as to need to despair.

Ibid.

Now a quarrel; now a reconciliation. Everlasting summers would be a grievance.

Richardson, *Sir Charles Grandison*, Two, III

Odd characters are needful to make even characters shine. Good girls would not be valued as they are, if there were not bad ones.

Ibid., Two, IV

We think of the plunderer with indignation till we hear of the assassin; and rail with severity against the flattery of the sycophant, till we hear of the ingratitude of the friend.

Roche, *Nocturnal Visit*, II

Well-constructed minds are never more sensible of the distresses of those whom they love than when their own situation forms a contrast with them.

Scott, *The Heart of Midlothian*, XLVI

There is no period at which men look worse in the eyes of each other, or feel more uncomfortable, than when the first dawn of daylight finds them watchers.
Scott, *Kenilworth*, XV

God only commands the issue. Man uses means. Scott, *Redgauntlet*, XVII

A valiant camel-driver is worthy to kiss the lip of a fair queen, when a cowardly prince is not worthy to salute the hem of her garment. Scott, *The Talisman*, XXVII

Say not that the food is lost unto thee which is given to the stranger. *Ibid.*

No two things are more different than the heart of a bully, at the times when he knows he shall be prevented from fighting, and when he knows he cannot.
Shebbeare, *Lydia*, III

A man will fight a lion on one day that will tremble at a mouse on another.
Shebbeare, *The Marriage Act*, I

Nothing is more different than the mind of a person before and after he has perpetrated an execrable action. *Ibid.*, II

The wants of men differ according to their moral natures, the moods, and changes of mind by which they are governed. Simms, *The Scout*, XXXII

What's bred in the bone will never come out of the flesh.
Smollett, *Ferdinand, Count Fathom*, XLIII

There's such a thing as a man being pious and honest, in the private way; and there's such a thing as a public virtue. Stevenson, *Prince Otto*, Book I, II

Nothing is great or little otherwise than by comparison.
Swift, *Gulliver's Travels*, Brobdingnag

As the approach of Death is not an unmingled sorrow, the approach of Life is not an unmingled joy. Taylor, *Hannah Thurston*, XXXVI

O brother-wearers of motley! Are there not moments when one grows sick of grinning and tumbling, and the jingling of caps and bells? This, dear friends and companions, is my amiable object—to walk with you through the Fair, to examine the shops and the shows there; and that we should all come home after the flare, and the noise, and the gaiety, and be perfectly miserable in private. Thackeray, *Vanity Fair*, XIX

Earrings like chandeliers. *Ibid.*, XX

A live dog is better than a dead lion. Tourgee, *Murvale Eastman*, X

It is so easy to condemn—and so pleasant too, for eulogy charms no listeners as detraction does. Trollope, *Barchester Towers*, XXI

Consider well the proportions of things. It is better to be a young Junebug than an old bird of paradise. Twain, *Pudd'nhead Wilson*, VIII

If you pick up a starving dog and make him prosperous, he will not bite you. This is the principal difference between a dog and a man. *Ibid.*, XVI

A devil born to a young couple is measurably recognizable by them as a devil before long, but a devil adopted by an old couple is an angel to them, and remains so, through thick and thin. *Ibid.*, XIX

There is a fatality about all physical and intellectual distinction. It is better not to be different from one's fellows. The ugly and the stupid have the best of it in this world. They can sit at their ease and gape at the play. If they know nothing of victory, they are at least spared the knowledge of defeat. Wilde, *The Picture of Dorian Gray*, I

He saw that there was no mood of the mind that had not its counterpart in the sensuous life. *Ibid.*, XI

What were the glories of the sun, if we knew not the gloom of darkness?
Wright, *A Few Days in Athens*, X

COMPARISON/CONTRAST; COUNTERPART; COUNTERPOINT (*continued*)

In retirement, reflection gloriously reigns; in the world, fancy and inclination as imperiously triumph.
Young, *The Adventures of Emmera*, I

COMPASSION

He was naturally scornful, unaffectedly condescending, as if from his height of six foot three he had surveyed all the vastness of human folly and had made up his mind not to be too hard on it.
Conrad, *The Nigger of the Narcissus*, I

If thoroughly examined, compassion will appear to be the fellow-feeling only of men of the same rank and degree of life for one another, on account of the evils to which they themselves are liable.
Fielding, H., *Amelia*, II

Much more does affliction demand our love when it proceeds from compassion for another's woes.
Jenner, *The Placid Man*, I

To take a thorn out of one's friend's foot, to put it into one's own.
Richardson, *Clarissa Harlowe*, I

A compassionate heart cannot habitually be an unjust one.
Richardson, *Sir Charles Grandison*, Two, IV

COMPENSATION: *see also* OBLIGATION

The compensation for injustice is that in that dark ordeal we gather the worthiest around us.
Meredith, *Ordeal of Richard Feverel*, IV

COMPETITION: *see also* CONTEST

Competition, which is the instinct of selfishness, is another word for dissipation of energy.
Bellamy, *Looking Backward*, XXII

Competition brings out the worst passions in man, punishes men for the finer qualities, as generosity, truthfulness, independence, magnanimity, and ranks him highest who has the least regard for his fellow-men.
Geissler, *Looking Beyond*, VII

Why will silly mortals strive to the painful pinnacle of championship?
Meredith, *Ordeal of Richard Feverel*, XV

It is so odd that men cannot amuse themselves without pitting themselves against each other. When a man tells me that he can shoot better than I, I tell him that my keeper can shoot better than he.
Trollope, *Phineas Finn*, XV

COMPLAINT: *see also* LAW

Those who do not complain are never pitied.
Austen, *Pride and Prejudice*, Volume I, XX

There is commonly something pitiful in a complaint.
Burney, *Cecilia*, III

It seemed impossible that past events should be so obstinate as to remain unmodified when they were complained against.
Eliot, *The Mill on the Floss*, Book I, VIII

Some folks rail against other folks because other folks have what some folks would be glad of.
Fielding, H., *Joseph Andrews*, 254

The complaint of a human heart, sorrow-laden, perchance guilty, telling its secret, whether of guilt or sorrow, to the great heart of mankind; beseeching its sympathy or forgiveness—at every moment—in each accent—and never in vain.
Hawthorne, *Scarlet Letter*, XXII

Passions which gain a vent by complaint evaporate much sooner than those which, by being partly smothered, prey continually on the mind.
Jenner, *The Placid Man*, I

Misfortune thinks itself entitled to speak and feels some consolation in the privilege of complaining.   Mackenzie, *Julia De Roubigné*, 17

Complainings debase her who suffers, and harden him who aggrieves.   *Ibid.*, 110

To rail against humanity for not being abstract perfection, and against human love for not realizing all the splendid visions of the poets of chivalry, is to rail at the summer for not being all sunshine, and at the rose for not being always in bloom.
                                                           Peacock, *Nightmare Abbey*, XI

How will injuries never honorably complained of be believed to grieve us?
                                                           Richardson, *Clarissa Harlowe*, IV

There is very little difference between a suppressed evidence and a false one.   *Ibid.*

We lose the right of complaining sometimes by forbearing.
                                                           Sterne, *Tristram Shandy*, II

COMPLETENESS; INCOMPLETENESS: *see also* WHOLENESS

Man was supposed to be incomplete.   Meredith, *Harry Richmond*, XXI

COMPLIMENTS; PRAISE

Praise, when closed with an exception, has been found the most successful means of blasting the credit of the most deserving.
                                                           Anonymous, *Tom Jones in His Married State*, 179

Man is surely a strange sort of creature, who never praises anyone more heartily than him who has spread destruction and ruin over the face of nations.
                                                           Godwin, *Caleb Williams*, II

Praise is to an old man an empty sound.   Johnson, *Rasselas*, 168

There is no more praise to be given to a fair face than to a false glass.
                                                           Lyly, *Euphues and His England*, 329

There is a wide distinction between the confidence which becomes a man and the simplicity that disgraces a simpleton: he who never trusts is a niggard of his soul who starves himself and by whom no other is enriched; but he who gives everyone his confidence and everyone his praise squanders the fund that should serve for the encouragement of integrity and the reward of excellence.
                                                           Mackenzie, *The Man of the World*, I

Be more sparing of your praise lest we should suspect that you secretly intend to praise yourself, while you would be thought only to commend another.
                                                           Richardson, *Clarissa Harlowe*, I

We are all apt to praise our benefactors because they *are* our benefactors, as if everybody did right or wrong as they obliged or disobliged us.   *Ibid.*

The man who is disposed immoderately to exalt himself cannot do it but by despising everybody else in proportion.   *Ibid.*, II

The man is more fond of praise than of deserving it.   *Ibid.*

Let your actions praise you.   *Ibid.*

Undeserved praise raises an emulation to deserve praise.   *Ibid.*, III

There is a secret pleasure one has to hear oneself praised.   Richardson, *Pamela*, 8

It is a great happiness to be praised of them that are most praiseworthy.
                                                           Sidney, *Arcadia*, I

The more power he hath to hurt, the more admirable is his praise, that he will not hurt.
                                                           Ibid., II

COMPLIMENTS; PRAISE (*continued*)

Empty praise will not supply the cravings of nature.

Smollett, Roderick Random, 416

Praise everybody: never be squeamish, but speak out your compliment both point-blank in a man's face, and behind his back, when you know there is a reasonable chance of his hearing it again.

Thackeray, Vanity Fair, XIX

COMPOSURE; DISCOMPOSURE

Do not discompose me by discomposing yourself!

Richardson, Clarissa Harlowe, I

COMPROMISE

The essence of compromise is littleness.

Disraeli, Sybil, Book V, I

COMPULSION: *see also* OBSESSION

There is a fatality, a feeling so irresistible and inevitable that it has the force of doom, which almost invariably compels human beings to linger around and haunt, ghostlike, the spot where some great and marked event has given the color to their lifetime; and still the more irresistibly, the darker the tinge that saddens it.

Hawthorne, The Scarlet Letter, V

Compulsion and fidelity are incompatible.

Johnstone, The History of Arsaces, II

Whenever I find myself growing grim about the mouth; whenever it is a damp, drizzly November in my soul; whenever I find myself involuntarily pausing before coffin warehouses, and bringing up the rear of every funeral I meet; and especially whenever my hypos get such an upper hand of me, that it requires a strong moral principle to prevent me from deliberately stepping into the street, and methodically knocking people's hats off—then, I account it high time to get to sea as soon as I can.

Melville, Moby Dick, I

I am tormented with an everlasting itch for things remote. I love to sail forbidden seas, and land on barbarous coasts.

Ibid.

I looked with sympathetic awe and fearfulness upon the man, who in midwinter just landed from a four years' dangerous voyage, could so unrestingly push off again for still another tempestuous term. The land seemed scorching to his feet.

Ibid., XXIII

Ah, God! what trances of torments does that man endure who is consumed with one unachieved revengeful desire. He sleeps with clenched hands; and wakes with his own bloody nails in his palms.

Ibid., XLIV

Such as can retain their senses after the first prostrating effect of the supernatural are apt to experience terror in one of its strangest forms—a wild desire to fling themselves upon the terrible object.

Reade, The Cloister and the Hearth, XI

All generous spirits hate compulsion.

Richardson, Clarissa Harlowe, I

Compulsion is often more tolerable than over-earnest entreaty.

Richardson, Sir Charles Grandison, Three, VI

CONCEALMENT

Varnish and gilding hide many stains.

Austen, Mansfield Park, Volume Three, XIV

There are many fine natures hidden under coarse forms.

Beecher, Norwood, XV

Surprise is the enemy of concealment.

Brown, C.B., Ormond, 99-100

There is something in every man's heart which, if we could know, would make us hate him.

Bulwer, The Caxtons, Book X, I

Much corn lies under the straw that is not seen.
Bulwer, *What Will He Do with It?*, Book V, II

Concealment is the foe of tranquillity.
Burney, *Evelina*, 250

Nothing in this world is hidden forever.
Collins, *No Name*

I say what other people only think; and when all the rest of the world is in a conspiracy to accept the mask for the true face, mine is the rash hand that tears off the plump pasteboard and shows the bare bones beneath.
Collins, *The Woman in White*, Part I, Second Epoch

Often the soul is ripened into fuller goodness while age has spread an ugly film, so that mere glances can never divine the preciousness of the fruit.
Eliot, *Silas Marner*, XVI

He was a man who kept his words well to the rear of his possible actions.
Hardy, *A Pair of Blue Eyes*, XX

There are some things over which nature herself commands to throw a veil.
Johnstone, *The Reverie*, I

She was young in suffering and thought, as the unseasoned and inexperienced do, that a mask is a concealment.
Meredith, *Beauchamp's Career*, XXVI

What serpent is there but hides his sting?
Nashe, *The Unfortunate Traveller*, 45

Ill-temper lies buried under a studied accumulation of smiles. Envy, hatred, and malice, retreat from the countenance, to entrench themselves more deeply in the heart. Treachery lurks under the flowers of courtesy. Ignorance and folly take refuge in that unmeaning gabble, "small talk." Small indeed!—the absolute minimum of the infinitely little.
Peacock, *Headlong Hall*, XIII

What she cannot conceal from herself, she will publish to all the world.
Richardson, *Clarissa Harlowe*, III

Does not concealment always imply somewhat wrong?
Richardson, *Sir Charles Grandison*, One, II

Convents seem calculated to make numbers really miserable, and only to hide from the world that they are so.
Scott, S., *The History of Cornelia*, 161

Courtesy of tongue, when it is used to veil churlishness of deed, is but a knight's girdle around the breast of a base clown.
Scott, *Ivanhoe*, XXIII

The mist hides the precipice from those who are doomed to fall over it.
Scott, *The Talisman*, XIV

Disguise is the spice of life.
Stevenson, *The Wrong Box*, VIII

He could not understand why nature should teach us to conceal what nature had given.
Swift, *Gulliver's Travels*, Houyhnhnms

Be cautious, young ladies; be wary how you engage. Be shy of loving frankly; never tell all you feel, or (a better way still) feel very little. See the consequences of being prematurely honest and confiding, and mistrust yourselves and everybody. Get yourselves married as they do in France, where the lawyers are the bridesmaids and confidantes. At any rate, never have any feelings which may make you uncomfortable, or make any promises which you cannot at any required moment command and withdraw.
Thackeray, *Vanity Fair*, XVIII

Sin writes itself across a man's face.
Wilde, *The Picture of Dorian Gray*, XII

CONCEIT

A conceited man never knows content.
Cooper, *The Prairie*, XXII

I've never any pity for conceited people, because I think they carry their comfort about with them.
Eliot, *Mill on the Floss*, Book V, IV

He liked so well to think how fond of him Marcia was, that it did not occur to him then to question whether he were as fond of her. Howells, *A Modern Instance*, VI

CONCENTRATION

Can a man that is looking at the stars mind what is under his feet?
Brackenridge, *Modern Chivalry*, Part II, Volume II

It is in the nature of exasperation gradually to concentrate itself. Eliot, *Felix Holt*, XV

The secret of success is concentration; wherever there has been a great life, or a great work, that has gone before. Taste everything a little, look at everything a little; but live for one thing. Anything is possible to a man who knows his end and moves straight for it, and for it alone. Schreiner, *Story of an African Farm*, Part II, VI

Men and things are plastic; they part to the right and left when one comes among them moving in a straight line to one end. *Ibid.*

Behold, the fool saith, "Put not all thine eggs in one basket"—which is but a manner of saying, "Scatter your money and your attention"; but the wise man saith, "Put all your eggs in the one basket and—WATCH THAT BASKET."
Twain, *Pudd'nhead Wilson*, XV

CONCEPTION; IDEA: *see* THOUGHT

CONCESSION

Individual concessions are like political; when you once begin, there is no saying where you will stop. Bulwer, *What Will He Do with It?*, Book XI, VI

Where a concession is made without pain, it is also made without meaning, for it is not in human nature to project any amendment without a secret repugnance.
Burney, *Cecilia*, II

They that yield when they are asked are one step before them that were never asked to yield, and two steps before them that yield before they are asked.
Defoe, *Moll Flanders*, 39

The thunder is driven away by ringing of bells, the lion's wrath qualified by a yielding body. Deloney, *Thomas of Reading*, 251

There are yielding moments in the lives of the sternest and harshest men.
Dickens, *Dombey and Son*, XXXV

What the right side gives up, the left may be better for.
Richardson, *Clarissa Harlowe*, II

CONDESCENSION

Condescension is not meanness. There is a glory in yielding, that hardly any violent spirit can judge of. Richardson, *Clarissa Harlowe*, II

Condescension implies dignity. *Ibid.*

CONDITION

The pigs is well, the cows is well, and the boys is bobbish.
Dickens, *Nicholas Nickleby*, LVII

He has gone to the demnition bow-wows. *Ibid.*, LXIV

CONFESSION: *see also* ACKNOWLEDGMENT

His countenance confessed faster than his tongue denied. Fielding, H., *Amelia*, I

It is more meritorious to stop in the midst of a bad design, and confess the fault, than even not to have erred. Marishall, *Miss Clarinda Cathcart*, II

He asked himself if confession were not inveterate in man. Moore, *Evelyn Innes*, VI

Confessing a mistake requires a greatness of soul. Richardson, *Clarissa Harlowe*, I

After-pretenses serve but for tacit confessions of vile usage. *Ibid.*, II

I get so little by my confessions, I had a good mind to try to defend myself. *Ibid.*, IV

It is a merit next in degree to that of having avoided error frankly to own an error.
Ibid.

CONFIDENCE; CONFIDENTIALITY: *see also* TRUST

We seldom appear considerable to others when we appear of no consequence to ourselves. Anonymous, *Memoirs of a Coquet*, 30

The simple confidence of a child, and the natural reliance of a child upon superior years (qualities I am very sorry any children should prematurely change for worldly wisdom).
Dickens, *David Copperfield*, V

No experiment can be more precarious than that of a half-confidence.
Godwin, *St. Leon*, 140

Confide in few, or rather none; yet behave obligingly to all.
McCarthy, *The Fair Moralist*, 4-5

I have sometimes thought that confidence between man and man—more particularly between stranger and stranger—is fled; that confidence is the New Astrea—emigrated —vanished—gone. Melville, *Confidence-Man*, V

Here and there, with a curious expression, one is reading a small sort of handbill of anonymous poetry, rather wordily entitled: "ODE ON THE INTIMATIONS OF DISTRUST IN MAN, UNWILLINGLY INFERRED FROM REPEATED REPULSES, IN DISINTERESTED ENDEAVORS TO PROCURE HIS CONFIDENCE."
Ibid., X

Distrust is a stage to confidence. *Ibid.*, XVI

"Pray, sir, who or what may you have confidence in?" "I have confidence in distrust."
Ibid., XXI

Misanthropy and infidelity are co-ordinates. For misanthropy, springing from the same root with disbelief of religion, is twin with that. Set aside materialism and what is an atheist, but one who does not, or will not, see in the universe a ruling principle of love; and what a misanthrope, but one who does not, or will not, see in man a ruling principle of kindness? In either case the vice consists in a want of confidence. *Ibid.*, XXVIII

Assurance is in presence of the assured. Melville, *Pierre*, Book III, I

A confident man must think as meanly of his company as highly of himself.
Richardson, *Clarissa Harlowe*, II

A confident man talks of more than he is master of. *Ibid.*

Noble confidence arises from a mind unconscious of having deserved reproach.
Ibid., III

CONFLICT: *see also* WAR AND PEACE

The old well-established grievance of duty against will, parent against child.
Austen, *Sense and Sensibility*, Volume I, XIX

CONFLICT (*continued*)

What a life of struggle between the head and the heart!　　　　Burney, *Cecilia*, III

How cruel, how unnatural a war between the intellects and the feelings!　　　*Ibid.*

Is it the good or the evil fortune of mortals that the comic side of life, and the serious side of life, are perpetually in collision with each other?
　　　　　　　　　　　　　　　　Collins, *The Legacy of Cain*, XXXV

There are two sorts of people that there is no contending with: a wise body and a fool.
　　　　　　　　　　　　　　　　Defoe, *Moll Flanders*, 48

As the flame consumes the candle, so men through discord waste themselves.
　　　　　　　　　　　　　　　　Deloney, *Jack of Newbury*, 369

Painful collisions come of this contrast between the outward and the inward.
　　　　　　　　　　　　　　　　Eliot, *Mill on the Floss*, Book III, V

A good heart will at times betray the best head in the world.　　Fielding, H., *Amelia*, I

Even when most elevated, the human mind is not equal to the influence of two opposing passions.　　　　　　　　　　　　　　　　　　Lee, *The Recess*, III

This tremendous conflict of opening manhood, which is to our life here what is the landing of a soul to the life to come.　　　　　Meredith, *Sandra Belloni*, XXX

All mankind is to be plagued by its contrary.　　Richardson, *Clarissa Harlowe*, III

Poor nations are hungry, and rich nations are proud; and pride and hunger will ever be at variance.　　　　　　　　　　　Swift, *Gulliver's Travels*, Houyhnhnms

CONJECTURE

Everybody liked better to conjecture how the thing was, than simply to know it; for conjecture soon became more confident than knowledge, and had a more liberal allowance for the incompatible.　　　　Eliot, *Middlemarch*, Book VII, LXXI

Conjecture is constantly guided by feeling.　　　Eliot, *Romola*, Book II, XXXIX

CONQUEST

Tell me if there ever, even in the ages most favorable to glory, could be a triumph more exalted and elating than the conquest of one noble heart?
　　　　　　　　　　　　　　　　Bulwer, *Pompeii*, Book Two, IV

The firmness of man should be adequate to conquer the weakness of his heart.
　　　　　　　　　　　　　　　　Dacre, *Passions*, Letter LXXXI

Even of perpetual conquest the heart of man will grow weary.　　Dacre, *Zofloya*, II

A small conquest it is to overthrow those that never resisteth.　　Lyly, *Euphues*, 119

What is there in an easy conquest? Hudibras questions well, "What mad lover ever died to gain a soft and easy bride?"　　　　Richardson, *Clarissa Harlowe*, II

[In marriage,] the conqueror once is generally the conqueror forever after.
　　　　　　　　　　　　　　　　Trollope, *Barchester Towers*, XVII

CONSCIENCE

When bread and conscience are weighed against each other in time of calamity, it is not to be wondered at that the former will preponderate.　　Annesley, *Memoirs*, II

The tribunal in his own bosom.　　　　　　　　　　　　　　　*Ibid.*

Custom and the fashion of the world will not always stifle the voice of conscience.
　　　　　　　　　　　　　　　　Anonymous, *Fatal Friendship*, II

No war finishes without far-reaching results, and the conscience of a country, like the conscience of a man, may be too severely tried.
Atherton, Senator North, Book II, XIII

More sin is the only anodyne for sin, and the only way to cure the ache of conscience is to harden it.
Bellamy, Dr. Heidenhoff's Process, XI

The pangs of conscience, so much vaunted by some, do most certainly drive ten deeper into sin where they bring one back to virtue.
Ibid.

Strong wind, earthquake-shock, and fire may pass by: but I shall follow the guiding of that still small voice which interprets the dictates of conscience.
Bronte, C., Jane Eyre, XIX

Whenever a lie was necessary for their occasions, they brought it out with a careless ease and breadth altogether untroubled by the rebuke of conscience.
Bronte, C., Villette, IX

God within the mind, this internal monitor.
Brown, W.H., The Power of Sympathy, 123

It is a devil of a thing to have too nice a conscience!   Bulwer, The Caxtons, Book VI, II

We are apt to connect the voice of conscience with the stillness of midnight. But we wrong that innocent hour. It is that terrible "next morning," when reason is wide awake, upon which remorse fastens its fangs.
Bulwer, Ernest Maltravers, Part I, VII

Be for a clear conscience, and for no bills without receipts to them.   Burney, Cecilia, II

Little is the boast of insolence when it is analyzed by the conscience.   Ibid., III

Man has the conscience of an angel and the impulses of a devil; and reason sits between them, for an umpire, with a fool's cap upon her head.
Caruthers, The Kentuckian in New-York, Volume I, VI

Impulse bribes reason, and reason laughs at conscience.
Ibid.

Bribed conscience makes hypocrites—frightened conscience makes fanatics,—but reason-drilled conscience makes incarnate devils.
Ibid.

Once self-supported by conscience, once embarked on a career of manifest usefulness, the true Christian never yields. Neither public nor private influences produce the slightest effect on us when we have once got our mission.
Collins, The Moonstone, Second Period, IV

Perhaps there is no time in which the ingenuity of man is more active than in those moments when he has a sensitive consciousness of being wrong, and consequently, a feverish desire to vindicate his works or acts to himself, as well as to others.
Cooper, Heidenmauer, XVIII

It is not an easy matter to hit a conscience exactly between wind and water.
Cooper, Homeward Bound, XXX

Spike groaned, for the past, blended fearfully with the future, gleamed on his conscience with a brightness that appalled him. And what is that future, which is to make us happy or miserable through an endless vista of time?   Cooper, Jack Tier, XVII

It is better for a man to die at peace with himself than to live haunted by an evil conscience.
Cooper, The Last of the Mohicans, VIII

I had the conscience of an assassin, and was haunted by a vague sense of enormous wickedness.
Dickens, David Copperfield, XLIV

"A jog-trot life, the same from day to day, would reconcile one to anything. One don't see anything, one don't hear anything. We go on taking everything for granted, and so we go on, until whatever we do, good, bad, or indifferent, we do from habit. Habit is all I shall have to report, when I am called upon to plead of my conscience, on my deathbed.

'Habit,' says I; 'I was deaf, dumb, blind, and paralytic, to a million things, from habit.'
'Very business-like indeed,' says Conscience, 'but it don't do here!'"

Dickens, *Dombey and Son*, XXXIII

Conscience is a dreadful thing when it accuses. Dickens, *Great Expectations*, II

My conscience is my bank. Dickens, *Martin Chuzzlewit*, XX

In the majority of cases, conscience is an elastic and very flexible article, which will
bear a deal of stretching and adapt itself to a great variety of circumstances.

Dickens, *Old Curiosity Shop*, VI

To those who have never wavered in conscience, the predicament of the individual
whose mind is less strongly constituted and who trembles in the balance between duty
and desire is scarcely appreciable, unless graphically portrayed.

Dreiser, *Sister Carrie*, XXVII

Nemesis can seldom forge a sword for herself out of our consciences—out of the suffering we feel in the suffering we may have caused: there is rarely metal enough there to
make an effective weapon. Eliot, *Adam Bede*, XXIX

Europe adjusts itself to a *fait accompli*, and so does an individual character—until the
placid adjustment is disturbed by a convulsive retribution. *Ibid.*

Were uneasiness of conscience measured by extent of crime, human history had been
different. Eliot, *Daniel Deronda*, Book V, XXXV

His conscience was large and easy, like the rest of him: it did only what it could do
without any trouble. Eliot, *Middlemarch*, Book I, VIII

His was one of the natures in which conscience gets the more active when the yoke of life
ceases to gall them. *Ibid.*, Book V, LII

If we regard this world only, it is the interest of every man to be either perfectly good or
completely bad. He had better destroy his conscience than gently wound it.

Fielding, H., *Amelia*, I

My great comfort in all my afflictions is that it is in the power of no enemy to rob me of
my conscience, nor will I ever be so much my own enemy to destroy it.

Fielding, H., *Jonathan Wild*, 142

In the conscience, honor and honesty pull one way, and a bribe and necessity another.

Fielding, H., *Joseph Andrews*, 37

Many arbitrary acts are daily committed by magistrates who have not the excuse of
conscience to plead for them. Fielding, H., *Tom Jones*, 142

Conscience, like a good lawyer. *Ibid.*, 262

This excellent method of conveying a falsehood with the heart only, without making the
tongue guilty of an untruth, by the means of equivocation and imposture, hath quieted
the conscience of many a notable deceiver. *Ibid.*, 286

A good conscience is never lawless in the worst regulated state, and will provide those
laws for itself, which the neglect of legislators hath forgotten to supply. *Ibid.*, 788

Conscience represents a fetish to which good people sacrifice their own happiness, bad
people their neighbors'. Glasgow, *The Descendant*, Book III, IV

The pain which conscience gives the man who has already done wrong is soon got over.

Goldsmith, *The Vicar of Wakefield*, 64

Conscience is a coward; and those faults it has not strength enough to prevent, it seldom
has justice enough to accuse. *Ibid.*

An evil and reproaching conscience who can bear?

Helme, *St. Margaret's Cave*, Volume I, XVIII

What armor so strong as an applauding conscience, and the certainty of truth on our side?   *Ibid.*, Volume II, X

Of all liars and false accusers, a sick conscience is the most inventive and indefatigable.
                                    Holmes, *Elsie Venner*, XII

Conscience itself requires a conscience, or nothing can be more unscrupulous. It told Saul that he did well in persecuting the Christians. It has goaded countless multitudes of various creeds to endless forms of self-torture.   *Ibid.*

Conscience won't be reasoned with.   *Ibid.*, XXII

"This is an age of conscience." "That's a part of your cant. It's an age of unspeakable shams, as Carlyle says."   James, H., *The Bostonians*, XXXIV

All that virtue can afford is quietness of conscience and a steady prospect of a happier state; this may enable us to endure calamity with patience, but remember that patience must suppose pain.   Johnson, *Rasselas*, 106

No evil is insupportable, but that which is accompanied with consciousness of wrong.
                                    Ibid., 131

Were it not stifled (sometimes by false and spurious honor), conscience would lead directly to liberal construction of the rules of morality.
                                    Mackenzie, *The Man of the World*, I

Conscience the awarder of its own doom.   Melville, *Mardi*, CLXII

A conscience is a kind of Tic-dolly-row, worse nor a toothache. The Lord keep me from catching it.   Melville, *Moby Dick*, XXIX

It will be found a common case, that when we have yielded to our instincts, and then have to soothe conscience, we must slaughter somebody, for a sacrificial offering to our sense of comfort.   Meredith, *Beauchamp's Career*, XII

The conscience is, like the spleen, a function whose uses are only to be understood in its derangement.   Meredith, *Harry Richmond*, XXXVIII

When women change their affections, they become a prey to scruples of conscience.
                                    Moore, *Evelyn Innes*, XXI

A good conscience is the best of all narcotics.   *Ibid.*, XXXI

That thing which is to the Utopians no profit to take from another to whom it is profitable they think it no right nor conscience.   More, *Utopia*, II

Change not your color, none can slander a clear conscience to itself; receive all your draught of misfortune in at once.   Nashe, *The Unfortunate Traveller*, 38

Her conscience was eloquent.   Radcliffe, *The Italian*, II

The luxury of a pure conscience, the health of the soul.
                                    Radcliffe, *The Mysteries of Udolpho*, II

It would be well if those who stifle their consciences, and commit crimes, would set up a sort of medico-moral diary, and record their symptoms minutely day by day. Such records might help to clear away some vague, conventional notions.
                                    Reade, *Griffith Gaunt*, XXIX

In strong and involuntary bias, the heart is conscience.
                                    Richardson, *Clarissa Harlowe*, I

What a foolish teaser is thy conscience!   *Ibid.*, II

Conscience has made me of party against myself.   *Ibid.*

Conscience, though it may be temporarily stifled, cannot die, and when it dare not speak aloud, will whisper.   *Ibid.*, III

His conscience begins to find him.   *Ibid.*, IV

CONSCIENCE (*continued*)

Conscience is the conqueror of souls. *Ibid.*

Conscience will make women speak out; there is vanity in very humility.
Richardson, *Sir Charles Grandison*, One, I

Your conscience is a law to you. *Ibid.*, Three, VII

What a thing is conscience, that through its means even such a thick-witted Northern lord as thou canst bring thy sovereign to confess his folly. Scott, *The Talisman*, VI

Remember thy beast, always, if thou wouldst sleep with a good conscience.
Simms, *Vasconselos*, XXXII

If there is anything which a man may depend upon, and to the knowledge of which he is capable of arriving upon the most indisputable evidence, it must be, whether he has a good conscience or no. Sterne, *Tristram Shandy*, II

Conscience is nothing else but the knowledge which the mind has within herself. *Ibid.*

Conscience is not a law. No, God and reason made the law, and have placed conscience within you to determine—like a British judge in this land of liberty and good sense, who makes no new law, but faithfully declares that law which he knows already written.
Ibid.

We may bid conscience "Down, dog," like an ill-trained puppy yapping at shadows.
Stevenson, *Prince Otto*, Book III, II

Conscience is not an infallible guide. It may impel to wrongdoing as well as to righteousness. Tourgée, *Murvale Eastman*, XLII

There are some points on which no man can be contented to follow the advice of another—some subjects on which a man can consult his own conscience only.
Trollope, *The Warden*, XVI

It don't make no difference whether you do right or wrong, a person's conscience ain't got no sense, and just goes for him *anyway*. If I had a yaller dog that didn't know no more than a person's conscience does, I would pison him. It takes up more room than all the rest of a person's insides, and yet ain't no good, nohow.
Twain, *Huckleberry Finn*, XXXIV

Conscience and cowardice are really the same things. Conscience is the trade-name of the firm. That is all. Wilde, *The Picture of Dorian Gray*, I

Nothing makes one so vain as being told that one is a sinner. Conscience makes egotists of us all. *Ibid.*, VIII

CONSCIENTIOUSNESS

Society as a body does not expect one to be so strictly conscientious in emptying one's glass as to turn it bottom upwards with the rim on one's nose.
Dickens, *Great Expectations*, XXII

Conscientious people are apt to see their duty in that which is the most painful course.
Eliot, *Mill on the Floss*, Book VII, V

CONSECRATION

What we did had a consecration of its own. Hawthorne, *The Scarlet Letter*, XVII

CONSEQUENCE: *see also* CAUSE AND EFFECT; DESTINY; etc.

What would we think of a general who should mount the rostrum in the presence of the enemy and explain the order of his battle? The less speaking, the better for a cause.
Brackenridge, *Modern Chivalry*, Part II, Volume I

Let us all think well before anything is added that may make what is already bad still more bitter.
Cooper, *The Prairie*, VIII

Consequences are unpitying.
Eliot, *Adam Bede*, XVI

As we brew, we must bake.
Godwin, *Caleb Williams*, I

When two people are once parted—have abandoned a common domicile and a common environment—new growths insensibly bud upward to fill each vacated place; unforeseen accidents hinder intentions, and old plans are forgotten.
Hardy, *Tess*, XXXVI

There are very few incidents that are not attended with favorable consequences to somebody.
Hill, *Adventures of Mr. George Edwards*, 171

The evil of any pleasure is not in the act itself, but in its consequences.
Johnson, *Rasselas*, 181

After violent emotions most people and all boys demand food.
Kipling, *Captains Courageous*, IX

As thou hast reaped where another hath sown, so another may thresh that which thou hast reaped.
Lyly, *Euphues*, 144

One knows not how it is, but it sometimes happens that, where earnestness is, there, also, is melancholy.
Melville, *Confidence-Man*, V

It is with the best of hearts as with the best of pears—a dangerous experiment to linger too long upon the scene.
Ibid., XXX

The young who avoid Romance escape the title of Fool at the cost of a celestial crown.
Meredith, *Diana of the Crossways*, I

We live and learn; but it is odd that, when we whip her, Madam should love us the more.
Meredith, *Ordeal of Richard Feverel*, I

There are questions in this life with which we must grapple, or be lost; and when, hunted by that cold eye of intense inner-consciousness, the clearest soul becomes a cunning fox, if it have not courage to stand and do battle.
Ibid., XXIX

If we sin we must needs avoid the consequences of our sin.
Moore, *Evelyn Innes*, XXXI

Honey is none the worse for passing through the bees' bellies.
Reade, *The Cloister and the Hearth*, XXIV

What must become of the lady whom love itself gives up, and conscience cannot plead for?
Richardson, *Clarissa Harlowe*, III

Assume airs of consequence, and you will be treated as a man of consequence.
Ibid.

People who are to act for themselves should be always left to judge for themselves.
Richardson, *Sir Charles Grandison*, One, II

We have been so blinded by thinking and feeling that we have never seen the world.
Schreiner, *The Story of an African Farm*, Part II, VII

The consequences of a little mind and small understanding are jealousy and suspicion.
Scott, *The History of Cornelia*, 59

Talk of the devil, and you shall see his horns.
Shebbeare, *The Marriage Act*, I

Nothing is more painful to the human mind than, after the feelings have been worked up by a quick succession of events, the dead calmness of inaction and certainty which follows and deprives the soul both of hope and fear.
Shelley, *Frankenstein*, IX

Fear breedeth wit; anger is the cradle of courage; joy openeth and enableth the heart; sorrow, as it closeth, so it draweth it inward to look to the correcting of itself; and all of them have power towards some good by the direction of reason.
Sidney, *Arcadia*, I

Slumbers once broken—visions intruded upon—seldom return in their original felicity. Glimpses only come back to us, telling us not so much what to enjoy, as what we have lost the enjoyment of.
Simms, *The Partisan*, Volume II, XVIII

CONSEQUENCE (*continued*)

How many clever minds have faltered in a noble aim by the sarcasm of the witling and the worldling!
Simms, *The Scout*, XXXI

I have arrayed before my mind's eye all my annoyances, and the consequence is that I snap my fingers at them.
Simms, *Woodcraft*, XIX

Waste breeds want.
Ibid., LIII

Grief and resentment, the natural consequence of unexpected gratitude.
Sleath, *The Orphan of the Rhine*, I

Seldom do we meet sensitiveness of conscience or discriminating reflection as the indigenous growth of a very vigorous physical development.
Stowe, *Orr's Island*, XVI

Novel-reading and vanity had turned her brain.
Thackeray, *Barry Lyndon*, XIX

She had been in France, and loved, ever after, French novels, French cookery, and French wines.
Thackeray, *Vanity Fair*, X

It is those who injure women who get the most kindness from them—they are born timid and tyrants, and maltreat those who are humblest before them.
Ibid., L

People who think they have been wronged are apt to be unreasonable, and people who have never tried to put themselves in the place of those who suffer are apt to think them extravagant in their views.
Tourgee, *Murvale Eastman*, XLIII

The world is too rough and too hard for people to allow their feelings full play.
Trollope, *The Way We Live Now*, LXXXIV

To be, or not to be; that is the bare bodkin/That makes calamity of so long life.
Twain, *Huckleberry Finn*, XXI

Small matters are of no consequence.
Young, *The Adventures of Emmera*, I

CONSERVATISM

Conservatism discards Prescription, shrinks from Principle, disavows Progress; having rejected all respect for Antiquity, it offers no redress for the Present, and makes no preparation for the Future.
Disraeli, *Coningsby*, Book II, V

It seems to me a barren thing—this Conservatism—an unhappy crossbreed, the mule of politics that engenders nothing.
Ibid., Book III, V

CONSISTENCY; INCONSISTENCY

Consistency is the first of Christian duties.
Bronte, C., *Jane Eyre*, IV

There is often a strange inconsistency in the mind of man; he shall have sufficient virtue to condemn what he shall not have fortitude to resist.
Dacre, *The Libertine*, III

Fast and loose in one thing, fast and loose in everything.
Dickens, *Bleak House*, LVII

You are a man of false weights and measure. You have one scale for women, another for men; one for princes, and one for farmer-folk.
Stevenson, *Prince Otto*, Book I, III

CONSOLATION: *see also* COMFORT

"My comfort is, I am sure Jane will die of a broken heart, and then he will be sorry for what he has done." As Elizabeth could not receive comfort from any such expectation, she made no answer.
Austen, *Pride and Prejudice*, Volume II, XVII

It's over, and can't be helped, and that's one consolation, as they always says in Turkey, ven they cuts the wrong man's head off.
Dickens, *Pickwick Papers*, XXIII

Premature consolation is but the remembrancer of sorrow.

Goldsmith, *The Vicar of Wakefield*, 9

Rome has a certain species of consolation readier at hand, for all the necessitous, than any other spot under the sky.

Hawthorne, *The Marble Faun*, XXXVIII

Heiresses soon get consoled.

Meredith, *Harry Richmond*, XXII

No melon is so bad but hath its rind, and although a tyrant may pluck out a beard by the roots, yet still the chin is left upon which it grew.

Morier, *Hajji Baba*, XXXIV

To soothe a man's weakness is to increase it.

Richardson, *Clarissa Harlowe*, IV

It is poor consolation to think that one might be worse off; because it is equally true that one might be better off.

Shaw, *The Irrational Knot*, XIV

CONTEMPLATION: *see* DELIBERATION; THOUGHT; etc.

CONTEMPT: *see also* ADMIRATION; RESPECT

Those who shew contempt, even though they are the most contemptible, always seem on the higher ground.

Burney, *Camilla*, Three, VI

Dislike is always associated with contempt.

Collins, *The Woman in White*, Part I, Second Epoch

By being contemptible we set men's minds to the tune of contempt.

Eliot, *Middlemarch*, Book IV, XL

Contempt may be said to be its own object; none so despicable as those who despise others.

Fielding, H., *Amelia*, II

Contempt is as frequently produced at first sight as love.

Melville, *Omoo*, XX

When the laugh is raised upon a great man, he never fails to dwindle into contempt.

Smollett, *Ferdinand, Count Fathom*, XXXVII

CONTENTMENT; DISCONTENT

He who is content with less gets nothing.

Glasgow, *The Voice*, Book III, II

A contented mind is a continual feast.

Hardy, *Jude the Obscure*, Part Five, VIII

Moralists who declaim so copiously on the duty of contentment betray an ignorance of human nature. No situation, however splendid, in which one is compelled to remain fixed and stationary, can long afford pleasure.

Hildreth, *Slave*, Volume I, XV

The minds of these simple savages, unoccupied by matters of graver moment, were capable of deriving the utmost delight from circumstances which would have passed unnoticed in more intelligent communities.

Melville, *Typee*, XIX

Discontent increases with the increase of information.

Peacock, *Crotchet Castle*, XVIII

CONTEST: *see also* COMPETITION

Notwithstanding Solomon, in a race speed must win.

Disraeli, *Coningsby*, Book IV, XIV

CONTRACT

There can be no bargain where both be not agreed.

Lyly, *Euphues*, 138

CONTRADICTION: *see also* AMBIVALENCE; COMPARISON/CONTRAST; etc.

As the fire dies without air, so whim without contradiction.

Brackenridge, *Modern Chivalry*, Part I, Volume I

There is no portion of human wisdom so select and faultless that it does not contain the seeds of its own refutation.   Cooper, *The Monikins*, Conclusion

Does his heart say one thing and his tongue another?   Cooper, *The Prairie*, XVIII

What would I forfeit to have the days of my childhood restored, or to be able to forget them forever!   Dickens, *Pickwick Papers*, V

Who supposes that it is an impossible contradiction to be superstitious and rationalizing at the same time?   Eliot, *Daniel Deronda*, Book I, II

The abomination of men calling themselves religious while living in splendor on ill-gotten gains.   Eliot, *Felix Holt*, Address to Working Men

Will magistrates who punish lewdness, or parsons who preach against it, make any scruple of committing it?   Fielding, H., *Joseph Andrews*, 33

Circumspection and devotion are a contradiction in terms.   Hardy, *Hand of Ethelberta*, XX

Unhappy is the man who bears about him a thorough conviction of what is regular and fit and, at the same time, transgresses against his knowledge and even the bent of his natural disposition.   Kimber, *Joe Thompson*, I

It is the common weakness of humanity to bend the attention solely to minute objects, while the leading ones come upon us totally unawares.   Lee, *The Recess*, I

We can live in contradiction to our theories, but not in contradiction to our feelings.   Moore, *Evelyn Innes*, XXI

You have shown yourself so silly, and so wise; so young, and so old; so gentle, and so obstinate; so meek and so violent; that never was there so mixed a character.   Richardson, *Clarissa Harlowe*, I

A shy, un-shy girl; another of your contradictory qualities.   *Ibid.*

People who deal in contradiction ought to pay for it.   *Ibid.*, II

What a contradiction: weakness of heart with strength of will!   *Ibid.*

Is it not a pity that people who are bright and clever should so often be exceedingly improper, and that those who are never improper should so often be dull and heavy?   Trollope, *Barchester Towers*, XXXIII

CONTROL

Who is there in the whole world that can pretend to assert his thoughts, words, and actions are exempt from control?   Burney, *Cecilia*, III

All things are not in the power of all.   Fielding, *Tom Jones*, 130

Women are the properest to manage women.   *Ibid.*, 264

Bridle your appetites, rein your mind, guard your lips, and purify your soul.   Kimber, *David Ranger*, I

The man is above control who wants not either to borrow or flatter.   Richardson, *Clarissa Harlowe*, II

Once subdued, always subdued—but some are never subdued.   *Ibid.*, III

I have often more than half ruined myself by my complaisance; and, being afraid of control, have brought control upon myself.   *Ibid.*

CONVENIENCE

A man must pay for his convenience.   Austen, *Sense and Sensibility*, Volume II, XI

CONVENTIONALITY; CUSTOM; USE

Tyrant custom adds a sanction to practices neither justifiable on principles of nature, reason, nor religion.　　　Anonymous, *Adventures of a Kidnapped Orphan*, 191

The remotest precedent cannot justify a bad custom, nor can numberless examples evince the propriety of an iniquitous conduct.　　　*Ibid.*

We cannot appear to advantage when out of our proper sphere.
　　　Anonymous, *The Birmingham Counterfeit*, II

The customs of the world must be complied with.　　Anonymous, *Fatal Friendship*, II

The opinion of the world should never be slighted.
　　　Anonymous, *Memoirs of a Coquet*, 102-103

Custom may account for the continuance, but not for the origin, of manners.
　　　Brown, C.B., *Alcuin*, III

Customs long established, and habits long indulged, assume an empire despotic, though their power is but prescriptive. Opposing them is vain. Nature herself, when forced aside, is not more elastic in her rebound.　　　Burney, *Cecilia*, III

The power of custom is enormous.　　　Butler, *Erewhon*, XXV

The bird that would soar above the level plain of tradition and prejudice must have strong wings. It is a sad spectacle to see the weaklings bruised, exhausted, fluttering back to earth.　　　Chopin, *The Awakening*, XXVII

The chains of convention, an external life grown out of all proportion with that of the heart and mind.　　　Disraeli, *Sybil*, Book II, XI

While that blind guide, Custom, is allowed to mislead, the great, as well as poor, man must never hope for happiness unalloyed with suspicion, or unclouded with care.
　　　Harley, *Priory of St. Bernard*, I

Custom has in no one point a greater sway than over our modes of wreaking our wild passions.　　　Hawthorne, *The Blithedale Romance*, IX

Tradition—which sometimes brings down truth that history has let slip, but is oftener the wild babble of the time, such as was formerly spoken at the fireside, and now congeals in newspapers—tradition is responsible for all contrary averments.
　　　Hawthorne, *The House of the Seven Gables*, I

It is remarkable that persons who speculate the most boldly often conform with the most perfect quietude to the external regulations of society.
　　　Hawthorne, *The Scarlet Letter*, XIII

Neither money nor prayers would get a man a bed to himself here; custom forbade it sternly. You might as well have asked to monopolize a seesaw.
　　　Reade, *The Cloister and the Hearth*, XXIV

Custom is a prodigious thing.　　　Richardson, *Clarissa Harlowe*, II

Use reconciles everything to us.　　　*Ibid.*, IV

Tyrant custom makes a daughter change her name in marriage, and gives to a son, for the sake of name only, the estate of the common ancestor of both.
　　　Richardson, *Sir Charles Grandison*, One, II

CONVERSATION

People who have no ideas out of the common road are generally the greatest talkers, because all their thoughts are low enough for common conversation; whereas those of more elevated understandings have ideas which they cannot easily communicate except to persons of equal capacity with themselves.　　　Brooke, *Emily Montague*, III

CONVERSATION (continued)

No ingenuous person ever thinks much of the particular subject of conversation.
Cooper, *Homeward Bound*, XVI

At the shrine of barbarous custom, the happiness and lives of individuals are daily immolated, society becomes in consequence more corrupt, and the aggregate of human misery increased.
Dacre, *The Libertine*, XXX

The art of conversation consists of the exercise of two fine qualities. You must originate, and you must sympathize; you must possess at the same time the habit of communicating, and the habit of listening.
Disraeli, *Coningsby*, Book III, III

There are few things in life more interesting than an unrestrained interchange of ideas with a congenial spirit; and there are few things more rare.
Ibid., Book VII, II

If a man has by any chance what he conceives an original idea, he hoards it as if it were old gold; and rather avoids the subject with which he is most conversant, from fear that you may appropriate his best thoughts.
Ibid.

One of the principal causes of our renowned dullness in conversation is our extreme intellectual jealousy.
Ibid.

The French do more commonly dance to talk, than entreat to dance.
Gascoigne, *Master F. J.*, 23

Conversation may be divided into two classes—the familiar and the sentimental.
Radcliffe, *A Sicilian Romance*, I

Common subjects afford only commonplace, and are soon exhausted: Why, then, should conversation be confined to narrow limits and to continual repetition?
Richardson, *Sir Charles Grandison*, Three, VI

The fellow loved to advise, or rather to hear himself talk.   Sterne, *Tristram Shandy*, II

Conversation is seldom witty or eloquent in private societies, or anywhere except in very high-flown and ingenious novels.
Thackeray, *Vanity Fair*, IV

A man had better be silent if he can only say today what he will stand by tomorrow, or if he may not launch into the general talk the whim and fancy of the moment.
Warner, *A Little Journey*, I

CONVICTION: *see also* OPINION

The only convictions a man of sense should entertain are those that adjust themselves to circumstances.
Glasgow, *The Descendant*, Book II, III

A man always had good spirits when he had acted in harmony with a conviction.
James, H., *Confidence*, XIV

A man with convictions may be wrong.
Page, *Red Rock*, II

Conviction is half way to amendment.
Richardson, *Clarissa Harlowe*, I

Better to retrench upon conviction than compulsion.
Smollett, *Peregrine Pickle*, 473

COQUETRY

A coquet never is anxious to make a conquest for the sake of the man; her chief intention is to prevent his being conquered by a rival.
Anonymous, *Memoirs of a Coquet*, 6

The whole business of the coquet, the supreme delight of her life, is to interrupt the felicity of others.
Ibid., 7

The arts of coquetry require but slender parts where the love of admiration is potent.
Burney, *Camilla*, Five, IX

I am the veriest coquet in nature, and take an infinite pleasure in making a wise man look and talk like a fool.
Lennox, *Henrietta*, I

CORRECTION; AMENDMENT

Look backward only to correct an error of conduct for the next attempt.
Meredith, *Amazing Marriage*, XXX

Evermore be sure of being in the right, when thou presumest to sit down to correct thy master.
Richardson, *Clarissa Harlowe*, II

He is in possession of a good estate, which makes amends for many defects.
Richardson, *Sir Charles Grandison*, One, I

CORRUPTION

The word *corruption* is the father of more platitudes than any word in the American language.
Atherton, *Senator North*, Book I, V

The nation that is corrupt deserves to fall.
Disraeli, *Coningsby*, Book VII, II

The grand corrupter, man.
Fielding, S., *The History of Ophelia*, II

It is more important to detect corruption than fiction.
Lennox, *The Female Quixote*, II

Corrupt as Lima.
Melville, *Moby Dick*, LIV

Good people may be corrupted.
Richardson, *Clarissa Harlowe*, III

It is an aggravation that they who are so capable of mending the heart should in any places show a corrupt one in themselves.
Ibid., IV

COST: *see* VALUE

COUNTERPART: *see* COMPARISON/CONTRAST

COURAGE: *see also* COWARDICE

There is a higher sort of bravery, the bravery of self-control.
Aldrich, *Stillwater*, XIII

Of all human accomplishments, none is more counterfeited than courage.
Anonymous, *The Birmingham Counterfeit*, I

We often find courage among the common occurrences of a domestic life.
Ibid.

Fortune is ever favorable to the brave.
Anonymous, *The Life of Sir Richard Perrott*, 39

Death can be met with fortitude by any strong brain, but not a lifetime of miserable invalidism.
Atherton, *Senator North*, Book III, XII

Great delicacy becomes brave men, and they will not insult the accused or triumph over the unfortunate.
Brackenridge, *Modern Chivalry*, Part II, Volume I

Courage is no definite or steadfast principle.
Brown, C.B., *Wieland*, 165

As man at first is exposed to all dangers from wild beasts, and from men as savage as himself, courage becomes the first quality mankind must honor.
Bulwer, *The Caxtons*, Book III, II

Bowels becometh pilgrims.
Bunyan, *Pilgrim's Progress*, 194

Courage meets death with steadiness; but it prepares for immortality with reverence and emotion.
Burney, *Camilla*, Four, VIII

At least in females, courage frequently becomes potent as an agent where it has been feeble as a principal.
Ibid.

How cool, how quiet, is true courage!
Burney, *Evelina*, 96

My courage was still more in my head than in my heart.
Cleland, *Memoirs of a Woman of Pleasure*, 171

Circumstances try the metal a man is really made of.
Collins, *The Moonstone*, First Period, Chapter XI

With that courage which women lose so often in the small emergency and so seldom in the great.
Collins, *The Woman in White*, Part I, First Epoch

One may get on knowing very well that one's courage does not come of itself.
Conrad, *Lord Jim*, XIII

Men are endowed with every gradation of courage, from the calm energy of reflection, which is rendered still more effective by physical firmness, to the headlong precipitation of reckless spirit; from the resolution that grows more imposing and more respectable, as there is greater occasion for its exercise, to the fearful and ill-directed energies of despair.
Cooper, *The Headsman*, XXIII

Courage is both a comparative and an improvable virtue.
Cooper, *Wish-ton-Wish*, XXX

Reassume your courage, not the courage to *die*, but to live.
Dacre, *Passions*, Letter LXXI

People glorify all sorts of bravery except the bravery they might show on behalf of their nearest neighbors.
Eliot, *Middlemarch*, Book VIII, LXXII

Men whose manners have been once thoroughly corrupted are apt to return, from any dawn of an amendment, into the dark paths of vice.
Fielding, H., *Amelia*, II

The seat of valor is not the countenance.
Fielding, H., *Joseph Andrews*, 95

Many a grave and plain man will, on a just provocation, betake himself to cold iron; while men of a fiercer brow will more prudently decline it.
Ibid.

A man might be a coward at one time, and brave at another.
Ibid., 114

Courage is a capricious property.
Godwin, *Caleb Williams*, III

Fortitude is not the virtue of a populace.
Godwin, *St. Leon*, 379

A man of courage is so far from being dismayed by an appearance of danger that he generally becomes more resolute.
Graves, *The Spiritual Quixote*, III

You can't expect a man to be brave in his [night]shirt.
Hardy, *The Trumpet-Major*, V

Fortitude springs as much from superiority to our enmities, as from superiority to our enemies.
Judd, *Margaret*, Volume II, III

Courage in most comes from a mechanical acquired habit of reasoning themselves out of their fear.
Kimber, *Joe Thompson*, II

It is not an easy matter for a man to find out how far his courage will carry him.
Lawrence, *The Contemplative Man*, II

It must be a wily mouse that shall breed in the cat's ear.
Lyly, *Euphues*, 119

As great a shame to be valiant and courtly without learning as to be studious and bookish without valor.
Lyly, *Euphues and His England*, 269

To fortitude there is no sting in adversity, and in death no evil to the valiant.
Mackenzie, *The Man of the World*, II

It is better that we slay a coward, than through a coward be slain.
Malory, *Le Morte DArthur*, One, I

Bravery in a poor cause is the height of simplicity.
Melville, *Israel Potter*, VII

He who is ready to despair in solitary peril, plucks up a heart in the presence of another.
Melville, *Mardi*, XXXIV

The most reliable and useful courage is that which arises from the fair estimation of the encountered peril.

Melville, *Moby Dick*, XXVI

An utterly fearless man is a far more dangerous comrade than a coward.   *Ibid.*

Brave as he might be, it was that sort of bravery chiefly, visible in some intrepid men, which, while generally abiding firm in the conflict with seas, or winds, or whales, or any of the ordinary irrational horrors of the world, yet cannot withstand those more terrific, because more spiritual terrors, which sometimes menace you from the concentrating brow of an enraged and mighty man.   *Ibid.*

It is a thing most sorrowful; nay shocking, to expose the fall of valor in the soul.   *Ibid.*

That immaculate manliness we feel within ourselves bleeds with keenest anguish at the undraped spectacle of a valor-ruined man.   *Ibid.*

Health is the body's virtue; truth, the soul's; valor springs but from the unison of these twain.

Meredith, *Ordeal of Richard Feverel*, IV

Want of courage is want of sense.   Meredith, *The Tragic Comedians*, XI

Fortitude stamps upon those who possess it an unfading lustre.

Moore, *Grasville Abbey*, I

Fortitude forsakes the breast which is governed by terror and self-interest.   *Ibid.*

The force of desperate calamity sometimes affords us fortitude.

Radcliffe, *A Sicilian Romance*, I

The courage, like the talent, of common men runs in a narrow groove. Take them but an inch out of that, and they are done.   Reade, *The Cloister and the Hearth*, XX

Courage, le diable est mort!   *Ibid.*, XXIV

One man's courage is not another's.   *Ibid.*, XXXII

What so fair as winter's lilies, snow yclept [covered], and what so brave as roses?

Ibid., LIII

Your courage is skin deep.   Reade, *Griffith Gaunt*, VII

Whoever knew a brave man, a base man?   Richardson, *Clarissa Harlowe*, I

He had hemmed himself into more courage.   *Ibid.*

There is a sort of valor in the face which, by its over-bluster, shows fear in the heart.

Ibid., II

A man's passiveness to a beloved object of the female sex does not argue want of courage on proper occasions.   *Ibid.*, III

The true bravery of spirit is to be above doing a vile action.   *Ibid.*, IV

He wants to be taught the difference between courage and bluster.   *Ibid.*

The empty, the false glory, that men have to be thought brave, and the apprehension of being deemed cowards among men, and among women too, very few men aim to get above.   Richardson, *Sir Charles Grandison*, One, II

Courage is a virtue; passion is a vice; passion, therefore, cannot be courage.   *Ibid.*

There may be as much courage in enduring as in acting.

Scott, *Redgauntlet*, Letter VI

There is a sort of glowworm courage that shows only by night.

Scott, *The Talisman*, XI

He was only valiant when he was angry.   Sidney, *Arcadia*, II

Sagacity and presence of mind very often supplied in our hero the place of courage.

Smollett, *Ferdinand, Count Fathom*, XXIX

'Tis as brave to kill a kitten as a man that defends not himself.

Stevenson, *The Black Arrow*, Book I, VI

COURAGE (*continued*)

A brave woman far more readily accepts a change of circumstances than the bravest man.
Stevenson, *Prince Otto*, Book III, I

I wonder is it because men are cowards in heart that they admire bravery so much, and place military valor so far beyond every other quality for reward and worship?
Thackeray, *Vanity Fair*, XXX

How can a man be manly when the manliness is knocked out of him? A man's courage lies in his heart;—but if his heart is broken where will his courage be then?
Trollope, *The American Senator*, LIX

There are girls so cold-looking whom to attack seems to require the same sort of courage, and the same sort of preparation, as a journey in quest of the northwest passage.
Trollope, *Phineas Finn*, II

Courage is resistance to fear, mastery of fear—not absence of fear. Except a creature be part coward it is not a compliment to say it is brave; it is merely a loose misapplication of the word. Consider the flea!—incomparably the bravest of all the creatures of God, if ignorance of fear were courage.
Twain, *Pudd'nhead Wilson*, XII

Courage has gone out of our race. Perhaps we never really had it.
Wilde, *The Picture of Dorian Gray*, II

The bravest man amongst us is afraid of himself.
Ibid.

COURTESY

Men are apt to be very courteous to those who have property.
Arthur, *Ten Nights in a Bar-Room*, Night The First

True courtesy is very often inattention.
Kipling, *Kim*, XII

Much courtesy, much subtlety.
Nashe, *The Unfortunate Traveller*, 34

Courtesy is a gallant gay, a courtier by name and by profession.
Scott, *Rob Roy*, X

Hail ye small sweet courtesies of life, for smooth do ye make the road of it! like grace and beauty which beget inclinations to love at first sight.
Sterne, *A Sentimental Journey*, 54

Courtesy and cordiality are not only not the same, but they are incompatible. Courtesy is an effort, and cordiality is free.
Trollope, *He Knew He Was Right*, LVI

COURTSHIP: *see also* LOVE; MALE AND FEMALE; MARRIAGE; etc.

All young ladies have been, or at least all have believed themselves to be, in danger from the pursuit of someone whom they wished to avoid; and all have been anxious for the attentions of someone whom they wished to please.
Austen, *Northanger Abbey*, X

Ladies frown in courtship as a thing of course; it's just like a man swearing at a coachman: he's not a bit more in a passion, only he thinks he sha'n't be minded without it.
Burney, *Cecilia*, III

It becometh not maidens to be wooers, though willingly they could wish to wed where they best fancy.
Deloney, *The Gentle Craft*, 145

A flat denial is meet for a saucy suitor.
Deloney, *Jack of Newbury*, 330

Men who come courting are just like bad cooks: if you are kind to them, instead of ascribing it to an exceptional courtesy on your part, they instantly set it down to their own marvelous worth.
Hardy, *The Hand of Ethelberta*, VI

All fish are not caught with flies; all women are not allured with personage.
Lyly, *Euphues and His England*, 350

He wooeth well that meaneth no ill, and he speedeth sooner that speaketh what he should than he that uttereth what he will.
Ibid., 350

Here's to the cock who makes love to the hen,/ Crows till he's hoarse and makes love again./ Here's to the hen that never refuses,/ Lets the cock pay compliment whenever he chooses.
Marryat, *Peter Simple*, XXXI

Favor destroys courtship. Distance increases it. Its essence is distance.
Richardson, *Clarissa Harlowe*, I

Women having it not in their power to begin a courtship lend an ear where their hearts incline not.
Ibid., 356

But this is horrid romancing!
Richardson, *Pamela*, 188

Courtship and marriage cannot be talked seriously of by a lady before company.
Richardson, *Sir Charles Grandison*, Two, III

He can court without speech; he can take one's heart, and say never a word.
Ibid., Three, VI

COVETOUSNESS

There is no method so sure by which a man can be made to covet a tail as by supplying all his neighbors and excluding him by an especial edict.
Cooper, *The Monikins*, Conclusion

Better thought covetous than careless.
Deloney, *The Gentle Craft*, 145

Thwackum was encouraged to the courting of the widow by reflecting that to covet your neighbor's sister is nowhere forbidden.
Fielding, H., *Tom Jones*, 93

Covetous people have every one's ill word: and so indeed they ought, because they are only solicitous to keep that which they prefer to every one's good one. Covetous indeed would they be who deserved neither, yet expected both!
Richardson, *Clarissa Harlowe*, I

Covetousness bursts the sack, and spills the grain.
Scott, *Kenilworth*, IV

COWARDICE: *see also* COURAGE

Cowards are always cruel.
Anonymous, *The Egg*, 67

All women despise a coward.
Bridges, *The Adventures of a Bank-Note*, II

Who but a coward would pass his whole life in hamlets, and forever abandon his faculties to the eating rust of obscurity?
Bronte, C., *Villette*, VI

What suffering it costs to be a coward!
Cable, *Bonaventure*, Book III, XVI

The most unendurable reproach that a woman can address to a man [is to call him a coward].
Collins, *The Moonstone*, Third Narrative, VII

The swaggerer is ever a coward at heart, however well he may wear a mask for a time.
Cooper, *Satanstoe*, Volume II, II

It is natural to an Englishman to hate a coward.
Defoe, *Captain Singleton*, 8

A coward made desperate is one of the worst of men in the world to encounter with.
Defoe, *Colonel Jack*, 202

It is mere cowardice to seek safety in negations.
Eliot, *Mill on the Floss*, Book V, III

Says Mr. Osborne, "A woman is the most cowardly of all the creatures God ever made."—a sentiment more remarkable for its bluntness than for its truth.
Fielding, H., *Tom Jones*, 152

Cowards kick and abuse the person who is known to be a degree more timorous than themselves, as much as they tremble at the frown of anyone who has more courage.
Fielding, S., *David Simple*, I

The cowards were the exception in battle; the man that were ready to die, the rule.
Howells, *Silas Lapham*, XIV

COWARDICE (*continued*)

It's a coward's trick to do nothing.   Kingsley, *Westward Ho!*, XX

Very few men are physical cowards in battle.   Lawrence, *Guy Livingstone*, XIII

Shame on the coward soul, which wants the courage neither to be a firm friend, or an open enemy.   Lewis, *The Monk*, 214

The grain of common sense in cowardice.   Meredith, *Beauchamp's Career*, XXV

Cowardice is even worse for nations than for individual men, though the consequences come on us more slowly.   *Ibid.*, XXVIII

The more I know of the world the more clearly I perceive that its top and bottom sin is cowardice, physically and morally alike.   Meredith, *Diana of the Crossways*, XVIII

A coward hardly objects to drag in his accomplice.
                                    Meredith, *Ordeal of Richard Feverel*, X

Which is the coward among us?—He who sneers at the failings of humanity.
                                                            Ibid., XLVIII

There never was a spirit in the world that would insult where it dared but would creep and cringe where it dared not.   Richardson, *Clarissa Harlowe*, I

Cowardice is a distemper as well as madness; for nobody would be afraid if he could help it.   Smollett, *Sir Launcelot Greaves*, 65

Cowardice, though sometimes the effect of natural imbecility, is generally a prejudice of education, or bad habit contracted from misinformation, or misapprehension, and may certainly be cured by experience, and the exercise of reason: but this remedy cannot be applied in madness, which is a privation or disorder of reason itself.   *Ibid.*

In a station of authority, the coward is more dangerous than fire.
                                        Stevenson, *Prince Otto*, Book II, VIII

The average man's a coward. The average man don't like trouble and danger.
                                            Twain, *Huckleberry Finn*, XXII

COXCOMBRY

A national coxcombry that pretends to an independence of human sensations, and makes a motto of our dandiacal courage, is more perilous to the armies of the nation than that of a few heroes.   Meredith, *Beauchamp's Career*, IV

COYNESS

Counsel those that be coy that they weave not the web of their own woe, nor spin the thread of their own thraldom by their own overthwartness.   Lyly, *Euphues*, 111

CRAFTINESS

The crafty person is always in danger.
                            Anonymous, *Tom Jones in His Married State*, 53

Artifice is more like Italian subtlety than English simplicity.
                                        Richardson, *Clarissa Harlowe*, IV

CREATION; CREATIVITY: *see also* ART; EXPRESSION; GOD; etc.

I often give writers credit for more creative ability than they possess, for I always am seeing someone in real life whose entire type I had supposed had come straight out of their genius.   Atherton, *Senator North*, Book III, XII

God's first creature, which was light.   Bacon, *The New Atlantis*, 207

A sow's ear is a much finer work of art than a silk purse.
Bulwer, *What Will He Do with It?*, Book VI, VIII

God has made nothing in vain.
Bunyan, *Pilgrim's Progress*, 210

It would seem to be strange that any human being should find more to wonder at in any one of the phenomena of the earth than in the earth itself; or, should specially stand astonished at the might of Him who created the world, when each night brings into view a firmament studded with other worlds, each equally the work of His hands!
Cooper, *Oak Openings*, I

There is a motive for adoration, in the study of the lowest fruits of the wisdom and power of God.
Ibid.

This conviction of power in the midst of despair was a revelation of intrinsic strength. It is indeed the test of a creative spirit.
Disraeli, *Coningsby*, Book IX, IV

Creation is always preceded by chaos.
Holmes, *The Guardian Angel*, XIX

Holy and delightsome is the Earth. God saw that every thing he had made was very good.
Judd, *Margaret*, Volume III

As well hate a seraph, as a shark. Both were made by the same hand.
Melville, *Mardi*, XIII

He whose intense thinking makes him a Prometheus; a vulture feeds upon that heart for ever; that vulture the very creature he creates.
Melville, *Moby Dick*, XLIV

She's got the creating mouth as well as the seeing eye.
Twain, *Joan of Arc*, Book II, XI

CREDIT

Beautiful credit! The foundation of modern society. Who shall say that this is not the golden age of mutual trust, of unlimited reliance upon human promises?
Twain and Warner, *The Gilded Age*, Volume I, XXVI

Credit cards were the symbols of wealth.
Vinton, *Looking Further Backward*, XIV

CREDULITY; INCREDULITY: *see also* BELIEF; FAITH; etc.

Nothing in this world is probable unless it appeals to our trumpery experience; and we only believe in a romance when we see it in a newspaper.
Collins, *The Moonstone*, First Period, VI

That brain-fed fancy, credulity.
Lawrence, *Common Sense*, I

The credulous man, abstractly and unconnected with mankind, is a harmless, inoffensive creature; but when mixed with the community, if he happen to have a lively imagination and an alluring tongue, he becomes a more dangerous animal than a mad ox in a crowd.
Ibid.

Credulity is the child of irrationality, and the parent of fiction. Faith is the offspring of judgment, and the mother of religion.
Ibid.

As incredulous as those who think none bald till they see his brains.
Lyly, *Euphues and His England*, 267

Credulity is the god of love's prime minister; and they never are asunder.
Richardson, *Clarissa Harlowe*, II

The youthful heart is ready to believe that what it wishes will happen. Alas, how doubly sharp does this readiness render the barb of disappointment.
Roche, *Clermont*, II

These birds which tell us news are seldom very credible—and are often not very creditable. You must take a bird's word for what it may be worth.
Trollope, *Phineas Finn*, LIX

Credulity is always a ridiculous, often a dangerous, failing: it has made of many a clever man, a fool; and of many a good man, a knave.   Wright, *A Few Days in Athens*, III

CRIME: *see also* GOOD AND EVIL

Do not commit a greater crime in order to retrieve a lesser one.
August, Horrid Mysteries, I

Many crimes grow more imperceptible the greater they are.
Ibid.

If agreeing to wrong is criminal, is not performing it worse?
Burney, Cecilia, II

The man makes the crime.   Cable, *The Grandissimes*, XXXVIII

It is my conviction, or my delusion, no matter which, that crime brings its own fatality with it.   Collins, *Moonstone*, Prologue

The fool's crime is the crime that is found out; and the wise man's crime is the crime that is *not* found out.   Collins, *The Woman in White*, Part I, Second Epoch

Crimes cause their own detection.
Ibid.

It is truly wonderful how easily Society can console itself for the worst of its short-comings with a little bit of clap-trap.
Ibid.

The hiding of a crime, or the detection of a crime, what is it? A trial of skill between the police on one side, and the individual on the other.
Ibid.

English society is as often the accomplice, as it is the enemy, of crime.
Ibid.

The real significance of crime is in its being a breach of faith with the community of mankind.   Conrad, *Lord Jim*, XIV

A crime is no less a crime, committed in the darkness of night, than if committed in the face of noon; neither is an act of dishonor which may never be published.
Dacre, Passions, Letter XC

Having committed a crime once is a sad handle to the committing of it again. All the reflections wear off when the temptation renews itself.   Defoe, *Moll Flanders*, 244

The criminal intellect its own professed students perpetually misread, because they persist in trying to reconcile it with the average intellect of average men instead of identifying it as a horrible wonder apart.   Dickens, *The Mystery of Edwin Drood*, XX

The turnkey was not unnaturally cruel or hard-hearted. He had come to look upon felony as a kind of disorder, like the scarlet fever or erysipelas: some people had it—some hadn't—just as it might be.   Dickens, *The Old Curiosity Shop*, LXI

A police officer is generally the last person to arrive in [the investigation of a crime].
Dickens, Oliver Twist, X

In many cases it is inevitable that the shame is felt to be the worst part of crime.
Eliot, Middlemarch, Book VIII, LXXV

I shall always insist that crime was his true vocation.
Frederic, The Market-Place, XXVII

The commission of one vice hurries sinful creatures into innumerable crimes.
Gibbes, Mr. Francis Clive, II

Every crime is made to be the agony of many innocent persons, as well as of the single guilty one.   Hawthorne, *The Marble Faun*, XI

Crime is for the iron-nerved, who have their choice either to endure it, or, if it press too hard, to exert their fierce and savage strength for a good purpose, and fling it off at once.   Hawthorne, *The Scarlet Letter*, XII

Their language is almost entirely destitute of terms to express the delightful ideas conveyed by our endless catalogue of civilized crimes. Melville, *Typee*, XVII

Crimes die when money dies. More, *Utopia*, II

It ain't no crime in a prisoner to steal the thing he needs to get away with. Twain, *Huckleberry Finn*, XXXV

Nobody ever commits a crime without doing something stupid. Wilde, *The Picture of Dorian Gray*, XIV

All crime is vulgar, just as all vulgarity is crime. *Ibid.*, XIX

I should fancy that crime is to the lower orders what art is to us, simply a method of procuring extraordinary sensations. *Ibid.*

CRITIC; CRITICISM: *see also* ART; FICTION; POETRY; etc.

Critics are the men who have failed in literature and art. Disraeli, *Lothair*

A critic in the republic of letters is the same as a constable in the government of England. Donaldson, *Sir Bartholomew Sapskull*, II

Great scholars who have shown the most pitiless acerbity in their criticism of other men's scholarship have yet been of a relenting and indulgent temper in private life. Eliot, *Adam Bede*, XIV

Wash your face before you mention aversion of another's. Fielding, H., *Joseph Andrews*, 270

Till critics produce the authority by which they are constituted judges, I shall not plead to their justification. Fielding, H., *Tom Jones*, 5

The world have paid too great a compliment to critics, and have imagined them men of much greater profundity than they really are. *Ibid.*, 160

The critic is no more than the clerk, whose office it is to transcribe the rules and laws laid down by those great judges whose vast strength of genius hath placed them in the light of legislators, in the several sciences over which they presided. *Ibid.*

While some critics are ready to allow that the same thing which is impossible may be yet probable, others have so little historic or poetic faith that they believe nothing to be either possible or probable the like to which hath not occurred to their own observation. *Ibid.*, 332

A morose, snarling critic may be suspected to be a bad man. *Ibid.*, 490

Memory is the only qualification necessary to make a critic. Fielding, S., *David Simple*, I

True critics are more rare than true poets. Melville, *Mardi*, CLXXX

A beautiful woman choosing to rhapsodize has her way, and is not subjected to the critical commentary within us. Meredith, *Diana of the Crossways*, XVI

Your criticism sounds more sincere than your admiration. Shaw, *The Irrational Knot*, XV

Criticism is ever held the truest and best when it is the first result of the critic's mind. Swift, *A Tale of a Tub*, III

A true critic, in the perusal of a book, is like a dog at a feast, whose thoughts and stomach are wholly set upon what the guests fling away, and consequently, is apt to snarl most, when there are the fewest bones. *Ibid.*

What can be so easy as [condemnation] when the critic has to be responsible for nothing? Trollope, *Barchester Towers*, XXI

There is the review intended to sell a book,—which comes out immediately after the appearance of the book, or sometimes before it; the review which gives reputation, but does not affect the sale, and which comes a little later; the review which snuffs a book out quietly; the review which is to raise or lower the author a single peg, or two pegs, as the case may be; the review which is suddenly to make an author, and the review which is to crush him.   Trollope, *The Way We Live Now*, XI

When the rumor goes abroad that some notable man has been actually crushed, then a real success has been achieved.   *Ibid.*

One mustn't criticize other people on grounds where he can't stand perpendicular himself.   Twain, *A Connecticut Yankee*, XXVI

They get down on a thing when they don't know nothing about it.
                                                     Twain, *Huckleberry Finn*

CRUELTY

That base prompting which makes a woman more cruel to a rival than to a faithless lover.   Eliot, *Middlemarch*, Book VIII, LXXX

Show me a man who has no pity on his horse and I will show you one who is a cruel husband, if he is married, and a tyrannical parent, if he has children; a man that would be a Nero if he had the power. He is a coward by nature and a fiend by practice.
                                                     Falkner, *Little Brick Church*, XI

The malicious disposition of mankind is well known, and they take cruel pleasure in destroying the reputations of others.   Fielding, H., *Amelia*, I

Can cruelty and beauty dwell together?   Fielding, S., *The History of Ophelia*, I

All malice arises from an opposition of interest.   Graves, *The Spiritual Quixote*, II

Cruelty is the law pervading all nature and society.
                                                     Hardy, *Jude the Obscure*, Part Five, VIII

The cruelty of fooled honesty is often great after enlightenment.   Hardy, *Tess*, XXXV

There are few uglier traits of human nature than this tendency to grow cruel, merely because they possessed the power of inflicting harm.
                                        Hawthorne, *The Scarlet Letter*, Introductory

The nature of man is in itself benevolent. Cruelty is ever the consequence of error in opinion or of bad example.   Johnstone, *The History of Arsaces*, I

The vicious are as bad as they can be; and do the devil's work without looking after.
                                                     Richardson, *Clarissa Harlowe*, III

The unmanlike cruelty of mankind.   Sidney, *Arcadia*, I

Human beings *can* be awful cruel to one another.   Twain, *Huckleberry Finn*, XXXIV

CULTURE

Culture is halfway to heaven.   Meredith, *Ordeal of Richard Feverel*, XV

CUNNING

There is always something offensive in the details of cunning.
                                                     Austen, *Persuasion*, XXI

Whatever bears affinity to cunning is despicable.
                                        Austen, *Pride and Prejudice*, Volume I, VIII

Such is deservedly the frequent fate of cunning, that, while it plots surprise and detection of others, commonly overshoots its mark and ends in its own disgrace.
                                                     Burney, *Cecilia*, I

Arts that I could never forgive, I never will practice. *Ibid.*, II

Nature has the deep cunning which hides itself under the appearance of openness, so that simple people think they can see through her quite well, and all the while she is secretly preparing a refutation of their confident prophecies.
Eliot, *Mill on the Floss*, Book I, V

Where we British ain't quite successful we're cunning.
Meredith, *Harry Richmond*, III

There are hours when the clearest soul becomes a cunning fox.
Meredith, *Ordeal of Richard Feverel*, XXXVII

Cunning is the wisdom of women. Richardson, *Sir Charles Grandison*, One, II

To be circumvented by cunning must ever be the fate, but never the disgrace, of the artless. Scott, S., *A Description of Millenium Hall*, 100

The cunning of the madman is a singular feature of his sometime disorder.
Simms, *The Partisan*, Volume II, X

CURIOSITY

Curiosity is an imperious tyrant, and will be obeyed.
Anonymous, *The Fruitless Repentance*, I

Curiosity has no rest till it is gratified.
Anonymous, *Memoirs of the Court of H—*, 10

Provided we are let into a secret, we care not how dearly we pay for it. *Ibid.*, 11

Curiosity is a dangerous petition. Bronte, C., *Jane Eyre*, XXIV

Curiosity is vicious, if undisciplined by reason and inconducive to benefit.
Brown, C.B., *Edgar Huntley*, 16

Curiosity, like virtue, is its own reward. *Ibid.*

Curiosity always leads to disagreeable questions. Burney, *Camilla*, Five, IX

Curiouser and curiouser! Carroll, *Alice's Adventures in Wonderland*, II

We are poor erring creatures, and however well established a woman's principles may be, she cannot always keep on her guard against the temptation to exercise an idle curiosity. Collins, *The Woman in White*, Part I, Second Epoch

Curiosity is the most obvious of sentiments. Conrad, *Lord Jim*, V

Curiosity is a passion that is rather quickened than destroyed by seclusion.
Cooper, *The Prairie*, Two

One is constantly wondering what sort of lives other people lead, and how they take things. Eliot, *Middlemarch*, Book IV, XXXIV

Curiosity hath its votaries among all ranks of people. Fielding, H., *Amelia*, II

Curiosity is a restless propensity, and often does but hurry us forward the more irresistibly, the greater is the danger that attends its indulgence.
Godwin, *Caleb Williams*, II

Curiosity is a principle that carries its pleasures as well as its pains along with it.
Ibid.

Curiosity is an incessant impulse to youth. Holcroft, *Hugh Trevor*, I

There is no knowledge in search of which people in general are more eager, than that of what others have been doing in the world. Jenner, *The Placid Man*, I

Under the direction of reason, curiosity is the strongest and most extensive cause of human knowledge. Johnstone, *The Reverie*, I

Curiosity begets curiosity. Richardson, *Clarissa Harlowe*, I

The curiosity of a prying person is governed by pride, which is not gratified but by whispering about a secret till it becomes public, in order to show either his consequence or his sagacity. *Ibid.*, III

Nothing is too shocking for women to look upon that has but novelty and curiosity in it. *Ibid.*, IV

Curiosity is a nail that will fasten to the ground the foot of an inquisitive person. Richardson, *Sir Charles Grandison*, Three, VII

Curiosity is one of those insatiable passions that grow by gratification. Scott, S., *A Description of Millenium Hall*, 6

My curiosity was stronger than my fear. Stevenson, *Treasure Island*, V

He had no curiosity. It was his chief defect. Wilde, *The Picture of Dorian Gray*, XIX

CURSE; CURSING

A little friendly curse or two is a very innocent refreshment to a man's mind. Burney, *Camilla*, Three, V

Oh, for a curse to kill with! Richardson, *Clarissa Harlowe*, II

CYNICISM: *see also* BELIEF; FAITH; etc.

Cynicism is intellectual dandyism without the coxcomb's feathers. Meredith, *The Egoist*, VII

Cynics are only happy in making the world as barren to others as they have made it for themselves. *Ibid.*

DANCING

It may be possible to do without dancing entirely. Instances have been known of young people passing many, many months successively without being at any ball of any description, and no material injury accrue either to body or mind; but when a beginning is made—when the felicities of rapid motion have once been, though slightly, felt—it must be a very heavy set that does not ask for more. Austen, *Emma*, XXIX

DANGER: *see also* COURAGE

The danger, when not seen, has the imperfect vagueness of human thought. The fear grows shadowy; and Imagination, the enemy of men, the father of all terrors, unstimulated, sinks to rest in the dullness of exhausted emotion. Conrad, *Lord Jim*, II

It is unsafe to wound the wild-boar, unless the wound be mortal. Cooke, *Mohun*, Book V, XVII

It is seldom danger is so pressing, that there is not time enough for reason to do its work. Cooper, *The Prairie*, XXIII

There are hazards in all voyages whether by sea or land. Dickens, *Dombey and Son*, XXXII

It is a dangerous thing to laugh at the wrong man. Dickens, *Pickwick Papers*, XXV

It would appear like presumption to say that a man who hath been just run through the body is in no manner of danger. Fielding, H., *Amelia*, I

Danger is often the best counter-irritant in cases of mental suffering. Holmes, *Elsie Venner*, XX

Delays breed dangers, nothing so perilous as procrastination. Lyly, *Euphues*, 121

The sweeter the more dangerous. Arsenic is sweeter than sugar.
Melville, *Israel Potter*, IX

All men live enveloped in whale-lines. All are born with halters round their necks; but it is only when caught in the swift, sudden turn of death, that mortals realize the silent, subtle, ever-present perils of life.
Melville, *Moby Dick*, LX

Familiarity with danger makes a brave man braver, but less daring.
Melville, *White Jacket*, XXIV

Danger will put wit into any man.
Nashe, *The Unfortunate Traveller*, 44

As dangerous a creature to herself and others as ever tied on a bonnet.
Reade, *Griffith Gaunt*, XVIII

A moment of peril is often also a moment of open-hearted kindness and affection. We are thrown off our guard by the general agitation of our feelings, and betray the intensity of those, which, at more tranquil periods, our prudence at least conceals, if it cannot altogether suppress them.
Scott, *Ivanhoe*, XXIX

Threatened men live long.
Scott, *A Legend of Montrose*, X

There are some dangers which, when they are braved, disappear, and which yet, when there is an obvious and apparent dread of them displayed, become certain and inevitable.
Scott, *Quentin Durward*, X

A neutral has a perilous part to sustain.
Ibid.

Youth seldom thinks of dangers; and bred up free, and fearless, and self-confiding, Quentin only thought of them to defy them.
Ibid., XIII

Times of danger have always, and in a peculiar degree, their seasons of goodwill and of security.
Scott, *The Talisman*, II

Danger is a part of the contract [of war]. It is to be counted on, but not considered. He who stops to consider the danger never goes into battle. No wise man, embarking in such an amusement as war, ever considers its mischances as likely to occur in his own case.
Simms, *Woodcraft*, XXI

To dash, with a sort of frenzy, into the worst of dangers, totally heedless of them all, as if bearing a charmed life—such a practice is very apt to carry with it its own securities.
Ibid.

Danger and dangerous men are always more attractive than safety and safe men.
Trollope, *Phineas Finn*, XVII

How fond you are of saying dangerous things!
Wilde, *The Picture of Dorian Gray*, XVIII

DARING: *see also* COURAGE

Though they had kicked me downstairs every day I presented myself at her door. That is my way of fascinating women. Let the man who has to make his fortune in life remember this maxim. *Attacking* is his only secret. Dare, and the world always yields: or, if it beat you sometimes, dare again, and it will succumb.
Thackeray, *Barry Lyndon*, XIII

DEATH: *see also* LIFE; SUICIDE; etc.

Death, lover of the peerless.
Allen, *Kentucky Cardinal*, II

Wise is the man who prepares both for his own death and the death of his friends; who makes use of the foresight of troubles so as to abate the uneasiness of them.
Amory, *The Life of John Buncle*, II

The dread of death seems implanted in the nature of human kind as a peculiar curse, since no other species of created beings are capable of it.
Annesley, *Memoirs of an Unfortunate Young Nobleman*, I

Death, that tremendous change. *Ibid.*

Death is a great traitor, a great tyrant. Anonymous, *Maria Brown*, II

[Memory of them] is the only revenge the dead have; and doubtless it is this vivid afterlife of theirs in memory that is at the root of the belief in ghosts.
Atherton, *Senator North*, Book III, IV

No man is dead whose inspiration lives on. *Ibid.*, Book III, XV

How can any man of ability submit to death without protest? *Ibid.*

"The death of your daughter would have been a blessing in comparison of this [scandal]."
Austen, *Pride and Prejudice*, Volume III, VI

Death is but the projection of a sin-burdened conscience upon the mists of the unknown.
Bates, *Puritans*, VI

Death is but the prophet of life. Beecher, *Norwood*, LII

There appears nothing remarkable, that one whose life has been a scene of folly, should become changed by the near approach of death. Bennett, *The Prairie Flower*, XVII

Why should we ever sink overwhelmed with distress, when life is soon over, and death is so certain an entrance to happiness—to glory? Bronte, C., *Jane Eyre*, VII

I lingered round them, under that benign sky; watched the moths fluttering among the heath and hare-bells; listened to the soft wind breathing through the grass; and wondered how anyone could ever imagine unquiet slumbers for the sleepers in that quiet earth. Bronte, E., *Wuthering Heights*, XXIV

Death is but a shifting of the scene; and the endless progress of eternity, which to the good is merely the perfection of felicity, is to the wicked an accumulation of woe.
Brown, C.B., *Edgar Huntley*, 83

We can never escape ghosts. They haunt us always. We cannot think or act, but the soul of some man who has lived before points the way. The dead never die.
Bulwer, *The Caxtons*, Book IV, I

It is not life that is sweet, but death that is awful. Bulwer, *Pompeii*, Book V, I

To go back is nothing but death; to go forward is fear of death, and life everlasting beyond it. Bunyan, *Pilgrim's Progress*, 44

If a man would live well, let him fetch his last day to him, and make it always his company-keeper. *Ibid.*, 213

It is better to go up the ladder to life, than down the hill to death. *Ibid.*, 226

If death is an offense at all, it is one beyond the reach of the law, which is therefore silent on the subject; but the Erewhonians insist that the greater number of those who are commonly said to die, have never yet been born—not, at least, into that unseen world which is alone worthy of consideration. Butler, *Erewhon*, XIII

The mere knowledge that we shall one day die does not make us very unhappy; no one thinks that he or she will escape, so that none are disappointed. *Ibid.*

My father heard him say "Good-bye, sun; good-bye, sun," as the sun sank, and saw by his tone and manner that he was feeling very feeble. Before the next sunset he was gone.
Butler, *The Way of All Flesh*, III

The most absolute life contains death, and the corpse is still in many respects living.
Ibid., XIX

Eulogies of the departed are in most cases both unnecessary and untrue.
Ibid., LXXXIII

Can a man who dies peacefully away during his sleep be said to have died at all?
Ibid., LXXXVI

Who is he that looketh upon the features of the dead and looketh not up to the giver and recipient of life? Caruthers, *Cavaliers*, Volume II, XI

The most ancient statuary of all nations is an image of death; not of sleeping energy. The arms adhere rigidly to the sides, the feet form one block; and even in the face, the divine ideal seems struggling hard to enter the reluctant form. Child, *Philothea*, III

Oh, Death, thou hast thy sting! Oh, Grave, thou hast thy victory! Collins, *The Woman in White*, Part II, Second Epoch

"Torn in her own lifetime from the list of the living, the daughter of Philip Fairlie and the wife of Percival Glyde might still exist for her sister, might still exist for me, but to all the world besides she was dead. Dead to her uncle, who had renounced her; dead to the servants of the house, who had failed to recognize her; dead to the persons in authority who had transmitted her fortune to her husband and her aunt; dead to my mother and my sister, who believed me to be the dupe of an adventuress and the victim of a fraud; socially, morally, legally—dead." *Ibid.*, Third Epoch, Walter Hartright's Narrative

What is it that makes the idea of death supportable? End! Finis! The potent word that exorcises from the house of the life the haunting shadow of fate. Conrad, *Lord Jim*, XVI

We are all equal before death. *Ibid.*, XLI

Death is better than strife. Conrad, *Outcast of the Islands*, Part I, VII

There is one feature connected with death in this country that we could gladly see altered. It is the almost indecent haste to get rid of the dead. Cooper, *Sea Lions*, XXX

It seemed that the dead men must have fallen from some great height to get into such positions. They looked to be dumped out upon the ground from the sky. Crane, *The Red Badge of Courage*, V

Death about to thrust him between the shoulder blades was far more dreadful than death about to smite him between the eyes. *Ibid.*, VI

He had been to touch the great death, and found that, after all, it was but the great death. *Ibid.*, XXIV

How miserable is the fate of the wretch who is not aroused to repentance till death gives the alarm! Dacre, *Passions*, Letter LXXXIV

To think of death is to die, and to be always thinking of it is to be all one's life long a-dying. It is time enough to think of it when it comes. Defoe, *Captain Singleton*, 293–294

They that never think of dying, often die without thinking of it. *Ibid.*, 294

It is because men live as if they were never to die, that so many die before they know how to live. *Ibid.*

What care they to die that cannot tell how to live? Defoe, *Moll Flanders*, 263

We all shall choose anything rather than death, especially when 'tis attended with an uncomfortable prospect beyond it. *Ibid.*, 305

It is not the least evil attendant upon the frequent exhibition of this last dread punishment, of Death, that it hardens the minds of those who deal it out, and makes them, though they be amiable men in other respects, indifferent to, or unconscious of, their great responsibility. Dickens, *Barnaby Rudge*, LXXVI

I know no more than the dead. Perhaps the dead know better, if they could only tell us. Dickens, *Bleak House*, XXXI

The Lord Chancellor of that Court has died the death of all Lord Chancellors in all Courts, and of all authorities in all places under all names soever, where false pretenses are made, and where injustice is done. *Ibid.*, XXXII

A countenance as imperturbable as Death. *Ibid.*, XXXIV

The light is come upon the dark benighted way. Dead!   *Ibid.*, XLVII

As all partings foreshadow the great final one,—so, empty rooms, bereft of a familiar presence, mournfully whisper what your room and what mine must one day be.
Ibid., LVIII

"Why do people spend more money upon a death than upon a birth?" "Hearts want binding, and spirits want balming when people die: not when people are born."
Dickens, *Martin Chuzzlewit*, XIX

That's a ve-ry shrewd woman. That's a woman whose intellect is immensely superior to her station in life. That's a woman who observes and reflects in an uncommon manner. She's the sort of woman one would almost feel disposed to bury for nothing: and do it neatly, too!   *Ibid.*, XXV

Ah! He'd make a lovely corpse.   *Ibid.*

There are three hundred and sixty-five days in the year—three hundred and sixty-six in leap year—and he may die on any one of 'em.   *Ibid.*, XLVI

When Death strikes down the innocent and young, for every fragile form from which he lets the panting spirit free, a hundred virtues rise, in shapes of mercy, charity, and love, to walk the world, and bless it.   Dickens, *Old Curiosity Shop*, LXXII

He had grown so like death in life, that they knew not when he died.
Dickens, *Pickwick Papers*, XLIV

"We all pity his loss, and are ready to do anything for him; and there's no situation in life so bad, that it can't be mended. Which is what a very worthy person said to me when my husband died."   *Ibid.*, LII

Death is Nature's remedy for all things.   Dickens, *A Tale of Two Cities*, Book II, I

For haste, for unadulterated despatch, commend me to the county burying. The body politic is busy and has no time to waste on an inert human body. It does its duty to the dead when the body is dropped with all celerity into the ground. The county is philosophical: it says, "Poor devil, the world was unkind to him: he'll be glad to get out of it: we'll be doing him a favor to put him at the earliest moment out of sight and sound and feeling of the things that wounded him. Then, too, the quicker the cheaper, and that will make it easier on the taxpayers."   Dunbar, *The Uncalled*, II

The faint odor which pervades the chamber of death—an odor that is like the reminiscence of sorrow.   *Ibid.*

I've a great fancy to see my own funeral afore I die.   Edgeworth, *Castle Rackrent*, 55

After the old women have continued their wailing at the wake for a decent time, with all the necessary accompaniments of wringing their hands, wiping or rubbing their eyes with the corners of their gowns or aprons, etc., one of the mourners suddenly suspends her lamentable cries, and, turning to her neighbor, asks, "Arrah now, honey, who is it we're crying for?"   *Ibid.*, 70

Our dead are never dead to us until we have forgotten them.   Eliot, *Adam Bede*, X

When our indignation is borne in submissive silence, we are apt to feel twinges of doubt afterwards as to our own generosity, if not justice; how much more when the object of our anger has gone into everlasting silence, and we have seen his face for the last time in the meekness of death.   *Ibid.*, XVIII

"In the midst of life we are in death." The present moment is all we can call our own for works of mercy, of righteous dealing, and of family tenderness. All very old truths—but what we thought the oldest truth becomes the most startling to us in the week when we have looked on the dead face of one who has made a part of our own lives.   *Ibid.*

When the commonplace "We must all die" transforms itself suddenly into the acute consciousness "I must die—and soon," then death grapples us, and his fingers are cruel;

afterwards, he may come to fold us in his arms as our mother did, and our last moment of dim earthly discerning may be like the first.   Eliot, *Middlemarch*, Book IV, XLII

Death was not to be a leap; it was to be a long descent under thickening shadows.
Eliot, *Mill on the Floss*, Book III, IV

Life is never sweeter than when we are near losing it.   Fielding, H., *Amelia*, I

It is not death, but dying, which is terrible.   *Ibid.*

Just at the very instant when Captain Blifil's heart was exulting in meditations on the happiness which would accrue to him by Mr. Allworthy's death, he himself—died of an apoplexy.   Fielding, H., *Tom Jones*, 69

Captain Blifil took measure of that proportion of soil which was now become adequate to all his future purposes, and he lay dead on the ground, a great (though not a living) example of the truth of that observation of Horace: "You provide the noblest materials for building, when a pickaxe and a spade are only necessary; and build houses of five hundred by a hundred feet, forgetting that of six by two."   *Ibid.*, 69–70

Death, that inexorable judge, had passed sentence on him, and refused to grant him a reprieve, though two doctors who arrived, and were fee'd at one and the same instant, were his counsel.   *Ibid.*, 72

Unwillingness to quit our friends is the most amiable motive from which we can derive the fear of death.   *Ibid.*, 189

Few men think of death till they are in its jaws.   *Ibid.*

However gigantic and terrible an object death may appear when it approaches men, they are nevertheless incapable of seeing it at any distance.   *Ibid.*

He who escapes from death is not pardoned; he is only reprieved, and reprieved to a short day.   *Ibid.*

Death ought neither to occasion our surprise nor our lamentation.   *Ibid.*, 190

[Thinking he was near death, Mr. Allworthy said,] "Bless you all. I am setting out a little before you."   *Ibid.*, 191

The great use of philosophy is to learn to die.   *Ibid.*, 830

The ever-gaping grave speedily swallows up the air-built fabrics of imagination.
Gentleman, *A Trip to the Moon*, I

In human life men plan and build as though it were eternal, forgetting that death is in the world.   Gilman, *The Story of a Western Claim*, XIII

Death in any form, brought upon us by surprise, and for which the mind has had no time to prepare, is inexpressibly terrible.   Godwin, *Caleb Williams*, III

There is no such thing as death, only a change.   Haggard, *She*, I

There is no such thing as Death, although there be a thing called Change.   *Ibid.*, XIII

Death is but Life's Night. Out of the Night is the Morrow born anew, and doth again beget the Night.   *Ibid.*, XVI

Why should Death alone lend what Life is compelled to borrow—rest?
Hardy, *Woodlanders*, XXVII

Death should take me while I am in the mood.
Hawthorne, *The Blithedale Romance*, VI

Has not the world come to an awfully sophisticated pass, when, after a certain degree of acquaintance with it, we cannot even put ourselves to death, in whole-hearted simplicity?
Ibid., XXVII

Alas, that the vanity of dress should extend even to the grave!
Hawthorne, *Fanshawe*, IX

A Dead Man, if he happen to have made a will, disposes of wealth no longer his own; or, if he die intestate, it is distributed in accordance with the notions of men much longer dead than he. We must be dead ourselves, before we can begin to have our proper influence on our own world, which will then be no longer our world, but the world of another generation, with which we shall have no shadow of a right to interfere.

Hawthorne, *The House of the Seven Gables*, XII

Of all the events which constitute a person's biography, there is scarcely one to which the world so easily reconciles itself, as to his death.　　　　　　　　　*Ibid.*, XXI

It is very singular, how the fact of a man's death often seems to give people a truer idea of his character, whether for good or evil, than they have ever possessed while he was living and acting among them.　　　　　　　　　　　　　　　　　　　*Ibid.*

No great mistake, whether acted or endured, in our mortal sphere, is ever really set right. Time, the continual vicissitude of circumstances, and the invariable inopportunity of death, render it impossible.　　　　　　　　　　　　　　　　　　　*Ibid.*

What a strange efficacy there is in death!　　　　Hawthorne, *The Marble Faun*, XIII

Death has probably a peculiar horror and ugliness, when forced upon the contemplation of a person naturally joyous.　　　　　　　　　　　　　　　　　　　*Ibid.*, XX

The many deaths that make up the one glory of a victory.　　　　　　*Ibid.*, XXI

Death was too definite an object to be wished for, or avoided.

Hawthorne, *The Scarlet Letter*, XVI

Preach! Write! Act! Do anything, save to lie down and die!　　　　*Ibid.*, XVII

Why should we pamper our bodies for the worms that will devour us?

Helme, *St. Margaret's Cave*, Volume I, VIII

[Far behind the hearse] there is often good and reasonably cheerful conversation going on about the virtues of the deceased, the probable amount of his property, or the little slips he may have committed, and where occasionally a subdued pleasantry at his expense sets the four waistcoats shaking that were lifting with sighs a half-hour ago in the house of mourning.　　　　　　　Holmes, *The Guardian Angel*, XXXVI

Mortality is an event by which a wise man can never be surprised.

Johnson, *Rasselas*, 78

We know that death is always near, and it should therefore always be expected.　　*Ibid.*

It is a great gift—Amiability. And, when the possessor dies, it is profoundly true that better men might be better spared.　　　　Lawrence, *Guy Livingstone*, XXXIII

One point of fleeting time past, and death reduces all to an equality.

Lennox, *Sophia*, II

Did we sit down to number the calamities of this world, we should change one idea of evil, and learn to look on death as a friend.　　Mackenzie, *Julia De Roubigné*, 113-114

He who wishes to die must leave the city [of Monterey: because life there is so healthful].

Marryat, *Monsieur Violet*, V

Talk not against mummies. Pharaoh's poorest brickmaker lies proudlier in his rags than the Emperor of all the Russias in his hollands; for death, though in a worm, is majestic; while life, though in a king, is contemptible.

Melville, *Confidence-Man*, XXXVI

In a theocracy, what is to fear? Let us compose ourselves to death as fagged horsemen sleep in the saddle. Let us welcome even ghosts when they rise.

Melville, *Mardi*, III

The consciousness of being deemed dead is next to the presumable unpleasantness of being so in reality. One feels like his own ghost unlawfully tenanting a defunct carcass.

Ibid., IX

Death has a mouth as black as a wolf's, and to be thrust into his jaws is a serious thing. But true it is that to sailors, as a class, the grisly king seems not half so hideous as he appears to those who have only regarded him on shore, and at a deferential distance.

Ibid.

Since death is the last enemy of all, valiant souls will taunt him while they may. Yet rather, should the wise regard him as the inflexible friend, who, even against our own wills, from life's evils triumphantly relieves us.   *Ibid.*

There is but little difference in the manner of dying. To die, is all. And death has been gallantly encountered by those who never beheld blood that was red, only its light azure seen through the veins. And to yield the ghost proudly, and march out of your fortress with all the honors of war, is not a thing of sinew and bone. The last end of a butterfly shames us all.   *Ibid.*

Watery obsequies.   *Ibid.*, LXIII

If our dead fathers somewhere and somehow live, why not our unborn sons? For backward or forward, eternity is the same; already have we been the nothing we dread to be.   *Ibid.*, LXXVIII

Death is but a mode of life.   *Ibid.*, CXXIII

Death is the deadest of all things.   *Ibid.*, CLXIII

[I am risen] from the buried dead within me; not from myself.   *Ibid.*, CLXXVI

Could we gain one glimpse of the great calendar of eternity, all our names would there be found, glued against their dates of death.   *Ibid.*, CLXXVIII

We die, because we live.   *Ibid.*

Let us be gay, if it be only for an hour, and Death hand us the goblet.   *Ibid.*, CLXXXIII

There is much to be learned from the dead, more than you may learn from the living.
                                                                          Ibid.

Death is Life's last despair.   *Ibid.*, CLXXXV

That all have died, makes it not easier for me to depart.   *Ibid.*

I have long been the tomb of my youth. And more has died out of me, already, than remains for the last death to finish.   *Ibid.*

Death! Must I be not, and millions be? Must I go, and the flowers still bloom?   *Ibid.*

I have marked what it is to be dead;—how shouting boys, of holidays, hide-and-seek among the tombs, which must hide all seekers at last.   *Ibid.*

Why not leap your graves, while ye may?   *Ibid.*

More valiant dying, than dead. The last wisdom is dumb.   *Ibid.*

Is a life of dying worth living o'er again?   *Ibid.*, CXCV

In what census of living creatures, the dead of mankind are included; why it is that a universal proverb says of them, that they tell no tales, though containing more secrets than the Goodwin Sands; how it is that to his name who yesterday departed for the other world, we prefix so significant and infidel a word, and yet do not thus entitle him, if he but embarks for the remotest Indies of this living earth; why the Life Insurance Companies pay death-forfeitures upon immortals; in what eternal, unstirring paralysis, and deadly, hopeless trance, yet lies antique Adam who died sixty round centuries ago; how it is that we still refuse to be comforted for those who we nevertheless maintain are dwelling in unspeakable bliss; why all the living so strive to hush all the dead; wherefore but the rumor of a knocking in a tomb will terrify a whole city. All these things are not without their meanings.   Melville, *Moby Dick*, VII

Methinks we have hugely mistaken this matter of Life and Death. Methinks that what they call my shadow here on earth is my true substance. Methinks that in looking at things spiritual, we are too much like oysters observing the sun through the water, and thinking that thick water the thinnest of air. Methinks my body is but the lees of my better being. In fact take my body who will, take it I say, it is not myself.

Melville, *Moby Dick*, VII

Whatever is truly wondrous and fearful in man, never yet was put into words or books. And the drawing near of Death, which alike levels all, alike impresses all with a last revelation, which only an author from the dead could adequately tell.   *Ibid.*, CX

Queequeg had changed his mind about dying: he could not die yet, he averred.   *Ibid.*

Oh, Death, why canst thou not sometimes be timely?   *Ibid.*, CXII

Death is only a launching into the region of the strange Untried; it is but the first salutation to the possibilities of the immense Remote, the Wild, the Watery, the Un-shored; to the death-longing eyes of men who still have left in them some interior compunctions against suicide does the all-contributed and all-receptive ocean alluringly spread forth his whole plain of unimaginable, taking terrors, and wonderful, new-life adventures; and from the hearts of infinite Pacifics, the thousand mermaids sing to them—"Come hither, brokenhearted; here is another life without the guilt of inter-mediate death; here are wonders supernatural, without dying for them. Come hither! bury thyself in a life which, to your now equally abhorred and abhorring, landed world, is more oblivious than death. Come hither! put up thy gravestone, too, within the churchyard, and come hither, till we marry thee!"   *Ibid.*

Death-glorious ship.   *Ibid.*, CXXXV

Oh, lonely death on lonely life! Oh, now I feel my topmost greatness lies in my topmost grief.   *Ibid.*

The most mighty of nature's laws is this, that out of Death she brings Life.

Melville, *Pierre*, Book I, III

Decreed by God Omnipotent it is, that Death should be the last scene of the last act of man's play;—a play, which begin how it may, in farce or comedy, ever hath its tragic end; the curtain inevitably falls upon a corpse.   *Ibid.*, Book XII, III

As suddenly as the bravest and fleetest ships, while careering in pride of canvas over the sea, have been struck, as by lightning, and quenched out of sight; even so do some lordly men, with all their plans and prospects gallantly trimmed to the fair, rushing breeze of life, and with no thought of death and disaster, suddenly encounter a shock unforeseen, and go down, foundering, into death.   Melville, *Redburn*, XIX

Why this gloom at the thought of the dead? And why should we not be glad? Is it that we ever think of them as departed from all joy? Is it that we believe that indeed they are dead?   *Ibid.*, L

Except in extraordinary instances of exposure, there are few living men who, at bottom, are not very slow to admit that any other living men have ever been very much nearer death than themselves.   *Ibid.*, LVIII

What a world of life and death, what a world of humanity and its woes, lies shrunk into a three-worded obituary sentence!   *Ibid.*

In a chronicle of sickness the event is death.   Meredith, *Beauchamp's Career*, L

To strangle craving is to go through a death before you reach your immortality.

Meredith, *Harry Richmond*, LV

Death is always next door.   Meredith, *Lord Ormont*, XXX

He that hath no grave is covered with the sky.   More, *Utopia*, I

Whatsoever is born is born to have an end.   Nashe, *The Unfortunate Traveller*, 114

Death is not an end, but a beginning of a real life. May I not as well undergo a change from this to a different state of life when I leave this world, as be born into it I know not from whence?   Paltock, *Peter Wilkins*, 47

Truth and innocence only can make a death-bed easy.
                                                    Parsons, *The Mysterious Warning*, IV

I've been crowded enough in my lifetime—I'll have room enough after I'm dead.
                                                    Payson, *Golden Dreams*, I

All tortures are equal if death is the end.
                                                    Radcliffe, *The Castles of Athlin and Dunbayne*, 52

To live in shame, and in the consciousness of guilt, is a living death.   *Ibid.*, 241-242

In death there is nothing new nor surprising, since we all know that we are born to die.
                                                    Radcliffe, *The Mysteries of Udolpho*, I

Many things are the better for being set to rights, but everything is not. Everything is the one thing that won't stand being set to rights, except in that calm and cool retreat, the grave.   Reade, *The Cloister and the Hearth*, LXXIII

Dying men are known to have a strange sight.   *Ibid.*, LXXXII

The old folk all say dying men can see more than living wights.   *Ibid.*

Death, to one in health, is a very terrible thing. We pity the person for what he suffers; and we pity ourselves for what we must some time hence in like sort suffer; and so are doubly affected.   Richardson, *Clarissa Harlowe*, I

Death endears.   *Ibid.*, II

Do not prefer a shroud when persons cannot die when they will.   *Ibid.*

Old men, when they marry young women, make much of death.   *Ibid.*

Death only can be dreadful to the bad: To innocence 'tis like a bugbear dressed to frighten children. Pull but off the mask, and he'll appear a friend.   *Ibid.*, III

One who fears not death will not be intimidated into a meanness unworthy of heart and principles.   *Ibid.*

Death-bed repentance is a precarious and ineffectual thing.   *Ibid.*

Death is her wooer. Nay, she is so forward a girl that she woos him: but I hope it never will be a match.   *Ibid.*

What is death? 'Tis but a cessation from mortal life: 'tis but the finishing of an appointed course: the refreshing inn after a fatiguing journey: the end of a life of cares and troubles; and, if happy, the beginning of a life of immortal happiness.   *Ibid.*

A death desired merely from worldly disappointment shows not a right mind.
                                                                          Ibid., IV

Merely to die, no man of reason fears.   *Ibid.*

The bed of death is rocking under him like a cradle.   *Ibid.*

As to the respect that is supposed to be shown to the memory of a deceased friend in a funeral, why should we do anything to reflect upon those who have made it a fashion to leave this parade to people whom they hire for that purpose?   *Ibid.*

Death does what nothing else can do: it teaches, by strengthening in us the force of the divinest example, to forgive injuries and to shut out from the soul the remembrance of past evils.   *Ibid.*

Death from grief is the slowest of deaths.   *Ibid.*

What is dying but the common lot?   *Ibid.*

It is not so hard to die. The preparation is the difficulty.   *Ibid.*

All the sentiments of worldly grandeur vanish at that unavoidable moment which decides the destiny of men.   *Ibid.*

Says the wise man, "There is no inquisition in the grave, whether we lived ten or a hundred years; and the day of death is better than the day of our birth."   *Ibid.*

We had rather see you covered with rags, and even follow you to the churchyard, than have it said, a child of ours preferred any worldly conveniences to her virtue.
                                                    Richardson, *Pamela*, 6-7

Arm yourself, my dear child, for the worst; and resolve to lose your life sooner than your virtue.   *Ibid.*, 13

May I never survive one moment that fatal one in which I shall forfeit my innocence!
                                                        Ibid., 25

The man that dare not think of dying is unfit to live.   Ridley, *James Lovegrove*, II

Many a foul deed has death forced people to reveal.   Roche, *Clermont*, II

The paths of fame and fortune lead but to the coffin and the grave.   *Ibid.*

All dies. The roses are red with the matter that once reddened the cheek of the child; the flowers bloom the fairest on the last year's battleground; the work of death's finger cunningly wreathed over is at the heart of all things, even of the living. Death's finger is everywhere. The rocks are built up of a life that was.
                        Schreiner, *The Story of an African Farm*, Part II, XIII

There is that which never dies—which abides. It is but the individual that perishes, the whole remains.   *Ibid.*

Death is the father of all life and beauty.   Schreiner, *Undine*, XX

I live by two trades: fiddle, and spade; filling the world, and emptying of it.
                            Scott, *The Bride of Lammermoor*, XXIV

Death is change, not consummation; and the commencement of a new existence, corresponding in character to the deeds which we have done in the body.
                            Scott, *The Heart of Midlothian*, LI

Men speak not of hawk and hound when there is but an hour betwixt them and death.
                            Scott, *The Talisman*, XIV

No sure dungeon but the grave.   *Ibid.*, XIX

A man at the point of death does not stop to think of etiquette.
                            Shaw, *The Irrational Knot*, I

What death is so evil as unworthy servitude?   Sidney, *Arcadia*, I

Let death first die.   *Ibid.*, II

No way to be rid from death but by death.   *Ibid.*, III

Death, the only period of all respects, doth dispense with a free speech.   *Ibid.*

Death with more mercy kills than love doth save.   *Ibid.*

Death, the last of revenges.   *Ibid.*, V

The idea of death is one of terrible contemplation. We should always esteem the danger, however boldly we may advance to meet it.   Simms, *The Partisan*, Volume II, X

He was one of those people who never think of death until he knocks at the door, and then earnestly entreat him to excuse them for the present, and be so good as to call another time.   Smollett, *Ferdinand, Count Fathom*, LVIII

Death is a debt that every man owes.   Smollett, *Peregrine Pickle*, 265

In his opinion, a man of virtue and common sense could not possibly be afraid of death, which is not only the peaceful harbor that receives him shattered on the tempestuous sea of life, but also the eternal seal of his fame and glory, which it is no longer in his power to forfeit and forego. *Ibid.*, 267-268

We all owe Heaven a death. Smollett, *Roderick Random*, 173

'Tis little matter how a rascal dies. Sterne, *Tristram Shandy*, II

To die is the great debt and tribute due unto nature. *Ibid.*, V

When we are, death is not; and when death is, we are not. *Ibid.*

'Tis worthy to recollect, continued my father, how little alteration, in great men, the approaches of death have made. Vespasian died in a jest upon his close-stool. Galba with a sentence. Septimus Severus in a dispatch. Tiberius in dissimulation, and Caesar Augustus in a compliment.—I hope 'twas a sincere one, quoth my uncle Toby. 'Twas to his wife, said my father. *Ibid.*

That eternal separation which we are shortly to make. *Ibid.*, IX

Is it not a misuse of words to call a heavenly translation *death*? and to call most things that are lived out on this earth *life*? Stowe, *Orr's Island*, XXXVIII

Sir Pitt was forgotten [after his death], like the kindest and best of us—only a few weeks sooner. Thackeray, *Vanity Fair*, XLI

Whoever has lived long enough to find out what life is, knows how deep a debt of gratitude we owe to Adam, the first great benefactor of our race. He brought death into the world. Twain, *Pudd'nhead Wilson*, III

Let us endeavor so to live that when we come to die even the undertaker will be sorry. *Ibid.*, VI

Pity is for the living, envy is for the dead. *Ibid.*

All say, "How hard it is that we have to die"—a strange complaint to come from the mouths of people who have had to live. *Ibid.*, X

Ah, if he could only die temporarily! Twain, *Tom Sawyer*, VIII

"When good Americans die they go to Paris." "And where do bad Americans go to when they die?" "They go to America." Wilde, *The Picture of Dorian Gray*, II

I have no terror of death. It is the coming of death that terrifies me. *Ibid.*, XVIII

Death's monstrous wings seem to wheel in the leaden air around me. *Ibid.*

One can survive everything nowadays except death. *Ibid.*, XIX

Death and vulgarity are the only two facts in the nineteenth century that one cannot explain away. *Ibid.*

Death is never our foe. When not a friend, he cannot be worse than indifferent. *For while we are, death is not; and when death is, we are not.* Wright, *A Few Days in Athens*, X

DECEIT: *see also* TREACHERY; TRUST; etc.

Her nature, too truthful to deceive others, was too noble to deceive itself.
Collins, *The Woman in White*, Part I, First Epoch

There are two things I have lived long enough to receive as truths established by my own experience, and they are these: I never knew a man who made large professions of a love for the people, and of his wish to serve them on all occasions, whose aim was not to deceive them to his own advantage; and the other is, that I never knew a man who was compelled to come much in contact with the people, and who at the same time was personally popular, who had anything in him, at the bottom.
Cooper, *The Chainbearer*, XXVIII

Ask no questions that may lead to deceitful answers. Cooper, *The Prairie*, XXXI

To have been deceived implies a trusting nature. Dickens, *Martin Chuzzlewit*, LII

If I wasn't to take a fool in now and then, he'd niver get any wiser.
Eliot, *Mill on the Floss*, Book III, VI

There is no killing the suspicion that deceit has once begotten.
Eliot, *Romola*, Book III, LVIII

Happy is the deceived party between true lovers, and wretched indeed is the author of the deceit!
Fielding, H., *Amelia*, II

From having long deceived their acquaintance, practicers of deceit gain at last a power of deceiving themselves, and acquire that very opinion, however false, of their own abilities, excellencies, and virtues, into which they have for years perhaps endeavored to betray their neighbors.
Fielding, H., *Joseph Andrews*, 256

The general practice of deceit makes people appear so much better at first than on long acquaintance they prove to be, that to continue to love them, rather than cease to do so, should be termed inconstancy.
Fielding, S., *The History of Ophelia*, I

Nothing can be so impolitic as to mention the word deceit or treachery to those whom we intend to deceive or betray; for what more likely than that they may hereafter turn those very suspicions on ourselves, with which we have armed them against others? It is the interest of all those who practice such arts, as much as possible, to conceal and to deny them.
Fielding, S., *The Lives of Cleopatra and Octavia*, 61

Oh! Ridicule, thou great friend of us the deceitful! who givest us more effectual assistance to impose our fallacies on our dupes, than all the other instruments of deceit in the world.
Ibid., 68

Deception seldom draws admiration, especially when it fails.
Hardy, *A Pair of Blue Eyes*, XXVII

Transparent natures are often deceptive in their depth; those pebbles at the bottom of the fountain are farther from us than we think.
Hawthorne, *The House of the Seven Gables*, XII

It is treason against human nature to make any man's virtues the means of deceiving him.
Johnson, *Rasselas*, 172

One is always certain to find people who will lend their assistance in cheating their fellow citizens, and it is almost incredible how willing everyone is to assist any impostor in deceiving others.
Kahlert, *The Necromancer*, III

We hate to be deceived; we therefore hate those that deceive us. We desire not to be hated, and therefore we know that we are not to deceive.
Lennox, *The Female Quixote*, II

We are better deceived by having some truth told us than none.
Lennox, *Henrietta*, II

Deceive thy friend, be deceived of thy foe.
Lyly, *Euphues*, 148

When we would deceive, we smile.
Melville, *Pierre*, Book IV, V

Many by showing their jealous suspect of deceit have made men seek more subtle means to deceive them.
Nashe, *The Unfortunate Traveller*, 121

If deceit is at any time excusable, it is when we practice it in self-defense.
Radcliffe, *The Italian*, I

Did ever any man deceive but at the expense of his veracity? How otherwise can he be said to deceive?
Richardson, *Clarissa Harlowe*, II

A man generally judges of the disposition of others by his own. A deceiver fears deception.
Roche, *Clermont*, IV

Deceit cannot otherwise be maintained but by deceit.
Sidney, *Arcadia*, III

DECISION: *see also* CHOICE

He felt that he should die of indecision. The perdition of a man of his stamp is to have to make up his mind.   Eggleston, *The Hoosier Schoolmaster*, XXXI

There is nothing in the world so difficult as that task of making up one's mind.
Trollope, *Phineas Finn*, LX

DEDUCTION: *see also* THOUGHT

If it was so, it might be; and if it were so, it would be; but as it isn't, it ain't. That's logic.
Carroll, *Through the Looking Glass*, IV

What is college logic? Conclusions without premises, ends without means; and opinions without experience.   Caruthers, *The Kentuckian in New-York*, Volume I, V

The data which life furnishes, toward forming a true estimate of any being, are as insufficient to that end as in geometry one side given would be to determine the triangle.
Melville, *Confidence-Man*, XXXVI

The best way to get out of a labyrinth is to retrace one's steps.   *Ibid.*

In no affairs to mere prejudice, *pro* or *con*, do we deduce inferences with entire certainty, even from the most simple data.   Poe, *Arthur Gordon Pym*, II

DEFECT: *see also* PERFECTION

Try not to associate bodily defects with mental.   Dickens, *David Copperfield*, XXXII

There is something wrong about the man who wants help. There is somewhere a defect, a want, in brief, a need, a crying need, somewhere about that man.
Melville, *Confidence-Man*, XXXIX

DEFENSE

Too much pains taken to defend a right often renders it suspected.
Kidgell, *The Card*, I

There never was a creature so criminal who had not some weak heads to pity and side with her.   Richardson, *Clarissa Harlowe*, IV

Defense is guarded; offense exposes itself.
Richardson, *Sir Charles Grandison*, One, II

Fortify yourself against seductive eloquence.   Roche, *Clermont*, I

Both in public and private respects, who stands only upon defense stands upon no defense.   Sidney, *Arcadia*, II

DELAY

What is delayed is not lost.   Cooke, *Surry of Eagle's-Nest*, X

DELIBERATION: *see* THOUGHT

DELICACY

A delicate mind has other considerations to satisfy than those of justice.
Jenner, *The Placid Man*, I

Delicacy is often a misleader; an idol, at whose shrine we sometimes offer up our sincerity; but, in that case, it should be called indelicacy.
Richardson, *Sir Charles Grandison*, Two, III

Nothing can be delicate that is not true or that gives birth to equivocation.   *Ibid.*

DELIVERANCE

Deliverance from sin a much greater blessing than deliverance from affliction.
Defoe, *Robinson Crusoe*, 91

How frequently, in the course of our lives, the evil which in itself we seek most to shun, and which, when we are fallen into, is the most dreadful to us, is oftentimes the very means or door of our deliverance, by which alone we can be raised again from the affliction we are fallen into.
Ibid., 166

DELUSION

Men, and women too, must have delusion of some sort; if not made ready to their hand, they will invent exaggeration for themselves.
Bronte, C., *Villette*, XXX

We are all of us, more or less, subject to the delusions of vanity, or hope, or love.
Edgeworth, *The Absentee*, V

DEMAGOGUERY

The demagogue flatters the clown, and finds fault with the sage.
Brackenridge, *Modern Chivalry*, Part II, Volume I

DEMAND

He who demands little gets it.　　　Glasgow, *The Voice of the People*, Book III, II

DEMOCRACY: *see also* GOVERNMENT; etc.

Democracy asserts the fact that the masses are now raised to a higher intelligence than formerly. All our civilization aims at this mark.
Adams, *Democracy*, IV

Democracy is a great institution in spite of its nuisances.
Atherton, *Senator North*, Book II, V

A democracy is beyond all question the freest government: because under this, every man is equally protected by the laws, and has equally a voice in making them. But I do not say an equal voice; because some men have stronger lungs than others and can express more forcibly their opinions of public affairs.
Brackenridge, *Modern Chivalry*, Part I, Volume I

Mutual toleration and forbearance, in our sentiments, with regard to the legality, or expedience of measures, is the soul of democracy.
Ibid., Part II, Volume II

DEMON; DEVIL: *see also* ANGEL; CHRISTIANITY; GOD; GOOD AND EVIL; etc.

There are no devils but those which are begotten upon selfishness and reared by cunning.
Brown, C. B., *Wieland*, 151

He that is shipped with the devil must sail with the devil.　　Defoe, *Captain Singleton*, 8

The devil is an unwearied tempter; he never fails to find opportunity for that wickedness he invites to.
Defoe, *Moll Flanders*, 21

The devil used to say that it was better to reign in Hell, than be a valet de chambre in Heaven.
Fielding, H., *Jonathan Wild*, 26

Pray what sort of a gentleman is the devil? For I have heard some say there is no such person; and that it is only a trick of the parsons to prevent their being broke; for, if it was publicly known that there was no devil, the parsons would be of no more use than soldiers in peace.
Fielding, H., *Tom Jones*, 439

Methought, if there be no devil, how can wicked people be sent to him?　　*Ibid.*

If he closed his eyes in sleep, Margaret, or Satan in her shape, beset him, a seeming angel of light. She came glowing with two beauties never before united—in angel's radiance and woman's blushes. Angels cannot blush, so he knew it was a fiend.
Reade, *The Cloister and the Hearth*, XCIII

Devils believe and tremble.   Richardson, *Clarissa Harlowe*, II

Satan has faithful instruments, and the bond of wickedness is a stronger bond than the ties of virtue.   *Ibid.*, III

Anywhere rather than at home the devil's at home.
Richardson, *Sir Charles Grandison*, One, I

Because men are by nature prone to sin, is therefore the devil a good being, who eternally solicits and prompts them to it?   Shebbeare, *The Marriage Act*, II

London is the devil's drawing-room.   Smollett, *Roderick Random*, 118

DENIAL: *see also* INJUSTICE/JUSTICE

Who deniges of it?   Dickens, *Martin Chuzzlewit*, XLIX

To deny a man the preferment which he merits, and to give it to another man who doth not, is a manifest act of injustice, and is consequently inconsistent with both honor and honesty.   Fielding, H., *Amelia*, II

If we deny everything which we do not clearly comprehend, our knowledge will be reduced within very narrow bounds.   Johnstone, *The History of Arsaces*, I

DENUNCIATION

It is next to idle merely to denounce an iniquity.   Melville, *White Jacket*, XXXV

DEPARTURE

The necessity of departure is like looking on the necessity of death.
Bronte, C., *Jane Eyre*, XXIII

Departures should be sudden.   Disraeli, *Coningsby*, Book IV, XV

DEPENDENCE: *see* INDEPENDENCE

DEPRAVITY: *see also* GOOD AND EVIL

Is there such depravity in man as that he should injure another without benefit to himself?   Johnson, *Rasselas*, 44

There is no human institution, however wise and salutary in its natural effects, which the depravity of man can not pervert to the most pernicious purposes.
Johnstone, *The History of Arsaces*, I

Men will not be depraved beyond the persuasion of some motive, and self-interest will often be the parent of social obligation.   Mackenzie, *Julia De Roubigné*, 127

DEPRIVATION: *see also* POVERTY

To be depriving themselves of the advantage of other eyes and other judgments might be an evil even beyond the loss of present pleasure.
Austen, *Mansfield Park*, Volume One, IX

Privation is a sharp graver. It carves deep and strong.
Beard, *Bristling With Thorns*, IV

People who seem to enjoy their ill temper have a way of keeping it in fine condition by inflicting privations on themselves.   Eliot, *Mill on the Floss*, Book I, XII

DEPRIVATION (*continued*)

It is not a denial of anything to have been always without it, and what Troy had never enjoyed he did not miss; but, being fully conscious that what sober people missed he enjoyed, his capacity, though really less, seemed greater than theirs.
Hardy, *Far From the Madding Crowd*, XXV

DERISION: *see also* CONTEMPT

A man in public life expects to be sneered at—it is the fault of his elevated situation, and not of himself.
Dickens, *Nicholas Nickleby*, XIV

DESCRIPTION

Even the best description of a person falls so short of the reality.
Collins, *The Black Robe*, Book I, I

Attempts at description are stupid: who can all at once describe a human being? Even when he is presented to us we only begin that knowledge of his appearance which must be completed by innumerable impressions under differing circumstances. We recognize the alphabet; we are not sure of the language. Eliot, *Daniel Deronda*, Book II

I describe not men, but manners; not an individual, but a species.
Fielding, H., *Joseph Andrews*, 159

The poor Bella has a plump high-fed face. Richardson, *Clarissa Harlowe*, I

It is a shame to give a description of the morning at the end of a chapter.
Ridley, *James Lovegrove*, II

DESERTION: *see also* ABANDONMENT

Who does not remember vaguely having been deserted in the fullness of possession by some one or something more precious than life? Conrad, *Lord Jim*, XXVIII

The humblebee having sucked honey out of the fair flower doth leave it and loathe it, the spider in the finest web doth hang the fairest fly. Lyly, *Euphues*, 144

Who shall befriend a person who forsakes herself? Richardson, *Clarissa Harlowe*, I

A falling house is best known by the rats leaving it; a falling state, by the desertion of confederates and allies; and a falling man, by the desertion of his friends.
Scott, *St. Ronan's Well*, XXV

DESIGN: *see* FORM; METHOD

DESIRE: *see also* LOVE

The tumult of desire is the fever of the soul. Brooke, *Emily Montague*, IV

As a stream of water being stopped, overfloweth the bank, so smothered desire doth burst out into a great flame of fire. Deloney, *The Gentle Craft*, 73

The more fond lovers are denied, the hotter is their desire.
Deloney, *Jack of Newbury*, 375

She did not grow in knowledge so much as she awakened in the matter of desire.
Dreiser, *Sister Carrie*, XII

I have already enjoyed too much; give me something to desire. Johnson, *Rasselas*, 23

Some desire is necessary to keep life in motion, and he whose real wants are already supplied must then admit those of fancy. *Ibid.*, 40

Our desire for anything is always in proportion to the difficulty which attends the attainment of it.   Johnstone, *The History of Arsaces*, II

Attachments of mere desire lose their force when the object is no longer present.   *Ibid.*

Unlawful desires are punished after the effect of enjoying; but impossible desires are punished in the desire itself.   Sidney, *Arcadia*, II

DESPAIR; DESPERATION: *see also* AFFLICTION; MISERY; etc.

Absolute despair is the first step towards the cure of love.
                                   Brackenridge, *Modern Chivalry*, Part I, Volume I

How shall a man who is desperate be prudent and circumspect?   Burney, *Cecilia*, III

There is a sublime stimulus in despair.   Caruthers, *Cavaliers*, Volume II, I

There is a strength of self-possession which is the sign that the last hope has departed. Despair no more leans on others than perfect contentment, and in despair pride ceases to be counteracted by the sense of dependence.   Eliot, *Adam Bede*, XXXVII

There is no hopelessness so sad as that of early youth, when the soul is made up of wants, and has no long memories, no superadded life in the life of others.
                                   Eliot, *The Mill on the Floss*, Book III, V

No human condition should inspire men with absolute despair.
                                   Fielding, H., *Amelia*, I

It is the nature of despair to blind us to all the means of safety, however easy and apparent they may be.   *Ibid.*, II

We decline great pursuits not from contempt, but from despair.
                                   Fielding, H., *Jonathan Wild*, 27

The mind that sinks under its suffering does not by that conduct shake off its burden.
                                   Godwin, *St. Leon*, 69-70

Despair will drive to anything a man whose sense of shame is stronger than that of guilt.
                                   Johnstone, *The Pilgrim*, I

Desperate men really can't be dainty.   Kingsley, *Alton Locke*, XXXIII

All colors disappear in the night, and despair has no diary—monotony is her essence and her curse.   Maturin, *Melmoth*, VII

Moles and bats alone should be skeptics; and the only true infidelity is for a live man to vote himself dead.   Melville, *Mardi*, XIII

The prince on his throne is not safe if a mind so desperate can be found that values not its own life.   Richardson, *Clarissa Harlowe*, II

Despair of recovery allows not room for cure.   *Ibid.*, IV

What is to be expected for or from a despairing man?
                                   Richardson, *Sir Charles Grandison*, Three, VI

Despair gives courage.   Scott, *The Heart of Midlothian*, L

Despair made fear valiant, and revenge gave shame countenance.
                                   Sidney, *Arcadia*, II

Vain is their pain who labor in despair.   *Ibid.*

Despair is perfectly compatible with a good dinner.
                                   Thackeray, *Lovel the Widower*, VI

DESPOTISM: *see also* GOVERNMENT

What despotism is so black as one the mind cannot challenge?
                                   Meredith, *Ordeal of Richard Feverel*, XXXVIII

DESTINATION

Not a soul on board of us knows whither we may be gliding—not even the commodore himself; assuredly not the chaplain; even our professor's surmisings are vain. On that point, the smallest cabin boy is as wise as the captain.   Melville, *White Jacket*, The End

"All roads take to Rome." "Aye, but the shortest road thither is my way."
Reade, *The Cloister and the Hearth*, XXIV

DESTINY; FATE; FORTUNE: *see also* CAUSE AND EFFECT; CHANCE; etc.

A man who is born to be hanged will never be drowned.
Anonymous, *The Adventures of an Author*, I

Fortune may be both a whimsical and perverse jade, but be persuaded she will bless us with some happy opportunity when we least expect it.
Anonymous, *The Fruitless Repentance*, I

Fortune is the key to every felicity.   *Ibid.*

What providence means to do with us is an anxious though presumptuous inquiry.
Ibid., II

Heaven has kindly closed from our eyes the book of future events, that we may not be guilty of repining at its ordinations.   Anonymous, *The Life of Jemmy Twitcher*, 3

We are short-sighted mortals; and while we stop one leak, the water rushes in at another. The very means that we use to save ourselves from one evil leads us to a worse.
Brackenridge, *Modern Chivalry*, Part I, Volume II

It is hard work to control the workings of inclination, and turn the bent of nature: but it may be done. God has given us, in a measure, the power to make our own fate.
Bronte, C., *Jane Eyre*, XXXI

I had wanted to compromise with Fate: to escape occasional great agonies by submitting to a whole life of privation and small pains. Fate would not so be pacified; nor would Providence sanction this shrinking sloth and cowardly indolence.
Bronte, C., *Villette*, IV

Fate was of stone, and Hope a false idol—blind, bloodless, and of granite core.
Ibid., XV

Dr. John himself was one of those on whose birth benign planets have certainly smiled. Adversity might set against him her most sullen front: he was the man to beat her down with smiles. Strong and cheerful, and firm and courteous; not rash, yet valiant; he was the aspirant to woo Destiny herself, and to win from her stone eyeballs a beam almost loving.   *Ibid.*, XVI

There are some human beings so born, so reared, so guided from a soft cradle to a calm and late grave, that no excessive suffering penetrates their lot, and no tempestuous blackness overcasts their journey. And often these are not pampered, selfish beings, but Nature's elect, harmonious and benign; men and women mild with charity, kind agents of God's kind attributes.   *Ibid.*, XXXVII

The destiny of man frequently hangs upon the lapse of a minute.
Brown, C. B., *Arthur Mervyn*, II

When any uncommon event happens to us, we often have a presentiment of it.
Brown, W. H., *The Power of Sympathy*, 175

All that is certain is the unkindness of Fortune.   Burney, *Camilla*, Five, IX

Providence is too good to make the mind necessarily deformed with the body.   *Ibid.*

Who can point out the road to his own felicity, or decide upon the spot where his peace will be insured?   Burney, *Cecilia*, II

Fortune is a blind and fickle fostermother, who showers her gifts at random upon her nurslings. But we do her a grave injustice if we believe such an accusation. Trace a man's career from his cradle to his grave and mark how Fortune has treated him. You will find that when he is once dead she can for the most part be vindicated from the charge of any but very superficial fickleness. Her blindness is the merest fable; she can espy her favorites long before they are born. Butler, *The Way of All Flesh*, V

"It is we who make thee, Fortune, a goddess," exclaimed the poet; and so it is, after Fortune has made us able to make her. *Ibid.*

A certain kind of good fortune generally attends self-made men to the last. *Ibid.*

Chemists might sway, if they pleased, the destinies of humanity.
Collins, *The Woman in White*, Part II, Third Epoch

Truth shall prevail when it gets a chance. Conrad, *Lord Jim*, XXXIV

He that is to be saved will be saved, and he that is predestined to be damned will be damned. This is the doctrine of truth, and most consoling and refreshing it is to the true believer. Cooper, *The Last of the Mohicans*, XII

There is a destiny in war, to which a brave man knows how to submit, with the same courage that he faces his foes. *Ibid.*, XVI

There is a fate in love, as in war. Cooper, *Satanstoe*, Volume II, XV

Human beings are in all cases the creatures of predicament. They are involuntary agents in the grand drama, which leads them to their destiny.
Dacre, *Passions*, Letter XXXIX

Will you tell me of a fate, of a destiny, *willing* you to become base?—*pre-ordaining* your weakness and guilt?—Impossible! *Ibid.*, Letter XLI

Destiny is absolute, and influencing every event through the life of man. When most he thinks he is pursuing his own will, he merely fulfills that of destiny.
Ibid., Letter XLV

Not even the suicide expires an instant before the period marked out by his destiny.
Ibid.

Man is a short-sighted creature at best, and in nothing more than in that of fixing his own felicity; or, as we may say, choosing for himself. Defoe, *Colonel Jack*, 263

I saw the cloud, though I did not foresee the storm. Defoe, *Moll Flanders*, 25

The world is before you; and it is most probable that as you enter it, so it will receive you. Trust in nothing but in Providence and your own efforts. Never separate the two, like the heathen waggoner. Dickens, *Bleak House*, XIII

"And how does the world use you?" "Pretty much as usual. Like a football."
Ibid., XXI

Shaken out of destiny's dice-box. Dickens, *Little Dorrit*, Book I, XI

No man knocks himself down; if his destiny knocks him down, his destiny must pick him up again. Dickens, *Old Curiosity Shop*, XXXIV

Heaven is above all. The curtain of our fate is still undrawn.
Disraeli, *Coningsby*, Book VII, II

Among the forces which sweep and play throughout our universe, untutored man is but a wisp in the wind. Our civilization is still in a middle stage, scarcely beast, in that it is no longer wholly guided by instinct; scarcely human, in that it is not yet wholly guided by reason. Dreiser, *Sister Carrie*, VIII

Carrie was an apt student of fortune's ways—of fortune's superficialities. *Ibid.*, XI

When Fate is fighting with all her might against a human soul, the greatest victory that the soul can win is to reconcile itself to the unpleasant, which is never quite unpleasant afterwards. Dunbar, *The Uncalled*, X

Our deeds determine us, as much as we determine our deeds.
Eliot, *Adam Bede*, XXIX

There is a terrible coercion in our deeds, which may first turn the honest man into a deceiver and then reconcile him to the change, for this reason—that the second wrong presents itself to him in the guise of the only practicable right. *Ibid.*

"He means always to be a poor man." "Means? But what a man means usually depends on what happens." Eliot, *Felix Holt*, XLIII

Starting a long way off the true point, and proceeding by loops and zigzags, we now and then arrive just where we ought to be. Eliot, *Middlemarch*, Book I, III

Destiny stands by sarcastic with our *dramatis personae* folded in her hand. *Ibid.*, Book I, XI

There is no creature whose inward being is so strong that it is not greatly determined by what lies outside it. *Ibid.*, Book VIII, Finale

To adopt a child, because children of your own have been denied you, is to try and choose your lot in spite of Providence. Eliot, *Silas Marner*, XVII

The public voice hath, in all ages, done much injustice to Fortune, and hath convicted her of many facts in which she had not the least concern. Fielding, H., *Amelia*, I

Perhaps men accuse Fortune with no less absurdity than a bad player complains of ill luck at the game of chess. *Ibid.*

A man can no more resist the impulse of fate than a wheelbarrow can the force of its driver. *Ibid.*

The arrows of fortune derive their force from the velocity with which they are discharged; for, when they approach you by slow and perceptible degrees, they have but little power to do you mischief. *Ibid.*, II

Fortune seems to take a delight in thwarting good temper, to which human life, with its many crosses and accidents, is by no means fitted. *Ibid.*

However Fortune may be reported to favor fools, she never shows them any countenance when they play at cards. *Ibid.*

He that is born to be hanged will never be drowned. Fielding, H., *Jonathan Wild*, 116

Providence will, sooner or later, procure the felicity of the virtuous and innocent. *Ibid.*, 239

Men do not make themselves. Fielding, H., *Joseph Andrews*, 114

I was one whom Fortune could not save if she would. *Ibid.*, 185

As we know not future events, so neither can we tell to what purpose any accident tends; and that which at first threatens us with evil may in the end produce our good. *Ibid.*, 224

As we know not to what purpose any event is ultimately directed, so neither can we affirm from what cause it originally sprung. *Ibid.*, 224-225

Fortune seldom doth good or ill. It makes men happy or miserable, by halves. *Ibid.*, 293

Fortune is a tender parent, and often doth more for her favorite offspring than either they deserve or wish. Fielding, H., *Tom Jones*, 32

Fortune at length took pity on this miserable couple, and considerably lessened the wretched state of Partridge by putting a final end to that of his wife, who caught the smallpox and died. *Ibid.*, 63

The number three, even from ancient times, has been suspected by the superstitious to involve in it some fatal mystery of ill-boding destiny. Fielding, S., *The Countess of Dellwyn*, I

The prosperity of fortune is like the blossoms of spring, or the golden hue of the evening cloud. It delighteth the spirit, and passeth away.　　　　Galt, *Annals*, XXVII

All human events are under the immediate direction of an over-ruling providence.
　　　　　　　　　　　　　　　　　Gibbes, *Mr. Francis Clive*, II

One man is born to the inheritance of every superfluity, while the whole share of another, without any demerit of his, is drudgery and starving.
　　　　　　　　　　　　　　　　　Godwin, *Caleb Williams*, I

Travelling after Fortune is not the way to secure her.
　　　　　　　　　　　　　Goldsmith, *The Vicar of Wakefield*, 107

A fancy some people hold, when in a bitter mood, is that inexorable circumstance only tries to prevent what intelligence attempts. Renounce a desire for a long-contested position, and go on another tack, and after a while the prize is thrown at you, seemingly in disappointment that no more tantalizing is possible.
　　　　　　　　　　　　　　　　　Hardy, *A Pair of Blue Eyes*, XXIII

He did sometimes think he had been ill-used by fortune, so far as to say that to be born is a palpable dilemma, and that instead of men aiming to advance in life with glory they should calculate how to retreat out of it without shame.
　　　　　　　　　　　　　　　Hardy, *The Return of the Native*, Book VI, I

In the ill-judged execution of the well-judged plan of things the call seldom produces the comer, the man to love rarely coincides with the hour for loving.　　Hardy, *Tess*, V

Nature does not often say 'See!' to her poor creature at a time when seeing can lead to happy doing; or reply 'Here!' to a body's cry of 'Where?' till the hide-and-seek has become an irksome, outworn game.　　　　　　　　　　　　　　*Ibid.*

How unexpected were the attacks of destiny!　　　　　　　*Ibid.*, XXXVIII

Bygones would never be complete till she was a bygone herself.　　　*Ibid.*, XLV

Little as we know of our life to come, we may be very sure, for one thing, that the good we aim at will not be attained.　　　　Hawthorne, *The Blithedale Romance*, IX

Destiny, it may be,—the most skillful of stage managers,—seldom chooses to arrange its scenes, and carry forward its drama, without securing the presence of at least one calm observer.　　　　　　　　　　　　　　Hawthorne, *Ibid.*, XI

Like busts in marble, so does our individual fate exist in the limestone of time.
　　　　　　　　　　　　　　　　Hawthorne, *The Marble Faun*, XIII

Chance and change love to deal with men's settled plans, not with their idle vagaries.
　　　　　　　　　　　　　　　　　　Ibid., XXXII

Incidents little in human speculation are great in the eye of fortune.
　　　　　　　　　　　　　　　　　Kidgell, *The Card*, I

All things fulfill their destiny.　　　　　　Kingsley, *Alton Locke*, XXII

The very just Providence who delights in causing pain.
　　　　　　　　　　　　Kipling, *The Light That Failed*, XIV

Time, patience, and fortitude often conquer fate herself.　　　Lee, *The Recess*, II

There is something very pleasing in supposing oneself the peculiar care of Providence.
　　　　　　　　　　　　　　　　　Lennox, *Henrietta*, I

Should it cease raining immediately before she is to go out, either to church or a visit, it is all one, she supposes that Providence is at that moment at work for her, and has cleared the skies that she may walk with convenience.　　　　　　　　*Ibid.*

When two noble men encounter needs must the one have the worse, like as God will suffer at that time.　　　　　　Malory, *Le Morte DArthur*, One, IX

Fortune loves to mingle herself in all events.　　　　Manley, *Rivella*, II

There is no bent of heart or turn of thought which any man holds by virtue of an unalterable nature or will.   Melville, *Confidence-Man*, XLI

There is no development in opinion and feeling but the developments of time and tide.
Ibid.

The soil decides the man.   Melville, *Mardi*, CLXII

Fate laughs at prophets.   *Ibid.*, CLXIV

If the great sun move not of himself; but is as an errand-boy in heaven; nor one single star can revolve, but by some invisible power; how then can this one small heart beat; this one small brain think thoughts; unless God does that beating, does that thinking, does that living, and not I. By heaven, man, we are turned round and round in this world, like yonder windlass, and Fate is the handspike.   Melville, *Moby Dick*, CXXXII

If the gods think to speak outright to man, they will honorably speak outright; not shake their heads, and give an old wife's darkling hint.   *Ibid.*, CXXXIII

Ahab is forever Ahab. This whole act's immutably decreed. 'Twas rehearsed by thee and me a billion years before this ocean rolled. I am the Fates' lieutenant; I act under orders.   *Ibid.*, CXXXIV

Not entirely untempered to human nature are the most direful blasts of Fate.
Melville, *Pierre*, Book V, V

Eternally inexorable and unconcerned is Fate, a mere heartless trader in men's joys and woes.   *Ibid.*

He was an uncommonly fine, cheerful, clever, arch little fellow, only six years old, and it was a thousand pities that he should be abandoned, as he was. Who can say whether he is fated to be a convict in New South Wales, or a member of Parliament for Liverpool?
Melville, *Redburn*, XXIII

Everyone in this world has his own fate intrusted to himself.   *Ibid.*, XLIV

All events are mixed in a fusion indistinguishable. What we call Fate is even, heartless, and impartial; not a fiend to kindle bigot flames, nor a philanthropist to espouse the cause of Greece.   Melville, *White Jacket*, LXXV

In our own hearts, we mould the whole world's hereafters; and in our own hearts, we fashion our own gods.   *Ibid.*

The automatic creature is subject to the laws of its construction. It can this, it can that, but it cannot leap out of its mechanism.   Meredith, *Beauchamp's Career*, XI

One may be as a weed of the sea while one's fate is being decided.   *Ibid.*, XXXV

It has been established that we do not wax diviner by dragging down the gods to our level.   *Ibid.*, XXXVIII

We cannot be entirely wise when we have staked our fate.   *Ibid.*, XL

How fortunate it is for us that here and there we do not succeed in wresting our temporary treasure from the grasp of the Fates!   *Ibid.*, LVI

The Fates are within us.   Meredith, *Vittoria*, XLV

Those which are the forces of the outer world are as shadows to the power we have created within us.   *Ibid.*

Our destiny is of our own weaving.   *Ibid.*

It is in the staging of her comedies that Fate shows herself superior to mere human invention.   Merriman, *In Kedar's Tents*, I

We are at once the creatures and the arbiters of destiny.   Moore, *Evelyn Innes*, XIX

Even now my destiny is accomplishing.   *Ibid.*, XXVI

The wisdom of man is unavailing, when opposed to the decrees of God.

Morier, *Hajji Baba*, XXXI

Destiny never defames herself but when she lets an excellent poet die.

Nashe, *The Unfortunate Traveller*, 64

You have no right to dispose of your future destiny whilst there is the least probable chance you may be reclaimed.

Parsons, *Castle of Wolfenbach*, II

Fate is just even to rival storytellers, and balances matters.

Reade, *The Cloister and the Hearth*, XLVII

Fortune will help will.

Richardson, *Clarissa Harlowe*, III

While weak souls are crushed by fortune, the brave mind maketh the fickle deity afraid of it.

Ibid., IV

It is not what is done to us, but what is made of us, that wrongs us. No man can be really injured but by what modifies himself.

Schreiner, *Story of an African Farm*, Part II, IV

Existence is a great pot, and the old Fate who stirs it round cares nothing what rises to the top and what goes down, and laughs when the bubbles burst.

Ibid., Part II, VII

The privilege of free action belongs to no mortal.

Scott, *Redgauntlet*, IX

In doing and suffering, we play but the part allotted by Destiny.

Ibid.

Amidst his most swift and easy pace the rider must guard himself against a fall, and it is when prosperity is at the highest that our prudence should be awake and vigilant to prevent misfortune.

Scott, *The Talisman*, XXII

Fortune may raise up or abuse the ordinary mortal, but the sage and the soldier should have minds beyond her control.

Ibid.

Fortune, that jilting jade.

Shebbeare, *Lydia*, IV

Blind fortune hates sharp sighted inventions.

Sidney, *Arcadia*, III

The fates are busy always to beguile with pleasant auguries those whom they would involve beyond their depths.

Simms, *Woodcraft*, LIX

There is a fatality attends the actions of some men.

Sterne, *Tristram Shandy*, I

A long tongue is a fault beloved by fortune.

Stevenson, *St. Ives*, XXI

The way of fate is often highly entertaining to the looker-on.

Stevenson, *The Wrong Box*, III

We are the sport of destiny.

Thackeray, *Barry Lyndon*, III

It is the lot of sensibility to suffer, and of confiding tenderness to be deceived.

Thackeray, *Pendennis*, XXIII

If the best men do not draw the great prizes in life, we know it has been so settled by the Ordainer of the lottery.

Ibid., LXXV

Think, what right have you to be scornful, whose virtue is a deficiency of temptation, whose success may be a chance, whose rank may be an ancestor's accident, whose prosperity is very likely a satire?

Thackeray, *Vanity Fair*, LVII

Eight years are not many in the life of a nation or the history of a state, but they may be years of destiny that shall fix the current of the century following.

Twain and Warner, *The Gilded Age*, Volume I, XVIII

One's days were too brief to take the burden of another's errors on one's shoulders. Each man lived his own life and paid his own price for living it. The only pity was one had to pay so often for a single fault. In her dealings with man, destiny never closed her accounts.

Wilde, *The Picture of Dorian Gray*, XVI

There is no such thing as an omen. Destiny does not send us heralds. She is too wise or too cruel for that.

Ibid., XVIII

DESTRUCTION

It is easier to destroy than to substitute.

Brackenridge, *Modern Chivalry*, Part II, Volume II

One leak will sink a ship; and one sin will destroy a sinner.

Bunyan, *Pilgrim's Progress*, 212

What is one man's safety is another man's destruction.   Defoe, *Robinson Crusoe*, 171

DETERMINATION

I am not inclined to halt before I am lame.   Bunyan, *Pilgrim's Progress*, 286

What power is able to hold in chains a mind ardent and determined? What power can cause that man to die, whose whole soul commands him to continue to live?

Godwin, *Caleb Williams*, II

In battles there ought to be a doubtful fight and desperate end; in pleading a difficult entrance and a diffused determination; in love a life without hope and a death without fear.   Lyly, *Euphues*, 119

The gentlest spirits when provoked are the most determined.

Richardson, *Clarissa Harlowe*, I

It is natural for people, when they set their hearts upon anything, to think everybody must see with their eyes.   *Ibid.*

It is unwise to look back when the journey lieth forward.

Scott, *The Talisman*, XXII

DEVELOPMENT: *see also* GROWTH; PROGRESS; etc.

Even Caesar's fortune at one time was but a grand presentiment. We know what a masquerade all development is, and what effective shapes may be disguised in helpless embryos. The world is full of hopeful analogies and handsome dubious eggs called possibilities.   Eliot, *Middlemarch*, Book I, X

DEVIATION

How hard to avoid many lesser deviations when we are betrayed into a capital one!

Richardson, *Clarissa Harlowe*, III

DEVIL: *see also* DEMON

The Devil is very sagacious. To judge by the event, he appears to have understood man better even than the Being who made him.   Melville, *Confidence-Man*, XXII

Doesn't the devil live forever; who ever heard that the devil was dead? Did you ever see any parson wearing mourning for the devil?   Melville, *Moby Dick*, LXXIII

I baptize thee not in the name of God, but in the name of the Devil.   *Ibid.*, CXIII

The devil is apt to keep an eye on exceptions.   Scott, *Ivanhoe*, XVII

DEVOTION: *see also* RELIGION; WORSHIP; etc.

You will rarely find the sternest or wisest of men disposed to be harsh towards errors that spring from a devotion to themselves.   Lawrence, *Guy Livingstone*, XXVII

DIFFERENCE: *see also* SIMILARITY

Different liquors, when put into the same cask, fall to fretting before they will take a quiet nap together.   Bridges, *Adventures of a Bank-Note*, II

Many men, many minds.   Cooper, *The Redskins*, IX

We are not accustomed to carry things with the same hand, or to look at 'em from the
same point.   Dickens, *Bleak House*, LXIII

So uncertain are our tempers, we at different times differ from ourselves.
                                                         Fielding, H., *Tom Jones*, 295

So many men, so many minds.   Gascoigne, *Master F. J.*, 28

It is impossible for two persons to be constituted so much alike, but that one of them
should have a more genuine and instantaneous relish for one sort of excellence, and
another for another.   Godwin, *St. Leon*, 41

It contributes greatly towards a man's moral and intellectual health, to be brought into
habits of companionship with individuals unlike himself, who care little for his pursuits,
and whose sphere and abilities he must go out of himself to appreciate.
                                       Hawthorne, *The Scarlet Letter*, Introductory

I could mingle at once with men of altogether different qualities and never murmur at
the change.   *Ibid.*

It would be taking up the pen of eternity were I to attempt to describe the boundless
difference that we discovered between the manners and sentiments of these people and
ourselves.   Morier, *Hajji Baba*, LXXVII

Does the difference of the time of the day at Paris make a difference in the sin? It makes
a difference, it is said, in the scandal.   Sterne, *A Sentimental Journey*, 103

The mortgager and mortgagee differ the one from the other, not more in length of purse
than the jester and jestee do in that of memory.   Sterne, *Tristram Shandy*, I

How many shades there are between love and indifference, and how little the graduated
scale is understood!   Trollope, *Barchester Towers*, XXIV

DIFFICULTY

Even in good weather there are bad roads.
                                       Brackenridge, *Modern Chivalry*, Part II, Volume II

There are situations in which it is as difficult to go back as to go forward.
                                                         Cooper, *Heidenmauer*, II

It is as hard to find sense in his speeches as to discover three eagles on the same tree.
                                                         Cooper, *The Prairie*, XVII

There is one thing worse even than getting into difficulties—patching them up. The
patching-up system is fatal; it is sure to break down; you never get clear.
                                                         Disraeli, *Sybil*, Book II, VI

It is more difficult to catch a bird than a lady.   Richardson, *Clarissa Harlowe*, II

Difficulty gives poignancy to our enjoyments; which are apt to lose their relish with us
when they are over-easily obtained.   *Ibid.*, IV

The troubles of property, the rascality of agents, the quibbles of lawyers, are endless.
                                                         Thackeray, *Barry Lyndon*, XVII

The statements [in *Pilgrim's Progress*] was interesting, but tough.
                                                         Twain, *Huckleberry Finn*, XVII

DIGNITY

Dignity robes the man who is filled with a lofty thought.
                                                         Bulwer, *The Caxtons*, Book XVII, III

Dignity is very expensive.   Bulwer, *Pompeii*, Book IV, III

Dignity is the dullest thing in the world.   Burney, *Cecilia*, III

DIGNITY (*continued*)

There is scarcely a less dignified entity than a patrician in a panic.
>Disraeli, *Coningsby*, Book I, III

It is certainly trying to a man's dignity to reappear when he is not expected to do so: a first farewell has pathos in it, but to come back for a second lends an opening to comedy.
>Eliot, *Middlemarch*, Book VI, LXII

When I have seen a man strutting in a procession, after others whose business was only to walk before him, I have conceived a higher notion of his dignity than I have felt on seeing him in a common situation.
>Fielding, H., *Tom Jones*, 108

Dignity and danger go hand in hand.
>Melville, *Moby Dick*, CX

What a dignity it gives an old lady, that balance at the banker's!
>Thackeray, *Vanity Fair*, IX

DIGRESSION

If I should seem now and then to trifle upon the road,—or should sometimes put on a fool's cap with a bell to it, for a moment or two as we pass along,—don't fly off,—but rather courteously give me credit for a little more wisdom than appears from my outside;—and as we jog on, either laugh with me, or at me, or in short do anything,— only keep your temper.
>Sterne, *Tristram Shandy*, I

Though my digressions are all fair, and I fly off from what I am about, as far, and as often too, as any writer in Great Britain; yet I constantly take care to order affairs so that my main business does not stand still in my absence.
>*Ibid.*

My work is digressive and progressive at the same time.
>*Ibid.*

Digressions, incontestably, are the sunshine;—they are the life, the soul of reading!— take them out of this book, for instance,—you might as well take the book along with them;—one cold eternal winter would reign in every page of it; restore them to the writer;—he steps forth like a bridegroom,—bids All-hail; brings in variety, and forbids the appetite to fail.
>*Ibid.*

DINING: *see also* DRINK

The Southerners are the only cooks in the United States. The real difference between the South and the North is that one enjoys itself getting dyspepsia and the other does not.
>Atherton, *Senator North*, Book I, XIV

Five is the very awkwardest of all possible numbers to sit down to table.
>Austen, *Mansfield Park*, Volume Two, V

Who would ever dine, however hungry, if required to eat everything brought on the table?
>Bellamy, *Looking Backward*, XI

I take care never to eat anything without knowing what it is.
>Day, *The History of Sandford and Merton*, 252

Polly put the kettle on, we'll all have tea.
>Dickens, *Barnaby Rudge*, XVII

Town seems to sharpen a man's appetite. A man is hungry all day long. A man is perpetually eating.
>Dickens, *David Copperfield*, XXIV

Conquer your passions, boys, and don't be eager after vittles. Subdue your appetites, my dears, and you've conquered human natur. This is the way we inculcate strength of mind.
>Dickens, *Nicholas Nickleby*, V

"You disliked the killibeate taste, perhaps?" "I don't know much about that 'ere. I thought they'd a wery strong flavor o' warm flat irons." "That *is* the killibeate," observed Mr. Smauker, contemptuously.
>Dickens, *Pickwick Papers*, XXXVI

A man shouldn't send away his plate till he has eaten his fill.
>James, H., *The American*, II

Little a love of fame can brook delay, a love of pudding less.
Jenner, *The Placid Man*, II

The most interesting thing in the world is to find out how the next man gets his vittles.
Kipling, *Captains Courageous*, IX

Never speak to a white man till he is fed.
Kipling, *Kim*, V

Pastry is poisoned bread. Never eat pastry. Be a plain man, and stick to plain things.
Melville, *Israel Potter*, IX

There is a savor of life and immortality in substantial fare. Like balloons, we are nothing till filled.
Melville, *Mardi*, LV

Who has but once dined his friends, has tasted what it is to be Caesar.
Melville, *Moby Dick*, XXXIV

He who dines latest is the greatest man; and he who dines earliest is accounted the least.
Melville, *White Jacket*, VII

What were a day without a dinner? A dinnerless day! Such a day had better be a night.
Ibid.

Drinking, and no thinking, at dinner.
Meredith, *Harry Richmond*, IX

If we could by any means appropriate to our use some of the extraordinary digestive power that a boa constrictor has in his gastric juices, there is really no manner of reason why we should not comfortably dispose of as much of an ox as our stomachs will hold, and one might eat French dishes without the wretchedness of thinking what's to follow.
Meredith, *Ordeal of Richard Feverel*, XXIX

The general prayer should be for a full stomach, and the individual for one that works well; for on that basis only are we a match for temporal matters, and able to contemplate eternal.
Ibid., XXX

When the parlor fire gets low, put coals on the kitchen fire. Such is man: no use in having their hearts, if ye don't have their stomachs.
Ibid., XXXII

Kissing don't last: Cookery do!
Ibid.

German cookery is an education for the sentiment of hogs.
Meredith, *Sandra Belloni*, XLIII

Quantity in food is more to be regarded than quality: a full meal is the great enemy both to study and industry.
Richardson, *Clarissa Harlowe*, IV

Eating is ignoble. Nature should have managed it differently.
Trollope, *Ayala's Angel*, XXI

A man must live, even though his heart be broken, and living he must dine.
Trollope, *Phineas Finn*, LIII

The true Southern watermelon is a boon apart, and not to be mentioned with commoner things.
Twain, *Pudd'nhead Wilson*, XIV

No gentleman dines before seven.
Wilde, *The Picture of Dorian Gray*, IV

DIRECTION: *see also* PLACE

One would think that, as since the beginning of the world almost, the tide of emigration has been setting west, the needle would point that way; whereas, it is forever pointing its fixed forefinger toward the Pole, where there are few inducements to attract a sailor, unless it be plenty of ice for mint-juleps.
Melville, *Redburn*, XXV

DISAPPOINTMENT

We mortals, men and women, devour many a disappointment between breakfast and dinnertime.
Eliot, *Middlemarch*, Book I, VI

DISAPPOINTMENT (*continued*)

The disappointments of human life are written legibly on every page of our existence.
Foster, *The Coquette*, Letter VII

The disappointed heart will catch at the next good to that it has lost.
Richardson, *Sir Charles Grandison*, Two, V

DISCARD

Nothing can be thrown quite away.
Howells, *Silas Lapham*, XXVII

DISCOMFITURE

The moment when a man's head drops off is seldom or never precisely the most agreeable of his life.
Hawthorne, *The Scarlet Letter*, Introductory

Well-bred people dislike few things more than a scene.
Melville, *Confidence-Man*, V

DISCOMFORT

Mrs. Varden was a lady of what is commonly called an uncertain temper—a phrase which being interpreted signifies a temper tolerably certain to make everybody more or less uncomfortable.
Dickens, *Barnaby Rudge*, VII

DISCORD: *see also* CONFLICT

When we are deeply mournful, discordant above all others is the voice of mirth.
Bulwer, *Pompeii*, Book IV, II

DISCOURSE: *see* EXPRESSION

DISCRETION

Carefulness—discretion—should not be confined to elderly ladies or to a second choice.
Austen, *The Watsons*, I

Discretion is a conciliation to virtue.
Burney, *Camilla*, Three, V

Those who have not in strict keeping that rare winter fruit, called discretion, must lay their account with having the forfeit of it exacted from them in some shape or another.
Cleland, *Memoirs of a Coxcomb*, 194

Think you that a man who has spent more than threescore years in the wilderness, has not learned the virtue of discretion?
Cooper, *The Prairie*, XXXI

Were not the powers of nature stronger than those of discretion, few people would have children.
Richardson, *Clarissa Harlowe*, II

Discretion is often most seen in minutenesses.
Richardson, *Sir Charles Grandison*, One, II

Discretion never boils over.
Ibid., Three, VI

DISGRACE

To men who only aim at escaping felony, nothing short of the prisoner's dock is disgrace.
Eliot, *Middlemarch*, Book V, LIII

I would rather follow you to the grave, than I would see you disgrace yourself and your family by such a match.
Fielding, *Tom Jones*, 231-232

DISOBEDIENCE: *see also* OBEDIENCE

There are some few instances in which it is virtuous to disobey.
Radcliffe, *The Italian*, I

Disobedience lets in every evil.   Richardson, *Sir Charles Grandison*, One, I

DISPOSITION

A teachableness of disposition in a young lady is a great blessing.
Austen, *Northanger Abbey*, XXII

No circumstance of time, place, or station, made a man absolutely either good or bad, but the disposition of his own mind.   Fielding, S., *David Simple*, I

It is the disposition of the thought that altereth the nature of the thing.
Lyly, *Euphues*, 100-101

DISTINCTION: *see also* COMPARISON/CONTRAST

Distinction does not consist in the facile use of a contemptible set of conventions, but in being numbered among those who are true, and honest, and just, and pure, and lovely, and of good report.   Hardy, *Tess*, XXIX

All men are like dust, but there are distinctions in society that it befits us to keep.
Helme, *St. Margaret's Cave*, Volume II, XII

DISTRESS: *see also* AFFLICTION; DESPAIR; MISERY

The perplexed mind is ever ready to suggest distressing thoughts.
Anonymous, *A Kidnapped Orphan*, 176

A man in distressed circumstances has not time for all those elegant decorums which other people may observe.   Austen, *Pride and Prejudice*, Volume II, IV

He little thinks of distress of others who has been afflicted with none himself.
Burney, *Cecilia*, I

A time of distress is a time of temptation.   Defoe, *Moll Flanders*, 195

There are very few moments in a man's existence when he experiences so much ludicrous distress, or meets with so little charitable commiseration, as when he is in pursuit of his hat.   Dickens, *Pickwick Papers*, IV

The eloquence of heart-felt distress.   Duff, *Rhedi*, 285

Some of our greatest distresses arise from trifles.   Fielding, H., *Amelia*, I

The distresses of mankind are mostly imaginary, and it would be rather folly than goodness to relieve them.   Fielding, H., *Joseph Andrews*, 233

Distress is more apt to excite contempt than commiseration, especially among men of business, with whom poverty is understood to indicate want of ability.
Fielding, H., *Tom Jones*, 191

Distress heightens devotion, which in prosperity is apt to grow languid.
Fielding, S., *Ophelia*, II

Bursts of universal distress are more dreaded than felt.   Johnson, *Rasselas*, 108

The enthusiasm of feeling will sometimes overcome distresses which the cold heart of prudence had been unable to endure.   Mackenzie, *Julia De Roubigné*, 109

'Tis our own feelings that constitute great part of our distress.
Parsons, *Castle of Wolfenbach*, II

DISTRESS (*continued*)

Such is the fluctuation of a mind overcome by distress, that if for a moment a ray of hope cheers its darkness, it vanishes at the touch of recollection.
Radcliffe, *Athlin and Dunbayne*, 101

The first natural impulses of the distressed heart often point out the best alleviation.
Richardson, *Sir Charles Grandison*, Two, III

DIVERSION: *see also* AMUSEMENT

The sooner every party breaks up the better.
Austen, *Emma*, XXV

DIVERSITY

Diversity is not inconsistency.
Johnson, *Rasselas*, 40

DIVINENESS; DIVINITY: *see also* GOD

True poets and true women have the native sense of the divineness of what the world deems gross material substance.
Meredith, *Diana of the Crossways*, XLIII

DOCTRINE: *see also* BELIEF

"I tell you," said Macchiavelli, "my doctrine is the doctrine of all men who seek an end a little farther off than their own noses."
Eliot, *Romola*, Book III, LX

Successful propagandists have succeeded because the doctrine they bring into form is that which their listeners have for some time felt without being able to shape.
Hardy, *The Return of the Native*, Book III, II

Our Stoics would teach us that wealth and wordly comfort and happiness on earth are not worth the search. Alas, for a doctrine which can find no believing pupils and no true teachers!
Trollope, *Barchester Towers*, XX

You preach a doctrine which you know you don't believe. It is the way with you all. If you know that there is no earthly happiness, why do you long to be a bishop or a dean? Why do you want lands and income?
Ibid., XXVII

DOMESTICITY

So large a ranger, would at home be a stranger.
Deloney, *Jack of Newbury*, 319

In the narrow sphere of domestic arrangements, sorrow may be made to smile and poverty to feel the diffusive power of benevolence.
Sleath, *Orphan of the Rhine*, IV

DOMINANCE

Life had not taught her domination—superciliousness of grace, which is the lordly power of some women.
Dreiser, *Sister Carrie*, XV

The mistakes that we male and female mortals make when we have our own way might fairly raise some wonder that we are so fond of it.
Eliot, *Middlemarch*, Book I, IX

As it is the nature of a kite to devour little birds, so it is the nature of some persons to insult and tyrannize over little people.
Fielding, H., *Tom Jones*, 13

Nothing can make the metaphor that the stage is a picture of life more strong, than the observing every theatrical performance spoiled by the great desire each performer shows of playing the top part.
Fielding, S., *David Simple*, II

He who reduces all beneath him to a state of servitude becomes himself the slave of his establishment, and of all his domestics.
Godwin, *St. Leon*, 85

As sure as your groom rides your horses, because he is a cunninger animal than they, so surely will the animal that is cunninger or stronger than he sit upon his shoulders in turn.
Goldsmith, *The Vicar of Wakefield*, 99-100

A club will beat down a sword.
Richardson, *Clarissa Harlowe*, I

'Tis very hard to subdue an embittered spirit!
Ibid.

The upbraider is in some sense a superior; while the upbraided, if with reason upbraided, must make a figure as spiritless as conscious.
Ibid.

Why will she not, once subdued, be always subdued?
Ibid., II

Once subdued, always subdued.
Ibid.

The greater malady generally swallows up the less.
Ibid.

DOUBT: *see also* BELIEF: FAITH; RELIGION; etc.

It is sometimes a folly to remain perplexed in doubts, since we often have it in our power to remove them.
Anonymous, *The Birmingham Counterfeit*, I

It is better to die by a frown than to live in perpetual silence and unavailing doubt.
Anonymous, *The History of the Human Heart*, 94

Little doubts grew into big ones—big doubts resolved themselves into downright negations.
DuMaurier, *Trilby*, V

Whenever knowledge obliges us to doubt, we are always safe in doubting.
Holmes, *Elsie Venner*, XXII

As there are some people with whom once to be in doubt is to have resolved, and once to have resolved is to have executed; so there are others who doubt even after they think they have resolved and resolve without ever executing.
Jenner, *The Placid Man*, I

Ifs will always stumble in the way of mortals.
Marishall, *Miss Clarinda Cathcart*, II

There are doubts which, if man have them, it is not man that can solve them.
Melville, *Confidence-Man*, XLV

The undoubting doubter believes the most.
Melville, *Mardi*, CIX

It is one of the most exquisite tortures of a noble mind, to doubt the sincerity of those in whom it has confided.
Radcliffe, *Athlin and Dunbayne*, 55

He doubts nothing but what he ought to believe.
Richardson, *Clarissa Harlowe*, II

Doubt is defiance.
Ibid.

When formalists are put out of their road, they are filled with doubts of themselves, and can never get into it again.
Ibid., III

Those who doubt most always err least.
Richardson, *Pamela*, 350

Doubt of a person's merit is the first step to disrespect.
Richardson, *Sir Charles Grandison*, One, I

Good fortune is never more doubtful than when it wears the sweetest and most promising countenance.
Simms, *The Scout*, XXXV

Nothing is more uneasy than doubt.
Smollett, *Roderick Random*, 119

DREAM(S): *see also* HOPE; IMAGINATION; etc.

The most perfect dream is the dream that never comes true.
Atherton, *Senator North*, Book II, XX

There never was a man so strong as to choose the dream when Reality cast off her shackles and beckoned. Imagination we regard as a compensation, not as the supreme gift.
Ibid.

If we awake in the morning to find rain when we vividly had anticipated sunshine, it is only the common mind who would regret the compensation of the dream. *Ibid.*

How is it that in our sleep events are made known to us, that really are, or are about taking place? Can it be that the spirit then roams at will, in all the freedom of disembodiment, and returns freighted with intelligence to communicate to the physical senses?
Bennett, *The Prairie Flower*, XXVII

I've dreamt in my life dreams that have stayed with me ever after, and changed my ideas; they've gone through and through me, like wine through water, and altered the color of my mind.
Bronte, E., *Wuthering Heights*, IX

Dreams are the gifts of the saints.
Bulwer, *Harold*, Book IV, VII

It's no use your talking about waking him, when you're only one of the things in his dream. You know very well you're not real.   Carroll, *Through the Looking Glass*, IV

A dream is the reproduction, in the sleeping state of the brain, of images and impressions produced on it in the waking state.   Collins, *Armadale*, Book I, V

He loved these dreams and the success of his imaginary achievements. They were its best parts of life, its secret truth, its hidden reality.   Conrad, *Lord Jim*, III

What is real in this world except your reveries and dreams?
Cooke, *Surry of Eagle's-Nest*, XCIV

What secret of happiness is greater than to follow your illusions?   *Ibid.*

Life is so short and dull that there is little in it worth our notice, save its illusions—so cold and sad that I wonder we are not all dreamers.   *Ibid.*

What queer things we do in our sleep, and how supremely selfish a dreamer is.
Cowan, *Daybreak*, XXXIX

A little trance of astonishment.   Crane, *The Red Badge of Courage*, I

I remember how I seemed to float, then, down the melancholy glory of that track upon the sea, away into the world of dreams.   Dickens, *David Copperfield*, XIII

Dreams are the bright creatures of poem and legend, who sport on earth in the night season, and melt away in the first beam of the sun, which lights grim care and stern reality on their daily pilgrimage through the world.
Dickens, *Nicholas Nickleby*, XIII

Day too often destroys an air-built castle at the moment of its completion, without the least ceremony or remorse.   Dickens, *The Old Curiosity Shop*, I

Oh, Carrie, Carrie! Oh, blind strivings of the human heart! Onward, onward, it saith, and where beauty leads, there it follows. Whether it be the tinkle of a lone sheep bell o'er some quiet landscape, or the glimmer of beauty in sylvan places, or the show of soul in some passing eye, the heart knows and makes answer, following. It is when the feet weary and hope seems vain that the heartaches and the longings arise. Know, then, that for you is neither surfeit nor content. In your rocking-chair, by your window dreaming, shall you long, alone. In your rocking-chair, by your window, shall you dream such happiness as you never feel.   Dreiser, *Sister Carrie*, XLVII

The whole cosmos is in a man's brains; perhaps it is nowhere else. And when sleep relaxes the will, and there are no earthly surroundings to distract attention—no duty, pain, or pleasure to compel it—riderless Fancy takes the bit in its teeth, and the whole cosmos goes mad and has its wild will of us.   DuMaurier, *Peter Ibbetson*, Part Second

That vivid dreaming which makes the margin of our deeper rest.
Eliot, *The Mill on the Floss*, Book VI, XIV

Dreams are generally the effects of excesses, or of feverish hearts.
Fielding, S., *Ophelia*, I

His dreams were as gigantic as his surroundings were small.   Hardy, *Jude*, Part I, III

Let us acknowledge it wiser, if not more sagacious, to follow one's daydream to its natural consummation, although, if the vision have been worth the having, it is certain never to be consummated otherwise than by a failure.
Hawthorne, *Blithedale Romance*, II

In dreams, the conscience sleeps, and we often stain ourselves with guilt of which we should be incapable in our waking moments.   Hawthorne, *The Marble Faun*, XXII

It must be a very dear and intimate reality for which people will be content to give up a dream.   *Ibid.*, XLIV

Fast in the wilds, and you will dream of spirits.   Marryat, *Monsieur Violet*, XXXVIII

Dreams are so wonderful that some people stop not short of ascribing them directly to heaven.   Melville, *Confidence-Man*, XL

We dream not ourselves, but the thing within us.   Melville, *Mardi*, CLXXII

Fedallah was such a creature as civilized, domestic people in the temperate zone only see in their dreams, and that but dimly.   Melville, *Moby Dick*, L

This dream-house of the earth.   Melville, *Pierre*, Book II, V

We dream that we dreamed we dream.   *Ibid.*, Book XIX, II

Dreams were to him the true realities; externals he accepted as other people accepted dreams—with diffidence.   Moore, *Evelyn Innes*, XII

The inconsistency so common in dreams.   Radcliffe, *The Romance of the Forest*, 381

What unaccountable things are dreams!   Richardson, *Clarissa Harlowe*, III

As quick as thought are dreams.   *Ibid.*

Dreams do not confine themselves to the rules of drama.   *Ibid.*

Dreams have no regard to consanguinity.   *Ibid.*

What is the reason, that though we know these dreams, these fleeting shadows of the night, to be no more than dreams, illusions of the working mind, fettered and debased as it is by the organs through which it conveys its confined powers to the grosser matter, body, then sleeping, inactive, as in the shades of death; yet that we cannot help being strongly impressed by them, and meditating interpretation of the flying vapors, when reason is broad awake and tells us that it is weakness to be disturbed at them?
Richardson, *Sir Charles Grandison*, Three, VI

Do not ask us how we make our dream tally with facts. The glory of a dream is this— that it despises facts, and makes its own. Our dream saves us from going mad; that is enough.   Schreiner, *The Story of an African Farm*, Part II, V

We are sparks, we are shadows, we are pollen, which the next wind will carry away. We are dying already; it is all a dream.   *Ibid.*, Part II, VI

Tell me what a man dreams, and I will tell you what he loves.   *Ibid.*, Part II, XIII

From the earliest childhood to the latest age, day by day, and step by step, the busy waking life is followed and reflected by the life of dreams—waking dreams, sleeping dreams.   *Ibid.*

Men *will* dream; the most that can be asked of them is but that the dream be not in too glaring discord with the thing they know.   *Ibid.*

Dreamers see the heavens open every day.   *Ibid.*

The bars of the real are set close about us; we cannot open our wings but they are struck against them, and drop bleeding. But, when we glide between the bars into the great unknown beyond, we may sail forever in the glorious blue, seeing nothing but our own shadows. So age succeeds age, and dream succeeds dream, and of the joy of the dreamer no man knoweth but he who dreameth. Our fathers had their dream; we have ours; the generation that follows will have its own. Without dreams and phantoms man cannot exist.   *Ibid.*

I have thought more and my daydreams are more extended and magnificent, but they want (as the painters call it) *keeping.*   Shelley, *Frankenstein*, Letter II

She dreamed she was delivered of a tennis-ball, which the devil (who, to her great surprise, acted the part of midwife) struck so forcibly with a racket that it disappeared in an instant.   Smollett, *Roderick Random*, 21

The man is himself, and the woman herself: that dream of love is over as everything else is over in life; as flowers and fury, and griefs and pleasures are over.
                                                      Thackeray, *Henry Esmond*, Book I, VII

"A dream of form in days of thought."   Wilde, *The Picture of Dorian Gray*, I

DRESS: *see also* APPEARANCE; BEAUTY; etc.

Dress is at all times a frivolous distinction, and excessive solicitude about it often destroys its own aim.   Austen, *Northanger Abbey*, X

It would be mortifying to the feelings of many ladies could they be made to understand how little the heart of man is affected by what is costly or new in their attire.   *Ibid.*

Woman is fine for her own satisfaction alone.   *Ibid.*

Dress shows blood, as much as anything else.
                                              Meredith, *Ordeal of Richard Feverel*, XXXIII

DRINK: *see also* DINING

Strong drink makes every hidden seed sprout up in the soul and show itself.
                                           Anonymous, *Tom Jones in His Married State*, 228

Wine is a leveller. It either raises the man to the master, or throws down the master to the man.   *Ibid.*, 230

Most quarrels that end in bloodshed begin in wine.   *Ibid.*, 232

The English phrase for a man's spending his estate is *running out his fortune*; the French, *eating his fortune*; the German, *drinking his fortune.*
                                           Anonymous, *Peregrinations of Jeremiah Grant*, 122-23

A cheerful glass is the first pleasure in life; the most convivial, the most exhilarating, the most friendly joy of a true honest soul.   Burney, *Camilla*, Three, VI

The man who really thinks much, seldom drinks much.   Cooper, *Two Admirals*, VIII

There is nothing so absurd, so surfeiting, so ridiculous, as a man heated by wine in his head and a wicked gust in his inclination together. He is in the possession of two devils at once, and can no more govern himself by his reason than a mill can grind without water.   Defoe, *Moll Flanders*, 232

Light hearts and merry minds live long without gray hairs, but seldom without red noses.   Deloney, *Jack of Newbury*, 354

To hint at any little delicate thing to drink and it came like magic in a pint bottle it was not ecstacy but it was comfort.   Dickens, *Little Dorrit*, Book I, XXIV

Leave the bottle on the chimley-piece, and don't ask me to take none, but let me put my lips to it when I am so dispoged, and then I will do what I'm engaged to do, according to the best of my ability.   Dickens, *Martin Chuzzlewit*, XIX

In some cases of drunkenness, and in others of animal magnetism, there are two states of consciousness which never clash, each of which pursues its separate course as though it were continuous instead of broken. Thus, if I hide my watch when I am drunk, I must be drunk again before I can remember where.   Dickens, *Mystery of Edwin Drood*, III

Most public characters have their failings; and the truth is that Mr. Snevellicci was a little addicted to drinking; or, if the whole truth must be told, that he was scarcely ever sober. He knew in his cups three distinct stages of intoxication,—the dignified—the quarrelsome—the amorous.   Dickens, *Nicholas Nickleby*, XXX

Bring in the bottled lightning, a clean tumbler, and a corkscrew.   *Ibid.*, XLIX

Fan the sinking flame of hilarity with the wing of friendship; and pass the rosy wine!
Dickens, *Old Curiosity Shop*, VII

A double glass o' the inwariable, my dear.   Dickens, *Pickwick Papers*, XXXIII

It's my opinion that this meeting is drunk.   *Ibid.*

I rather like bad wine; one gets so bored with good wine.   Disraeli, *Sybil*, Book I, I

The Irish sometimes make and keep a vow against whiskey; these vows are usually limited to a short time.   Edgeworth, *Castle Rackrent*, 29

We drank Sir Condy's good health and the downfall of his enemies till we could stand no longer ourselves.   *Ibid.*, 38

Drunkenness shows the mind of a man, as a mirror reflects his person.
Fielding, H., *Tom Jones*, 197

To be drunk with joy—an intoxication which greatly forwards the effects of wine.
Ibid.

Drink doth not reverse nature, nor create passions in men which did not exist in them before.   *Ibid.*, 199

Wine is often the forerunner of incontinency.   *Ibid.*, 202

Tom was in a condition, in which, if reason had interposed, though only to advise, she might have received the answer which one Cleostratus gave many years ago to a silly fellow who asked him if he was not ashamed to be drunk. "Are not you," said Cleostratus, "ashamed to admonish a drunken man?"   Fielding, H., *Tom Jones*, 204

In a court of justice drunkenness must not be an excuse, yet in a court of conscience it is greatly so; and therefore Aristotle, who commends the laws of Pittacus, by which drunken men receive double punishment for their crimes, allows there is more of policy than justice in that law.   *Ibid.*

The whimsical sallies of wit are the natural productions of Champagne.
Fielding, S., *The Countess of Dellwyn*, I

The God-forgive-me was a two-handled tall mug. Such a class of mug is called a God-forgive-me for uncertain reasons; probably because its size makes any given toper feel ashamed of himself when he sees its bottom in drinking it empty.
Hardy, *Far From the Madding Crowd*, VIII

Drinking was the regular, stereotyped resource of the despairing worthless.
Hardy, *Jude*, Part One, XI

Drunkenness is a peculiar privilege.   Helme, *St. Margaret's Cave*, Volume III, II

Drunkenness, which degrades the freeman to the level with the brutes, raises, or seems to raise the slave, to the dignity of a man.   Hildreth, *Slave*, Volume I, XV

Throw the lumber over, man! Let your boat of life be light, packed with only what you need—a homely home and simple pleasures, one or two friends, worth the name, someone to love and someone to love you, a cat, a dog, and a pipe or two, enough to eat and enough to wear, and a little more than enough to drink; for thirst is a dangerous thing.   Jerome, *Three Men in a Boat*, III

While a man is their favorite, people are continually getting drunk with drinking his health; when he is out of favor with them they get drunk with drinking his confusion.
Johnstone, *The Reverie*, I

DRINK (*continued*)

These people can see no fault in the man who makes them drunk; they will see no virtue in him who will not. *Ibid.*

The harangues of orators, the promises of patriots, make no impression, unless the head is warmed with wine, to receive them with proper force. *Ibid.*

The glass comes very quick about when a man drinks by himself.
Lawrence, *Common Sense*, II

Wine is the mirror of the mind. Lyly, *Euphues and His England*, 308

Disguised with liquor. Marryat, *Peter Simple*, II

How delightful to think that the word [conviviality] which among men signifies the highest pitch of geniality, implies, as indispensable auxiliary, the cheery benediction of the bottle. To live together in the finest sense, we must drink together.
Melville, *Confidence-Man*, XXX

"Wine opens the heart." "Opens it! It thaws it right out." *Ibid.*

Plain water is very good drink for plain men. Melville, *Israel Potter*, VII

Of all blessed fluids, the juice of the grape is the greatest foe to cohesion. True, it tightens the girdle; but then it loosens the tongue, and opens the heart.
Melville, *Mardi*, XCV

When wild with much thought, 'tis to wine I fly, to sober me. *Ibid.*, CLI

The study of astronomy is wonderfully facilitated by wine. *Ibid.*

Upon the opening of that fatal cork, forth flew the fiend, the Bottle Conjuror, and shrivelled up his home. Melville, *Moby Dick*, CXII

Drink is the death's river of women. Meredith, *Amazing Marriage*, XVIII

Men sit and talk despondently of this extraordinary disease of the vine, and not one of them seems to think it incumbent on him to act, and do his best to stop it.
Meredith, *Ordeal of Richard Feverel*, XX

Too much wine is decidedly bad. But just the quantum makes men of us. *Ibid.*

There's great virtue belongs to a cup of cider. Nashe, *The Unfortunate Traveller*, 34

Good drink is a medicine for all diseases. *Ibid.*, 69

He hath learning enough that hath learned to drink to his first man. *Ibid.*, 71

Wine certainly kills some, but it saves the lives of others. Peacock, *Headlong Hall*, V

If your heart fail you, another cup of wine will set all to rights.
Peacock, *The Misfortunes of Elphin*, XIV

This discourse [against drinking] caused quite an uproar. The hearers formed knots; the men were indignant; so the women flattered them, and took their part openly against the preacher. A married man had a right to a drop; he needed it, working for all the family. And for their part they did not care to change their men for milksops. The double faces! That very evening a band of men caught near a hundred of them round Brother Clement, filling his wallet with the best, and offering him the very roses off their heads, and kissing his frock, and blessing him "for taking in hand to mend their sots." Reade, *The Cloister and the Hearth*, LXXX

Drunkenness is not heresy, that a whole sermon should be preached against it. *Ibid.*

As drunk as a fiddler. Reade, *Griffith Gaunt*, IX

As drunk as the Baltic Ocean. Scott, *Redgauntlet*, XIV

Dipsomaniacs are always intending to reform; but they rarely succeed.
Shaw, *The Irrational Knot*, XV

How men should beware of wicked punch! Thackeray, *Vanity Fair*, VIII

Wine is a dangerous thing, and should not be made the exponent of truth, let the truth be good as it may; but it has the merit of forcing a man to show his true colors. A man who is a gentleman in his cups may be trusted to be a gentleman at all times.
Trollope, *He Knew He Was Right*, LI

How grand a thing would wine really be, if it could make glad the heart of man.
Ibid., LXXXVI

There is an intoxication that makes merry in the midst of affliction; and there is an intoxication that banishes affliction by producing oblivion. But again there is an intoxication which is conscious of itself though it makes the feet unsteady, and the voice thick, and the brain foolish; and which brings neither mirth nor oblivion.
Trollope, *The Way We Live Now*, L

He was a teetotaler sometimes—when it was judicious to be one.
Twain, *Pudd'nhead Wilson*, XI

Even a sober person does not like to have a human being emptied on him when he is not doing any harm; a person who is not sober cannot endure such an attention at all. *Ibid.*

"What dost thou know but war?" "The taste of good wine."
Wallace, *The Fair God*, Volume I, Book V, IV

DUEL

An honest savage has more sense than to practice duelling—he takes his bow or his gun and shoots his enemy from behind a bush. There can, in that case, be only one man's death between them.
Scott, *St. Ronan's Well*, XXXIV

DULLNESS

A late facetious writer told the public that whenever he was dull they might be assured there was a design in it.
Fielding, H., *Tom Jones*, 163

The dullest fellows may learn to be comical for a night or two.
Goldsmith, *The Vicar of Wakefield*, 28

Alone he was rather dull, as a man who beholds but one thing must naturally be.
Meredith, *Ordeal of Richard Feverel*, XXXVI

Dullness gets on as well as any other quality with women.
Thackeray, *Vanity Fair*, XI

Always to be right, always to trample forward, and never to doubt, are not these the great qualities with which dullness takes the lead in the world? *Ibid.*, XXXV

DUTY: *see also* OBLIGATION

A life of duty must be empty, cold, and wrong. It was not that we were made for.
Atherton, *Doomswoman*, XVI

A mistaken sense of duty has been the cause of quite one fourth of the unhappiness of mankind, and few have been so bigoted as not to acknowledge this when too late.
Atherton, *Senator North*, Book III, XIX

To do the best for himself passed as a duty. Austen, *Persuasion*, XXI

It is always agreeable to get an unpleasant duty deferred.
Cooper, *Satanstoe*, Volume I, VIII

Our chief duty on this earth is to help our fellow man. Crane, *The O'Ruddy*, XXIX

Duty, before every consideration in the universe. Dickens, *David Copperfield*, XLV

I have heard some talk about duty first and last; but it has always been of my duty to other people. I have wondered now and then whether no one ever owed any duty to me.
Dickens, *Dombey and Son*, XXXIV

The essence of all tenure is the performance of duty.
Disraeli, Coningsby, Book VIII, III

The duty which we owe to the weak overrides all other duties and is superior to all circumstances.
Doyle, Micah Clarke, XXX

Each position has its corresponding duties.
Eliot, Middlemarch, Book I, IX

Can man or woman choose duties? No more than they can choose their birthplace or their father and mother.
Eliot, Romola, Book II, XL

Every bond of your life is a debt.
Ibid.

The question where the duty of obedience ends, and the duty of resistance begins, could in no case be any easy one.
Ibid., Book III, LV

What signifies knowing your duty, if you do not perform it?
Fielding, Joseph Andrews, 225

It is one of our most imperious duties to seek our happiness.   Godwin, St. Leon, 295

This stale excuse of duty signifies bigotry; self-conceit; an insolent curiosity; a meddlesome temper; a cold-blooded criticism, founded on a shallow interpretation of half-perceptions; a monstrous scepticism in regard to any conscience or any wisdom, except one's own; a most irreverent propensity to thrust Providence aside, and substitute oneself in its awful place.
Hawthorne, Blithedale Romance, XX

The first duty of a great man is justice.   Helme, St. Margaret's Cave, Volume III, IV

Many good women are suffered to perish by that form of spontaneous combustion in which the victim goes on toiling day and night with the hidden fire consuming her, until all at once her cheek whitens, and, as we look upon her, she drops away, a heap of ashes.
Holmes, Elsie Venner, XII

A man's foremost duty is not to get collared.   James, H., Princess Casamassima, XXI

Duty to a father is the best assurance of loyalty to a sovereign.   Johnstone, Arsaces, I

It is a duty to qualify ourselves to fill properly whatever station is appointed for us.
Ibid.

The bare performance of duty merits not reward.
Ibid., II

Duty must not wait for private quarrels, even though they be just over.
Kingsley, Westward Ho!, VII

In the Enthusiast to Duty, the heaven-begotten Christ is born; and will not own a mortal parent, and spurns and rends all mortal bonds.   Melville, Pierre, Book V, V

A man owes a duty to his class as long as he sees his class doing its duty to the country.
Meredith, Beauchamp's Career, XVI

The clear duty of a man of any wealth is to serve the people as he best can.
Meredith, Ordeal of Richard Feverel, XXIX

Since your heart is free let your duty govern it.   Richardson, Clarissa Harlowe, I

When young ladies fall out with their own duty, it is not much to be wondered at that they are angry at anybody who do theirs.
Ibid.

The filial duty must be a duty prior to all other duties; a duty anterior to birth.
Ibid., II

What is the precise stature and age at which a good child shall conclude herself absolved from the duty she owes to a parent?
Ibid.

Duty should be the conqueror of inclination.
Ibid.

One who is dutiful to parents will be dutiful to a spouse: since duty upon principle is a uniform thing.
Ibid., IV

Not doing a duty does not warrant another's not doing his.   *Ibid.*

A man, moving in the exalted sphere of society, has his public duties to perform before he consults his private affections.   Thackeray, *Barry Lyndon*, XV

There are listeners who show by their mode of listening that they listen as a duty, not because they are interested.   Trollope, *Eustace Diamonds*, III

The path of duty leads but to the grave.   Trollope, *Phineas Finn*, XXXVIII

The highest duty, the duty that one owes to one's self.
                    Wilde, *The Picture of Dorian Gray*, II

EARNESTNESS

Can one in earnest be other than careless?   Meredith, *Sandra Belloni*, XXXVII

ECONOMICS; ECONOMY

Female economy will do a great deal, but it cannot turn a small income into a large one.
                    Austen, *The Watsons*, II

"You set no value on the right principles of rent, profit, wages, and currency?" "My principles in these things are, to take as much as I can get, and to pay no more than I can help. These are every man's principles, whether they be the right principles or no. There is political economy in a nutshell." "The principles which regulate production and consumption are independent of the will of any individual as to giving or taking, and do not lie in a nutshell by any means."   Peacock, *Crotchet Castle*, II

Without economy, no estate is large enough. With it, the least is not too small.
                    Richardson, *Clarissa Harlowe*, II

EDUCATION: *see also* EXPERIENCE; KNOWLEDGE; etc.

Nothing is to be done in education without steady and regular instruction.
                    Austen, *Pride and Prejudice*, Volume II, VI

No amount of education can cure natural dullness or make up for original mental deficiencies.   Bellamy, *Looking Backward*, XXI

When we can afford it better, we can pull down the college.
                    Brackenridge, *Modern Chivalry*, Part II, Volume I

It is absurd to require of youth thoughts before they have any.
                    Ibid., Part II, Volume II

I do not approve of taking notes. You read your lectures, and the student must take notes. It spoils his hand; for trying to keep up with you he writes fast, and runs into scratches like shorthand, or the Coptic alphabet.   *Ibid.*

How to make Virtue practicable, Instruction desirable, and Religion lovely and comprehensible.   Bronte, A., *Agnes Grey*, I

The business of education is less to give us good impressions, which we have from nature, than to guard us against bad ones, which are generally acquired.
                    Brooke, *Emily Montague*, III

You might as well expect a Laplander to write Greek spontaneously, and without instruction, as that anyone should be wise or skillful, without suitable opportunities.
                    Brown, C. B., *Alcuin*, I

They cannot read who never saw an alphabet. They who know no tool but the needle cannot be skillful at the pen.   *Ibid.*

A scholar is of all persons the most unfit to teach young children. A mother is the infant's true guide to knowledge.   Bulwer, *The Caxtons*, Book I, IV

The two great teachers, Nature and Love. *Ibid.*

The ordeal for talent is school. *Ibid.*, Book I, VI

Students, whatever their age, are rarely young. *Ibid.*, Book IV, I

The ordinary run of scholars and of readers are, in their superstitious homage to the dead, always willing enough to sacrifice the living. *Ibid.*, Book VII, I

We are here but as schoolboys, whose life begins where school ends; and the battles we fought with our rivals, and the toys that we shared with our playmates, and the names that we carved, high or low, on the wall, above our desks—will they so much bestead us hereafter? *Ibid.*, Book XVI, X

Could we know by what strange circumstances a man's genius became prepared for practical success, we shoud discover that the most serviceable items in his education were never entered in the bills which his father paid for it.
Bulwer, *What Will He Do with It?*, Book V, III

O schoolmasters—if any of you read this book—bear in mind when any particularly timid, drivelling urchin is brought by his papa into your study, and you treat him with the contempt which he deserves, and afterwards make his life a burden to him for years—bear in mind that it is exactly in the disguise of such a boy as this that your future chronicler will appear. Butler, *The Way of All Flesh*, XXVIII

Never learn anything until you find you have been made uncomfortable for a long while by not knowing it. *Ibid.*, XXXI

There are understandings that expand, not imperceptibly hour by hour, but as certain flowers do, by little explosive ruptures, with periods of quiescence between.
Cable, *The Grandissimes*, XVIII

When a man's social or civil standing is not dependent on his knowing how to read, he is not likely to become a scholar. *Ibid.*, XXIV

The regular course was Reeling and Writhing, of course, to begin with; and then the different branches of Arithmetic—Ambition, Distraction, Uglification, and Derision.
Carroll, *Alice in Wonderland*, IX

College discipline should imitate the world in this respect: it should develop every man's peculiar genius. Neglect of this is the true reason why so many men distinguish themselves in the world, who were considered asses in college, and why so many who were considered amazingly clever in college, are found to be little better than asses in the world. Caruthers, *Kentuckian in New-York*, Volume I, XIV

My native purity had taken no root in education. Cleland, *Fanny Hill*, 28

Like most self-taught men, he overestimated the value of an education.
Dana, *Two Years Before the Mast*, XXIII

He that undertakes the education of a child undertakes the most important duty in society, and is severely answerable for every voluntary omission.
Day, *Sandford and Merton*, 247

Under the forcing system [of education], a young gentleman usually took leave of his spirits in three weeks. He had all the cares of the world on his head in three months. He conceived bitter sentiments against his parents or guardians in four; he was an old misanthrope, in five; envied Curtius that blessed refuge in the earth, in six; and at the end of the first twelvemonth had arrived at the conclusion, from which he never afterwards departed, that all the fancies of the poets, and lessons of the sages, were a mere collection of words and grammar, and had no other meaning in the world.
Dickens, *Dombey and Son*, XI

The books comprised a little English, and a deal of Latin—names of things, declensions of articles and substantives, exercises thereon, and preliminary rules—a trifle of orthography, a glance at ancient history, a wink or two at modern ditto, a few tables, two or three weights and measures, and a little general information. When poor Paul had spelt out number two, he found he had no idea of number one; fragments whereof afterwards obtruded themselves into number three, which slided into number four, which grafted itself on to number two. So that whether twenty Romuluses made a Remus, or hic haec hoc was troy weight, or a verb always agreed with an ancient Briton, or three times four was Taurus a bull, were open questions with him.   *Ibid.*, XII

Train up a fig-tree in the way it should go, and when you are old sit under the shade of it.
Ibid., XIX

You must be a common scholar afore you can be a oncommon one.
Dickens, *Great Expectations*, IX

EDUCATION.—At Mr. Wackford Squeers's Academy, Dotheboys Hall, at the delightful village of Dotheboys, near Great Bridge in Yorkshire, Youth are boarded, clothed, booked, furnished with pocket-money, provided with all necessaries, instructed in all languages living and dead, mathematics, orthography, geometry, astronomy, trigonometry, the use of the globes, algebra, fortification, and every other branch of classical literature. Terms, twenty guineas per annum. No extras, no vacations, and diet unparalleled. Mr. Squeers is in town, and attends daily, from one till four, at the Saracen's Head, Snow Hill. N. B. An able assistant wanted. Annual salary five pounds. A Master of Arts would be preferred.   Dickens, *Nicholas Nickleby*, III

When he has learned that bottinney means a knowledge of plants, he goes and knows 'em [by weeding the garden]. That's our system.   *Ibid.*, VIII

A horse is a quadruped, and quadruped's Latin for beast, as everybody that's gone through the grammar knows, or else where's the use of having grammars at all?   *Ibid.*

We've got a private master comes to teach us at home, but we ain't proud, because ma says it's sinful.   *Ibid.*, XVI

The influence of the individual is nowhere so sensible as at school. There the personal qualities strike without any intervening and counteracting causes.
Disraeli, *Coningsby*, Book I, IX

Polite education qualifies a man for the social duties of life.
Donaldson, *Sir Bartholomew Sapskull*, I

All the learnin' *my* father ever paid for was a bit o' birch at one end and the alphabet at th' other.   Eliot, *Mill on the Floss*, Book I, II

How very slightly do we commonly find the heart improved by genteel education!
Fielding, H., *Amelia*, II

Public schools are the nurseries of all vice and immorality.
Fielding, H., *Joseph Andrews*, 194

Great schools are little societies.   *Ibid.*, 195

If a boy be of a mischievous, wicked inclination, no school will ever make him good.
Ibid.

Thwackum considered a sick-bed to be a convenient scene for lectures.
Fielding, H., *Tom Jones*, 164

Education and behavior put all upon a level.   Graves, *The Spiritual Quixote*, I

He held that education had as yet but little affected the beats of emotion and impulse on which domestic happiness depends.   Hardy, *Tess*, XXVI

The secret of productive study is to avoid well.   Hardy, *Two on a Tower*, VII

Those who have the charge of youth should watch the first attempts of dawning reason, and fix, in their youthful hearts, such sentiments of truth and honor as might defy the hand of time to efface.   Harley, *Priory of St. Bernard*, I

That education is the most effectual which commences earliest.
Hildreth, *Slave*, Volume I, III

A knowledge of the world so seldom falls to the share of a tutor that when, in consequence of his employment, he follows his pupil into the world, it is oftener the pupil that carries the tutor, than the tutor the pupil.   Jenner, *The Placid Man*, I

Hard knocks in good humor, strict rules, fair play, and equal justice for high and low; this was the old outlaw spirit, which has descended to their inlawed descendants; and makes, to this day, the life and marrow of an English public school.
Kingsley, *Hereward the Wake*, XXXIV

It is not a pleasant epoch in one's life—the first forty-eight hours at a large public school.
Lawrence, *Guy Livingstone*, I

He that coveteth to have a straight tree, must not bow him being a twig.
Lyly, *Euphues*, 94

It is too late to shut the stable door when the steed is stolen.   *Ibid.*, 95

A whale ship was my Yale College and my Harvard.   Melville, *Moby Dick*, XXIV

English young ladies seem to be educated to conceal their education.
Meredith, *Harry Richmond*, XXVIII

"Education can give purposes, but not powers." "No, education makes the man, powers, purposes, and all."   Peacock, *Crotchet Castle*, IV

If learning get nothing but honor; and if the good things of this world, which ought to be the rewards of learning, become the mere gifts of self-interested patronage; you must not wonder if, in the finishing of education, the science which takes precedence of all others should be the science of currying favor.   *Ibid.*, IX

Colleges are classes of tyrants, from the upper-students over the lower, and from them to the tutor.   Richardson, *Clarissa Harlowe*, I

Reading and writing, though not too much for the wits of you young girls, are too much for your judgments.   *Ibid.*

We are all apt to turn teachers.   *Ibid.*, II

How shall so young a scholar in the school of affliction be able to bear such heavy and such various evils?   *Ibid.*, III

College novices, who think they know everything in their cloisters, and that all learning lies in books, make dismal figures when they come into the world.   *Ibid.*, IV

People of fortune are generally educated wrong.   Richardson, *Pamela*, 470

The education of youth is professed by many, but executed by few.
Ridley, *James Lovegrove*, I

It requires a great knowledge of books and sciences to instruct a pupil properly; nor will every soil take kindly the laborious cultivation.   *Ibid.*

Of all cursed places under the sun, where the hungriest soul can hardly pick up a few grains of knowledge, a girl's boarding-school is the worst. They are called finishing schools, and the name tells accurately what they are. They finish everything but imbecility and weakness, and that they cultivate.
Schreiner, *The Story of an African Farm*, Part II, IV

Apt scholars need little teaching.   Shebbeare, *The Marriage Act*, I

Schooling and education are meant for this very purpose, to give us an ear for music—the music of birds as well as men, the music of the soul, as well as of the throat—music which fills the heart as well as the ear—music which is not only sweet, but wise—which not only pleases but makes good; for the great secret of education is to open all the ears—which we call *senses*—of a man, so that he can drink in all the harmonies of that world of music, which we commonly call life.   Simms, *Woodcraft*, XLI

Whatever may amuse a man is an important agent in his education. *Ibid.*

The Sunday paper is one of the features of the age. In America, it supersedes all other literature, the bone and sinew of the nation finding their requirements catered for; hundreds of columns will be occupied with interesting details of the world's doings, such as water-spouts, elopements, conflagrations, and public entertainments; there is a corner for politics, ladies' work, chess, religion, and even literature; and a few spicy editorials serve to direct the course of public thought. It is difficult to estimate the part played by such enormous and miscellaneous repositories in the education of the people.
Stevenson, *The Wrong Box*, XIV

It is common for people who write treatises on education to give forth their rules and theories with a self-satisfied air, as if a human being were a thing to be made up, like a batch of bread, out of a given number of materials combined by an infallible recipe.
Stowe, *Orr's Island*, XX

Torture in a public school is as much licensed as the knout in Russia.
Thackeray, *Vanity Fair*, V

Education is a great thing. This was the same youth who had come to West Point so ignorant that when I asked him, "If a general officer should have a horse shot under him on the field of battle, what ought he to do?" answered up naïvely and said: "Get up and brush himself." Twain, *Connecticut Yankee*, XXV

Training is everything. The peach was once a bitter almond; cauliflower is nothing but cabbage with a college education. Twain, *Pudd'nhead Wilson*, V

Examinations are pure humbug from beginning to end. If a man is a gentleman, he knows quite enough, and if he is not a gentleman, whatever he knows is bad for him.
Wilde, *The Picture of Dorian Gray*, III

EFFECTIVENESS

Subtle courses are more effective than violence. Scott, *The Talisman*, XI

EFFORT

What battle was ever won without an effort? What great act achieved without resolution?
Helme, *St. Margaret's Cave*, Volume II, X

You make a long harvest for a little corn, and angle for the fish that is already caught.
Lyly, *Euphues*, 149

The endlessness, the intolerableness of all earthly effort. Melville, *Moby Dick*, XIII

EGOTISM: *see also* SELF and SELF-_____

Self-love dreads a blunder. Bronte, C., *Jane Eyre*, XIV

Man's natural tendency is to egotism. In his infancy of knowledge he thinks that all creation was formed for him. Bulwer, *Zanoni*, Book IV, IV

EMOTIONS: *see also* specific emotions such as ANGER; LOVE; etc.

There is a time when, in extremities, the most violent agitations and transports of the mind are more serviceable than hurtful. Anonymous, *The Wanderer*, II

Allow me to feel no more than I profess.
Austen, *Sense and Sensibility*, Volume I, XVIII

Feeling and I turned Reason out of doors. Bronte, C., *Villette*, XXIII

Was this feeling dead? I do not know, but it was buried. Sometimes I thought the tomb unquiet, and dreamed strangely of disturbed earth, and of hair, still golden and living, obtruded through coffin-chinks. *Ibid.*, XXXI

In the feelings of the heart there can be no dissimulation.
Brown, W. H., *The Power of Sympathy*, 78

Virtue should be the sovereign of the feelings, not their destroyer.
Bulwer, *Devereux*, Book I, XV

Do not think him without feeling who is not always crying.
Burney, *Camilla*, Five, IX

The narrowest human limits are wide enough to contain the grandest human emotions.
Collins, *Poor Miss Finch*, I

I have heard of a poet who remarked that feelings were the common lot of all. If he could have been a pig, and have uttered that sentiment, he would still have been immortal.
Dickens, *Old Curiosity Shop*, LXVI

Men feel less deeply than of old and act with less devotion.   Disraeli, *Sybil*, Book II, XI

It isn't notions sets people doing the right thing—it's feelings.
Eliot, *Adam Bede*, XVII

We've no right t' intermeddle with people's feelings when they wouldn't tell 'em themselves.
Ibid., LI

To have in general but little feeling, seems to be the only security against feeling too much on any particular occasion.   Eliot, *Middlemarch*, Book I, VII

Personal feeling is not always in the wrong if you boil it down to the impressions which make it simply an opinion.   *Ibid.*, Book V, XLV

Shallow natures dream of an easy sway over the emotions of others, trusting implicitly in their own petty magic to turn the deepest streams, and confident, by pretty gestures and remarks, of making the thing that is not as though it were.
Ibid., Book VIII, LXXVIII

Our naked feelings make haste to clothe themselves in propositions which lie at hand among our store of opinions, and to give a true account of what passes within us something else is necessary besides sincerity, even when sincerity is unmixed.
Eliot, *Romola*, Book III, LXIV

Feeling does not stay to calculate with weights and a balance the importance and magnitude of every object that excites it; it flows impetuously from the heart, without consulting the cooler responses of the understanding.   Godwin, *St. Leon*, 274

What an instrument is the human voice! How wonderfully responsive to every emotion of the human soul!   Hawthorne, *House of the Seven Gables*, VI

The feelings of the human heart are as different as the tinctures of the skin.
Johnstone, *The Pilgrim*, I

There are some feelings which are too tender to be suffered by the world.
Mackenzie, *The Man of Feeling*, 128

In their precise tracings-out and subtile causations, the strongest and fieriest emotions of life defy all analytical insight.   Melville, *Pierre*, Book IV, I

There is no more grievous sight, as there is no greater perversion, than a wise man at the mercy of his feelings.   Meredith, *Ordeal of Richard Feverel*, XLVIII

What we feel matters much more than what we know.   Moore, *Evelyn Innes*, XXVI

My heart is on my lips. I speak just what I think.   Peacock, *Crotchet Castle*, III

Whatever our hearts are in, our heads will follow.   Richardson, *Clarissa Harlowe*, II

Other people's emotions were much more delightful than their ideas, it seemed to him.
Wilde, *Picture of Dorian Gray*, I

The advantage of the emotions is that they lead us astray, and the advantage of science is that it is not emotional. *Ibid.*, III

There is always something ridiculous about the emotions of people whom one has ceased to love. *Ibid.*, VII

ENCOURAGEMENT: *see also* APPROBATION

Never encourage beggars. Burney, *Camilla*, One, II

Encouragement is the food of talent; without cheering, no one can say what an author's faculty naturally is. Galt, *Annals*, XLVIII

Providence seldom vouchsafes to mortals any more than just that degree of encouragement, which suffices to keep them at a reasonably full exertion of their powers.
Hawthorne, *House of the Seven Gables*, III

I never see a modest man, but I am sure that he has a treasure in his mind which requires nothing but the key of encouragement to unlock it, to make him shine.
Richardson, *Clarissa Harlowe*, II

ENDURANCE

Nothing very long abides. Blackmore, *Lorna Doone*, XLVII

There is a limit to the length of the inspection which a man can endure, under certain circumstances. Collins, *Moonstone*, Third Narrative, III

Never say die. Dickens, *Barnaby Rudge*, XLVII

Some common things are hard to die. Dickens, *David Copperfield*, XLVI

There is a point beyond which endurance becomes ridiculous, if not culpable.
Dickens, *Dombey and Son*, XXIX

Art thou to put a bound to the divine will, and to say, Thus much will I bear, and no more? Richardson, *Pamela*, 182

Nothing in this world is made to last forever. Sterne, *Tristram Shandy*, VIII, 507

The elastic heart of youth cannot be compressed into one constrained shape long at a time.
Twain, *Tom Sawyer*, VIII

Shallow sorrows and shallow loves live on. The loves and sorrows that are great are destroyed by their own plenitude. Wilde, *Picture of Dorian Gray*, XVIII

ENERGY

Liveliness is a pleasant thing—when it don't lead to spending money.
Dickens, *Martin Chuzzlewit*, XI

Energy is perhaps of all qualities the most valuable. Godwin, *Caleb Williams*, III

Unskilled labor wastes in beating against the bars ten times the energy exerted by the practiced hand in the effective direction. Hardy, *Desperate Remedies*, XVIII

Laden with that superabundant energy which makes a fool of a man, and a scapegrace of a boy. Meredith, *Ordeal of Richard Feverel*, IV

ENJOYMENT: *see also* JOIE DE VIVRE; LIFE

It is something to look upon enjoyment, so that it be free and wild and in the face of nature, though it is but the enjoyment of an idiot. Dickens, *Barnaby Rudge*, XXV

Ye men of gloom and austerity, who paint the face of Infinite Benevolence with an eternal frown; read in the Everlasting Book, wide open to your view, the lesson it would teach. *Ibid.*

ENJOYMENT (*continued*)

When we enjoy most, we have least to tell.
Galt, *Annals*, XXV

To enjoy the blessing of a willing prize is everything.
Simms, *The Scout*, XXXV

ENNUI

At home, one is killed with meditation; abroad, one is overpowered by ceremony.
Burney, *Cecilia*, II

What can be the gifts worthy of acceptance of a man who, while he possesses them, is tired of life, and desires to die, or what the wealth of him who bears about him every external symptom of poverty and desolation?
Godwin, *St. Leon*, 129

ENTERTAINMENT

When Mary had finished her second song, he said aloud, "That will do extremely well, child. You have delighted us long enough. Let the other young ladies have time to exhibit."
Austen, *Pride and Prejudice*, Volume I, XVIII

The trouble in civilized life of entertaining company, as it is called too generally without much regard to strict veracity, is so great that it cannot but be matter of wonder that people are so fond of attempting it.
Trollope, *Barchester Towers*, XXXVI

Who shall have sufficient self-assurance, who shall feel sufficient confidence in his own powers to dare to boast that he can entertain his company?
Ibid.

ENTHUSIASM: *see also* ZEAL

Nothing is so contagious as enthusiasm; it moves stones, it charms brutes. Enthusiasm is the genius of sincerity, and truth accomplishes no victories without it.
Bulwer, *Pompeii*, Book One, VIII

A philanthropist is necessarily an enthusiast; for without enthusiasm what was ever achieved but commonplace?
Melville, *Confidence-Man*, VII

If a drunkard in a sober fit is the dullest of mortals, an enthusiast in a reason-fit is not the most lively.
Ibid., VIII

An overmastering fervor upsets the vessel we float in.
Meredith, *Beauchamp's Career*, X

Enthusiasm has the privilege of not knowing monotony.
Meredith, *Diana of the Crossways*, XL

Chivalry is only another name for enthusiasm.
Simms, *Vasconselos*, XV

ENVY

Envy is a kind of turnkey by birth, and an executioner by profession.
Anonymous, *Tom Jones in His Married State*, 304

Envy has its rise from emulation, than which there cannot be a greater incentive to laudable actions.
Anonymous, *The Lady's Drawing Room*, 8

The pointed darts of envy are generally thrown against any exalted merit.
Anonymous, *The Theatre of Love*, 124

Handsome women ought to be too vain to be envious.
Brooke, *Emily Montague*, III

Envy will be a science when it learns the use of a microscope.
Bulwer, *What Will He Do with It?*, Book V, I

The worst and most rancorous kind of envy, the envy of superiority of understanding.
Fielding, H., *Tom Jones*, 514

Envy feels not its own happiness but when it may be compared with the misery of others.   Johnson, *Rasselas*, 44

Envy is commonly reciprocal.   *Ibid.*, 72

EQUALITY

Who are willing to be domestic servants in a community where all are social equals?
                                                  Bellamy, *Looking Backward*, XI

Equal education and opportunity must needs bring to light whatever aptitudes a man has, and neither social prejudices nor mercenary considerations hamper him in the choice of his life work.   *Ibid.*, XII

It is the worst thing about any system which divides men, or allows them to be divided, into classes and castes, that it weakens the sense of a common humanity.   *Ibid.*, XIV

The physician must sell his healing and the apostle his preaching like the rest.   *Ibid.*

The lie of fear is the refuge of cowardice, and the lie of fraud the device of the cheat. The inequalities of men and the lust of acquisition offer a constant premium on lying.
                                                                          Ibid., XIX

It is making a devil of a man to lift him up to a state to which he is not suited.
                                          Brackenridge, *Modern Chivalry*, Part I, Volume I

Less light, more equality of vision.   *Ibid.*, Part II, Volume I

Men of this earth, of similar forms, and of like passions with ourselves, what have I to fear from them? What right have we to exclude them? We are not born for ourselves; nor did we achieve the revolution for ourselves only.   *Ibid.*, Part II, Volume II

The power of mischief is given to every one of us. It is the true, the only Equality of Man—we can all destroy.   Collins, *Blind Love*, XLIX

There is but one birth and one death to all things, be it hound or be it deer; be it redskin or white. Both are in the hands of the Lord, it being as unlawful for man to strive to haste the one, as impossible to prevent the other.   Cooper, *The Prairie*, XXVII

Worldly goods are divided unequally, and man must not repine.
                                                          Dickens, *Bleak House*, XLIX

Equality is the soul of real and cordial society.   Godwin, *St. Leon*, 210–211

Fools and wise men all come to one end.   Haggard, *People of the Mist*, V

If every one was equal, where would be the gratification I feel in getting a visit from a grandee?   James, H., *Princess Casamassima*, XXXII

Were all equal in beauty, there would be no beauty, for beauty is only by comparison. Were all equal in strength, conflicts would be interminable. Were all equal in rank, and power, and possessions, the greatest charms of existence would be destroyed: generosity, gratitude, and half the finer virtues would be unknown.
                                                  Marryat, *Mr. Midshipman Easy*, XXXVI

Games in which all may win remain as yet in this world uninvented.
                                                          Melville, *Confidence-Man*, X

No custom is strange; no creed is absurd; no foe, but who will in the end prove a friend. In heaven, at last, our good, old, white-haired father Adam will greet all alike, and sociality forever prevail.   Melville, *Mardi*, III

A king on his throne! After all, but a gentleman seated.   *Ibid.*, LX

Civilization has not ever been the brother of equality.   *Ibid.*, CLXI

Freedom was born among the wild eyries in the mountains; and barbarous tribes have sheltered under her wings, when the enlightened people of the plain have nestled under different pinions.   *Ibid.*

EQUALITY (*continued*)

In kings, mollusca, and toadstools, life is one thing and the same. *Ibid.*, CLXIII

In all things, equality is not for all. *Ibid.*, CLXXXVII

In some things, we Americans leave to other countries the carrying out of the principle of equality that stands at the head of our Declaration of Independence.
Melville, *Redburn*, XLI

To be efficacious, Virtue must come down from aloft, even as our blessed Redeemer came down to redeem our whole man-of-war world; to that end, mixing with its sailors and sinners as equals. Melville, *White Jacket*, LIV

Equality implies sentiments of the most noble and generous kind; instead of pulling down laws, and levelling the whole class of mankind, it would confirm unity, peace, and good order. Moore, *Grasville Abbey*, II

Vain equality is but contention's field. Sidney, *Arcadia*, III

It is the instinct of fallen man to hate equality, desire ascendancy, to crush, to oppress, to tyrannize, to enslave. Then, when the slave is at last free, and in his freedom demands equality, man is not great enough to take his enfranchised brother to his bosom.
Trollope, *He Knew He Was Right*, LVI

The tendency of all law-making and of all governing should be to reduce the inequalities.
Trollope, *Phineas Finn*, XIV

The natural liking of a young woman for a man in a station above her, because he is softer and cleaner and has better parts of speech—just as we keep a pretty dog if we keep a dog at all,—is one of the evils of the inequality of mankind.
Trollope, *The Way We Live Now*, XLII

If men were equal tomorrow and all wore the same coats, they would wear different coats the next day. *Ibid.*

ERROR

What avail reflections on our errors past, when wisdom itself is at a loss to find a remedy to repair them? Anonymous, *The Ladies Advocate*, 34

Who is ever displeased with a person that has been in the same error with himself?
Brackenridge, *Modern Chivalry*, Part II, Volume I

Error is always weakness. Integrity cannot save error. It can only reduce it from misdemeanor to frailty. *Ibid.*, Part II, Volume II

Error is often strong, and government is often weak. Eliot, *Felix Holt*, XIV

Error, once committed, has a fascinating power, like that ascribed to the rattlesnake, to draw us into a second error. It deprives us of that proud confidence in our own strength, to which we are indebted for so much of our virtue. Godwin, *Caleb Williams*, II

"There are no such things as mistakes." "Very true—for those who are not clever enough to perceive them. Not to recognize one's mistakes—that would be happiness in life."
James, H., *The Europeans*, I

Let us respect even error when it has its source in virtue. Lee, *The Recess*, III

The chief art of life is to learn how best to remedy mistakes.
Melville, *Israel Potter*, VII

When a wise man makes a false step, will he not go further than a fool?
Meredith, *Ordeal of Richard Feverel*, XXVI

A man who errs with his eyes open, and against conviction, is a thousand times worse for what he knows, and ten thousand times harder to be reclaimed, than if he had never known anything at all. Richardson, *Clarissa Harlowe*, II

We all err in some things. *Ibid.*, III

By our errors we see deeper into life.
Schreiner, *Story of an African Farm*, Part II, VI

Error creeps in through the minute holes and small crevices which human nature leaves unguarded. Sterne, *Tristram Shandy*, II

ESCAPE

There is commonly something extraordinary in the fortunes of those who fly from society. Fielding, H., *Tom Jones*, 378

Even in the worst of the calamities that befell patient Job, some *one* at least of his servants escaped to report it. Melville, *Redburn*, LIX

The moment had not come when she could escape from herself.
Moore, *Evelyn Innes*, XXIII

One cannot run away from a malady within. Richardson, *Clarissa Harlowe*, III

Though of all parties a garden party is the nicest, everybody is always anxious to get out of the garden as quick as may be. Trollope, *Phineas Finn*, LXIII

ESSENTIALS

The three great essentials: matter, form, and place. Sterne, *Tristram Shandy*, I

ESTEEM

Cold, lifeless esteem may grow from a long tasteless acquaintance; but real affection makes a sudden and lively impression. Brooke, *Emily Montague*, IV

People of title are less gratified with the sound of their own honors, than people of no title in pronouncing them. Burney, *Camilla*, Three, VI

Esteem is the groundwork of happiness. Gibbes, *Mr. Francis Clive*, I

Esteem people for what we find them, not what they may have been. *Ibid.*

Mutual esteem is the only substantial basis of love. Godwin, *St. Leon*, 41

Mutual esteem produces mutual desire to please. Johnson, *Rasselas*, 113

ETERNALITY; ETERNITY: *see also* TIME; PAST-PRESENT-FUTURE

I am seldom otherwise than happy while watching in the chamber of death, should no frenzied or despairing mourner share the duty with me. I see a repose that neither earth nor hell can break, and I feel an assurance of the endless and shadowless hereafter—the Eternity they have entered—where life is boundless in its duration, and love in its sympathy, and joy in its fullness. Bronte, E., *Wuthering Heights*, XVI

The immense volumes of Eternity. Burney, *Camilla*, Five, X

Eternity represented itself with all its incomprehensible additions.
Defoe, *Moll Flanders*, 298

That which long endures full-fledged, must have long lain in the germ. And duration is not of the future, but of the past; and eternity is eternal, because it has been; and though a strong new monument be builded today, it only is lasting because its blocks are old as the sun. Melville, *Mardi*, LXXV

Deeper and deeper into Time's endless tunnel, does the winged soul, like a night-hawk, wend her wild way; and finds eternities before and behind; and her last limit is her everlasting beginning. *Ibid.*

Each age thinks its own is eternal. *Ibid.*, CLXI

Throughout all eternity, the parts of the past are but parts of the future reversed.
Ibid.

The eternity to come is but a prolongation of time present: and the beginning may be more wonderful than the end.   *Ibid.*, CLXXV

Time is Eternity; and we live in Eternity now.   *Ibid.*, CLXXXV

Eternity is in his eye.   *Ibid.*, CXCV

Oh! the metempsychosis! Oh! Pythagoras, that in bright Greece, two thousand years ago, did die, so good, so wise, so mild; I sailed with thee along the Peruvian coast last voyage—and, foolish as I am, taught thee, a green simple boy, how to splice a rope!
Melville, *Moby Dick*, XCVIII

To have the sense of the eternal in life is a short flight for the soul. To have had it is the soul's vitality.   Meredith, *Diana of the Crossways*, I

And what is this poor needle's point of NOW to a boundless ETERNITY?
Richardson, *Clarissa Harlowe*, III

The terror of eternity.   Wilde, *Picture of Dorian Gray*, VIII

ETIQUETTE

Duelling was an inhuman practice always, and it is now worse—it is a breach of manners.   Meredith, *Beauchamp's Career*, XXVI

EVASION

There's nothing like a metaphor for an evasion.   Meredith, *Beauchamp's Career*, XVI

EVENTUALITY

Before the sun rises, the dew may eat your eyes out.   King, *Zalmonah*, I

EXAGGERATION

He that hath gone through many perils and returned safe from them, makes but a merriment to dilate them.   Nashe, *The Unfortunate Traveller*, 118

EXAMPLE; STANDARD: *see also* ILLUSTRATION

If there be a mirror in the world worthy to hold men's eyes, it is that country [Atlantis].
Bacon, *The New Atlantis*, 207

Example is apt to be catching, and one lady's crying makes another think she must do the same, for a little thing serves for a lady's tears, being they can cry at any time.
Burney, *Cecilia*, III

A man likes to assume superiority over himself, by holding up his bad example and sermonizing on it.   Eliot, *Middlemarch*, Book V, XLV

The general course of nature only can be a fit standard of example.
Gentleman, *A Trip to the Moon*, I

Individuals must always begin by setting the examples, which the state too slowly, though surely, will learn to copy.   Kingsley, *Alton Locke*, XL

A virtuous mind need not be shown the deformity of vice, to make it be hated and avoided; the more pure and uncorrupted our ideas are, the less shall we be influenced by example.   Lennox, *The Female Quixote*, II

Few things are harder to put up with than the annoyance of a good example.
Twain, *Pudd'nhead Wilson*, XIX

EXCELLENCE: *see also* MERIT

The best maxim that ever came into the mind of man: *one thing at once.*
Brackenridge, *Modern Chivalry*, Part I, Volume I

In America, excellence in nothing is justly appreciated, nor is it often recognized; and the suffrages of the nation are pretty uniformly bestowed on qualities of a second class. Numbers have sway, and it is as impossible to resist them in deciding on merit, as it is to deny their power in the ballot boxes. Cooper, *Sea Lions*, I

You have constantly acquired some new excellence, like a snowball.
Fielding, H., *Joseph Andrews*, 221

EXCEPTION

Every man thinks he will be the exception. Disraeli, *Sybil*, Book II, XVI

EXCESS

Nothing is bad, but as far as it is practiced to excess, or attended with accidental evils which defeat the promised end; or, in short, when the abuse of it is greater than its use.
Anonymous, *The Adventures of a Jesuit*, II

Excesses carry with them the principles of their own destruction.
Cleland, *Memoirs of a Coxcomb*, 311

All passions are criminal in their excess; and even love itself, if it is not subservient to our duty, may render us blind to it. Fielding, H., *Joseph Andrews*, 265

All excess is vicious; even that sorrow which is amiable in its origin, becomes a selfish and unjust passion if indulged at the expense of our duties.
Radcliffe, *The Mysteries of Udolpho*, I

EXCHANGE

A fair day's wage for a fair day's work. Disraeli, *Sybil*, Book VI, VI

EXCITATION: *see also* ANXIETY; EMOTIONS; etc.

Mrs. Bennet was quite in the fidgets. Austen, *Pride and Prejudice*, Volume III, XI

EXCUSE

Women will suggest a thousand excuses to themselves for the folly of those they like.
Fielding, H., *Tom Jones*, 509

A plaster is a small amends for a broken head, and a bad excuse will not purge an ill accuser. Lyly, *Euphues and His England*, 324

Are not excuses confessions of excuses inexcusable?
Richardson, *Clarissa Harlowe*, I

What poor excuses will good heads make for the evils they are put upon by bad hearts!
Ibid., IV

He who can sit down premeditatedly to do a bad action will content himself with a bad excuse: and yet, what fools must he suppose the rest of the world to be, if he imagines them as easy to be imposed upon as he can impose upon himself? *Ibid.*

The offering of an excuse in a blamable matter is the undoubted mark of a disingenuous, if not of a perverse mind. *Ibid.*

EXCUSE (*continued*)

Excuses are more than tacit confessions.

Richardson, *Sir Charles Grandison*, Two, III

EXECUTION: *see also* DEATH

He who is taken out to pass through a fair scene to the scaffold, thinks not of the flowers that smile on his road, but of the block and axe-edge; of the disseverment of bone and vein; of the grave gaping at the end. Bronte, C., *Jane Eyre*, XXVII

Off with their heads! Carroll, *Alice in Wonderland*, VIII

They're dreadfully fond of beheading people here: the great wonder is, that there's any one left alive! *Ibid.*

Our Saxon ancestors, fierce as they were in war, had but few executions in times of peace. Goldsmith, *The Vicar of Wakefield*, 160

It is not necessary that we should know a man's name in order to hang him.

Simms, *Woodcraft*, XXV

EXILE

The Bostonian who leaves Boston ought to be condemned to perpetual exile.

Howells, *Silas Lapham*, V

EXPECTATION; REALIZATION: *see also* HOPE

It is always the unexpected that happens. Conrad, *Lord Jim*, VIII

No one thinks of certain habits, opinions, manners, and tastes, in the circle where they are expected to be found. Cooper, *Satanstoe*, Volume I, III

Nothing ever happens but the *un*foreseen. DuMaurier, *Trilby*, IV

Nothing is so good as it seems beforehand. Eliot, *Silas Marner*, XVIII

All earthly enjoyments promise mountains in the expectation, but are only shadows in the possession. Kirkby, *The Capacity of Human Understanding*, 222-223

One likes to know the worst, and what's possible.

Meredith, *Beauchamp's Career*, XXIX

Certainty must be preferable to suspense. Richardson, *Clarissa Harlowe*, I

Very seldom is it that high expectations are so much as tolerably answered. *Ibid.*, II

To dwell long in expectation of an event that may be decided in a quarter hour is grievous. *Ibid.*, IV

Impending evil is always the most terrible.

Richardson, *Sir Charles Grandison*, Three, VII

'Tis by looking forward to future pleasures we are enabled to bear present ills; without hope, none of us could boast of enduring spirits to support misfortunes.

Roche, *Nocturnal Visit*, I

EXPERIENCE: *see also* EDUCATION; KNOWLEDGE AND LEARNING; LIFE

Experience is a severe mistress, but she makes her scholars truly wise.

Anonymous, *Memoirs of a Coquet*, 106

One cannot reason with inexperience. Atherton, *Doomswoman*, XXIV

How can you form an idea of the enjoyment of a refreshing draught if you have never been dry? August, *Horrid Mysteries*, I

Experience is a great softener of the mind; it gives knowledge.
Brackenridge, *Modern Chivalry*, Part II, Volume I

It is foolish to wish for beauty. Sensible people never either desire it for themselves, or care about it in others. If the mind be but well cultivated, and the heart well disposed, no one ever cares for the exterior. All very judicious and proper, no doubt; but are such assertions supported by actual experience? Bronte, A., *Agnes Grey*, XVII

Alas, Experience! No other mentor has so wasted and frozen a face as yours: none wears a robe so black, none bears a rod so heavy, none with hand so inexorable draws the novice so sternly to his task, and forces him with authority so resistless to its acquirement.
Bronte, C., *Shirley*, VII

The longer we live, the more our experience widens; the less prone are we to judge our neighbor's conduct, to question the world's wisdom. Bronte, C., *Villette*, XXVII

Neither man nor wood comes to the uses of life till the green leaves are stripped and the sap gone. Bulwer, *The Caxtons*, Book VII, VII

Were I asked what best dignifies the present, and consecrates the past; what enables us alone to draw a just moral from the tale of life; what sheds the purest light upon our reason; what gives the firmest strength to our religion; and, whether our remaining years pass in seclusion or in action, is best fitted to soften the heart of man, and to elevate the soul to God, I would answer, "Experience."
Bulwer, *Devereux*, Book VI, VIII

No man can tell what in combat attends us, but he that hath been in the battle himself.
Bunyan, *Pilgrim's Progress*, 133

The saddest things that are left to one of a bitter experience are the knowledge and distrust that come of it. Burnett, *Through One Administration*, XXX

'Tis in the bitterness of personal proof alone that experience comes home with conviction.
Burney, *Camilla*, One, I

Man develops but little, though he experiences much. *Ibid.*, Five, X

Though discernment teaches us the folly of others, experience singly can teach us our own. Burney, *Cecilia*, I

He jests at scars who never felt a wound. *Ibid.*, II

There's many a good tune played on an old fiddle. Butler, *The Way of All Flesh*, LXI

Where is the faultless human creature who can persevere in a good resolution without sometimes failing and falling back? Where is the woman who has ever really torn from her heart the image that has been once fixed in it by a true love? Books tell us that such unearthly creatures have existed; but what does our own experience say in answer to books? Collins, *The Woman in White*, Part I, Second Epoch

Your young man, who gathers his learning from books and can measure what he knows by the page, may conceit that his knowledge, like his legs, outruns that of his father; but where experience is the master, the scholar is made to know the value of years, and respects them accordingly. Cooper, *The Last of the Mohicans*, XXI

Every trail has its end, and every calamity brings its lesson. *Ibid.*, XXV

He that has seen much is apt to think much. Cooper, *The Prairie*, XXIX

Men never know themselves till they are tried, and courage is acquired by time and experience. Defoe, *Colonel Jack*, 208

I bought all my experience before I had it. Defoe, *Robinson Crusoe*, 98

Experientia does it. Dickens, *David Copperfield*, XI

When men are young, they want experience; and when they have gained experience, they want energy. Disraeli, *Coningsby*, Book III, I

Great men never want experience. *Ibid.*

Experience is the child of Thought, and Thought is the child of Action. We cannot learn men from books.   Disraeli, *Vivian Grey*, Book V, I

Experience is an article that may be borrowed with safety, and is often dearly bought.
                                                      Edgeworth, *The Absentee*, IV

In the chequered area of human experience the seasons are all mingled as in the golden age: fruit and blossom hang together; in the same moment the sickle is reaping and the seed is sprinkled; one tends the green cluster and another treads the wine-press.
                                                      Eliot, *Daniel Deronda*, LXX

Has it not by this time ceased to be remarkable—is it not rather what we expect in men, that they should have numerous strands of experience lying side by side and never compare them with each other?   Eliot, *Middlemarch*, Book VI, LVIII

Without use and experience, the strongest minds and bodies both will stagger under a weight which habit might render easy and even contemptible.
                                                      Fielding, H., *Amelia*, II

When thou art a father, thou wilt be capable then only of knowing what a father can feel.
                                                      Fielding, H., *Joseph Andrews*, 267

Experience, long conversant with the wise, the good, the learned, and the polite. Nor with them only, but with every kind of character, from the minister at his levee, to the bailiff in his sponging-house; from the duchess at her drum, to the landlady behind her bar.   Fielding, H., *Tom Jones*, 599

Experience teaches fools.   Galt, *Annals*, XLIII

Experience is as to intensity, and not as to duration.   Hardy, *Tess*, XIX

Sheer experience had already taught her that, in some circumstances, there was one thing better than to lead a good life, and that was to be saved from leading any life whatever.   *Ibid.*, XXXVI

The past of one's experience doesn't differ a great deal from the past of one's knowledge.
                                                      Howells, *Silas Lapham*, XIV

The cup of experience is a poisoned drink.   James, H., *Portrait of a Lady*, XV

We can never describe what we have not seen.   Johnson, *Rasselas*, 48

That some places may operate upon our own minds in an uncommon manner is an opinion which hourly experience will justify.   *Ibid.*, 53

Experience is the only teacher.   Melville, *Confidence-Man*, IX

Experience, the only true knowledge.   *Ibid.*, XL

I have swum through libraries and sailed through oceans.
                                                      Melville, *Moby Dick*, XXXII

"Has experience the same opinion of the world as ignorance?" "It should have more charity."   Meredith, *The Egoist*, VII

Years are the teachers of the great rocky natures, whom they round and sap and pierce in caverns, having them on all sides, and striking deep inward at moments. There is no resisting the years, if we have a heart and a common understanding.
                                                      Meredith, *Lord Ormont*, XXX

Experience, old Time's fruit, hateful to the palate of youth.
                                                      Meredith, *Ordeal of Richard Feverel*, IX

Experience of trouble has made me older.   Meredith, *Vittoria*, XLIV

The experience of the world, being learned, cannot easily be forgotten.
                                                      More, *Utopia*, I

Experience will inevitably teach us that the laws for a wise and noble life have a foundation infinitely deeper than the fiat of any being, God or man, even in the groundwork of human nature.   Schreiner, *Story of an African Farm*, Part II, II

All is but lip-wisdom which wants experience.   Sidney, *Arcadia*, I

Was ever any dazzled with the moon that used his eyes to the beams of the sun?
Ibid., III

The experience which tutors pride to a just humility is perhaps the best sort of lessoning.
Simms, *Vasconselos*, XXXII

An uninitiated man cannot take upon himself to portray the great world accurately, and had best keep his opinions to himself whatever they are.
Thackeray, *Vanity Fair*, LI

Experience, that unvarying and rational order of the world which has been the appointed instrument of man's training since life and thought began.
Ward, *Robert Elsmere*, Book V, XL

Experience is of no ethical value. It is merely the name men give to their mistakes.
Wilde, *The Picture of Dorian Gray*, IV

There is no motive power in experience. It is as little of an active cause as conscience itself.   *Ibid.*

We can have in life but one great experience at best, and the secret of life is to reproduce that experience as often as possible.   *Ibid.*, XVII

Variety of disappointments ought to give more penetration.
Young, *The Adventures of Emmera*, I

EXPLANATION: *see also* EDUCATION; LEARNING AND KNOWLEDGE; etc.

Explanations take such a dreadful time.   Carroll, *Alice in Wonderland*, X

In our eagerness to explain impressions, we often lose our hold of the sympathy that comprehends them.   Eliot, *Adam Bede*, IV

The actual experience of even the most ordinary life is full of events that never explain themselves, either as regards their origin or their tendency.
Hawthorne, *Marble Faun*, L

What nuisance can be so great to a man busied with immense affairs, as to have to explain, or to attempt to explain, small details to men incapable of understanding them?
Trollope, *The Way We Live Now*, XXXVII

If there be a proceeding which an official man dislikes worse than another, it is a demand for a written explanation.   Trollope, *The Eustace Diamonds*, LVI

EXPLORATION: *see also* ADVENTURE

Exploring is delightful to look forward to and back upon, but it is not comfortable at the time, unless it be of such an easy nature as not to deserve the name.
Butler, *Erewhon*, IV

EXPRESSION: *see also* ARGUMENTATION; PREACHMENT; etc.

A *bon mot* is a *bon mot* only because it represents a thing which everyone thinks, and expresses it in a lively, delicate, and new manner.
Anonymous, *The Peregrinations of Jeremiah Grant*, 92–93

Those speeches look best in the Record which make no appeal to the gallery.
Atherton, *Senator North*, Book I, XV

I cannot speak well enough to be unintelligible.   Austen, *Northanger Abbey*, XVI

The portraits seemed to be staring in astonishment.　　　　Austen, *Persuasion*, V

A person who can write a long letter with ease cannot write ill.
　　　　　　　　　　　　　　Austen, *Pride and Prejudice*, Volume I, X

He studies too much for words of four syllables.　　　　　　　　*Ibid.*

We are each of an unsocial, taciturn disposition, unwilling to speak, unless we expect to say something that will amaze the whole room, and be handed down to posterity with all the eclat of a proverb.　　　　　　　　　　　*Ibid.*, Volume I, XVIII

It was impossible for her to say what she did not feel.
　　　　　　　　　　　　Austen, *Sense and Sensibility*, Volume I, XXI

Their tongues quivered like aspen leaves.　　　　　Beckford, *Vathek*, 178

There is a great difference between a vulgar term or phrase, and that which is common, and comes first upon the tongue, in easy and familiar conversation. Ought not language to be precisely the same whether spoken or written?
　　　　　　　　　　Brackenridge, *Modern Chivalry*, Part I, Volume III

What is eloquence but good sense expressed in clear language?
　　　　　　　　　　　　　　　　Ibid., Part II, Volume IV

And now I think I have said sufficient.　　　Bronte, A., *Agnes Grey*, last line

"I only know three phrases of English, and a few words; par exemple, de sonn, de mone, de stare—est ce bien dit?"　　　　　　　Bronte, C., *Villette*, XV

Expression is feeble when emotions are exquisite.
　　　　　　　　　　　　Brown, W. H., *The Power of Sympathy*, 48

With the cultivation of the masses the literature of the affections has awakened. Every sentiment finds an expositor, every feeling an oracle.
　　　　　　　　　　　　　　Bulwer, *The Caxtons*, Book VII, I

I was born with many of the sentiments of the poet, but without the language to express them.　　　　　　　　　Bulwer, *The Pilgrim of the Rhine*, XXIII

A good tongue is a good weapon.　　Bulwer, *What Will He Do with It?*, Book II, II

Notwithstanding his fine tongue Talkative is but a sorry fellow.
　　　　　　　　　　　　　　Bunyan, *Pilgrim's Progress*, 80

To them who have not thorough acquaintance with him, Talkative seems to be a very pretty man; for he is best abroad; near home he is ugly enough.　　　　*Ibid.*

Talkative is for any company and for any talk.　　　　　　　　*Ibid.*

Religion hath no place in Talkative's heart, or house, or conversation.　　*Ibid.*

All Talkative hath lieth in his tongue, and his religion is to make a noise therewith.
　　　　　　　　　　　　　　　　　　　　　Ibid.

A happy citation of one *bon mot* is worth any ten offenses.　Burney, *Camilla*, Five, IX

Ill usage is as hard to relate as to be endured.　　　　Burney, *Cecilia*, III

Those wrongs, which though too trifling to resent, are too humiliating to be borne, speech can convey no idea of; the soul must feel, or the understanding can never comprehend them.　　　　　　　　　　　　　　　*Ibid.*

The language of gems is as much more important than that of flowers as the imperishable gem is itself more enduring than the withering, the evanescent blossom.
　　　　　　　　　　　　　Cable, *Bonaventure*, Book III, III

Speak in French when you can't think of the English for a thing—turn out your toes as you walk—and remember who you are!　Carroll, *Through the Looking Glass*, II

Language is worth a thousand pounds a word!　　　　　　*Ibid.*, III

The power of sentences has nothing to do with their sense or the logic of their construction.   Conrad, *Lord Jim*, VI

A word carries far—very far—deals destruction through time as the bullets go flying through space.   *Ibid.*, XV

There is a vast difference between understanding and speaking a foreign tongue.
                                              Cooper, *The Last of the Mohicans*, XVI

When a man has told all he has to say, the sooner he is silent the better.
                                                            Cooper, *Ned Myers*, XIX

A talking man is no better than a barking dog.   Cooper, *The Prairie*, VIII

Woman's rhetoric, tears.   Defoe, *Moll Flanders*, 314

It is not meet that every nice offense should bear its comment.
                                              Dickens, *David Copperfield*, LVII

"I'm gormed—and I can't say no fairer than that!"   *Ibid.*, LXIII

I dispense with style!   Dickens, *Little Dorrit*, Book I, XXX

I could have bore it with a thankful art. But the words she spoke, lambs could not forgive, nor worms forget.   Dickens, *Martin Chuzzlewit*, XLIX

Which fiddle-strings is weakness to expredge my nerves!   *Ibid.*, LI

They are very charming apartments. They command an uninterrupted view of—of over the way, and they are within one minute's walk of—of the corner of the street.
                                              Dickens, *Old Curiosity Shop*, XXXIV

It was a maxim with Mr. Brass that the habit of paying compliments kept a man's tongue oiled without any expense; and, as that useful member ought never to grow rusty or creak in turning on its hinges in the case of a practitioner of the law, in whom it should be always glib and easy, he lost few opportunities of improving himself by the utterance of handsome speeches and eulogistic expressions.   *Ibid.*, XXXV

An ordinary exclamation often denotes that the mind is more stirring than it cares to acknowledge, or at the moment is capable to express.   Disraeli, *Sybil*, Book II, V

It is wonderful how soon a man falls into the cant of his position and learns to dole out the cut-and-dried phrases of ministerial talk like a sort of spiritual phonograph.
                                              Dunbar, *The Uncalled*, XIII

Much of human speech is mere purposeless impulse or habit.   Eliot, *Adam Bede*, V

He was an amateur of superior phrases, and never used poor language without immediately correcting himself.   Eliot, *Middlemarch*, Book III, XXXII

All phrases of mere compliment have their turn to be true. A man is occasionally grateful when he says "Thank you."   Eliot, *Mill on the Floss*, Book VI, II

No compliment can be eloquent, except as an expression of indifference.   *Ibid.*

Nature adorns the peacock with various colored beauties; but hath left the choice in the bird's own power, either to drop down its feathers in almost one indistinguishable lump, or to open and display their lustre in the sun.
                                  Fielding, S., *History of the Countess of Dellwyn*, I

It is only in books that people taken by surprise adjure each other in polished phraseology.
                                              Harrison, *The Anglomaniacs*, III

Many words of deep significance, many entire sentences, and those possibly the most important ones, have flown too far on the winged breeze to be recovered.
                                              Hawthorne, *The Marble Faun*, XI

He was convinced of the emptiness of rhetorical sound, and the inefficacy of polished periods and studied sentences.   Johnson, *Rasselas*, 79

His discourse was cheerful without levity and pious without enthusiasm.   *Ibid.*, 86

There are a thousand familiar disputes which reason never can decide.
Ibid., 113-114

The empty vessel giveth a greater sound than the full barrel.   Lyly, *Euphues*, 102

The sincere affection of the mind cannot be expressed by the mouth, and no art can unfold the entire love of the heart.   *Ibid.*, 106

I beseech you not to measure the firmness of my faith, by the fewness of my words, but rather think that the overflowing waves of good will will leave no passage for many words.   *Ibid.*

His favorite author, Carlyle, was one writing of Heroes, in a style resembling either early architecture or utter dilapidation, so loose and rough it seemed.
Meredith, *Beauchamp's Career*, II

Renee's gift of speech counted unnumbered strings which she played on with a grace that clothed the skill, and was her natural endowment—an art perfected by the education of the world. Who cannot talk!—but who can? Discover the writers in a day when all are writing! It is as rare an art as poetry, and in the mouths of women as enrapturing, richer than their voices in music.   *Ibid.*, XXIV

It is not high flying, which usually ends in heavy falling.   *Ibid.*

The habitually and professedly cynical should not deliver themselves at length: for as soon as they miss their customary incision of speech they are apt to aim to recover it in loquacity, and thus it may be that the survey of their ideas becomes disordered.
Ibid., XXXVI

Time goes forward, and you go round. Speak to the point.   *Ibid.*, XLIII

Between the vulgarity of romantic language, and the baldness of commonplace, it seemed that English gives us no choice; that we cannot be dignified in simplicity.
Ibid., XLVII

The expressions seemed the labored sentiments of a man fearful he should not say enough and therefore ran into the contrary extreme, and said too much.
Parsons, *The Mysterious Warning*, IV

Man does not speak by words alone. A mute glance of reproach has pierced the heart a tirade would have left untouched; and even an inarticulate cry may utter volumes.
Reade, *Griffith Gaunt*, X

Air and manner often express more than the accompanying words.
Richardson, *Clarissa Harlowe*, I

True respect, true value, lies not in words: words cannot express it. The silent awe, the humble, the doubting eye, and even the hesitating voice, better show it by much than, as Shakespeare says, "The rattling tongue/Of saucy and audacious eloquence."   *Ibid.*

Short sentences drive themselves into the heart and stay there.   *Ibid.*, II

In long discourses, one good thing drives out another, till all is forgotten.   *Ibid.*

Do not write with too much violence to be clear.   *Ibid.*, III

Words are weak.   *Ibid.*

Must not a person be capable of premeditated art who can sit down to write, and not write from the heart?   *Ibid.*

Little said is soon amended.   *Ibid.*

This *innocent* house: long have my ears been accustomed to such inversions of words.
Ibid.

French expression professes more than it performs.
Sterne, *A Sentimental Journey*, 53

Writing, when properly managed, is but a different name for conversation.
Sterne, Tristram Shandy, II

In writing it is as in travelling. If a man is in haste to be at home, if his horse be tired with long riding and ill ways, I advise him clearly to make the straightest and commonest road.
Swift, A Tale of a Tub, XI

I am now trying an experiment very frequent among modern authors; which is, to write upon nothing: When the subject is utterly exhausted, to let the pen still move on; by some called, the ghost of wit, delighting to walk after the death of its body.
Ibid., "The Conclusion"

When a man can say what he likes with the certainty that every word will be reported, and can speak to those around him as one manifestly their superior, he always looms large.
Trollope, The Eustace Diamonds, XXXV

Do what one may, there is no getting an air of variety into a court circular. There is a profound monotonousness about its facts that baffles and defeats one's sincerest efforts to make them sparkle and enthuse.
Twain, Connecticut Yankee, XXVI

Clarence's way [of reporting in the court circular] was good, it was simple, it was dignified, it was direct and businesslike; all I say is, it was not the best way:

COURT CIRCULAR.

On Monday, the King rode in the park.
 " Tuesday, "   "   "   " "   "
 " Wednesday,   "   "   " "   "
 " Thursday,   "   "   " "   "
 " Friday, "   "   "   " "   "
 " Saturday,"   "   "   " "   "
 " Sunday, "   "   "   " "   "

Ibid.

Words are only painted fire; a look is the fire itself.
Ibid., XXXV

Everything was dead quiet, and it looked late, and smelt late. You know what I mean—I don't know the words to put it in.
Twain, Huckleberry Finn, VII

Eloquence was a native gift of Joan of Arc; it came from her lips without effort and without preparation. Her words were as sublime as her deeds, as sublime as her character; they had their source in a great heart and were coined in a great brain.
Twain, Joan of Arc, Book III, XI

EXTERMINATION

Extermination is good doctrine.   Dickens, A Tale of Two Cities, Book III, XII

EXTREMES: see also AMBIVALENCE; COMPARISON/CONTRAST; etc.

Everlasting flame, or everlasting dishonor—nothing between!
DuMaurier, Trilby, V

Extremes inevitably meet. The bear can dance, and the monkey, which is one of the most sportive, if not the most formidable, is one of the most malignant of the wild tribes of the forest. A frivolous people is apt to be a savage people; and the most desperate Indian warriors prefer the looking-glass worn about their necks to any other ornament.
Simms, The Scout, XXVII

Gratitude and treachery are merely the two extremities of the same procession.
Twain, Pudd'nhead Wilson, XVIII

EXTROVERTEDNESS; INTROVERTEDNESS

Reserved people often really need the frank discussion of their sentiments and griefs more than the expansive. The sternest-seeming stoic is human after all; and to "burst" with boldness and good will into "the silent sea" of their souls, is often to confer on them the first of obligations.
Bronte, C., Jane Eyre, XXXII

EYES

The eye, though it does not tell all, tells much. It is the key of character, the mirror of the soul.
Cable, *Bonaventure*, Book III, III

I have a pair of eyes, and that's just it. If they wos a pair o' patent double million magnifyin' gas microscopes of hextra power, p'raps I might be able to see through a flight o' stairs and a deal door; but bein' only eyes, you see, my wision's limited.
Dickens, *Pickwick Papers*, XXXIV

Thou lookest far into eternity, with those bright eyes! Then tell me what thou seest?
Hawthorne, *Scarlet Letter*, XXIII

The eye only sees that which brings with it the power of seeing.
Kingsley, *Alton Locke*, I

Watch your enemy's eyes, not his blade.
Lawrence, G., *Guy Livingstone*, XIX

The eye is the index of the soul, and expresses every passion of the mind.
Lawrence, H., *The Contemplative Man*, I

True love lacketh a tongue, and is tried by the eyes, which in a heart that meaneth well, are as far from wanton glances as the mind is from idle thoughts.
Lyly, *Euphues and His England*, 392

The eye is the messenger of love, not the master; the ear is the carrier of news, the heart the digester.
Ibid., 397

What is it that makes the front of a man—what, indeed, but his eyes?
Melville, *Moby Dick*, LXXIV

Man may be said to look out on the world from a sentry-box with two joined sashes for his window.
Ibid.

Gazing into the depths of her strange blue eyes, when she was in a contemplative mood, they seemed most placid yet unfathomable; but when illuminated by some lively emotion, they beamed upon a beholder like stars.
Melville, *Typee*, XI

The rivals held their pistols lowered, but fixed their deadly eyes on each other. The eye, in such a circumstance, is a terrible thing: it is literally a weapon of destruction, for it directs the deadly hand that guides the deadly bullet.
Reade, *Griffith Gaunt*, VI

Should the eye be disgusted when the heart is to be engaged?
Richardson, *Clarissa Harlowe*, I

The eye, the wicked eye, has such a strict alliance with the heart, and both have such enmity to the understanding!
Ibid., II

The eye is a traitor, and ought ever to be mistrusted.
Ibid.

A pretty country within the eye.
Ibid.

The eye is the casement at which the heart generally looks out.
Ibid., III

The eye, rather than the judgment, is usually the director of a young woman's affections.
Richardson, *Sir Charles Grandison*, Three, VI

Eyes which threatened they would drown his face.
Sidney, *Arcadia*, I

An eye is like a cannon in this respect: It is not so much the eye or the cannon, in themselves, as it is the carriage of the eye—and the carriage of the cannon, by which both the one and the other are enabled to do so much execution.
Sterne, *Tristram Shandy*, VIII

FACT

Entrenching himself behind an undeniable fact.
Alcott, *Little Women*, XXXV

They demanded facts from him, as if facts could explain anything.
Conrad, *Lord Jim*, IV

It is impossible to lay the ghost of a fact. *Ibid.*, XIX

The language of facts, that are so often more enigmatic than the craftiest arrangement of words. *Ibid.*, XXXVI

Arranging a fact by reason is embarrassing, and admits of cavilling; while adapting a reason to a fact is a natural, easy, everyday, and sometimes necessary, process.
Cooper, *The Monikins*, Conclusion

Facts make life long—not years. Crawford, *Don Orsino*, XV

Facts alone are wanted in life. Dickens, *Hard Times*, Book I, I

An unaccommodating grasp, like a stubborn fact. *Ibid.*

What is called Taste is only another name for Fact. *Ibid.*, Book I, II

You are to be in all things regulated and governed by fact. We hope to have, before long, a board of fact, composed of commissioners of fact, who will force the people to be a people of fact, and of nothing but fact. You must discard the word Fancy altogether. You have nothing to do with it. *Ibid.*

Mrs. Gradgrind's stock of facts in general was woefully defective; but Mr. Gradgrind in raising her to her high matrimonial position, had been influenced by two reasons. Firstly, she was most satisfactory as a question of figures; and, secondly, she had "no nonsense" about her. *Ibid.*, Book I, IV

It is so very rarely that facts hit that nice medium required by our own enlightened opinions and refined taste. Eliot, *Adam Bede*, XVII

We are all humiliated by the sudden discovery of a fact which has existed very comfortably and perhaps been staring at us in private while we have been making up our world entirely without it. Eliot, *Middlemarch*, Book IV, XXXV

Italian asseverations of any questionable fact, however true they may chance to be, have no witness of their truth in the faces of those who utter them.
Hawthorne, *The Marble Faun*, XLIV

Minutiae are of more service than a thousand oaths, vows, and protestations made to supply the neglect of them. Richardson, *Clarissa Harlowe*, II

All true facts of nature or the mind are related.
Schreiner, *The Story of an African Farm*, Part II, II

It ain't a philosophy at all—it's a fact. Twain, *Pudd'nhead Wilson*, XIX

Facts fled before philosophy like frightened forest things.
Wilde, *The Picture of Dorian Gray*, III

FAILURE: *see also* SUCCESS

Men who can talk freely, but do nothing, fail in everything they attempt. There is too much vision mixed with the fact. Brackenridge, *Modern Chivalry*, Part II, I

Failure after long perseverance is much grander than never to have a striving good enough to be called a failure. Eliot, *Middlemarch*, Book II, XXII

There is no sorrow I have thought more about than that—to love what is great, and try to reach it, and yet to fail. *Ibid.*, Book VIII, LXXVI

A man has no business to fail; least of all can he expect others to have time to look back upon him or pity him if he sink under the stress of conflict.
Gissing, *New Grub Street*, XIX

FAINTING

The fainting of a person in a crowd is a signal for everybody else to make fools of themselves. Eggleston, *The Hoosier Schoolmaster*, XXXI

FAINTING (*continued*)

Faintness is such a queer thing that to think of it is to have it.
Hardy, *The Hand of Ethelberta*, VI

FAITH: *see also* BELIEF; RELIGION; TRUTH; etc.

The more religious faith is shaken, the greater is the temptation to supply its place by a ritual.
Bates, *Puritans*, XIII

His heart assured him that a want of faith was a want of nature.
Disraeli, *Coningsby*, Book III, II

Where can we find faith in a nation of sectaries?
Ibid., Book IV, XIII

Love is faith, and faith, like a gathered flower, will rootlessly live on.
Hardy, *A Pair of Blue Eyes*, XXIII

Loss of faith is ever one of the saddest results of sin.
Hawthorne, *Scarlet Letter*, V

The faith of men though it try in their words, it freezeth in their works.
Lyly, *Euphues*, 127

A thing may be incredible and still be true; sometimes it is incredible because it is true. And many infidels but disbelieve the least incredible things; and many bigots reject the most obvious.
Melville, *Mardi*, XCVII

Let us not turn round upon friends, confounding them with foes. For dissenters only assent to more than we.
Ibid.

Though we be all Christians now, the best of us had perhaps been otherwise in the days of Thomas.
Ibid.

The higher the intelligence, the more faith, and the less credulity: Gabriel rejects more than we, but outbelieves us all.
Ibid.

The greatest marvels are first truths; and first truths the last unto which we attain. Things nearest are furthest off. Though your ear be next-door to your brain, it is forever removed from your sight.
Ibid.

Man has a more comprehensive view of the moon, than the man in the moon himself.
Ibid.

'Tis not the dying for a faith that's so hard—every man of every nation has done that—
'tis the living up to it that is difficult.
Thackeray, *Henry Esmond*, Book I, VI

Faith laughs at the impossible.
Tourgée, *Bricks Without Straw*, LXII

Scepticism is the beginning of faith.
Wilde, *The Picture of Dorian Gray*, XVII

The things one feels absolutely certain about are never true. That is the fatality of faith, and the lesson of romance.
Ibid., XIX

FALLACY: *see also* ERROR; FALSEHOOD; TRUTH; etc.

A common fallacy: to imagine a measure will be easy because we have private motives for desiring it.
Eliot, *Silas Marner*, XVII

FALSEHOOD; IMPROBABILITY: *see also* FALLACY; TRUTH; etc.

Falsehood triumphed. It triumphed through doubt, through stupidity, through pity, through sentimentalism.
Conrad, *Nigger of the Narcissus*, V

The strong, effective and respectable bond of a sentimental lie.
Ibid.

Truth and falsehood, inseparable companions, it would seem, throughout all time.
Cooper, *Mercedes of Castile*, XI

Lies is lies. Howsever they come, they didn't ought to come, and they come from the father of lies, and work round to the same. Dickens, *Great Expectations*, IX

Falsehood is so easy, truth so difficult. Eliot, *Adam Bede*, XVII

The prevarication and white lies which a mind that keeps itself ambitiously pure is as uneasy under as a great artist under the false touches that no eye detects but his own, are worn as lightly as mere trimmings when once the actions have become a lie. Eliot, *Silas Marner*, XIII

He made many shuffling and evasive answers, not boldly lying out, which, perhaps, would have succeeded, but poorly and vainly endeavoring to reconcile falsehood with truth; an attempt which seldom fails to betray the most practiced deceiver. Fielding, H., *Amelia*, I

Those who will tell one fib will hardly stick at another. Fielding, H., *Tom Jones*, 87

Thwackum then applied himself to the vice of lying, on which head he was altogether learned. *Ibid.*, 88

This artful and refined distinction between communicating a lie and telling one. *Ibid.*, 286

It is possible for a man to convey a lie in the words of truth. *Ibid.*, 853

Falsehood learns people to disregard truth, and we cannot expect those whom we teach to lie for our convenience should forbear it when it may turn to their advantage. Fielding, S., *The History of Ophelia*, I

It is only by following a falsehood through all its doublings that it can be effectually destroyed. Godwin, *St. Leon*, 320

A compact that is false between two is equally so between a hundred or a hundred thousand; for as ten millions of circles can never make a square, so the united voice of myriads cannot lend the smallest foundation to falsehood. It is thus that reason speaks, and untutored nature says the same thing. Goldsmith, *The Vicar of Wakefield*, 159

Nobody has any conscience about adding to the improbabilities of a marvellous tale. Hawthorne, *The Marble Faun*, IV

He had spoken the very truth, and transformed it into the veriest falsehood. Hawthorne, *The Scarlet Letter*, XI

To the untrue man, the whole universe is false—it is impalpable—it shrinks to nothing within his grasp. And he himself, in so far as he shows himself in a false light, becomes a shadow, or, indeed, ceases to exist. *Ibid.*

A lie is never good, even though death threaten on the other side. *Ibid.*, XVII

Tongues were made to lie. Hudson, *The Purple Land*, XX

I knew a young man once, he was a most conscientious fellow and, when he took to fly-fishing, he determined never to exaggerate his hauls by more than twenty-five per cent.

"When I have caught forty fish," said he, "then I will tell people that I have caught fifty, and so on. But I will not lie any more than that, because it is sinful to lie."

But the twenty-five per cent plan did not work well at all. He never was able to use it. The greatest number of fish he ever caught in one day was three, and you can't add twenty-five per cent to three—at least, not in fish.

So he increased his percentage to thirty-three-and-a-third, but that, again, was awkward, when he had only caught one or two; so, to simplify matters, he made up his mind to double the quantity.

He stuck to this arrangement for a couple of months, and then he grew dissatisfied with it. Nobody believed him when he told them that he only doubled, and he, therefore, gained no credit that way whatever, while his moderation put him at a disadvantage among the other anglers. When he had really caught three small fish, and said he had caught six, it used to make him quite jealous to hear a man, whom he knew for a fact had only caught one, going about telling people he had landed two dozen.

So, eventually he made one final arrangement with himself, which he has religiously held to ever since, and that was to count each fish that he caught as ten, and to assume ten to begin with. For example, if he did not catch any fish at all, then he said he had caught ten fish—you could never catch less than ten fish by his system; that was the foundation of it. Then, if by any chance he really did catch one fish, he called it twenty, while two fish would count thirty, three forty, and so on.

It is a simple and easily worked plan, and there has been some talk lately of its being made use of by the angling fraternity in general. Indeed, The Committee of the Thames Anglers' Association did recommend its adoption about two years ago, but some of the older members opposed it. They said they would consider the idea if the number were doubled, and each fish counted as twenty. Jerome, *Three Men in a Boat*, XVII

Falsehood is a species of corruption, and no falsehood is more hateful than the falsehood of history. Lennox, *The Female Quixote*, II

The only excellence of falsehood is its resemblance to truth. *Ibid.*

The whale, like all things that are mighty, wears a false brow to the common world. Melville, *Moby Dick*, LXXX

Falsehood hemmed him in to the narrowest ring that ever statue stood on, if he meant to be stone. Meredith, *Beauchamp's Career*, XLI

The liar must eat his lie. Meredith, *Ordeal of Richard Feverel*, XIII

Where is the thief that cannot lie with a smooth face?
Reade, *The Cloister and the Hearth*, XXXIII

Is a thief never a liar? Is he not aye a liar? *Ibid.*, XXXV

Our lies are as inferior to the lies of the ancients as our statues, and for the same reason; we do not study nature as they did. We are imitators, servum pecus. *Ibid.*, LXXII

A lie has no bounds at all. The nature of the thing is to ramify beyond human qualifications. *Ibid.*, LXXVIII

Who do falsehood to their superiors teach falsehood to their inferiors.
Sidney, *Arcadia*, III

He replied that I must needs be mistaken, or that I said the thing which was not.
Swift, *Gulliver's Travels*, A Voyage to the Houyhnhnms

The general belief which often seizes upon the world in regard to some special falsehood is very surprising. Everybody on a sudden adopts an idea that some particular man is over head and ears in debt, so that he can hardly leave his house for fear of the bailiffs;—or that some ill-fated woman is cruelly ill-used by her husband;—or that some eldest son has ruined his father; whereas the man doesn't owe a shilling, the woman never hears a harsh word from her lord, and the eldest son in question has never succeeded in obtaining a shilling beyond his allowance. Trollope, *The Eustace Diamonds*, XVII

Statistics are always false. *Ibid.*, XXIV

There are certain statements which, though they are false as hell, must be treated as though they were true as gospel. *Ibid.*, LXXVIII

Laurence Fitzgibbon possessed the rare accomplishment of telling a lie with a good grace. Trollope, *Phineas Finn*, XXXVIII

There are some circumstances so distressing as to make lying almost a necessity.
Trollope, *The Way We Live Now*, LXXII

One of the most striking differences between a cat and a lie is that a cat has only nine lives. Twain, *Pudd'nhead Wilson*, VII

It is often the case that the man who can't tell a lie thinks he is the best judge of one.
Ibid., Conclusion

He was a falsehood done in flesh and blood.
Twain and Warner, *The Gilded Age*, Volume II, XXVII

FAME: *see also* AMBITION; etc.

Posthumous fame must be about as satisfactory as a draught of ice-water poured down the throat of a man who has died on Sahara.　　　　Atherton, *Doomswoman*, XIX

Fame compensates for a column of wants.　　　　Atherton, *Los Cerritos*, Interlude

O Fame! Fame that rescues a Jane Austen and passes an Emily Bronte by! Fame that is oftener spelt with nine letters than with four! Fame that is as kind to cleverness as to genius!　　　　*Ibid.*

Fame in itself is certainly no good; but the desire of attaining it is the criterion of an exalted mind.　　　　August, *Horrid Mysteries*, II

Fame and power are the objects of all men. Even their partial fruition is gained by very few; and that too at the expense of social pleasure, conscience, life.
Disraeli, *Coningsby*, Book II, VII

The schoolboy, when he becomes a man, finds that power, even fame, like everything else, is an affair of party.　　　　*Ibid.*

Remarkable what a number of illustrious obscure are going about.
Gissing, *New Grub Street*, VI

You have to become famous before you can secure the attention which would give fame.
Ibid., XXVIII

I was the fool of fame.　　　　Godwin, *Caleb Williams*, II

Of what value is a fair fame? It is the jewel of men formed to be amused with baubles.
Ibid.

The world judges by events; success is necessary to procure the palm of fame.　　*Ibid.*

A man should be only partially before his time: to be completely to the vanward in aspirations is fatal to fame.　　　　Hardy, *The Return of the Native*, Book III, II

Swift as ill-judging fame.　　　　McCarthy, *The Fair Moralist*, 54

Fame is not always honest. Not seldom to be famous is to be widely known for what you are not.　　　　Melville, *Mardi*, CXXVI

Of what available value reputation, unless wedded to power, dentals, or place?　　*Ibid.*

Fame, the chief retainer of distinguished families.
Meredith, *Ordeal of Richard Feverel*, II

Do not confound noise with fame. The man who is remembered is not always honored.
Wright, *A Few Days in Athens*, XI

FAMILIARITY; ACQUAINTANCE

Familiarity is the sure destroyer of reverence.　　　　Brown, C. B., *Alcuin*, III

In our own hearts we trust for our salvation in the men that surround us, in the sights that fill our eyes, in the sounds that fill our ears, and in the air that fills our lungs.
Conrad, *Lord Jim*, III

Ugliness and svindlin' never ought to be formiliar with elegance and wirtew.
Dickens, *Pickwick Papers*, XXV

So shy are the English of letting a stranger into their houses, that one would imagine they regarded all such as thieves.　　　　Fielding, H., *Amelia*, I

To argue upon the possibility of culture before luxury to the bucolic world may be to argue truly, but it is an attempt to disturb a sequence to which humanity has been long accustomed.   Hardy, *Return of the Native*, Book III, II

We form the truest judgment of persons by their behavior on the most familiar occasions.   Richardson, *Clarissa Harlowe*, IV

FAMILY; BLOOD: *see also* CHILDHOOD; MATERNALITY; etc.

Happy the son whose faith in his mother remains unchanged, and who, through all his wanderings, has kept some filial token to repay her brave and tender love.
Alcott, *Little Men*, XII

Families are the most beautiful things in all the world.   Alcott, *Little Women*, XLVII

There are few parents who are under obligations to their children, and we all are obliged to our parents for our lives.   Anonymous, *The Adventures of a Corkscrew*, 114

The exultation of mind which parents feel from the consciousness of having children participates of somewhat divine.   Anonymous, *The Birmingham Counterfeit*, II

Pretty women in the family are a nuisance.   Atherton, *The Californians*, Book I, IX

Nobody who has not been in the interior of a family can say what the difficulties of any individual of that family may be.   Austen, *Emma*

Mothers certainly have not yet got quite the right way of managing their daughters.
Austen, *Mansfield Park*, Volume One, V

Sir Walter Elliot, of Kellynch Hall, in Somersetshire, was a man who, for his own amusement, never took up any book but the Baronetage; there he found occupation for an idle hour, and consolation in a distressed one; there his faculties were roused into admiration and respect, by contemplating the limited remnant of the earliest patents; there any unwelcome sensations, arising from domestic affairs, changed naturally into pity and contempt, as he turned over the almost endless creations of the last century—and there, if every other leaf were powerless, he could read his own history with an interest which never failed.   Austen, *Persuasion*, I

A sick child is always the mother's property, her own feelings generally make it so.
Ibid., VII

Even the smooth surface of family union seems worth preserving, though there may be nothing durable beneath.   *Ibid.*, XXI

"Don't keep coughing so, Kitty, for heaven's sake! Have a little compassion on my nerves. You tear them to pieces." "Kitty has no discretion in her coughs," said her father; "she times them ill."   Austen, *Pride and Prejudice*, Volume I, II

Your father of course may spare you, if your mother can.—Daughters are never of so much consequence to a father.   *Ibid.*, Volume II, XIV

It was very well known that no affection was ever supposed to exist between the children of any man by different marriages.
Austen, *Sense and Sensibility*, Volume I, II

The women of a family give the tone and place to it.   Barr, *Squire*, II

Villages are family groups.   Barrie, *The Little Minister*, IV

I think that when women are too fond of other people's babies they never have any of their own.   Barrie, *Tommy and Grizel*, XXXV

None deserve so well of the world as good parents.
Bellamy, *Looking Backward*, XXV

The duty we owe a parent is sacred.   Brown, W. H., *The Power of Sympathy*, 136

We inherit other things besides gout and consumption.
Bulwer, *The Caxtons*, Book IV, V

He who sees his heir in his own child, carries his eyes over hopes and possessions lying far beyond his gravestone, viewing his life, even here, as a period but closed with a comma. He who sees his heir in another man's child, sees the full stop at the end of the sentence.
Bulwer, *What Will He Do with It?*, Book II, XIII

Papas and mamas are ever most egregiously in the way.
Burney, *Camilla*, Two, III

The family is a survival of the principle which is more logically embodied in the compound animal—and the compound animal is a form of life which has been found incompatible with high development. I would do with the family among mankind what nature has done with the compound animal, and confine it to the lower and less progressive races. Certainly there is no inherent love for the family system on the part of nature herself.
Butler, *The Way of All Flesh*, XXIV

If there are one or two good ones in a very large family, it is as much as can be expected.
Ibid., LXVI

A man first quarrels with his father about three-quarters of a year before he is born.
Ibid., LXXIX

It often happens that if the son is right, the father is wrong, and the father is not going to have this if he can help it.
Ibid., LXXXVI

"There are so many Grandissimes I cannot distinguish between—I can scarcely count them." "Well, now, let me tell you, don't try. They can't do it themselves. Take them in the mass—as you would shrimps."
Cable, *The Grandissimes*, V

She pictured to herself how this same little sister of hers would, in the after-time, be herself a grown woman; and how she would keep, through all her riper years, the simple and loving heart of her childhood; and how she would gather about her other little children, and make their eyes bright and eager with many a strange tale, perhaps even with the dream of Wonderland of long ago; and how she would feel with all their simple sorrows, and find a pleasure in all their simple joys, remembering her own child-life, and the happy summer days.
Carroll, *Alice in Wonderland*, XII

The mother-women seemed to prevail that summer at Grand Isle. It was easy to know them, fluttering about with extended, protecting wings when any harm, real or imaginary, threatened their precious brood. They were women who idolized their children, worshiped their husbands, and esteemed it a holy privilege to efface themselves as individuals and grow wings as ministering angels.
Chopin, *The Awakening*, IV

The force of blood.
Cleland, *Memoirs of a Coxcomb*, 343

"She is the child of the universe." "The universe makes rather an indifferent parent, I am afraid."
Dickens, *Bleak House*, VI

Some men rarely revert to their father, but seem, in the bankbooks of their remembrance, to have transferred all their stock of filial affection into their mother's name.
Ibid., XLIX

What is public life without private ties?
Ibid.

Reginald Wilfer is a name with rather a grand sound, suggesting on first acquaintance brasses in country churches, scrolls in stained-glass windows, and generally the De Wilfers who came over with the Conqueror. For, it is a remarkable fact in genealogy that no De Any ones ever came over with anybody else.
Dickens, *Our Mutual Friend*, Book I, IV

Family likeness has often a deep sadness in it. Nature, that great tragic dramatist, knits us together by bone and muscle, and divides us by the subtler web of our brains; blends yearning and repulsion; and ties us by our heartstrings to the beings that jar us at every movement.
Eliot, *Adam Bede*, IV

It hath been many an honest man's hap to pass for the father of children he never begot.
Fielding, H., *Tom Jones*, 7

The beggarly question of parentage—what is it, after all? What does it matter, when you come to think of it, whether a child is yours by blood or not? All the little ones of our time are collectively the children of us adults of the time, and entitled to our general care.
Hardy, *Jude the Obscure*, Part Five, III

Decrepit families imply decrepit wills, decrepit conduct.　　　　Hardy, *Tess*, XXXV

A perplexing and ticklish possession is a daughter.　　　Hardy, *Woodlanders*, XII

There is no one thing which men so rarely do, whatever the provocation or inducement, as to bequeath patrimonial property away from their own blood.
Hawthorne, *The House of the Seven Gables*, I

To plant a family: this idea is at the bottom of most of the wrong and mischief men do. The truth is, that, once in every half-century, at longest, a family should be merged into the great, obscure mass of humanity, and forget all about its ancestors.　　*Ibid.*, XII

What we call real estate is the broad foundation on which nearly all the guilt of this world rests.　　　　　　　　　　　　　　　　　　　　　　*Ibid.*, XVII

The brief duration of our families, as a hereditary household, renders it next to a certainty that the great-grandchildren will not know their father's grandfather, and that half a century hence at furthest, the hammer of the auctioneer will thump its knock-down blow against his blockhead, sold at so much for the pound of stone.
Hawthorne, *The Marble Faun*, XIII

Men, and especially women and children, cannot have anything much about them, be it a dog, a cat, or even a slave, without insensibly contracting some interest in it and regard for it.　　　　　　　　　　Hildreth, *Slave*, Volume I, XVI

Good families are generally worse than any others.　　Hope, *The Prisoner of Zenda*, I

A son-in-law or brother-in-law does not enter the family; he need not be caressed or made anything of; but the son's or brother's wife has a claim upon his mother and sisters which they cannot deny.　　　　　　　　　　Howells, *Silas Lapham*, XII

In families where there is not poverty, there is commonly discord.
Johnson, *Rasselas*, 100

If a kingdom be a great family, a family likewise is a little kingdom, torn with factions and exposed to revolutions.　　　　　　　　　　　　　　　　　　　*Ibid.*

Parents and children seldom act in concert.　　　　　　　　　　　　　*Ibid.*

How can children credit the assertions of parents, which their own eyes show to be false?
Ibid., 101

He that leaveth his own home is worthy no home.
Lyly, *Euphues and His England*, 240

Surely a gentle sister is the second best gift to a man; and it is first in point of occurrence; for the wife comes after. He who is sisterless, is as a bachelor before his time. For much that goes to make up the deliciousness of a wife, already lies in the sister.　　　　　　　　　　　　　　　　　　Melville, *Pierre*, Book I, II

Adam and Eve! If indeed ye are yet alive and in heaven, may it be no part of your immortality to look down upon the world ye have left. For as all these sufferers and cripples are as much your family as young Abel, so, to you, the sight of the world's woes would be a parental torment indeed.　　　　　　　　Melville, *Redburn*, XXXVIII

There is no first claim. A man's wife and children have a claim on him for bread. A man's parents have a claim on him for obedience while he is a child. A man's uncles, aunts, and cousins have no claim on him at all, except for help in necessity, which he can grant and they require. None—wife, children, parents, relatives—none have a claim to bar his judgment and his actions. Sound the conscience, and sink the family! With a clear conscience, it is best to leave the family to its own debates.

Meredith, *Beauchamp's Career*, XII

A generation is but a large family, united by ties of impulse and idea.

Moore, *Evelyn Innes*, XVIII

The whole island is one family, or household.

More, *Utopia*, II

A man who has sons brings up chickens for his own table whereas daughters are chickens brought up for the tables of other men.

Richardson, *Clarissa Harlowe*, I

Who could bear to lighten herself by loading a father?

Ibid.

She is grown so much into mother that she has forgotten she ever was a daughter.

Ibid.

A prudent daughter will not wilfully err, because her parents err, if they were to err: if she do, the world which blames the parents will not acquit the child.

Ibid.

Could but my parents have let go as fast as I pulled, I should have been a very happy creature.

Ibid.

There cannot be a father in the world who would sell his child's virtue.

Ibid.

What is the precise stature and age at which a parent, after the example of the dams of the brute creation, is to lay aside all care and tenderness for her offspring?

Ibid., II

Parents must always love the child they once loved.

Ibid., IV

A man's best brother nowadays is the thing he fights with. His best friend is his rifle. You may call his jackknife a first-cousin, and his two pistols his eldest sons.

Simms, *The Scout*, II

A little management is necessary in all families.

Thackeray, *Lovel the Widower*, III

Blood's the word. Nothing like blood, in hosses, dawgs, *and* men.

Thackeray, *Vanity Fair*, XXXIV

Fathers always have bowels of compassion at last.

Trollope, *Ayala's Angel*, XLI

In calamity, trouble, sorrow, it is wonderful how the ties of blood assert themselves.

Warner, *A Little Journey*, XXII

FANATICISM: *see also* INSANITY; OBSESSION; RELIGION; etc.

Fanaticism is a more powerful combatant than avarice.

Atherton, *Doomswoman*, XXIX

Fanatics cling to their dream, and would not give it for gold.

Bronte, C., *Shirley*, IV

FASHION

Fashion is a thing that anyone may want who does not happen to be in vogue.

Cooper, *Satanstoe*, Volume I, VII

Fashions are like human beings. They come in, nobody knows when, why, or how; and they go out, nobody knows when, why, or how.

Dickens, *David Copperfield*, IX

The old, old fashion! The fashion that came in with our first garments, and will last unchanged until our race has run its course, and the wide firmament is rolled up like a scroll. The old, old fashion—Death!

Dickens, *Dombey and Son*, XVI

People of fashion are the slaves of custom.

Fielding, H., *Joseph Andrews*, 253

Fashion, by which what is really fantastic becomes for a moment universal.

Wilde, *The Picture of Dorian Gray*, XI

Fat men are the salt and savor of the earth; full of good humor, high spirits, fun, and all manner of jollity. Their breath clears the atmosphere: their exhalations air the world. Of men, they are the good measures; brimmed, heaped, pressed down, piled up, and running over. Melville, *Mardi*, XCV

FAULT; FAULTINESS: *see also* ERROR; GOOD AND EVIL; etc.

The usual style of letter-writing among women is faultless, except in three particulars: a general deficiency of subject, a total inattention to stops, and a very frequent ignorance of grammar. Austen, *Northanger Abbey*, III

The secret of opposition is to find fault with whatever may be done.
Brackenridge, *Modern Chivalry*, Part II, II

The event of discovered faults is more frequently callousness than amendment; and propriety of example is as much a duty to our fellow creatures, as purity of intention is a debt to ourselves. Burney, *Camilla*, Three, V

We all acknowlege our faults: but the acknowledgment passes for current payment; and therefore we never amend them. *Ibid.*, Three, VI

The quickest at finding out the faults that are his neighbors', and the slowest at finding out the faults that are his own. Collins, *The Woman in White*, Part I, Second Epoch

The whole people is not infallible, neither is a part of the people infallible.
Cooper, *The Monikins*, Conclusion

One would not be worrying people with too many words, which is a great fault in a man who is recounting his own affairs. Crane, *The O'Ruddy*, XIV

He is all fault that hath no fault at all. DuMaurier, *The Martian*, Part Ninth

He held it no virtue to frown at irremediable faults. Eliot, *Adam Bede*, V

Blameless people are always the most exasperating. Eliot, *Middlemarch*, Book I, XII

A man who is really concerned for another's frailties will keep them as much as possible even from his own thoughts, as well as endeavor to hide them from the rest of the world.
Fielding, H., *David Simple*, II

Instead of blaming herself she laid the fault upon the shoulders of some indistinct, colossal Prince of the World, who had framed her situation and ruled her lot.
Hardy, *The Return of the Native*, Book IV, VIII

It would have been a fault in her not to have been faulty. Manley, *Rivella*, II

Any human being supposed to be complete, must for that very reason infallibly be faulty.
Melville, *Moby Dick*, XXXII

The fault of a blameable person cannot warrant a fault in a more perfect person.
Richardson, *Clarissa Harlowe*, II

We have all of us something to amend. *Ibid.*, III

Irreconcilableness is her family fault. *Ibid.*

An awkward fellow will do everything awkwardly: and when he has done foolishly, will rack his unmeaning brain for excuses as awkward as his first fault. Ibid., IV

Fair looks hide many a fault, where a person has the art to behave obligingly.
Richardson, *Pamela*, 70

Has not every faulty inclination something to plead in its own behalf?
Richardson, *Sir Charles Grandison*, Two, III

Some strand of our own misdoing is involved in every quarrel.
Stevenson, *Prince Otto*, Book III, II

No one is willing to acknowledge a fault in himself when a more agreeable motive can be found for the estrangement of his acquaintances.

Twain and Warner, *The Gilded Age*, Volume II, XIII

It is easy to find fault, if one has that disposition. There was once a man who, not being able to find any other fault with his coal, complained that there were too many prehistoric toads in it.

Twain, *Pudd'nhead Wilson*, IX

FAVOR: *see also* REWARD

To request a favor is one thing; to challenge it as our due is another.

Richardson, *Clarissa Harlowe*, II

Favors speedily conferred are the most graceful and obliging.

Ibid., IV

FEAR: *see also* COURAGE; COWARDICE; etc.

It is only the living enemies we fear; the dead and their past are beautiful unrealities to the smarting ego.

Atherton, *The Californians*, Book II, XXX

It is dreadful to appear unprepared before men whom one has learnt to fear.

August, *Horrid Mysteries*, I

Fear shackles the mind, and suffers the soul to unfold herself but slowly.

Ibid.

Prudence is another name for fear.

Barrie, *The Little Minister*, XVIII

The priest is an adjunct of fear, because he holds out the horror of what is to come, or is invisible.

Brackenridge, *Modern Chivalry*, Part II, II

It is a very strange sensation to inexperienced youth to feel itself quite alone in the world, cut adrift from every connection, uncertain whether the port to which it is bound can be reached, and prevented by many impediments from returning to that it has quitted. The charm of adventure sweetens that sensation, the glow of pride warms it; but then the throb of fear disturbs it; and fear with me became predominant, when half an hour elapsed and still I was alone.

Bronte, C., *Jane Eyre*, XI

To see and know the worst is to take from Fear her main advantage.

Bronte, C., *Villette*, XXXIX

Fear sometimes imagines a vain thing.

Ibid., XLII

Intense dark is always the parent of fears.

Brown, C. B., *Edgar Huntley*, 96

Fear followed me so hard that I fled.

Bunyan, *Pilgrim's Progress*, 16

Fear tends much to men's good, and to make them right, at their beginning to go on pilgrimage.

Ibid., 154

The felon that standeth before the judge quakes and trembles, and seems to repent most heartily; but the bottom of all is the fear of the halter, not that he hath any detestation of the offense.

Ibid., 157

Who will throw the best out first? None but he that feareth not God.

Ibid., 212

Do you love to go before when no danger doth approach, and love to come behind so soon as the lions appear?

Ibid., 228

He that is down needs fear no fall; he that is low, no pride.

Ibid., 249

He was so chicken-hearted a man.

Ibid., 263

Mr. Fearing was tender of sin. He was so afraid of doing injuries to others that he often would deny himself of that which was lawful, because he would not offend.

Ibid., 266

No fears, no grace.

Ibid., 267

Hope with a grave face always means fear.

Burney, *Camilla*, Five, IX

Fear is stronger than hope.

Child, *Philothea*, XIV

FEAR (*continued*)

All-mastering fear.

Collins, Blind Love, XXXIX

Fear of Danger is ten thousand times more terrifying than Danger itself, when apparent to the Eyes; and we find the Burden of Anxiety greater, by much, than the Evil which we are anxious about.

Collins, Moonstone, First Period, X

That fear of finality which lurks in every human breast and prevents so many heroisms and so many crimes.

Conrad, Almayer's Folly, X

One is always afraid.

Conrad, Lord Jim, XIII

Nothing easier than to say, Have no fear! Nothing more difficult. How does one kill fear?

Ibid., XXXIII

Nothing is so contagious as alarm.

Cooper, Jack Tier, XIV

Fear transforms the creatures of the world and the craft of man, making that which is ugly, seemly in our eyes, and that which is beautiful, unsightly.

Cooper, The Prairie, XXIV

To be fear'd like a lion, like a tyrant, is a violence upon nature every way, and is the most disagreeable thing in the world to a generous mind.

Defoe, Colonel Jack, 144

It was all fear and dark within.

Defoe, Moll Flanders, 197

Few people know what secrecy there is in the young, under terror. No matter how unreasonable the terror, so that it be terror.

Dickens, Great Expectations, II

I would not have you be virtuous out of fear.

Doyle, Micah Clarke, III

Secrets are rarely betrayed or discovered according to any program our fear has sketched out. Fear is almost always haunted by terrible dramatic scenes, which recur in spite of the best-argued probabilities against them.

Eliot, The Mill on the Floss, Book V, V

The courage as well as cowardice of fools proceeds from not knowing what is or what is not the proper object of fear; we may account for the extreme hardiness of some men in the same manner as for the terrors of children at a bugbear. The child knows not but that the bugbear is the proper object of fear, the blockhead knows not that a cannonball is so.

Fielding, H., Amelia, I

Fear is never more uneasy than when it doth not certainly know its object.

Ibid.

If fear has too much ascendance in the mind, the man is rather to be pitied than abhorred.

Fielding, H., Joseph Andrews, 114

Fear easily runs into madness.

Fielding, H., Tom Jones, 186

Nothing is so captious as a man who is acting a part, it being very natural for him to be in a continual fear of being found out.

Fielding, S., David Simple, II

There is perhaps no greater difficulty than to enter into conversation under the terror of betraying any hidden secret of the heart.

Fielding, S., History of the Countess of Dellwyn, I

The man who has nothing to lose has nothing to fear.

Gibbes, Mr. Francis Clive, II

Nothing is so potent as fear well maintained.

Hardy, A Laodicean, Book II, V

Stare the ugly horror right in the face; never a sidelong glance, nor half-look, for those are what show a frightful thing in its frightfullest aspect.

Hawthorne, The Marble Faun, XX

Is there no virtue in woman, save what springs from a wholesome fear of the gallows?

Hawthorne, The Scarlet Letter, II

A base and dastard fear is the sole principle of human nature to which the slaveholder appeals.

Hildreth, Slave, Volume II, X

Fear quickens the flight of guilt. Johnson, *Rasselas*, 26

Apprehension doubles every evil. Johnstone, *Arsaces*, II

Fear is the child of ignorance. Johnstone, *Pilgrim*, II

Fear always accompanies love when it is great, as flames burn highest when they tremble most. Lennox, *Henrietta*, I

A true and faithful heart standeth more in awe of his superior whom he loveth for fear than of his prince whom he feareth for love. Lyly, *Euphues and His England*, 256

It is slender affection which either the fear of law or care of religion may diminish.
Ibid., 338

The present evil we dread is always the worst. Marishall, *Miss Clarinda Cathcart*, I

I will have no man in my boat who is not afraid of a whale.
Melville, *Moby Dick*, XXVI

There lurks an elusive something in the innermost idea of whiteness, which strikes more of panic to the soul than that redness which affrights in blood. *Ibid.*, XLII

Fear plucks the feathers from the wings of the soul and sits it naked and shivering in a vault, where the passing of a common hodman's foot above sounds like the king of terrors coming. Meredith, *Beauchamp's Career*, XXIX

Nothing confounds like to sudden terror, it thrusts every sense out of office.
Nashe, *The Unfortunate Traveller*, 144

Poison wrapped up in sugared pills is but half a poison: the fear of death's looks are more terrible than his stroke. *Ibid.*

The whilst I view death, my faith is deaded: where a man's fear is, there his heart is.
Ibid., 144–145

Fear never engenders hope. *Ibid.*, 145

It is not from death I request thee to deliver me, but from this terror of torment's eternity. *Ibid.*

What will not slaves do for fear? *Ibid.*, 148

Whom we fear more than love, we are not far from hating.
Richardson, *Clarissa Harlowe*, I

Shall it be said that fear makes more gentle obligers than love? *Ibid.*

It is good, when calamities befall us, that we should look into ourselves, and fear. *Ibid.*

How may noises unlike be made like what one fears! *Ibid.*

Let us look into ourselves, and fear. *Ibid.*, II

Fear comes with a fear. *Ibid.*, III

What is feared generally happens, because there is generally occasion for the fear.
Ibid.

Fear brings one into more dangers than the caution that goes along with it delivers one from. Richardson, *Pamela*, 158

Terror does but add to her frost; but she is a charming girl, and may be thawed by kindness; and I should have melted her by love, instead of freezing her by fear.
Ibid., 218

Something must be done by a man who refuses a challenge to let a challenger see that he has better motives than fear for a refusal.
Richardson, *Sir Charles Grandison*, One, II

Apprehensiveness, the child of prudence, is as characteristic in women as courage in men. *Ibid.*

FEAR (*continued*)

Fear makes cowards loving. *Ibid.*

Fear is but bad diet for the young. Ridley, *James Lovegrove*, II

I would rather feel the sword than behold it suspended. Roche, *Nocturnal Visit*, II

Fear is more painful to cowardice than death to courage. Sidney, *Arcadia*, IV

Fear is more pain than is the pain it fears. *Ibid.*, V

The remote fear is no fear with the vulgar. They seldom think in advance of the necessity. Simms, *The Partisan*, Volume I, IX

Evil-doers are evil-dreaders. Stevenson, *Kidnapped*, XXVII

I screamed as loud as fear could make me. Swift, *Gulliver's Travels*, Brobdingnag

FEROCITY: *see also* ANGER; WAR; etc.

The gentlest creatures are fierce when they have young to provide for.
Bellamy, *Looking Backward*, XXVI

FEUDALISM: *see also* SOCIETY

Feudalism is not an objectionable thing if you can be sure of the lord.
Meredith, *The Egoist*, IX

FICKLENESS

Fickleness means getting weary of a thing while the thing remains the same.
Hardy, *The Well-Beloved*, Part I, VII

FICTION; NARRATION; NOVELS; STORY-TELLING: *see also* ART; AUTHORSHIP; EXPRESSION; etc.

The greatest misfortune attending novels is that as soon as you have made the hero tolerably easy, you have no further business with him. The vicissitudes, perturbations, and misfortunes of life are the only things that are attractive in narration.
Anonymous, *The Adventures of an Author*, II

A novel should be an exact representation of simple nature as she appears while the sun is in its meridian glory, but a modern novel is an ill-drawn picture of distorted nature, delineated while the sun is in eclipse. Anonymous, *The Egg*, 37

The persons who generally employ themselves in novel writing are as properly qualified for that purpose as the deaf man is to teach music. *Ibid.*

A faithful memoir-writer must exhibit his principal character with all its lights and shades, and it is not his fault if the former are eclipsed by the latter.
Anonymous, *Memoirs of a Coquet*, 67

One book about the good of the nation is worth all the romances under the sun. *Ibid.*, 91

A novel, in short, only some work in which the greatest powers of the mind are displayed, in which the most thorough knowledge of human nature, the happiest delineation of its varities [*sic*], the liveliest effusions of wit and humor, are conveyed to the world in the best-chosen language. Austen, *Northanger Abbey*, V

Anyone can write the campaign of a great prince, because the subject sustains the narrative. But it is a greater praise to give a value to the rambles of private persons, or the dissensions of a borough town. Brackenridge, *Modern Chivalry*, Part II, II

Begin at the beginning, and go on till you come to the end: then stop.
Carroll, *Alice in Wonderland*, XII

The universal love of the marvelous, which causes most people to insist on having it introduced into a story, if it do not happen to come in legitimately.

Cooper, *The Chainbearer*, XV

Ever since I began to write this story, I have been anxious to know how it was going to come out.

Eggleston, *The Hoosier Schoolmaster*, XXXIV

With a single drop of ink for a mirror, the Egyptian sorcerer undertakes to reveal to any chance comer far-reaching visions of the past.

Eliot, *Adam Bede*, I

It is our business to discharge the part of a faithful historian, and to describe human nature as it is, not as we would wish it to be.

Fielding, H., *Amelia*, II

Without interruptions the best narrative of plain matter of fact must overpower every reader; for nothing but the everlasting watchfulness, which Homer has ascribed only to Jove himself, can be proof against a newspaper of many volumes.

Fielding, H., *Tom Jones*, 107

The meeting of the man and the woman—it is to this that every story in the world goes back for its beginning.

Frederic, *Gloria Mundi*, Part I, I

Fiction has not yet outgrown the influence of the stage on which it originated.

Gissing, *New Grub Street*, X

Think of the very words "novel," "romance"—what do they mean but exaggeration of one bit of life?

Ibid., XXVI

The action of a teller is wanted to give due effect to all stories of incident.

Hardy, *The Hand of Ethelberta*, XIII

That coarse touch is to my mind a recommendation; for it do always prove a story to be true.

Hardy, *Under the Greenwood Tree*, Part One, VIII

The choicest egg that ever was laid was not as big as the nest that held it. If a story were so interesting that a maiden would rather hear it than listen to the praise of her own beauty, or a poet would rather read it than recite his own verses, still it would have to be wrapped in some tissue of circumstance, or it would lose half its effectiveness.

Holmes, *A Mortal Antipathy*, VI

Novelists and lawyers understand the art of "cramming" better than any other persons in the world.

Ibid.

Novelists might be the greatest possible help to us if they painted life as it is, and human feelings in their true proportion and relation, but for the most part they have been and are altogether noxious.

Howells, *Silas Lapham*, XIV

What lady in Romance ever married the man that was chosen for her?

Lennox, *The Female Quixote*, I

One never has the idea of an heroine older than eighteen, though her history begins at that age and the events which compose it contain the space of twenty more.

Ibid.

Love is the business, the sole business of ladies in romances.

Ibid., II

It is with fiction as with religion: it should present another world, and yet one to which we feel the tie.

Melville, *Confidence-Man*, XXXIII

The purpose of every storyteller—to amuse.

Ibid., XXXV

This history goes forward and goes backward, as occasion calls. Nimble center, circumference elastic you must have.

Melville, *Pierre*, Book III, III

Ancedotes are portable; they can be carried home, they are disbursable at other tables.

Meredith, *Diana of the Crossways*, XIV

The pleasant narrator in the first person is the happy bubbling fool, not the philosopher who has come to know himself and his relations toward the universe. The words of this last are one to twenty; his mind is bent upon the causes of events rather than their progress.

Meredith, *Harry Richmond*, LVI

The end, and the delivery of reader and writer alike, should not be dallied with.   *Ibid.*

All attestation favors the critical dictum that a novel is to give us copious sugar and no cane.
                                                                    Meredith, *Sandra Belloni*, LI

The art of a storyteller (and it is that which marks a genius) is to make his tale interminable, and still to interest his audience.   Morier, *Hajji Baba*, XLV

I don't approve of a man ending off neatly like a novel.
                                                    Oliphant, *The Perpetual Curate*, XLVIII

Suspense is the soul of narrative.   Reade, *The Cloister and the Hearth*, XLVII

Caesar performed great actions by day and wrote them down at night.
                                                            Richardson, *Clarissa Harlowe*, I

It is much better to tell your own story than to have an adversary tell it for you.
                                                                                    Ibid., III

One story is good till another is heard.   *Ibid.*, IV

Glossing over one part of a story, and omitting another, will make a bad cause a good one at any time.
                                                                                    Ibid.

AN OWER TRUE TALE.   Scott, *Bride of Lammermoor*, XXXIV

Works of fiction, if only well gotten up, have always their advantages in the hearts of listeners over plain, homely truth.   Stowe, *Orr's Island*, V

Novels give false views of life. Is there not an eternal novel, with all these false, cheating views, written in the breast of every beautiful and attractive girl whose witcheries make every man that comes near her talk like a fool?   *Ibid.*, XXXI

Why do I make zigzag journeys [in my narrative]? 'Tis the privilege of old age to be garrulous, and its happiness to remember early days.   Thackeray, *Denis Duval*, IV

Novelists are supposed to know everything, even the secrets of female hearts, which the owners themselves do not perhaps know.   Thackeray, *Pendennis*, XXIII

There are scenes of all sorts; some dreadful combats, some grand and lofty horse-riding, some scenes of high life, and some of very middling indeed; some love-making for the sentimental, and some light comic business; the whole accompanied by appropriate scenery, and brilliantly illuminated with the Author's own candles.
                                        Thackeray, *Vanity Fair*, Before the Curtain

In novels the most indifferent hero comes out right at last.
                                                    Trollope, *Ayala's Angel*, XXXVIII

The sorrows or our heroes and heroines, they are your delight, oh public!—their sorrows, or their sins, or their absurdities; not their virtues, good sense, and consequent rewards.
                                                        Trollope, *Barchester Towers*, LI

The end of a novel, like the end of a children's dinner party, must be made up of sweetmeats and sugar-plums.   *Ibid.*, LIII

It is a matter of thankfulness that neither the historian nor the novelist hears all that is said by their heroes or heroines, or how would three volumes or twenty suffice! In the present case so little of this sort have I overheard, that I live in hopes of finishing my work within 300 pages, and of completing that pleasant task—a novel in one volume.
                                                                Trollope, *The Warden*, VI

What story was ever written without a demon?   *Ibid.*, XVI

Most people who have the narrative gift—that great and rare endowment—have with it the defect of telling their choice things over the same way every time, and this injures them and causes them to sound stale and wearisome after several repetitions.
                                                        Twain, *Joan of Arc*, Book II, VII

The story could not go much further without becoming the history of a man. When one writes a novel about grown people, he knows exactly where to stop—that is, with a marriage; but when he writes of juveniles, he must stop where he best can.

Twain, *Tom Sawyer*, Conclusion

Every man is bound to leave a story better than he found it.

Ward, *Robert Elsmere*, Book I, III

"What are American dry-goods?" "American novels."

Wilde, *The Picture of Dorian Gray*, II

Medieval art is charming, but medieval emotions are out of date. One can use them in fiction, of course. But then the only things that one can use in fiction are the things that one has ceased to use in fact.

Ibid., VI

FIDELITY; INFIDELITY: *see also* TRUST

History is full of instances of men who have given one woman the devoted love of a lifetime and been unfaithful to her every week in the year.

Atherton, *Doomswoman*, XXIV

I pitied poor Ivanhoe for his misplaced constancy.

DuMaurier, *The Martian*, Part Third

The breath of infidelity goes forth like a two-edged sword to destroy.

Gentleman, *A Trip to the Moon*, I

There are men whose hearts insist upon a dogged fidelity to some image or cause thrown by chance into their keeping, long after their judgment has pronounced it no rarity.

Hardy, *The Mayor of Casterbridge*, XLII

What atheistic, anti-Christian fear pervades Church and State! How much men pay and do, to demonstrate their infidelity.

Judd, *Margaret*, Volume III

Faithless to one, faithful to none.

Lyly, *Euphues*, 114

A faithful fool is the best servant of great schemes.

Meredith, *Ordeal of Richard Feverel*, XXVI

To vow fidelity is to show that there is reason for doubt of it.

Richardson, *Clarissa Harlowe*, II

Do not let even honest people blame anyone for fidelity in a bad cause.

Ibid., III

Scepticism, the parent of infidelity.

Richardson, *Sir Charles Grandison*, Three, VI

The deil be in my feet gin I leave ye.

Scott, *Rob Roy*, XXIV

Ought fidelity to reckon furlongs, or miles, or leagues—like the poor courier, who is paid for his labor by the distance he traverses?

Scott, *The Talisman*, XII

"I thought they always swore by each other." "It's at each other they swear."

Trollope, *Phineas Finn*, I

My kind of loyalty was loyalty to one's country, not to its institutions or its office-holders.

Twain, *Connecticut Yankee*, XIII

Those who are faithful know only the trivial side of love: it is the faithless who know love's tragedies.

Wilde, *The Picture of Dorian Gray*, I

Even in love fidelity is purely a question for physiology. It has nothing to do with our own will. Young men want to be faithful, and are not; old men want to be faithless, and cannot.

Ibid., II

The people who love only once in their lives are really the shallow people. What they call their loyalty, and their fidelity, I call either the lethargy of custom or their lack of imagination. Faithfulness is to the emotional life what consistency is to the life of the intellect—simply a confession of failure.

Ibid., IV

FIDELITY; INFIDELITY (*continued*)

There are many things that we would throw away if we were not afraid that others might pick them up. *Ibid.*

FIGHTING; FEUDING: *see also* WAR

A Frenchman fights best fasting, a Dutchman drunk, an Englishman full, and a Spaniard when the devil is in him, and that's always. Kingsley, *Westward Ho!*, XX

When two parties are watching to see who strikes the first blow, they are sure to come to fisticuffs from mere fear of each other. *Ibid.*, XXIII

"A skirmish lost counts for nothing in a battle without end: it must be incessant." "But does incessant battling keep the intellect clear?"
Meredith, *Beauchamp's Career*, XXVII

A feud is this way. A man has a quarrel with another man, and kills him; then that other man's brother kills *him*; then the other brothers, on both sides, goes for one another; then the *cousins* chip in—and by-and-by everybody's killed off, and there ain't no more feud.
Twain, *Huckleberry Finn*, XVIII

FIRE

I am scorched all over. I am past scorching; not easily canst thou scorch a scar.
Melville, *Moby Dick*, CXIII

FIRMNESS

The censure of the world, though sometimes too severe, is rarely misplaced, and in general there is foundation for their opinions. But the world, though it have discrimination, has not always firmness; it cannot resist those, who, by their graces or wit, blind them to their own imperfections, or amuse their vacant hours.
Dacre, *Passions*, LXXXIX

FITNESS: *see also* RIGHTNESS

Fitness is governed by the nature of things, and not by customs, forms, or municipal laws. Nothing is indeed unfit which is not unnatural. Fielding, H., *Tom Jones*, 180

Things may be fitting to be done, which are not fitting to be boasted of. *Ibid.*

FLATTERY

Flattery is the one general master key to all hearts, and a well-timed compliment has sometimes gained a man more in a minute than all his schemes of industry could have procured him in an age. Anonymous, *The Adventures of a Jesuit*, I

We never fail to like the person who flatters our self-love.
Anonymous, *Fatal Friendship*, I

Flattery is a meanness in the undesigning, and the grand engine of the base and ungenerous; it cannot have any place where truth and faith become the question.
Anonymous, *The Fruitless Repentance*, I

Flattery is generally the greatest friend to love, and the easiest way of gaining a place in a woman's affections. Anonymous, *The Ladies Advocate*, 13

Your eyes looked so many pretty flatteries, love might have borrowed language from them. Anonymous, *Memoirs of an Oxford Scholar*, 35

No tongue flatters like a lover's. Bulwer, *Pompeii*, Book Three, IX

If a man makes you a great many compliments, always suspect him of some bad design, and never believe him your friend till he tells you of some of your faults.

Burney, *Camilla*, Two, IV

He that feels not love must learn to flatter.   Caruthers, *Cavaliers*, Volume II, VI

We are always ready to apply in one's own favor examples which flatter our weakness.

Cleland, *Memoirs of a Coxcomb*, 194

If flattery easily insinuates itself into our hearts, it is chiefly because it soothes our desire of pleasing.   Collyer, *Felicia to Charlotte*, I

That man which needeth neither to flatter with his friends, nor borrow of his neighbors, hath riches sufficient.   Deloney, *The Gentle Craft*, 144

Fair words make fools fain.   *Ibid.*, 269

Nothing can be more reasonable, than that slaves and flatterers should exact the same taxes on all below them which they themselves pay to all above them.

Fielding, H., *Tom Jones*, 14

There is no kind of flattery so irresistible as at second hand.   *Ibid.*, 91

There is scarce any man, how much soever he may despise the character of a flatterer, but will condescend in the meanest manner to flatter himself.   *Ibid.*, 216

Healing balsam of self-flattery.   Fielding, S., *The Countess of Dellwyn*, I

It was a favorite opinion of his that all mankind are, on some blind side or other, to be cajoled and flattered.   *Ibid.*

How delusive are the flatteries of fortune!   Galt, *Ayrshire*, VI

Flattery is the incense always offered to female beauty, and love the only language which it hears.   Johnstone, *The Reverie*, I

Flattery is always mean; but to flatter folly is criminal.   Lennox, *Henrietta*, II

Our flatterers will tell us anything sooner than our faults, or what they know we do not like to hear.   Richardson, *Clarissa Harlowe*, I

Language of flattery looks always as if the flatterer thought to find a woman a fool or hoped to make her one.   *Ibid.*

What can be done with a woman who is above flattery, and despises all praise but that which flows from the approbation of her own heart?   *Ibid.*, II

Do you flatter? Then are you a man.   *Ibid.*, III

Flattery is the vice of men.   Richardson, *Sir Charles Grandison*, One, I

Flattery is dearer to a woman than her food.   *Ibid.*

Flattery is never so successfully administered, as to those who stand in need of friendship, assent, and approbation.   Smollett, *Ferdinand, Count Fathom*, XXX

Who was the blundering idiot who said that "fine words butter no parsnips"? Half the parsnips of society are served and rendered palatable with no other sauce.

Thackeray, *Vanity Fair*, XIX

Substantial benefits often sicken some stomachs; whereas, most will digest any amount of fine words, and be always eager for more of the same food.   *Ibid.*

FOIBLES: *see also* FOOL; SOCIETY; etc.

Our foibles are our manias.   Reade, *Griffith Gaunt*, II

FOOL; FOLLY: *see also* EDUCATION; EXPERIENCE; INTELLIGENCE; WISDOM; etc.

Unfortunately most people don't know when they have made fools of themselves; that is one reason the world grows wise so slowly.   Atherton, *Senator North*, Book III, VII

Fools are more dangerous in the United States than elsewhere, because they are just bright enough to think that they know more than the Almighty ever knew in His best days.   *Ibid.*, Book III, XII

The advantages of natural folly in a beautiful girl.   Austen, *Northanger Abbey*, XIV

The notions of a young man of one or two and twenty as to what is necessary in manners to make him quite the thing, are more absurd than those of any other set of beings in the world. The folly of the means they often employ is only to be equalled by the folly of what they have in view.   Austen, *Persuasion*, XV

We have the sage and the fool, interspersed in society, and the fool gives occasion for the wise man to make his reflections.   Brackenridge, *Modern Chivalry*, Part II, II

There is no folly so besotted that the idiotic rivalries of society, the prurience, the rashness, the blindness of youth, will not hurry a man to its commission.
                                        Bronte, C., *Jane Eyre*, XXVII

Folly does not amuse, or even employ one's notice long.
                                        Cleland, *Memoirs of a Coxcomb*, 130

The saddest of all confessions that a man can make—the confession of his own folly.
                                        Collins, *The Woman in White*, Part I, First Epoch

Man is so blinded in his folly as to go on, ages on ages, doing harm chiefly to himself.
                                        Cooper, *The Prairie*, XXII

The secret of the transmutation of metals may possibly be yet discoverable, but we must nevertheless account him a fool who should expend his life and substance in the search.
                                        Dacre, *Passions*, Letter XIII

If men deny us the prerogative of being rational creatures, they give us ample liberty to range in the wide precincts of folly.   *Ibid.*, Letter XXXI

Fools can never take delight in men more wise and capable than themselves; and that makes them converse with scoundrels, drink belch with porters, and keep company always below themselves.   Defoe, *Roxana*, 15

The world goes its way past all who will not partake of its folly.
                                        Dreiser, *Sister Carrie*, XLVII

Folly and vanity create abundantly more wants than nature.
                                        Fielding, H., *Tom Jones*, 36

There is, perhaps, no surer mark of folly than an attempt to correct the natural infirmities of those we love.   *Ibid.*, 68

It hath always been the sport and privilege of folly to laugh at men of sense; and the characteristic of understanding calmly and steadily to submit to such laughter with an undisturbed tranquility.   Fielding, S., *The Countess of Dellwyn*, I

Give me a wise man of science in love. No one beats him in folly.
                                        Gaskell, *Wives and Daughters*, LX

If one man is foolish enough to fight a windmill, like Don Quixote, you cannot suppose any nation of men would be.   Howland, *Papa's Own Girl*, XVI

It is quite within a man's rights to be a fool once in a while.
                                        James, H., *Confidence*, XXX

A long discourse argueth folly, and delicate words incur the suspicion of flattery.
                                        Lyly, *Euphues*, 106

Follies past are sooner remembered than redressed, and time lost may well be repented, but never recalled.   *Ibid.*, 297

It is a blind goose that knoweth not a fox from a fern bush, and a foolish fellow that cannot discern craft from conscience, being once cozened. *Ibid.*, 319

One must be somewhat hated to be independent of folly.
Mackenzie, *Julia De Roubigné*, 29

People of feeling would do well to acquire a certain respect for the follies of mankind.
Mackenzie, *The Man of Feeling*, 11

Give me the folly that dimples the cheek rather than the wisdom that curdles the blood.
Melville, *Confidence-Man*, XLV

Solomon more than hints that all men are fools; and every wise man knows himself to be one. Melville, *Mardi*, XV

How wondrous familiar is a fool. Melville, *Moby Dick*, CXV

Duelling is sickening folly. We go too far in pretending to despise every insult pitched at us. Meredith, *Beauchamp's Career*, I

It's the mark of a fool to take everybody for a bigger fool than himself. *Ibid.*, XI

To anchor the heart by an object, ere we have half traversed the world, is youth's foolishness. Meredith, *Ordeal of Richard Feverel*, XXV

What expect out of a folly but fools? *Ibid.*, XXVII

Folly's a new name for fashions. *Ibid.*

"How should you define the Monument of Folly?" "All the human race on one another's shoulders." *Ibid.*, XXXVI

Great is that day when we see our folly! *Ibid.*, XLVII

Adam never fell till God made fools. Nashe, *The Unfortunate Traveller*, 48

In medicine or law, as in divinity, to be wiser than the All-wise is to be a fool.
Reade, *The Cloister and the Hearth*, XXIX

Things foolishly worded are not always foolish. *Ibid.*, L

What is worldly wisdom but the height of folly? Richardson, *Clarissa Harlowe*, I

If a fool can be made sensible that there is a man who has more understanding than himself, he is ready enough to conclude that such a man must be a very extraordinary creature. *Ibid.*, II

No man is always a fool, every man sometimes. *Ibid.*

By continually laughing at his own absurdities, he left us at liberty to suppose that his folly was his choice. Richardson, *Sir Charles Grandison*, One, I

That weed, folly, is a native of the soil. A very little watering will make it sprout, and choke the noble flowers that education has planted. *Ibid.*, One, II

Fool and madman we often join as terms of reproach; but fools seldom run really mad.
Ibid., Two, IV

There are more fools and fewer hypocrites than the wise world dreams of.
Schreiner, *The Story of an African Farm*, Part II, I

There are folks before whom one should take care how they play the fool—because they have either too much malice, or too little wit. Scott, *Guy Mannering*, XXXVI

When one does a foolish thing, it is right to do it handsomely. Scott, *Kenilworth*, XXX

A fool will ever grasp rather at the appearance than the reality of authority.
Scott, *Quentin Durward*, XXX

Like a fool, he would be both swordsman and philosopher. *Ibid.*, XXXVI

Yes and *but* are words for fools: wise men neither hesitate nor retract—they resolve and they execute. Scott, *The Talisman*, XIX

197

FOOL; FOLLY (*continued*)

O fool that I am, that thought I could grasp water and bind the wind.
Sidney, Arcadia, II

A fool can do an immense deal of mischief with the tail-end of a truth.
Simms, The Scout, XXXII

A fool would rather you see him as a fool than not see him at all. *Ibid.*, XXXV

The briefest follies are the best. Smollett, *Peregrine Pickle*, 219

A fool is more mischievous than famine, pestilence, and war. *Ibid.*, 488

I have seen wicked men and fools, a great many of both; and I believe they both get paid in the end; but the fools first. Stevenson, *Kidnapped*, XIV

Fools must live in the world. Trollope, *Ayala's Angel*, LVII

It is very hard for a fool not to be a fool. Trollope, *Barchester Towers*, XV

Any man who is willing to sacrifice his interest to get possession of a pretty face is a fool. Pretty faces are to be had cheaper than that. *Ibid.*

Blessed be the capacity of being fond and foolish! Warner, *A Little Journey*, X

FORBEARANCE

The person who will bear much shall have much to bear all the world through.
Richardson, Clarissa Harlowe, I

To bear and forbear is the duty of those who pretend to have most sense. *Ibid.*

To bear much is to be obliged to bear more. *Ibid.*, III

FORCE

He that stoppeth the stream forceth it to swell higher. Lyly, *Euphues*, 117

The rattling thunderbolt hath but his clap, the lightning but his flash, and as they both come in a moment, so do they both end in a minute. *Ibid.*

You have just so much force: when the one channel runs over the other runs dry.
Schreiner, The Story of an African Farm, Part II, VII

FORESIGHT

Give us foresightful minds; give us minds to obey what foresight tells.
Sidney, Arcadia, II

FORGETFULNESS

Forgetfulness is not to be purchased with a wish.
Bronte, A., Tenant of Wildfell Hall, XXXV

What can be more unkind than forgetfulness? Brown, C. B., *Arthur Mervyn*, II

FORGIVENESS; PARDON: *see also* LAW

Forgiving sins is not blotting them out. The blood of Christ only turns them red instead of black. It leaves them in the record. Bellamy, *Dr. Heidenhoff's Process*, I

Forgiveness is a man's duty, but that can only mean as you're to give up all thoughts o' taking revenge; it can never mean as you're t' have your old feelings back again, for that's not possible. Eliot, *Adam Bede*, XXIX

A dissolute and selfish mind is commonly an unforgiving one.
Griffin, *The Duke of Monmouth*, XXX

Damnatory doctrines best pleased him. He was ready to pardon, as a Christian should, but he did want his enemy before him on his knees.
Meredith, *Ordeal of Richard Feverel*, XXVII

Forgiveness is never denied to sincere repentance.
Radcliffe, *A Sicilian Romance*, I

Too ready forgiveness does but encourage offenses. There would not be so many head-strong daughters as there are if this maxim were kept in mind.
Richardson, *Clarissa Harlowe*, I

How much nobler it is to forgive, and even how much more manly to despise, than to resent, an injury.   *Ibid.*

Once forgiven, forever forgiven.   *Ibid.*, III

The inconsistence of her forgiving unforgivingness.   *Ibid.*

Nothing can be more wounding to a spirit not ungenerous than a generous forgiveness.
Ibid.

Where would be our triumph if our enemies deserved our forgiveness?   *Ibid.*, IV

To forgive a crime readily is a weakness that would induce one to suspect the virtue of the forgiver.   *Ibid.*

How wounding a thing is a generous and well-distinguished forgiveness!   *Ibid.*

Forgiveness comes of loose views and (what is if anything more dangerous) a regular life.   Stevenson, *Prince Otto*, Book III, II

The man who cannot forgive any mortal thing is a green hand in life.   *Ibid.*

It is ourselves that we cannot forgive, when we refuse forgiveness to our friend.   *Ibid.*

Are there not offenses that disgrace the pardoner?   *Ibid.*

There is nothing that a woman will not forgive a man, when he is weaker than she is herself.   Trollope, *He Knew He Was Right*, XCIII

One does not become angry with a madman; but while a man has power in his hands over others, and when he misuses that power grossly and cruelly, who is there that will not be angry?   *Ibid.*, XCVIII

Ennui is the one sin for which there is no forgiveness.
Wilde, *The Picture of Dorian Gray*, XVIII

FORM; FORM AND FUNCTION; METHOD

Do not bring in a supernatural agent when you can do without him.
Fielding, H., *Jonathan Wild*, 117

Whatever is done with design is always overdone.   Lennox, *Henrietta*, I

Write as you talk and it will do.   Meredith, *Diana of the Crossways*, XVIII

Form is deceitful: a fine person is seldom paired by a fine mind.
Richardson, *Clarissa Harlowe*, II

Buildings should be fitted to grace the sculpture, not the sculpture to grace the building.
Trollope, *Barchester Towers*, XLII

The canons of good society are, or should be, the same as the canons of art. Form is absolutely essential to it. It should have the dignity of a ceremony, as well as its unreality, and should combine the insincere character of a romantic play with the wit and beauty that make such plays delightful to us. Is insincerity such a terrible thing? I think not. It is merely a method by which we can multiply our personalities.
Wilde, *The Picture of Dorian Gray*, XI

FORTUNE: *see also* DESTINY; WEALTH; etc.

A fortune, like a man, is an organism which draws to itself other minds and other strength than that inherent in the founder. Dreiser, *Sister Carrie*, XXXIII

Fortune is a woman and capricious. But sometimes she is a good woman and gives to those who merit. Eliot, *Middlemarch*, Book VI, LIV

Fortune is the worst of mistresses, or the best, for she laughs ever behind her frown and mingles stripes with kisses. Haggard, *People of the Mist*, V

Not seldom in this life, when, on the right side, fortune's favorites sail close by us, we, though all adroop before, catch somewhat of the rushing breeze, and joyfully feel our baggin sails fill out. Melville, *Moby Dick*, CXVI

FRANKNESS: *see also* SINCERITY

Affectation, or coldness, or stupid, coarse-minded misapprehension of one's meaning are the usual rewards of candor. Bronte, C., *Jane Eyre*, XIV

How can a man's candor be seen in all its lustre unless he has a few failings to talk of?
Eliot, *Adam Bede*, XII

The man of candor and of true understanding is never hasty to condemn.
Fielding, H., *Tom Jones*, 268

Frankness begets frankness. Jenner, *The Placid Man*, I

It is natural for a candid nature to recoil from duplicity.
Shaw, *The Irrational Knot*, V

The human soul will be generally found most defective in the article of candor.
Smollett, *Humphry Clinker*, 113

FRAUD

Cry but a pickpocket, and, by the alacrity of the mob to secure him, you would imagine that the whole nation held the least act of fraud in the most utter detestation.
Jenner, *The Placid Man*, I

Caught by fraud, kept by force. Lyly, *Euphues*, 146

FREEDOM; SLAVERY: *see also* SLAVERY under separate heading

Hungry men may fight for a bone—not for liberty.
Adams, F., *President John Smith*, XI

A free government is a noble possession to a people: and this freedom consists in an equal right to make laws, and to have benefit of the laws when made.
Brackenridge, *Modern Chivalry*, Part I, I

There is a natural alliance between liberty and letters. *Ibid.*, Part II, I

It takes a man half an age to enjoy liberty, before he can know how to use it.
Ibid., Part II, II

What avails it to be told by anyone that he is an advocate for liberty? We must first know what he means by the word. We shall generally find that he intends only freedom to himself, and subjection to all others. Brown, C. B., *Alcuin*, II

Our liberty consists in the choice of our governors. *Ibid.*, II

Homely liberty is better than splendid servitude. Brown, C. B., *Ormond*, 69

Liberty without peril can never exist. *Ibid.*, 170

All men who are not free are fearfully selfish. Freedom alone makes men sacrifice to each other. Bulwer, *Pompeii*, Book IV, III

200

More bounteous run rivers when the ice that locked their flow melts into their waters. And when fine natures relent their kindness is swelled by the thaw.

Bulwer, *What Will He Do with It?*, Book XII, V

Why should the better half of a man's actions be always under the dominion of some prescriptive slavery?

Burney, *Camilla*, Three, VI

Liberty is sweeter when founded securely on the law.

Chesnutt, *House Behind the Cedars*, XVIII

The most pardonable of all liberties—the liberty of composing your mind.

Collins, *The Moonstone*, Second Period, VII

Every man loves liberty for his own sake, and very few for the sake of other people.

Cooper, *The Monikins*, Conclusion

Liberty is a convertible term, which means exclusive privileges in one country, no privileges in another, and inclusive privileges in all.

Ibid.

Oh! 'tis pleasant to be free,/ The sweetest miss is liberty.

Defoe, *Roxana*, 145

The butterflies are free. Mankind will surely not deny to [a man] what it concedes to the butterflies.

Dickens, *Bleak House*, VI

By the law of nature, everything hath a right to liberty.

Fielding, H., *Tom Jones*, 115

What but the sublime idea of virtue could inspire a human mind with the generous thought of giving liberty?

Ibid., 116–117

Liberty is one of the rights that I put on when I put on the form of a man, and no event is of power to dissolve or abdicate that right.

Godwin, *St. Leon*, 428

Liberty, that attribute of gods.

Goldsmith, *The Vicar of Wakefield*, 99

The foremost result of a broken law is ever an ecstatic sense of freedom.

Hawthorne, *The Marble Faun*, XIX

He knows but little of human nature who has not discovered that, to all who rise one step above the brutes, it is far pleasanter to starve and freeze after their own fashion than to be fed and clothed and worked upon compulsion.

Hildreth, *Slave*, Volume I, XV

Liberty is often a heavy burden on a man. It involves that necessity for perpetual choice which is the kind of labor men have always dreaded. In common life we shirk it by forming habits, which take the place of self-determination.

Holmes, *Elsie Venner*, XVIII

Man, born free, knows no superior.

Johnstone, *The Pilgrim*, II

It is not the prime end, and chief blessing, to be politically free. And freedom is only good as a means; is no end in itself.

Melville, *Mardi*, CLXI

Freedom is the name for a thing that is *not* freedom.

Ibid.

A man must earn his freedom daily, or he will become a slave in some form or another: and the way to earn it is by work and obedience to right direction.

Meredith, *Beauchamp's Career*, XXVI

Never say your heart is free.

Richardson, *Clarissa Harlowe*, I

When acknowledged, love authorizes freedom; and freedom begets freedom.

Ibid., II

He wants to build up a merit for sincerity or plain-dealing, by saying free things.

Richardson, *Sir Charles Grandison*, One, I

Liberty is the life of all pleasure.

Shebbeare, *The Marriage Act*, I

Freedom is my infirmity. It leads to sad irreverences.

Simms, *The Yemassee*, VII

Like every other privilege, the liberty of the press must be restrained within certain bounds; for if it is carried to a breach of law, religion, and charity, it becomes one of the greatest evils that ever annoyed the community.

Smollett, *Humphry Clinker*, 111

I go free to prison.

Stevenson, *Prince Otto*, Book II, XIV

Dolls are safe companions. Alcott, *Old-Fashioned Girl*, IV

Exalted minds enter more rapidly and closely into the connections of friendship than those of a vulgar stamp. Anonymous, *The Adventures of a Kidnapped Orphan*, 230

Friendship is so nearly allied to happiness, that one can hardly exist without the other.
Anonymous, *The Birmingham Counterfeit*, I

Friendship must not overturn generosity. Anonymous, *The Egg*, 220

Violent friendships are never permanent; and female friendship, the least durable of any. Anonymous, *Memoirs of a Coquet*, 167

A man may be contented with one woman's love, but not with one woman's friendship.
Atherton, *The Californians*, Book II, XIX

Love is nothing in comparison with the intimacy of two congenial friends.
August, *Horrid Mysteries*, IV

The flame of passion lasts for months; whereas the tranquil, modest and unassuming warmth of friendship unites two congenial souls forever. *Ibid.*

Business may bring money, but friendship hardly ever does. Austen, *Emma*, XXXIV

Friendship is certainly the finest balm for the pangs of disappointed love.
Austen, *Northanger Abbey*, IV

Affection between two men is much more likely to be mutual than that between two women. Bates, *Puritans*, XXXIV

Friends always forget those whom fortune forsakes. Bronte, C., *Jane Eyre*, XXVII

What was become of that curious one-sided friendship which was half marble and half life; only on one hand truth, and on the other perhaps a jest?
Bronte, C., *Villette*, XXXI

People hate their wives, sometimes, but not their sisters and brothers.
Bronte, E., *Wuthering Heights*, XXIII

Friendship, like love, is the child of sympathy, not of complaint.
Brooke, *Emily Montague*, II

Equality is the soul of friendship. *Ibid.*

Nothing shows the value of friendship more than the envy it excites. *Ibid.*, IV

The world will sooner pardon us any advantage, even wealth, genius, or beauty, than that of having a faithful friend. *Ibid.*

It is better to be the dupe of a thousand false professions of friendship than, for fear of being deceived, give up the pursuit of it. *Ibid.*

Friendship is a mighty pretty invention, and, next to love, gives of all things the greatest spirit to society. *Ibid.*

Friendship is an affection of earth. Bulwer, *Pompeii*, Book Two, IV

There is no man so friendless but what he can find a friend sincere enough to tell him disagreeable truths. Bulwer, *What Will He Do with It?*, Book III, XV

In life it is difficult to say who do you the most mischief, enemies with the worst intentions, or friends with the best. *Ibid.*, Book III, XVII

Whatever the number of a man's friends, there will be times in his life when he has too few; but if he has only one enemy, he is lucky indeed if he has not one too many.
Ibid., Book IX, III

When amicable relations between two men happen to be in jeopardy, there is least danger of an ensuing quarrel if the friendly intercourse has been of artificial growth, on either side. Collins, *Blind Love*, XXX

In a true attachment, there is an innocent familiarity implied, which is forgetful of ceremony, and blind to consequences. *Ibid.*

The enemies who have once loved each other are the bitterest enemies of all. *Ibid.*

True friendship disregards selfish considerations, and rather risks to offend by endeavoring to serve, than aims to please by concurring in what is injurious.
Dacre, *Passions*, Letter XIII

Friendship between woman and woman, what is it but a refined and disinterested species of love? *Ibid.*, Letter XXX

"Wal'r, my boy," replied the Captain, "in the Proberbs of Solomon you will find the following words, 'May we never want a friend in need, nor a bottle to give him!' When found, make a note of." Dickens, *Dombey and Son*, XV

The stranger who looks into ten thousand faces for some answering look and never finds it, is in cheering society as compared with him who passes ten averted faces daily, that were once the countenances of friends. Dickens, *Hard Times*, Book II, IV

What is the odds so long as the fire of soul is kindled at the taper of conwiviality, and the wing of friendship never moults a feather! Dickens, *Old Curiosity Shop*, II

"Every man's his own friend." "Except sometimes some people are nobody's enemies but their own." Dickens, *Oliver Twist*, XLIII

When a man's his own enemy, it's only because he's too much his own friend; not because he's careful for everybody but himself. *Ibid.*

It is the fate of most men who mingle with the world, and attain even the prime of life, to make many real friends, and lose them in the course of nature. It is the fate of all authors or chroniclers to create imaginary friends, and lose them in the course of art.
Dickens, *Pickwick Papers*, LVII

At school, friendship is a passion. It entrances the being; it tears the soul. All loves of after life can never bring its rapture, or its wretchedness; no bliss so absorbing, no pangs of jealousy or despair so crushing and so keen! Disraeli, *Coningsby*, Book I, IX

Though her heart was not large enough to harbor more than one light love at a time, it had room for many warm friendships; and she was the warmest, most helpful, and most compassionate of friends, far more serious in friendship than in love.
DuMaurier, *Trilby*, I

Perhaps the most delightful friendships are those in which there is much agreement, much disputation, and yet more personal liking. Eliot, *Felix Holt*, X

That new sense which is the gift of sorrow,—that susceptibility to the bare offices of humanity which raises them into a bond of loving fellowship, as to haggard men among the icebergs the mere presence of an ordinary comrade stirs the deep fountains of affection. Eliot, *Mill on the Floss*, Book II, VII

There are jilts in friendship as well as in love; and, by the behavior of some men in both, one would almost imagine that they industriously sought to gain the affections of others with a view only of making the parties miserable. Fielding, H., *Amelia*, I

Out of love to one's self, one must speak better of a friend than an enemy.
Fielding, H., *Joseph Andrews*, 81

A treacherous friend is the most dangerous enemy. Fielding, H., *Tom Jones*, 85

No wonder that one idle fellow should love another. *Ibid.*, 122

Friendship makes us warmly espouse the interest of others; but it is very cold to the gratification of their passions. *Ibid.*, 168

The beauty and loveliness of friendship is too strong for dim eyes. *Ibid.*, 194

Every profession of friendship easily gains credit with the miserable. *Ibid.*, 350

In his friendships and affections, man is subject to some inscrutable moral law, similar in its effects to what the chemists call affinity. Galt, *Ayrshire*, VI

He found that such friends as benefits had gathered round him were little estimable; he found that a man's own heart must be ever given to gain that of another.

Goldsmith, *The Vicar of Wakefield*, 14

Disproportioned friendships ever terminate in disgust. *Ibid.*, 23

To discover evil in a new friend is to most people only an additional experience: to him it was ever a surprise. Hardy, *Desperate Remedies*, I

That false mirror called friendship. Harley, *Priory of St. Bernard*, II

If you would try a friend, lead him to the scenes of distress. *Ibid.*

Admire that friend who freely chides your faults and reproves you when wrong. *Ibid.*

In the time of trial, the man who is selfish enough to feel personal fear is unworthy the name of friend. Helme, *St. Margaret's Cave*, Volume III, V

He looked like a person who would willingly shake hands with anyone.

James, H., *The American*, II

The rubs of life may occasionally loosen the cohesion of friendship; but it is very good to feel that, with a little direct contact, it may easily be re-established.

James, H., *Confidence*, XXV

The process of falling in love at first sight is as final as it is swift in such a case, but the growth of true friendship may be a lifelong affair.

Jewett, *The Country of Pointed Firs*, I

Congenial virtues attract each other. Johnstone, *Arsaces*, II

The transition from friendship to love is imperceptible, and seldom fails between the different sexes. Johnstone, *The Reverie*, I

In a good mind friendship often arises from the same cause which would have produced envy in one of a different cast. *Ibid.*, II

An offended friend is no common enemy. Kidgell, *The Card*, I

Better is old wine than new, and old friends likewise.

Kingsley, *Hereward the Wake*, XXVII

Love and friendship, the wise say, exclude each other. Lennox, *Henrietta*, I

Friendship, the jewel of human joy. Lyly, *Euphues*, 105

A friend is long a-getting and soon lost, like a merchant's riches, who by tempest loseth as much in two hours as he hath gathered together in twenty years.

Lyly, *Euphues and His England*, 324

The admonition of a friend should be like the practice of a wise physician, who wrappeth his sharp pills in fine sugar. *Ibid.*, 328

Water is praised for that it savoreth of nothing; fire, for that it yieldeth to nothing; and such should the nature of a true friend be, that it should not savor of any rigor, and such the effect, that it may not be conquered with any offense. *Ibid.*, 382

Friends must be used as the musicians tune their strings, who finding them in a discord, do not break them, but either by intention or remission, frame them to a pleasant consent: or as riders handle their young colts, who finding them wild and untractable, bring them to a good pace, with a gentle rein, not with a sharp spur, or as the Scythians ruled their slaves not with cruel weapons but with the shew of small whips.

Ibid., 382–383

Beware of pretended friendship, that cloak to mischief.

McCarthy, *The Fair Moralist*, 4

Love may do much, but friendship shall do wonders; friendship, the nobler passion of the mind, born with the soul, must still with that survive, when love, the silly baby of the fancy, can be no more. *Ibid.*, 63-64

Much less pleasure in being the master of acres than the friend of man.

Mackenzie, *Julia De Roubigné*, 30

Reciprocal friendship seldom exists in a strong degree between superiors and inferiors.

Meeke, *Count St. Blanchard*, I

True friendliness, like true religion, is independent of words.

Melville, *Confidence-Man*, XI

The same may be said of friendship at first sight as of love at first sight: it is the only true one, the only noble one. It bespeaks confidence. Who would go sounding his way into love or friendship, like a strange ship by night, into an enemy's harbor? *Ibid.*, XXIX

When the whole world shall have been genialized, it will be as out of place to talk of murderers, as in a Christianized world to talk of sinners. *Ibid.*, XXX

True friendship, like other precious things, is not rashly to be meddled with. And what more meddlesome between friends than a loan? A regular marplot. *Ibid.*, XLI

It is but well to be on friendly terms with all the inmates of the place one lodges in.

Melville, *Moby Dick*, I

I'll try a pagan friend, thought I, since Christian kindness has proved but hollow courtesy. *Ibid.*, X

All professors of the arts love to fraternize. Melville, *Omoo*, VIII

It is false that in point of policy a man should never make enemies. As well-wishers some men may not only be nugatory but positive obstacles in your peculiar plans; but as foes you may subordinately cement them into your general design.

Melville, *Pierre*, Book XV, I

An exchange of names is equivalent to a ratification of good will and amity among these simple people; and as we were aware of this fact, we were delighted that it had taken place. Melville, *Typee*, X

Friends may laugh: I am not roused. My enemy's laugh is a bugle blown in the night.

Meredith, *Amazing Marriage*, XXVIII

It is in absence that we desire our friends to be friendship itself.

Meredith, *Beauchamp's Career*, XXIII

Friendship is the holiday of those who can be friends. Meredith, *The Egoist*, IV

Wives are plentiful, friends are rare. *Ibid.*

No man ought to be counted an enemy which hath done no injury. More, *Utopia*, II

The fellowship of nature is a strong league; and men be better and more surely knit together by love and benevolence than by covenants of leagues; by hearty affection of minds than by words. *Ibid.*

Friendship should never give a bias against justice.

Richardson, *Clarissa Harlowe*, I

It is natural for a person to be the more desirous of making new friends in proportion as she loses the favor of old ones. *Ibid.*

Spare me not because I am your friend. For that very reason spare me not. *Ibid.*

A faithful friend is the medicine of life. *Ibid.*, II

As money is said to increase money, so does the countenance of persons of character increase friends. *Ibid.*

High-souled and noble friendship has often been the ground of apprehension, because of its unbridled fervor. *Ibid.*

God send me a friend that may tell me of my faults: if not, an enemy, and he will. *Ibid.*

All experience confirms that friendship between women never holds to the sacrifice of capital gratifications, or to the endangering of life, limb, or estate, as it often does in the nobler male sex. *Ibid.*, III

Faithful are the wounds of a friend. *Ibid.*

It is impossible but the errors of the dearest friend must weaken our inward opinion of that friend. *Ibid.*

There are friendships which are only bottle-deep. *Ibid.*

Our friendships and intimacies are only calculated for strong life and health. *Ibid.*, IV

So warm, yet so cool a friend! *Ibid.*

Friendship is the balm, as well as seasoning, of life; and a man cannot be defective in any of the social duties who is capable of it.
Richardson, *Sir Charles Grandison*, Two, III

How much more glorious a character is that of the friend of mankind than that of the conqueror of nations! *Ibid.*

Friendship begins at home. Scott, *St. Ronan's Well*, X

I love friendly deeds better than fair words. Scott, *The Talisman*, III

It is an ill-judged friendship that does not correct its friend's mistakes before they are given to the world, and are irrevocable. Shebbeare, *The Marriage Act*, II

Friendship is an idle title of a thing which cannot be where virtue is not established.
Sidney, *Arcadia*, I

Times change; but they shouldn't change friends. Simms, *The Scout*, III

True friendship seldom suspects, and is the last to yield to the current, when its course bears against the breast it loves. *Ibid.*, VIII

We are all unwilling to be disappointed in our friends, not because they are so, but because it is our judgment which has made them so. *Ibid.*, XXXIII

Friendship has two garments, an outer and an under one.
Sterne, *Tristram Shandy*, IX

Get a friend, sir, and that friend a woman—a good household drudge, who loves you. *That* is the most precious sort of friendship; for the expense of it is all on the woman's side. Thackeray, *Barry Lyndon*, XIII

When you and your brother are friendly, his doings are indifferent to you. When you have quarrelled, all his outgoings and incomings you know, as if you were his spy.
Thackeray, *Vanity Fair*, XI

What is the secret mesmerism which friendship possesses, and under the operation of which a person ordinarily sluggish, or cold, or timid, becomes wise, active, and resolute, in another's behalf? *Ibid.*, XXIII

One's friend has no right to decide for one what is, and what is not, dangerous.
Trollope, *He Knew He Was Right*, LVI

I must be allowed to contradict the friend that I love. *Ibid.*

The holy passion of Friendship is of so sweet and steady and loyal and enduring a nature that it will last through a whole lifetime, if not asked to lend money.
Twain, *Pudd'nhead Wilson*, VIII

You don't understand what friendship is—or what enmity is. You like everyone; that is to say, you are indifferent to everyone. Wilde, *The Picture of Dorian Gray*, I

A man cannot be too careful in the choice of his enemies. *Ibid.*

FRIVOLITY

One has a right to be frivolous, if it's one's nature.   James, H., *The Europeans*, VIII

Frivolity is the fruit of that training that is all for the flesh.
         Meredith, *Harry Richmond*, XIII

GAIN

To carry on two controversies at the same time is favorable to neither.
         Holcroft, *Hugh Trevor*, II

In finding nothing, thou shalt gain all things.   Lyly, *Euphues and His England*, 229

All is not gain that is got into the purse.   Sterne, *Tristram Shandy*, III

GALLANTRY

Young men of open, generous dispositions are naturally inclined to gallantry, which, if they have good understandings, exerts itself in an obliging complacent behavior to all women in general.   Fielding, H., *Tom Jones*, 119

GAMBLING: *see also* CHANCE; DESTINY; FORTUNE; LUCK; etc.

What ecstasy not to know if, in dice and betting, one mayn't in two seconds be worth ten thousand pounds or else without a farthing!   Burney, *Camilla*, Three, VI

Gambling requires as much coolness as the most austere school of philosophy.
         Fielding, H., *Tom Jones*, 394

Nothing more aggravates bad luck than the near approach to good luck. The gamester who loses by a single point laments his bad luck ten times as much as he who never came within a prospect of the game.   *Ibid.*, 602

Losers never despair retrieving all by the last stake.   Jenner, *The Placid Man*, I

A right sense of gaming enlarges the faculties of the mind.   Kidgell, *The Card*, I

Very high mysteries may be couched under the character of a gambler.
         Kimber, *David Ranger*, II

Gambling is a sordid vice; an immorality; the child of avarice; and a direct breach of that commandment which forbids us to covet what is our neighbor's.
         Richardson, *Clarissa Harlowe*, IV

An honorable card hand should go with an honorable heart.
         Richardson, *Pamela*, 428

GENEROSITY: *see also* GIFT; GIVING AND RECEIVING; etc.

Good fortune opens the hand as well as the heart wonderfully; and to give somewhat when we have largely received, is but to afford a vent to the unusual ebullition of the sensations.   Bronte, C., *Jane Eyre*, XXXIV

Every generous rich man deserves to be worshipped.   Bulwer, *Pompeii*, Book Two, II

Generosity, the most eager and active of the virtues.
         Bulwer, *The Pilgrims of the Rhine*, VI

Generosity without delicacy, like wit without judgment, generally gives as much pain as pleasure.   Burney, *Evelina*, 76

Generosity is the stamp of greatness.   Donaldson, *Sir Bartholomew Sapskull*, II

It is always disagreeable to a generous mind to disappoint the expectations of those who trust to their felicity.   Duff, *The History of Rhedi*, 169

Nothing can be more irksome to a generous mind than to discover that it hath thrown away all its good offices on a soil that bears no other fruit than ingratitude.
                                                                Fielding, H., *Amelia*, II

When the mighty Caesar had with wonderful greatness of mind destroyed the liberties of his country, and gotten all the power into his own hands, we receive, as an evidence of his generosity, his largeness to his followers and tools, by whose means he had accomplished his purpose, and by whose assistance he was to establish it.
                                                        Fielding, H., *Jonathan Wild*, 11-12

The man of generosity roams above all thought to the realms of pleasure.
                                                            Harley, *Priory of St. Bernard*, I

No change of condition can alter the sentiments of a generous heart.
                                                                Johnstone, *Arsaces*, II

He is humane who helps the needy.   Judd, *Margaret*, Volume II, III

If I had a fortune as large as my heart, there should not be one distressed person in the world.   Lennox, *Sophia*, II

True good-breeding is the sister of philanthropy, with feelings perhaps not so serious or tender, but equally inspired by a fineness of soul and open to the impressions of social affection.   Mackenzie, *The Man of the World*, I

To a generous mind few circumstances are more afflicting than a discovery of perfidy in those whom we have trusted.   Radcliffe, *The Romance of the Forest*, 431

They make use of your own generosity to oppress you.
                                                            Richardson, *Clarissa Harlowe*, I

Who is able to give a heart, if a heart be wanting?   *Ibid.*

Undue generosity does as much mischief to the noble-minded as love to the ignobler.
                                                                                Ibid.

A generous mind is not to be forced.   *Ibid.*

A generous mind scorns to abuse a generous confidence.   *Ibid.*, II

A just man will keep his promise; a generous man will go beyond it.   *Ibid.*

True generosity is not confined to pecuniary instances.   *Ibid.*

True generosity is greatness of soul.   *Ibid.*

Generosity will not surely permit a worthy mind to doubt of its honorable and beneficent intentions: much less will it allow itself to shock, to offend any one; and, least of all, a person thrown by adversity, mishap, or accident, into its protection.   *Ibid.*

His generosity is more owing to pride and vanity than to that philanthropy which distinguishes a beneficent mind.   *Ibid.*

People even of narrow tempers are ready to praise generous ones: such persons generally find it to their purpose, that all the world should be open-minded but themselves.
                                                                                Ibid., IV

Generosity is the happy medium between parsimony and profusion.   *Ibid.*

A generous mind will not scruple to give advantage to a person of merit, though not always to his own advantage.   *Ibid.*

There is, where the power is wanting, as much generosity in the will as in the action.
                                                            Richardson, *Pamela*, 354

Generosity will not be confined to obligations.

Richardson, *Sir Charles Grandison*, Two, III

Intelligent unselfishness ought to be wiser than intelligent selfishness.

Sheldon, *In His Steps*, IX

Who feels injustice; who shrinks before a slight; who has a sense of wrong so acute, and so glowing a gratitude for kindness as a generous boy?

Thackeray, *Vanity Fair*, V

People are very fond of giving away what they need most themselves. It is the depth of generosity.　　　　　Wilde, *The Picture of Dorian Gray*, IV

GENIUS; ORIGINALITY: *see also* FOLLY; GREATNESS; INTELLECT; KNOWL-
EDGE AND LEARNING; WISDOM

We are all of us great geniuses. We never say so, because we are as modest as we are great.　　　　　Adams, H., *Esther*, IV

It takes people a long time to learn the difference between talent and genius, especially ambitious young men and women.　　　　Alcott, *Little Women*, XXVI

Michelangelo affirms, "Genius is eternal patience."　　　　　*Ibid.*

Talent isn't genius, and you can't make it so.　　　　　*Ibid.*, XLI

Genius is arbitrary. All attempts to force it are ineffectual.

Anonymous, *The Adventures of an Author*, II

Genius and virtue are independent of rank and fortune.

Brackenridge, *Modern Chivalry*, Part I, I

Genius is self-conscious.　　　　　Bronte, C., *Jane Eyre*, XVII

Poetry is not dead, nor genius lost; nor has Mammon gained power over either, to bind or slay: they will both assert their existence, their presence, their liberty and strength. Powerful angels, safe in heaven! they smile when sordid souls triumph, and feeble ones weep over their destruction.　　　　　*Ibid.*, XXXII

Genius will never mount high, where the faculties of the mind are benumbed half the year.　　　　　Brooke, *Emily Montague*, I

Genius is like the sensitive plant; it shrinks from the touch.　　　　*Ibid.*, IV

It is the proud consciousness of certain qualities that it cannot reveal to the everyday world that gives to genius that shy, and reserved, and troubled air, which puzzles and flatters you when you encounter it.　　　　Bulwer, *Pompeii*, Book Two, IV

Deviations from common rules, when they proceed from genius, are not merely pardonable, but admirable.　　　　　Burney, *Cecilia*, I

The pitiful prevalence of general conformity extirpates genius and murders orginality.

Ibid.

Of genius Erewhonians make no account, for they say that everyone is a genius, more or less. No one is so physically sound that no part of him will be even a little unsound, and no one is so diseased but that some part of him will be healthy—so no man is so mentally and morally sound, but that he will be in part both mad and wicked; and no man is so mad and wicked but he will be sensible and honorable in part. In like manner there is no genius who is not also a fool, and no fool who is not also a genius.

Butler, *Erewhon*, XXII

He thought that ideas came into clever people's heads by a kind of spontaneous germination, without parentage in the thoughts of others or the course of observation; for as yet he believed in genius, of which he well knew that he had none, if it was the fine frenzied thing he thought it was.　　　　Butler, *The Way of All Flesh*, XLVI

Every man of true genius has his peculiarity. Sir, the peculiarity of my friend Slyme is, that he is always waiting round the corner. He is perpetually round the corner, sir. He is round the corner at this instant.　　　　　　Dickens, *Martin Chuzzlewit*, IV

Eccentricities of genius.　　　　　　Dickens, *Pickwick Papers*, XXX

Ascendant power is the destiny of genius.　　　　Disraeli, *Coningsby*, Book II, VII

Genius is necessarily intolerant of fetters.　　　Eliot, *Middlemarch*, Book I, X

Men of great genius easily discover one another.　　Fielding, H., *Jonathan Wild*, 22

Genius, thou gift of Heaven, without whose aid in vain we struggle against the stream of nature.　　　　　　　　Fielding, H., *Tom Jones*, 598

Humanity, almost the constant attendant on true genius.　　　　*Ibid.*, 599

Wherever there is genius, there is pride.　　Goldsmith, *The Vicar of Wakefield*, 110

Genius is modest.　　　　　　Hardy, *The Hand of Ethelberta*, XXI

Youthful genius may produce nothing visible to the world's eye, and yet may complete its development within to a very perfect degree.　　Hardy, *Two on a Tower*, XXV

Let not a moderate genius be too much ashamed of a guide.
　　　　　　　　　　　　　　Jenner, *The Placid Man*, I

The point-blank piercing eye of genius, and the laughter-loving face of humor.
　　　　　　　　　　　　　　Lawrence, *Common Sense*, I

The followers of genius are not always the enemies of prudence.　　　*Ibid.*, II

Genius must be somewhat like us kings—calm, content, in consciousness of power.
　　　　　　　　　　　　　　Melville, *Mardi*, CLXXX

Genius is full of trash. But genius essays its best to keep it to itself; and giving away its ore, retains the earth; whence, the too frequent wisdom of its works, and folly of its life.
　　　　　　　　　　　　　　Ibid.

Genius in the Sperm Whale? Has the Sperm Whale ever written a book, spoken a speech? No, his great genius is declared in his doing nothing particular to prove it. It is moreover declared in his pyramidical silence.　　　Melville, *Moby Dick*, LXXIX

Genius is unacquainted with wrinkles.　　　　Meredith, *The Egoist*, XIV

The sign of genius is the power of recognizing and assimilating that which is necessary to the development of oneself.　　　　　Moore, *Evelyn Innes*, XIII

Genius is merely the power of assimilation; only the fool imagines he invents.　*Ibid.*

The most ingenious minds are easiest moved.　Nashe, *The Unfortunate Traveller*, 83

If genius arises, encourage it; there will be rustics enough to do the common services for the finer spirits.　　　　　Richardson, *Sir Charles Grandison*, Two, V

Genius without deep learning makes a much more shining figure than learning without genius.　　　　　　　　　　　　*Ibid.*, Three, VI

Genius, whether in man or woman, will push itself into light.　　　　*Ibid.*

Genius can see more in one moment than those who have it not can in seven years.
　　　　　　　　　　　　　　Shebbeare, *The Marriage Act*, II

She is one of those geniuses who find some diabolical enjoyment in being dreaded and detested by their fellow-creatures.　　　Smollett, *Humphry Clinker*, 70

The great geniuses are, and have been, essentially savages in all but the breech-clout.
　　　　　　　　　　　　　　Webber, *Old Hicks*, XXIII

Genius lasts longer than beauty. That accounts for the fact that we all take such pains to over-educate ourselves.　　　　Wilde, *The Picture of Dorian Gray*, I

GENTILITY; GENTLEMANLINESS

A real gentleman is as polite to a little girl as to a woman.

Alcott, *Old-Fashioned Girl*, II

There is a manner of doing even a genteel thing, and that is to do it genteelly. I much doubt if a genteel thing *can* be done ungenteelly.   Cooper, *Satanstoe*, Volume I, V

In those days there was little the people feared but a gentleman, and small wonder.

Crane, *The O'Ruddy*, II

A gentleman is known by the ways of his servants.   *Ibid.*, XIII

I know what a gentleman is, and what a gentleman is capable of. A gentleman can bear a shock, when it must come, boldly and steadily. A gentleman can make up his mind to stand up against almost any blow.   Dickens, *Bleak House*, LIV

It is a principle of his that no man who was not a true gentleman at heart, ever was, since the world began, a true gentleman in manner.

Dickens, *Great Expectations*, XXII

Once a gentleman, and, always a gentleman. A gentleman from the beginning, and a gentleman to the end.   Dickens, *Little Dorrit*, Book II, XXVIII

A mean man never agrees to anything without deliberately turning it over, so that he may see its dirty side, and, if he can, sweating the coin he pays for it. If an archangel should offer to save his soul for sixpence he would try to find a sixpence with a hole in it. A gentleman says yes to a great many things without stopping to think: a shabby fellow is known by his caution in answering questions, for fear of compromising his pocket or himself.   Holmes, *Elsie Venner*, XXVIII

Gentlemaning as a profession has got to play out in a generation or two.

Howells, *Silas Lapham*, II

GHOSTS: *see also* DEATH

If the ghost of a man's own father cannot be allowed to claim his attention, what can?

Dickens, *Great Expectations*, XXVII

If ghos'es want me to believe in 'em, let 'em leave off shulking i' the dark and i' lon places—let 'em come where there's company and candles.   Eliot, *Silas Marner*, VI

Goblins and spirits have no more to do with darkness than with light.

Graves, *The Spiritual Quixote*, I

Your ghosts are very rude unsociable folks.   Parsons, *The Castle of Wolfenbach*, I

GIFT; TALENT: *see also* GENIUS; GIVING AND RECEIVING; GREATNESS; etc.

It is no shame to use God's gifts for our credits.   Deloney, *Jack of Newbury*, 384

Of all silly things in the world, the silliest is a present that is not wanted.

Disraeli, *Sybil*, Book IV, II

Excellent always are the gifts which are made acceptable by the virtue of the giver.

Lyly, *Euphues*, 129

To excel in theory and to excel in practice generally require different talents, which are not always met in the same person.   Richardson, *Clarissa Harlowe*, I

A gift that is begrudged is already recalled.   Scott, *The Talisman*, XIV

There is many a trifle I would deny you. There is many a great gift I would give you willingly.   Trollope, *Phineas Finn*, LX

GIVING AND RECEIVING: *see also* GENEROSITY; GIFT; etc.

To have to spare is to have to give away.   Melville, *Israel Potter*, VIII

GIVING AND RECEIVING (*continued*)

The giver and the accepter are principally answerable in an unjust donation.
Richardson, Clarissa Harlowe, I

The petitioned has as good a right to reject as the petitioner to ask.　　*Ibid.*, IV

It is a godlike power to confer benefits rather than to be obliged to receive them.　　*Ibid.*

GLORY: *see also* HONOR

A nobleman's glory appeareth in nothing so much as in the pomp of his attendants.
What is the glory of the sun, but that the moon and so many millions of stars borrow
their light from him?　　　　　Nashe, *The Unfortunate Traveller*, 91

Would that the whole world were wrong that you might have the glory of setting it
right!　　　　　　Radcliffe, *The Italian*, I

Though glory always follows virtue, yet it is only its shadow.
Richardson, Clarissa Harlowe, IV

The word and thing called glory, what mischief has it not occasioned!
Richardson, Sir Charles Grandison, One, II

Each was the constant center of a group of breathless listeners; each recognized that she
knew now for the first time the real meaning of that great word Glory, and perceived
the stupendous value of it, and understood why men in all ages had been willing to
throw away meaner happinesses, treasure, life itself, to get a taste of its sublime and
supreme joy. Napoleon and all his kind stood accounted for—and justified.
Twain, Pudd'nhead Wilson, VI

GLUTTONY

"Swine," pursued Mr. Wopsle, in his deepest voice, and pointing his fork at my blushes,
as if he were mentioning my Christian name, "Swine were the companions of my
prodigal. The gluttony of Swine is put before us, as an example to the young." (I thought
this pretty well in him who had been praising up the pork for being so plump and juicy.)
"What is detestable in a pig, is more detestable in a boy."
Dickens, Great Expectations, IV

GOD; CHRIST: *see also* DEMON; RELIGION; etc.

God winds you up, and you go till He stops you.　　　Alcott, *Little Women*, XLV

We are here in God's bosom, a land unknown.　　Sir Francis Bacon, *Atlantis*, 214

The only coin current is the image of God.　　Bellamy, *Looking Backward*, XII

It is very easy to believe in the fatherhood of God in the twentieth century.　　*Ibid.*, XXVI

God can make the basest passions serve the most worthy ends.　　Bierce, *Monk*, XVI

The human and fallible should not arrogate a power with which the divine and perfect
alone can be safely entrusted.　　　Bronte, C., *Jane Eyre*, XIV

God, who does the work, ordains the instrument.　　　　*Ibid.*, XX

We know that God is everywhere; but certainly we feel His presence when His works
are on the grandest scale spread before us; and it is in the unclouded night-sky, where
His worlds wheel their silent course, that we read clearest His infinitude, His omnipotence, His omnipresence.　　　　　*Ibid.*, XXVIII

Do you think God will be satisfied with half an oblation? Will He accept a mutilated
sacrifice?　　　　　　　*Ibid.*, XXXIV

God sees not as man sees; *His* will be done.　　　　*Ibid.*, XXXV

Some lives are blessed; it is God's will: it is the attesting trace and lingering evidence of Eden. Other lives run from the first another course. Other travellers encounter weather fitful and gusty, wild and variable—breast adverse winds, are belated and overtaken by the early closing winter night.   Bronte, C., *Villette*, XXXII

The man worthy of God is a god among men.   Bulwer, *Pompeii*, Book One, VI

When God wills, all winds bring rain.
                         Bulwer, *What Will He Do with It?*, Book IV, XV

This shame tells me what men are; but it tells me nothing what God or the Word of God is.   Bunyan, *Pilgrim's Progress*, 75

What God says is best, is best, though all the men in the world are against it.   *Ibid.*

What thing is so pleasant, and what so profitable, as to talk of the things of God?
                                                 Ibid., 78

Christ is one that has not his fellow.   *Ibid.*, 219

Christ has two natures in one person, plain to be distinguished, impossible to be divided.
                                                     Ibid.

Mention but the word divinity, and our sense of the divine is clouded.
                                           Butler, *Erewhon*, XIV

When you would conceive of that great Being truly and fully, you must be able to realize the duration of eternity, obliterate the little periods of time and chronology, which require a starting and a resting-place in our human minds—soar out of the reach of the sickly atmospheres which surround these little planets, and stand erect in the broad and fathomless light of God's own atmosphere.
                       Caruthers, *Kentuckian in New-York*, Volume I, XVII

God is too often a convenient stalking horse for human selfishness.
                         Chesnutt, *The House Behind the Cedars*, XIX

Any man who calls any human individual "divine" is a profane man.
                             Collins, *The Dead Secret*, Book IV, III

The true peace of God begins at any spot a thousand miles from the nearest land.
                             Conrad, *Nigger of the Narcissus*, II

There are men who read in books to convince themselves there is a God.
                             Cooper, *The Last of the Mohicans*, XII

Nothing but vast wisdom and unlimited power should dare to sweep off men in multitudes; for it is only the one that can know the necessity of the judgment; and what is there, short of the other, that can replace the creatures of the Lord?   *Ibid.*, XVIII

God implants in the bosom of his servants a desire to advance his ends, but human agents are compelled to employ natural means.   Cooper, *Mercedes of Castile*, XVII

Human folly is not needed to fill up the great design of God. There is no stature, no beauty, no proportions, nor any colors in which man himself can well be fashioned, that is not already done to his hands.   Cooper, *The Prairie*, XXII

Men reap only the harvest they have sown in the world. Even in this life, God is just.
                         Davis, R. H., *Waiting for the Verdict*, XXVI

How do I know what God himself judges?   Defoe, *Robinson Crusoe*, 157

Our Maker is a good borrower. Never fear making a bad debt there.
                                           Defoe, *Roxana*, 25

God never comes where knaves are present.   Deloney, *Thomas of Reading*, 231

Long may it remain in this mixed world a point not easy of decision, which is the more beautiful of the Almighty's goodness—the delicate fingers that are formed for sensitive-

ness and sympathy of touch, and made to minister to pain and grief, or the rough hard hand, that the heart teaches, guides, and softens in a moment.
Dickens, *Dombey and Son*, XLVIII

Her sorrows were known to man; her virtues to God.   Dickens, *Pickwick Papers*, VI

The great magician who majestically works out the appointed order of the Creator never reverses his transformations.   Dickens, *Tale of Two Cities*, Book III, XV

It is very wicked and most immoral to believe, or affect to believe, and tell others to believe, that the unseen, unspeakable, unthinkable Immensity we're all part and parcel of, source of eternal, infinite, indestructible life and light and might, is a kind of wrathful, glorified, and self-glorifying ogre in human shape, with human passions, and most inhuman hates—who suddenly made us out of nothing, one fine day—just for a freak—and made us so badly that we fell the next—and turned us adrift the day after—damned us from the very beginning—and ever since never gave us a chance.
DuMaurier, *Trilby*, V

All-merciful Father, indeed! Why, the Prince of Darkness was an angel in comparison (and a gentleman into the bargain).   *Ibid.*

Shocky has given his spare time to making outcasts feel that God has not forgot.
Eggleston, *The Hoosier Schoolmaster*, XXXIV

We are in sad want of good news about God; and what does other good news signify if we haven't that? For everything else comes to an end, and when we die we leave it all. But God lasts when everything else is gone. What shall we do if he is not our friend?
Eliot, *Adam Bede*, II

We are overhasty to speak—as if God did not manifest himself by our silent feeling, and make his love felt through ours.   *Ibid.*, XLV

No accident happens to us without the Divine permission.
Fielding, H., *Joseph Andrews*, 224

With God all things are possible. But ofttimes He does His work with awful instruments. There is a peacemaker whose name is Death.   Gaskell, *Sylvia's Lovers*, XLIV

The mind wearies easily when it strives to grapple with the Infinite, and to trace the footsteps of the Almighty as He strides from sphere to sphere, or deduce His purpose from His works.   Haggard, *She*, X

God's *not* in his heaven: all's *wrong* with the world!   Hardy, *Tess*, XXXVII

The broad, sunny smile of God.   Hawthorne, *The Marble Faun*, XXVIII

God gives years, but the devil gives increase.   Hope, *Prisoner of Zenda*, XIII

God has never been imagined at all. But if you suppose an unselfish patriot was Authorized, it will help you to imagine what God must be.
Howells, *Silas Lapham*, XIV

What service can the Deity receive from the works of man?   Johnstone, *Arsaces*, II

What opinion can be intelligible concerning the nature of the Deity, which exceeds the powers of the human mind to understand?   Johnstone, *The Pilgrim*, II

There are four persons in the Godhead—There is God the Father, God the Son, God the Holy Ghost, and God Buonaparte.   Judd, *Margaret*, Volume I, XIV

Beauty and pureness are everlasting; they are of God, and can never die. They may for a moment be obscured, but they shall reappear in brighter lustre. Angels have charge over them that they dash not their foot against a stone. Let us turn to the pleasant face of God in what is about us.   *Ibid.*, Volume II, V

Have you not reflected that Christ was a singer? At the Last Supper "they sang a hymn."
Ibid., Volume III

Are we not more saved by a living, than a dead Christ? *Ibid.*

God produces light from the womb of darkness. Kahlert, *The Necromancer*, II

Anything is good, however bitter, which shows us that there is such a law as retribution, that we are not the sport of blind chance or a triumphant fiend, but that there is a God who judges the earth—righteous to repay every man according to his works.
Kingsley, *Alton Locke*, XXVII

There can be no religion without some previous knowledge of a God.
Kirkby, *The Capacity of Human Understanding*, 92

For wise and good reasons, God made the knowledge of Himself scarce any otherwise attainable by us, than that of the existence of other beings absent to sense. *Ibid.*, 92-93

To talk of imitating God is blasphemy. His Providence is extended to collective bodies only; He has no regard to individuals: nor is the soul a distinct substance from the body.
Lennox, *Henrietta*, II

The will is placed in the soul, and who can enter there but he that created the soul?
Lyly, *Euphues and His England*, 349

The immeasurable's altitude is not heightened by the arches of Mahomet's heavens; and were all space a vacuum, yet would it be a fullness; for to Himself His own universe is He. Melville, *Mardi*, LXXV

Indefinite as God. Melville, *Moby Dick*, XXIII

What are the comprehensible terrors of man compared with the interlinked terrors and wonders of God! *Ibid.*, XXIV

The great God absolute! The centre and circumference of all democracy! His omnipresence, our divine equality! *Ibid.*, XXVI

De god wat made shark must be one dam Ingin. *Ibid.*, LXVI

We lie in nature very close to God; and though, further on, the stream may be corrupted by the banks it flows through; yet at the fountain's rim, where mankind stand, there the stream infallibly bespeaks the fountain. Melville, *Pierre*, Book V, VII

Human life partakes of the unravelable inscrutableness of God.
Ibid., Book VII, VIII

That love of earth which is recognition of God. Meredith, *Beauchamp's Career*, LV

Love leads to God, through art or in acts. *Ibid.*

The God of this world is in the machine—not out of it.
Meredith, *Ordeal of Richard Feverel*, XXXVII

The brotherhood greeted each other with, "Man is God, and son of God, and there is no God but man." Moore, *Evelyn Innes*, XVIII

Once we are convinced that there is a God, and that we are here to save our souls, it were surely folly in the extreme to think of anything except him. *Ibid.*, XXXIII

He sought God in art, while she sought him in dogma. *Ibid.*, XXXV

He that sees himself sees God, and in him there is neither I nor thou. *Ibid.*

God sees at one view the whole thread of our existence, not only that part which we have already passed through, but that which runs forward into all the depths of eternity.
Moore, *Grasville Abbey*, II

Does God concern Himself with us who can do Him no service?
Paltock, *The Life and Adventures of Peter Wilkins*

Him whose name is but a syllable, but whose hand is over all the earth.
Reade, *The Cloister and the Hearth*, XXVII

God Almighty is just and gracious, and gives not His assent to rash and inhuman curses.
Richardson, *Clarissa Harlowe*, II

None but God can curse. *Ibid.*

God's justice cannot let His mercy operate for the comfort of one person. *Ibid.*, IV

God does not desire the spiritual death of a sinner. *Ibid.*

Little by little, in a gradual sensible death, God dies away in us, in order to subdue His poor creatures to Himself. *Ibid.*

God deadens all other sensations, or rather absorbs them all in the love of Him. *Ibid.*

Some are drawn by love, others are driven by terrors, to their Divine refuge. *Ibid.*

The divine grace is not divined to space. Richardson, *Pamela*, 64

A godlike power is that of doing good. *Ibid.*, 329

The fear of God is the beginning of wisdom.
Richardson, *Sir Charles Grandison*, Three, VII

The highest glory of man is that he was created in the image of God.
Roberts, *Looking Within*, XXXI

God wounds but to heal. Roche, *Clermont*, IV

I love Jesus Christ, but I hate God. Schreiner, *The Story of an African Farm*, Part I, I

Gold and love, what are they? The great gods that rule us! Gold, god of the body with its lusts and its clay; Love, god of the soul with its fire and its passions.
Schreiner, *Undine*, VII

God is the only father of the fatherless. Scott, *The Heart of Midlothian*, IX

God is the disposer of all. He can turn back the captivity of Judah, even by the weakest instrument. To execute his message the snail is as sure a messenger as the falcon.
Scott, *Ivanhoe*, XXXVIII

The gifts of God are to be enjoyed, when the Giver is remembered.
Scott, *The Talisman*, III

The finest perception may err in its estimate of the inscrutable work of the Almighty.
Shaw, *The Irrational Knot*, I

The God which is God of nature doth never teach unnaturalness. Sidney, *Arcadia*, I

Would you have an inconstant God, since we count a man foolish that is inconstant?
Ibid., III

God sees the deepest dissembled thoughts, nay sees the thoughts before they be thought.
Ibid.

God is just to exercise his might, and mighty to perform his justice. *Ibid.*

None should take life but him who gives it. Simms, *The Partisan*, Volume I, XII

God is good security for all the debts of the poor. Simms, *Woodcraft*, XLI

There is no cause but one why one man's nose is longer than another's, but because that God pleases to have it so. Sterne, *Tristram Shandy*, III

The devil may work against us, but God sends us men when we want them.
Stoker, *Dracula*, XII

God has always been to me not so much like a father as like a dear and tender mother.
Stowe, *Orr's Island*, XXXII

He turneth the shadow of death into morning. *Ibid.*, XLIV

Mistress says that when all things go wrong to us, we must believe that God is doing the very best. Stowe, *Uncle Tom's Cabin*, III

For the weak, God's providence is always human. Tourgee, *Murvale Eastman*, I

How much kinder is God to us than we are willing to be to ourselves!

Trollope, *Barchester Towers*, II

How can we argue about God's power in the other stars from the laws which he has given for our rule in this one?

Ibid., XIX

Surely the absurdity of all the doctrines of religion, and the iniquity of man, are sufficiently evident. To fear a being on account of his power is degrading; to fear him if he be good, ridiculous.

Wright, *A Few Days in Athens*, XVI

GOOD AND EVIL: *see also* ERROR; RIGHTNESS; etc.

Badness always gets found out.

Alcott, *Little Men*, XX

As the best institutions are liable to be abused, so are the best people to be vilified.

Anonymous, *The Adventures of Sylvia Hughes*, 55

As poisonous adders lurk beneath the cover of the most delightful shrubberies, so falsity and deceit are concealed under alluring language.

Anonymous, *The Birmingham Counterfeit*, II

Darkness is more eligible than light to those whose deeds are evil.

Anonymous, *The Fruitless Repentance*, II

The world might be prosaic without sin, but it is right positive that women would suffer less.

Atherton, *The Californians*, Book I, XI

Man, in his gropings down through the centuries, has concocted, shivered, and patched certain social conditions well enough calculated to develop the best and the worst that is in us, making it easier for us to be bad than good, that good might be the standard.

Atherton, *Doomswoman*, XX

Sin has a habit of persisting, and is remorseless in its choice of vehicles.

Atherton, *Senator North*, Book II, XXI

Every noisy evil is missed when it is taken away.

Austen, *Mansfield Park*, Volume Two, XI

From whence our greatest good springs, our greatest evils arise.

Brackenridge, *Modern Chivalry*, Part II, I

No man is wholly bad all at once.

Bulwer, *The Caxtons*, Book III, VII

The evil that takes false nobility, by garbing itself in the royal magnificence of good.

Ibid., Book III, VIII

Wickedness, like a flood, is like to drown our world.

Bunyan, *The Life and Death of Mr. Badman*, 145

Why should a man so carelessly cast away himself, by giving heed to a stranger?

Bunyan, *Pilgrim's Progress*, 19

A man may cry out against sin, of policy, but he cannot abhor it but by virtue of a godly antipathy against it.

Ibid., 84

Some cry out against sin even as the mother cries out against her child in her lap, when she calleth it slut and naughty girl, and then falls to hugging and kissing it.

Ibid.

A work of grace in the soul discovereth itself either to him that hath it, or to standers by.

Ibid., 85

Sins are all Lords and great ones.

Ibid., 97

Whispering and change of thoughts proves that sin is in the world.

Ibid., 213

'Tis difficult getting of good doctrine in erroneous times.

Ibid., 224

Though to let loose the bridle to lusts, while our opinions are against such things, is bad; yet to sin, and plead a toleration so to do, is worse.

Ibid., 270

Evils inevitable are always best supported, because known to be past amendment, and felt to give defiance to struggling.   Burney, *Cecilia*, III

Half the vices which the world condemns most loudly have seeds of good in them and require moderate use rather than total abstinence.
                Butler, *The Way of All Flesh*, LII

The father of lies is the Devil—mischief and the Devil are never far apart.
                Collins, *The Moonstone*, First Period, XV

There are more ways than one of sowing the good seed.   *Ibid.*, Second Period, IV

All sinners are more or less miserable sinners.   Collins, *The New Magdalen*, XIII

The best men are not consistent in good—why should the worst men be consistent in evil?   Collins, *The Woman in White*, Part II, Third Epoch

The most sacred engagements are daily violated; friendship and love, the most endearing bonds of society, are made a cloak to perpetrate the most execrable villainies, the ruin of innocence, the destruction of the most unsuspecting and honest man.
                Collyer, *Felicia to Charlotte*, I

There are different degrees of turpitude, as there are different tempers to commit it.
                Cooper, *Red Rover*, XXII

It is a heathenish and atheistical dogma, to assert, that man is born evil; that evil is implanted in, and is co-existent with his nature; and that an inevitable combination of circumstance makes the commission of what is termed crime unavoidable to him.
                Dacre, *Passion*, Letter XLI

Either we must suppose that the love of evil is born with us (which would be an insult to the Deity), or we must attribute them to the suggestions of infernal influence.
                Dacre, *Zofloya*, XXXIII

I was exactly fitted for their evil society indeed; for I had no sense of virtue or religion upon me.   Defoe, *Captain Singleton*, 7

The subtile devil is never absent from his business, but ready at all occasions to encourage his servants.   Defoe, *Colonel Jack*, 17

Every ill turn has some good in it.   Defoe, *Moll Flanders*, 187

For me to do wrong, that never did right, was no great wonder.
                Defoe, *Robinson Crusoe*, 34

All evils are to be considered with the good that is in them, and with what worse attends them.   *Ibid.*, 63

There is nothing base, but that which is basely used.   Deloney, *Jack of Newbury*, 369

All good things perverted to evil purposes are worse than those which are naturally bad.
                Dickens, *Barnaby Rudge*, LI

Evil often stops short at itself and dies with the doer of it; but good, never.
                Dickens, *Our Mutual Friend*, IX

Not evil, but longing for that which is better, more often directs the steps of the erring.
                Dreiser, *Sister Carrie*, XLVII

Not evil, but goodness more often allures the feeling mind unused to reason.   *Ibid.*

It is curious to observe how good and bad are mingled in human institutions.
                Edgeworth, *Castle Rackrent*, 78

No man falls like Lucifer from heaven—the progress of evil is slow and not easily perceived. If thou hast defeated Circe, and escaped all swinish transformations then mayest thou proceed in safety and resist the sirens.   Eggleston, *Roxy*, XXXIX

There is no sort of wrong deed of which a man can bear the punishment alone; you can't isolate yourself and say the evil which is in you shall not spread. Men's lives are as thoroughly blended with each other as the air they breathe: evil spreads as necessarily as disease.
Eliot, *Adam Bede*, XLI

When a man's spoiled his fellow creatur's life, he's no right to comfort himself with thinking good may come out of it. Somebody else's good doesn't alter her [his victim's] shame and misery.
Ibid., XLVI

We must learn to see the good in the midst of much that is unlovely.
Ibid., L

By desiring what is perfectly good, even when we don't quite know what it is and cannot do what we would, we are part of the divine power against evil—widening the skirts of light and making the struggle with darkness narrower.
Eliot, *Middlemarch*, Book IV, XXXIX

Cold and nakedness are evils introduced by luxury and custom.
Fielding, H., *Joseph Andrews*, 233

The good or evil we confer on others very often recoils on ourselves.
Fielding, H., *Tom Jones*, 673

It is evil to limp before a cripple.
Gascoigne, *Master F. J.*, 22

A man, while he practices every vice that can disgrace human nature, may imagine he is doing God service.
Godwin, *St. Leon*, 334

The vermin race are ever treacherous, cruel, and cowardly, whilst those endowed with strength and power are generous, brave, and gentle.
Goldsmith, *The Vicar of Wakefield*, 75

In all human institutions a smaller evil is allowed to procure a greater good.
Ibid., 128

The greater the sinner, the greater the saint.
Graves, *The Spiritual Quixote*, II

To every bad there is a worse.
Hardy, *Woodlanders*, XXXIV

Every human being, when given over to the devil, is sure to have the wizard mark upon him, in one form or another.
Hawthorne, *Blithedale Romance*, XVIII

The ghost of a dead progenitor—perhaps as a portion of his own punishment—is often doomed to become the Evil Genius of his family.
Hawthorne, *The House of the Seven Gables*, I

You do not know, for you could never learn it from your own heart, which is all purity and rectitude, what a mixture of good there may be in things evil; and how the greatest criminal, if you look at his conduct from his own point of view, or from any side point, may seem not so unquestionably guilty, after all.
Hawthorne, *The Marble Faun*, XLII

Sin has really become an instrument most effective in the education of intellect and soul.
Ibid., XLVII

To bear with impatience the state in which it has pleased Providence to place us, is sinful.
Helme, *St. Margaret's Cave*, Volume I, XIII

We are never nearer to evil than when we believe a person is incapable of wrongdoing.
James, H., *The Europeans*, V

Parents, are there not real sins enough in the world already, without your defiling it, over and above, by inventing new ones?
Kingsley, *Alton Locke*, II

Fiends we are all, till God's grace comes.
Kingsley, *Hereward the Wake*, XXXVII

Providence allots a certain portion of triumph to the machinations of the wicked.
Lathom, *The Midnight Bell*, II

The works of evil-doers are as acceptable in the eyes of God as the actions of the best men; for vice would not be permitted in the world, if it were not to answer some wise purposes, though our understandings are too shallow to fathom or find them out.
Lawrence, *The Contemplative Man*, I

Conceive a greater hope of a man who in the beginning of his life is hurried away by some evil habit than one who fastens on nothing.　　Lennox, *The Female Quixote*, II

As sinful as ever I was are saints in heaven.　　Malory, *Le Morte DArthur*, Two, XXI

Money, you think, is the sole motive to pains and hazard, deception and deviltry, in this world. How much money did the devil make by gulling Eve?
Melville, Confidence-Man, VI

What creature but a madman would not rather do good than ill, when it is plain that, good or ill, it must return upon himself.　　*Ibid.*, VII

It appeared that the unfortuante man had had for a wife one of those natures, anomalously vicious, which would almost tempt a metaphysical lover of our species to doubt whether the human form be, in all cases, conclusive evidence of humanity, whether, sometimes, it may not be a kind of unpledged and indifferent tabernacle, and whether, once for all to crush the saying of Thrasea (an unaccountable one, considering that he himself was so good a man), that "he who hates vice, hates humanity," it should not, in self-defense, be held for a reasonable maxim, that none but the good are human.
Ibid., XII

Are not foul streams often traced to pure fountains?　　Melville, *Mardi*, CXXXVII

The essence of all good and all evil is in us, not out of us.　　*Ibid.*

It is easier for some men to be saints, than for others not to be sinners.　　*Ibid.*, CXLIII

At bottom, men wear no bonds that other men can strike off; and have no immunities, of which other men can deprive them. Tell a good man that he is free to commit murder—will he murder? Tell a murderer that at the peril of his soul he indulges in murderous thoughts—will that make him a saint?　　*Ibid.*

Though all evils may be assuaged; all evils cannot be done away. For evil is the chronic malady of the universe; and checked in one place, breaks forth in another.　　*Ibid.*, CLXI

In this world, sin that pays its way can travel freely, and without a passport; whereas Virtue, if a pauper, is topped at all frontiers.　　Melville, *Moby Dick*, IX

Thought Queequeg, it's a wicked world in all meridians; I'll die a pagan.　　*Ibid.*, XII

Somehow I felt that all good, harmless men and women were human things, placed at cross-purposes, in a world of snakes and lightnings, in a world of horrible and inscrutable inhumanities.　　Melville, *Pierre*, Book VI, V

What man does not feel livelier and more generous emotions toward the great god of Sin—Satan,—than toward yonder haberdasher, who only is a sinner in the small and entirely honorable way of trade?　　*Ibid.*, Book X, II

There is no dignity in wickedness, whether in purple or rags; and hell is a democracy of devils, where all are equals.　　Melville, *Redburn*, LV

Sin is an alien element in our blood. 'Tis the Apple-Disease with which Nature has striven since Adam. To treat Youth as naturally sinful, is, therefore, false, and bad; as it is bad, and false, to esteem it radically pure. We must consider that we have forfeited Paradise, but were yet grown there.　　Meredith, *Ordeal of Richard Feverel*, I

The triumph of man's intellect, the proof of his power, is to make the serpent who inhabits us fight against himself, till he is destroyed.　　*Ibid.*

A truly good man is possible upon earth: a thoroughly bad man is not possible.　　*Ibid.*

When the sins of the fathers are multiplied by the sons, is not perdition the final sum of things? And is not life, the boon of heaven, growing to be the devil's game utterly?
Ibid., XX

As nice as sin, without the knowledge that you are sinning.
Meredith, Sandra Belloni, XXXI

Below the fine fabric of all that was good in him ran the foul stream of hereditary evil,
like a sewer. Norris, *McTeague*, II

She never suffered any good to pass unnoticed because it came attended with evil.
Radcliffe, *The Romance of the Forest*, 277

Things good and evil balance themselves in a remarkable manner; and almost universally. Reade, *The Cloister and the Hearth*, XXVII

The good and the ill are all one while their lids are closed. *Ibid.*, XXXII

To do evil that good may come of it is forbidden: and shall I do evil yet know not whether
good may come of it or not? Richardson, *Clarissa Harlowe*, I

Why should I, who have such real evils to contend with, regard imaginary ones? *Ibid.*

Good often comes when evil is expected. *Ibid.*, II

Evils self-caused, and avoidable, admit not of palliation or comfort. *Ibid.*, III

Good actions are remembered but for a day: bad ones for many years after the life of the
guilty. *Ibid.*

The evil risk more to serve evil than the good risk to serve good. *Ibid.*

Even persons who have bad hearts will have a veneration for those who have good ones.
Ibid.

No bad is not *good*. Richardson, *Sir Charles Grandison*, One, I

If the human mind is not actively good, it will generally be actively evil. *Ibid.*, One, II

People seldom commit a sin without intending to derive benefit from it.
Roche, *Clermont*, IV

The greatest devil among us has his white spots, and the purest saint has ink-black
stains which will be clearly visible if he do not keep his white clothing too tight about
him. Schreiner, *Undine*, XI

Ignorance and prejudice are the only real evils. Scott, *Quentin Durward*, XXIX

Sin is never in season; and—alas!—it is never out of season when the devil is master.
Shaw, *The Irrational Knot*, V

A people universally debauched is certainly undone. Shebbeare, *The Marriage Act*, II

The evil spirits always hate the good ones. Trollope, *Ayala's Angel*, LXI

"You would doubt his teaching who had gone astray himself." "Then I must doubt all
human teaching, for all have gone astray." Trollope, *Dr. Wortle's School*, IV

It is seldom that a bad person expects to be accounted good. It is the general desire of
such a one to conquer the existing evil impression; but it is generally presumed that the
evil impression is there. Trollope, *The Eustace Diamonds*, IX

It is a great mistake to think that anybody is either an angel or a devil.
Trollope, *He Knew He Was Right*, XLIII

Men don't begin either very good or very bad. Trollope, *Phineas Finn*, V

There is but little evil that has not in it some seed of what is goodly.
Trollope, *The Warden*, XV

Laura was not much changed. The lovely woman had a devil in her heart. That was all.
Twain and Warner, *The Gilded Age*, Volume I, XVIII

Sin is the only real color-element left in modern life.
Wilde, *The Picture of Dorian Gray*, II

The leprosies of sin. *Ibid.*, XIII

There were sins whose fascination was more in the memory than in the doing of them,
strange triumphs that gratified the pride more than the passions, and gave to the

221

intellect a quickened sense of joy, greater than any joy they brought, or could ever bring, to the senses.   *Ibid.*, XIV

One should never do anything that one cannot talk about after dinner.   *Ibid.*, XIX

GOOD-HEARTEDNESS; GOOD-NATUREDNESS: *see also* EMOTION; HEART; etc.

It is with some an unalterable maxim, that the good-natured man must be a fool.
                                                                Anonymous, *The Birmingham Counterfeit*, I

A good heart will help you to a bonny face; and a bad one will turn the bonniest into something worse than ugly.   Bronte, E., *Wuthering Heights*, VII

The heart must appear in the book too, as well as the learning. For though it is full of things I don't understand, every now and then there *is* something I do understand: that seems as if that heart spoke out to all the world.   Bulwer, *The Caxtons*, Book II, V

If a good face is a letter of recommendation, a good heart is a letter of credit.
                                                            Bulwer, *What Will He Do with It?*, Book II, XI

Good-nature gives pleasure without any allay; ease, confidence, and happy carelessness, without the pain of obligation, with the exertion of gratitude.
                                                                Burney, *Camilla*, Three, V

Evil's evil, and sorrow's sorrow, and you can't alter its natur by wrapping it up in other words. Other folks were not created for my sake, that I should think all square when things turn out well for me.   Eliot, *Adam Bede*, LIV

A man with the milk of human kindness in him can scarcely abstain from doing a good-natured action, and one cannot be good-natured all round.
                                                                Eliot, *Mill on the Floss*, Book I, III

Good nature and generosity are always the same.   Fielding, S., *David Simple*, I

All good-natured men are passionate; and a sincere man cannot hide it.
                                                                Richardson, *Clarissa Harlowe*, I

It is very difficult for a good-natured young person to give a negative where it disesteems not.   *Ibid.*

Politeness, even to excess, is necessary on men's part, to bring us to listen to their first addresses, in order to induce us to bow our necks to a yoke so unequal.   *Ibid.*, II

Good manners are so little natural, that we ought to be composed to observe them: politeness will not live in a storm.   *Ibid.*

A man may afford to shew politeness to those he has resolved to keep at a distance.
                                                            Richardson, *Sir Charles Grandison*, One, II

GOODNESS: *see also* GENEROSITY; GOOD AND EVIL; GOOD-HEARTEDNESS; KINDNESS; etc.

Nature meant me to be, on the whole, a good man.   Bronte, C., *Jane Eyre*, XIV

A good man is no more to be feared than a sheep.
                                                            Bulwer, *What Will He Do with It?*, Book XII, II

Nothing good is difficult to you.   Dickens, *David Copperfield*, LX

That glorious vision of doing good is often the sanguine mirage of many good minds.
                                                            Dickens, *A Tale of Two Cities*, Book II, XXIV

Goodness is of a modest nature, easily discouraged, and when much elbowed in early life by unabashed vices, is apt to retire into extreme privacy.
                                                            Eliot, *Middlemarch*, Book IV, XXXIV

A sentiment in some Latin book, "I am a man myself, and my heart is interested in whatever can befall the rest of mankind." That is the sentiment of a good man, and whoever thinks otherwise is a bad one.   Fielding, H., *Amelia*, II

Writers have endeavored to confound the ideas of greatness and goodness, whereas no two things can possibly be more distinct from each other.
                                                Fielding, H., *Jonathan Wild*, 11

Greatness consists in bringing all manner of mischief on mankind, and goodness in removing it from them.   *Ibid.*, 13

A good man is a standing lesson to all his acquaintance, and of far greater use in that narrow circle than a good book.   Fielding, H., *Joseph Andrews*, 13

Nobody scarce doth any good, yet they all agree in praising those who do.   *Ibid.*, 198

It is strange that all men should consent in commending goodness, and no man endeavor to deserve that commendation; whilst, on the contrary, all rail at wickedness, and all are as eager to be what they abuse.   *Ibid.*

Good, but not religious-good.   Hardy, *Under the Greenwood Tree*, II

You was a good man, and did good things.
                                    Hardy, *The Woodlanders*, XLVIII, last line

Good men ever interpret themselves too meanly.   Hawthorne, *The Scarlet Letter*, IX

Whether perfect happiness would be procured by perfect goodness, this world will never afford an opportunity of deciding.   Johnson, *Rasselas*, 106

Goodness affords the only comfort which can be enjoyed without a partner.   *Ibid.*, 133

Goodness is no such rare thing among men. The world familiarly know the noun, a common one in every language.   Melville, *Confidence-Man*, VII

A good deed never dies.   Meredith, *Ordeal of Richard Feverel*, XXVI

Good in a strong many-compounded nature is of slower growth than any other mortal thing, and must not be forced.   *Ibid.*, XXVII

Who ever heard of the good man saying he was unhappy? The tedium of life the good man never knows.   Moore, *Evelyn Innes*, XVII

The less he deserves of you, the more will be your goodness.   Richardson, *Pamela*, 379

What have good men, engaged in a right cause, to fear?
                                        Richardson, *Sir Charles Grandison*, One, I

There is a kind of magnetism in goodness.   *Ibid.*, Two, III

Goodness and greatness are synonymous words.   Ibid.

He cannot be good that knows not why he is good.   Sidney, *Arcadia*, I

A prince, that measured his greatness by his goodness; and if for anything he loved greatness it was because therein he might exercise his goodness.   *Ibid.*, II

The eye of goodness espieth all things.   Sterne, *Tristram Shandy*, VIII

You are too good to be forgiving.   Stevenson, *Prince Otto*, Book III, II

To be good is to be in harmony with one's self. Discord is to be forced to be in harmony with others.   Wilde, *The Picture of Dorian Gray*, VI

GOVERNMENT: *see also* SOCIETY

No representative government can long be much better or much worse than the society it represents. Purify society if you purify the government. But try to purify the government artificially and you only aggravate failure.   Adams, H., *Democracy*, IV

The people are a sovereign, and greatly despotic; but, in the main, just.
                                        Brackenridge, *Modern Chivalry*, Part I, I

How difficult to link man with man; how difficult to preserve a free government! The easiest thing in the world, says the clown, if the sage will only let it alone. It is the philosopher that ruins all. *Ibid.*, Part II, I

Servility creates despotism. Bronte, C., *The Professor*, XV

The daringness of female curiosity is seldom so adventurous as to attempt to penetrate into the mysteries of government. Brown, C. B., *Alcuin*, I

All despotism subsists by virtue of the errors and supineness of its slaves. *Ibid.*, II

The chief purpose of the wise is to make men their own governors, to persuade them to practice the rules of equity without legal constraint. *Ibid.*

Of all modes of government, is not the sovereignty of the people, however encumbered with inconveniences, yet attended by the fewest? *Ibid.*

You must have many weapons in use, if you would govern that strange animal called man. Burney, *Camilla*, Three, VI

Men have in all ages required to be ruled strongly, and often tyrannically. Despots are disagreeable, but necessary. Cooke, *The Virginia Comedians*, Volume I, XXIII

A strict legal representation of all its interests is far more necessary to a worldly than to a simple people, since responsibility, which is the essence of a free government, is more likely to keep the agents of a nation near to its own standard of virtue than any other means. Cooper, *The Bravo*, XXVII

It is one thing to have a king, another to have a throne, and another to have neither. Cooper, *The Monikins*, Conclusion

He governs over his realm most surely that ruleth justice with mercy: for he ought to fear many, whom many do fear. Deloney, *Thomas of Reading*, 226

England has been in a dreadful state for some weeks. Lord Coodle would go out, Sir Thomas Doodle wouldn't come in, and there being nobody in Great Britain (to speak of) except Coodle and Doodle, there has been no Government. Dickens, *Bleak House*, XL

Your sister is given to government. Dickens, *Great Expectations*, VII

The Circumlocution Office was the most important Department under Government. Dickens, *Little Dorrit*, Book I, X

Human bees will swarm to the beating of any old tin kettle; in that fact lies the complete manual of governing them. When they can be got to believe that the kettle is made of the precious metals, in that fact lies the whole power of [those who can take them in]. *Ibid.*, Book II, XXVIII

It is an old prerogative of kings to govern everything but their passions. Dickens, *Pickwick Papers*, XXXVI

No government can be long secure without a formidable opposition. Disraeli, *Coningsby*, Book II, I

The arch-mediocrity presided, rather than ruled, over this cabinet of mediocrities. *Ibid.*

That fatal drollery called a representative government. Disraeli, *Tancred*

I am sure we are very good friends to the Government: and so we are for sartain, for we pay a mint of money to 'um. And yet I often think to myself the Government doth not imagine itself more obliged to us, than to those that don't pay 'um a farthing. Ay, ay, it is the way of the world. Fielding, H., *Tom Jones*, 316

Most nations, free ones especially, should be dealt with like a spirited horse, whom a judicious rider will keep steady, by maintaining an exact balance in his seat, showing neither fear nor cruelty, occasionally giving and checking the rein, while he prudently and resolutely corrects with the spur, or kindly blandishes with his hand.

Gentleman, *A Trip to the Moon*, I

No form of government has been yet discovered by which cruelty can be wholly prevented.

Johnson, *Rasselas*, 39

There can be no pleasure equal to that of feeling the joy of thousands, all made happy by wise administration.

Ibid., 95

Those who have kingdoms to govern have understandings to cultivate.

Ibid., 118

A state in which the power of the sovereign can be counterbalanced by that of his subjects is like a body without an head, and must necessarily fall to ruin.

Johnstone, *Arsaces*, I

The meanest mechanic will undertake to mend the state; and if he can but harangue with noise and virulence, will find fools of all denominations to listen to what he says.

Johnstone, *The Reverie*, I

Unhappy the people whose king is governed by a favorite.

Ibid., II

A prince is to his court what the sun is to the firmament: if he shines, every object is gilded; if clouded, all is gloomy.

Lyttleton, *The Court Secret*, 16–17

Human government, being subordinate to the divine, must needs, therefore, in its degree, partake of the characteristics of the divine.

Melville, *Confidence-Man*, XIX

In no stable democracy do all men govern themselves. Though an army be all volunteers, martial law must prevail.

Melville, *Mardi*, CLXI

Numbers win in the end: proof of small wisdom in the world.

Meredith, *Beauchamp's Career*, XXIX

Too many time-servers rot the State.

Ibid., XXXVII

To find citizens ruled by good and wholesome laws, that is an exceeding rare and hard thing.

More, *Utopia*, I

From the prince, as from a perpetual well spring, cometh among the people the flood of all that is good or evil.

Ibid.

The most part of all princes have more delight in warlike matters and feats of chivalry than in the good feats of peace; and employ much more study, how by right or by wrong to enlarge their dominions, than how well and peaceably to rule and govern that they have already.

Ibid.

The king ought to take more care for the wealth of his people than for his own wealth.

Ibid.

If any king were so little regarded and so lightly esteemed, yea so hated of his subjects, that other ways he could not keep them in awe, but only by open wrongs and by bringing them to beggary, surely it were better for him to forsake his kingdom, than to hold it by means whereby though the name of a king be kept, yet the majesty is lost.

Ibid.

It is against the dignity of a king to have rule over beggars, but rather over rich and wealthy men.

Ibid.

Verily, one man to live in pleasure and wealth, while all other weep and smart for it, that is the part, not of a king but of a jailer.

Ibid.

Women make better sovereigns than men: because the women sovereigns are governed by men; the men sovereigns by women.

Richardson, *Clarissa Harlowe*, II

Louis XI was careful in disguising his real sentiments and purposes from all who approached him, and frequently used the expressions "The king knows not how to reign who knows not how to dissemble" and "If I thought my very cap knew my secrets, I would throw it into the fire."

Scott, *Quentin Durward*, I

A man may govern the Mandarins and yet live in comparative idleness. To do such governing work well a man should have a good presence, a flow of words which should mean nothing, an excellent temper, and a love of hospitality.

Trollope, *He Knew He Was Right*, LXII

All governments are mortal, and Conservative governments in England are especially prone to die.   Trollope, *Phineas Finn*, V

Unlimited power *is* the ideal thing when it is in safe hands. The despotism of heaven is the one absolutely perfect government.   Twain, *Connecticut Yankee*, X

Men write many fine and plausible arguments in support of monarchy, but the fact remains that where every man in a state has a vote, brutal laws are impossible.

Ibid., XXV

The master minds of all nations, in all ages, have sprung in affluent multitude from the mass of the nation, and from the mass of the nation only—not from its privileged classes.

Ibid.

A man *is* a man, at bottom. Whole ages of abuse and oppression cannot crush the manhood clear out of him.   *Ibid.*, XXX

GRACE

Crimes are human errors, and signify but little; perhaps the worse a man is by nature, the more room there is for grace.   Fielding, H., *Amelia*, I

Nature is one thing, and grace another.   Graves, *The Spiritual Quixote*, II

GRATITUDE; INGRATITUDE

Ingratitude is the native offspring of Satan.

Anonymous, *Genuine Memoirs of Maria Brown*, I

Gratitude is not a passion, but a sentiment of the soul.

Anonymous, *The Life of Sir Richard Perrott*, 63

Can you think of any service constituting a stronger claim on the nation's gratitude than bearing and nursing the nation's children?   Bellamy, *Looking Backward*, XXV

Ingratitude is constitutional, and inseparable from human nature.

Brown, W. H., *The Power of Sympathy*, 158

Gratitude is a debt that never ceases while the benefit received remains.

Defoe, *Colonel Jack*, 276

There is nothing so rare as gratitude in males, especially in husbands.

Fielding, H., *Amelia*, I

Ingratitude never so thoroughly pierces the human breast as when it proceeds from those in whose behalf we have been guilty of transgressions.

Fielding, H., *Tom Jones*, 38

Let no man build on the expected gratitude of those he spends his strength to serve!

Godwin, *St. Leon*, 382

There is a levity in the generality of men that entails on them a continual oblivion of past benefits, and makes one recent disappointment of more importance in their eyes than an eternity of kindnesses and condescension.   *Ibid.*, 382–383

The poorer the guest, the better pleased he ever is with being treated.

Goldsmith, *The Vicar of Wakefield*, 2

Gratitude was surely implanted in our hearts by our great Creator, and to fail in its observance, is acting against the dictates of conscience and humanity.

Helme, *St. Margaret's Cave*, Volume II, VI

How inconsiderate are persons who, from the absence of its officious manifestations in the world, complain that there is not much gratitude extant; when the truth is, that there is as much of it as there is of modesty.　　　　Melville, *Confidence-Man*, V

Gratitude cannot be too much towards God, but towards man, it should be limited. No man can possibly so serve his fellow, as to merit unbounded gratitude.
　　　　Melville, *Israel Potter*, VII

You must not construe common gratitude into love.　　Richardson, *Clarissa Harlowe*, I

Can a right heart be ungrateful?　　　　Richardson, *Sir Charles Grandison*, Two, IV

I would have no more mercy on an ungrateful man than I would on a woodcock.
　　　　Scott, *Guy Mannering*, XXXV

Abuse not the steed which hath borne thee from the battle.
　　　　Scott, *The Talisman*, XVIII

There is no wretch so ungrateful as he whom you have most generously obliged, and no enemy so implacable as those who have done you most wrong.
　　　　Smollett, *Roderick Random*, 42

Ingratitude is among them a capital crime: for the reason that whoever makes ill returns to his benefactors must needs be a common enemy to the rest of mankind, from whom he hath received no obligation.　　　　Swift, *Gulliver's Travels*, "Lilliput"

GRAVITY: *see also* SERIOUSNESS

Gravity is not always agreeable, and there are moments when folly becomes pleasing and we find a delight in being ridiculous.　　　　Collyer, *Felicia to Charlotte*, II

Serious minds are adapted to serious subjects.
　　　　Donaldson, *Sir Bartholomew Sapskull*, II

Those things which we call heavy do not sink toward the center of the earth, as their natural place, but as drawn by a secret property of the globe of the earth, or rather something within the same, in like sort as the loadstone draweth iron, being within the compass of the beams attractive.　　　　Godwin, *The Man in the Moon*, 46–47

Gravity is a mysterious carriage of the body to cover the defects of the mind.
　　　　Sterne, *Tristram Shandy*, I

GREATNESS; GRANDNESS: *see also* GENIUS; NOBILITY; ORIGINALITY

What is greatness, when purchased at the expense of all that can render the possessor deservedly respected by the world, or easy in himself?
　　　　Annesley, *Memoirs of an Unfortunate Young Nobleman*, I

Great endowments cannot long be concealed.
　　　　Anonymous, *The Life of Sir Richard Perrott*, 16

The Southern sun has prevented many a man from becoming great.
　　　　Atherton, *Senator North*, Book I, XVII

Nothing can be great, the contempt of which is great.
　　　　Brackenridge, *Modern Chivalry*, Part II, I

Three things are necessary to constitute a great man: judgment, fortitude, and self-denial.　　　　*Ibid.*

Great souls know each other.　　　　Beecher, *Norwood*, LVI

A man who becomes great is often but made so by a kind of sorcery in his own soul.
　　　　Bulwer, *Rienzi*, Book X, VIII

The true greatness wears an invisible cloak, under cover of which it goes in and out among men without being suspected; if its cloak does not conceal it from itself always, and from all others for many years, its greatness will ere long shrink to very ordinary dimensions. What, then, is the good of being great? The answer is that you may

understand greatness better in others, whether alive or dead, and choose better company from these and enjoy and understand that company better when you have chosen it—also that you may be able to give pleasure to the best people and live in the lives of thsoe who are yet unborn.
Butler, The Way of All Flesh, XXII

It is no uncommon event, in the experience of us all, to see the possessors of exalted ability occasionally humbled to the level of the most poorly-gifted people about them.
Collins, The Moonstone, Second Period, VII

Great men are urged on to the abuse of power by their flatterers and dependents.
Dickens, Barnaby Rudge, XXX

The sea has no appreciation of great men, but knocks them about like the small fry.
Dickens, Bleak House, XII

Mr. Pickwick's mind, like those of all truly great men, was open to conviction.
Dickens, Pickwick Papers, X

Great minds must trust to great truths and great talents for their rise, and nothing else.
Disraeli, Coningsby, Book II, I

A great man is one who affects the mind of his generation.
Ibid., Book III, II

Man is only truly great when he acts from the passions; never irresistible but when he appeals to the imagination.
Ibid., Book IV, XIII

If you wish to be great, you must give men new ideas, you must teach them new words, you must modify their manners, you must change their laws, you must root out prejudices, subvert convictions. Greatness no longer depends on rentals: the world is too rich; nor on pedigrees: the world is too knowing.
Ibid., Book IX, IV

Reduce the grandest type of man hitherto known to an abstract statement of his qualities and efforts, and he appears in dangerous company.
Eliot, Daniel Deronda, Book VI, XLI

There are so many things wrong and difficult in the world, that no man can be great—he can hardly keep himself from wickedness—unless he gives up thinking much about pleasure or rewards, and gets strength to endure what is hard and painful.
Eliot, Romola, Epilogue

Tho' Master Wild was by no means to be terrified into compliance, yet might he by a sugar-plum be brought to your purpose. Indeed, to say the truth, he was to be bribed to anything, which made many say he was certainly born to be a great man.
Fielding, H., Jonathan Wild, 17

I am far from agreeing that great parts are often buried in oblivion; I am convinced, on the contrary, it is impossible they should be so.
Ibid., 25

The truest mark of greatness is insatiability.
Ibid., 75

A great man ought to do his business by others.
Ibid., 167

Nothing truly great was ever achieved that was not executed or planned in solitary seclusion.
Godwin, St. Leon, 138

The truly great stand upon no middle ledge; they are either famous or unknown.
Hardy, Desperate Remedies, III

There is much littleness in trying to be great. A man must think a good deal of himself, and be conceited enough to believe in himself, before he tries at all.
Hardy, A Pair of Blue Eyes, XVII

Worldy greatness requires so much littleness to grow up in, that an infirmity more or less is not a matter for regret.
Ibid., XIX

A great man attains his normal condition only through the inspiration of one great idea.
Hawthorne, The Blithedale Romance, XIX

A great cause makes great souls, or reveals them to themselves.

Holmes, *Guardian Angel*, XXXVI

Great men are not always wise.

Judd, *Margaret*, III

There have been certain men so great, that he who describes them in words—much more pretends to analyze their inmost feelings—must be a very great man himself, or incur the accusation of presumption.

Kingsley, *Hereward the Wake*, XXV

All men tragically great are made so through a certain morbidness. Be sure of this, O young ambition, all mortal greatness is but disease.

Melville, *Moby Dick*, XVI

Small erections may be finished by their first architects; grand ones, true ones, ever leave the copestone to posterity. Heaven keep me from ever completing anything. This whole book is but a draught—nay, but the draught of a draught. Oh, Time, Strength, Cash, and Patience!

Ibid., XXXII

Oh, Ahab, what shall be grand in thee, it must needs be plucked at from the skies, and dived for in the deep, and featured in the unbodied air!

Ibid., XXXIII

There's something ever egotistical in mountaintops and towers, and all other grand and lofty things.

Ibid., XCIX

Like a pyramid, a great man stands on a broad base. It is only the brittle porcelain pagoda that tottles on a toe.

Melville, *Redburn*, LVI

Great minds cannot avoid doing extraordinary things.

Richardson, *Clarissa Harlowe*, IV

Great people think they must not do right things in the common way.

Richardson, *Sir Charles Grandison*, Two, IV

There was never a great man who had not a great mother.

Schreiner, *Story of an African Farm*, Part II, IV

The greatness of the man who labors.

Schreiner, *Undine*, XVI

Great men of all nations talk and stalk so much alike, that I would not give nine-pence to choose amongst them.

Sterne, *A Sentimental Journey*, 53

The way to be great lies through books now, and not through battles.

Stowe, *Orr's Island*, XV

Great souls cannot avoid great thoughts.

Tourgee, *Murvale Eastman*, XXI

GRIEF

She grieved because she could not grieve.   Austen, *Mansfield Park*, Volume One, III

They encouraged each other now in the violence of their affliction. The agony of grief which overpowered them at first was voluntarily renewed, was sought for, was created again and again. They gave themselves up wholly to their sorrow, seeking increase of wretchedness in every reflection that could afford it, and resolved against ever admitting consolation in future.   Austen, *Sense and Sensibility*, Volume I, I

A grief inexpressible over a loss unendurable.   Bronte, C., *Villette*, XXXVIII

The pressure of grief is sometimes such as to prompt us to seek a refuge in voluntary death.   Brown, C. B., *Ormond*, 21-22

All grief is unavailing, and it is our duty to submit.   Dickens, *Dombey*, XVIII

The blank that follows death, when every household god becomes a monument and every room a grave.   Dickens, *Old Curiosity Shop*, LXXII

Soothing uneasiness, always the first physic to be given to grief.

Fielding, H., *Amelia*, II

The sublimest grief will eat at last.   Fielding, H., *Tom Jones*, 748

Everybody thinketh their own grief greatest.   Gascoigne, *Master F. J.*, 53

Greater is the grief that is sustained without desert, and much more is the wrong that is offered without cause. *Ibid.*, 58

Grief does not commonly lay a strong and invincible hold of us in the morning of our days. Godwin, *St. Leon*, 296

Grief is dry; let us have a bottle of the best gooseberry wine, to keep up our spirits. Goldsmith, *The Vicar of Wakefield*, 86

The great fault of elegiasts is that they are in despair for griefs that give the sensible part of mankind very little pain. A lady loses her muff, her fan, or her lap-dog, and so the silly poet runs home to verify the disaster. *Ibid.*, 88

The grief of the passing moment takes upon itself an individuality, and a character of climax, which it is destined to lose, after awhile, and to fade into the dark gray tissue, common to the grave or glad events of many years ago. It is but for a moment, comparatively, that anything looks strange or startling. Hawthorne, *The House of the Seven Gables*, XVI

She could no longer borrow from the future to help her through the present grief. Hawthorne, *The Scarlet Letter*, V

The pungency of extreme grief acts as a temporary opiate. Holcroft, *Hugh Trevor*, IV

Lay your hand upon your heart, reader, and ask yourself seriously, whether, for one real misfortune, you have not grieved for ten imaginary ones, all through your life? Jenner, *The Placid Man*, I

A fool has not sense enough to grieve. Kimber, *Joe Thompson*, II

Grief shows the strongest in those countenances where tears never make their appearance. Lawrence, *The Contemplative Man*, I

Grief makes the most violent impression in youth; but 'tis the most transient. Lee, *The Recess*, I

Grief, not Joy, is a moralizer. Melville, *Pierre*, Book II, V

When divided, griefs become less poignant. Parsons, *The Castle of Wolfenbach*, I

Only the humble, silent grief deserves pity. Richardson, *Clarissa Harlowe*, II

The voice of grief is alike in all. *Ibid.*, IV

It is natural to interest all in our grief. *Ibid.*, IV

Heavy grief gives way to milder melancholy. *Ibid.*

Friendly grief mellowed by time. *Ibid.*

Grief produces pity for another; pity, love. Richardson, *Sir Charles Grandison*, Three, VI

Who grieves not hath but a blockish brain, since cause of grief no cause from life removes. Sidney, *Arcadia*, II

Griefs are like usurpers: the most powerful deposes all the rest. Smollett, *Roderick Random*, 149-150

There are griefs which grow with years. Stowe, *Orr's Island*, XXVIII

GROUP PSYCHOLOGY: *see also* HUMAN NATURE; MIND; PSYCHOLOGY; SOCIETY

Like all men renowned for eloquence, Godwin went with the popular feeling of his times. He embodied its passions, its prejudices—but also that keen sense of self-interest which is the invariable characteristic of a multitude. He *was* the sense of the commonalty carried to the highest degree. Bulwer, *Harold*, Book III, II

GROWTH; DEVELOPMENT: *see also* PROGRESS

A man's fortune or material progress is very much the same as his bodily growth.
Dreiser, *Sister Carrie*, XXXIII

The growth of higher feeling within us is like the growth of faculty, bringing with it a sense of added strength. We can no more wish to return to a narrow sympathy than a painter or a musician can wish to return to his cruder manner, or a philosopher to his less complete formula.
Eliot, *Adam Bede*, LIV

Our consciousness rarely registers the beginning of a growth within us any more than without us: there have been many circulations of the sap before we detect the smallest sign of the bud.
Eliot, *Silas Marner*, VII

If he could only prevent himself growing up! He did not want to be a man.
Hardy, *Jude the Obscure*, Part I, II

Human nature will not flourish, any more than a potato, if it be planted and replanted for too long a series of generations in the same worn-out soil.
Hawthorne, *The Scarlet Letter*, Introductory

No fine, firm fabric ever yet grew like a gourd.
Melville, *Mardi*, LXXV

Man lives months ere his Maker deems him fit to be born; and ere his proud shaft gains its full stature, twenty-one long Julian years must elapse. And his whole mortal life brings not his immortal soul to maturity; nor will all eternity perfect him.
Ibid.

Out of the trunk, the branches grow; out of them, the twigs. So, in productive subjects, grow the chapters.
Melville, *Moby Dick*, LXIII

Good seed is long ripening.
Meredith, *Ordeal of Richard Feverel*, XIII

When one ceases to be an ardent youth, the genius of the family, master of his functions, one is no longer man. It is the tendency of very fast people to grow organically downward.
Ibid., XXIV

It is Nature's way to make first a healthy animal, and then develop in it gradually higher faculties.
Stowe, *Orr's Island*, XVII

Fortune does not change men and women. It but develops their character.
Thackeray, *Henry Esmond*, Book II, I

Men may move forward from little work to big work; but they cannot move back and do little work, when they have had tasks which were really great.
Trollope, *Phineas Finn*, LXXII

No life is spoiled but one whose growth is arrested.
Wilde, *The Picture of Dorian Gray*, VI

GUIDANCE: *see also* EDUCATION; INSTRUCTION; KNOWLEDGE AND LEARNING

Nothing can be more unfortunate for youth and beauty, than to be left to its own guidance and discretion.
Lennox, *Henrietta*, I

GUILT: *see also* INNOCENCE

Guilt confounds even its strongest votaries.
Anonymous, *The Fruitless Repentance*, I

Shall we impute guilt where there is no design?
Brown, C. B., *Edgar Huntley*, 87

The poor not impoverished by their own guilt are equals of the affluent not enriched by their own virtue.
Burney, *Cecilia*, I

Guilt is alone the basis of lasting unhappiness.
Ibid., III

The guilty fly from those who remind them of their sins, and hate those who were the partners of their guilt.
Dacre, *The Libertine*, XXX

When deep intrigues are close and shy,/ The guilty are the first that spy.
Defoe, *Roxana*, 68

Circumstances may accumulate so strongly even against an innocent man, that directed, sharpened, and pointed, they may slay him. One wanting link discovered by perseverance against a guilty man, proves his guilt, however slight its evidence before, and he dies.
Dickens, *The Mystery of Edwin Drood*, XIX

Guilt, like a base thief, suspects every eye that beholds him to be privy to his transgressions, and every tongue that mentions his name to be proclaiming them.
Fielding, H., *Amelia*, I

Tom's guilt now flew in his face more than any severity could make it. He could more easily bear the lashes of Thwackum than the generosity of Allworthy.
Fielding, H., *Tom Jones*, 81

Equally culpable, the buyer and the seller were alike to be driven out of the temple.
Ibid., 101–102

The first time the very best may err; art may persuade, and novelty spread out its charm. The first fault is the child of simplicity, but every other, the offspring of guilt.
Goldsmith, *The Vicar of Wakefield*, 91

None but the guilty can be long and completely miserable.   *Ibid.*, 136

Conscious of his own guilt, he ever mistrusted appearance in others.
Harley, *Priory of St. Bernard*, I

Lonely—lonely as guilt could wish.   Hawthorne, *Fanshawe*, VIII

The ever-increasing loathsomeness of a union that consists in guilt.
Hawthorne, *The Marble Faun*, XIX

Guilt has its moment of rapture too.   *Ibid.*

An individual wrongdoing melts into the great mass of human crime.   *Ibid.*

At no time are people so sedulously careful to keep their trifling appointments, attend to their ordinary occupations, and thus put a commonplace aspect on life, as when conscious of some secret that if suspected would make them look monstrous in the general eye.
Ibid., XX

The young and pure are not apt to find out that miserable truth that sin is in the world until it is brought home to them by the guiltiness of some trusted friend.   *Ibid.*, XXIII

While there is a single guilty person in the universe, each innocent one must feel his innocence tortured by that guilt.   *Ibid.*

Sin has darkened the whole sky.   *Ibid.*

Who more need the tender succor of the innocent, than wretches stained with guilt?
Ibid., XLII

The breach which guilt has once made into the human soul is never, in this mortal state, repaired.   Hawthorne, *The Scarlet Letter*, XVIII

Guilty minds are soon alarmed.   Helme, *St. Margaret's Cave*, Volume II, IX

If there is anything that can excite one's compassion in a more than ordinary degree, it is the sight of a man made not only unfortunate, but even guilty in spite of himself.
Jenner, *The Placid Man*, I

No man was ever hurt at hearing a fault reproved of which he was not guilty himself.
Johnstone, *The Reverie*, I

Guilt is stubborn.   Lathom, *The Midnight Bell*, II

The guilty, if unhappy, are doubly so.   Lennox, *Sophia*, I

When a person is found less guilty than he is suspected, he is concluded more innocent than he really is.   *Ibid.*, II

Guilt and courage are incompatible.   Lewis, *The Monk*, 94

The guilty are ever in terror.   Lyttleton, *The Court Secret*, 15–16

Where no guilt is, nought is to be feared.   McCarthy, *The Fair Moralist*, 8

Is the sun of blue heavens guilty of the shadow it casts?
                                                        Meredith, *Harry Richmond*, XXVII

It is better to suffer from the follies or vices of others than to feel self-condemnation from a sense of your own.   Parsons, *The Castle of Wolfenbach*, I

Can tortures make one guilty?   Radcliffe, *The Italian*, II

What could be expected from a person who could feel the pain of guilt without the humility of repentance?   Radcliffe, *The Mysteries of Udolpho*, I

There is no bond of kindness among the guilty.   *Ibid.*, II

There would hardly be a guilty person in the world, were each suspected or accused person to tell his or her own story and be allowed any degree of credit.
                                                        Richardson, *Clarissa Harlowe*, I

Guilt makes the most lofty spirit look like the miscreant he is.   *Ibid.*, IV

Who will take the part of a man that condemns himself? He that pleads guilty leaves no room for aught but the sentence.   *Ibid.*

In duelling the more guilty often has been the vanquisher of the less guilty.   *Ibid.*

Why should the guiltless tremble so, when the guilty can possess their minds in peace?
                                                        Richardson, *Pamela*, 191

Of how many falsehoods does politeness make guilty people who are called polite!
                                                Richardson, *Sir Charles Grandison*, Two, IV

There is nothing more terrible to a guilty heart, than the eye of a respected friend.
                                                        Sidney, *Arcadia*, I

Guilt is a thing of isolation always, even when most surrounded by its associates and operations. Its very insecurity tends to its isolation as completely as its selfishness.
                                                        Simms, *The Scout*, XV

What hangs people is the unfortunate circumstance of guilt.
                                                        Stevenson, *The Wrong Box*, VII

The sensitiveness to eyebeams is one of the earliest signs of conscious, inward guilt.
                                                        Stowe, *Orr's Island*, XXII

Can guilt dwell with innocent beauty and virtuous modesty?
                                                        Walpole, *The Castle of Otranto*, 98

Guilt has a vital power, which gives it life, until it is held up to scorn.
                                                        Whitman, *Franklin Evans*, XXII

HABIT

Any habit can be acquired.   Atherton, *Senator North*, Book II, VII

Habit is a second nature.   Burney, *Cecilia*, I

They who have used a dialect different from the common forms of speech in their youth, and come afterwards to correct it, by intercourse with the world usually fall back into their early infirmities in moments of trial, perplexity, or anger. Habit has become a sort of nature, in their childhood, and it is when most tried that we are the most natural.
                                                        Cooper, *Afloat and Ashore*, XXX

Habit is invincible.   Cooper, *The Monikins*, Conclusion

How hell should become by degrees so natural, and not only tolerable but even agreeable, is a thing unintelligible but by those who have experienced it.
Defoe, *Moll Flanders*, 286

A citizen of the world has no habits.   Dickens, *Little Dorrit*, Book I, XXX

The most glutinously indefinite minds enclose some hard grains of habit; and a man has been seen lax about all his own interests except the retention of his snuffbox, concerning which he was watchful, suspicious, and greedy of clutch.
Eliot, *Middlemarch*, Book I, I

It is not from nature, but from education and habit, that our wants are chiefly derived.
Fielding, H., *Amelia*, I

Habit teaches men to bear the burdens of the mind, as it inures them to bear heavy burdens on their shoulders.   *Ibid.*, II

Habit hath so vast a prevalence over the human mind, that there is scarce anything too strange or too strong to be asserted of it.   Fielding, H., *Joseph Andrews*, 256

Habit is more potent than any theoretical speculation.   Godwin, *St. Leon*, 165

Habit has a resistless empire over the human mind.   *Ibid.*, 300

There is nothing so extravagant or absurd but habit will reconcile.
Johnstone, *The Reverie*, I

Long habit has the art of giving charms to places; or, rather, 'tis the people who inhabit them.   Lee, *The Recess*, I

What cannot habit accomplish?   Melville, *Moby Dick*, LX

The habit of the defensive paralyzes will.   Meredith, *The Amazing Marriage*, XXXVI

There is scarcely any condition so bad, but we may one time or other wish we had not quitted it.   Radcliffe, *The Romance of the Forest*, 282

Habits are not so easily changed.   Richardson, *Clarissa Harlowe*, I

Bad habits are of the Jerusalem artichoke-kind; once planted, there is no getting them out of the ground.   Richardson, *Sir Charles Grandison*, Three, VI

Man is a creature born to habitudes.   Sterne, *Tristram Shandy*, VII

Habit is habit, and not to be flung out of the window by any man, but coaxed downstairs a step at a time.   Twain, *Pudd'nhead Wilson*, VI

Nothing so needs reforming as other people's habits.   *Ibid.*, XV

HANDSOMENESS: *see also* BEAUTY

Nobody can call such an undersized man handsome. He is not five foot nine.
Austen, *Mansfield Park*, Volume One, X

You should tell your father that Mr. Crawford is not above five feet eight, or he will be expecting a well-looking man.   *Ibid.*, Volume Two, I

HAPPINESS; UNHAPPINESS: *see also* MISERY; etc.

Perhaps it is the instinctive trait of most of us to seek an explanation for any great happiness as we are always prone to discuss the causes of our adversity.
Allen, *The Choir Invisible*, VI

Imagination may form fine pictures of felicity from an indulgence in every wish; but, so blind are mankind to their own happiness, that it is oftener to the gratification than to the disappointment of their wishes that their misery is owing.   Amory, *John Buncle*, I

Of all things in this world, moral dominion, or the empire over ourselves, is not only the most glorious, as reason is the superior nature of man, but the most valuable, in respect of real human happiness.   *Ibid.*, II

It is sometimes a happiness to be ignorant of our destiny.
                                                Anonymous, *The Birmingham Counterfeit*, I

There is no such thing as happiness without alloy.   Anonymous, *Fatal Friendship*, I

We ought not to flatter ourselves with undisturbed repose. Happiness is not the lot of mortals.   *Ibid.*, II

Self-approbation is the highest honor, and the highest happiness, of a reasonable being.
                                                Anonymous, *The History of Betty Barnes*, II

The only chance of happiness lies in the isolated companionship of mated souls.
                                                Atherton, *Los Cerritos*, Part II

A large income is the best recipe for happiness.
                                                Austen, *Mansfield Park*, Volume Two, IV

Her happiness was of a quiet, deep, heart-swelling sort; she was always more inclined to silence when feeling most strongly.   *Ibid.*, Volume Three, VI

I must learn to brook being happier than I deserve.   Austen, *Persuasion*, XXIII

She was now in an irritation as violent from delight, as she had ever been fidgetty from alarm and vexation.   Austen, *Pride and Prejudice*, Volume III, VII

I am happier even than Jane; she only smiles, I laugh.   *Ibid.*, Volume III, XVIII

Wealth has much to do with happiness.
                                                Austen, *Sense and Sensibility*, Volume I, XVII

Money can only give happiness where there is nothing else to give it.   *Ibid.*

The happiness of some lives is distributed pretty evenly over the whole stretch from the cradle to the grave, while that of others comes all at once, glorifying some particular epoch and leaving the rest in shadow.   Bellamy, *Miss Ludington's Sister*, I

True happiness can be found only in congruity, and what is natural.
                                                Brackenridge, *Modern Chivalry*, Part I, II

The best of happiness is mine—the power and the will to be useful.
                                                Bronte, A., *Agnes Grey*, XIII

There is no happiness like that of being loved by your fellow-creatures, and feeling that your presence is an addition to their comfort.   Bronte, C., *Jane Eyre*, XXII

No mockery in this world ever sounds so hollow as that of being told to cultivate happiness.   Bronte, C., *Villette*, XXI

A new creed became mine—a belief in happiness.   *Ibid.*, XXIII

He was a man whom it made happy to see others happy.   *Ibid.*, XXXIII

To be happy in this world, it is necessary not to raise one's ideas too high.
                                                Brooke, *Emily Montague*, I

Love, the gay child of sympathy and esteem, is, when attended by delicacy, the only happiness worth a reasonable man's pursuit, and the choicest gift of heaven.   *Ibid.*

Happiness is not to be found in a life of intrigue.   *Ibid.*, II

We are formed to be happy, and to contribute to the happiness of our fellow creatures. There are no real virtues but the social ones.   *Ibid.*, III

In the same proportion as we lose our confidence in the virtue of others, we lose our proper happiness.   *Ibid.*, IV

The wise order of providence has ordained that we shall make others happy in being so ourselves.   *Ibid.*

Before we act, we must consider not only the misery produced, but the happiness precluded by our measures.   Brown, C. B., *Ormond*, 130

A great proportion of our happiness depends on our own choice.
                Brown, W. H., *The Power of Sympathy*, 19

Inequality among mankind is a foe to happiness.   *Ibid.*, 53

Unfortunate is the man who trusts his happiness to the precarious friendship of the world.   *Ibid.*, 159

Happy he who combines the enthusiast's warmth with the worldly man's light.
                Bulwer, *The Caxtons*, Book II, II

Happy the man who is an early riser.   *Ibid.*, Book IV, I

Laugh at forebodings of evil, but tremble after daydreams of happiness.
                Bulwer, *What Will He Do with It?*, Book III, XXIV

The pure design of benevolence is to bestow happiness upon others, but its intrinsic reward is bringing happiness home.   Burney, *Camilla*, Four, VII

The true secret of happiness, Labor with Independence.   Burney, *Cecilia*, III

People reason and refine themselves into a thousand miseries, by choosing to settle that they can only be contented one way.   *Ibid.*

The true art of happiness in this most whimsical world seems nothing more nor less than this: Let those who have leisure find employment and those who have business find leisure.   *Ibid.*

Some people say that their school days were the happiest of their lives. They may be right, but I always look with suspicion upon those I hear saying this. It is hard enough to know whether one is happy or unhappy now, and still harder to compare the relative happiness or unhappiness of different times of one's life; the utmost that can be said is that we are fairly happy so long as we are not distinctly aware of being miserable.
                Butler, *The Way of All Flesh*, XLV

Happiness is negative. Misery positive. There is always a subtle doubt lingering upon our most substantial scenes of happiness; but with misery it is slow, certain and enduring; the proof conclusive and damning. It is more real than our existence, and exists when it is no more.   Caruthers, *Cavaliers*, Volume II, III

Unhappiness soon makes us indifferent to mere locality.
                Caruthers, *Kentuckian in New-York*, Volume I, VII

How easy it is to be happy, if you will only be good.
                Collins, *The Moonstone*, Second Period, IV

Felicity is quaffed out of a golden cup in every latitude: the flavor is with you—with you alone—and you can make it as intoxicating as you please.   Conrad, *Lord Jim*, XVI

Do you imagine that if mortals had power over events, or were in reality free and uncontrollable agents in the history of their own existence, that you would see so many unhappy beings?—no certainly, for who would do that which would render him miserable, if he had the power of avoiding it? And if he had that power, yet chose nevertheless to be miserable, who would pity him?   Dacre, *Passions*, Letter XXXIX

Happiness is the sole end of existence.   *Ibid.*, XLIII

Those philosophers deal in nothing but falsehood, who assert that virtue is happiness. Why then are [the virtuous] not happy?   *Ibid.*

I was happy; but the happiness I had vaguely anticipated was not the happiness I enjoyed, and there was always something wanting.
                Dickens, *David Copperfield*, XLVIII

To remember happiness which cannot be restored is pain, but of a softened kind.
Dickens, *Nicholas Nickleby*, VI

"You will be well and happy." "I hope so. After I am dead, but not before."
Dickens, *Oliver Twist*, VII

Undertakers are the merriest fellows in the world.   Dickens, *Pickwick Papers*, XXIX

Happiness is a mental enjoyment, and he that wilfully thinks ill or indifferently of his neighbor is a disturber of his own tranquillity.
Donaldson, *Sir Bartholomew Sapskull*, I

Sin and sadness are never far apart.   Doyle, *Micah Clarke*, III

All earthly happiness is fleeting and uncertain as the sunbeams which play upon the lake.   Duff, *The History of Rhedi*, 215

The best happiness I shall ever know, will be to escape the worst misery.
Eliot, *Felix Holt*, I

It is only a poor sort of happiness that could ever come by caring very much about our own narrow pleasures.   Eliot, *Romola*, Epilogue

Never think those men wise who, for any worldly interest, forego the greatest happiness of their lives.   Fielding, H., *Amelia*, I

None deserve happiness, or are capable of it, who make any particular station a necessary ingredient.   *Ibid.*

There is nothing more difficult than to lay down any fixed and certain rules for happiness; or to judge with any precision of the happiness of others from the knowledge of external circumstances.   *Ibid.*

He to whom content is given need ask no more.   Fielding, H., *Joseph Andrews*, 140

To be content with a little is greater than to possess the world; which a man may possess without being so.   *Ibid.*

Do not give too much way to thy passions, if thou dost expect happiness.   *Ibid.*, 266

There are a set of religious, or rather moral writers, who teach that virtue is the certain road to happiness, and vice to misery, in this world. A very wholesome and comfortable doctrine, and to which we have but one objection, namely, that it is not true.
Fielding, H., *Tom Jones*, 690

If a man could make himself happy by imagining himself six feet tall, though he was but three, it certainly would be ill-natured in anyone to take that happiness from him.
Fielding, S., *David Simple*, I

He that loves, and is loved by, a race of pure and virtuous creatures, and that lives continually in the midst of them, is an idiot if he does not think himself happy.
Godwin, *St. Leon*, 93

I was never much displeased with those harmless delusions that tend to make us more happy.   Goldsmith, *The Vicar of Wakefield*, 15

She whose youth had seemed to teach that happiness was but the occasional episode in a general drama of pain.   Hardy, *The Mayor of Casterbridge*, XLV

Happiness frequently has reason for haste, but it is seldom that desolation need scramble or strain.   Hardy, *A Pair of Blue Eyes*, XXV

Heart-dilating happiness.   Harley, *Priory of St. Bernard*, I

Happiness never comes but incidentally.
Hawthorne, *The Blithedale Romance*, XV

If a stray sunbeam steal in, the shadow is all the better for its cheerful glimmer.
Hawthorne, *The Marble Faun*, V

Their lives were rendered blissful by an unsought harmony with nature.
Ibid., XXVI

Mankind are getting so far beyond the childhood of their race that they scorn to be happy any longer. *Ibid.*

A simple and joyous character can find no place for itself among the sage and sombre figures that would put his unsophisticated cheerfulness to shame. *Ibid.*

A happy person is such an unaccustomed and holy creature in this sad world. *Ibid.*, XXXV

We have yet to learn again the forgotten art of gaiety. Hawthorne, *The Scarlet Letter*, XXI

The human mind, in its eager, though too often unavailing, struggle after happiness, will still make the most of its means. Hildreth, *Slave*, Volume I, XIII

Human happiness is never in fruition, but always in prospect of pursuits. *Ibid.*, Volume I, XV

Happiness and brains seldom go together. Howe, *Story of a Country Town*, XXX

Every day is the day of small things, with people who are happy. Howells, *A Modern Instance*, XXVII

When I tried to be a philosopher, "happiness was always breaking in." Hudson, *The Purple Land*, XXVIII

Unhappiness is according as one takes things. James, H., *The American*, VIII

Agreeable circumstances, arising in a disagreeable prospect, convey the greatest happiness that can be imagined. Jenner, *The Placid Man*, I

Happy the man whose amusement depends upon trifles, whose curiosity keeps such an even pace with the common occurrences of life, as to bid far for being satisfied without much trouble. *Ibid.*

That kind of ideal happiness which arises from the contemplation of imaginary objects is in the power of everyone. *Ibid.*, II

The sight of the miseries of the world is necessary to happiness. Johnson, *Rasselas*, 23

Happiness he could enjoy only by concealing it. *Ibid.*, 25

There is so much infelicity in the world, that scarce any man has leisure from his own distresses to estimate the comparative happiness of others. *Ibid.*, 54

We are long before we are convinced that happiness is never to be found, and each believes it possessed by others, to keep alive the hope of obtaining it for himself. *Ibid.*, 72

Whatever may be the general infelicity of man, one condition is more happy than another, and wisdom surely directs us to take the least evil in the choice of life. *Ibid.*, 73

Happiness must be something solid and permanent, without fear and without certainty. *Ibid.*, 75

Nothing is more idle than to inquire after happiness, which nature has kindly placed within our reach. *Ibid.*, 90

We do not always find visible happiness in proportion to visible virtue. *Ibid.*, 106

Nature seeks happiness. Johnstone, *Arsaces*, I

It is better not to be, than be unhappy. *Ibid.*

The human heart is so fond of happiness, that we give easy credit to what we wish. *Ibid.*

Happy are they who are blessed with the power of making happy. Johnstone, *The Pilgrim*, II

It is better to condescend to be happy than to aspire to be miserable.

Kidgell, *The Card*, II

Undeserved happiness sits very heavy upon the mind.   Kimber, *David Ranger*, II

One can be very happy with much less trouble, than very wise.

Mackenzie, *Julia De Roubigné*, 40–41

In all cases man must eventually lower, or at least shift, his conceit of attainable felicity; not placing it anywhere in the intellect or the fancy; but in the wife, the heart, the bed, the table, the saddle, the fireside, the country.   Melville, *Moby Dick*, XCIV

There is nothing so slipperily alluring as sadness; we become sad in the first place by having nothing stirring to do; we continue in it, because we have found a snug sofa at last.   Melville, *Pierre*, Book XVIII, I

The mistake of the world is to think happiness possible to the senses.

Meredith, *Diana of the Crossways*, XXXVIII

Too happy to be sentimental.   Meredith, *Harry Richmond*, XXIV

Is not happiness like another circulating medium? When we have a very great deal of it, some poor hearts are aching for what is taken away from them. When we have gone out and seized it on the highways, certain inscrutable laws are sure to be at work to bring us to the criminal bar, sooner or later.   Meredith, *Ordeal of Richard Feverel*, XXXVI

Happiness and intelligence are seldom sisters.   Peacock, *Headlong Hall*, V

None so happy as the versatile, provided they have not their bread to make by it.

Reade, *The Cloister and the Hearth*, LIX

Happiness and riches are two things and very seldom meet together.

Richardson, *Clarissa Harlowe*, I

My relations cannot be happy unless they make me unhappy.   *Ibid.*

My sunshine darts but through a drizzly cloud.   *Ibid.*

To know your own happiness, and that it is now, nor to leave it to after-reflection to look back upon the preferable past with a heavy and self-accusing heart, that you did not choose it when you might have chosen it, is all that is necessary to complete your felicity.

Ibid.

Happy is the man who knows his follies in his youth.   *Ibid.*, II

In being well deceived consists the whole of human happiness.   *Ibid.*

Those least bear disappointment who love most to give it.   *Ibid.*, III

The unhappy never want for enemies.   *Ibid.*, IV

That only is happiness which we think so.

Richardson, *Sir Charles Grandison*, Two, IV

If we cannot be as happy as we wish, we should rejoice in the happiness we can have.

Richardson, *Sir Charles Grandison*, Two, IV

To rush the world over seeking for happiness is a fool's work.   Schreiner, *Undine*, XV

Nothing is perhaps more dangerous to the future happiness of men of deep thought and retired habits, than the entertaining an early, long, and unfortunate attachment.

Scott, *Kenilworth*, XXVII

Will men prefer the happiness of others at the neglect of their own?

Shebbeare, *The Marriage Act*, II

Shepherds: a happy people, wanting little, because they desire not much.

Sidney, *Arcadia*, I

A light heart and a thin pair of breeches goes through the world.

Smollett, *Roderick Random*, 36

Happy and happy, there are so many hundred ways. A man may be happy in revolt; he may be happy in sleep; wine, change, and travel make him happy; virtue will do the like—and in old, quiet, and habitual marriages there is yet another happiness.

Stevenson, *Prince Otto*, Book II, VI

Whether mankind is really partial to happiness is an open question.

Stevenson, *The Wrong Box*, III

A broad back with a heavy weight upon it gives the best chance of happiness here below.

Trollope, *Ayala's Angel*, LXIV

When we are happy, we are always good, but when we are good, we are not always happy.
Wilde, *The Picture of Dorian Gray*, VI

I have never searched for happiness. Who wants happiness? I have searched for pleasure.
Ibid., XVII

The carelessness of happiness, the high indifference of joy.   *Ibid.*, XVIII

A happy life is like neither to a roaring torrent, nor a stagnant pool, but to a placid and crystal stream, that glows gently and silently along.

Wright, *A Few Days in Athens*, X

HARM

Do no harm to others for the sake of any good it may do to you.

Burney, *Camilla*, Two, IV

An injury is the object of anger, danger of fear, and praise of vanity; goodness is the object of love.   Fielding, H., *Amelia*, II

Never trust the man who hath reason to suspect that you know he hath injured you.

Fielding, H., *Jonathan Wild*, 138

Certainly it is less wicked to hurt all the world than one's own dear self.

Fielding, H., *Tom Jones*, 288

Harm watch, harm catch.   Kimber, *David Ranger*, I

Injury a church rite will at any time repair.   Richardson, *Clarissa Harlowe*, III

Injuries only come from the heart.   Sterne, *Tristram Shandy*, III

HATE: *see also* LOVE

I love a dog, but I hate a bitch.   Anonymous, *Jeremiah Grant*, 98

The devil and a Portuguese equally my aversion.   Defoe, *Captain Singleton*, 8

The embitterment of hatred is often as unaccountable to onlookers as the growth of devoted love, and it not only seems but is really out of direct relation with any outward causes to be alleged.   Eliot, *Daniel Deronda*, Book VII, LIV

The intensest form of hatred is that rooted in fear.   *Ibid.*

Whence can all the quarrels, and jealousies, and jars, proceed, in people who have no love for each other, unless from that noble passion, that desire of curing each other of a smile?   Fielding, H., *Jonathan Wild*, 157-158

Hatred is not the effect of love, even through the medium of jealousy.

Fielding, H., *Tom Jones*, 278

No innocence, and no merit, can defend a man from the unrelenting antipathy of his fellows.   Godwin, *St. Leon*, 289

Nothing is more common than for persons to hate those whom they have injured.

Lennox, *Sophia*, II

We know not what we do when we hate. Hate is a thankless thing. So, let us only hate hatred; and once give love play, we will fall in love with a unicorn. Ah! the easiest way is the best; and to hate, a man must work hard.   Melville, *Mardi*, XIII

Love is a delight; but hate a torment.   *Ibid.*

Haters are thumbscrews, Scotch boots, and Spanish inquisitions to themselves. He who hates is a fool.   *Ibid.*

Though we should hate naught, yet some dislikes are spontaneous; and disliking is not hating.   *Ibid.*

Hatred appeased is love begun; or love renewed if love ever had a footing.
                                                  Richardson, *Clarissa Harlowe*, III

If thou really hatedst me, thou wouldst not venture to tell me so.   *Ibid.*

Hate often begetteth victory, love commonly is the instrument of subjection.
                                                                    Sidney, *Arcadia*, III

HEALTH; SICKNESS: *see also* MEDICINE

Fevers are never at their height at once. They must get on by degrees.
                                                          Dickens, *Barnaby Rudge*, LII

Health first, and honesty afterwards.   Disraeli, *Sybil*, Book III, III

Health loses its relish to one who knows not what it is to be sick.
                                                          Fielding, S., *David Simple*, II

Neither love nor valor can withstand the influence of that sea-demon, [seasickness].
                                                                    Galt, *Ayrshire*, IV

When a man of robust and vigorous constitution has a fit of sickness, it produces a much more powerful effect than the same indisposition upon a delicate valetudinarian.
                                                        Godwin, *Caleb Williams*, I

Nature is health; for health is good, and nature cannot work ill. As little can she work error. Get nature, and you get well.   Melville, *Confidence-Man*, XVI

The maxim of the healthy man is: up, and have it out in exercise when sleep is for foisting base coin of dreams upon you. And as the healthy only are fit to live, their maxims should be law.   Meredith, *Beauchamp's Career*, LI

Too much health is inductive disease.   Meredith, *Ordeal of Richard Feverel*, IV

Health's everything.   *Ibid.*, XXIX

Sickness palls every appetite and makes us hate what we loved.
                                                  Richardson, *Clarissa Harlowe*, III

Health is the normal condition.   Tourgee, *Murvale Eastman*, XXIII

HEART: *see also* EMOTIONS; GOOD-HEARTEDNESS; etc.

Nature has made the heart the magnetic point of mutual attraction in affairs of a first and mutual passion, and the head of the wisest man is here out of its sphere.
                                          Caruthers, *Kentuckian in New-York*, Volume I, XVII

Few men have not their secret moments of deep feeling.   Collins, *Basil*, Part One, V

What is the hardness of stone? Nothing compared to the hardness of the unregenerate human heart.   Collins, *The Moonstone*, Second Period, II

The human heart is unsearchable. Who is to fathom it?   *Ibid.*, Second Period, III

The human heart is vast enough to contain all the world.   Conrad, *Lord Jim*, XXXIV

He who denies an American girl a heart, knows nothing about her. She is *all* heart.
                                                        Cooper, *Satanstoe*, Volume II, IV

Men have stronger arms, and heads for harder work, but they have no such hearts as women. And the world has been led by the heart in all the ages.

Crawford, *A Rose of Yesterday*, IV

It is a poor heart that never rejoices.   Dickens, *Barnaby Rudge*, XIX

There are strings in the human heart that had better not be vibrated.   *Ibid.*, XXII

The heart is an ingenious part of our formation—the center of the blood vessels and all that sort of thing—which has no more to do with what you say or think, than your knees have.   *Ibid.*, XXXII

His manner is the gravely impressive manner of a man who has not committed himself in life, otherwise than as he has become the victim of a tender sorrow of the heart.

Dickens, *Bleak House*, XX

To this mind of the heart, some bright ray of the truth shot straight.

Dickens, *David Copperfield*, XLII

The first mistaken impulse of an undisciplined heart.   *Ibid.*, XLV

"What I want," drawled Mrs. Skewton, pinching her shrivelled throat, "is heart." It was frightfully true in one sense, if not in that in which she used the phrase. "What I want, is frankness, confidence, less conventionality, and freer play of soul. We are so dreadfully artificial." We were, indeed.   Dickens, *Dombey and Son*, XXI

My heart is a desert island, and she lives in it alone.   *Ibid.*, XLVIII

Some people have no hearts to break.   Dickens, *Nicholas Nickleby*, III

He never offended anyone's self-love. His good breeding sprang from the only sure source of gentle manners—a kind heart.   Disraeli, *Coningsby*, Book II, II

An English heart is not easily broken.   Disraeli, *Sybil*, Book II, XVI

The heart of man is the same everywhere.   Eliot, *Adam Bede*, X

Love and prudence are deadly foes, and when one gets possession of the heart he instantly expels the other.   Falkner, *Little Brick Church*, XXV

What a man is to the world, and to his own heart, is a very different thing.

Galt, *Ayrshire*, VII

My heart is in the happy position of a country which has no history or debt.

Hardy, *The Hand of Ethelberta*, XXI

My heart comes back to its old anchorage.   Hardy, *Trumpet-Major*, XXXVII

Her heart was deep, but of small compass; it had room but for a very few dearest ones.

Hawthorne, *The Blithedale Romance*, XVI

That cold tendency, between instinct and intellect, which made me pry with a speculative interest into people's passions and impulses, appeared to have gone far towards unhumanizing my heart.   *Ibid.*, XVIII

A man cannot always decide for himself whether his own heart is cold or warm.   *Ibid.*

Groping for human emotions in the dark corners of the heart.   *Ibid.*, XXV

Next to the lightest heart, the heaviest is apt to be most playful.

Hawthorne, *The House of the Seven Gables*, XVI

Wherever there is a heart and an intellect, the diseases of the physical frame are tinged with the peculiarities of these.   Hawthorne, *The Scarlet Letter*, IX

He has violated, in cold blood, the sanctity of a human heart.   *Ibid.*, XVII

As, in spite of seeming discouragement, some mathematicians are yet in hopes of hitting upon an exact method of determining the longitude, the more earnest psychologists may, in the face of previous failures, still cherish expectations with regard to some mode of infallibly discovering the heart of man.   Melville, *Confidence-Man*, XIV

Compassion the heart decides for itself.   *Ibid.*, XXXVI

Unauthorized and abhorrent thoughts will sometimes invade the best human heart.
     Melville, *Israel Potter*, V

There are those who like not to be detected in the possession of a heart.
     Melville, *Mardi*, CL

Many of us are but sorry hosts to ourselves. Some hearts are hermits.   *Ibid.*, CLI

We are all good and bad. Give me the heart that's huge as all Asia; and unless a man be a villain outright, account him as one of the best tempered blades in the world.
     Ibid., CLXXXI

Nothing like a cold heart; warm ones are ever chafing, and getting into trouble.   *Ibid.*

I have found that the heart is not whole, but divided; that it seeks a soft cushion whereon to repose; that it vitalizes the blood; which else were weaker than water: I have found that we cannot live without hearts; though the heartless live longest. Yet hug your hearts, ye handful that have them; 'tis a blessed inheritance!   *Ibid.*, CLXXXIII

Deep, deep, and still deep and deeper must we go, if we would find out the heart of a man.   Melville, *Pierre*, Book XXI, II

Nothing is surer [than] the heart.   Meredith, *Beauchamp's Career*, VII

Daily the body changes, daily the mind—why not the heart?
     Meredith, *Harry Richmond*, XXXI

There's a many ways of showing the heart.   Reade, *Griffith Gaunt*, XXVI

Our hearts are often larger than our wills.   Schreiner, *Undine*, VII

The heart knoweth its own bitterness.   Stowe, *Uncle Tom's Cabin*, XXVII

Hearts that break are not worth mending.   Tourgee, *Murvale Eastman*, XLVII

I don't know what heart means. I sometimes fancy that it is a talent for getting into debt, and running away with other men's wives.   Trollope, *The Eustace Diamonds*, XIX

HEAVEN; EARTH; HELL

Heaven at distance does not attract us so forcibly as a fool's paradise in sight.
     Anonymous, *Memoirs of the Court of H—*, 76

I am dying in Paradise.   Bronte, C., *Villette*, IV

Long are the "times" of Heaven.   *Ibid.*, XVII

All sinners would be miserable in heaven.   Bronte, E., *Wuthering Heights*, IX

Every human act, good or ill, is an angel to guide or to warn.
     Bulwer, *Lucretia*, Epilogue to Part II

There was a way to hell, even from the gates of heaven.
     Bunyan, *Pilgrim's Progress*, 168

The way to heaven is as up a ladder, and the way to hell is as down a hill.   *Ibid.*, 226

And earth was heaven a little the worse for wear. And heaven was earth, done up again to look like new.   Collins, *The Moonstone*, First Period, X

The ugly women have a bad time of it in this world; let's hope it will be made up to them in another.   *Ibid.*, First Period, XIV

The heaven and the earth must not be shaken.   Conrad, *Lord Jim*, XXI

For myself, it would be no great indulgence to be kept shut up in those mansions of which they preach, having a natural longing for motion and the chase.
     Cooper, *The Last of the Mohicans*, XIX

It is fortunate "all will come right in heaven," for it is certain too much goes wrong on earth.
Cooper, *The Monikins*, Conclusion

Why do mortals talk continually of the joys of Heaven, yet so anxiously endeavor to prolong life?
Dacre, *Passions*, Letter LXX

If once we pushed on to the coast and separated, we should never be able to see that place again with our eyes, or do any more than sinners did with heaven,—wish themselves there, but know they can never come at it.
Defoe, *Captain Singleton*, 150

Man proposes, Heaven disposes.
Dickens, *The Mystery of Edwin Drood*, IV

A man may go to heaven with half the pains which it costs him to purchase hell.
Fielding, H., *Jonathan Wild*, 263-264

Hell is but the chimera of priests, to bubble idiots and cowards.
Godwin, *St. Leon*, 56

Heaven promotes its purposes without aiming at the stage effect of what is called miraculous interposition.
Hawthorne, *The Scarlet Letter*, IX

Heaven doesn't always make the right men kings.
Hope, *The Prisoner of Zenda*, XXI

Were I persuaded that all the devils in hell were women, I would never live devoutly to inherit heaven, or that they were all saints in heaven, I would live more strictly for fear of hell.
Lyly, *Euphues*, 125

To have used prosperity well is the first favored lot of heaven; the next is his whom adversity has not smitten in vain.
Mackenzie, *The Man of the World*, II

To live at all is a high vocation; to live forever may truly appal us. Toil we not here? and shall we be forever slothful elsewhere?
Melville, *Mardi*, CLXXV

Peradventure at this instant, there are beings gazing up to this very world as their future heaven. But the universe is all over a heaven: nothing but stars on stars, through-out infinities of expansion.
Ibid.

All Heaven's a sun.
Ibid., CLXXXVII

If man were wholly made in heaven, why catch we hell-glimpses?
Melville, *Pierre*, Book V, VII

The way to heaven out of all places is of like length and distance.
More, *Utopia*, I

Heavens will not always come to witness when they are called.
Nashe, *The Unfortunate Traveller*, 81

Celestial sounds have sometimes been heard on earth.
Radcliffe, *The Mysteries of Udolpho*, II

Honest folk get to heaven by different roads.
Reade, *Griffith Gaunt*, I

Who knows what the justice of Heaven may inflict in order to convince us that we are not out of the reach of misfortune; and to reduce us to a better reliance, than that we have hitherto presumptuously made?
Richardson, *Clarissa Harlowe*, I

If Heaven will afford time for repentance, why should not man?
Ibid., IV

No heretic can learn the language of Heaven.
Richardson, *Sir Charles Grandison*, Two, III

Heaven might keep its angels if men were but left to men.
Schreiner, *Story of an African Farm*, Part II, XIII

We dream of heaven, but would laugh to scorn the man who offered to show it us.
Schreiner, *Undine*, VII

To be just is to deserve celestial aid.
Shebbeare, *Excellence and Decline of the Sumatrans*, II

Nothing wins heaven but what doth earth forsake.
Sidney, *Arcadia*, II

Nought can reason avail in heavenly matters. *Ibid.*

When a man thinks of anything which is past, he looks down upon the ground, but when he thinks of something that is to come, he looks up towards the heavens.
Sterne, *Tristram Shandy*, II

Every exaltation must have its depression. God will not let us have heaven here below.
Stowe, *The Minister's Wooing*, XXXVII

The treasury of heaven, where all things that are divine belong.
Twain, *Connecticut Yankee*, XXXV

When I reflect upon the number of disagreeable people who I know have gone to a better world, I am moved to lead a different life. Twain, *Pudd'nhead Wilson*, XIII

Heaven mocks the short-sighted views of man. Walpole, *The Castle of Otranto*, 48

Heaven will not be trifled with. *Ibid.*, 58

Heaven does not send heralds to question earthly titles. *Ibid.*, 59

Heaven does nothing in vain. *Ibid.*, 83

It is sinful to cherish those whom Heaven has doomed to destruction. *Ibid.*, 98

Will Heaven visit the innocent for the crimes of the guilty? *Ibid.*, 99

Heaven often plans more mercifully for us than we plan for ourselves.
Warner, *A Little Journey*, XXII

Each of us has heaven and hell in him. Wilde, *The Picture of Dorian Gray*, XIII

HERITAGE; INHERITANCE: *see also* FAMILY

Nothing comes out in a man but one of his forefathers possessed it before him.
Schreiner, *Story of an African Farm*, Part II, IV

HEROISM: *see also* COURAGE

The heroism of principle. Austen, *Mansfield Park*, Volume Two, IX

When a young lady is to be a heroine, the perverseness of forty surrounding families cannot prevent her. Something must and will happen to throw a hero in her way.
Austen, *Northanger Abbey*, I

The man is a hero who can withstand unjust opinion.
Brackenridge, *Modern Chivalry*, Part II, I

There are heroes in words as well as heroes in blows.
Bridges, *The Adventures of a Bank-Note*, I

There are heroes in smallware and heroes in great matters. *Ibid.*

I was not heroic enough to purchase liberty at the price of caste.
Bronte, C., *Jane Eyre*, III

Give thy sinews a mind that conceives the heroic, and what noble things thou mayst do! But value thy sinews for strength alone, and that strength may be turned to thy shame and thy torture. Bulwer, *What Will He Do with It?*, Book X, VII

Is it not time to begin to take more counsel of humanity, and less of your courage?
Cooper, *The Last of the Mohicans*, XIV

To believe in the heroic makes heroes. Disraeli, *Coningsby*, Book III, I

Heroes think with their hands. Fielding, H., *Joseph Andrews*, 220

Players are heroes upon the stage; but beggars, sots, or prostitutes in their private lodgings. Graves, *The Spiritual Quixote*, III

The greatest obstacle to being heroic is the doubt whether one may not be going to prove one's self a fool; the truest heroism is, to resist the doubt; and the profoundest wisdom, to know when it ought to be resisted, and when to be obeyed.
Hawthorne, *The Blithedale Romance*, II

There can be no truer test of the noble and heroic, in any individual, than the degree in which he possesses the faculty of distinguishing heroism from absurdity.
Ibid., XIX

To heroic tempers, to fight a battle with the world is a martyrdom that is the richest meed in the world's gift.
Hawthorne, *The House of the Seven Gables*, VII

Occasion inspires heroes.
Howells, *Silas Lapham*, XIV

We shall have heroism if we have the occasion.
Ibid.

No woman could endure to live in the same house with a perfect hero.
Ibid., XXVII

Not to be afraid of what may happen to you when you've no more to say for yourself than a steamer without a light—that is the highest heroism.
James, H., *The Awkward Age*, Book VI, I

The law has no power over heroes.
Lennox, *The Female Quixote*, I

A hero in one age will be a hero in another.
Ibid., II

There are heroes without armies, who hear martial music in their souls.
Melville, *Mardi*, CXXVI

Easy for a man to think like a hero; but hard for man to act like one.
Melville, *Pierre*, Book IX, IV

All imaginable audacities readily enter into the soul; few come boldly forth from it.
Ibid.

There is an inevitable keen cruelty in the loftier heroism.
Ibid., Book X, II

Women will have a hero.
Meredith, *The Amazing Marriage*, XVIII

Heroism seems partly a matter of training.
Meredith, *Ordeal of Richard Feverel*, XXVI

Though every man of us may be a hero for one fatal minute, very few remain so after a day's march.
Ibid., XXXIII

Think ye a hero one to be defeated in his first battle?
Ibid.

Like women, heroes trust to instinct, and graft on it the muscle of men.
Ibid., XLII

Outrage upon outrage they have endured, and that deadens—or rather makes their heroism unscrupulous.
Meredith, *Sandra Belloni*, XLVIII

Not a day passes over the earth but men and women of no note do great deeds, speak great words, and suffer noble sorrows.
Reade, *The Cloister and the Hearth*, I

The greater cowardice, the greater delight in subjects of heroism.
Richardson, *Clarissa Harlowe*, I

He who is too proud ever to admit a mean thought—who is ambitious only of ideal excellence—who has an inflexible will only in the pursuit of truth and righteousness— may be a saint and a hero.
Stowe, *Orr's Island*, XXIV

If this is a novel without a hero, at least let us lay claim to a heroine.
Thackeray, *Vanity Fair*, XXX

We cannot have heroes to dine with us. There are none. And were these heroes to be had, we should not like them.
Trollope, *The Eustace Diamonds*, XXXV

The heroes of life are so much better than the heroes of romance.
Trollope, *He Knew He Was Right*, LXXXV

HIDEOUSNESS: *see also* BEAUTY; HANDSOMENESS; etc.

Virtuous and gifted animals, whether man or beast, always are so very hideous.
Dickens, *Barnaby Rudge*, XXIII

HISTORY; BIOGRAPHY: *see also* ETERNALITY; PAST-PRESENT-FUTURE; TIME; etc.

The fact that a thing is old makes me suspicious of it. I believe in the present. I have no veneration for the past and study it only to avoid mistakes.
Adams, F., *President John Smith*, X

Many grave histories are as dangerous as the most absurd fictions.
Anonymous, *The Ladies Advocate*, 297

Everyone is engaged in history.
Anonymous, *Private Letters from an American in England*, 112

I read history a little as a duty, but it tells me nothing that does not either vex or weary me.
Austen, *Northanger Abbey*, XIV

Historians are not happy in their flights of fancy. They display imagination without raising interest.
Ibid.

I am fond of history, and am very well contented to take the false with the true.
Ibid.

I have often wondered at the person's courage that could sit down on purpose to labor only for the torment of little boys and girls [by writing history].
Ibid.

That little boys and girls should be tormented [by reading history] is what no one at all acquainted with human nature in a civilized state can deny.
Ibid.

Historians are not accountable for the difficulty of learning to read.
Ibid.

Human history, like all great movements, is cyclical, and returns to the point of beginning.
Bellamy, *Looking Backward*, I

History has been well said to be the Romance of the human mind and Romance the history of the heart.
Brackenridge, *Modern Chivalry*, Part II, I

All true histories contain instruction.
Bronte, A., *Agnes Grey*, I

Though a scholar is often a fool, he is never a fool so supreme, so superlative, as when he is defacing the first unsullied page of the human history, by entering into it the commonplaces of his own pedantry.
Bulwer, *The Caxtons*, Book I, IV

Was it enough to write quartos upon the past history of Human Error? Was it not his duty, when the occasion was fairly presented, to enter upon that present, daily, hourly war with Error—which is the sworn chivalry of Knowledge!
Ibid., Book VII, I

History reveals men's deeds, men's outward characters, but not themselves.
Bulwer, *The Pilgrims of the Rhine*, XXII

There is a secret self that hath its own life "rounded by a dream," unpenetrated, unguessed.
Ibid.

It is the interval between our first repinings and our final resignation, in which, both with individuals and communities, is to be found all that makes a history worth telling.
Bulwer, *What Will He Do with It?*, Book III, XIV

The years pass and repeat each other; the same events revolve in the cycles of time.
Collins, *The Moonstone*, Epilogue

History, like love, is apt to surround her heroes with an atmosphere of imaginary brightness.
Cooper, *The Last of the Mohicans*, XVIII

History is not a prediction, but a record of the past.
Cooper, *The Monikins*, XI

The loftiest interests of man are made up of a collection of those that are lowly; he who makes a faithful picture of only a single important scene in the events of a single life, is doing something towards painting the greatest historical piece of his day.

Cooper, *Satanstoe*, Volume I, I

The historian who would wish his lessons to sink deep into the heart, thereby essaying to render mankind virtuous and more happy, must not content himself with simply detailing a series of events—he must ascertain causes, and follow progressively their effects; he must draw deductions from incidents as they arise, and ever revert to the actuating principle.

Dacre, *Zofloya*, I

It was the best of times, it was the worst of times, it was the age of wisdom, it was the age of foolishness, it was the epoch of belief, it was the epoch of incredulity, it was the season of Light, it was the season of Darkness, it was the spring of hope, it was the winter of despair, we had everything before us, we had nothing before us, we were all going direct to Heaven, we were all going direct the other way—in short, the period was so far like the present period, that some of its noisiest authorities insisted on its being received, for good or for evil, in the superlative degree of comparison only.

Dickens, *A Tale of Two Cities*, Book the First, I

Read no history: nothing but biography, for that is life without theory.

Disraeli, *Contarini Fleming*

It is with nations as it is with individuals. A book of history is a book of sermons.

Doyle, *Micah Clarke*, III

Every history has one quality in common with eternity. Begin where you will, there is always a beginning back of the beginning. And, for that matter, there is always a shadowy ending beyond the ending.

Eggleston, *The Circuit Rider*, III

Men, like planets, have both a visible and an invisible history.

Eliot, *Daniel Deronda*, Book II, XVI

What elegant historian would neglect a striking opportunity for pointing out that his heroes did not foresee the history of the world, or even of their own actions?

Eliot, *Middlemarch*, Book I, VII

The growing good of the world is partly dependent on unhistoric acts.

Ibid., Book VIII, Finale

There are many little circumstances too often omitted by injudicious historians, from which events of the utmost importance arise. The world may indeed be considered as a vast machine, in which the great wheels are originally set in motion by those which are very minute, and almost imperceptible to any but the strongest eyes.

Fielding, H., *Tom Jones*, 172-173

Impartiality is the very essence of history.

Gentleman, *A Trip to the Moon*, I

To be at one moment active, gay, penetrating, with stores of knowledge at one's command, capable of delighting, instructing and animating mankind, and the next, lifeless and loathsome, an incumbrance upon the face of the earth—such is the history of many men, and such will be mine.

Godwin, *Caleb Williams*, I

What's the use of learning that I am one of a long row only—finding out that there is set down in some old book somebody just like me, and to know that I shall only act her part; making me sad, that's all. The best is not to remember that your nature and your past doings have been just like thousands' and thousands', and that your coming life and doings'll be like thousands' and thousands'.

Hardy, *Tess*, XIX

Books will not tell me why the sun do shine on the just and the unjust alike.

Ibid.

Romance, as it sets out in utter defiance of truth, and commonly of reason too, may make its own way to the magnificent; history, as it is nothing, if not founded on facts, is tied down to much narrower limits.

Hill, *George Edwards*, 11

If we act only for ourselves, to neglect the study of history is not prudent; if we are entrusted with the care of others, it is not just.   Johnson, *Rasselas*, 118

There is no part of history so generally useful as that which relates the progress of the human mind.   *Ibid.*

In the history of individuals, as well as in nations, there is often a period of sudden blossoming—a short, luxuriant summer, not without its tornadoes and thunder-glooms, in which all the buried seeds of past observation leap forth together into life, and form, and beauty.   Kingsley, *Alton Locke*, IX

War and disorder, ruin and death, cannot last forever.
        Kingsley, *Hereward the Wake*, XLII

Why should a mark be set upon those whom history has condemned unrighteously?
        Lawrence, *Guy Livingstone*, XIX

The great end of history is to show how much human nature can endure or perform.
        Lennox, *The Female Quixote*, II

The ends meet.   Melville, *Israel Potter*, XXVI

Nothing changes, though much be new-fashioned: new fashions but revivals of things previous. In the books of the past we learn naught of the present; in those of the present, the past. All history was written out in capitals in the first page penned. The whole story is told in a title-page. An exclamation point is entire Mardi's [the world's] autobiography.
        Melville, *Mardi*, CLXXVI

With these unsophisticated savages the history of a day is the history of a life.
        Melville, *Typee*, XX

The stench of the trail of Ego in our History. It is ego—ego, the fountain cry, origin, sole source of war.   Meredith, *Beauchamp's Career*, XXIX

The proper defense for a nation is its history.   Meredith, *Harry Richmond*, XXVIII

The history of mankind shows our painful efforts to find a middle course, but they have invariably resolved themselves into asceticism, or laxity, acting and reacting. The moral question is, If a naughty little man, by reason of his naughtiness, releases himself from foolishness, does a foolish little man, by reason of his foolishness, save himself from naughtiness?   Meredith, *Ordeal of Richard Feverel*, XXXVI

The fortune, or misfortune, to which men attribute their successes and reverses are useful impersonations to novelists; but my opinion is that we make our own history without intervention.   *Ibid.*, XXXVII

Former times are constant informers.   Nashe, *The Unfortunate Traveller*, 83

Every calm is succeeded by a storm, as is every storm by its calm.
        Paltock, *Peter Wilkins*, 101

We are the cream of all that have gone before us. We really live their life; we begin where they ended; we stand on their shoulders; their whole learning is only our alphabet; they laid the foundation, we build the superstructure.   Payson, *Golden Dreams*, I

History is but a tiresome thing in itself; it becomes more agreeable the more romance is mixed with it.   Peacock, *Crotchet Castle*, IX

History, a far more daring storyteller than romance.
        Reade, *The Cloister and the Hearth*, XCVI

What does a man read history for, if he cannot profit by the examples he finds in it?
        Richardson, *Clarissa Harlowe*, III

Jails, like other places, have their ancient traditions, known only to the inhabitants, and handed down from one set of the melancholy lodgers to the next who occupy their cells.
        Scott, *The Heart of Midlothian*, I

In all the difficulties which attend an historian, there is none which is greater than that of steering free from offense.   Shebbeare, *Lydia*, I

Instruction in the knowledge of mankind is the most useful part of history.
Shebbeare, *The Marriage Act*, I

The knowledge of a paltry historian is circumscribed. Infinitely superior would the fund of information be of one who should be an eyewitness to extraordinary events through all time, in the vast round of eternity. Sheridan, *Nourjahad*, 135–136

When a man sits down to write a history, he knows no more than his heels what lets and confounded hindrances he is to meet with in his way, or what a dance he may be led, by one excursion or another, before all is over. Sterne, *Tristram Shandy*, I

The history of a soldier's wound beguiles the pain of it. *Ibid.*

How many of us begin a new record with each day of our lives? Stoker, *Dracula*, VI

Why shall History go on kneeling to the end of time? I am for having her rise up off her knees, and take a natural posture: not to be forever performing cringes and congees like a court-chamberlain, and shuffling backwards out of doors in the presence of the sovereign. In a word, I would have history familiar rather than heroic.
Thackeray, *Henry Esmond*, Book I, The History

While in science and religion humanity is making stupendous strides, in government as in art, it turns ever to the model of the antique and approves the wisdom only of the ancient. Tourgee, *Bricks Without Straw*, XXVII

History is never a trustworthy guide to the thinker. It is, at the best, only a staff, and a most unreliable one at that. Despite the adage, it never repeats itself. The butterfly of today can never again be the chrysalid of yesterday. Analogies the past may furnish, but patterns for the future never. Tourgee, *Murvale Eastman*, VII

It is impossible for the historian, with even the best intentions, to control events or compel the persons of his narrative to act wisely or to be successful. It is easy to see how things might have been better managed; a very little change here and there would have made a very different history. Twain and Warner, *The Gilded Age*, Volume II, XIX

HOLINESS

Hands off from that holiness! Melville, *Moby Dick*, CXXV

HOME: *see also* FAMILY

We said there warn't no home like a raft. Other places do seem so cramped up and smothery, but a raft don't. You feel mighty free and easy and comfortable on a raft.
Twain, *Huckleberry Finn*, XVIII

HONESTY: *see also* HONOR; TRUTH; etc.

Modesty is very well in its way; but really a little common honesty is sometimes quite as becoming. Austen, *Northanger Abbey*, XVIII

An honest man will avow himself and his opinions.
Brackenridge, *Modern Chivalry*, Part II, I

The want of honesty is want of sense. *Ibid.*, Part II, II

It is right to look our life-accounts bravely in the face now and then, and settle them honestly. And he is a poor self-swindler who lies to himself while he reckons the items, and sets down under the head happiness that which is misery.
Bronte, C., *Villette*, XXXI

How does a mercenary divine, or lawyer, or physician, differ from a dishonest chimney-sweep? The most that can be dreaded from a chimney-sweep is the spoiling of our dinner, or a little temporary alarm; but what injuries may we not dread from the abuses of law, medicine, or divinity! Brown, C. B., *Alcuin*, I

Honesty is the best policy. Whatever it be, it is not the road to wealth. *Ibid.*

It is not permitted to an honest man to corrupt himself for the sake of others.
Bulwer, *The Caxtons*, Book XVI, X

An honest heart fears no danger from any earthly source.
Caruthers, *Kentuckian in New-York*, Volume I, VI

Honesty is no guard against external danger in this world, whether moral or physical.
Ibid.

Think all men rogues, till we find them honest. Collyer, *Felicia to Charlotte*, II

All honest men are worthy. Cooke, *Virginia Comedians*, Volume II, XXIX

Honesty is a great advantage. Cooper, *The Deerslayer*, XXIV

Honesty lies deeper than the skin. Cooper, *The Prairie*, XXVI

My pride, not my principle, my money, not my virtue, kept me honest.
Defoe, *Moll Flanders*, 57

Honesty is out of the question when starvation is the case. Defoe, *Roxana*, 31

Honesty and honor are the same. *Ibid.*, 194

He mistrusted the honesty of all poor people who could read and write.
Dickens, *Barnaby Rudge*, XLVII

This vicious assumption of honesty in dishonesty—a vice so dangerous, so deadly, and so common. Dickens, *Hard Times*, Book II, II

Flora had a decided tendency to be always honest when she gave herself time to think about it. Dickens, *Little Dorrit*, Book I, XXIV

"Honesty is the best policy.—I always find it so. I lost forty-seven pound ten by being honest this morning. But it's all gain, it's gain!" "A man who loses forty-seven pound ten in one morning by his honesty is a man to be envied. If it had been eighty pound, the luxuriousness of feeling would have been increased. Every pound lost would have been a hundredweight of happiness gained." Dickens, *Old Curiosity Shop*, LVII

You had better be an honest man than half a rogue. Fielding, H., *Jonathan Wild*, 134

The honest part of mankind would be much too hard for the knavish, if they could bring themselves to incur the guilt, or thought it worth their while to take the trouble.
Fielding, H., *Tom Jones*, 296–297

There is a kind of sympathy in honest minds, by means of which they give an easy credit to each other. *Ibid.*, 667

One's impression of his honesty was almost like carrying a bunch of flowers; the perfume was most agreeable, but they were occasionally an inconvenience.
James, H., *The Europeans*, VI

He that loseth his honesty hath nothing else to lose. Lyly, *Euphues*, 118

There are many more honest dealings than honest men; there are more honest men than knaves; common sense will keep them so, even exclusive of principle, but all may be vanquished by adequate temptation. Mackenzie, *Julia De Roubigné*, 127

Honesty's best voucher is honesty's face. Melville, *Confidence-Man*, XV

One remedy for mistakes is honesty. Melville, *Israel Potter*, VII

A man can be honest in any sort of skin. Melville, *Moby Dick*, III

In reserves men build imposing characters; not in revelations. He who shall be wholly honest, though nobler than Ethan Allen; that man shall stand in danger of the meanest mortal's scorn. Melville, *Pierre*, Book V, VII

That which the ass wants in wit, he hath in honesty; who ever saw him kick or winch, or use any jade's tricks? Nashe, *The Unfortunate Traveller*, 44–45

251

HONESTY (*continued*)

Many are honest because they know not how to be dishonest. *Ibid.*, 83

There are more honest low people than honest high. Richardson, *Clarissa Harlowe*, I

It is difficult for an honest man to act in disguises. As the poet says, "Thrust Nature back with a pitchfork, it will return." *Ibid.*, II

An honest man will not wish to have it in his power to do hurt. *Ibid.*

My countenance is an honest picture of my heart. *Ibid.*, IV

An honest man fears not inspection. Richardson, *Sir Charles Grandison*, One, II

The honest heart aims not at secrets. *Ibid.*, Three, VI

I have found brutes ofttimes the honester animals. Scott, *The Talisman*, XXVII

You seem to think honesty as easy as Blind Man's Buff: I don't. It's some difference of definition. Stevenson, *The Wrecker*, V

There is a cringing and almost contemptible littleness about honesty, which hardly allows it to assert itself. The really honest man can never say a word to make those who don't know of his honesty believe that it is there. Honesty goes about with a hang-dog look about him, as though knowing that he cannot be trusted till he be proved. Dishonesty carries his eyes high, and assumes that any question respecting him must be considered to be unnecessary. Trollope, *The Eustace Diamonds*, LIII

A man who is ready to vote black white because somebody tells him is dishonest. Trollope, *Phineas Finn*, LXIII

HONOR; DISHONOR: *see also* GLORY; HONESTY; TRUTH

Honor is more valuable than life. Anonymous, *The Birmingham Counterfeit*, I

Honor is the acknowledgment which the world makes of a man's respectability. Brackenridge, *Modern Chivalry*, Part I, I

Man recreates himself by the principle of honor. Bulwer, *The Caxtons*, Book III, II

Honor is the foundation of all improvement in mankind. *Ibid.*

A man looks horrid small, walking about, when he can't pay his debts of honor. Burney, *Camilla*, Five, IX

Even libertinism has its laws of honor at least. Cleland, *Memoirs of a Coxcomb*, 111

Honors are sweet even to the most humble. Cooper, *The Monikins*, Conclusion

Men are never greater simpletons, than when they let the secret consciousness of their love of life push them into swaggering about their honor; when their honor has nothing to do with the matter in hand. Cooper, *Satanstoe*, Volume II, II

Mistaken ideas of honor lead men readily to excuse in others that which on similar false and destructive principles, they would feel no remorse in being guilty of themselves. Dacre, *The Libertine*, XXX

All good ends can be worked out by good means. Those that cannot, are bad; and may be counted so at once, and left alone. Dickens, *Barnaby Rudge*, LXXIX

Whoever offends against the laws of honor in the least instance is treated as the highest delinquent. Here is no excuse, no pardon; and he doth nothing who leaves anything undone. Fielding, H., *Amelia*, I

Nothing is so tender as a man's honor. *Ibid.*, II

Honor is a word of such sovereign use and virtue, of so uncertain and various an application, that scarce two people mean the same thing by it. Fielding, H., *Jonathan Wild*, 56

The honor of a man consists in receiving no affront from his own sex, and that of woman in receiving no kindness from men. *Ibid.*, 232

While it is in the power of every man to be perfectly honest, not one in a thousand is capable of being a complete rogue. *Ibid.*, 289

Can honor teach any one to tell a lie, or can any honor exist independent of religion?
Fielding, H., *Tom Jones*, 82

Honor is a creature of the world's making, and the world hath the power of a creator over it, and may govern and direct it as they please. *Ibid.*, 686

Did reason ever authorize such principles as hereditary honors?
Gentleman, *A Trip to the Moon*, I

I can only be dishonored by perpetrating an unjust action.
Godwin, *Caleb Williams*, I

My honor is in my own keeping, beyond the reach of all mankind. *Ibid.*

Every man is in his different mode susceptible to a sense of honor. *Ibid.*, III

Honor is my only dower. Helme, *St. Margaret's Cave*, Volume I, XVIII

Honor binds a woman, too. Hope, *The Prisoner of Zenda*, XXI

Honor is the word of fools, or of those wiser men who cheat them.
Mackenzie, *The Man of Feeling*, 61

I hope there are not many in this world to whom the thought of honor being tied to money ever appears possible. Meredith, *Sandra Belloni*, XXXVI

Honor sat as easy as his glove. Richardson, *Clarissa Harlowe*, I

All young honor is supercilious and touchy. *Ibid.*, II

There is honor in being related to ladies as eminent for their virtue as for their descent.
Ibid., III

Honors change manners. *Ibid.*, IV

To die like a man of honor, you must have lived like one.
Richardson, *Sir Charles Grandison*, One, II

Nothing in the world makes a fool of a man so soon as honor.
Ridley, *James Lovegrove*, I

Honor is a term much used but little understood. Roche, *Nocturnal Visit*, IV

The sense of honor is often stronger than all reasoning. Stowe, *Orr's Island*, XXVI

HOPE: *see also* ASPIRATION; FAITH; etc.

Hope is a charming passion, the only real friend of human thought.
Annesley, *Memoirs of an Unfortunate Young Nobleman*, I

You want nothing but patience; or give it a more fascinating name: call it hope.
Austen, *Sense and Sensibility*, Volume I, XIX

The most precious gift of heaven, hope. Beckford, *Vathek*, 242

Can anything amuse more than fair hopes?
Brackenridge, *Modern Chivalry*, Part II, II

I believe in some blending of hope and sunshine sweetening the worst lots. I believe that this life is not all; neither the beginning nor the end. I believe while I tremble; I trust while I weep. Bronte, C., *Villette*, XXXI

There is no love without a ray of hope. Brooke, *Emily Montague*, I

While thou art free hope yet survives—a phantom, haply, but hope still.
Bulwer, *Harold*, Book IV, IV

Pause and ask thyself if all the true happiness thou hast known is not bounded to hope. As long as thou hopest, thou art happy. *Ibid.*, Book IV, VI

If we were enabled minutely to examine the mental organization of men who have risked great dangers, whether by the impulse of virtue or in the perpetration of a crime, we should probably find therein a large preponderance of hope.
Bulwer, *Pausanias*, Book III, VI

That which the foolish-wise call fanaticism, belongs to the same part of us as hope.
Bulwer, *Rienzi*, Book X, VIII

Is there no hope, but you must be kept in the iron cage of despair?
Bunyan, *Pilgrim's Progress*, 35

Few criminals at the moment of receiving sentence of death, realize more than a horrid and oppressive sense of present calamity—all hope has not yet entirely forsaken them.
Caruthers, *Cavaliers*, Volume II, IX

So long as we possess the power to struggle, hope is the last feeling to desert the human mind. Cooper, *The Headsman*, XXIII

I like not that principle of the natives, which teaches them to submit without a struggle, in emergencies that appear desperate; our own maxim, "while life remains there is hope," is more consoling, and better suited to a soldier's temperament.
Cooper, *The Last of the Mohicans*, IX

Hope is indispensable to love, and hope is allied to confidence.
Cooper, *Satanstoe*, Volume II, XII

Hope, Heaven's own gift to struggling mortals; pervading, like some subtle essence from the skies, all things, both good and bad; as universal as death, and more infectious than disease. Dickens, *Nicholas Nickleby*, XIX

She was saved in that she was hopeful. Dreiser, *Sister Carrie*, XXIX

The fairest blossoms in the garden of hope. Duff, *Rhedi*, 115

Exiles notoriously feed much on hopes, and are unlikely to stay in banishment unless they are obliged. Eliot, *Middlemarch*, Book VIII, LXXXII

The falsehood of a common assertion, that the greatest human happiness consists in hope. Fielding, H., *Joseph Andrews*, 87–88

Of all the powers exercised by passion over our minds, one of the most wonderful is that of supporting hope in the midst of despair. Fielding, H., *Tom Jones*, 730

Hope never faileth to recomfort an afflicted mind. Gascoigne, *Master F. J.*, 44

There is scarcely anything that produces such a sickness of the heart as the repeated prorogation of hope. Godwin, *St. Leon*, 60

What we place most hopes upon generally proves most fatal.
Goldsmith, *The Vicar of Wakefield*, 20

Hope is from within, and not from without—man himself must work out his own salvation. Haggard, *She*, XVII

It may be argued that reminiscence is less an endowment than a disease, and that expectation in its only comfortable form—that of absolute faith—is practically an impossibility; whilst in the form of hope and the secondary compounds, patience, impatience, resolve, curiosity, it is a constant fluctuation between pleasure and pain.
Hardy, *Far From the Madding Crowd*, XXV

The unhappy are continually tantalized by delusions of succor near at hand; the despair is very dark that has no will-o'-the-wisp to glimmer in it.
Hawthorne, *The Marble Faun*, XXXVIII

Who has no one to love or trust has little to hope. Johnson, *Rasselas*, 133

Hope, the cordial of life. Lawrence, H., *The Contemplative Man*, II

Hope is slowly extinguished and swiftly revived. Lee, *The Recess*, II

Hope, sweet substitute for happiness. *Ibid.*

The sunbeams of hope, the dews of disappointment. *Ibid.*

Where the mind is past hope, the face is past shame.
Lyly, *Euphues and His England*, 341

Not easily may hope be awakened in one long tranced into hopelessness by a chronic complaint. Melville, *Confidence-Man*, XVI

There he sat, holding up that candle in the heart of that almighty forlornness. There he sat, the sign and symbol of a man without faith, hopelessly holding up hope in the midst of despair. Melville, *Moby Dick*, XLVIII

Great hopes have lean offspring. Meredith, *Ordeal of Richard Feverel*, XXII

Inelastic hope. Murfree, *The Story of Old Fort Loudon*, XI

If there is a human being I could envy, it would be the one who can raise the desponding heart to hope and peace. Parsons, *The Castle of Wolfenbach*, II

While there is life there is hope: while there is hope there is joy.
Reade, *The Cloister and the Hearth*, XVII

To hope for better days is half to deserve them. Richardson, *Clarissa Harlowe*, I

What likelihood of corrupting a man who has no hope, no ambition? *Ibid.*, II

Hope gives an ardor which subsides in certainty.
Richardson, *Sir Charles Grandison*, One, II

Hope is more complete than even possession; because we may hope for twenty times more than we can possibly possess. Ridley, *James Lovegrove*, II

A lover's hope resembles the bean in the nursery tale—let it once take root, and it will grow so rapidly, that in the course of a few hours the giant Imagination builds a castle on the top and by and by comes Disappointment with the "curtal axe," and hews down both the plant and the superstructure. Scott, *The Heart of Midlothian*, XXXIX

Hope will catch at the most feeble twig. Scott, *Redgauntlet*, X

Hope is the fawning traitor of the mind, while under color of friendship it robs it of his chief force of resolution. Sidney, *Arcadia*, III

I felt what kind of sickness of the heart arises from hope deferred.
Sterne, *A Sentimental Journey*, 78

Each bitter cup must be drained in the hope that the next might be sweeter.
Trollope, *The Eustace Diamonds*, LXIX

The great sheet-anchor, Hope! Whitman, *Franklin Evans*, III

HORSEBACK

The great advantage of dialogue on horseback: it can be merged any minute into a trot or a canter, and one might escape from Socrates himself in the saddle.
Eliot, *Adam Bede*, IX

HOSPITALITY

Hospitality is one of the first Christian duties.
Goldsmith, *The Vicar of Wakefield*, 25

HUMANKIND: *see also* HUMAN NATURE; MALE AND FEMALE; etc.

The generality of mankind are too corrupt to be governed by the great universal law of social nature.
Amory, *John Buncle*, I

Out of the innumerable multitude of human creatures which are every day coming into the world, by far the greater part seems born for no other purpose but merely to go out of it again.
Anonymous, *Oxymel Classic*, I

What a wretch is man! What a connection of inconsiderable and ridiculous circumstances generally combine to produce the most important events of his whole life!
Ibid., II

What is a man without information? In form only above a beast. What is a man, negligent of moral duty? Worse than a beast.
Brackenridge, *Modern Chivalry*, Part I, II

The power and the malice of demons have been a thousand times exemplified in human beings.
Brown, C. B., *Wieland*, 151

What an important little thing is man!   Brown, W. H., *The Power of Sympathy*, 158

What so diversified as man? What so little to be judged by his fellow?
Burney, *Camilla*, Five, X

A man's a man, and for one man to worship another is quite out of law.
Burney, *Cecilia*, III

There are two classes of people in this world, those who sin, and those who are sinned against; if a man must belong to either, he had better belong to the first than to the second.
Butler, *The Way of All Flesh*, XXVI

The rough animal, man.   Collins, *The Legacy of Cain*, XLVII

Man is amazing, but he is not a masterpiece.   Conrad, *Lord Jim*, XIX

The normal condition [of man] is animal.
Cooke, *Virginia Comedians*, Volume I, XVIII

Mankind are a species of civilized monsters, without hearts.
Dacre, *The Libertine*, II

The world—a conventional phrase which, being interpreted, often signifieth all the rascals in it.   Dickens, *Nicholas Nickleby*, III

There is disinterestedness in the world, I hope? We are not all arrayed in two opposite ranks: the *of*fensive and the *de*fensive. Some few there are who walk between; who help the needy as they go; and take no part with either side? Umph?
Dickens, *Martin Chuzzlewit*, II

Every human creature is constituted to be [a] profound secret and mystery to every other.   Dickens, *A Tale of Two Cities*, Book I, III

Man comes out of darkness into light. He tarries a while and then passes into darkness again.   Doyle, *Micah Clarke*, XXII

Man in Mars is, it appears, a very different being from what he is here. He is amphibious, and descends from no monkey, but from a small animal that seems to be something between our seal and our sealion.   DuMaurier, *The Martian*, Part Eighth

A human being in this aged nation of ours is a very wonderful whole, the slow creation of long interchanging influences; and charm is a result of two such wholes, the one loving and the one loved.   Eliot, *Middlemarch*, Book IV, XL

All mankind almost are villains in their hearts.   Fielding, *Amelia*, II

No mortal, after a thorough scrutiny, can be a proper object of our adoration.
Fielding, *Jonathan Wild*, 11

Mankind are properly to be considered under two grand divisions, those that use their hands, and those who employ hands.   *Ibid.*, 62

What is a man? He is a feather, but a feather blown by the wind. He is a fire, but a fire born of the fuel. He is a spirit having wings wherewith to sail to either destiny. He may choose the good, and on him doth rest the evil that he does. He is the helm unto the boat of Fate; he is the shadow that goes before the sword; he is the dream that presages the truth. Haggard, *Cleopatra*, I

The gods made men only to laugh at them. Fielding, *Joseph Andrews*, 133

There are two kinds of description of people, the partial and the unfavorable. Gibbes, *Mr. Francis Clive*, II

Self-importance of man, upon how slight a basis do thy gigantic erections repose! Godwin, *St. Leon*, 367

The arising sun the setting sun: There we have the symbol and the type of humanity, and of all things with which humanity has to do. The sun that rises today for us set last night for our fellow-voyagers. Haggard, *She*, IV

It is impossible to hail the slave as a Christian brother, without first acknowledging his rights as a fellow man. Hildreth, *Slave*, Volume I, XIX

If we compare the population of two villages of the same race and region, there is such a regularly graduated distribution and parallelism of character, that it seems as if Nature must turn out human beings in sets like chessmen. Holmes, *Elsie Venner*, XII

Flying is a lost art among men and reptiles. Bats fly, and men ought to. Holmes, *The Guardian Angel*, XXXV

A man with a brain large enough to understand mankind is always wretched, and ashamed of himself. Howe, *The Story of a Country Town*, XXX

I look upon mankind as one great book; and sometimes meet with much instruction in a page which does not happen to be so fair as some others may be. Jenner, *The Placid Man*, II

In every bone, there is a marrow, and beneath every jacket lives a man. Judd, *Margaret*, Volume III

Mankind, in the gross, is a gaping monster that loves to be deceived and has seldom been disappointed. Mackenzie, *The Man of Feeling*, 39

Learn from me that, though the sorrows of the world are great, its wickedness—that is, its ugliness—is small. Melville, *Confidence-Man*, V

Much cause to pity man, little to distrust him. *Ibid.*

Mankind are not reasoning beings, if reason won't do with them. *Ibid.*, VII

To what vicissitudes of light and shade is man subject! *Ibid.*, XXIII

Brick is no bad name for any son of Adam. Eden was but a brickyard. What is a mortal but a few luckless shovelfuls of clay, moulded in a mould, laid out on a sheet to dry, and ere long quickened into his queer caprices by the sun? Are not men built into communities just like bricks into a wall? Melville, *Israel Potter*, XXIII

As a carpenter's nails are divided into wrought nails and cut nails; so mankind may be similarly divided. Melville, *Moby Dick*, XXVII

Consider them both, the sea and the land; and do you not find a strange analogy to something in yourself? For as this appalling ocean surrounds the verdant land, so in the soul of man there lies one insular Tahiti, full of peace and joy, but encompassed by all the horrors of the half-known life. God help thee! Push not off from that isle, thou canst never return! Melville, *Moby Dick*, LVIII

We are all in the hands of the Gods. *Ibid.*, XCIII

Oh God! that man should be a thing for immortal souls to sieve through! *Ibid.*, CXXV

What a vile juggler and cheat is man! Melville, *Pierre*, Book XIX, II

HUMANKIND (*continued*)

Exhibit humanity as it is, wallowing, sensual, wicked, behind the mask.
Meredith, *Diana of the Crossways*, XXIV

It is useless to base any system on a human being.
Meredith, *Ordeal of Richard Feverel*, XXXVII

Man lives between two desires—his desire of spiritual peace and happiness, and his desire of earthly experience.
Moore, *Evelyn Innes*, XXIII

All men are monkeys more or less.
Richardson, *Clarissa Harlowe*, I

Man is a pragmatical, foolish creature; and the more we look into him the more we must despise him. "Lord of creation!" he is not. What has he of his own but a mischievous, monkey-like, bad nature?
Ibid., IV

The whole world is but one great Bedlam!
Ibid.

Man is as frail a piece of machinery as any clockwork whatever; and, by irregularity, is as subject to be disordered.
Richardson, *Pamela*, 390

The universe is so large, and man is so small.
Schreiner, *Story of an African Farm*, Part II, VI

It's no fish ye're buying—it's men's lives.
Scott, *The Antiquary*, XI

This man, this talking beast, this walking tree.
Sidney, *Arcadia*, II

We are creatures of two lives, two principles, neither of which have perfect play at any time in the case of a man not absolutely a fanatic or a brute. The animal restrains the moral man, the moral man checks the animal.
Simms, *Woodcraft*, XIX

The characters of mankind are everywhere the same; common sense and honesty bear an infinitely small proportion to folly and vice; and life is at best a paltry province.
Smollett, *Peregrine Pickle*, 302

There is no best in man.
Stevenson, *Prince Otto*, Book III, II

Till we can become divine, we must be content to be human, lest in our hurry for a change we sink to something lower.
Trollope, *Barchester Towers*, XLIII

The pilgrims were human beings. Otherwise they would have acted differently. There is no accounting for human beings.
Twain, *Connecticut Yankee*, XXII

I believe that some day it will be found out that peasants are people.
Twain, *Joan of Arc*, Book II, XXXVII

I wonder who it was defined man as a rational animal. It was the most premature definition ever given. Man is many things, but he is not rational.
Wilde, *The Picture of Dorian Gray*, II

HUMAN NATURE: *see also* HUMANKIND; MALE AND FEMALE; etc.

What would men do in this melancholy world if they had not inherited gaiety from the monkeys—as well as oratory.
Adams, *Democracy*, V

Men are naturally more watchful in matters dear to them.
Amory, *John Buncle*, I

The good, honest man will pass unnoticed, unrespected; while the insignificant rake is courted and caressed.
Anonymous, *Fatal Friendship*, II

If a man should happen to be successful in the course of his villainy, he will be cherished and esteemed by those who class themselves among the honest and worthy.
Anonymous, *Genuine Memoirs of Maria Brown*, I

We pass one half our lives in doing nothing, and the other half in ruminating upon what we have done.
Ibid., II

It is the still sow that drinks up all the draught.
Anonymous, *The History of Betty Barnes*, I

There is no calamity in life that falls heavier upon human nature than a disappointment in love.　　　　　　　　Anonymous, *The History of Tom Jones in His Married State*, 23

None are more industrious in publishing the blemishes of an extraordinary reputation than such as lie open to the same censures in their own characters.　　　*Ibid.*, 179-180

The world is busy and malicious by nature.

Anonymous, *The Life of Sir Richard Perrott*, 27

She was human first and mental afterward.　　　Atherton, *Senator North*, Book III, XIX

Dark and dreadful things are hid in the human heart.　　　August, *Horrid Mysteries*, I

The nature of man and humanity resemble each other everywhere.　　　　　　*Ibid.*

Weak and inconsequential is the human heart. It always assumes the shape of the present moment, painting futurity either gloomy or smiling, guided merely by external circumstances.　　　　　　　　　　　　　　　　　　　　*Ibid.*, II

Human nature is so well disposed towards those who are in interesting situations, that a young person, who either marries or dies, is sure of being kindly spoken of.

Austen, *Emma*, XXII

Here and there, human nature may be great in times of trial, but generally speaking it is its weakness and not its strength that appears in a sick chamber; it is selfishness and impatience rather than generosity and fortitude that one hears of.

Austen, *Persuasion*, XVII

It is natural for the human mind, when it observes a great security and confidence in another, to imagine there must be some ground for it.

Brackenridge, *Modern Chivalry*, Part I, I

All men, taken singly, are more or less selfish; and taken in bodies they are intensely so.

Bronte, C., *Shirley*, X

Human beings are distinguished by nothing more than by a propensity to imitation.

Brown, C. B., *Alcuin*, III

Human affairs will never be reduced to that state in which the decisions of the wisest man will be immutable.　　　　　　　　　　　　　　　　　　　　　　　*Ibid.*

Some must pipe and some must weep.　　　Bunyan, *Pilgrim's Progress*, 266

The historian of human life finds less of difficulty and of intricacy to develop, in its accidents and adventures, than the investigator of the human heart in its feelings and its changes.　　　　　　　　　　　　　　　　Burney, *Camilla*, One, I

How futile an animal is man, without some decided character and principle! Wise, foolish; virtuous, vicious; active, indolent; prodigal and avaricious—no contrast is too strong for him while guided but by accident or impulse.　　　*Ibid.*, Three, VI

What is so hard to judge as the human heart?　　　　*Ibid.*, Five, IX

There seems in human nature a worthlessness not to be conquered.

Burney, *Cecilia*, III

Man is not a sentimental animal where his material interests are concerned.

Butler, *Erewhon*, XXV

Most men are fond of making a parade of those qualifications with which they are least endowed by nature.　　　Caruthers, *Kentuckian in New-York*, Volume I, XIX

There is not a crime which ever was committed, but what lurks in the breast of every man, as he is formed by nature, and to which he is particularly inclined.

Collyer, *Felicia to Charlotte*, I

It is when we try to grapple with another man's intimate need that we perceive how incomprehensible, wavering, and misty are the beings that share with us the sight of the stars and the warmth of the sun.　　　　　　　Conrad, *Lord Jim*, XVI

And yet is not mankind itself, pushing on its blind way, driven by a dream of its greatness and its power upon the dark paths of excessive cruelty and of excessive devotion.   *Ibid.*, XXXVII

Men have always been radically false and unworthy.
                                        Cooke, *Virginia Comedians*, Volume I, XXIII

Men are not by nature destitute of truth and love, nobility and purity—the annals of the world show how untrue it is.   *Ibid.*

We live in a world of transgressions and selfishness, and no pictures that represent us otherwise can be true; though happily for human nature, gleamings of that pure spirit in whose likeness man has been fashioned, are to be seen, relieving its deformities, and mitigating, if not excusing its crimes.   Cooper, *The Deerslayer*, XXXII

It is not the swiftest leaping deer that gives the longest chase.
                                        Cooper, *The Last of the Mohicans*, XVIII

When food is scarce, and when food is plenty, a wolf grows bold.   *Ibid.*, XIX

The tendency of human nature is not very directly to charity.
                                        Cooper, *Satanstoe*, Volume I, VIII

Mankind is a mass of depravity, cruelty, and illiberality; it does no justice to motives; it decides by effect, and not by cause; it condemns misfortune, as if it were a crime; it worships greatness, as if it were a virtue; it is uninterested in your miseries, and interested in your welfare only, in hopes of pleasure or benefit to self.
                                        Dacre, *The Libertine*, II

Man has it within his power to reflect, to weigh, and to appreciate, before he acts.
                                        Dacre, *Passions*, XLI

The faculties cannot bear to be forever on the stretch.   *Ibid.*, Conclusion

It is but too often an ungenerous principle in human nature, first most ardently to desire the possession of a certain object, and despise it when obtained.
                                        Dacre, *Zofloya*, III

May not all human characters frequently be traced back to impressions made at so early a period, that none but discerning eyes would ever suspect their existence?
                                        Day, *The History of Sandford and Merton*, 248

If you save a thief from the gallows, he shall be the first to cut your throat.
                                        Defoe, *Colonel Jack*, 145

The thoughts of worldly men are forever regulated by a moral law of gravitation, which, like the physical one, holds them down to earth.   Dickens, *Barnaby Rudge*, XXIX

A Bank Director, reputed to be able to buy up anything—human Nature generally, if he should take it in his head to influence the money market in that direction.
                                        Dickens, *Dombey and Son*, XXXVI

Use is second nature.   Dickens, *Martin Chuzzlewit*, XIX

The instability of human nature appears in every second action of a man's life.
                                        Donaldson, *Sir Bartholomew Sapskull*, I

Poor human nature, so richly endowed with nerves of anguish, so splendidly organized for pain and sorrow, is but slenderly equipped for joy.
                                        DuMaurier, *Peter Ibbetson*, Part Second

It is our habit to say that while the lower nature can never understand the higher, the higher nature commands a complete view of the lower. But the higher nature has to learn this comprehension, as we learn the art of vision, by a good deal of hard experience, often with bruises and gashes incurred in taking things up the wrong end, and fancying our space wider than it is.   Eliot, *Adam Bede*, XV

If we're men and have men's feelings, we must have men's troubles.   *Ibid.*, XVI

In so complex a thing as human nature, it is hard to find rules without exceptions.

Ibid., XXXIII

The greatest of painters only once painted a mysteriously divine child; he couldn't have told how he did it, and we can't tell why we feel it to be divine. There are stores laid up in our human nature that our understandings can make no complete inventory of.

Eliot, *Mill on the Floss*, Book V, I

Such is the nature of men, that whoever denies himself to do you a favor is unwilling that it should be done to you by any other.   Fielding, H., *Amelia*, I

As the great man hath his different kinds of salutation, so the porter to some bows with respect, to others with a smile, to some he bows more, to others less low, to others not at all. Some he lets in, and others he shuts out.   *Ibid.*

The nature of man is far from being in itself evil; it abounds with benevolence, charity, and pity, coveting praise and honor, and shunning shame and disgrace. Bad education, bad habits, and bad customs, debauch our nature, and drive it headlong as it were into vice.   *Ibid.*, II

No man is born into the world without his particular allotment.

Fielding, H., *Jonathan Wild*, 118

How apt men are to hate those they injure. How unforgiving they are of the injuries they do themselves.   *Ibid.*, 137

Nature equips all creatures with what is most expedient for them.

Fielding, H., *Joseph Andrews*, 116

A man naturally wants clothes no more than a horse or any other animal.   *Ibid.*, 233

Do some natures delight in evil, as others are thought to delight in virtue? Or is there a pleasure in being accessory to a theft when we cannot commit it ourselves?

Fielding, H., *Tom Jones*, 29

Doth the man who recognizes in his own heart no traces of avarice or ambition, conclude that there are no such passions in human nature?   *Ibid.*, 216

The pleasures, honors, and misfortunes of those who are denominated rational beings are generally imaginary; they frequently rejoice at what is no benefit, and grieve for what is no evil; they eagerly pursue trifles which are not worth a thought, and neglect matters of the highest importance.   Fielding, S., *The History of Ophelia*, II

The nature of human affairs will not suffer us to be often or long together.

Gentleman, *A Trip to the Moon*, II

The human heart is replete with a strong bias and propensity to every vice and folly.

Gibbes, *Mr. Francis Clive*, I

The pride of philosophy has taught us to treat man as an individual. He is no such thing. He holds, necessarily, indispensably, to his species.

Godwin, *Caleb Williams*, III

Human nature is so constituted, that the highest degree of anguish can be felt but for a few instants.   Godwin, *St. Leon*, 91

The human mind is easily induced to forget those benefits with which we are constantly surrounded, and our possession of which we regard as secure.   *Ibid.*, 93

Human nature can't help being itself.   Hardy, *Jude*, Part Six, III

Human nature at bottom is romantic rather than ascetic.

Hardy, *A Laodicean*, Book III, V

Egdon Heath was at present a place perfectly accordant with man's nature—neither ghastly, hateful, nor ugly: neither commonplace, unmeaning, nor tame; but, like man, slighted and enduring; and withal singularly colossal and mysterious in its swarthy monotony.   Hardy, *Return of the Native*, Book I, I

261

Young men and boys play, according to recognized law, old, traditionary games, permitting no caprioles of fancy, but with scope enough for the outbreak of savage instincts. For, young or old, in play or in earnest, man is prone to be a brute.
Hawthorne, *The Blithedale Romance*, IX

The propensity of human nature to tell the very worst of itself.
Hawthorne, *The Scarlet Letter*, XIII

Even provincial human nature sometimes has a touch of sublimity about it.
Holmes, *Elsie Venner*, VIII

There is something in human nature which causes man in his shirt-sleeves to wish all other men to appear in the same dishabille.	Howells, *Silas Lapham*, VI

It isn't well for us to see human nature at white heat habitually. It would make us vain of our species.	*Ibid.*, XIV

It seems to be the rule of this world. Each person has what he doesn't want, and other people have what he does want.	Jerome, *Three Men in a Boat*, VI

That all men are equal in their nature reason will infallibly show; as it will also show that they have an equal right to the same stations if they can arrive at them by just means.	Johnstone, *Arsaces*, I

There are natures, who, instead of rejoicing in the strength of men of greater prowess than themselves, look at such with irritation, dread, at last, spite; expecting, perhaps, that the stronger will do to them what they feel they might have done in his place.
Kingsley, *Westward Ho!*, III

We are none of us better than we should be.	Lawrence, H., *The Contemplative Man*, I

It is a great reproach to human nature that whatever is reported to the disadvantage of an individual shall meet with more credit and be better received than any circumstance advanced in his favor.	*Ibid.*, II

That the infirmities and failings of our fellow creatures should furnish matter of entertainment to mankind is a reflection upon human nature.
Lawrence, H., *Common Sense*, II

Man is an animal equally selfish and vain. Vanity, indeed, is but a modification of selfishness.	Mackenzie, *The Man of Feeling*, 42

He who, in view of its inconsistencies, says of human nature the same that, in view of its contrasts, is said of the divine nature, that it is past finding out, thereby evinces a better appreciation of it than he who, by always representing it in a clear light, leaves it to be inferred that he clearly knows all about it.	Melville, *Confidence-Man*, XIV

The grand points of human nature are the same today as they were a thousand years ago.
Ibid.

The greater idiot ever scolds the lesser.	Melville, *Moby Dick*, CXXV

Unwashed human nature, though it is natural to us to wash, is the most human.
Meredith, *The Amazing Marriage*, XIX

It is English as well as common human nature to feel an interest in the dog that has bitten you.	Meredith, *Diana of the Crossways*, I

Human nature. Strange as it may appear to the unobservant, our hearts warm more readily to those we have benefited than to our benefactors.
Reade, *The Cloister and the Hearth*, XXXIX

Brutes do not deliberately slaughter their species; it remains for man only, man, proud of his prerogative of reason, and boasting of his sense of justice, to unite the most terrible extremes of folly and wickedness.	Radcliffe, *The Italian*, II

One half of mankind tormenting the other, and being tormented themselves in tormenting!
Richardson, *Clarissa Harlowe*, I

It is in nature. I can't help it. Nay, for that matter, I love it, and wish not to help it.   *Ibid.*

You partake of the common weakness of human nature in being apt to slight what is in your own power.   *Ibid.*, II

What a vile corruptible rogue, whether in poor or in rich, is human nature!   *Ibid.*

'Tis human to err, but not to persevere.   *Ibid.*

It is more a satire upon human nature than upon the clergy if we suppose those who have the best opportunities to be good less perfect than other people.   *Ibid.*, III

Power and riches never want tools to promote their vilest ends, and there is nothing so hard to be known as the heart of man.   Richardson, *Pamela*, 122

I have found more fools in the world than I have made.
     Richardson, *Sir Charles Grandison*, One, II

There is hardly a greater difference in intellect between angel and man, than there is between man and man.   *Ibid.*, Two, IV

Human nature, a vile rogue.   *Ibid.*, Two, V

Human nature is rarely uniform.   Scott, *Quentin Durward*, I

The different accidents of life are not so changeable as the feelings of human nature.
     Shelley, M., *Frankenstein*, V

Our nature is never so legitimately employed as when it is inventing, contriving, multiplying images and offices, the purposes and pleasures of which are to keep us from stagnation.   Simms, *The Partisan*, Volume II, X

The desire of life and health is implanted in man's nature; the love of liberty and enlargement is a sister-passion to it.   Sterne, *Tristram Shandy*, II

The world is in conspiracy to drive out what little wit God has given us.   *Ibid.*

Human nature is the same in all professions.   *Ibid.*, III

Inconsistent soul that man is!—languishing under wounds, which he has the power to heal!—his whole life a contradiction to his knowledge!—his reason, that precious gift of God to him, serving but to sharpen his sensibilities—to multiply his pains, and render him more melancholy and uneasy under them!   *Ibid.*

There are in this world two kinds of natures—those that have wings, and those that have feet—the winged and the walking spirits.   Stowe, *The Minister's Wooing*, XVIII

There are two classes of human beings in this world: one class seem made to give love, and the other to take it.   Stowe, *Orr's Island*, XI

Human nature is the same everywhere: it deifies success, it has nothing but scorn for defeat.   Twain, *Joan of Arc*, Book I, VIII

A life of retirement and innocence is as consistent with human nature as one of dissipation and luxury.   Young, *The Adventures of Emmera*, II

HUMBLENESS; HUMILIATION; HUMILITY: *see also* PRIDE

Nothing is more deceitful than the appearance of humility. It is often only carelessness of opinion, and sometimes an indirect boast.
     Austen, *Pride and Prejudice*, Volume I, X

Humility is the groundwork of Christian virtues.   Bronte, C., *Jane Eyre*, XXXIV

Humility in a man of the world is worse than the hypocrisy of the saints.
     Brooke, *Emily Montague*, I

Men are all spoilt by humility, and all conquered by gaiety.
     Burney, *Camilla*, Three, VI

Men are not very scrupulous touching the humility due to God, but are so tenacious of their own privileges in this particular, they will confide in plausible rogues rather than in plain-dealing honesty.　　　　　　　　　　　　　　Cooper, *The Monikins*, Conclusion

"I am well aware that I am the umblest person going," said Uriah Heep, modestly; "let the other be where he may. My mother is likewise a very umble person. We live in a numble abode."　　　　　　　　　　　　　　　　Dickens, *David Copperfield*, XVI

The umblest persons may be the instruments of good.　　　　　　　　　　　*Ibid.*, XXV

That noble bearing which comes from humility itself when it has fairly triumphed.
　　　　　　　　　　　　　　　　　　　　　　　　Freeman, *Pembroke*, XIV

Of all the garbs I ever saw pride put on, that of her humility is to me the most disgusting.　　　　　　　　　　　　　　　Mackenzie, *The Man of Feeling*, 80

Humbleness does not win multitudes or women.　　　　　　Meredith, *The Egoist*, II

The parson's horse was as lean, and as lank, and as sorry a jade as Humility herself could have bestrided.　　　　　　　　　　　　Sterne, *Tristram Shandy*, I

No one is the better for a humiliation.　　　　　Stevenson, *Prince Otto*, Book III, IV

The magnificence of men has become so intolerable now that one is driven to be humble in one's self-defense.　　　　　　　Trollope, *He Knew He Was Right*, XLIX

HUMOR: *see also* LAUGHTER

A good funeral needs a joke. If mine is not more amusing than my friends', I would rather not go to it.　　　　　　　　　　　　　　Adams, H., *Esther*, II

Even professional humorists seldom enjoy jokes at their own expense.　　　*Ibid.*

Every man, even the wisest, is to be managed by consulting his humor, and the foolishest husband upon earth grows stubborn by crossing it.
　　　　　　　　　　　　　　　　　　　　　　　Anonymous, *Sophronia*, 6

An agony of ill humor.　　　　　Austen, *Pride and Prejudice*, Volume I, XXIII

It was necessary to laugh, when she would rather have cried.　　*Ibid.*, Volume III, XV

In all true humor lies its germ, pathos.　　　Bulwer, *The Caxtons*, Book IV, II

There are many varieties of sharp practitioners in this world, but the hardest of all to deal with are the men who overreach you under the disguise of inveterate good-humor.
　　　　　　　　　　　　　　Collins, *Woman in White*, Part I, First Epoch

Religious dread of a disastrous infection of good humor.
　　　　　　　　　　　　　　　　　Dickens, *David Copperfield*, XLIII

He achieved that performance which is designated in melodramas "laughing like a fiend,"—it seems that fiends always laugh in syllables, and always in three syllables, never more nor less.　　　　　　　　　　Dickens, *Old Curiosity Shop*, LVI

As some things are too sad and too deep for tears, so some things are too grotesque and too funny for laughter.　　　　　　　　　　　　DuMaurier, *Trilby*, I

A difference of taste in jokes is a great strain on the affections.
　　　　　　　　　　　　　　　　Eliot, *Daniel Deronda*, Book II, XV

Men overrate the necessity for humoring everybody's nonsense, till they get despised by the very fools they humor.　　　　　　Eliot, *Middlemarch*, Book II, XVII

Humor everybody's weak place.　　　　　　　　*Ibid.*, Book V, XLV

The advantage of seldom joking is that people remember the joke, and it gets repeated.
　　　　　　　　　　　　Ford, *The Honorable Peter Stirling*, XXIX

Life is a huge farce, and the advantage of possessing a sense of humor is that it enables one to defy fate with mocking laughter. Gissing, *New Grub Street*, X

The jests of the rich are ever successful. Goldsmith, *The Vicar of Wakefield*, 28

All laughing comes from misapprehension. Rightly looked at, there is no laughable thing under the sun. Hardy, *Jude the Obscure*, Part Five, III

Humor is a thing of so delicate a nature that, if it is not felt, it is impossible to point it out. Jenner, *The Placid Man*, II

A poignant jest often shames a man out of an opinion which no argument could make him give up. Johnstone, *The Reverie*, II

There is no resource for one who cannot laugh at a jest. Mackenzie, *Julia De Roubigné*, 164

Humor is so blessed a thing, that even in the least virtuous product of the human mind, if there can be found but nine good jokes, some philosophers are clement enough to affirm that those should redeem all the wicked thoughts, though plenty as the populace of Sodom. Melville, *Confidence-Man*, XXIX

It is said that a man may smile and be a villain; but it is not said that a man may laugh and be one. *Ibid.*

Never joke at funerals, or during business transactions. Melville, *Israel Potter*, VII

Humor, thy laugh is divine. Melville, *Mardi*, CLXXXIII

A laugh's the wisest, easiest answer to all that's queer. Melville, *Moby Dick*, XXXIX

One definition of the arts is, humor made easy. Meredith, *Beauchamp's Career*, XI

A sense of humor solves nothing. Moore, *Evelyn Innes*, XXVI

Reason is in no way essential to mirth. No man should ask another why he laughs, or at what, seeing that he does not always know, and that, if he does, he is not a responsible agent. Laughter is an involuntary action of certain muscles, developed in the human species by the progress of civilization. The savage never laughs. Peacock, *Crotchet Castle*, II

His first three years must have been one continual fit of crying; and his muscles have never yet been able to recover a risible tone. Richardson, *Clarissa Harlowe*, I

All we say, all we do, all we wish for, is a jest. *Ibid.*, II

He that makes life not a jest is a sad fellow. *Ibid.*

I cannot let sorrow touch my heart. I cannot be grave six minutes together. I should not forbear to cut a joke, were I upon the scaffold. *Ibid.*, III

Who can laugh, and be angry, in the same moment? Richardson, *Sir Charles Grandison*, Two, IV

Humor is a gentle, a decent, a lively thing. *Ibid.*, Three, VII

There is no humor to which impudent poverty can not make itself serviceable. Sidney, *Arcadia*, II

The humor in the farce of life. Smollett, *Humphry Clinker*, 58

There is no regular reasoning upon the ebbs and flows of our humors; they may depend upon the same causes which influence the tides themselves. Sterne, *A Sentimental Journey*, 5

A man who laughs will never be dangerous. *Ibid.*, 93

Too oft a person laughed at considers himself in the light of a person injured, with all the rights of such a situation belonging to him. Sterne, *Tristram Shandy*, I

Humor lies in contrast, and a wag will find more subject in a synod of grave sages than a crew of laughing wits. Wright, *A Few Days in Athens*, XII

HUNGER

Hunger is as leisurely a death as breaking upon the wheel.

Defoe, *Colonel Jack*, 194

Empty platters make greedy stomachs, and where scarcity is kept, hunger is nourished.

Deloney, *Jack of Newbury*, 386

Hanging is an easier death than starving.   Donaldson, *Sir Bartholomew Sapskull*, II

It is a wonderful subduer, this need of love,—this hunger of the heart,—as peremptory as that other hunger by which Nature forces us to submit to the yoke, and change the face of the world.   Eliot, *Mill on the Floss*, Book I, V

A man may be as easily starved in Leadenhall Market as in the deserts of Arabia.

Fielding, H., *Tom Jones*, 389

Very often there is an insatiable instinct that demands friendship, love, and intimate communion, but is forced to pine in empty forms; a hunger of the heart, which finds only shadows to feed upon.   Hawthorne, *The Marble Faun*, XIII

It takes much more than you think to starve a man. Starvation is very little when you are used to it. Some people even live on it quite comfortably, and make their daily bread by it.   Thackeray, *Catherine*, VI

HUNTING: *see also* all the novels of Robert Smith Surtees.

There is a passion *for hunting something* deeply implanted in the human breast.

Dickens, *Oliver Twist*, X

In the warmth of a chase, sportsmen are too much engaged to attend to any manner of ceremony, nay, even to the offices of humanity.   Fielding, H., *Tom Jones*, 542

To ride to hounds is very glorious; but to have ridden to hounds is more glorious still.

Trollope, *Phineas Finn*, XXIV

HYPOCRISY

Without the vice of hypocrisy, all the other vices are of no use.

Anonymous, *Jeremiah Grant*, 66

A saint abroad and a devil at home.   Bunyan, *Pilgrim's Progress*, 81

I have heard many cry out against sin in the pulpit who yet can abide it well enough in the heart, house, and conversation.   *Ibid.*, 84

That vice pays homage to virtue is notorious; we call this hypocrisy; there should be a word found for the homage which virtue not unfrequently pays, or at any rate would be wise in paying, to vice.   Butler, *The Way of All Flesh*, XIX

Of all the 'ocracies (aristocracy and democracy included) hypocrisy is the most flourishing.   Cooper, *The Monikins*, Conclusion

Is a Paleface always made with two tongues?   Cooper, *The Prairie*, XXVI

His cloak of religion was always ready to cover the dirty stable.   Davis, *Verdict*, XVI

Men who are thoroughly false and hollow seldom try to hide those vices from themselves; and yet in the very act of avowing them, they lay claim to the virtues they feign most to despise.   Dickens, *Barnaby Rudge*, XXIII

I found that the most professing men were the greatest objects of interest: and that their conceit, their vanity, their want of excitement, and their love of deception all prompted to these professions, and were all gratified by them.

Dickens, *David Copperfield*, LXI

We must have humbug, we all like humbug, we couldn't get along without humbug. A little humbug, and a groove, and everything goes on admirably, if you leave it alone.

Dickens, *Little Dorrit*, Book II, XXVIII

There are some men who, living with the one object of enriching themselves, no matter by what means, and being perfectly conscious of the baseness and rascality of the means which they will use every day towards this end, affect nevertheless—even to themselves —a high tone of moral rectitude, and shake their heads and sigh over the depravity of the world.   Dickens, *Nicholas Nickleby*, XLIV

Both religion and virtue have received more real discredit from hypocrites than the wittiest profligates or infidels could ever cast upon them.
                                                   Fielding, H., *Tom Jones*, 85

Ah! child, you should read books which would teach you a little hypocrisy, which would instruct you how to hide your thoughts a little better.   *Ibid.*, 229–230

Some have considered the larger part of mankind in the light of actors, as personating characters no more their own, and to which they have no better title than the player hath to be in earnest thought the king or emperor whom he represents. Thus the hypocrite may be said to be a player; and indeed the Greeks called them both by one and the same name.   *Ibid.*, 266

He was not of the opinion that the more ignorant a man is of any subject, the more necessary it is to talk of it.   Fielding, S., *David Simple*, I

A man of forms and phrases and postures.   James, H., *The American*, XII

There is no crime so dangerous, so detestable, as hypocrisy; it has the complicated guilt of every crime that it conceals.   Jenner, *The Placid Man*, I

Everything may be dreaded from a hypocrite.   Lennox, *Henrietta*, I

What he wanted in purity of heart, he supplied by exterior sanctity.
                                                          Lewis, *The Monk*, 180

There he sat, his very indifference speaking a nature in which there lurked no civilized hypocrisies and bland deceits.   Melville, *Moby Dick*, X

The French make no pretenses, and thereby escape one of the main penalties of hypocrisy.
                                        Meredith, *Ordeal of Richard Feverel*, XXI

It is generally the conscious over-fulness of conceit that makes the hypocrite most upon his guard to conceal it.   Richardson, *Clarissa Harlowe*, III

With hypocrites, proudly humble as they are, vanity will break out sometimes in spite of their cloaks, though but in self-denying, compliment-begging self-degradation.   *Ibid.*

A little pretense served the wolf when he had a mind to quarrel with the lamb.
                                            Richardson, *Clarissa Harlowe*, III

Hypocrisy is capable of firmness to promote her ends.
                                                   Shebbeare, *The Sumatrans*, II

The falsest men will yet bear outward shows of a pure mind.   Sidney, *Arcadia*, III

Of all the cants which are canted in this canting world—though the cant of hypocrites may be the worst—the cant of criticism is the most tormenting!
                                                   Sterne, *Tristram Shandy*, III

The best of women are hypocrites.   Thackeray, *Vanity Fair*, XVII

She was not willfully a hypocrite.   Trollope, *He Knew He Was Right*, LVI

We are in the native land [England] of the hypocrite.
                                          Wilde, *The Picture of Dorian Gray*, XII

Nothing is so provoking as that a man should preach viciously and act virtuously.
                                          Wright, *A Few Days in Athens*, II

ICONOCLASM

A sensible man doesn't tear down idols. Let the world alone and it'll let you alone.
                                          Glasgow, *The Descendant*, Book II, II

IDEA; THEME: *see also* IMAGINATION; KNOWLEDGE AND LEARNING; THOUGHT; etc.

An exciting idea is like a venomous microbe; it bites into the brain, and if circumstances do not occur to expel it, it produces a form of mania.

Atherton, *Senator North*, Book III, IX

She was not a woman of many words; for, unlike people in general, she proportioned them to the number of her ideas.   Austen, *Sense and Sensibility*, Volume II, XII

The ruling idea of any mind assumes the foreground of thought.

Barr, *The Maid*, VIII

The mind loves ease, and does not wish to be at the trouble of thinking. It is hard to collect ideas, and still harder to compose them; it is like rowing a boat: whereas, acting without thought, it is like sailing before the wind, and the tide in our favor.

Brackenridge, *Modern Chivalry*, Part I, II

The minutest animalcule on earth is a large subject to expatiate upon.

Bridges, *The Adventures of a Bank-Note*, IV

Ideas, no less than the living beings in whose minds they arise, must be begotten by parents not very unlike themselves, the most original still differing but slightly from the parents that have given rise to them. Life is like a fugue, everything must grow out of the subject and there must be nothing new.   Butler, *The Way of All Flesh*, XLVI

One of the rarest of all the intellectual accomplishments that a man can possess is the grand faculty of arranging his ideas.

Collins, *Woman in White*, Part II, Third Epoch

Hang ideas! They are tramps, vagabonds, knocking at the back-door of your mind, each taking a little of your substance, each carrying away some crumb of that belief in a few simple notions you must cling to if you want to live decently and would like to die easy!

Conrad, *Lord Jim*, V

Ideas, like ghosts, must be spoken to a little before they will explain themselves.

Dickens, *Dombey and Son*, XII

The more the mind takes in, the more it has space for, and all one's ideas are like the Irish people who live in the different corners of a room and take boarders.

James, H., *Roderick Hudson*, V

Every idea is useful for the enforcement or decoration of moral or religious truth.

Johnson, *Rasselas*, 49

One idea is a bullet, good for the day of battle to beat the foe.

Meredith, *The Amazing Marriage*, XXX

There was a half sigh floating through his pages for those days of intellectual coxcombry, when Ideas come to us affecting the embraces of Virgins, and swear to us, they are ours alone, and no one else have they ever visited: and we believe them.

Meredith, *Ordeal of Richard Feverel*, I

There are ideas language is too gross for, and shape too arbitrary, which come to us and have a definite influence upon us, and yet we cannot fasten on the filmy things and make them visible and distinct to ourselves, much more to others.   *Ibid.*, XXVI

The narrow, barren soul is narrow and barren because it cannot acquire.

Moore, *Evelyn Innes*, XIII

We come into the world with nothing in our own right except the capacity for the acquisition of ideas.   *Ibid.*

IDEAL: *see also* DREAM; PERFECTION; etc.

If we did but recognize them aright, these ideals at the close of life would become one with the ideals of our youth. We lose them as we left mortal youth behind; we regain them as we enter upon youth immortal.   Allen, J. L., *The Choir Invisible*, XXIII

All earthly forms are but the clothing of some divine ideal; and this truth we *feel*, though we *know* it not. Child, *Philothea*, XVII

One thing alone can cure us from being ourselves. Submit yourself to the destructive element, and follow the dream, and again follow the dream. Conrad, *Lord Jim*, XX

To do nothing and get something formed a boy's ideal of a manly career.
Disraeli, *Sybil*, Book I, V

As harps in the wind, dreamers respond to every breath of fancy, voicing in their moods all the ebb and flow of the ideal. Dreiser, *Sister Carrie*, XLVII

Idealism, that gaudy coloring matter of passion, fades when it is brought beneath the trenchant white light of knowledge. Ideals, like mountains, are best at a distance.
Glasgow, *The Descendant*, Book III, II

To be sure, she was almost an ideality to him still. Perhaps to know her would be to cure himself of this unexpected and unauthorized passion. A voice whispered that, though he desired to know her, he did not desire to be cured.
Hardy, *Jude the Obscure*, Part Two, IV

Let us reflect, that the highest path is pointed out by the pure Ideal of those who look up to us, and who, if we tread less loftily, may never look so high again.
Hawthorne, *The Marble Faun*, XXXVI

The best righteousness of our world seems but an unrealized ideal; and those maxims which, in the hope of bringing about a millennium, we busily teach to the heathen, we Christians ourselves disregard. Melville, *White Jacket*, LXXVI

Only in dreams do men set forth in quest of the ideal. Moore, *Evelyn Innes*, XIX

The roughest and most matter-of-fact minds have a craving for the ideal somewhere.
Stowe, *Orr's Island*, XXXVII

No man comes across two ideal things. Few come across one.
Wilde, *The Picture of Dorian Gray*, IX

IDENTITY: *see also* NAME

Heathcliff's more myself than I am. Whatever our souls are made of, his and mine are the same; and Linton's is as different as a moonbeam from lightning, or frost from fire.
Bronte, E., *Wuthering Heights*, IX

If the lion ever wear the fox's hide, still he wears it on the lion.
Bulwer, *What Will He Do With It?*, X, II

A good archer is not known by his arrows, but by his aim. *Ibid.*, XII, II

Why should I complain of being among the mediocrities? If a man is not absolutely below mediocrity let him be thankful. Butler, *The Way of All Flesh*, LXXXVI

It's no use to pretend to be two people. Why, there's hardly enough of me left to make *one* respectable person! Carroll, *Alice in Wonderland*, I

I've often seen a cat without a grin; but a grin without a cat! *Ibid.*, VI

Be what you would seem to be—or, if you'd like it put more simply—Never imagine yourself not to be otherwise than what it might appear to others that what you were or might have been was not otherwise than what you had been would have appeared to them to be otherwise. *Ibid.*, IX

The [fox] chase, like misfortune, is a wonderful leveller of distinctions.
Caruthers, *Cavaliers*, Volume I, XI

Breeding shines through sackcloth. Churchill, *Richard Carvel*, XIX

He was one of us. Conrad, *Lord Jim*, V

It was solemn, and a little ridiculous, too, as they always are, those struggles of an individual trying to save from the fire his idea of what his moral identity should be.
Ibid., VII

Every Irishman is a boy until he has grandchildren. Crane, *The O'Ruddy*, XXI

What he whispers sounds like what it is—mere jumble and jargon.

Dickens, *Bleak House*, LVI

Whenever a person says to you that they are as innocent as lambs in all concerning money, look well after your own money, for they are dead certain to collar it, if they can. Whenever a person proclaims to you "In worldly matters I'm a child," you consider that that person is only a crying off from being held accountable, and that you have got that person's number, and it's Number One. Dickens, *Bleak House*, LVII

"The name of those fabulous animals (pagan, I regret to say) who used to sing in the water, has quite escaped me." "Swans." "Not swans. Very like swans, too." "Oysters." "No, nor oysters. But by no means unlike oysters. A very excellent idea. Wait! Sirens. Dear me! sirens, of course." Dickens, *Martin Chuzzlewit*, IV

Some people may be Rooshans, and others may be Prooshans; they are born so, and will please themselves. Them which is of other naturs thinks different. *Ibid.*, XIX

Our fellow-countryman is a model of a man, quite fresh from Natur's mould! He is a true-born child of this free hemisphere! Verdant as the mountains of our country; bright and flowing as our mineral Licks; unspiled by withering conventionalities as air our broad and boundless Perearers! Rough he may be. So air our Barrs. Wild he may be. So air our Buffalers. But he is a child of Natur', and a child of Freedom; and his boastful answer to the Despot and the Tyrant is, that his bright home is in the Settin' Sun.

Ibid., XXXIV

I don't believe there's no sich a person! *Ibid.*, XLIX

Every bullet has its billet. Dickens, *Pickwick Papers*, XIX

I perceive your tongue is English. And what the tongue is, I suppose the man is.

Dickens, *A Tale of Two Cities*, XVI

Some gentlemen have made an amazing figure in literature by general discontent with the universe as a trap of dullness into which their great souls have fallen by mistake; but the sense of a stupendous self and an insignificant world may have its consolations.

Eliot, *Middlemarch*, Book VII, LXIV

A fly's a fly, though it may be a hoss fly. Eliot, *Silas Marner*, VII

Every village has its idiosyncrasy, its constitution, often its own code of morality.

Hardy, *Tess*, X

I am only a peasant by position, not by nature. *Ibid.*, XXXV

How easy it is to be unknown! Lee, *The Recess*, III

A cunning archer is not known by his arrow but by his aim; neither a friendly affection by the tongue, but by the faith. Lyly, *Euphues and His England*, 333

A person may be known in many ways, though never seen. Macnie, *The Diothas*, VI

America is, or may yet be, the John Paul Jones of nations.

Melville, *Israel Potter*, XIX

This gaining a name is but the individualizing of a man; as well achieved by an extraordinary nose, as by an extraordinary epic. Far better, indeed; for you may pass poets without knowing them. Melville, *Mardi*, CXXII

Loud lungs are a blessing; a lion is no lion that cannot roar. *Ibid.*, CXXXVI

There are birds of divinest plumage, and most glorious song, yet singing their lyrics to themselves. *Ibid.*

There are men eloquent who never babble in the market-place. *Ibid.*

Call me Ishmael.	Melville, *Moby Dick*, I

A purse is but a rag unless you have something in it. *Ibid.*

The man that has anything bountifully laughable about him, be sure there is more in that man than you perhaps think for. *Ibid.*, V

Queequeg was George Washington cannibalistically developed. *Ibid.*, X

Captain Ahab's a grand, ungodly, god-like man. *Ibid.*, XVI

Dark Ahab. *Ibid.*

That great America on the other side of the sphere, Australia. *Ibid.*, XXIV

Reality outran apprehensions; Captain Ahab stood upon his quarterdeck. There seemed no sign of common bodily illness about him, nor of the recovery from any. He looked like a man cut away from the stake, when the fire has overrunningly wasted all the limbs without consuming them, or taking away one particle from their compacted aged robustness. *Ibid.*, XXVIII

In essence whiteness is not so much a color as the visible absence of color, and at the same time the concrete of all colors. *Ibid.*, XLII

In the midst of the personified impersonal, a personality stands here. *Ibid.*, CXIX

Ahab, lord of the level loadstone. *Ibid.*, CXXIV

Is Ahab, Ahab? Is it I, God, or who, that lifts this arm? *Ibid.*, CXXXII

England is a cushion on springs. Meredith, *Beauchamp's Career*, LV

A woman who is not quite a fool will forgive your being but a man, if you are surely that. Meredith, *Ordeal of Richard Feverel*, XXXVII

If we pretend to be what we are not, women, for whose amusement the farce is performed, will find us out and punish us for it. *Ibid.*

If a flower grows on a dunghill, 'tis still a flower, and not a part of the dunghill. Reade, *Griffith Gaunt*, XLVI

There is nothing diviner about a king than there is about a tramp. He is just a cheap and hollow artificiality when you don't know he is a king. But reveal his quality, and dear me it takes your very breath away to look at him. I reckon we are all fools. Born so, no doubt. Twain, *Connecticut Yankee*, XXXIV

A king is a mere artificiality, and so a king's feelings, like the impulses of an automatic doll, are mere artificialities; but as a man, he is a reality, and his feelings, as a man, are real, not phantoms. *Ibid.*, XXXV

The king was a good deal more than a king, he was a man; and when a man is a man, you can't knock it out of him. *Ibid.*

"Is a Frenchman a man?" "Yes." "*Well*, den! Dad blame it, why doan' he *talk* like a man?" Twain, *Huckleberry Finn*, XIV

It took six thousand years to produce her; her like will not be seen in the earth again in fifty thousand. Twain, *Joan of Arc*, Book III, VI

To all intents and purposes Roxy was as white as anybody, but the one-sixteenth of her which was black out-voted the other fifteen parts and made her a Negro. Twain, *Pudd'nhead Wilson*, II

[Remark concerning upstarts:] We don't care to eat toadstools that think they are truffles. *Ibid.*, V

They think the Koran is a Bible, and people that knows better knows enough to not let on. Twain, *Tom Sawyer Abroad*, XIII

When I asked him what a Moslem was, he said it was a person that wasn't a Presbyterian. *Ibid.*

IDLENESS; LAZINESS

Laziness is the mother of all vice.   Anonymous, *Maria Brown*, II

Idleness is the root of all evil, and the nurse of love.   Brooke, *Emily Montague*, I

The world is so lazy that the person most easy of access, however valueless, is preferred to the most perfect, who must be pursued with any trouble.
                                              Burney, *Camilla*, Three, VI

The vacant mind is ever on the watch for relief and ready to plunge into error to escape from the languor of idleness.   Radcliffe, *The Mysteries of Udolpho*, I

Never think. It does no good. It simply means doubting, and doubt always leads to error. The safest way in the world is to do nothing.   Trollope, *Phineas Finn*, LX

IGNORANCE; STUPIDITY: *see also* KNOWLEDGE AND LEARNING; etc.

Ignorance is the mother of devotion.   Anonymous, *The Modern Fine Gentleman*, I

She was heartily ashamed of her ignorance—a misplaced shame. Where people wish to attach, they should always be ignorant. To come with a well-informed mind is to come with an inability of administering to the vanity of others, which a sensible person would always wish to avoid. A woman, especially, if she have the misfortune of knowing anything, should conceal it as well as she can.   Austen, *Northanger Abbey*, XIV

Stupid men are the only ones worth knowing.
                                    Austen, *Pride and Prejudice*, Volume II, IV

Ignorance and folly breed the phantoms by which ignorance and folly are perplexed and terrified.   Brown, C. B., *Ormond*, 30

What are the bounds of human imbecility!   Brown, C. B., *Wieland*, 121

Man is arrogant in proportion to his ignorance.   Bulwer, *Zanoni*, Book IV, IV

Some boys are born stupid; some achieve stupidity; and some have stupidity thrust upon them.   Butler, *The Way of All Flesh*, I

Her ignorance made the unknown infinitely vast.   Conrad, *Lord Jim*, XXXIII

The statesman who cannot look beyond the petty hatreds and rivalries of the present is a ninny.   Cooke, *Surry of Eagle's-Nest*, XCI

The ignorant soul is the prey of demagogues and false leaders—it is a sea which any wind will lash into foam.   Cooke, *Virginia Comedians*, Volume I, XVIII

If men will not allow us the use of reason, and reduce us to mere animals, of no discrimination, they must take the consequences of our ignorance; and if occasionally we commit slight errors, they have no right to arraign us—for we are fools, and incapable of distinguishing good from evil.   Dacre, *Passions*, Letter XXXI

He was exceedingly distrustful, as ignorance usually was.
                                              Dickens, *Bleak House*, XIV

Ignorance is relative.   Disraeli, *Sybil*, Book III, IV

Mr. Kremlin was distinguished for ignorance, for he had only one idea,—and that was wrong.   *Ibid.*, Book IV, V

No political institution will alter the nature of Ignorance, or hinder it from producing vice and misery. Let Ignorance start how it will, it must run the same round of low appetites, poverty, slavery, and superstition.
                                    Eliot, *Felix Holt*, Address to Working Men

Where mere ignorance is to decide a point between two litigants, it will always be an even chance whether it decides right or wrong.   Fielding, H., *Amelia*, I

Where men are ignorant, every man thinks himself at liberty to report what he pleases.
                                              Ibid., I

The ignorant peasant without fault is greater than the philosopher with many; for what is genius or courage without an heart?   Goldsmith, *The Vicar of Wakefield*, 74

Ignorance is mere privation, by which nothing can be produced; it is a vacuity in which the soul sits motionless and torpid for want of attraction.   Johnson, *Rasselas*, 54

Ignorance, when it is voluntary, is criminal; and he may properly be charged with evil who refused to learn how he might prevent it.   *Ibid.*, 118

The ignorance of mankind hath been brought to believe the pleasures of nature to be crimes against its author.   Johnstone, *Arsaces*, II

It is dangerous to arm the enraged and the ignorant.   Lee, *The Recess*, II

Ignorance is the parent of fear.   Melville, *Moby Dick*, III

That empire some think the safest which is founded in ignorance.
Richardson, *Sir Charles Grandison*, One, I

Even ignorance is pretty in a woman.   *Ibid.*

Ignorance is of all things the most apprehensive in nature.
Simms, *The Partisan*, Volume I, XVIII

The darker the ignorance, the more praise to the sage who dispels it; the deeper the prejudice, more fame to the courage which braves it.
Wright, *A Few Days in Athens*, XI

ILLEGITIMACY

You have not the worse opinion of a young fellow for getting a bastard, have you, girl? No, no, the women will like un the better for't.   Fielding, H., *Tom Jones*, 140

ILLUSION: *see also* APPEARANCE; TRUTH; etc.

Perhaps it is better to wake up, even to suffer, rather than to remain a dupe to illusions all one's life.   Chopin, *The Awakening*, XXXVIII

All our illusions: visions of remote unattainable truth, seen dimly.
Conrad, *Lord Jim*, XXXIV

What we call illusions are often a wider vision of past and present realities—a willing movement of a man's soul with the larger sweep of the world's forces.
Eliot, *Felix Holt*, XVI

Confirmed dyspepsia is the apparatus of illusions.
Meredith, *Ordeal of Richard Feverel*, XXXVIII

All ways end at the same point, disillusion.
Wilde, *The Picture of Dorian Gray*, XVIII

ILLUSTRATION: *see also* EXAMPLE; STANDARD; etc.

Words are gas till you condense them into pictures.
Schreiner, *Story of an African Farm*, Part II, VI

It is a dangerous thing to trust to an illustration.   Scott, *The Heart of Midlothian*, XII

ILLUSTRIOUSNESS: *see also* GRANDNESS; GREATNESS; etc.

Of all the illustrious mortals, there are but very few who would not gladly have exchanged their immortality for the comforts and conveniences which are bestowed on the meanest of mankind.   Anonymous, *Oxymel Classic*, I

IMAGINATION: *see also* ART; IDEA; THOUGHT; etc.

Imagination is the child of inherited and living impressions.
Atherton, *Doomswoman*, XXXI

The curse of human nature is imagination. When a long anticipated moment comes, we always find it pitched a note too low, for the wings of imagination are crushed into its withering sides under the crowding hordes of petty realities.
Atherton, *Los Cerritos*, Part I, IV

Imagination has the instinct of a nun in its depths and loves the cloister of a picturesque solitude. It is a Fool's Paradise, but not inferior to the one which mortals are at liberty to enter and ruin.
Atherton, *Senator North*, Book III, XIX

One cannot fix one's eyes on the commonest natural production without finding food for a rambling fancy.
Austen, *Mansfield Park*, Volume Two, IV

Imagination governs the world.
Brackenridge, *Modern Chivalry*, Part I, I

Our imagination dresses up a phantom to impose on our reason. We fall in love with the offspring of our brain.
Brown, W. H., *The Power of Sympathy*, 167

The play of imagination, in the romance of early youth, is rarely interrupted with scruples of probability.
Burney, *Camilla*, One, II

Three hundred miles beyond the end of telegraph cables and mail-boat lines, the haggard utilitarian lies of our civilization wither and die, to be replaced by pure exercises of imagination, that have the futility, often the charm, and sometimes the deep hidden truthfulness, of works of art.
Conrad, *Lord Jim*, XXIX

On the human imagination events produce the effects of time.
Cooper, *The Deerslayer*, I

Of all delusions, beware those of the imagination, the heart is readily seduced by them.
Dacre, *Passions*, Letter XIII

Mind and matter glide swift into the vortex of immensity.
Dickens, *Martin Chuzzlewit*, XXXIV

Perhaps the biggest and most benighted fools have been the best hell-makers. Whereas the best of our heavens is but a poor perfunctory conception, for all that the highest and cleverest amongst us have done their very utmost to decorate and embellish it, and make life there seem worth living. So impossible it is to imagine or invent beyond the sphere of our experience.
DuMaurier, *Peter Ibbetson*, Part Second

Imagination is a licensed trespasser: it has no fear of dogs, but may climb over walls and peep in at windows with impunity.
Eliot, *Adam Bede*, VI

To glory in a prophetic vision of knowledge covering the earth is an easier exercise of believing imagination than to see its beginning in newspaper placards, staring at you from a bridge beyond the cornfields; and it might well happen to most of us dainty people that we were in the thick of the battle of Armageddon without being aware of anything more than the annoyance of a little explosive smoke and struggling on the ground immediately about us.
Eliot, *Daniel Deronda*, Book IV, XXX

Many men have been praised as vividly imaginative on the strength of their profuseness in indifferent drawing or cheap narration:—reports of very poor talk going on in distant orbs; or portraits of Lucifer coming down on his bad errands as a large ugly man with bat's wings and spurts of phosphorescence; or exaggerations of wantonness that seem to reflect life in a diseased dream.
Eliot, *Middlemarch*, Book II, XVI

We are all of us imaginative in some form or other, for images are the brood of desire.
Ibid., Book IV, XXXIV

Those slight indirect suggestions which are dependent on apparently trivial coincidences and incalculable states of mind, are the favorite machinery of Fact, but are not the stuff in which Imagination is apt to work.
Eliot, *Mill on the Floss*, Book V, V

The nets woven by the human imagination, although they are composed of the smallest materials, are perhaps full as difficult to be broken as the strongest real bonds.
Fielding, S., *The Countess of Dellwyn*, II

Masquerades are the produce of a strange excess of fancy, an overheated imagination, set to work by a wild desire of amusement.   Fielding, S., *The History of Ophelia*, I

So long as we have faith in our fairy tales we are none the worse.
Glasgow, *The Descendant*, Book III, II

Life itself would be insipid; nor could human nature support itself upon merely rational pleasures, did not fancy enlarge our sphere of enjoyment, not only by giving an additional gloss to the most substantial objects but also by stamping an imaginary value upon the most trifling.   Graves, *The Spiritual Quixote*, I

My empire is of the imagination.   Haggard, *She*, XV

It is too often assumed that a person's fancy is a person's real mind.
Hardy, *The Hand of Ethelberta*, X

By long brooding over our recollections, we subtilize them into something akin to imaginary stuff, and hardly capable of being distinguished from it.
Hawthorne, *The Blithedale Romance*, XII

My imagination was a tarnished mirror. It would not reflect, or only with miserable dimness, the figures with which I did my best to people it.
Hawthorne, *The Scarlet Letter*, The Custom House Introductory

Your imagination prevails over your skill, and you tell rather what you wish than what you know.   Johnson, *Rasselas*, 32

Let us not imagine evils which we do not feel, nor injure life by misrepresentations.
Ibid., 107

There is no man whose imagination does not sometimes predominate over his reason, who can regulate his attention wholly by his will and whose ideas will come and go at his command.   *Ibid.*, 163

He who has nothing external that can divert him must find pleasure in his own thoughts, and must conceive himself what he is not, for who is pleased with what he is?
Ibid., 164

Fancy grows first imperious and, in time, despotic. Then fictions begin to operate as realities, false opinions fasten upon the mind, and life passes in dreams of rapture or of anguish.   *Ibid.*

When we first form visionary schemes, we know them to be absurd, but familiarize them by degrees, and in time lose sight of their folly.   *Ibid.*, 166

Gloomy dismal fancies, the usual companions of solitary bachelors.
Kahlert, *The Necromancer*, I

Imagination can surpass the wonders of art, but those of nature leave all imagination far behind.   Lee, *The Recess*, I

Your imaginations are too quick for language. You conjecture too soon what you do not wait to hear and reason upon suppositions which cannot be allowed you.
Lennox, *The Female Quixote*, II

Dissemble thy fancy, or desist from thy folly.   Lyly, *Euphues*, 130

The imagination is the unical, rudimental, and all-comprehending abstracted essence of the infinite remoteness of things. Without it, we were grasshoppers.
Melville, *Mardi*, CLI

All the great books in the world are but the mutilated shadowings-forth of invisible and eternally unembodied images in the soul.   Melville, *Pierre*, Book XX, I

Gentlemen of an unpracticed imaginative capacity cannot vision for themselves exactly what they would, being unable to exercise authority over the proportions and the hues of the objects they conceive, which are very much at the mercy of their sportive caprices.
Meredith, *Beauchamp's Career*, XXXIII

I find no pleasure in rash imaginations, and undigested schemes built upon the mere instinct of principles.　　　　　Meredith, *Ordeal of Richard Feverel*, XXIX

Fancy will not be bridled.　　　　　Reade, *The Cloister and the Hearth*, LXXIX

Imagination, unnaturally heightened, may change into one altitude from another.
　　　　　Richardson, *Sir Charles Grandison*, Two, V

The evils of life are sufficiently great without adding to them those of the imagination.
　　　　　Roche, *Clermont*, III

We fools of fancy have this advantage over the wise ones of the earth, that we have our whole stock of enjoyments under our own command, and can dish for ourselves an intellectual banquet with most moderate assistance from external objects.
　　　　　Scott, *Redgauntlet*, Letter XII

All men, in situations of peculiar doubt and difficulty, when they have exercised the reason to little purpose, are apt, in a sort of despair, to abandon the reins to their imagination, and be guided either altogether by chance, or by those whimsical impressions which take possession of the mind, and to which we give way as if to involuntary impulses.　　　　　Scott, *Rob Roy*, XXI

That mischievous fertility of fancy.　　　　　Smollett, *Peregrine Pickle*, 72

Fancy, thou art a seduced and a seducing slut.　　　Sterne, *A Sentimental Journey*, 18

Fancy is capricious. Wit must not be searched for. Pleasantry will not come in at a call, were an empire to be laid at her feet.　　　　　Sterne, *Tristram Shandy*, IX

There are those people who possess a peculiar faculty of mingling in the affairs of this life as spectators as well as actors.　　　　　Stowe, *Orr's Island*, X

Actual life was chaos, but there was something terribly logical in the imagination.
　　　　　Wilde, *The Picture of Dorian Gray*, XVIII

IMITATION

Those whose actions are forever before our eyes, whose words are ever in our ears, will naturally lead us, albeit against our will, slowly, gradually, imperceptibly, perhaps, to act and speak as they do.　　　　　Bronte, A., *Agnes Grey*, XI

Nothing is so plebeian as imitation.　　　　　Bulwer, *Pelham*, LXVII

Any strongly marked expression of face on the part of a chief actor in a scene of great interest to whom many eyes are directed will be unconsciously imitated by the spectators.　　　　　Dickens, *A Tale of Two Cities*, Book II, III

The pretense to imitate Pindar is as if a dwarf should undertake to step over wide rivers and stride over mountains, because he has seen a giant do it.
　　　　　Fielding, S., *David Simple*, I

A good imitation is often not inferior to a tolerable original, and always superior to a bad one.　　　　　Jenner, *The Placid Man*, I

No man was ever great by imitation.　　　　　Johnson, *Rasselas*, 48

There is nothing that betrays a weak head into more or grosser absurdities than imitation.　　　　　Johnstone, *The Reverie*, II

Imitation of the great is more dangerous, if less ridiculous, in man than in woman.
　　　　　Ibid.

Once a spirit of emulation is inspired, great things are accomplished.
　　　　　Moore, *Evelyn Innes*, XVII

IMMOBILITY: *see also* ACTION; etc.

Mrs. Vesey looked the personification of human composure and female amiability. A calm enjoyment of a calm existence beamed in drowsy smiles on her plump, placid face. Some of us rush through life, and some of us saunter through life. Mrs. Vesey *sat* through life.　　　　　　　　　　　　　　Collins, *The Woman in White*, First Epoch

IMMORALITY: *see* GOOD AND EVIL

IMMORTALITY: *see also* DEATH; ETERNALITY; HEAVEN; LIFE; etc.

The word *individual*, as applied here on earth, is a misuse of language. It is absurd to call that an individual which every hour divides. The earthly stage of human life is so small that there is room for but one of the persons of an individual upon it at one time. The past and future selves have to wait in the side scenes.
　　　　　　　　　　　　　　　　　　Bellamy, *Miss Ludington's Sister*, XI

The past is good or bad for itself, and the present good or bad for itself, and an evil past can more shadow a virtuous present than a virtuous present can retroact to brighten or redeem an ugly past. It is the soul that repents which is ennobled by repentance. The soul that did the deed repented of is past forgiving.　　　　　*Ibid.*, Last Chapter

The mansions of immortality.　　　　　　Duff, *The History of Rhedi*, 278

A man who, like Melchisedec, is without end of life, may well consider himself as being also, like him, without father, without mother, and without descent.
　　　　　　　　　　　　　　　　　　　　Godwin, *St. Leon*, 165

Your immortality is annihilation, your Hereafter is a lie.
　　　　　　　　　　Schreiner, *The Story of an African Farm*, Part II, XIII

IMPARTIALITY

It is difficult to be impartial in our own cause.　　Godwin, *St. Leon*, 317

In cases of right and wrong, we ought not to know either relation or friend.
　　　　　　　　　　　Richardson, *Sir Charles Grandison*, Two, III

IMPENETRABLENESS

She saves herself many griefs by her impenetrableness.
　　　　　　　　　　　Richardson, *Clarissa Harlowe*, I

IMPERTINENCE: *see also* IMPUDENCE

There is nothing which requires more immediate notice than impertinence, for it ever encroaches when it is tolerated.　　　　　　Burney, *Evelina*, 95

He had not that vivacity, or rather impertinence, which frequently passes for wit with superficial people.　　　　Day, *The History of Sandford and Merton*, 284

IMPORTANCE; UNIMPORTANCE: *see also* GRANDNESS; GREATNESS; etc.

We are strangers to our own inconsiderableness, and imagine the annihilation of a being so perfect as ourselves would derogate from all nature.
　　　　　　　　　　　　　Anonymous, *Jeremiah Grant*, 152-153

The man was too insignificant to be dangerous.　　Conrad, *Lord Jim*, XXXIV

Most men like to have a secret to tell which may exalt their own importance.
　　　　　　　　　　　　　Dickens, *Barnaby Rudge*, XXXIII

The little words, like the little folks in a nation, are the most significant.

Richardson, *Clarissa Harlowe*, II

The least trifles will set princes and children at loggerheads. *Ibid.*

IMPOSITION

We are liable to be imposed upon, and to confer our choicest favors often on the undeserving. Fielding, H., *Tom Jones*, 56

Lay yourself but the least open to imposition, and you will find so many ready to make their advantage of it that you would imagine justice was never in the land.

Jenner, *The Placid Man*, I

The man who checks the inclination which he feels in his breast to do a humane action, from a fear of being imposed on, but little deserves to have opportunities of doing good thrown in his way. *Ibid.*, I

There is nothing easier than for artful people to impose upon simple ones, except it is to persuade them to impose upon themselves. *Ibid.*, II

Tame spirits must always be imposed upon. Richardson, *Clarissa Harlowe*, III

IMPOSSIBILITY: *see also* POSSIBILITY

One thing is not consistent with another, the same proposition cannot be at once true and false, the same number cannot be even and odd, cogitation cannot be conferred on that which is created incapable of cogitation. Johnson, *Rasselas*, 185

It is impossible that contrary things should meet to make up a perfection without force and wisdom above their powers. Sidney, *Arcadia*, III

IMPOSTURE

Time and ignorance, the two great supporters of imposture.

Fielding, H., *Tom Jones*, 160

All imposture weakens confidence and chills benevolence. Johnson, *Rasselas*, 172

IMPRESSION

People capable of the deepest and most enduring impressions often receive these impressions upon apparently shallow waters. They feel the blow, but it skims the surface at the moment, to choose its place and sink slowly, surely, into the thinking brain.

Atherton, *Senator North*, Book III, I

There are some people who leave impressions not so lasting as the imprint of an oar upon the water. Chopin, *The Awakening*, XXIV

Our first impressions are almost always received through the senses.

Cooper, *Heidenmauer*, VII

Events, however terrible and strange at the moment of their occurrence, lose by degrees their impression over the mind, for the ideas failing to identify the point at which they aim, relax their attempts, and revert to the consideration of objects more familiar to them. Dacre, *Zofloya*, XXVI

Carrie was possessed of that sympathetic, impressionable nature which, ever in the most developed form, has been the glory of the drama. Dreiser, *Sister Carrie*, XVI

There is something so massive, stable, and almost irresistibly imposing, in the exterior presentment of established rank and great possessions, that their very existence seems to give them a right to exist. Hawthorne, *The House of the Seven Gables*, I

There are few first impressions fit to be encouraged.

Richardson, *Clarissa Harlowe*, I

IMPRISONMENT

All closely imprisoned forces rend and destroy. The air that would be healthful to the earth, the water that would enrich it, the heat that would ripen it, tear it when caged up.

Dickens, *Hard Times*, Book III, I

A bird cage: veels vithin veels, a prison in a prison.   Dickens, *Pickwick Papers*, XL

IMPROVEMENT: *see also* PROGRESS

Every generation has its improvements.   Austen, *Mansfield Park*, Volume One, IX

The betterment of mankind from generation to generation, physically, mentally, morally, is recognized as the one great object supremely worthy of effort and of sacrifice.

Bellamy, *Looking Backward*, XXVI

There is nothing in the flattened skull and the ebon aspect that rejects God's law—improvement.   Bulwer, *The Caxtons*, Book IV, II

Know thyself, said the old philosophy. Improve thyself, saith the new.

Ibid., Book XVI, X

The railways will do as much for mankind as the monasteries did.

Disraeli, *Sybil*, Book II, VIII

If a thing can be done better in three hours than in one, there is no reason why three hours should not be spent on it.   Moore, *Evelyn Innes*, XXXV

IMPUDENCE: *see also* IMPERTINENCE

No limits to the impudence of an impudent man.

Austen, *Pride and Prejudice*, Volume III, IX

Impudence has always an advantage over innocence.   Jenner, *The Placid Man*, I

IMPULSE: *see also* INSTINCT; NATURE; etc.

Blind impulse is Nature's highest wisdom. We make our great jump, and then she takes the bandage off our eyes.   Holmes, *Elsie Venner*, XIX

INCIDENT: *see also* ACTION; IMMOBILITY; etc.

What wonderful things are events! The least are of greater importance than the most sublime and comprehensive speculations.   Disraeli, *Coningsby*, Book I, X

INCONSISTENCY: *see also* LOGIC; TRUTH; etc.

The inconsistency of false delicacy.   Burney, *Cecilia*, I

INDEPENDENCE

I should not put myself into the hands of an improver.

Austen, *Mansfield Park*, Volume One, VI

If you would have your son to walk honorably through the world, you must not attempt to clear the stones from his path, but teach him to walk firmly over them—not insist upon leading him by the hand, but let him learn to go alone.

Bronte, A., *The Tenant of Wildfell Hall*, III

INDEPENDENCE (*continued*)

Under every cloud, no matter what its nature, she called out lustily for sympathy and aid. She had no notion of meeting any distress single-handed. In some shape, from some quarter or other, she was pretty sure to obtain her will, and so she got on—fighting the battle of life by proxy.
Bronte, C., *Villette*, XL

I hold that man to be independent who treats the great as the little, and the little as the great, who neither exults in riches nor blushes in poverty, who owes no man a groat, and who spends not a shilling he has not earned.
Burney, *Cecilia*, III

Men who will not shrink from the danger and toil of penetrating the polar basin will shrink from the trouble of doing their own thinking.
Cooper, *The Monikins*, Conclusion

In this world people must climb their own trees.
Crane, *The O'Ruddy*, XXIII

It is a great thing for a lad, when he is first turned into the independence of lodgings.
Gaskell, *Cousin Phillis*, I

To diminish the cases in which the assistance of others is felt necessary is the only genuine road to independence.
Godwin, *St. Leon*, 85

The period in which he is his own master is all which can properly be called a man's life.
Jenner, *The Placid Man*, I

The Remora has little power in swimming; hence its sole locomotion is on the backs of larger fish. Leech-like, it sticketh closer than a false brother in prosperity; closer than a beggar to the benevolent; closer than Webster to the Constitution.
Melville, *Mardi*, XVIII

He looked like a man who had never cringed and never had a creditor.
Melville, *Moby Dick*, X

Glimpses do ye seem to see of that mortally intolerable truth; that all deep, earnest thinking is but the intrepid effort of the soul to keep the open independence of her sea; while the wildest winds of heaven and earth conspire to cast her on the treacherous, slavish shore?
Ibid., XXIII

Talk not to me of blasphemy, man; I'd strike the sun if it insulted me. For could the sun do that, then could I do the other; since there is ever a sort of fair play herein, jealously presiding over all creations.
Ibid., XXXVI

You young creatures covet independency; but those who wish most for it are seldom the fittest to be trusted either with the government of themselves or with power over others.
Richardson, *Clarissa Harlowe*, I

It is not fit a woman should, of any age, or in any state of life, be in a state of independency.
Ibid., III

To beg from the public at large he considers as independence, in comparison to drawing his whole support from the bounty of an individual.
Scott, *Antiquary*, XXXV

One man is enough to right his own wrong.
Scott, *Bride of Lammermoor*, VI

To face the enemy's cannon is a less effort of courage than to put our happiness into the hands of a person who will not once reflect on the importance of the trust committed to his care.
Scott, S., *A Description of Millenium Hall*, 145

There are women who, even amidst their strongest efforts at giving assistance to others, always look as though they were asking aid themselves.
Trollope, *He Knew He Was Right*, VIII

It is not ours to make election for ourselves; Heaven, our fathers, and our husbands, must decide for us.
Walpole, *The Castle of Otranto*, 95

The object of the sage is to make himself independent of all that he cannot command within himself.
Wright, *A Few Days in Athens*, XI

INDIFFERENCE

Reader, do you know, as I do, what terror those cold people can put into the ice of their questions? How much of the fall of the avalanche is in their anger? of the breaking up of the frozen sea in their displeasure? Bronte, C., *Jane Eyre*, XXXV

Indifference to obloquy because we are habituated to it is a token of peculiar baseness.
Brown, C. B., *Ormond*, 103

We are mostly accustomed to look upon all opposition which is not animate as that of the stolid, inexorable hand of indifference, which wears out the patience more than the strength. Hardy, *A Pair of Blue Eyes*, XXII

Philosophy never had any remedy that can cure an indifferent mind.
Lennox, *The Female Quixote*, II

Indifference is generally the inseparable companion of a weak and imperfect judgment.
Ibid., II

Indifference next to hatred. Richardson, *Clarissa Harlowe*, II

INDIGNATION

Honest indignation does sometimes counsel us wisely.
Collins, *The Legacy of Cain*, LXII

INDIVIDUALITY: *see also* INDEPENDENCE; IMITATION; etc.

No animal is more gregarious than a fashionable man, who, whatever may be his abilities to think, rarely decides, and still less frequently acts for himself.
Burney, *Camilla*, Five, IX

Servility of imitation has ever been as much my scorn as servility of dependence.
Burney, *Cecilia*, III

Nothing is great but the personal. As civilization advances, the accidents of life become each day less important. The power of man, his greatness and his glory, depend on essential qualities. Brains every day become more precious than blood.
Disraeli, *Coningsby*, Book IX, IV

The frigid theories of a generalizing age have destroyed the individuality of man.
Ibid., Book IX, VII

To have lost the godlike conceit that we may do what we will, and not to have acquired a homely zest for doing what we can, shows a grandeur of temper which cannot be objected to in the abstract, for it denotes a mind that, though disappointed, forswears compromise. Hardy, *Return of the Native*, Book I, VII

Though all men be made of one metal, yet they be not cast in one mold.
Lyly, *Euphues*, 98

Nothing abideth; the river of yesterday floweth not today; the sun's rising is a setting; living is dying; the very mountains melt; and all revolve:—systems and asteroids; the sun wheels through the zodiac, and the zodiac is a revolution. Ah gods! in all this universal stir, am *I* to prove one stable thing? Melville, *Mardi*, LXXVIII

We cannot feel, or if we feel we cannot so intensely feel, our oneness, except by dividing ourselves from the world. Meredith, *The Egoist*, VII

Every man thinks *that* perfection, that he is himself; *that* the only knowledge that he possesses; and *that* the only pleasure that he pursues.
Wright, *A Few Days in Athens*, XII

Trust me, there are as many ways of living as there are men, and one is no more fit to lead another, than a bird to lead a fish, or a fish a quadruped. *Ibid.*

INDULGENCE

When the mind is under the pressure of affliction, every indulgence tends to soften it.

Kelly, *The Abbey of St. Asaph*, I

INDUSTRY

When self is at the bottom, how industrious it renders us.

Anonymous, *The Fruitless Repentance*, I

I was ruined by a piece of good fortune—or rather, by trusting more to the smiles of fortune than to industry.

Graves, *The Spiritual Quixote*, I

To give to the necessitous may sometimes be a weakness in the man; to encourage industry is a duty to the citizen.

Mackenzie, *The Man of Feeling*, 46

INEVITABILITY: *see also* DESTINY

Night will fall: stories must end: best friends must part.

Thackeray, *Philip*, last lines

INFATUATION: *see also* LOVE

Infatuations are next to being possessed of the devil.

Defoe, *Roxana*, 152

INFERIORITY: *see also* IMPORTANCE; PRIDE; etc.

Shyness is only the effect of a sense of inferiority.

Austen, *Sense and Sensibility*, Volume I, XVII

How can one be at ease with a man when his yes or no may be success or destruction to you? It makes him of too much consequence. A fellow finds himself crying to please, and it spoils his manner.

Burnett, *Through One Administration*, XXVIII

He held that power over the passing moment was a sign of inferiority.

Moore, *Evelyn Innes*, XVIII

INFLUENCE: *see also* CAUSE AND EFFECT

The man who feels himself prosperous and happy will not easily be persuaded by factious declamation that he is undone.

Brooke, *Emily Montague*, IV

The influence of innocence and beauty is universal.

Cooper, *The Headsman*, XVI

There are some books, when we close them—our minds seem to have made a great leap.

Disraeli, *Coningsby*, Book III, II

'Tis the same with human beings as with books. All of us encounter, at least once in our life, some individual who utters words that make us think forever. A great thing is a great book; but greater than all, is the talk of a great man!

Ibid.

Guanoed her mind by reading French novels.

Disraeli, *Tancred*

Clever sons, clever mothers.

Eliot, *Middlemarch*, Book I, V

Our deeds still travel with us from afar,/ And what we have been makes us what we are.

Ibid., Book VII, LXX

To talk nonsense, or poetry, or the dash between the two, in a tone of profound sincerity, and to enunciate solemn discordances with received opinion so seriously as to convey the impression of a spiritual insight, is the peculiar gift by which monomaniacs, having first persuaded themselves, contrive to influence their neighbors, and through them to make conquest of a good half of the world, for good or for ill.

Meredith, *Ordeal of Richard Feverel*, XV

Rhetoric in a worthy cause has good chances of carrying the gravest.

Meredith, *The Tragic Comedians*, V

Mara had from nature a good endowment of that kind of innocent hypocrisy which is needed as a staple in the lives of women who bridge a thousand awful chasms with smiling unconscious looks, and walk, singing and scattering flowers, over abysses of fear, while their hearts are dying within them.

Stowe, *Orr's Island*, XXII

She's been reading novels till she has learned to think she couldn't settle down quietly till she had run off with somebody.

Trollope, *The Way We Live Now*, LIII

There is no such thing as a good influence. All influence is immoral—immoral from a scientific point of view. To influence a person is to give him one's own soul.

Wilde, *The Picture of Dorian Gray*, II

INGENUITY: *see also* GENIUS

Able fowlers put one bird in a trap to take another.

Anonymous, *The Temple-beau*, 208

It is not in the power of ingenuity to subvert the distinctions of right and wrong.

Godwin, *Caleb Williams*, II

INJUSTICE: *see* JUSTICE; LAW; etc.

INNATENESS: *see also* NATURE

A thing has got to be born in a man; and if it ain't born in him, all the privations in the world won't put it there, and if it is, all the college training won't take it out.

Howells, *Silas Lapham*, IX

INNOCENCE; CHASTITY: *see also* GUILT; IGNORANCE; PURITY; VIRTUE; etc.

How awful is innocence, and how timid guilt!

Annesley, *Memoirs of an Unfortunate Young Nobleman*, II

Despair seldom reigns long in the breast of the innocent.

Anonymous, *The Birmingham Counterfeit*, II

The cause of injured innocence will not go unpunished.

Anonymous, *The Fruitless Repentance*, I

The only way to be safe is to be innocent.

Anonymous, *The Ladies Advocate*, 300

Innocence in a man who is prosecuted is the very worst thing that can attend him, the surest symptom, and often the only cause of his ruin, for he is apt to trust to his innocence, which a rogue never can do, by which means the proof is apt to run all on the side against him, which being the only thing the law looks upon, he is consequently condemned.

Anonymous, *Memoirs of the Life of Tsonnonthouan*, II

Cheerfulness is the native garb of innocence.

Brooke, *Emily Montague*, II

Happy are the dreams of infancy, and happy their harmless pursuits!

Brown, W. H., *The Power of Sympathy*, 140

Very near are two hearts that have no guile between them.

Bulwer, *The Caxtons*, Book XVIII, VIII

Firmness given by the ascendance of innocence over guilt.

Burney, *Camilla*, Five, X

Life's only blessing, Innocence.

Burney, *Cecilia*, III

Guileless yourself, how can you prepare against the duplicity of another?

Burney, *Evelina*, 250

Her understanding is excellent; but she is too young for suspicion, and has an artlessness of disposition.

Ibid., 321

We often hear that guilt can look like innocence. I believe it to be infinitely the truer axiom that innocence can look like guilt.
Collins, *The Moonstone*, Third Narrative, VI

Innocence and peace do not always bless the cottage. Vice sometimes finds an entrance under the lowest roof, and care and sorrow can hover over the brow of humble virtue.
Collyer, *Felicia to Charlotte*, II

While she was full of pity for the visible mistakes of others, she had not yet any material within her experience for subtle constructions and suspicions of hidden wrong.
Eliot, *Middlemarch*, Book VIII, LXXVII

That is a rare and blessed lot which some greatest men have not attained, to know ourselves guiltless before a condemning crowd—to be sure that what we are denounced for is solely the good in us.
Ibid., Book VIII, LXXXV

Innocence fears neither the eyes nor the tongues of men.   Fielding, H., *Amelia*, I

It is not want of sense, but want of suspicion, by which innocence is often betrayed.
Ibid., II

As he had never any intention to deceive, so he never suspected such a design in others.
Fielding, H., *Joseph Andrews*, 17

Mrs. Deborah Wilkins, though in the fifty-second year of her age, vowed she had never beheld a man without his coat.   Fielding, H., *Tom Jones*, 6–7

Innocence and guilt are too much confounded in human life.
Godwin, *Caleb Williams*, II

The Inquisitors strip innocence of those consecrated weapons by which only it can be defended.   Godwin, *St. Leon*, 320

The innocent may have heard much of the evil of the world, and seem to know it, but only as an impalpable theory. In due time, some mortal, whom they reverence too highly, is commissioned by Providence to teach them this direful lesson; he perpetrates a sin; and Adam falls anew, and Paradise, heretofore in unfaded bloom is lost again, and closed forever, with the fiery swords gleaming at its gates.
Hawthorne, *The Marble Faun*, XXIII

Bad as the world is said to have grown, innocence continues to make a paradise around itself, and keep it still unfallen.   *Ibid.*, XLII

As calm as innocence.   Helme, *St. Margaret's Cave*, Volume III, III

The sword of the magistrate is no terror to the innocent.   Kidgell, *The Card*, I

He is reported to be so strict an observer of chastity that he knows not in what consists the difference of man and woman.   Lewis, *The Monk*, 9

You should not seem to remember that there is such a thing as a man in the world, and you ought to imagine everybody to be of the same sex with yourself.   *Ibid.*, 9–10

When we are innocent of an accusation, we hardly feel it.
Meeke, *Count St. Blanchard*, II

Innocence is my redress.   Melville, *Confidence-Man*, XVII

The liking of strangers best is a curious exemplification of innocence.
Meredith, *Diana of the Crossways*, XII

Can innocence issue of the guilty?   Meredith, *One of Our Conquerors*, XXVI

The rich have this comfort, that, let them be ever so guilty, they can buy themselves innocent again, in the twinkling of a ducat. Now a poor man might be a month before he recovered his innocence.   Radcliffe, *The Italian*, II

All earthly innocence is but comparative. Yet still how wide asunder are the extremes of guilt.   Radcliffe, *The Mysteries of Udolpho*, II

Naked innocence is unequal to armed guilt.   Richardson, *Clarissa Harlowe*, II

Why, said he, there was never a girl of your innocence, that set a large family in such an
uproar, surely.   Richardson, *Pamela*, 231

More innocence in your hearts, less shame in your countenances.
    Richardson, *Sir Charles Grandison*, One, II

Innocence is confident.   Scott, *Bride of Lammermoor*, XVII

Sophia followed me to India. She was as innocent as gay; but, unfortunately for us both,
as gay as innocent.   Scott, *Guy Mannering*, XII

Blessed is the man who is not pricked with the multitude of his sins.
    Sterne, *Tristram Shandy*, II

Blessed is the man whose heart hath not condemned him.   *Ibid.*

The innocent have aye a chance to get assoiled in court.
    Stevenson, *Kidnapped*, XVIII

Ignorance is no bad security of innocence.   Young, *The Adventures of Emmera*, II

INQUIRY; INVESTIGATION: *see also* INQUISITION

To prevent inquiry is among the worst of evils.   Holcroft, *Hugh Trevor*, VI

The more we inquire, the less we resolve.   Johnson, *Rasselas*, 103

Look into faces only to know whether a man's nose be a long or a short one.
    Mackenzie, *The Man of Feeling*, 53

INQUISITION: *see also* INQUIRY

The Inquisition claims the bodies and souls of all heretics all over the world; and none
that it catches, whether peaceable merchants, or shipwrecked mariners, but must turn
or burn.   Kingsley, *Westward Ho!*, VII

INSANITY; MANIA; SANITY: *see also* EMOTIONS; MIND; etc.

Insanity: its alternative, suicide.   Bellamy, *Looking Backward*, XXI

Every man is mad once or twice in his life.   Bronte, C., *Shirley*, VII

We're all mad here. I'm mad. You're mad.   Carroll, *Alice in Wonderland*, VI

Nature in her wildest moods has no terrors for those who have nothing to love or win; no
terrors for them who laugh and play with the very elements of her destruction; they are
wildly, madly independent. It is the sublimity of the manias.
    Caruthers, *Cavaliers*, Volume II, I

Her mind, brooding solitary, had grown diseased, as all minds do and must and will that
reverse the appointed order of their Maker.   Dickens, *Great Expectations*, XLIX

Madness and moonshine.   Dickens, *Our Mutual Friend*, Book IV, Chapter the Last

The maniac can hardly be held accountable for the enormities to which his madness
prompts him, even though that madness be self-created.
    Hildreth, *Slave*, Volume I, XIX

All power of fancy over reason is a degree of insanity.   Johnson, *Rasselas*, 163

It is full as absurd to suppose that the moon is in the man, as that the man is in the moon.
    Lawrence, H., *The Life and Adventures of Common Sense*, II

Is this thing of madness conscious to thyself? If ever thou art sane again, wilt thou have
reminiscences?   Melville, *Mardi*, CLXXXIV

INSANITY; MANIA; SANITY (*continued*)

I am madness maddened! That wild madness that's only calm to comprehend itself!
Melville, *Moby Dick*, XXXVII

Human madness is oftentimes a cunning and most feline thing. When you think it fled, it may have but become transfigured into still subtler form.
Ibid., XLI

The sea had jeeringly kept his finite body up, but drowned the infinite of his soul. . . . Man's insanity is heaven's sense; and wandering from all mortal reason, man comes at last to that celestial thought, which, to reason, is absurd and frantic; and weal or woe, feels then uncompromised, indifferent as his God.
Ibid., XCIII

One daft with strength, the other daft with weakness.
Ibid., CXXV

The eloquence of frenzy, madness.
Meredith, *Beauchamp's Career*, X

Martyrs of love or religion are madmen.
Ibid., XI

Favorable circumstances—good air, good company, two or three good rules rigidly adhered to—keep the world out of Bedlam. But let the world fly into a passion, and is not Bedlam its safest abode?
Meredith, *Ordeal of Richard Feverel*, VII

We are mad; and we make life the disease, and death the cure.
Ibid.

I must either be merry, or mad.
Richardson, *Clarissa Harlowe*, III

The tae half of the warld thinks the tither daft.
Scott, *Redgauntlet*, VII

Madness is fond of schemes.
Simms, *The Partisan*, Volume II, X

It was sufficient for him to have been a madman [only] once in his life.
Smollett, *Peregrine Pickle*, 219

In some cases madness is catching.
Smollett, *Sir Launcelot Greaves*, 51

One half of the nation is mad—and the other not very sound.
Ibid., 52

There is perhaps no great social question so imperfectly understood among us as that which refers to the line which divides sanity from insanity.
Trollope, *He Knew He Was Right*, XXXVIII

Threats are seldom of avail to bring a man back to reason. One does not become angry with a madman.
Ibid., XCVIII

In one sense all misconduct is proof of insanity.
Ibid.

There's nothing in the world easier than calling a man mad. It's what we do to dogs when we want to hang them.
Trollope, *Phineas Redux*, XXII

INSATIABILITY: *see also* CURIOSITY

Hope and curiosity are no sooner satisfied, than they begin a new search.
Ridley, *James Lovegrove*, I

INSIGHT: *see also* KNOWLEDGE AND LEARNING

The seership of a poet's heart, the insight that is given to faith.
Bellamy, *Looking Backward*, XIII

Love gives insight, and insight often gives foreboding.
Eliot, *Mill on the Floss*, Book V, III

INSPIRATION: *see also* ART; POETRY; etc.

Do we not all agree to call rapid thought and noble impulse by the name of inspiration?
Eliot, *Adam Bede*, X

The tenth Muse now governs the periodical press.
Trollope, *The Warden*, XIV

INSTINCT; SENSES: *see also* NATURE; etc.

The voice of instinct ought to be obeyed.　　Anonymous, *The Fruitless Repentance*, II

Instinct is the ultimate court of appeal. What is instinct? It is a mode of faith in the evidence of things not actually seen.　　　　　Butler, *The Way of All Flesh*, LXV

What is the instinct of brutes but God's ever present and supporting hand; but man—he has neither perfect reason nor instinct.
Caruthers, *Kentuckian in New-York*, Volume I, VI

Our senses are not dupes.　　　　　Cleland, *Memoirs of a Coxcomb*, 198

The gift of instinct: an inferior gradation of reason. A sort of mysterious combination of thought and matter.　　　　　　Cooper, *The Prairie*, XVII

Man is not a beast to follow the gift of instinct, and to snuff up his knowledge by a taint in the air, or a rumbling in the sound; but he must see and reason, and then conclude.
Ibid., XXIII

Instinct is a keener expert than reason at interpreting covert under-meanings.
Davis, R. H., *Waiting for the Verdict*, XXII

Instinct, though knowing, is yet a teacher set below reason.
Melville, *Confidence-Man*, III

It is not so much outer temptations that prevail over mortals; but inward instincts.
Melville, *Mardi*, CXLIII

Surely there is something divine in instinct.
Meredith, *Ordeal of Richard Feverel*, XLII

Our actions obey an unknown law, implicit in ourselves, but which does not conform to our logic.　　　　　　　Moore, *Evelyn Innes*, IX

Wings were in the air and every instinct was homeward.
Murfree, *The Prophet of the Great Smoky Mountains*, I

Instinct is never off its guard.　　　Reade, *The Cloister and the Hearth*, XXIII

For all the brag you hear about knowledge being such a wonderful thing, instink [sic] is worth forty of it for real unerringness.　　Twain, *Tom Sawyer Abroad*, XIII

INSTITUTION

"What are American institutions?" "Everything is an institution. Having iced water to drink in every room of the house is an institution. Having hospitals in every town is an institution. Travelling altogether in one class of railway cars is an institution. Saying sir is an institution. Plenty of food is an institution. Getting drunk is an institution in a great many towns. Lecturing is an institution."
Trollope, *He Knew He Was Right*, XLVI

INSTRUCTION: *see also* EDUCATION; KNOWLEDGE AND LEARNING; etc.

The greatest men may sometimes overshoot themselves, but their very mistakes are so many lessons of instruction to teach others the art of over-reaching.
Fielding, H., *Jonathan Wild*, 114

The mysterious process by which our earthly life instructs us for another state of being.
Hawthorne, *The Marble Faun*, XXXV

There are some sages whom we understand less as we hear them longer.
Johnson, *Rasselas*, 92

INTEGRITY: *see also* HONESTY; HONOR; etc.

Both wit and understanding are trifles, without integrity.
Goldsmith, *The Vicar of Wakefield*, 74

There seems to be less pride than folly in being ashamed of having been deceived; for it more generally argues an undesigning integrity of heart, than a weakness of head.
Jenner, *The Placid Man*, I

Integrity without knowledge is weak and useless, and knowledge without integrity is dangerous and dreadful.
Johnson, *Rasselas*, 156

INTELLECT; INTELLIGENCE: *see also* COMMON SENSE; WISDOM; etc.

The average intelligence is always shallow, and in electric climates very excitable.
Atherton, *Senator North*, Book III, IX

Only those who know the supremacy of the intellectual life—the life which has a seed of ennobling thought and purpose within it—can understand the grief of one who falls from that serene activity into the absorbing soul-wasting struggle with worldly annoyances.
Eliot, *Middlemarch*, Book VIII, LXXIII

Men of sense are frequently over-persuaded by their friends, and over-ruled by their servants.
Kidgell, *The Card*, I

We prefer the rapier thrust, to the broad embrace, of intelligence.
Meredith, *Ordeal of Richard Feverel*, XXVI

Intellect is in itself a mode of exaggeration, and destroys the harmony of any face. The moment one sits down to think, one becomes all nose, or all forehead, or something horrid.
Wilde, *The Picture of Dorian Gray*, I

INTENSITY

None of us can stand more than just so much intensity.
Atherton, *Senator North*, Book II, III

The bow always strung will not do.
Eliot, *Middlemarch*, Book I, VII

Men of uncommon intellect, who have grown morbid, possess this occasional power of mighty effort, into which they throw the life of many days, and then are lifeless for as many more.
Hawthorne, *The Scarlet Letter*, XXII

INTERDEPENDENCE: *see also* INDEPENDENCE

A wanderer's repose or a sinner's reformation should never depend on a fellow-creature.
Bronte, C., *Jane Eyre*, XX

Foreign artisans and servants do everything by couples: it would take two Labasse-courien carpenters to drive a nail.
Bronte, C., *Villette*, XLI

Every desire man has links him with others. Man is not a machine. He is a part of one.
Bulwer, *The Caxtons*, Book VI, I

One part of a community must inevitably hang upon another, and it is a farce to call either independent, when to break the chain by which they are linked would prove destruction to both.
Burney, *Cecilia*, III

We exist only in so far as we hang together.
Conrad, *Lord Jim*, XXI

We are bound to think well of one another in this world.
Dickens, *Dombey and Son*, XXIX

Our mental business is carried on much in the same way as the business of the State: a great deal of hard work is done by agents who are not acknowledged.
Eliot, *Adam Bede*, XVI

In natural science there is nothing petty to the mind that has a large vision of relations, and to which every single object suggests a vast sum of conditions. It is surely the same with the observation of human life.
Eliot, *The Mill on the Floss*, Book IV, I

But nobody did come, because nobody does.   Hardy, *Jude the Obscure*, Part I, IV

One subject is but the reverberation of the other.
                    Hawthorne, *The House of the Seven Gables*, XII

A time comes to every one of us when we can't help ourselves, and then we must get others to help us.   Howells, *Silas Lapham*, XVIII

All men are inspired; for the essence of all ideas is infused.
                                            Melville, *Mardi*, CLXXX

If rich men want what poor men can perform, though the poor men also want what the rich only can bestow; yet there is want on either side.   Morris, *John Daniel*, 241-242

The fox's case must help when the lion's skin is out at the elbows.
                            Nashe, *The Unfortunate Traveller*, 34

There is no such thing as living without being beholden to somebody.
                            Richardson, *Clarissa Harlowe*, III

It is an age so full of light, that there is scarce a country or corner of Europe, whose beams are not crossed and interchanged with others.
                            Sterne, *A Sentimental Journey*, 13

INTEREST; INTERESTINGNESS; SELF-INTEREST

Interest sometimes perverts the noblest minds.
                    Annesley, *Memoirs of an Unfortunate Young Nobleman*, II

Trade promotes the love of self-interest, which is the destruction of society.
                            Anonymous, *The Birmingham Counterfeit*, I

Gentlemen are too apt to think nothing ruin that promotes their own inclinations.
                            Anonymous, *The History of Betty Barnes*, I

Nothing, next to curiosity, makes a man so true to his appointment as interest.
                    Anonymous, *Private Letters from an American in England*, 57

I would as soon trust a man whose interest binds him to be just to me as a man whose principle binds himself.   Defoe, *Captain Singleton*, 228

We are ready to imagine that all the business of the world should stand still on an occasion interesting to us.   Richardson, *Clarissa Harlowe*, IV

The end of uncertainty is the death of interest.   Scott, *The Heart of Midlothian*, I

Every man will speak of the fair as his own market has gone in it.
                            Sterne, *Tristram Shandy*, I

There are people who never do anything that is not worth watching; they cannot eat an apple or button a shoe in an unnoticeable, unsuggestive manner. If they undertake to be awkward, they do it so symbolically that you feel in debt to them for it.
                            Ward, *The Silent Partner*, I

INTERPRETATION: *see also* JUDGMENT; PERSPECTIVE; etc.

The texts of scripture are not to be strained, but are to be construed naturally.
                            Cooper, *Satanstoe*, Volume II, XV

Many of us would read in the stars, if we could, something hidden from us; but none of us so much as know our letters in the stars yet—or seem likely to do it, in this state of existence—and few languages can be read until their alphabets are mastered.
                    Dickens, *The Mystery of Edwin Drood*, XVII

Signs are small measurable things, but interpretations are illimitable, and in girls of sweet, ardent nature, every sign is apt to conjure up wonder, hope, belief, vast as a sky, and colored by a diffused thimbleful of matter in the shape of knowledge.
                            Eliot, *Middlemarch*, Book I, III

INTERPRETATION (*continued*)

There is reason to suspect that a people are waning to decay and ruin the moment that their life becomes fascinating either in the poet's imagination or the painter's eye.
Hawthorne, *The Marble Faun*, XXXII

There is a class of spectators whose sympathy will help them to see the perfect through a mist of imperfection. Nobody ought to read poetry, or look at pictures or statues, who cannot find a great deal more in them than the poet or artist has actually expressed. Their highest merit is suggestiveness. *Ibid.*, XLI

To a girl everything a young man does is of significance; and if he holds a shaving down with his foot while she pokes through it with her parasol, she must ask herself what he means by it. Howells, *Silas Lapham*, IX

The novelist who could interpret the common feelings of commonplace people would have the answer to "the riddle of the painful earth" on his tongue. *Ibid.*, XIV

There's another rendering now; but still one text. All sorts of men in one kind of world.
Melville, *Moby Dick*, XCIX

Stating amounts in sounding fractional sums conveys a much fuller notion of their magnitude than by disguising their immensity in such aggregations of value as doubloons, sovereigns, and dollars. Who would not rather be worth 125,000 francs in Paris than only 5000 pounds in London? Melville, *Redburn*, LXI

We who interpret things heavenly by things earthly must not hope to juggle with them for our pleasures, and can look to no absolution of evil acts.
Meredith, *Beauchamp's Career*, XXXIX

INVOLVEMENT

His finger was in every man's palm, his mouth was in every man's ear.
Scott, *Quentin Durward*, XXXI

Why is it that we rejoice at a birth and grieve at a funeral? Is it because we are not the person involved? Twain, *Pudd'nhead Wilson*, IX

ISOLATION: *see also* LONELINESS

He was protected by his isolation, alone of his own superior kind, in close touch with Nature, that keeps faith on such easy terms with her lovers. Conrad, *Lord Jim*, XVI

Isolation seemed only the effect of his power. His loneliness added to his stature.
Ibid., XXVII

Who can be said to live that is isolated on the earth, never experiencing the joys of paternity? Dacre, *Passions*, Letter XXXI

In the life of each of us, there is a place remote and islanded, and given to endless regret or secret happiness; we are each the uncompanioned hermit and recluse of an hour or a day; we understand our fellows of the cell to whatever age of history they may belong.
Jewett, *Country of the Pointed Firs*, XV

People may talk of the solitude of forests, but there is company in trees which one misses upon the prairie. It is in the prairie, with its ocean-like waving of grass, like a vast sea without landmarks, that the traveller feels a sickly sensation of loneliness.
Marryat, *Monsieur Violet*, XXI

JEALOUSY: *see also* LOVE

When a man becomes jealous without a cause, a woman resolves to justify his suspicions.
Anonymous, *The Fruitless Repentance*, II

You never felt jealousy, did you? Of course not: I need not ask you; because you never felt love. Bronte, C., *Jane Eyre*, XV

His veins were dark with a livid belladonna tincture, the essence of jealousy—not merely the tender jealousy of the heart, but that sterner, narrower sentiment whose seat is in the head. Bronte, C., *Villette*, XXX

Nothing kindles the fire of love like a sprinkling of the anxieties of jealousy; it takes then a wilder, a more resistless flame; it forgets its softness; it ceases to be tender; it assumes something of the intensity—of the ferocity—of hate.
Bulwer, *Pompeii*, Book Two, VIII

The right hand jealous of the left! The heart jealous of the soul!
Chopin, *The Awakening*, V

Jealousy varies. Collins, *Blind Love*, XXXV

Jealousy is the wrath of a man. Defoe, *Colonel Jack*, 225

Many women are jealous without cause: I knew a woman that was ready to hang herself, for seeing but her husband's shirt hang on a hedge with her maid's smock.
Deloney, *Jack of Newbury*, 320

'Tis a bitter pang under any circumstances to find another preferred to yourself. It is about the same blow as one would probably feel if falling from a balloon.
Disraeli, *Coningsby*, Book VII, I

Too often jeajousy is the quality upon which it feeds. Dreiser, *Sister Carrie*, XXIII

There is a sort of jealousy which needs very little fire: it is hardly a passion, but a blight bred in the cloudy, damp despondency of uneasy egoism.
Eliot, *Middlemarch*, Book II, XXI

A happy rival is an odious sight to an unfortunate lover. Fielding, H., *Amelia*, I

Jealousy is a familiar kind of heat which disfigures, licks playfully, clouds, blackens, and boils a man as a fire does a pot. Hardy, *The Hand of Ethelberta*, VIII

Fly that vice, jealousy: for if thou suspect without cause, it is the next way to have cause.
Lyly, *Euphues and His England*, 474–475

Senile jealousy is anxious to be deceived. Meredith, *Beauchamp's Career*, XLIII

The jealousy of a mean mind, when conscious of its deficiencies, is natural enough. We cannot be hurt by malice any more than we can be gratified by undue praises at the expense of others. Parsons, *The Castle of Wolfenbach*, I

What hell can give torments to what a jealous man feels? *Ibid.*, II

Marriage would not cure this madness [of jealousy], for wives do not escape admiration any more than maids. Reade, *Griffith Gaunt*, II

Jealousy is doubt. Richardson, *Sir Charles Grandison*, Three, VII

Jealous in all the tenses and moods of that amiable passion. Scott, *Rob Roy*, XVII

Boys and girls prate themselves into love; and when their love is like to fall asleep, they prate and tease themselves into jealousy. *Ibid.*

Jealousy, the filthy traitor to true affection, and yet disguising itself in the raiment of love. Sidney, *Arcadia*, III

A dog-in-the-manger jealousy is a thing the dogs may laugh at.
Stevenson, *Prince Otto*, Book II, VI

A man need not be mad because he is jealous, even though his jealousy be ever so absurd.
Trollope, *He Knew He Was Right*, XCV

One of those dark gloomy minds in which love always leads to jealousy.
Trollope, *Phineas Finn*, LXIV

I am jealous of everything whose beauty does not die.
Wilde, *The Picture of Dorian Gray*, II

JOIE DE VIVRE: *see also* HAPPINESS; LIFE; etc.

For what end are the blessings of life granted us, but to enjoy them?
Anonymous, *The Birmingham Counterfeit*, I

The love of life increases with age.   Brown, W. H., *The Power of Sympathy*, 165

We love life because we know it.   *Ibid.*

This gentleman desired to know little more of the world than its pleasures.
Goldsmith, *The Vicar of Wakefield*, 11

Nature prescribes to us a joyful life, that is to say, pleasure as the end of all our operations.   More, *Utopia*, II

When the mind is made easy, the body will not long suffer; and the love of life is a natural passion that is soon revived when fortune turns about and smiles.
Richardson, *Clarissa Harlowe*, IV

Good cheer unites good company.   Smollett, *Humphry Clinker*, 68–69

JOKING: *see also* HUMOR

There's nothing upon earth I hate like a joke; unless it's against another person.
Burney, *Camilla*, Two, III

The same thing we philosophize into an admirable good joke for our neighbors, we moralize into a crime against ourselves.   *Ibid.*, Five, IX

JOY AND SORROW: *see also* HAPPINESS; JOIE DE VIVRE; LIFE; etc.

Sorrow and joy are nearly allied.   Anonymous, *The Wanderer*, I

Sorrows are only for a time.   Cleland, *Memoirs of a Woman of Pleasure*, 69

Joy is as extravagant as grief.   Defoe, *Colonel Jack*, 26

Nicholas was one of those whose joy is incomplete unless it is shared by the friends of adverse and less fortunate days.   Dickens, *Nicholas Nickleby*, LXIV

We said that we would make a virtue of joy.
Hardy, *Jude the Obscure*, Part Six, II

Disposition to make a joy of grief.   Hawthorne, *Fanshawe*, IX

He that grudges a poor man joy ought to have none himself.
Richardson, *Clarissa Harlowe*, II

I will not lie abed when anything joyous is going forward.   *Ibid.*, III

Joyful people are not always wise ones. When the heart is open, silly things will be said.
Richardson, *Sir Charles Grandison*, Two, V

Joy is the parent of many a silly thing.   *Ibid.*

JUDGMENT: *see also* JUSTICE; LAW; etc.

The judgment is weak that is built on rumor, or guided by appearances.
Annesley, *Memoirs of an Unfortunate Young Nobleman*, I

How happy would it be for mankind, could they behold their foibles and vices with the piercing eyes that others can.   Anonymous, *The Adventures of Sylvia Hughes*, 63

There are few people whose judgment is a true mirror to themselves.
Anonymous, *The Lady's Drawing Room*, 287

It is not in fine preaching only that a good clergyman will be useful in his parish and his neighborhood, where the parish and neighborhood are of a size capable of knowing his private character, and observing his general conduct.
Austen, *Mansfield Park*, Volume One, IX

Where any one body of educated men, of whatever denomination, are condemned indiscriminately, there must be a deficiency of information.

Ibid., Volume One, XI

We are all in the habit of judging men as if their degradation was deliberate, which as a matter of fact it never is.

Bates, *Puritans*, IX

The application of the rule to the case is the province of judgment.

Brackenridge, *Modern Chivalry*, Part II, II

Twelve judges do not make a half dozen honest men.

Bridges, *The Adventures of a Bank-Note*, II

His judgment of art is a hasty pudding of words, gleaned from dissertations on painting, and applied with as much propriety as a piece of broken glass to a broken shin.

Ibid.

Are we not to be judged according to the deeds done in the body? Where's the use of a probationary existence, if a man may spend it as he pleases, just contrary to God's decrees, and then go to heaven with the blest, if the vilest sinner may win the reward of the holiest saint merely by saying, "I repent"?

Bronte, A., *Tenant of Wildfell Hall*, XLIX

Sense would resist delirium: judgment would warn passion.

Bronte, C., *Jane Eyre*, XV

Feeling without judgment is a washy draught indeed; but judgment untempered by feeling is too bitter and husky a morsel for human deglutition.

Ibid., XXI

I had rather judge ill, than not judge for myself.

Brooke, *Emily Montague*, II

We are apt to judge of others by ourselves.

Brown, C. B., *Arthur Mervyn*, I

Men must judge from what they see: they must build their conclusions on their knowledge.

Ibid., II

We must judge men not so much by what they do, as by what they make us feel that they have it in them to do.

Butler, *The Way of All Flesh*, I

I do not know whether his epitaph was written by one of his children, or whether they got some friend to write it for them. I do not believe that any satire was intended. I believe that it was the intention to convey that nothing short of the Day of Judgment could give anyone an idea how good a man Mr. Pontifex had been, but at first I found it hard to think that it was free from guile. The last lines run as follows: HE NOW LIES AWAITING A JOYFUL RESURRECTION AT THE LAST DAY. WHAT MANNER OF MAN HE WAS THAT DAY WILL DISCOVER.

Butler, *The Way of All Flesh*, XVIII

Men most remarkable for discretion and judgment have trusted too much to their judgments, and too little to their hearts, to be happy.

Caruthers, *Kentuckian in New-York*, Volume I, XVII

He knew himself well, and choosing to imagine that all mankind were cast in the same mould, hated them; for, though no man hates himself, the coldest among us having too much self-love for that, yet most men unconsciously judge the world from themselves, and it will be very generally found that those who sneer habitually at human nature, and affect to despise it, are among its worst and least pleasant samples.

Dickens, *Nicholas Nickleby*, XLIV

Skepticism can never be thoroughly applied, else life would come to a standstill: something we must believe in and do, and whatever that something may be called, it is virtually our own judgment, even when it seems like the most slavish reliance on another.

Eliot, *Middlemarch*, Book III, XXIII

Hear everything and judge for yourself.

Ibid., Book V, XLV

How little we know what would make paradise for our neighbors! We judge from our own desires, and our neighbors themselves are not always open enough even to throw out a hint of theirs.

Ibid., Book V, LIII

The terror of being judged sharpens the memory.   *Ibid.*, Book VI, LXI

People will talk. Even if a man has been acquitted by a jury, they'll talk, and nod and wink—and as far as the world goes, a man might often as well be guilty as not.
Ibid., Book VIII, LXXIV

To the common run of mankind it has always seemed a proof of mental vigor to find moral questions easy, and judge conduct according to concise alternatives.
Eliot, *Romola*, Book III, LXIV

Hath the block any preference to the gallows, or the ax to the halter, but what is given them by the ill-guided judgment of men?   Fielding, H., *Jonathan Wild*, 26

The more our judgments err, the less we are willing to own it.
Fielding, H., *Joseph Andrews*, 274

Why will we not modestly observe the same rule in judging of the good as well as the evil of others?   Fielding, H., *Tom Jones*, 216

We must examine the different tempers of men, and see how much they will bear, before we attempt the dealing with them at all.   Fielding, S., *David Simple*, II

God judges of men by what they are at the period of arraignment, and, whatever be their crimes, if they have seen and abjured the folly of those crimes, receives them to favor.   Godwin, *Caleb Williams*, III

As men are most capable of distinguishing merit in women, so the ladies often form the truest judgments of men. The two sexes seem placed as spies upon each other, and are furnished with different abilities, adapted for mutual inspection.
Goldsmith, *The Vicar of Wakefield*, 40

When the heart flies out before the understanding, it saves the judgment a world of pains.   Hardy, *The Hand of Ethelberta*, VII

I cannot be fairly tried and judged before an earthly tribunal.
Hawthorne, *The Marble Faun*, XXIII

When an uninstructed multitude attempts to see with its eyes, it is exceedingly apt to be deceived. When, however, it forms its judgment, as it usually does, on the intuitions of its great and warm heart, the conclusions thus attained are often so profound and so unerring, as to possess the character of truths supernaturally revealed.
Hawthorne, *The Scarlet Letter*, IX

Sins and sorrows require different expiations, and must be judged, according to the sources from where they arise.   Helme, *St. Margaret's Cave*, Volume I, VIII

Let those who have not wit enough to speak have judgment enough to hold their tongue.
Jenner, *The Placid Man*, I

To judge rightly of the present, we must oppose it to the past, for all judgment is comparative, and of the future nothing can be known.   Johnson, *Rasselas*, 117

Suddenly change as people may in their dispositions, it is not always waywardness, but improved judgment, which operates with them.   Melville, *Confidence-Man*, III

It is a human weakness to take pleasure in sitting in judgment upon one in a box.
Ibid.

Never a sound judgment without charity. When man judges man, charity is less a bounty from our mercy than just allowance for the insensible leeway of human fallibility.
Ibid., XXVIII

Take the whole populace for a judge, and you will long wait for a unanimous verdict.
Melville, *Mardi*, LX

As unerring justice dwells in a unit, and as one judge will at last judge the world beyond all appeal; so—though often here below justice be hard to attain—does man come nearest the mark, when he imitates that model divine. Hence, one judge is better than twelve.   *Ibid.*

There is more likelihood of being overrated while living, than of being underrated when dead.   *Ibid.*, LXIX

There is no supreme standard yet revealed, whereby to judge of ourselves. Our very instincts are prejudices. Our very axioms and postulates are far from infallible. In respect of the universe, mankind is but a sect, and first principles are dogmas.
Ibid., CLXXV

An incessant struggle of one man with the world, which position usually ranks his relatives against him, does not conduce to soundness of judgment.
Meredith, *Beauchamp's Career*, XXXIX

What so kind as the eyes of the lady who loves? Yet are they very rigorous, those soft watchful woman's eyes. If you fall below the measure they have made of you, you will feel it in the fullness of time.   Meredith, *Ordeal of Richard Feverel*, XXXVII

The world is wiser than its judges.   *Ibid.*, XLI

An error *against* judgment is worse, infinitely worse, than an error *in* judgment.
Richardson, *Clarissa Harlowe*, I

We love to keep ourselves in countenance for a rash judgment.   *Ibid.*

Does not the person who will vindicate, or seek to extenuate, a faulty step in another give an indication either of a culpable will or a weak judgment?   *Ibid.*, II

Exalt not into judges those who are prepared to take lessons and instructions from you.
Ibid., III

Human depravity may oftener justify those who judge harshly than human rectitude can those who judge favorably.   *Ibid.*, IV

If thou fearest an unjust judge when thou art innocent, what would'st thou do before a just one if thou wert guilty?   Richardson, *Pamela*, 28

The wise world, that never is wrong itself, judges always by events.   *Ibid.*, 265

Where the world is inclined to favor, it is apt to over-rate, as much as it will under-rate where it disfavors.   Richardson, *Sir Charles Grandison*, One, I

No one can judge of another, that cannot be that very other in imagination, when he takes the judgment seat.   *Ibid.*, One, II

The world will not see with our eyes, nor judge as we would have it, and as we sometimes know it ought to judge.   *Ibid.*, Two, V

Singularity in dress is usually the indication of something wrong in judgment.
Ibid., Three, VI

The world can judge of others better than it can act itself.   *Ibid.*

We judge of a man according to his own manliness.   *Simms, The Scout*, XXXV

When the heart flies out before the understanding, it saves the judgment a world of pains.   Sterne, *A Sentimental Journey*, 17

Men of least wit are reported to be men of most judgment.
Sterne, *Tristram Shandy*, III

We all know how constantly hope and expectation will rise high within our own bosoms in opposition to our own judgment—how we become sanguine in regard to events which we almost know can never come to pass.   Trollope, *He Knew He Was Right*, LVII

JUSTICE; JUSTNESS; INJUSTICE: *see also* LAW; etc.

It is half the battle to fight in a just cause.
Anonymous, *The History of Tom Jones in His Married State*, 79

Though justice has leaden heels, her hands are made of iron; and perhaps her motion is the slower because she is always sure of overtaking.
Anonymous, *The Ladies Advocate*, 301

Internal graces conquer the souls of the judicious.
Anonymous, *The Theatre of Love*, 125

I meant to be uncommonly clever in taking so decided a dislike to him, without any reason. It is such a spur to one's genius, such an opening for wit to have a dislike of that kind. One may be continually abusive without saying anything just; but one cannot be always laughing at a man without now and then stumbling on something witty.
Austen, *Pride and Prejudice*, Volume II, XVII

There is no such thing as moral responsibility for past acts, no such thing as real justice in punishing them, for the reason that human beings are not stationary existences, but changing, growing, incessantly progressive organisms, which in no two moments are the same. Therefore justice, whose only possible mode of proceeding is to punish in present time for what is done in past time, must always punish a person more or less similar to, but never identical with, the one who committed the offense, and therein must be no justice.
Bellamy, *Dr. Heidenhoff's Process*, XI

Providence is sometimes pleased to manifest his justice, even in this world of imperfection where we are not always to expect it.
Boswell, *Dorando*, 17

Let the sovereign, like that of all the people of the earth, do justice; and consider that the possession of power is upheld by justice.
Brackenridge, *Modern Chivalry*, Part II, I

Where parties exist in a republic, that party will predominate eventually which pursues justice.
Ibid.

The knowledge of all law goes but a little way to the discerning the justice of the cause.
Ibid., Part II, II

What a singularly deep impression her injustice seems to have made on your heart! No ill usage so brands its record on my feelings.
Bronte, C., *Jane Eyre*, VI

Human approbation or censure can never be exempt from injustice, because our limited perceptions debar us from a thorough knowledge of any actions and motives but our own.
Brown, C. B., *Ormond*, 217

Justice is relative.
Butler, *Erewhon*, XII

Retributive justice pursues and overtakes the guilty to the ends of the earth.
Caruthers, *Cavaliers*, Volume II, XI

"Poetical justice." "Poetical fiddlesticks."
Collins, *The Legacy of Cain*, LXII

Under extreme provocation men will be just—whether they want to be so or not.
Conrad, *Nigger of the Narcissus*, II

On men reprieved by its disdainful mercy, the immortal sea confers in its justice the full privilege of desired unrest.
Ibid., IV

Justice, like liberty, has great reservations.
Cooper, *Heidenmauer*, XVIII

Is it justice to make evil, and then punish for it?
Cooper, *Last of the Mohicans*, XI

Justice is the master of a redskin.
Ibid., XXVIII

The philanthropy which is dependent on buying land by the square mile, and selling it by the square foot, is stench in the nostrils of the just.
Cooper, *The Monikins*, Conclusion

Fortunate is the gentleman that can obtain even a reluctant and meagre justice.
Cooper, *The Redskins*, XXVIII

Men in masses, when goaded by disappointment, are never just.
Cooper, *Satanstoe*, Volume II, IX

Just appreciation of motives and acts can only proceed from those who feel and think alike; and this is morally impossible where there exist broad distinctions in social classes.   *Ibid.*, Volume II, XV

Proof must be built up stone by stone. The end crowns the work. It is not enough that Justice should be morally certain; she must be immorally certain—legally, that is.
Dickens, *The Mystery of Edwin Drood*, XVIII

When men are about to commit, or to sanction the commission of some injustice, it is not uncommon for them to express pity for the object either of that or some parallel proceeding, and to feel themselves, at the time, quite virtuous and moral, and immensely superior to those who express no pity at all.   Dickens, *Nicholas Nickleby*, LIV

The world, being in the constant commission of vast quantities of injustice, is a little too apt to comfort itself with the idea that if the victim of its falsehood and malice have a clear conscience, he cannot fail to be sustained under his trials, and somehow or other to come right at last; "in which case," say they who have hunted him down, "—though we certainly don't expect it—nobody will be better pleased than we." Whereas, the world would do well to reflect, that injustice is in itself, to every generous and properly constituted mind, an injury, of all others the most insufferable, the most torturing, and the most hard to bear; and that many clear consciences have gone to their account elsewhere, and many sound hearts have broken, because of this very reason; the knowledge of their own deserts only aggravating their sufferings, and rendering them the less endurable.   Dickens, *The Old Curiosity Shop*, LXI

Even justice makes its victims.   Eliot, *The Mill on the Floss*, Book III, VII

Who shall put his finger on the work of justice, and say, "It is there"? Justice is like the Kingdom of God—it is not without us as a fact, it is within us as a great yearning.
Eliot, *Romola*, Book III, LXVII

Thwackum was for doing justice, and leaving mercy to Heaven.
Fielding, H., *Tom Jones*, 103

Justice is certain and inflexible.   Gaskell, *Ruth*, XXI

I hate the man in whom kindness produces no responsive affection, and injustice no swell, no glow of resentment.   Godwin, *St. Leon*, 416

What men call justice lies chiefly in outward formalities.
Hawthorne, *The Marble Faun*, XXIII

There is no such thing as earthly justice, and especially none under the head of Christendom.   *Ibid.*, XLVII

The public is despotic in its temper; it is capable of denying common justice when too strenuously demanded as a right; but quite as frequently it awards more than justice when the appeal is made, as despots love to have it made, entirely to its generosity.
Hawthorne, *The Scarlet Letter*, XIII

Kings are accountable for injustice permitted as well as done.
Johnson, *Rasselas*, 39

Prudence is a virtue, equally with generosity; and a man may be unjust to himself, no less than to another.   Johnstone, *Arsaces*, I

Nothing, humanely speaking, can deserve higher respect than a profession in which a man devotes the labors of his life to the support of justice.
Johnstone, *The Pilgrim*, II

Would it not be justice to oblige every man who proposes a medicine to sale, first to make proof that it is harmless at least, by taking it himself?   *Ibid.*

Isn't anything fair in a good cause?   Kingsley, *Alton Locke*, XXXIII

Offended justice is diligent in detecting the breakers of her law.
Lathom, *The Midnight Bell*, II

It is easy to be just when our own inclinations do not oppose it.
Lennox, *Henrietta*, II

In the cold courts of justice the dull head demands oaths, and holy writ proofs; but in the warm halls of the heart one single, untestified memory's spark shall suffice to enkindle such a blaze of evidence, that all the corners of conviction are as suddenly lighted up as a midnight city by a burning building, which on every side whirls its reddened brands.
Melville, *Pierre*, Book IV, III

If women understood justice they would be the first to proclaim, that when two are tied together, the one who does the other serious injury is more naturally excused than the one who calls up the grotesque to extinguish both.
Meredith, *Amazing Marriage*, XXXI

Seldom do they prove patient martyrs who are punished unjustly.
Nashe, *The Unfortunate Traveller*, 86

Strong minds perceive that justice is the highest of the moral attributes; mercy is only the favorite of weak ones.
Radcliffe, *The Italian*, I

Calling sternness justice, he extolled that for strength of mind which was only callous insensibility.
Ibid.

Justice does not the less exist, because her laws are neglected. A sense of what she commands lives in our breasts; and when we fail to obey that sense, it is to weakness, not to virtue, that we yield.
Ibid., II

When justice happens to oppose prejudice, we are apt to believe it virtuous to disobey her.
Ibid.

Half justice is injustice.
Reade, *Griffith Gaunt*, XLI

"May I not be unjust to myself?" "Certainly not; you have no right to be unjust to anybody."
Ibid., XLII

Who does most injustice, a prodigal man or a saving man? The one saves his own money; the other spends other people's.
Richardson, *Clarissa Harlowe*, I

If the world is unjust, or rash, in one man's case, why may it not be so in another's?
Ibid.

Nothing can be polite that is not just.
Ibid., III

Is not the man guilty of a high degree of injustice who is more apt to give contradiction than able to bear it?
Ibid., IV

Justice is a severe thing.
Richardson, *Sir Charles Grandison*, One, II

To do justice in another's case against oneself is making at least a second merit for oneself.
Ibid., Three, VI

Mercy to a criminal may be gross injustice to the community.
Scott, *Waverley*, XXXII

Though we cannot o'ercome, our cause is just.
Sidney, *Arcadia*, II

Justice teacheth us not to love punishment, but to fly to it for necessity.
Sidney , *Arcadia*, V

Nothing, to the noble heart, is so afflicting as the consciousness of having done injustice.
Simms, *The Scout*, VIII

A just medium prevents all conclusions.
Sterne, *Tristram Shandy*, VIII

The Christian idea of justice never gets across the color line. It counts it wicked to rob the strong, but no crime to mulct the weak under the form of law. Right is always white in Christian law.
Tourgee, *Pactolus Prime*, VIII

Justice today pays all the debts of yesterday and nothing else will.
Ibid.

A man must be an idiot or else an angel who, after the age of forty, shall attempt to be just to his neighbors.
Trollope, *Barchester Towers*, XXXVII

Justice may be purchased too dearly.   Trollope, *The Eustace Diamonds*, XXVIII

JUSTIFICATION

Her not objecting does not justify *him*.
                              Austen, *Pride and Prejudice*, Volume II, IV

The right of a man to maintenance at the nation's table depends on the fact that he is a man, and not on the account of health and strength he may have.
                              Bellamy, *Looking Backward*, XII

Justifiable is a suspicion that a man is capable of doing what he hath done already, and that it is possible for one who hath been a villain once to act the same part again.
                              Fielding, H., *Tom Jones*, 534

Your greatness wants to be justified by my lowness.   Richardson, *Pamela*, 72

There is something in stooping to justification which the pride of innocence does not at all times willingly submit to.   Scott, *The Heart of Midlothian*, XIV

The caricaturist, who draws only caricatures, is held to be justifiable, let him take what liberties he may with a man's face and person. It is his trade, and his business calls upon him to vilify all that he touches. But were an artist to publish a series of portraits, in which two out of a dozen were made to be hideous, he would certainly make two enemies, if not more.   Trollope, *The Way We Live Now*, I

KIND; TYPE; CLASS: *see also* COMPARISON/CONTRAST; DIFFERENCE; etc.

Streets with only one side to them.   Holmes, *Elsie Venner*, II

There are two sorts of men in this world—them that axes questions, and them that won't answer questions.   Kennedy, *Horse-Shoe Robinson*, XV

Many damn-my-eyes humbugs there are in this man-of-war world of ours.
                              Melville, *White Jacket*, LXXIII

The people all walk in lines in England.   Meredith, *Beauchamp's Career*, XL

The burlesque Irishman can't be caricatured. Nature strained herself in a fit of absurdity to produce him, and all that Art can do is to copy.
                              Meredith, *Diana of the Crossways*, III

To be both generally blamed and generally liked evinces a peculiar construction of mortal.   Meredith, *Evan Harrington*, I

Fat, fair, and forty.   Scott, *St. Ronan's Well*, VII

KINDNESS; *see also* CRUELTY; GENEROSITY; GOODNESS; etc.

It is charitable to lend a hand to lift those up who come to pluck you down.
                              Annesley, *Memoirs of an Unfortunate Young Nobleman*, II

I learned in time that this benignity, this cordiality, this music, belonged in no shape to me: it was a part of himself; it was the honey of his temper: it was the balm of his mellow mood; he imparted it, as the ripe fruit rewards with sweetness the rifling bee; he diffused it about him, as sweet plants shed their perfume. Does the nectarine love either the bee or bird it feeds? Is the sweet-briar enamored of the air?
                              Bronte, C., *Villette*, XXXI

The greatest merit any person could have is to be good and useful.
                              Day, *The History of Sandford and Merton*, 338

How much better it is to be useful than rich or fine; how much more amiable to be good than to be great.   *Ibid.*, 364

To do a kindness to a bad man is like sowing your seed in the sea.
                              Fielding, H., *Amelia*, II

KINDNESS (*continued*)

What I would not do for kindness, I would not do for money.   Johnson, *Rasselas*, 46

Our hearts warm more to those we have been kind to, than to those who have been kind to us.   Reade, *Griffith Gaunt*, XXVI

He wants a heart: and if he does, he wants everything.
Richardson, *Clarissa Harlowe*, I

Divine grace, working a miracle, or next to a miracle, can only change a bad heart.
Ibid.

Let not even the faulty have cause to complain of unkindness from us.
Richardson, *Sir Charles Grandison*, Two, III

One can always be kind to people about whom one cares nothing.
Wilde, *The Picture of Dorian Gray*, VIII

KISSING: *see also* AFFECTION; LOVE

A kiss for a blow is always best, though not very easy.   Alcott, *Little Women*, XXX

I've never been kissed by a pure woman in my life—except by my dear mother and sister; and mothers and sisters don't count, when it comes to kissing.
DuMaurier, *Trilby*, V

Kissing is a prologue to a play. There is no woman who grants that, but will grant more.
Fielding, H., *Joseph Andrews*, 32

There are certain words of provocation which men of honor hold can properly be answered only by a blow. Among lovers possibly there may be some expressions which can be answered only by a kiss.   Fielding, H., *Tom Jones*, 716

KNIGHTHOOD

The very perfect knight is a lamb among ladies and a lion among lances.
Scott, *Quentin Durward*, XIV

KNOWLEDGE AND LEARNING: *see also* EDUCATION; GUIDANCE; INSTRUCTION; INTELLIGENCE; WISDOM; etc.

A fellow can't live on books.   Alcott, *Little Women*, V

The ancients are the true sons of knowledge; whose piercing eyes, with boundless glances, could penetrate into the whole universe, and whose matchless pens are unrivalled.   Anonymous, *The Adventures of Sylvia Hughes*, 35

We blame people who go to see foreign countries without first acquiring some knowledge of their own. What a figure most of us will make in the next world if questioned by its inhabitants about that we have left.   Anonymous, *Fatal Friendship*, I

Disappointments and adversity are excellent schoolmasters.
Anonymous, *The Fruitless Repentance*, I

A man's brain accumulates naturally all widely diffused impressions.
Atherton, *Senator North*, Book I, IV

The light of knowledge is sometimes so powerful that it will kill the beholder.
August, *Horrid Mysteries*, I

The things which men cannot perform teach them far more than the things which they can easily do.   Beecher, *Norwood*, LVI

It is a mistake to suppose that a man cannot learn man by reading him in a corner, as well as on the widest space of transaction.
Brackenridge, *Modern Chivalry*, Part I, Volume I

All learning is a nuisance. *Ibid.*, Part II, Volume I

Politicians say that though they have no learning, they feel no want of it. Is it to be supposed that a workman does not know whether he wants tools? *Ibid.*

Were I the master of an academy, the first and continual lesson would be, to attain science and be learned; but as to seeming so, to consider it as of no account. Science would discover itself. *Ibid.*

Everyone is to be trusted in that thing of which he has some knowledge. *Ibid.*

Learning must go somewhere, as a river that sinks in one place rises in another. *Ibid.*

Learning is not a thing that will grow upon you all at once. It is a generous enemy; like a rattlesnake, it gives warning. *Ibid.*, Part II, Volume II

Nothing can be so great a discouragement to learning as to find a fellow with only simple nature to guide him who shall have the impudence to know the same things that learned men have studied so many years to attain the knowledge of.
Bridges, *The Adventures of a Bank-Note*, I

The foresight of man is in proportion to his knowledge.
Brown, C. B., *Arthur Mervyn*, I

Good intentions unaided by knowledge will perhaps produce more injury than benefit.
Ibid., II

We must not be inactive because we are ignorant. Our good purposes must hurry to performance, whether our knowledge be greater or less. *Ibid.*

Justice and compassion are the fruit of knowledge. Brown, C. B., *Ormond*, 203

Human scrutiny is neither to be solicited nor shunned. *Ibid.*, 217

The human mind is an extensive plain, and knowledge is the river that should water it.
Brown, W. H., *The Power of Sympathy*, 30

It is a glorious fever, that desire to know. Bulwer, *My Novel*, Book IV, XVIII

The higher we mount in knowledge the more wonders we behold.
Bulwer, *Pompeii*, Book Two, VIII

The great impediments to knowledge are, first, the want of a common language; and next, the short duration of existence. Bulwer, *Zanoni*, Book I, VI

It is sense that makes punishment heavy.
Bunyan, *The Life and Death of Mr. Badman*, 151

A man may know like an angel, and yet be no Christian.
Bunyan, *Pilgrim's Progress*, 84

To know is a thing that pleaseth talkers and boasters; but to do that which pleaseth God.
Ibid., 84–85

The heart cannot be good without knowledge. *Ibid.*, 85

There is knowledge and knowledge. Knowledge that resteth in the bare speculation of things; and knowledge that is accompanied with the grace of faith and love. *Ibid.*

There is something in men of learning, prodigious nice to deal with.
Burney, *Camilla*, One, II

I don't see the greast superiorness of learning, if it can't keep a man's temper out of a passion. *Ibid.*, Two, III

Where intellect is uncultivated, what is man better than a brute, or woman than an idiot? *Ibid.*, Five, IX

Dull and heavy characters, incapable of animating from wit or from reason, because unable to keep pace with them, and void of all internal sources of entertainment, require the stimulation of show, glare, noise, and bustle, to interest or awaken them.
Burney, *Cecilia*, I

A mind which has once been opened by knowledge can ill endure the contraction of dark and perpetual ignorance.   *Ibid.*, III

What cruel maxims are we taught by a knowledge of the world!
                                                                                                                                    Burney, *Evelina*, 239

The venerable Professor of Worldly Wisdom, a man verging on eighty but still hale, said, "It is not our business to help students to think for themselves. Surely this is the very last thing which one who wishes them well should encourage them to do. Our duty is to ensure that they shall think as we do, or at any rate, as we hold it expedient to say we do."   Butler, *Erewhon*, XXII

It is far safer to know too little than too much. People will condemn the one, though they will resent being called upon to exert themselves to follow the other.
                                                                                                           Butler, *The Way of All Flesh*, V

It is the fashion to say that young people must find out things for themselves, and so they probably would if they had fair play to the extent of not having obstacles put in their way.   *Ibid.*, LXXII

Learning is divided into reading, writing, and figures; and a man may well understand one, without knowing a word of the others.   Cooper, *The Bravo*, III

With all your bookish larning and hard words, you are farther from the truth than you are from the settlements.   Cooper, *The Prairie*, IX

The sin of wasted learning.   *Ibid.*, XIII

Man may be degraded to the very margin of the line which separates him from the brute, by ignorance; or he may be elevated to a communion with the great Master-spirit of all, by knowledge; nay, I know not, if time and opportunity were given him, but he might become the master of all learning, and consequently equal to the great moving principle.   *Ibid.*, XVII

Knowledge is [God's] plaything.   *Ibid.*

Learned men make one headful of brains go a long way by poaching on each other's knowledge.   Crane, *The O'Ruddy*, XIV

The purser and one of the gunners were hanged immediately, and I expected it with the rest. I do not remember any great concern I was under about it, only that I cried very much, for I knew little then of this world, and nothing at all of the next.
                                                                                                       Defoe, *Captain Singleton*, 12

But knowledge isn't to be got with paying sixpence. If you're to know figures, you must turn 'em over in your head and keep your thoughts fixed on 'em. There's nothing you can't turn into a sum, for there's nothing but what's got number in it—even a fool.
                                                                                                                      Eliot, *Adam Bede*, XXI

The more knowledge a man has, the better he'll do's work; and feeling's a sort o' knowledge.   *Ibid.*, LII

It is a common sentence that Knowledge is power; but who hath duly considered or set forth the power of Ignorance? Knowledge slowly builds up what Ignorance in an hour pulls down.   Eliot, *Daniel Deronda*, Book III, XXI

Knowledge, through patient and frugal centuries, enlarges discovery and makes record of it; Ignorance, wanting its day's dinner, lights a fire with the record, and gives a flavor to its one roast with the burnt souls of many generations.   *Ibid.*

Knowledge, instructing the sense, refining and multiplying needs, transforms itself into skill and makes life various with a new six days' work; comes Ignorance drunk on the seventh, with a firkin of oil and a match and an easy, "Let there not be"—and the many-colored creation is shrivelled up in blackness.   *Ibid.*

Of a truth, Knowledge is power, but it is a power reined by scruple, having a conscience of what must be and what may be; whereas Ignorance is a blind giant who, let him but wax unbound, would make it a sport to seize the pillars that hold up the long-wrought fabric of human good, and turn all the places of joy dark as a buried Babylon.   *Ibid.*

Thoughts, opinions, knowledge, are only a sensibility to facts and ideas.
Eliot, *Felix Holt*, X

To find right remedies and right methods. Here is the great function of knowledge.
Ibid., Address to Working Men

Knowledge seemed to him a very superficial affair, easily mastered: judging from the conversation of his elders, he had apparently got already more than was necessary for mature life.   Eliot, *Middlemarch*, Book II, XV

It is very difficult to be learned; it seems as if people were worn out on the way to great thoughts, and can never enjoy them because they are too tired.
Ibid., Book IV, XXXVII

It is but once that we can know our worst sorrows.   Eliot, *Romola*, Epilogue

A weaver who finds hard words in his hymn-book knows nothing of abstractions; as the little child knows nothing of parental love, but only knows one face and one lap towards which it stretches its arms for refuge and nurture.   Eliot, *Silas Marner*, II

Learning has the same effect on the mind that strong liquors have on the constitution; both tending to eradicate all our natural fire and energy.   Fielding, H., *Amelia*, II

Were we to believe nothing but what we can comprehend, every man upon the face of the earth would be an atheist.   Fielding, H., *Jonathan Wild*, 114

People that don't see all, often know nothing.   Fielding, H., *Joseph Andrews*, 83

It is as possible for a man to know something without having been at school, as it is to have been at school and to know nothing.   Fielding, H., *Tom Jones*, 311

Men of true learning, and almost universal knowledge, always compassionate the ignorance of others; but fellows who excel in some little, low, contemptible art, are always certain to despise those who are unacquainted with that art.   *Ibid.*, 399

Think of the sunny spaces in the world's history, in each of which one could linger forever—to become a citizen of any one age means a lifetime of endeavor.
Gissing, *A Life's Morning*, I

Might one not learn more in one instant of unreflecting happiness than by toiling on to a mummied age, only to know in the end the despair of never having lived?   *Ibid.*

Knowledge is to the strong.   Haggard, *She*, X

What is the first result of man's increased knowledge interpreted from Nature's book by the persistent effort of his purblind observation? Is it not but too often to make him question the existence of his Maker, or, indeed, of any intelligent purpose beyond his own?   *Ibid.*

Growing up brought responsibilities, he found. Events did not rhyme quite as he had thought. Nature's logic was too horrid for him to care for. That mercy towards one set of creatures was cruelty towards another sickened his sense of harmony.
Hardy, *Jude the Obscure*, Part I, II

All knowledge is dangerous. It matters not that the law prohibits teaching [slaves] to read. Oral instruction is as dangerous as written; and the catechism is nothing but a Bible in disguise.   Hildreth, *Slave*, Volume I, XIX

People who are long before they see a thing, when once it strikes them, see it in the strongest light.   Jenner, *The Placid Man*, I

The fields of air are open to knowledge. Only ignorance and idleness need crawl upon the ground.   Johnson, *Rasselas*, 32

The life devoted to knowledge passes silently away and is little diversified by events.
Ibid., 38

To talk in public, to think in solitude, to read and to hear, to inquire and answer inquiries, is the business of a scholar. *Ibid.*

The scholar wanders about the world without pomp or terror, and is neither known nor valued but by men like himself. *Ibid.*

We can not hope to move those with delight or terror whose interests and opinions we do not understand. *Ibid.*, 48

Knowledge will always predominate over ignorance, as man governs the other animals.
Ibid., 52

Knowledge is one of the means of pleasure, as is confessed by the natural desire which every mind feels of increasing its ideas. *Ibid.*, 54

We always rejoice when we learn and grieve when we forget. *Ibid.*

If nothing counteracts the natural consequence of learning, we grow more happy as our minds take a wider range. *Ibid.*

Knowledge is more than equivalent to force. *Ibid.*, 63

Knowledge is nothing but as it is communicated. *Ibid.*, 133

Men advanced far in knowledge do not love to repeat the elements of their art.
Ibid., 172

Open your heart to the influence of the light which from time to time breaks in upon you. *Ibid.*, 177

If that which is known may be overruled by that which is unknown, no human being can arrive at certainty. *Ibid.*, 185

An uninformed man is a monster.
Lawrence, H., *The Life and Adventures of Common Sense*, II

Is it not far better to abhor sins by the remembrance of others' faults, than by repentance of thine own follies? Lyly, *Euphues*, 96

When we reach the summit of knowledge, we begin to discover that human knowledge is so imperfect, as not to warrant any vanity upon it.
Mackenzie, *The Man of the World*, I

The knowledge which teaches men to live among people of civility and manners is preferable to any other. Manley, *Zarah*, II

Suspect first and know next. True knowledge comes but by suspicion and revelation.
Melville, *Confidence-Man*, XVII

Since a wise man will keep even some certainties to himself, much more some suspicions, at least he will at all events so do till they ripen into knowledge. *Ibid.*

I seldom care to be consistent. In a philosophical view, consistency is a certain level at all times, maintained in all the thoughts of one's mind. But, since nature is nearly all hill and dale, how can one keep naturally advancing in knowledge without submitting to the natural inequalities in the progress? *Ibid.*, XXXVI

In this world, men must provide knowledge before it is wanted.
Melville, *Israel Potter*, IX

Much of the knowledge we seek, already we have in our cores. Yet so simple it is, we despise it; so bold, we fear it. Melville, *Mardi*, CLXXV

The ocean we would sound is unfathomable; and however much we add to our line, when it is out, we feel not the bottom. *Ibid.*

Wherefore have Gloom and Grief been celebrated of old as the selectest chamberlains to knowledge? Wherefore is it, that not to know Gloom and Grief is not to know aught than an heroic man should learn?
Melville, *Pierre*, Book IX, III

The uninstructive are the humanly deficient: they remain with us like the tolerated old aristocracy, which may not govern, and is but socially seductive.
Meredith, *The Amazing Marriage*, XX

You always learn something new from educated people.
Meredith, *The Ordeal of Richard Feverel*, XXV

Our most diligent pupil learns not so much as an earnest teacher.
Ibid.

Can one learn to convey consolation to the dying, to teach the ignorant, to comfort the sorrowful? Are these matters to be acquired by study, like Greek verbs or intricate measures?
Oliphant, *The Rector*, III

They supplied the place of knowledge by converting conjectures into dogmas; an art which is not yet lost.
Peacock, *The Misfortunes of Elphin*, VI

Great knowledge of the world, or, what is often mistaken for it, an acquaintance with the higher circles and with the topics of the day.
Radcliffe, *The Romance of the Forest*, 368

We have all much to learn: let us try and teach one another as kindly as we can.
Reade, *Griffith Gaunt*, XVI

I have heard famous scholars often and often say very silly things; but I thought they did it out of humility, and in condescension to those who had not their learning.
Richardson, *Clarissa Harlowe*, I

Her knowledge must be all theory.
Ibid., II

Knowledge by theory only is a vague uncertain light: a will-o'-the-wisp, which as often misleads the doubting mind as puts it right.
Ibid., III

Those who know least are the greatest scoffers.
Ibid., IV

Early love of roguery makes rakes run away from instruction; and so they become mere smatterers in the sciences they are put to learn; and, because they *will* know no more, think there is no more to be known.
Ibid.

Is it a necessary consequence that knowledge, which makes a man shine, should make a woman vain and pragmatical? May not two persons, having the same taste, improve each other?
Richardson, *Sir Charles Grandison*, One, I

No one despises learning that has pretensions to it.
Ibid.

Shakespeare is an adept in the superior learning, the knowledge of nature.
Ibid., Three, VI

A little knowledge leads to vanity and conceit.
Ibid.

The condescending magnanimity which superior knowledge can always afford to show to ignorance.
Schreiner, *The Story of an African Farm*, Part II, IV

A mind of moderate capacity which closely pursues one study must infallibly arrive at great proficiency in that study.
Shelley, *Frankenstein*, IV

Of what a strange nature is knowledge! It clings to the mind when it has once seized on it like a lichen on the rock.
Ibid., XIII

Knowledge in most of its branches and in most affairs is like music in an Italian street, whereof those may partake who pay nothing.
Sterne, *A Sentimental Journey*, 13

Let no man say from what tags and jags hints may not be cut out for the advancement of human knowledge.
Sterne, *Tristram Shandy*, VI

Little knowledge is got by mere words.
Ibid., IX

The most accomplished way of using books at present is twofold: Either first, to serve them as some men do lords, learn their titles exactly, and then brag of their acquaintance. Or secondly, which is indeed the choicer, the profounder, and politer method, to get a thorough insight into the index, by which the whole book is governed and turned, like fishes by the tail. For to enter the palace of learning at the great gate requires an expense of time and forms; therefore men of much haste and little ceremony are content to get in by the back door. Swift, *A Tale of a Tub*, VII

A knowledge of the world cures one of unreasonable pride.
Taylor, *Hannah Thurston*, VIII

There is no royal road to learning, no short cut to the acquirement of any valuable art.
Trollope, *Barchester Towers*, XX

You should know a man seven years before you poke his fire.
Trollope, *The Eustace Diamonds*, XXVI

You do not ask a child whether he would like to learn his lesson. At any rate, you do not wait till he cries for his book. Trollope, *Phineas Finn*, XXXV

There are only two kinds of people who are really fascinating—people who know absolutely everything, and people who know absolutely nothing.
Wilde, *The Picture of Dorian Gray*, VII

Knowledge is the best riches that man can possess. Without it, he is a brute; with it, he is a god. But like happiness, he often pursues it without finding it; or, at best, obtains of it but an imperfect glimpse. It is not that the road to it is either dark or difficult, but that he takes a wrong one; or if he enters on the right, he does so unprepared for the journey. Wright, *A Few Days in Athens*, IX

Knowledge of the world is not knowledge of man. *Ibid.*

That only is real, is sterling knowledge, which goes to make us better and happier men, and which fits us to assist the virtue and happiness of others. *Ibid.*

All learning is useful, all the sciences are curious, all the arts are beautiful; but more useful, more curious, and more beautiful, is the perfect knowledge and perfect government of ourselves. Wright, *Ibid.*

True knowledge embraces the whole universe. Young, *The Adventures of Emmera*, I

LABOR: *see also* ACTION; ACTIVITY; PROFESSION

A man's field of labor is his country. Meredith, *Harry Richmond*, XXVIII

Men shall never live wealthily where all things be common. For how can there be abundance of goods, or of anything, where every man withdraweth his hand from labor?
More, *Utopia*, I

He cannot be happy who involuntarily is bound either to work, or starve; and yet he may be said to be happier whose daily labor supplies his daily want than one obliged to want for years together. Morris, *John Daniel*, 243

In labor, the more one doth exercise it, the more by the doing one is enabled to do, strength growing upon the work. Sidney, *Arcadia*, III

Labor is the seed of idleness. Swift, *A Tale of a Tub*, VIII

LANGUAGE: *see also* EXPRESSION; etc.

His face was its language. Collins, *The Woman in White*, Part II, Third Epoch

She was dry and sandy with working in the graves of deceased languages. None of your live languages for Miss Blimber. They must be dead—stone dead—and then Miss Blimber dug them up like a ghoul. Dickens, *Dombey and Son*, XI

"What's the water in French, sir?" "*L'Eau*," replied Nicholas. "Ah!" said Mr. Lillyvick, shaking his head mournfully, "I thought as much. Lo, eh? I don't think anything of that language—nothing at all."   Dickens, *Nicholas Nickleby*, XVI

There is a language in the kindly eye and the honest brow which all men may understand.
                                                    Doyle, *Micah Clarke*, XXXIV

The voice of the inanimate! Who shall translate for us the language of the stones?
                                                    Dreiser, *Sister Carrie*, XI

One language helps another; even the smattering of a dead language is better than no extra language at all.   DuMaurier, *The Martian*, Part Ninth

"Ah, there are so many things monsieur must want to say: difficult things!" "Everything I want to say is difficult. But you give [French] lessons?"   James, H., *The American*, I

Informal language on formal subjects is altogether contrary to logic.
                                                    Judd, *Margaret*, Volume II, II

A feature of the Typee language is the different senses in which one and the same word is employed; its various meanings all have a certain connection, which only makes the matter more puzzling. So one brisk, lively little word is obliged, like a servant in a poor family, to perform all sorts of duties.   Melville, *Typee*, XXX

Language is not fitted to express emotion. Passion rejects it.
                                                    Meredith, *The Egoist*, VII

There is an art can speak without words; unfettered by the penman's limits, it can steal through the eye into the heart and brain alike of the learned and unlearned; and it can cross a frontier or a sea, yet lose nothing. It is at the mercy of no translator; for it writes an universal language.   Reade, *The Cloister and the Hearth*, XL

Thy language hath in its indifferent bluntness something which cannot be reconciled with the horrors it seems to express.   Scott, *Ivanhoe*, XXIII

LAUGHTER: *see also* EMOTION; HUMOR; etc.

Take care not to laugh, when there is nothing to laugh at.
                                                    Brackenridge, *Modern Chivalry*, Part II, I

Weeds are put off at a fair; no heart bursts but in secret; it is good to laugh, though the laugh be hollow; and wise to make merry, now and for aye. Laugh, and make friends: weep, and they go. Women sob, and are rid of their grief: men laugh, and retain it. There is laughter in heaven, and laughter in hell. And a deep thought whose language is laughter. Though wisdom be wedded to woe, though the way thereto is by tears, yet all ends in a shout. But wisdom wears no weeds; woe is more merry than mirth; 'tis a shallow grief that is sad. Ha! ha! how demoniacs shout; how all skeletons grin; we all die with a rattle.   Melville, *Mardi*, CLXXXIII

We must laugh or we die; to laugh is to live. Not to laugh is to have the tetanus. Will you weep? then laugh while you weep. For mirth and sorrow are kin; are published by identical nerves.   *Ibid.*

Laughter, let it be but genuine, is of a common nationality, indeed a common fireside; and profound disagreement is not easy after it.
                                                    Meredith, *The Amazing Marriage*, XXXIV

They laugh who win.   Meredith, *The Ordeal of Richard Feverel*, II

Devils dare not laugh at whom angels crowd to contemplate.   *Ibid.*, XXXIII

Though angels smile, shall not devils laugh!   *Ibid.*

LAW: *see also* JUSTICE; etc.

Law and equity are of little weight, where force is supreme.
                                                    Anonymous, *Memoirs of the Court of H—*, 69

The will of sovereigns is generally admitted as a law. *Ibid.*

Even when a defenseless town is given up to be sacked and pillaged, military men do not put helpless women and children to the sword with that just proportion of coolness with which a hangman ties the fatal noose, or a lawyer draws up a brief by which he beggars the wretched family he is employed against.

Anonymous, *Memoirs of the Life of Tsonnonthouan*, II

Law does not seem like law at all when one knows the makers of it.

Atherton, *Senator North*, Book II, IX

The law as a special science is obsolete. Bellamy, *Looking Backward*, XIX

When a witness has answered well, let the answer rest.

Brackenridge, *Modern Chivalry*, Part II, I

Law is an image of war; and as in war, the greatest praise is to discharge your duty wherever it may be assigned. *Ibid.*

It were better to have no judges than to have no laws, or at least as bad. Arbitrary discretion is a blind guide. *Ibid.*

What necessity on a point of law to read all cases, that have relation to the subject? To give a lecture on the elementary principle, and adduce cases, from the first decision to the last. *Ibid.*

It is the practice that makes the law. *Ibid.*, Part II, Volume II

The least suspicion in the minds of a jury that the passions are attempted will excite distrust of even a good argument. *Ibid.*, Part II, Volume IV

Safe behind that impenetrable shield the law, the scurviest rascals upon earth make a scurvy use of their scurvy tongues. Bridges, *The Adventures of a Bank-Note*, I

Is it better to drive a fellow-creature to despair than to transgress a mere human law— no man being injured by the breach? Bronte, C., *Jane Eyre*, XXVII

Laws and principles are not for the times when there is no temptation: they are for moments when body and soul rise in mutiny against their rigor; stringent are they; inviolate they shall be. If at my individual convenience I might break them, what would be their worth? *Ibid.*

The law is very obliging, but more polite than efficient.

Bulwer, *Pompeii*, Book IV, XVII

Woman *versus* lawyer: In the courts, lawyer would win; but in a private parlor, foot to foot, and tongue to tongue, lawyer has not a chance.

Bulwer, *What Will He Do With It?*, Book X, III

This Legality is not able to set thee free from thy burden.

Bunyan, *Pilgrim's Progress*, 24

The law was made for poltroons: a man of honor does not know what it means.

Burney, *Camilla*, Three, VI

Ill luck of any kind, or even ill treatment at the hands of others, is considered an offense against society [in Erewhon], inasmuch as it makes people uncomfortable to hear of it. Loss of fortune, therefore, or loss of some dear friend on whom another was much dependent, is punished hardly less severely than physical delinquency.

Butler, *Erewhon*, X

You may say that it is your misfortune to be criminal; I answer that it is your crime to be unfortunate. *Ibid.*, XI

The crime of having been maligned unjustly. *Ibid.*

What is the offense of a lamb that we should rear it, and tend it, and lull it into security, for the express purpose of killing it? Its offense is the misfortune of being something which society wants to eat, and which cannot defend itself. *Ibid.*, XII

Rule Forty-two. *All persons more than a mile high to leave the court.*
Carroll, *Alice in Wonderland*, XII

Sentence first—verdict afterwards. *Ibid.*

The Law is still, in certain inevitable cases, the pre-engaged servant of the long purse.
Collins, *The Woman in White*, Part I, First Epoch

It is the great beauty of the Law that it can dispute any human statement, made under any circumstances, and reduced to any form. *Ibid.*

He who is in the clutches of the law may think himself lucky if he escape with the loss of his tail. Cooper, *The Monikins*, Conclusion

Nature has created inequalities in men and things, and, as human institutions are intended to prevent the strong from oppressing the weak, *ergo*, the laws should encourage natural inequalities as a legitimate consequence. *Ibid.*

The laws of nature having made one man wise and another man foolish, this strong and that weak, human laws should reverse it all by making another man wise and one man foolish, that strong and this weak. *Ibid.*

When the law of the land is weak, it is right the law of nature should be strong.
Cooper, *The Prairie*, VIII

The arm of the law reaches far, and though its movements are sometimes slow, they are not the less certain. *Ibid.*, XXXI

Juries have the effect of placing the control of the law in the hands of those who would be most apt to abuse it. Cooper, *The Redskins*, IX

Society is doing very well in its work of bravely lawing away at Nature.
Crane, *The Third Violet*, XXXII

Law and all forms of law are only deductions made by the intelligence from the right instincts of the people's heart. Crawford, *A Rose of Yesterday*, XIII

I look upon many of our courts as one huge machinery for legalizing injustice.
Daniel, *Ai*, XXVIII

The man who has had an injustice done him in the name of the law is generally a poor man—that is the reason he has been squeezed. He had no money, and could not hold out.
Ibid.

"Suffer any wrong that can be done you, rather than come here!" (to the Court of Chancery) Dickens, *Bleak House*, I

This scarecrow of a suit has, in course of time, become so complicated, that no man alive knows what it means. The parties to it understand it least; but it has been observed that no two Chancery lawyers can talk about it for five minutes, without coming to a total disagreement as to all the premises. *Ibid.*

Jarndyce and Jarndyce still drags its dreary length before the Court, perennially hopeless. *Ibid.*

The Court is, by solemn settlement of law, our grim old guardian, and we are to suppose that what it gives us (when it gives us anything) is our right. It is not necessary to quarrel with our right. *Ibid.*, XIV

I expect a Judgment. On the day of Judgment. *Ibid.*

It is only by resenting [wrongs done to me], and by revenging them in my mind, and by angrily demanding the justice I never get, that I am able to keep my wits together. It's in my nature to do it, and I must do it. There's nothing between doing it, and sinking into the smiling state of the poor little mad woman that haunts the Court. If I was to sit down under it, I should become imbecile. *Ibid.*, XV

Women are at the bottom of all that goes wrong in the world, though, for the matter of that, they create business for lawyers. *Ibid.*, XVI

The one great principle of the English law is, to make business for itself. *Ibid.*, XXXIX

Chancery knows no wisdom but in Precedent. *Ibid.*

Even an innocent man must take ordinary precautions to defend himself. *Ibid.*, LII

It does not become us, who assist in making the laws, to impede or interfere with those who carry them into execution. Or who vindicate their outraged majesty. *Ibid.*, LIII

We are not musical in the law. *Ibid.*, LX

To a man possessed of the higher imaginative powers, the objection to legal studies is the amount of detail which they involve. Dickens, *David Copperfield*, XXXIX

In the taking of legal oaths, deponents seem to enjoy themselves mightily when they come to several good words in succession, for the expression of one idea; as, that they utterly detest, abominate, and abjure, or so forth. *Ibid.*, LII

The nature of the law: immoral. Dickens, *The Mystery of Edwin Drood*, XVIII

The arm of the law is a strong arm, and a long arm. *Ibid.*

The long arm of the law will reach, and the strong arm will strike. *Ibid.*

One of nature's beacons, warning off those who navigated the shoals and breakers of the World, or of that dangerous strait the Law, and admonishing them to seek less treacherous harbors and try their fortune elsewhere.
Dickens, *The Old Curiosity Shop*, XXXV

"You are the more guilty of the two, in the eye of the law; for the law supposes that your wife acts under your direction." "If the law supposes that, the law is a ass—a idiot. If that's the eye of the law, the law is a bachelor; and the worst I wish the law is, that his eye may be opened by experience—by experience."
Dickens, *Oliver Twist*, LI

Never mind the character, and stick to the alleybi. Nothing like a alleybi, nothing.
Dickens, *Pickwick Papers*, XXXIII

"Take the book in your right hand this is your name and handwriting you swear that the contents of this your affidavit are true so help you God a shilling you must get change I haven't got it." *Ibid.*, XL

The have-his-carcase, next to the perpetual motion, is the vun of the blessedest things as wos ever made. *Ibid.*, XLIII

Laws say: "Be allured, if you will, by everything lovely, but draw not nigh unless by righteousness." Convention says: "You shall not better your situation save by honest labor." Dreiser, *Sister Carrie*, XLVII

The Irish all love law. It is a kind of lottery, in which every man, staking his own wit or cunning against his neighbor's property, feels that he has little to lose, and much to gain.
Edgeworth, *Castle Rackrent*, 75

Nothing can be more demoralizing in the long run than lynch law. And yet lynch law often originates in a burst of generous indignation which is not willing to suffer a bold oppressor to escape by means of corrupt and cowardly courts. It is oftener born of fear.
Eggleston, *The Hoosier Schoolmaster*, XXXII

There's no rules so wise but what it's a pity for somebody or other.
Eliot, *Adam Bede*, Epilogue

I wouldn't make a downright lawyer o' the lad,—I should be sorry for him to be a raskill.
Eliot, *The Mill on the Floss*, Book I, II

Mr. Tulliver was a strictly honest man, and proud of being honest, but he considered that in law the ends of justice could only be achieved by employing a stronger knave to frustrate a weaker. Law was a sort of cock-fight, in which it was the business of injured honesty to get a game bird with the best pluck and the strongest spurs.

Ibid., Book II, II

There are men whose brains have not yet been dangerously heated by the loss of a lawsuit, who are apt to see in their own interest or desires a motive for other men's actions. *Ibid.*, Book III, I

There are certain animals to which tenacity of position is a law of life,—they can never flourish again, after a single wrench: and there are certain human beings to whom predominance is a law of life,—they can only sustain humiliation so long as they can refuse to believe in it, and, in their own conception, predominate still.

Ibid., Book III, I

The law's made to take care o' raskills. *Ibid.*, Book III, IV

We should have no law but the inclination of the moment. *Ibid.*, Book VI, XIV

It will probably be objected that imperfections do not lie in the laws themselves, but in the ill execution of them; but this appears to be no less an absurdity than to say of any machine that it is excellently made, though incapable of performing its functions.

Fielding, H., *Amelia*, I

Good laws should execute themselves in a well-regulated state. *Ibid.*

The judge was never indifferent in a cause but when he could get nothing on either side.
Ibid.

There are none whose conduct should be so strictly watched as that of bailiffs, these necessary evils in the society, as their office concerns for the most part those poor creatures who cannot do themselves justice, and as they are generally the worst of men who undertake it. *Ibid.*, II

A man of honor wears his law by his side. *Ibid.*

The lawyer I write of is not only alive, but hath been so these four thousand years. He hath not confined himself to one profession, one religion, or one country; but when the first mean selfish creature appeared upon the human stage, who made self the centre of the whole creation, would give himself no pain, incur no danger, advance no money, to assist or preserve his fellow-creatures; then was our lawyer born; and, whilst such a person exists on earth, so long shall he remain upon it.

Fielding, H., *Joseph Andrews*, 159

A hundred lawyers could not alter the law. *Ibid.*, 242

The utmost in the power of a lawyer is to prevent the law's taking effect. *Ibid.*

The depusition of James Scout, on of his magesty's justasses. *Ibid.*, 274

Here, reader, I beg your patience a moment, while I make a just compliment to the great wisdom and sagacity of our law, which refuses to admit the evidence of a wife for or against her husband. This would be the means of creating an eternal dissension between them. It would, indeed, be the means of much perjury, and of much whipping, fining, imprisoning, transporting, and hanging. Fielding, *Tom Jones*, 61

When a lawgiver sets down plainly his whole meaning, we are prevented from making him mean what we please ourselves. *Ibid.*, 93

It will be much wiser to submit to a few inconveniences arising from the dispassionate deafness of laws, than to remedy them by applying to the passionate open ears of a tyrant. *Ibid.*, 587

That greatest of evils—the giving of different sentences for the same crimes.
Fuller, *A. D. 2000*, XIV

There is no such thing as irrelevant testimony. *Ibid.*

311

I have heard a lawsuit compared to a country dance, in which, after a great bustle and regular confusion, the parties stand still, all tired, just on the spot where they began.
Galt, *Ayrshire*, I

Wealth and despotism easily know how to engage those laws as the coadjutors of their oppression which were perhaps at first intended for the safeguards of the poor.
Godwin, *Caleb Williams*, I

We, who are thieves without a license, are at open war with another set of men, who are thieves according to law.
Ibid., III

To make laws complete they should reward as well as punish.
Goldsmith, *The Vicar of Wakefield*, 151

The law does not consult the ease of individuals, but the good of the whole.
Graves, *The Spiritual Quixote*, II

The law never varies. The cases never agree. The law is general. The case is individual. The penalty of the law is uniform. The justice or injustice of the case is continually different.
Holcroft, *Hugh Trevor*, III

The English law never began to get hold of the idea that a crime was not necessarily a sin, till Hadfield, who thought he was the Saviour of mankind, was tried for shooting at George the Third.
Holmes, *Elsie Venner*, XV

Treat bad men exactly as if they were insane. They are *in-sane*, out of health, morally.
Ibid.

The quickest way to get rid of a bad law is to enforce it.
Howells, *A Modern Instance*, XXIV

The road is like a lawsuit; round-about, full of puddles and pitfalls, and long to travel.
Hudson, *The Purple Land*, X

It's a poor rule that won't work both ways.
James, H., *The American*, XXIV

When we pursue our end by lawful means, we may always console our miscarriage by the hope of future recompense.
Johnson, *Rasselas*, 129

The judicial delay is often a severer grievance than the wrong could have been.
Johnstone, *The Pilgrim*, I

Lawyers may say anything for their fee.
Johnstone, *The Reverie*, I

The law holds people answerable when they are sober for what they do when they are intoxicated.
Judd, *Margaret*, Volume II, IX

The laws are the guardians of human happiness.
Kahlert, *The Necromancer*, III

I know law too well in practice to be moved by any theories about it.
Kingsley, *Alton Locke*, XXXIV

Laws are no law, but tyranny, when the few make them, in order to oppress the many by them.
Ibid.

Doth not law accuse if it be not rightly interpreted?
Lyly, *Euphues*, 152

To lawyers we owe the wonderful style of oratory known as "congressional," that unique combination of inflated verbiage with appeals to the lowest considerations of self-interest and prejudice.
Macnie, *The Diothas*, Conclusion

A good defense is not always good against a bad accusation.
Marryat, *Peter Simple*, LXII

There seems a reason in all things, even in law.
Melville, *Moby Dick*, XC

As at sea no appeal lies beyond the captain, he too often makes unscrupulous use of his power. And as for going to law with him at the end of the voyage, you might as well go to law with the Czar of Russia.
Melville, *Redburn*, LII

A law should be universal, and include in its possible penal operations the very judge himself who gives decisions upon it; nay, the very judge who expounds it.

Melville, *White Jacket*, XXXV

The law was not made for the captain. *Ibid.*, LXXII

The Law is always, and must ever be, the Law of the stronger.

Meredith, *One of Our Conquerors*, I

Among boys there are laws of honor and chivalrous codes, not written, or formally taught, but intuitively understood by all, and invariably acted upon by the loyal and the true. The race is only half-civilized, we must remember.

Meredith, *Ordeal of Richard Feverel*, VI

Rank was much: money was much: but law was more. In this country, law was above the sovereign. To tamper with the law was treason to the realm. *Ibid.*, XI

There's no law possible without wine. Law is an occupation which dries the blood.

Ibid., XX

The law of the Church coincides very closely with the law of Nature.

Moore, *Evelyn Innes*, XXXI

In Utopia every man is a cunning lawyer. For they have very few laws; and the plainer and grosser that any interpretation is, that they allow as most just.　More, *Utopia*, II

Justice was with him, but the law was against him.　Peacock, *Nightmare Abbey*, III

The law in this land slays an honest man, an' if he do but steal. What follows? He would be pitiful, but is discouraged therefrom; pity gains him no pity, and doubles his peril; an' he but cut a purse, his life is forfeit; therefore cutteth he the throat to boot, to save his own neck; dead men tell no tales.　Reade, *The Cloister and the Hearth*, XXV

The case against me is like a piece of rotten wood varnished all over. It looks fair to the eye, but will not bear handling.　Reade, *Griffith Gaunt*, XLII

She had learned that the law will not allow even a woman to say anything and everything with impunity. She had been in a court of justice, and seen how gravely, soberly, and fairly, an accusation is sifted there, and, if false, annihilated; which, elsewhere it never is.　*Ibid.*, XLV

The law asserts not itself till it is offended.　Richardson, *Clarissa Harlowe*, I

To demand is not to litigate.　*Ibid.*

Law-breakers have the advantage of law-keepers all the world over.　*Ibid.*, II

Who so proper to assist in making new laws as those no law could hold?　*Ibid.*

Law and Gospel are two very different things.　*Ibid.*

In courts of justice, character acquits or condemns as often as facts, and sometimes even in spite of facts.　*Ibid.*, III

The laws of truth and justice are always the same.

Richardson, *Sir Charles Grandison*, One, II

Laws were not made so much for the direction of good men, as to circumscribe the bad.

Ibid., Two, III

"*Dies inceptus* means that a term-day is not begun till it's ended." "That sounds like nonsense." "Maybe so; but it may be very good law for all that."

Scott, *Guy Mannering*, IX

A lawyer without history or literature is a mechanic, a mere working mason; if he possesses some knowledge of these, he may venture to call himself an architect.

Ibid., XXXVII

As the law binds us, the law should loose us.　Ibid., XXXIX

In civilized society, law is the chimney through which all that smoke discharges itself that used to circulate through the whole house and put everyone's eyes out—no wonder, therefore, that the vent itself should sometimes get a little sooty.　*Ibid.*

The blow which the law aims cannot be broken by directly encountering it, but it may
be turned aside. Scott, *The Heart of Midlothian*, XV

Lawyers are necessary evils. Scott, *Redgauntlet*, VI

Law is a lickpenny—no counselor like the pound in purse.
Scott, *St. Ronan's Well*, XXVIII

He whom ambition or hope of personal advantage has led to disturb the peace of a well-
ordered government, let him fall a victim to the laws. Scott, *Waverley*, XXXII

It's agin natur' and reason, and a man's own seven senses, to reckon on any man's right
to make laws for another, when he don't live in the same country with him.
Simms, *The Scout*, XIII

The laws of the land don't follow out the laws of God. Simms, *Woodcraft*, XLII

In a democracy, you may pull the nose of the law, at pleasure, but you must be prepared
to pay well for any such liberty taken with the nose of its officer.
Ibid., LIX

Shun going to law as you would shun the devil; and look upon all attorneys as devouring
sharks or ravenous fish of prey. Smollett, *Peregrine Pickle*, 305

Ignorance, idleness, and vice are the proper ingredients for qualifying a legislator; laws
are best explained, interpreted, and applied by those whose interest and abilities lie in
perverting, confounding, and eluding them. Swift, *Gulliver's Travels*, Brobdingnag

I said there was a society of men among us, bred up from their youth in the art of
proving by words multiplied for the purpose, that white is black, and black is white,
according as they are paid. To this society all the rest of the people are slaves.
Ibid., Houyhnhnms

Neither society nor religion requires men to do right always. Such a rule might do for
angels, but not men. Society and religion merely demand that men shall obey the law.
Tourgee, *Murvale Eastman*, XLII

The law's mysterious authority. Trollope, *He Knew He Was Right*, LII

He knew his own laws just as other people so often know the laws; by words, not by
effects. They take a *meaning*, and get to be very vivid, when you come to apply them to
yourself. Twain, *Connecticut Yankee*, XXXIV

LEADING/FOLLOWING

The sun lets every planet take its course; and so did George Washington. His forte was
"the not doing too much." Brackenridge, *Modern Chivalry*, Part II, I

The virtue of the world is not mainly in its leaders. In the midst of the multitude which
follows there is often something better than in the one that goes before.
Holmes, *Elsie Venner*, VI

No one who aspires to the honorable office of leading another by the nose can tolerate a
party to his ambition. Meredith, *Ordeal of Richard Feverel*, XXIV

To be far in advance of the mass is as fruitless to mankind as straggling in the rear. For
how do we know that they move behind us at all? Or move in our track? What we win for
them is lost; and where we are overthrown we lie. *Ibid.*, XXXVII

LEISURE: *see also* LABOR

Old Leisure was quite a different personage. He only read one newspaper, innocent of
leaders, and was free from that periodicity of sensations which we call post-time. He
was a contemplative, rather stout gentleman, of excellent digestion; of quiet perceptions, undiseased by hypothesis; happy in his inability to know the causes of things,

preferring the things themselves. He lived chiefly in the country, among pleasant seats and homesteads, and was fond of sauntering by the fruit-tree wall and scenting the apricots when they were warmed by the morning sunshine, or of sheltering himself under the orchard boughs at noon, when the summer pears were falling. He knew nothing of weekday services, and thought none the worse of the Sunday sermon if it allowed him to sleep from the text to the blessing; liking the afternoon service best, because the prayers were the shortest, and not ashamed to say so; for he had an easy, jolly conscience, broad-backed like himself, and able to carry a great deal of beer or port-wine, not being made squeamish by doubts and qualms and lofty aspirations. Life was not a task to him, but a sinecure. He fingered the guineas in his pocket, and ate his dinners, and slept the sleep of the irresponsible, for had he not kept up his character by going to church on the Sunday afternoons? Eliot, *Adam Bede*, LII

LEVITY: *see also* HUMOR; LAUGHTER; etc.

Nothing like a little judicious levity. Stevenson, *The Wrong Box*, VII

LIBERALISM; LIBERALITY: *see also* DEMOCRACY; FREEDOM; GENEROSITY

He had liberality, and he had the means of exercising it.
Austen, *Pride and Prejudice*, Volume III, X

The most liberal studies may be pursued to an illiberal excess.
Brackenridge, *Modern Chivalry*, Part I, IV

There are few doors through which liberality, joined with good humor, cannot find its way. Johnson, *Rasselas*, 97

What is called liberality is often no more than the vanity of giving, of which some persons are fonder than of what they give. Lennox, *Sophia*, II

Liberalism stakes too much on the chance of gain.
Meredith, *Beauchamp's Career*, XXVIII

LIBERTINISM

It is one characteristic of the libertine that he detests marriage, for it is the immutable consequence attendant on the long pursuit of vicious and ignoble pleasures, which unhinge the mind, and unfit the soul for the calm delights of virtue.
Dacre, *The Libertine*, XVII

The errors of the libertine are too frequently so imbued with the character, as to be invincible to the operation of time, experience, conscience, or reason, and to end but with the life of the wretched being they tyrannize over. *Ibid.*, XIX

He in a few minutes ravished this fair creature, or at least would have ravished her, if she had not, by a timely compliance, prevented him.
Fielding, H., *Jonathan Wild*, 147

Man and libertine are synonymous terms. Gibbes, *Francis Clive*, II

Libertines are nicer than other men. Richardson, *Clarissa Harlowe*, II

Though I am a rake, I am not a rake's friend. *Ibid.*

Libertines hardly ever reform but by miracle, or by incapacity. *Ibid.*

A libertine must be remorseless—unjust he must always be. *Ibid.*

Hard-heartedness is an essential of the libertine's character. *Ibid.*

Familiarized to the distresses he occasions, the libertine is seldom betrayed by tenderness into a complaisant weakness unworthy of himself. *Ibid.*

Who expects consistency in libertines? *Ibid.*

There never were libertines so vile but purposed to set about reforming. *Ibid.*

Libertines put no other bound to their views than what want of power gives them.
Ibid.

An honest prowling fellow is a necessary evil on many accounts. It is highly requisite that a sweet girl should be now and then drawn aside by him. The more eminent the girl, in the graces of person, mind, and fortune, the more efficacious is the example likely to be. *Ibid.*, III

If he could not make sport, he would spoil none. *Ibid.*

As a rake, I have done no more than prosecute the maxims by which rakes are governed; maxims which I have pursued from pretty girl to pretty girl, as fast as I had set one down, taking another up; just as the fellows do with the flying coaches and flying horses at a country fair, with a "Who rides next! Who rides next!" *Ibid.*

The rake is used to indifference and coldness in the very midst of his happiest prospects. *Ibid.*, III

What others call blame, the rake calls praise; and discharges shame, that cold-water damper to an enterprising spirit. *Ibid.*

A young rake is hardly tolerable; but an old rake, and an old beau, are two very sad things. Richardson, *Pamela*, 396

LIFE; LIVING: *see also* DEATH; *JOIE DE VIVRE*; etc.

We have got to get by the lions, first. Alcott, *Little Women*, V

People don't have fortunes left them nowadays; men have to work, and women to marry for money. It's a dreadfully unjust world. *Ibid.*, XV

Life is like plumcakes. In some the plums are all on the top, and we eat them gaily, till we suddenly find they are gone. In others the plums sink to the bottom, and we look for them in vain as we go on, and often come to them when it is too late to enjoy them. But in the well-made cake, the plums are wisely scattered all through, and every mouthful is a pleasure. We make our own cakes, in a great measure. Alcott, *Old-Fashioned Girl*, XVII

All that the world gives may be taken away. Anonymous, *The History of Tom Jones in His Married State*, 270

Books are too heterogeneous an interest to furnish a vital soul in life, a reason for being alive. Atherton, *The Californians*, Book I, XII

One of life's compensations is that there is always something ahead. Atherton, *Senator North*, Book III, VII

Life could do nothing for her beyond giving time for a better preparation for death. Austen, *Sense and Sensibility*, Volume II, IX

The life of every man is a diary in which he means to write one story, and writes another; and his humblest hour is when he compares the volume as it is with what he vowed to make it. Barrie, *The Little Minister*, I

He did not think that it was necessary to make a hell of this world to enjoy paradise in the next. Beckford, *Vathek*, 127

Your soul sleeps; the shock is yet to be given which shall awaken it. You think all existence lapses in as quiet a flow as that in which your youth has hitherto slid away. Floating on with closed eyes and muffled ears, you neither see the rocks bristing not far off in the bed of the flood, nor hear the breakers boil at their base. But I tell you—you will come some day to a craggy pass of the channel, where the whole of life's stream will be broken up into whirl and tumult, foam and noise: either you will be dashed to atoms on crag points, or lifted up and borne on by some master wave into a calmer current. Bronte, C., *Jane Eyre*, XV

Life is still life, whatever its pangs. Bronte, C., *Villette*, XXIV

If life be a war, it seemed my destiny to conduct it single-handed. *Ibid.*, XXVI

Life is said to be all disappointment. *Ibid.*, XXXII

Life is so constructed that the event does not, cannot, will not match the expectation.
Ibid., XXXVI

What is life but an intermitted pool at quadrille? Brooke, *Emily Montague*, IV

Life, like poverty, has strange bedfellows. Bulwer, *The Caxtons*, Book IV, IV

Life is a drama, not a monologue. *Ibid.*, Book VI, I

In every life, go it fast, go it slow, there are critical pausing-places. When the journey is renewed the face of the country is changed.
Bulwer, *What Will He Do With It?*, Book V, X

Dig but deep enough, and under all earth runs water, under all life runs grief.
Ibid., Book VI, IV

Sensible people get the greater part of their own dying done during their own lifetime. A man at five and thirty should no more regret not having had a happier childhood than he should regret not having been born a prince of the blood.
Butler, *The Way of All Flesh*, XXIV

Life is not a donkey race in which everyone is to ride his neighbor's donkey and the last is to win. *Ibid.*, XXXIII

Ever drifting down the stream—/ Lingering in the golden gleam—/ Life, what is it but a dream? Carroll, *Through the Looking Glass*, last lines

We must not soar too far above the earth, while she offers us the rich treasures of her fruit trees and vines. Child, *Philothea*, III

The taste of life's delirium. Chopin, *The Awakening*, XVIII

She felt as if a mist had been lifted from her eyes, enabling her to look upon and comprehend the significance of life, that monster made up of beauty and brutality.
Ibid., XXVIII

In this curious little world of ours, we enjoy our lives on infernally hard terms. We live on condition that we die. Collins, *Blind Love*, XLIV

Never think of anything until you have first asked yourself if there is an absolute necessity for doing it, at that particular moment. Thinking of things, when things needn't be thought of, is offering an opportunity to Worry; and Worry is the favorite agent of Death when the destroyer handles his work in a lingering way, and achieves premature results. Never look back, and never look forward, as long as you can possibly help it. Looking back leads the way to sorrow. And looking forward ends in the cruelest of all delusions: it encourages hope. The present time is the precious time. Live for the passing day: the passing day is all that we can be sure of.
Collins, *The Legacy of Cain*, XLII

It is one of my rules in life never to notice what I don't understand.
Collins, *The Moonstone*, First Period, VI

Human life is a sort of target—misfortune is always firing at it, and always hitting the mark. *Ibid.*, First Period, XV

The problem of life seemed too voluminous for the narrow limits of human speech, and by common consent it was abandoned to the great sea that had from the beginning enfolded it in its immense grip; to the sea that knew all, and would in time infallibly unveil to each the wisdom hidden in all the errors, the certitude that lurks in doubts, the realm of safety and peace beyond the frontiers of sorrow and fear.
Conrad, *Nigger of the Narcissus*, V

Land draws life away. *Ibid.*

Life is but a graver sort of mummery, and the second of its rarest secrets is to make others fancy us what we wish to appear—the first being, without question, the faculty of deceiving ourselves.   Cooper, *The Headsman*, XVI

What is the life of man, that he desires to prolong it?—What imperious duty can compel us to be miserable?   Dacre, *Passions*, Letter XCII

On the rampage, and off the rampage—such is life!   Dickens, *Great Expectations*, XV

The wayfarer in the toilsome path of human life sees, with each returning sun, some new obstacle to surmount, some new height to be attained. Distances stretch out before him which, last night, were scarcely taken into account, and the light which gilds all nature with its cheerful beams, seems but to shine upon the weary obstacles that yet lie strewn between him and the grave.   Dickens, *Nicholas Nickleby*, LIII

Life in a wig is, to a large class of people, much more terrifying and impressive than life with its own head of hair.   Dickens, *The Old Curiosity Shop*, LXIII

Living by his wits means by the abuse of every faculty that, worthily employed, raises man above the beasts, and so degraded, sinks him far below them.
                                        Ibid., Chapter the Last

Strange life mine—rather curious history—not extraordinary, but singular.
                                        Dickens, *Pickwick Papers*, II

People need to rise early, to see the sun in all his splendor, for his brightness seldom lasts the day through. The morning of day and the morning of life are but too much alike.   *Ibid.*, V

Recalled to life.   Dickens, *A Tale of Two Cities*, Book I, II

Life's a tumbleabout thing of ups and downs.   Disraeli, *Sybil*, Book VI, VIII

Life is a feudal tenure, for which nature exacts homage.
                                        Donaldson, *Sir Bartholomew Sapskull*, II

Life isn't cast in a mould—not cut out by rule and line, and that sort of thing.
                                        Eliot, *Middlemarch*, Book I, IV

The clue of life.   Eliot, *The Mill on the Floss*, Book VI, XIV

Life may as properly be called an art as any other; and the greast incidents in it are no more to be considered as mere accidents than the several members of a fine statue or a noble poem.   Fielding, H., *Amelia*, I

The most useful of all arts, the art of life.   *Ibid.*

As sweet as life is, people ought to take care to live sweetly.   *Ibid.*

There are moments of life worth purchasing with worlds.   *Ibid.*

The actual means of existence are the property of all.   Godwin, *Caleb Williams*, III

A life of leisure is often an active and a busy life.   Godwin, *St. Leon*, 257

Life is a battle; but it is so only in the sense that a game of chess is—there is no seriousness in it; it may be put an end to at any inconvenient moment by owning yourself beaten, with a careless "Ha-ha!" and sweeping your pieces into the box.
                                        Hardy, *The Hand of Ethelberta*, XVII

A just conception of life is too large a thing to grasp during the short interval of passing through it.   Hardy, *A Pair of Blue Eyes*, XIX

Nobody's life is altogether a failure.   *Ibid.*

Anybody's life may be just as romantic and strange and interesting if he or she fails as if he or she succeed. All the difference is, that the last chapter is wanting in the story.
                                                       Ibid.

Real life never arranges itself exactly like a romance.

Hawthorne, *The Blithedale Romance*, XII

Life and death together make sad work for us all. *Ibid.*, XXVII

Life is made up of marble and mud. Hawthorne, *The House of the Seven Gables*, II

Life is only estimable as it is useful. Of what value is a jewel locked up in a casket, or a light burning in a dead man's tomb? Helme, *St. Margaret's Cave*, Volume II, X

Life is a game of calculation; and he that plays the best of it is the cleverest fellow.

Holcroft, *Hugh Trevor*, III

Wisdom, science, power, learning—all these are as blind and impotent before the great problem of life as ignorance and weakness. Holland, *Arthur Bonnicastle*, XXVII

Never was a galley-slave so chained as we are to these four and twenty oars, at which we must tug day and night all our life long! Holmes, *A Mortal Antipathy*, XXIII

I hate all dreams of perpetual peace, all wonderful cities of the sun, where people consume their joyless monotonous years in mystic contemplations, or find their delight like Buddhist monks in gazing on the ashes of dead generations of devotees. The state is one unnatural, unspeakably repugnant: the dreamless sleep of the grave is more tolerable to the active, healthy mind than such an existence.

Hudson, *The Purple Land*, XXVIII

Life is full of cares and anxieties; man has occasion for, and a right to make use of, many expedients to make it pass on with tolerable ease. Jenner, *The Placid Man*, II

If a man will live in the world, he must live like the world. *Ibid.*

Human life is everywhere a state in which much is to be endured, and little to be enjoyed. Johnson, *Rasselas*, 55

To him that lives well every form of life is good, nor can there be given any other rule for choice than to remove from all apparent evil. *Ibid.*, 86

Let us cease to dispute, and learn to live. *Ibid.*, 91

He that attempts to change the course of his own life very often labors in vain.

Ibid., 113

While you are making the choice of life, you neglect to live. *Ibid.*, 116

Commit yourself to the current of the world. *Ibid.*, 134

Nothing is more common than to call our own condition the condition of life.

Ibid., 170

They were contented to be driven along the stream of life, without directing their course to any particular port. *Ibid.*, 189

Human life is like a shadow, no sooner seemingly enjoyed than vanished.

McCarthy, *The Fair Moralist*, 3

Life takes its complexion from inferior things; and providence has wisely placed its real blessings within the reach of moderate abilities. Mackenzie, *Julia De Roubigné*, 41

Life is a picnic *en costume*. Melville, *Confidence-Man*, XXIV

Toil is man's allotment. Melville, *Mardi*, LXIII

One moment lived, is a life. *Ibid.*, CLXXXV

Our lives are our Amens. *Ibid.*, CLXXXVII

The mingled, mingling threads of life are woven by warp and woof: calms crossed by storms, a storm for every calm. There is no steady unretracing progress in this life.

Melville, *Moby Dick*, CXIV

This world hath a secret deeper than beauty, and Life some burdens heavier than death.

Melville, *Pierre*, Book I, II

Not always doth life's beginning gloom conclude in gladness; wedding-bells peal not ever in the last scene of life's fifth act. *Ibid.*, Book VII, VIII

Man's life seems but an acting upon mysterious hints. *Ibid.*, Book X, I

If man must wrestle, perhaps it is well that it should be on the nakedest possible plain. *Ibid.*, Book XXII, I

With the Marquesans [sleep] might almost be styled the great business of life, for they pass a large portion of their time in the arms of Somnus. The native strength of their constitutions is no way shown more emphatically than in the quantity of sleep they can endure. To many of them, indeed, life is little else than an often interrupted and luxurious nap. Melville, *Typee*, XX

In our man-of-war world, Life comes in at one gangway and Death goes overboard at the other. Melville, *White Jacket*, LXXXIII

Though long ages should elapse, and leave our wrongs unredressed, yet, shipmates and worldmates, let us never forget, that "Whoever afflict us, whatever surround, Life is a voyage that's homeward bound." *Ibid.*, The End

There is a princely view of life which is a true one; but it is a false one if it is the sole one. Meredith, *Harry Richmond*, XXVIII

Life is a tedious process of learning we are fools. Meredith, *Ordeal of Richard Feverel*, I

Life is a game of cross-purposes. *Ibid.*, XXXIII

If monotonous, the one note of the drum is very correct. Like the speaking of great Nature, what it means is implied by the measure. When the drum beats to the measure of a common human pulsation it has a conquering power: inspiring us neither to dance nor to trail the members, but to march as life does, regularly, and in hearty good order, and with a not exhaustive jollity. It is a sacred instrument. Meredith, *Sandra Belloni*, IX

United to the eternal idea of generation, he perceived the congenital idea which in remotest time seems to have sprung from it—that life is sin and must be atoned for by prayer. Moore, *Evelyn Innes*, XV

Life without a moral purpose is but a passing spectre, and our immortality lies in our religious life. *Ibid.*, XXI

As life dwindles like a flame that a breath will quench, the spirit attains its maximum, and the abiding and unchanging life that lies beyond death waxes till it becomes the real life. *Ibid.*, XXVI

Life is but a continual hypnotism; and the thoughts of others reach us from every side, determining in some measure our actions. *Ibid.*, XXXV

Our lives run in grooves; we get into one and we follow it out to the end. Moore, *A Mummer's Wife*, XXVIII

It is not possible for all things to be well, unless all men were good. More, *Utopia*, I

"The original unsophisticated man was by no means constructive. He lived in the open air, under a tree." "The tree of life." Peacock, *Headlong Hall*, V

Life is a school, and the lesson never done. Reade, *The Cloister and the Hearth*, XLIII

Those who want the fewest earthly blessings most regret that they want any. Richardson, *Clarissa Harlowe*, I

A handful of good life is better than a whole bushel of learning. *Ibid.*, II

He that lives well, lives long. *Ibid.*

He that lives ill one year, will sorrow for it seven. *Ibid.*

Who lives well, sees afar off. *Ibid.*

Who lives well sees into eternity. *Ibid.*

Life is a short stage where longest. *Ibid.*, IV

Life I would not put upon the perhaps involuntary twitch of a finger.
Richardson, *Sir Charles Grandison*, One, II

Can life be life, when there is no hope? *Ibid.*, Three, VII

This thing we call existence; is it not a something which has its roots far down below in the dark, and its branches stretching out into the immensity above, which we among the branches cannot see? Not a chance jumble; a living thing, a *One*. The thought gives us intense satisfaction, we cannot tell why.
Schreiner, *The Story of an African Farm*, Part II, VII

There will always be something worth living for while there are shimmery afternoons.
Ibid., Part II, XIV

Every house has its smoky chimney, its draughty room, its creaky door; every life its own haunting shadows; and every state of life its own small troubles.
Schreiner, *Undine*, IV

What a small thing it is sometimes that makes life's kiss sweeter than death's to us.
Ibid., XI

Death took the mother and Life the child. *Ibid.*, XVII

Life is obstinate and clings closest where it is most hated.
Shelley, *Frankenstein*, XXIII

Life or death is a trifling matter. Simms, *The Scout*, XXXVIII

A life's only a life. It's what we all have to pay one day or another. *Ibid.*, XXXIX

Nature asserts for herself some happy hours, even in a life which is one of unfailing sorrows. Simms, *Vasconselos*, VIII

Is life less loathsome because one learns to laugh at it as well as hate it?
Simms, *Woodcraft*, XIX

Life is a constant warfare. *Ibid.*, LVII

Life is too short to be long about the forms of it. Sterne, *A Sentimental Journey*, 62

What is the life of man? Is it not to shift from side to side?—from sorrow to sorrow?—to button up one cause of vexation—and unbutton another?
Sterne, *Tristram Shandy*, IV

Show me the man who knows what life is, who dreads it, and I'll show thee a prisoner who dreads his liberty. *Ibid.*, V

Unlike is life to novels! Stevenson, *The Wrong Box*, XIII

Lives are run in different lengths, and nobody can say what's the matter with some folks, only that their thread's run out; there's more on one spool and less on another.
Stowe, *Orr's Island*, XXXVI

In a novel, people's hearts break, and they die, and that is the end of it; and in a story this is very convenient. But in real life we do not die when all that makes life bright dies to us. Stowe, *Uncle Tom's Cabin*, XV

Are not there little chapters in everybody's life, that seem to be nothing, and yet affect all the rest of the history? Thackeray, *Vanity Fair*, VI

The true picture of life as it is, if it could be adequately painted, would show men what they are, and how they might rise, not, indeed, to perfection, but one step first, and then another on the ladder. Trollope, *The Eustace Diamonds*, XXXV

Life will not run in harmonies. Trollope, *Phineas Finn*, LI

She had been reduced, and kept in order, and made to run in a groove—and was now almost inclined to think that the world was right, and that grooves were best.

Ibid., LXII

"Are we never to get out of the old groove?" "Not if the groove is good." *Ibid.*, LXV

Who can say, in the broader view and the more intelligent weight of values, that the life of one man is not more than that of a nationality, and that there is not a tribunal where the tragedy of one human soul shall not seem more significant than the overturning of any human institution whatever?

Twain and Warner, *The Gilded Age*, Volume I, XVIII

Repute not those slain in God's cause to be dead; nay, alive with God, they are provided for. Wallace, *The Prince of India*, Volume II, Book VI

Our lives are largely made up of the things we do not have.

Warner, *A Little Journey*, XIV

There is something terribly morbid in the modern sympathy with pain. One should sympathize with the color, the beauty, the joy of life. The less said about life's sores, the better. Wilde, *The Picture of Dorian Gray*, III

He had begun by vivisecting himself, as he had ended by vivisecting others. Human life—that appeared to him the one thing worth investigating. Compared to it there was nothing else of any value. *Ibid.*, IV

One should absorb the color of life, but one should never remember its details. Details are always vulgar. *Ibid.*, VIII

The girl never really lived, and so she has never really died. *Ibid.*

Pace gives life. *Ibid.*, XVII

Life is not governed by will or intention. *Ibid.*, XIX

To walk through life innocently and tranquilly: and to look on death as its gentle termination, which it becomes us to meet with ready minds, neither regretting the past, nor anxious for the future. Wright, *A Few Days in Athens*, X

Is life short? It is an evil: But render life happy, its shortness is the *only* evil.

Ibid., XVI

To bury oneself in woods and wilds consists in nothing more than flying from those enemies we have not the courage to encounter. How much superior is the life of him who lives in the midst of vice and temptation, uncontaminated by example, untainted by the sad influence of the age! Young, *The Adventures of Emmera*, I

It is no contemptible opinion that the wisest plan, in an age so corrupted as this, is to glide through life, rather avoiding the shoals of vice than combating with them; rather attempting to preserve oneself free from infection, than empirically prescribing for the diseases of others. *Ibid.*

Suppose you were on the plan of a desert island, you might nearly put it in practice at home, and that in the midst of society. *Ibid.*

Try retirement at home. *Ibid.*

LIGHT: *see also* COMPARISON/CONTRAST

Light is the first essential. Light stimulates, nourishes, preserves. You can no more do without it, than if you were a flower.

Collins, *The Woman in White*, Part I, Second Epoch

To light a fire is the instinctive and resistant act of man when, at the winter ingress, the curfew is sounded throughout Nature. It indicates a spontaneous, Promethean rebelliousness against the fiat that this recurrent season shall bring foul times, cold darkness, misery and death. Black chaos comes, and the fettered gods of the earth say, Let there be light. Hardy, *Return of the Native*, Book I, III

What may not be expected in a country of eternal light?
Shelley, *Frankenstein*, Letter I

LIKE; DISLIKE

One is apt to say more than one would of a person one dislikes, when more is said in his favor than he can possibly deserve. Richardson, *Clarissa Harlowe*, I

Our likings and dislikings are seldom governed by prudence or with a view to happiness.
Ibid., II

Their qualifying remarks showed in their very dispraises too much liking. *Ibid.*, IV

LIMITATION

Man's gifts are not equal to his wishes. Cooper, *The Prairie*, XXII

Why have we not the wings of the pigeon, the eyes of the eagle, and the legs of the moose, if it had been intended that man should be equal to all his wishes? *Ibid.*

Every limit is a beginning as well as an ending.
Eliot, *Middlemarch*, Book VIII, Finale

LISTENING; HEARING

Sir William Lucas, and his daughter Maria, a good humored girl, but as emptyheaded as himself, had nothing to say that could be worth hearing, and were listened to with about as much delight as the rattle of the chaise.
Austen, *Pride and Prejudice*, Volume II, IV

She seldom listened to anybody for more than half a minute. *Ibid.*, Volume II, XVI

Listeners never hear anything good. Ford, *The Great K. & A. Train Robbery*, XIV

Nature has formed our ears open; but enabled us to shut up our mouths.
Kimber, *David Ranger*, I

Folks will always listen when the tale is their own.
Mackenzie, *The Man of Feeling*, 21-22

Listeners seldom hear good of themselves. Richardson, *Clarissa Harlowe*, III

LITERATURE: *see also* AUTHORSHIP; EDUCATION; KNOWLEDGE AND LEARNING; POETRY

Everything in print is right.
Anonymous, *Life and Memoirs of Ephraim Tristram Bates*, 141

There *are* books of which the backs and covers are by far the best parts.
Dickens, *Oliver Twist*, XIV

The copy that sells best will be always the best copy.
Fielding, H., *Joseph Andrews*, 67

A little space between chapters may be looked upon as an inn or resting-place.
Ibid., 73

A volume without places of rest resembles the opening of wilds or seas, which tires the eye and fatigues the spirit when entered upon. *Ibid.*

Good books always survive the bad. Fielding, H., *Tom Jones*, 266

All great books are called a great evil. *Ibid.*, 282

No man can paint a distress well which he doth not feel while he is painting it; the most pathetic and affecting scenes have been writ with tears. *Ibid.*, 418

The old Roman literature survives, and creates for us an intimacy with the classic ages, which we have no means of forming with the subsequent ones.

Hawthorne, *The Marble Faun*, XVIII

A bad composition carries with it its own punishment.   Lewis, *The Monk*, 157

Light literature is the garden and the orchard, the fountain, the rainbow, the far view; the view within us as well as without. The choice public will have good writing for light reading.   Meredith, *The Tragic Comedians*, VI

To brand a book with infamy is to insure its sale.   Ridley, *James Lovegrove*, I

Tell me, ye learned, shall we forever be adding so much to the bulk, so little to the stock?

Sterne, *Tristram Shandy*, V

LOGIC: *see also* DEDUCTION; REASON; etc.

Trust a boat on the high seas to bring out the Irrational that lurks at the bottom of every thought, sentiment, sensation, emotion.   Conrad, *Lord Jim*, X

The person who can join ideas with the most propriety will separate them with the greatest nicety.   Fielding, S., *David Simple*, I

There is no logic like the logic of the heart.   Lennox, *Henrietta*, I

Hers was a nature more reasoning than creative and poetic; and whatever she believed bound her mind in strictest claims to its logical results. She delighted in the regions of mathematical knowledge and walked them as a native home.

Stowe, *The Minister's Wooing*, XXIII

LONELINESS: *see also* COMPANY; SOLITUDE

What loneliness is more lonely than distrust?   Eliot, *Middlemarch*, Book V, XLIV

It is very lonesome at the summit, like a man's life, when he has climbed to eminence.

Hawthorne, *The Marble Faun*, XXVIII

There might be a more miserable torture than to be solitary forever. Think of having a single companion in eternity, and instead of having any consolation, or at all events variety of torture, to see your own weary, weary sin repeated in that inseparable soul.

Ibid., XXXIII

In calm weather, to swim in the open ocean is as easy to the practiced swimmer as to ride in a spring-carriage ashore. But the awful lonesomeness is intolerable. The intense concentration of self in the middle of such a heartless immensity, my God! who can tell it?   Melville, *Moby Dick*, XCIII

Ahab stands alone among the millions of the peopled earth, nor gods nor men his neighbors!   *Ibid.*, CXXXIII

LOSS

Small things are more easily lost than great.

Brackenridge, *Modern Chivalry*, Part II, I

LOVE; AFFECTION: *see also* FRIENDSHIP; HATE; MARRIAGE; etc.

Love is the great magnet of life, and religion is love.   Adams, H., *Esther*, VII

Love is a flower that grows in any soil.   Alcott, *Little Men*, XXI

Gentlemen are sometimes seized with sudden fits of admiration for the young relatives of ladies whom they honor with their regard; but this counterfeit philoprogenitiveness sits uneasily upon them, and does not deceive anybody a particle.

Alcott, *Little Women*, XLV

Honesty is the best policy in love as in law. *Ibid.*

Love and labor, two beautiful old fashions that began long ago, with the first pair in Eden. Alcott, *Old-Fashioned Girl*, XIX

Love and a bottle were his taste. Amory, *John Buncle*, II

So fearful is love, so bashful is virginity, that neither has the courage to reveal what each languishes to make known. Annesley, *An Unfortunate Young Nobleman*, I

The path of poetry is the direct road to love.
Anonymous, *The Adventures of an Author*, I

Love, which softens the heart of the most savage and obdurate tyrant, sometimes tempts the most generous mind to wander from the path that leads to virtue and honor.
Anonymous, *The Birmingham Counterfeit*, II

Love is of every age. *Ibid.*

Love, in general, arises from the pleasure which all men naturally take in whatever they judge or perceive to be good and perfect. *Ibid.*

To be wise and love is hardly granted to the gods above. Anonymous, *The Egg*, 55

Love is capricious and involuntary; reason cannot direct its choice.
Anonymous, *Fatal Friendship*, I

Love levels all distinction. *Ibid.*, II

Love is an encroacher. *Ibid.*

Charity and religion can be made to fit every shape.
Anonymous, *The Fruitless Repentance*, I

Every moment of time solicits to be employed in the important business of love.
Anonymous, *The History of the Human Heart*, 105

Love is as ingenious to torment as to flatter.
Anonymous, *Memoirs of an Oxford Scholar*, 28

My love is subject to fear, but a stranger to suspicion. *Ibid.*, 41-42

Old people may talk of subjecting love to reason, young ones cannot. *Ibid.*, 119

Self-love is our ruling passion. Anonymous, *The Modern Fine Gentleman*, I

We are no more able to direct the choice upon which our love is fixed than we can alter our taste for a pineapple, or a nectarine, into an aversion for those fruits, or into a liking or fondness for wormwood or rhubarb.
Anonymous, *Peregrinations of Jeremiah Grant*, 296

Nothing can add to a woman's looks like a lover. Anonymous, *Sophronia*, 17

Love is the soul of harmony, the connecting chain that links the whole frame of being; it is the glory of nature, and the very perfection of human kind.
Anonymous, *The Wanderer*, II

A man to love one woman must love all women. Atherton, *Doomswoman*, XXIV

The last test of highest love, passion without sensuality. *Ibid.*, XXV

Love is not passion, for one may feel that for many women; not affection, for friendship demands that. Not even sympathy and comradeship; one can find either with men.
Ibid., XXVI

As soon as a man awakens a woman's passions she begins to idealize him and there is no limit to the virtues he will be made to carry. Atherton, *Senator North*, Book I, XVIII

If love is the very best thing in life, it is not the only thing. *Ibid.*, Book II, VII

If a woman does not love at once, it takes a long time to teach her what love is.
Ibid., Book II, X

Any man can make a woman of feeling love him if he loves her enough and she has no antipathy to him. *Ibid.*, Book III, V

When a man loves, he has no past. There are no experiences alive in his memory to help him to philosophy. *Ibid.*, Book III, VII

One cannot love hopelessly and look one's best. Nature demands some tribute in spite of the strongest will. *Ibid.*, Book III, X

Love unblended with any kind of ambition is unnatural, and the latter is frequently the father of the former. August, *Horrid Mysteries*, III

Chance is as unpropitious as favorable to lovers. *Ibid.*, IV

The enthusiasm of a woman's love is even beyond the biographer's.
Austen, *Mansfield Park*, Volume Two, IX

If it be true that no young lady can be justified in falling in love before the gentleman's love is declared, it must be very improper that a young lady should dream of a gentleman before the gentleman is first known to have dreamt of her.
Austen, *Northanger Abbey*, III

Where the heart is really attached, one can be little pleased with the attention of anybody else. Everything is insipid, uninteresting, that does not relate to the beloved object. *Ibid.*, VI

To be fond of dancing was a certain step towards falling in love.
Austen, *Pride and Prejudice*, Volume I, III

There is so much of gratitude or vanity in almost every attachment, that it is not safe to leave any to itself. *Ibid.*, Volume I, VI

In nine cases out of ten, a woman had better shew *more* affection than she feels. *Ibid.*

Next to being married, a girl likes to be crossed in love a little now and then. It is something to think of, and gives her a sort of distinction among her companions.
Ibid., Volume II, I

That expression of "violently in love" is as often applied to feelings which arise from an half-hour's acquaintance, as to a real, strong attachment.
Ibid., Volume II, II

Is not general incivility the very essence of love? *Ibid.*

You are too sensible to fall in love merely because you are warned against it.
Ibid., Volume II, III

I was in the middle [of love] before I knew that I had begun.
Ibid., Volume III, XVIII

Is nothing due to the man whom we have all so much reason to love and no reason in the world to think ill of? Austen, *Sense and Sensibility*, Volume I, XV

Hush! Love is here. Barr, *Maid*, XIV

At twenty-one a man is a musical instrument given to the other sex, but it is not as instruments learned at school, for when she sits down to it she cannot tell what tune she is about to play. That is because she has no notion of what the instrument is capable.
Barrie, *The Little Minister*, XV

A young man thinks that he alone of mortals is impervious to love, and so the discovery that he is in it suddenly alters his views of his own mechanism. It is thus not unlike a rap on the funnybone. *Ibid.*, XIX

Is not love God's doing? *Ibid.*, XXIII

To know him is to love him. Barrie, *Tommy and Grizel*, XXXV

To be is an irregular verb in all languages, but always regular is the verb *to love*.

Bates, *Puritans*, XII

Love is liable to ten million suits for breach of warranty.

Bellamy, *Dr. Heidenhoff's Process*, V

Surely the spiritual and the carnal love are not so widely different as I have been taught to think them. They are, perhaps, not antagonistic, and are but expressions of the same will.

Bierce, *Monk*, XVII

In all matters of love there is a vast amount of luck.

Blackmore, *Dariel: A Romance of Surrey*, XIV

Love is a phrenzy.

Brackenridge, *Modern Chivalry*, Part I, Volume I

Coolness in love is a great secret of success.

Ibid., Part I, Volume III

There is a kind of natures in the world—and very noble, elevated natures, too—whom love never comes near.

Bronte, C., *Shirley*, XII

A girl's affections should never be won unsought.

Bronte, A., *The Tenant of Wildfell Hall*, XVI

It does good to no woman to be flattered by her superior, who cannot possibly intend to marry her; and it is madness in all women to let a secret love kindle within them, which, if unreturned and unknown, must devour the life that feeds it; and, if discovered and responded to, must lead, *ignis-fatuus*-like, into miry wilds whence there is no extrication.

Bronte, C., *Jane Eyre*, XVI

Keep to your caste; and be too self-respecting to lavish the love of the whole heart, soul, and strength, where such a gift is not wanted and would be despised.   *Ibid.*, XVII

"Prove yourself true ere I cherish you," was his ordinance.

Bronte, C., *Villette*, XXX

Deeper than melancholy lies heartbreak.

Ibid., XXXVII

Love is an intellectual pleasure, and even the senses will be weakly affected where the heart is silent.

Brooke, *Emily Montague*, I

If moralists would improve human nature, they should endeavor to expand, not to contract the heart. They should build their system on the passions and affections, the only foundations of the nobler virtues.   *Ibid.*, III

There is always some injustice mixed with love.   *Ibid.*

Love throws round beauty almost the rays of divinity.   *Ibid.*

Love has a thousand ways of making himself understood.   *Ibid.*, IV

Your love is from the imagination, not the heart.   *Ibid.*

Love, like virtue, is not only its own reward, but sometimes entitles us to other rewards too.   *Ibid.*

Love seldom visits us but at the sober invitation of our judgment. It speedily takes its leave when its presence becomes uneasy, and its gratification ineligible or impossible.

Brown, C. B., *Alcuin*, III

Love has made many a patient.   Brown, C. B., *Arthur Mervyn*, II

For those who know that life is made up of business and care, spun out in long years, not counted by the joys of an hour, love is a folly.   Bulwer, *Harold*, Book IV, V

She loves melancholy and subduing music; she sighs without an outward cause. This may be the beginning of love—it may be the want of love.

Bulwer, *Pompeii*, Book One, IV

In every time, in every state, love can find space for its golden altars.

Ibid., Book Two, IV

The love which visits the happy and the hopeful hath but freshness on its wings; its violence is but sportive. *Ibid.*, Book Three, IV

Love in a woman must destroy her rights of equality—it gives to her a sovereign even in one who would be inferior to her if her love did not glorify and crown him.
Bulwer, *The Parisians*, Part I, Book I

Why is it that the noblest of our passions should be also the most selfish?
Bulwer, *Pelham*, LXVIII

Dame Nature, raise thine arm somewhat out of everyday reach, and bring me down that obsolete, neglected, unconsidered thing, love between Age and Childhood.
Bulwer, *What Will He Do With It?*, Book III, XXIII

The most submissive where they love may be the most stubborn where they do not love.
Ibid., Book IV, V

The learned compute that seven hundred and seven millions of millions of vibrations have penetrated the eye before the eye can distinguish the tints of a violet. What philosophy can calculate the vibrations of the heart before it can distinguish the colors of love? *Ibid.*, Book VIII, II

"The course of true love never does run smooth." May it not be because when there are no obstacles, there are no tests to the truth of love? Ships fitted for rough weather are those built and stored for long voyage. *Ibid.*, Book XI, I

He's a girl's man, just the very thing, all sentiment and poetry and heroics.
Burney, *Camilla*, Two, III

Is being in love anything beyond being very fond, and very silly, and with a little touch of melancholy? *Ibid.*, Three, VI

What is so credulous as self-love? *Ibid.*, Four, VIII

'Tis the very deuce and all for a man to be in love when he is poor. *Ibid.*, Five, IX

Love is prodigious for quickness. Burney, *Cecilia*, III

Who can love any man whose liver is out of order?
Butler, *The Way of All Flesh*, VI

'Tis better to have loved and lost, than never to have lost at all. *Ibid.*, LXXVII

Some boys are born lovers. From the time they can reach out from the nurse's arms, they must be billing and cooing and choosing a mate. Cable, *Bonaventure*, Book I, II

Man proposes, Cupid disposes. Cable, *Ibid.*, Book III, VII

God has written on every side of our nature,—on the mind, on the soul, yes, and in our very flesh,—the interdict forbidding love to have any one direction only, under penalty of being forever dwarfed. *Ibid.*, Book III, IX

God be praised for love's young dream. Cable, *The Grandissimes*, LX

"'Tis love, 'tis love, that makes the world go round!" "Somebody said that it's done by everybody minding their own business." Carroll, *Alice in Wonderland*, IX

There are times when, to a lover's mind, love dwarfs all ordinary laws.
Chesnutt, *The House Behind the Cedars*, XXX

Custom is tyranny; love is the only law. *Ibid.*, XXXIII

The fetters of love are a flowery bondage. Blossoms do not more easily unfold themselves to the sunshine. Child, *Philothea*, IV

Philothea had drunk freely from those abundant fountains of joy in the human soul, which remain hidden till love reveals their existence, as secret springs are said to be discovered by a magic wand. *Ibid.*, VI

Do you suppose a woman knows why she loves? Chopin, *The Awakening*, XXVI

When love is out of the question, the head, uninfluenced by the heart, is generally pretty cool, and numerical. Cleland, *Memoirs of a Coxcomb*, 84

Love, that made me timid, taught me to be tender too.
Cleland, *Memoirs of a Woman of Pleasure*, 42

Blind Love doth never wholly die. Collins, *Blind Love*, Epilogue

Successful love may sometimes use the language of flattery. But hopeless love always speaks the truth. Collins, *Moonstone*, Second Period, V

If love is a weakness, it is at least the noblest weakness we are liable to.
Collyer, *Felicia to Charlotte*, I

Can one imagine a loathsome insect in love? Conrad, *Lord Jim*, XXIX

Love does not express itself by tirade. Cooke, *Virginia Comedians*, Volume I, XII

Lovers are wholly destitute of conscience, magnanimity, common sense, and ordinary courtesy. *Ibid.*, Volume II, XXXVII

Heart-sickness is the worst kind of sickness. *Ibid*, Volume II, XXXVIII

The man who loves, and loves truly, should not long permit its object to remain in any doubt of his feelings and intentions. Cooper, *Satanstoe*, Volume I, XIII

Stratagems are excusable in love, as in war. *Ibid.*, Volume II, XII

He was thinking. To go to the devil—to go to the devil—to go to the devil with this girl was not a bad fate—not a bad fate—not a bad fate. Crane, *Active Service*, XVII

The mind of a lover moves in a circle, or at least on a more circular course than other minds, some of which at times even seem to move almost in a straight line.
Ibid., XXVIII

No man of middle-aged experience can ever be in love. Crane, *The O'Ruddy*, XXI

Irishmen are able to remain in love to a very great age. *Ibid.*

Love is beauty. Crawford, *Khaled*, III

Real love can only arise where there is either a void in the breast, occasioned by the falsehood or indifference of a once favorite object, or where love before has never been admitted. Dacre, *Passions*, Letter XLIII

The crime of loving is, when that love leads us on to the injury of others. *Ibid.*, LX

He repeated it several times, that he was in love with me, and my heart spoke as plain as a voice, that I liked it. Defoe, *Moll Flanders*, 16

I acted as if there was no such thing as any kind of love but that which tended to matrimony. *Ibid.*, 19

Where love is the case, the doctor's an ass. *Ibid.*, 43

She loves enough that does not hate. *Ibid.*, 77

In wars the sorer the fight is, the greater is the glory of the victory; and the harder a woman is to be won, the sweeter is her love when it is obtained.
Deloney, *The Gentle Craft*, 73

A true hearted lover forgets all trespasses, and a smile cureth the wounding of a frown.
Ibid., 82

Fire in straw will not be hidden, and the flames of affection will burst forth at length, though it be long kept under. *Ibid.*, 143

It is small discretion for a woman to disclose her secret affection in an open assembly.
Deloney, *Jack of Newbury*, 327

Real love and truth are stronger in the end than any evil or misfortune.
Dickens, *David Copperfield*, XXXV

Love must suffer in this stern world. *Ibid.*, XXXVIII

My love was founded on a rock, and it endures. *Ibid.*, XLV

It is not in the nature of pure love to burn so fiercely and unkindly long.
Dickens, *Dombey and Son*, XVIII

Filial love, in its stern beauty. *Ibid.*, XXXVII

Real love is blind devotion, unquestioning self-humiliation, utter submission, trust and belief against yourself and against the whole world, giving up your heart and soul to the smiter. *Dickens, Great Expectations*, XXIX

The true lover's mind is completely permeated by the beloved object of his affections.
Dickens, *Mystery of Edwin Drood*, XI

Mystery and disappointment are not absolutely indispensable to the growth of love, but they are, very often, its powerful auxiliaries. Dickens, *Nicholas Nickleby*, XL

Is selfishness a necessary ingredient in the composition of that passion called love, or does it deserve all the fine things which poets, in the exercise of their undoubted vocation, have said of it? *Ibid.*, XLIII

I always loved that boy as if he'd been my-my-my own grandfather.
Dickens, *Oliver Twist*, LI

At this stage of the affair the poor girl respectfully intimated that she was secretly engaged to that popular character whom the novelists and versifiers call Another, and that such a marriage would make Dust of her heart and Dust of her life.
Dickens, *Our Mutual Friend*, Book I, II

Love, though said to be afflicted with blindness, is a vigilant watchman.
Ibid., Book II, XI

Love is in all things a most wonderful teacher. *Ibid.*, Book IV, XI

The most interesting and pardonable of human weaknesses—love.
Dickens, *Pickwick Papers*, I

The recollection of what he had been to her awakened feelings of forbearance and meekness under suffering in her bosom, to which all God's creatures, but women, are strangers. *Ibid.*, VI

Never sign a walentine with your own name. *Ibid.*, XXXIII

Sam was not to be dissuaded from the poetical idea that had occurred to him, so he signed the letter, "Your love-sick Pickwick." *Ibid.*

Tobacco is the tomb of love. Disraeli, *Sybil*, Book II, XVI

We are all born for love. It is the principle of existence, and its only end.
Ibid., Book V, IV

Love is all a woman has to give, but it is the only thing which God permits us to carry beyond the grave. Dreiser, *Sister Carrie*, XIX

She might have been said to be imagining herself in love, when she was not. Women frequently do this. It flows from the fact that in each exists a bias toward affection, a craving for the pleasure of being loved. The longing to be shielded, bettered, sympathized with, is one of the attributes of the sex. This, coupled with sentiment and a natural tendency to emotion, often makes refusing difficult. It persuades them that they are in love. *Ibid.*, XXIII

Love is a stronger passion than vanity. Edgeworth, *The Absentee*, VI

A man does not always love most what he admires. Eggleston, *Roxy*, LVI

It's a deep mystery—the way the heart of man turns to one woman out of all the rest he's seen i' the world, and makes it easier for him to work seven year for *her*, like Jacob did for Rachel, sooner than have any other woman for th' asking.   Eliot, *Adam Bede*, III

We canna love just where other folks 'ud have us. There's nobody but God can control the heart of man.   *Ibid.*, IV

Love has a way of cheating itself consciously, like a child who plays at solitary hide-and-seek; it is pleased with assurance that it all the while disbelieves.   *Ibid.*, XI

The vainest woman is never thoroughly conscious of her own beauty till she is loved by the man who sets her own passion vibrating in return.   *Ibid.*, XV

It is hardly an argument against a man's general strength of character that he should be apt to be mastered by love. A fine constitution doesn't insure one against smallpox or any other of those inevitable diseases.   *Ibid.*, XVI

Adam was mistaken about her. Like many other men, he thought the signs of love for another were signs of love towards himself.   *Ibid.*, XX

We are all very much alike when we are in our first love.   *Ibid.*, XXVI

A woman may get to love by degrees—the best fire dosna flare up the soonest.
     Ibid., XXX

In all ages it hath been a favorite text that a potent love hath the nature of an isolated fatality, whereto the mind's opinions and wonted resolves are altogether alien. Yet all love is not such, even though potent; nay, this passion hath as large scope as any for allying itself with every operation of the soul: so that it shall acknowledge an effect from the imagined light of unproven firmaments, and have its scale set to the grander orbits of what hath been and shall be.   Eliot, *Daniel Deronda*, XXXII

Even a man who has practiced in lovemaking till his own glibness has rendered him skeptical, may at last be overtaken by the lover's awe.   *Ibid.*, LXIII

The beloved lover is always called happy, and happiness is considered as a well-fleshed indifference to sorrow outside it.   *Ibid.*, LXIX

The remote worship of a woman throned out of their reach plays a great part in men's lives, but in most cases the worshipper longs for some queenly recognition, some approving sign by which his soul's sovereign may cheer him without descending from her high place.   Eliot, *Middlemarch*, Book II, XXII

If I loved, I should love at once and without change.   *Ibid.*, Book III, XXXI

Young lovemaking—that gossamer web!   *Ibid.*, IV, XXXVI

That simple, primitive love which knits us to the beings who have been nearest to us, in their times of helplessness or of anguish.   Eliot, *Mill on the Floss*, Book III, I

The need of being loved would always subdue her.   *Ibid.*, Book VI, IV

Love does not aim simply at the conscious good of the beloved object: it is not satisfied without perfect loyalty of heart; it aims at its own completeness.
     Eliot, *Romola*, Book II, XXVIII

Perfect love has a breath of poetry which can exalt the relations of the least-instructed human beings.   Eliot, *Silas Marner*, XVI

Men are often blind to the passions of women; but every woman is as quick-sighted as a hawk on these occasions, nor is there one article in the whole science of love which is not understood by all women.   Fielding, H., *Amelia*, I

Every virtue is often made the instrument of effecting the most atrocious purpose of this all-subduing tyrant, love.   *Ibid.*

There is no greater vulgar error than that it is impossible for a man who loves one woman ever to love another. On the contrary, it is certain that a man who can love one woman so well at a distance will love another better that is nearer to him.   *Ibid.*, II

Love can make a molehill appear as a mountain, a Jew's-harp sound like a trumpet, and a daisy smell like a violet.   Fielding, H., *Joseph Andrews*, 29

Love has wings.   *Ibid.*, 40

Lady Booby loved Joseph long before she knew it; and now loved him much more than she suspected.   *Ibid.*, 257

No woman will plead the passion of love for an excuse.   Fielding, H., *Tom Jones*, 19

All persons are doomed to be in love once in their life.   *Ibid.*, 30

Out of strict conformity with the Stoic philosophy, we shall here treat the affair of love as a disease.   *Ibid.*, 149

Mr. Western grew every day fonder and fonder of his daughter, insomuch that his beloved dogs themselves almost gave place to her in his affections.   *Ibid.*, 149-150

Love may be likened to a disease in this, that when it is denied a vent in one part, it will certainly break out in another.   *Ibid.*, 166

Certain philosophers, among many other wonderful discoveries, pretend to have found out that there is no such passion as love in the human breast.   *Ibid.*, 214

Esteem and gratitude are the proper motives to love, as youth and beauty are to desire.
                                                                              Ibid., 216

Love frequently preserves from the attacks of hunger.   *Ibid.*, 435

The too inordinate fondness of a father, an amiable weakness.   *Ibid.*, 479

The passion of love is too restless to remain contented without the gratification which it receives from its object; and one can no more be inclined to love without loving than we can have eyes without seeing.   *Ibid.*, 518

Love is no more capable of allaying hunger than a rose is capable of delighting the ear, or a violin of gratifying the smell.   *Ibid.*, 620

Love is the child of love only; to love the creature who we are assured hates us is not in human nature.   *Ibid.*, 792

The professions of love must be highly esteemed where fallacious coin can pass for sterling worth.   Fielding, S., *The Countess of Dellwyn*, II

I have seen a woman wash her lover from her remembrance in less time than she could get a spot of ink out of her ruffle.   Fielding, S., *The History of Ophelia*, I

This is the only century in which love has obtained even a partial divorce from worldly and parental influences.   Ford, *The Honorable Peter Stirling*, I

The lover's fear of loss.   Garland, *Spirit*, Part III, I

Fair lady, my hand is on my heart, and yet my heart is not in mine own hands.
                                                          Gascoigne, *Master F. J.*, 17

It is hard to end the thing, whereof yet I have found no beginning.   *Ibid.*, 22

Is there any greater impediment to the fruition of a lover's delights than to be mistrusted?   *Ibid.*, 61

Where wicked lust doth bear the name of love, it doth not only infect the lightminded, but it may also become confusion to others which are vowed to constancy.   *Ibid.*, 81

I don't think love for one's mother quite comes by nature.
                                                    Gaskell, *Wives and Daughters*, XIX

It seems to be my fate never to be off with the old lover before I am on with the new.
                                                                              Ibid., LVI

Lover *versus* father! Lover wins.   *Ibid.*, LX

Love is not a passion that degrades, but exalts our nature.

Gibbes, *Mr. Francis Clive*, I

What silly nonsense love is! Why don't people write about the really important things of life?

Gissing, *New Grub Street*, XXVI

It has been said to be a peculiar felicity for anyone to be praised by a man who is himself eminently a subject of praise: how much happier to be prized and loved by a person worthy of love?

Godwin, *St. Leon*, 39

Love often entails imbecility on the noblest of mankind.

Ibid., 478

These fine sentiments, it seemed to me, had more of love than matrimony in them.

Goldsmith, *The Vicar of Wakefield*, 83

Offenses are easily pardoned where there is love at bottom.

Ibid., 131

There is no security against the encroachments of love, but by checking the first motions of the soul.

Graves, *The Spiritual Quixote*, II

Love is of the spirit and knows not death.

Haggard, *Cleopatra*, XXXI

Life is not worth the trouble of life, except when one is in love.

Haggard, *She*, I

There is only one perfect flower in the wilderness of Life, Love.

Ibid., XX

The man who works up a good income has had no time to learn love to its solemn extreme; the man who has learnt that has had no time to get rich.

Hardy, *Desperate Remedies*, III

Love, an extremely exacting usurer.

Hardy, *Far From the Madding Crowd*, IV

A lover is not a relative; and he isn't quite a stranger; but he may end in being either, and the way to reduce him to whichever of the two you wish him to be is to treat him like the other.

Hardy, *Hand of Ethelberta*, VI

New love is brightest, and long love is greatest; but revived love is the tenderest thing known upon earth.

Ibid., VIII

We don't need to know a man well in order to love him. That's only necessary when we want to leave off.

Ibid., XIX

A lover without indiscretion is no lover at all.

Ibid., XX

Lovemaking is an ornamental pursuit that matter-of-fact fellows are quite unfit for.

Ibid., XXI

These lovers—you find 'em out-o'-doors in all seasons and weathers—lovers and homeless dogs only.

Hardy, *Jude the Obscure*, Part I, VII

Sometimes a woman's *love of being loved* gets the better of her conscience, and though she is agonized at the thought of treating a man cruelly, she encourages him to love her while she doesn't love him at all. Then, when she sees him suffering, her remorse sets in, and she does what she can to repair the wrong.

Ibid., Part Four, V

Accessibility is a great point in matters of love.

Hardy, *A Laodicean*, Book I, X

Of all the miseries attaching to miserable love, the worst is the misery of thinking that the passion which is the cause of them all may cease.

Hardy, *A Pair of Blue Eyes*, IX

A man in love setting up his brains as a gauge of his position is as one determining a ship's longitude from a light at the masthead.

Ibid., XX

Love frequently dies of time alone—much more frequently of displacement.

Ibid., XXVII

Shrewdness in love usually goes with meanness in general.

Ibid., XXVIII

Fidelity in love for fidelity's sake had less attraction for her than for most women: fidelity because of love's grip had much. A blaze of love, and extinction, was better than a lantern glimmer of the same which should last long years.

Hardy, *The Return of the Native*, Book I, VII

Of love it may be said, the less earthly the less demonstrative. In its absolutely indestructible form it reaches a profundity in which all exhibition of itself is painful.

Ibid., Book III, III

Love dies, and it is just as well to strangle it in its birth; it can only die once.

Hardy, *Two on a Tower*, XIV

Many erroneous things have been written and said by the sages, but never did they float a greater fallacy than that love serves as a spur to win the loved one by patient toil.

Ibid., XV

Miss Hepzibah never had a lover—poor thing, how could she?—nor ever knew, by her own experience, what love technically means.

Hawthorne, *House of the Seven Gables*, II

People of high intellectual endowments do not require similar ones in those they love. They are just the persons to appreciate the wholesome gush of natural feeling, the honest affection, the simple joy, the fullness of contentment with what they love.

Hawthorne, *The Marble Faun*, XII

When women have other objects in life, they are not apt to fall in love.   *Ibid.*, XIII

We draw one breath; we live one life.   *Ibid.*, XIX

What a sweet reverence is that, when a young man deems his mistress a little more than mortal, and almost chides himself for longing to bring her close to his heart!   *Ibid.*, XL

It is to the credit of human nature, that, except where its selfishness is brought into play, it loves more readily than it hates. Hatred, by a gradual and quiet process will even be transformed to love, unless the change be impeded by a continually new irritation of the original feeling of hostility.   Hawthorne, *Scarlet Letter*, XIII

It is a curious subject of observation and inquiry, whether hatred and love be not the same thing at bottom. Each, in its utmost development, supposes a high degree of intimacy and heart-knowledge; each renders one individual dependent for the food of his affections and spiritual life upon another, each leaves the passionate lover, or the no less passionate hater, forlorn and desolate by the withdrawal of his subject.

Ibid., XXIV

There's nothing so good as a voyage to England to cure a love fit.

Hill, *Mr. George Edwards*, 39-40

There is no circumstance of life in which a man so much feels the advantage of having two strings to his bow as in a love affair.   *Ibid.*, 228

The study of love is very much like that of meteorology. We know that just about so much rain will fall in a season; but on what particular day it will shower is more than we can tell. We know that just about so much love will be made every year in a given population; but who will rain his young affections upon the heart of whom is not known except to the astrologers and fortune-tellers. And why rain falls as it does and why love is made just as it is are equally puzzling questions.   Holmes, *Elsie Venner*, XX

Many a woman rejects a man because he is in love with her, and accepts another because he is not.   Holmes, *Guardian Angel*, XVIII

Love is the master-key that opens the gates of happiness, of hatred, of jealousy, and, most easily of all, of *fear*.   Holmes, *A Mortal Antipathy*, XX

Love gives even to a dull man the knowledge of his lover's heart.

Hope, *Prisoner of Zenda*, XXI

When a man is in love, there's nothing else of him.   Howells, *A Modern Instance*, I

I don't see why, when it comes to falling in love, a man shouldn't fall in love with a rich girl as easily as a poor one.   Howells, *Silas Lapham*, V

The whole business of love, and lovemaking and marrying, is painted by the novelists in a monstrous disproportion to the other relations of life. *Ibid.*, XIV

Why shouldn't people in love behave sensibly? *Ibid.*, XVI

The loved object is always complicated. James, H., *Confidence*, VIII

One doesn't want a lover one pities. James, H., *Roderick Hudson*, XX

It is a mistaken notion to suppose that a third person is always an encumbrance to lovers. Jenner, *The Placid Man*, I

Formed by nature for love, the human heart sympathizes instinctively in the misfortunes too often occasioned by it. Johnstone, *Arsaces*, I

Cease to be astonished, and only learn to love—an important lesson, and one not too well learned. Judd, *Margaret*, Volume II, III

Love: an absorbing concentration on some one object, an intense movement to a single point, a gravitation of your whole being around a solitary centre. *Ibid.*, Volume II, V

When it is peculiarly fitting that some grandam, uncle, cousin, father, or guest, should retire early to bed, in order that some scheme of interest to young lovers might be successfully achieved; precisely on such nights is the perversity of fate most conspicuous, in inclining the mind of such grandam, uncle, cousin, and so forth, to sit up much longer than they are wont; thus showing that the grooves and dovetails of things in this world are not nicely fitted to the occasions of those who deal in the tender passion.
Kennedy, *Horse-Shoe Robinson*, XXXII

A true lover's blood is always at his finger's ends. Kingsley, *Westward Ho!*, VIII

One lovemaking is very like another. *Ibid.*, X

A lady was asked what she did when an admirer became too lover-like. Her answer was, "I never had such a case." I think she spoke the truth; yet she was a coquette renowned through a good part of two hemispheres. Lawrence, G. A., *Guy Livingstone*, XXXII

It is natural to wish to be beloved by those we love. Lennox, *Henrietta*, II

Where love beareth sway, friendship can have no shew. Lyly, *Euphues*, 118

The court of Cupid, wherein there be more sleights than stars in heaven. *Ibid.*, 130

Pardon me if in love I cast beyond the moon, which bringeth us women to endless moan.
Ibid., 131

As love knoweth no laws, so it regardeth no conditions. *Ibid.*, 137

He that cannot dissemble in love is not worthy to live. *Ibid.*, 146

They that kick oftenest against love are ever in love.
Lyly, *Euphues and His England*, 267

To love and to live well is wished of many , but incident to few. To live and to love well is incident to few, but indifferent to all. To love without reason is an argument of lust, to live without love, a token of folly. The measure of love is to have no mean, the end to be everlasting. *Ibid.*, 271

There is nothing in love more requisite or more delectable than pleasant and wise conference; neither can there arise any storm in love which by wit is not turned to a calm.
Ibid., 293

Tender love maketh greatest show of blossoms, but tried love bringeth forth sweetest juice. *Ibid.*, 300

Love is a poison and by poison must be maintained. *Ibid.*, 346

In love one letter is of more force than a thousand looks. *Ibid.*, 354

Nothing but love keeps maids awake. McCarthy, *The Fair Moralist*, 10

Falsehood increases love, and the true lover only is despised. *Ibid.*, 19

A knight may never be of prowess but if he be a lover.

Malory, *Le Morte DArthur*, Two, X

There was never worshipful man or worshipful woman, but they loved one better than another.   *Ibid.*, Two, XVIII

Boldness is ever a friend to love.   Manley, *Henry*, I

Cupid sometimes blinds people for their good.   Marishall, *Miss Clarinda Cathcart*, I

It is a hard thing to have loved; it is a hard thing not to have loved. But harder than all else is to lose (or fail to gain) one's lover.   Maturin, *Melmoth the Wanderer*, XXIX

I have loved ships, as I have loved men.   Melville, *Mardi*, XXXVII

Love, in the eye of its object, ever seeks to invest itself with some rare superiority.

Ibid., LI

Love is a fervent fire.   *Ibid.*, CLXXXVII

Love has more to do with posterities than with the past.

Melville, *Pierre*, Book II, IV

Man or woman who has never loved, nor once looked deep down into their own lover's eyes, they know not the sweetest and loftiest religion of this earth. Love is both Creator's and Saviour's gospel to mankind.   Melville, *Pierre*, Book II, IV

The extremest top of love is Fear and Wonder.   *Ibid.*, Book II, V

The audacious immortalities of divinest love.   *Ibid.*

A glorious, softly glorious, and most gracious evening, which seemed plainly a tongue to all humanity, saying: I go down in beauty to rise in joy; Love reigns throughout all worlds that sunsets visit; it is a foolish ghost-story; there is no such thing as misery. Would Love, which is omnipotent, have misery in his domain? Would the god of sunlight decree gloom? It is a flawless, speckless, fleckless, beautiful world throughout; joy now, and joy forever!

Ibid., Book III, III

Whatever some lovers may sometimes say, love does not always abhor a secret, as nature is said to abhor a vacuum. Love is built upon secrets, as lovely Venice upon invisible and incorruptible piles in the sea. Love's secrets, being mysteries, ever pertain to the transcendent and the infinite; and so they are as airy bridges, by which our further shadows pass over into the regions of the golden mists and exhalations; whence all poetical, lovely thoughts are engendered, and drop into us, as though pearls should drop from rainbows.   *Ibid.*, Book IV, IV

Letters of a lover in an extremity of love, crying for help, are as curious to cool strong men as the contortions of the proved heterodox tied to a stake must have been to their chastening clerical judges.   Meredith, *Beauchamp's Career*, XI

Old love reviving may be love of a phantom after all. We can, if it must revive, keep it to the limits of a ghostly love.   *Ibid.*, XXV

May not one love, not craving to be beloved? Such a love does not sap our pride, but supports it; increases rather than diminishes our noble self-esteem. To attain such a love the martyrs writhed up to the crown of saints.   *Ibid.*, XXVIII

The people verily thirst to love and reverence. Their love is the only love worth having, because it is disinterested love, and endures, and takes heart in adversity. So with a Church. It lives if it is at home with the poor.   *Ibid.*, XXIX

To love is to be on the sea, out of sight of land.   *Ibid.*, XXXV

Her instinct of love sounded her lover through, and felt the deficiency or the contrariety in him, as surely as musical ears are pained by a discord that they require no touchstone to detect.   *Ibid.*, XL

Where love exists there is goodness. *Ibid.*, LII

Does not love shun the world? Two that love must have their substance in isolation.
Meredith, *Egoist*, VII

The love of a young girl with the morning's mystery about her.
Meredith, *Harry Richmond*, XXII

There is no pure love but strong love. *Ibid.*, XXXI

Love is a dangerous malady for middle age. *Ibid.*, XXXIX

The love that survives has strangled craving; it lives because it lives to nourish and succor
like the heavens. *Ibid.*, LV

Nature and love are busy in conjunction. Meredith, *Lord Ormont*, XXIV

Love played on love in the woman's breast. *Ibid.*, XXV

Deep true love, proved by years, is the advocate. Meredith, *One of Our Conquerors*, II

Thou that thinkest thyself adored: O Fool! It is not Thou she loveth, but the Difficulty.
Meredith, *Ordeal of Richard Feverel*, I

If immeasurable love were perfect wisdom, one human being might almost impersonate
providence to another. *Ibid.*, VII

Love is that blessed wand which wins the waters from the hardness of the hearts.
Ibid., XIII

The Magnetic Age: the age of violent attractions: when to hear mention of love is
dangerous, and to see it, a communication of the disease. *Ibid.*, XVI

When Nature has made us ripe for love it seldom occurs that the Fates are behindhand in
furnishing a temple for the flame. *Ibid.*, XVII

Young love has a thousand eyes. *Ibid.*, XVIII

Love is still the cunning musician. *Ibid.*, XXIII

Every love tale is an epic war of the upper and lower powers. *Ibid.*, XXIV

Love of any human object is the soul's ordeal. *Ibid.*, XXV

Love the charioteer is easily tripped, while honest jog-trot Love keeps his legs to the end.
Ibid., XXXI

Love is love, and ever will be, in spite of fathers and mothers. *Ibid.*, XXXII

Love, with his accustomed cunning. Meredith, *Sandra Belloni*, XII

Love is the death of self. *Ibid.*, XXXVII

Love is an instrument like any other thing, and we must play on it with considerate
gentleness. *Ibid.*, XLIII

A case of a man who had two loves—a woman and his country; and both true to him.
Ibid., XLVIII

Who ever loved that loved not at first sight? Meredith, *The Tragic Comedians*, IV

The wishes of two lovers make a will. *Ibid.*, V

Strength in love is the sole sincerity. *Ibid.*, VI

At the age of forty, men that love love rootedly. If the love is plucked from them, the life
goes with it. *Ibid.*, XVI

The earth has grown weary of the sun and turns herself into the shadow, eager for rest.
The sun has been too ardent a lover. But the gaze of the sun upon the receding earth is
fonder than his look when she raised herself to his bright face.
Moore, *Evelyn Innes*, XVI

Illusions are the mirror of love. Moore, *Muslin*, IV

There is a little god called Love, that will not be worshiped of any leaden brains; one that proclaims himself sole king and emperor of piercing eyes, and chief sovereign of soft hearts. Nashe, *The Unfortunate Traveller*, 65

Many become passionate lovers only to win praise to their wits. *Ibid.*, 85

Will you cast out the devil whose name is Legion, when you cannot cast out the imp whose name is Love? Peacock, *Maid Marian*, III

Love cannot exist in a heart that has lost the meek dignity of innocence. Radcliffe, *The Mysteries of Udolpho*, I

"You know how foolish those are that love." "They are greater fools that don't." Reade, *The Cloister and the Hearth*, XXXVIII

Where pity and admiration meet, love is not far behind. Reade, *Griffith Gaunt*, XXVI

Love is not reason; love is not common sense. 'Tis a passion. *Ibid.*, XLV

Love takes the deepest root in the steadiest minds. Richardson, *Clarissa Harlowe*, I

People take high delight in finding out folks in love. *Ibid.*, I

Who knows what opportunities a man in love may give against himself? *Ibid.*, II

If I am guilty of a fault in my universal adorations of the sex, the women in general ought to love me the better for it. *Ibid.*, II

Love was ever a traitor to its harborer. *Ibid.*

Love within, and I without, she will be more than woman or I less than man if I succeed not. *Ibid.*

Love is ingenious. *Ibid.*

Love is not naturally a doubter; fear is. *Ibid.*

An acknowledged love sanctifies every freedom; and one freedom begets another. *Ibid.*

Smooth love—that is to say, a passion without rubs, a passion without passion—is like a sleepy stream that is hardly seen to give motion to a straw. *Ibid.*

True love only wishes; nor has it any active will but that of the adorable object. *Ibid.*

Love is but second to revenge. *Ibid.*

He can hardly bear your name; yet can think of nobody else. *Ibid.*

Love never goes backward. *Ibid.*, II

Nothing but the highest act of love can satisfy an indulged love. *Ibid.*

Those who most love are least set by. *Ibid.*

Are not lovers' oaths a jest of hundreds of years' standing? *Ibid.*

Love hides a multitude of faults, and diminishes those it cannot hide. *Ibid.*

Love is allowed to be an excuse for our most unreasonable follies. *Ibid.*

Love is always aspiring, always must aspire. *Ibid.*

Nothing but the highest act of love can satisfy an indulged love. *Ibid.*

Love satisfied is indifference begun. *Ibid.*

Love and compassion are hard to be separated: while anger converts what would be pity, without it, into resentment. *Ibid.*

How does this damned love unman me! *Ibid.*

Love is gentler than conscience. *Ibid.*, III

Love never was under the dominion of prudence or of any reasoning power. *Ibid.*

Love unmans and softens. *Ibid.*, IV

Love will draw an elephant through a keyhole. *Ibid.*

Where a woman loves, she seldom doubts enough for her own safety. *Ibid.*

This love is the d_____! In how many strange shapes does it make people shew themselves! Richardson, *Pamela*, 44

I should be ungrateful not to love them for their love. *Ibid.*, 102

None but the giddy love at first sight.
Richardson, *Sir Charles Grandison*, One, I

Love everybody; but not their faults. *Ibid.*

Love will creep, where it cannot go. *Ibid.*, One, II

Love is a selfish deity. *Ibid.*

Of what absurd things does love make its votaries guilty! *Ibid.*, Two, III

Love is a very subtle thing, and, like water, will work its way into the banks that are set up to confine it, if it be not watched, and dammed out in time. *Ibid.*

Platonic love is, in general, a dangerous allowance. *Ibid.*, Two, IV

Is love such a stayed, deliberate passion, as to allow a young creature to take time to ponder and weigh all the merits of its cause? *Ibid.*

Love at first sight must indicate a mind prepared for impression, and a sudden gust of passion, and that of the least noble kind; since there could be no opportunity of knowing the merit of the object. *Ibid.*

Love on one side and discretion on the other is enough in conscience; and, in short, much better than love on both sides: for what room can there be for discretion, in the latter case? *Ibid.*, Three, VI

Is not real and unaffected tenderness for the infirmities of another, the very essence of love? *Ibid.*, Three, VII

She argued poor love out of doors. She did not seem to allow the possibility of any persons being in love at all. *Ibid.*

A man's love is a fire of olive-wood. It leaps higher every moment.
Schreiner, *Story of an African Farm*, Part II, IV

There are different species of love that go under the same name. There is a love that begins in the head, and goes down to the heart, and grows slowly; but it lasts till death, and asks less than it gives. There is another love, that blots out wisdom, that is sweet with the sweetness of life and bitter with the bitterness of death, lasting for an hour; but it is worth having lived a whole life for that hour. *Ibid.*, Part II, VIII

There be loves many and gods many; and happy the man whose god and love are one— happy for the time being; most miserable of mortals when the time of revelation comes and at one stroke both god and lover crumble into dust. Schreiner, *Undine*, VII

Life is too wonderful to hate in. We are all too nearly bound for hating. *Ibid.*, XIII

The party that loves most is always most willing to acknowledge the greater fault.
Scott, *Kenilworth*, XXXV

Love, like despair, catches at straws. Scott, *Quentin Durward*, XXXV

Everyone can tell a love letter that has ever received one. One knows them without opening—They are always folded hurriedly and sealed carefully, and the direction manifests a kind of tremulous agitation, that marks the state of the writer's nerves.
Scott, *St. Roman's Well*, XXXI

Love exists not without hope. Scott, *The Talisman*, XXIII

Early love is frequently ambitious in choosing its object. Scott, *Waverley*, XIV

Love will subsist on wonderfully little hope, but not altogether without it.
Ibid., LIV

Guarded with poverty, and guided with love. Sidney, *Arcadia*, I

Love utterly subverts the course of nature in making reason give place to sense, and man to woman. *Ibid.*

True love hath that excellent nature in it, that it doth transform the very essence of the lover into the thing loved, uniting, and as it were, incorporating it with a secret and inward working. *Ibid.*

To define love is impossible, because no words reach to the strange nature of it: they only know it, which inwardly feel it. *Ibid.*

Love, the refiner of invention. *Ibid.*

Who will resist love must either have no wit or put out his eyes. Can any man resist his creation? Certainly by love we are made, and to love we are made. *Ibid.*

Love to a yielding heart is a king; but to a resisting, a tyrant. *Ibid.*

Love, since thou art so changeable in men's estates, how art thou so constant in their torments? *Ibid.*

Love is better than a pair of spectacles to make everything seem greater which is seen through it. *Ibid.*

Dove and love always go together. Simms, *The Scout*, XXXII

I am no player in love. I speak the language of my own heart; and have no prompter but nature. Smollett, *Humphry Clinker*, 26

Affection may exist independent of esteem; nay, the same object may be lovely in one respect, and detestable in another. The mind has a surprising faculty of accommodating, and even attaching itself, in such a manner, by dint of use, to things that are in their own nature disagreeable, and even pernicious, that it cannot bear to be delivered from them without reluctance and regret. *Ibid.*, 338

Lord, what a thing is love! Smollett, *Roderick Random*, 449

Grave people hate Love for the name's sake. Selfish people hate it for their own. Hypocrites for heaven's sake. Sterne, *A Sentimental Journey*, 28

To say a man is fallen in love,—or that he is deeply in love,—or up to the ears in love,—and sometimes even over head and ears in it,—carries an idiomatical kind of implication, that love is a thing below a man. Sterne, *Tristram Shandy*, VI

As the ancients agree that there are two different and distinct kinds of love, according to the different parts which are affected by it—the brain or the liver—when a man is in love, it behooves him a little to consider which of the two he is fallen into. *Ibid.*, VIII

What matters it how bad we are, if others can still love us, and we can still love others? Stevenson, *Prince Otto*, Book III, II

There is nothing in life more beautiful than that trancelike quiet dawn which precedes the rising of love in the soul. Stowe, *The Minister's Wooing*, VI

It may be that the love which is stronger than death has a power sometimes to make itself heard and felt through the walls of our mortality, when it would plead for the defenseless ones it has left behind. Stowe, *Orr's Island*, VII

He mistook his desire to be loved for an affectionate disposition. *Ibid.*, XXIV

Why should you love an unseen and distant Being more than you do one whom you can feel and see, who holds you in his arms, whose heart beats like your own?
Ibid., XXXII

He who has learned the paramount value of love has taken one step from an earthly to a spiritual existence. *Ibid.*, XLI

What is the meaning of fidelity in love, and whence the birth of it? 'Tis a state of mind that men fall into, and depending on the man rather than the woman. We love being in love, that's the truth on't. If we had not met Joan, we should have met Kate, and adored her. Thackeray, *Henry Esmond*, Book II, XV

Cupid is the father of invention. Thackeray, *Pendennis*, XXIII

Some cynical Frenchman has said that there are two parties to a love-transaction: the one who loves and the other who condescends to be so treated.
Thackeray, *Vanity Fair*, XIII

Love will play freaks with men who are silly enough to believe that love is not incompatible with civilization. Tourgee, *Murvale Eastman*, XXI

It is not a great thing in a man to be turned out of his course by some undefined feeling which he has to a young woman. Trollope, *Ayala's Angel*, XLVI

Love is as bad as drink when it knocks a man's courage out of him, and makes him unfit for work, and leaves him to bemoan himself. *Ibid.*, LXI

Never mind love. What is it? The dream of a few weeks. That is all its joy. The disappointment of a life is its Nemesis. Who was ever successful in true love? Success in love argues that the love is false. True love is always despondent or tragical.
Trollope, *Barchester Towers*, XXVII

For real true love we believe the best age is from forty-five to seventy; up to that, men are generally given to mere flirting. *Ibid.*, XXXVII

"It is as easy to love a girl who has something as one who has nothing." "No—it is not; because the girls with money are scarce, and those without it are plentiful."
Trollope, *The Eustace Diamonds*, IV

For love I could give up everything—but nothing from fear. *Ibid.*, XV

The persons whom you cannot care for in a novel, because they are so bad, are the very same that you so dearly love in your life, because they are so good. *Ibid.*, XXXV

A man cannot understand that love which induces a woman to sacrifice her pride simply for his advantage. *Ibid.*, LIII

What does love signify? How much real love do we ever see among married people?
Ibid., LXVII

You are the only woman whom my heart has stooped to love. *Ibid.*, LXXIII

Tender love should show itself by tender conduct.
Trollope, *He Knew He Was Right*, XXXI

How grand a thing it is to be equal with those whom you love! *Ibid.*, LVI

Jove smiles at lovers' perjuries. Trollope, *Phineas Finn*, XVI

Love and friendship know nothing of justice. The value of love is that it overlooks faults, and forgives even crimes. *Ibid.*, XX

Love is involuntary. It does not often run in a yoke with prudence. *Ibid.*, LXVI

Is there any inconstancy in ceasing to love when one is not loved? Is there inconstancy in changing one's love, and in loving again? *Ibid.*

It has been difficult with me to love. The difficulty with most girls is not to love.
Ibid., LXXI

In matters of love men do not see clearly in their own affairs.
Trollope, *The Warden*, VII

He was a man who might be loved;—but he was hardly a man for love.
Trollope, *The Way We Live Now*, II

Love, she said, was a woman's first necessity.
Twain and Warner, *The Gilded Age*, Volume II, XXIX

All right, then, I'll *go* to hell [rather than betray a loved one].
Twain, *Huckleberry Finn*, XXXI

If love levels ranks, it raises them too.
Walpole, *The Castle of Otranto*, 39

In love, or unhappy—it is the same thing. Is anybody unhappy about another unless they are in love with them?
Ibid., 41

Was there ever a young man who could see any reasons against the possession of the woman he loved?
Warner, *A Little Journey*, V

Was there ever any love worth the name that could be controlled by calculations of expediency?
Ibid.

The world is created anew for every person who is in love. There is therefore this constant miracle of a new heaven and a new earth.
Ibid., X

When one is in love, one always begins by deceiving one's self, and one always ends by deceiving others. That is what the world calls a romance.
Wilde, *Picture of Dorian Gray*, IV

Love is a more wonderful thing than art.
Ibid., VII

Love is an illusion.
Ibid., XVII

"We women can't bear mediocrities. We love with our ears, just as you men love with your eyes, if you ever love at all." "It seems to me that we never do anything else." "Then you never really love."
Ibid.

Romance lives by repetition, and repetition converts an appetite into an art. Each time that one loves is the only time one has ever loved. Difference of object does not alter singleness of passion.
Ibid.

Love is a passion which kindles honor into noble acts.
Woodfin, *The Auction*, II

The softest lover ever best succeeds.
Ibid.

Love laughs at parsons.
Woolson, *Anne*, VIII

Love's sweet violence.
Ibid., XXV

My only wickedness is that I love you; my only goodness, the same.
Ibid., XXVI

Cupid is a knavish god; he can pierce the hearts of others, and hold a shield before his own.
Wright, *A Few Days in Athens*, XII

LUCK: *see also* DESTINY; FORTUNE; etc.

The public man needs but one patron, the lucky moment.
Bulwer, *What Will He Do With It?*, Book VI, VI

How far a man has any right to be more lucky and hence more venerable than his neighbors is a point that always has been and always will be, settled proximately by a kind of higgling and haggling of the market, and ultimately by brute force; but however this may be, it stands to reason that no man should be allowed to be unlucky to more than a moderate extent.
Butler, *Erewhon*, XI

It is sinful to begrudge a man his lawful luck.
Cooper, *The Pilot*, XXXIV

The more easily a man takes life the more persistently does luck follow him.
Hardy, *Hand of Ethelberta*, XXV

Luck is all.
Johnstone, *The Reverie*, I

Experience, the only true knowledge, teaches me that, for everyone, good luck is in store.
Melville, *Confidence-Man*, XL

Jim said you mustn't count the things you are going to cook for dinner, because that would bring bad luck.   Twain, *Huckleberry Finn*, VIII

LUXURY

Luxury is the foundation of all national calamities.
                              Anonymous, *Memoirs of a Coquet*, 83

One must be poor to know the luxury of giving.   Eliot, *Middlemarch*, Book II, XVII

God often tempers the anguish of our sufferings, till there is a sort of luxury in feeling them.   Mackenzie, *Julia De Roubigné*, 109

MACHINERY

A machine is a slave that neither brings nor bears degradation; it is a being endowed with the greatest degree of excitement, yet free at the same time from all passion and emotion. It is therefore not only a slave, but a supernatural slave. And why should one say that the machine does not live? It breathes, for its breath forms the atmosphere of some towns. It moves with more regularity than man. And has it not a voice?
                              Disraeli, *Coningsby*, Book IV, II

A machine has no business to refuse its duty.   Gissing, *New Grub Street*, VIII

MAGIC

The purser is a conjurer; he can make a dead man chew tobacco.
                              Melville, *White Jacket*, XLVIII

MALE/FEMALE: *see also* LOVE; MARRIAGE; etc.

All women are more or less alike; but men are quite different, and even the silly ones may have brains somewhere.   Adams, H., *Esther*, IV

Men like to work alone. Women cannot work without company.   *Ibid.*, V

Girls are quiet, and like to play nurse.   Alcott, *Little Women*, V

Women should learn to be agreeable, particularly poor ones; for they have no other way of repaying the kindnesses they receive.   *Ibid.*, XXIX

Girls' quarrels are soon over.   *Ibid.*, XXX

Girls are so queer you never know what they mean. They say No when they mean Yes, and drive a man out of his wits just for the fun of it.   *Ibid.*, XXXV

Let the boys be boys, the longer the better, and let the young men sow their wild oats if they must; but mothers, sisters, and friends may help to make the crop a small one, and keep many tares from spoiling the harvest, by believing, and showing that they believe, in the possibility of loyalty to the virtues which make men manliest in good women's eyes.   *Ibid.*, XLI

Woman's special mission is supposed to be drying tears and bearing burdens.
                              Ibid., XLVI

It is my private opinion, that the little shifts and struggles we poor girls have to undergo beforehand, give a peculiar relish to our fun when we get it.
                              Alcott, *Old-Fashioned Girl*, XII

Men don't belong in a kitchen.   *Ibid.*, XVII

Every complete man embraces some of the qualities of a woman, for Nature does not mean that sex shall be more than a partial separation of one common humanity; otherwise we should be too much divided to be companionable.
                              Allen, J. L., *The Choir Invisible*, IV

Do not the faculties and imagination of women's minds, properly cultivated, equal those of the greatest men?
Amory, *John Buncle*, II

Why should reason be left to itself in the female sex, and be disciplined with so much care in the male?
Ibid.

Learning and knowledge are perfections in us not as we are men, but as we are rational creatures, in which order of beings the female world is upon the same level with the male. We ought to consider in this particular, not what is the sex, but what is the species they belong to.
Ibid.

As nature has made a great difference in the external appearance of man and woman, we may reasonably expect to find as remarkable a one in their moral characters.
Anonymous, *The Birmingham Counterfeit*, II

There are many actions becoming a woman that would disgrace a man.
Ibid., II

Men are designed to perform those offices, both of body and mind, which require more strength, labor, and application, than women are formed for.
Ibid.

We expect men to shew more prudence, wisdom and knowledge than women, in all the weighty concerns of life.
Ibid.

It is justly expected from men to provide for their families, defend their country, perform the laborious exercises, and engage in all the robust employments of life, for which they are fitted by their superior mental and corporal strength.
Ibid.

It is justly accounted shameful in a man who has a family to leave the support and maintenance of it to his wife; nor can he properly be called a father who takes no care or pains to provide for his children, but devolves that office entirely upon the mother.
Ibid.

Men are formed to stand firmer, and behave braver in dangers, than women.
Ibid.

The military virtues belong to men.
Ibid.

The conquering of the passions, and acting the strictly moral part, require a strength of mind and a firmness of resolution, more to be expected from the male than the female sex.
Ibid., II

If the female sex cannot boast of many heroines in the sublimer virtues, it is not deformed by so many monstrous vices and wicked characters as have appeared among men.
Ibid.

History is more ornamented by illustrious men than illustrious women.
Ibid.

Though men have a great superiority over women in respect to the qualifications for virtue, men sink greatly below them in vice.
Ibid.

Men being destined by their nature to exercise the highest virtues, and fitted for the greatest undertakings, are too robust for the minuter delicacies.
Ibid.

Paint and patches are intolerable things on a bearded face, but may be pleasingly placed upon a lady's.
Ibid.

Expertness and readiness in judging of lace and needlework is doubtless an accomplishment in women that will ill become a man. Men should not endeavor to acquire perfection in these and the like female prettinesses.
Ibid.

Fear does not ill become a woman; for no one expects great courage in that sex.
Ibid.

Fear and shamefacedness proceed from too great a want of fortitude and magnanimity to become the male character.
Ibid.

Superstition, credulity, prejudice, and hasty judgments better suit the softer female than the rough masculine sex.
Ibid.

We should particularly guard women, this amiable half of our species, where nature may seem to have left them weakest, or rendered them most accessible to their despisers, insulters and betrayers, vicious, guileful men, who, under pretense of adoring and idolizing female beauty, seek an opportunity of inhumanly triumphing over virtues and talents greatly superior to their own.   *Ibid.*

If we inquire into the causes that render the female character cheap and despicable, we shall find them chiefly owing to the gross vices, ignorance, and errors of men, who, in general, shamefully neglect the culture of female minds.   *Ibid.*, II

Many men cannot bear that women should be wiser than themselves.   *Ibid.*

The powers of women's minds are not derived from their bodies; women, in general, think and reflect as well, and quicker than men.   *Ibid.*

Some of the sciences are not suitable to women, particularly those which require long and abstruse meditation, and an uninterrupted series of reasoning.   *Ibid.*

Nature has formed the female sex for better purposes than solving difficult philosophical problems or searching after metaphysical subtleties, which would consume too much of their valuable time and interfere with the duties of their sex.   *Ibid.*

Though women cannot study so long, or so abstractedly, as male metaphysicians, it is highly unjust to pronounce them less intelligent, or less rational, in their nature than men.   *Ibid.*

Where wit and ingenuity, vivacity, delicacy, and quickness are required, women manifestly excel men.   *Ibid.*

If our daughters were early and properly instructed in the politer sciences, we should be surprised at the quick progress they would make and the degrees of knowledge they would arrive at. For men, therefore, to condemn women to ignorance, and despise them for that ignorance, is injustice, cruelty, inhumanity.   *Ibid.*

Women are usually bred up in too low, narrow, and servile a manner of thinking, by being made to believe that their principal objects are to ornament their person, improve their fortunes, and marry rich husbands.   *Ibid.*

As few husbands have little more knowledge than qualifies them for their professions and employments, they seldom require more in their wives than fits them for useful servants.   *Ibid.*, II

Women dress and adorn themselves to suit men's folly, and think the more about external ornament because they find men weak enough to be caught by it.   *Ibid.*

The proper dominion of a man over his wife is not to make her a slave. The use of this dominion is to preserve order and peace in the family; for which end the husband's will is to be obeyed, when it happens to differ from the wife's.   *Ibid.*

The greater good a man does, in proportion to what he is capable of doing, the more manly he is.   *Ibid.*

Women love themselves in men.   Anonymous, *Fatal Friendship*, I

Woman, the most beautiful of nature's flowers, is the most recreant to her laws, and starves with cold and unnecessary forms that divine flame her beauteous system was designed to kindle.   Anonymous, *The History of the Human Heart*, 171

A woman never dies of a distemper of the mind, when she can be brought to cry it out.
                            Anonymous, *History of Tom Jones in His Married State*, 168

What is folly and rashness in the woman is only fire, spirit, and gallantry in the man.
                                             Anonymous, *Memoirs of a Coquet*, 107

A female who is at the same time useful and agreeable is as rare as sincerity in a statesman, or humility in an author.   *Ibid.*, 115

It is the highest compliment to give every man his own way; to a lady it is an infallible one.   Anonymous, *Private Letters*, 7

Men ought to be very cautious of excluding the other sex from bearing a part in any entertainment—separate diversions, separate meals, and at last, separate beds.

Anonymous, *Sophronia*, 196

It is a melancholy thing to consider that a man's education is merely to qualify him to get a livelihood, but a woman's, to dissipate it. *Ibid.*, 232

Women forgive your beauty and brains so much more willingly if you divert their attention by the one thing their soul can admire without bitterness.

Atherton, *The Californians*, Book II, I

A man can know a woman fairly well, because her life, consequently the interests which mould her mind and conceive her thoughts, are more or less simple.

Atherton, *Doomswoman*, XIX

Passion is so largely mental in women that it reaches heights in the imagination that reality seldom justifies and mere propinquity quells. For this reason they often are recklessly unfair to men, who are made on simpler lines.

Atherton, *Senator North*, Book II, VII

The best of women are frauds. *Ibid.*, Book II, XVIII

I have enough of feminine insight to know that a woman is really happy only when she is making a man happy, and that she is almost ready to bless the troubles which give her the opportunity to console him. *Ibid.*, Book III, V

Ladies can never look ill. Austen, *Emma*, XXIV

Young ladies are delicate plants. *Ibid.*, XXXIV

Give a girl an education, and introduce her properly into the world, and ten to one but she has the means of settling well, without farther expense to anybody.

Austen, *Mansfield Park*, Volume One, I

Girls should be quiet and modest. One does not like to see a girl of eighteen or nineteen so immediately up to everything. *Ibid.*, Volume One, V

A woman can never be too fine when she is in white. *Ibid.*, Volume Two, V

Let him have all the perfections in the world, it ought not to be set down as certain that a man must be acceptable to every woman he may happen to like himself.

Ibid., Volume Three, IV

The talent of writing agreeable letters is peculiarly female.

Austen, *Northanger Abbey*, III

Though, to the larger and more trifling part of the male sex, imbecility in females is a great enhancement of their personal charms, there is a portion of men too reasonable, and too well-informed themselves, to desire anything more in woman than ignorance.

Ibid., XIV

Nursing does not belong to a man, it is not his province. Austen, *Persuasion*, VII

Man is more robust than woman, but he is not longer-lived. *Ibid.*, XXIII

Songs and proverbs all talk of woman's fickleness. But these were all written by men.

Ibid., XXIII

"It is very often nothing but our own vanity that deceives us. Women fancy admiration means more than it does." "And men take care that they should."

Austen, *Pride and Prejudice*, Volume II, I

A woman's intuition is like a leopard's spring: it seizes the truth at the first bound.

Barr, *Maid*, XI

An ugly man may generally be successful with women if he remains sufficiently indifferent to them. Bates, *Puritans*, V

Every woman with any brains knows what a man is the minute she claps eyes on him; only if he's good-looking, or awful wicked, or makes love to her, or forty thousand other things, she'll deny to herself that she knows any bad about him. *Ibid.*, XI

It is not the nature of the female tongue to be silent.
Brackenridge, *Modern Chivalry*, Part I, Volume I

Women are supposed to be very calm generally; but women feel just as men feel; they need exercise for their faculties, and a field for their efforts as much as their brothers do; they suffer from too rigid a constraint, too absolute a stagnation, precisely as men would suffer; and it is narrow-minded in their more privileged fellow-creatures to say that they ought to confine themselves to making puddings and knitting stockings, to playing on the piano and embroidering bags. It is thoughtless to condemn them, or laugh at them, if they seek to do more or learn more than custom has pronounced necessary for their sex. Bronte, C., *Jane Eyre*, XII

I had a theoretical reverence and homage for beauty, elegance, gallantry, fascination; but had I met those qualities incarnate in masculine shape, I should have known instinctively that they neither had nor could have sympathy with anything in me, and should have shunned them as one would fire, lightning, or anything else that is bright but antipathetic. *Ibid.*

Men never do consider economy and common sense. *Ibid.*, XVII

Young ladies have a remarkable way of letting you know that they think you a "quiz," without actually saying the words. *Ibid.*, XXI

He made no pretense of comprehending women, or comparing them with me; they were a different, probably a very inferior order of existence. Bronte, *Shirley*, IV

It is the nature of womenites to be spiteful. *Ibid.*, IX

Women have so few things to think about—men so many. *Ibid.*, XII

Men fancy women's minds something like those of children. *Ibid.*, XX

A "woman of intellect," it appeared, was a sort of luckless accident, a thing for which there was neither place nor use in creation, wanted neither as wife nor worker. Beauty anticipated her in the first office. Bronte, C., *Villette*, XXX

Be gentle, be pitying, be a woman. *Ibid.*, XLI

Custom has done enough to make the life of one half of our species, women, tasteless.
Brooke, *Emily Montague*, I

Women choose much oftener from affection than men. *Ibid.*, II

Bred in ignorance from one age to another, women can learn little of their own sex.
Ibid., III

That naughty creature, man. *Ibid.*, IV

Shallow and inexperienced as all women are known to be. Brown, C. B., *Alcuin*, I

Mere sex is a circumstance so purely physical; it has little essential influence beyond what has flowed from the caprice of civil institutions on the qualities of mind or person. If the law should exclude from all political functions everyone who had a mole on his right cheek, or whose statute did not exceed five feet six inches, who would not condemn without scruple so unjust an institution? Yet in truth the injustice would be less than in the case of women. The distinction is no less futile, but the injury is far greater, since it annihilates the political existence of at least one half of the community. *Ibid.*, II

Women are born to trouble, and tears are given them for their relief.
Brown, C. B., *Arthur Mervyn*, II

Women always exaggerate, and make realities of their own bugbears: it is the vice of their lively imaginations. Bulwer, *The Caxtons*, Book XI, I

Woman can best decoy woman. Bulwer, *My Novel*, Book XII, II

A woman too often reasons from her heart—hence two-thirds of her mistakes and her troubles. A man of genius, too, often reasons from his heart—hence, also, two-thirds of his troubles and mistakes. Wherefore, between woman and genius there is a sympathetic affinity; each has some intuitive comprehension of the secrets of the other, and the more feminine the woman, the more exquisite the genius, the more subtle the intelligence between the two.   Bulwer, *What Will He Do With It?*, Book VIII, IV

Women invariably fall victims to men who are big and a little lumbering. They like to persuade themselves that they are overawed and subjected.
                    Burnett, *Through One Administration*, XXII

I shouldn't like to be a woman, and have to follow my leader, and live in one groove from beginning to end.   *Ibid.*, XXXIV

The equanimity of her temper made her seem, though a female, born to be a practical philosopher.   Burney, *Camilla*, One, I

All men are at the disposition of women. If even the shrewd monied man cannot resist, what heart shall men find impenetrable?   *Ibid.*, Three, VI

A daring defiance of the world and its opinions is in a woman of all things the most odious.   Burney, *Cecilia*, II

Though gentleness and modesty are the peculiar attributes of women, yet fortitude and firmness, when occasion demands them, are virtues as noble and as becoming in them as in men.   Burney, *Evelina*, 202

In a woman the unbounded license of the tongue is intolerable.   *Ibid.*, 318

She is not, like most modern young ladies, to be known in half an hour.   *Ibid.*, 321

She does not, beautiful as she is, seize the soul by surprise, but, with more dangerous fascination, she steals it almost imperceptibly.   *Ibid.*, 322

I have an insuperable aversion to strength, either of body or of mind, in a female.
                    Ibid., 336

I'd as soon see a woman chop wood, as hear her chop logic.   *Ibid.*

No man ought to be connected with a woman whose understanding is superior to his own.   *Ibid.*

All young ladies are either very pretty or very clever or very sweet; they may take their choice as to which category they will go in for, but go in for one of the three they must.
                    Butler, *The Way of All Flesh*, XLVIII

The drawing-room is woman's element—realm—rather than man's.
                    Cable, *Bonaventure*, Book III, VII

The fiction of chivalry made man serve woman; the fact of human nature makes woman happiest when serving where she loves.   Chesnutt, *House Behind the Cedars*, IX

Woman is a very peculiar and delicate organism—a sensitive and highly organized woman is especially peculiar. It would require an inspired psychologist to deal successfully with them. And when ordinary fellows attempt to cope with their idiosyncrasies the result is bungling. Most women are moody and whimsical.
                    Chopin, *The Awakening*, XXII

Many women are rakes at their heart.   Cleland, *Memoirs of a Coxcomb*, 138

Women are not naturally born for liberties which dishonor them.   *Ibid.*, 201

The great point with women is to be taken notice of by them, no matter whether for one's good or bad qualities, if one has but the merit of a pleasing person. With that advantage, one may safely reply upon them, for turning even one's faults into recommendations.
                    Ibid., 286

Men know not in general how much they destroy of their own pleasure, when they break through the respect and tenderness due to women, and even to those who live only by pleasing them. Cleland, *Memoirs of a Woman of Pleasure*, 138

We live in an age when too many women appear to be ambitious of morally unsexing themselves before society by aping the language and manners of men.

Collins, *Basil*, Part One, V

The woman is always to blame. Collins, *Blind Love*, Prologue, IV

In all my experience, I never met a woman who declined to express an opinion.

Ibid., XVI

Fanny is a woman—that is to say, an inferior form of man. *Ibid.*, XLIX

Man hunts wild creatures; woman hunts man. *Ibid.*, L

To the most misanthropic female there sometimes comes a time when she must own that man has his uses. *Ibid.*, LIX

A young lady's tongue is a privileged member. Collins, *Moonstone*, First Period, XII

Men (being superior creatures) are bound to improve women—if they can.

Ibid., First Period, XVII

Mr. Abelewhite won't find the world quite so easy to convince as a committee of charitable ladies. *Ibid.*, Second Period, III

Absolute self-dependence is a great virtue in a man. In a woman, it has the serious drawback of morally separating her from the mass of her sex, and so exposing her to misconstruction by the general opinion. *Ibid.*, Second Narrative, I

This is the story of what a woman's patience can endure, and what a man's resolution can achieve. Collins, *Woman in White*, Part I, First Epoch

Being nothing but a woman, condemned to patience, propriety, and petticoats.

Ibid., Part I, Second Epoch

That sublime self-forgetfulness of women, which yields so much and asks so little.

Ibid., Part II, Third Epoch

One of those long looks that are a woman's most terrible weapon.

Conrad, *Almayer's Folly*, XI

War is your sex's natural state, madam. See, the artillery of your eyes—how fatal is it!

Cooke, *Virginia Comedians*, Volume II, III

Women are peculiarly apt to follow the bias of their affections, rather than of their reasons, in all cases connected with guilt. Cooper, *Chainbearer*, IV

There is no more sure sign that a young woman is all the while thinking of the beaux than her never mentioning them. Cooper, *Homeward Bound*, XVI

Even the most intellectual and refined women feel a disposition to judge handsome, manly, frank, flighty fellows somewhat leniently. Cooper, *Satanstoe*, Volume I, XIV

Women are slower than us men to admit totally novel impressions. *Ibid.*, Volume II, II

A woman's mind is not easily read. *Ibid.*, Volume II, III

Men must learn to wait [for women]. *Ibid.*

Make a nurse of a female, and she is yours. *Ibid.*, Volume II, XII

A woman's judgment and her feelings may not impel her the same way.

Ibid., Volume II, XIII

Any woman may fall a victim to a limber, manly, and courteous bow.

Crane, *The O'Ruddy*, III

A woman's meddling often results in the destruction of those she—those she don't care to have killed. *Ibid.*, VIII

Women are so constituted that they are able to misinterpret almost every one of their emotions. *Ibid.*, XX

Women are stronger to hate than to love. Crawford, *Khaled*, III

The reason why woman has privileges instead of rights is that all men tacitly acknowledge the future of humanity to be dependent on her from generation to generation. Crawford, *A Rose of Yesterday*, IV

It is bad for a man if a woman comes to know her strength before he has learned his weakness. *Ibid.*, X

If any man says that he understands women he is convicted of folly by his own speech, seeing that they are altogether incomprehensible. Crawford, *Sant' Ilario*, V

The female who has once erred, and who does not hate the author of her error, should beware of confiding in her own strength, or relying on the firmness of repentant virtue; for her, there is no safety but in flight; and if she desire to retrieve her path, she should never *behold* him who caused her to wander aside. Dacre, *The Libertine*, XIII

Womankind never cordially or sincerely forgive the man who has been so unfortunate as to slight their charms, or who has had the temerity to avow indifference in return for love. It is quite otherwise with man—he is seldom, if ever, vindictive against the woman he has been once attached to. Dacre, *Passions*, Letters XV

Ungenerous reports will often exist against a woman who is beautiful, and whose manners are unreserved, yet we should judge what credit to attach to them, when she is well received by society, whose sanction gives the lie to calumny. *Ibid.*

The pride and vanity of a man—his self-love—causes him to dread superiority in woman. He bears no rival near the throne. *Ibid.*, Letter XVI

I have so great a contempt for, and hatred of the injustice of the nobler [male] sex, that it is with the greatest reluctance, I enter into the society of which they inevitably compose so great a part. *Ibid.*, Letter XXXI

An overstrained sense of manliness is the characteristic of seafaring men, or, rather, of life on board ship. Dana, *Two Years Before the Mast*, XXVIII

Women are generally the leaders in social reform. Perhaps it is because evils press hardest in their direction. Daniel, *Ai*, XXVIII

[Women's] wire-drawn sympathies and affinities. Davis, *Verdict*, XXIX

Fondness is the last favor but one that a woman can grant, and lays her almost as low, lays her at the mercy of the man she shows it to. Defoe, *Colonel Jack*, 190

The market is against our sex; and if a young woman has beauty, birth, breeding, wit, sense, manners, modesty, and all to an extreme, yet if she has not money, she's nobody, she had as good want them all. Defoe, *Moll Flanders*, 15

The women had lost the privilege of saying no. *Ibid.*, 64

I would have despised a man that should think I ought to take him upon his own recommendation only. *Ibid.*, 65

It was my opinion a woman was as fit to govern and enjoy her own estate without a man as a man was without a woman, and that if she had a mind to gratify herself as to sexes, she might entertain a man as a man does a mistress. Defoe, *Roxana*, 145

Man has great power over a woman when he can touch that strongest part of her nature, her sentiments. DeForest, *Miss Ravenel's Conversion*, XXXV

Women are like shadows, for the more a man follows them, the faster they run away; but let a man turn his course, and then they will presently follow him. Deloney, *The Gentle Craft*, 75

Though roses have prickles, yet they are gathered; and though women seem forward, yet they will shew themselves kind and friendly. Neither is there any wax so hard but, by often tempering, is made apt to receive an impression. *Ibid.*, 82

Every carter may reach to the garter,/ A shoemaker he may reach to the knee,/ But he that creeps higher shall ask leave of me. *Ibid.*, 146

He that fears and doubts womankind cannot be counted mankind.
Deloney, *Jack of Newbury*, 318

The restraint of liberty enforceth women to be lewd: for where a woman cannot be trusted, she cannot think herself beloved. Deloney, *Thomas of Reading*, 217

As a general principle and abstract proposition, Miggs held the male sex to be utterly contemptible and unworthy of notice; to be fickle, false, base, sottish, inclined to perjury, and wholly undeserving. When particularly exasperated against them she was accustomed to wish with great emphasis that the whole race of women could but die off, in order that the men might be brought to know the real value of the blessings by which they set so little store; nay, her feelings for her order ran so high, that she sometimes declared, if she could only have good security for a fair, round number—say ten thousand—of young virgins following her example, she would, to spite mankind, hang, drown, stab, or poison herself, with a joy past all expression. Dickens, *Barnaby Rudge*, VII

Mrs. Varden was but a woman, and had her share of vanity, obstinacy, and love of power. *Ibid.*, XXVII

Women are all secret. Dickens, *Bleak House*, XVI

The society of girls is a very delightful thing. It's not professional but it's very delightful.
Dickens, *David Copperfield*, LIX

The ladies are great observers. *Ibid.*

Women like music, when you are paying your addresses to them.
Dickens, *Dombey and Son*, XLI

'Tis woman as seduces all mankind. *Ibid.*, LVI

Nature often enshrines gallant and noble hearts in weak bosoms—oftenest, in female breasts. Dickens, *Old Curiosity Shop*, XXIV

All women are angels. Dickens, *Pickwick Papers*, VIII

Fielding tells us that man is fire, and woman too, and the Prince of Darkness sets a light to 'em. *Ibid.*

Show me the man who says anything against women, as women, and I boldly declare he is not a man. *Ibid.*, XIV

Tongue: that's a wery good thing when it an't a woman's. *Ibid.*, XIX

He saw that women, the tenderest and most fragile of all God's creatures, were the oftenest superior to sorrow, adversity, and distress; and he saw that it was because they bore, in their own hearts, an inexhaustible well-spring of affection and devotion.
Ibid., XXIX

We know—we, who are men of the world—that a good uniform must work its way with the women, sooner or later. *Ibid.*, XXXVII

Women can kill as well as men when the place is taken.
Dickens, *Tale of Two Cities*, XXI

Women think everything to be suffering. Disraeli, *Coningsby*, Book III, III

Most women are vain, and some men are not. *Ibid.*, Book III, V

Women are the priestesses of predestination. *Ibid.*, Book IV, II

Man conceives fortune, but woman conducts it. *Ibid.*

It is the spirit of man that says, "I will be great"; but it is the sympathy of woman that usually makes him so. *Ibid.*

A reputation for success has as much influence with women, as a reputation for wealth has with men. *Ibid.*, Book IV, IX

The only useless life is woman's. *Ibid.*, Book IV, XV

Life is too short to be little. Man is never so manly as when he feels deeply, acts boldly, and expresses himself with frankness and with fervor. *Ibid.*, Book VII, II

Quarrels about women are always a mistake. One should make it a rule to give up to them, and then they are sure to give up to us. *Ibid.*, Book VIII, I

There is no end to the influence of woman on our life. It is at the bottom of everything that happens to us. *Ibid.*, Book VIII, VII

Nothing is of so much importance and of so much use to a young man entering life as to be well criticized by women.   Disraeli, *Contarini Fleming*, Part the First, XXIII

I don't care what women say, high or low, they always exaggerate.
Disraeli, *Sybil*, Book III, II

He was what man should be to woman ever—gentle, and yet a guide.   *Ibid.*, Book V, IV

I don't like these politics. They bayn't in a manner business for our [female] sex.
Ibid., Book VI, VIII

There is an indescribably faint line in the matter of man's apparel which somehow divides for a woman those who are worth glancing at and those who are not. Once an individual has passed this faint line on the way downward he will get no glance from her. There is another line at which the dress of a man will cause her to study her own.
Dreiser, *Sister Carrie*, I

He loved the thing that women love in themselves, grace.   *Ibid.*, XI

Good and happy women have no history.   DuMaurier, *The Martian*, Part Ninth

Girls are missionaries who convert boys. Boys are mainly heathens.
Dunbar, *The Uncalled*, VII

There is some subtle tie between tea-drinking and gossip. It is over their dainty cups that women dissect us men and damn their sisters. Some of the quality of the lemon they take in their tea gets into their tongues. Tea is to talk what dew is to a plant, a gentle nourishing influence, which gives to its product much of its own quality. There are two acids in the tea which cultured women make. There is only one in the beverage brewed by commonplace people. But that is enough. *Ibid.*, IX

Religion seems to be a necessary qualification of the female mind.
Eastman, *Aunt Phillis's Cabin*, XII

One of the lessons a woman most rarely learns is never to talk to an angry or a drunken man. Eliot, *Adam Bede*, IV

The commonest man, who has his ounce of sense and feeling, is conscious of the difference between a lovely, delicate woman and a coarse one. Even a dog feels a difference in their presence. *Ibid.*, XXV

Who can deny that bows and arrows are among the prettiest weapons in the world for feminine forms to play with? They prompt attitudes full of grace and power, where that fine concentration of energy seen in all marksmanship is freed from associations of bloodshed. Eliot, *Daniel Deronda*, Book I, X

Oh, child, men's men: gentle or simple, they're much of a muchness.
Ibid., Book IV, XXXI

A fine lady is a squirrel-headed thing, with small airs and small notions, about as applicable to the business of life as a pair of tweezers to the clearing of a forest.
Eliot, *Felix Holt*, V

If a woman really believes herself to be a lower kind of being, she should place herself in subjection: she should be ruled by the thoughts of her father or husband. If not, let her show her power of choosing something better.   *Ibid.*, X

A woman doesn't like a man who tells her the truth   *Ibid.*

Women were expected to have weak opinions; but the great safeguard of society and of domestic life was, that opinions were not acted on.   Eliot, *Middlemarch*, Book I, I

Young people should think of their families in marrying.   *Ibid.*, Book I, VI

A woman is never in love with anyone she has always known—ever since she can remember; as a man often is. It is always some new fellow who strikes a girl.
Ibid., Book II, XIV

"Women don't love men for their goodness." "Perhaps not. But if they love them, they never think them bad."   *Ibid.*

A girl should keep her heart within her own power.
Eliot, *Middlemarch*, Book III, XXXI

A man is seldom ashamed of feeling that he cannot love a woman so well when he sees a certain greatness in her: nature having intended greatness for men. But nature has sometimes made sad oversights in carrying out her intention.
Ibid., Book IV, XXXIX

When one sees a perfect woman, one never thinks of her attributes—one is conscious of her presence.   *Ibid.*, Book V, XLIII

A woman may venture on some efforts of sympathy which would hardly succeed if men undertook them.   *Ibid.*, Book VIII, LXXII

That simplicity of hers, holding up an ideal for others in her believing conception of them, was one of the great powers of her womanhood.   *Ibid.*, Book VIII, LXXVII

How can a man explain at the expense of a woman?   *Ibid.*, Book VIII, LXXVIII

A woman must not force her heart—she'll do a man no good by that.
Ibid., Book VIII, LXXXVI

An over-'cute woman's no better nor a long-tailed sheep,—she'll fetch none the bigger price for that.   Eliot, *Mill on the Floss*, Book I, II

I don't pretend to know anything about putting out money and all that. I could never see into men's business.   *Ibid.*, Book I, IX

Mr. Glegg had a double source of mental occupation, which gave every promise of being inexhaustible. On the one hand, he surprised himself by his discoveries in natural history. And his second subject of meditation was the "contrariness" of the female mind, as typically exhibited in Mrs. Glegg. That a creature made—in a genealogical sense— out of a man's rib, and in this particular case maintained in the highest respectability without any trouble of her own, should be normally in a state of contradiction to the blandest propositions and even to the most accommodating concessions, was a mystery in the scheme of things to which he had often in vain sought a clue in the early chapters of Genesis.   *Ibid.*, Book I, XII

Gentlemen are apt to impart imprudent confidences to ladies concerning their un-favorable opinion of sister fair ones. That is why so many women have the advantage of knowing that they are secretly repulsive to men who have self-denyingly made ardent love to them.   *Ibid.*, Book VI, II

The happiest women, like the happiest nations, have no history.   *Ibid.*, Book VI, III

It is a fact capable of an amiable interpretation that ladies are not the worst disposed toward a new acquaintance of their own sex because she has points of inferiority.
Ibid., Book VI, VI

Until every good man is brave, we must expect to find many good women timid—too timid even to believe in the correctness of their own best promptings, when these would place them in a minority.   *Ibid.*, Book VII, IV

When once a woman comes to ask herself, Is the man whom I like for some other reason handsome? her fate, and his too, strongly depend on her answering in the affirmative.

Fielding, *Amelia*, I

Women generally love to be of the obliging side.　　　　　　　　　　　*Ibid.*

She had contracted a hearty contempt for much the greater part of both sexes; for the women, as being idiots, and for the men, as the admirers of idiots.　　　　*Ibid.*, II

The knowledge that they are in the wrong is a very strong reason to some women to continue so.　　　　　　　　　　　　　　　　　　　　　　　　　　　*Ibid.*

Women who have learning can be contented without that qualification in a man.

Ibid.

Woman is a various and changeable animal.　　　　　　　　　　　　　*Ibid.*

Why should not a woman follow her mind as well as man?

Fielding, *Joseph Andrews*, 281

When a woman is not seen to blush, she doth not blush at all.　　Fielding, *Tom Jones*, 22

He looked on a woman as on an animal of domestic use, of somewhat higher consideration than a cat.　　　　　　　　　　　　　　　　　　　　　　　　　*Ibid.*, 66

Your men's bodies, and not your brains, are stronger than women's.　　*Ibid.*, 220

It was a maxim with Mr. Western, that women should come in with the first dish and go out after the first glass.　　　　　　　　　　　　　　　　　　　　*Ibid.*, 277

Women never give their consent if they can help it. 'Tis not the fashion.　*Ibid.*, 283

Her age was about thirty, for she owned six-and twenty.　　　　　　*Ibid.*, 732

I have got more wisdom, and know more of the world, than to take the word of a woman in a matter where a man is concerned.　　　　　　　　　　　　　　*Ibid.*, 745

He was charmed with her person, and thought women's souls were of no great consequence, nor did it signify much what they profess.　　Fielding, S., *David Simple*, I

Women cannot choose for themselves.　　　　　　　Gibbes, *Mr. Francis Clive*, I

Woman will have turned upon her real foe, and have rent the mask apart, and, lo! she will have looked into the face and have seen her own.

Glasgow, *The Descendant*, Book II, V

A noble woman has made many a man a blackguard.　　　　*Ibid.*, Book III, III

A woman is a fool until she falls in love, and then she's a damn fool.

Ibid., Book III, IV

One of the qualifications that women are early taught to look for in the male is that of a protector.　　　　　　　　　　　　　　　　Godwin, *Caleb Williams*, I

The temper of a woman is generally formed from the turn of her features.

Goldsmith, *The Vicar of Wakefield*, 4

Women are persistently imitative.　　　　　　　Hardy, *Desperate Remedies*, VIII

The only superiority in women that is tolerable to the rival sex is, as a rule, that of the unconscious kind; but a superiority which recognizes itself may sometimes please by suggesting possibilities of capture to the subordinated man.

Hardy, *Far From the Madding Crowd*, IV

If a woman did not invariably form an opinion of her choice before she has half seen him, and love him before she has half formed an opinion, there would be no tears and pining in the whole feminine world, and poets would starve for want of a topic.

Hardy, *Hand of Ethelberta*, XIX

A man must have courted at least half-a-dozen women before he's a match for one.

Ibid., XXI

More often than not "no" is said to a man's importunities because it is traditionally the correct modest reply, and for nothing else in the world.

Ibid., XXII

If all men took "no" superficially, women should die of decorum in shoals.

Ibid.

A woman who attempts a public career must expect to be treated as public property.

Ibid., XXXV

Were women, instead of more sensitive, as reputed, more callous, and less romantic; or were they more heroic?

Hardy, Jude the Obscure, Part Three, VII

If God disposed not, woman did.

Ibid., Part Four, II

Not being men, women don't know that in looking back on those he has had tender relations with, a man's heart returns closest to her who was the soul of truth in her conduct.

Ibid., Part Five, I

There's nothing like bondage and a stone-deaf taskmaster for taming us women.

Ibid., Part Five, VIII

'Tis hard for a woman to keep virtuous where there's so many young men.

Ibid., Part Six, VI

Strange difference of sex, that time and circumstance, which enlarge the views of most men, narrow the views of women almost invariably.

Ibid., Part Six, X

'Tis woman's nature to be false except to a man and man's nature to be true except to a woman.

Hardy, A Laodicean, VI, III

The worst women are those vain in their hearts, and not in their ways.

Hardy, A Pair of Blue Eyes, XIX

Woman's ruling passion—to fascinate and influence those more powerful than she.

Ibid., XX

Men may love strongest for a while, but women love longest.

Ibid., XXXVIII

What every woman says some women may feel.

Hardy, Tess, XII

Women whose chief companions are the forms and forces of outdoor Nature retain in their souls far more of the Pagan fantasy of their remote forefathers than of the systematized religion taught their race at later date.

Ibid., XVI

A woman should not be try'd beyond her Strength, and continual dropping will wear away a Stone—ay, more—a Diamond.

Ibid., LII

Who is himself when he's got a woman round his neck like a millstone?

Hardy, Trumpet-Major, XXVI

Men who love women the very best always blunder and give more pain than those who love them less.

Ibid., XXXVII

Women the most delicate get used to strange moral situations. Eve probably regained her normal sweet composure about a week after the Fall.

Hardy, Two on a Tower, XXXV

Whatever they may say about a woman's right to conceal where her love lies, and pretend it doesn't exist, it is not best. And an honest woman in that shines most brightly, and is thought most of in the long run.

Hardy, Under the Greenwood Tree, Part Three, I

'Tis a talent of the female race that low numbers should stand for high, more especially in matters of waiting, matters of age, and matters of money.

Ibid., Part Five, II

Women are always carried about like corks upon the waves of masculine desires.

Hardy, Woodlanders, XXVI

Triumph at any price is sweet to men and women—especially the latter.

Ibid., XLIII

All women under the sun be prettier one side than t'other. And the pains she would take to make me walk on the pretty side were unending. She could lead me with a cotton thread, like a blind ram. I don't think the women have got cleverer, for they was never otherwise. *Ibid.*, XLVIII

A female reformer, in her attacks upon society, has an instinctive sense of where the life lies, and is inclined to aim directly at that spot. Especially the relation between the sexes is naturally among the earliest to attract her notice.
Hawthorne, *Blithedale Romance*, VI

Nature thrusts some men into the world miserably incomplete on the emotional side, with hardly any sensibilities except what pertain to us as animals. No passions, save of the senses; no holy tenderness, nor the delicacy that results from this. Externally they bear a close resemblance to other men, and have perhaps all save the finest grace; but when a woman wrecks herself on such a being, she ultimately finds that the real womanhood within her has no corresponding part in him. Her deepest voice lacks a response; the deeper her cry, the more dead his silence. *Ibid.*, XII

It is my belief that, when my sex shall achieve its rights, there will be ten eloquent women where there is now one eloquent man. Thus far, no woman in the world has ever once spoken out her whole heart and her whole mind. The mistrust and disapproval of the vast bulk of society throttles us, as with two gigantic hands at our throats. We mumble a few weak words, and leave a thousand better ones unsaid. *Ibid.*, XIV

The pen is not for woman. Her power is too natural and immediate. It is with the living voice alone that she can compel the world to recognize the light of her intellect and the depth of her heart. *Ibid.*

Woman is the most admirable handiwork of God, in her true place and character. Her place is at man's side. *Ibid.*

The heart of true womanhood knows where its own sphere is, and never seeks to stray beyond it. *Ibid.*

Women possess no rights, or, at all events, only little girls and grandmothers would have the force to exercise them. *Ibid.*, XVI

Those pitiless rebukes which a woman always has at hand, ready for an offense (and which she so seldom spares, on due occasion). *Ibid.*, XVIII

I am a woman, with every fault that a woman ever had—weak, vain, unprincipled (like most of my sex; for our virtues, when we have any, are merely impulsive and intuitive), passionate, too, and pursuing my foolish and unattainable ends by indirect and cunning, though absurdly chosen means, as an hereditary bond-slave must; false, moreover, to the whole circle of good, in my reckless truth to the little good I saw before me—but still a woman! *Ibid.*, XXV

This is a woman's view, a woman's, whose whole sphere of action is in the heart, and who can conceive of no higher nor wider one. *Ibid.*

In the battlefield of life, the downright stroke, that would fall only on a man's steel head-piece, is sure to light on a woman's heart, over which she wears no breastplate, and whose wisdom it is, therefore, to keep out of the conflict. The whole universe, and Providence, or Destiny, to boot, make common cause against the woman who swerves one hair's breadth out of the beaten track. *Ibid.*, XXVI

Poor womanhood, with its rights and wrongs. *Ibid.*

Affection and sympathy for flowers is almost exclusively a woman's trait. Men, if endowed with it by nature, soon lose, forget, and learn to despise it, in their contact with coarser things than flowers. Hawthorne, *House of the Seven Gables*, X

A woman's days are so tedious that it is a boon to leave even one of them out of the account of her life. Hawthorne, *The Marble Faun*, II

There is something extremely pleasant, and even touching—at least, of very sweet, soft, and winning effect—in this peculiarity of needlework, distinguishing women from men.

Ibid., V

Why should not there be a woman to listen to the prayers of women? A mother in heaven for all motherless girls? In all God's thought and care, can he have withheld this boon, which female weakness so much needs?

Ibid., XXXVIII

You confuse yourself between right feelings and very foolish inferences, as is the wont of women.

Ibid., XXXIX

In ninety-nine cases out of a hundred, the apprehensiveness of women is gratuitous.

Ibid., XLII

Women are safer in perilous situations and emergencies than men; and might be still more so, if they trusted themselves more confidingly to the chivalry of manhood.

Ibid.

Women, poor simple creatures, are always to be pitied, never blamed.

Holcroft, *Hugh Trevor*, III

The devil himself is not half so cunning as women.

Ibid.

Women are cunning as serpents; but, though fond of cooing, not harmless as doves.

Ibid.

Women delight in being forced to follow their own inclinations.

Ibid.

Beware of the woman who cannot find free utterance for all her stormy life either in words or song! So long as a woman can talk, there is nothing she cannot hear.

Holmes, *Elsie Venner*, XXIII

She could not swear: she was not a boy.

Holmes, *Guardian Angel*, VIII

Most women seem to love for no other reason than that it is expected of them.

Howe, *Story of a Country Town*, XXX

I know too much about women to honor them more than they deserve; in fact, I know all about them. I visited a place once where doctors are made, and saw them cut up one.

Ibid.

A woman loses her power when she allows a man to find out all there is to her. *Ibid.*

If men would only tell what they actually know about women, instead of what they believe, or hear, they would receive more credit for chastity than is now the case, for they deserve more.

Ibid.

There is only one grade of men; they are all contemptible.

Ibid.

A woman's work is never done, for the reason that she does not go about it in time to finish it.

Ibid.

Men are virtuous because the women are; women are virtuous from necessity. *Ibid.*

One of the advantages of the negative part assigned to women in life is that they are seldom forced to commit themselves. They can, if they choose, remain perfectly passive while a great many things take place in regard to them; they need not account for what they do not do. From time to time a man must show his hand, but save for one supreme exigency a woman need never show hers. She moves in mystery as long as she likes; and mere reticence in her, if she is young and fair, interprets itself as good sense and bad taste.

Howells, *The Lady of the Aroostook*, VI

We can't do women a greater injustice than not to account for a vast deal of human nature in them.

Howells, *A Modern Instance*, XXVI

You women haven't risen yet—it's an evidence of the backwardness of your sex—to a conception of the Bismarck idea in diplomacy. If a man praises one woman, you still think he's in love with another.

Howells, *Silas Lapham*, XII

Women are not like men—implacable.

Hudson, *The Purple Land*, XXII

She considered men in general as so much in the debt of the opposite sex that any individual woman had an unlimited credit with them; she could not possibly overdraw the general feminine account.   James, H., *The Bostonians*, XVII

The suffering of women is the suffering of all humanity.   *Ibid.*, XXIV

Women have one source of happiness that is closed to us—the consciousness that their presence here below lifts half the load of *our* suffering.   *Ibid.*

The use of a truly amiable woman is to make some honest man happy.   *Ibid.*, XXV

The whole generation is womanized; the masculine tone is passing out of the world.
                          Ibid., XXXIV

Women are necessities.   James, *Confidence*, VII

Women are a sort of foliage. They are always rustling about and dropping off.   *Ibid.*, XI

In every disadvantage that a woman suffers at the hands of a man, there is inevitably, in what concerns the man, an element of cowardice.   *Ibid.*, XIX

Men are so stupid; it's only women that have real discernment.   *Ibid.*, XXIX

You should never ask a woman for dates [having to do with her history].
                          James, H., *The Europeans*, VI

Living with women helps to make a man a gentleman.   *Ibid.*, VII

"Women rarely boast of their courage. Men do so with a certain frequency." "Men have it to boast of."   James, H., *Portrait of a Lady*, XV

A woman's natural mission is to be where she's most appreciated.   *Ibid.*, XXIV

"I have always had a fear of clever women." "That's a part of your prudence. But you're the sort of man who ought to know how to use them."
                          James, H., *Princess Casamassima*, XXXVI

Women have more taste. They are more conciliating; they can persuade better.
                          James, H., *Washington Square*, X

Then we cleaned up, and put everything straight (a continual labor, which was beginning to afford me a pretty clear insight into a question that had often posed me—namely, how a woman with the work of only one house on her hands, manages to pass away her time).
                          Jerome, *Three Men in a Boat*, XV

Wise were our ancestors, to confine women to their proper sphere.
                          Johnstone, *The Pilgrim*, II

Woman is but a creature made for man's pleasure, and therefore every method for making her subservient to this original end of her creation is lawful for him to use.
                          Johnstone, *The Reverie*, I

The youth of man is devoted to profitable instruction; but that of woman to initiation into the paths of ruin.   *Ibid.*, *The Reverie*, II

A lady's nerves are as delicate as the strings of a harp, and must not be rudely struck.
                          Kennedy, J.P., *Horse-Shoe Robinson*, XLVIII

Rough to me, may be gracious to women.   Kingsley, C., *Hereward the Wake*, XXXVII

Women, like the world, are pretty sure to value a man (especially if there be any real worth in him) at his own price; and the more he demands for himself, the more they will give for him.   Kingsley, C., *Westward Ho!*, XII

Women are much more fond of worshipping than of being worshipped, and of obeying than of being obeyed.   *Ibid.*

I've often thought, when I've seen men die out in the desert, that if the news could be sent through the world, and the means of transport were quick enough, there would be one woman at least at each man's bedside.   Kipling, *The Light That Failed*, XII

A woman will forgive the man who has ruined her life's work so long as he gives her love: a man may forgive those who ruin the love of his life, but he will never forgive the destruction of his work. *Ibid.*, XIV

"Why are men so foolish?" "Because women are so fair."
Kirkland, *The Captain of Company K*, I

Oh credulity, bane of the female! Lathom, *The Midnight Bell*, I

Unravelling the cord of a man's existence, you will generally find the blackest hank in it twined by a woman's hand; but it is not less common to trace the golden thread to the same spindle. Lawrence, G. A., *Guy Livingstone*, XIV

Very old and very young women, in the plenitude of their benevolence, are good enough to sympathize with any tale of woe, however absurdly exaggerated; but men are most moved by the simple and quiet sorrows. *Ibid.*, XXXIII

A woman's opinion is never better known than when she speaks the very reverse of what she thinks. Lawrence, H., *The Life and Adventures of Common Sense*, I

As she affects to know nothing of those things which every woman ought to know, she knows very little of those things which no woman has occasion to know. *Ibid.*, II

Foolish and wretched is the man who builds his happiness on the frail and unstable affection of woman. Leland, *Longsword*, II

Must a man talk nonsense to be acceptable to women? Lennox, *Henrietta*, I

Women are ever readier to discover merit in the other sex than their own. *Ibid.*, II

No woman is envious of another's virtue who is conscious of her own.
Lennox, *Sophia*, I

Are women not more gentle, more witty, more beautiful than men? Lyly, *Euphues*, 125

If women knew what excellency were in them, men should never win them to their wills or wean them from their mind. *Ibid.*, 126

Women either love entirely or hate deadly. *Ibid.*, 147

Because of all creatures, the woman's wit is most excellent; therefore have the poets fained the Muses to be women, the Nymphs, the Goddesses: ensamples of rare wisdoms, and sharp capacities. Lyly, *Euphues and His England*, 281

The theft of a woman's affections is not so atrocious as that of her honor.
Mackenzie, *Julia De Roubigné*, 156

Manhood is not worthy but if it be medled with wisdom.
Malory, *Le Morte DArthur*, Two, X

No passion but that of extraordinary love can fix a woman's heart.
Manley, *Queen Zarah*, I

Pride and vanity are but too natural to our female sex.
Marishall, *Miss Clarinda Cathcart*, I

It requires great courage and great art for women to guard against so many invisible powers that war against them every moment. *Ibid.*

Women never look to consequences. Marryat, *Mr. Midshipman Easy*, II

What knows a philosopher about women? Melville, *Mardi*, XXXV

Ladies are like creeds; if you can not speak well of them, say nothing.
Melville, *Redburn*, LI

I was astonished to perceive that among the number of natives that surrounded us not a single female was to be seen. At that time I was ignorant of the fact that by the operation of the "taboo" the use of canoes in all parts of the island is rigorously prohibited to the entire sex, for whom it is death even to be seen entering one when hauled on shore; consequently, whenever a Marquesan lady voyages by water, she puts in requisition the paddles of her own fair body. Melville, *Typee*, II

Love, as a motive of action for a woman, she considered the female's lunacy and suicide. Men are born subject to it, happily, and thus the balance between the lordly half of creation and the frail is rectified. Meredith, *The Amazing Marriage*, XIII

We never can come to the exact motives of any extraordinary piece of conduct on the part of man or woman. Girls are to read, and the study of a boy starts from the monkey. *Ibid.*

Women are in and of Nature. *Ibid.*, XXXI

Women get an aid from their pride of maternity. *Ibid.*, XXXII

Is the man unsympathetic with women a hater of Nature deductively? *Ibid.*

Paris is the book of women. Meredith, *Beauchamp's Career*, X

Never pretend to know a girl by her face. *Ibid.*, XII

What does it matter what a woman thinks in politics? But he deemed it of great moment. Politically, he deemed that women have souls, a certain fire of life for exercise on earth. He appealed to reason in them; he would not hear of convictions. *Ibid.*, XVII

Women don't care uncommonly for the men who love them, though they like precious well to be loved. *Ibid.*, XIX

There may be women who think as well as feel. I don't know them. *Ibid.*

A thoroughly good-looking girl who takes a fellow for what he's doing in the world, must have ideas of him precious different from the adoration of six feet three and a fine seat in the saddle. *Ibid.*

Education for women is to teach them to rely on themselves. *Ibid.*

The less men and women know of one another, the happier for them. *Ibid.*, XX

Handsome men are rarities. And, by the way, they do not set *our* world on fire quite as much as beautiful women do yours. *Ibid.*, XXIII

The gallant man of the world feels paralyzed in his masculine sense of leadership the moment his lady assumes the initiative and directs him: he gives up at once; and thus have many nimble-witted dames from one clear start retained their advantage. *Ibid.*, XXIV

Name the two countries which alone have produced THE WOMAN, the ideal woman, the woman of art, whose beauty, grace, and wit offer her to our contemplation in an atmosphere above the ordinary conditions of the world: these two countries are France and Greece. *Ibid.*, XXV

An old spoiler of women is worse than one spoiled by them. *Ibid.*

The idea of a pretty woman exercising her mind independently, and moreover moving him to examine his own, made him smile. Could a sweet-faced girl originate a sentence that would set him reflecting? He was unable to forget it, though he allowed her no credit for it. *Ibid.*, XXVII

An heiress is a distinct species among women. *Ibid.*, XXIX

The superior strength of men to women seems to come from their examining all subjects, shrinking from none. *Ibid.*

She was one of the artificial creatures called women who dare not be spontaneous, and cannot act independently if they would continue to be admirable in the world's eye, and who for that object must remain fixed on shelves, like other marketable wares, avoiding motion to avoid shattering or tarnishing. *Ibid.*, XXXII

Telling the truth to women is an impertinence. *Ibid.*, XXXVIII

Sailors are credulous. Women are like them when they embark. *Ibid.*, XL

Women must have society, just as men must have exercise. *Ibid.*

You are unused to real suffering—that is for women!—and want to be doing instead of enduring. *Ibid.*, XLII

Women can read men by their power to love. *Ibid.*, LII

In their judgments upon women men are females.
Meredith, *Diana of the Crossways*, I

She could afford to say that the world was bad: not that women were. *Ibid.*, XXIV

The consciences of women are smooth deeps or running shallows. *Ibid.*, XXXIV

Women with brains are all heartless: they have no pity for distress, no horror of catastrophes, no joy in the happiness of the deserving. Brains in men advance a household to station; but brains in women divide it and are the wrecking of society.
Ibid., XXXVI

A man's power of putting on a face is not equal to a girl's. Men have to learn the arts which come to women by nature. Meredith, *The Egoist*, XXXIV

The only philosophic method of discovering what a young woman means, and what is in her mind, is that zigzag process of inquiry conducted by following her actions, for she can tell you nothing, and if she does not want to know a particular matter, it must be a strong beam from the central system of facts that shall penetrate her.
Meredith, *Evan Harrington*, XVII

Women are happier enslaved. Meredith, *Lord Ormont*, XXIV

To be patient in contention with women, one must have a continuous and an exclusive occupation; and the tax it lays on us conduces usually to impatience with men. *Ibid.*

I expect that Woman will be the last thing civilized by Man.
Meredith, *Ordeal of Richard Feverel*, I

Woman when she wrestles for supremacy with everyone she encounters, is but seeking her master. *Ibid.*

She's a tyrant till she's reduced to bondage, and a rebel till she's well beaten. *Ibid.*

Women are born pagans, ever on the look-out for material gods. *Ibid.*

Man is the speculative animal: woman the practical. *Ibid.*

Women esteem not easy game. *Ibid.*

The Amazon cut off a breast to battle: How will not Woman disfigure and unsex herself to gain her end? *Ibid.*

Not to have mastered a woman, he thought the meanest confession a man could make.
Ibid., II

Women are, by nature, our staunchest conservatives. We must look on them as the bulwarks of society. *Ibid.*, IV

How all but impossible it is to legislate where there are women! *Ibid.*, XVI

Whenever people of both sexes are thrown together, they will be silly, and where they are high-fed, uneducated, and barely occupied, it must be looked for as a matter of course. *Ibid.*

The self-devotion of a woman. *Ibid.*

"Girls are more innocent than boys." "Because of their education." *Ibid.*

Women who like and will have for hero a rake, how soon are you not to learn that you have taken bankrupts to your bosoms, and that the putrescent goal that attracted you is the slime of the Lake of Sin. *Ibid.*, XVIII

Man is a self-acting machine. He cannot cease to be a machine; but, though self-acting, he may lose the powers of self-guidance, and in a wrong course his very vitalities hurry him to perdition. *Ibid.*, XIX

I've always found the best fellows were wildish once. You can't expect to have a man, if he doesn't take a man's food. *Ibid.*, XXI

A sinful man—why Mrs. Caroline expected nothing better: but a sinful woman—Oh! what was a scandal, a shame! You met no sinful woman at Mrs. Caroline Grandison's parties. As a consequence, possibly, though one hardly dares suppose it, her parties were the dullest in London, and gradually fell into the hands of popular preachers, Specific Doctors, raw missionaries with their passage paid for, and a chance Dean or so; a non-dancing, stout-dining congregation. *Ibid.*, XXII

It is given to very few men to meet good women on the threshold. We find them after hard buffeting, and usually we find the one fitted for us, when our madness has mis-shaped our destiny, our lot is cast. For women are not the end, but the means, of life. *Ibid.*, XXV

"I think girls are very like boys. I am beginning to think that the subsequent immense distinction is less one of sex than of education. They are drilled into hypocrites." A girl so like a boy was quite his ideal of a girl. *Ibid.*, XXVI

Woman is nearer the vegetable than man. *Ibid.*

Women are cowards, and succumb to irony and passion, rather than yield their hearts to excellence and nature's inspiration. *Ibid.*

We women do not really care for humor. We have none ourselves, and cackle instead of laugh. *Ibid.*

Give me Nature—woman as she's made. *Ibid.*, XXVII

The ways of women, which are involution, and their practices, which are opposition, are generally best hit upon by guesswork and a bold word. *Ibid.*, XXVIII

The victims of Woman may do each other good. *Ibid.*

The always true instinct of woman, that they all worship strength in whatever form and seem to know it to be the child of heaven. *Ibid.*, XXIX

This is how the ranks of our enemies are thinned: no sooner do poor women put up a champion in their midst than she betrays them. *Ibid.*

Women are very much like men after all. *Ibid.*

Granted dear women are not quite in earnest, still the mere words they utter should be put to their good account. They do mean them, though their hearts are set the wrong way. *Ibid.*, XXXI

Women are the born accomplices of mischief. *Ibid.*, XXXII

Each woman is Eve throughout the ages: man grows, and woman does not. *Ibid.*, XXXVI

God's rarest blessing is a good woman. *Ibid.*, XXXVII

The female the practical animal. *Ibid.*, XXXVIII

Men are made to be managed, and women are born managers. *Ibid.*

To be passive in calamity is the province of no woman. *Ibid.*, XXXIX

"I don't like women to smoke." "Why mayn't they do what men do? I like the women who are brave enough not to be hypocrites." *Ibid.*, XL

Young men take joy in nothing so much as the thinking women angels: and nothing sours men of experience more than knowing that all are not quite so. *Ibid.*

There's something about a fine man on his knees that's too much for us women. *Ibid.*, XLV

Women are wonderfully quick scholars under ridicule, though it half-kills them. Meredith, *Sandra Belloni*, XVI

Women are never quite so mad in sentimentalism as men.   *Ibid.*, LV

I wonder whether girls have really an admonition of what is good for them while they are going their ways like destined machines?   Meredith, *Vittoria*, XLI

The happiest women are those who live in a small world.
                    Merriman, *In Kedar's Tents*, XXV

It is always a woman's fault.   Moore, G., *Esther Waters*, XII

A girl can't know what a man is thinking of, and we takes the worst for the best.
                    Ibid., XIV

Does not woman need the grosser aid of dogma to raise her sensual nature out of complete abjection?   Moore, G.,*Evelyn Innes*, VI

If one man isn't enough for a woman, twenty aren't too many.   *Ibid.*, XXI

The female is like a shadow: if you follow her, she runs from you; if you run, she pursues you.   Moore, G. *Muslin*, IV

A woman can't get enough of anything.   Murfree, *Story of Old Fort Loudon*, X

Why cannot women let a man go?   Page, *Red Rock*, XXXI

The way of a serpent on a rock is not harder than that of a maid with a man.
                    Ibid., XXXII

What has a woman to do with learning? And who ever heard a woman commended for valor?   Peacock, *Maid Marian*, I

A girl's mind is as hard to change as nature and the elements, and it is easier to make her renounce the devil than a lover.   *Ibid.*, III

It would be absurd to compliment a woman of refined understanding: she is above all praise.   Radcliffe, *The Mysteries of Udolpho*, I

Those contemptible foibles that frequently mark the female character—such as avarice and the love of power, which latter makes women delight to contradict and to tease when they cannot conquer.   *Ibid.*, II

Women are creatures brimful of courage. Theirs is not exactly the same quality as manly courage; that would never do, hang it all: we should have to give up trampling on them. No; it is a vicarious courage. Nothing can exceed the resolution with which they have been known to send forth men to battle; as some witty dog says, "Les femmes sont tres braves avec le peau d'autrui."   Reade, *The Cloister and the Hearth*, IX

Where is the woman who cannot act a part?   *Ibid.*, XV

Sweetest of all her charms is a woman's weakness to a manly heart.   *Ibid.*, XVII

A woman's tongue is her sword.   *Ibid.*, XXXII

We that are woman be notice-takers; and out of the tail of our eye see more than most men can glaring through a prospect glass.   *Ibid.*

None run women down but such as are too old, or too ill-favored, or too witless, to please them.   *Ibid.*, XXXVI

Wise men have not folly enough to please women, nor madness enough to desire to please them.   *Ibid.*

"I feel all a woman's weakness." "Then you are invincible."   *Ibid.*, XLVII

Each sex has its form of cruelty; man's is more brutal and terrible; but shallow women, that have neither read nor suffered, have an unmuscular barbarity of their own, when no feeling of sex steps in to overpower it.   *Ibid.*, LI

Power gives a feeble, furious woman male instruments. And the effect is as terrible as the combination is unnatural.   *Ibid.*, LXIV

A resolute woman is a very resolute thing.   *Ibid.*, XCI

Force is men's way of wooing, not women's.   *Ibid.*, XCVI

Women seem cleverer than men in this, that when they resign their wills, they do it graciously and not by halves. Perhaps they are more accustomed to knock under; and practice makes perfect.   Reade, *Griffith Gaunt*, XV

Men can't read men, but any woman can read a woman.   *Ibid.*, XXIV

'Twas my fault for making that personal which should be general. But women they are so. 'Tis our foible.   *Ibid.*, XLII

Prepossession and love have strange effects upon young ladies.
                                  Richardson, *Clarissa Harlowe*, I

I know not what wit in a woman is good for, but to make her overvalue herself, and despise every other person.   *Ibid.*

But the devil's in this female sex! Eternal misguiders! Who, that has once trespassed with them, ever recovered his virtue?   *Ibid.*

With some of the sex, insolent control is a more efficacious subduer than kindness or concession.   *Ibid.*

Women love to trade in surprises.   *Ibid.*

Females have so much advantage in smartness.   *Ibid.*

How familiar these men wretches grow upon a smile, what an awe they are struck into when we frown!   *Ibid.*

Pray, which would you have to have most sense, the woman or the man?   *Ibid.*

What if our governors should appoint churches for the women only, and others for the men? Full as proper for the promoting of true piety in both, as separate schools for their education.   *Ibid.*, II

A fine woman is too rich a jewel to hang about a poor man's neck.   *Ibid.*

Pride is perhaps the principal bulwark of female virtue.   *Ibid.*

Humble a woman, and may she not be effectually humbled?   *Ibid.*

Do not say that virtue, in the eye of Heaven, is as much a manly as a womanly grace.   *Ibid.*

The woman was made for the man, not the man for the woman. Virtue, then, is less to be dispensed with in the woman than in the man.   *Ibid.*

The female sex love to be called cruel.   *Ibid.*

Men must not let us see that we can make fools of them.   *Ibid.*

I do not think a man-woman a pretty character at all.   *Ibid.*

Men, no more than women, know how to make a moderate use of power.   *Ibid.*

Men are to ask; women are to deny.   *Ibid.*

Cunning women and witches we read of without number, but wisdom never entered into the character of a woman. It is not a requisite of the sex.   *Ibid.*

Women can't swear. They can only curse.   *Ibid.*

Women love ardors.   *Ibid.*

Man is the woman's sun; woman is the man's earth.   *Ibid.*

When the ice is once broken for these little sly rogues of females, how swiftly can they make to port!   *Ibid.*

Can education have stronger force in a woman's heart than nature? Sure it cannot.
                                  Ibid.

Many a pretty soul would yield were she not afraid that the man she favored would think the worse of her for it. *Ibid.*

I am willing to believe that women have no souls. And if so, to whom shall I be accountable for what I do to them? *Ibid.*

If women have souls, as there is no sex in ethereals, nor need of any, what plea can a lady hold of injuries done her in her lady-state when there is an end of her lady-ship? *Ibid.*

Females must seem satisfied with poor pretenses, if once they put themselves into the power of a designing man. *Ibid.*

A man who is gross in a woman's company ought to be knocked down with a club; for, like so many musical instruments, touch but a single wire, and the dear souls are sensible all over. *Ibid.*, III

Women tacitly acknowledge the inferiority of their sex, in the pride they take to behold a kneeling lover at their feet. *Ibid.*

Women love busy scenes. Still-life is their aversion. *Ibid.*

A woman will create a storm, rather than be without one. So as they can preside in the whirlwind, and direct it, they are happy. *Ibid.*

Women's tongues are licensed. *Ibid.*

Women have a high opinion of what they can do for a man. *Ibid.*

Delicate women *make* delicate women, as well as decent men. *Ibid.*

There have been more girls ruined, at least prepared for ruin, by their own sex than directly by the attempts and delusions of men. *Ibid.*

The first struggle with a woman is usually the last. *Ibid.*

The world can furnish mountainous proof of the imbecility of women. *Ibid.*

All women are cowards at bottom: only violent where they may. *Ibid.*

Women ought to be more scrupulous than men where they lodge. *Ibid.*

Revenge and obstinacy will make women, even the best of them, do very unaccountable things. Rather than not put out both eyes of the man they are offended with, they will give up one of their own. *Ibid.*

Many a woman who will not show herself at the door has tipped the sly, the intelligible wink, from the windows. *Ibid.*

The generality of ladies are rakes in their hearts. *Ibid.*, IV

To show any of you men a favor today, you would expect it as a right tomorrow. *Ibid.*

All that a woman can learn above the useful knowledge proper to her sex, let her learn. This will show that she is a good housewife of her time; and that she has not a narrow or confined genius. *Ibid.*

What can be more disgraceful to a woman, than either, through negligence of dress, to be found to be a learned slattern; or, through ignorance of household management, to be known to be a stranger to domestic economy? *Ibid.*

Women are inferior in nothing to men but in want of opportunities. *Ibid.*

It is demonstrable that a lady at eighteen, take the world through, is more prudent and conversable than a man at twenty-five. *Ibid.*

It is grown more a wonder that men are resisted, than that women comply.
Richardson, *Pamela*, 68

How much it behoves the fair sex to stand upon their guard against artful contrivances, especially when riches and power conspire against innocence and a low estate.
Ibid., 91

Why are poor foolish maidens tried with such dangers, when they have such weak minds to grapple with them?   *Ibid.*, 159

A woman shines not forth to the public as a man.   *Ibid.*, 274

I considered all intellectual attainments as either useless or impertinent in women.
Richardson, *Sir Charles Grandison*, One, I

Women know better how to be sorry than to amend.   *Ibid.*

At twenty, time always stands still with women.   *Ibid.*

A lady's age once known, will be always remembered; and that more for spite than love.   *Ibid.*

It is a sign, when women are so desirous to conceal their age, that they think they shall be good for nothing when in years.   *Ibid.*

An old head upon a young pair of shoulders would make rare work among women.
Ibid.

Where no duty is neglected for the acquirement; where modesty, delicacy, and a teachable spirit, are preserved, as characteristics of the sex, it need not be thought a disgrace for women to be supposed to know something.   *Ibid.*

A woman is a man's.   *Ibid.*

Young women are almost as unwilling to find out themselves as to be found out by others.   *Ibid.*, One, II

Men do not make women fools. They have folly deep-rooted within them.   *Ibid.*

One half of a woman's virtue is pride; the other half, policy.   *Ibid.*

Woman's weakness is man's strength.   *Ibid.*

Silly girls distinguish not between the would and the should.   *Ibid.*

The man who knows how to say agreeable things to a woman has her vanity on his side; since, to doubt his veracity, would be to question her own merit.   *Ibid.*

Women ought always to despise, and directly to break with the man, who offers to exact a promise from them.   *Ibid.*

Men and women are devils to one another. They need no other tempter.   *Ibid.*

It is not in woman to be unreserved.   *Ibid.*, Two, III

Affection or esteem between man and woman, once forfeited, hardly ever is recovered.
Ibid.

The most profligate of men love modesty in women, at the very time they are forming plots to destroy it in a particular object.   *Ibid.*

No woman is entitled to ridicule a lover whom she does not intend to encourage.
Ibid.

Woman is the glory of all created existence.   *Ibid.*

Ladies must not be easily won.   *Ibid.*

The cause of virtue, and of women, can hardly be separated.   *Ibid.*

In the pride of their hearts, men are apt to suppose that nature has designed them to be superior to women.   *Ibid.*

The woman who has been once wrong has reason to be always afraid of herself.   *Ibid.*

Very few causes can justify a woman's anger.   *Ibid.*, Two, IV

Women were given to delight, not torment men.   *Ibid.*

Women are of gentle natures; and, being accustomed to be humored, opposition sits not easy upon them. *Ibid.*

Whenever women know their own minds, then men need not be long doubtful of them. *Ibid.*

Flippant women are afraid of wise men. *Ibid.*

Meekness was never attributed to woman as a fault. *Ibid.*

Wise or foolish before, women are all equally foolish in love. *Ibid.*, Three, VI

Women are afraid of wise men, and seldom choose them when a fool offers. *Ibid.*

In common intercourse and conversation, why are we to be perpetually considering the sex of the person we are talking to? *Ibid.*

Why must women always be addressed in an appropriated language; and not treated on the common footing of reasonable creatures? And why must they, from a false notion of modesty, be afraid of shewing themselves to be such, and affect a childish ignorance? *Ibid.*

I would not have women enter into learned disputes, for which they are rarely qualified; but there is a degree of knowledge very compatible with their duties; therefore not unbecoming them, and necessary to make them fit companions for men of sense: a character in which they will always be found more useful than that of a plaything, the amusement of an idle hour. *Ibid.*

The advantages of education which men must necessarily have over women, if they have made the proper use of them, will have set them so forward on the race, that women can never overtake them. But then don't let men despise women for this, as if their superiority were entirely founded on a natural difference of capacity! Despise them as women, and value themselves merely as men; for it is not the hat or cap which covers the head that decides the merit of it. *Ibid.*

Women are women sooner than men are men. *Ibid.*

There is a difference in the constitution, in the temperament, of the two sexes, that gives to the one advantages it denies to the other. *Ibid.*

Why has nature made a difference in the beauty, proportion, and symmetry, in the persons of the two sexes? Why gave it delicacy, softness, grace, to that of the woman; strength, firmness, to men; a capacity to bear labor and fatigue; and courage, to protect the other? Why gave it a distinction, both in qualities and plumage, to the different sexes of the feathered race? Why in the courage of the male and female animals?—the surly bull, the meek, the beneficent, cow, for one instance? *Ibid.*

Can there be characters more odious than those of a masculine woman, and an effeminate man? *Ibid.*

Women, whose minds seem to be cast in a masculine mold: those married women who are so kind as to take the reins out of their husbands' hands, in order to save the honest men trouble. *Ibid.*

In the economy of Providence, weaker powers are given generally for weaker purposes. *Ibid.*

Both God and Nature have designed a very apparent difference in the minds of both sexes, as well as in the peculiar beauties of their persons. Were it not so, their offices would be confounded, and the women would not perhaps so readily submit to those domestic ones in which it is their province to shine, and the men would be allotted the distaff, or the needle. *Ibid.*

Supposing that all human souls are equal; yet the very design of the different machines in which they are inclosed is to super-induce a temporary difference on their original equality; a difference adapted to the different purposes for which they are designed by Providence in the transitory state. When those purposes are at an end, this difference will be at an end. *Ibid.*

When sex ceases, inequality of souls will cease; and women will be on a foot with men, as to intellectuals, in Heaven.   *Ibid.*

What woman who thinks but will prefer a good man to all others, however distinguished by rank, fortune, or person?   *Ibid.,* Three, VII

What wretched simpletons are we women! Daughters of gewgaw, folly, ostentation, trifle!   *Ibid.*

What is the inclemency of season, what are winds, mountains, seas, to a woman who has set her heart on an adventure?   *Ibid.*

It is delightful to be a woman; but every man thanks the Lord devoutly that he isn't one.   Schreiner, *The Story of an African Farm,* Part II, IV

The less a woman has in her head the lighter she is for climbing.   *Ibid.*

I shall be old and ugly one day, and I shall look for men's chivalrous help, but I shall not find it. The bees are very attentive to the flowers till their honey is done, and then they fly over them. I don't know if the flowers feel grateful to the bees; they are great fools if they do.   *Ibid.*

Do you think if Napoleon had been born a woman he would have been contented to give small tea-parties and talk small scandal?   *Ibid.*

There was never a man who said one word for woman but he said two for man, and three for the whole human race.   *Ibid.*

Men bring weighty arguments against us when we ask for the perfect freedom of women; but when you come to the objections, they are like pumpkin devils with candles inside, hollow, and can't bite.   *Ibid.*

Men say, "If the women have liberty, they will be found in positions for which they are not fitted!" If two men climb one ladder, did you ever see the weakest anywhere but at the foot?   *Ibid.*

Men say women have one great and noble work left them, and they do it ill. . . . And yet, thank God, we have this work: it is the one window through which we see into the great world of earnest labor.   *Ibid.*

The woman who does woman's work needs a many-sided, multiform culture; the heights and depths of human life must not be beyond the reach of her vision; she must have knowledge of men and things in many states, a wide catholicity of sympathy, the strength that springs from knowledge, and the magnanimity which springs from strength. We *women* bear the world, and *we* make it.   *Ibid.*

The first six years of our life make us; all that is added later is veneer; and yet some say, if a woman can cook a dinner or dress herself well she has culture enough.   *Ibid.*

When men and women are equals they will love no more.   *Ibid.*

If a man lets a woman do what he doesn't like *he's a muff.*   *Ibid.,* Part II, V

A woman to be womanly should have nothing striking or peculiar about her. Men may turn to one side or the other; woman never must.   Schreiner, *Undine,* VIII

It would be unnatural for a woman to quarrel with curiosity.
                              Scott, S., *A Description of Millenium Hall,* 91

We are always ready to esteem a woman who will give us leave to do so.   *Ibid.,* 210

Women are said to admire men of courage, on account of their own deficiency in that qualification.   Sir Walter Scott, *Heart of Midlothian,* IX

Meaner women, like the lesser lights of heaven, have revolutions and phases, but who shall impute mutability to the sun, or to Elizabeth?
                              Sir Walter Scott, *Kenilworth,* XXXVIII

Freedom is for man alone; woman must ever seek a protector, since nature made her incapable to defend herself.　　　　　Sir Walter Scott, *Quentin Durward*, XXIII

There is no sense in being too quiet with women folk.
Sir Walter Scott, *Redgauntlet*, V

Every woman that yields makes herself a slave to her seducer.
Sir Walter Scott, *St. Ronan's Well*, XXXII

Women's wits are quick in spying the surest means of avenging a slight.
Ibid., XXXIV

I am like all women: I love those best who deserve least.
Shaw, *The Irrational Knot*, XIV

It is twice as easy to make a woman happy as to feed a man.　　　　*Ibid.*, XVIII

"Not 'will not' but 'better not.'" "A very womanly distinction."　　　　*Ibid.*, XXIII

The glorious mystery of a woman's heart.　　　Shaw, *An Unsocial Socialist*, XIV

Man's experience is woman's best eyesight.　　　　Sidney, *Arcadia*, III

A fair woman shall not only command without authority, but persuade without speaking. She shall not need to procure attention, for the eyes of men will chain their ears unto it. Men venture lives to conquer, she conquers lives without venturing.　　*Ibid.*

No is no negative in a woman's mouth.　　　　*Ibid.*

A lover's modesty among women is much more praised than liked.　　　*Ibid.*

That imperious masterfulness which nature gives to men above women.　　*Ibid.*

Women very soon discern when they have to deal with a fool.
Simms, *The Scout*, XXVI

Devilish strange animal is woman.　　　　*Ibid.*, XXVIII

Women go by looks. Smooth flowing locks, big, bushy whiskers, and a bold, death-defying face will do much among a regiment of women.　　　*Ibid.*, XXXII

A woman is never more flattered by a man than when he solicits her advice.
Simms, *Woodcraft*, XXXI

Women are weak vessels that ain't expected to be reasonable, and things will tickle their ears that are only foolishness in the ears of a sensible man.　　　*Ibid.*, XLII

A woman of experience likes a man the better if he gives her no time for long thinking. Women naturally expect to be taken by storm. They like a good excuse for surrendering.
Ibid., XLIII

Women are naturally fruitful of expedients in cases of [domestic] emergency.
Smollett, *Peregrine Pickle*, 162

I have been unhappy because I loved, and was a woman.　　　　*Ibid.*, 335

A man has seldom an offer of kindness to make a woman, but she has a presentiment of it some moments before.　　　Sterne, *A Sentimental Journey*, 29

The nonsense of the old women (of both sexes) throughout the kingdom.
Sterne, *Tristram Shandy*, V

All the great negotiators, when they have not been women, have had women at their elbows.　　　Stevenson, *Prince Otto*, Book II, V

What boys men are! What lovers of big words!　　　　*Ibid.*

Who is born a woman is born a fool.　　　　*Ibid.*, Book II, XIII

In the old times, women did not get their lives written, though many of them were much better worth writing than the men's.　　　Stowe, *Orr's Island*, XV

Man's utter ignorance of woman's nature is a cause of a great deal of unsuspected cruelty which he practices toward her. *Ibid.*, XXII

A woman saint may be excused for a little gentle vindictiveness. *Ibid.*, XXIII

You men must have everything, the enterprise, the adventure, the novelty, the pleasure of feeling that you are something, and can do something in the world; and besides all this, you want the satisfaction of knowing that we women are following in chains behind your triumphal car. *Ibid.*, XXXI

The women were proposed to be taxed according to their beauty and skill in dressing; wherein they had the same privilege with the men, to be determined by their own judgment. But constancy, chastity, good sense, and good nature were not rated, because they would not bear the charge of collecting. Swift, *Gulliver's Travels*, Laputa

The pages of history do not prove the superiority of man. Taylor, *Hannah Thurston*, V

When we consider the position which man has forced woman to occupy, we should rather wonder that she has so often resisted his authority, and won possession of the empire which he had appropriated to himself. *Ibid.*

The first poet who sang may have been Homer, but the second was Sappho. *Ibid.*

When God calls a human being to be the discoverer of His eternal laws, or the illustrator of His eternal beauty, He does not stop to consider the question of sex. *Ibid.*

No man can be independent of woman's judgment, without loss to himself. Her purer nature is a better guide to him than his clouded instincts. *Ibid.*, XXXI

Since the days of Adam, there has been hardly a mischief done in this world but a woman has been at the bottom of it. Thackeray, *Barry Lyndon*, I

Women are born to be our greatest comforts and conveniences; our moral bootjacks, as it were. *Ibid.*, XIII

'Tis strange what a man may do, and a woman yet think him an angel. Thackeray, *Henry Esmond*, Book I, VII

Women do not always hate a man for scorning and despising them. Women do not revolt at the rudeness and arrogance of their natural superiors. Women, if properly trained, come down to heel at the master's bidding and lick the hand that has been often raised to hit them. Thackeray, *Lovel the Widower*, III

Woman forgives but too readily. Thackeray, *Vanity Fair*, XXIII

What do men know about women's martyrdoms? *Ibid.*, LVI

Every one of the dear sex is the rival of the rest of her kind. *Ibid.*, LXII

The female Inquisition. *Ibid.*

It is a woman's duty to be attractive. Tourgee, *Murvale Eastman*, XVII

God gave woman beauty to lighten the world. With it she is able to exorcise evil and strengthen the impulse for good. Man does not need it. He is the doer, the achiever. Woman is the inspirer, the consoler. Her beauty is the complement of his strength. *Ibid.*

A woman should rejoice in her beauty just as a man exults in his strength. It is her kingdom. *Ibid.*

Wealth, which hides a man's defects, is apt to magnify a woman's. *Ibid.*, XX

Are not girls always mercenary? Trollope, *Ayala's Angel*, XVIII

One acquirement will drive out others. A woman, if she cannot be beautiful, should at any rate be graceful, and if she cannot soar to poetry, should at least be soft and unworldly. *Ibid.*

A woman's hand is soft, but she can steel her heart when she thinks it necessary, as no man can do. *Ibid.*, XXVIII

A man can drop a word; but a girl is a different sort of thing. One can't drop a girl, even if one tries. *Ibid.*, XXX

It often happens that ladies mean that to be expressed which it does not become them to say out loud. *Ibid.*, XXXVIII

One lady never considers another to be divine. *Ibid.*, XXXIX

It is a young lady's special province to be ornamental. *Ibid.*, XLVI

To be self-denying is all that is necessary to a woman. *Ibid.*, LIX

It is the nature of young men to be much younger than young ladies. *Ibid.*, LXIV

That nice appreciation of the feelings of others which belongs of right exclusively to women. Trollope, *Barchester Towers*, LII

To be in love, as an absolute, well-marked, acknowledged fact, is the condition of a woman more frequently and more readily than of a man. Such is not the common theory on the matter, as it is the man's business to speak, and the woman's business to be reticient. Trollope, *The Eustace Diamonds*, IV

There are men by whom a woman, if she have wit, beauty, and no conscience, cannot be withstood. *Ibid.*, XIX

Women are never happy without men. Men can get along without women, and women can't without men. *Ibid.*, XXIII

There is always a savor of misfortune—or, at least, of melancholy—about a household which has no man to look after it. *Ibid.*, XXIV

"I hope I haven't kept you waiting," she said. "Women always do. It gives them importance." *Ibid.*, XLII

It is inexpressibly difficult for a man to refuse tender of a woman's love. *Ibid.*, LIII

So like a man's pride! *Ibid.*

Men don't know how sly women can be. *Ibid.*, LVI

There's nothing a pretty woman can't do when she has got rid of all sense of shame. *Ibid.*, LXXII

A man, to be a man in her eyes, should be able to swear that all his geese are swans;—should be able to reckon his swans by the dozen, though he have not a feather belonging to him, even from a goose's wing. *Ibid.*, LXXIII

Is it not the fate of women to play the tunes which men dictate—except in some rare case in which the woman can make herself the dictator? *Ibid.*, LXXVI

What lady will ever scruple to avoid her taxes? *Ibid.*, LXXIX

What woman ever understood her duty to the State? *Ibid.*

When girls have headaches it comes from tight-lacing, and not walking enough, and carrying all manner of nasty smells about with them. How is a woman not to have a headache, when she carries a thing on the back of her poll as big as a gardener's wheelbarrow? Trollope, *He Knew He Was Right*, VIII

Women are slow to burn their household gods. *Ibid.*, X

Women are so dependent on men. A woman can get nothing without a man. *Ibid.*, XXV

A man who is a nobody can perhaps make himself somebody—or, at any rate, he can try; but a woman has no means of trying. She is a nobody, and a nobody she must remain. *Ibid.*, LI

The commonest folly of man in regard to women is a weak taste for intrigue, with little or nothing on which to feed it—a worse than feminine aptitude for male coquetry, which never ascends beyond a desire that somebody shall hint that there is something peculiar; and which is shocked and retreats backwards into its boots when anything like a consequence forces itself on the apprehension. *Ibid.*, LXXXIII

The lad who talks at twenty as men should talk at thirty, has seldom much to say worth the hearing when he is forty; and the girl who at eighteen can shine in society with composure, has generally given over shining before she is a full-grown woman.
Ibid., XCVII

I prefer men who are improper, and all that sort of thing. If I were a man myself I should go in for everything I ought to leave alone. Trollope, *Phineas Finn*, X

I do not believe in girls being saviors to men. The man should be the savior to the girl. *Ibid.*, XIX

I hate a stupid man who can't talk to me, and I hate a clever man who talks me down. I don't like a man who is too lazy to make any effort to shine; but I particularly dislike the man who is always striving for effect. I abominate a humble man, but yet I love to perceive that a man acknowledges the superiority of my sex, and youth, and all that kind of thing. I want to be flattered without plain flattery. A man who would tell me that I am pretty, unless he is over seventy, ought to be kicked out of the room. But a man who can't show me that he thinks me so without saying a word about it, is a lout. *Ibid.*, XXII

She would teach herself to love him. Nay, she had taught herself to love him. *Ibid.*

A woman, and therefore guarded. *Ibid.*, XXXIX

What can a woman become if she remain single? The curse is to be a woman at all. *Ibid.*, LI

Women sympathize most effectually with men, as men do with women. *Ibid.*, LIV

A woman who is alone in the world is ever regarded with suspicion. *Ibid.*, LXII

A woman cannot transfer her heart. *Ibid.*, LXIV

Did any man in love ever yet find himself able to tell the lady whom he loved that he was very much disappointed on discovering that she had got no money? If so, his courage was greater than his love. Trollope, *The Small House*, XII

How is a girl to get along if she be not false? Trollope, *The Three Clerks*, XXII

How few women there are who can raise themselves above the quagmire of what we call love, and make themselves anything but playthings for men.
Trollope, *The Way We Live Now*, I

When a man has kissed a woman it goes against the grain with him to say the very next moment that he is sorry for what he has done. It is as much as to declare that the kiss had not answered his expectation. *Ibid.*

Nothing but age enables men and women to know each other intimately.
Ibid., XXXI

As long as there are men to fight for women, it may be well to leave the fighting to the men. *Ibid.*, LI

If woman be treated as prey, shall she not fight as a beast of prey? *Ibid.*

A man should kneel to a woman for love, not for pardon. *Ibid.*

What a box women are put into, measured for it, and put in young.
Twain and Warner, *The Gilded Age*, Volume I, XIV

The reason novelists nearly always fail in depicting women when they make them act, is that they let them do what they have observed some woman has done at some time or another. And that is where they make a mistake; for a woman will never do again what has been done before. *Ibid.*, Volume I, XXI

Men do not want women educated to do anything, to be able to earn an honest living by their own exertions.   *Ibid.*, Volume II, XVII

When a man becomes only an elegant piece of furniture in a woman's life, to be dusted at times, and admired at others, and shoved up garret at last by remorseless clean fingers that wipe the cobwebs of him off, it will be generally found that he endures the annoyance of neglected furniture . . . little more.

Ward, E.S.P., *The Silent Partner*, VII

Woman's happiness depends so much upon the continuation of the surroundings and sympathies in which she is bred.   Warner, *A Little Journey in the World*, IV

In our conventional life women must move behind a mask in a world of uncertainties.
Ibid., V

Who says that a woman cannot be as cruel as a man?   *Ibid.*, XVIII

Who knows what is in a woman? How many moods in a quarter of an hour, and which is the characteristic one?   *Ibid.*, XX

Woman, the consummate flower of civilization.   *Ibid.*, XXII

Women have no appreciation of good looks; at least, good women have not.
Wilde, *The Picture of Dorian Gray*, I

No woman is a genius.   *Ibid.*, IV

Women are a decorative sex. They never have anything to say, but they say it charmingly.   *Ibid.*

Women represent the triumph of matter over mind, just as men represent the triumph of mind over morals.   *Ibid.*

Women defend themselves by attacking, just as they attack by sudden and strange surrenders.   *Ibid.*, V

"Pleasure is to adore some one." "That is certainly better than being adored. Being adored is a nuisance. Women treat us just as humanity treats its gods. They worship us, and are always bothering us to do something for them." "I should have said that whatever they ask for they had first given to us. They create love in our natures. They have a right to demand it back."   *Ibid.*, VI

"Women give to men the very gold of their lives." "Possibly, but they invariably want it back in such very small change. Women inspire us with the desire to do masterpieces and always prevent us from carrying them out."   *Ibid.*

Women are better suited to bear sorrow than men. They live on their emotions.
Ibid., VII

Women never know when the curtain has fallen. They always want a sixth act.
Ibid., VIII

Ordinary women always console themselves. Some of them do it by going in for sentimental colors. Never trust a woman who wears mauve, whatever her age may be, or a woman over thirty-five who is fond of pink ribbons. It always means that they have a history. Others find a great consolation in suddenly discovering the good qualities of their husbands. They flaunt their conjugal felicity in one's face, as if it were the most fascinating of sins.   *Ibid.*

Religion consoles some ordinary women. Its mysteries have all the charm of a flirtation.
Ibid.

Women appreciate cruelty, downright cruelty, more than anything else. They have wonderfully primitive instincts. We have emancipated them, but they remain slaves looking for their masters, all the same.   *Ibid.*

Women love us for our defects. If we have enough of them, they will forgive us everything, even our intellects.   *Ibid.*, XV

I like men who have a future and women who have a past.   *Ibid.*

She is very clever, too clever for a woman. She lacks the indefinable charm of weakness. It is the feet of clay that make the gold of the image precious. Her feet are very pretty, but they are not feet of clay. White porcelain feet, if you like. They have been through the fire, and what fire does not destroy, it hardens. *Ibid.*

I am sick of women who love one. Women who hate one are much more interesting. *Ibid.*, XVI

"Describe us women as a sex." "Sphinxes without secrets." *Ibid.*, XVII

Women are not always allowed a choice. *Ibid.*

How fond women are of doing dangerous things! *Ibid.*, XVIII

A woman will flirt with anybody in the world as long as other people are looking on. *Ibid.*

It is impossible a woman should fall in love with a man that makes no advances. Young, *The Adventures of Emmera*, II

MARRIAGE: *see also* LOVE; MALE/FEMALE; etc.

Occasionally a matrimonial epidemic appears, especially towards spring, devastating society, thinning the ranks of bachelordom, and leaving mothers lamenting for their fairest daughters. Alcott, *Old-Fashioned Girl*, XIX

If you have acquired the divine habits, marriage may unhinge them. It often forces even the pious into immoralities. Amory, *Life of John Buncle*, II

Celibacy is popery and hell in perfection. It is the doctrine of devils, and a war with the Almighty. *Ibid.*

Though, for the sake of peace, the man's will is to be the rule, the wife is his natural adviser and counsellor, whose opinion he should always listen to and follow if he finds it more just and reasonable than his own. Anonymous, *The Birmingham Counterfeit*, II

It is contrary to the laws of God and nature for a husband to require blind obedience from his wife. *Ibid.*, II

Marriage becomes a state wherein man acquires a new set of conceptions, a new system of thoughts, which prove highly advantageous and suitable to his nature. *Ibid.*

Single persons who, without sufficient reason, refuse to marry are to be considered as half-men. *Ibid.*

Matrimony is the most delicious state of life a man can enjoy. When all other amusements grow dull and insipid, he can always find an inexhaustible fund of entertainment in tormenting his wife. Anonymous, *The Egg*, 229

Where young ladies blindly cast themselves away upon men who turn out bad husbands, they are seldom found to repine at their bad fortune. Anonymous, *History of Tom Jones in His Married State*, 23

Where there is not a union of minds, wedlock is but a more solemn prostitution. *Ibid.*

All marriages are alike in the eye of heaven. Anonymous, *The Lady's Drawing Room*, 145

Wherefore it should be praiseworthy in a woman to submit to ill treatment from her husband has always been a mystery. *Ibid.*, 270

Second marriages are happy. Anonymous, *The Modern Fine Gentleman*, II

Matrimony I look upon as a civil death, and people that have the misfortune to be in it as only the ghosts of men. Anonymous, *Peregrinations of Jeremiah Grant*, 97

There is nothing more displeasing to a man of sense than to see his wife make no difference between matters of the greatest moment, and those of no moment at all. When a good lady in the same tone of voice, and with equal concern, inquires after her husband's health, and how a spot came upon the floor, the consequence is natural that he thinks a spot upon the floor affects her as much as his own health.

Anonymous, *Sophronia*, 75

Some women unconsciously establish a habit of being proposed to.

Atherton, *Senator North*, Book I, XIII

Some men are tyrants in public life and slaves at home—to a beautiful woman.

Ibid., Book I, XIV

No woman is really satisfied in any other state [but marriage].   *Ibid.*, Book III, VI

She wanted nothing on earth but to be the wife of the man whom she had loved for a lifetime in a year.   *Ibid.*, Book III, XIX

There certainly are not so many men of large fortune in the world as there are pretty women to deserve them.   Austen, *Mansfield Park*, Volume One, I

I pay very little regard to what any young person says on the subject of marriage. If they profess a disinclination for it, I only set it down that they have not yet seen the right person.   *Ibid.*, Volume One, IV

An engaged woman is always more agreeable than a disengaged. She is satisifed with herself. Her cares are over, and she feels that she may exert all her powers of pleasing without suspicion.   *Ibid.*, Volume One, V

"Everybody is taken in at some period or another." "Not always in marriage." "In marriage especially."   *Ibid.*

Marriage is, of all transactions, the one in which people expect most from others, and are least honest themselves.   *Ibid.*

Marriage is a manoeuvring business.   *Ibid.*

You see the evil in marriage, but you do not see the consolation.   *Ibid.*

The admiral hated marriage, and thought it never pardonable in a young man of independent fortune.   *Ibid.*, Volume Two, XII

Some opposition is friendly to matrimonial happiness.   *Ibid.*, Volume Three, IV

When two sympathetic hearts meet in the marriage state, matrimony may be called a happy life.   *Ibid.*, Volume Three, V

In a review of the two houses, as they appeared to her before the end of a week, Fanny was tempted to apply to them Dr. Johnson's celebrated judgment as to matrimony and celibacy, and say, that though Mansfield Park might have some pains, Portsmouth could have no pleasures.   *Ibid.*, Volume Three, VIII

I consider a country-dance as an emblem of marriage. Fidelity and complaisance are the principal duties of both; and those men who do not choose to dance or marry themselves have no business with the partners or wives of their neighbors.

Austen, *Northanger Abbey*, X

People that marry can never part, but must go and keep house together. People that dance only stand opposite to each other in a long room for half an hour.   *Ibid.*

Going to one wedding brings on another.   *Ibid.*, XV

I hate the idea of one great fortune looking out for another.   *Ibid.*

Husbands and wives generally understand when opposition will be vain.

Austen, *Persuasion*, VII

The husband had not been what he ought, and the wife had been led among that part of mankind which made her think worse of the world than she hoped it deserved.

Ibid., XVII

When one lives in the world, a man or woman's marrying for money is too common to strike one as it ought. *Ibid.*, XXI

She gloried in being a sailor's wife, but she must pay the tax of quick alarm for belonging to that profession which is, if possible, more distinguished in its domestic virtues than in its national importance. *Ibid.*, XXIV

It is a truth universally acknowledged, that a single man in possession of a good fortune, must be in want of a wife. Austen, *Pride and Prejudice*, Volume I, I

I have a high respect for your nerves. They are my old friends. I have heard you mention them with consideration these twenty years [of marriage] at least. *Ibid.*

Happiness in marriage is entirely a matter of chance. *Ibid.*, Volume I, VI

A lady's imagination is very rapid; it jumps from admiration to love, from love to matrimony in a moment. *Ibid.*

"Well, my dear," said Mr. Bennet, "if your daughter should have a dangerous fit of illness, if she should die, it would be a comfort to know that it was all in pursuit of Mr. Bingley, and under your orders." *Ibid.*, Volume I, VII

The girls were not the only objects of Mr. Collins's admiration. The hall, the dining-room, and all its furniture were examined and praised; and his commendation of everything would have touched Mrs. Bennet's heart, but for the mortifying supposition of his viewing it all as his own future property. *Ibid.*, Volume I, XIII

Mr. Collins had only to change [his marriage proposal] from Jane to Elizabeth—and it was soon done—done while Mrs. Bennet was stirring the fire. *Ibid.*, Volume I, XV

Your portion is unhappily so small that it will in all likelihood undo the effects of your loveliness and amiable qualifications. As I must therefore conclude that you are not serious in your rejection of me, I shall choose to attribute it to your wish of increasing my love by suspense, according to the usual practice of elegant females. *Ibid.*, Volume I, XIX

From this day you must be a stranger to one of your parents.— Your mother will never see you again if you do *not* marry Mr. Collins, and I will never see you again if you *do*. *Ibid.*, Volume I, XX

Without thinking highly either of men or of matrimony, marriage had always been her object; it was the only honorable provision for well-educated young women of small fortune, and however uncertain of giving happiness, must be their pleasantest preservative from want. *Ibid.*, Volume I, XXII

The strangeness of Mr. Collins's making two offers of marriage within three days was nothing in comparison of his being now accepted. *Ibid.*

They are young in the ways of the world, and not yet open to the mortifying conviction that handsome young men must have something to live on, as well as the plain. *Ibid.*, Volmue II, III

What is the difference in matrimonial affairs, between the mercenary and the prudent motive? Where does discretion end, and avarice begin? *Ibid.*, Volume II, IV

Had Elizabeth's opinion been all drawn from her own family, she could not have formed a very pleasing picture of conjugal felicity or domestic comfort. *Ibid.*, Volume II, XIX

She was more alive to the disgrace which the want of new clothes must reflect on her daughter's nuptials than to any sense of shame at her eloping and living with Wickham, a fortnight before they took place. *Ibid.*, Volume III, VIII

You must go lower, because I am a married woman. *Ibid.*, Volume III, IX

Married women have never much time for writing. *Ibid.*, Volume III, XI

The loss of her daughter [to marriage] made Mrs. Bennet very dull for several days.

Ibid.

It is a delightful thing to have a daughter well married.

Ibid.

You are each of you so complying, that nothing will ever be resolved on; so easy, that every servant will cheat you; and so generous, that you will always exceed your income.

Ibid., Volume III, XIII

Do anything rather than marry without affection.

Ibid., Volume III, XVII

Your lively talents would place you in the greatest danger in an unequal marriage.

Ibid.

A woman may take liberties with her husband which a brother will not always allow in a sister more than ten years younger than himself.

Ibid., Volume III, XIX

She had only two daughters, both of whom she had lived to see respectably married, and she had now therefore nothing to do but to marry all the rest of the world.

Austen, *Sense and Sensibility*, Volume I, VIII

Thirty-five has nothing to do with matrimony.

Ibid.

A woman of seven and twenty can never hope to feel or inspire affection again, and if her home be uncomfortable, or her fortune small, I can suppose she might bring herself to submit to the offices of a nurse for the sake of the provision and security of a wife.

Ibid.

One never thinks of married men's being beaux; they have something else to do.

Ibid., Volume I, XXI

I would rather be a teacher than marry a man I did not like.

Austen, *The Watsons*, I

I should not like marrying a disagreeable man, but I do not think there *are* very many disagreeable men.

Ibid.

Elderly ladies should be careful how they make a second choice.

Ibid.

When an old lady plays the fool [in her choice of husbands], it is not in the course of nature that she should suffer from it many years.

Ibid.

If women didn't cheat themselves there wouldn't be no marriages.

Bates, *Puritans*, XI

In all times, and in all places, *matrimony* has been a *matter of money*.

Brackenridge, *Modern Chivalry*, Part II, Volume I

Whenever I marry, I am resolved my husband shall not be a rival, but a foil to me. I will suffer no competitor near the throne; I shall exact an undivided homage: his devotions shall not be shared between me and the shape he sees in his mirror.

Bronte, C., *Jane Eyre*, XVII

Reader, I married him.

Ibid., XXXVIII

To be together is for us to be at once as free as in solitude, as gay as in company. We talk, I believe, all day long: to talk to each other is but a more animated and an audible thinking.

Ibid.

When people love, the next step is they marry.

Bronte, C., *Shirley*, VII

Marriage and love are superfluities, intended only for the rich, who live at ease, and have no need to take thought for the morrow; or desperations, the last and reckless joy of the deeply wretched, who never hope to rise out of the slough of their utter poverty.

Ibid., IX

Marriage is never wholly happy. Two people can never literally be as one.

Ibid., XXI

A woman engaged loses all her attractions as a woman.

Brooke, *Emily Montague*, I

Marriage is seldom happy where there is a great disproportion of fortune.

Ibid.

Widows are fair prey, as being sufficiently experienced to take care of themselves.
Ibid.

Some men are weak enough to decline marrying the woman on earth most pleasing to themselves, because not thought handsome by the generality of their companions.
Ibid. II

To give delight, marriage must join two minds, not devote a slave to the will of an imperious lord.
Ibid.

Whatever conveys the idea of subjection necessarily destroys that of love, of which I am so convinced, that I have always wished the word OBEY expunged from the marriage ceremony.
Ibid.

Women by ill temper make husbands pay dear for their fidelity.
Ibid.

Do not lose the mistress in the wife.
Ibid.

In delicate minds, love is seldom the consequence of marriage.
Ibid., III

Marrying a man one dislikes is the most deliberate and shameful degree of vice of which the human mind is capable.
Ibid.

If people married from affection, there would be no such thing as gallantry at all.
Ibid., IV

Matrimony makes young ladies amazingly learned.
Ibid.

It is really cruel of papas and mamas to shut up two poor innocent creatures in a house together in marriage, to plague and torment one another, who might have been very happy separate.
Ibid.

Those who marry from love may grow rich; but those who marry to be rich will never love.
Ibid.

Marriage is sacred, but iniquitous laws, by making it a compact of slavery by imposing impracticable conditions and extorting impious promises have converted it into something flagititious and hateful.
Brown, C. B., *Alcuin*, III

Marriage is an union founded on free and mutual consent. It cannot exist without friendship. It cannot exist without personal fidelity. As soon as the union ceases to be spontaneous it ceases to be just. This is the sum, the completeness of this definition.
Ibid., III

Men choose a wife as they choose any household movable, and when the irritation of the senses has subsided, the attachment that remains is the offspring of habit.
Brown, C. B., *Ormond*, 104

A wife is generally nothing more than a household superintendent.
Ibid., 105

Marriage is an instrument of pleasure or pain in proportion as equality is more or less.
Ibid., 129

There are three great events in life—birth, marriage, and death. None know how they are born, few know how they die. But I suspect that many can account for the intermediate phenomenon.
Bulwer, *The Caxtons*, Book I, II

A wife is a good thing—when it belongs to another man.
Bulwer, *Pompeii*, Book Two, XI

Matrimony is a great change. One is astonished not to find a notable alteration in one's friend, even if he or she have been only wedded a week.
Bulwer, *My Novel*, Book IV, II

No coinage in circulation so fluctuates in value as the worth of a marriageable man.
Bulwer, *What Will He Do With It?*, Book VII, XVIII

Man is not permitted, with ultimate impunity, to exasperate the envies, and insult the miseries of those around him, by a systematic perseverance in willful celibacy.
Ibid., Book VIII, XIX

What gentleman will bear with a learned wife? Burney, *Camilla*, One, I

A very young man seldom likes a silly wife. It is generally when he is further advanced in life that he takes that depraved taste. He then flatters himself a fool will be easier to govern. *Ibid.*, Three, VI

No man is in love when he marries. He may have loved before; he has sometimes loved after: but at the time never. There is something in the formalities of the matrimonial preparations that drives away all the little cupidons. *Ibid.*

A man of any fashion never blushes for his wife, whatever she may be. For his mistress, indeed, he may blush: for if there are any small failings there, his taste may be called in question. *Ibid.*

Rich or poor, high or low, whatever be the previous distinction between the parties, on the hour of marriage they begin as equals. *Ibid.*, Four, VIII

A single woman is a thousand times more shackled than a wife, for she is accountable to everybody; and a wife, you know, has nothing to do but just to manage her husband.
Burney, *Cecilia*, III

If the course of true love never runs smooth, the course of true matchmaking sometimes does so. Butler, *The Way of All Flesh*, XI

There is no time at which what the Italians call *la figlia della Morte* lays her cold hand upon a man more awfully than during the first half hour that he is alone with a woman whom he has married but never genuinely loved. *Ibid.*, XIII

A man's friendships are, like his will, invalidated by marriage—but they are also no less invalidated by the marriage of his friends. *Ibid.*, LXXV

You have been inoculated for marriage, and have recovered. *Ibid.*, LXXVII

Marriage is a matter of the future, not of the past.
Chesnutt, *The House Behind the Cedars*, IX

To a woman with marriageable daughters all roads lead to matrimony. *Ibid.*, XV

She says a wedding is one of the most lamentable spectacles on earth. Nice thing for a woman to say to her husband! Chopin, *The Awakening*, XXII

I have become an Agnostic. The inevitable result of marrying an old man.
Collins, *I Say No*, IX

Economy—with a dash of love. Collins, *The Moonstone*, First Period, II

It will be cheaper to marry her than to keep her. *Ibid.*

When I wanted to go upstairs, there was my wife coming down; or when my wife wanted to go down, there was I coming up. That is married life, according to my experience of it. *Ibid.*

Study your wife closely for the next four-and-twenty hours. If your good lady doesn't exhibit something in the shape of a contradiction in that time, Heaven help you,—you have married a monster. *Ibid.*, First Period, VIII

Do you know many wives who respect and admire their husbands? And yet they and their husbands get on very well. How many brides go to the altar with hearts that would bear inspection by the men who take them there? And yet it doesn't end unhappily—somehow or other the nuptial establishment jogs on.
Ibid., Second Period, V

Nothing sets the odious selfishness of mankind in such a repulsively vivid light as the treatment, in all classes of society, which single people receive at the hands of married people. When you have once shown yourself too considerate and self-denying to add a family of your own to an already overcrowded population, you are vindictively marked out by your married friends, who have no similar consideration and no similar self-denial, as the recipient of half their conjugal troubles, and the born friend of all their children. Husbands and wives *talk* of the cares of matrimony, and bachelors and spinsters *bear* them. Collins, *The Woman in White*, Part I, Second Epoch

A woman always stands in some degree in the same light with her husband, and she cannot certainly make him appear infamous without throwing a load of disgrace upon herself. Collyer, *Felicia to Charlotte*, I

The sacrament of marriage is not of man. Cooper, *The Bravo*, XXIII

Can anything be more grave than wedlock? *Ibid.*

That is a wise regulation of the Church which makes the marriage ceremony brief, for the intensity of the feelings it often creates would frequently become too powerful to be suppressed, were it unnecessarily prolonged. Cooper, *Home as Found*, XXIX

Few women are jealous on their wedding-day. *Ibid.*

Wedding-days, like all formally prepared festivals, are apt to go off a little heavily. *Ibid.*

An affectionate wife will take her bias generally from her husband. Cooper, *Homeward Bound*, XX

To marry a man against the movements of his will is to do a violence to human nature. Cooper, *The Prairie*, XXI

I would not marry a woman who did not understand Picquet, to say nothing of Whist, and one or two other games. Cooper, *Satanstoe*, Volume II, V

They laughed at constancy in marriage as the most ridiculous thing in nature and exploded the very notion of matrimonial happiness. Coventry, *Pompey the Little*, 36

There is this little misfortune attending matrimony, that people cannot live together any time, without discovering each other's tempers. *Ibid.*, 41

A man is better with no wife at all than with three. Crawford, *Mr. Isaacs*, II

Novels often end in marriage, yet real life frequently begins there. Crawford, *A Rose of Yesterday*, VII

Civilization gave us marriage. Progress is giving us divorce. *Ibid.*, XIII

The wisdom of past ages perceived the necessity of decreeing holy ties—subsequent ages found it wisdom to abide by the law. Marriage became the bond of society—the strong, though imperceptible chain which linked mankind together. Dacre, *The Libertine*, XXXI

I will never please my pocket in marrying, and not please my fancy. Defoe, *Moll Flanders*, 32

No man is lost when a good wife has found him. *Ibid.*, 41

A woman should never be kept for a mistress that has money to keep herself a wife. *Ibid.*, 57

If ladies did not marry so soon, they would make themselves amends by marrying safer. *Ibid.*, 73

She is always married too soon who gets a bad husband, and she is never married too late who gets a good one. *Ibid.*

If a woman precipitates herself in marriage, it is ten thousand to one but she is undone. *Ibid.*

As a fool is the worst of husbands to do a woman good, so a fool is the worst husband a woman can do good to. Defoe, *Roxana*, 92

A wife is treated with indifference, a mistress with a strong passion. *Ibid.*, 129

A wife is looked upon as but an upper servant, a mistress is a sovereign. *Ibid.*

A wife must give up all she has, have every reserve she makes for herself be thought hard of, and be upbraided with her very pin-money, whereas a mistress makes the saying true, that what a man has is hers, and what she has is her own. *Ibid.*

The wife bears a thousand insults and is forced to sit still and bear it or part and be undone, a mistress insulted helps herself immediately and takes another. *Ibid.*

It is not you I suspect, but the law of matrimony puts power into your hands, commands you to command, and binds me, forsooth, to obey. You, that are now upon even terms with me, and I with you, are the next hour set up upon the throne, and the humble wife placed at your footstool. *Ibid.*, 146–147

After a man has lain with me as a mistress he ought never to lie with me as a wife; that's not only preserving the crime in memory, but it is recording it in the family. *Ibid.*, 148

Certainly it was never known that any woman refused to marry a man that had first lain with her. *Ibid.*, 151

Was ever woman so stupid to choose to be a whore where she might have been an honest wife? *Ibid.*, 152

I have tried both marriage and single life, and I cannot recommend either.
DeForest, *Miss Ravenel's Conversion*, XIII

The flesh and the spirit agree not. For the parson will be so bent to his book that he will have little mind of his marriage bed: for one month's studying for a sermon will make him forget his wife a whole year. Deloney, *Jack of Newbury*, 319

One swallow makes not a summer, nor one meeting a marriage. *Ibid.*, 326

Delays in love are dangerous, and he that will woo a widow must take time by the forelock and suffer none other to step before him, lest he leap without the widow's love. *Ibid.*, 398

He called the matrimonial alliance of Mrs. Jellyby with Mr. Jellyby the union of mind and matter. Dickens, *Bleak House*, IV

Mrs. Badger has been married to three husbands—two of them highly distinguished men, and, each time, upon the twenty-first of March at Eleven in the forenoon. *Ibid.*, XIII

My experience teaches me that most of the people I know would do far better to leave marriage alone. It is at the bottom of three-fourths of their troubles. *Ibid.*, XLI

"Barkis is willin' [to marry]." Dickens, *David Copperfield*, V

"Perhaps she fell in love with her second husband." "Fell in love! What do you mean? What business had she to do it?" "Perhaps she did it for pleasure." *Ibid.*, XIII

Estimate her by the qualities she has, and not by the qualities she may not have. This is marriage. *Ibid.*, XLIV

Child-wife. *Ibid.*

There can be no disparity in marriage like unsuitability of mind and purpose. *Ibid.*, XLV

It's very much to be wished that some mothers would leave their daughters alone after marriage, and not be so violently affectionate. They seem to think the only return that can be made them for bringing an unfortunate young woman into the world is full liberty to worry her out of it again. *Ibid.*

Have you ever had an opportunity of remarking that the children of not exactly suitable marriages are always most particularly anxious to be married?
Dickens, *Great Expectations*, XXX

You will be surprised to hear that he proposed seven times once in a hackney-coach once in a boat once in a pew once on a donkey at Tunbridge Wells and the rest on his knees.
Dickens, *Little Dorrit*, Book I, XXIV

Farewell! Be the proud bride of a ducal coronet, and forget me! Long may it be before you know the anguish with which I now subscribe myself—Unalterably, never yours, Augustus.
Dickens, *Martin Chuzzlewit*, LIV

My boy, be wery careful o' widders all your life.
Dickens, *Pickwick Papers*, XX

The gout is a complaint as arises from too much ease and comfort. If ever you're attacked with the gout, jist you marry a widder as has got a good loud woice, with a decent notion of usin' it, and you'll never have the gout agin. It's a capital prescription. I takes it reg'lar, and I can warrant it to drive away any illness as is caused by too much jollity.
Ibid.

I think he's the wictim of connubiality, as Blue Beard's domestic chaplain said, with a tear of pity, ven he buried him.
Ibid.

Widders are 'ceptions to ev'ry rule.
Ibid., XXIII

"You know what the counsel said, as defended the gen'lem'n as beat his wife with the poker, venever he got jolly. 'And arter all, my Lord,' says he, 'it's a amable weakness.'"
Ibid.

Wen you're a married man, you'll understand a good many thing as you don't understand now; but vether it's worth while goin' through so much, to learn so little, as the charity-boy said ven he got to the end of the alphabet, is a matter o' taste.
Ibid., XXVII

Every woman should marry—and no man.
Disraeli, *Lothair*

The ladies must settle it amongst themselves who was to be his second wife, and his third, and his fourth, whilst his first was still alive, to his mortification and theirs.
Edgeworth, *Castle Rackrent*, 21

Where's the use of a woman having brains of her own if she's tackled to a geck as everybody's a-laughing at? She might as well dress herself fine to sit backwards on a donkey.
Eliot, *Adam Bede*, IX

No gentleman, out of a ballad, could marry a farmer's niece.
Ibid., XIII

Add one fool to another fool, and in six years' time six fools more—they're all the same denomination, big and little's nothing to do with the sum.
Ibid., XXI

Old bachelors are wiser than married men, because they have time for more general contemplation.
Ibid., XXV

Your fine critic of woman must never shackle his judgment by calling one woman his own.
Ibid.

"The women are foolish: God Almighty made 'em to match the men." "Match! Aye, as vinegar matches one's teeth. If a man says a word, his wife'll match it with a contradiction; if he's a mind for hot meat, his wife'll match it with cold bacon; if he laughs, she'll match him with whimpering. She's such a match as the horsefly is to th' horse: she's got the right venom to sting him with."
Ibid., LIII

What greater thing is there for two human souls than to feel that they are joined for life—to strengthen each other in all labor, to rest on each other in all sorrow, to minister to each other in all pain, to be one with each other in silent unspeakable memories at the moment of the last parting?
Ibid., LIV

Her observation of matrimony had inclined her to think it rather a dreary state, in which a woman could not do what she liked, had more children than were desirable, was consequently dull, and became irrevocably immersed in humdrum.
Eliot, *Daniel Deronda*, Book I, IV

Marriage is a noose. Eliot, *Middlemarch*, Book I, IV

A woman dictates before marriage in order that she may have an appetite for submission afterwards. *Ibid.*, Book I, IX

The doorsill of marriage once crossed, expectation is concentrated on the present. *Ibid.*, Book II, XX

Having once embarked on your marital voyage, it is impossible not to be aware that you make no way and that the sea is not within sight—that, in fact, you are exploring an enclosed basin. *Ibid.*

On a wedding journey, the express object of which is to isolate two people on the ground that they are all the world to each other, the sense of disagreement is confounding and stultifying. *Ibid.*

To have a discussion coolly waived when you feel that justice is all on your own side is even more exasperating in marriage than in philosophy. *Ibid.*, Book III, XXIX

Some men must marry to elevate themselves a little. *Ibid.*, Book III, XXXII

Marriage must be the best thing for a man who wants to work steadily. He has every thing at home then—no teasing with personal speculations—he can get calmness and freedom. *Ibid.*, Book IV, XXXVI

A woman's choice usually means taking the only man she can get. *Ibid.*, Book VI, LIV

Priority is a poor recommendation in a husband if he has got no other. *Ibid.*, Book VI, LV

I would rather have a good second husband than an indifferent first. *Ibid.*

Marriage is so unlike everything else. There is something even awful in the nearness it brings. *Ibid.*, Book VIII, LXXXI

Marriage drinks up all our power of giving or getting any blessedness in that sort of love. It may be very dear—but it murders our marriage—and then the marriage stays with us like a murder. *Ibid.*

Husbands are an inferior class of men, who require keeping in order. *Ibid.*, Book VIII, LXXXVI

Marriage, which has been the bourne of so many narratives, is still a great beginning, as it was to Adam and Eve, who kept their honeymoon in Eden, but had their first little one among the thorns and thistles of the wilderness. It is still the beginning of the home epic—the gradual conquest or irremediable loss of that complete union which makes the advancing years a climax, and age the harvest of sweet memories in common. *Ibid.*, Book VIII, Finale

Some set out [in marriage], like Crusaders of old, with a glorious equipment of hope and enthusiasm, and get broken by the way, wanting patience with each other and the world. *Ibid.*

The possession of a wife conspicuously one's inferior in intellect is, like other high privileges, attended with a few inconveniences, and, among the rest, with the occasional necessity for using a little deception. Eliot, *Mill on the Floss*, Book III, I

I should like to know what is the proper function of women, if it is not to make reasons for husbands to stay at home, and still stronger reasons for bachelors to go out. *Ibid.*, Book VI, VI

A man must turn over a new leaf when he thinks of marrying. Eliot, *Silas Marner*, IX

Let even an affectionate Goliath get himself tied to a small, tender thing, dreading to hurt it by pulling, and dreading still more to snap the cord, and which of the two, pray, will be master? *Ibid.*, XIV

Wives set one on to abuse their husbands and then they turn round on one and praise 'em as if they wanted to sell 'em.   *Ibid.*, XVII

The vindication of the loved object is the best balm affection can find for its wounds: "A man must have so much on his mind," is the belief by which a wife often supports a cheerful face under rough answers and unfeeling words.   *Ibid.*

A woman can always be satisfied with devoting herself to her husband, but a man wants something that will make him look forward more.   *Ibid.*

That quiet mutual gaze of a trusting husband and wife is like the first moment of rest or refuge from a great weariness or a great danger—not to be interfered with by speech or action which would distract the sensations from the fresh enjoyment of repose.
                                                                              Ibid., XX

A woman who hath given her consent to marry can hardly be said to be safe till she is married.   Fielding, H., *Amelia*, I

When widows exclaim loudly against second marriages, I would always lay a wager that the man, if not the wedding-day, is absolutely fixed on.   *Ibid.*

Wherever there is great disparity of years between husband and wife, the younger is always possessed of absolute power over the elder.   *Ibid.*, II

One fool at least in every married couple.   *Ibid.*

Mind that, ladies; you are all the property of your husbands.   *Ibid.*

Domestic happiness is the end of almost all our pursuits, and the common reward of all our pains.   *Ibid.*

Honeymoon, the only moon in which it is fashionable or customary for the married parties to have any affection for each other.   Fielding, H., *Jonathan Wild*, 160

Will any woman hesitate a moment whether she shall ride in a coach, or walk on foot all the days of her life?   Fielding, H., *Joseph Andrews*, 92

Every woman, till she is married, ought to consider of, and provide against, the possibility of the affair's breaking off.   *Ibid.*, 97

It is hard to have two lovers, and get never a husband at all.   *Ibid.*, 108

He was one of those wise men who rather choose to possess every convenience of life with an ugly woman, than a handsome one without any of those conveniences.
                                                                Fielding, H., *Tom Jones*, 32

Marriage hath saved many a woman from ruin.   *Ibid.*, 233

Many a woman who shrieks at a mouse may be capable of poisoning a husband; or, what is worse, of driving him to poison himself.   *Ibid.*, 480

Can a man make a bad husband who is not a fool?   *Ibid.*, 521

If a marriage is made in heaven, all the justices of peace upon earth can't break it off.   *Ibid.*, 714

That monstrous animal, a husband and wife.   *Ibid.*, 726

To prevent a husband's surfeit or satiety in the matrimonial feast, a little acid is now and then very prudently thrown into the dish by the wife.
                                            Fielding, S., *Adventures of David Simple*, I

All the world is sensible of the beauty of a fine woman except her husband.
                                        Fielding, S., *History of the Countess of Dellwyn*, I

Marriage is of human invention; for was it a necessary ceremony we must be all bastards, as we have no reason to believe Adam and Eve had the sanction of the priest for their union. Theirs was the wedlock of hearts, the true matrimony of affection.   Fielding, S., *History of Ophelia*, II

Marriage is the tomb of friendship. Foster, *The Coquette*, Letter XII

Marriage appears a very selfish state. *Ibid.*

As long as people *will* marry in their teens, the wrong people will get yoked up together. Frederic, *Damnation of Theron Ware*, Part II, XIV

No married man can do well unless his wife will let him. Galt, *Ayrshire*, V

Marriage is like death—it's what we are all to come to. *Ibid.*, IX

Sacrificed to the minotaur, Matrimony, who devours so many of our bravest youths and fairest maidens. *Ibid.*

Of love and marriage, coarse men speak with sneers and obscene jests, while serious men express themselves in hints, with apologetic smiles, as if they were betraying a weakness. Garland, *Rose*, XVIII

I dislike planning marriages, or looking forward to deaths, about equally. Gaskell, *Wives and Daughters*, LVIII

Our females are taught to believe that complaisance, affection, and industry are essential to her that would obtain the amiable and exalted character of a good wife. Gentleman, *A Trip to the Moon*, I

No sooner does a husband betray a particular affection for or attachment to his wife, than he is considered an owl amongst the birds. Gibbes, *Mr. Francis Clive*, II

Once married, you must live up to the standard of the society you frequent; you can't be entertained without entertaining in return. Gissing, *New Grub Street*, III

The honest man who marries and brings up a large family does more service than he who continues single and only talks of population. Goldsmith, *The Vicar of Wakefield*, I

I chose my wife, as she did her wedding-gown, not for a fine glossy surface, but such qualities as would wear well. *Ibid.*

We had no revolutions to fear, nor fatigues to undergo; all our adventures were by the fireside, and all our migrations from the blue bed to the brown. *Ibid.*

Matrimony being usually considered as making a purchase at the expense of our liberty, nothing is more natural than the pride we take in finding our choice approved by the world. Graves, *The Spiritual Quixote*, II

The two classes into which gentle young women naturally divide: those who grow red at their weddings and those who grow pale. Hardy, *Hand of Ethelberta*, II

"The consciousness of a fellow-sufferer being in just such another hole is such a relief always, and softens the sense of one's folly so very much." "That's why married men advise others to marry." *Ibid.*, XXI

"Honest courtship cures a man of many evils he had no power to stem before." "By substituting an insurable matrimony!" *Ibid.*

A proposal of marriage can never be an insult. *Ibid.*, XXXVI

Is it wrong for a husband or wife to tell a third person that they are unhappy in their marriage? If a marriage ceremony is a religious thing, it is possibly wrong; but if it is only a sordid contract, based on material convenience in householding, rating, and taxing, and the inheritance of land and money by children, making it necessary that the male parent should be known—which it seems to be—why surely a person may say, even proclaim upon the housetops, that it hurts and grieves him or her? Hardy, *Jude the Obscure*, Part Four, II

If the marriage ceremony consisted in an oath and signed contract between the parties to cease loving from that day forward, in consideration of personal possession being given, and to avoid each other's society as much as possible in public, there would be more loving couples than there are now. Fancy the secret meetings between the perjuring husband and wife, the denials of having seen each other, the clambering in at bedroom windows, and the hiding in closets! There'd be little cooling them.   *Ibid.*, Part Five, I

People go on marrying because they can't resist natural forces, although many of them may know perfectly well that they are possibly buying a month's pleasure with a life's discomfort.   *Ibid.*

Weddings be funerals nowadays.   *Ibid.*, Part Six, IX

In matrimony you should be slow to decide, but quick to execute.
Hardy, *A Laodicean*, Book VI, III

The practical husbands and wives who take things philosophically are very humdrum.
Hardy, *A Pair of Blue Eyes*, XXX

Men who at first will not allow the verdict of perfection they pronounce upon their sweethearts or wives to be disturbed by God's own testimony to the contrary, will, once suspecting their purity, morally hang them upon evidence they would be ashamed to admit in judging a dog.   *Ibid.*, XXXIV

In a world where doing means marrying.   Hardy, *The Return of the Native*, Book I, VII

The light-minded woman had been discovering good matches for her daughter almost from the year of her birth.   Hardy, *Tess*, VI

The intuitive heart of woman knoweth not only its own bitterness, but its husband's, and even if these assumed reproaches were not likely to be addressed to him or to his by strangers, they might have reached his ears from his own fastidious brain.
Ibid., XXXVI

Wives be such a provoking class of society because, though they be never right, they be never more than half wrong.   Hardy, *Under the Greenwood Tree*, Part Two, VI

A loveless marriage is the worst sin, the worst sacrilege, that a human being can be guilty of.   Harland, *Mea Culpa*, Part Three, VIII

An Iliad of matrimonial woes.   Harrison, *The Anglomaniacs*, I

Calculation and action are husband and wife, married without a possibility of divorce.
Holcroft, *Hugh Trevor*, III

Ten years younger as a bride than she had seemed as a lone woman.
Holmes, *Guardian Angel*, XXXVI

In some communities the women were mean to their husbands; in others, the husbands were mean to their wives. It is usually the case that the friends of a wife believe her husband to be a brute, and the friends of the husband believe the wife to possess no other talent than to make him miserable. You can't tell how it is; the evidence is divided.
Howe, *Story of a Country Town*, XXX

We are sometimes unable to understand why a pretty little woman marries a fellow we know to be worthless; but the fellow, who knows the woman better than we do, considers that he has thrown himself away. We know the fellow, but we do not know the woman.
Ibid.

Women appear to think they marry a man's whole life—his past as well as his future.
Howells, *A Modern Instance*, VII

Many a woman who would be ready to die for her husband makes him wretched because she won't live for him.   *Ibid.*, XXVII

Most of us marry silly little girls grown up to look like women.
Howells, *Silas Lapham*, I

The silken texture of the marriage tie bears a daily strain of wrong and insult to which no other human relation can be subjected without lesion; and sometimes the strength that knits society together might appear to the eye of faltering faith the curse of those immediately bound by it. Two people by no means reckless of each other's rights and feelings, but even tender of them for the most part, may tear at each other's heartstrings in this sacred bond with perfect impunity; though if they were any other two they would not speak or look at each other again after the outrages they exchange.

Ibid., IV

We are altogether too delicate to arrange the marriages of our children; and when they have arranged them we don't like to say anything, for fear we should only make bad worse. The right way is for us to school ourselves to indifference. *Ibid.,* VIII

"Valentin holds that women should marry, and that men should not," said Madame de Cintré. "I don't know how he arranges it." James, H., *The American,* XIV

It is very wrong to make love to a woman who is engaged, but it is very wrong not to make love to a woman who is married. *Ibid.,* XVI

It's very jolly making love to married women, because they can't ask you to marry them.
Ibid.

"In England all the girls ask a fellow to marry them." "And a fellow brutally refuses." "Why, really, you know, a fellow can't marry any girl that asks him." *Ibid.*

Miss Chancellor was a signal old maid. That was her quality, her destiny; nothing could be more distinctly written. There are women who are unmarried by accident, and others who are unmarried by option; but Olive Chancellor was unmarried by every implication of her being. She was a spinster as Shelley was a lyric poet, or as the month of August is sultry. James, H., *The Bostonians,* III

We know so little about the women of the South; they are very voiceless. *Ibid.,* VII

Women marry—are given in marriage—less and less; that isn't their career, as a matter of course, any more. You can't tell them to go and mind their husband and children, when they have no husband and children to mind. *Ibid.,* XXXIV

"He wishes to put away his wife." "To put her away?" "To repudiate her, as the historians say." James, H., *Confidence,* XXIX

"I don't want to begin life by marrying. There are other things a woman can do." "There's nothing she can do so well." James, H., *Portrait of a Lady,* XV

One can't explain one's marriage. *Ibid.,* LIII

One doesn't want a husband who's a picturesque curiosity.
James, H., *Roderick Hudson,* XX

A life-long devotion [in marriage] is measured after the fact; and meanwhile it is usual in these cases to give a few material securities. James, H., *Washington Square,* XII

A wedding is the thing in the world upon which women love most to expatiate.
Jenner, *The Placid Man,* II

Marriage has many pains, but celibacy has no pleasures. Johnson, *Rasselas,* 103

Marriage is rather permitted than approved, and none, but by the instigation of a passion too much indulged, entangle themselves with indissoluble compacts.
Ibid., 109

We ought not conclude too hastily from the infelicity of marriage against its institution. Will not the misery of life prove equally that life cannot be the gift of heaven? The world must be peopled by marriage, or peopled without it. *Ibid.,* 110

The good of the whole is the same with the good of all its parts. If marriage be best for mankind, it must be evidently best for individuals. *Ibid.,* 111

The incommodities of a single life are, in a great measure, necessary and certain, but those of the conjugal accidental and avoidable. *Ibid.*

What can be expected but disappointment and repentance from a choice of a mate made in the immaturity of youth, in the ardor of desire, without judgment, without foresight, without inquiry after conformity of opinions, similarity of manners, rectitude of judgment, or purity of sentiment? *Ibid.*, 112

Those who marry discover what nothing but voluntary blindness before had concealed; they wear out life in altercations, and charge nature with cruelty. *Ibid.*

The evils of marriage may be avoided by that deliberation and delay which prudence prescribes to irrevocable choice. *Ibid.*

Those who marry late are best pleased with their children, and those who marry early, with their partners. *Ibid.*, 114

There is nothing more dangerous for a man than to raise a curiosity in his wife, the gratification of which can be to his disadvantage. Johnstone, *The Pilgrim*, II

She was the only child of an ill-assorted marriage. Judd, *Margaret*, Volume I

I believe in falling in love, spontaneously, ardently, but I do not believe in falling into a quagmire. I cannot approve of those marrying who have no points in common. *Ibid.*, Volume III

Women look for as much courtship after marriage as before it. Accustomed to an intoxicating round of fulsome adulation, they really believe themselves the wonders men represent them. Kelly, H., *Memoirs of a Magdalen*, I

That Gordian knot, marriage. Kimber, *David Ranger*, I

The world is a wedding. King, E., *Zalmonah*, IV

A doleful music—an ancient tale of wrong—the Song of the Brides! Lawrence, G. A. *Guy Livingstone*, XIV

Wedded love supplies the want of every other blessing in life; and as no condition can be truly happy without it, so none can be absolutely miserable with it. Lennox, *Henrietta*, I

The folly of marrying for love. *Ibid.*

The lover who marries his mistress only because he cannot gain her upon easier terms has just as much generosity as the highwayman who leaves a traveler in possession of his money because he is not able to take it from him. *Ibid.*, II

Man was not created for celibacy: were love a crime, God never would have made it so sweet, so irresistible. Lewis, *The Monk*, 178

A man isn't married but once in his life. Locke, *A Paper City*, VIII

If he find thee wanton before thou be wooed, he will guess thou wilt be wavering when thou art wedded. Lyly, *Euphues*, 115

Maidens commonly are no sooner born, but they begin to bride it. *Ibid.*, 136

I cannot but smile to hear, that a marriage should be solemnized, where never was any mention of assuring, and that the wooing should be a day after the wedding. *Ibid.*, 138

There can be no marrige made where no match was meant. *Ibid.*

Be not hasty to marry. It is better to have one plough going than two cradles: and more profit to have a barn filled than a bed. Lyly, *Euphues and His England*, 229

The husband should have two eyes, and the wife but one. *Ibid.*, 284

In governing thy household, use thine own eyes, and her hand, for housewifery consisteth as much in seeing things as settling things, and yet in that go not above thy latchet, for cooks are not to be taught in the kitchen, nor painters in their shops, nor housewives in their houses. *Ibid.*, 475

In the fate of a woman, marriage is the most important crisis: it fixes her in a state of all others the most happy, or the most wretched. Mackenzie, *Julia De Roubigné*, 106

Never consider a trifle what may tend to please a husband.   *Ibid.*, 107

It is not sufficient that the husband should never have occasion to regret the want of power; the wife must so behave that he may never be conscious of possessing it.
                                                                             Ibid., 108

The office of a wife includes the exertion of a friend: a good one must frequently strengthen and support that weakness which a bad one would endeavor to overcome.
                                                                             Ibid., 109

Comedies and romances always end with a marriage, because, after that, there is nothing to be said.   *Ibid.*, 161

How do the thoughts of marriage bring down the best spirits!
                                                Marishall, *Miss Clarinda Cathcart*, II

Marriages in France are not made in heaven.   Meeke, *Count St. Blanchard*, I

Better be an old maid, a woman with herself for a husband, than the wife of a fool.
                                                                Melville, *Mardi*, XV

Thinking the lady to his mind, being brave like himself, and doubtless well adapted to the vicissitudes of matrimony at sea, he meditated suicide—I would have said, wedlock —and the twain became one.   *Ibid.*, XXII

A widow with her husband alive!   Melville, *Moby Dick*, CXXXII

Every wedding where true lovers wed, helps on the march of universal Love. Who are brides here shall be Love's bridesmaids in the marriage world to come.
                                                    Melville, *Pierre*, Book II, IV

Do you dream that men ever have the marrying of themselves? Juxtaposition marries men.   *Ibid.*, Book III, III

A regular system of polygamy exists among the islanders; but of a most extraordinary nature,—a plurality of husbands, instead of wives; and this solitary fact speaks volumes for the gentle disposition of the male population. Where else, indeed, could such a practice exist, even for a single day?—Imagine a revolution brought about in a Turkish seraglio, and the harem rendered the abode of bearded men; or conceive some beautiful woman in our own country running distracted at the sight of her numerous lovers murdering one another before her eyes, out of jealousy for the unequal distribution of her favors.   Melville, *Typee*, XXVI

On the whole wedlock, as known among these Typees, seems to be of a more distinct and enduring nature than is usually the case with barbarous people.   *Ibid.*

Of all chamber furniture in the world, best calculated to cure a bad temper, and breed a pleasant one, is the sight of a lovely wife.   Melville, *White Jacket*, XII

Marriage—the Grandest Inquisitor, next to Death.
                                              Meredith, *Beauchamp's Career*, VII

Our girls are chess-pieces until they're married. Then they have life and character: sometimes too much.   *Ibid.*

His opinion was that young unmarried women were incapable of the passion of love, being but half-feathered in that state, and unable to fly.   *Ibid.*, VIII

After forty, men have married their habits, and wives are only an item in the list, and not the most important.   *Ibid.*, XX

Men who are open to passion have to be taught reflection before they distinguish between the woman they should sue for love because she would be their best mate, and the woman who has thrown a spell on them.   *Ibid.*, XXXII

For a beggared man to think of running away with a wife, or of marrying one, the folly is as big as the worldly offense.   *Ibid.*, XXXIX

No young man is ever jilted; he is allowed to escape.   Meredith, *The Egoist*, IV

Marriage represents facts, courtship fancies. *Ibid.*, XXXIV

Husbands exist who refuse the right of breathing to their puppet wives.
Meredith, *Lord Ormont*, XXV

Marriage is more than a creation of the laws. As the solemn deed of life, the culminating act of our existence, an anticipation of its ordinances is not to be cancelled by seeking their countenance; which endeavor may expose penitence in the offender, but generates for him retribution rather than absolution, in lives unborn, misbegotten, in a callous companion, in an outraged future bearing with it a lifelong ill-assortedness.
Meredith, *Ordeal of Richard Feverel*, IV

Birth and death are natural accidents: marriage we can avoid. *Ibid.*

Heaven knows what forms of torture and self-denial are smilingly endured by that greatest of voluntary martyrs, a mother with a daughter to marry. *Ibid.*, XVI

In a dissension between man and wife, that one is in the right who has most friends.
Ibid., XXII

Marriage is made in Heaven, they say; and if that's the case, I say they don't take much account of us below. *Ibid.*, XXXII

There's as much difference in wedding rings as there is in wedding people.
Ibid., XXXIV

Do you mean to tell me a boy can go and marry when he pleases, and any trull he pleases, and the marriage is good? *Ibid.*, XXXVI

Who knows the honeymoon that did not steal somebody's sweetness? *Ibid.*

Young girls should be glad to have those who will take them. If they can't make a good marriage let them make a bad marriage. Moore, G., *Muslin*, IX

Married people stand up for each other, however they may fight between themselves.
Oliphant, *The Doctor's Family*, VII

Have not women been incomprehensible since ever there was in this world a pen with sufficient command of words to call them so? And is it not certain that, whether it may be to their advantage or disadvantage, every soul of them is plotting to marry somebody? Never was there a man, however ugly, disagreeable, or penniless, but he could tell of a narrow escape he had, some time or other. Oliphant, *The Rector*, II

Luxury, despotism, and avarice have so seized and entangled nine hundred and ninety-nine out of every thousand of the human race, that the matrimonial compact, which ought to be the most easy, the most free, and the most simple of all engagements, is become the most slavish and complicated,—a mere question of finance,—a system of bargain, and barter, and commerce, and trick, and chicanery, and dissimulation, and fraud. Peacock, *Headlong Hall*, XV

What is marriage, but the most sordid of bargains, the most cold and slavish of all the forms of commerce? Peacock, *Melincourt*, VII

Marriage is a lottery, and the less choice and selection a man bestows on his ticket the better. Peacock, *Nightmare Abbey*, I

A man who has quarrelled with his wife is absolved from all duty to his country.
Ibid., XI

Love is a union of loveliness with truth. Porter, *Thaddeus of Warsaw*, XXIX

A vile heresy, celibacy of the clergy, an invention truly fiendish.
Reade, *The Cloister and the Hearth*, XCIX

If persons about to marry were compelled to inscribe their names and descriptions in a Matrimonial Weekly Gazette, and a copy of this were placed on a desk in ten thousand churches, perhaps we might stop one lady per annum from marrying her husband's brother, and one gentleman from wedding his neighbor's wife. But the crying of banns in a single parish church is a waste of the people's time and the parson's breath.

Reade, *Griffith Gaunt*, XXIX

There is no article so proper for parents to govern in as marriage.

Richardson, *Clarissa Harlowe*, I

Men were the framers of the matrimonial office. *Ibid.*

Fear is a better security than love for a woman's good behavior to her husband. *Ibid.*

Fondness spoils more wives than it makes good. *Ibid.*

Many are mere babies in matrimony: perverse fools, when too much indulged and humored; creeping slaves, when treated harshly. *Ibid.*

If love and fear must be separated in matrimony, the man who makes himself feared fares best. *Ibid.*

What a degree of patience, what a greatness of soul is required in the wife not to despise a husband who is more ignorant, more illiterate, more low-minded, than herself. *Ibid.*

There hardly ever was a very handsome and a very sprightly man who made a good husband. *Ibid.*

Husbands are sometimes jealous of their authority with witty wives. *Ibid.*

Daughters should implicitly submit to the will of their parents in the great article of marriage. *Ibid.*

Who will presume to look upon such an act of violence, a forced marriage, as marriage? *Ibid.*

Is not a wife the keeper of a man's honor? And do not her faults bring more disgrace upon a husband than even upon herself? *Ibid.*, II

Am I not justified in my resolutions of trying her virtue, who is resolved, as I may say, to try mine? Who has declared that she will not marry me till she has hopes of my reformation? *Ibid.*

It is necessary for complete happiness in the married state that one should be a fool. But the fool should know that he is so, else the obstinate one will disappoint the wise one. *Ibid.*

None but the impudent little rogues who can name the parson and the church before you ask them for either, and undress and go to bed before you the next hour, should think of running away with a man. *Ibid.*

A notable wife is more impatient of control than an indolent one. *Ibid.*

Marriage is the highest state of friendship. *Ibid.*

If marriage is happy, it lessens our cares by dividing them, at the same time that it doubles our pleasures by a mutual participation. *Ibid.*

Antiquated bachelors (old before they believe themselves to be so) imagine that when they have once persuaded themselves to think of marriage, they have nothing more to do than to make their minds known to the woman. *Ibid.*

The ardent, the complaisant gallant is often preferred to the cold, the unadoring husband. *Ibid.*

Married people prevent abundance of quarrels by seeing one another but seldom. *Ibid.*

God forbid marrying in hopes of burying. *Ibid.*

A man should be in the wrong now and then, to make his wife shine. *Ibid.*

Better anybody expose a man than his wife. *Ibid.*

A perverse wife makes a listening husband. *Ibid.*, III

Two maidenheads meeting together in wedlock, the first child must be a fool.   *Ibid.*

Women love to be married twice at least; though not indeed to the same man.   *Ibid.*

In unequal unions, tolerable creatures frequently incur censure when, more happily yoked, they might be entitled to praise.   *Ibid.*

I have no patience with the pretty fools who use strong words such as ruined, undone, and such sort of stuff to describe a transitory evil; an evil which a mere church form makes none!   *Ibid.*

Could a man do as the birds do, change wives every Valentine's Day, there would be nothing at all in marriage.   *Ibid.*

If partners in marriage could change their spouses each year, such a change would be a means of annihilating four or five atrocious capital sins. What a multitude of domestic quarrels would be avoided, since both sexes would bear with each other, in the view that they could help themselves in a few months.   *Ibid.*

Were marriages to be for one year at a time, every one would be married a dozen times at least. Both men and women would be careful of their characters, and polite in their behavior, as well as delicate in their persons and elegant in their dress, either to induce a renewal with the old love or to recommend themselves to a new.   *Ibid.*

A wife at any time.   *Ibid.*

If a man gives himself up to the company of women, they never let him rest till he either suspect or hate his wife.   *Ibid.*

The catastrophe of every story that ends in wedlock is accounted happy, be the difficulties in the progress to it ever so great.   *Ibid.*

If there be a union of hearts and an intention to solemnize, what is there wanting but the foolish ceremony?   *Ibid.*

Marriage with these women is an atonement for all we men can do to them.   *Ibid.*

Matrimony is the grave of love, because it allows of the end of love.   *Ibid.*

A husband is a charming cloak, a fig-leafed apron, for a wife.   *Ibid.*

What a punishment would it come out to be upon the rake, that, marrying the object of his wiles, had been plundering his own treasury.   *Ibid.*

Matrimony is a bottomless pit, a gulf.   *Ibid.*, IV

Many worthy women are betrayed, by that false and inconsiderate notion, raised and propagated, no doubt, by the author of all delusion, that a reformed rake makes the best husband.   *Ibid.*

The dreadful yet delightful wedding day.   Richardson, *Pamela*, 351

Marriage is the highest consideration which the law knows.   *Ibid.*, 370

Happy yet awful moment: the wedding night.   *Ibid.*, 372

There are fewer instances of men's loving better after matrimony than of women's.   *Ibid.*, 472

If the wife would overcome, it must be by sweetness and complaisance; that is, by yielding.   *Ibid.*, 477

The words *command* and *obey* shall be blotted out of the vocabulary of marriage.   *Ibid.*

Whose leavings is it that a virtuous woman takes, who marries a profligate?
   Richardson, *Sir Charles Grandison*, One, I

If a woman resolves not to marry till she finds herself addressed to by a man of strict virtue, she must be for ever single.   *Ibid.*

A woman out of wedlock is half useless to the end of her being. *Ibid.*

The duties of a good wife, of a good mother, and a worthy matron, well performed, dignify a woman. *Ibid.*

Many a woman has married a man to get rid of his importunity. *Ibid.*

A woman is more a husband's than a man is a wife's. *Ibid.*

A man of quality confers quality on his wife. *Ibid.*

Marriage is a duty, whenever it can be entered into with prudence. *Ibid.*, One, II

If women were sure men would not think the worse of them for it, they would not wait a second proposal. *Ibid.*

Bachelors, cousins, and maids, when long single, are looked upon as houses long empty, which nobody cares to take. *Ibid.*

Marriage is every day more and more out of fashion; and even virtuous women give not the institution so much of their countenance as to discourage by their contempt the free-livers. *Ibid.*, Two, III

A good woman has but few chances for happiness in marriage. *Ibid.*

Women's sphere is the house, and their shining-place the sick chamber, in which they can exert all their amiable and lenient qualities. *Ibid.*

Courtship and marriage cannot be talked seriously of by a lady before company. *Ibid.*

A wife, in general, may allow of a husband's superior judgment. *Ibid.*

Can there be a greater difference between any two men in the world, than there often is between the same man as a lover and a husband? *Ibid.*, Two, IV

Every woman who marries imprudently furnishes a strong argument in favor of a parent's authority over a maiden daughter. *Ibid.*

In what can men and women, who are much together, employ themselves, but in proving and defending, quarreling and making-up? *Ibid.*

Married people would have enough to do, if they were to trouble their friends every time they misunderstood one another. *Ibid.*

A marriage of convenience, when that's the motive, will hold out its comforts, while a gratified love quickly evaporates. *Ibid.*

Private weddings, doubtful happiness. *Ibid.*, Three, VI

Husband: unfashionable as the word is, it is a pretty word. The *house-band*, that ties all together. *Ibid.*

Young folks are too apt to think of matrimony before they know how to keep a wife.
Ridley, *James Lovegrove*, I

Marriage is the highest of all wordly engagements. *Ibid.*, II

The dignity of superior knowledge so universally affected by affianced and married women in discussing man's nature with their uncontracted sisters.
Schreiner, *The Story of an African Farm*, Part II, IV

If the beloved Redeemer didn't mean men to have wives what did He make women for? That's what I say. If a woman's old enough to marry, and doesn't, she's sinning against the Lord—it's a wanting to know better than Him. What, does she think the Lord took all that trouble in making her for nothing? It's evident He wants babies, otherwise why does He send them? *Ibid.*, Part II, XIV

You can't love a man till you've had a baby by him. *Ibid.*

As for a husband, it's very much the same who one has. Some men are fat, and some men are thin; some drink brandy, and some men drink gin; but it all comes to the same thing in the end; it's all one. A man's a man. *Ibid.*

Man and wife are often nothing better than assistants in each other's ruin.
Scott, S., *A Description of Millenium Hall,* 146

The vivacity which pleases in the mistress is often a fatal vice in a wife.   *Ibid.,* 252

"There is a difference betwixt ruin and marriage." "Some people are said to have found them synonymous."   Scott, W., *St. Ronan's Well,* XXXII

The shrewdest of us don't know what marriage is until we are wives.
Shaw, *The Irrational Knot,* XIV

There are not nearly so many good men in the world as there are women who want to marry them; and some must get the bad ones.   *Ibid.*

Pretty ladies whose husbands are never seen often get talked about in the world.
Ibid., XVI

The attentions of a husband are stale, unsuited to holiday time.   *Ibid.*

Leaving husbands will soon become so common that it will be as little singular as living with them.   Shebbeare, *Lydia,* IV

Putting children in the power of parents and guardians to marry them to whom they please will wed them to their destruction.   *Ibid.*

There is no conjurer that can foretell a marriage or guess at a man and woman's designs so shrewdly as a milliner or mantua-maker.   Shebbeare, *The Marriage Act,* I

Your only happy marriages are those where people do not care a farthing for each other, each pursuing his own way.   *Ibid.*

A dead husband is of no sort of use in this world. That the widow has found one husband grateful is good reason why she should try another.   Simms, *Woodcraft,* XXX

A man who can stand hard usage may safely venture upon matrimony.   *Ibid.*

Marriage is business; not love. It's earnest work; not sport.   *Ibid.,* XLIII

A sensible marriage, for a man, means the bettering of his circumstances.   *Ibid.,* XLIV

One does not want an equal, but an ally in marriage.   *Ibid.,* L

A man ought to be wise enough for his wife and himself.   *Ibid.*

To get a woman who shall best comprehend one is the sufficient secret; and no woman can properly comprehend her husband, who is not prepared to recognize his full superiority.   *Ibid.*

The disease of being henpecked was epidemic in the parish.
Smollett, *Peregrine Pickle,* 128

A man can't talk to a woman but she immediately thinks of a midwife.
Smollett, *Roderick Random,* 353

We live in a world beset on all sides with mysteries and riddles—and so 'tis no matter— else it seems strange, that Nature, who makes everything so well to answer its destina- tion, and seldom or never errs, unless for pastime, in giving such forms and aptitudes to whatever passes through her hands, that whether she designs for the plough, the caravan, the cart—or whatever other creature she models, be it but an ass's foal, you are sure to have the thing you wanted; and yet at the same time should so eternally bungle it as she does, in making so simple a thing as a married man.
Sterne, *Tristram Shandy,* IX

It was a scene of high comedy, such as is proper to unhappy marriages.
Stevenson, *Prince Otto,* Book II, IX

To be a true helpmeet to Man, Woman must know all that Man knows.
Taylor, *Hannah Thurston,* V

Every man imprisons his wife to a certain degree; the world would be in a pretty condition if women were allowed to quit home and return to it whenever they had a mind.
Thackeray, *Barry Lyndon*, XIX

It is not your feeble easy husbands who are loved best in the world; according to my experience of it. I do think the women like a little violence of temper, and think no worse of a husband who exercises his authority pretty smartly. *Ibid.*

A good wife is the best diamond a man can wear in his bosom.
Thackeray, *Samuel Titmarsh*, XIII

What causes young people to "come *out*," but the noble ambition of matrimony?
Thackeray, *Vanity Fair*, III

A woman with fair opportunities, and without an absolute hump, may marry *whom she likes*. *Ibid.*, IV

Like almost all women who are worth a pin, she was a matchmaker in her heart. *Ibid.*

Of what else have young ladies to think, but husbands? Of what else do their dear mammas think? *Ibid.*, X

Lord Nelson went to the deuce for a woman. There *must* be good in a man who will do that. I adore all imprudent matches. *Ibid.*, XI

If people only made prudent marriages, what a stop to population there would be!
Ibid., XVI

No woman ever was really angry at a romantic marriage. *Ibid.*, XXIII

A virtuous woman is a crown to her husband. *Ibid.*, LV

If a girl accept a man all at once when she has had no preparation for such a proposal, she must always surely be in a state of great readiness for matrimonial projects. When there has been a prolonged period of spooning then of course it is quite a different thing. The whole thing has in fact been arranged before the important word has been spoken.
Trollope, *Ayala's Angel*, XLVI

Infinite trouble has been taken not only in arranging these marriages but in joining like to like—so that, if not happiness, at any rate sympathetic unhappiness, might be produced. *Ibid.*, LXIV

He is to be nobody until he comes forth from the church as your husband. Then he is to be everybody. That is the very theory of marriage. *Ibid.*

A girl does so often raise herself in her lover's estimation by refusing him half-a-dozen times. *Ibid.*

On the eve of committing matrimony. *Ibid.*

On the eve of matrimony, there is always a feeling of weakness, as though the man had been subdued, brought at length into a cage and tamed, so as to be made fit for domestic purposes, and deprived of his ancient freedom amongst the woods; whereas the girl feels herself to be the triumphant conqueror, who has successfully performed this great act of taming. Such being the case, the man had perhaps better keep away till he is forced to appear at the church-door. *Ibid.*

He assured her that he would be her lover just the same, even though they were husband and wife. Alas, no! There he had promised more than it is given to a man to perform.
Ibid.

Marriage means tyranny on one side and deceit on the other.
Trollope, *Barchester Towers*, XV

It so often happens that one's husband is the last person to understand one.
Trollope, *The Eustace Diamonds*, XII

If a man marries for money, he should have the money. *Ibid.*, XVII

A female Prometheus, even without a vulture, would indicate cruelty worse even than Jove's. *Ibid.*, XXIV

A woman should marry—once, twice, and thrice if necessary. *Ibid.*

Women can't marry without men to marry them. *Ibid.*

When a man has shown himself to be so far amenable to feminine authority as to have put himself in the way of matrimony, ladies will bear a great deal from him.
Ibid., XLIII

Who can believe that a woman will always love her husband because she swears she will?
Ibid., XLIV

Women must marry. *Ibid.*

A woman can marry without consulting her heart. Women do so every day.
Ibid., LXII

What is life till a man has met and obtained the partner of his soul? *Ibid.*, LXIX

She felt that a woman by herself in the world can do nothing, and that an unmarried woman's strength lies only in the expectation that she may soon be married.
Ibid., LXXIX

If a woman is to marry, she had better marry a fool. After all, a fool generally knows that he is a fool, and will trust someone, though he may not trust his wife.
Trollope, *He Knew He Was Right*, V

Wives are bound to obey their husbands, but obedience cannot be exacted from wives, as it may from servants, by aid of law and with penalties, or as from a horse, by punishments, and manger curtailments. *Ibid.*

"I am as likely to be taken bodily to heaven, as to become any man's wife." "Most women think so of themselves at some time, and yet they are married." *Ibid.*, XVI

Is it not manifestly God's ordinance that a man should live together with a woman?
Ibid., XXXIII

Seven years of flirtation with a young lady is more trying to the affection than any duration of matrimony. *Ibid.*, XXXVI

Women who don't get married are intended to be desolate; and perhaps it is better for them, if they bestow their time and thoughts properly. A woman with a family of children has almost too many of the cares of this world, to give her mind as she ought to the other. *Ibid.*, LXVI

An old maid is nothing if she be not kind and good. *Ibid.*

Widows' practices do not always tally with wives' vows. *Ibid.*, XCIX

A husband is very much like a house or a horse. You don't take your house because it's the best house in the world, but because just then you want a house. You go and see a house, and if it's very nasty you don't take it. But if you think it will suit pretty well, and if you are tired of looking about for houses, you take it. That's the way one buys one's horses—and one's husbands. Trollope, *Phineas Finn*, X

I like a fast man, but I know that I must not dare to marry the sort of man that I like.
Ibid.

If he were married tomorrow, his vices would fall from him like old clothes. *Ibid.*

"Is there to be no prudence in marriage?" "There may be a great deal too much prudence." *Ibid.*, XIX

All the virtues in the calendar, though they exist on each side, will not make a man and woman happy together, unless there be sympathy. *Ibid.*, XXIII

Do men never ask for a hand more than three times? *Ibid.*, XXXIX

To change a love is better than to marry without love. *Ibid.*

There are moments when even a married woman must be herself rather than her husband's wife. *Ibid.*

There are men who cannot guard themselves from the assertion of marital rights at most inappropriate moments. *Ibid.*, XL

Lord Cantrip lived with his wife most happily; yet you should pass hours with him and her together, and hardly know that they knew each other. *Ibid.*

Between husband and wife a warm word now and then matters but little, if there be a thoroughly good understanding at bottom. *Ibid.*, LVIII

Of almost all these royal and luxurious sinners it was the chief sin that in some phase of their lives they consented to be playthings without being wives.
Trollope, *The Way We Live Now*, I

It was now his business to marry an heiress. He was well aware that it was so, and was quite prepared to face his destiny. *Ibid.*, II

Women have a natural love for speaking, especially on the subject of weddings.
Walcot, *The New Pilgrim's Progress*, 221-222

The level that we strike in the soul that touches us most nearly is almost sure to be the highwater mark of our own. Ward, E. S. P., *The Silent Partner*, VII

Married women have the oddest habit of going about the world picking out the men they would not like to have married. Do they need continually to justify themselves?
Warner, *A Little Journey*, XI

"Polygamy! So men only dropped the *e pluribus unum* method on account of the expense?" "Not at all. Women are so much better now than formerly that one wife is quite enough." *Ibid.*, XXII

The one charm of marriage is that it makes a life of deception absolutely necessary for both parties. Wilde, *The Picture of Dorian Gray*, I

Men marry because they are tired; women, because they are curious: both are disappointed. *Ibid.*, IV

I have a distinct remembrance of being married, but I have no recollection at all of being engaged. I am inclined to think that I never was engaged. *Ibid.*, VI

The real drawback to marriage is that it makes one unselfish. And unselfish people are colorless. They lack individuality. *Ibid.*

There are certain temperaments that marriage makes more complex. They retain their egotism, and add to it many other egos. They are forced to have more than one life.
Ibid.

Every experience is of value, and whatever one may say against marriage, it is certainly an experience. *Ibid.*

There are other and more interesting bonds [than marriage] between men and women.
Ibid.

It is always the women who propose to us, and not we who propose to the women. *Ibid.*

"Four husbands is *trop de zèle*." "*Trop de'audace*." *Ibid.*, XV

The husbands of very beautiful women belong to the criminal classes. *Ibid.*

When a woman marries again, it is because she detested her first husband. When a man marries again, it is because he adored his first wife. Women try their luck; men risk theirs. *Ibid.*

If we women did not love you for your defects, where would you all be? Not one of you would ever be married. You would be a set of unfortunate bachelors. Not, however, that that would alter you much. Nowadays all the married men live like bachelors, and all the bachelors like married men. *Ibid.*

MARRIAGE (*continued*)

What nonsense people talk about happy marriages! A man can be happy with any woman, as long as he does not love her. *Ibid.*

Ten years of marriage with Monmouth must have been like eternity, with time thrown in. *Ibid.*

Married life is merely a habit, a bad habit. But then one regrets the loss even of one's worst habits. Perhaps one regrets them the most. They are such an essential part of one's personality. *Ibid.*, XIX

A wife had need bring money, when they cost such a plaguy deal to get rid of!
Young, *The Adventures of Emmera*, I

MARTYRDOM: *see also* CHRISTIANITY; DEATH; etc.

It is surely nothing less than martyrdom, to a man of cosmopolitan sympathies, to absorb in silent resignation the news of a country town.
Collins, *The Moonstone*, Third Narrative, VIII

Is martyrdom a lot to displease a Christian? Cooper, *Heidenmauer*, XXXVI

He who perishes in needless dangers is the devil's martyr.
Richardson, *Clarissa Harlowe*, II

The pathetic uselessness of martyrdom, its wasted beauty.
Wilde, *The Picture of Dorian Gray*, IX

MATCHING: *see also* LOVE; MALE AND FEMALE; MARRIAGE

Far unfit it is that the turtledove should match with the eagle. Though her love be never so pure, her wings are unfit to mount so high. Deloney, *Thomas of Reading*, 250

More matches are made at wakes than at weddings. Edgeworth, *Castle Rackrent*, 79

Marriage and hanging go by destiny. Gibbes, *Mr. Francis Clive*, II

This man is not *the* man. Richardson, *Clarissa Harlowe*, I

MATERIALISM; PHILISTINISM

I'm a Philistine, and not ashamed; so was Moliere—so was Cervantes. We're of all sorts in Philistia, the great and the small, the good and the bad.
DuMaurier, *The Martian*, Part Ninth

MEANING; DEFINITION: *see also* INTERPRETATION; PERSPECTIVE

Your verbosity, founded upon your memory of what others have said, proves that you retain words without ever having considered their meaning.
Anonymous, *The Adventures of an Author*, II

Take care of the sense and the sounds will take care of themselves.
Carroll, *Alice in Wonderland*, IX

A Mock Turtle is the thing Mock Turtle Soup is made from. *Ibid.*

Even a joke should have some meaning. *Ibid.*

Where much talk is, must needs be some offense. Deloney, *Jack of Newbury*, 378

There's a moral in everything, if we would only avail ourselves of it.
Dickens, *Dombey and Son*, II

Meanin' goes but a little way i' most things, for you may mean to stick things together and your glue may be bad, and then where are you? Eliot, *Silas Marner*, VI

If sentences have little meaning when they are writ, when they are spoken they have less.
Fielding, H., *Joseph Andrews*, 221

Mercenary is a big word, but it means a low thing.   James, H., *Washington Square*, X

"Many young men are [political mystics], before they have written out a fair copy of their meaning," said Mr. Austin. Cecilia laughed to herself at the vision of the fiery Nevil engaged in writing out a fair copy of his meaning. How many erasures! what footnotes!   Meredith, *Beauchamp's Career*, XVIII

Meaning, subtle as odor.   Meredith, *Harry Richmond*, XXVII

Innumerable meanings wreathed away unattainable to thought.   *Ibid.*

Long-worded, long-winded, obscure, affirmatizing by negatives, confessing by implication!—Where's the beginning and end of you, and what's your meaning?
                                                    Meredith, *Vittoria*, XLII

MEANS

The man who prefers the highroad to a more reputable way of making his fortune, doth it because he imagines the one easier than the other.   Fielding, H., *Jonathan Wild*, 27

To drive out one nail with another.   Gascoigne, *Master F. J.*, 23

MEASURE: *see also* VALUE

A thing cannot be weighed in a scale incapable of containing it.
                                                    Aldrich, *Stillwater*, XIII

The person who has not pleasure in a good novel must be intolerably stupid.
                                                    Austen, *Northanger Abbey*, XIV

The length of the sun's journeying can no more tell us how far life has advanced than the acreage of a field can tell us what growths may be active within it.
                                            Eliot, *Daniel Deronda*, Book VIII, LVIII

Measurement of life should be proportioned rather to the intensity of the experience than to its actual length.   Hardy, *A Pair of Blue Eyes*, XXVII

Resources do not depend upon gross amounts, but upon the proportion of spendings to takings.   Hardy, *The Return of the Native*, Book VI, I

There is no place but the universe; no limit but the limitless; no bottom but the bottomless.
                                                    Melville, *Mardi*, CXLIII

MEDIA: *see also* NEWS

The press is the palladium of liberty.   Brackenridge, *Modern Chivalry*, Part II, I

The common law protects the press. It is the right of the tongue transferred to the hand: it ought to be as free as the air that we breathe: The privilege as unfettered as the organs of articulation.   *Ibid.*

I take the pulpit, the courts of judicature, and the press, to be the three great means of sustaining and enlightening a republic   *Ibid.*

Good breeding is as necessary in print as in conversation. The press can have no more license than the tongue.   *Ibid.*

A newspaper is a battery, and it must have something to batter at.   *Ibid.*, Part II, II

A paper published weekly is a poor thing, out of the tide, behind the date, mainly a literary periodical, no foremost combatant in politics, no champion in the arena; hardly better than a commentator on the events of the six past days; an echo, not a voice. It sits on a Saturday bench and pretends to sum up. Who listens? The verdict knocks dust out of a cushion. It has no steady continuous pressure of influence. It is the organ of sleepers. Of all the bigger instruments of money, it is the feeblest.
                                            Meredith, *Beauchamp's Career*, XLIV

Gravity is the most practical qualification of the physician.
Brackenridge, *Modern Chivalry*, Part II, I

When the patient is dead, it was the disease killed him, not the doctor. Dead men tell no tales. *Ibid.*

Without good sense, the physician is as likely to kill as to cure. *Ibid.*, Part II, II

Doctors are so opinionated, so immovable in their dry, materialist views.
Bronte, C., *Villette*, XXIII

The physicians there are so modest, that they attribute the recovery of a person to divine Providence, and are ready to accuse themselves of ignorance or negligence should he die under their hands. Brunt, *A Voyage to Cacklogallinia*, 49

A good surgeon must have an eagle's eye, a lion's heart, and a lady's hand.
Bulwer, *What Will He Do With It?*, Book XII, II

It is seldom a medical man has true religious views—there is too much pride of intellect.
Eliot, *Middlemarch*, Book III, XXXI

Gout, a disease which has a good deal of wealth on its side. *Ibid.*, Book VIII, Finale

The sick man doth ill for himself, who makes his physician his heir.
Fielding, H., *Jonathan Wild*, 115

These two doctors, whom, to avoid my malicious applications, we shall distinguish by the names of Dr. Y and Dr. Z, having felt his pulse; to wit, Dr. Y his right arm and Dr. Z his left; both agreed that he was absolutely dead; but as to the distemper, or cause of his death, they differed; Dr. Y holding that he died of an apoplexy, and Dr. Z of an epilepsy.
Fielding, H., *Tom Jones*, 72

Every physician almost hath his favorite disease, to which he ascribes all the victories obtained over human nature. *Ibid.*

Instead of endeavoring to revive the patient, the learned gentlemen fell immediately into a dispute on the occasion of his death. *Ibid.*

There is nothing more unjust than the vulgar opinion, by which physicians are misrepresented as friends to death. On the contrary, if the number of those who recover by physic could be opposed to that of the martyrs to it, the former would rather exceed the latter. Nay, some are so cautious on this head, that, to avoid a possibility of killing the patient, they abstain from all methods of curing, and prescribe nothing but what can neither do good nor harm. I have heard some of these, with great gravity, deliver it as a maxim that Nature should be left to do her own work, while the physician stands by as it were to clap her on the back and encourage her when she doth well. *Ibid.*, 73

So little did the doctors delight in death that they discharged the corpse after a single fee. *Ibid.*

The gentlemen of the Aesculapian art are in the right in advising, that the moment the disease has entered at one door, the physician should be introduced at the other.
Ibid., 187

Doctor Misaubin used very pathetically to lament the late applications which were made to his skill, saying, "Bygar, me believe my pation take me for de undertaker, for dey never send for me till de physician have kill dem." *Ibid.*, 188

As a wise general never despises his enemy, however inferior that enemy's force may be, so neither doth a wise physician ever despise a distemper, however inconsiderable.
Ibid., 196

Doctors have that anxious manner; it's professional. Gaskell, *North and South*, XVIII

Many things are uncertain in this world, and among them the effect of a large proportion of the remedies prescribed by physicians. Holmes, *The Guardian Angel*, XI

Even medical families cannot escape the more insidious forms of disease.

James, H., *Washington Square*, I

It is a most extraordinary thing, but I never read a patent medicine advertisement without being impelled to the conclusion that I am suffering from the particular disease therein dealt with in its most virulent form.　　Jerome, *Three Men in a Boat*, I

I remember going to the British Museum one day to read up the treatment for some slight ailment of which I had a touch. I got down the book, and read all I came to read; and then, in an unthinking moment, I idly turned the leaves, and began to indolently study diseases. Bright's disease, I was relieved to find, I had only in a modified form, and, so far as that was concerned, I might live for years. Cholera I had, with severe complications; and diphtheria I seemed to have been born with. I plodded conscientiously through the twenty-six letters, and the only malady I could conclude I had not got was housemaid's knee.　　*Ibid.*

It is a curious fact, but nobody ever is seasick—on land. At sea, you come across plenty of people very bad indeed, whole boat-loads of them; but I never met a man yet, on land, who had ever known at all what it was to be seasick.　　*Ibid.*

To discuss medicine before the ignorant is of one piece with teaching the peacock to sing.

Kipling, *Kim*, XII

The young student of medicine, who is brim full of theory, though he has not yet begun to visit the sick, thinks it high time to appear in print. He calls upon Hippocrates and others so easily and familiarly that those readers who knew not when these folks lived would swear he was their intimate friend and companion.

Lawrence, H., *The Contemplative Man*, II

No one has a digestion who is in the doctor's hands. They prescribe from dogmas, and don't count on the system.　　Meredith, *Ordeal of Richard Feverel*, XXIV

Doctors are such fools! They don't know headaches from apoplexy.　　*Ibid.*, XXV

If coroner's inquests sat on horses, those doctors would be found guilty of mareslaughter.
Ibid.

No man of sense believes in medicine for chronic disorder.　　*Ibid.*, XXIX

When medical men are at a loss what to prescribe, they inquire what their patients best like and forbid them that.　　Richardson, *Clarissa Harlowe*, IV

Who would regard physicians, whose art is to cheat us with hopes while they help to destroy us, and who, not one of them, know anything but by guess?　　*Ibid.*

If a physician give me over, I give him over.　　*Ibid.*

There is nothing at all but pickpocket parade in the physician's art; and the best guesser is the best physician.　　*Ibid.*

Fond of life and fearful of death, what do we do when we are taken ill but call physicians in? And what do they do, when called in, but nurse our distempers, till from pygmies they make giants of them?　　*Ibid.*

If physicians could make mortal men immortal, and would not, it would be just to find fault with them.　　*Ibid.*

Physicians should be more moderate in their fees, or take more pains to deserve them; for generally they come into a room, feel the sick man's pulse, ask the nurse a few questions, inspect the patient's tongue, and perhaps his water; then sit down, look plaguy wise, and write. The golden fee finds the ready hand, and they hurry away, as if the sick man's room were infectious.　　*Ibid.*

This lovely creature is my doctor, as her absence was my disease.

Richardson, *Pamela*, 268

Male nurses are unnatural creatures.　　Richardson, *Sir Charles Grandison*, Two, III

When a patient has money, it is hard for a physician to be honest, and to say, till the last extremity, that the parson and sexton may take him.   *Ibid.*, Three, VI

We are angels when we come to cure—devils when we ask payment.
                                                                        Scott, The Abbot, VI

The physician hath free access to the bedside of his patient.
                                                            Scott, *The Talisman*, XXIII

The sick man, while he is yet infirm, knoweth the physician by his step; but when he is recovered, he knoweth not even his face.   *Ibid.*, XXVII

When a physician becomes the town talk, he generally concludes his business more than half done, even though his fame should wholly turn upon his malpractice; insomuch that some members of the faculty have been heard to complain that they never had the good fortune to be publicly accused of homicide.   Smollett, *Ferdinand, Count Fathom*, LIII

A certain famous physician never flourished to any degree of wealth and reputation till after he had been attacked in print and fairly convicted of having destroyed a good number of the human species.   *Ibid.*

Physick is no mystery of your making. It is a mystery in its own nature; and, like other mysteries, requires a strong gulp of faith to make it go down.
                                                            Smollett, *Humphry Clinker*, 54

A man's skull is not to be bored every time his head is broken.   *Ibid.*, 171

A seasonable fit of illness is an excellent medicine for the turbulence of passion.
                                                        Smollett, *Peregrine Pickle*, 328

The character of a physician not only supposes natural sagacity, and acquired erudition, but also implies every delicacy of sentiment, every tenderness of nature, and every virtue of humanity.   Smollett, *Sir Launcelot Greaves*, 192

Life short, and the art of healing tedious!   Sterne, *Tristram Shandy*, V

It isn't mere love and good-will that is needed in a sick-room; it needs knowledge and experience.   Stowe, *Orr's Island*, XXXIX

Whether medicine is a science, or only an empirical method of getting a living out of the ignorance of the human race, Ruth found before her first term was over at the medical school that there were other things she needed to know quite as much as that which is taught in medical books, and that she could never satisfy her aspirations without more general culture.   Twain and Warner, *The Gilded Age*, Volume I, XXI

Should we catch disease, that we may show our skill in curing it?
                                                    Young, *The Adventures of Emmera*, II

MEDITATION: *see also* PRAYER; RELIGION; THOUGHT

Thwackum's meditations were full of birch.   Fielding, H., *Tom Jones*, 88

Meditation and water are wedded forever.   Melville, *Moby Dick*, I

Beware of enlisting in your vigilant fisheries any lad with lean brow and hollow eye; given to unseasonable meditativeness; and who offers to ship with Phaedon instead of Bowditch in his head.   *Ibid.*, XXXV

Meditation makes the head dizzy and foot unsteady, as if the stomach were filled with new wine.   Scott, *Ivanhoe*, XLIII

MELANCHOLIA: *see also* HAPPINESS; JOY AND SORROW; MISERY, etc.

To the melancholy, as well as the philosophic mind, all dwellings are indifferent.
                                            Anonymous, *Memoirs of the Court of H—*, 118

Employment, even melancholy, may dispel melancholy.
Austen, *Mansfield Park*, Volume Three, XV

That darkest foe of humanity—constitutional melancholy. Bronte, C., *Villette*, XX

A feeling of melancholy, even of uneasiness, attends our first entrance into a great town, especially at night. Disraeli, *Coningsby*, Book IV, II

Baffled sympathy is the secret spring of most melancholy.
Disraeli, *Sybil*, Book VI, II

Melancholy shrinks from communication. Johnson, *Rasselas*, 178

Her melancholy was a sort of voluptuous meditation. Moore, *Evelyn Innes*, VIII

Sorrow wears; grief tears; melancholy soothes. Richardson, *Clarissa Harlowe*, IV

No infliction can be so distressing to a mind absorbed in melancholy, as being plunged into a scene of mirth and revelry, forming an accompaniment so dissonant from its own feelings. Scott, *Kenilworth*, XXV

Melancholy, even love-melancholy, is not so deeply seated, at least in minds of a manly and elastic character, as the soft enthusiasts who suffer under it are fond of believing.
Scott, *Quentin Durward*, XIX

There are few more melancholy sensations than those with which we regard scenes of past pleasure, when altered and deserted. Scott, *Rob Roy*, XXXVIII

Melancholy, only rich in unfortunate remembrances. Sidney, *Arcadia*, III

MEMORY; COMMEMORATION: *see also* DREAM; FORGETFULNESS; REFLECTION

If any one faculty of our nature may be called *more* wonderful than the rest, I do think it is memory. Austen, *Mansfield Park*, Volume Two, IV

Think only of the past as its remembrance gives you pleasure.
Austen, *Pride and Prejudice*, Volume III, XVI

Perhaps I did not always love him so well as I do now. But in such cases as these, a good memory is unpardonable. *Ibid.*, Volume III, XVII

Memory is the principle of moral degeneration. Remembered sin is the most utterly diabolical influence in the universe. Bellamy, *Dr. Heidenhoff's Process*, XI

Commit to memory now, what you will understand afterwards.
Brackenridge, *Modern Chivalry*, Part II, II

To have a sullied memory is a perpetual bane. Bronte, C., *Jane Eyre*, XIV

I love memory. I prize her as my best friend. Brone, C., *Villette*, IV

What a fool a man is to remember anything that happened more than a week ago unless it was pleasant, or unless he wants to make some use of it.
Butler, *The Way of All Flesh*, XXIV

It's a poor sort of memory that only works backwards.
Carroll, *Through the Looking Glass*, V

Little that I have ever seen is forgotten. I am at the close of many weary days, but there is not one among them all that I could wish to overlook. Cooper, *The Prairie*, XXXIII

The great remembrance by which that time is marked in my mind seems to have swallowed up all lesser recollections, and to exist alone.
Dickens, *David Copperfield*, IX

All this is yesterday's event. Events of later date have floated from me to the shore where all forgotten things will reappear, but this stands like a high rock in the ocean. *Ibid.*

I have stood aside to see the phantoms of those days go by me. They are gone, and I resume the journey of my story. *Ibid.*, XLIII

Memory, however sad, is the best and purest link between this world and a better. Dickens, *Nicholas Nickleby*, VI

There is nothing innocent, or good, that dies, and is forgotten. Dickens, *The Old Curiosity Shop*, LIV

It was to Adam the time that a man can least forget in afterlife, the time when he believes that the first woman he has ever loved betrays by a slight something—a word, a tone, a glance, the quivering of a lip or an eyelid—that she is at least beginning to love him in return. Eliot, *Adam Bede*, XX

The memory has as many moods as the temper, and shifts its scenery like a diorama. Eliot, *Middlemarch*, Book V, LIII

All long-known objects, even a mere window fastening or a particular door-latch, have sounds which are a sort of recognized voice to us,—a voice that will thrill and awaken, when it has been used to touch deep-lying fibres. Eliot, *The Mill on the Floss*, Book III, IV

It will be a fresher and better world when it flings off this great burden of stony memories [monuments], which the ages have deemed it a piety to heap upon its back. Hawthorne, *The Marble Faun*, XIII

Dead emperors have very little delight in their monuments. *Ibid.*, XVI

A Frenchman, in the midst of a mixed assembly, remembering that on that day ten years he had lost a dear friend, instantly went out and wept bitterly. He was so charmed with the happiness of the thought that, as he says, "I took the resolution henceforth to weep for all whom I have loved each on the anniversary of their death." Lawrence, G. A., *Guy Livingstone*, XXXI

My memory is a life beyond birth; my memory, my library of the Vatican, its alcoves all endless perspectives, eve-tinted by cross-lights from Middle-Age oriels. Melville, *Mardi*, CXIX

Memory was like a heavy barrel on my breast, rolling with the sea. Meredith, *Harry Richmond*, XII

There are as many monuments in Rome as there have been emperors, consuls, orators, conquerors, famous painters or players in Rome. Till this day not a Roman will kill a rat, but he will have some registered remembrance of it. Nashe, *The Unfortunate Traveller*, 102

As it is not possible for any man to learn the art of memory, except he have a natural memory before: so is it not possible for any man to attain any great wit by travel, except he have the grounds of it rooted in him before. *Ibid.*, 121

If only reasonable actions are to be reckoned among my doings, I am sure I have done little worth recording. Paltock, *Peter Wilkins*, 47

What a god is memory, to keep in life—to endow with an unslumbering vitality beyond that of our own nature—its unconscious company—the things that seem only born for its enjoyment. Simms, *The Partisan*, Volume I, XI

I've a grand memory for forgetting. Stevenson, *Kidnapped*, XVIII

MERCY; "MERCY KILLING"

You come in by yourselves without his direction, and shall go out by yourselves without his mercy. Bunyan, *Pilgrim's Progress*, 41

If repentance for ill actions calls for mercy, has not repentance for ill intentions a yet higher claim? Burney, *Cecilia*, II

Men come nearest unto God in shewing mercy and compassion.
Deloney, *Jack of Newbury*, 372

You need no mercy, and therefore know not how to show any.
Hawthorne, *The Marble Faun*, XLII

In our nature, there is a provision, alike marvellous and merciful, that the sufferer should never know the intensity of what he endures by its present torture, but chiefly by the pang that rankles after it.
Hawthorne, *The Scarlet Letter*, II

Mercy is for the merciful.
Kelly, *The Abbey of St. Asaph*, III

To look with mercy on the conduct of others is a virtue no less than to look with severity on your own.
Lewis, *The Monk*, 356

A knight without mercy is dishonored.
Malory, *Le Morte DArthur*, One, III

Ever will a coward show no mercy.
Ibid., Two, XVIII

I was sorry to find more mercy in a heathen than in a brother Christian.
Swift, *Gulliver's Travels*, A Voyage to Laputa

If there be rejoicing in heaven over one sinner that repenteth, should there not also be mercy and forgiveness at least upon earth?
Webber, *Old Hicks*, XXIII

MERIT: *see also* REWARD

Desert is a moral question.
Bellamy, *Looking Backward*, IX

The worst class of sum worked in the everyday world is cyphered by the diseased arithmeticians who are always in the rule of Subtraction as to the merits and successes of others, and never in Addition as to their own.
Dickens, *Little Dorrit*, Book II, VI

A man nearly fifty who is not always quite well is seldom ardently hopeful: he is aware that this is a world in which merit is often overlooked.
Eliot, *Felix Holt*, XII

If you are not proud of your cellar, there is no thrill of satisfaction in seeing your guest hold up his wine-glass to the light and look judicial. Such joys are reserved for conscious merit.
Eliot, *Middlemarch*, Book II, XIII

When a man gets a good berth, half the deserving must come after.
Ibid., Book V, LII

He was doctrinally convinced that there was a total absence of merit in himself; but that doctrinal conviction may be held without pain when the sense of demerit does not take a distinct shape in memory and revive the tingling of shame or the pang of remorse.
Ibid., Book V, LIII

If rank were the result of approved merit only, it would much more justly and universally claim respect. Now, however, it serves to awe the vulgar; in the view of sensible men it does but reflect scandal upon the unworthy possessors.
Gentleman, *A Trip to the Moon*, I

We should not conclude that a man who strives earnestly for success does so with a strong sense of his own merit. He may see how little success has to do with merit, and his motive may be his very humility.
Hardy, *A Pair of Blue Eyes*, XVII

The holiest among us has but attained so far above his fellows as to discern more clearly the Mercy which looks down, and repudiate more utterly the phantom of human merit which would look aspiringly upward.
Hawthorne, *The Scarlet Letter*, XXIV

He that sees inferior desert advanced above him will naturally impute that preference to partiality or caprice; and, indeed, it can scarcely be hoped that any man, however magnanimous by nature or exalted by condition, will be able to persist forever in the fixed and inexorable justice of distribution.
Johnson, *Rasselas*, 105

What claims our wonder does not always merit our regard.
Mackenzie, *The Man of the World*, I

To implore help is itself the proof of undesert of it.
Melville, *Confidence-Man*, XXXIX

Fame is an accident; merit a thing absolute.   Melville, *Mardi*, CXXVI

Far better to perish meriting immortality, than to enjoy it unmeritorious.
    Ibid., CLXXV

The only man in the world that could offer so much and deserve so little!
    Richardson, *Clarissa Harlowe*, I

Merits but aggravate fault.   *Ibid.*, II

He from whom no good is expected is not allowed the merit of the good he does.
    Ibid., III

Never say that is severe that is deserved.   *Ibid.*, IV

He gave it for his opinion that whoever could make two ears of corn or two blades of grass to grow upon a spot of ground where only one grew before would deserve better of mankind, and do more essential service to his country, than the whole race of politicians put together.   Swift, *Gulliver's Travels*, Brobdingnag

We may be pretty certain that the persons whom all the world treats ill, deserve entirely the treatment they get. The world is a looking-glass, and gives back to every man the reflection of his own face.   Thackeray, *Vanity Fair*, II

MESSAGE; MESSENGER: *see also* EXPRESSION

The bearer of evil tidings hath but a losing office.   Melville, *Typee*, XXVI

MICROCOSM: *see also* WORLD

The best introduction to astronomy is to think of the nightly heavens as a little lot of stars belonging to one's homestead.   Eliot, *Daniel Deronda*, Book I, III

MIDDLE CLASS: *see also* POVERTY; SOCIETY; WEALTH; etc.

Perhaps, what this world can give may be found in the modest habitations of middle fortune, too low for great designs and too high for penury and distress.
    Johnson, *Rasselas*, 94

It is the poor and the middling that must save the rest of the world, if the rest are to be saved.   Richardson, *Clarissa Harlowe*, II

MILITARY SERVICE: *see also* WAR AND PEACE

Soldiers and sailors are always acceptable in society. Nobody can wonder that men are soldiers and sailors.   Austen, *Mansfield Park*, Volume One, XI

Promptitude is a military virtue.   Cooper, *The Two Admirals*, XIX

The sergeant was describing a military life. It was all drinking, he said, except that there were frequent intervals of eating and love-making. A battle was the finest thing in the world—when your side won it—and Englishmen always did that.
    Dickens, *Barnaby Rudge*, XXXI

Military trainings—a sort of New England holiday.   Judd, *Margaret*, Volume I, XIII

In the army a man's boots is his castle.
    Peck, *How Private George W. Peck Put Down the Rebellion*, XXVII

MIND: *see also* BODY; INTELLECT; THOUGHT; etc.

Since women have the same improvable minds as the male part of the species, why should they not be cultivated by the same method?   Amory, *John Buncle*, II

Sudden transitions are apt to make the mind giddy.   Anonymous, *Betty Barnes*, II

Every man's mind is his best friend, and every man's memory better than a memorandum book.   Anonymous, *The Ladies Advocate*, 298-299

There are as many minds as men.   Anonymous, *Memoirs of an Oxford Scholar*, 15

The right of a lively mind, seizing whatever may contribute to its own amusement or that of others: perfectly allowable, when untinctured by ill humor or roughness.
Austen, *Mansfield Park*, Volume One, VII

When the body becomes diseased, it is not uncommon for the mind to be affected also.   Bennett, *The Prairie Flower*, XVII

Strength of mind is improvable; hence strength of mind differs more than strength of body. The aggregate of mind is one thing and a distinguished mind another.
Brackenridge, *Modern Chivalry*, Part II, I

Pain of mind is relieved by an abstraction of solid thought.   *Ibid.*, Part II, II

The great secret of managing the mind of man is to find employment for it.
Ibid., Part II, IV

Cheerfulness depends as much on the state of things within, as without.
Bronte, C., *Shirley*, III

In vast cycles, age after age, the human mind marches on—like the ocean, receding here, but there advancing.   Bulwer, *The Caxtons*, Book IV, II

Despise the body to make wise the mind.   Bulwer, *Pompeii*, Book Three, X

There are two lives to each of us, gliding on at the same time, scarcely connected with each other—the life of our actions, the life of our minds.
Bulwer, *The Pilgrims of the Rhine*, XXII

The heart loves repose and the soul contemplation, but the mind needs action.
Bulwer, *A Strange Story*, LX

What does it matter where my body happens to be? My mind goes on working all the same.   Carroll, *Through the Looking Glass*, VIII

What man has ever felt that all his thinking powers were absorbed, even by the most poignant mental misery that could occupy them? In moments of imminent danger, the mind can still travel of its own accord over the past in spite of the present—in moments of bitter affliction, it can still recur to everyday trifles in spite of ourselves.
Collins, *Basil*, Part Three, III

There is a curious want of system in the English mind. When we are not occupied in making machinery, we are (mentally speaking) the most slovenly people in the universe.
Collins, *The Moonstone*, First Period, VI

The mind cannot be forever on the stretch, the calm and social pleasures of intellectual intercourse are necessary to refresh, and to invigorate it.   Dacre, *The Libertine*, XV

The real superiority, even of manners, must be placed in the mind.
Day, *The History of Sandford and Merton*, 238

What a felicity it is to mankind, that they cannot see into the hearts of one another!
Defoe, *Moll Flanders*, 185

A man's mind is a kingdom to himself.   Deloney, *Jack of Newbury*, 362

There are chords in the human mind.   Dickens, *Bleak House*, XX

There is a drowsy state, between sleeping and waking, when you dream more in five minutes with your eyes half open, and yourself half conscious of everything that is passing around you, than you would in five nights with your eyes fast closed, and your senses wrapt in perfect unconsciousness. At such times, a mortal knows just enough of what his mind is doing, to form some glimmering conception of its mighty powers, its bounding from earth and spurning time and space, when freed from the restraint of its corporeal associate.   Dickens, *Oliver Twist*, IX

The caverns of my mind are open, and they will not close.   Disraeli, *Sybil*, Book V, IV

These janglings and wranglings are but on the surface, and spring from the infinite variety of the human mind, which will ever adapt a creed to suit its own turn of thought.   Doyle, *Micah Clarke*, III

In life there is ever the intellectual and the emotional nature—the mind that reasons, and the mind that feels. Of one come the men of action—generals and statesmen; of the other, the poets and dreamers—artists all.   Dreiser, *Sister Carrie*, XLVII

He had that mental combination which is at once humble in the region of mystery and keen in the region of knowledge.   Eliot, *Adam Bede*, IV

The mind of a man is as a country which was once open to squatters, who have bred and multiplied and become masters of the land. But then happeneth a time when new and hungry comers dispute the land; and there is a trial of strength, and the stronger wins.   Eliot, *Felix Holt*, VIII

It is usual with the human mind to skip from one extreme to its opposite, as easily, and almost as suddenly, as a bird from one bough to another.   Fielding, H., *Joseph Andrews*, 257

Philosophy and religion may be called the exercises of the mind, and when this is disordered, they are as wholesome as exercise can be to a distempered body.   Fielding, H., *Tom Jones*, 398

His mind deceives itself by its own acuteness.   Galt, *Ayrshire*, IX

The mind is master of itself; and is endowed with powers that might enable it to laugh at the tyrant's vigilance.   Godwin, *Caleb Williams*, II

I have ever perceived, that where the mind was capacious, the affections were good.   Goldsmith, *The Vicar of Wakefield*, 75

A well-proportioned mind is one which shows no particular bias; one of which we may safely say that it will never cause its owner to be confined as a madman, tortured as a heretic, or crucified as a blasphemer. Also, on the other hand, that it will never cause him to be applauded as a prophet, revered as a priest, or exalted as a king. Its usual blessings are happiness and mediocrity.   Hardy, *The Return of the Native*, Book III, II

The mind unfettered from the body is still the same, and those impressions which nature first stamps upon the infant mind are seldom or ever obliterated.   Harley, *Priory of St. Bernard*, I

It is a certain elevation of mind alone, a sensibility of what is great and good, a comprehensive view of what is desirable or contemptible, which sets a man above the common level, and shows him everything in its true light.   Jenner, *The Placid Man*, I

To the mind, as to the eye, it is difficult to compare with exactness objects vast in their extent and various in their parts.   Johnson, *Rasselas*, 109

A virtuous mind soon finds consolation in itself.   Johnstone, *The Pilgrim*, II

The most agreeable food of the mind, taken in by the eyes and ears, does not always prove nutritious to the understanding.   Lawrence, H., *The Life and Adventures of Common Sense*, II

A good mind ought to be incited, a bad mind restrained.   Lennox, *The Female Quixote*, II

The qualities that are required of the mind are good conditions, as temperance not to exceed in diet; chastity not to sin in desire; constancy not to covet change; wit to delight; wisdom to instruct; mirth to please without offense; and modesty to govern without preciseness.   Lyly, *Euphues and His England*, 407

He whose treasure is in his mind is richer than the walking mine, who carries all his honors on his back, and when Fortune is pleased to divest him of them, what is he fit for? McCarthy, *The Fair Moralist*, 16

There is a certain kind of trifling in which a mind not much at ease can sometimes indulge itself. One feels an escape, as it were, from the heart, and is fain to take up with lighter company. It is like the theft of a truant boy, who goes to play for a few minutes while his master is asleep, and throws the chiding for his task upon futurity. Mackenzie, *Julia De Roubigné*, 161

The mind that is often employed about little things will be rendered unfit for any serious exertion. Mackenzie, *The Man of the World*, I

The mind is ductile: but images, ductilely received into it, need a certain time to harden and bake in their impressions. Melville, *Confidence-Man*, IV

The mind does not exist unless leagued with the soul. Melville, *Moby Dick*, XLIV

The beginning of a motive life must be in the head. Meredith, *Diana of the Crossways*, I

A mind that after a long season of oblivion in pain returns to wakefulness without a keen edge for the world is much in danger of souring permanently. *Ibid.*, XXXIX

I have seen, have seen ahead, seen where all is dark, read the unwritten. The brain of man is Jove's eagle and his lightning on earth—the title to majesty henceforth. Meredith, *The Tragic Comedians*, VII

A well-informed mind is the best security against the contagion of folly and vice. Radcliffe, *The Mysteries of Udolpho*, I

It is the first proof of a superior mind to liberate itself from prejudices of country or of education. Radcliffe, *The Romance of the Forest*, 479-480

He seemed to have more in his head than could come out at his mouth. Richardson, *Clarissa Harlowe*, I

What mind is superior to calamity? *Ibid.*, II

What an unequal union, the mind and body! *Ibid.*

The mind is strongly indicated by its outward dress. *Ibid.*

The mind will run away with the body at any time. *Ibid.*, IV

Suffering minds will be partial to their own cause and merits. *Ibid.*

If the mind be not engaged, there is hardly any confinement sufficient for the body! Richardson, *Pamela*, 282

Can delicate minds be united to each other but by delicate observances? Richardson, *Sir Charles Grandison*, Two, IV

Your mind is the unsullied book of nature. *Ibid.*, Three, VII

Virtues better apparel the mind, than clothes the body. Sidney, *Arcadia*, I

That calm dignity of mind that accompanies conscious rectitude. Sleath, *The Orphan of the Rhine*, II

I am shocked to find a man have sublime ideas in his head, and nothing but illiberal sentiments in his heart. Smollett, *Humphry Clinker*, 113

To think the man, whose ample mind must grasp whatever yonder stars survey—what is your opinion of that image of the mind's grasping the whole universe? Smollett, *Peregrine Pickle*, 204

The mind sits terrified at the objects she has magnified herself and blackened; reduce them to their proper size and hue, she overlooks them. Sterne, *A Sentimental Journey*, 75

MIND (*continued*)

Our minds shine not through the body.   Sterne, *Tristram Shandy*, I

There is a North-west passage to the intellectual world.   *Ibid.*, V

There is a sympathetic power in all states of mind, and they who have reached the deep secret of eternal rest have a strange power of imparting calm to others.
Stowe, *Orr's Island*, XLII

Can the mind forget the history of its own life?
Trollope, *He Knew He Was Right*, XXXV

It is very hard to see into the minds of men, but we can see the results of their minds' work.   Trollope, *The Way We Live Now*, LV

The mind of the thoroughly well-informed man is a dreadful thing. It is like a bric-a-brac shop, all monsters and dust, with everything priced above its proper value.
Wilde, *The Picture of Dorian Gray*, I

It has been said that the great events of the world take place in the brain. It is in the brain, and the brain only, that the great sins of the world take place also.   *Ibid.*, II

MIRACLE: *see also* GOD; IMPOSSIBILITY; POSSIBILITY; RELIGION; etc.

Miracles seem impossible, just because they break the laws of Nature. There seems something blasphemous in supposing that God can mar His own order.
Kingsley, *Alton Locke*, XXXVIII

MISANTHROPY: *see also* LOVE; HATE; HUMANKIND; HUMAN NATURE; etc.

Misanthropy is sometimes the natural characteristic of the mind; but more generally the offspring of extreme benevolence, hurt by ingratitude.
Brackenridge, *Modern Chivalry*, Part II, II

The despisers of mankind—apart from the mere fools and mimics, of that creed—are of two sorts. They who believe their merit neglected and unappreciated, make up one class; they who receive adulation and flattery, knowing their own worthlessness, compose the other. Be sure that the coldest-hearted misanthropes are ever of this last order.   Dickens, *Barnaby Rudge*, XXIV

Black-visaged misanthropy.   Lee, *The Recess*, III

There is no misanthrope like a boy disappointed; and such was I, with the warm soul of me flogged out by adversity.   Melville, *Redburn*, II

He seemed to be full of hatred and gall against everything and everybody in the world; as if all the world was one person, and had done him some dreadful harm, that was rankling and festering in his heart.   *Ibid.*, XII

Misanthropy is sometimes the product of disappointed benevolence; but it is more frequently the offspring of overweening and mortified vanity, quarrelling with the world for not being better treated than it deserves.   Peacock, *Nightmare Abbey*, VII

The worst of all disease—a low idea of humanity.
Trollope, *The Eustace Diamonds*, XXVIII

MISCHIEF; WICKEDNESS: *see also* GOOD AND EVIL

The man who is reported to have done most mischief is received with most kindness by women.   Fielding, S., *David Simple*, I

Mischief is seldom so weak but that worth may be stung by it.
Mackenzie, *The Man of the World*, I

The greatest half of my wickedness is vapor, to show my invention and to prove that I *could* be mischievous if I would.   Richardson, *Clarissa Harlowe*, II

410

To know a designed mischief is to disappoint it and to turn it upon the contriver's head. *Ibid.*

In a piece of mischief, execution, with its swiftest feet, is seldom three paces behind projection, which hardly ever limps neither. *Ibid.*

Even good folks love to have the power of doing mischief, whether they make use of it or not. *Ibid.*, III

Mischief is of such nature that it cannot stand but with strengthening one evil by another, and so multiply in itself till it come to the highest and then fall with his own weight. Sidney, *Arcadia*, II

MISERLINESS

The miser, who thinks himself respectable merely because he possesses wealth, and thus mistakes the means of doing good for the actual accomplishment of it, is not more blameable than the man of sentiment without active virtue.
Radcliffe, *The Mysteries of Udolpho*, I

The miser's feast is often the most splendid.
Richardson, *Sir Charles Grandison*, Two, V

MISERY: *see also* HAPPINESS; MISFORTUNE; etc.

There is no rectitude in being miserable.
Anonymous, *The Adventures of an Author*, I

The road to misery is often through the most pleasing paths.
Anonymous, *The Birmingham Counterfeit*, II

Thoughtless words are the fruitful seed of misery.
Beard, *Bristling With Thorns*, XIV

Misery generates hate. Bronte, C., *Shirley*, II

'Tis the enemy of human kind who has taught that austerity and voluntary misery are virtue. Brooke, *Emily Montague*, III

The misery that overspreads so large a part of mankind exists chiefly because those who are able to relieve it do not know that it exists. Brown, C. B., *Ormond*, 203

It is the peculiar, not the general evil, that constitutes all hardship.
Burney, *Camilla*, Two, IV

It is suspense, it is hope, that make the food of misery; certainty is always endured, because known to be past amendment, and felt to give defiance to struggling.
Burney, *Cecilia*, II

Misery seeks not man, but man misery. *Ibid.*, III

Bitter is the agony of self-reproach, where misery follows hardness of heart! *Ibid.*

Miseries have power over men, and not men over miseries.
Deloney, *The Gentle Craft*, 80

Haggard anxiety and remorse are bad companions to be barred up with.
Dickens, *Little Dorrit*, Book II, XXIX

It is seldom that the miserable can help regarding their misery as a wrong inflicted by those who are less miserable. Eliot, *Silas Marner*, XII

What can be more miserable than to see anything necessary to the preservation of a beloved creature, and not be able to supply it? Fielding, H., *Amelia*, I

No condition, however destitute or degraded, out of which one has a fair prospect, or anything like a rational hope of rising, can justly be considered as utterly miserable.
Hildreth, *Slave*, Volume I, XV

The unhappy are never pleasing, and all naturally avoid the contagion of misery.

Johnson, *Rasselas*, 132

Who that is struggling under his own evils will add to them the miseries of another?

Ibid.

The evils of our own creating are infinitely more intolerable than those real misfortunes which it is not in our power to prevent.   Lawrence, H., *The Contemplative Man*, II

Consummate misery has a moral use.   Lee, *The Recess*, I

The infinite cliffs and gulfs of human mystery and misery.

Melville, *Pierre*, Book III, III

A bucketful of misery now saves an ocean in time to come.

Meredith, *Harry Richmond*, XII

The child of misery receives great addition to his woes by the sneers and scandal of his neighbors.   Moore, G., *Grasville Abbey*, II

Miserable is that mouse that lives in a physician's house.

Nashe, *The Unfortunate Traveller*, 127

There is a certain point of misery beyond which the mind becomes callous and acquires a fort of artificial calm.   Radcliffe, *The Castles of Athlin and Dunbayne*, 223

Gloomy is my soul; and all nature round me partakes of my gloom!

Richardson, *Clarissa Harlowe*, I

Prosperity and independence are charming things on this account, that they give force to the counsels of a friendly heart; while it is thought insolence in the miserable to advise, or so much as to remonstrate.   *Ibid.*, III

If the human mind will busy itself to make the worst of every disagreeable occurrence, it will never want woe.   *Ibid.*, IV

MISFORTUNE: *see also* HAPPINESS; LUCK; MISERY; etc.

Ill news soon reaches the unwelcome ear.   Anonymous, *The Fruitless Repentance*, I

The Italians use the same word for "disgrace" and "misfortune." I once heard an Italian lady speak of a young friend whom she described as endowed with every virtue under heaven. "*Ma*," she exclaimed, "*povero disgraziatio, ha ammazzato suo zio.*" ("Poor unfortunate fellow, he has murdered his uncle.")   Butler, *Erewhon*, X

'Tis very seldom that the unfortunate are so but for a day.   Defoe, *Colonel Jack*, 4

To be discouraged is to yield to the misfortune.   Defoe, *Moll Flanders*, 152

Of all misfortunes it is most unhappy to be fortunate.   Deloney, *Thomas of Reading*, 222

Misfortunes are not always coupled with vice and ignorance, but too often complicated with virtue and learning.   Donaldson, *Sir Bartholomew Sapskull*, II

His misfortune made him more interesting, and even helped him to be the fashion.

James, H., *Washington Square*, I

Misfortunes give us room to hope.   Kidgell, *The Card*, I

Misfortune is not always misery.   Mackenzie, *Julia De Roubigné*, 109

With misfortune a good heart easily makes an acquaintance.

Mackenzie, *The Man of the World*, II

We are all apt to magnify our own troubles and think them superior to what others feel.

Parsons, *The Castle of Wolfenbach*, II

People in misfortune are always in doubt.   Richardson, *Clarissa Harlowe*, I

My misfortunes had taught me how little the caresses of the world during a man's
prosperity are to be valued by him.   Smollett, *Roderick Random*, 50

MIST

England, that dear land of mists.   Bronte, C., *Villette*, XIV

MOB

A mob is usually a creature of very mysterious existence, particularly in a large city.
Where it comes from or whither it goes, few men can tell.
                                        Dickens, *Barnaby Rudge*, LII

"It's always best on these occasions to do what the mob do." "But suppose there are two
mobs?" "Shout with the largest."   Dickens, *Pickwick Papers*, XIII

Wherever this word *mob* occurs in our writings, it intends persons without virtue or
sense, in all stations; and many of the highest rank are often meant by it.
                                        Fielding, H., *Tom Jones*, 25

The pitifulest thing out is a mob; that's what an army is—a mob; they don't fight with
courage that's born in them, but with courage that's borrowed from their mass, and from
their officers.   Twain, *Huckleberry Finn*, XXII

MODERATION

The best men are the most moderate.   Brackenridge, *Modern Chivalry*, Part II, II

There is moderation even in excess.   Disraeli, *Vivian Grey*, Book VI, I

Magnificence is cumbrous. The moderate man is the only free.   Godwin, *St. Leon*, 85

Sparing is good getting.   Lyly, *Euphues and His England*, 229

Put no more clothes on thy back than will expel cold; neither any more meat in thy belly
than may quench hunger.   *Ibid.*

Long quaffing maketh a short life; fond lust causeth dry bones; and lewd pastimes,
naked purses.   *Ibid.*, 229–230

Galen, being asked what diet he used that he lived so long, answered, "I have drunk no
wine, I have touched no woman, I have kept myself warm."   *Ibid.*, 275

The merit of moderation is most apt to be extolled by the losing party. The winner holds
in more esteem the prudence which calls on him not to leave an opportunity unimproved.
                                        Scott, *Quentin Durward*, XXX

Moderation is a fatal thing. Enough is as bad as a meal. More than enough is as good as a
feast.   Wilde, *The Picture of Dorian Gray*, XV

MODESTY: *see also* PRIDE

Modesty with regard to dress is a mere chimera of the imagination.
                          Anonymous, *The History of the Human Heart*, 126

Genuine modesty is alive to every sensation that can affect it; shame, one of its guards,
rushes upon duty on the slightest attack.   Anonymous, *The Modern Fine Gentleman*, I

Those who hide their knowledge acquire a double glory; for to instruction, they join
modesty.   Anonymous, *The Temple-beau*, 121

Retiring modesty, that seemingly negative virtue, is the index by which all others are
supposed to be foretold.   Caruthers, *Kentuckian in New-York*, Volume II, XI

How rare modesty is in this world!   Collins, *The Moonstone*, First Period, XV

True greatness and true courage are ever modest.   *Ibid.*, Second Period, II

MODESTY (*continued*)

Ruined modesty acts her part in the natural government of mankind.
Donaldson, *Sir Bartholomew Sapskull*, II

False modesty always attends false honor as its shadow.   Fielding, H., *Tom Jones*, 675

Modesty is the shield of virtue, and, if once penetrated by the stings of vice, scarce admits repair.   Gentleman, *A Trip to the Moon*, I

Though modesty is praised by everybody, immodesty is much oftener successful.
Johnstone, *The Reverie*, I

Modesty is that accomplishment which young gentlemen generally first affect to lose.
Kidgell, *The Card*, II

It is better to die without money than to live without modesty.
Lyly, *Euphues and His England*, 229

To own in some instances our limited knowledge is a piece of modesty in which lies the truest wisdom.   Mackenzie, *The Man of the World*, I

A modest woman cannot break through a well-tested modesty.
Richardson, *Clarissa Harlowe*, II

Doubt of one's own abilities is a fault owing to natural modesty.   *Ibid.*

It becomes not a modest man to pry into secrets a modest man cannot reveal.   *Ibid.*, III

A modest man should no more be made little in his own eyes than in the eyes of others.
Ibid., IV

Modesty is easily alarmed.   Richardson, *Sir Charles Grandison*, One, I

Modesty never forgets duty.   *Ibid.*, One, II

That modesty which has kept you silent is more often a grace than a disgrace.
Trollope, *Phineas Finn*, XX

MONEY: *see also* POVERTY; WEALTH; etc.

Money is the locomotive power of all things.   Anonymous, *The Egg*, 225

A rich heiress is always in danger.   *Ibid.*, 227

They who are slaves to money command conscience, and scorn to truckle to the unchangeable commands of good and evil.
Anonymous, *The History of Tom Jones in His Married State*, 270

Money begets money.   Anonymous, *The Life of Sir Richard Perrott*, 46

When the money is once parted with, it never can return.
Austen, *Sense and Sensibility*, Volume I, II

People always live forever when there is any annuity to be paid them.   *Ibid.*

An annuity is a very serious business; it comes over and over every year, and there is no getting rid of it.   *Ibid.*

One's fortune is *not* one's own.   *Ibid.*

"Money," the Erewhonian says "is the symbol of duty, it is the sacrament of having done for mankind that which mankind wanted. Mankind may not be a very good judge, but there is no better."   Butler, *Erewhon*, XX

It has been said that the love of money is the root of all evil. The want of money is so quite as truly.   *Ibid.*

When a man is very fond of his money it is not easy for him at all times to be very fond of his children also. The two are like God and Mammon.   Butler, *The Way of All Flesh*, V

Loss of money is not only the worst pain in itself, but it is the parent of all others.
                                                                    Ibid., LXVI

We both wanted money. Immense necessity! Universal want! Is there a civilized human
being who does not feel for us? How insensible must that man be! Or how rich!
                              Collins, *The Woman in White*, Part II, Third Epoch

Money commonly purifies the spirit as wine quenches thirst; and therefore it is wise to
commit all our concerns to the keeping of those who have most of it.
                                        Cooper, *The Monikins*, Conclusion

Money's virtue, gold is fate.   Defoe, *Moll Flanders*, 76

With money in the pocket one is at home anywhere.   *Ibid.*, 182

His treasure is little enough to maintain wars against the butterflies.
                                        Deloney, *Jack of Newbury*, 370

I think that mischeevious consequences is always meant when money's asked for.
                                        Dickens, *Bleak House*, XXXIV

Mr. Dombey expounded to him how that money, though a very potent spirit, never to be
disparaged on any account whatever, could not keep people alive whose time was
come to die; and how that we must all die, unfortunately, even in the City, though we
were never so rich. But how that money caused us to be honored, feared, respected,
courted, and admired, and made us powerful and glorious in the eyes of all men; and
how that it could, very often, even keep off death, for a long time together.
                                        Dickens, *Dombey and Son*, VIII

Money will bring about unlikely things.   *Ibid.*, LII

The true meaning of money yet remains to be popularly explained and comprehended.
                                        Dreiser, *Sister Carrie*, VII

Try and keep clear of wanting small sums that you haven't got.
                                        Eliot, *Middlemarch*, Book V, XLV

There is not anything worth our regard besides money.
                                        Fielding, H., *Joseph Andrews*, 92

Money, the common mistress of all cheats, makes them regard each other in the light of
rivals.   Fielding, *Tom Jones*, 826

Without money, one spends the best part of one's life in toiling for that first foothold
which money could at once purchase.   Gissing, *New Grub Street*, III

To have money is to have friends.   *Ibid.*

A million dollars is a kind of golden cheese.   Holmes, *Elsie Venner*, I

The millionocracy is not an affair of persons and families, but a perpetual fact of money
with a variable human element.   *Ibid.*

With the generality of mankind, money will purchase respect as well as everything else.
                                        Jenner, *The Placid Man*, I

Money, the law-maker.   Keenan, *The Money-Makers*, XXVII

A difference in income, as you go lower, makes more and more difference in the supply
of the common necessaries of life; and worse—in education and manners, in all which
polishes the man.   Kingsley, *Alton Locke*, II

Our money is most truly ours, when it ceases being in our possession.
                                        Mackenzie, *The Man of Feeling*, 44

That old fatted iniquity, that tyrant, that tempter, that legitimated swindler cursed of
Christ, that palpable Satan whose name is Capital!
                                        Meredith, *Beauchamp's Career*, XII

I do not care for money, except that it gives wings.   *Ibid.*, XL

MONEY (*continued*)

Never mind how money comes.

Ibid., LIV

Money's the weapon of war.

Ibid.

It is the nature of money that you never can tell if the boarding's sound, once be dependent upon it.

Meredith, *Harry Richmond*, XXII

Where money beareth all the swing, there many vain and superfluous occupations must needs be used, to serve only for riotous superfluity and unhonest pleasure.

More, *Utopia*, II

Where money is not to be had the king must lose his right.

Nashe, *The Unfortunate Traveller*, 34

Money is like the marigold, which opens and shuts with the sun.

Ibid., 42

Gold is the only physic for the eyesight.

Ibid., 100

Money makes the mare to go.

Richardson, *Clarissa Harlowe*, II

People who have money never want assistants in their views.

Ibid., III

Youth and learning and love, they are all convertible into terms of cash, and have their equivalents.

Schreiner, *Undine*, XII

Few fortunes are sufficient to stand a double expense.

Scott, *A Description of Millenium Hall*, 145

The great mover of all treasons—money.

Thackeray, *Barry Lyndon*, XIX

How to live well on nothing a year.

Thackeray, *Vanity Fair*, XXXVI

When we say of a gentleman that he lives elegantly on nothing a year, we use the word *nothing* to signify something unknown.

Ibid.

Money is a thing which none of us can afford to hate.

Trollope, *Ayala's Angel*, IX

Doan't thou marry for munny, but goa where munny is.

Trollope, *The Eustace Diamonds*, XIII

I hate money. It is the only thing that one has that one cannot give to those one loves.

Ibid., LXXVI

Money is neither god nor devil, that it should make one noble and another vile.

Trollope, *Phineas Finn*, LXXII

Presents of money are always bad. They stain and load the spirit, and break the heart.

Ibid.

Rank squanders money; trade makes it;—and then trade purchases rank by re-gilding its splendor.

Trollope, *The Way We Live Now*, LVII

Her hurts were too deep for money to heal.

Twain, *Pudd'nhead Wilson*, Conclusion

There is no difficulty in digging a hole in the ground, if you have money enough to pay for the digging, but those who try this sort of work are always surprised at the large amount of money necessary to make a small hole. The earth is never willing to yield one product, hidden in her bosom, without an equivalent for it; and when a person asks of her coal, she is quite apt to require gold in exchange.

Twain and Warner, *The Gilded Age*, Volume II, XVII

A man wants riches in his youth, when the world is fresh to him.

Ibid., Volume II, XVIII

It is only people who pay their bills who want money, and I never pay mine.

Wilde, *The Picture of Dorian Gray*, III

Credit is the capital of a younger son, and one lives charmingly upon it.

Ibid.

MOOD: *see also* EMOTIONS

My nature varies: the mood of one hour is sometimes the mockery of the next.
Bronte, C., *Villette*, XXI

She had different moods for different people.   *Ibid.*, XXVI

Our moods are apt to bring with them images which succeed each other like the magic-lantern pictures of a doze.   Eliot, *Middlemarch*, Book II, XX

We color according to our moods the objects we survey.
Hardy, *A Pair of Blue Eyes*, XXIII

There are moods of man which no one will dare to describe, unless like Shakespeare, he is Shakespeare, and like Shakespeare knows it not.
Kingsley, C., *Hereward the Wake*, XXXVI

A forced, interior quietude, in the midst of great outward commotion, breeds moody people.   Melville, *White Jacket*, XII

He was in that humor which converts outward bodily sufferings almost into a relief.
Trollope, *Ayala's Angel*, XLIV

People who go in for being consistent have just as many moods as others have.
Wilde, *The Picture of Dorian Gray*, IX

MORALITY: *see also* GOOD AND EVIL

A moral lunatic.   Adams, H., *Democracy*, XIV

Are we to countenance things and people we detest, merely because we are not belles and millionaires? That's a nice sort of morality.   Alcott, *Little Women*, XXIX

There is no moral law governing the animal kingdom.
Atherton, *The Californians*, Book I, XI

Expediency is the root of all morality. It is stupid to be unmoral, and that is the long and the short of it.   Atherton, *Senator North*, Book III, VI

We do not look in great cities for our best morality.
Austen, *Mansfield Park*, Volume One, IX

All the rules of morality are but maxims of prudence.
Brackenridge, *Modern Chivalry*, Part II, II

There is no moral truth, the weight of which can be felt without experience.
Ibid., Part II, IV

When the world was younger and haler than now, moral tricks were a deeper mystery: perhaps in all the land of Israel there was but one Saul—certainly but one David to soothe or comprehend him.   Bronte, C., *Villette*, XXIV

If morality is that which, on the whole, brings a man peace in his declining years—if, that is to say, it is not an utter swindle, can you under these circumstances flatter yourself that you have led a moral life?   Butler, *The Way of All Flesh*, IX

The world has long ago settled that morality and virtue are what bring men peace at the last. Unfortunately, though we are all of a mind about the main opinion that virtue is what tends to happiness, and vice what ends in sorrow, we are not so unanimous about details—that is to say as to whether any given course, such, we will say, as smoking, has a tendency to happiness or the reverse.   *Ibid.*, XIX

"Is there any human character that is always consistently good?" "One reads of them sometimes in books." "In the worst books you could possibly read—the only really immoral books written in our time." "Why are they immoral?" "For this plain reason, that they deliberately pervert the truth."   Collins, *The Evil Genius*, LII

Oh, my young friends and fellow sinners! beware of presuming to exercise your poor carnal reason. Oh, be morally tidy! Let your faith be as your stockings, and your stockings as your faith. Both ever spotless, and both ready to put on at a moment's notice!
Collins, *The Moonstone*, Second Period, I

Communities always establish a higher standard of justice and truth, than is exercised by their individual members. We commend the virtue we cannot imitate. Thus it is that those countries, in which public opinion has most influence, are always of the purest public practice. It follows that a representation should be as real as possible, for its tendency will be inevitably to elevate national morals. Miserable is the condition of that people whose maxims and measures of public policy are below the standard of its private integrity.
Cooper, *The Bravo*, XXVII

In America, our morals were, and long have been, separated into three great and very distinct classes: New England, or puritan-morals; middle colonies, or liberal morals; and southern colonies, or latitudinarian morals.
Cooper, *Satanstoe*, Volume II, III

All morality is but the shadow cast on one side or the other of a definition.
Crawford, *Don Orsino*, XI

That it is at least as difficult to stay a moral infection as a physical one; that such a disease will spread with the malignity and rapidity of the Plague; that the contagion, when it has once made head, will spare no pursuit or condition, but will lay hold on people in the soundest health, and become developed in the most unlikely constitutions; is a fact as firmly established by experience as that we human creatures breathe an atmosphere.
Dickens, *Little Dorrit*, Book II, XIII

Perhaps there never was a more moral man than Mr. Pecksniff.
Dickens, *Martin Chuzzlewit*, II

Eggs, even they have their moral. See how they come and go! Every pleasure is transitory.
Ibid.

There is nothing personal in morality.
Ibid.

Scanty food and hard labor are in their way, if not exactly moralists, a tolerably good police.
Disraeli, *Sybil*, Book III, IV

Immorality implies some forethoughts.
Ibid.

For all the liberal analysis of Spencer and our modern naturalistic philosophers, we have but an infantile perception of morals.
Dreiser, *Sister Carrie*, X

We are all of us born in moral stupidity, taking the world as an udder to feed our supreme selves.
Eliot, *Middlemarch*, Book II, XXI

There is no general doctrine which is not capable of eating out our morality if unchecked by the deep-seated habit of direct fellow-feeling with individual fellow-men.
Ibid., Book VI, LXI

Our lives make a moral tradition for our individual selves, as the life of mankind at large makes a moral tradition for the race; and to have once acted nobly seems a reason why we should always be noble.
Eliot, *Romola*, Book II, XXXIX

Square taught that the end was immaterial, so that the means were fair and consistent with moral rectitude.
Fielding, H., *Tom Jones*, 285

Though to visit the sins of the fathers upon the children may be a morality good enough for divinities, it is scorned by average human nature; and it therefore does not mend the matter.
Hardy, *Tess*, XI

Because men without exception are more or less tainted with error, all pretensions to superior moral principles are laughed at as false and ridiculous.
Holcroft, *Hugh Trevor*, V

Our libraries are crammed with books written by spiritual hypochondriacs, who inspected all their moral secretions a dozen times a day. They are full of interest, but they should be transferred from the shelf of the theologian to that of the medical man who makes a study of insanity. Holmes, *Elsie Venner*, XII

It is very singular that we recognize all the bodily defects that unfit a man for military service, and all the intellectual ones that limit his range of thought, but always talk at him as if all his moral powers were perfect. *Ibid.*, XV

That great doctrine of moral insanity has done more to make men charitable and soften legal and theological barbarism than any one doctrine that I can think of since the message of peace and good-will to men. *Ibid.*

Death comes and it goes; but this moral problem looks as if it was one of those things that had come to stay. Howells, *Silas Lapham*, XVIII

We can trace the operation of evil in the physical world, but I'm more and more puzzled about it in the moral world. There its course is often so very obscure; and often it seems to involve, so far as we can see, no penalty whatever. *Ibid.*, XXVII

Teachers of morality discourse like angels, but they live like men. Johnson, *Rasselas*, 78

Immorality brings its punishment. Meredith, *Beauchamp's Career*, XLVII

The Wild Oats plea is a torpedo that seems to have struck the world, and rendered it morally insensible. Meredith, Ordeal of Richard Feverel, XXI

As a shell from the sea, man is murmurous with morality. Moore, G., *Evelyn Innes*, XVII

It is true that man is a moral animal, but it is not true that there is one morality; there are a thousand, the morality of each race is different, the morality of every individual differs. *Ibid.*, XXVI

A sort of monster in morals. Mozeen, *Young Scarron*, 10

Well-greased morality. Reade, *The Cloister and the Hearth*, XCVI

Faulty morals deservedly level all distinction and bring down rank and birth to the canaille. Richardson, *Clarissa Harlowe*, I

Persons of little strictness in their own morals take it not into their heads to be very inquisitive after the morals of others. *Ibid.*, IV

I believe there are few young men, and those very sturdy moralists, who would not rather be taxed with some moral peccadillo than with want of knowledge in horsemanship. Scott, *Rob Roy*, VII

There's more moral science in physical science than people think. Shaw, *Cashel Byron's Profession*, IV

As we can have no dependence upon morality without religion, so, on the other hand, there is nothing better to be expected from religion without morality. Sterne, *Tristram Shandy*, II

For any man of culture to accept the standard of his age is a form of the grossest immorality. Wilde, *The Picture of Dorian Gray*, VI

You are really beginning to moralize. You will soon be going about like the converted, and the revivalist, warning people against all the sins of which you have grown tired. *Ibid.*, XIX

Moral truth, resting entirely upon the ascertained consequences of actions, supposes a process of observation and reasoning. Wright, *A Few Days in Athens*, XV

MOTHERHOOD; MOTHERLINESS; MATERNALITY: *see also* FAMILY; LOVE; etc.

The mother's eyes are not always deceived in their partiality: she at least can best judge who is the tender, filial-hearted child. Eliot, *Middlemarch*, Book II, XIV

MOTHERHOOD; MOTHERLINESS; MATERNALITY (*continued*)

All the earth, though it were full of kind hearts, is but a desolation and a desert place to a mother when her only child is absent.　Gaskell, *My Lady Ludlow*, VI

What woman, among the most faithful adherents of the truth, believes the promises and threats of the Word in the sense in which she believes in her own children, or would not throw her theology to the wind if weighed against their happiness?　Hardy, *Tess*, LIII

You may despise your mother's leading-strings, but they are the manropes by which many youngsters have steadied the giddiness of youth, and saved themselves from lamentable falls.　Melville, *White Jacket*, LIV

To withstand them, must we first annihilate our mothers within us: die half!　Meredith, *Ordeal of Richard Feverel*, I

A mother's love perceives no impossibilities.　Paddock, *Fate*, III

Mercy was in that condition which appeals to a man's humanity, and masculine pity, as well as to his affection. To use the homely words of Scripture, she was great with child.　Reade, *Griffith Gaunt*, XXIX

Most mothers are instinctive philosophers.　Stowe, *The Minister's Wooing*, XXI

Mother is the name for God in the lips and hearts of little children.　Thackeray, *Vanity Fair*, XXXVII

MOTION; REST: *see also* ACTION; ACTIVITY

I must move. Resting fatigues me.　Austen, *Mansfield Park*, Volume One, IX

A state of rest is ungraceful; all nature is most beautiful in motion: trees agitated by the wind, a ship under sail, a horse in the course, a fine woman dancing.　Brooke, *Emily Montague*, I

Motion and sound inevitably go together.　Brown, C. B., *Arthur Mervyn*, I

In the heart, as in the ocean, the great tides ebb and flow.　Bulwer, *Alice*, Book II, IV

No longer pipe, no longer dance.　Gentleman, *A Trip to the Moon*, II

Motion without intelligence, like windmills.　Murfree, *The Story of Old Fort Loudon*, IV

MOTIVATION; MOTIVE

In no case, perhaps, is the decision of a human being impartial, or totally uninfluenced by sinister and selfish motives.　Brown, C. B., *Ormond*, 130

There is no sensible difference between motives in the polar region and motives anywhere else.　Cooper, *The Monikins*, Conclusion

We are most of us brought up in the notion that the highest motive for not doing a wrong is something irrespective of the beings who would suffer the wrong.　Eliot, *Middlemarch*, Book III, XXIV

It is one of those cases on which a man is condemned on the ground of his character—it is believed that he has committed a crime in some undefined way, because he had the motive for doing it.　*Ibid.*, Book VIII, LXXVI

He was one of those men who can be prompt without being rash, because their motives run in fixed tracks, and they have no need to reconcile conflicting aims.　Eliot, *Mill on the Floss*, Book III, VII

We never choose to assign motives to the actions of men, when there is any possibility of our being mistaken.　Fielding, H., *Tom Jones*, 205

Our motives are always pretty badly mixed.　Howells, *Silas Lapham*, XIV

The motives even of our best actions will not always bear examination.

Lennox, Sophia, II

Have there not been some, who, looking back on the motives of their crimes, were scarce able to understand how they should have had such temptation as to seduce them from virtue?

Scott, The Heart of Midlothian, I

The hope of fame, desire of honor and preferment, envy, emulation, and the dread of disgrace, are motives which co-operate in suppressing that aversion to death or mutilation, which nature hath implanted in the human mind.

Smollett, Ferdinand, Count Fathom, XVIII

My father was a great motive-monger, and consequently a very dangerous person for a man to sit by, either laughing or crying,—for he generally knew your motive for doing both, much better than you knew it yourself.

Sterne, Tristram Shandy, VI

People are so prejudiced and so used to humbug that for the most part they do not in the least know their own motives for what they do.

Trollope, Phineas Finn, XLIX

MURDER; KILLING: *see also* DEATH

Mortals are easily tempted to pinch the life out of their neighbor's buzzing glory, and think that such killing is no murder.

Eliot, Middlemarch, Book II, XXI

Murder is catching.

Melville, Mardi, XXXV

No doubt the first man that ever murdered an ox was regarded as a murderer; perhaps he was hung; and if he had been put on his trial by oxen, he certainly would have been; and he certainly deserved it if any murderer does.

Melville, Moby Dick, LXV

Is heaven a murderer when its lightning strikes a would-be murderer in his bed, tindering sheets and skin together?

Ibid., CXXIII

Poets murder men's reputations; and that is a worse sort of killing than the doctor's.

Morier, Hajji Baba, XXXII

Murder is wide-mouthed and will not let God rest till he grant revenge.

Nashe, The Unfortunate Traveller, 142

Murder is a house divided within itself: it suborns a man's own soul to inform against him: his soul, being his accuser, brings forth his two eyes as witnesses against him; and the least eyewitness is unrefutable.

Ibid., 145

One murder begetteth another: was never yet bloodshed barren from the beginning of the world to this day.

Ibid., 149

He who kills a man has all his sins to answer for as well as his own, because he gave him not the time to repent of them that Heaven designed to allow him.

Richardson, Clarissa Harlowe, III

Giving him a sound blow, I sent him to feed fishes.

Sidney, Arcadia, II

I wish I owned half of that dog. I would kill my half.

Twain, Pudd'nhead WIlson, I

MUSIC

Have you ever thought how much of life can be expressed in terms of music? Every civilization has given out its distinct musical quality; the ages have their peculiar tones; each century its key, its scale. For generations in Greece you can hear nothing but the pipes; during other generations nothing but the lyre. Think of the long, long time among the Romans when your ear is reached by the trumpet alone.

Allen, J. L., The Choir Invisible, XII

There is a fine old saying, "Keep your breath to cool your porridge,"—and I shall keep mine to swell my song.

Austen, Pride and Prejudice, Volume I, VI

If you cannot teach me to fly, teach me to sing.

Barrie, Tommy, IX

Music is half of life.   Bellamy, *Looking Backward*, XI

I soon forgot storm in music.   Bronte, C., *Jane Eyre*, XXXIII

Music is the friend of love.   Collins, *Jezebel's Daughter*, Book I, III

The master brought out his flute, and began immediately to play. My impression is, after many years of consideration, that there never can have been anybody in the world who played worse. He made the most dismal sounds I have ever heard produced by any means, natural or artificial. I don't know what the tunes were—if there were such things in the performance, which I doubt—but the influence of the strain upon me was, first, to make me think of all my sorrows until I could hardly keep my tears back; then to take away my appetite; and lastly, to make me so sleepy that I couldn't keep my eyes open.   Dickens, *David Copperfield*, V

Not all the words in all the tongues that ever were can ever pierce to the uttermost depths of the soul of man, and let in a glimpse of the Infinite, as do the inarticulate tremblings of those sixteen strings.   DuMaurier, *Peter Ibbetson*, Part Third

Is it any weakness to be wrought on by exquisite music? To feel its wondrous harmonies searching the subtlest windings of your soul, the delicate fibres of life where no memory can penetrate, and binding together your whole being past and present in one unspeakable vibration, melting you in one moment with all the tenderness, all the love that has been scattered through the toilsome years, concentrating in one emotion of heroic courage or resignation all the hard-learnt lessons of self-renouncing sympathy, blending your present joy with past sorrow and your present sorrow with all your past joy?
                                           Eliot, *Adam Bede*, XXXIII

Her sensibility to the supreme excitement of music was only one form of that passionate sensibility which belonged to her whole nature, and made her faults and virtues all merge in each other; made her affections sometimes an impatient demand, but also prevented her vanity from taking the form of mere feminine coquetry and device, and gave it the poetry of ambition.   Eliot, *Mill on the Floss*, Book VI, VI

There's people set up their own ears for a standard, and expect the whole choir to follow 'em.   Eliot, *Silas Marner*, VI

From love proceeds music, and to love it returns.   Fielding, H., *Tom Jones*, 109

Music—light and airy, wild and passionate, or the full harmony of stately marches, in accordance with her varying mood—should have attended Zenobia's footsteps.
                                    Hawthorne, *The Blithedale Romance*, XVIII

Of all the pleasures of sense, that which captivates the soul most strongly is music. By its command over the passions, it commands the heart, while it silences reason by its union with sentiment.   Johnstone, *Arsaces*, I

Music is a holy thing, and its instruments, however humble, are to be loved and revered. Whatever was made, or does make, or may make music, should be held sacred as the golden bridle-bit of the Shah of Persia's horse, and the golden hammer, with which his hoofs are shod.   Melville, *Redburn*, XLIX

Music makes me childish.   Meredith, *Beauchamp's Career*, XXXII

There are times when soft music hath not charms: when it is put to as base uses as Imperial Caesar's dust as is simply taken to fill horrid pauses.
                                   Meredith, *Ordeal of Richard Feverel*, XXXVI

Angelica Forey thumped the piano, and sang: *"I'm a laughing Gitana, ha-ha! Ha-ha!"* Nobody believed her.   *Ibid.*

Military music—twenty thousand doors jam on horrid hinge.
                                              Meredith, *Vittoria*, XLII

A great voice is an ocean. You cannot drain it. It is something found—an addition to the wealth of this life.   *Ibid.*, XLV

In the center of the green was a Maypole hidden in boughs and garlands; and a multitude of round-faced bumpkins and cherry-cheeked lassies were dancing around it, to the quadruple melody of Scrapesqueak, Whistlerap, Trumtwang, and Muggledrone; harmony we must not call it; for, though they had agreed to a partnership in point of tune, each, like a true painstaking man, seemed determined to have his time to himself; Muggledrone played *allegretto*, Trumtwang *allegro*, Whistlerap *presto*, and Scrapesqueak *prestissimo*. There was a kind of mathematical proportion in their discrepancy; while Muggledrone played the tune four times, Trumtwang played it five, Whistlerap six, and Scrapesqueak eight; for the latter completely distanced all his competitors, and indeed worked his elbow so nimbly that its outline was scarcely distinguishable through the mistiness of its rapid vibration.   Peacock, *Maid Marian*, VI

Music, like beauty, is often most delightful, or at least most interesting to the imagination, when its charms are but partially displayed, and the imagination is left to fill up what is from distance but imperfectly detailed.   Scott, *Quentin Durward*, X

Superior music is purity itself; it clears the air.   Ward, E. S. P., *The Silent Partner*, II

MYSTERY

I talk like a Sphynx.   Bronte, C., *Jane Eyre*, XIV

It is my rule never to make unnecessary mysteries, and never to set people suspecting me for want of a little seasonable candor on my part.
                         Collins, *The Woman in White*, Part II, Third Epoch

To surround anything, however monstrous or ridiculous, with an air of mystery, is to invest it with a secret charm, and power of attraction which to the crowd is irresistible. False priests, false prophets, false doctors, false patriots, false prodigies of every kind, veiling their proceedings in mystery, have always addressed themselves at an immense advantage to the popular credulity, and have been, perhaps, more indebted to that resource in gaining and keeping for a time the upper hand of Truth and Common Sense, than to any half-dozen items in the whole catalogue of imposture.
                                          Dickens, *Barnaby Rudge*, XXXVII

What is a country village without its mysterious personage?
                                          Holmes, *A Mortal Antipathy*, IV

From without, no wonderful effect is wrought within ourselves, unless some interior, responding wonder meets it.   Melville, *Pierre*, Book III, II

Seek not to mystify the mystery.   *Ibid.*

Far sweeter are mysteries than surmises: though the mystery be unfathomable, it is still the unfathomableness of fullness; but the surmise, that is but shallow and unmeaning emptiness.   *Ibid.*, Book VIII, IV

Sailing with sealed orders, we ourselves are the repositories of the secret packet, whose mysterious contents we long to learn. There are not mysteries out of ourselves.
                                      Melville, *White Jacket*, The End

Mystery is the great danger to youth. Mystery is woman's redoubtable weapon.
                                  Meredith, *Ordeal of Richard Feverel*, XXIX

Our lives are enveloped in mystery, and the woof of which the stuff of life is woven is shot through with many a thread of unknown origin, untraceable to any earthly shuttle.
                                          Moore, G., *Evelyn Innes*, VI

Mystery was his mental element. He lived in the midst of that visionary world in which nothing is but what is not.   Peacock, *Nightmare Abbey*, I

Light is a great enemy to mystery, and mystery is a great friend to enthusiasm.
                                                        Ibid., VI

Nothing is so becoming to a man as an air of mystery.   *Ibid.*, VIII

Mysteries which must explain themselves are not worth the loss of time which a conjecture about them takes up. Sterne, *A Sentimental Journey*, 92

We live amongst riddles and mysteries. Sterne, *Tristram Shandy*, IV

A ship is a beauty and a mystery wherever we see it. Stowe, *Orr's Island*, XXX

There are souls sent into this world who seem to have mysterious affinities for the invisible and the unknown—who see the face of everything beautiful through a thin veil of mystery and sadness. *Ibid.*

A mystery is good for nothing if it remains always a mystery. Trollope, *Phineas Finn*, XLI

A mystery is good for nothing at all when it is found out. *Ibid.*

Uncertainty charms one. A mist makes things wonderful. Wilde, *The Picture of Dorian Gray*, XVIII

MYSTICISM: *see also* RELIGION

Mysticism, with its marvellous power of making common things strange to us. Wilde, *The Picture of Dorian Gray*, XI

NAME: *see also* IDENTITY

He that hath an ill name is half hanged. Bulwer, *What Will He Do With It?*, Book VIII, III

What's the use of [insects'] having names, if they won't answer to them? Carroll, *Through the Looking Glass*, III

Must a name mean something? *Ibid.*, VI

Names are far more useful than things, being more generally understood, less liable to objections, of greater calculation, besides occupying much less room. Cooper, *The Monikins*, Conclusion

My man Friday. Defoe, *Robinson Crusoe*, 184

He avowed that among his intimate friends he was better known by the sobriquet of "The Artful Dodger." Dickens, *Oliver Twist*, VIII

Our names are the names of the past. Disraeli, *Coningsby*, Book IV, XI

Tears, Idle Tears ought to have been called *Slop, Silly Slop*. Howells, *Silas Lapham*, XIV

Sailors are great hands for false names; they have a trick of using them when they have money to leave ashore, for fear their shipmates will go and draw it out. Jewett, *Deephaven*, Captain Sands

Judge not things by their names. To be called one thing, is oftentimes to be another. Melville, *Mardi*, LXXXIX

The entire merit of a man can never be made known; nor the sum of his demerits, if he have them. We are only known by our names; as letters sealed up, we but read each other's superscriptions. *Ibid.*, CXXVI

Names make not distinctions. *Ibid.*, CLXI

It is really wonderful how many names there are in the world. Melville, *Redburn*, XIII

To know a great many names seems to look like knowing a good many things; though I should not be surprised, if there were a great many more names than things in the world. *Ibid.*

Christian names are coin that seem to have an indifferent valuation of the property they claim.   Meredith, *Diana of the Crossways*, XL

Names beginning with "Cl" I prefer. The "Cl's" are always gentle and lovely girls you would die for!   Meredith, *Ordeal of Richard Feverel*, XVII

We like the names of the people we like best.   *Ibid.*

Names are but the signs of things.   Reade, *The Cloister and the Hearth*, LXXII

There must be something more than a name in virtue.
                                               Richardson, *Clarissa Harlowe*, III

Must family names, without nature, be preferred to love?   *Ibid.*, IV

There is so much in a name.   Trollope, *The Eustace Diamonds*, LV

When I like people immensely, I never tell their names to anyone. It is like surrendering a part of them.   Wilde, *The Picture of Dorian Gray*, I

We have lost the faculty of giving lovely names to things. Names are everything.
                                                                    Ibid., XVII

From a label there is no escape.   *Ibid.*

NARCOTICS: *see also* MEDICINE; OBSESSION

Opium is so far like a human creature that you always hear what can be said against it, but seldom what can be said in its praise.
                                       Dickens, *The Mystery of Edwin Drood*, XXIII

When applied to the purposes of indulgence and debauchery, opium rends the nerves, destroys the strength, weakens the intellect, and undermines life. But fear not to use its virtues in the time of need, for the wise man warms him by the same firebrand with which the madman burneth the tent.   Scott, *The Talisman*, XXII

NARRATION; NOVELS: *see* FICTION

NATION: *see also* GOVERNMENT; SOCIETY

No nation ever was loved while it lived.   Meredith, *Beauchamp's Career*, XLVI

A nation's much too big for refined feelings and affections. It must be powerful or out of the way, or down it goes.   *Ibid.*

NATURALNESS: *see also* NATURE

The naturalest way is the best way.   Dickens, *Bleak House*, LVII

With all those yearnings, and gushings, and impulsive throbbings that we have implanted in our souls, and which are so very charming, why are we not more natural?
                                               Dickens, *Dombey and Son*, XXI

It might be worth while, sometimes, to inquire what Nature is, and how men work to change her, and whether, in the enforced distortions so produced, it is not natural to be unnatural.   *Ibid.*, XLVII

Are there so few things in the world about us most unnatural, and yet most natural in being so!   *Ibid.*

Men talk of nature as an abstract thing, and lose sight of what is natural while they do so.   Dickens, *Nicholas Nickleby*, XLVI

Parents who never showed their love, complain of want of natural affection in their children; children who never showed their duty, complain of want of natural feeling in their parents; lawmakers who find both so miserable that their affections have never had enough of life's sun to develop them, are loud in their moralizings over parents and children too, and cry that the very ties of nature are disregarded.   *Ibid.*

There be grains of sense in a simpleton, so long as he be natural.
Melville, *Mardi*, CXXXI

It is as natural for a human being to swim as it is for a duck.   Melville, *Typee*, XXXI

Being natural is simply a pose, and the most irritating pose.
Wilde, *The Picture of Dorian Gray*, I

NATURE: *see also* ART; HUMANKIND; HUMAN NATURE; NATURALNESS

Nature loves to do a gentle thing even in her most savage moods.
Aldrich, *Queen of Sheba*, IX

Nature is always uniform, consistent, and true to her own designs.
Anonymous, *The Birmingham Counterfeit*, II

Nature constantly tempers one gift with another, in order to maintain a proper
equality.   *Ibid.*

All nature is but one continued *memento mori.*
Anonymous, *The History of the Human Heart*, 126

Nature cannot bear perpetual transports.
Anonymous, *The Lady's Drawing Room*, 211

It is a pretty trick of authors to make nature ever in sympathy with man, but as a
matter of fact she seldom is.   Atherton, *Los Cerritos*, Part II, XI

Nature is a wicked old matchmaker.   Atherton, *Senator North*, Book II, VII

Nature is inexorable.   *Ibid.*, Book II, X

Nature commands union.   *Ibid.*

Everything in nature presses and urges the other; and a new life originates from every
death.   August, *Horrid Mysteries*, I

How astonishing a variety of nature!—In some countries we know the tree that sheds its
leaf is the variety, but that does not make it less amazing, that the same soil and the
same sun should nurture plants differing in the first rule and law of their existence.
Austen, *Mansfield Park*, Volume Two, IV

Nature ever has a voice.   Bennett, *The Prairie Flower*, III

Nature is more faithful than reason.   Brackenridge, *Modern Chivalry*, Part II, I

The universal mother, Nature.   Bronte, C., *Jane Eyre*, XXVIII

The blindness and partiality of nature.   Brooke, *Emily Montague*, III

Nature is everywhere liberal in dispensing her beauties and her variety.
Brown, W. H., *The Power of Sympathy*, 19

The head and the heart are at variance, but when nature pleads, the voice of reason is
feeble.   *Ibid.*, 154

Nature's loving proxy, the watchful mother.   Bulwer, *The Caxtons*, Book I, IV

Nature's ever-variable mould.   *Ibid.*, Book III, V

Nature, who casts nothing in stereotype.   *Ibid.*

Nature orders each of us how to use her gifts.   *Ibid.*, Book IV, V

To push on is the law of nature.   *Ibid.*, Book VI, I

Nature is the great agent of the external universe.   Bulwer, *Pompeii*, Book One, VIII

The lifeless symmetry of architecture no man would be so mad as to put in competition
with the animated charms of nature.   Burney, *Evelina*, 100

Shall we ever subdue Nature and make her always submissive and compliant? Who knows what man may do with her when once he has got self, the universal self, under perfect mastery? Cable, *Bonaventure*, Book III, XVIII

The book of nature is a catechism. But, after it answers the first question with "God," nothing but questions follow. Cable, *Madame Delphine*, V

Nature is of itself a wonderful instructress: One has but to abandon oneself to its impulses and there is no fear of making any very wide mistakes.
Cleland, *Memoirs of a Coxcomb*, 89

Nature is hardly ever seen to yield to the efforts of art. *Ibid.*, 199

All art, when it is not exact enough to be mistaken for nature, is sure to turn doubly to the disadvantage of those who employ it. *Ibid.*, 257

The pure language of nature. *Ibid.*, 343

A mild, a compliant, an unutterably tranquil and harmless old lady, who never by any chance suggested the idea that she had been actually alive since the hour of her birth. Collins, *The Woman in White*, Part I, First Epoch

Nature has so much to do in this world, and is engaged in generating such a vast variety of co-existent productions, that she must surely be now and then too flurried and confused to distinguish between the different processes that she is carrying on at the same time. *Ibid.*

At any time, and under any circumstances of human interest, is it not strange to see how little real hold the objects of the natural world can gain on our hearts and minds?
Ibid.

We go to Nature for comfort in trouble, and sympathy in joy, only in books. *Ibid.*

Admiration of those beauties of the inanimate world, which modern poetry so largely and so eloquently describes, is not, even in the best of us, one of the original instincts of our nature. As children, we none of us possess it. No uninstructed man or woman possesses it. *Ibid.*

Nature, the balance of colossal forces. Nature, the great artist.
Conrad, *Lord Jim*, XIX

Nature has given to every man enough of frailty to enable him to estimate the workings of selfishness and fraud, but her truly privileged are those who can shroud their motives and intentions in a degree of justice and disinterestedness, which surpass the calculations of the designing. Cooper, *The Bravo*, XXIV

All hours and all seasons are alike to the genuine lover of nature.
Cooper, *The Prairie*, VI

There is no mistaking the expression of a death-wound on the human countenance, when the effect is direct and not remote. Nature appears to admonish the victim of his fate. Cooper, *Satanstoe*, Volume II, XIV

On the whole, the ocean is capricious, rather than malignant.
Cooper, *The Two Admirals*, XVII

Nature had gone tranquilly on with her golden process in the midst of so much devilment. Crane, *The Red Badge of Courage*, V

He conceived Nature to be a woman with a deep aversion to tragedy. *Ibid.*, VII

The sun was pasted in the sky like a wafer. *Ibid.*, IX

Nature will often become exhausted by the intenseness of its own sensations.
Dacre, *Zofloya*, XIII

There are times when, the elements being in unusual commotion, those who are bent on daring enterprises, or agitated by great thoughts, whether of good or evil, feel a mysterious sympathy with the tumult of nature, and are roused into corresponding violence. Dickens, *Barnaby Rudge*, II

427

We are all children of one great mother, Nature. Dickens, *Bleak House*, XLIII

I sought out nature, never sought in vain. Dickens, *David Copperfield*, LVIII

There is always a charm in nature. Dickens, *Dombey and Son*, XXVI

Time and tide will wait for no man. But all men have to wait for time and tide.
Dickens, *Martin Chuzzlewit*, X

Nature will smile though priests may frown. Dickens, *Nicholas Nickleby*, VI

The sun does not shine upon this fair earth to meet frowning eyes. *Ibid.*

Natur is more easier conceived than described. O what a blessed thing to be in a state o' natur! *Ibid.*, XLV

The morning's too fine to last. Dickens, *Pickwick Papers*, V

"It does not take a long time to strike a man with lightning." "How long does it take to make and store the lightning?" Dickens, *A Tale of Two Cities*, Book II, XVI

The great grindstone, Earth, had turned. *Ibid.*, Book III, II

Nature, like man, sometimes weeps from gladness. It is the joy and tenderness of her heart that seek relief. Disraeli, *Coningsby*, Book VII, V

There is no rebel like Nature. She is an iconoclast. Dunbar, *The Uncalled*, VI

Nature has a language of her own, which she uses with strict veracity.
Eliot, *Adam Bede*, XV

Nature has her language, and she is not unveracious; but we don't know all the intricacies of her syntax just yet, and in a hasty reading we may happen to extract the very opposite of her real meaning. *Ibid.*

If it be true that Nature at certain moments seems charged with a presentiment of one individual lot, must it not also be true that she seems unmindful, unconscious of another? *Ibid.*, XXVII

You will be thrown into the world some day, and then every rational satisfaction of your nature that you deny now will assault you like a savage appetite.
Eliot, *Mill on the Floss*, Book V, III

Nature repairs her ravages—repairs them with her sunshine, and with human labor. Nature repairs her ravages, but not all. The uptorn trees are not rooted again; the parted hills are left scarred; if there is a new growth, the trees are not the same as the old, and the hills underneath their green vesture bear the marks of the past rending. To the eyes that have dwelt on the past, there is no thorough repair.
Ibid., Book VII, Conclusion

Nature seldom produces any one who is afterwards to act a notable part on the stage of life, but she gives some warning of her intention. Fielding, H., *Jonathan Wild*, 15

Nature is remarked to give us no appetites without furnishing us with the means of gratifying them. *Ibid.*, 16–17

The great *alma mater* Nature is of all other females the most obstinate, and tenacious of her purpose. *Ibid.*, 117

Whatever Nature purposes to herself, she never suffers any reason, design, or accident, to frustrate. *Ibid.*

Nature generally imprints such a portraiture of the mind in the countenance, that a skillful physiognomist will rarely be deceived. Fielding, H., *Joseph Andrews*, 155

The law of nature is a jargon of words, which means nothing.
Fielding, H., *Tom Jones*, 115

There is a certain air of natural gentility which it is neither in the power of dress to give nor to conceal. *Ibid.*, 604

Nature has wisely contrived that some satiety and languor should be annexed to all our real enjoyments, lest we should be so taken up by them as to be stopped from further pursuits. *Ibid.*, 618

Man and nature are ever at variance. In the issue nature wins. Man boasts continually of his conquests over her, her instincts, her terrors, and her hopes. But let him escape from out his cities and the fellowship of his kind, let him be alone with her for a while, and where is his supremacy? Haggard, *People of the Mist*, V

Why should Nature's law be mutual butchery?
Hardy, *Jude the Obscure*, Part Five, VI

There was a natural instinct to abjure man as the blot on an otherwise kindly universe; till it was remembered that all terrestrial conditions were intermittent, and that mankind might some night be innocently sleeping when these quiet objects were raging loud. Hardy, *The Mayor of Casterbridge*, I

To musing weather-beaten West-country folk who pass the greater part of their days and nights out of doors, Nature seems to have moods in other than a poetical sense: predilections for certain deeds at certain times, without any apparent law to govern or season to account for them. She is read as a person with a curious temper; as one who does not scatter kindnesses and cruelties alternately, impartially, and in order, but heartless severities or overwhelming generosities in lawless caprice.
Hardy, *A Pair of Blue Eyes*, XXII

The storm, in its evening aspect, was decidedly dreary. It seemed to have arisen for our especial behoof—a symbol of the cold, desolate, distrustful phantoms that invariably haunt the mind, on the eve of adventurous enterprises to warn us back within the boundaries of ordinary life. Hawthorne, *The Blithedale Romance*, III

Nature, in beast, fowl, and tree, and earth, flood, and sky, is what it was of old; but sin, care, and self-consciousness have set the human portion of the world askew; and thus the simplest character is ever the soonest to go astray.
Hawthorne, *The Marble Faun*, XXVI

Broad as the sympathies of nature. *Ibid.*, XXVII

Birds act according to the simple dictates of nature, and cannot err, nor would they be sensible if they did. Helme, *St. Margaret's Cave*, Volume II, I

Nature, though you push her off with a pitchfork, will return upon you.
Hill, *Mr. George Edwards*, 100

Nature's republicanism. Holmes, *Elsie Venner*, I

Deviation from nature is deviation from happiness. Johnson, *Rasselas*, 91

Nature sets her gifts on the right hand and on the left. *Ibid.*, 115

He does nothing who endeavors to do more than is allowed to humanity. *Ibid.*

No man can, at the same time, fill his cup from the source and from the mouth of the Nile. *Ibid.*

Nature's deepest laws, her own true laws, are her invisible ones.
Kingsley, C., *Alton Locke*, XXXVIII

You may blow up a bubble, but it will be only a bubble. Soap and water will not harden into marble and granite. Locke, *A Paper City*, XXXVI

Art nothing toucheth nature. Lyly, *Euphues*, 98

If we follow and obey nature, we shall never err. *Ibid.*, 99

Nature frameth or maketh nothing in any point rude, vain, and unperfect. *Ibid.*

If nature can no way resist the fury of affection, how should it be stayed by wisdom?
Ibid., 140

As nature must of necessity pay her debt to death, so must she also shew her devotion to youth. Lyly, *Euphues and His England*, 227

Nature has made nothing in vain.   Manley, *The New Atalantis*, I

If reason be judge, no writer has produced such inconsistent characters as nature herself has.   Melville, *Confidence-Man*, XIV

Natur is good Queen Bess; but who's responsible for the cholera?   *Ibid.*, XXI

No cannonade, naught that mad man can do, molests the stoical imperturbability of Nature, when Nature chooses to be still.   Melville, *Israel Potter*, XVII

Nature is an immaculate virgin, forever standing unrobed before us.
                    Melville, *Mardi*, CXXXVII

Life or death, weal or woe, the sun stays not his course. On: over battlefield and bower; over tower, and town, he speeds,—peers in at births, and death-beds; lights up cathedral, mosque, and pagan shrine;—laughing over all;—a very Democritus in the sky; and in one brief day sees more than any pilgrim in a century's round.   *Ibid.*, CLXXXIV

Not only is the sea such a foe to man who is an alien to it, but it is also a fiend to its own offspring; worse than the Persian host who murdered his own guests; sparing not the creatures which itself hath spawned. Like a savage tigress that tossing in the jungle overlays her own cubs, so the sea dashes even the mightiest whales against the rocks, and leaves them there side by side with the split wrecks of ships. No mercy, no power but its own controls it. Panting and snorting like a mad battle steed that has lost its rider, the masterless ocean overruns the globe.
                    Melville, *Moby Dick*, LVIII

O Nature, and O soul of man! how far beyond all utterance are your linked analogies! not the smallest atom stirs or lives on matter, but has its cunning duplicate in mind.   *Ibid.*, LXX

Most all fighting creatures sport either whiskers or beards; it seems a law of Dame Nature. Witness the boar, the tiger, the cougar, man, the leopard, the ram, the cat—all warriors, and all whiskerandoes. Whereas, the peace-loving tribes have mostly enamelled chins.   Melville, *White Jacket*, LXXXVII

The world imagines those to be at our nature's depths who are impudent enough to expose its muddy shallows. The dredging of nature is the miry form of art.
                    Meredith, *Diana of the Crossways*, XXIV

Away with systems! Away with a corrupt world! Let us breathe the air of the Enchanted Island! Golden lie the meadows: golden run the streams: red gold is on the pine-stems. The sun is coming down to earth, and walks the fields and the waters.
                    Meredith, *Ordeal of Richard Feverel*, XXIII

Nature, though heathenish, reaches at her best to the footstool of the highest. She is not all dust, but a living portion of the spheres. In aspiration it is our error to despise her, forgetting that through Nature only can we *ascend*. Cherished, trained, and purified, she is then partly worthy the divine mate who is to make her wholly so. St. Simeon saw the hog in nature, and took nature for the hog.   *Ibid.*, XXVI

Nature never forgives.   *Ibid.*, XLVIII

After a time Nature stops, and says to us "Thou art now what thou wilt be."
                    Meredith, *Sandra Belloni*, LIX

Nature is always on my side.   Merriman, *In Kedar's Tents*, XXVII

Nature does not take long.   Moore, G., *Esther Waters*, XLVI

Though nature be contrary inclined, it may be altered.
                    Nashe, *The Unfortunate Traveller*, 44

Those whom nature denies her ordinary gifts in one thing, she doubles them in another.   *Ibid.*

Art may disguise complexions, but never improve them.

Parsons, *The Castle of Wolfenbach*, I

Nothing grows old but man and his inventions. Who ever heard of a decrepit rose, a superannuated violet, or a greyheaded butterfly?   Payson, *Golden Dreams*, I

Nature is satisfied with a very little nourishment.   Richardson, *Clarissa Harlowe*, I

God Almighty is very kind in making much not necessary to the support of life.   *Ibid.*

The wolf that runs away from a lion will devour a lamb the next moment.   *Ibid.*, II

Nature was her art, her art was nature.   *Ibid.*, IV

That smaller people we make acquaintance with, who live in the flowers. Every bluebell has its inhabitant.   Schreiner, *The Story of an African Farm*, Part II, VII

There are only rare times when a man's soul can see Nature. So long as any passion holds its revel there, the eyes are holden that they should not see her.

Ibid., Part II, XIV

Nature, ever, like the old Hebrew God, cries out, "Thou shalt have no other gods before me."   *Ibid.*

Some of her children die every day, and Nature might go about forever in deep weeds and mourning if she took the trouble to lament for them; so she goes on smiling, though the best loved and the dearest have just gone—smiling, smiling, when our hearts are breaking. Why should the sky be clouded and the birds fly home hungry, because in one small tent a man lay stiff and white? Men whom women's hearts had yearned over died just so every week, and the world rocked on the same.   Schreiner, *Undine*, XIX

Few people have the art of making the most of nature's bounty.

Scott, S., *A Description of Millenium Hall*, 226

It is better to hear the lark sing than the mouse squeak.

Scott, W., *Fair Maid of Perth*, XXX

It is from the great book of Nature, the same through a thousand editions, whether of black-letter, or wire-woven, and hot-pressed, that I have venturously essayed to read a chapter to the public.   Scott, W., *Waverley*, I

Nature is shy, and hates to act before spectators.   Sterne, *A Sentimental Journey*, 114

The laws of nature will defend themselves.   Sterne, *Tristram Shandy*, II

The sun that sails overhead, ploughing into gold the fields of daylight azure and uttering the signal to man's myriads, has no word apart for man the individual; and the moon, like a violin, only praises and laments our private destiny. The stars alone, cheerful whisperers, confer quietly with each of us like friends; they give ear to our sorrows smilingly, like wise old men, rich in tolerance; and by their double scale, so small to the eye, so vast to the imagination, they keep before the mind the double character of man's nature and fate.   Stevenson, *Prince Otto*, Book III, I

Zephaniah had read many wide leaves of God's great book of Nature.

Stowe, *Orr's Island*, III

You must be very despairing indeed, when Nature is doing her best, to look her in the face sullen and defiant. So long as there is a drop of good in your cup, a penny in your exchequer of happiness, a bright day reminds you to look at it, and feel that all is not gone yet.   *Ibid.*, XLIII

Condemned by nature and fortune to an active and restless life.

Swift, *Gulliver's Travels*, A Voyage to Brobdingnag

Nature never duplicates her products, however persistently she may adhere to types.

Tourgee, *Murvale Eastman*, XXXII

Nature alone will not lead us always aright.   Trollope, *The Eustace Diamonds*, LXVI

Nature must needs be lavish with the mother and creator of men, and center in her all the possibilities of life.   Twain and Warner, *The Gilded Age*, Volume I, XVIII

The sky looks ever so deep when you lay down on your back in the moonshine; I never knowed it before. And how far a body can hear on the water such nights! I heard people talking at the ferry land. I heard what they said, too, every word of it.
Twain, *Huckleberry Finn*, VII

It's lovely to live on a raft. We had the sky, up there, all speckled with stars, and we used to lay on our backs and look up at them, and discuss about whether they was made, or only just happened—Jim he allowed they was made, but I allowed they happened; I judged it would have took too long to *make* so many. Jim said the moon could a *laid* them; well, that looked kind of reasonable, so I didn't say nothing against it, because I've seen a frog lay most as many, so of course it could be done. We used to watch the stars that fell, too, and see them streak down. Jim allowed they'd got spoiled and was hove out of the nest.
Ibid., XIX

God's own presence is felt lingering yet, as if, in love with his own work, he stayed to touch it again—creating new charms in multiplied duration.
Webber, *Old Hicks*, VIII

NECESSITY: *see also* CHANCE; DESTINY; NATURE

Necessity is the scourge of genius and the bane of merit.
Anonymous, *The Adventures of an Author*, I

The devil's maxim: "Your necessity is my opportunity."
Bellamy, *Looking Backward*, IX

A wound in the head is of all places the most dangerous; because there can be no amputation to save life. There being but one head to a man, and that being the residence of the five senses, it is impossible to live without it.
Brackenridge, *Modern Chivalry*, Part I, I

Necessity is the mother of invention, and impels to labor.   *Ibid.*, Part II, II

Necessity is the ruler of all we see.   Bulwer, *Pompeii*, Book One, VIII

The evidence of Necessity is all around us—its name is Nature.   *Ibid.*

Amusement is the first necessity of civilized man.
Bulwer, *The Parisians*, Book XII, II

I made a vice of necessity, from the constant fears I had of being turned out to starve.   Cleland, *Memoirs of a Woman of Pleasure*, 28

Necessity knows no law.   Collins, *Blind Love*, Epilogue

People in high life have all the luxuries to themselves—among others the luxury of indulging their feelings. People in low life have no such privilege. Necessity, which spares our betters, has no pity on us.   Collins, *The Moonstone*, First Period, XX

Necessity is a spur to ingenuity and the motion of invention.
Defoe, *Captain Singleton*, 35

To be reduced to necessity is to be wicked; for necessity is not only the temptation, but is such a temptation as human nature is not empowered to resist.
Defoe, *Colonel Jack*, 161

Prove to a man that his will is governed by something outside of himself, and you have lost all hold on his moral and religious nature. There is nothing bad men want to believe so much as that they are governed by necessity.
Holmes, *Elsie Venner*, XXII

Necessities usually are odious. But women meet them. Men evade them and shirk them.   James, H., *Confidence*, VII

The natural wants of man are few, and easily supplied; but the artificial are infinite, and insatiable. Johnstone, *Arsaces*, I

Necessity knows no law, and heeds no risk. Melville, *Confidence-Man*, IV

The straight warp of necessity, not to be swerved from its ultimate course—its every alternating vibration, indeed, only tending to that; freewill still free to ply her shuttle between given threads; and chance, though restrained in its play within the right lines of necessity, and sideways in its motions modified by freewill, though thus prescribed to by both, chance by turns rules either, and has the last featuring blow at events. Melville, *Moby Dick*, XLVII

Many times extreme necessity turneth cowardice into prowess and manliness. More, *Utopia*, II

Necessity is as a strong rider with sharp stirrups, who maketh the sorry jade do that which the strong horse sometimes will not do. Morier, *Hajji Baba*, LXXIV

A virtue of necessity. Richardson, *Clarissa Harlowe*, I

What you *will* do, you *must* do. *Ibid.*, II

He who does what he will, seldom does what he ought. *Ibid.*

All that is more than necessary is too much. *Ibid.*

What ought to be done, must be done. Richardson, *Sir Charles Grandison*, One, II

What will be, must be. *Ibid.*

Necessity is the mother of courage. Scott, *Quentin Durward*, XXIII

Necessity is the mother of the arts. Stevenson, *The Wrong Box*, XIII

I told him that we ate when we were not hungry, and drank without the provocation of thirst. Swift, *Gulliver's Travels*, Houyhnhnms

The necessity of sitting still in the boat with one's enemies is in itself irksome. And then there comes some crisis in which a man cannot sit still. Trollope, *Phineas Finn*, LXIII

It is not necessary to be able to lecture in order to go into the lecture field. Twain and Warner, *The Gilded Age*, Volume II, XXVII

NEIGHBOR; NEIGHBORHOOD; *see also* SOCIETY

Why should a man want to be better than his neighbors? Let him be thankful if he is no worse. Butler, *Erewhon*, XXII

It is no small feather in a man's cap if he has been no worse than his neighbors. Butler, *The Way of All Flesh*, XIX

Neighbors should be neighborly. Meredith, *Sandra Belloni*, VII

NERVES; NERVOUSNESS: *see also* EMOTION

I am nothing but a bundle of nerves dressed up to look like a man. Collins, *The Woman in White*, Part I, Second Epoch

There are some situations in life, such for instance as entering the room of a dentist, when the prostration of the nervous system is absolute. Disraeli, *Coningsby*, Book I, III

NEWS: *see also* MEDIA

Lady Middleton exerted herself to ask Mr. Palmer if there was any news in the paper. "None, none at all," he replied, and read on. Austen, *Sense and Sensibility*, Volume I, XIX

When a public clamor is once raised, there is no resisting it. People will have the thing be so, lest there should be no news. The stagnation of intelligence is equal to the want of breath.   Brackenridge, *Modern Chivalry*, Part II, I

The news of the day is commonly a lie, and that lie a stupid one: somebody in, somebody out, a new chariot, a new play, a hand at quadrille described to a pip.
                                                                    Jenner, *The Placid Man*, I

Good news travels fast, sometimes, as well as bad.
                                                                    Twain, *Joan of Arc*, Book II, XXIII

NICETY: *see also* GOOD AND EVIL; PERFECTION

Nice people may have the grossest ideas.   Graves, *The Spiritual Quixote*, I

NIGHT: *see also* DREAM; SLEEP; etc.

Night is the pilgrim's day.   Bulwer, *Pompeii*, Book IV, IV

Do we not fail to accord to our nights their true value? Our nights are the keys to our days. They explain them. They are also the day's correctors. Night's leisure untangles the mistakes of day's haste. We should not attempt to comprise our pasts in the phrase, "in those days"; we should rather say "in those days and nights."
                                                                    Cable, *The Grandissimes*, XVII

The night sat lightly upon the sea and the land. There was no weight of darkness; there were no shadows. The white light of the moon had fallen upon the world like the mystery and the softness of sleep.   Chopin, *The Awakening*, X

The nights descended like a benediction.   Conrad, *Lord Jim*, II

What a night it was! There was no moon, and a veil of dark vapor was drawn across the vault of the heavens, concealing most of the mild summer stars, that ought to have been seen twinkling in their Creator's praise.   Cooper, *Satanstoe*, Volume II, IX

Night, like a giant, fills the church, from pavement to roof, and holds dominion through the silent hours.   Dickens, *Dombey and Son*, XXXI

Evening—that mystic period between the glare and gloom of the world when life is changing from one sphere or condition to another. Ah, the promise of the night. What does it not hold for the weary! What old illusion of hope is not here forever repeated!
                                                                    Dreiser, *Sister Carrie*, I

Nightfall, which in the frost of winter comes as a fiend and in the warmth of summer as a lover, came as a tranquillizer on this March day.   Hardy, *Tess*, L

Night, that strange personality, within walls brings ominous introspectiveness and self-distrust, but under the open sky banishes such subjective anxieties as too trivial for thought.   Hardy, *The Woodlanders*, III

Moonlight, and the sentiment in man's heart responsive to it, is the greatest of renovators and reformers.   Hawthorne, *The House of the Seven Gables*, XIV

Moonlight is a medium the most suitable for a romance writer to get acquainted with his illusive guests.   Hawthorne, *The Scarlet Letter*, The Custom House Introductory

Night brings counsel: men are cooler and wiser by night.
                                                                    Meredith, *Beauchamp's Career*, XLV

As secret as the night.   Richardson, *Sir Charles Grandison*, One, II

Nothing lasts forever not even the night.
                                                                    Schreiner, *The Story of an African Farm*, Part I, XII

NOBILITY; NOBLENESS: *see also* GRANDNESS; GREATNESS

The world is full of mortifications, and to endure, or to sink under them, makes all the distinction between the noble or the weak-minded. Burney, *Cecilia*, II

The noblest nature is often the most blinded to the character of the woman's soul that beauty clothes. Eliot, *Adam Bede*, XXXIII

It is much more noble to rescue mankind from famine and death, than to violate the honest pride of their nature with the exhibition of victories and trophies.
Godwin, *St. Leon*, 410

It is a misfortune for a man who has a living to get, to be born of a truly noble nature. A high soul will bring a man to the workhouse. Hardy, *A Pair of Blue Eyes*, XIX

Noble souls alone can see and cherish worth. Harley, *Priory of St. Bernard*, I

True nobleness of soul always shines brightest in adversity. Johnstone, *Arsaces*, II

The noble mind suspecteth no guile without cause, neither condemneth any wight without proof. Lyly, *Euphues*, 127

All noble things are touched with melancholy. Melville, *Moby Dick*, XVI

A thin joist of a spine never yet upheld a full and noble soul. I rejoice in my spine, as in the firm audacious staff of that flag which I fling half out to the world. *Ibid.*, LXXX

In an instant's compass, great hearts sometimes condense to one deep pang, the sum-total of those shallow pains kindly diffused through feebler men's whole lives.
Ibid., CXXXIII

Pride gave to her her nameless nobleness. Melville, *Pierre*, Book X, I

Don Quixote—what end can be served in making a noble mind ridiculous?
Meredith, *Ordeal of Richard Feverel*, XXVI

More noble, more humble. Richardson, *Clarissa Harlowe*, II

It is nobler not to offend, than to be obliged to atone.
Richardson, *Sir Charles Grandison*, Two, III

Man never looks so noble as when he contends calmly with the obvious danger.
Simms, *The Scout*, XL

NON-CONFORMITY: *see also* INDEPENDENCE

A non-conformist in fashion is always an affected character.
Lawrence, H., *The Life and Adventures of Common Sense*, II

NONSENSE

Twaddle is not good for the soul. Reade, *Griffith Gaunt*, XVII

NOSTALGIA: *see also* MEMORY; PAST-PRESENT-FUTURE; etc.

The remembrance of past pleasures affects us with a kind of tender grief, like what we suffer for departed friends; and the ideas of both may be said to haunt our imaginations.
Fielding, H., *Tom Jones*, 500

NOVELTY: *see also* SINGULARITY

If erudition is lost with men, it is well to find it with pigs. The extraordinaries are always pleasing. Brackenridge, *Modern Chivalry*, Part II, I

The love of novelty, the delight in acquiring new ideas, is the first passion of the human mind, and the last. Brooke, *Emily Montague*, III

Novelty ever makes the strongest impressions, and in pleasures, especially.
Cleland, *Memoirs of a Woman of Pleasure*, 90

Let a man preach like an angel in his own church and no one regards him; but as soon as one says he is preaching on a mountain, the multitude flocks out to hear him. It is the uncommonness of the thing that recommends it. Graves, *The Spiritual Quixote*, I

Mere novelty gives a preacher no small advantage, if there is nothing vilely dull or ungracious in his manner. *Ibid.*, II

The world is not yet exhausted; let me see something tomorrow which I never saw before. Johnson, *Rasselas*, 179

All mankind are fond of novelty, and everything is new to us that we do not understand.
Lawrence, H., *The Contemplative Man*, II

If a man should bring forth anything new in a company where some disdain and have despite at other men's inventions, there the hearers fare as though the whole estimation of their wisdom were in jeopardy—as if to say it were a dangerous matter if a man in any point should be found wiser than his forefathers were. More, *Utopia*, I

New faces will draw more attention than fine faces constantly seen.
Richardson, *Clarissa Harlowe*, IV

Ennui finds entrance into every scene, when the gloss of novelty is over.
Scott, *St. Ronan's Well*, XVI

There is nothing more desirous of novelties than a man that fears his present fortune.
Sidney, *Arcadia*, V

Every age has its own fund of interesting novelty, so that when it has been once exhausted, there must of necessity be an interval of rest, until time has accumulated a new supply of materials. Tucker, *A Century Hence*, Letter XI

Unquestionably, the popular thing in this world is novelty.
Twain, *Connecticut Yankee*, XXXIX

NUDITY

Nowadays people are as good as born in their clothes, and there is practically not a nude human being in existence. Hawthorne, *The Marble Faun*, XIV

An artist cannot sculpture nudity with a pure heart, if only because he is compelled to steal guilty glimpses of hired models. The marble inevitably loses its chastity under such circumstances. *Ibid.*

OBEDIENCE: *see also* DUTY; OBLIGATION

Tacit obedience implies no force upon the will, and consequently may be easily, and without any pains, preserved. Fielding, H., *Tom Jones*, 12

Tardy obedience is of the house of mutiny. Johnston, *To Have and to Hold*, VI

The unalterable essence of virtue, which is pure obedience. Johnstone, *The Reverie*, I

If love don't carry me to the altar, obedience never shall.
Meeke, *Count St. Blanchard*, I

If we obey God, we must disobey ourselves; and it is in this disobeying ourselves, wherein the hardness of obeying God consists. Melville, *Moby Dick*, IX

Obey orders, though you break owners. Melville, *Redburn*, VI

In time of peril, like the needle to the loadstone, obedience, irrespective of rank, generally flies to him who is best fitted to command. Melville, *White Jacket*, XXVII

Physic is an immense ally in bringing about filial obedience.

Meredith, *Ordeal of Richard Feverel*, XXII

Excess of obedience is as bad as insurrection. *Ibid.*, XXXIII

Obedience is a divine sensualism; it is the sensualism of the saints; its lassitudes are animated with deep pauses and thrills of love and worship. We lift our eyes, and a great joy fills our hearts, and we sink away into blisses of remote consciousness. The delights of obedience are the highest felicities of love. Moore, G., *Evelyn Innes*, X

Is it morality to obey where the command is criminal? Radcliffe, *The Italian*, I

I have no child, I *will* have no child, but an obedient one.

Richardson, *Clarissa Harlowe*, I

Obedience is better than sacrifice. *Ibid.*

The virtue of obedience lies not in obliging when you can be obliged again—but give up an inclination, and there is some merit in that. *Ibid.*

Where is the praiseworthiness of obedience, if it be only paid in instances where we give up nothing? *Ibid.*

To obey your parents is to serve God. Richardson, *Sir Charles Grandison*, Two, V

Obeying God never brings on public evils. Stowe, *Uncle Tom's Cabin*, IX

All sins are sins of disobedience. When that high spirit, that morning star of evil, fell from heaven, it was as a rebel that he fell. Wilde, *The Picture of Dorian Gray*, XVI

OBLIGATION: *see also* DUTY; OBEDIENCE

It was painful to know that they were under obligations to a person who could never receive a return. Austen, *Pride and Prejudice*, Volume III, X

A man that would speak with any weight should first pay his debts.

Bridges, *Adventures of a Bank-Note*, IV

There are obligations which every man owes to society and to human nature.

Cooper, *The Prairie*, XXXIII

To whom nothing is given, of him can nothing be required.

Fielding, H., *Joseph Andrews*, 113

No man is obliged to impossibilities. *Ibid.*, 267

It is a secret well known to great men, that, by conferring an obligation they do not always procure a friend, but are certain of creating many enemies.

Fielding, H., *Tom Jones*, 24

There is a principle in the human breast that easily induces people to regard everything that can be done for them as no more than their due, and speedily discharges them from the oppressive consciousness of obligation. Godwin, *St. Leon*, 382

When any one of our relations was found to be a person of very bad character, a troublesome guest, or one we desired to get rid of, upon his leaving my house I ever took care to lend him a riding-coat or a pair of boots, or sometimes an horse of small value, and I always had the satisfaction of finding he never came back to return them.

Goldsmith, *The Vicar of Wakefield*, 2

The churlishness which cannot oblige is little more selfish than the haughtiness which will not be obliged. Mackenzie, *The Man of the World*, I

Possession without obligation to the object possessed approaches felicity. It is the rarest condition of ownership. Meredith, *The Egoist*, XIV

The whole world have a claim upon the active fortitude of those who are placed between the alternative of confirming a wrong by consent, or preventing it by resistance.

Radcliffe, *The Italian*, I

OBLIGATION (*continued*)

Much only is required where much is given.　　　　Richardson, *Clarissa Harlowe*, I

An undesigning open heart, where it is loth to disoblige, is easily drawn in to oblige more than ever it designed.　　　　*Ibid.*

An obliging temper is a very dangerous temper. By endeavoring to gratify others it is evermore disobliging itself.　　　　*Ibid.*

Do not think that a favor, which is but a due.
　　　　Richardson, *Sir Charles Grandison*, One, II

If a man must pay his debt or go to jail, it signifies but little whether he goes as a debtor or a rebel.　　　　Scott, *Antiquary*, XXXIX

They will never allow that a child is under any obligation to his father for begetting him or to his mother for bringing him into the world; which, considering the miseries of human life, was neither a benefit in itself, nor intended so by his parents, whose thoughts in their love-encounters were otherwise employed.
　　　　Swift, *Gulliver's Travels*, Lilliput

A child ought to have no ears or eyes but as a parent directs.
　　　　Walpole, *The Castle of Otranto*, 36

OBSCURITY: *see also* MYSTERY

The most incessant and undaunted exertions may be shadowed by the veil of obscurity.
　　　　Godwin, *St. Leon*, 441

OBSESSION

Those who are eternally on the watch to accomplish an object of which they never lose sight have a peculiar advantage over every moment of time, and cannot be forever circumvented.　　　　Dacre, *Passions*, Conclusion

I am thrown away by society. Cows are my passion. What I have ever sighed for, has been to retreat to a Swiss farm, and live entirely by cows—and china.
　　　　Dickens, *Dombey and Son*, XXI

A man leading a monotonous life and getting his nerves, or his stomach, out of order, dwells upon an idea until it loses its proportions.
　　　　Dickens, *The Mystery of Edwin Drood*, XIV

When a man rides an amiable hobby that shies at nothing and kicks nobody, it is only agreeable to find him riding it with a humorous sense of the droll side of the creature. When the man is a cordial and an earnest man by nature, and withal is perfectly fresh and genuine, it may be doubted whether he is ever seen to greater advantage than at such a time.　　　　*Ibid.*, XXII

When one idea has got possession of the soul, it is scarcely possible to keep it from finding its way to the lips.　　　　Godwin, *Caleb Williams*, II

A person may be guilty of idolatry by setting his affections too much upon any one thing.
　　　　Graves, *The Spiritual Quixote*, III

Who has much that has given up his brains for a lodging to a single idea? It is at once a devouring dragon, and an intractable steamforce; it is a tyrant that has eaten up a senate, and a prophet with a message. Inspired of solitariness and gigantic size it claims divine origin. The world can have no peace for it.
　　　　Meredith, *Beauchamp's Career*, XXXVIII

Have not the wisest of men in all ages had their hobby horses?
　　　　Sterne, *Tristram Shandy*, I

The thing that you can't get is the thing that you want, mainly.
　　　　Twain, *Connecticut Yankee*, XII

OBSTACLE

The most terrible obstacles are such as nobody can see except oneself.
Eliot, *Middlemarch*, Book VIII, LXXVI

Each man has, one time or other, a little Rubicon—a clear, or a foul, water to cross.
Meredith, *Ordeal of Richard Feverel*, XXXIII

Barriers are for those who cannot fly. Meredith, *The Tragic Comedians*, II

OBSTINACY

An argument against anything is an argument in its favor—for obstinacy is a delicious thing to a person of spirit. Anonymous, *The Egg*, 194

Sooner marry a devil, in contradiction to those who proscribe, than an angel with their approbation. The most sublime pleasure is to do what we please ourselves, not what other people would have us. *Ibid.*

Obstinacy, the greatest and most substantial perfection of the human mind. *Ibid.*, 195

Nothing so obstinate as a young man's hope; nothing so eloquent as a lover's tongue.
Bulwer, *What Will He Do With It?*, Book XI, III

Your stomachfulness swallowed up your stomach; obstinacy is meat, drink, and cloth to you. Richardson, *Clarissa Harlowe*, I

Obstinacy will defend her from harm. *Ibid.*

Obstinacy in a weak man must be worse than tyranny in a man of sense.
Richardson, *Sir Charles Grandison*, One, I

OCCUPANCY

Whatever is built by man for man's occupation, must, like natural creations, fulfill the intention of its existence, or soon perish. A certain leanness falls upon houses not sufficiently imbued with life, as if they were nourished upon it.
Dickens, *Our Mutual Friend*, XV

OCCUPATION: *see* PROFESSION

OCEAN: *see also* GRANDNESS; NATURE; etc.

The Ocean, that hospital friend to the wretched. Fielding, H., *Tom Jones*, 270

The Pacific is populous [with creatures] as China. Melville, *Mardi*, XIII

Oh, Ocean, when thou choosest to smile, more beautiful thou art than flowery mead or plain! *Ibid.*, XVI

This mysterious, divine Pacific zones the world's whole bulk about; makes all coasts one bay to it; seems the tide-beating heart of earth. Melville, *Moby Dick*, CXI

The great shroud of the sea rolled on as it rolled five thousand years ago.
Ibid., CXXXV

Give me this glorious ocean life, this salt-sea life, this briny, foamy life, when the sea neighs and snorts, and you breathe the very breath that the great whales respire! Let me roll around the globe, let me rock upon the sea; let me race and pant out my life, with an eternal breeze astern, and an endless sea before! . . . But how soon these raptures abated, when after a brief idle interval, I had a vile commission to clean out the chicken coops, and make up the beds of the pigs in the long-boat. Melville, *Redburn*, XIII

OMISSION

We shall strictly adhere to a rule of Horace; by which writers are directed to pass over all those matters which they despair of placing in a shining light.
Fielding, H., *Tom Jones*, 282

OMNISCIENCE: *see also* GOD; KNOWLEDGE AND LEARNING; etc.

As mere human knowledge can split a ray of light and analyze the manner of its composition, so sublimer intelligences may read in the feeble shining of this earth of ours, every thought and act, every vice and virtue, of every responsible creature on it.
Dickens, *A Tale of Two Cities*, Book II, XVI

It is only what we are vividly conscious of that we can vividly imagine to be seen by Omniscience.
Eliot, *Middlemarch*, Book VII, LXVIII

Perfect scheming demands omniscience.
Eliot, *Romola*, Book III, LXIII

OPINION: *see also* ARGUMENTATION; BELIEF; IDEA; JUDGMENT; KNOWLEDGE AND LEARNING; THOUGHT; etc.

Nothing is more common than to endeavor to make proselytes to our opinion.
Anonymous, *Private Letters from an American in England*, 5–6

Where an opinion is general, it is usually correct.
Austen, *Mansfield Park*, Volume One, XI

It is particularly incumbent on those who never change their opinion, to be secure of judging properly at first.
Austen, *Pride and Prejudice*, Volume I, XVIII

If my opinions are wrong, I must correct them; if they are above my situation, I must endeavor to conceal them.
Austen, *The Watsons*, I

We admire learning in a pig; and undervalue it in a man. Learning endangers a man's neck. The man that can read goes to the wall; not him that is ignorant.
Brackenridge, *Modern Chivalry*, Part II, I

We find from the voice of history that those men are thought to have deserved best of their country who have occasionally withstood the intemperance of opinion.
Ibid.

Where a government is founded on opinion, it is of the essence of its preservation that opinion be free. It is not enough that no inquisition exists; that no lettre de cachet can issue; but that no man shall attempt to *frown* another out of his exercise of private judgment.
Ibid., Part II, II

In a government founded on opinion, nothing ought to be a reproach, that is the exercise of private judgment. It is subversive of the essence of liberty. A frown is the shadow of force, and he that uses the one would have recourse to the other.
Ibid.

We are greatly inclined to think nobody in the right, but those who are of the same opinion with ourselves.
Brooke, *Emily Montague*, IV

The fiend that ever whispers to the heart of man, "Dread men's opinions more than God's law."
Bulwer, *The Caxtons*, Book III, VIII

A man's business, they hold, is to think as his neighbors do, for Heaven help him if he thinks good what they count bad. And really it is hard to see how the Erewhonian theory differs from our own, for the word "idiot" only means a person who forms his opinions for himself.
Butler, *Erewhon*, XXII

No man's opinions can be worth holding unless he knows how to deny them easily and gracefully upon occasion in the cause of charity.
Butler, *The Way of All Flesh*, LXXXVI

Nothing wheels about with a quicker step than the sort of public opinion that is got up under a cry, and runs itself out of breath at the start.
Cooper, *The Ways of the Hour*, VII

Opinion is arbitrary, and various as religion.
Dacre, *Passions*, Letter XXXIX

An opinion brighter than diamonds.
Dickens, *Dombey and Son*, XXXIX

Perfect breeding forms no opinions, and is never demonstrative.
Dickens, *Little Dorrit*, Book II, V

"What is an individual against a vast public opinion?" "Divine. God made man in his own image; but the public is made by newspapers, members of parliament, excise officers, poor law guardians."
Disraeli, *Coningsby*, Book III, I

Opinions: men's thoughts about great subjects. Taste: their thoughts about small ones: dress, behavior, amusements, ornaments.
Eliot, *Felix Holt*, X

A prig is a fellow who is always making you a present of his opinions.
Eliot, *Middlemarch*, Book I, XI

There's allays two 'pinions; there's the 'pinion a man has of himsen, and there's the 'pinion other folks have on him. There'd be two 'pinions about a cracked bell, if the bell could hear itself.
Eliot, *Silas Marner*, VI

A fig for custom and nonsense! What vails what people say? Shall I be afraid of eating sweetmeats because people may say I have a sweet tooth?
Fielding, H., *Joseph Andrews*, 281

No man fully realizes what opinions he acts upon, or what his actions mean.
Hardy, *A Pair of Blue Eyes*, XIII

There are as many points of view in the world as there are people of sense to take them.
James, H., *Portrait of a Lady*, VII

When wrong opinions are entertained, they mutually destroy each other, and leave the mind open to truth.
Johnson, *Rasselas*, 109

Professions are idle things when contradicted by the incontestable evidence of facts.
Kelly, H., *Memoirs of a Magdalen*, I

There is nothing more effectual in showing us the weakness of any habitual fallacy or assumption than to hear it sympathetically, through the ears, as it were, of a skeptic.
Oliphant, *Phoebe Junior*, Volume II, XII

In every age there are a few men who hold the opinions of another age, past or future.
Reade, *The Cloister and the Hearth*, LIX

Never give more than a second place to the world's opinion.
Richardson, *Clarissa Harlowe*, IV

It is not good manners to despise the world's opinion, though we should regard it only in the second place.
Richardson, *Sir Charles Grandison*, Two, III

The world is generally mistaken in their opinions of the understanding of common men.
Shebbeare, *Lydia*, I

There is no independence and pertinacity of opinion like that of these seemingly soft, quiet creatures, whom it is easy to silence, and so difficult to convince.
Stowe, *Orr's Island*, XVI

Opinions, no matter how powerfully they may operate to shape our lives, are external circumstances, compared with the deep, original springs of character.
Taylor, *Hannah Thurston*, XXXI

The ballot-box is the grave of all political opinion.
Trollope, *Phineas Finn*, XX

It were not best that we should all think alike; it is difference of opinion that makes horse-races.
Twain, *Pudd'nhead Wilson*, XIX

It is difficult to condemn a person who goes with the general opinion of his generation.
Warner, *A Little Journey*, XIX

An opinion, right or wrong, can never constitute a moral offense, nor be in itself a moral obligation. It may be mistaken; it may involve an absurdity, or a contradiction. It is a truth; or it is an error; it can never be a crime or a virtue.
Wright, *A Few Days in Athens*, XIV

OPPORTUNITY

'Tis impossible but that to one that is vigilant and industrious many opportunities must happen.
Defoe, Moll Flanders, 278

As with many men, their opportunities of observation were not so good as their opportunities of expression.
Hardy, Tess, XXVI

If every man had opportunity for his desires, this would be a nation of murderers and disgraced women.
Howe, The Story of a Country Town, XXX

A man's duties will rise with his opportunities.
Richardson, Sir Charles Grandison, Two, III

My maxim is to bear all, to put up with water if you cannot get burgundy, and if you have no velvet to be content with frieze. But burgundy and velvet are the best, <i>bien entendu</i>, and the man is a fool who will not seize the best when the scramble is open.
Thackeray, Barry Lyndon, VI

OPPOSITION: see also COMPARISON/CONTRAST; CONFLICT; WAR AND PEACE; etc.

Nobody outwardly disbelieves or opposes a gentleman at the head of his own table.
Anonymous, Private Letters from an American in England, 62

Violent evils require violent remedies.
Beckford, Vathek, 199

Struggle against yourself as you would struggle against an enemy.
Burney, Camilla, Three, V

Nothing gives so much strength to an adversary as the view of timidity in his opponent.
Ibid., Four, VIII

The opposition of an individual to a community is always dangerous in the operation, and seldom successful in the event.
Burney, Cecilia, I

If the one proposed any amusement, the other constantly objected to it: they never loved or hated, commended or abused, the same person.
Fielding, H., Tom Jones, 66

A thousand naked men are nothing to one pistol; for though it is true it will kill but one at a single discharge, yet who can tell but that one may be himself?
Ibid., 596

As gold is tried by fire, and virtue by temptation, so is sterling wit by opposition.
Richardson, Clarissa Harlowe, II

Indiscreet opposition does frequently as much mischief as giddy love.
Ibid., IV

OPPRESSION

"As a rule, man everywhere oppresses his weaker fellow." "True; but he betrays consciousness of his error, directly or indirectly. One can show his sense of the magnitude of his crime even by the manner of defending it."
Cooper, Homeward Bound, XXIX

Man lording it over man, man kneeling to man, is a spectacle that Gabriel might well travel hitherward to behold; for never did he behold it in heaven.
Melville, Mardi, LX

OPTIMISM: see also HOPE

The reason we all like to think so well of others is that we are all afraid for ourselves. The basis of optimism is sheer terror.
Wilde, The Picture of Dorian Gray, VI

ORATORY: see also EXPRESSION; PREACHMENT

My friends, peace be on this house! On the master thereof, on the young maidens, and on the young men! My friends, why do I wish for peace? What is peace? Is it war? No. Is it strife? No. Is it lovely, and gentle, and beautiful, and pleasant, and serene, and joyful? O yes! Therefore, my friends, I wish for peace, upon you and upon yours.

Dickens, *Bleak House*, XIX

Mr. Chadband stalks to the table, and, before, taking a chair, lifts up his admonitory hand. "My friends," says he, "what is this which we now behold as being spread before us? Refreshment. Do we need refreshment then, my friends? We do. And why do we need refreshment, my friends? Because we are but mortal, because we are but sinful, because we are but of the earth, because we are not of the air. Can we fly, my friends? We cannot. Why can we not fly, my friends?" Mr. Snagsby ventures to observe in a cheerful and rather knowing tone, "No wings." But, is immediately frowned down by Mrs. Snagsby. "I say, my friends," pursues Mr. Chadband, utterly rejecting and obliterating Mr. Snagsby's suggestion, "why can we not fly? Is it because we are calculated to walk? It is. Could we walk, my friends, without strength? We could not. What should we do without strength, my friends? Our legs would refuse to bear us, our knees would double up, our ankles would turn over, and we should come to the ground. Then from whence, my friends, in a human point of view, do we derive the strength that is necessary to our limbs? Is it from bread in various forms, from butter which is churned from the milk which is yielded untoe [*sic*] us by the cow, from the eggs which are laid by the fowl, from ham, from tongue, from sausage, and from such like? It is. Then let us partake of the good things which are set before us!"

Ibid.

Piling verbose flights of stairs, one upon another, the Chadband style of oratory is widely received and much admired.

Ibid.

Peace, my friends. Peace be with us! My friends, why with us? Because it cannot be against us, because it must be for us: because it is not hardening, because it is softening; because it does not make war like the hawk, but comes home untoe[sic] us like the dove. Therefore, my friends, peace be with us!

Ibid., XXV

My friends, we are now in the mansions of the rich and great. Why are we now in the mansions of the rich and great, my friends? Is it because we are invited? Because we are bidden to feast with them, because we are bidden to rejoice with them, because we are bidden to play the lute with them, because we are bidden to dance with them? No. Then why are we here, my friends? Air we in possession of a sinful secret, and doe [*sic*] we require corn, and wine, and oil—or, what is much the same thing, money—for the keeping thereof? Probably so, my friends.

Ibid., LIV

The most innocent echo has an impish mockery in it when it follows a gravely persistent speaker.

Eliot, *Middlemarch*, Book V, LI

Oratory will not work against the stream, or on languid tides.

Meredith, *Beauchamp's Career*, XIV

ORDER: *see also* FORM

In the animal and vegetable world there would be full as much confusion as there is in human life, was not everything kept in its proper place.   Fielding, S., *David Simple*, II

Method or order constitutes the beauty of good writing.

Richardson, *Clarissa Harlowe*, IV

No one can spend his time properly who does not live by some rule.   *Ibid.*

ORDINARINESS

The Egremonts had never said anything that was remembered, or done anything that could be recalled.   Disraeli, *Sybil*, Book I, III

We are on a perilous margin when we begin to look passively at our future selves, and see our own figures led with full consent into insipid misdoing and shabby achievement.

Eliot, *Middlemarch*, Book VIII, LXXIX

There is always something infinitely mean about other people's tragedies.

Wilde, *The Picture of Dorian Gray*, IV

ORIGIN; SOURCE

If money is fairly and honestly earned, why should we pretend to care what it comes out of?
Howells, *Silas Lapham*, VIII

No mere mortal who has at all gone down into himself will ever pretend that his slightest thought or act solely originates in his own defined identity.
Melville, *Pierre*, Book X, I

ORIGINALITY: *see also* GENIUS; INDEPENDENCE; INDIVIDUALITY

He was one of those who carried most weight in the university, and had the reputation of having done more perhaps than any other living man to suppress any kind of originality.
Butler, *Erewhon*, XXII

I am not fond of anything original; I don't like it; don't see the necessity for it.
Dickens, *Pickwick Papers*, XXII

Heaven has taken care that everybody shall not be an originator.
Eliot, *Middlemarch*, Book V, XLV

In all the universe is but one original; and the very suns must to their source for their fire; and we Prometheuses must to them for ours; which, when had, only perpetual Vestal tending will keep alive.
Melville, *Mardi*, LXXV

The world is forever babbling of originality; but there never yet was an original man, in the sense intended by the world; the first man himself not being an original.
Melville, *Pierre*, Book XVIII, I

There is nothing very great or striking about most of the people one meets anywhere.
Oliphant, *Phoebe Junior*, Volume II, I

OSTENTATION: *see also* PRIDE

Ostentation is ostentation, whether it shows itself in the shape of ermine over a senator's shoulders; or in a multiplicity of hairs flowing from a judge's pericranium; or in shape of a great star on the breast of a Bath-metal knight; or a broad brimmed beaver upon the noddle of a stiff-rumped Quaker.
Bridges, *The Adventures of a Bank-Note*, I

PAIN: *see also* PLEASURE

An aching scar is often covered with the laurel.
Amory, *The Life of John Buncle*, I

Pain and impatience are no uncommon companions.
Anonymous, *The Fruitless Repentance*, I

We get accustomed to mental as well as bodily pain, without losing our sensibility to it.
Eliot, *Adam Bede*, L

Sometimes, our pain is very deep and real, and we stand before her [Night] very silent, because there is no language for our pain, only a moan. Night's heart is full of pity for us: she cannot ease our aching; she takes our hand in hers, and the little world grows very small and very far away beneath us, and, borne on her dark wings, we pass for a moment into a mightier Presence than her own, and in the wondrous light of that great Presence, all human life lies like a book before us, and we know that Pain and Sorrow are but the angels of God.
Jerome, *Three Men in a Boat*, X

All pains are ever most acute in the time of suffering: for how easy sit upon the reflection the heaviest misfortunes when they have been surmounted!
Richardson, *Clarissa Harlowe*, IV

Pain rather seemed to increase life than to weaken life in these champions.
Sidney, *Arcadia*, III

PAINTING: *see also* ART

There are only two styles of portrait painting: the serious and the smirk; and we always use the serious for professional people, and the smirk for private ladies and gentlemen who don't care so much about looking clever.   Dickens, *Nicholas Nickleby*, X

PANIC: *see also* FEAR

Panic we will, for the sake of convenience, assume to be of the feminine gender and a spinster, though properly she should be classed with the large mixed race of mental and moral neuters which are the bulk of comfortable nations.
                                        Meredith, *Beauchamp's Career*, I

PARABLE; EXAMPLE: *see also* EXAMPLE; ILLUSTRATION

Here the parable ends, as all parables end—incomplete, disappointing.
                                        Keenan, *The Money-Makers*, XXVII

PARASITES

Big fleas have little fleas.   DuMaurier, *The Martian*, Part Ninth

PARDON: *see also* FORGIVENESS; JUDGMENT; etc.

He never pardoned because the offender himself, or his friends, were unwilling that he should be punished.   Fielding, H., *Tom Jones*, 63

PARTING: *see also* SEPARATION

Many a man and woman looks with some impatience for the last good-bye to be said, so sweet is the prospect of sadness, of suffering, of resignation.
                                        Atherton, *Doomswoman*, XX

Death, self-interest, and fortune's changes, are every day breaking up many a happy group, and scattering them far and wide; and the boys and girls never come back again.
                                        Dickens, *Pickwick Papers*, XXX

Leave-takings in novels are as disagreeable as they are in real life; not so sad, indeed, for they want the reality of sadness; but quite as perplexing, and generally less satisfactory.
                                        Trollope, *Barchester Towers*, LI

PASSION: *see also* DESIRE; EMOTION; LOVE; etc.

The passion of thin, wizened old souls is avarice; that of plump ones a well-furnished table.   Anonymous, *Fatal Friendship*, I

A real passion is too mighty for words.   Anonymous, *The Lady's Drawing Room*, 209

It is not in the power of the wisest, or most resolute mind, to prescribe bounds to any passion it ventures to encourage.   Anonymous, *Philamour and Philamena*, 72

Passion blows a man up like a bladder. He grows as big as himself. His hair rises on his head, and his breast heaves. Will rules give a man passion? Will a man that feels stand in need of rules?   Brackenridge, *Modern Chivalry*, Part II, II

In the voyage of life, passion is the tempest, love the gentle gale.
                                        Brooke, *Emily Montague*, IV

No misery can equal the struggles of a virtuous mind wishing to act in a manner becoming its own dignity, yet carried by passions to do otherwise.   *Ibid.*

The poetry of passion.   Bulwer, *The Pilgrims of the Rhine*, II

Passion seemed to be much discontented; but Patience was very quiet.

Bunyan, *Pilgrim's Progress*, 31

Our passions are but loose casuists, and what is worse, our reason is often too bribed over to their side; in which case we fall like a client sold by his attorney, or a prince murdered by his guards.

Cleland, *Memoirs of a Coxcomb*, 92

Passions are unconsequential.

Ibid., 191

Violent passions seldom last long, and those of women least of any.

Cleland, *Memoirs of a Woman of Pleasure*, 71

That sweet fury, that rage of active delight which crowns the enjoyments of a mutual love-passion.

Ibid., 75

When guilty passion is let loose, who shall name its boundaries? Is not guilty passion as the flame, or the torrent?

Dacre, *Passions*, Letter XLIII

Passion seemed not only to do wrong and violence to the memory of the dead, but to be infected by death, and to droop and decline beside it. All the living knaves and liars in the world were nothing to the honesty and truth of one dead friend.

Dickens, *Dombey and Son*, XXXII

There is no such passion in human nature as the passion for gravy among commercial gentlemen.

Dickens, *Martin Chuzzlewit*, IX

This majesty of passion is possessed by nearly every man once in his life, but it is usually an attribute of youth and conduces to the first successful mating.

Dreiser, *Sister Carrie*, XXIII

The first passion may be but the enthusiasm of discovery.

Dunbar, *The Uncalled*, VII

Our passions do not live apart in locked chambers, but, dressed in their small wardrobe of notions, bring their provisions to a common table and mess together, feeding out of the common store according to their appetite.

Eliot, *Middlemarch*, Book II, XVI

There were passions at war in Maggie to have made a tragedy, if tragedies were made by passion only.

Eliot, *Mill on the Floss*, Book I, X

Of all passions there is none against which we should so strongly fortify ourselves as love.

Fielding, H., *Amelia*, I

Passions operate differently on the human mind, as diseases on the body, in proportion to the strength or weakness, soundness or rottenness, of the one and the other.

Fielding, H., *Joseph Andrews*, 27

The little god passion lay lurking in her heart, though anger and disdain so hoodwinked her, that she could not see him.

Ibid., 36

Passions, the managers and directors of the theatre of Nature.

Fielding, H., *Tom Jones*, 268

As no smoke ariseth where no coal is kindled, so without cause of affection the passion is easy to be cured.

Gascoigne, *Master F. J.*, 10

What has passion to do with knowledge?

Glasgow, *The Descendant*, Book III, II

The corpses of those old fitful passions which had lain inanimate amid the lines of his face ever since his reformation seemed to wake and come together as in a resurrection.

Hardy, *Tess*, XLVI

Honesty and wisdom are such a delightful passion, at another person's expense.

Hawthorne, *The Blithedale Romance*, XVI

How icy cold is the heart, when the fervor, the wild ecstasy of passion, has faded away, and sunk down among the dead ashes of the fire that blazed so fiercely, and was fed by the very substance of its life!

Hawthorne, *The Marble Faun*, XX

The music, the painting, the poetry of the passions, is the property of everyone who has a heart to be moved. Mackenzie, *The Man of the World*, I

If passion is to invade, surely science must evacuate. Melville, *Confidence-Man*, XXII

Passion has the sensitiveness of fever, and is as cruelly chilled by a tepid air. Meredith, *Beauchamp's Career*, XL

The tenacity of true passion is terrible. It will stand against the hosts of heaven, God's great array of facts, rather than surrender its aim, and must be crushed before it will succumb—sent to the lowest pit. Meredith, *Ordeal of Richard Feverel*, XXVII

Honest passion has an instinct that can be safer than conscious wisdom. *Ibid.*, XXXIII

Passion thinks willfully when it thinks at all. Meredith, *Sandra Belloni*, XXX

In France passion is virtue. Radcliffe, *The Romance of the Forest*, 376

In order to have a due command of our passions, it is necessary to subject them to early obedience. Radcliffe, *A Sicilian Romance*, I

Passion, in its undue influence, produces weakness as well as injustice. *Ibid.*

A person who has any over-ruling passion will compound by giving up twenty secondary or under-satisfactions, though more laudable ones, in order to have that gratified. Richardson, *Clarissa Harlowe*, I

My predominant passion is girl, not gold. *Ibid.*, II

Women are never angry at bottom for being disobeyed through excess of love. They like an uncontrollable passion. *Ibid.*

Ill will and passion are dreadful misrepresenters. *Ibid.*

Some one passion predominating in every human breast breaks through principle and controls us all. *Ibid.*, III

Is not passion a universally allowed extenuator of violence? *Ibid.*

A rake in passion is not a rake in love. Richardson, *Sir Charles Grandison*, One, II

When a person can rave, the passion is not dangerous. *Ibid.*, Two, V

The passions are intended for our servants, not our masters, and we have, within us, a power of controlling them, which it is the duty and the business of our lives to exert. *Ibid.*, Three, VII

Passion has eyes, as far-seeing in the dark as love's. Schreiner, *Undine*, XI

How little do they know human nature who think they can say to passion, so far shalt thou go, and no further! Scott, S., *The History of Cornelia*, 193

The language of passion is almost always pure as well as vehement. Scott, W., *Rob Roy*, XXXV

It is better that a man should be the servant of a kind master than the slave of his own wild passion. Scott, W., *The Talisman*, XXII

Passions yield at length to Reason's strokes. Sidney, *Arcadia*, II

Passion acts upon the human mind in a ratio compounded of the acuteness of sense and constitutional heat. Smollett, *Peregrine Pickle*, 110

When a man gives himself up to the government of a ruling passion—or, in other words, when his hobby horse grows headstrong—farewell cool reason and fair discretion! Sterne, *Tristram Shandy*, II

There is no passion so serious as lust. *Ibid.*, VIII

To inspire hopeless passion is my destiny. Thackeray, *Pendennis*, XXIII

PASSION (*continued*)

Thin-lipped wisdom spoke at her from the worn chair, hinted at prudence, quoted from that book of cowardice whose author apes the name of common sense. She did not listen. She was free in her prison of passion.　　Wilde, *The Picture of Dorian Gray*, V

Passion makes one think in a circle.　　*Ibid.*, XVI

PAST-PRESENT-FUTURE: *see also* ETERNALITY; TIME

There is no way of joining the past with the present, and there is no difference between what is a moment past and what is eternally past.
　　Bellamy, *Dr. Heidenhoff's Process*, XI

What necessity is there to dwell on the Past, when the Present is so much surer—the Future so much brighter?　　Bronte, C., *Jane Eyre*, XXVII

I have only to do with the present.　　Bronte, E., *Wuthering Heights*, IX

The Future!—what mystery in the very word! Had we lived all *through* the Past, since Time was, our profoundest experience of a thousand ages could not give us a guess of the events that wait the very moment we are about to enter!
　　Bulwer, *Rienzi*, Book X, VIII

The only reason why we cannot see the future as plainly as the past, is because we know too little of the actual past and actual present; these things are too great for us, otherwise the future, in its minutest details, would lie spread out before our eyes, and we should lose our sense of time present by reason of the clearness with which we should see the past and future; perhaps we should not be even able to distinguish time at all.
　　Butler, *Erewhon*, XXV

The rule is, jam tomorrow and jam yesterday—but never jam *today*.
　　Carroll, *Through the Looking-Glass*, V

The past was nothing to her; offered no lesson which she was willing to heed. The future was a mystery which she never attempted to penetrate. The present alone was significant, was hers, to torture her as it was doing then with the biting which her impassioned, newly awakened being demanded.　　Chopin, *The Awakening*, XV

[In memory] the Past comes into the Present, and possesses it.
　　Cooke, *Surry of Eagle's-Nest*, CXXXII

Troubled as the future was, it was the unknown future, and in its obscurity there was ignorant hope.　　Dickens, *A Tale of Two Cities*, Book III, I

One likes to be done well by in every tense, past, present, and future.
　　Eliot, *Middlemarch*, Book IV, XXXV

The present time was like the level plain where men lose their belief in volcanoes and earthquakes, thinking tomorrow will be as yesterday, and the giant forces that used to shake the earth are forever laid to sleep.　　Eliot, *Mill on the Floss*, Book I, XII

Would you never think the present made amends for the past?
　　Eliot, *Silas Marner*, XI

The citizen's Then is the rustic's Now.　　Hardy, *Far From the Madding Crowd*, XXII

She dismissed the past—trod upon it and put it out, as one treads on a coal that is smouldering and dangerous.　　Hardy, *Tess*, XXIX

There is sad confusion when the spirit flits away into the past, or into the more awful future, or, in any manner, steps across the spaceless boundary betwixt its own region and the actual world; where the body remains to guide itself, as best it may, with little more than the mechanism of animal life. It is like death, without death's quiet privilege; its freedom from mortal care. Worst of all, when the actual duties are comprised in petty details.　　Hawthorne, *The House of Seven Gables*, IV

The Past lies upon the Present like a giant's dead body.　　*Ibid.*, XII

The past is but a coarse and sensual prophecy of the present and the future.
Ibid., XVII

In that fortunate land [America], each generation has only its own sins and sorrows to bear. Here [Rome], it seems as if all the weary and dreary Past were piled upon the back of the Present. Hawthorne, *The Marble Faun*, XXXIII

The past is a prophet. Be the future, its prophecy fulfilled. Melville, *Mardi*, CLIX

Could time be reversed, and the future change places with the past, the past would cry out against us, and our future, full as loudly, as we against the ages foregone. All the Ages are his children, calling each other names. *Ibid.*, CLXI

The future is all hieroglyphics. *Ibid.*, CLXII

The copestone of today is the cornerstone of tomorrow. Melville, *Redburn*, XXX

However ignorant man may be, he still feels within him his immortal spirit yearning after the unknown future. Melville, *Typee*, XXIV

The world has arrived at a period which renders it the part of Wisdom to pay homage to the prospective precedents of the Future in preference to those of the Past. The Past is dead, and has no resurrection; but the Future is endowed with such a life, that it lives to us even in anticipation. The Past is, in many things, the foe of mankind; the Future is, in all things, our friend. In the Past is no hope; the Future is both hope and fruition. The Past is the textbook of tyrants; the Future the Bible of the Free. Those who are solely governed by the Past stand like Lot's wife, crystallized in the act of looking backward, and forever incapable of looking before. Melville, *White Jacket*, XXXVI

The future not being born, we will abstain from baptizing it. For me, less privileged than my fellows, I have never seen the future. Meredith, *Beauchamp's Career*, X

I say that men who do not live in the present chiefly, but hamper themselves with giant tasks in excess of alarm for the future, however devoted and noble they may be, reduce themselves to the dimensions of pigmies; they have the cry of infants. You reply, Foresight is an element of love of country and mankind. But how often is not the foresight guesswork? *Ibid.*, LV

The future his bejewelled and expectant bride.
Meredith, *Diana of the Crossways*, XXIV

Today is like an eagle we have sent an arrow to shoot and know not if he will come down.
Meredith, *Harry Richmond*, XV

We are sons of yesterday, not of the morning. The past is our mortal mother, no dead thing. Our future constantly reflects her to the soul. Nor is it ever the new man of today which grasps his fortune, good or ill. We are pushed to it by the hundreds of days we have buried, eager ghosts. And if you have not the habit of taking counsel with them, you are but an instrument in their hands. *Ibid.*, XXXII

We have a rich or a barren future, just as we conceive it. *Ibid.*, XLIII

It is not till the past has receded many steps that before the clearest eyes it falls into co-ordinate pictures. It is not till the I we tell of has ceased to exist that it takes its place among other objective realities, and finds its true niche in the picture. The present and the near past is a confusion, whose meaning flashes on us as it slinks away into the distance. Schreiner, *The Story of an African Farm*, Part II, II

Why sacrifice the living to the dead, the present to the past? The past is a fruitless dream, the present only is living and demands all things. Schreiner, *Undine*, XVIII

The doubts of the past may be as nothing to the dangers of the future.
Simms, *The Scout*, VIII

On the trestle-board of the Present, Liberty forever sets before the Future some new query. The Wise Man sweats drops of blood. The Greatheart abides in his strength. The King makes Commandment. The Fool laughs. Tourgee, *Bricks Without Straw*, LXII

He would care for today, and not try to put a yoke upon tomorrow.

Tourgee, *Murvale Eastman*, VII

That grim Sphinx, the Future, whose secret no man knoweth.

Tourgee, *A Royal Gentleman*, XLVII

The future is a vast ignorance. Wells, *The Time Machine*, Epilogue

The one charm of the past is that it is the past.

Wilde, *The Picture of Dorian Gray*, VIII

What has the actual lapse of time got to do with the past? *Ibid.*, IX

"I give the truths of tomorrow." "I prefer the mistakes of today." *Ibid.*, XVII

PASTIME: *see also* ENTERTAINMENT

The frolicsome company had begun to practice the ancient and now forgotten pastime of high-jinks. Scott, *Guy Mannering*, XXXVI

All primitive periods, in all countries, are distinguished by the passions for gaming and drinking, and by such a degree of invention as will enable men to gratify both. The fact illustrates the necessity of the race for mental exercise, and for the excitement of the nervous system. Simms, *Woodcraft*, XXXVI

PATIENCE

Patience will cure all evils. Anonymous, *The Adventures of a Jesuit*, I

The usual satisfaction of preaching patience to a sufferer is denied me.

Austen, *Pride and Prejudice*, Volume III, XI

Can you, like patience on a monument, smile in the midst of disappointment?

Burney, *Evelina*, 37

The wisdom of patience. Cooper, *The Prairie*, XXIX

It is the nature of all mankind, authors as well as others, to abuse the patience of their friends. Coventry, *The History of Pompey the Little*, 58

A patient man is better than a strong man. Deloney, *The Gentle Craft*, 92

Fellow mortals, every one, must be accepted as they are: you can neither straighten their noses, nor brighten their wit, nor rectify their dispositions; and it is these people—amongst whom your life is passed—that it is needful you should tolerate, pity, and love: it is these more or less ugly, stupid, inconsistent people whose movements of goodness you should be able to admire—for whom you should cherish all possible hopes, all possible patience. Eliot, *Adam Bede*, XVII

Patience is a virtue which is very apt to be fatigued by exercise.

Fielding, H., *Tom Jones*, 16

Man little knows what calamities are beyond his patience to bear till he tries them.

Goldsmith, *The Vicar of Wakefield*, 95

Patience, that blending of moral courage with physical timidity. Hardy, *Tess*, XLIII

Patience was not made for men in love. Jenner, *The Placid Man*, II

Do not confound impatience with resentment, or unsuccessfulness with negligence.

Johnson, *Rasselas*, 132

Patience needs no prophet. Melville, *Mardi*, CLIII

Patience never yet was a solitary virtue. Richardson, *Sir Charles Grandison*, One, II

PATRIOTISM

Love for country, whilst it has occasioned some men to do noble deeds, has caused others to commit wild extravagances.   Anonymous, *The Adventures of a Jesuit*, II

What is love of our country, but a love to our countrymen?
                              Anonymous, *The Peregrinations of Jeremiah Grant*, 213

It is in small states that glory is most active and pure—the more confined the limits of the circle, the more ardent the patriotism.   Bulwer, *Pompeii*, Book Two, IV

In love of home, the love of country has its rise.
                              Dickens, *The Old Curiosity Shop*, XXXVIII

A true patriot will lament the necessity of war.   Gentleman, *A Trip to the Moon*, II

There is no character more admirable than the patriot-yeoman, who unites with the utmost simplicity of garb and manners an understanding fraught with information and sentiment and a heart burning with the love of mankind.   Godwin, *St Leon*, 86

How many club men do you know who would think it sweet and fitting to die for their country?   Howells, *Silas Lapham*, XIV

My patriotism is modified by an indisposition to generalize.
                              James, H., *Confidence*, IX

The common motive of patriotism is the price for which a man can sell himself and his party.   Johnstone, *The Reverie*, I

A man may do for his country what he wouldn't do for himself.
                              Meredith, *Beauchamp's Career*, I

The woman who keeps you from serving your country, she's your country's enemy.
                              Meredith, *Lord Ormont*, XXIX

Whose patriotism would not grow warmer on the plains of Marathon?
                              Scott, *Antiquary*, IV

True patriotism is of no party.   Smollett, *Sir Launcelot Greaves*, 71

With Joan of Arc love of country was more than sentiment—it was a passion. She was the Genius of Patriotism—she was Patriotism embodied, concreted, made flesh, and palpable to the touch and visible to the eye.   Twain, *Joan of Arc*, Book III, Conclusion

PAUSE

That cold awkward pause so common with sullen spirits and barren brains.
                              Disraeli, *Coningsby*, Book III, III

PEACE: *see also* CONFLICT; WAR AND PEACE

Is it the region inside a man, or out, that gives him peace?
                              Meredith, *Beauchamp's Career*, XII

PEDIGREE: *see also* FAMILY; SOCIETY; etc.

Pedigree is of no avail. Do we not find that sages have had blockheads for their sons; and that blockheads have had sages?   Brackenridge, *Modern Chivalry*, Part I, I

PERCEPTION: *see also* JUDGMENT; OPINION; PERSPECTIVE; etc.

The art of reading the inner human nature by the outer aspect is of immeasurable interest and boundless practical value, and the man who can practice it skillfully and apply it sagaciously is on the high road to fortune.   Cable, *Bonaventure*, Book III, III

451

Perhaps a man never sees so much at a glance as when he is in a situation of extremity.
Dickens, *Barnaby Rudge*, LVIII

There is a subtlety of perception in real attachment, even when it is borne towards man by one of the lower animals, which leaves the highest intellect behind.
Dickens, *David Copperfield*, XLII

There are times when, the mind being painfully alive to receive impressions, a great deal may be noted at a glance.
Dickens, *Nicholas Nickleby*, LIII

Some men endeavor so long to blind other men's eyes, that at last they quite darken their own; and although in their nature they are certainly daws, yet they find a method of persuading themselves that they are peacocks.
Fielding, S., *David Simple*, I

The mind's eye is not formed to take in many ideas, no more than the body's eyes many objects at once.
Ibid., II

What is beauty at one time is deformity at another.
Gentleman, *A Trip to the Moon*, I

The rudest exhibition of art is at first admired; till a nobler is presented, and we are taught to wonder at the facility with which before we had been satisfied.
Godwin, *Caleb Williams*, I

It is very easy to criticize other people's modes of dealing with their children. Outside observers see results; parents see processes.
Holmes, *Elsie Venner*, XIX

We have perceptions of the outer forms of things, but that is all we know of them. The only thing we are sure of is what is in ourselves.
Moore, G., *Evelyn Innes*, XXXV

A stander-by is often a better judge of the game than those that play.
Richardson, *Clarissa Harlowe*, I

We young girls think, if we put our hands before our eyes, nobody can see us.
Richardson, *Sir Charles Grandison*, Three, VII

The common eye sees only the outside of things, and judges by that, but the seeing eye pierces through and reads the heart and the soul, finding there capacities which the outside didn't indicate or promise, and which the other kind couldn't detect.
Twain, *Joan of Arc*, Book II, XI

Even the clearest and most perfect circumstantial evidence is likely to be at fault, after all, and therefore ought to be received with great caution. Take the case of any pencil, sharpened by any woman: if you have witnesses, you will find she did it with a knife; but if you take simply the aspect of the pencil, you will say she did it with her teeth.
Twain, *Pudd'nhead Wilson*, XX

A bystander often sees more of the game than those who play.
Walpole, *The Castle of Otranto*, 40

PERFECTION; WHOLENESS: *see also* COMPLETENESS

Perfect characters are just as uncommon in the moral, as perfect performances in the literary world.
Anonymous, *The Wanderer*, I

The first step leading to perfection, and real activity, is to wander through the world unknown, and subject to few wants.
August, *Horrid Mysteries*, IV

Never yet was mortal created so perfect, that every wish was virtuous, or every impulse wise.
Burney, *Camilla*, Three, V

A man who piques himself upon his perfections finds no mode so convenient and ready for displaying them as proving all about him to be constantly in the wrong.
Ibid.

Nothing perfect is natural. I hate everything out of nature.
Burney, *Cecilia*, I

There are many who have some recommendations, but who is there wholly unexceptionable?
Ibid., II

Perfection is not flattered when it is called perfect.　　Crawford, *Don Orsino*, XV

They should only write and sing for each other, these impeccables, who so despise success and revile the successful. How do they live, I wonder? Do they take in each other's washing, or review each other's books?　　DuMaurier, *The Martian*, Part Ninth

The very best of mortals are so far from the standard of perfection that great room indeed is left for improvement.　　Harley, *Priory of St. Bernard*, II

She is a saint, and a persecution is all that she needs to bring out her saintliness and make her perfect.　　James, H., *The American*, VI

In all perfect shapes, a blemish bringeth rather a liking every way to the eyes, than a loathing any way to the mind.　　Lyly, *Euphues*, 91

The freshest colors soonest fade, the keenest razor soonest turneth his edge, the finest cloth is soonest eaten with moths, and the cambric sooner stained than the coarse canvas.　　*Ibid.*, 92

Not to do things wholly is worse than not to do things at all.
　　Meredith, *Harry Richmond*, LV

Belonging by birth to Paradise, our tendency should ever be towards it: allowing no lower standard than its Perfection.　　Meredith, *Ordeal of Richard Feverel*, I

Noble minds emulative of perfection may be allowed a little generous envy.
　　Richardson, *Clarissa Harlowe*, I

Felicitate thyself then upon thy defects; which are evidently thy principal perfections; and which occasion thee a distinction which otherwise thou wouldst never have.
　　Ibid., II

A perfect woman must interest gods and men in her cause.　　*Ibid.*

Partial mortals take their measures of right and wrong from what they find themselves to be, and cannot help being. So awkwardness is a perfection in the awkward.
　　Richardson, *Clarissa Harlowe*, IV

PERFORMANCE: *see also* ACTION

The power of doing anything with quickness is always much prized by the possessor, and often without any attention to the imperfection of the performance.
　　Austen, *Pride and Prejudice*, Volume I, X

Many things difficult in design prove easy in performance.　　Johnson, *Rasselas*, 64

PERSECUTION: *see also* OPPRESSION

Persecution is a tempest raised by the breath of hell.　　Collyer, *Felicia to Charlotte*, II

Persecution and discouragement depress ingenuous minds, and blunt the edge of lively imaginations.　　Richardson, *Clarissa Harlowe*, I

PERSEVERANCE; PERSISTENCE

It is astonishing how large a hole a woodpecker makes with so small a beak: it is owing to successive impressions.　　Brackenridge, *Modern Chivalry*, Part II, I

Perseverance is the surest road to success.　　Dacre, *Passions*, Letter XVI

I never give up anything that I choose to do.　　Eliot, *Middlemarch*, Book IV, XXXVI

Great works are performed, not by strength, but perseverance.
　　Johnson, *Rasselas*, 64

You must not forsake the ship in a tempest, because you cannot rule and keep down the winds.　　More, *Utopia*, I

PERSEVERANCE; PERSISTENCE (*continued*)

Attention, love, admiration, cannot be always kept at the stretch.
Richardson, *Sir Charles Grandison*, Two, IV

Persevere in what is well begun.
Ibid., Three, VII

A ship is not counted strong by biding one storm.
Sidney, *Arcadia*, III

PERSONALNESS

It is the personal that interests mankind; that fires their imagination, and wins their hearts.
Disraeli, *Coningsby*, Book II, VII

PERSPECTIVE: *see also* PERCEPTION

What is sport to one may be death to another.
Bronte, C., *Villette*, XXI

There is such a thing as making nothing out of a molehill, in consequence of your head being too high to see it.
Collins, *The Moonstone*, First Period, XII

The onlookers see most of the game.
Conrad, *Lord Jim*, XXI

If I could live another fifty years, I should be blind to everything that wasn't out of other people's sight, like a man who stands in a well and sees nothing but the stars.
Eliot, *Adam Bede*, XXV

Will not a tiny speck very close to our vision blot out the glory of the world, and leave only a margin by which we see the blot?
Eliot, *Middlemarch*, Book IV, XLII

Who can know how much of his most inward life is made up of the thoughts he believes other men to have about him, until that fabric of opinion is threatened with ruin?
Ibid., Book VII, LXVIII

To other eyes than ours evil may be good and darkness more beautiful than day, or all alike be fair.
Haggard, *She*, XVIII

There are those who falter in the common tongue, because they think in another; and these are accounted stutterers and stammerers.
Melville, *Mardi*, CXXVI

Oh, ye laurels! to be visible to me, ye must be removed from my brow!
Ibid.

It is pleasant to read about whales through their own spectacles.
Melville, *Moby Dick*, LXVIII

It is the not impartially bestowed privilege of the more final insights, that at the same moment they reveal the depths, they do, sometimes, also reveal—though by no means so distinctly—some answering heights. But when only midway down the gulf, its crags wholly conceal the upper vaults, and the wanderer thinks it all one gulf of downward dark.
Melville, *Pierre*, Book IX, III

The reason why men and women are mysterious to us, and prove disappointing is, that we will read them from our own book: just as we are perplexed by reading ourselves from theirs.
Meredith, *Ordeal of Richard Feverel*, XXXIII

Everything has two sides—the outside that is ridiculous, and the inside that is solemn.
Schreiner, *Story of an African Farm*, Part II, IV

If the ploughboy knew how the worm suffers that writhes beneath his foot, surely he would not crush it. If we saw the work of the cruel word, surely we should not utter it. If we could see the light of a life vanish and die out, surely we should be loath to extinguish it. But we never can see, never know, never watch these things; therefore blighting, cursing, and inflicting suffering, we go on our way rejoicing.
Schreiner, *Undine*, XI

A wink's as good as a nod to a blind horse.
Scott, *The Heart of Midlothian*, XVI

There's always a hole in theories somewheres, if you look close enough.
Twain, *Tom Sawyer Abroad*, IX

PERSUASION: *see also* ARGUMENTATION

Persuasion is not at command.   Austen, *Northanger Abbey*, XIX

Men can resist the remonstrances that wound them, and so irritate them, better than they can those gentle appeals that rouse no anger, but soften the whole heart.
Reade, *Griffith Gaunt*, XXIX

Drawn by gentle words into the perpetration of the most violent acts.
Richardson, *Clarissa Harlowe*, I

There is great cruelty in persuasion, and still more to a soft and gentle temper, than to a stubborn one.   Richardson, *Sir Charles Grandison*, Three, VI

PERVERSITY

The best institutions may be perverted to vilest purposes.
Anonymous, *The Fruitless Repentance*, II

There is a perverse mood of the mind which is rather soothed than irritated by misconstruction; and in quarters where we can never be rightly known, we take pleasure in being consummately ignored. What honest man, on being casually taken for a housebreaker, does not feel rather tickled than vexed at the mistake?   Bronte, C., *Villette*, X

Nothing is beyond mortal perversity; and anything is credible when our fallen natures get the better of us.   Collins, *The Moonstone*, Second Period, III

They who do not understand that a man may be brought to hope that which of all things is the most grievous to him have not observed with sufficient closeness the perversity of the human mind.   Trollope, *He Knew He Was Right*, XXXVIII

PETITION

What right has a petitioner to be angry at a repulse, if he has not a right to demand what he sues for as a debt?   Richardson, *Clarissa Harlowe*, II

PHILANTHROPY: *see also* GENEROSITY

We Irishmen are all of us true philanthropists. That is why we have nothing, although in other countries I have seen philanthropists who had a great deal.
Crane, *The O'Ruddy*, XI

We hope by this time next year to have from a hundred and fifty to two hundred healthy families cultivating coffee and educating the natives of Borrioboola-Gha, on the left bank of the Niger.   Dickens, *Bleak House*, IV

A pretty thing, indeed, to marry a Philanthropist.   *Ibid.*, XIV

It is a most extraordinary thing that these philanthropists are always denouncing somebody. And it is another most extraordinary thing that they are always so violently flush of miscreants. And it is another most extraordinary thing that these philanthropists are so given to seizing their fellow-creatures by the scruff of the neck, and bumping them into the paths of peace.   Dickens, *The Mystery of Edwin Drood*, VI

He has an obderrate [*sic*] bosom. Who else could have resisted the pleading of sixteen of our fairest sisters, and withstood their exhortations to subscribe to our noble society for providing the infant negroes in the West Indies with flannel waistcoats and moral pocket handkerchiefs?   Dickens, *Pickwick Papers*, XXVII

The besetting sin of a philanthropist is apt to be a moral obliquity. His sense of honor ceases to be the sense of other honorable men.
Hawthorne, *The Blithedale Romance*, XV

Admitting what is called philanthropy, when adopted as a profession, to be often useful by its energetic impulse of society at large, it is perilous to the individual whose ruling passion, in one exclusive channel, it thus becomes.   *Ibid.*, XXVIII

Modern philanthropy is the cause of much trouble and vexation.
Marryat, *Mr. Midshipman Easy*, XXX

Philanthropists know better what goodness is than what men are.
Melville, *Confidence-Man*, XLIII

Almost for the first time in the history of earth, national selfishness is unbounded philanthropy; for we cannot do a good to America, but we give alms to the world.
Melville, *White Jacket*, XXXVI

Philanthropic people lose all sense of humanity. It is their distinguishing characteristic.
Wilde, *The Picture of Dorian Gray*, II

PHILOSOPHY: *see also* IDEA; MIND; RELIGION; etc.

Transcendental philosophers are mostly elderly men, usually married, and, when engaged in business, somewhat apt to be sleepy towards evening.
Adams, H., *Democracy*, I

Philosophy gives no indulgence to vice, makes no allowance for any crime.
Amory, *John Buncle*, I

The philosophy of life is nothing but an accurate ocular knowledge of the vicissitude of all things.
August, *Horrid Mysteries*, II

An age of philosophy succeeds an age of poetry. What succeeds philosophy? Cynicism or infidelity—next a utilitarian age, and lastly we have a mongrel compound of all—then we have revolution, bloodshed, sentiment, religion, and spinning-jennies.
Caruthers, *Kentuckian in New-York*, Volume I, VIII

I have never yet seen a woman who preferred philosophy to princes.
Child, *Philothea*, XII

Kings are less fortunate than philosophers.
Ibid.

There is nothing like a disappointment for throwing one into the arms of philosophy for consolation.
Cleland, *Memoirs of a Coxcomb*, 237

Philosophy, sound principles, and virtue are really delightful; but, after all, they are no more than so many slaves of the belly; a man usually preferring to eat his best friend, to starving.
Cooper, *The Monikins*, Conclusion

True philosophy is superior to the refinements of fancy; and, when it is accompanied with a sound understanding, and a virtuous heart, it seldom errs in its judgments or definitions.
Dacre, *Passions*, Letter II

A philosopher, one of that stern and rigid school who are far above the weaknesses of mankind in general.
Dickens, *Barnaby Rudge*, LXXXI

Measles, rheumatics, hooping-cough, fevers, agers, and lumbagers is all philosophy together; that's what it is. The heavenly bodies is philosophy; and if there's a screw loose in a earthly body, that's philosophy too; or it may be that sometimes there's a little metaphysics in it, but that's not often. Philosophy's the chap for me.
Dickens, *Nicholas Nickleby*, LVII

It is the invariable practice of many mighty philosophers, in carrying out their theories, to evince great wisdom and foresight in providing against every possible contingency which can be supposed at all likely to affect themselves. Thus, to do a great right, you may do a little wrong; and you may take any means which the end to be attained will justify; the amount of the right, or the amount of the wrong, or indeed the distinction between the two, being left entirely to the philosopher concerned, to be settled and determined by his clear, comprehensive, and impartial view of his own particular case.
Dickens, *Oliver Twist*, XII

It has somehow or other happened, from time immemorial, that many of the best and ablest philosophers, who have been perfect lights of science in matters of theory, have been wholly unable to reduce them to practice.   Dickens, *Pickwick Papers*, XIX

Repression is the only lasting philosophy.   Dickens, *A Tale of Two Cities*, Book II, IX

The word *philosophy* is a commodity very unfairly smuggled by the ignorant, who, by not taxing it with any duty either to God or man, undervalue its consequence by disposing of it inconsiderately. It is the wealthiest citizen robbed of his property, and become the poorest bankrupt.   Donaldson, *Sir Bartholomew Sapskull*, II

Philosophy: not the bare knowledge of right and wrong, but an energy, a habit, superior to all the attacks of fortune.   Fielding, H., *Amelia*, II

Though such great beings, philosophers, think much better and more wisely, they always act exactly like other men.   Fielding, H., *Tom Jones*, 177

What would a teacher be without her own philosophy?   Haggard, *She*, XVII

I am weary of Blithedale, and sick to death of playing at philanthropy and progress. Of all varieties of mock-life, we have surely blundered into the very emptiest mockery, in our effort to establish the one true system.
         Hawthorne, *The Blithedale Romance*, XXVI

In knowledge and philosophy be careful to distinguish that the purpose of research should ever be fixed on making simple what is abstruse, not abstruse what is simple; and that difficulty in acquisition will no more sanctify its inexpediency than the art of tumblers, who have learned to stand on their heads, will prove that to be the proper posture for man.   Mackenzie, *The Man of the World*, I

Mr. Easy turned philosopher, the very best profession a man can take up, when he is fit for nothing else; he must be a very incapable person indeed who cannot talk nonsense.
         Marryat, *Mr. Midshipman Easy*, I

To every philosophy are certain rear parts, very important parts, and these, like the rear of one's head, are best seen by reflection.   Melville, *Confidence-Man*, XXXVII

Since we philosophers bestow so much wisdom upon others, it is not to be wondered at, if now and then we find what is left in us too small for our necessities. It is from our very abundance that we want.   Melville, *Mardi*, CXXXI

Endurance is the test of philosophy.   *Ibid.*, CLI

Here was a man some twenty thousand miles from home, by the way of Cape Horn thrown among people as strange to him as though he were in the planet Jupiter; and yet he seemed entirely at his ease; preserving the utmost serenity; content with his own companionship; always equal to himself. Surely this was a touch of fine philosophy; though no doubt he had never heard there was such a thing as that. But, perhaps, to be true philosophers, we mortals should not be conscious of so living or so striving. So soon as I hear that such or such a man gives himself out for a philosopher, I conclude that, like the dyspeptic old woman, he must have "broken his digester."
         Melville, *Moby Dick*, X

There are certain queer times and occasions in this strange mixed affair we call life when a man takes this whole universe for a vast practical joke, though the wit thereof he but dimly discerns, and more than suspects that the joke is at nobody's expense but his own.   *Ibid.*, XLIX

As much as legs are wanted for the dance, philosophy is required to make our human nature credible and acceptable.   Meredith, *Diana of the Crossways*, I

A young philosopher's an old fool.   Meredith, *Ordeal of Richard Feverel*, XXIX

There is one who comes to all feasts that have their basis in folly, whom criminals of trained instinct are careful to provide against: who will speak, and whose hateful voice must somehow be silenced while the feast is going on. This personage is THE PHILOSOPHER.   *Ibid.*, XXXIV

PHILOSOPHY (*continued*)

No philosopher would resign his mental acquisitions for the purchase of any terrestrial good. Peacock, *Headlong Hall*, V

He is so far a true philosopher, as to be a contemner of all ordinary rules of hours and times. Scott, *Antiquary*, XXXV

Those who philosophize yet go forward—a race of which the world has comparatively few. Simms, *The Scout*, XXXIV

He prided himself upon the fact that he could extract his morals always from his appetites. He took philosophy with him to his table, and grew wise over his wine. Simms, *Woodcraft*, XVIII

The philosophy which today has brought will reconcile me tomorrow. *Ibid.*, XIX

'Tain't philosophy, but it's mighty good sense. *Ibid.*, XXX

People in general are so misled by vulgar prejudices that philosophy is hardly sufficient to undeceive them. Smollett, *Humphry Clinker*, 27

Aristotle was a pedantic blockhead, and still more knave than fool. Smollett, *Sir Launcelot Greaves*, 79

Philosophy has a fine saying for everything. For death it has an entire set. Sterne, *Tristram Shandy*, V

Philosophy speaks freely of everything. *Ibid.*, IX

If you want to be a philosopher, never find an eye for painting, a finger for music, or a brain for poetry. Any one of these will keep a man from wisdom. Wright, *A Few Days in Athens*, III

Philosophy cannot change the laws of nature; but she may teach us to accommodate to them. *Ibid.*, X

PHYSIQUE: *see also* BODY

High-stomached sheiks. Beckford, *Vathek*, 226

PIETY: *see also* PURITY; RELIGION

Pious harpooneers never make good voyagers. Melville, *Moby Dick*, XVIII

PITY: *see also* COMPASSION; LOVE

Pity is a great cordial to distress. Annesley, *Memoirs of an Unfortunate Young Nobleman*, I

Pity has a distant resemblance to love. Anonymous, *Fatal Friendship*, II

The indignities of stupidity, and the disappointments of selfish passion, can excite little pity. Austen, *Mansfield Park*, Volume III, XVII

Pity from some people is a noxious and insulting sort of tribute, which one is justified in hurling back in the teeth of those who offer it; but that is a sort of pity native to callous, selfish hearts: it is a hybrid, egotistical pain at hearing of woes, crossed with ignorant contempt for those who have endured them. Bronte, C., *Jane Eyre*, XXVII

Pity is not for angels. Collyer, *Felicia to Charlotte*, II

There are few moments more dangerous to man or woman than those when pity dissolves the heart; love may then easily enter, and would scarcely be detested or repulsed. Dacre, *Passions*, Letter IV

Pity is a sentiment so natural, so appropriate to the female character, that it is scarcely a merit for a woman to possess it; but to be without it is a grievous crime. Lewis, *The Monk*, 184

The agony of pity is keener than any other, except that of remorse, and even in remorse, it is, perhaps, the mingling unavailing pity that points the sting.

Radcliffe, *The Italian*, I

How despicable is that humanity which can be contented to pity where it might assuage! Radcliffe, *The Mysteries of Udolpho*, I

Pity is but one remove from love. Richardson, *Clarissa Harlowe*, I

He who pities another, remembers himself. *Ibid.*, II

Pity from one begets pity from another. *Ibid.*

What the unpenetrating world calls humanity is frequently self-pity. *Ibid.*, III

Pity cannot restore to one a lost reputation. *Ibid.*, IV

Pity melts the soul to love. Richardson, *Sir Charles Grandison*, One, I

In a man's pity there is, too probably, a mixture of insult or contempt. *Ibid.*, Two, III

Pity from a lady of a man is noble. The declaration of pity from a man for a woman may be thought a vanity bordering upon insult. *Ibid.*, Three, VI

Pity and love are neighbors, and will call in to ask kindly how a sufferer does. *Ibid.*

PLACE: *see also* DIRECTION

If you were sensible of your own good, you would not wish to quit the sphere in which you have been brought up. Austen, *Pride and Prejudice*, Volume III, XIV

One place is as good as another; for so as what one does is good, 'tis no matter for where it may be. Burney, *Cecilia*, II

May not the complaint that common people are above their station often take its rise in the fact of *un*common people being below theirs? Dickens, *Nicholas Nickleby*, XVII

London is a roost for every bird. Disraeli, *Lothair*, XI

London—a nation, not a city. *Ibid.*

As the season advances, London gradually unfolds, like Nature, all the variety of her powers and pleasures. Galt, *Ayrshire*, VI

How is it possible to say an unkind or irreverential word of Rome? The city of all time, and of all the world! Hawthorne, *The Marble Faun*, XII

The way to live in New York is to move every three or four years. Then you always get the last thing. James, H., *Washington Square*, V

The world's one Lima. Melville, *Moby Dick*, LIV

Paris is the central hotel on the highroad of civilization.

Meredith, *Harry Richmond*, XIX

London is a narrow place to one not caring to be seen. *Ibid.*, XLII

Nothing lasts in Ireland but the priests. Moore, *Muslin*, XXIX

Observe that great, mean, brown bird in the zoological gardens, which sits so tame on its perch, and droops and slouches like a drowsy duck. That is the great and soaring eagle. Who would believe it, to look at him? Yet all he wants is to be put in his right place instead of his wrong. He is not himself in man's cages, belonging to God's sky. Reade, *Griffith Gaunt*, XV

There is no worse place to starve than in Paris. The appearances of life are there so especially gay, it is so much a magnified beer-garden, the houses are so ornate, the theatres so numerous, the very pace of the vehicles is so brisk, that a man in any deep concern of mind or pain of body is constantly driven in upon himself.

Stevenson, *The Wrecker*, V

PLACE (*continued*)

There is something good and motherly about Washington, the grand old benevolent National Asylum for the Helpless.
Twain and Warner, *The Gilded Age*, Volume I, XXIV

"Why can't American women stay in their own country? They are always telling us that it is the paradise for women." "It is. That is the reason why, like Eve, they are so excessively anxious to get out of it." Wilde, *The Picture of Dorian Gray*, II

Perhaps, after all, America never has been discovered. I myself would say that it had merely been detected. *Ibid.*

It is an odd thing, but everyone who disappears is said to be seen at San Francisco. It must be a delightful city, and possess all the attractions of the next world. *Ibid.*, XIX

PLEASANTNESS; PLEASINGNESS

Have always the idea of pleasing before you, and you cannot fail to please.
Brooke, *Emily Montague*, II

Who strives to please the world will be deservedly rewarded.
Brown, W. H., *The Power of Sympathy*, 167

Uniform pleasantness is rather a defect than a faculty. It shows that a man hasn't sense enough to know whom to despise. Hardy, *A Pair of Blue Eyes*, IX

It is pleasant to live where one is much desired, and very useful.
Hawthorne, *The House of the Seven Gables*, XIV

Life would be very pleasant if it were not for its enjoyments.
Surtees, *Mr. Facey Romford's Hounds* , XXXII

PLEASURE: *see also* PAIN

Pleasure and pain are the night and day of life, and succeed one another as duly.
Anonymous, *Memoirs of the Court of H—*, 86

The pleasure of assuaging hunger. Atherton, *Senator North*, Book II, III

One half of the world cannot understand the pleasures of the other.
Austen, *Emma*, IX

When pain is over, the remembrance of it often becomes a pleasure.
Austen, *Persuasion*, XX

It is painful to be frustrated in what we propose as our pleasure. I have known a good man wish to have bad news true, merely because he had related them: and we may conceive a saint vexed at not finding a man dead, when he had digested a funeral sermon in his mind, and was ready to bury him.
Brackenridge, *Modern Chivalry*, Part I, III

Every pleasure worth a wish is in the power of almost all mankind.
Brooke, *Emily Montague*, IV

To make life pleasant, we must have our trifling amusements as well as our sublime transports. *Ibid.*

Pleasure unites strange varieties. Bulwer, *Pompeii*, Book IV, III

Pleasure given in society, like money lent in usury, returns with interest to those who dispense it. Burney, *Cecilia*, I

My pleasure is my business, and my business is my pleasure. *Ibid.*, III

It is but natural to be most pleased with what is most familiar. Burney, *Evelina*, 102

Pleasure is the safest test of virtue. Butler, *The Way of All Flesh*, XIX

Pleasure is a safer guide than either right or duty. *Ibid.*

Of all the pleasures which a man finds in the society of a woman whom he loves, are there any superior, are there many equal to the pleasure of reading out of the same book with her? Collins, *Basil*, Part Two, I

Pursuing the phantom, Pleasure, through the guilty mazes of Dissipation. Collins, *The Moonstone*, Second Period, IV

This world giveth the pleasure of an hour, but the sorrow of many days. Deloney, *Thomas of Reading*, 271

As many know what an exquisite delight there is in conveying pleasure to a beloved object, so some few may have experienced the satisfaction of tormenting one we hate. Fielding, *Tom Jones*, 66

All pleasures seem painful to them that take no delight therein, and likewise all toil seemeth pleasant to such as set their felicity in the same. Gascoigne, *Master F. J.*, 53

Every class has its pleasures. James, H., *Princess Casamassima*, XXIV

Pleasure has ceased to please. Johnson, *Rasselas*, 22

Pleasures never can be so multiplied or continued as not to leave much of life unemployed. *Ibid.*, 25

Flatter not yourself with contrarieties of pleasure. Of the blessings set before you, make your choice, and be content. *Ibid.*, 115

To be deprived of one pleasure is no very good reason for rejection of the rest. *Ibid.*, 133

In the state of future perfection, there will be pleasure without danger and security without restraint. *Ibid.*, 181

The love of pleasure and the fear of pain are the ruling principles of the human heart, in which they maintain an uninterrupted struggle for superiority. Johnstone, *Arsaces*, II

Concealed pleasures are the greatest. Lee, *The Recess*, I

Pleasure is subservient to virtue. Mackenzie, *The Man of the World*, I

At the prospect of pleasure never be elated; but without depression respect the omens of ill. Melville, *Israel Potter*, XIII

Every moment of pleasure that you enjoy, account it gain. Morier, *Hajji Baba*, VIII

The near approach of pleasure frequently awakens the heart to emotions which would fail to be excited by a more remote and abstracted observance. Radcliffe, *A Sicilian Romance*, I

The pleasure which attends noble aims remunerates not the pains they bring with them. Richardson, *Clarissa Harlowe*, II

I have ever had more pleasure in my contrivances than in the end of them. *Ibid.*

All pleasures are greater in the expectation, or in the reflection, than in fruition. *Ibid.*, IV

The mere feast is nothing to the pleasure of its preparation—its attainment. Simms, *The Partisan*, Volume II, X

How our pleasures slip from under us in this world! Sterne, *Tristram Shandy*, IX

The world seems to experience a lively pleasure in holding a man to his early follies. Warner, *A Little Journey*, VI

Pleasure is the only thing worth having a theory about. Wilde, *The Picture of Dorian Gray*, VI

Pleasure in Nature's test, her sign of approval. *Ibid.*

PLEASURE (*continued*)

No civilized man ever regrets a pleasure, and no uncivilized man ever knows what a pleasure is. *Ibid.*

Anything becomes a pleasure if one does it too often. *Ibid.*, XIX

PLIABILITY: *see also* AGREEABLENESS; PLEASANTNESS

Sweet pliability of man's spirit, that can at once surrender itself to illusions, which cheat expectation and sorrow of their weary moments!
Sterne, *A Sentimental Journey*, 92

PLOT: *see also* FICTION; FORM; etc.

The plot was most interesting. It belonged to no particular age, people, or country, and was perhaps the more delightful on that account, as nobody's previous information could afford the remotest glimmering of what would ever come of it. An outlaw had been very successful in doing something somewhere, and came home, in triumph, to the sound of shouts and fiffles, to greet his wife—a lady of masculine mind, who talked a great deal about her father's bones, which it seemed were unburied, though whether from a peculiar taste on the part of the old gentleman himself, or the reprehensible neglect of his relations, did not appear. The outlaw's wife was, somehow or other, mixed up with a patriarch, living in a castle a long way off, and this patriarch was the father of several of the characters, but he didn't exactly know which, and was uncertain whether he had brought up the right ones in his castle, or the wrong ones; he rather inclined to the latter opinion, and, being uneasy, relieved his mind with a banquet, during which solemnity somebody in a cloak said "Beware!" which somebody was known by nobody (except the audience) to be the outlaw himself, who had come there, for reasons unexplained, but possibly with an eye to the spoons.
Dickens, *Nicholas Nickleby*, XXIV

POETRY: *see also* ART; GENIUS; IMAGINATION; INDEPENDENCE; LITERATURE; etc.

How strangely should we be deceived, if we should take a poet in the literal sense?
Anonymous, *The Temple-beau*, 144

"I wonder who first discovered the efficacy of poetry in driving away love." "I have been used to consider poetry as the *food* of love." "Of a fine, stout, healthy love it may. Everything nourishes what is strong already. But if it be only a slight, thin sort of inclination, I am convinced that one good sonnet will starve it entirely away."
Austen, *Pride and Prejudice*, Volume I, IX

Who cares for learning—who cares for fine words in poetry? And who does not care for feeling—however simply, even rudely expressed? Bronte, C., *Shirley*, XII

Those poets are always odd. Bulwer, *Pompeii*, Book IV, III

Some poets always begin to get groggy about the knees after running for seven or eight lines. Butler, *The Way of All Flesh*, IV

Poetry is but the shadow or reflection of chivalry, heroism, action. First an age of deeds, and then an age of song. Caruthers, *Kentuckian in New-York*, Volume I, VIII

Is not the noblest poetry of prose fiction the poetry of everyday truth?
Collins, *Basil*, Letter of Dedication

Poetry, like virtue, is its own reward.
Coventry, *The History of Pompey the Little*, 217

The mission of the poet is to soothe. Davis, R. H., *Waiting for the Verdict*, IV

Neither poet nor woman should look into the morbid depths of human nature. *Ibid.*

" . . . It were my intentions to have had put upon his tombstone that Whatsume'er the failings on his part, Remember reader he were that good in his hart." Joe recited this couplet with such manifest pride and careful perspicuity, that I asked him if he had made it himself. "I made it," said Joe, "my own self. I made it in a moment. It was like striking out a horseshoe complete, in a single blow. It were my intentions to have had it cut over him; but poetry costs money, cut it how you will, small or large, and it were not done." Dickens, *Great Expectations*, VII

There is a poetry in wildness, and every alligator basking in the slime is in himself an Epic, self-contained. Dickens, *Martin Chuzzlewit*, XXII

Poetry makes life what lights and music do the stage—strip the one of its false embellishments, and the other of its illusions, and what is there real in either to live or care for? Dickens, *Pickwick Papers*, III

Poetry's unnat'ral; no man ever talked poetry 'cept a beadle on boxin' day, or Warren's blackin', or Rowland's oil, or some o' them low fellows; never you let yourself down to talk poetry. *Ibid.*, XXXIII

Wot's the good o' callin' a young 'ooman a Wenus or a angel? *Ibid.*

Time was, when a poet sat upon a stool in a public place, and mused in the sight of men. Dickens, *A Tale of Two Cities*, Book II, XIV

How is it that the poets have said so many fine things about our first love, so few about our later love? Eliot, *Adam Bede*, LI

Here undoubtedly lies the chief poetic energy:—in the force of imagination that pierces or exalts the solid fact, instead of floating among cloud-pictures.
Eliot, *Daniel Deronda*, Book IV, XXX

To be a poet is to have a soul so quick to discern that no shade of quality escapes it, and so quick to feel, that discernment is but a hand playing with finely-ordered variety on the chords of emotion—a soul in which knowledge passes instantaneously into feeling, and feeling flashes back as a new organ of knowledge. One may have that condition by fits only. Eliot, *Middlemarch*, Book II, XXII

Poems are wanted to complete the poet. *Ibid.*

You are a poem—and that is to be the best part of a poet—what makes up the poet's consciousness in his best moods. *Ibid.*

The poet must know how to hate. *Ibid.*

Rhymes are difficult things; they are stubborn things. Fielding, H., *Amelia*, II

A great poet ought to comprehend all perfections. Fielding, H., *Joseph Andrews*, 166

The muses, like vines, may be pruned, but not with a hatchet. *Ibid.*, 220

The great art of all poetry is to mix truth with fiction, in order to join the credible with the surprising. Fielding, H., *Tom Jones*, 338

There's a deal to be said as cannot be put into poetry. Gaskell, *Sylvia's Lovers*, XXX

Poetry and romance ought to be an imitation of real life.
Graves, *The Spiritual Quixote*, I

Writing rhymes is a stage people pass through, as they pass through the stage of shaving for a beard, or thinking they are ill-used, or saying there's nothing in the world worth living for. Hardy, *Desperate Remedies*, III

The difference between a common man and a poet is, that one has been deluded, and cured of his delusion, and the other continues deluded all his days. *Ibid.*

You are a poet, and must be allowed to make an opera-glass of your imagination, when you look at women. Hawthorne, *The Blithedale Romance*, XX

What is called poetic insight is the gift of discerning, in this sphere of strangely mingled elements, the beauty and the majesty which are compelled to assume a garb so sordid.　　　　　　　　　　　　Hawthorne, *The House of the Seven Gables*, II

Why are poets so apt to choose their mates, not for any similarity of poetic endowment, but for qualities which might make the happiness of the rudest handicraftsman, as well as that of the ideal craftsman of the spirit? Because, probably, at his highest elevation, the poet needs no human intercourse; but he finds it dreary to descend, and be a stranger.　　　　　　　　　　　　　　　　　　　　　　　*Ibid.*, IX

A sculptor, to meet the demands which our preconceptions make upon him, should be even more indispensably a poet than those who deal in measured verse and rhyme.　　　　　　　　　　　　　　　　　Hawthorne, *The Marble Faun*, XV

A place for a poet to dream in, and people it with the beings of his imagination.　　　　　　　　　　　　　　　　　　　　　　　　　　*Ibid.*, XXVII

This young gentleman had the enormous advantage of that all-subduing accomplishment, the poetical endowment. No woman can resist the youth or man who addresses her in verse.　　　　　　　　　　　Holmes, *The Guardian Angel*, XVIII

Poets—Sausage-makers! Empty skins of old phrases!　　　　　　　　　*Ibid.*

To a poet nothing can be useless.　　　　　　　　　Johnson, *Rasselas*, 48

The business of a poet is to examine not the individual, but the species; to remark general properties and large appearances. He does not number the streaks of the tulip, or describe the different shades in the verdure of the forest.　　　　*Ibid.*, 49

The poet must content himself with the slow progress of his name, contemn the applause of his own time, and commit his claims to the justice of posterity.　　　*Ibid.*, 50

The poet must write as the . . . legislator of mankind.　　　　　　　*Ibid.*

No human being can ever be a poet.　　　　　　　　　　　　　*Ibid.*, 51

A poet never kept a secret yet.　　　　　　　　Johnstone, *The Reverie*, I

You cannot employ your time worse than in making verses.　　Lewis, *The Monk*, 157

Vanity has been immemorially the charter of poets.　　　　　　　　　　　　　　　　　　　　　Mackenzie, *The Man of Feeling*, 80

The poetical inclination is an incentive to philanthropy. There is a certain poetic ground on which a man cannot tread without feelings that enlarge the heart.　　　　　　　　　　　　　　　　　　　　　　　　　　*Ibid.*, 81

Poetry is not a thing of ink and rhyme, but of thought and act, and, in the latter way, is by anyone to be found anywhere, when in useful action sought.　　　　　　　　　　　　　　　　　Melville, *Confidence-Man*, XXXVII

Poets are omnipresent.　　　　　　　　　　Melville, *Mardi*, CXXXVII

"Tell me how you poets spend so many hours in meditation." "It is because, that when we think, we think so little of ourselves."　　　　　　　　　　　*Ibid.*, CLI

Of all mortals, poets are most subject to contrary moods. Now, heaven over heaven in the skies; now layer under layer in the dust.　　　　　　　　　　　*Ibid.*, CLXX

Poets are only seen when they soar.　　　　　　　　　　　　　　*Ibid.*

We madmen are all poets.　　　　　　　　　　　　　*Ibid.*, CLXXXIII

Poetry, however erratic, is less a servant of the bully Present, or pompous Past, than History.　　　　　　　　　　Meredith, *Amazing Marriage*, XXXIV

The early morning always has this touch . . . whisper . . . gleam . . . beat of wings of Eden. Prose can paint evening and moonlight, but poets are needed to sing the dawn.

Prose is equal to melancholy stuff. Gladness requires the finer language. Otherwise we have it coarse—anything but a reproduction.   Meredith, *Diana of the Crossways*, XVI

As we to the brutes, poets are to us.   *Ibid.*

Poetic men take aim at maidens.   *Ibid.*, XL

Nothing but poetry makes romances passable: for poetry is the everlastingly and embracingly human.   Meredith, *Harry Richmond*, XXXIV

Having one's name to a volume of poems is as bad as to an advertising pill.
                                          Meredith, *Ordeal of Richard Feverel*, XXIX

All's game to the poet.   *Ibid.*

Poets are always poor, and live upon what they can cozen from others. Who will ransom a poet?   Morier, *Hajji Baba*, VI

Poets are sometimes very rich, and can, if they choose, become rich at all times, for they carry their wealth in their heads.   *Ibid.*

If there be any spark of Adam's paradised perfection yet embered up in the breasts of mortal men, certainly God hath bestowed that his perfectest image on poets.
                                          Nashe, *The Unfortunate Traveller*, 64

None come so near to God in wit, none more contemn the world, than poets.   *Ibid.*

Seldom have you seen any poet possessed with avarice. Only verses he loves, nothing else he delights in.   *Ibid.*

As poets contemn the world, so contrarily of the mechanical world are none more contemned.   *Ibid.*

Despised are poets of the world, because they are not of the world: their thoughts are exalted above the world of ignorance and all earthly conceits.   *Ibid.*

As sweet angelical queristers poets are continually conversant in the heaven of arts: heaven itself is but the highest height of knowledge.   *Ibid.*, 64-65

He that knows himself and all things else, knows the means to be happy: happy, thrice happy, are they whom God hath doubled his spirit upon, and given a double soul unto to be poets.   Nashe, *The Unfortunate Traveller*, 65

Chaste life, wanton verse.   *Ibid.*, 88

That high enthusiasm which wakes the poet's dream.
                                          Radcliffe, *The Mysteries of Udolpho*, I

The fire of the poet is in vain if the mind of his reader is not tempered like his own, however it may be inferior to his in power.   *Ibid.*, II

To be a poet requires an heated imagination, which often runs away with the judgment.
                                          Richardson, *Sir Charles Grandison*, One, II

Are poets not inflamers of the worst passions? Would Alexander have been so much a madman, had it not been for Homer? Of what violences, murders, depredations, have not the epic poets been the occasion, by propagating false honor, false glory, and false religion?   *Ibid.*, Three, VI

It takes more to make a poet than nature has poured into my mold.
                                          Schreiner, *Undine*, XIV

In poetry there is always fallacy, and sometimes fiction.
                                          Scott, *Bride of Lammermoor*, XXI

She wrote rather doubtful grammar sometimes, and in her verses took all sorts of liberties with the metre. But oh, mesdames, if you are not allowed to touch the heart sometimes in spite of syntax, and are not to be loved until you all know the difference between trimeter and tetrameter, may all Poetry go to the deuce, and every school-master perish miserably!   Thackeray, *Vanity Fair*, XII

POETRY (*continued*)

Poetry is usually false. The difficulty is to know when it is false and when it is true.
Trollope, *Phineas Finn*, XIV

The very best background for a poem of deep and refined sentiment and pathetic melancholy is one where great and satisfying merriment has prepared the spirit for the powerful contrast.
Twain, *Joan of Arc*, Book II, XV

Most people become bankrupt through having invested too heavily in the prose of life. To ruin one's self over poetry is an honor.
Wilde, *The Picture of Dorian Gray*, IV

Artists who are personally delightful are bad artists. Good artists exist simply in what they make, and consequently are perfectly uninteresting in what they are.
Ibid.

POLITENESS

His civilities were worn out like his information.
Austen, *Pride and Prejudice*, Volume II, IV

There is no great difference between politeness and affection.
Bulwer, *Caxtons*, Book II, III

While it is the easiest thing in the world to throw a human court into commotion by a violation of etiquette, matters of mere life and death are not at all of a nature to disturb its tranquillity. There, everything is a matter of routine and propriety; and nothing is so unseemly as to appear to possess human sympathies.
Cooper, *Monikins*, XVIII

Appearances are ever to be consulted in cases of morals, and it is a minor virtue to be decent in matters of manners.
Cooper, *Satanstoe*, Volume I, X

Politeness is compelled to throw off cloak and jacket when it steps into the arena to meet the encounter of a bull.
Meredith, *Beauchamp's Career*, XXV

POLITICS: *see also* GOVERNMENT

Congressmen are like birds of the air, which are caught only by the early worm.
Adams, H., *Democracy*, III

At no other season [as in February] is there so much guile. This is the moment when the two whited sepulchres at either end of the Avenue [in Washington] reek with the thick atmosphere of bargain and sale. The old is going; the new is coming.
Ibid., VI

If the Senate makes a weak man weaker, it makes a strong man stronger, owing to the very temptations he must resist from the day he enters, the compromises he is forced to make, and the danger to his convictions from the subtler brains of older men.
Atherton, *Senator North*, Book I, XX

Hysterical members of the House are only too representative, unfortunately, but they are more hysterical than the average because they have the opportunity their constituents lack, of shouting in public. The House is America let loose.
Ibid., Book II, VII

Party spirit, a magnificent thing at its best, warps and withers the little brain in the party out of power.
Ibid.

There is one fact that the second-rate politician never grasps. That is, that the true American respects convictions; no matter how many fads he may conceive nor how loud he may clamor for their indulgence, when his mind begins to balance methodically again, he respects the man who told him he was wrong and imperilled his own re-election rather than vote against his convictions.
Ibid., Book III, III

Many a Senator has lost re-election through yielding to pressure.
Ibid.

No party could exist five minutes unless it had some good in it.
Ibid., Book III, V

No arrangement could be worse than to entrust the politicians with control of the wealth-producing machinery of the country.
Bellamy, *Looking Backward*, VI

A wise man will weigh what he undertakes; what his shoulders can bear, and what they cannot. He will consider whether the office is fit for him, or whether he is fit for the office. He will reflect that the shade is oftentimes the most desirable situation.

Brackenridge, Modern Chivalry, Part II, I

The man that has given his vote will conceive that he has turned the election, that daylight springs because he has croaked. Ibid.

Self-seekers only are all things to all men. Ibid.

Those who are conscious that they cannot please by great actions attempt it by small.
Ibid.

The people-pleaser is not always the friend of the people. Ibid.

Do we find him in war the best general who consults the ardor of his troops and fights when they cry out for battle? Ibid.

"Who serves the people best?" "Not always him that pleases them most." Ibid.

The term *democrat* has ceased to be a stigma; and begins to be assumed by our public writers, and claimed by our patriots, as characteristic of a good citizen. That of *republican*, which alone has been vented on for some time, is now considered cold, and equivocal, and has given way, pretty generally, to that of democratic republican. In a short time, it will be simply, the *democracy*, and *a democrat*. Ibid., Part II, II

The most upright discharge of a public function will not atone for the engrossing money in one's own person, or that of connections. Ibid., Part II, IV

Select political wisdom, like select schools, propagates much questionable knowledge.
Cooper, The Monikins, Conclusion

One thoroughly imbued with [political expediency] invariably squeezes himself into a little wheel, in order to show how small he can become at need. Ibid.

The man who enters public life has to choose between political infidelity and a destructive creed. Disraeli, Coningsby, Book VII, II

Politics belong to men; and petticoats should not meddle.
Fielding, H., Tom Jones, 219

Males, that wise sex which Heaven hath formed for politicians. Ibid., 221

The pity is that politics are looked on as being a game for politicians, just as cricket is a game for cricketers; not as the serious duties of political trustees.
Hardy, The Well-Beloved, Part II, I

There can be only one best course at all times, and the wisdom of the nation should be directed to finding it, instead of zigzagging in two courses, according to the will of the party which happens to have the upper hand. Ibid.

In politics party organization saves us the pains of much thinking before deciding how to cast our vote. Holmes, Elsie Venner, XVIII

Politics involves the doing of lots of disagreeable things to ourselves and our relations.
Meredith, Beauchamp's Career, XIV

Those Liberals, those temporizers, compromisers, a concourse of atoms, glorify themselves in the animal satisfaction of sucking the juice of the fruit, for which they pay with their souls. They have no true cohesion, for they have no vital principle. Ibid., XXVII

The Liberals are the professors of the practicable in politics. Ibid.

He is the earnest man, and flies at politics as uneasy young brains fly to literature, fancying they can write because they can write with a pen. Ibid., XXXVII

Politics is the first business of men, the school to mediocrity, to the covetously ambitious a sty, to the dullard his amphitheatre, arms of Titans to the desperately enterprising, Olympus to the genius. Meredith, Diana of the Crossways, I

POLITICS (*continued*)

It is one of the weaknesses of nations, as well as of children, that they come to consider their political fathers as saints.   Mitchell, *Hugh Wynne*, VI

Our vulgar reputed politicians are but flies swimming on the stream of subtlety superficially. Their blind narrow eyes cannot pierce into the profundity of hypocrisy.
                                            Nashe, *The Unfortunate Traveller*, 45

Politics is the one subject that goes to the vitals of every rural American; and a Hoosier will talk politics after he is dead.   Tarkington, *The Gentleman from Indiana*, I

Nowhere is there the same good-humored, affectionate, prize-fighting ferocity in politics [as in England].   Trollope, *Phineas Finn*, IX

If there be any man unfitted by his previous career for office, it is he who has become, or who has endeavored to become, a popular politician—an exponent of public opinion. Office is offered to such men with one view only—that of clipping their wings.
                                            Ibid., LXV

A man in office must be a slave.   *Ibid.*

The chances are that a man cannot get into Congress now without resorting to arts and means that should render him unfit to go there.
                              Twain and Warner, *The Gilded Age*, Volume II, XIX

POPULARITY: *see also* AGREEABLENESS; PLEASANTNESS; POLITICS; etc.

Nothing will so certainly perish as the talk of the town.
                                            Barrie, *Tommy and Grizel*, XXXV

Popular! How broad has the signification of this word got to be! In the eyes of two thirds of the population it already means, "what is right."   Cooper, *The Redskins*, XVI

Oglethorpe contended that the men who made the most money from books were the best authors. Hollanden contended that they were the worst. Oglethorpe said that such a question should be left to the people. Hollanden said that the people habitually made wrong decisions on questions that were left to them. "That is the most odiously aristo-cratic belief," said Oglethorpe. "No," said Hollanden, "I like the people. But, considered generally, they are a collection of ingenious blockheads." "But they read your books," said Oglethorpe, grinning. "That is through a mistake," replied Hollanden.
                                            Crane, *The Third Violet*, XVII

It edifies one to see what a lot of trouble these deriders of other people's popularity will often take to advertise themselves, and how they yearn for that popular acclaim they so scornfully denounce.   DuMaurier, *The Martian*, Part Ninth

Uncertain is the air of popular applause, and a moment suffices to make him today the detestation of the world who yesterday was its idol.   Lewis, *The Monk*, 238

The artist who paints for the million must use glaring colors.
                                            Trollope, *The Warden*, XVI

Even popularity can be overdone. In Rome, along at first, you are full of regrets that Michelangelo died; but by and by you only regret that you didn't see him do it.
                                            Twain, *Pudd'nhead Wilson*, XVII

Every effect that one produces gives one an enemy. To be popular one must be a mediocrity.   Wilde, *The Picture of Dorian Gray*, XVII

POPULATION

No industrious people can [afford to] be too populous.   Brooke, *Emily Montague*, II

POSSESSION; PROPERTY: *see also* POVERTY; WEALTH

Let me see property acknowledging as in the old days of faith, that labor is his twin brother.   Disraeli, *Coningsby*, Book VIII, III

It is a very good quality in a man to have a trout-stream.
Eliot, *Middlemarch*, Book I, VIII

A good place in possession is better than one in expectation.
Fielding, H., *Joseph Andrews*, 35

Possession, which cloys man, only increases the affection of women.
Lewis, *The Monk*, 187

What availeth it to be a cunning lapidary and have no stones? or a skillful pilot and have no ship? or a thrifty man and have no money?   Lyly, *Euphues and His England*, 231

He that hath little to spend hath not much to lose, and he that hath nothing in his own country cannot have less in any.   *Ibid.*, 243

All men are possessed by devils; but as these devils are sent into men, and kept in them, for an additional punishment; not garrisoning a fortress, but limboed in a Bridewell; so, it may be more just to say, that the devils themselves are possessed by men, and not men by them.   Melville, *Mardi*, CIV

Often possession is the whole of the law.   Melville, *Moby Dick*, LXXXIX

Property and titles are worth having, whether you are worthy of them or a disgrace to your class. The best way of defending them is to keep a strong fist, and take care you don't draw your forefoot back more than enough.   Meredith, *Beauchamp's Career*, III

Property's pretty much in *thinking*, unless you've got to raise money on it.
Taylor, *Hannah Thurston*, XXXVI

POSSIBILITY; IMPOSSIBILITY: *see also* MIRACLE

Everything that is, is possible.   Peacock, *The Misfortunes of Elphin*, XI

It is as impossible to learn science from hearsay as to gain wisdom from proverbs.
Shaw, *Cashel Byron's Profession*, IV

POSTERITY: *see also* AGE AND YOUTH; FAMILY; etc.

Every man who is at his ease in his moneyed affairs feels a disposition to make some provision for his posterity.   Cooper, *Satanstoe*, Volume II, V

POVERTY: *see also* WEALTH; etc.

We all like to read and cry over the troubles of the poor in books, but when we have the real thing before us, we think it is uninteresting and disagreeable.
Alcott, *Old-Fashioned Girl*, XI

The rich are no less discontented amidst their superfluities than the poor man involved in poverty.   Anonymous, *The Birmingham Counterfeit*, I

The iron hand of poverty.   Anonymous, *The Fruitless Repentance*, I

Nobody will pretend to contradict that we make a shocking figure in this world when we are poor. No money, no pleasure, no contentment in this life.
Anonymous, *Genuine Memoirs of Maria Brown*, II

He is not poor that has enough; but he that has millions, if he desires more.
Anonymous, *The History of Tom Jones in His Married State*, 270–271

If he gets richer, somebody will be poorer.
Arthur, *Ten Nights in a Bar-Room*, Night the First

Poverty and crime have their origin in the corrupt heart.   *Ibid.*, Night the Fifth

I see no present solution of a great and intricate problem but that the rich should realize their duty to the poor.   Atherton, *Los Cerritos*, Part II, XIV

The rich are at the mercy of the poor, not the poor at that of the rich. Who permits us to be rich if not the poor? *Ibid.*

Where people are really attached, poverty itself is wealth.
Austen, *Northanger Abbey*, XV

Poverty is a great evil, but to a woman of education and feeling it ought not, it cannot be the greatest. Austen, *The Watsons*, I

Poverty looks grim to grown people; still more so to children: they have not much idea of industrious, working, respectable poverty; they think of the word only as connected with ragged clothes, scanty food, fireless grates, rude manners, and debasing vices: poverty for me was synonymous with the degradation. Bronte, C., *Jane Eyre*, III

I could not see how poor people had the means of being kind. *Ibid.*

Poverty is ever the inseparable companion of indolence. Brooke, *Emily Montague*, II

Indigence, as well as wealth, is comparative. Brown, C. H., *Ormond*, 71

Poverty is the master-ill of the world. Bulwer, *The Caxtons*, Book IV, V

People are generally ill-natured when they see a poor one in need.
Burney, *Camilla*, Two, IV

If destruction and death have heard the sound of wisdom, to a certain extent poverty has done so also. Butler, *Erewhon*, XXII

Poverty, a state of labor and frequent self-denial, is the natural state of man.
Day, *The History of Sanford and Merton*, 242

A thousand cottages are thrown down to afford space for a single palace. *Ibid.*

That worst of devils, poverty. Defoe, *Moll Flanders*, 192

He is most poor that hath least wit. Deloney, *The Gentle Craft*, 144

Poverty has its whims and shows of taste, as wealth has.
Dickens, *Barnaby Rudge*, XLIV

Utilitarian economists, skeletons of schoolmasters, Commissioners of Fact, genteel and used-up infidels, gabblers of many little dog's-eared creeds, the poor you will always have with you. Cultivate in them, while there is yet time, the utmost graces of the fancies and affections, to adorn their lives so much in need of ornament; or, in the day of your triumph, when romance is utterly driven out of their souls, and they are a bare existence stand face to face, Reality will take a wolfish turn, and make an end of you.
Dickens, *Hard Times*, Book II, VI

What have paupers to do with soul or spirit? It's quite enough that we let 'em have live bodies. Dickens, *Oliver Twist*, VII

Poverty and pride don't go at all well together. It stands to reason. A man being poor, has nothing to be proud of. Dickens, *Our Mutual Friend*, Book III, V

It's a wery remarkable circumstance that poverty and oysters always seem to go together. Dickens, *Pickwick Papers*, XXII

Their history [that of the poor] has been written by their enemies: they were condemned without a hearing. Disraeli, *Sybil*, Book II, V

The voice of want made answer for her. Dreiser, *Sister Carrie*, X

Poverty is always superstitious. Eggleston, *Roxy*, XII

There is a chill air surrounding those who are down in the world, and people are glad to get away from them, as from a cold room. Eliot, *Mill on the Floss*, Book IV, II

Simply to be poor was not held scandalous by the wise Athenians, but highly so to owe that poverty to our own indiscretion. Fielding, H., *Amelia*, I

Those poor wretches who make visits to the great to solicit favors or the payment of a debt are alike treated as beggars. *Ibid.*

Worse than poverty, or rather what is the worst consequence of poverty, is attendance and dependence on the great. Fielding, H., *Joseph Andrews*, 181

Every man who is greatly destitute of money is on that account entirely excluded from all means of acquiring it. Fielding, H., *Tom Jones*, 270

Gentlemen oft not to kill poor folks without answering for it. A poor man hath a soul to be saved as well as his betters. *Ibid.*, 315

Poverty is the root of all social ills; its existence accounts even for the ills that arise from wealth. The poor man is a man laboring in fetters. Gissing, *New Grub Street*, III

The nakedness of the indigent world may be clothed from the trimmings of the vain. Goldsmith, *The Vicar of Wakefield*, 19

Such as are poor, and will associate with none but the rich, are hated by those they avoid, and despised by those they follow. Unequal combinations are always disadvantageous to the weaker side, the rich having the pleasure, and the poor the inconveniences that result from them. *Ibid.*, 61

Poverty in the country is a sadness, but poverty in town is a horror. Hardy, *The Hand of Ethelberta*, XXIV

I see no more harm in killing a man than taking his property; marry, I think it the least sin of the two; for poverty is a greater evil than death. Helme, *St. Margaret's Cave*, Volume III, X

Don't joke about your poverty. That is quite as vulgar as to boast about it. James, H., *The Europeans*, I

Poverty has, in large cities, very different appearances; it is often concealed in splendor, and often in extravagance. Johnson, *Rasselas*, 99

It is the care of a very great part of mankind to conceal their indigence from the rest; they support themselves by temporary expedients, and every day is lost in contriving for the morrow. *Ibid.*

The fortune of the poor is seldom distinguished by any incidents worthy of recital. Johnstone, *Arsaces*, II

That feeling which prevents the acquisition of wealth is formed for the support of poverty. Mackenzie, *The Man of the World*, I

There is perhaps nothing more bitter in the lot of poverty than the distance to which it throws a man from the woman he loves. *Ibid.*

The poor must ever be cautious, and there is a certain degree of pride which is their safest virtue. *Ibid.*

Nothing is more enviable, nothing richer to the mind, than the aspect of a cheerful poverty. Meredith, *Diana of the Crossways*, XXIV

The search for pleasure at the expense of discomfort, as frantic lovers woo their mistresses to partake the shelter of a hut and batten on a crust, Adrian deemed the bitterness of beggarliness. Meredith, *Ordeal of Richard Feverel*, XXXVI

Poverty in the end parts friends. Nashe, *The Unfortunate Traveller*, 34

Want cannot be withstood, men can do no more than they can do. *Ibid.*

Poverty is the mother of health. Richardson, *Clarissa Harlowe*, I

The pleasures of the mighty are obtained by the tears of the poor. *Ibid.*

Better a bare foot than not to be able to walk. *Ibid.*

Nothing sooner brings down a proud spirit than a sense of lying under pecuniary obligations. Richardson, *Clarissa Harlowe*, II

POVERTY (*continued*)

I long to go back to my poverty and distress; though I am sure of the poverty, I shall not have half the distress. Richardson, *Pamela*, 33

"No shame in honest poverty, I hope." "That is according as folks have used their prosperity." Scott, *St. Ronan's Well*, XXXV

Nothing so effectually subdues a spirit unused to supplicate as want.
Smollett, *Peregrine Pickle*, 393

To die of want is very indecent. Trollope, *He Knew He Was Right*, V

Poverty will show itself to be meagre, dowdy, and draggled in a woman's dress, let the woman be ever so simple, ever so neat, ever so independent, and ever so high-hearted.
Ibid., LVIII

The real tragedy of the poor is that they can afford nothing but self-denial. Beautiful sins, like beautiful things, are the privilege of the rich.
Wilde, *The Picture of Dorian Gray*, VI

POWER: *see also* STRENGTH; WEAKNESS

Too much power is not good for any man. Atherton, *Senator North*, Book II, XX

The natural rights of man are finally resolvable, as in the inanimate world, into power on the one hand, and weakness on the other.
Brackenridge, *Modern Chivalry*, Part I, II

The duration of power will always be in proportion to the discrete [*sic*] use of it.
Ibid., Part II, I

If you confer independence any more than in a ministerial officer, the judge becomes impudent. Power corrupts. It is natural to count too much upon a man's standing. Everyone overrates his own importance; much more his own services. Self-love, and self-consequence, swells. *Ibid.*

Most men have more or less the passion for power. Bulwer, *Pompeii*, Book Two, VIII

We scarce ever use power one way, but what we are sorry we did not use it another.
Burney, *Camilla*, Two, IV

Power that loves to tyrannize over its slaves by playing with their chains.
Ibid., Four, VIII

That love of power which hides itself beneath the mask of Democracy, until a corrupt public can endure its undistinguished features without execration.
Child, *Philothea*, IX

There is a weird power in a spoken word. Conrad, *Lord Jim*, XV

The depositary of power is always unpopular; all combine against it, always it falls.
Disraeli, *Coningsby*, Book IV, XIII

All power is a trust. We are accountable for its exercise. From the people, and for the people, all springs, and all must exist. Disraeli, *Vivian Grey*, Book VI, VII

It is not advisable to make it that man's interest to hurt you, who has the power.
Fielding, H., *Jonathan Wild*, 115

The examples of all ages show us that mankind in general desire power only to do harm, and, when they obtain it, use it for no other purpose. Fielding, H., *Tom Jones*, 587

There's nothing else in the world so big as power-strength. If you have that, you can get everything else. But if you have it, and don't use it, then it rusts and decays on your hands. It's like a thoroughbred horse. You can't keep it idle in the stable. If you don't exercise it, you lose it. Frederic, *The Market-Place*, XVIII

Power does not answer to the will. Gissing, *New Grub Street*, IV

Every man is in some degree influenced by the love of power.

Godwin, *Caleb Williams*, III

Power is ever dangerous and intoxicating. Human nature cannot bear it. It must be constantly checked, controled and limited, or it declines inevitably into tyranny.

Hildreth, *Slave*, Volume II, VIII

Subordination supposes power on one part and subjection on the other.

Johnson, *Rasselas*, 39

If power be in the hands of men, it will sometimes be abused. *Ibid.*

Is power without any efficacy to do good? *Ibid.*, 96

The weight of power too often intoxicates the best head and warps the best heart.

Johnstone, *Arsaces*, I

Is the insolence of ill-gotten power to know no control? Leland, *Longsword*, II

Of the highest order of genius, it may be truly asserted, that to gain the reputation of superior power, it must partially disguise itself; it must come down, and then it will be applauded for soaring. Melville, *Mardi*, CXXVI

What signifies power, if we do not exert it? Richardson, *Clarissa Harlowe*, II

A spark may do more than a hundred cannon. *Ibid.*

Power loves to be trusted. *Ibid.*

Who is covetous of power or wealth for the sake of making a right use of it? *Ibid.*, III

The valued have it in power to insult. *Ibid.*

When we enter upon a devious course, we think we shall have it in our power when we will to return to the right path. *Ibid.*

It is not in a man's own power to reform when he will. *Ibid.*, IV

Power to the powerful is the law. Stevenson, *Prince Otto*, Book II, V

I think these vast powers and capacities were born in her, and that she applied them by an intuition which could not err. Twain, *Joan of Arc*, Book II, XXVII

PRACTICALITY

In the language of this defunct school of statesmen, a practical man is a man who practices the blunders of his predecessors. Disraeli, *Coningsby*, Book II, I

The practical wants of our nature guide us best. Meredith, *Sandra Belloni*, X

PRAISE: *see* COMPLIMENTS; HONOR; etc.

What praise is more valuable than the praise of an intelligent servant?

Austen, *Pride and Prejudice*, Volume III, I

The advantage of doing one's praising for oneself is that one can lay it on so thick and exactly in the right places. Butler, *The Way of All Flesh*, XXXIV

In America, no man is much praised for himself, but for the purposes of party, or to feed national vanity. Cooper, *Home as Found*, XVIII

No praise so much elates me, as censure depresses. Melville, *Mardi*, CIII

Bravos but induce flatulency. *Ibid.*, CXXVI

A newspaper that wishes to make its fortune should never waste its columns and weary its readers by praising anything. Eulogy is invariably dull.

Trollope, *The Way We Live Now*, I

Abuse from those who occasionally praise is considered to be personally offensive, and they who give personal offense will sometimes make the world too hot to hold them.

Ibid.

PRAISE (*continued*)

We think that we are generous because we credit our neighbor with the possession of those virtues that are likely to be a benefit to us. We praise the banker that we may overdraw our account, and find good qualities in the highwayman in the hope that he may spare our pockets.   Wilde, *The Picture of Dorian Gray*, VI

PRAYER

God gives us more than, were we not over-bold, we should have to ask for, and yet how often (perhaps after saying "Thank God" so curtly that it is only a form of swearing) we are supplicants again within the hour.   Barrie, *The Little Minister*, XXIX

Tennyson has said that more things are wrought by prayer than this world dreams of, but he has wisely refrained from saying whether they are good things or bad things. It might perhaps be well if the world were to dream of, or even become wide awake to, some of the things that are being wrought by prayer.
                                   Butler, *The Way of All Flesh*, VIII

Think over your prayers; for He to whom you make them knows all tongues; that of the heart as well as those of the mouth.   Cooper, *The Last of the Mohicans*, XX

Does anyone suppose that private prayer is necessarily candid—necessarily goes to the roots of action? Private prayer is inaudible speech, and speech is representative: who can represent himself just as he is, even in his own reflections?
                                   Eliot, *Middlemarch*, Book VII, LXX

Prayer is for the just, the softened heart.
                     Gibbes, *The Life and Adventure of Mr. Francis Clive*, II

Can mortal prayers ensure immortal happiness?   Lee, *The Recess*, II

Prayer draws us near to our own souls, and purifies our thoughts.
                                                      Melville, *Mardi*, CXI

Oh, thou big white God aloft there somewhere in yon darkness, have mercy on this small black boy down here; preserve him from all men that have no bowels to feel fear!
                                             Melville, *Moby Dick*, XL

If there be anything a man might well pray against, that thing is the responsive gratification of some of the devoutest prayers of his youth.   Melville, *Pierre*, Book I, II

He who has the fountain of prayer in him will not complain of hazards. Prayer is the recognition of laws; the soul's exercise and source of strength; its thread of conjunction with them. Prayer for an object is the cajolery of an idol; the resource of superstition.
                                   Meredith, *Beauchamp's Career*, XXIX

We that fight the living world must have the universal for succor of the truth in it. Cast forth the soul in prayer, you meet the effluence of the outer truth, you join with the creative elements giving breath to you.   *Ibid.*

Prayer, the soul's overflow, the heart's resignation.   *Ibid.*

Prayer is power within us to communicate with the desired beyond our thirsts.
                                             Meredith, *Lord Ormont*, XIV

Who rises from prayer a better man, his prayer is answered.
                                   Meredith, *Ordeal of Richard Feverel*, XV

One should choose one's company for prayer as for everything else.
                                   Moore, G., *Esther Waters*, XLV

These women could only speak in prayer.   Moore, G., *Evelyn Innes*, XXXIV

Were it not for our prayers, God would have long ago destroyed the world.
                                                      Ibid., XXXV

We know what to pray for when we pray, that God's will may be done, and that we may be resigned to it.   Richardson, *Clarissa Harlowe*, IV

474

She prayed for me; but her prayers were meant for herself.

Richardson, *Sir Charles Grandison*, Three, VI

Some men must think the Almighty very ignorant, for they never kneel down to speak to him without feeling themselves called upon to explain to him the whole plan of salvation, creation, and damnation: subjects on which, one might suppose, he would be better informed than themselves.

Schreiner, *Undine*, II

Every grace [prayer at a meal] must come to an end, so philosophizes the hungry child.

Schreiner, *Undine*, XVI

To think that those powers above are moved either by the eloquence of our prayers, or in a chafe at the folly of our actions, carries as much reason as if flies should think that men take great care which of them hums sweetest and which of them flies nimblest.

Sidney, *Arcadia*, III

There's something in it when a body like the widow or the parson prays, but it don't work for me, and I reckon it don't work for only just the right kind.

Twain, *Huckleberry Finn*, VIII

"If I be not in a state of Grace, I pray God place me in it; if I be in it, I pray God keep me so."

Twain, *Joan of Arc*, Book III, VII

Not "Forgive us our sins" but "Smite us for our iniquities" should be the prayer of man to a most just God.

Wilde, *The Picture of Dorian Gray*, XX

PREACHMENT: *see also* ART; EXPRESSION; METHOD; ORATION; ORATORY; etc.

That is very cunning of you to turn our own stories against us, and give us a sermon instead of a romance.

Alcott, *Little Women*, IV

How can two sermons a week, even supposing them worth hearing, govern the conduct and fashion the manners of a large congregation for the rest of the week? One scarcely sees a clergyman out of his pulpit.

Austen, *Mansfield Park*, Volume One, IX

A sermon, well delivered, is more uncommon even than prayers well read.

Ibid., Volume Three, III

A simple delivery is much better calculated to inspire devotion, and shows a much better taste.

Austen, *The Watsons*, I

It appeared to me an unconscionable thing in a man to speak too long when it was left to himself how long he should speak.

Brackenridge, *Modern Chivalry*, Part I, IV

Elocution has its place, and noble praise. It is delightful to hear one speak well where he ought to speak.

Ibid., Part II, I

Brevity is the soul of eloquence, and amplification, the usual fault.

Ibid.

Few err in saying too little. Tediousness is the more common extreme: padding, and beating on the point.

Ibid.

After a passion is excited, there is danger of tearing it to rags.

Ibid.

Self-preservation is at the bottom of long speaking. Or is it in accommodation to false opinion?

Ibid.

In order to speak short upon any subject, think long.

Ibid.

Much reflection is the secret of all that is excellent in oratory.

Ibid.

No man that speaks just enough, and no more, ever wearies those that hear him. And that is enough which exhausts the subject before the patience of the audience.

Ibid.

What occasion can little misses have to harangue?

Ibid., Part II, II

The art of oratory consists not in length of speech, or melody of voice, or beauty of diction; but in wise thoughts.

Ibid.

Is there not a sublimity in the obscure? I want something that I cannot understand. Give me the divine that will speak through his nose, whack the pulpit, and make the whole

house ring; who will shut his eyes, and open his mouth, and stamp with his foot. It is of no moment whether I understand his words or not; or rather, I would not wish to understand him, for if I did, I would take it for granted that it was not so deep as it ought to be.
Ibid.

When a man moralizes, it is a sign that he has known error. Because I have been a trifler I rail against triflers.   Bulwer, *What Will He Do With It?*, Book III, VIII

A magnificent sermon was preached on the heathen indifference of the world to the sinfulness of little sins. I said to Rachel, "Has it found its way to your heart, dear?" And she answered, "No; it has only made my head ache."
Collins, *The Moonstone*, Second Period, VII

In few things are the credulous more imposed on that in sermons. A clergyman shall preach the workings of other men's brains for years, and not one of his hearers detect the imposition, purely on account of the confiding credit it is customary to yield to the pulpit. In this respect, preaching is very much like reviewing—the listener, or the reader, being too complaisant to see through the great standing mystifications of others.
Cooper, *Sea Lions*, XXX

I am not to preach, but to relate.   Defoe, *Roxana*, 50

Eloquence is the child of Knowledge.   Disraeli, *The Young Duke*, Book V, VI

Nature is a silent preacher which holds forth upon weekdays as on Sabbaths.
Doyle, *Micah Clarke*, XXII

He has the art of saying bitter things in a sweet way.   Galt, *Ayrshire*, VII

He lacks that occasional accent of passion, the melody of oratory.   *Ibid.*, IX

When a preacher reads his sermon with as much coldness and indifference as he would read a newspaper or an act of parliament, he must not be surprised if his audience discover the same indifference, or even take a nap.   Graves, *The Spiritual Quixote*, III

Writing a sermon is very much like playing that game called "When is it? where is it? what is it?" You take the text. You think, why is it? what is it? and so on. You put that down under "Generally." Then you proceed to the First, Secondly, and Thirdly. Fourthlys are all my eye. Then you have a final Collectively, several pages of this being put in great black brackets, writing opposite, *"Leave this out if the farmers are falling alseep."* Then comes your In Conclusion, then A Few Words And I Have Done.
Hardy, *A Pair of Blue Eyes*, IV

There are sermons in stones.   Hawthorne, *The Marble Faun*, XVI

A good orator in a bad cause will always raise such images in the minds of his audience, as are most likely to predispose them to favorable sentiments.
Jenner, *The Placid Man*, I

Lectures which please only while they were new, to become new again, must be forgotten.   Johnson, *Rasselas*, 21

Why is it that the great proportion of our pastors seem to conspire together with one consent to make the periodical duty of listening to them as hard as possible?
Lawrence, G. A., *Guy Livingstone*, VII

The best orators, spiritual and mundane, have been brief sometimes.   *Ibid.*

Never have I heard religious discourses better adapted to an audience of men, who, like sailors, are chiefly, if not only, to be moved by the plainest of precepts, and demonstrations of the misery of sin, as conclusive and undeniable as those of Euclid. No mere rhetoric avails with such men; fine periods are vanity. You can not touch them with tropes. They need to be pressed home by plain facts.   Melville, *Redburn*, XXXV

The natural exaggeration which eloquence produces, rather, as a rule, to assure itself of the overwhelming justice of the cause it pleads than to deceive the adversary.
Meredith, *Beauchamp's Career*, XIX

He had bruised his eloquence, for though you may start a sermon from stones to hit the stars, he must be a practiced orator who shall descend out of the abstract to take up a heavy lump of the concrete without unseating himself.

Ibid., XXVI

There came on him a thirst for the haranguing of crowds. They agree with you or they disagree; exciting you to activity in either case. They do not interpose cold exclusiveness and inaccessibility.   *Ibid.*, XXXVIII

Oratory is always the more impressive for the spice of temper which renders it untrustworthy.   Meredith, *Diana of the Crossways*, I

The hand of the preacher is against every man, and every man's hand is against him.
Nelson, *The Case of John Nelson*, 11

Men of talents are sooner to be convinced by short sentences than by long preachments.
Richardson, *Clarissa Harlowe*, II

He preaches by action.   Richardson, *Sir Charles Grandison*, Two, V

There are times when a sermon has a value and power due to conditions in the audience rather than to anything new or startling or eloquent in the words said or arguments presented.   Sheldon, *In His Steps*, X

To preach, to show the extent of our reading, or the subtleties of our wit—to parade in the eyes of the vulgar with the beggarly accounts of a little learning, tinselled over with a few words which glitter, but convey little light and less warmth—is a dishonest use of the poor single half hour in a week which is put into our hands. 'Tis not preaching the gospel, but ourselves. For my own part, continued Yorick, I had rather direct five words point-blank to the heart.   Sterne, *Tristram Shandy*, IV

He preached his sermon in the manner which men are wont to use when they know that they are preaching in vain. There is a tone of refusal, which, though the words used may be manifestly enough words of denial, is in itself indicative of assent.
Trollope, *Ayala's Angel*, XI

In his sermons he deals greatly in denunciations, excites the minds of his weaker hearers with a not unpleasant terror, and leaves an impression on their minds that all mankind are in a perilous state, and all womankind, too, except those who attend regularly to the evening lectures.   Trollope, *Barchester Towers*, IV

There is, perhaps, no greater hardship at present inflicted on mankind in civilized and free countries than the necessity of listening to sermons.

Ibid., VI

That anxious longing for escape is the common consequence of common sermons.

Ibid.

With what complacency will a young parson deduce false conclusions from misunderstood texts, and then threaten us with all the penalties of Hades if we neglect to comply with the injunctions he has given us!   *Ibid.*

The Bible is good, the prayer-book is good, nay, you yourself would be acceptable, if you would read to me some portion of those time-honored discourses which our great divines have elaborated in the full maturity of their powers. But you must excuse me, my insufficient young lecturer, if I yawn over your imperfect sentences, your repeated phrases, your false pathos, your drawlings and denouncings, your humming and hawing, your ohing and ahing, your black gloves and your white handkerchief. To me, it all means nothing: and hours are too precious to be so wasted—if one could only avoid it.

Ibid.

I must make a protest against the pretence, so often put forward by the working clergy, that they are overburdened by the multitude of sermons to be preached. We are all too fond of our own voices, and a preacher is encouraged in the vanity of making his heard by the privilege of a compelled audience. His sermon is the pleasant morsel of his life, his delicious moment of self-exaltation.   *Ibid.*

PREACHMENT (*continued*)

The best of clergymen cannot but be influenced by their audience.

Trollope, *The Warden*, XVI

He preached a prayer-meeting sermon that night that give him a rattling ruputation [*sic*], because the oldest man in the world couldn't a understood it.

Twain, *Huckleberry Finn*, XLII

Inattention dies a quick and sure death when a speaker stops and stands silent.

Twain, *Pudd'nhead Wilson*, XXI

A prevalent feature in these compositions was a nursed and petted melancholy; another was a wasteful and opulent gush of "fine language"; another was a tendency to lug in by the ears particularly prized words and phrases until they were worn entirely out; and a peculiarity that conspicuously marked and marred them was the inveterate and intolerable sermon that wagged its crippled tail at the end of each and every one of them. No matter what the subject might be, a brain-racking effort was made to squirm it into some aspect or other that the moral and religious mind could contemplate with edification. The glaring insincerity of these sermons was not sufficient to compass the banishment of the fashion from the schools, and it is not sufficient today; it never will be sufficient while the world stands, perhaps. There is no school in all our land where the young ladies do not feel obliged to close their compositions with a sermon; and you will find that the sermon of the most frivolous and the least religious girl in the school is always the longest and the most relentlessly pious. But enough of this. Homely truth is unpalatable.

Twain, *Tom Sawyer*, XXI

PREDICTION; PROPHECY; FORECAST; FOREWARNING: *see also*
PAST-PRESENT-FUTURE

"I am always conscious of an uncomfortable sensation now and then when the wind is blowing in the east." "Rheumatism, sir?" "I dare say it is. I believe it is."

Dickens, *Bleak House*, VI

Among all forms of mistake, prophecy is the most gratuitous.

Eliot, *Middlemarch*, Book I, X

You shall see men to fly from place to place in the air; you shall be able (without moving or travailing of any creature) to send messages in an instant many miles off and receive answer again immediately; you shall be able to declare your mind presently unto your friend, being in some private and remote place of a populous city. You shall have notice of a new world, of many most rare and incredible secrets of nature, that all the philosophers of former ages could never so much as dream of.

Godwin, *The Man in the Moon*, 10–11

Most warnings are warnings which do not forewarn, but in mockery come after the fact.

Melville, *Confidence-Man*, XXXVI

Outward portents and inward presentiments were his.   Melville, *Moby Dick*, XXVI

PREFERENCE

Our likings are regulated by our circumstances. The artist prefers a hilly country because it is picturesque; the engineer a flat one because it is convenient.

Bronte, C., *The Professor*, XIV

PREJUDICE; BIGOTRY

To exaggerate beauties, and aggravate deformities is no uncommon practice where interest or prejudice governs the pen.   Anonymous, *The Fruitless Repentance*, II

The prejudice of education goes a great way, and it is not the work of an hour to remove it.   Anonymous, *Genuine Memoirs of Maria Brown*, I

The prejudice against lawyers stands upon the ground with the prejudice against learning. The majority are not lawyers, or learned men.

Brackenridge, *Modern Chivalry*, Part II, I

It is hard to root from the mind its favorite principles or prejudices.
Burney, Evelina, 214

The man who is a bigot and yet disclaims infallibility is a contradiction to himself.
Collyer, Felicia to Charlotte, II

It is out of the power of any individual, however strenuous may be his endeavors, to prevent the mass of mankind from acquiring prejudices and corruptions.
Day, The History of Sandford and Merton, 247–248

In almost every country, a pale color in animals is considered as a mark of weakness and inferiority. Why then should a certain race of men imagine themselves superior to the rest, for the very circumstance they despise in other animals?
Ibid., 354

People of poor capacities are apt to be deluded by vulgar prejudices.
Donaldson, Sir Bartholomew Sapskull, I

To minds strongly marked by the positive and negative qualities that create severity—strength of will, conscious rectitude of purpose, narrowness of imagination and intellect, great power of self-control, and a disposition to exert control over others—prejudices come as the natural food of tendencies which can get no sustenance out of that complex, fragmentary, doubt-provoking knowledge which we call truth.
Eliot, The Mill on the Floss, Book VI, XII

Like the religious bigot, she was sufficiently disposed to avenge a hostility against her opinions with the weapons of sublunary warfare.
Godwin, Caleb Williams, III

Ancient prejudice, wherewith was linked much of ancient principle.
Hawthorne, The Scarlet Letter, XIII

While we can think to maintain the rights of our own individuality against every human combination, let us not forget to caution all who are disposed to waver that there is a cowardice which is criminal, and a longing for rest which it is baseness to indulge.
Holmes, Elsie Venner, XVIII

Attachment to a favorite system will make the best informed mind blind.
Johnstone, Arsaces, I

The darkness of prejudice and ancient pride.
Radcliffe, The Castles of Athlin and Dunbayne, 249

If every man's private life were searched into by prejudiced people, set on for that purpose, I know not whose reputation should be safe.
Richardson, Clarissa Harlowe, I

A prejudice in favor is as hard to be totally overcome as a prejudice in disfavor.
Ibid., II

Why should narrowness run away with the praises due to a noble expansion of heart?
Ibid.

It is hard to remove early-taken prejudices, whether of liking or distaste: people will hunt for reasons to confirm first impressions, in compliment to their own sagacity: nor is it every mind that has the ingenuousness to confess itself mistaken, when it finds itself to be wrong.
Ibid., IV

We are the fools of prejudice.
Smollett, Humphry Clinker, 59

Prejudices of education are never wholly eradicated, even when they are discovered to be erroneous and absurd.
Ibid., 270

Prejudice of education is the devil.
Sterne, Tristram Shandy, V

PREPARATION; PREPAREDNESS

The bow will not be forever bent.
Godwin, Caleb Williams, Appendix II

The first years of man must make provision for the last.
Johnson, Rasselas, 75

PREPARATION; PREPAREDNESS (*continued*)

Two arrows in the quiver are better than one; and three are better still.

Kipling, *Kim*, V

PREVENTION: *see also* CAUSE AND EFFECT; CAUTION; PREPAREDNESS; etc.

What is impossible to undo might be easily prevented.   Brown, C. B., *Ormond*, 141

PRIDE: *see also* MODESTY

Pride is in some instances a virtue.   Anonymous, *The Fruitless Repentance*, I

Applause is the strongest motive of all our actions, and that we may enjoy it with less scandal, we have found out names to disguise it, and risk life, peace, and everything that is dear to us to have the pleasure of it.

Anonymous, *The History of the Human Heart*, 118

Our pride hinders us from being made wise by the remarks of our friends.

Anonymous, *The Ladies Advocate*, 299

A person may be proud without being vain. Pride relates more to our opinion of ourselves, vanity to what we would have others think of us.

Austen, *Pride and Prejudice*, Volume I, V

Pride—where there is a real superiority of mind—will be always under good regulation.

Ibid., Volume I, XI

She was proud of him, proud that in a cause of compassion and honor, he had been able to get the better of himself.   *Ibid.*, Volume III, X

Pride, when it arises in a modest nature, is the proper power to keep it sweet.

Blackmore, *Dariel*, XXXVI

There is a certain pride in man which leads him to elevate the low and pull down the high.   Brackenridge, *Modern Chivalry*, Part I, I

No man will own himself weak and uninformed. In fact, he has not humility to think he is: or, if he should be conscious of a want of knowledge, he is unwilling that others should have the same opinion: and he will not submit to be instructed, as that would imply that he is not already so.   *Ibid.*, Part I, II

It is natural for us to suppose that the world cannot do without us. O what will they do when we are gone is the language of almost every man's heart.   *Ibid.*, Part II, I

Proud people breed sad sorrows for themselves.   Bronte, E., *Wuthering Heights*, VII

He was not proud even of not being proud.   Bulwer, *The Caxtons*, Book III, V

Pride is a sin that sticks close to nature, and is one of the first follies wherein it shows itself to be polluted.   Bunyan, *The Life and Death of Mr. Badman*, 253

He that is proud must be distanced; he that is vain must be flattered. This is paying them with their own coin; but they hold no other to be current. Pride, if not humbled, degenerates into contempt; vanity, if not indulged, dissolves into indifference.

Burney, *Camilla*, Three, VI

In the first pride of youth and beauty, our attention is all upon how we are looked at. But when those begin to be on the wane, our ambition is how we are listened to.

Ibid., Five, IX

The whole of this unfortunate business has been the result of PRIDE and PREJUDICE.

Burney, *Cecilia*, III

There are few people so debased in their own opinion as not to be proud of their peculiar origin and character.   Cooper, *The Headsman*, XXVI

We have so little right to value ourselves on anything, that pride is a sentiment of very doubtful service, and one certainly, that is unable to effect any useful results which will not equally flow from good principles.   Cooper, *Precaution*, XXXV

It is a great mistake to think oneself necessary to anyone.   Crawford, *Don Orsino*, XV

Oh! self-love!—dangerous and resistless flatterer!—thou immolated at thy shrine more victims than all the artifices of man!   Dacre, *Zofloya*, II

Human pride and sensuality, two passions the most fatal in their effects, and the most apt to desolate the world.   Day, *The History of Sandford and Merton*, 242

There is nothing Pride can so little bear with as Pride itself.
Dickens, *Bleak House*, XVIII

I'd rather be knocked down by a man who had got Blood in him, than I'd be picked up by a man who hadn't.   Dickens, *David Copperfield*, XXV

There is a kind of pride which is mere duty.   Dickens, *Dombey and Son*, XXXIII

It was not in the nature of things that the cold hard armor of pride in which he lived encased should be made more flexible by constant collision with haughty scorn and defiance.   *Ibid.*, XL

Their pride, however different in kind and object, was equal in degree; and, in their flinty opposition, struck out fire between them which might smoulder or might blaze, as circumstances were, but burned up everything within their mutual reach, and made their marriage way a road of ashes.   *Ibid.*, XLVII

Pride is one of the seven deadly sins; but it cannot be the pride of a mother in her children, for that is a compound of two cardinal virtues—faith and hope.
Dickens, *Nicholas Nickleby*, XLIII

Pride and meanness, like man and wife, are always coupled together.
Donaldson, *Sir Bartholomew Sapskull*, I

Pride and cowardice are concomitants in the character of a soldier, and you may be ever certain when pride appears in the front of a general, cowardice skulks in the rear.
Ibid.

Pride is not a bad thing when it only urges us to hide our own hurts—not to hurt others.
Eliot, *Middlemarch*, Book I, VI

Pride only helps us to be generous; it never makes us so, any more than vanity makes us witty.   *Ibid.*, Book I, VIII

The pride of poverty that will not be ashamed of itself.
Eliot, *The Mill on the Floss*, Book VI, II

Few men want a good opinion of themselves.   Fielding, H., *Amelia*, I

No woman who hath any great pretensions to admiration is ever well pleased in a company where she perceives herself to fill only the second place.   *Ibid.*

Of all kinds of pride, there is none so unchristian as that of station.   *Ibid.*, II

There is not in the universe a more ridiculous nor a more contemptible animal than a proud clergyman.   *Ibid.*

I have an awkward pride in my nature, which is better pleased with being at the head of the lowest class, than at the bottom of the highest.
Fielding, H., *Jonathan Wild*, 25

I had rather stand on the summit of a dunghill, than at the bottom of a hill in Paradise.
Ibid.

Some people have been noted to be able to read in no book but their own.
Fielding, H., *Tom Jones*, 101

That sort of pride, by fools mistaken for greatness of mind, which makes people disdain the receiving obligations.   Fielding, S., *David Simple*, I

PRIDE (*continued*)

It is the nature of pride to throw the human mind into confusion and perturbation, and to rob it of all its steadiness.　　　Fielding, S., *The History of the Countess of Dellwyn*, II

When pride intervenes, compassion must subside.
　　　　　　　　　　　　Fielding, S., *The Lives of Cleopatra and Octavia*, 88

No man can at once feel his pride piqued, and his compassion moved, by the same object.
　　　　　　　　　　　　Ibid.

Love, when it is only the consequence of pride gratified, will vanish as soon as that pride is piqued; and will surrender up its place to aversion.　　　　　　　*Ibid.*, 207

False pride insinuates itself into the human breast under innumerable disguises.
　　　　　　　　Gibbes, *The Life and Adventures of Mr. Francis Clive*, II

It is a strange experience, to a man of pride and sensibility, to know that his interests are within the control of individuals who neither love nor understand him, and by whom, since one or the other must needs happen, he would rather be injured than obliged.　　　　　Hawthorne, *The Scarlet Letter*, The Custom House Introductory

Lapham had the pride which comes of self-making.　　　Howells, *Silas Lapham*, IX

"Pride's all right when it helps one to bear things." "But that's only when one wants to take the least from them."　　　　　　James, H., *The Awkward Age*, Book X, IV

Pride is seldom delicate. It will please itself with very mean advantages.
　　　　　　　　　　　　Johnson, *Rasselas*, 44

It gratifies the pride of some people to appear difficult of access, and consequently more significant than they really are.　　　　　　Kidgell, *The Card*, II

The pride of affronted virtue.　　　　　　　　Lennox, *Henrietta*, I

When true friendship is the motive for giving, it is pride, not generosity, to refuse.
　　　　　　　　　　　　Ibid., II

There is a pride which becomes every man; a poor man, of all others, should possess it.
　　　　　　　　　　Mackenzie, *Julia De Roubigné*, 29

The pride of knowledge often labors to gain what if gained would be useless, and wastes exertion upon objects that have been left unattained from their futility.
　　　　　　　　　　Mackenzie, *The Man of the World*, I

One whose unwonted self-respect in the hour of need, and in the act of being aided, might have appeared to some not wholly unlike pride out of place; and pride, in any place, is seldom very feeling. But the truth, perhaps, is, that those who are at least touched with that vice, besides being not unsusceptible to goodness, are sometimes the ones whom a ruling sense of propriety makes appear cold, if not thankless, under a favor.
　　　　　　　　　　　　Melville, *Confidence-Man*, V

Pride's priestess.　　　　　　　　　　Melville, *Pierre*, Book V, I

A proud man ever holds but lightly those things, however beneficent, which he did not for himself procure.　　　　　　　　　　*Ibid.*, Book XVIII, II

A proud man likes to feel himself in himself, and not by reflection in others.　　*Ibid.*

His pride had been shocked by that stupefying rejection of him. Conceive the highest bidder at an auction hearing the article announce that it will not have *him*!
　　　　　　　　　　Meredith, *Beauchamp's Career*, XXIX

Pride, our volcano-peak that sinks us in a crater.　　　　　　　*Ibid.*

An injured pride that strikes not out will strike home.　　Meredith, *The Egoist*, XVII

A man's pride is the front and headpiece of his character, his soul's support or snare.
　　　　　　　　　　Meredith, *Harry Richmond*, XXXIII

One who takes the trouble to sit and write his history for as large a world as he can obtain, and shape his style to harmonize with every development of his nature, can no longer have much of the hard grain of pride in him. *Ibid.*

Human pride is a well-adjusted mixture of good and evil.
Meredith, *The Ordeal of Richard Feverel*, I

A check to the pride of a boy will frequently divert him to the path where lie his subtlest powers. *Ibid.*, XV

It is naturally given to all men to esteem their own inventions best. So both the raven and the ape think their own young ones fairest. More, *Utopia*, I

Do not indulge in the pride of fine feeling, the romantic error of amiable minds.
Radcliffe, *The Mysteries of Udolpho*, I

Beware of priding yourself on the gracefulness of sensibility. *Ibid.*

Pride and meanness are as nearly allied as wit and madness.
Richardson, *Clarissa Harlowe*, I

Pride, when it is native, will show itself sometimes in the midst of mortifications.
Ibid., II

His pride has eaten up his prejudice. *Ibid.*

Pride is an excellent substitute where virtue shines not out, as the sun, in its own unborrowed lustre. *Ibid.*

Why should some men think themselves above giving beautiful proofs of a feeling heart?
Ibid.

Appeals give pride and superiority to the persons appealed to, and are apt to lessen the appellant, not only in their eye, but in her own. *Ibid.*, III

Better fall with pride than stand with meanness. *Ibid.*

Pride hardly ever fails to bring forth its mortifying contrary. *Ibid.*, IV

Jays will strut in peacocks' feathers. *Ibid.*

There is but one pride pardonable: that of being above doing a base or dishonorable action. *Ibid.*

Your poverty is my pride, as your integrity shall be my imitation.
Richardson, *Pamela*, 50

Pride is not my talent. *Ibid.*, 92

Proud people never think what a short stage life is. *Ibid.*, 271

If I can not conquer my pride, I will endeavor to make it innocent at least.
Richardson, *Sir Charles Grandison*, One, II

Pride and petulance must go down by degrees. *Ibid.*, Two, IV

Debasement is the child of pride. *Ibid.*

Pride will do greater things for women than reason can. *Ibid.*

Pride makes man claim immortality for himself, but deny it to others.
Scott, S., *A Description of Millenium Hall*, 198

When was the pride of woman too lofty to overlook the passionate devotion of a lover, however inferior in degree? Scott, W., *The Talisman*, IV

A proper pride may not be a pleasant thing at all times; but I should be sorry to see anyone I cared for without it. Shaw, *The Irrational Knot*, XIV

Pride is half the time in favor of philosophy. Simms, *The Scout*, XXVIII

Pride discourses of humility with moist lips; selfishness becomes eloquent in its exhortations to self-sacrifice; and the good preacher will possess himself of the fattest ewe lamb of the flock while insisting on the beauties of a perpetual lent.

Simms, *Woodcraft*, XLIII

Some men cannot bear to be out-gone. Sterne, *Tristram Shandy*, II

It was ordained as a scourge upon the pride of human wisdom that the wisest of us all should outwit ourselves. *Ibid.*, V

Pride in skepticism is a peculiar distinction of young men. Stowe, *Orr's Island*, XXIV

As vain as a girl. . . . As vain as a man. Thackeray, *Vanity Fair*, III

Pride must bear pain; but pain is recompensed by pride.

Trollope, *He Knew He Was Right*, LXV

That pride of individualism that is half the fascination of sin.

Wilde, *The Picture of Dorian Gray*, XI

The madness of pride. *Ibid.*, XII

PRINCIPLE: *see also* BELIEF; MORALITY; RELIGION; etc.

Principles are not always the only means of rendering man capable to face every storm of life with tranquillity. August, *Horrid Mysteries*, I

I have been a selfish being all my life, in practice, though not in principle. As a child I was taught what was *right*, but I was not taught to correct my temper. I was given good principles, but left to follow them in pride and conceit.

Austen, *Pride and Prejudice*, Volume III, XVI

Let every man speak his maxim. Burney, *Cecilia*, II

Where there is so much stability in morals, there must be permanent principles, and something surely is worthy to be saved from the wreck of the past. I doubt if all this craving for change has not more of selfishness in it than either of expediency or of philosophy. Cooper, *Satanstoe*, Volume II, XV

Perhaps no surer test of high principles, as it is certain no more accurate test of high breeding can be found, than a distaste for injurious gossip.

Cooper, *The Ways of the Hour*, XIX

Remember principle: no expediency, no compromise. Disraeli, *Sybil*, Book II, II

Envy and strife are the first principle of all things. Kimber, *David Ranger*, II

An unprincipled as the gods. Melville, *Moby Dick*, CXXXVII

We know not to what inconveniences a small departure from principle will lead.

Richardson, *Sir Charles Grandison*, One, II

I like persons better than principles, and I like persons with no principles better than anything else in the world. Wilde, *The Picture of Dorian Gray*, I

PRIORITIES

Placed on Crusoe's Island, his first cry would have been for clean linen: his next for the bill-of-fare: and then, for that grand panorama of the Mistress of the World falling to wreck under the barbarians, which had been the spur and the seal to his mind.

Meredith, *Ordeal of Richard Feverel*, IV

PRISONERS: *see also* CRIME; FREEDOM; etc.

Prisoners of long date do not hope. They do not calculate. Air, light, they say; to breathe freely and drop down. They are reduced to the instincts of beasts.

Meredith, *Beauchamp's Career*, XL

PRIVILEGE: *see also* FAVOR

A cat may look at a king. I've read that in some book, but I don't remember where.
Carroll, Alice in Wonderland, VIII

The evil one has his privileges, as well as the public.   Cooper, *The Chainbearer*, XVI

Men are apt to think what they have once enjoyed is their indisputable right.
Gentleman, A Trip to the Moon, I

[Addressed to one who has subdued the speaker by assault:] Unloose me—this passes thy privilege.   Scott, W., *The Talisman*, III

PROBABILITY: *see also* CAUSE AND EFFECT; IMPOSSIBILITY; POSSIBILITY; etc.

Are no probabilities to be accepted merely because they are not certainties?
Austen, Sense and Sensibility, Volume I, XV

I feign probabilities, I record improbabilities.   Reade, *A Terrible Temptation*

PROCESS: *see also* CAUSE AND EFFECT; FORM; etc.

A vast deal of coolness, and a peculiar degree of judgment, are requisite in catching a hat.   Dicken, *Pickwick Papers*, IV

Great engines are moved by small springs.   Richardson, *Clarissa Harlowe*, II

There was a most ingenious architect who had contrived a new method for building houses, by beginning at the roof, and working downwards to the foundation; which he justified by the like practice of those two prudent insects the bee and the spider.
Swift, Gulliver's Travels, Laputa

PROFESSION; EMPLOYMENT

"An employer owes a good workman something beyond the wages paid." "And a workman owes a good employer something beyond the work done."
Aldrich, Stillwater, XIV

No man likes to acknowledge that he has made a mistake in the choice of his profession, and every man, worthy of the name, will row long against wind and tide before he allows himself to cry out, "I am baffled!" and submits to be floated passively back to land.   Bronte, C., *The Professor*, IV

Every man's work is always a portrait of himself.   Butler, *The Way of All Flesh*, XIV

Pike-keepers're all on 'em men as has met vith some disappointment in life. Consequence of vich, they retires from the world, and shuts themselves up in pikes; partly vith the view of being solitary, and partly to rewenge themselves on mankind, by takin' tolls. If they was gen'lm'n you'd call 'em misanthropes, but as it is, they only takes to pike-keepin'.   Dickens, *Pickwick Papers*, XXII

There's nothing but what's bearable as long as a man can work.
Eliot, Adam Bede, XI

There's no work so tirin' as danglin' about and starin' an' not rightly knowin' what you're goin' to do next; and keepin' your face i' smilin' order like a grocer o' market-day for fear people shouldna think you civil enough.   *Ibid.*, XXVI

Every man's work, pursued steadily, tends to become an end in itself, and so to bridge over the loveless chasms of his life.   Eliot, *Silas Marner*, II

It is noble to see a man's hands subdued to what he works in.
Hardy, Jude the Obscure, Part III, I

There is at least this good in a life of toil, that it takes the nonsense and fancy-work out of a man, and leaves nothing but what truly belongs to him.
Hawthorne, The Blithedale Romance, VIII

The sweet weariness that follows accustomed toil. *Ibid.*, X

George goes to sleep at a bank from ten to four each day, except Saturdays, when they wake him up and put him outside at two. Jerome, *Three Men in a Boat*, II

It always does seem to me that I am doing more work than I should do. It is not that I object to the work, mind you; I like work; it fascinates me. I can sit and look at it for hours. I love to keep it by me; the idea of getting rid of it nearly breaks my heart. *Ibid.*, XV

No man's profession can exempt him from the misfortunes incident to his nature. Kidgell, *The Card*, II

He who hath a trade in his hand is like a vineyard that is fenced about. King, E., *Joseph Zalmonah*, I

Peddlers are their own best advertisements. *Ibid.*, II

Whatever his private sorrows may be, a multimillionaire, like any other workingman, should keep abreast of his business. Kipling, *Captains Courageous*, IX

There seems to be no calamity overtaking man that can not be rendered merchantable. Undertakers, sextons, tomb-makers, and hearse-drivers get their living from the dead; and in times of plague most thrive. Melville, *Redburn*, XXXVI

Printers are mad whoresons. Nashe, *The Unfortunate Traveller*, 31

To manipulate millions [of pounds] till they should breed other millions is the meanest occupation of a life's energy. Trollope, *Ayala's Angel*, XXXIII

To puff and to get one's self puffed have become different branches of a new profession. Trollope, *The Way We Live Now*, I

The fire-boys mounted to the hall and flooded it with water enough to annihilate forty times as much fire as there was there; for a village fire company does not often get a chance to show off, and so when it does get a chance it makes the most of it. Such citizens of that village as were of thoughtful and judicious temperament did not insure against fire; they insured against the fire company. Twain, *Pudd'nhead Wilson*, XI

A good knight cannot go to the grave with more satisfaction than when falling and dying in his vocation. Walpole, *The Castle of Otranto*, 68

PROFIT

Profit brings honor, and is, indeed, the most substantial support of it. Brackenridge, *Modern Chivalry*, Part I, I

Straightforward dealings don't bring profit—'tis the sly and the underhand that get on in these times. Hardy, *The Mayor of Casterbridge*, III

When godliness is gain, I believe in serving ourselves as well as others. Locke, *A Paper City*, XV

PROGRESS: *see also* CIVILIZATION; IMPROVEMENT; PROGRESSION; etc.

Grasshoppers never stand still; they are always hopping and jumping, and making what they think "progress," till they die of exhaustion. Bulwer, *Kenelm*, Book II, IX

Has the theory of the solar system been advanced by graceful manners and conversational tact? Eliot, *Middlemarch*, Book I, X

There is a principle in the human mind destined to be eternally at war with improvement and science. Godwin, *St. Leon*, 289-290

No sooner does a man devote himself to the pursuit of discoveries which, if ascertained, would prove the highest benefit to his species, than his whole species becomes armed against him.   *Ibid.*, 290

Progress is the law of human existence only because there are more poor than rich, more weak than strong, more who suffer by wrong than enjoy by injustice.
Tourgee, *Murvale Eastman*, XLII

Often it is not the first step that costs, but the waiting for the second.
Webster, *The Banker and the Bear*, XII

PROGRESSION

Everything in the world is conducted by gradual process. This seems to be the great principle of harmony in the universe. Nothing is abrupt; one thing is so blended and softened into another, that it is impossible to say where the former ends and the latter begins.   Godwin, *St. Leon*, 169

All things are progressive.   Reade, *Griffith Gaunt*, XIX

PROHIBITION: *see also* RESTRAINT

To do what is forbidden always has its charms, because we have an indistinct apprehension of something arbitrary and tyrannical in the prohibition.
Godwin, *Caleb Williams*, II

The sin of a prohibited correspondence!   Richardson, *Clarissa Harlowe*, I

Adam was but human—this explains it all. He did not want the apple for the apple's sake, he wanted it only because it was forbidden. The mistake was in not forbidding the serpent: then he would have eaten the serpent.   Twain, *Pudd'nhead Wilson*, II

PROMISE: *see also* FAITH; FIDELITY; TRUTH

Some folks think a promise ought to be expressed, while others think it may be understood.   Cooper, *Sea Lions*, XXX

You know what being a reference means. A person who can't pay, gets another person who can't pay, to guarantee that he can pay. Like a person with two wooden legs, getting another person with two wooden legs, to guarantee that he has got two natural legs.
Dickens, *Little Dorrit*, Book I, XXIII

Promises are dangerous things to ask or to give.   Edgeworth, *The Absentee*, II

The promise is sweeter when this life is so dark and weary, and the soul gets more hungry when the body is ill at ease.   Eliot, *Adam Bede*, VIII

A man cannot make a vow not to quarrel.   Eliot, *Felix Holt*, IX

Instead of money, he gave promises.   Goldsmith, *The Vicar of Wakefield*, 14

Oaths are foolish.   Meredith, *Beauchamp's Career*, XL

Promises are pie-crusts.   Reade, *The Cloister and the Hearth*, LXXIX

A promise once given the promised only can dispense with; except in cases of a very apparent necessity imposed upon the promiser which leaves no power to perform it.
Richardson, *Clarissa Harlowe*, I

What honest man is obliged to keep his promise with a highwayman?   *Ibid.*, IV

PROOF: *see also* CAUSE AND EFFECT; LAW; TRUTH; etc.

He came near to convincing them by disdaining to produce proofs.
Crane, *The Red Badge of Courage*, I

PROOF (*continued*)

Mr. Gradgrind sat writing in the room with the deadly statistical clock, proving something no doubt—probably, in the main, that the Good Samaritan was a Bad Economist.
Dickens, *Hard Times*, Book II, XII

Do not waste time in repeating the proofs of principles self-evident.
Johnstone, *Arsaces*, I

No matter whether a man is innocent or guilty, he must depend upon proof. Instead of innocence being sufficient to defend a man, it is much oftener the cause of his being condemned; because trusting to that, he does not take care to provide proof, for which reason ten innocent men suffer for one who is really guilty.
Johnstone, *The Pilgrim*, II

Man requires but weak proof to convince him of what he wishes to be true.
Johnstone, *The Reverie*, I

PROPHECY: *see also* PREDICTION

Who can see an inch into futurity, beyond his nose?
Hawthorne, *The Scarlet Letter*, The Custom House Introductory

Long foretold, long past;/ Short notice, soon past.   Jerome, *Three Men in a Boat*, V

Who wants to be foretold the weather? It is bad enough when it comes, without our having the misery of knowing about it beforehand.   *Ibid.*

If often happens that those who are gifted with prophetic knowledge have not the power of foreseeing those events in which they themselves are personally interested. They cannot see their own features by the light which shows the faces of others.
Scott, *Quentin Durward*, XII

Strange and mysterious science [divination], which, pretending to draw the curtain of futurity, misleads those whom it seems to guide, and darkens the scene which it pretends to illuminate.   Scott, *The Talisman*, XXVIII

When a great calamity is hanging over a man he has frequently many strange and awful forebodings of it.   Thackeray, *Barry Lyndon*, XIX

PROPRIETY: *see also* RIGHTNESS

The pleasantness of an employment does not always evince its propriety.
Austen, *Sense and Sensibility*, Volume I, XIII

Great propriety of mind can only result from the union of good sense with virtue.
Burney, *Cecilia*, II

Propriety, another word for nature, is the foundation of all true judgment.
Richardson, *Clarissa Harlowe*, IV

PROSPECT: *see also* PREDICTION; PROPHECY

I like a fine prospect, but not on picturesque principles.
Austen, *Sense and Sensibility*, Volume I, XVIII

The hours we pass with happy prospects in view are more pleasing than those crowned with fruition. In the first case, we cook the dish to our own appetite; in the latter Nature cooks it for us.   Goldsmith, *The Vicar of Wakefield*, 46

PROSPERITY: *see also* WEALTH

It is not less difficult to preserve equanimity in a prosperous situation than to sustain with fortitude a depression of fortune.   Brackenridge, *Modern Chivalry*, Part I, IV

Prosperity depends in great measure upon energy and good sense, but it also depends not a little upon pure luck—that is to say, upon connections which are in such a tangle that it is more easy to say that they do not exist than to try to trace them.
Butler, *The Way of All Flesh*, LXXII

There is a pale shade of bribery which is sometimes called prosperity.
Eliot, *Middlemarch*, Book VIII, LXXV

We're never so prosperous as when we can't remember what happened last Monday.
Howells, *A Modern Instance*, XXVII

It is the curse of prosperity that it takes work away from us, and shuts that door to hope and health of spirit.
Howells, *Silas Lapham*, XVII

One's standard was the ideal of one's own good-humored prosperity, the prosperity which enabled one to give as well as take.
James, H., *The American*, V

Pietro Vanucci was one of those who bear prosperity worse than adversity.
Reade, *The Cloister and the Hearth*, LXIII

The poorest man's house has a glory, where there are true hands, a divine heart, and an honest fame.
Scott, *The Heart of Midlothian*, XXVII

PROSTITUTION: *see also* LIBERTINISM; MALE/FEMALE; PROFESSION

No whore in the world was ever worth fighting for.
Anonymous, *Memoirs of an Oxford Scholar*, 54

PROSTRATION

Nothing so abject as the behavior of a man canvassing for a seat in parliament. This mean prostration has contributed in a great measure to raise that spirit of insolence among the vulgar; which, like the devil, will be found very difficult to lay.
Smollett, *Humphry Clinker*, 85

PROTECTION; PROTECTIVENESS

It will always happen that these men of the world, who go through it in armor, defend themselves from quite as much good as evil; to say nothing of the inconvenience and absurdity of mounting guard with a microscope at all times, and of wearing a coat of mail on the most innocent occasions.
Dickens, *The Old Curiosity Shop*, LXVI

Seafaring natures be very good shelter for shorn lambs.
Hardy, *The Mayor of Casterbridge*, I

When did the murderous tyger protect the lamb? Or when did the fell kite preserve the dove?
Helme, *St. Margaret's Cave*, Volume I, X

Needful is the protection of the brave to the fair.
Richardson, *Clarissa Harlowe*, IV

They who protect the injured should be strong themselves.
Trollope, *He Knew He Was Right*, XXIX

"You disarm me." "Of your shield, not of your spear."
Wilde, *The Picture of Dorian Gray*, XVII

PROVERBS; QUOTATIONS; SAYINGS: *see also* EXPRESSION; PREACHMENT; TRUTH; etc.

Proverbs are the deductions of experience, and to which we assent as soon as expressed; containing in them an obvious truth, which the simplest understand.
Brackenridge, *Modern Chivalry*, Part I, II

Whenever a thought leads me into a quotation, I do not make a scruple of conscience to run after it; especially if I have any reason to think, upon the small reflection I can give it, that the quotation will be better than the original idea that might have taken place of it.   *Ibid.*, Part II, IV

I read with great pleasure oftentimes a book which has not a single idea in it except in the quotations.   *Ibid.*

Quotations are good for nothing but to mislead people and show that the user of them is a man of reading.   Bridges, *The Adventures of a Bank-Note*, IV

A capital proverb, and sometimes even a true one.   DuMaurier, *Trilby*, VIII

All people of broad, strong sense have an instinctive repugnance to the men of maxims; because such people early discern that the mysterious complexity of our life is not to be embraced by maxims, and that to lace ourselves up in formulas of that sort is to repress all the divine promptings and inspirations that spring from growing insight and sympathy.   Eliot, *The Mill on the Floss*, Book VII, II

Proverbs: short aphorisms, in which men of great genius have wrapt up some egregious discovery, either in nature or science, making it thus easily portable for the memory, which is apt to fail under the burden of voluminous erudition.
                                       Fielding, H., *Jonathan Wild*, 113

Sayings are all made by men, for their own advantages. Women who use public proverbs as a guide through events are those who have not ingenuity enough to make private ones as each event occurs.   Hardy, *The Hand of Ethelberta*, XX

Quotations judiciously chosen and properly introduced elucidate and heighten discourse.
                                       Lawrence, H., *The Contemplative Man*, II

He took to proverbs; sure sign of the sere leaf in a man's mind.
                                       Meredith, *Beauchamp's Career*, XX

Modern Aphorists are accustomed to make their phrases a play of wit, flashing antithetical brilliancies, rather than condensing profound truths.
                                       Meredith, *The Ordeal of Richard Feverel*, I

A maker of proverbs—what is he but a narrow mind the mouthpiece of narrower?
                                       Ibid., XLVIII

A proverb is the halfway house to an ideal; and the majority rest there content: can the keeper of such a house be flattered by his company?   *Ibid.*

A book that furnishes no quotations is no book—it is a plaything.
                                       Peacock, *Crotchet Castle*, IX

Proverbs put old heads on young men's shoulders.
                                       Reade, *The Cloister and the Hearth*, XXIV

Proverbs are the wisdom of whole nations and ages collected into a small compass.
                                       Richardson, *Clarissa Harlowe*, II

Proverbs often contain more wisdom in them than the tedious harangues of most parsons and moralists.   *Ibid.*

Leave old saws to old men.   *Ibid.*

Proverbs may be set against proverbs.   Richardson, *Sir Charles Grandison*, One, I

Not to wear best things every day was a maxim of New England thrift as little disputed as any verse of the catechism.   Stowe, *Orr's Island*, XIII

When poverty creeps in at the door, love flies in through the window. Our proverbs want rewriting. They were made in winter, and it is summer now.
                                       Wilde, *The Picture of Dorian Gray*, V

You would sacrifice anybody for the sake of an epigram.   *Ibid.*, XVIII

Where is a greater absurdity to be found than in general maxims founded in private opinions?   Young, *The Adventures of Emmera*, II

PRUDENCE: *see also* CAUTION

Prudence can only direct us to take more cautious measures for the future, and so, if possible, frustrate the bad effects which our imprudence has occasioned.
Anonymous, The Ladies Advocate, 34

There is nothing so pernicious as an imprudent connection.
Anonymous, Memoirs of a Coquet, 165

A prudent modest woman never loves anything but herself.
Brooke, Emily Montague, IV

The imprudence of our thoughts recoils upon our heads.   Conrad, *Lord Jim*, XXXVI

The world is always on the side of prudence.   Fielding, H., *Joseph Andrews*, 92

Prudence is always readiest to go on duty where there is the least danger.
Fielding, H., Tom Jones, 4–5

No man can be good enough to enable him to neglect the rules of prudence; nor will virtue herself look beautiful unless she be bedecked with the outward ornaments of decency and decorum.   *Ibid.*, 98

The voice of prudence is salutary to the young and inexperienced.
Gibbes, The Life and Adventures of Mr. Francis Clive, I

Prudence is too often the only virtue that is left us at seventy-two.
Goldsmith, The Vicar of Wakefield, 8

The opinion a man forms of his own prudence is measured by that of the company he keeps.   *Ibid.*, 65

If prudence consists in wishing well to one's self, young flirts are as prudent as old souls.   Richardson, *Clarissa Harlowe*, II

Prudent people in other's matters are not always prudent in their own.
Richardson, Sir Charles Grandison, Three, VI

PSYCHOLOGY: *see also* HUMAN NATURE; MIND: etc.

The agitation of the mind baffles all the power of medicine, and till the mind is relieved, the body can never be restored.   Burney, *Cecilia*, I

It is impossible to study the human frame without a little studying the human mind.
Ibid., III

The Doctor knew his fellow creatures better than most men, knew that inner life which so seldom unfolds itself to unanointed eyes.   Chopin, *The Awakening*, XXIII

PUBLIC: *see also* SOCIETY

There is nothing so difficult as to manage the public mind.
Brackenridge, Modern Chivalry, Part II, II

There is often something poisonous in the air of public rooms.
Eliot, Middlemarch, Book VIII, LXXIV

Private vices are public benefits.   Richardson, *Clarissa Harlowe*, III

This incongruous monster, the public.   Smollet, *Humphry Clinker*, 96

PUNISHMENT: *see also* MERIT; REWARD

Are there as many hells as there are crimes? If not, all punishments are alike.
Anonymous, Genuine Memoirs of Maria Brown, I

"If you are a good girl for the next ten years, I will take you to a [military] review at the end of them."   Austen, *Pride and Prejudice*, Volume III, VI

Newgate Prison was a place that seldom made penitents, but often made villains worse, till they learned to defy God and Devil. Defoe, *Colonel Jack*, 164

Sin is always punished in this world, whatever may come in the next. There is always some penalty in health, in comfort, or in peace of mind to be paid for every wrong.
Doyle, *Micah Clarke*, III

Fines and imprisonments and corporal punishments operate more forcibly on the human mind than all the fears of damnation. Fielding, H., *Amelia*, II

Happy is it for those few who are detected in their sins, and brought to exemplary punishment for them in this world. Fielding, H., *Jonathan Wild*, 247

Jonathan Wild the Great was, what so few great men are, though all in propriety ought to be—hanged by the neck till he was dead. *Ibid.*, 262

As for the thought of eternal punishment, what signifies matters so far off? The mug is out, shall I draw another? Fielding, H., *Joseph Andrews*, 82

Thwackum could, with the utmost propriety, repeat this old flogging line, "I chastise thee not out of hatred, but out of love." Fielding, H., *Tom Jones*, 94

The breech, the place to which Thwackum always applied for information on every doubtful occasion. *Ibid.*, 98

You cannot legally commit any one to Bridewell only for illbreeding. *Ibid.*, 295

God hath given him blood to drink! Hawthorne, *The House of the Seven Gables*, I

Perhaps this is to be the punishment of sin, not that it shall be made evident to the universe, which can profit nothing by such knowledge, but that it shall insulate the sinner from all sweet society by rendering him impermeable to light, and, therefore, unrecognizable in the abode of heavenly simplicity and truth.
Hawthorne, *The Marble Faun*, XXXIII

The supreme magistrate can never know all the crimes that are committed, and can seldom punish all that he knows. Johnson, *Rasselas*, 39

He who has been driven by necessity to rob another of a few pieces of silver, or break open a door, to come at some victuals for the instant relief of nature, will rather slay the man who attempts to prevent him, than be apprehended, because he knows that his life is already forfeited by the first crime; whereas, were the former crimes punished in another manner, and only murder punished with death, few or none would ever be guilty of the atrocious crime. Johnstone, *The Pilgrim*, II

'Tis not the crime which holds your hand, but the punishment; 'tis not respect for God which restrains you, but the terror of his vengeance. Fain would you offend him in secret, but you tremble to profess yourself his foe. Lewis, *The Monk*, 214

In the punishments of the divinity there is no idea of vengeance; and the infliction of what we term evil serves equally the purpose of universal benignity, with the dispensation of good. Mackenzie, *The Man of the World*, II

In all cases where two have joined to commit an offense, punish one of the two lightly. Meredith, *Ordeal of Richard Feverel*, XXXI

Hanging is too extreme and cruel a punishment for theft, and yet not sufficient to refrain, and withhold men from theft. More, *Utopia*, I

I think it not right nor justice, that the loss of money should cause the loss of man's life. For all the goods in the world are not able to countervail man's life. *Ibid.*

They often hang their female malefactors, instead of drowning them decently, as other nations use. Reade, *The Cloister and the Hearth*, LIV

Punishments are of service to offenders. Rewards should be only to the meriting, and the former are to be dealt out rigorously in willful cases.
Richardson, *Clarissa Harlowe*, I

A deviation from propriety scarcely ever escapes punishment.

Roche, *Nocturnal Visit*, I

The hand of man cannot punish like the reproaches of conscience. *Ibid.*

No man because he hath done well before should have his present evil spared, but rather so much the more punished, as having showed he knew how to be good, yet would against his knowledge be naught. Sidney, *Arcadia*, V

The bird that can sing, and won't sing, must be made to swing.

Simms, *Woodcraft*, XXV

PURIFICATION

All towns should be made capable of purification by fire, or of decay, within each half-century. Hawthorne, *The Marble Faun*, XXXIII

Is sin, like sorrow, merely an element of human education, through which we struggle to a higher and purer state than we could otherwise have attained? Did Adam fall, that we might ultimately rise to a far loftier paradise than his? *Ibid.*, L

PURITY: *see also* INNOCENCE; PERFECTION

To the pure all things are pure. Kingsley, *Alton Locke*, VI

Purity is but a characteristic, a garment, and can be spotted.

Meredith, *Ordeal of Richard Feverel*, XXIX

A pure heart, whether in man or woman, will be always, in every company, on every occasion, pure. Richardson, *Sir Charles Grandison*, One, I

Chastity is so very essential to the female sex that she who violates it seldom preserves any other virtue. Scott, S., *Millenium Hall*, 174

The spotless virgin fears not the raging lion. Scott, W., *The Talisman*, XVII

Chastity, by nature, the gentlest of all affections—give it but its head—'tis like a ramping and a roaring lion. Sterne, *Tristram Shandy*, V

The purity of your heart prevents your seeing the depravity of others.

Walpole, *The Castle of Otranto*, 93

PURPOSE

Who can prove that the enjoyment of the moment also is the purpose of the existence of that moment? August, *Horrid Mysteries*, I

Let other pens dwell on guilt and misery. I quit such odious subjects as soon as I can, impatient to restore everybody, not greatly in fault themselves, to tolerable comfort, and to have done with all the rest. Austen, *Mansfield Park*, Volume Three, XVII

Everything's got a moral, if only you can find it. Carroll, *Alice in Wonderland*, IX

How fond she is of finding morals in things! *Ibid.*

"If any misanthrope were to put the question 'Why were we born?' I should reply, 'To make an effort.'" Dickens, *Dombey and Son*, XVIII

Some purpose or other is so natural to everyone, that a mere loiterer always looks and feels remarkable. Dickens, *Hard Times*, Book II, VI

A cause is a great abstraction, and fit only for students; embodied in a party, it stirs men to action; but place at the head of that party a leader who can inspire enthusiasm, he commands the world. Disraeli, *Coningsby*, Book II, VII

Harold was quick at translating other men's generalities into his own special and immediate purposes. Eliot, *Felix Holt*, XVI

It is the iron rule in our day to require an object and a purpose in life. We go all wrong, by too strenuous a resolution to go all right. Hawthorne, *The Marble Faun*, XXVI

His heaven-insulting purpose, God may wedge aside.
Melville, Moby Dick, XXXVIII

Even the high-lifted and chivalric Crusaders of old times were not content to traverse two thousand miles of land to fight for their holy sepulchre, without committing burglaries, picking pockets, and gaining other pious perquisites by the way.
Ibid., XLVI

To what purpose live we, if not to grow wiser, and to subdue our passions?
Richardson, Sir Charles Grandison, Two, V

Could he say what purpose the fiery comet answers? Scott, S., Millenium Hall, 200

Nothing contributes so much to tranquillize the mind as a steady purpose.
Shelley, Frankenstein, Letter 1

Persons attempting to find a motive in this narrative will be prosecuted; persons attempting to find a moral in it will be banished; persons attempting to find a plot in it will be shot. Twain, Huckleberry Finn, NOTICE

To be highly organized is the object of man's existence.
Wilde, The Picture of Dorian Gray, VI

PURSUIT

Though all men have not the same objects of pursuit, all are impelled by the same love of pursuing. Hildreth, Slave, Volume I, XV

There are two pursuits that never pall—making money and making love.
Warner, A Little Journey, IX

PUSHINESS

The English race represents the survival of the pushing.
Wilde, The Picture of Dorian Gray, XVII

QUACKERY: *see also* MEDICINE; PROFESSION

Germany has quacks in religion, quacks in physic, quacks in law, quacks in politics; quacks in patriotism; quacks in government; high German quacks that have blistered, sweated, bled, and purged the nation into an atrophy.
Smollett, Sir Launcelot Greaves, 79

QUERULOUSNESS

How uneasily that man must pass his time who sits, like a spider in the midst of his feeling web, ready to catch the minutest occasion for quarrel and resentment.
Mackenzie, The Man of the World, I

QUESTIONS: *see also* CAUSE AND EFFECT; INQUIRY; KNOWLEDGE AND LEARNING; etc.

Questions are always easy. Disraeli, Sybil, Book IV, IX

I've thought it all over, and there ain't no way to find out why a snorer can't hear himself snore. Twain, Tom Sawyer Abroad, X

RAIN: *see also* NATURE

People who have pleasant homes get indoor enjoyments that they would never think of but for the rain. Eliot, Adam Bede, V

The rainiest nights, like the rainiest lives, are by no means the saddest.
Ward, *The Silent Partner*, I

RAISING; REARING

I had cherished a profound conviction that her bringing me up by hand gave her no right to bring me up by jerks. Dickens, *Great Expectations*, VIII

RAPE: *see also* LIBERTINISM; MALE/FEMALE; VIOLENCE

Rapes are unnatural things, and more rare than imagined.
Richardson, *Clarissa Harlowe*, II

To rakes, a rape is far from being an undesirable thing. *Ibid.*, III

RARITY

A rare bird upon the earth, and very like a black swan. Fielding, H., *Tom Jones*, 138

Rare as epic song is the man who is thorough in what he does.
Meredith, *Evan Harrington*, VII

RASCALITY: *see also* GOOD AND EVIL; LIBERTINISM

As all boys are rascals, so are all men. Melville, *Confidence-Man*, XXII

A rascal never goes straight to his business. If he has to shake hands with you he does it with a sort of twist, and a twirl, and sometimes a squint, that looks every which way but the right one. Simms, *The Scout*, XXXIV

REACTION: *see also* CAUSE AND EFFECT

She didn't know which to be most shocked at—my language or my principles.
Collins, *The Moonstone*, First Period, II

Who was ever awestruck about a testator, or sang a hymn on the title to real property?
Eliot, *Middlemarch*, Book III, XXXI

READING: *see also* LITERATURE; POETRY; etc.

To dip into any book burthens the mind with unnecessary lumber, and may rather be called a disadvantage than a benefit. Brown, W. H., *The Power of Sympathy*, 29

Among all kinds of knowledge which arise from reading, self-knowledge is eminent.
Ibid., 40

What is the use of a book without pictures or conversation?
Carroll, *Alice in Wonderland*, I

Haven't I seen you the reader with the greatest authors in your hands, and don't I know how ready your attention is to wander when it's a book that asks for it, instead of a person? Collins, *The Moonstone*, First Period, V

No one who can read ever looks at a book, even unopened on a shelf, like one who cannot. Dickens, *Our Mutual Friend*, Book I, III

He is a sagacious reader who can see two chapters before him.
Fielding, H., *Joseph Andrews*, 39

Books, the only way of travelling by which any knowledge is to be acquired.
Ibid., 155

Every book ought to be read with the same spirit and in the same manner as it is writ. Thus the famous author of Hurlothrumbo told a learned bishop, that the reason his lordship could not taste the excellence of his piece was, that he did not read it with a fiddle in his hand; which instrument he himself had always had in his own, when he composed it. Fielding, H., *Tom Jones*, 106

Reading is like setting a mirror before us. Fielding, S., *The Countess of Dellwyn*, I

There is a wide difference between reading with the attention which is necessary to digest, and extract utility from writings, and skimming over the surface of authors, with the view only of filling up a chasm of time, which is not so fortunate as to be engaged to some more entertaining amusement. *Ibid.*, II

If the vulgar were to be told that anything which is in a book is in nature also, they would be astonished, and give no credit to such an assertion.
Fielding, S., *The Countess of Dellwyn*, II

I never care much for reading what one ought to read.
Hardy, *The Hand of Ethelberta*, IX

We have great opportunities at the university of knowing human nature from books, the calm result of the wise men's wisdom. Richardson, *Clarissa Harlowe*, IV

REALITY; REALISM: *see also* FICTION; ROMANCE; TRUTH; etc.

By a good and strong root her graces held to the firm soil of reality.
Bronte, C., *Villette*, XXVII

Not one man in ten thousand, living in the midst of reality, has discovered that he is also living in the midst of romance. Collins, *Heart and Science*, II

Most men will be found sufficiently true to themselves to be true to an old idea. It is no proof of an inconstant mind, but exactly the opposite, when the idea will not bear close comparison with the reality, and the contrast is a fatal shock to it.
Dickens, *Little Dorrit*, Book I, XIII

In real life we are content with oats that are really middling, are very glad to have a useful horse, and know that if we drink port at all we must drink some that is neither good nor sound. Trollope, *The Eustace Diamonds*, XXXV

If one doesn't talk about a thing, it has never happened. It is simply expression that gives reality to things. Wilde, *The Picture of Dorian Gray*, IX

Ugliness was the one reality. *Ibid.*, XVI

The man who could call a spade a spade should be compelled to use one. *Ibid.*, XVII

REASON; REASONABLENESS: *see also* LOGIC; PASSION; etc.

People reason very differently when danger is near and unavoidable, from what they do when it is yet doubtful, and only threatens at a distance.
Anonymous, *The Birmingham Counterfeit*, II

Reason, that unerring light within us which, when we are not blinded by passion, will always teach us to distinguish right from wrong. Anonymous, *Fatal Friendship*, II

When reason sleeps, extravagance breaks loose: quality and peasantry pig together: and there is no difference between the lord and his footman.
Anonymous, *The History of Tom Jones in His Married State*, 230

When once reason is drowned, passion always swims on the surface. *Ibid.*, 232

While mankind are continually boasting of their reason, they seldom make use of it. Anonymous, *The Ladies Advocate*, 301

Let a man be endowed by Nature with every noble and elevated attribute she has in her power to bestow, if he lacks sensuality a woman will see him in the clear cold light of reason. Atherton, *Senator North*, Book I, XVIII

Every impulse of feeling should be guided by reason; and exertion should always be in proportion to what is required. Austen, *Pride and Prejudice*, Volume I, VII

Reason is the only argument that belongs to man.
Brackenridge, *Modern Chivalry*, Part I, Volume II

General reason is a safer ground than doubtful decisions. *Ibid.*, Part II, Volume I

There is nothing that alarms a dunce so much as the idea of reason.
Ibid., Part II, Volume II

A vein of reason ever ran through her passion: she was logical even when fierce.
Bronte, C., *Villette*, IV

Miserable reasoners are we all. Brown, W. H., *The Power of Sympathy*, 167

The closet reasoner is always refined in his sentiments, and always confident in his virtue; but when he mixes with the world, when he thinks less and acts more, he soon finds the necessity of accommodating himself to such customs as are already received, and of pursuing quietly the track that is already marked out. Burney, *Cecilia*, I

Deep reasoners, when they are also nice casuists, frequently resolve with a tardiness which renders their resolutions of no effect. *Ibid.*, II

So much stronger is our reason than our virtue, so much higher our sense of duty than our performance! *Ibid.*, III

Who teaches man's reason, but the inward devils of his impulses?
Caruthers, *Kentuckian in New-York*, Volume I, VI

Men who have elected to govern their lives by principles of abstract right and reason, which happen, perhaps, to be at variance with what society considers equally right and reasonable, should, for fear of complications, be careful about descending from the lofty heights of logic to the common level of impulse and affection.
Chesnutt, *The House Behind the Cedars*, II

Nothing preaches so powerfully or leads more surely into a return to reason than the experienced insufficiency of a course of folly and vice, even to the end of pleasure aimed at in it. Cleland, *Memoirs of a Coxcomb*, 329

Cultivate a superiority to reason, and see how you pare the claws of all the sensible people when they try to scratch you for your own good.
Collins, *The Moonstone*, First Period, XX

Before this time I have always especially disliked corpulent humanity. I have always maintained that the popular notion of connecting excessive grossness of size and excessive good-humor as inseparable allies was equivalent to declaring either that no people ever get fat, or that the accidental addition of so many pounds of flesh has a directly favorable influence over the disposition of the person on whose body they accumulate. I have invariably combated both these absurd assertions by quoting examples of fat people who were as mean, vicious, and cruel as the leanest and worst of their neighbors. I have asked whether Henry the Eighth was an amiable character? Whether Pope Alexander the Sixth was a good man? Whether hired nurses, proverbially as cruel a set of women as are to be found in all England, were not, for the most part, also as fat a set of women as are to be found in all England?
Collins, *The Woman in White*, Part I, Second Epoch

There is reason in your words, for they are bottomed on religion and honesty.
Cooper, *The Last of the Mohicans*, XX

The reasoning which is drawn from particular abuses, is no reasoning for general uses. Cooper, *The Monikins*, Conclusion

He reasoned me out of my reason. Defoe, *Moll Flanders*, 53

As reason is the substance and original of the mathematics, so by stating and squaring everything by reason, and by making the most rational judgment of things, every man may be in time master of every mechanic art. Defoe, *Robinson Crusoe*, 66

Reasoning is worse than scolding.   Dickens, *David Copperfield*, XLIV

How limited is human reason, the profoundest inquirers are most conscious. We are not indebted to the reason of man for any of the great achievements which are the landmarks of human action and human progress.   Disraeli, *Coningsby*, Book IV, XIII

There's rasons in things as nobody knows on.   Eliot, *Silas Marner*, VI

Reason, however we flatter ourselves, hath not such despotic empire in our minds, that it can, with imperial voice, hush all our sorrow in a moment.
         Fielding, H., *Jonathan Wild*, 127

Reason is known to be a very idle fellow and seldom to exert himself.
         Fielding, H., *Tom Jones*, 268

One of those secret spontaneous emotions of the soul to which the reason is often a stranger.   *Ibid.*, 500

There are few persons of so phlegmatic a constitution as to content themselves with merely rational pursuits.   Graves, *The Spiritual Quixote*, II

The reason of man is bounded. He sees only the present, and deems it evil, because his narrow comprehension can understand no further; whereas, could his contracted sight extend, he would view himself but as one atom, suffered to act for the universal good of the whole.   Helme, *St. Margaret's Cave*, Volume II, V

Why can't they let people have a chance to behave reasonably in stories?
         Howells, *Silas Lapham*, XVI

Do not disturb your mind with other hopes or fears than reason may suggest.
         Johnson, *Rasselas*, 64

He thought it unsuitable to a reasonable being to act without a plan, and to be sad or cheerful only by chance.   *Ibid.*, 74

He compared reason to the sun, of which light is constant, uniform, and lasting; and fancy to a meteor, of bright but transitory lustre, irregular in its motion and delusive in its direction.   *Ibid.*, 77

Few can be supposed to act upon any occasions with all the reasons of action present to their minds.   *Ibid.*, 114

Wretched would be those who should be doomed to adjust by reason, every morning, all the minute detail of a domestic day.   *Ibid.*

The original of ancient customs is commonly unknown, for the practice often continues when the cause has ceased, and concerning superstitious ceremonies it is vain to conjecture, for what reason did not dictate, reason cannot explain.   *Ibid.*, 183

He who will determine against that which he knows, because there may be something which he knows not—he that can set hypothetical possibility against acknowledged certainty—is not to be admitted among reasonable beings.   *Ibid.*, 185

Disgrace not reason by making an excuse for virtue.   Johnstone, *Arsaces*, I

I asked for reasons, not sermons.   Kingsley, *Hereward the Wake*, XXXII

What is the beginning of reason but the beginning of sorrow?
     Kirkby, *The Capacity of Human Understanding*, 116

There is no fire so hot but it is quenched with water, neither affection so strong but is weakened with reason.   Lyly, *Euphues*, 147

To give reason for fancy were to weigh the fire and measure the wind.   *Ibid.*, 155

Let reason be the pilot when passion blows the gale.
     Marishall, *Miss Clarinda Cathcart*, I

Is not reason subtile as quicksilver—live as lightning—a neighing charger to advance, but a snail to recede?
Melville, *Mardi*, CXXXV

Reason was the first revelation; and so far as it tests all others, it has precedence over them.
Ibid., CLXXV

Deliver yourself by permit of your cheque on the Bank of Reason, and your account is increased instead of lessened.
Meredith, *The Amazing Marriage*, XXXIV

To be pointedly rational is a greater difficulty to me than a fine delirium.
Meredith, *Diana of the Crossways*, I

Our reason is our own. Our feelings we inherit.
Moore, *Evelyn Innes*, XIII

He doth follow the course of nature who, in desiring and refusing things, is ruled by reason.
More, *Utopia*, II

There is a period when all reasoning must yield to nature.
Radcliffe, *The Mysteries of Udolpho*, I

Those who follow the banners of Reason are like the well-disciplined battalion, which, wearing a more sober uniform, and making a less dazzling show, than the light troops commanded by Imagination, enjoy more safety, and even more honor, in the conflicts of human life.
Scott, *Redgauntlet*, XVIII

Reason hath eyes to see his own ill case.
Sidney, *Arcadia*, II

Is not Reason dim with Passion's might?
Ibid.

Reason shrunk before the thronging ideas of his fancy.
Smollett, *Ferdinand, Count Fathom*, LXIII

A fig for reason. I laugh at reason; give me ocular demonstration.
Smollett, *Roderick Random*, 110

Reason's between two people.
Stevenson, *The Wrecker*, XXIV

Lunatics always reason well within their own scope.
Stoker, *Dracula*, VI

No person can disobey reason without giving up his claim to be a rational creature.
Swift, *Gulliver's Travels*, Houyhnhnms, X

I can stand brute force, but brute reason is quite unbearable. There is something unfair about its use. It is hitting below the intellect.
Wilde, *The Picture of Dorian Gray*, III

REBUKE

It is not in the words others say to us, but in those other words which these make us say to ourselves, that we find our gravest lessons and our sharpest rebukes.
Holmes, *Guardian Angel*, XV

Young men are naturally impatient of rebuke. They reprove the reprover, and instruct their teachers in their turn.
Kidgell, *The Card*, I

RECEPTIVENESS; RECIPROCITY

The eagerness of a listener quickens the tongue of a narrator.
Bronte, C., *Jane Eyre*, XIX

Nothing gives such life and soul to youthful gaiety as the consciousness that it is successfully received.
Scott, *Quentin Durward*, XVIII

RECONCILIATION

Reconciliation is the tenderest part of love and friendship: the soul here discovers a kind of elasticity, and, being forced back, returns with an additional violence.
Brooke, *Emily Montague*, IV

RECONCILIATION (*continued*)

People who really love will grant anything in the moment of reconciliation.
Fielding, S., *David Simple*, II

Face to face many a quarrel is made up, which distance will keep alive and widened.
Richardson, *Clarissa Harlowe*, IV

Those reconciliations are the most durable in which the lady makes the advances.
Richardson, *Sir Charles Grandison*, Two, IV

REFINEMENT: *see also* IMPROVEMENT

It is not an infallible sign of great mental refinement to bespatter our fellow-creatures, while every nerve is writhing in honor of our pigs, our cats, our stocks, and our stones.
Cooper, *The Monikins*, Conclusion

Super-refinements put a man out of sympathy with much that is basic in humanity.
Ford, *The Honorable Peter Stirling*, XLVI

REFLECTION: *see also* MEMORY

A man capable of reflection, where a beautiful young creature is in question, can have no soul nor vitals.
Burney, *Camilla*, Two, III

It is curious to imagine people of the world, busy in thought, turning their eyes towards the countless spheres that shine above us, and making them reflect the only images their minds contain. The man who lives but in the breath of princes, has nothing in his sight but stars for courtiers' breasts. The envious man beholds his neighbors' honors even in the sky; to the money-hoarder, and the mass of worldly folk, the whole great universe above glitters with sterling coin—fresh from the mint—stamped with the sovereign's head coming always between them and heaven, turn where they may. So do the shadows of our own desires stand between us and our better angels, and thus their brightness is eclipsed.
Dickens, *Barnaby Rudge*, XXIX

The common reflection among old bachelors is whether they have lived in vain.
Gibbes, *Mr. Francis Clive*, I

There is not one who does not dread the moment when solitude shall deliver him to the tyranny of reflection.
Johnson, *Rasselas*, 73

Banish reflection, or be lost.
Richardson, *Clarissa Harlowe*, II

Recollection is my enemy!
Ibid.

The morning after a debauch is usually one of reflection, even to the most determined boon companion.
Scott, *St. Ronan's Well*, XXIII

The art of those whose minds have been troubled with the malady of reverie.
Wilde, *The Picture of Dorian Gray*, XI

REFORM; REFORMATION

It is natural to distrust him who proposes to stop short of what seems a complete reform.
Brackenridge, *Modern Chivalry*, Part II, I

Down with the lawyers has been the language of the human heart ever since the first institution of society. A spirit of reform is a salutary temper of the times; because there is at all times need of reformation.
Ibid., Part II, II

The spirit of reform is terrible in its excess. It is a matter of great judgment to stay it at a proper point.
Ibid.

What man can set the world right?
Ibid.

A reformed mind is more valuable than one that has plodded on in a continued beaten path, merely from being exempt from the same temptations which may have misled a less unworthy person.
Gibbs, *Mr. Francis Clive*, I

The first step to reformation is to subdue sudden gusts of passion, from which frequently the greatest evils arise, and to learn to bear disappointments.

Richardson, *Clarissa Harlowe*, I

Reformation cannot be sudden work.   *Ibid.*, II

We hope to live to sense, as long as sense can relish, and purpose to reform when we can sin no longer.   *Ibid.*

Reformation is oftentimes generated from unsuccessful vice.

Smollett, *Ferdinand, Count Fathom*, LVI

If you want to mar a nature, you have merely to reform it.

Wilde, *The Picture of Dorian Gray*, VI

REFUGE: *see also* SECURITY

There is a sort of refuge which always comes with the prostration of thought under an overpowering passion.   Eliot, *Silas Marner*, V

A hermitage in the forest is the refuge of the narrow-minded misanthrope; a hammock on the ocean is the asylum for the generous distressed. The ocean brims with natural griefs and tragedies; and into that watery immensity of terror, man's private grief is lost like a drop.   Melville, *Israel Potter*, II

REGARD

There are so many drawbacks to regard and intimacy, from pride, from propriety, and various other collateral causes, that rarely as we meet with people of brilliant parts, there is almost ever some objection to our desire of meeting them again.

Burney, *Cecilia*, I

REGENERATION: *see also* BIRTH

He who would regenerate society must first regenerate himself, and then his virtues must act as a contagion acts, by contact of man with man.   Daniel, *Ai*, XXXIV

REGRET

There are some landmarks on the road to the tomb, which, but for the impiety of the aspiration, a man would wish never to have passed.

Dickens, *David Copperfield*, XLIX

What cannot be repaired is not to be regretted.   Johnson, *Rasselas*, 28

REJOICING: *see also* HAPPINESS

"Hurrah for nothing!" seems to embody the full amount of most men's matter for rejoicing.   Simms, *Woodcraft*, XIX

RELIEF

The geatest object in the universe, says a certain philosopher, is a good man struggling with adversity; yet there is still a greater, which is the good man that comes to relieve it.

Goldsmith, *The Vicar of Wakefield*, 182

Nothing is more dangerous than flying for relief from any distress to folly.

Johnstone, *The Reverie*, I

Harassed beyond its bearing, the mind seeks insensibly the balm designed by nature for its restoration.   Lathom, *The Midnight Bell*, I

RELIGION; REVERENCE: *see also* BELIEF; GOD; etc.

Religion is a terrible battle, to be won or lost. Adams, H., *Esther*, V

Religion is passion. To reach Heaven you must go through hell, and carry its marks on your face and figure. *Ibid.*

Religion is so far from being rightly understood, that it is rendered by some explainers the most doubtful and disputable thing in the world. Amory, *John Buncle*, I

The practice of reason and truth is the rule of action to God himself, and the foundation of all true religion. *Ibid.*, II

When the pleasures of the world elude our pursuits, we fly naturally to devotion. Anonymous, *Fatal Friendship*, II

Avoid what religion calls temptation and the world opportunities. Anonymous, *The History of Tom Jones in His Married State*, 292

The best of men strive more or less constantly toward an ideal which, if realized, would make this world a very different place. It is this instinct alone which is responsible for religions. Atherton, *The Californians*, Book I, XI

Men drop religion the moment the wings on their mind grow fast. Atherton, *Doomswoman*, V

Is religion impossible without fanaticism? Atherton, *Los Cerritos*, Part II, XVI

The camp-meeting is probably to the Methodist what the confessional is to the Catholic. Both must ease one's mind a lot. Atherton, *Senator North*, Book II, XXI

What has Puritanism resulted in? Its whole struggle has come to an end in doubt and agnosticism and flippancy. Intellectual curiosity has taken the place of spiritual stress; ethical casuistry or theological amusements seem to stand instead of religious conviction. Bates, *Puritans*, XXXII

It is true that, formerly in the infancy of the church, a knowledge of languages and sciences might be requisite. But the case is altered now. The Scripture has been well explained, and frequently preached over; every text and context examined, and passages illustrated. The Hebrew roots, so to speak, have been all dug up; and there is scarcely a new etymology to be made. Are there any new doctrines to discover? I should think it impossible. At any rate, I should conceive it unnecessary. These are enough in all conscience. In state affairs, ignorance does very well, and why not in church? Brackenridge, *Modern Chivalry*, Part I, I

Religion is of no government. *Ibid.*, Part II, I

In the propagation of a new religion, or in a new tenet of a particular faith, what is moderate will be less likely to prevail in the opinions of men. The absurd is always the most popular, and this upon the principle that artificial tastes are stronger than the natural; and what produces the greatest excitement is most pleasing to the mind. *Ibid.*, Part II, IV

The end of religion is not to teach us how to die, but how to live. Bronte, A., *Agnes Grey*, XXIII

A religious man does not want to reason about his religion—religion is not mathematics. Religion is to be felt, not proved. There are a great many things in the religion of a good man which are not in the catechism. Bulwer, *The Caxtons*, Book III, IV

His house is as empty of religion as the white of an egg is of savor. Bunyan, *Pilgrim's Progress*, 80

The soul of religion is the practic part. *Ibid.*, 82

We love much to walk with Religion in the street, if the sun shines and the people applaud him. *Ibid.*, 102

That man that takes up religion for the world will throw away religion for the world. *Ibid.*, 108-109

Some have spoken well of a pilgrim's life at first that after a while have spoken as much against it. *Ibid.*, 271

I have loved to hear my Lord spoken of; and wherever I have seen the print of his shoe in the earth, there I have coveted to set my foot too. *Ibid.*, 328–329

They had no sense of a hereafter, and their only religion was that of self-respect and consideration for other people. Butler, *Erewhon*, XVII

I like religion well enough of a Sunday.
Caruthers, *Kentuckian in New-York*, Volume I, II

Have purgatorial fires no purifying power, that we can be purified as much by repeating a few words of devotion at certain altars as by centuries of agony in the flames? Charles, *Chronicles of the Schonberg-Cotta Family*, X

The sentiment of religion is so high and pure, depends so completely upon the untrammelled operation of the human heart, that any legislation which tends to circumscribe it and reduce it to a rule must eternally fail, and operate woefully for the great interest of mankind. Cooke, *Virginia Comedians*, Volume II, XIII

Religious toleration is the first and most important duty of a state. *Ibid.*

Religion is a paradox, in which self-denial and humility are proposed as tenets, in direct contradiction to every man's senses. Cooper, *The Monikins*, Conclusion

Goot men have no neet of so much religion. Vhen a man is *really* goot, religion only does him harm. I mean Yankee religion. Cooper, *Satanstoe*, Volume I, II

An old-fashioned theologian might say that a man who has no good in him is not properly fit to be damned. Such a man would have no free-will, and could not, therefore, logically be punished for anything he did. Crawford, *Corleone*, XXV

As I knew nothing about religion, neither Protestant from Papist, or either of them from a Mahometan, I could never be a heretic. Defoe, *Captain Singleton*, 9

There is priestcraft even amongst the most blinded ignorant pagans in the world.
Defoe, *Robinson Crusoe*, 193

Religion should be a faith and not a form. Disraeli, *Coningsby*, Book III, V

The character of a church is universality. *Ibid.*, Book VII, II

"Sensible men are all of the same religion." "And pray, what is that?" "Sensible men never tell." Disraeli, *Endymion*

Let us take religion upon its broadest base, for the truth must be broader than aught which we can conceive. Doyle, *Micah Clarke*, XXII

Long ere Religion had made up her mind to meet Science halfway, and hobnob and kiss and be friends. DuMaurier, *Trilby*, V

Poor, blind, conceited humanity! Interpreters of God, indeed! We reduce the Deity to vulgar fractions. We measure infinity with a foot-rule. Dunbar, *The Uncalled*, IX

I'm not for laughing at no man's religion. Let 'em follow their consciences, that's all. Only I think it 'ud be better if their consciences 'ud let 'em stay quiet i' the church— there's a deal to be learnt there. And there's such a thing as being oversperitial; we must have something beside Gospel i' this world. Eliot, *Adam Bede*, I

It isn't for men to make channels for God's Spirit, as they make channels for the watercourses, and say, "Flow here, but flow not there." *Ibid.*, VIII

Sometimes both men and women fancy themselves channels for God's Spirit, and are quite mistaken, so that they set about a work for which they are unfit and bring holy things into contempt. *Ibid.*

Religion can only change when the emotions which fill it are changed; and the religion of personal fear remains nearly at the level of the savage.
Eliot, *Middlemarch*, Book VI, LXI

Thwackum held that if the end proposed was religious, it mattered not how wicked were the means. Fielding, H., *Tom Jones*, 285

Almost every religion had its Immaculate Conception. What does it all come to, except to show us that man turns naturally toward the worship of the maternal idea? Frederic, *The Damnation of Theron Ware*, Part III, XXIV

That religion which is supported by infamy is viler than atheism. Godwin, *St. Leon*, 320

There is no necessary connection between religion and virtue; and people may be good moral men, and good members of society, without the belief of a God. Graves, *The Spiritual Quixote*, III

Mankind asks ever of the skies to vision out what lies behind them. It is terror for the end, and but a subtler form of selfishness—this it is that breeds religion. Haggard, *She*, XVII

There are states of our spiritual system when the throb of the soul's life is too faint and weak to render us capable of religious aspiration. Hawthorne, *The Blithedale Romance*, XXI

In Italy religion jostles along side by side with business and sport, after a fashion of its own, and people are accustomed to kneel down and pray, or see others praying, between two fits of merriment, or between two sins. Hawthorne, *The Marble Faun*, XVII

Catholicism is such a miracle of fitness for its own ends, many of which might seem to be admirable ones, that it is difficult to imagine it a contrivance of mere man. *Ibid.*, XXXVIII

In religious matters there are great multitudes watching us perpetually, each propagandist ready with his bundle of finalities, which having accepted we may be at peace. Holmes, *Elsie Venner*, XVIII

The supreme self-indulgence is to surrender the will to a spiritual director. Holmes, *Guardian Angel*, XXXV

My father's religion would have been unsatisfactory without a hell. Howe, *The Story of a Country Town*, II

"Our religion sometimes gives us very difficult duties." "The duty of sitting in a white-washed meeting-house and listening to a nasal Puritan! That's difficult. But it's not sublime." James, H., *Roderick Hudson*, XVII

Can any duty be more incumbent on man than to propagate the true religion, even by force, where persuasion fails? Is not every man who refuses to receive it an enemy to God, and as such to be cut off from among men? Johnstone, *Arsaces*, I

True piety cannot be represented to sense. *Ibid.*, II

Whenever you see a man perform religious exercises in public, and especially if he affects to exceed in them, you may safely conclude either that his reason is disordered or that he acts from motives different from those which he professes. *Ibid.*

Nothing is made a greater cloak for wickedness than religion. Kimber, *Maria*, II

In the awful day of retribution, God will dreadfully distinguish the bigoted dictators in religion. Lee, *The Recess*, II

Out of itself, Religion has nothing to bestow. Nor will she save us from aught, but from the evil in ourselves. Her one grand end is to make us wise; her only, but ample reward, herself. Melville, *Mardi*, CXXIV

Any poor sinner may go to church wherever he pleases. Melville, *Redburn*, XLI

You speak of the Lord loving his own; you make out the Lord to be *your* own, and use your religion like a drug. Meredith, *Beauchamp's Career*, XIX

The religion of this vast English middle-class ruling the land is Comfort.   *Ibid.*, XXIX

She relapsed upon religion and little dogs.

Meredith, *Ordeal of Richard Feverel*, XXII

I believe everything except Atheism, and unthinking contentment. I believe in Christianity, but I am not so foolish as to limit myself to Christianity; I look upon Christianity as part of the truth, but not the whole truth. There is a continuous revelation: before Christ Buddha, before Buddha Krishna, who was crucified in mid-heaven, and the Gods of my race live too.   Moore, G., *Evelyn Innes*, XIV

We are not atheists, except in practice.   Richardson, *Clarissa Harlowe*, III

No religion teaches a man evil.   Richardson, *Sir Charles Grandison*, One, II

Religion is like love. It flourishes best in silence, and is to be felt, not spoken of.

Schreiner, *Undine*, VII

Nobody's *nothing*. You aren't a Unitrinitarian, are you?   *Ibid.*, XV

There are some remains of religion left in the human mind, even after every moral sentiment hath abandoned it; the most exercrable ruffian finds means to quiet the suggestions of his conscience, by some reversionary hope of Heaven's forgiveness.

Smollett, *Ferdinand, Count Fathom*, VII

There can be no religion without mercy.   Sterne, *Tristram Shandy*, II

Whenever a man talks loudly against religion, always suspect that it is not his reason, but his passions, which have got the better of his creed.   *Ibid.*

There was no God in his estimate of life—and a sort of secret unsuspected determination at the bottom of his heart that there should be none. He feared religion, from a suspicion which he entertained that it might hamper some of his future schemes. He did not wish to put himself under its rules, lest he might find them in some future time inconveniently strict.   Stowe, *Orr's Island* XXIV

Religion being the best of things, its corruptions are likely to be the worst.

Swift, *A Tale of a Tub*, Apology

What though his head be empty, provided his Commonplace Book be full.

Ibid., Section VII

I'm not much on religion; but I'm strong on humanity.

Tourgee, *Murvale Eastman*, IX

The religious "boomer" is sometimes a man who is supposed to be especially good because he has aforetime been especially bad.   *Ibid.*, XXVII

I am an enemy of everything that calls itself religion, which lifts one man above another in earthly privilege or opportunity.   Tourgee, *Pactolus Prime*, XI

It is piety alone that can distinguish us from the dust whence we sprung and whither we must return.   Walpole, *The Castle of Otranto*, 56

Religion is the fashionable substitute for belief.

Wilde, *The Picture of Dorian Gray*, XVII

Many are called impious, not for having a worse, but a different religion from their neighbors; and many atheistical, not for the denying of God, but for thinking somewhat peculiarly concerning him.   Wright, *A Few Days in Athens*, I

The leading error of the human mind, the bane of human happiness, the perverter of human virtue, is religion, that dark coinage of trembling ignorance. It is religion, that poisoner of human felicity. It is religion, that blind guide of human reason. It is religion, that dethroner of human virtue, which lies at the root of all the evil and all the misery that pervade the world.   *Ibid.*, XVI

The world is full of religion, and full of misery and crime.   *Ibid.*

It is not that religion is merely useless, it is mischievous. It is mischievous by its idle terrors; it is mischievous by its false morality; it is mischievous by its hypocrisy; by its fanaticism; by its dogmatism; but its threats; by its hopes; by its promises.   *Ibid.*

It is a sad misfortune that anything of such great and real importance to mankind as religion should ever become the favorite study and topic of people whose striking characteristics are ignorance and bigotry.   Young, *The Adventures of Emmera*, I

REMEDY: *see also* CAUSE AND EFFECT; IMPROVEMENT; etc.

The knowledge that one has a remedy within reach is often as effectual as the remedy itself.   Anstey, *Tourmalin's Time Cheques*, II

There is no one want or weakness of human nature for which Catholicism will own itself without a remedy.   Hawthorne, *The Marble Faun*, XXXVIII

Thou canst cut off the head, but not cure the aching tooth.   Scott, *The Talisman*, XIX

REMORSE: *see also* REGRET

Remorse is the poison of life.   Bronte, C., *Jane Eyre*, XIV

Remorse is very busy.   Trowbridge, *Neighbor Jackwood*, IX

RENUNCIATION

The mind should be entirely disengaged from all worldly hopes before it can renounce it properly.   Parsons, *Castle of Wolfenbach*, II

REPARATION

There's a sort of wrong that can never be made up for.   Eliot, *Adam Bede*, Epilogue

It's foolish work, tearing things to pieces to sew 'em together again.
          Eliot, *The Mill on the Floss*, Book I, II

A knot that is unloosed may again be fastened, but not so the cord which has been cut to pieces.   Scott, *The Talisman*, XI

Things sometimes are fixed which must be unfixed.
          Trollope, *The Eustace Diamonds*, XXX

REPENTANCE: *see also* REFORM; REFORMATION

There are degrees of vice that repentance cannot reach.
          Anonymous, *The Life of Sir Richard Perrott*, 33

"Repentance is said to be the cure of remorse." "It is not its cure. Reformation may be."
          Bronte, C., *Jane Eyre*, XIV

Remorse is an ample and proper expiation for all offenses.
          Brown, C. B., *Edgar Huntley*, 24

Confession is a token of repentance.   Brown, C. B., *Ormond*, 122

Sick-bed repentance is seldom good for anything.
          Bunyan, *The Life and Death of Mr. Badman*, 273

Sparing thieves from the gallows makes more penitents than the gallows itself.
          Defoe, *Colonel Jack*, 166

I was a penitent not that I had sinned, but that I was to suffer.
          Defoe, *Moll Flanders*, 284-285

The true penitent, hating his self-besotted error, asks from all coming life duty instead of joy, and service instead of ease.　　　　　　　　　Eliot, *Felix Holt*, XV

Repentance never failed to follow his transgressions; and yet so perverse is our judgment, and so slippery is the descent of vice when once we are entered into it, the same crime which he now repented of became a reason for doing that which was to cause his future repentance; and he continued to sin on because he had begun.　　　Fielding, H., *Amelia*, I

Repentance, from a just sense of the crime committed, gives an humility which renders the grief less turbulent, and makes way for the rise of some comfortable considerations, even from suffering the punishment which naturally follows the indulgence of violent passions.　　　　　　　　　Fielding, S., *The Countess of Dellwyn*, II

He was a John the Baptist who took ennoblement rather than repentance for his text.
　　　　　　　　　　　　　　Hardy, *Return of the Native*, Book III, II

What repentance, what self-sacrifice, can atone for infinite wrong?
　　　　　　　　　　　　　　Hawthorne, *The Marble Faun*, XXXV

Is there no reality in the penitence sealed and witnessed by good works?
　　　　　　　　　　　　　　Hawthorne, *The Scarlet Letter*, XVII

Here had been her sin; here, her sorrow; and here was yet to be her penitence.
　　　　　　　　　　　　　　Ibid., XXIV

As we have youth and health in hand, we hope to have time for repentance.
　　　　　　　　　　　　　　Richardson, *Clarissa Harlowe*, II

Foolish is the penitent who has nothing to repent of.　　　　　　　*Ibid.*, III

How transitory is penitence!　　　　　　　　　　　　　　　*Ibid.*

A man cannot repent when he will.　　　　　　　　　　　　　*Ibid.*

By fits and starts I have repented a thousand times.　　　　　　　*Ibid.*

Reparation follows repentance.　　　　　　　　　　　　　*Ibid.*, IV

No false colorings, no glosses, does a true penitent aim at.　　　　　*Ibid.*

Debasement, diffidence, mortification, contrition, are all near of kin; and inseparable from a repentant spirit.　　　　　　　　　　　　　　*Ibid.*

There is no use in wailing and repentance here: the next world is the place for that; this life is too short.　　　　　　Schreiner, *The Story of an African Farm*, Part II, VI

Cool repentance.　　　　　　　　　　　　　　Scott, *Rob Roy*, XII

If we were to attempt to reform all our bad ways at once, we should never do any good thing.　　　　　　　　　　　Trollope, *The Way We Live Now*, I

REPERCUSSION: *see also* CAUSE AND EFFECT

Everything has its drawbacks, as the man said when his mother-in-law died, and they came down upon him for the funeral expenses.　　Jerome, *Three Men in a Boat*, III

REPETITION

There is scarcely anything when a man is in difficulties that he is more disposed to look upon with abhorrence than a right-about retrograde movement—a systematic going over of the already trodden ground.　　　　　　　Melville, *Typee*, VIII

REPRESENTATION: *see also* SIGN; SYMBOL; TYPE; etc.

A great city, whose image dwells in the memory of man, is the type of some great idea. Rome represents Conquest; Faith hovers over the towers of Jerusalem; and Athens embodies the pre-eminent quality of the antique world—Art.
　　　　　　　　　　　　　　Disraeli, *Coningsby*, Book IV, I

REPRESENTATION (*continued*)

The fragment of a life, however typical, is not the sample of an even web: promises may not be kept, and an ardent outset may be followed by declension; latent powers may find their long-waited opportunity; a past error may urge a grand retrieval.
Eliot, *Middlemarch*, Book VIII, Finale

REPRIMAND; REPROACH; REPROOF

Where reproof takes any effect, it is not received with easiness.   Burney, *Cecilia*, II

If people never did anything to reproach themselves for, they would seldom meet with the reproach of the world.   Jenner, *The Placid Man*, II

Do not reproach yourself for virtue or consider that as blamable by which evil has accidentally been caused.   Johnson, *Rasselas*, 129

The conscious heart is easily alarmed. Too ready sensibility takes the imputation that was never meant, and turns general satire into particular reproach.
Johnstone, *The Reverie*, I

It is for the injured to reproach.   Richardson, *Clarissa Harlowe*, III

Reproof seldom amends a determined spirit.
Richardson, *Sir Charles Grandison*, Two, IV

REPUTATION

To take upon credit is a blur to a gentleman's reputation.
Anonymous, *The History of Tom Jones in His Married State*, 271

To murder one's own reputation is a kind of suicide, a detestable and odious vice.
Fielding, H., *Tom Jones*, 180

You have to obtain reputation before you can get a fair hearing for that which would justify your repute.   Gissing, *New Grub Street*, XXVIII

One's good name is one's livelihood.   Graves, *The Spiritual Quixote*, II

One man had better steal a horse than another look over the hedge at it.
Lawrence, G. A., *Common Sense*, II

To a mind of any delicacy, nothing is so shocking as to have a reputation to defend.
Lennox, *Henrietta*, I

I could not avoid thinking that I had fallen in with a greatly traduced people, and I moralized not a little upon the disadvantage of having a bad name, which in this instance had given a tribe of savages, who were as pacific as so many lambkins, the reputation of a confederacy of giantkillers.   Melville, *Typee*, XVII

There is only one thing in the world worse than being talked about, and that is not being talked about.   Wilde, *The Picture of Dorian Gray*, I

"All good hats are made out of nothing." "Like all good reputations."   *Ibid.*, XVII

RESCUE

If you save a man's life he'll make you rue it.   Reade, *Griffith Gaunt*, XXVI

RESENTMENT

We call in question the understanding of a man when he wrongs us; and say, if he had the reflection of a reasonable being, he would have conducted himself in a different manner. And yet the consideration that he had not reflection does not mitigate, but increases our resentment.   Brackenridge, *Modern Chivalry*, Part II, I

Do not suffer extravagant resentment to operate against true interests.

Radcliffe, *The Romance of the Forest*, 406

RESERVE: *see also* FRANKNESS; LIBERALITY

Reserve is a most repulsive quality. Oftentimes very convenient, no doubt, but never pleasing. There is safety in reserve, but no attraction. One cannot love a reserved person.

Austen, *Emma*, XXIV

Reserve is painful to an open and liberal mind.

Jenner, *The Placid Man*, I

RESIGNATION

Where resignation is voluntary, to give up a higher place may denote more greatness of mind than to retain it; but where imposed by others, few things are less exhilarating to the principal, or impress less respect upon the bystander.

Burney, *Camilla*, Five, IX

Resignation is sublime.

Collins, *The Woman in White*, Part II, Third Epoch

Resignation is the willing endurance of a pain that is not allayed, that you don't expect to be allayed.

Eliot, *The Mill on the Floss*, Book V, III

The lowest depth of resignation is not to be found in martyrdom; it is only to be found when we have covered our heads in silence and felt, "I am worthy to be a martyr; the Truth shall prosper, but not by me."

Eliot, *Romola*, Book III, LXVI

She resigned her position—which hath been always held a synonymous expression with being turned out, or turned away.

Fielding, H., *Tom Jones*, 297

To resign a real good with contentment is less an effort of reason than of temper.

Radcliffe, *The Romance of the Forest*, 347

Every wise man, when he sees a rock giving way, withdraws from the bootless attempt of preventing the fall.

Scott, *Quentin Durward*, XXX

RESISTANCE: *see also* REVOLT; REVOLUTION; WAR; etc.

The influence of climate no resistance can overcome.

Eliot, *Adam Bede*, X

Evils we have never experienced we are unprepared to resist.

Harley, *Priory of St. Bernard*, I

It is always the way of those who intend not to mend, to set their hearts against their correctors.

Richardson, *Sir Charles Grandison*, Two, V

Passive resistance.

Scott, *The Heart of Midlothian*, VI

RESOLUTION

A meeting without resolutions is an ocean without froth.

Beard, *Bristling With Thorns*, XXX

Resolution is necessary to decision unequivocal and satisfactory, unawed by forensic opinion or the influence of individuals.

Brackenridge, *Modern Chivalry*, Part II, I

To sustain life, under certain circumstances, calls for more resolution than to commit suicide.

Ibid.

All human resolution has its limits.

Collins, *The Woman in White*, Part II, Third Epoch

Resolutions taken in the absence of the beloved object are very apt to vanish in its presence.

Fielding, H., *Joseph Andrews*, 27

When a lady hath once taken a resolution to run to a lover, or to run from him, all obstacles are considered as trifles.

Fielding, H., *Tom Jones*, 290

RESOLUTION (*continued*)

Resolutions are easily formed when the heart suggests them.　　Lennox, *Henrietta*, I

Wrought up to a half-resolution.　　Richardson, *Clarissa Harlowe*, II

To fail of one's resolutions is to become the scoff of men, and the triumph of devils.
　　Ibid., IV

There is a fatality about good resolutions—they are always made too late.
　　Wilde, *The Picture of Dorian Gray*, VIII

Good resolutions are useless attempts to interfere with scientific laws. Their origin is pure vanity.　　*Ibid.*

RESOURCE; RESOURCEFULNESS

It is a strange, but no uncommon feature in the human mind, that the very resource of which we stand in greatest need in a critical situation fails to present itself at the time when it should be called into action.　　Godwin, *Caleb Williams*, II

Youth has wonderful resources against every evil but the sense of shame.
　　Simms, *Vasconselos*, XXIV

RESPECT; RESPECTABILITY

Ceremony is odious, but little tokens of respectful consideration cannot be dispensed with.　　Anonymous, *The Fruitless Repentance*, I

Be honest and poor—but I shall not envy you; I do not much think I shall even respect you. I have a much greater respect for those that are honest and rich.
　　Austen, *Mansfield Park*, Volume Two, IV

The great secret of preserving respect, is the cultivating and shewing to the best advantage the powers that we possess, and the not going beyond them.
　　Brackenridge, *Modern Chivalry*, Part I, I

I never knew a worsted man any the more respected for his mishap.
　　Cooper, *Satanstoe*, Volume II, VIII

A man may be respectable and yet have a good hunger on him.
　　Crane, *The O'Ruddy*, XIII

Mr. Vholes is a very respectable man. He has not a large business, but he is a very respectable man. He is allowed by the greater attorneys who have made good fortunes, or are making them, to be a most respectable man. He never misses a chance in his practice; which is a mark of respectability. He never takes any pleasure; which is another mark of respectability. He is reserved and serious, which is another mark of respectability. His digestion is impaired, which is highly respectable.
　　Dickens, *Bleak House*, XXXIX

There seemeth to be implanted in the human mind a natural delight in borrowing the forms, and mimicking the manners, of those persons for whom we have any degree of respect.　　Fielding, S., *The Countess of Dellwyn*, I

Respectable means rich, and decent means poor.　　Peacock, *Crotchet Castle*, III

For persons to endeavor to gain respect by a haughty behavior is to give a proof that they mistrust their own merit: to make confession that they know that their actions will not attract it.　　Richardson, *Clarissa Harlowe*, I

Reverence is too apt to be forgotten by children, where the reverends forget first what belongs to their own characters.　　*Ibid.*, II

No person can live happily with another simply upon esteem.
　　Trollope, *Phineas Finn*, XXIII

Nothing tends so much to respect as a good income.

Trollope, *The Way We Live Now*, XIX

There is that about earthly pomps which doth ever move to reverence.

Twain, *Connecticut Yankee*, XXXII

RESPONSIBILITY

Over the unborn our power is that of God, and our responsibility like His toward us. As we acquit ourselves toward them, so let Him deal with us.

Bellamy, *Looking Backward*, XXV

"You look as if you held me responsible for his death." "Innocently responsible."

Collins, *I Say No*, LXVI

Everybody is obliged to be responsible.   Dickens, *Bleak House*, XXXVII

RESTRAINT; RESTRICTION

It is an uneasy lot at best, to be what we call highly taught and yet not to enjoy: to be present at this great spectacle of life and never to be liberated from a small hungry shivering self—never to be fully possessed by the glory we behold, never to have our consciousness rapturously transformed into the vividness of a thought, the ardor of a passion, the energy of an action, but always to be scholarly and uninspired, ambitious and timid, scrupulous and dimsighted.   Eliot, *Middlemarch*, Book III, XXIX

Nothing shows the natural right of the human soul to liberty so strongly as the reluctance with which it bears every semblance of restraint.   Johnstone, Arsaces, I

It's a dangerous experiment, that of bringing up flesh and blood in harness.

Meredith, *Ordeal of Richard Feverel*, XXI

Decency and a sense of honor restrain most of us from being wise, and miserable, forever.   *Ibid.*, XXVIII

It is possible for young heads to conceive proper plans of action, and occasionally, by sheer force of will, to check the wild horses that are ever fretting to gallop off with them. But when they have given the reins and the whip to another, what are they to do? They may go down on their knees, and beg and pray the furious charioteer to stop, or moderate his speed. Alas! each fresh thing they do redoubles his ardor. Lucy submitting, he chooses his pace. Lucy remonstrating, he is fired to madness.

Ibid., XXXI

Needless watchfulness and undue restraint produce artifice and contrivance.

Richardson, *Clarissa Harlowe*, I

The less restraint, the less affectation.   *Ibid.*, II

RETALIATION

When we are struck at without a reason, we should strike back again very hard.

Bronte, C., *Jane Eyre*, VI

I must dislike those who, whatever I do to please them, persist in disliking me; I must resist those who punish me unjustly.   *Ibid.*

I do not think that under any provocation a woman should use a horsewhip.

Trollope, *The Way We Live Now*, LI

RETRIBUTION: *see also* VENGEANCE

Hanging is too good for him.   Bunyan, *Pilgrim's Progress*, 100

If men cannot stand before the sentence of men, what will they do with the sentence of God?   *Ibid.*, 109

RETRIBUTION (*continued*)

Retribution may come from any voice; the hardest, cruelest, most imbruted urchin at the street-corner can inflict it; surely help and pity are rarer things, more needful for the righteous to bestow.   Eliot, *The Mill on the Floss*, Book VII, II

As the Utopians seek to use good men well, so they seek to abuse evil and vicious men.   More, *Utopia*, II

REVELATION

Be true! Show freely to the world, if not your worst, yet some trait whereby the worst may be inferred!   Hawthorne, *The Scarlet Letter*, XXIV

Let a man be ever so elevated, he must undergo the censure of the world, and after death his real countenance will be unveiled.   Kimber, *David Ranger*, II

Some revelations show best in a twilight.   Melville, *Mardi*, XIX

Let not your face arraign your heart.   Richardson, *Clarissa Harlowe*, III

Green woods have ears.   Scott, *Fair Maid of Perth*, XXIX

REVOLT; REVOLUTION: *see also* RESISTANCE; WAR

In a revolution every man thinks he has done all.   Brackenridge, *Modern Chivalry*, Part II, I

Every system has got to be knocked over by something.   Butler, *The Way of All Flesh*, LXIX

The man who seriously maintains that any pursuit in which he can engage is independent of moral restraint is a man in a state of revolt against God.   Collins, *Heart and Science*, LIX

There is a rebellious soul in things which must be overcome by powerful charms and incantations.   Conrad, *Lord Jim*, XXVII

It does not take a long time for an earthquake to swallow a town. Tell me how long it takes to prepare an earthquake? When it is ready, it takes place, and grinds to pieces everything before it.   Dickens, *Tale of Two Cities*, Book II, XVI

"We shall not see the triumph." "We shall have helped it."   *Ibid.*

I have ever been of opinion that revolutions are not to be evaded.   Disraeli, *Coningsby*, Book IV, XI

Revolt is the forerunner of all great change.   Glasgow, *The Descendant*, Book II, IV

Youth and beauty can never be paired with age and coldness without danger of revolt.   Kimber, *David Ranger*, I

Whoso storms the sky gives best proof he came from thither!   Melville, *Pierre*, Book XXV, V

Rebellion against Society, and advocacy of Humanity, run counter.   Meredith, *Beauchamp's Career*, XXIX

Wilfrid stood like a machine with a thousand wheels in revolt.   Meredith, *Sandra Belloni*, XXX

How can one be such a reptile as not to turn when tramped upon!   Richardson, *Clarissa Harlowe*, I

REWARD: *see also* MERIT

There is a wide distinction between voluntary favors and rewards.   Fielding, H., *Tom Jones*, 193

Deeds worthy of reward often meet with it, while they seem to disdain it.
Hill, *Mr. George Edwards*, 41

This at least is the present reward of virtuous conduct, that no unlucky consequence can oblige us to repent it.
Johnson, *Rasselas*, 130

Stolen fruits are said to be sweet. Undeserved rewards are very exquisite.
Meredith, *Ordeal of Richard Feverel*, IV

There is no manner of act nor deed that gifts and rewards do not enforce men unto.
More, *Utopia*, II

Would anyone commit errors, and expect to be rewarded of them?
Richardson, *Clarissa Harlowe*, III

RIDICULE; SATIRE

What a powerful engine is ridicule! It is the battering-ram of the mind, and will often destroy by a single blow the mightiest fabric of reason. It is used by fools and men whose minds are too imbecile to cope with the edifice of thought which towers above the limited grasp; and yet the very architect of such construction fears it, as does the poor red-man the annihilating artillery of the pale-face.
Bennett, *The Prairie Flower*, X

Mankind is naturally delighted with ridicule.
Brackenridge, *Modern Chivalry*, Part I, I

Everybody is ready to dislike and ridicule any invention.
Dickens, *Little Dorrit*, Book II, XXVIII

An ounce of ridicule is often more potent than a hundred-weight of argument.
Trollope, *The Eustace Diamonds*, LV

There is no character, howsoever good and fine, but it can be destroyed by ridicule, howsoever poor and witless. Observe the ass, for instance: his character is about perfect, he is the choicest spirit among all the humbler animals, yet see what ridicule has brought him to. Instead of feeling complimented when we are called an ass, we are left in doubt.
Twain, *Pudd'nhead Wilson*, A Whisper to the Reader

RIGHT AND WRONG; RIGHTEOUSNESS; RIGHTNESS: *see also* GOOD AND EVIL

Right is a dull weapon, unless skill and good luck manage it.
Anonymous, *The History of Tom Jones in His Married State*, 77

Down with all law, and give us a free government, that every man may do that which is right in his own eyes.
Brackenridge, *Modern Chivalry*, Part II, I

It is an evil that men should do that which is right in their own eyes.
Ibid.

A man is not a proper judge of right in his own cause.
Ibid.

The people are not always right.
Ibid.

Men had rather be suffered to be wrong than to be set right against their wills.
Ibid.

There is a natural rectitude in your heart that the ablest casuists could not mend.
Burney, *Cecilia*, II

Sectarians are prone to substitute their own narrow notions of right and wrong for the Law of God, confounding acts that are perfectly innocent in themselves with sin.
Cooper, *Satanstoe*, Volume I, X

That parent does not sincerely love his child, who to avoid paining him for an instant, by reproving him when he is wrong, does him eternal injury in permitting him to retain the impression that he is right.
Dacre, *Passions*, Letter XIII

An ancient proverb warns us that we should not expect to find old heads upon young shoulders; to which it may be added that we seldom meet with that unnatural combination, but we feel a strong desire to knock them off; merely from an inherent love we have of seeing things in their right places. Dickens, *Martin Chuzzlewit*, XI

A man may wish to be right, and yet be a sort of parchment code. Eliot, *Middlemarch*, Book I, VIII

Giants have an immemorial right to stupidity and insolent abuse. Eliot, *Mill on the Floss*, Book V, V

Parsons and doctors know everything by heart, like so as they aren't worreted wi' thinking what's the rights and wrongs o' things. Eliot, *Silas Marner*, VI

Nothing in this world is worth doing wrong for. *Ibid.*, XVIII

To do right, for the pure love of right, or the love of God, is a very difficult thing. Hale, *Liberia*, II

To act right simply because it is one's duty is proper; but a good action which is the result of no law of reflection shines more than any! Hardy, *Desperate Remedies*, XIX

The people who have always gone right don't know half as much about the nature and ways of going right as those do who have gone wrong. Hardy, *A Pair of Blue Eyes*, XIX

There is only one right and one wrong; and I do not understand, and may God keep me from ever understanding, how two things so totally unlike can be mistaken for one another. Hawthorne, *The Marble Faun*, XLII

How utterly nugatory is the choicest of man's own righteousness. Hawthorne, *The Scarlet Letter*, XXIV

The grand principles of virtue and honor, however they may be distorted by arbitrary codes, are the same all the world over. Melville, *Typee*, XXVII

A gentleman in the right engaged with a fellow in the wrong has nothing to apprehend; is in the position of a game preserver with a poacher. Meredith, *Beauchamp's Career*, XXXIII

There is a too much as well as a too little, even in righteousness, so that we can be wicked in piety. Richardson, *Clarissa Harlowe*, IV

No consideration should influence us to act contrary to our sense of right. Roche, *Nocturnal Visit*, I

The hour's come, but not the man. Scott, *The Heart of Midlothian*, IV

There are rights of nature. Stevenson, *Prince Otto*, Book II, V

Wise people, when they are in the wrong, always put themselves right by finding fault with the people against whom they have sinned. Trollope, *Barchester Towers*, XXXVII

A man in the right relies easily on his rectitude and therefore goes about unarmed. His very strength is his weakness. *Ibid.*

What's the use you learning to do right, when it's troublesome to do right and ain't no trouble to do wrong, and the wages is just the same? Twain, *Huckleberry Finn*, XVI

Right is right, and wrong is wrong, and a body ain't got no business doing wrong when he ain't ignorant and knows better. *Ibid.*, XXXVI

It seems that some people do not belong in the country where they were born. Warner, *A Little Journey*, IV

The right lies with all men in our democracy to sit in a tub, or to walk in a dirty tunic. Wright, *A Few Days in Athens*, IV

RISK: *see also* DANGER; SALVATION; etc.

Men seldom risk their lives where an escape is without hope of recompense.
Burney, *Cecilia*, I

The miminum of risk with the maximum of profit is my motto.   Conrad, *Lord Jim*, XV

To move at his ease, he needed so imperatively the sense of great risks and great prizes.   James, H., *The American*, IV

One never knows when one's taking one's biggest risks.
Kipling, *Captains Courageous*, IX

To divide my affections was to lessen them; to expose them was to risk them: where there is risk, there may be loss.   Sterne, *A Sentimental Journey*, 46

ROMANCE: *see also* ADVENTURE; LOVE; REALITY

There is a romance in every life.   Disraeli, *Coningsby*, Book VII, V

To preserve Romance (we exchange a sky for a ceiling if we let it go), we must be inside the heads of our people as well as the hearts, more than shaking the kaleidoscope of hurried spectacles, in days of a growing activity of the head.
Meredith, *The Amazing Marriage*, XX

A romantic tale on her eyelashes.   Meredith, *The Egoist*, II

Romances are the destruction of human interest. The moment you begin to move the individuals, they are puppets.   Meredith, *Harry Richmond*, XXXIV

The worst of having a romance of any kind is that it leaves one so unromantic.
Wilde, *The Picture of Dorian Gray*, I

Romantic art begins with its climax.   *Ibid.*, XVII

ROUTINE

Man must ever be the slave of routine; but in old days it was a routine of great thoughts, and now it is a routine of little ones.   Disraeli, *Coningsby*, Book IV, XI

ROYALTY: *see also* GOVERNMENT

I would have all men kings.   Goldsmith, *The Vicar of Wakefield*, 99

A real king's life is perhaps a hard one; but a pretended king's is much harder.
Hope, *The Prisoner of Zenda*, VIII

Kings differ in character like other folk; but there is one trait they have in common; they are mightily inclined to be affable to men of very low estate.
Reade, *The Cloister and the Hearth*, XXXVIII

All kings is mostly rapscallions.   Twain, *Huckleberry Finn*, XXIII

RUINATION

I think I rather wished for ruin than studied to avoid it.   Defoe, *Moll Flanders*, 21

When a man lays the foundation of his own ruin, others will be too apt to build upon it.   Fielding, H., *Tom Jones*, 863

He had no idea of a woman's being ruined any way but one.
Fielding, S., *David Simple*, I

If people who seek their own ruin could be the only sufferers by their headstrong doings, it were something.   Richardson, *Clarissa Harlowe*, III

If success is rare and slow, everybody knows how quick and easy ruin is.
Thackeray, *Vanity Fair*, XVI

RULE; SUBORDINATION: *see also* LAW; ROYALTY

Such is the fate of the human race, that one order of men lords it over another.
Brown, W. H., *The Power of Sympathy*, 53

A ruler should never forget that his foes are his fellow creatures; that his very victories are purchased with the inevitable miseries of his own subjects.   Johnstone, *Arsaces*, I

No man would rather resign by love than by fear.   Paltock, *Peter Wilkins*, 309

RUMOR; REPORT

We should never incline to believe the uncharitable, more than the good-natured report.
Anonymous, *The History of Tom Jones in His Married State*, 180–181

Common report is seldom wrong in a matter where to be right is so easy.
Burney, *Cecilia*, III

Rumor hath a nimbler foot than the mule.   Cooper, *The Headsman*, XX

Rumor, busy overmuch, persists in flitting and chattering about town. It hears all sorts of shocking things. It makes the world of five miles round, quite merry.
Dickens, *Bleak House*, LVIII

Ill news flies fast enough all the world over.   Edgeworth, *Castle Rackrent*, 39

That talkative maiden, Rumor, though in the interest of art she is figured as a youthful winged beauty with flowing garments, soaring above the heads of men, and breathing world-thrilling news through a gracefully-curved trumpet, is in fact a very old maid, who puckers her silly face by the fireside, and really does no more than chirp a wrong guess or a lame story in the ear of a fellow-gossip.   Eliot, *Felix Holt*, VIII

Rumor, with her hundred babbling tongues.
Fielding, S., *The History of the Countess of Dellwyn*, I

There is no species of news which does not enlarge, in proportion to the space through which it is carried.   Hill, *Mr. George Edwards*, 60

What reason cannot collect and what experiment has not yet taught can be known only from the report of others.   Johnson, *Rasselas*, 112

Rumor is seldom at a loss for answers.   Melville, *Confidence-Man*, XXXIV

In maritime life, far more than in that of *terra firma*, wild rumors abound, wherever there is any adequate reality for them to cling to.   Melville, *Moby Dick*, XLI

Rumors violently blow the sails of popular judgments.   Sidney, *Arcadia*, III

Rumor, though she flies so fast and so far, is often slow in reaching those ears which would be most interested in her tidings.   Trollope, *Phineas Finn*, XL

Rumors always lie.   *Ibid.*, LXV

SACRIFICE

If one could only make a sacrifice all at once, and be done with it, it would seem easier; but to keep up a daily sacrifice of one's wishes, tastes, and pleasures is a hard task.   Alcott, *Old-Fashioned Girl*, IX

It is madness to sacrifice an hundred to one dream.   August, *Horrid Mysteries*, I

. . . . . t he might die, he went from life to death, and then from death to death,
atural to death eternal.   Bunyan, *Pilgrim's Progress*, 39

ne rest by his sorrow, and life by his death.   *Ibid.*

'p the unessential, but she would never sacrifice herself for her
Chopin, *The Awakening*, XXXIX

It is a far, far better thing that I do, than I have ever done; it is a far, far better rest that I go to than I have ever known. Dickens, *Tale of Two Cities*, XV

Past sacrifices are nothing. Disraeli, *Coningsby*, Book II, IV

Never yet did man lay down his heroic life for so great a cause: the cause of the Church and the cause of the Poor. Disraeli, *Sybil*, Book IV, VI

A man who won't sacrifice his life for his country deserves to be hanged. Fielding, H., *Joseph Andrews*, 110

He who would not die for his country, he would not be worthy to live in it. *Ibid.*, 114

Had Abraham so loved his son Isaac as to refuse the sacrifice required, is there any of us who would not condemn him? *Ibid.*, 265

He wished to raise the class at the expense of individuals rather than individuals at the expense of the class. What was more, he was ready at once to be the first unit sacrificed. Hardy, *The Return of the Native*, Book III, II

The self-sacrifice painted in most novels like *Tears, Idle Tears* is nothing but psychical suicide, and is as wholly immoral as the spectacle of a man falling upon his sword. Howells, *Silas Lapham*, XIV

We are all blinded, we are all weakened, by a false ideal of self-sacrifice. *Ibid.*, XVIII

So sacred are the laws of hospitality among the Comanches, that a dozen lives would be sacrificed if required, to save that of a guest. Marryat, *Monsieur Violet*, XXVII

For God's sake, be economical with your lamps and candles! not a gallon you burn, but at least one drop of man's blood was spilled for it. Melville, *Moby Dick*, XLV

Sacrifice of self is the sin that cries loudest to Nature for vengeance. To discover our best gift from Nature, and to cultivate that gift, is the first law of life. Moore, *Evelyn Innes*, VIII

Men may sacrifice rams and goats, but not honor and conscience. Scott, *The Talisman*, XXVI

Sacrifice, the holiest joy of love. Taylor, *Hannah Thurston*, XXXVI

SADNESS: *see* HAPPINESS; MISERY; etc.

SAINTS; SAINTLINESS: *see also* GOOD AND EVIL; RELIGION; etc.

Saints make the finest bed-fellows in the world. Anonymous, *Oxymel Classic*, I

An unsainted lion [, a desperado, especially one without compassion]. Morier, *Hajji Baba*, XXXIII

A saint's bastard may be no saint himself. Walpole, *The Castle of Otranto*, 56

SANITY: *see also* INSANITY

SARCASM: *see also* RIDICULE; SATIRE

Sarcasm confers a title of aristocracy straightway and sharp on the sconce of the man who does but imagine that he is using it. Meredith, *Beaucham's Career*, XVIII

Beware of the ironical mood. It is a dangerous instrument. Stevenson, *St. Ives* , IV

SATIRE: *see also* RIDICULE; SARCASM

Ridicule is a two-edged weapon, and may be made to cut and mangle anything, particularly whatever is grave and solemn. Anonymous, *Tsonnonthouan*, I

Of all human dealings, satire is the very lowest, and most mean and common. It is the equivalent in words for what bullying is in deeds; and no more bespeaks a clever man, than the other does a brave one.　　　　　　　　　　Blackmore, *Lorna Doone*, XLVI

It is astonishing with what avidity we look for the application of satire which is general, and never had a prototype.　　　　Brackenridge, *Modern Chivalry*, Part II, I

The strongest admirers of female eyes are frequently the most austere satirists of their conduct.　　　　　　　　　　　　　　　Burney, *Camilla*, Three, VI

My satire shall be general. I would as much disdain to be personal with an anonymous pen, as to attack an unarmed man in the dark with the dagger I had kept concealed.
　　　　　　　　　　　　　　　　　　　　　　　　　　Burney, *Cecilia*, III

Satirists speak of things as they are, rather than as they ought to be.
　　　　　　　　　　　　　　　　　　　　　Cooper, *Satanstoe*, Volume I, VI

All universal satires against humankind are false.　　　　Fielding, H., *Amelia*, I

To hold the glass to thousands in their closets, that they may contemplate their deformity, and endeavor to reduce it, and thus by suffering private mortification may avoid public shame.　　　　　　　　　　Fielding, H., *Joseph Andrews*, 159

The satirist privately corrects the fault for the benefit of the person, like a parent; the libeller publicly exposes the person himself, as an example to others, like an executioner.　　　　　　　　　　　　　　　　　　　　　　　　　　　*Ibid.*

In most of our particular characters we mean not to lash individuals, but all of the like sort.　　　　　　　　　　　　　　　　　　　　　　　　　*Ibid.*, 160

As he was entirely well satisfied with his own person and parts, so he was very apt to ridicule and laugh at any imperfection in another.　　　　　　　*Ibid.*, 269

It is the unkindness of the person who levels the satire at us, and not the satire itself, that pierces the soul.　　　　　Fielding, S., *Cleopatra and Octavia*, 200–201

It is ignorantly inhuman to dart the strings of ridicule at a person for taking steps too long or too short; turning toes in instead of out; drooping the head instead of holding it erect; or dangling the arms instead of disposing them according to art.
　　　　　　　　　　　　　　　　　　　　　　Gentlemen, *A Trip to the Moon*, I

To rake into filth is more likely to propagate vice, and to taint, than purify the mind of the reader. It gives a large majority the knowledge of what otherwise they would not, and indeed should not, know.　　　　　　　　　　　　　　　　　*Ibid.*, II

The behavior of the generality of mankind is ungenerous, in ridiculing what they ought to applaud.　　　　　　　　　　　　　　　　Gibbes, *Mr. Francis Clive*, II

Ridicule is the severest weapon with which truth can be attacked.
　　　　　　　　　　　　　　　　　　　　　　　Johnstone, *The Pilgrim*, II

The sting of ridicule is always poisoned.　　　　　Johnstone, *The Reverie*, II

In the more important articles of belief or conviction, let not the flow of ridicule be mistaken for the force of argument.　　　　Mackenzie, *The Man of the World*, I

Nothing is so easy as to excite a laugh, at that time of life, when seriousness is held to be an incapacity of enjoying it; and no wit so subtle, or so dangerous, as that which is drawn from the perverted attitudes of what is in itself momentous.
　　　　　　　　　　　　　　　　　　　　　　　　　　　　　　Ibid., I

Permitted or desired satire may be apt in a generous satirist to turn too soon into panegyric.　　　　　　　　　　　　　　Richardson, *Clarissa Harlowe*, I

Satire must be founded in good nature, and directed by a right heart.　　　*Ibid.*

An impartial person may suspect that the satirist sometimes has a natural spleen to gratify; which may be as great a fault in him as any of those which he pretends to censure and expose in others. *Ibid.*, III

Who will ridicule a personal imperfection in one that seems conscious that it is an imperfection? Richardson, *Clarissa Harlowe*, II

Nothing so effectually blunts the shafts or ridicule, and defeats the aims of slander, as humorous self-criticism. Smollett, *Ferdinand, Count Fathom*, L

SAVAGERY: *see also* ANIMAL AND INSECT LIFE; CIVILIZATION; etc.

A savage is free all over the world. Brooke, *Emily Montague*, I

All barbarians are rakes. Melville, *Israel Potter*, XI

Savages have an innate sense of delicacy; it is marvellous how essentially polite they are. Melville, *Moby Dick*, IV

At first [savages] are overawing; their calm self-collectedness of simplicity seems a Socratic wisdom. *Ibid.*, X

Men who sojourn amidst savagery fear the mosquito more than the lion. Trollope, *Phineas Finn*, LXIX

SCANDAL: *see also* REPUTATION; RUMOR; etc.

Evil fame and scandal are always new. When the offender has forgot a vile fact, it is often told to one and to another, who, having never heard of it before, trumpet it about as a novelty. Richardson, *Clarissa Harlowe*, III

Scandal is the atmosphere in which we live, we princes; it is what a prince should know. Stevenson, *Prince Otto*, Book II, VI

Scandal lied, as she so often does. Trollope, *The Warden*, I

"There is never any basis for scandal." "The basis of every scandal is an immoral certainty." Wilde, *The Picture of Dorian Gray*, XVIII

SCHEME: *see also* PLOT

Captain Cuttle, in the exercise of that surprising talent for deep-laid and unfathomable scheming, with which (as is not unusual in men of transparent simplicity) he sincerely believed himself to be endowed by nature, . . . Dickens, *Dombey and Son*, XVII

SCIENCE: *see also* KNOWLEDGE AND LEARNING; etc.

Science is not a club, it is an ocean. Who can exhaust the sea? Who say to intellect, the deeps of philosophy are pre-occupied? Bulwer, *The Caxtons*, Book IV, III

What is scientific knowledge now may be scientific ignorance in some years more. Collins, *Heart and Science*, LIV

What Art was to the ancient world, Science is to the modern; the distinctive faculty. Disraeli, *Coningsby*, Book IV, I

Science is properly more scrupulous than dogma. Dogma gives a charter to mistake, but the very breath of science is a contest with mistake, and must keep the conscience alive. Eliot, *Middlemarch*, Book VIII, LXXIII

Science is notoriously of slow movement. Meredith, *Ordeal of Richard Feverel*, XLIV

The modern masters of chemistry promise very little; they know that metals cannot be transmuted and that the elixir of life is a chimera. But these philosophers, whose hands seem only made to dabble in dirt, and their eyes to pore over the microscope or crucible, have indeed performed miracles. They penetrate into the recesses of nature and show how she works in her hiding places. They ascend into the heavens; they have discovered how the blood circulates, and the nature of the air we breathe. They have acquired new and almost unlimited powers; they can command the thunders of heaven, mimic the earthquake, and even mock the invisible world with its own shadows.

Shelley, M., Frankenstein, III

SCRIPTURES: *see also* BOOK; INTERPRETATION; LITERATURE; RELIGION; etc.

The Holy Scriptures impart to us the knowledge and assurance of things much more worthy our attention than all which this world can offer to our acceptance; of things which Heaven itself hath condescended to reveal to us, and to the smallest knowledge of which the highest human wit unassisted could never ascend.

Fielding, Tom Jones, 398

SEASONS: *see also* CHANGE; NATURE; TIME; etc.

March is a month when the needle of my nature dips towards the country.
Allen, J. L., Kentucky Cardinal, III

In May I am of the earth earthy.
Ibid., V

Youth is like spring, an overpraised season—delightful if it happen to be a favored one, but in practice very rarely favored and more remarkable, as a general rule, for biting east winds than genial breezes.
Butler, The Way of All Flesh, VI

There are seasons when we should leave our griefs and concerns at home.
Gibbes, Mr. Francis Clive, I

No summer ever came back, and no two summers ever were alike.
Hawthorne, The Blithedale Romance, XVI

Married Summer, matronly Autumn, virgin Spring.
Hawthorne, The Marble Faun, XII

The prodigal must take his chance if he comes back out of season.
Howells, Silas Lapham, V

The sorrows of Autumn have no warning for April.
Meredith, Ordeal of Richard Feverel, XXXII

Each virtue hath its time.
Sidney, Arcadia, III

October. This is one of the peculiarly dangerous months to speculate in stocks in. The others are July, January, September, April, November, May, March, June, December, August, and February.
Twain, Pudd'nhead Wilson, XIII

We know all about the habits of the ant, we know all about the habits of the bee, but we know nothing at all about the habits of the oyster. It seems almost certain that we have been choosing the wrong time for studying the oyster.
Ibid., XVI

July 4. Statistics show that we lose more fools on this day than in all the other days of the year put together. This proves, by the number left in stock, that one Fourth of July per year is now inadequate, the country has grown so.
Ibid., XVII

Thanksgiving Day. Let all give humble, hearty, and sincere thanks, now, but the turkeys. In the island of Fiji they do not use turkeys; they use plumbers. It does not become you and me to sneer at Fiji.
Ibid., XVIII

April 1. This is the day upon which we are reminded of what we are on the other three hundred and sixty-four.
Ibid., XXI

SECRETS; SECRECY: *see also* MYSTERY

Few secrets of a family are unknown to the servants belonging to it.
Anonymous, *The Adventures of a Corkscrew*, 13

When a female reposes her secrets in the breast of one of her sex, how secure must the cabinet be which every man can unlock.
Anonymous, *The Egg*, 210

How wonderfully well people behave whose common secret would set their world by the ears.
Atherton, *Senator North*, Book II, VIII

The Pacific is the most discreet of live, hot-tempered oceans: the chilly Antarctic can keep a secret too, but more in the manner of a grave.
Conrad, *Lord Jim*, XVI

Confidences are sometimes blinding, even when they are sincere.
Eliot, *Mill on the Floss*, Book VI, III

When God Almighty wills it, our secrets are found out.
Eliot, *Silas Marner*, XVIII

Few secrets are divulged to one person only.
Fielding, H., *Tom Jones*, 53

Secrets between man and wife is like not letting the left hand know what the right hand does.
Gibbes, *Mr. Francis Clive*, II

Few secrets can escape an investigator who has opportunity and license to undertake such a quest and skill to follow it up.
Hawthorne, *The Scarlet Letter*, IX

A man burdened with a secret should especially avoid the intimacy of his physician.
Ibid.

There can be no power short of the Divine mercy, to disclose, whether by uttered words, or by type or emblem, the secrets that may be buried with a human heart.
Ibid., X

I do not know how it is that clergymen and physicians keep from telling their wives the secrets confided to them; perhaps they can trust their wives to find them out for themselves whenever they wish.
Howells, *Silas Lapham*, XXVII

What is there in the world that more delighteth a lover than secrecy, which is void of fear without suspicion, free from envy: the only hope a woman hath to build both her honor and honesty upon.
Lyly, *Euphues and His England*, 416

He that hath a privy hurt is loath to have a shame outward.
Malory, *Le Morte DArthur*, One, VIII

There is no place like a bed for confidential disclosures between friends. Man and wife, they say, there open the very bottom of their souls to each other.
Melville, *Moby Dick*, X

It is the easiest thing in the world for a man to look as if he had a great secret in him.
Ibid., XIX

The discovery of a secret implies no obligation to retain it.
Meredith, *Ordeal of Richard Feverel*, I

In love, it is said, all stratagems are fair, and many little ladies transverse the axiom by applying it to the secrets of their friends.
Ibid., XIV

Secret as the grave.
Reade, *Griffith Gaunt*, XXVII

A person fond of prying into the secrets of others is not fit to be trusted.
Richardson, *Clarissa Harlowe*, III

Keyholes are the occasions of more sin and wickedness than all other holes in this world put together.
Sterne, *Tristram Shandy*, IX

There are some moments in life in which both men and women feel themselves imperatively called on to make a confidence, in which not to do so requires a disagreeable resolution and also a disagreeable suspicion.
Trollope, *Barchester Towers*, XLI

A secret is always accompanied by more or less of fear, and produces more or less of cowardice.
Trollope, *Dr. Wortle's School*, V

Perhaps, on the whole, more power is lost than gained by habits of secrecy.

Trollope, *The Eustace Diamonds*, LVII

The earth and the sea are always giving up their secrets.

Wallace, *The Prince of India*, Volume II, I

Secrecy seems to be the one thing that can make modern life mysterious or marvellous to us. The commonest thing is delightful if one only hides it.

Wilde, *The Picture of Dorian Gray*, I

SECURITY: *see also* REFUGE

Imagined security is the forerunner of destruction.

Anonymous, *A Court Intrigue*, 43-44

The word of a gentleman is as good as his bond—sometimes better, where his bond might prove but a doubtful sort of security.   Dickens, *Old Curiosity Shop*, LVIII

A man's own safety is a good that sometimes makes very grim demands.

Eliot, *Romola*, Book III, LX

Where no wealth is, we can sleep secure.   McCarthy, *The Fair Moralist*, 8-9

Assured morality in a husband is a great thing. Assured good temper is very excellent. Assured talent, religion, amiability, truth, honesty, are all desirable. But an assured income is indispensable.   Trollope, *He Knew He Was Right*, XXXIX

What teacher is safe from malevolence, what system from misconstruction?

Wright, *A Few Days in Athens*, VII

SEDUCTION: *see also* LIBERTINISM

Seduction opens the door to a dismal train of innumerable miseries.

Brown, W. H., *The Power of Sympathy*, 66

The voice of the sea is seductive; never ceasing, whispering, clamoring, murmuring, inviting the soul to wander for a spell in abysses of solitude; to lose itself in mazes of inward contemplation.   Chopin, *The Awakening*, VI

If you take seven hairs of hyena's lips, and carry them six days in your teeth, or a piece of her skin next your bare heart, or her belly girded to your left side, if a woman suffer you not to obtain your purpose with her, certainly she cannot choose but thank you for your pains.   Lyly, *Euphues and His England*, 346

She did not seduce, she ravished.   Meredith, *Diana of the Crossways*, VII

What but remorse can follow a forcible attempt?   Richardson, *Clarissa Harlowe*, II

How many ways are there to undo poor creatures!   Richardson, *Pamela*, 83

SELF

The reverence of a man's self is, after religion, the chiefest bridle of all vices.

Bacon, *The New Atlantis*, 209

Self is the predominant idea, self is the darling theme, self is the focus to which every principle converges.   Dacre, *The Libertine*, II

No speck so troublesome as self.   Eliot, *Middlemarch*, Book IV, XLII

His humanity—his sense of his own interest.   Hildreth, *Slave*, Volume I, XV

We are always apt to think more highly of ourselves than we ought to.

Kirkby, *The Capacity of Human Understanding*, 256

I have striven to be Thine, more than to be this world's or mine own. Yet this is nothing; I leave eternity to Thee; for what is man that he should live out the lifetime of his God?
Melville, *Moby Dick*, IX

The wide-mouthed old dragon Ego.   Meredith, *Diana of the Crossways*, XXIV

What care ought we to take not to confound the distinctions of right and wrong when self comes into the question.   Richardson, *Clarissa Harlowe*, I

Self, which is at the bottom of all we do, and of all we wish, is the grand misleader.
Ibid., II

A devilish thing for a man to be so little himself, when he has most occasion for himself!
Ibid., III

Self is an odious devil, that reconciles to some people the most cruel and dishonest actions.   *Ibid.*, IV

When a man is discontented with himself, it has one advantage, that it puts him into an excellent frame of mind for making a bargain.   Sterne, *A Sentimental Journey*, 9

"Surely, if one lives merely for one's self, one pays a terrible price for doing so?" "Yes, we are overcharged for everything nowadays."   Wilde, *The Picture of Dorian Gray*, VI

SELF-COMMAND; SELF-CONTROL

He was a man whose self-control was absolute or non-existent.
Atherton, *Senator North*, Book III, IV

Self-control is not deceit.   Bulwer, *Pompeii*, Book Three, IV

Self-command is dominion.   Cable, *Bonaventure*, Book III, XII

Unsought self-possession is a sure sign of good breeding.
Collins, *The Moonstone*, Third Narrative, IX

When each individual has subdued his own spirit, then there will be no war and no other enemies to conquer.   Cowan, *Daybreak*, XXXIX

Over their passions and their weaknesses, mortals cannot keep a curb too strong.
Dacre, *Zofloya*, XXXIII

Not quite in a good temper? Take a little time—count five-and-twenty.
Dickens, *Little Dorrit*, Book I, XVI

Keep yourself *to* yourself.   Dickens, *Pickwick Papers*, XXXII

The noblest of all victories, that over ourselves.   Harley, *Priory of St. Bernard*, I

Our souls are not our own. We convey a property in them to those with whom we associate; but to what extent can never be known, until we feel the tug, the agony, or our abortive effort to resume an exclusive sway over ourselves.
Hawthorne, *The Blithedale Romance*, XXIII

Men with poignant feelings, buried under an air of carefree self-command, are never proof to the sudden incitements of passion. Though in the main they may control themselves, yet if they but once permit the smallest vent, then they may bid adieu to all self-restraint, at least for that time.   Melville, *Israel Potter*, XIV

A man who is master of himself can end a sorrow as easily as he can invent a pleasure.
Wilde, *The Picture of Dorian Gray*, IX

SELF-CONSCIOUSNESS

As the sore palate findeth grit, so an uneasy consciousness heareth innuendoes.
Eliot, *Middlemarch*, Book III, XXXI

SELF-DECEPTION; SELF-CONTRADICTION

None are oftener deceived than bad men; nor is it any wonder, since they entrust only those as wicked as themselves. Anonymous, *The Birmingham Counterfeit*, I

We deceive others far less than we deceive ourselves. Bulwer, *Falkland*, Book I

Though the mind may be set on a very improper and base object, it will not fail to seek a good motive for its justification, few men being so hardened in any grovelling passion, that they will not endeavor to deceive themselves, as well as their neighbors.
Cooper, *The Monikins*, Conclusion

In things we wish, 'tis easy to deceive;/ What we would have, we willingly believe.
Defoe, *Roxana*, 69

There are characters which are continually creating collisions and nodes for themselves in dramas which nobody is prepared to act with them. Their susceptibilities will clash against objects that remain innocently quiet. Eliot, *Middlemarch*, Book II, XIX

When the heart does not dictate a probability of evil in others, the owner is easier deceived into a good opinion of mankind. Fielding, H., *The History of Ophelia*, II

But for the power of deceiving ourselves, we couldn't live at all.
Gissing, *The Whirlpool*, Part III, I

SELF-DENIAL: *see also* SACRIFICE

Self-denial is the great virtue of a republic. It is the opposition of ambition. Self-denial looks only at justice. It looks at the public good.
Brackenridge, *Modern Chivalry*, Part II, II

As he looked back upon man moving through history, he was haunted by a feeling of loss. So much had been surrendered! and to such little purpose! There had been made willful rejections, monstrous forms of self-torture and self-denial, whose origin was fear and whose result was a degradation infinitely more terrible than that fancied degradation from which, in their ignorance, they had sought to escape; Nature, in her wonderful irony, driving out the anchorite to feed with the wild animals of the desert and giving to the hermit the beasts of the field as his companions.
Wilde, *The Picture of Dorian Gray*, XI

SELF-DESTRUCTION: *see also* SUICIDE

A baker is not to be called venal if he sells his loaves—he is venal if he sells himself.
Bulwer, *The Caxtons*, Book VI, VIII

A man cannot fight against himself for long. That deadly enemy is certain to slay.
Caine, *The Manxman*, Part I, I

Men often court their destruction, from ignorance of their own interests.
Cooper, *Red Rover*, XVI

The stratagems of the base recoil upon their authors and cover their confusion.
Dacre, *Passions*, Letter LV

I was born to be my own destroyer. Defoe, *Robinson Crusoe*, 39

The yoke a man creates for himself by wrong-doing will breed hate in the kindliest nature. Eliot, *Silas Marner*, III

It would be extreme weakness to compassionate the misfortunes of a man who runs headlong to his own destruction. Fielding, H., *Joseph Andrews*, 185

How cheerfully we consign ourselves to perdition! Melville, *Moby Dick*, I

SELF-DISPLEASURE

Nothing can be so bad as to be displeased with one's self. Jackson, *Ramona*, IV

SELF-ESTEEM; SELF-RESPECT: *see also* PRIDE

A man who has any good reason to believe in himself never flourishes himself before the faces of other people in order that they may believe in him.
Dickens, *David Copperfield*, XLVIII

There is harm in a man's thinking a good deal of himself when it is proved he has been thinking wrong.
Hardy, *Pair of Blue Eyes*, XVII

We do ourselves wrong, and too meanly estimate the Holiness above us, when we deem that any act or enjoyment, good in itself, is not good to do religiously.
Hawthorne, *The Marble Faun*, XXXII

It is hard to have one's last prop of self-respect cut away just when we are suffering a martyr's agony at the stake.
Meredith, *Ordeal of Richard Feverel*, XV

There is no better antidote against entertaining too high an opinion of others, than having an excellent one of ourselves at the same time.
Scott, *Waverly*, V

SELF-EXAMINATION: *see also* SELF-KNOWLEDGE

Whenever we discover a dislike in us toward anyone, we should ever be a little suspicious of ourselves.
Melville, *Redburn*, LI

A man is never the best judge of his own position.
Trollope, *The Warden*, XVII

It is better to correct ourselves than to find fault with our neighbors.
Wright, *A Few Days in Athens*, XI

SELF-EXPOSURE: SELF-REVELATION

To aim at shining in company is generally to expose ourselves to contempt.
Anonymous, *Memoirs of a Coquet*, 10

Through an eagerness to outwit others, many are apt to outwit themselves.
Ibid., 28

Those who pinch themselves at home in order to puff away abroad take a great deal of pains to be laughed at.
Ibid., 164–165

Thou art quarreling with the light of thine own eyes.
Caruthers, *Cavaliers*, Volume I, VIII

The man who reviews his own life had need to have been a good man indeed, if he would be spared the sharp consciousness of many talents neglected, many opportunities wasted, many erratic and perverted feelings constantly at war within his breast, and defeating him.
Dickens, *David Copperfield*, XLII

We don't make ourselves, except it be worse by our dress.
Richardson, *Clarissa Harlowe*, IV

They who open suspect others, of secret condemn themselves.
Sidney, *Arcadia*, I

SELF-IMPROVEMENT; SELF-REALIZATION

The aim of life is self-development. To realize one's nature perfectly—that is what each of us is here for.
Wilde, *The Picture of Dorian Gray*, II

SELF-INDULGENCE

Your disapprobation is a great defect of temper, made worse by a very faulty habit of self-indulgence.
Austen, *Mansfield Park*, Volume One, XI

Others seldom regard us in the same light we regard ourselves.
Cooper, *The Monikins*, Conclusion

No man should have more than two attachments—the first, to number one, and the second to the ladies.
Dickens, *Pickwick Papers*, LIII

SELF-INFLICTION: *see also* SELF-DESTRUCTION

The worst of our evils we blindly inflict upon ourselves.
Melville, *White Jacket*, The End

SELFISHNESS; UNSELFISHNESS: *see also* AVARICE

Selfishness is so predominant, that when we hear of benevolence, we consider it a curiosity.
Anonymous, *Memoirs of a Coquet*, 40

Selfishness must always be forgiven, because there is no hope of a cure.
Austen, *Mansfield Park*, Volume One, VII

There is no task so unselfish, so necessarily without return, though the heart is well rewarded, as the nurture of the children who are to make the world for one another when we are gone.
Bellamy, *Looking Backward*, XXV

Selfishness is the master-key to unlock every heart; it is the great passion upon which all others have their foundation.
Caruthers, *Kentuckian in New-York*, Volume II, IV

It is easy for generous sentiments, high courtesy, and chivalrous courage to lose their influence beneath the chilling blight of selfishness, and to exhibit to the world a man great in all the minor attributes of character, but found wanting when it becomes necessary to prove how much principle is superior to policy.
Cooper, *The Last of the Mohicans*, XVIII

Some philosophers tell us that selfishness is at the root of our best loves and affections.
Dickens, *Dombey and Son*, VIII

There is a kind of selfishness which is constantly upon the watch for selfishness in others; and holding others at a distance by suspicions and distrusts, wonders why they don't approach, and don't confide, and calls that selfishness in them.
Dickens, *Martin Chuzzlewit*, LII

'Tis a genial regard for the feelings of others that springs from an absence of selfishness.
Disraeli, *Coningsby*, Book II, II

Cheerful, successful worldliness has a false air of being more selfish than the acrid, unsuccessful kind, whose secret history is summed up in the terrible words, "Sold, but not paid for."
Eliot, *Daniel Deronda*, Book I, III

All men, as well the best as the worst, act alike from the principle of self-love.
Fielding, H., *Amelia*, II

There is a temper of mind which borrows a degree of virtue even from self-love.
Fielding, H., *Tom Jones*, 127

Unselfishness is a word that none may speak without calling into question the entire conduct of his or her life.
Moore, G., *Evelyn Innes*, XXXV

Those who aim at more than their due will be refused the honors they may justly claim.
Richardson, *Clarissa Harlowe*, I

Selfish are the hearts of poor mortals, that they are ready to change as favor goes.
Richardson, *Pamela*, 266

Selfishness is the language of the world.
Scott, *The Antiquary*, XI

When is a mental argument conducted without some reference to selfish considerations?
Scott, *Quentin Durward*, XVII

The selfishness of man's nature soars triumphant above all other considerations, in a time of war; and life becomes as small a subject of consideration as any one of its circumstances.
Simms, *The Scout*, XXI

Do we never perceive our own foibles? It is happy we can find consolation in the follies of
our neighbors.   Anonymous, *The Peregrinations of Jeremiah Grant*, 58

All of us possess every good and bad instinct in the whole book of human nature, but few
of us have imagination enough to find it out. And the less we know of ourselves the
better.   Atherton, *Senator North*, Book I, XXII

She knows her own worth too well for false shame.
                                     Austen, *Sense and Sensibility*, Volume I, XVII

She saw that there is no great man on this earth except the man who conquers self, and
that in some the accursed thing, which is in all of us, may be so strong that to battle with
it and be beaten is not altogether to fail.   Barrie, *Tommy and Grizel*, XXXV

I enjoyed the "giftie" of seeing myself as others see me.   Bronte, C., *Villette*, XX

To scrutinize and ascertain our own principles is abundantly difficult. To exhibit those
principles to the world with absolute sincerity can scarcely be expected.
                                     Brown, C. B., *Ormond*, 92

We are not judges of our own ailments: physicians do not often prescribe for themselves.
                                     Caruthers, *Kentuckian in New-York*, Volume I, VI

No man ever understands quite his own artful dodges to escape from the grim shadow of
self-knowledge.   Conrad, *Lord Jim*, VII

The first point is to know one's own mind. The next is, to act up to the decision.
                                     Cooper, *The Last of the Mohicans*, II

No man knows till the time comes, what depths are within him.
                                     Dickens, *Our Mutual Friend*, Book II, XV

People may really have in them some vocation which is not quite plain to themselves.
                                     Eliot, *Middlemarch*, Book I, IX

He had two selves within him apparently, and they must learn to accommodate each
other and bear reciprocal impediments.   *Ibid.*, Book II, XV

Every man may, by examining his own mind, guess what passes in the minds of others.
When you feel that your own gaiety is counterfeit, it may justly lead you to suspect that
of your companions not to be sincere.   Johnson, *Rasselas*, 72

Self-knowledge is thought by some not so easy. Who knows but for a time you may have
taken yourself for somebody else? Stranger things have happened.
                                     Melville, *Confidence-Man*, IV

The danger of a little knowledge of things is disputable, but beware the little knowledge
of one's self!   Meredith, *Ordeal of Richard Feverel*, XXXIII

So well do we know ourselves that we one and all determine to know a purer.
                                     Meredith, *Diana of the Crossways*, I

It is more eligible to hear what a man says of himself than what another says of him.
                                     Morris, *John Daniel*, 275–276

No son of Adam ever reads his own heart at all except by the habit acquired, and the
light gained, from some years' perusal of other hearts; and even then, with his acquired
sagacity and reflected light, he can but spell and decipher his own heart, not read it
fluently.   Reade, *The Cloister and the Hearth*, VI

The darkest and most contemptible ignorance is that of not knowing oneself.
                                     Richardson, *Clarissa Harlowe*, IV

He could not be angry with others for seeing him in a light in which he so strongly saw
himself.   Sterne, *Tristram Shandy*, I

SELF-LOVE: *see also* SELF-ESTEEM; SELFISHNESS; etc.

There is a pleasure in writing, which only the man who writes knows. Yet no man would write, unless he expected somebody to read. His own reading would be small if he did not expect to have it found out that he had read. Thus self-love is, in a great degree, the spring of all things. Brackenridge, *Modern Chivalry*, Part II, II

That glorified self-love requires the touch upon imagination of strangeness and un-accustomed grace, to subdue it and make it pardon an outrage to its temples and altars, and its happy reading of the heavens, the earth too: earth foremost, we ought perhaps to say. Meredith, *Beauchamp's Career*, XXIV

The secret of the heart is its pressing love of self. Meredith, *The Egoist*, XXXVII

A regard for personal appearance is a species of self-love, from which the wisest are not exempt, and to which the mind clings so instinctively, that not only the soldier, advancing to almost inevitable death, but even the doomed criminal who goes to certain execution, shows an anxiety to array his person to the best advantage.
Scott, *Kenilworth*, XXX

I cannot conceive anything better calculated to excite sympathy than the spectacle of a man devoting his life to self-worship. Shaw, *The Irrational Knot*, I

Which of us is there can tell how much vanity lurks in our warmest regard for others, and how selfish our love is? Thackeray, *Vanity Fair*, XXXV

SELF-PRESERVATION

The contempt of life is not meritorious in itself; on the contrary, self-preservation is enjoined by the law of nature. Anonymous, *The Birmingham Counterfeit*, I

Self-preservation operates pretty equally through the whole species.
Anonymous, *The Fruitless Repentance*, I

Her instinct of self-preservation was stronger than her candor. Hardy, *Tess*, XXIX

Self-preservation first united mankind in civil society. Johnstone, *The Pilgrim*, I

From the last ills no being can save another; therein each man must be his own savior.
Melville, *White Jacket*, The End

SELF-REPROACH

The keenest of all anguish, self reproach. Austen, *Pride and Prejudice*, Volume III, V

The power of self-torture which the human heart possesses is well-nigh infinite.
Bates, *Puritans*, XI

SELF-RESPECT: *see also* PRIDE; SELF-ESTEEM

Though the Scriptures obliges me to remain contented, it does not enjoin me to shut my eyes to my own merit, nor restrain me from seeing when I am injured by an unjust comparison. Fielding, H., *Tom Jones*, 194

Self-applause is our principal support in every liberal and elevated act of virtue.
Godwin, *St. Leon*, 137

A man can never be respectable in the eyes of the world or in his own, except so far as he stands by himself and is truly independent. *Ibid.*, 138

The man who has ceased to respect himself must look for no respect from others.
Ibid., 218

When nature biddeth thee to be good and gentle to others, she commands thee not to be cruel and ungentle to thyself. More, *Utopia*, II

SELF-SUPPORT: *see also* INDEPENDENCE

There is no such thing in a civilized society as self-support.
Bellamy, *Looking Backward*, XII

SENSE(S); SENSIBLENESS: *see also* SENSIBILITY; SENTIMENT

You might as well expect good liquors without fermentation, as a man of real sense without experience in life.
Brackenridge, *Modern Chivalry*, Part II, II

Sense is but an afterbirth; we eat and drink many months before we are conscious of thoughts.
Melville, *Mardi*, CXLIII

The worship of the senses has often, and with much justice, been decried, men feeling a natural instinct of terror about passions and sensations that seem stronger than themselves, and that they are conscious of sharing with the less highly organized forms of existence.
Wilde, *The Picture of Dorian Gray*, XI

The senses, no less than the soul, have their spiritual mysteries to reveal.
Ibid.

SENSIBILITY; SENSITIVITY; INSENSIBILITY: *see also* SENSE(S); SENTIMENT

It is not everyone who has your passion for dead leaves.
Austen, *Sense and Sensibility*, Volume I, XVI

A man without sensibility exhibits no sign of a soul.
Brown, W. H., *The Power of Sympathy*, 179

When the human—the physical—system is put under the effect of an excessive stimulant, whether grape, opium, or poison, taken in a quantity not sufficient to produce death, there is for a time, an unnatural exaltation, a tremendous accession of velocity in all the wheels of life.
Cooke, *Virginia Comedians*, Volume II, X

Hidden things were visible to her (at least, so the people inferred from obscure hints escaping unawares out of her mouth), and silence was audible.
Hawthorne, *The Blithedale Romance*, XXII

Whatever may be the evils resulting from a too susceptible heart, nothing can be hoped from an insensible one.
Radcliffe, *The Mysteries of Udolpho*, I

The finer sensibilities make not happy!
Richardson, *Clarissa Harlowe*, II

Some are as sensible of a scratch from a pin as others from a push of a sword.
Ibid., IV

There would be no supporting life, if we felt quite as poignantly for others as we do for ourselves.
Richardson, *Sir Charles Grandison*, One, II

Why does man boast of sensibilities superior to those apparent in the brute? It only renders them more necessary beings.
Shelley, M., *Frankenstein*, X

The peace of life is insensibility—the suicide of mind or affection.
Simms, *The Yemassee*, XXXI

Nothing renders the soul so callous and insensible as the searing brands of infamy and disgrace.
Smollett, *Ferdinand, Count Fathom*, LXI

All comes from thee, great, great Sensorium of the world, which vibrates, if a hair of our heads but falls upon the ground, in the remotest desert of thy creation.
Sterne, *A Sentimental Journey*, 125–126

SENTIMENT: *see also* SENSIBILITY

It is one of the paradoxes of human nature that young women with all the world before them delight in singing retrospective melodies about an auld-lang-syne concerning which, in the very nature of the case, they cannot well know anything, but in regard to which they seem to entertain sentiments so distressful.
Eggleston, *The Graysons*, IV

The most pious sentiments will affect us but little when delivered by those who appear to have no religion in their hearts. Graves, *The Spiritual Quixote*, I

"You want to see, but not to feel." "I don't think that if one's a sentient being one can make the distinction." James, H., *Portrait of a Lady*, XV

After science comes sentiment. Melville, *Mardi*, XXXVIII

All's plain in history and fact, so long as we do not obtrude sentimentalism. Nothing mixes well with that stuff—except poetical ideas. Meredith, *Beauchamp's Career*, XLVI

The lady's difficulty [in expression of her feelings] was peculiar to sweet natures that have no great warmth of passion; it can only be indicated. Like others of the kind, it is traceable to the most delicate of sentiments, and to the flattest. *Ibid.*, XLVII

Sentimental people fiddle harmonics on the strings of sensualism. Meredith, *Diana of the Crossways*, I

Sentimentalists are they who seek to enjoy reality without incurring the immense debtorship for a thing done. Meredith, *Ordeal of Richard Feverel*, XXVIII

One who could set down Dying for Love as a Sentimentalism can hardly be accepted as a clear authority. *Ibid.*

Sentimental people are sure to live long and die fat. *Ibid.*, XLV

Sentiment is the cajolery of existence: the soft bloom which whoso weareth, he or she is enviable. *Ibid.*

Eclipsed as they may be in the gross appreciation of the world by other people, who excel in this and that accomplishment, persons that nourish Nice Feelings and are intimate with the Fine Shades carry their own test of intrinsic value. Meredith, *Sandra Belloni*, I

Sentimentalists are a perfectly natural growth of a fat soil. *Ibid.*

Take it as an axiom, when you utter a sentimentalism, that more than one pair of ears makes a cynical critic. A sentimentalism requires secrecy. *Ibid.*, II

Sentiment above all—*true* rhyming to *you*, *regret* to *forget*, *part* to *heart*—is sufficient to force the peasant woman to tears, to produce a gross exultation of the senses. The wording may be simple, the substance commonplace; but the mere statement that two people are separated and love each other is sufficient. For her the art is never deficient, and the same singsong cry will never fail to give her the same sensations of regret and longing. Moore, G., *A Mummer's Wife*, VII

Sentiment is a disgrace instead of an ornament, unless it lead us to good actions. Radcliffe, *The Mysteries of Udolpho*, I

Sentimental commerce is always against the expatriated adventurer: he must buy what he has little occasion for, at their own price. Sterne, *A Sentimental Journey*, 10

The heart is for saving what it can. *Ibid.*, 25

Love is nothing without sentiment. *Ibid.*, 51

Sentiment is even less without love. *Ibid.*

An injury sharpened by an insult, be it to whom it will, makes every man of sentiment a party. *Ibid.*, 65

It fares better with sentiments, not to be in a hurry with them. *Ibid.*, 129

Sentiment increases by self-indulgence. Thackeray, *Pendennis*, XXIII

Of all such reformers Mr. Sentiment is the most powerful. It is incredible the number of evil practices he has put down: it is to be feared he will soon lack subjects, and that when

he has made the working classes comfortable, and got bitter beer put into proper-sized pint bottles, there will be nothing further for him left to do.
Trollope, *The Warden*, XVI

It may be better for the world that there are these women to whom life has still some mysteries, who are capable of illusions and the sweet sentimentality that grows out of a romance unrealized.
Warner, *A Little Journey*, II

The sentiment which gets a man into a difficulty rarely stays around to help him out of it.
Webster, *The Banker and the Bear*, XII

I cannot repeat an emotion. No one can, except sentimentalists.
Wilde, *The Picture of Dorian Gray*, IX

SEPARATION: *see also* ABANDONMENT; ABSENCE; PARTING; etc.

The separation was rather noisy than pathetic.
Austen, *Pride and Prejudice*, Volume II, XVIII

The pain of parting is nothing to the joy of meeting again.
Dickens, *Nicholas Nickleby*, III

Life is constant separation.
Disraeli, *Coningsby*, Book III, I

The desire for distances betokens emptiness and undirected hunger: when the heart is possessed by an image we fly to wood and forest, like the guilty.
Meredith, *Ordeal of Richard Feveral*, XVI

Who can part, forever; only when we come so close that nothing separates us can we meet again, only when what binds us is not my need of you or your need of me nor any chance circumstance, but a deep ingrained likeness of nature that cannot pass away.
Schreiner, *Undine*, XIX

SERENITY

Querulous serenity.
Austen, *Pride and Prejudice*, Volume II, XIX

You may cut off my existence, but you cannot disturb my serenity.
Godwin, *Caleb Williams*, II

Men are extremely provoked by a polite serenity, where their hearts are deeply interested in the issue of a debate.
Kelly, *Memoirs of a Magdalen*, I

'Tis the use we make of comforts, and the manner in which we support their loss, that fixes the peace or misery of our last moments.
Roche, *Clermont*, II

A heart at ease flies into no extremes—'tis ever on its center.
Sterne, *A Sentimental Journey*, 81

SERIOUSNESS: *see also* GRAVITY; IMPORTANCE; etc.

There are so many who forget to think seriously till it is almost too late.
Austen, *Persuasion*, XVII

There is nothing serious in mortality.
Collins, *The Woman in White*, Part II, Third Epoch

It seems that human beings compounded especially for happiness have no longer any business on earth, or elsewhere. Life has grown so sadly serious, that such must change their nature, or else perish, like the antediluvian creatures, that required, as the condition of their existence, a more summer-like atmosphere than ours.
Hawthorne, *The Marble Faun*, L

The increasing seriousness of things—the great opportunity of jokes.
James, H., *Portrait of a Lady*, I

There is such a thing as gravity, and in condemned felons it may be genuine; but of long faces there are three sorts: that of grief's drudge, that of the lantern-jawed man, and that of the impostor. Melville, *Confidence-Man*, VI

Thoughtful men will not spend their lives acquiring sleight-of-hand.
Shaw, *An Unsocial Socialist*, XII

I speak with the bluntness of gravity. Stevenson, *Prince Otto*, Book II, VIII

Gravity is the world's original sin. If the caveman had known how to laugh, history would have been different. Wilde, *The Picture of Dorian Gray*, III

SERVANT; SERVICE; SERVITUDE: *see also* SLAVERY

How could I live without service to the world? Bellamy, *Looking Backward*, I

That punctual servant of all work, the sun. Dickens, *Pickwick Papers*, II

Service is our destiny in life or in death. Meredith, *Diana of the Crossways*, I

The years may freeze, but otherwise they do not alter a working woman's heart; and should a thaw come, the simple sentiments of her youth again burst into blossom. Her choice of books shows how little time has taught her. The same grotesque adventures enrapture her as they did before. She is as incapable at thirty as at twenty to distinguish between the false and the true;—apparently even less so, for if experience has influenced her taste at all, it has rendered it more childish and ignorant, and now more than before is her imagination the palpitating prey of the absurd fiction, and now more than ever does she relish the stories of supernatural heroism, abnegation, and sacrifice.
Moore, G., *A Mummer's Wife*, VII

A servant's calamity will increase good will with a generous master or mistress.
Richardson, *Clarissa Harlowe*, II

Servants boast of their master's pedigree and descent as if they were related to him.
Ibid.

Anything servants know of their master, or of his affairs, is not a secret to one another, if it would hang him. *Ibid.*

Men of family should take care to give servants subjects worth boasting of. *Ibid.*

Always find fault with servants, so to have no reason to find fault. *Ibid.*

Servants are fond of deriving collateral honors and distinctions from the quality or rank of those they serve. *Ibid.*, III

Servants should see all and say nothing. Smollett, *Humphry Clinker*, 17

We get forwards in the world, not so much by doing services, as receiving them; you take a withering twig, and put it in the ground; and then you water it because you have planted it. Sterne, *A Sentimental Journey*, 117

SEXUALITY: *see also* LIBERTINISM; MALE AND FEMALE; SEDUCTION; etc.

The hen knows the barleycorn was not all the rooster called her for.
Richardson, *Clarissa Harlowe*, II

SHADOW; SUBSTANCE

Such as seek the pleasure of the world follow a shadow wherein is no substance: and as the adder Aspis tickleth a man to death, so doth vain pleasure flatter us, till it makes us forget God, and consume our substance. Deloney, *Thomas of Reading*, 267

In arguing of the shadow, we forgo the substance. Lyly, *Euphues*, 108-109

As a good root is known by a fair blossom, so is the substance of the heart noted by the shew of the countenance. Lyly, *Euphues and His England*, 318

The shadow honor; the substance virtue. Mackenzie, *The Man of Feeling*, 39

The shadows of things are greater than themselves; and the more exaggerated the shadow, the more unlike to the substance. Melville, *Mardi*, CXVII

When the substance is gone, men cling to the shadow.
Melville, *Pierre*, Book XIX, I

Beauty is an angel that no man ever caught; truth is a deception that changes to falsehood while you finger it. We are shadows among shadows.
Schreiner, *Undine*, XVII

While we walk in this misty valley of humanity, men will mistake shadows for substances. Scott, *The Talisman*, XX

SHALLOWNESS: *see also* IMPORTANCE; ORDINARINESS; SHADOW; SUBSTANCE

Shallowness [of nature and intellect] has this advantage, that you can't be drowned there. Hardy, *Pair of Blue Eyes*, XXX

All flounces and frills and nothing to say. Ward, *Robert Elsmere*, Book I, I

SHAME

If Shame was not himself audacious, he would never attempt to do as he does. But let us still resist him; for notwithstanding all his bravadoes he promoteth the fool and none else. Bunyan, *Pilgrim's Progress*, 76

Shame and distress are natural to every unhackneyed mind, in any necessity of soliciting a pecuniary favor. Burney, *Camilla*, Three, VI

Sin and shame follow one another. Defoe, *Colonel Jack*, 164

It is a most miserable thing to feel ashamed of home.
Dickens, *Great Expectations*, XIV

He must be a fool who is ashamed of being hanged who is not weak enough to be ashamed of having deserved it. Fielding, H., *Jonathan Wild*, 288

Mortifications are often more painful than calamities.
Goldsmith, *The Vicar of Wakefield*, 55

Men often are ashamed of what is best in them.
Hawthorne, *The Blithedale Romance*, VI

There can be no outrage against our common nature more flagrant than to forbid the culprit to hide his face for shame. Hawthorne, *The Scarlet Letter*, II

Mortification is not virtuous in itself, nor has any other use, but that it disengages us from the allurements of sense. Johnson, *Rasselas*, 181

Where embarrassments prevail, they affect the most disembarrassed.
Melville, *Pierre*, Book III, I

If everybody would give praise where only praise is due, dispraise where due likewise, shame, if not principle, would mend the world—shame would introduce principle.
Richardson, *Clarissa Harlowe*, II

Shame not the past by future behavior. *Ibid.*, III

Many a man has been ashamed of his wicked attempts when he has been repulsed, that would never have been ashamed of them had he succeeded.
Richardson, *Pamela*, 37

SHAME (*continued*)

Nature or custom has bequeathed to the assistance of reason the passion of shame, to support it in its combating the influences of unlawful love.
Shebbeare, *The Marriage Act*, II

Shame is a haunting spectre that will down at no man's bidding.
Simms, *Vasconselos*, XXIV

What false shame is the inheritance of fashionable politeness!
Young, *The Adventures of Emmera*, II

SIGN; SYMBOL; IMAGE: *see also* MEANING; REPRESENTATION

Presentiments are strange things, and so are sympathies, and so are signs: and the three combined make one mystery to which humanity has not yet found the key.
Bronte, C., *Jane Eyre*, XXI

Gold, the dumb symbol of organized matter's great mystery, storing in itself, according as mind, the informer of matter, can distinguish its uses, evil and good, bane and blessing. Bulwer, *A Strange Story*, LXXXI

All signs fail in dry weather. Howells, *Silas Lapham*, VIII

This ring, this speaking picture. Kimber, *Joe Thompson*, II

All that most maddens and torments; all that stirs up the lees of things; all truth with malice in it; all that cracks the sinews and cakes the brain; all the subtle demonisms of life and thought; all evil, to crazy Ahab, were visibly personified, and made practically assailable in Moby Dick. He piled upon the whale's white hump the sum of all the general rage and hate felt by his whole race from Adam down; and then, as if his chest had been a mortar, he burst his hot heart's hell upon it. Melville, *Moby Dick*, XLI

Omens are as impassible as heroes. Meredith, *Ordeal of Richard Feverel*, XXX

How hard it is not to bewray a man's fault by his forehead.
Nashe, *The Unfortunate Traveller*, 116

SIGNIFICANCE: *see also* MEANING; SIGN; etc.

Some certain significance lurks in all things, else all things are little worth, and the round world itself but an empty cipher, except to sell by the cartload, as they do hills about Boston, to fill up some morass in the Milky Way. Melville, *Moby Dick*, XCIX

SILENCE; STILLNESS: *see also* SERENITY

The music of the spheres consists in a profound silence.
Anonymous, *The Lady's Drawing Room*, 192

He is no fool, but his sense consists chiefly in holding his tongue.
Anonymous, *Memoirs of an Oxford Scholar*, 154

Is it ever a complaint in common life that men want tongues? Are you obliged to urge them to write in newspapers? The difficulty is to keep them from it. They will be talking and scribbling before they know what to say, or to write.
Brackenridge, *Modern Chivalry*, Part II, II

Silence composes the nerves. Bronte, C., *Jane Eyre*, XV

Silence is of different kinds, and breathes different meanings.
Bronte, C., *Villette*, XXIX

Is not silence as good a cloak as sleep? Bulwer, *The Caxtons*, Book XI, I

The strong man armed is the devil, and quietness is his security.
Bunyan, *The Life and Death of Mr. Badman*, 297

There are so many ways of communication independent of speech, that silence is but one point in the ordinances of discretion.   Burney, *Camilla*, Three, V

Those who are most silent to strangers commonly talk most fluently to their intimates.
                                                                Burney, *Cecilia*, II

Dumb as a drum with a hole in it.   Dickens, *Pickwick Papers*, XXV

Speech is often barren; but silence also does not necessarily brood over a full nest.
                                                                Eliot, *Felix Holt*, XVI

Great joy is, especially after a sudden change and revolution of circumstances, apt to be silent, and dwells rather in the heart than in the tongue.   Fielding, H., *Tom Jones*, 882

That man's silence is wonderful to listen to.   Hardy, *Under the Greenwood Tree*, XIV

Quiet is not the daughter of grandeur or of power, is not to be bought by wealth, nor enforced by conquest.   Johnson, *Rasselas*, 104

The silence of a man who loves to praise is a censure sufficiently severe.
                                                        Lennox, *The Female Quixote*, II

It is better to sit still than to arise and fall.   Lyly, *Euphues and His England*, 419

Pauses precede the earthquake, and every other terrible commotion.
                                                            Melville, *Pierre*, Book II, II

All profound things, and emotions of things are preceded and attended by Silence.
                                                                Ibid., Book XIV, I

Silence is the only Voice of our God.   *Ibid.*

Silence is the general consecration of the universe.   *Ibid.*

Speech is the small change of silence.   Meredith, *Ordeal of Richard Feverel*, XXXVIII

Silence is sometimes eloquence.   Radcliffe, *The Italian*, II

The silence of terror.   Radcliffe, *The Romance of the Forest*, 268

The difficulty is not to speak; the difficulty is to keep silence.
                                            Schreiner, *The Story of an African Farm*, Part II, IV

There are cases in which silence implies other things than consent.
                                                            Scott, *Redgauntlet*, Letter V

Shallow brooks murmur most; deep, silent slide away.   Sidney, *Arcadia*, I

Whatsoever in great things will think to prevent all objections must lie still and do nothing.   *Ibid.*, III

Few words are best.   Smollett, *Ferdinand, Count Fathom*, XXXIX

He shunned all superfluity of speech, as much as he avoided any other unnecessary expense.   Smollett, *Peregrine Pickle*, 13

A man of few words speaks few in vain.   Young, *The Adventures of Emmera*, I

SILLINESS

All sorts of silly things are to be found in Old England, as well as some that are wise.
                                                        Cooper, *Satanstoe*, Volume II, IV

SIMILARITY: *see also* COMPARISON/CONTRAST; DIFFERENCE; etc.

Nothing can differ more widely than wise men and fools in their estimation of things; but, as both act from their uppermost passion, they both often act alike.
                                                            Fielding, H., *Amelia*, II

The same parts, the same actions often promote men to the head of superior societies, which raise them to the head of lower.   Fielding, H., *Jonathan Wild*, 26

Her nature had a great deal of color, and, in accordance with it, so likewise had her pictures. Hawthorne, *The Marble Faun*, III

Two ends of a stick are pretty much alike: they're all that length apart.
Meredith, *Beauchamp's Career*, LIII

SIMPLICITY

Simplicity is beyond the reach of almost every actress by profession. It requires a delicacy of feeling which they have not. It requires a gentlewoman.
Austen, *Mansfield Park*, Volume One, XIV

Language being the vestment of thought, it comes within the rules of other dress; so that as slovenliness, on the one hand, or foppery, on the other, is to be avoided in our attire; so also in our speech, and writing. Simplicity in the one and the other is the greatest beauty. Brackenridge, *Modern Chivalry*, Part I, I

Perspicuity is the natural result of simplicity. *Ibid.*, Part I, III

A man there was, though some did count him mad,/ The more he cast away, the more he had. Bunyan, *Pilgrim's Progress*, 277

He complicated matters by being so simple. Conrad, *Lord Jim*, VIII

Simplicity, when set on its guard, is often a match for cunning.
Fielding, H., *Tom Jones*, 282

That innocent untempted simplicity which is more than half the grace of virtue.
Galt, *Ayrshire*, VII

Simplicity verges on coquetry. Hardy, *Pair of Blue Eyes*, XX

Simplicity increases in value the longer we can keep it, and the further we carry it onward into life. Hawthorne, *The Marble Faun*, XXVII

There are some cases in which simplicity is the greatest refinement of art.
Lennox, *Henrietta*, II

To simplify expression is always the effect of the deepest knowledge and of the clearest discernment. Mackenzie, *The Man of the World*, I

I am one of those that never take on about princely fortunes, and am quite content if the world is ready to board and lodge me. Melville, *Moby Dick*, XVI

Simplicity is the keenest weapon and a beautiful refinement of cleverness.
Meredith, *Harry Richmond*, IX

Though ordinary, I am as clean as a penny. Richardson, *Pamela*, 272

Simplicity only can be elegance. Richardson, *Sir Charles Grandison*, Three, VI

As simple as a sum. Stevenson, *Prince Otto*, Book II, V

Amiable simplicity, ten thousand times more charming than all the polished elegance of the world's art. Young, *The Adventures of Emmera*, II

SINCERITY: *see also* HONESTY; HYPOCRISY; etc.

Sincerity cannot be called sincerity but upon proof, nor virtue virtue.
Anonymous, *The Fruitless Repentance*, I

Frank customers are worthy of good ware. Deloney, *The Gentle Craft*, 147

Human converse is not rigidly sincere. Eliot, *Adam Bede*, XVII

A person who persists in the willful breach of any one moral virtue cannot be sincere in the profession of any other. Johnstone, *The Reverie*, I

Politeness is sometimes a great tax upon sincerity.   Lennox, *Henrietta*, I

Often I so incline to a distrust of my powers, that I am far more keenly alive to censure, than to praise; and always deem it the more sincere of the two.
                                                        Melville, *Mardi*, CIII

Sincerity glows in the simple words of nature.   Parsons, *The Mysterious Warning*, IV

Too often vehemence passes for sincerity.   Radcliffe, *The Romance of the Forest*, 396

Be thought perverse rather than insincere.   Richardson, *Clarissa Harlowe*, I

No vows are less sincere than those made in anger.
                                                Scott, S., *The History of Cornelia*, 217

Sincerity is the true knight.   Scott, W., *Rob Roy*, X

A dupe to the sincerity of your own heart.
                                        Smollett, *Ferdinand, Count Fathom*, LIX

The value of an idea has nothing whatsoever to do with the sincerity of the man who expresses it.   Wilde, *The Picture of Dorian Gray*, I

SINGULARITY; UNIQUENESS: *see also* NOVELTY

There are in most societies a set of self-important young men who borrow consequence from singularity and take precedency in wisdom from the unfeeling use of the ludicrous; this is at best a shallow quality; in objects of eternal moment, it is poisonous to society.   Mackenzie, *The Man of the World*, I

SLANDER

The worst kind of slander is to speak well of everybody.
                                        Barr, *The Maid of Maiden Lane*, XI

Those are generally the best people whose characters have been most injured by slanderers, as we usually find that the best fruit which the birds have been pecking at.
                                        Brooke, *Emily Montague*, IV

Slander: a lot that often falls from bad men's mouths upon good men's names and professions.   Bunyan, *Pilgrim's Progress*, 81

The tongue of a viper is less hurtful than that of a slanderer.
                                        Fielding, H., *Jonathan Wild*, 134

Vice hath not a more abject slave; society produces not a more odious vermin; nor can the devil receive a guest more worthy of him, nor possibly more welcome to him, than a slanderer.   Fielding, H., *Tom Jones*, 488

Slander is a more cruel weapon than a sword, as the wounds which the former gives are always incurable.   *Ibid.*

There can be no greater sign of want of merit than where a man seeks to pull down another's character, in order to build up his own.   Richardson, *Clarissa Harlowe*, I

SLAVERY: *see also* FREEDOM; SERVICE; etc.

Frequently do we labor to secure the things that debase us into slaves, and overwhelm us with calamity.   Amory, *The Life of John Buncle*, I

Nothing is more strange than that any who have known a better state can support with life the hardships of an American slavery.
                                        Annesley, *Memoirs of an Unfortunate Young Nobleman*, I

There is no man who pretends to humanity, much less to religion, would be safe in being the possessor of a slave.   Brackenridge, *Modern Chivalry*, Part I, II

Hiring a mistress is the next worst thing to buying a slave: both are often by nature, and always by position, inferior: and to live familiarly with inferiors is degrading.

Bronte, C., *Jane Eyre*, XXVII

A slave here, a saint hereafter.

Eastman, *Aunt Phillis's Cabin*, XII

It is the lot of the slave to be exposed, in common with other men, to all the calamities of chance and all the caprices of fortune. But unlike other men, he is denied the consolation of struggling against them.

Hildreth, *Slave*, Volume I, XVI

What sort of liberty is it whose chosen city (Washington) is its slave-market?

Ibid.

Men born and bred in slavery are not men but children.

Ibid.

That single word *slave*, what volumes it does speak! It speaks of chains, of whips and tortures, compulsive labor, hunger and fatigues and all the miseries our wretched bodies suffer. It speaks of haughty power, and insolent commands; of insatiate avarice; of pampered pride and purse proud luxury; and of the cold indifference and scornful unconcern with which the oppressor looks down upon his victims. It speaks of crushing fear, and base servility; of low, mean cunning and treacherous revenge. It speaks of humanity outraged; manhood degraded; the social charities of life, the sacred ties of father, wife and child trampled under foot; of aspirations crushed; of hope extinguished; and the light of knowledge sacrilegiously put out. It speaks of man deprived of all that makes him amiable or makes him noble; stripped of his soul and sunk into a beast.

Ibid., Volume II, III

I cannot be a slave the second time.

Ibid., Volume II, XVI

We are but the veriest, sorriest slaves of our stomach.

Jerome, *Three Men in a Boat*, IX

The world is a tyrant; they are slaves who obey it.

Mackenzie, *The Man of Feeling*, 61

Abolitionism but expresses the fellow-feeling of slave for slave.

Melville, *Confidence-Man*, XXI

Who is not a slave?

Melville, *Moby Dick*, I

Though thousands in all ages have been made to drink of thee, Slavery, thou art no less bitter on that account.

Sterne, *A Sentimental Journey*, 77

No tint of words can spot thy snowy mantle, Liberty, or chymic power turn thy sceptre into iron; with thee to smile upon him as he eats his crust, the swain is happier than his monarch, from whose court thou art exiled.

Ibid.

Grant me but health and give me but this fair goddess Liberty as my companion.

Ibid.

"Here, Topsy," he said, giving a whistle, as a man would to call the attention of a dog, "give us a song, now, and show us some of your dancing."

Stowe, *Uncle Tom's Cabin*, XX

"Don't know how old you are? Didn't anybody ever tell you? Who was your mother?" "Never had none!" "Never had any mother? What do you mean? Where were you born?" "Never was born!"

Ibid.

Of the forces which have balefully touched life, the chief is that monster which has been the source of so many woes—the idea that God created one human being inferior to another, and destined to be forever subordinate and subservient. It is the cloak and cover of all enormity—the shield of oppression, and the ready excuse for unutterable infamy.

Tourgee, *Pactolus Prime*, XXIV

Wisdom cannot be grafted on the stock of slavery: justice cannot be established without denunciation and disapproval of the wrong.

Ibid.

Slavery sought to hide its deformity with the veil of faith, and take refuge with religion in the sanctuary of simple belief. It would not do. Reason was jealous of her attributes, and religion fearful of too much companionship in her sacred seclusion. So reason and religion—in the main—struck hands in denying the claims of slavery.
Tourgee, A Royal Gentleman, XXIV

SLEEP: see also DREAMS

Sleep does not commonly end of itself.   Brown, C. B., Arthur Mervyn, I

The incapacity of sound sleep denotes a mind sorely wounded.
Brown, C. B., Edgar Huntley, 13

Sleep is sweet to the laboring man.   Bunyan, Pilgrim's Progress, 140

Our heart ofttimes wakes when we sleep, and God can speak to that, either by words, by proverbs, by signs and similitudes, as well as if one was awake.   Ibid., 233

In the case of the wiser animals, the person submits to sleep. It is only the superior human being who tries the hopeless experiment of making sleep submit to the person.
Collins, I Say No, XXIV

"'Tis the woice," said the Captain, impressively, and announcing a quotation with his hook, "of the sluggard, I heerd him complain, you have woke me too soon, I must slumber again."   Dickens, Dombey and Son, LVI

Sleep is generally the epilogue to a good entertainment.
Donaldson, Sir Bartholomew Sapskull, I

Heroes must sleep, and lovers too; or they soon will cease to be heroes or lovers.
Edgeworth, The Absentee, XVI

Sleep, that powerful friend to the distressed, though, like other powerful friends, not always ready to give assistance to those who want it most.   Fielding, H., Amelia, I

When sorrow ceases to be speculative sleep sees her opportunity.
Hardy, Tess, XXXV

Fine weather's good sleepin'.   Kipling, Captains Courageous, II

It was the forty-fathom slumber that clears the soul and eye and heart, and sends you to breakfast ravening.   Ibid., III

Go to bed with the lamb, and rise with the lark. Late watching in the night breedeth unquiet; long sleeping in the day, ungodliness. Fly both: this, as unwholesome; that, as unhonest.   Lyly, Euphues and His England, 229

Sound sleep, like hearty dining, endows men with a sense of rectitude, and sunlight following the former, as a pleasant spell of conversational ease or sweet music the latter, smiles a celestial approval of the performance.   Meredith, Beauchamp's Career, LII

Sleep, the gentle sister of that awful power which shrouds man in its cold bosom, and bears him in still repose to the blissful wakefulness of eternal life.
Porter, Scottish Chiefs, XIX

People who have plots in their heads as seldom have good nights as deserve them.
Richardson, Clarissa Harlowe, III

Sleep has a long time quarrelled with me, and will not be friends, although I have made the first advances.   Ibid., IV

Sleep, the shades of death.   Ibid.

That sleep which only attends innocence and truth.   Shebbeare, Lydia, I

Sleep, the elder brother of death.   Sidney, Arcadia, I

God's blessing be upon the man who first invented this self-same thing called sleep—it covers a man all over like a cloak.   Sterne, Tristram Shandy, IV

SMOKING: *see also* HABIT; PLEASURE

If the smoking of tobacco were permitted in public places, the fumes of it would be communicated to numbers of people who have a great dislike to the smell of it.
Lawrence, H., *The Contemplative Man*, I

Like a good wife, a pipe is a friend and companion for life. And whoso weds with a pipe, is no longer a bachelor.
Melville, *Mardi*, CXXI

Once ignited, nothing like longevity pertains to cigars or cigarettes. They never grow old. The stump of a cigarette is an abomination; and two of them crossed are more of a *memento-mori*, than a brace of thighbones at right angles.
Ibid.

Life itself is a puff and a wheeze. Our lungs are two pipes which we constantly smoke.
Ibid.

In every puff [of a pipe], there hangs a wreath. In every puff, off flies a care.
Ibid.

When Stubb dressed, instead of first putting his legs into his trousers, he put his pipe into his mouth.
Melville, *Moby Dick*, XXVII

I shall not have time to wash before I am laid out. My time is short. I want tobacco. The washing can be done by-and-by, but not the smoking.
Meredith, *Vittoria*, XLII

To smoke is to contemplate. Contemplation implies calm, repose, and an easy position for the body.
Simms, *Woodcraft*, XXX

If I saw a young woman smoking, I should blush for my sex; and though she were the nearest and dearest that I had, I would never speak to her—never.
Trollope, *He Knew He Was Right*, XXXI

I cannot understand what pleasure it is that men take in making chimneys of themselves, and going about smelling so that no one can bear to come near them.
Ibid.

A cigarette is the perfect type of a perfect pleasure. It is exquisite, and it leaves one unsatisfied. What more can one want?
Wilde, *The Picture of Dorian Gray*, VI

SOCIETY; SOCIALNESS

Society in America means all the honest, kindly mannered, pleasant-voiced women, and all the good, brave, unassuming men, between the Atlantic and the Pacific. Each of these has a free pass in every city and village "good for this generation only," and it depends on each to make use of this pass or not as it may happen to suit his or her fancy. To this rule there are *no* exceptions, and those who say "Abraham is our father" will surely furnish food for that humor which is the staple product of our country.
Adams, H., *Democracy*, III

No plea arising from the preservation of property can justify actions repugnant to the general interest and happiness of society.
Anonymous, *The Adventures of a Kidnapped Orphan*, 249

Money and position will cover up a good many indiscretions in a married woman or a widow, but the world always has demanded that a girl should be immaculate; and if she permits Society to think she is not, it punishes her for violating one of its pet standards.
Atherton, *Senator North*, Book III, VI

In London, society has learned to combine the maximum of pleasure with the minimum of work. Washington society is its antithesis; and although many of the most brilliant men in America are in its official set, and the brightest and most charming women in its fashionable as well as political set, they are, through the exigencies of the old social structure, of little use to each other.
Ibid., Book III, VII

"I consider dancing as one of the first refinements of polished societies." "And it has the advantage of being in vogue amongst the less polished societies of the world. Every savage can dance."
Austen, *Pride and Prejudice*, Volume I, VI

Trial by battle must regulate society.   Brackenridge, *Modern Chivalry*, Part II, I

A general and indiscriminate acquaintance, by levelling all ranks, does injury to the rites of society.   Burney, *Cecilia*, I

Who shall limit the right of society except society itself?   Butler, *Erewhon*, XII

He who makes a collosal fortune in the hosiery trade, and by his energy has succeeded in reducing the price of woolen goods by the thousandth part of a penny in the pound—this man is worth ten professional philanthropists.   *Ibid.*, XX

Society, at its very best, always needs, and at its best or worst always contains, a few superior members, who make themselves a blessing by working a constant, tactful redistribution of individuals by their true values, across the unworthy lines upon which society ever tends to stratify.   Cable, *Bonaventure*, Book III, VII

The expediency of establishing the base of society on a principle of the most sordid character, one that is denounced by the revelations of God, and proved to be insufficient by the experience of man, may at least be questioned without properly subjecting the dissenter to the imputation of being a sheep-stealer.
                                       Cooper, *The Monikins*, Conclusion

At table, seated close together, there is a whole language in one's neighbor's elbow and an unlimited power of expression in its way of avoiding collisions.
                                       Crawford, *A Rose of Yesterday*, IX

Society corrupts the heart.   Dacre, *The Libertine*, I

Society is the hot-bed of crimes and vices.   *Ibid.*, II

The whole social system is a system of Prince's nails.
                                       Dickens, *David Copperfield*, XXII

Of all mysteries the social mysteries are the most appalling. Going to an assembly for the first time is more alarming than the first battle.   Disraeli, *Coningsby*, Book IV, VI

If a society created by labor suddenly becomes independent of it, that society is bound to maintain the race whose only property is labor, from the proceeds of that property, which has not ceased to be productive.   Disraeli, *Sybil*, Book II, XIII

The beast-men of society.   Dreiser, *Sister Carrie*, XIII

In the society of men we must have something to endure, as well as to enjoy.
                                       Godwin, *Caleb Williams*, I

No man must think that the world was made for him.   *Ibid.*

It is only with a social enjoyment that a man is truly pleased—when pulse replies to pulse, when the eyes discourse eloquently to each other, when in responsive tones and words the soul is communicated.   Godwin, *St. Leon*, 63

Man was not born to live alone. He is linked to his brethren by a thousand ties; and, when those ties are broken, he ceases from all genuine existence.   *Ibid.*, 282

In society, a genuine American never dreams of stepping across the inappreciable air-line which separates one class from another.
                                       Hawthorne, *The Blithedale Romance*, XX

If society took in all the people of right ideas and good sense, it would expand beyond the calling capacity of its most active members. Society is a very different thing from good sense and right ideas.   Howells, *Silas Lapham*, XI

If it did not happen that a bad man generally defeats his own purposes, society must be very uncomfortable.   Jenner, *The Placid Man*, I

There may be community of material possessions, but there can never be community of love or of esteem.   Johnson, *Rasselas*, 59

Mankind is by nature designed for society.
                                       Kirkby, *The Capacity of Human Understanding*, 89

What are the qualifications of a General Favorite? Good looks, good birth, good humor, and good assurance will do much; but the want of one or more of these will not invalidate the election, nor the union of all four ensure it.
Lawrence, G. A., *Guy Livingstone*, XXXIII

Society, that first of blessings, brings with it evils death only can cure.
Lee, *The Recess*, I

Even among animals, where there is a society, there is a great tyrant and a pariah.
Marryat, *Monsieur Violet*, XLIV

In all societies, you will invariably meet with a bully.
Marryat, *Mr. Midshipman Easy*, X

There are classes of men in the world who bear the same relation to society at large that the wheels do to a coach: and are just as indispensable.   Melville, *Redburn*, XXIX

Society is our one tangible gain, our one roofing and flooring in a world of most uncertain structures built on morasses. Toward the laws that support it men hopeful of progress give their adhesion. If it is martyrdom, what then? Let the martyrdom be. Contumacy is animalism.   Meredith, *Beauchamp's Career*, XXIX

Tell me Society is the whited sepulchre, that it is blotched, hideous, hollow: and I say, add not another disfigurement to it; add to the purification of it.   *Ibid.*

Society is the protection of the weaker, therefore a shield of women, who are our temple of civilization, to be kept sacred; and he that loves a woman will assuredly esteem and pity her sex, and not drag her down for another example of their frailty.   *Ibid.*

Society is the best thing we have, but it is a crazy vessel worked by a crew that formerly practiced piracy, and now, in expiation, professes piety, fearful of a discovered omnipotence, which is in the image of themselves and captain.
Meredith, *Diana of the Crossways*, XVIII

Her practiced play upon the social instrument, surely the grandest of all, the chords being men and women.   Meredith, *Sandra Belloni*, X

Society will get the better of us unless we get the better of society.
Moore, G., *Evelyn Innes*, VII

Nothing is so easy as to lay down the outlines of perfect society. There wants nothing but money to set it going.   Peacock, *Crotchet Castle*, VI

A ballroom is an epitome of all that is most worthless and unamiable in the great sphere of human life.   Peacock, *Headlong Hall*, XIII

No two things are more opposite than a crowd and society.
Scott, S., *A Description of Millenium Hall*, 76

You can't make a life over—society wouldn't let you if you would.
Twain and Warner, *The Gilded Age*, Volume II, XIII

A salutary sense has begun to penetrate even modern provincial society, that no man may tell a ghost story without leave.   Ward, Mrs. H., *Robert Elsmere*, Book I, III

SOLDIERY; THE MILITARY: *see also* WAR

There is no heaven for soldiers.   Anonymous, *Ephraim Tristram Bates*, 18-19

'Tis not a red coat makes a soldier; patience of fatigue and firmness are the things.
Ibid., 39

When an army composed of a great number of men moves slowly on at a distance, nobody thinks of considering a single soldier.
Brown, W. H., *The Power of Sympathy*, 49

I cannot see why the coat of the soldier should harden the heart of the man.
Doyle, *Micah Clarke*, XXX

Military man disguises to himself the real nature of his occupation.
Godwin, *St. Leon*, 22

Battles (as soldiers know, and newspaper editors do not) are usually fought, not as they ought to be fought, but as they can be fought.   Kingsley, C., *Westward Ho!*, IX

Soldiers: like dolls all with one face.   Meredith, *Vittoria*, XLII

A soldier is a Yahoo hired to kill in cold blood as many of his own species, who have never offended him, as possibly he can.   Swift, *Gulliver's Travels*, Houyhnhnms

SOLIDITY: *see also* SUBSTANCE

A well-built house requires but little repairs.   Richardson, *Clarissa Harlowe*, IV

SOLITUDE: *see also* LONELINESS

It is only the shallow mind that dislikes and fears the lonely places of Nature: the intellect, no matter what vapors may be sent up from the heart, finds not only solace in retirement, but another form of that companionship of the ego which the deeply religious find in retreat.   Atherton, *Senator North*, Book III, XIX

No one can enjoy solitude better than a man who is bent down with the burthen of age, and has made a wise use of his life.   August, *Horrid Mysteries*, II

Solitude: Cold abstraction—fleshless skeleton—daughter—mother—and mate of Death!
Bronte, C., *Shirley*, XXIX

Solitude imposes least restraint upon the fancy. Dark is less fertile of images than the feeble lustre of the moon.   Brown, C. B., *Wieland*, 105

In solitude we shrink up. No plant so much as man needs the sun and the air.
Bulwer, *The Caxtons*, Book VII, IX

To a heart formed for friendship and affection the charms of solitude are very short-lived.   Burney, *Cecilia*, I

It is a dreadful feeling that of being cut off from all one's kind. I do not believe that any man could long retain his reason in solitude. One begins doubting one's own identity.
Butler, *Erewhon*, IV

In solitude alone can we be free from the contagion of example, and enjoy a comparative felicity.   Dacre, *The Libertine*, II

More solitary than Robinson Crusoe, who had nobody to look at him, and see that he was solitary.   Dickens, *David Copperfield*, V

Perfect solitude can never be reconciled to a social mind, but when it relieves you from the company of those you hate.   Fielding, H., *Tom Jones*, 516

It is absurd, it may be termed profanation, to talk of solitary pleasure. No sensation ordinarily distinguished by that epithet can endure the test of a moment's inspection, when compared with a social enjoyment.   Godwin, *St. Leon*, 62-63

In circumstances of profound feeling and passion, there is often a sense that too great a seclusion cannot be endured; there is an indefinite dread of being quite alone with the object of our deepest interest. The species of solitude that a crowd harbors within itself is felt to be preferable, in certain conditions of the heart, to the remoteness of a desert or the depths of an untrodden wood.   Hawthorne, *The Marble Faun*, XXXV

In solitude, if I escape the example of bad men, I want likewise the counsel and conversation of the good.   Johnson, *Rasselas*, 87

He that lives well in the world is better than he that lives well in a monastery.
Ibid., 180

543

SOLITUDE (*continued*)

They who never enter into public life can not possibly have the same feeling as those who are fond of society; at least, we don't have many examples of their doing generous actions. Their purses are generally as contracted as their minds, and both, as it were, are confined to a corner.　　　　　　　　Marishall, *Miss Clarinda Cathcart*, II

Solitude breeds taciturnity. Who so taciturn as authors, taken as a race?
　　　　　　　　　　　　　　　　　　Melville, *White Jacket*, XII

Solitariness is a common human fate and the one chance of growth, like space for timber.　　　　　　　　　　Meredith, *Diane of the Crossways*, I

Solitude is only the nurse of discontent.　　　Parsons, *The Mysterious Warning*, III

There is nothing more remarkable in human nature than the strength it gains from solitude.　　　　　　　　　　　Tourgee, *Murvale Eastman*, XXI

The greatest natures have always been lovers of solitude. Shallow ones do not require it; they need often to be refilled.　　　　　　　　　　　　　*Ibid.*

To the great, solitude is the antechamber of the Infinite, the place where the soul renews its strength.　　　　　　　　　　　　　　　　　　*Ibid.*

SONG: *see also* MUSIC

A serenade is an every-day affair, and in the street one voice sounds about as well as another.　　　　　　　　　　Crawford, *A Roman Singer*, VII

Ah, songs without words are the best!　　DuMaurier, *Peter Ibbetson*, Part Third

There's no way to stop my singing in this world but to cut my throat. And when that's done, ten to one I sing ye the doxology for a wind-up.　　Melville, *Moby Dick*, CXIX

A sweet thing is a song.　　　　　　　　　　Melville, *Redburn*, LVI

Who would listen to the thrush when the nightingale is singing?
　　　　　　　　　　　　　　　　　　Scott, *Kenilworth*, VII

SOPHISTRY: *see also* EDUCATION; LOGIC; KNOWLEDGE AND LEARNING; etc.

We may call that sophistry which, having been previously heard, fails to produce conviction.　　　　　　　　　　Brown, C. B., *Alcuin*, III

SORDIDNESS

So sordid are the lives of such low natures, who are not only not heroic to their valets and waiting-women, but have neither valets nor waiting-women to be heroic to withal.
　　　　　　　　　　　　　　　　　　Dickens, *Dombey and Son*, XXXIII

Remorse drives man away from man? How came Cain, after the first murder, to go and build the first city? And why is it that the modern Cain dreads nothing so much as solitary refinement? No one goes into the crowd but for his end; and the end of too many is the same as the pickpocket's.　　　　　　Melville, *Confidence-Man*, XXIV

In times of strong emotion mankind disdain all base considerations; but such times are evanescent. The permanent constitutional condition of the manufactured man is sordidness.　　　　　　　　　　　　Melville, *Moby Dick*, XLVI

SORROW: *see also* HAPPINESS

Personal size and mental sorrow have certainly no necessary proportions. A large bulky figure has as good a right to be in deep affliction, as the most graceful set of limbs in the world.　　　　　　　　　　　　Austen, *Persuasion*, VIII

Sorrow cometh with years, and to live is to mourn.
Bulwer, *The Pilgrims of the Rhine*, XXVI

Better great sorrow than small delight.   Cable, *Bonaventure*, Book III, XXI

In a mind wherein strong sympathies are at work, where there is no supreme sense of right to which the agitated nature can cling and steady itself to quiet endurance, one of the first results of sorrow is a desperate vague clutching after any deed that will change the actual condition.   Eliot, *Adam Bede*, XXXI

All things are dark to sorrow.   Evans, *Inez*, XXX

So passed away Sorrow the Undesired—that intrusive creature, that bastard gift of shameless Nature who respects not the social law; a waif to whom eternal Time had been a matter of days merely, who knew not that such things as years and centuries ever were; to whom the cottage interior was the universe, the week's weather climate, new-born babyhood human existence, and the instinct to suck human knowledge.
Hardy, *Tess*, XIV

Sorrow may be a softening medicine at last, but at first it is apt to be a hardening one.
Kingsley, C., *Hereward the Wake*, XXXVI

That mortal man who hath more of joy than sorrow in him, that mortal man cannot be true—not true, or undeveloped. With books the same. The truest of all men was the Man of Sorrows, and the truest of all books is Solomon's, and Ecclesiastes is the fine-hammered steel of woe.   Melville, *Moby Dick*, XCVI

There is a wisdom that is woe; but there is a woe that is madness.   *Ibid.*

The sacredness of sorrow.   Radcliffe, *The Italian*, I

Little incidents affect a mind enervated by sorrow.
Radcliffe, *The Mysteries of Udolpho*, I

Sorrow is divine. Sorrow is reigning on the throne of the Universe, and the crown of all crowns has been one of thorns.   Stowe, *The Minister's Wooing*, XXIV

SOUL; SOULFULNESS: *see also* BODY; MIND; SPIRIT

A soul is like a bird, and needs a sharp tap on its shell to open it.
Adams, H., *Esther*, IV

My soul is straight if my back isn't.   Alcott, *Little Men*, II

When my soul shall be separated from my body, will there exist less order or perfection in the creation?   Anonymous, *Jeremiah Grant*, 152

The holiness of the soul is immortal.   Bates, *Puritans*, VI

The whole world pulls at the body, and will have it an animal. Therefore the heavens must draw upon the spirit.   Beecher, *Norwood*, LVI

The soul has an interpreter—often an unconscious, but still a truthful interpreter—in the eye.   Bronte, C., *Jane Eyre*, XXVII

"*Here*! and *here*!" replied Catherine, striking one hand on her forehead and the other on her breast, "in whichever place the soul lives."   Bronte, E., *Wuthering Heights*, IX

My soul's bliss kills my body, but does not satisfy itself.   *Ibid.*, XXXIV

Our souls should be as stars on earth, not as meteors and tortured comets.
Bulwer, *The Caxtons*, Book VII, VI

The soul really grand is only tested in its errors.   Bulwer, *Harold*, Book XI, VII

The soul asleep in the arms of love.   Bulwer, *Pompeii*, Book V, Chapter the Last

The soul of man seems to have been constructed for another sphere of existence.
Caruthers, *Kentuckian in New-York*, Volume II, VI

The face is but a reflecting surface for the soul. *Ibid.*, Volume II, XII

You can't expect the constituted authorities to inquire into the state of a man's soul—or is it only of his liver? Conrad, *Lord Jim*, VI

A narrow life demands a narrow soul. Davis, *Verdict*, XXXV

The absence of the soul is far more terrible in a living man than in a dead one.
Dickens, *Barnaby Rudge*, III

His soul is a great deal too large for his frame. Dickens, *Dombey and Son*, VIII

The light had dawned on his soul. Disraeli, *Coningsby*, Book VI, III

How can the soul progress save through the cultivation of virtue and self-mastery?
Doyle, *Micah Clarke*, XXII

We must learn to accommodate ourselves to the discovery that some of those cunningly fashioned instruments called human souls have only a very limited range of music, and will not vibrate in the least under a touch that fills others with tremulous rapture or quivering agony. Eliot, *Adam Bede*, IX

Men's muscles move better when their souls are making merry music, though their merriment is of a poor blundering sort, not at all like the merriment of birds.
Ibid., XIX

To know intense joy without a strong bodily frame, one must have an enthusiastic soul.
Eliot, *Middlemarch*, Book III, XXIX

The energy that would animate a crime is not more than is wanted to inspire a resolved submission, when the noble habit of the soul reasserts itself. *Ibid.*, Book IV, XLII

As a strong boy struggles against fumes with the more violence when they begin to be stifling, a strong soul struggles against phantasies with all the more alarmed energy when they threaten to govern in the place of thought. Eliot, *Romola*, Book II, XXXVI

Like the sunbeams, the soul of man pervades and enlightens surrounding matter.
Gentleman, *A Trip to the Moon*, II

There is a species of intuition—either a spiritual lie, or the subtle recognition of a fact—which comes to us in a reduced state of the corporeal system.
Hawthorne, *The Blithedale Romance*, VI

The yearning of a soul, formed by Nature in a peculiar mould, for communion with those to whom it bore a resemblance, yet of whom it was not.
Hawthorne, *Fanshawe*, IX

The soul needs air; a wide sweep and frequent change of it. Morbid influences, in a thousand-fold variety, gather about hearths, and pollute the life of households.
Hawthorne, *The House of the Seven Gables*, XVII

A river is strangely like a human soul. It has its dark and bright days, its troubles from within, and its disturbances from without. It often runs over ragged rocks with a smooth surface, and is vexed with ripples as it slides over sands that are level as a floor. It betrays its various moods by aspects which are the commonplaces of poetry, as smiles and dimples and frowns. Its face is full of winking eyes, when the scattering raindrops, as with knitted brows, when the winds are let loose. It talks, too, in its own simple dialect, murmuring, as it were, with busy lips all the way to the ocean, as children seeking the mother's breast and impatient of delay.
Holmes, *The Guardian Angel*, VIII

Your soul was in a hurry, and made a rush for a body. There are patient spirits that have waited from eternity, and never found parents fit to be born of. *Ibid.*, XXXV

The soul, as you conceive it, is not a spiritual conception, but some kind of organization—a ghost, in short, having functions, but the Devil himself cannot define its structure.
Howland, *Papa's Own Girl*, IV

The soul is a more tender organism than the body, and it shrinks from the prospect of being subjected to violence.   James, H., *Confidence*, XXI

All things die not: while the soul lives, love lives: the song may be now gay, now plaintive, but it is deathless.   Johnston, *To Have and to Hold*, end

In purity and love have we genius; the Gospel gives beauty and holiness to the soul.
                    Judd, *Margaret*, Volume III

The human soul is finite and not in the least under its own command.
                    Kipling, *The Light That Failed*, IV

Lukewarmness of soul, which sends forth but feeble desires, sends also but feeble lights; so that those who are guilty of it, not knowing anything clearly, cannot fasten on anything with perseverance.   Lennox, *The Female Quixote*, II

If there is not a sex in the soul, custom and education have established one in our idea.
                    Mackenzie, *Julia De Roubigné*, 157

The two great movements of the soul are the desire of honor and the fear of shame.
                    Mackenzie, *The Man of the World*, I

Man is no poor drifting seaweed of the universe. Man has a soul; which, if he will, puts him beyond fortune's finger and the future's spite.
                    Melville, *Confidence-Man*, XXXIX

Waves know the last secret of many a stout ship, never heard of from the days she left port. Every wave in my eyes seems a soul.   Melville, *Mardi*, XVI

Samoa had a soul in his eye; looking out upon you there, like somebody in him.
                    Ibid., XXX

Many, many souls are in me.   *Ibid.*, CXIX

Better slay the body than the soul; and if it be the direst of sins to be the murderers of our own bodies, how much more to be a soul-suicide.   *Ibid.*, CXXXV

I am my own soul's emperor; and my first act is abdication!   *Ibid.*, CXCV

You cannot hide the soul.   Melville, *Moby Dick*, X

For the third time my soul's ship starts upon this voyage.   *Ibid.*, CXXXV

The food of thy soul is light and space.   Melville, *Pierre*, Book XXII, I

Foolish, to think that by starving thy body, thou shalt fatten thy soul.   *Ibid.*

Man's aim has been to keep men from having a soul for *this* world.
                    Meredith, *Beauchamp's Career*, XII

Seed sown in faith day by day is the nightly harvest of the soul, and with the soul we work. With the soul we see.   *Ibid.*, XXIX

We have in history durable testification that our seasons come in the souls of men, yea, as a planet that we have set in motion.   *Ibid.*

That crust of habit which is the soul's tomb.   *Ibid.*

Custom, the soul's tyrant.   *Ibid.*

There is no home for the soul where dwells a shadow of untruth.
                    Meredith, *Ordeal of Richard Feverel*, XXV

Just as every variation of habit, of fashion is noticeable to those who live outside themselves, so the changes and complexities in the life of the soul are perceived by them who live within themselves.   Moore, G., *Evelyn Innes*, XXXV

Souls differ like locks, and preachers must differ like keys, or the fewer should the Church open for God to pass in.   Reade, *The Cloister and the Hearth*, LXXX

Souls will not be saved by brute force.   *Ibid.*, LXXXII

The less soul, the more sensual.   Richardson, *Clarissa Harlowe*, II

Have not women souls as well as men, and souls as capable of the noblest attainments, as theirs?　　　　　　　　　　　　　　　　　Richardson, *Sir Charles Grandison*, One, I

Souls may be near when bodies are distant.　　　　　　　　　　　　　*Ibid.*, Three, VI

Has a new soul crept into this old body, that even our intellectual faculties are changed?
　　　　　　　　　　　　　Schreiner, *The Story of an African Farm*, Part II, VII

Tell me what a soul desires, and I will tell you what it is.　　　　　*Ibid.*, Part II, XIII

The things of life are very little, and the soul is great.　　　　Schreiner, *Undine*, XV

Is there a moment before the hour of dissolution when the mortal is vouchsafed communion, a close communion and converse with its God? It is, it must be so. The dim confine, the heavy earth, cannot always be around us.
　　　　　　　　　　　　　　　　　　Simms, *The Partisan*, Volume II, V

A soul is a something that has eluded all the search of the anatomist.
　　　　　　　　　　　　　　　　　　Simms, *The Scout*, XXVIII

All souls are by nature equal.　　　　　　　　　Sterne, *Tristram Shandy*, II

In that half-waking doze, when the outer senses are at rest, and the mind is all the more calm and clear for their repose, a spiritual clairvoyance often seems to lift for a while the whole stifling cloud that lies like a confusing mist over the problems of life, and the soul has sudden glimpses of things unutterable which lie beyond.
　　　　　　　　　　　　　　　　　　Stowe, *Orr's Island*, XXXVII

The soul does not measure time by seconds, nor yet by heart-beats, but by modifications in its own quality and character. The watches of the world may stop; the planets may cease to measure the flight of time; the body may retain its pristine vigor—but in an hour, a moment almost, the heart may grow old, the man be transformed.
　　　　　　　　　　　　　　　　　　Tourgee, *Murvale Eastman*, X

Make his soul immortal, but don't disturb the Negro as he is.
　　　　　　　　　　　　　Twain and Warner, *The Gilded Age*, Volume I, XX

Nothing can cure the soul but the senses, just as nothing can cure the senses but the soul.
　　　　　　　　　　　　　　　Wilde, *The Picture of Dorian Gray*, II

Is the soul a shadow seated in the house of sin? Or is the body really in the soul? The separation of spirit from matter is a mystery, and the union of spirit with matter is a mystery also.　　　　　　　　　　　　　　　　　　　　　*Ibid.*, IV

To cure the soul by means of the senses, and the senses by means of the soul.
　　　　　　　　　　　　　　　　　　　　　　　　　Ibid., XVI

The soul is a terrible reality. It can be bought, and sold, and bartered away. It can be poisoned, or made perfect. There is a soul in each one of us.　　　*Ibid.*, XIX

It was the living death of his own soul that troubled him.　　　　*Ibid.*, XX

SPIRIT: *see also* SOUL; SUBSTANCE

The divorced mates, Spirit and Substance, were hard to reunite: they greeted each other, not in an embrace, but a racking sort of struggle.　　Bronte, C., *Villette*, XVI

Man's heart is more strong in the flesh than true to the spirit.
　　　　　　　　　　　　　　　　　　Bulwer, *Harold*, Book X, IX

It is because the spirit is inestimable that the lifeless body is so little valued.
　　　　　　　　　　　　　Hawthorne, *The Blithedale Romance*, XXVIII

The human spirit does not perish of a single wound, nor exhaust itself in a single trial of life.　　　　　　　　　　　　　　Hawthorne, *The Marble Faun*, XI

A bodily disease, which we look upon as whole and entire within itself, may, after all, be but a symptom of some ailment in the spiritual part.

Hawthorne, *The Scarlet Letter*, X

A sickness in your spirit hath immediately its appropriate manifestation in your bodily frame. *Ibid.*

Which is flesh and which is spirit? Kingsley, C., *Alton Locke*, I

Palliation of a sin is the hunted creature's refuge and final temptation. Our battle is ever between spirit and flesh. Spirit must brand the flesh that it may live.

Meredith, *Diana of the Crossways*, I

I feel myself almost a spirit when I gaze upon stars. Thackeray, *Vanity Fair*, XI

SPITE: *see also* HATE; LOVE

What we despise we always neglect. Gentleman, *A Trip to the Moon*, II

He that lives well cannot be despised. Johnson, *Rasselas*, 102

Men of sense rarely obtain satisfactory answers: they are provoked to despise their kind.

Meredith, *Beauchamp's Career*, II

To be despised by her sex is a very great compliment to a woman.

Thackeray, *Vanity Fair*, XII

SPYING

In business, as in war, spies and informers are necessary evils, which all good men detest; but which yet all prudent men must use, unless they mean to fight and act blindfold. Scott, *Redgauntlet*, IX

STARS: *see also* HEAVEN; NATURE; etc.

Wondrous worlds on worlds! Lo, round and round me, awful spells: all glorious, vivid constellations, God's diadem ye are! To you, ye stars, man owes his subtlest raptures, thoughts unspeakable, yet full of faith. Melville, *Mardi*, LVIII

STATE; STATESMANSHIP: *see also* GOVERNMENT

Amongst the various qualifications necessary to form a complete statesman, presence of mind is the most essential. Bridges, *The Adventures of a Bank-Note*, II

States and empires have their periods of declension, and feel in their turns what distress and poverty is. Sterne, *A Sentimental Journey*, 85

STATUS: *see also* SOCIETY; etc.

Why should not we have low life above stairs as well as high life below stairs?

Edgeworth, *Castle Rackrent*, 78

Many a great gentleman is sometimes found in places that don't become them well.

Fielding, H., *Amelia*, I

There are many worse men in the world than highwaymen; no more genteeler way than the road. *Ibid.*

Very high persons know us in one place and not in another, today and not tomorrow.

Fielding, H., *Joseph Andrews*, 133

Maidservants are no less practiced in the highest feminine arts than their fair superiors in quality and fortune. Fielding, H., *Tom Jones*, 128

He reverenced the inborn divinity that attends upon rank, as Indians worship the devil.

Godwin, *Caleb Williams*, I

STATUS (*continued*)

Rank and station are the homage of the multitude and the applause of fools.
Godwin, *St. Leon*, 93

The highest stations cannot hope to be abodes of happiness.
Johnson, *Rasselas*, 105–106

The king can make lords, but he cannot make gentlemen.
Lawrence, H., *The Contemplative Man*, II

Were the succession of modern fine ladies to be extinct, it might be supplied from those whom they place in the next rank to themselves, their chambermaids and confidants.
Richardson, *Clarissa Harlowe*, I

It is one of the distinctions of persons of condition and well-bred people to put bashful bodies out of countenance.
Richardson, *Pamela*, 300

The highest things are ever said by men of the lowest understandings.
Richardson, *Sir Charles Grandison*, Three, VI

Every idle vagabond who has neither home nor habitation, trade nor profession, designs himself a gentleman.
Smollett, *Sir Launcelot Greaves*, 94

STRANGER: *see also* FRIENDSHIP; etc.

What truth can there be found in a traveler? what stay in a stranger?
Lyly, *Euphues*, 131

STRATEGY: *see also* METHOD

The way to manage your Englishman is to dine him.
Meredith, *Beauchamp's Career*, XXX

When a general must regulate himself by the motions of a watchful adversary, how can he say beforehand what he will, or what he will not do?
Richardson, *Clarissa Harlowe*, II

There are some things that can beat smartness and foresight. Awkwardness and stupidity can. The best swordsman in the world doesn't need to fear the second best swordsman in the world; no, the person for him to be afraid of is some ignorant antagonist who has never had a sword in his hand before; he doesn't do the thing he ought to do, and so the expert isn't perpared for him; he does the thing he ought not to do; and often it catches the expert out and ends him on the spot.
Twain and Warner, *Connecticut Yankee*, XXXIV

Nothing shows the splendor and wisdom of her military genius like her instant comprehension of the size of the change which has come about, and her instant perception of the right and only right way to take advantage of it.
Twain, *Joan of Arc*, Book II, XXVI

STRENGTH; WEAKNESS

Weak men, who, meddling with things too high for them, do suddenly fall into distractions; which distractions do not only unman men, but they run upon desperate ventures to obtain they know not what.
Bunyan, *Pilgrim's Progress*, 19

Is it meet to think that a little child should handle Goliath as David did? Or that there should be the strength of an ox in a wren?
Ibid., 133

There is something almost pathetic in the humbleness of a young man's strength before the object of his first true love. It is the abasement of the real before the ideal; but if the ideal fails, the real takes vengeance of the man for having trodden it under.
Crawford, *A Rose of Yesterday*, X

The strength of a king is the love and friendship of his people.

Deloney, *Thomas of Reading*, 226

Physical force, that unmistakable evidence of sovereignty.

Hawthorne, *The Blithedale Romance*, XIV

Strength is incomprehensible by weakness, and therefore the more terrible.

Hawthorne, *The House of the Seven Gables*, XI

I am equal to any trial, any sacrifice, day after tomorrow; but when it comes today it's another thing.

Howells, *Silas Lapham*, XX

Heaven always proportions our strength to the trials which it lays before us.

Johnstone, *Arsaces*, II

No man is strong enough to take liberties with his public.

Kipling, *The Light That Failed*, IV

Real strength never impairs beauty or harmony, but it often bestows it; and in everything impossibly beautiful, strength has much to do with the magic.

Melville, *Moby Dick*, LXXXVI

Strength is the brute form of truth.

Meredith, *Beauchamp's Career*, II

Strength indicates a boundless nature—like the Maker. Strength is a God to you: Purity a toy.

Meredith, *Ordeal of Richard Feverel*, XXIX

It requires much personal strength, standing alone against the well-armed batteries of all one's friends.

Trollope, *Phineas Finn*, LXII

I am not strong enough to put the world straight.

Trollope, *The Way We Live Now*, I

STRUGGLE

Struggles with the natural character, the strong native bent of the heart, may seem futile and fruitless, but in the end they do good. They tend, however slightly, to give the actions, the conduct, that turn which Reason approves, and which Feeling, perhaps, too often opposes: they certainly make a difference in the general tenor of a life, and enable it to be better regulated, more equable, quieter on the surface; and it is on the surface only the common gage will fall. As to what lies below, leave that with God.

Bronte, C., *Villette*, XVII

STUDY: *see also* EDUCATION; KNOWLEDGE AND LEARNING; etc.

Plumb not the height of the house that feasts you.

Melville, *Mardi*, LV

Beware of prosecuting study too excitedly.

Meredith, *Ordeal of Richard Feverel*, XIX

STUPIDITY: *see also* IGNORANCE; INTELLIGENCE; KNOWLEDGE AND LEARNING; etc.

No stupid man ever suspected himself of being anything but clever.

Aldrich, *Stillwater*, VIII

STYLE: *see also* ART; EXPRESSION; LITERATURE; METHOD; etc.

It is the secret of good taste and perfection in behavior to conceal that you ever think of it all. So it is the most perfect proof of a good style, that when you read the composition, you think of nothing but the sense; and are never struck with the idea that it is otherwise expressed than everybody would express it.

Brackenridge, *Modern Chivalry*, Part I, III

SUBJECT: *see also* IDEA; MIND; THEME; THOUGHT

The gloomiest and truthfulest dramatist seldom chooses for his theme the calamities, however extraordinary, of inferior and private persons; least of all, the pauper's; admonished by the fact, that to the craped palace of the king lying in state, thousands of starers shall throng; but few feel enticed to the shanty, where, like a peeled knuckle-bone, grins the unupholstered corpse of the beggar.   Melville, *Israel Potter*, XXV

SUBJUGATION: *see also* OPPRESSION; SUBMISSION

Mistresses are wonderful subjugators.   Reade, *The Cloister and the Hearth*, XXXII

SUBLIMITY

The sublimity connected with vastness.   Cooper, *The Pathfinder*, I

SUBMISSION

The party then gathered round the fire to hear Lady Catherine determine what weather they were to have on the morrow.   Austen, *Pride and Prejudice*, Volume II, VI

Whatever is inevitable, submit to it.   Cable, *The Grandissimes*, V

The innate submissiveness of the goose as beautifully corresponding to the strength of the gander.   Eliot, *Middlemarch*, Book IV, XXXVI

Strange, that men from age to age should consent to hold their lives at the breath of another, merely that each in his turn may have a power of acting the tyrant according to law.   Godwin, *Caleb Williams*, III

The more absolute the submission demanded, the stronger the temptation becomes to those who have been tossed among doubts and conflicts.
Holmes, *Elsie Venner*, XVIII

Hard obtaining is the excuse of woman's granting.   Sidney, *Arcadia*, III

There are men who take other men at the price those other men put upon themselves.
Trollope, *The Way We Live Now*, LIV

If I never learnt nothing else out of pap, I learnt that the best way to get along with his kind of people is to let them have their own way.   Twain, *Huckleberry Finn*, XIX

SUBSTANCE: *see also* SHADOW; SPIRIT

I am no wrangler, to quarrel with a shadow.   Cooper, *Satanstoe*, Volume II, II

I find nothing so singular in life, as that everything appears to lose its substance, the instant one actually grapples with it.   Hawthorne, *The House of the Seven Gables*, III

The displeasure of his fellows is a slight and ephemeral matter to a man whose mind is fixed on a great essential question, charged with moral gravity and imperishable consequence.   Murfree, *The Prophet of the Great Smoky Mountains*, X

SUBTLETY

The defense of the purest innocence is often difficult, sometimes impossible, against the artfulness of a malicious tale, or the fortuitous concurrence of unfavorable appearances.
Godwin, *St. Leon*, 320

It is common and lamentable to behold simplicity entrapped by subtility.
Lyly, *Euphues*, 320

SUCCESS: *see also* FAILURE

To despair of success, is to prevent our succeeding.

Anonymous, The Life of Sir Richard Perrott, 35

Success supposes endeavor.

Austen, Emma, I

It is foolish to demand complete success of those we want to love; we should rejoice when they rise for a moment above themselves and sympathize with them when they fall.

Barrie, Tommy and Grizel, XXXV

We seldom find in men a strong desire of obtaining anything which depends on human power who have not been able to obtain it.

Brackenridge, Modern Chivalry, Part I, III

Old generals are not always the most successful, because they are afraid of accident and leave too little to chance, while the know-nothing, fear-nothing, has oftentimes been the secret of fortunate adventure.

Ibid., Part II, II

Victory depends upon ardor more than numbers.

Bulwer, Harold, Book XII, II

A certainty of success in many destroys, in all weakens, its charm: the bashful excepted, to whom it gives courage; and the indolent, to whom it saves trouble.

Burney, Camilla, Three, V

A man may find success in one direction or another; but a woman has got to be a social success, or she's a complete failure.

Cable, Bonaventure, Book III, VII

Alas for those who succeed too well!

Cable, The Grandissimes, XXVIII

Success is the most rare of results. Thousands fail; units triumph.

Disraeli, Coningsby, Book IX, IV

Versatility is the foundation of success.

Eggleston, The Faith Doctor, II

The best augury of a man's success in his profession is that he thinks it the finest in the world.

Eliot, Daniel Deronda, Book VIII, LVIII

There is no state of satisfaction, because to himself no man is a success.

Glasgow, The Descendant, Book II, III

Make ambition your business and indifference your relaxation, and you will fail; but make indifference your business and ambition your relaxation, and you will succeed. So impish are the ways of the gods.

Hardy, The Hand of Ethelberta, XVII

Nothing is so dangerous, especially to those who are not much accustomed to it, as a little success.

Jenner, The Placid Man, II

Success is a very poor proof of merit.

Johnstone, The Reverie, I

Absolute success often bears in it the seeds of its own destruction.

Page, Red Rock, XX

Success in projects is everything.

Richardson, Clarissa Harlowe, III

Moderation in success is necessary to its ultimate advantage.

Scott, Quentin Durward, XXX

Success at first is as likely to attend the hideous as the handsome; that is, if it be coupled with a good wit and a rare audacity.

Simms, The Scout, XXXII

I have seen too much of success to take off my hat and huzza to it as it passes in its gilt coach.

Thackeray, Henry Esmond, Book I, The History

It is the heart that gives success.

Trollope, The Last Chronicle of Barset, Volume II, XXII

There's many a way to win in this world, but none of them is worth much without good hard work back of it.

Twain, Joan of Arc, Book II, XXVII

SUDDENNESS

All really delightful things are sudden.   Wilde, *The Picture of Dorian Gray*, VI

SUFFERING: *see also* MISERY; SORROW

One does not love a place the less for having suffered in it, unless it has been all
suffering.   Austen, *Persuasion*, XX

Suffering can, and does, develop the latent evil that there is in humanity, as well as the
latent good.   Collins, *Armadale*, Book III, I

Deep unspeakable suffering may well be called a baptism, a regeneration, the initiation
into a new state.   Eliot, *Adam Bede*, XLII

It is not the persecution, but the catastrophe which is annexed to it, that makes the
difference between the tyrant and the sufferer. In mere corporal exertion the hunter
perhaps is upon a level with the miserable animal he pursues.
                                                  Godwin, *Caleb Williams*, III

We are born to suffer—and to bear it.   James, H., *The Bostonians*, XXIV

For one of your pangs another bosom is racked by ten.
                                                  Meredith, *The Egoist*, XXXIV

No one is to blame for suffering an evil he cannot avoid.
                                                  Richardson, *Clarissa Harlowe*, III

Who would not rather be the sufferer than the defrauder?
                                                  Richardson, *Sir Charles Grandison*, Two, V

Men live fast who suffer.   Tourgee, *Pactolus Prime*, XXI

SUICIDE: *see also* DEATH; KILLING; SELF-DESTRUCTION

Don Roberto had hanged himself with the American flag.
                                                  Atherton, *The Californians*, Book II, XXXI

The self-destroyer is his own enemy.   Brown, C. B., *Edgar Huntley*, 83

He that kills another can but commit murder upon his body; but for one to kill himself is
to kill body and soul at once.   Bunyan, *Pilgrim's Progress*, 118–119

They who commit suicides never talk of them; they who talk of suicides never commit
them.   Defoe, *Moll Flanders*, 102

He that dedicates his days to an endless sorrow is the worst and most degraded of
suicides.   Godwin, *St. Leon*, 295

Suicide is contrary to the first law of nature, self-preservation; and it shocks the natural
feelings and common apprehensions of all mankind.
                                                  Graves, *The Spiritual Quixote*, III

He supposed he was not a sufficiently dignified person for suicide.
                                                  Hardy, *Jude the Obscure*, Part One, XI

A sign: "No suicides permitted here, and no smoking in the parlour."
                                                  Melville, *Moby Dick*, XVII

There is nothing the body suffers that the soul may not profit by.
                                                  Meredith, *Diana of the Crossways*, XLIII

Who gave thee a power over thy life?   Richardson, *Pamela*, 181

SUPERINTENDENCE

There should always be one steady head to superintend many young ones.
                                                  Austen, *Mansfield Park*, Volume One, XV

554

SUPERIORITY: *see also* DOMINANCE; STATUS; etc.

Mankind are not so depraved to hate anyone for being possessed of superior qualities, but when they find them worn with an assuming air.
Annesley, *Memoirs of an Unfortunate Young Nobleman*, II

It's only in books that the officers of the detective force are superior to the weakness of making a mistake.
Collins, *The Moonstone*, Fifth Narrative, I

Be a man's intellectual superiority what it will, it can never assume the practical, available supremacy over other men, without the aid of some sort of external arts and entrenchments, always, in themselves, more or less paltry and base.
Melville, *Moby Dick*, XXXIII

SUPERSTITION: *see also* BELIEF; RELIGION

Whatever philosophy and experience may pretend on such subjects, it is certain that man is disposed to be superstitious in respect to the secret influences that guide his fortunes, in the dark passage of the world.
Cooper, *Heidenmauer*, IV

SUPPOSITION: *see also* BELIEF; LOGIC; MIND; THOUGHT

A man may be puffed and belauded, envied, ridiculed, counted upon as a tool and fallen in love with, or at least selected as a future husband, and yet remain virtually unknown —known merely as a cluster of signs for his neighbors' false suppositions.
Eliot, *Middlemarch*, Book II, XV

SUPPRESSION

The wound that bleedeth inward is most dangerous, the fire kept close burnest most furious, the oven dammed up baketh soonest, sores having no vent fester inwardly.
Lyly, *Euphues*, 118-119

SURPRISE

Surprise is an emotion that enfeebles, not invigorates.
Brown, C. B., *Wieland*, 125

Surprises, like misfortunes, rarely come alone.
Dickens, *Dombey and Son*, VI

There is nothing so dangerous as a question which comes by surprise on a man whose business it is to conceal truth or to defend falsehood.
Fielding, H., *Tom Jones*, 835

Great surprises are to me never pleasures.
James, H., *Confidence*, XIX

SURRENDER; COMPLIANCE: *see also* SUBMISSION

It is the first surrender that decides.
Allen, J. L., *Kentucky Cardinal*, XII

To sink under the weight is but to increase the weight.
Defoe, *Moll Flanders*, 287

SUSPENSE

Suspense is irksome, disappointment bitter.
Bronte, C., *Shirley*, VI

The worst of certainties is better than suspense.
DuMaurier, *Peter Ibbetson*, Part Fifth

The suspense we love to give is the greatest torment to us to receive.
Richardson, *Clarissa Harlowe*, IV

SUSPICION: *see also* TRUST

It is the nature of an anonymous correspondence to be attended with very disadvantageous circumstances: surprise and suspicion.
Anonymous, *A Court Intrigue*, 34

SUSPICION (*continued*)

Suspicion, once run wild, might run wilder. Dickens, *Bleak House*, LII

Banks are always suspicious, and officially must be. Dickens, *Hard Times*, Book II, I

It was a maxim with Foxey—"Always suspect everybody." That's the maxim to go through life with! Dickens, *Old Curiosity Shop*, LXVI

Suspicion is the foundation of a misery. Harley, *Priory of St. Bernard*, I

Always suspect a man who endeavors officiously to be acquainted. Jenner, *The Placid Man*, I

As suspicion is the source of crimes, it is also the worst of crimes, attaching itself with equal mischief to the guilty and the innocent; it is the influence of evil that breeds suspicion, the noble spirit of charity that subdues it. Lathom, *The Midnight Bell*, III

They who always suspect will often be mistaken and never be happy. Mackenzie, *The Man of the World*, I

Shallow as it is, yet, how subtle a thing is suspicion, which at times can invade the humanest of hearts and wisest of heads. Melville, *Confidence-Man*, IV

In some moods, the movements of an entire street, as the suspicious man walks down it, will seem an express pantomimic jeer at him. In short, the suspicious man kicks himself with his own foot. *Ibid.*, VI

There are some persons who, unable to give better proof of being wise, take a strange delight in showing what they think they have sagaciously read in mankind by uncharitable suspicions of them. *Ibid.*

Too much suspicion is as bad as too little sense. Melville, *Israel Potter*, VII

When a man suspects any wrong, it sometimes happens that if he be already involved in the matter, he insensibly strives to cover up his suspicions even from himself. Melville, *Moby Dick*, XX

We are naturally disposed to regard everything like an exposure of ecclesiastical misconduct as the offspring of malevolence or irreligious feeling. Melville, *Typee*, XXVI

I don't sympathize with suspicion, from having none myself. Meredith, *The Egoist*, XXXIV

People suspiciously treated are never at a loss for invention. Richardson, *Clarissa Harlowe*, I

It is a grievous thing to an honest man to be suspected. *Ibid.*, II

Evermore is parade and obsequiousness suspectable: it must show either a foolish head, or a knavish heart. *Ibid.*, III

SYMBOL: *see* SIGN

SYMPATHY: *see also* GENEROSITY; KINDNESS; LOVE; PITY

Knowledge is sympathy and sympathy is love, and to learn it the Son of God became a man. Barrie, *Tommy and Grizel*, XXXV

Sympathy—the one poor word which includes all our best insight and our best love. Eliot, *Adam Bede*, L

There is a companionship of ready sympathy, which might get the advantage even over the longest associations. Eliot, *Middlemarch*, Book VII, LXVI

Sympathies of all kinds are apt to beget love. Fielding, H., *Tom Jones*, 28

Practical sympathy is good. Howells, *Silas Lapham*, XIV

Perhaps there is no true sympathy but between equals; and it may be, that we should distrust that man's sincerity, who stoops to condole with us.

Melville, *Redburn*, LVI

There is no sympathy between good and bad fortune, except as the one is apt to desire that survey of the other which will best enable it to comprehend the superior benefits of its own position.

Simms, *The Partisan*, Volume I, XVIII

The old man said that what a man wanted that was down, was sympathy.

Twain, *Huckleberry Finn*, V

SYSTEM: *see also* METHOD

"This is a great system, and would you wish a great country to have a little system?" He said this at the stair-head, gently moving his right hand as if it were a silver trowel, with which to spread the cement of his words on the structure of the system, and consolidate it for a thousand ages.

Dickens, *Bleak House*, LXII

TACT

Good-looking, refined-looking, quick-witted girls can be grown; but the nimble sense of fitness, ineffable lightning-footed tact, comes of race and breeding.

Meredith, *Beauchamp's Career*, XII

TALENT: *see also* GENIUS

Is not the talent of the artist shown as much in painting a fly as a wagon wheel?

Brackenridge, *Modern Chivalry*, Part I, II

All men of talent, whether they be men of feeling or not; whether they be zealots, or aspirants, or despots—provided only they be sincere—have their sublime moments: when they subdue and rule.

Bronte, C., *Jane Eyre*, XXXV

As much talent as was ever compressed into one young person's body: she's the only sylph *I* ever saw, who could stand upon one leg, and play the tambourine on her other knee, *like* a sylph.

Dickens, *Nicholas Nickleby*, XXV

TALK: *see also* EXPRESSION

Who was ever cured by talk?

Melville, *Confidence-Man*, XVI

It is the peculiar vocation of a teacher to talk. What's wisdom itself but table-talk? The best wisdom in this world.

Ibid., XXII

In [France] speaking is fencing.

Meredith, *Beauchamp's Career*, XXIV

Like all good talkers, he knew how to delude his listeners into the belief that they were taking an important part in the conversation.

Moore, *Evelyn Innes*, X

People who talk to themselves always talk to the Devil.

Schreiner, *The Story of an African Farm*, Part I, XI

If only people would not talk till they knew, the world would be a much nicer place.

Schreiner, *Undine*, I

TASTE: *see also* OPINION; PERSPECTIVE

Each generation has its own critical canons in poetry as well as in political creeds, financial systems, or whatever other changeable matters of taste are called "settled questions" and "fixed opinions."

Bulwer, *What Will He Do with It?*, Book VII, XX

Taste and distinction, if they do not justify, they at least ennoble weakness.

Cleland, *Memoirs of a Coxcomb*, 324

TASTE (*continued*)

The nature of a man's tastes is, most times, as opposite as possible to the nature of a man's business.   Collins, *The Moonstone*, First Period, XII

Faces are matters of taste.   Dickens, *Barnaby Rudge*, IV

"Did you ever taste beer?" "I had a sip of it once." "Here's a state of things! She *never* tasted it—it can't be tasted in a sip!"   Dickens, *Old Curiosity Shop*, LVII

"Do you spell Weller with a 'V' or a 'W'?" "That depends upon the taste and fancy of the speller, my lord. I never had occasion to spell it more than once or twice in my life, but I spells it with a 'V'."   Dickens, *Pickwick Papers*, XXXIV

A taste for marriages and public executions.   Disraeli, *Lothair*

We never quite understand why another dislikes what we like.
                                                     Eliot, *Middlemarch*, Book IV, XL

A truly elegant taste is generally accompanied with an excellency of heart; true virtue is nothing else but true taste.   Fielding, H., *Amelia*, II

People of brains are justified in supplying the mob with the food it likes.
                                                     Gissing, *New Grub Street*, I

To please the vulgar you must, one way or another, incarnate the genius of vulgarity.
                                                     Ibid.

The evil of the time is the multiplication of ephemerides. Hence a demand for essays, descriptive articles, fragments of criticism, out of all proportion to the supply of even tolerable work.   *Ibid.*, III

Good work succeeds—now and then.   *Ibid.*, IV

All that a theater has to do is to keep even with the public.
                                                     Howells, *A Modern Instance*, XXIV

Though a taste for the fine arts may not always be a mark of a great mind, yet a contempt for them always indicates the contrary.   Jenner, *The Placid Man*, I

Nothing is serviceable except what the public is pleased to think so, and the value of a new book can never be determined till 'tis sold.   Kidgell, *The Card*, II

Virtue is little more than active taste; and the most delicate affections of each combine in real love.   Radcliffe, *The Mysteries of Udolpho*, I

TAXES

Nothing's truer than taxes.   Dickens, *David Copperfield*, XXI

TEACHING: *see also* EDUCATION; INSTRUCTION; KNOWLEDGE AND LEARNING

We all love to instruct, though we can teach only what is not worth knowing.
                                                     Austen, *Pride and Prejudice*, Volume III, XII

I would rather do anything than be a teacher.   Austen, *The Watsons*, I

TEARS: *see also* MISERY; SORROW

I cannot see the interest of a secretion from a sentimental point of view.
                                                     Collins, *The Woman in White*, Part I, Second Epoch

Heaven knows we need never be ashamed of our tears, for they are rain upon the blinding dust of earth, overlying our hard hearts.   Dickens, *Great Expectations*, XIX

Of all fruitless errands, sending a tear to look after a day that is gone, is the most fruitless.   Dickens, *Nicholas Nickleby*, X

Her effort to bring tears into her eyes issued in an odd contraction of her face.

Eliot, *Mill on the Floss*, Book I, IX

That pressure of the heart which forbids tears. *Ibid.*, Book II, VII

Tears are as critical discharges of nature as any of those which are so called by the physicians, and do more effectually relieve the mind than any remedies with which the whole materia medica of philosophy can supply it. Fielding, H., *Amelia*, I

If I ever shed tears, they are the tears of indignation. *Ibid.*

Those tears which the innocent heart pours forth with the first actual discovery that sin is in the world. Hawthorne, *The Marble Faun*, XXIII

The strongest figure in female rhetoric to excite compassion is a flood of tears.

Jenner, *The Placid Man*, I

Through tears never did man see his way in the dark.

Melville, *Confidence-Man*, XXXIX

Tears are the way of women and their comfort. Meredith, *Harry Richmond*, LV

A good cry [before sleep is] better than the best of medicine.

Meredith, *Ordeal of Richard Feverel*, XXXII

Her tears indicated rather a yielding than a perverse temper.

Richardson, *Clarissa Harlowe*, III

Those who weep in the wrong place ought not to go to a tragedy. *Ibid.*

Nothing dries sooner than tears. *Ibid.*

Tears are the prerogative of manhood. *Ibid.*, IV

Tears are no proof of cowardice. Sterne, *Tristram Shandy*, IV

TEMPERANCE: *see also* DRINKING; MODERATION; etc.

Temperance makes men lords over those pleasures that intemperance enslaves them to.

Cleland, *Memoirs of a Woman of Pleasure*, 213

TEMPTATION

Gentlemen are subject to more and greater temptations than their inferiors.

Anonymous, *The History of Tom Jones in His Married State*, 282

There is bound to be a certain percentage of scoundrels and of men too weak to resist a bribe in a great and shifting body like the House of Representatives.

Atherton, *Senator North*, Book I, XIV

The most perfect being must owe his exemption from vice to the absence of temptation.

Brown, C. B., *Wieland*, 260

A remembrance of former chastisements is an help against present temptations.

Bunyan, *Pilgrim's Progress*, 139

Temptation is very easy of resistance in theory. Burney, *Cecilia*, I

Reason and will are more than adequate to oppose the strongest temptations. The *wish* to resist more than half accomplishes the object. Dacre, *Passions*, XLI

There are temptations which it is not in the power of human nature to resist.

Defoe, *Moll Flanders*, 192

So far does fooling and toying sometimes go, that I know nothing a young woman has to be more cautious of. Defoe, *Roxana*, 45

If your destiny leads you into public life, and public station, you must expect to be subjected to temptations which other people are free from.

Dickens, *Pickwick Papers*, XXXVI

The city has its cunning wiles, no less than the infinitely smaller and more human tempter. There are large forces which allure with all the soulfulness of expression possible in the most cultured human. The gleam of a thousand lights is often as effective as the persuasive light in a wooing and fascinating eye. Half the undoing of the unsophisticated and natural mind is accomplished by forces wholly superhuman.
Dreiser, *Sister Carrie*, I

There are temptations to which no wise, no good man will expose himself.
Edgeworth, *The Absentee*, XIV

No woman could ever safely say, "so far only will I go."
Fielding, H., *Joseph Andrews*, 33

Everybody likes to be tempted. And, after all, it's very easy to resist temptation, if one wishes.
Gaskell, *Wives and Daughters*, LX

An embittered man is a man beset by evil temptations.
Gissing, *New Grub Street*, VII

Scarcely any virtue is found to resist the power of long and pleasing temptation.
Goldsmith, *The Vicar of Wakefield*, 84

Men are faithful for so long only as temptations pass them by.   Haggard, *She*, XVIII

Pomp, noise, and show may be the voice of death; and sirens sing the sweeter to allure the unwary traveller to meet his fate.   McCarthy, *The Fair Moralist*, 21

I don't believe in temptations that one doesn't yield to.   Moore, G., *Evelyn Innes*, XXI

What blessed things are trials and temptations, when we have the strength to resist and subdue them!
Richardson, *Pamela*, 32

Let us thank our lowliness, since it secures us from temptation.
Scott, *The Fair Maid of Perth*, II

The devil is an adversary, whom if we resist he will fly from us. But I seldom resist him at all, from a terror that though I may conquer, I may still get a hurt in the combat—so I give up the triumph for security; and instead of thinking to make him fly, I generally fly myself.
Sterne, *A Sentimental Journey*, 98

The only way to get rid of a temptation is to yield to it.
Wilde, *The Picture of Dorian Gray*, II

TENDERNESS

There is no true tenderness but in a woman of spirit.   Fielding, H., *Amelia*, I

Tenderness for women is a true manly character.   *Ibid.*

Except in love, or the attachments of kindred, or other very long and habitual affection, we really have no tenderness.   Hawthorne, *The Blithedale Romance*, VI

Your tenderness seems the reflection of God's own love.   *Ibid.*

Instruments sound sweetest when they be touched softest, women wax wisest when they are used mildest.   Lyly, *Euphues and His England*, 473

What is a tender heart good for? Who can be happy that has a feeling heart?
Richardson, *Clarissa Harlowe*, III

THEATER; ACTING: *see also* ART; LITERATURE; etc.

A love of the theatre is general, an itch for acting strong, among young people.
Austen, *Mansfield Park*, Volume One, XIII

Shakespeare one gets acquainted with without knowing how.
Ibid., Volume Three, III

Threadbare is the simile which compares the world to a stage.
Bulwer, What Will He Do With It?, Book IV, VI

I confess I seldom listen to the players on stage: one has so much to do, in looking about and finding out one's acquaintance, that, really, one has no time to mind the stage.
Burney, Evelina, 74–75

I have no time to read play-bills; one merely comes to a play to meet one's friends, and show that one's alive.
Ibid., 75

The transitions in real life from well-spread boards to death-beds, and from mourning-weeds to holiday garments, are not a whit less startling [than similar actions on the stage].
Dickens, Oliver Twist, XVII

Where nothing particular is going on, one incident makes a drama.
Hardy, The Hand of Ethelberta, III

The world, being earnest itself, likes an earnest scene, and an earnest man, very well, but only in their place—the stage.
Melville, Confidence-Man, V

Comedy is a game played to throw reflections upon social life, and it deals with human nature in the drawing-room of civilized men and women, where we have no dust of the struggling outer world, no mire, no violent crashes, to make the correctness of the representation convincing.
Meredith, The Egoist, Prelude

The stage is the pastime of great minds.   Meredith, Ordeal of Richard Feverel, IX

Every man loves in his soul to play the part of the stage deity.
Stevenson, Prince Otto, Book I, III

The best actors cannot act well before empty benches.   Trollope, The Warden, XVI

Delightful illusion of paint and tinsel and silk attire, of cheap sentiment and high and mighty dialogue!   Twain and Warner, The Gilded Age, Volume I, XII

Lips that Shakespeare taught to speak have whispered their secret in my ear. I have had the arms of Rosalind around me, and kissed Juliet on the mouth.
Wilde, The Picture of Dorian Gray, VI

Acting is so much more real than life.
Ibid.

It is not good for one's morals to see bad acting.
Ibid., VII

THEME: see also IDEA; SUBJECT; THOUGHT

Give me a condor's quill! Give me Vesuvius' crater for an inkstand! Friends, hold my arms! For in the mere act of penning my thoughts of this Leviathan, they weary me, and make me faint with their outreaching comprehensiveness of sweep, as if to include the whole circle of the sciences, and all the generations of whales, and men, and mastodons, past, present, and to come, with all the revolving panoramas of empire on earth, and throughout the whole universe, not excluding its suburbs. Such, and so magnifying, is the virtue of a large and liberal theme! We expand to its bulk. To produce a mighty book, you must choose a mighty theme. No great and enduring volume can ever be written on the flea, though many there be who have tried it.
Melville, Moby Dick, CIV

THEORY: see also BELIEF; IDEA; LOGIC; etc.

Theories have nothing to do with life.   Glasgow, The Descendant, Book II, II

THIEVERY

To accept a service from another which we would be unwilling to return in kind, if need were, is like borrowing with the intention of not repaying, while to enforce such a service by taking advantage of the poverty or necessity of a person would be an outrage like forcible robbery.   Bellamy, Looking Backward, XIV

THIEVERY (*continued*)

I would rather be a beggar than know my son a thief.
Bulwer, *The Caxtons*, Book III, VII

A thief is a man living among his equals.   Godwin, *Caleb Williams*, III

One man steals in one way, and another in another.   *Ibid.*

If fidelity and honor be banished from thieves, where shall they find refuge upon the face of the earth?   *Ibid.*

Thieves spend loosely what they have gotten lightly.
Nashe, *The Unfortunate Traveller*, 61

A thief mistakes every bush for a true man.   *Ibid.*, 141

The mountain sheep are sweeter,/ But the valley sheep are fatter;/ We therefore deemed it meeter/ To carry off the latter.   Peacock, *The Misfortunes of Elphin*, XI

Pap always said it warn't no harm to borrow things, if you was meaning to pay them back, sometime; but the widow said it warn't anything but a soft name for stealing, and no decent body would do it. Jim said he reckoned the widow was partly right and pap was partly right; so the best way would be for us to pick out two or three things from the list and say we wouldn't borrow them any more—then he reckoned it wouldn't be no harm to borrow the others.   Twain, *Huckleberry Finn*, XII

A robber is more high-toned than what a pirate is—as a general thing. In most countries they're awful high up in the nobility—dukes and such.
Twain, *Tom Sawyer*, XXXV

THIRST: *see also* DRINK; HUNGER

Thirst is not enjoyment, and a satiated thirst that we insist on over-satisfying to drown the recollection of past anguish, is baneful to the soul.
Meredith, *Beauchamp's Career*, XLVI

THOUGHT; CONTEMPLATION: *see also* IDEA; MIND

What is a new, brilliant, and extraordinary thought? It is not, as ignorant people think, a thought which nobody has ever had; it is, on the contrary, a thought which anyone may hit upon, and which someone has been so lucky as to be the first person that uttered it.
Anonymous, *Jeremiah Grant*, 92

How can you conceive a notion of a height which never has been seen nor measured?
August, *Horrid Mysteries*, I

Thought rarely grows out of great suffering. Thinking is consumed in the furnace of pain. There is sensation. No more.   Beard, *Bristling With Thorns*, XXXVI

It is wonderful what a breadth of life can be encompassed in a moment's thought.
Ibid., XXXIX

Consciousness itself is the malady, the pest, of which he only is cured who ceases to think.   Brown, C. B., *Edgar Huntley*, 266

Ideas exist that can be accounted for by no established laws.
Brown, C. B., *Wieland*, 106

Earnest men never think in vain, though their thoughts be errors.
Bulwer, *The Caxtons*, Book IV, II

If a man must always be stopping to consider what foot he is standing upon, he had need have little to do, being the right does as well as the left, and the left as well as the right.
Burney, *Cecilia*, II

Thought has a cruel spite against happiness.   *Ibid.*, III

How little do we know our thoughts—our reflex actions indeed, yes; but our reflections.
Butler, *The Way of All Flesh*, V

What is a sensation compared with a thought?   Crawford, *A Roman Singer*, VII

To think is one real advance from hell to heaven.   Defoe, *Moll Flanders*, 292

He that is restored to his thinking, is restored to himself.   *Ibid.*

It is written, that we shall give an account for every idle word, and that ill thoughts are as bad as wanton deeds.   Deloney, *The Gentle Craft*, 151

Thoughtfulness begets wrinkles.   Dickens, *Barnaby Rudge*, XXIX

A man's thoughts is like the winds, and nobody can't answer for 'em for certain.
Dickens, *Dombey and Son*, XXXIX

All places are holy with holy thoughts.   Disraeli, *Sybil*, Book II, VIII

Great thoughts have very little to do with the business of the world.   *Ibid.*, V, I

A thought will color a world for us.   Dreiser, *Sister Carrie*, VI

Thoughts are so great. They seem to lie upon us like a deep flood.
Eliot, *Adam Bede*, VIII

If a man has a capacity for great thoughts, he is likely to overtake them before he is decrepit.   Eliot, *Middlemarch*, Book IV, XXXVII

All yielding is attended with a less vivid consciousness than resistance; it is the partial sleep of thought; it is the submergence of our own personality by another.
Eliot, *Mill on the Floss*, Book VI, XIII

Thought was busy though the lips were silent.   *Ibid.*, Book VII, V

Excessive rumination and self-questioning is perhaps a morbid habit inevitable to a mind of much moral sensibility when shut out from its due share of outward activity and of practical claims on its affections.   Eliot, *Silas Marner*, XVII

Dancers think with their heels.   Fielding, H., *Joseph Andrews*, 220

There is something indescribably delicious in concentration of the mind. It raises a man above himself and makes him feel a certain nobleness and elevation of character, of the possession of which he was to that hour unconscious.   Godwin, *St. Leon*, 22

Nothing is more singular in a state of great mental effervescence, than the rapidity with which our ideas succeed each other.   *Ibid.*, 243

Thinking can only serve to measure out the helplessness of thought. What is the purpose of our feeble crying in the silences of space? Can our dim intelligence read the secrets of that star-strewn sky?   Haggard, *She*, X

When a person's thoughts are turned steadily in one direction, it is wonderful how much can be seen in a short space of time.   Hale, *Liberia*, IV

There exists, as it were, an outer chamber to the mind, in which, when a man is occupied centrally with the most momentous question of his life, casual and trifling thoughts are just allowed to wander softly for an interval, before being banished altogether.
Hardy, *Desperate Remedies*, XVI

Thinking is causing in not a few cases.   Hardy, *Two on a Tower*, XVIII

It is a great mistake to try to put our best thoughts into human language.
Hawthorne, *The Marble Faun*, XXVIII

When we ascend into the higher regions of emotion and spiritual enjoyment, our best thoughts are expressible only by grand hieroglyphics [of nature].   *Ibid.*

The best thought, like the most perfect digestion, is done unconsciously.
Holmes, *The Guardian Angel*, XXXV

We are long before we are able to think, and we soon cease from the power of acting.
Johnson, *Rasselas*, 27

What space does the idea of a pyramid occupy more than the idea of a grain of corn?
Ibid., 186

Think ten minutes before you answer a question. Kimber, *David Ranger*, I

He never thought about thinking, or felt about feeling.
Kingsley, C., *Westward Ho!*, I

Is your mind on your meat? A penny for your thought. Lyly, *Euphues*, 133

Our thoughts are not our own. Melville, *Mardi*, CIX

All thought is a puff. *Ibid.*, CXXI

The catalogue of true thoughts is but small; they are ubiquitous; no man's property; and unspoken, or bruited, are the same. When we hear them, why seem they so natural, receiving our spontaneous approval? Why do we think we have heard them before? Because they but reiterate ourselves; they were in us, before we were born. The truest poets are but mouthpieces; and some men are but duplicates of each other.
Ibid., CXXXVI

Ten thoughts for one act. *Ibid.*, CLXXVII

Every thought's a soul of some past poet, hero, sage. *Ibid.*, CLXXX

How immaterial are all materials! What things real are there, but imponderable thoughts? Melville, *Moby Dick*, CXXXVII

Ahab never thinks; he only feels, feels, feels, *that's* tingling enough for mortal man! to think's audacity. God only has that right and privilege. *Ibid.*, CXXXV

Is there not a pleasure in contemplating that which is characteristic?
Meredith, *Beauchamp's Career*, XXVIII

Brains are never the worse for activity; they subsist on it. *Ibid.*, XLV

To begin to think is the beginning of disgust of the world. Meredith, *The Egoist*, III

Our new thoughts have thrilled dead bosoms. Meredith, *Ordeal of Richard Feverel*, I

I like to know of what you were thinking when you composed this or that saying—what *suggested* it. May not one be admitted to inspect the machinery of wisdom? I feel curious to know how thoughts—*real* thoughts are born. *Ibid.*, XXVI

The world exists not in itself, but in man's thought. Moore, G., *Evelyn Innes*, XXXV

Like most men, Wilbur had to walk when he was thinking hard.
Norris, *Moran of the Lady Letty*, XIII

My own thoughts are the worst company you could leave me in at present.
Parsons, *Castle of Wolfenbach*, II

Thought cannot always be controlled by will. Radcliffe, *The Mysteries of Udolpho*, II

Unthinking creatures have some comfort in the shortness of their views; in their unapprehensiveness; and that they penetrate not beyond the present moment: in short, that they *are* unthinking. Richardson, *Clarissa Harlowe*, I

What are words, but the body and dress of thought? *Ibid.*, II

A man cannot begin to think, but causes for thought crowd in upon him. *Ibid.*, IV

When we are not happy in our own thoughts, it is a relief to carry them out of ourselves.
Richardson, *Sir Charles Grandison*, Three, VII

Contemplation is a very stingy lady. She loves to make the most of everything, rummaging old hoards and patching new and old together.
Ridley, *James Lovegrove*, II

If people were to allow themselves a little time to consider, half the bad actions that are committed would be left undone. Roche, *Clermont*, II

Too much thinking doth consume the spirits, and oft it falls out that while one thinks too much of his own doing, he leaves to do the effect of his thinking.   Sidney, *Arcadia*, I

They are never alone that are accompanied with noble thoughts.   *Ibid.*

Company confirms resolutions, and loneliness breeds a weariness of one's thoughts.
Ibid., III

The thoughts are but overflowings of the mind, and the tongue is but a servant of the thoughts.   *Ibid.*

Quick as thought.   Simms, *The Partisan*, Volume II, XXVIII

If a man thinks at all, he must be privy to his own thoughts and desires; he must remember his past pursuits, and know certainly the true springs and motives which, in general, have governed the actions of his life.   Sterne, *Tristram Shandy*, II

A great part of this life consists in contemplating what we cannot cure.
Stevenson, *The Master of Ballantrae*, VI

It is hard to tell how a man arrives at conclusions and solves knotty problems without consciously thinking of them at all. Yet it is one of the most familiar facts of every man's experience.   Tourgee, *Murvale Eastman*, XXI

A man's mind will very generally refuse to make itself up until it be driven and compelled by emergency.   Trollope, *Ayala's Angel*, XLI

In nothing is procrastination so tempting as in thought.   *Ibid.*

THREAT

Threatened men live long.   Dickens, *The Mystery of Edwin Drood*, XIV

THRIFT: *see also* MONEY; POVERTY; WEALTH

Thrift never yet brought any one to want.   Cooper, *The Water-Witch*, I

I know not how to get a shilling, nor how to keep it in my pocket if I had it.
Fielding, H., *Amelia*, II

Many a person hath lost his cattle by saving a half-penny.
Fielding, H., *Tom Jones*, 578

Thrift consisteth not in gold, but grace.   Lyly, *Euphues and His England*, 229

TIME: *see also* ETERNALITY; PAST-PRESENT-FUTURE

Time, time, to what spot in the compass of folly wilt thou point next?
Anonymous, *The Egg*, 232

When time's curtain drops.   Anonymous, *The Modern Fine Gentleman*, II

Time develops all of us, one way or another.   Atherton, *Senator North*, Book I, I

When hours are no longer possible, minutes become precious, and the more precious the more dangerous.   *Ibid.*, Book III, I

Life has a chronology quite independent of the almanac. The heart divides it into periods.   Barr, *Squire*, III

Time is a babbler, and speaks ever when no question is put.   *Ibid.*, XI

Time is measured only by the slower or quicker succession of ideas. A sparrow that dies of old age at the end of four or five years performs some particular feats oftener than any man that lives to the age of fourscore, and has been as useful to his generation.
Bridges, *Adventures of a Bank-Note*, II

Time will obliterate the deepest impressions.   Brown, C. B., *Wieland*, 253

Moments make the hues in which years are colored.   Bulwer, *Devereux*, Book III, VII

TIME (*continued*)

'Tis better late than never.   Bunyan, *Pilgrim's Progress*, 201

If you knew Time as well as I do, you wouldn't talk about wasting *it*. It's *him*.
                                                               Carroll, *Alice in Wonderland*, VII

Time touches all things with destroying hand.
                                                               Chesnutt, *The House Behind the Cedars*, I

Time, that great comforter in ordinary.   Cleland, *Memoirs of a Woman of Pleasure*

When are we most acutely sensible of the shortness of life? When do we consult our
watches in perpetual dread of the result? When does the night steal on us unawares, and
the morning take us by surprise? When we are going on a journey.
                                                               Collins, *Heart and Science*, XX

The author of the saying *Tempus fugit* was, I think, an idle man. The more I have to do,
the readier Time is to wait for me.   Collins, *Legacy of Cain*, LII

How tedious is time, when his wings are loaded with expectation!
                                                               Collyer, *Felicia to Charlotte*, II

There is never time to say our last word—the last word of our love, of our desire, faith,
remorse, submission, revolt.   Conrad, *Lord Jim*, XXI

[Ancient monuments] are gone. Time has lasted too long for them. For why? Time was
made by the Lord, and they were made by man.   Cooper, *The Prairie*, XXII

Care and suffering are devils—secret, stealthy, undermining devils—who tread down
the brightest flowers in Eden, and do more havoc in a month than Time does in a year.
                                                               Dickens, *Barnaby Rudge*, XXVI

Old Time lay snoring, and the world stood still.   *Ibid.*, LV

With them who stood upon the brink of the great gulf which none can see beyond, Time,
so soon to lose itself in vast Eternity, rolled on like a mighty river, swoln and rapid as it
nears the sea.   *Ibid.*, LXXVI

All times are alike to me.   Dickens, *Bleak House*, LIII

Time is the only thing that can't be spared.   *Ibid.*, LVII

Time, sure of foot and strong of will.   Dickens, *Dombey and Son*, XXXIX

Time, consoler of affliction and softener of anger.   *Ibid.*, XLVII

Time went on in Coketown like its own machinery: so much material wrought up, so
much fuel consumed, so many powers worn out, so much money made. Time, with his
innumerable horsepower, worked away.   Dickens, *Hard Times*, Book I, XIV

After long delay, every minute is an age.   Dickens, *Old Curiosity Shop*, LXV

Thou powerful enchanter, Time.   Dickens, *A Tale of Two Cities*, Book III, XV

Time is the great physician.   Disraeli, *Endymion*

The restless mind creates and observes at the same time. Indeed there is scarcely any
popular tenet more erroneous than that which holds that when time is slow, life is dull.
It is very often and very much the reverse. If we look back on those passages of our life
which dwell most upon the memory, they are brief periods full of action and novel
sensation.   Disraeli, *Sybil*, Book III, X

Time, like money, is measured by our needs.   Eliot, *Middlemarch*, Book II, XV

Time, the sure friend of justice.   Fielding, H., *Jonathan Wild*, 165

Time, the best physician of the mind.   Fielding, H., *Tom Jones*, 398

Time, the great healer of the unfortunate mind.
                                                  Fielding, S., *The Countess of Dellwyn*, I

With him the past was yesterday; the future, tomorrow; never, the day after.
Hardy, *Far From the Madding Crowd*, XXV

Some great Atlantic of time.
Hardy, *Jude the Obscure*, Part Five, III

Time, the magician, had wrought much here.
Hardy, *The Mayor of Casterbridge*, V

Of all human characteristics, a low opinion of the value of his own time by an individual must be among the strangest to find.
Hardy, *A Pair of Blue Eyes*, XXIX

Time ruthlessly destroys his own romances.
Hardy, *Tess*, XLIX

Time, that is never to be recalled or stayed, blots out the memory of the greatest worth.
Harley, *Priory of St. Bernard*, II

Sculpture, and the delight which men naturally take in it, appear a proof that it is good to work with all time before our view.
Hawthorne, *The Marble Faun*, XIII

Time alone can smooth all obstacles.
Helme, *St. Margaret's Cave*, Volume I, III

In a long time much must be endured.
Johnson, *Rasselas*, 24

No mind is much employed upon the present; recollection and anticipation fill up almost all our moments.
Ibid., 117

Time is the mightiest mason of all. And a tutor, and a counselor, and a physician, and a scribe, and a poet, and a sage, and a king.
Melville, *Mardi*, LXXV

Time truly works wonders. It sublimates wine; it sublimates fame; nay, is the creator thereof; of fables distills truths; and smooths, levels, glosses, softens, melts, and meliorates all things.
Ibid., LXXXIX

It is Time, old midsummer Time, that has made the old world what it is.
Ibid.

Time—all-healing Time—Time, great Philanthropist!
Ibid., CLXII

Time and tide flow wide.
Melville, *Moby Dick*, XXXVIII

The winged minute.
Meredith, *Beauchamp's Career*, XXII

Reverence Time!
Meredith, *Ordeal of Richard Feverel*, XXV

Could we see Time's full face we were wise of him.
Ibid., XXVIII

To see Time's full face, it is sometimes necessary to look through keyholes, the veteran having a trick of smiling peace to you on one cheek, and grimacing confusion on the other, behind the curtain.
Ibid.

It goes as Time himself, and Time has the intention of going a great way.
Meredith, *Vittoria*, XLII

Time heightened their blessings, and their declining years were like a setting sun, which gathers fresh splendor, as it gradually vanishes from our sight.
Moore, G., *Grasville Abbey*, III

Time subdues all things.
Ibid., IV

Those who will not keep a strict account of their time seldom long keep any.
Ibid.

Time is the only thing of which we can be allowably covetous.
Ibid.

Time is the pacifier of every woe, the qualifier of every disappointment.
Richardson, *Sir Charles Grandison*, Three, VII

The soul's life has seasons of its own; periods not found in any calendar, times that years and months will not scan.
Schreiner, *The Story of an African Farm*, Part II, I

Men have set their mark on mankind forever, as they thought, but time has washed it out as it has washed out mountains and continents.
Ibid., Part II, VI

Mankind is only an ephemeral blossom on the tree of time.
Ibid.

Time—I see it not, I feel it not: it is but a shadowy name—a succession of breathings measured forth by night by the clank of a bell, by day by a shadow crossing along a dialstone. Scott, *The Talisman*, XII

Gaining time is gaining everything in love, trade, and politics.
Shebbeare, *The Marriage Act*, I

Time is the best capital in morals as in war. Simms, *Woodcraft*, XIX

He put this engine to our ears, which made an incessant noise like that of a water mill. We conjecture it is either some unknown animal or the God that he worships. We are more inclined to the latter opinion, because he said he never did anything without consulting it. He called it his oracle, and said it pointed out the time for every action of his life. Swift, *Gulliver's Travels*, A Voyage to Lilliput

There is no difference between Time and of the three dimensions of Space except that our consciousness moves along it. Wells, *The Time Machine*, I

Time is not so all-erasing as we think. Woolson, *Anne*, X

TIMIDITY

Acadian maidens are shy as herons. They always see you first. They see you first, silently rise, and are gone from the galérie. Cable, *Bonaventure*, Book II, IX

The timidity natural to minds of quick and delicate perception.
Sleath, *The Orphan of the Rhine*, II

TOLERANCE; TOLERATION

What a mighty pleasant virtue toleration should be when we are right, to be so very pleasant when we are wrong, and quite unable to demonstrate how we come to be invested with the privilege of exercising it! Dickens, *Dombey and Son*, V

Charity would beget toleration, which is a kind of implied permitting, and in effect a kind of countenancing; and that which is countenanced is so far furthered.
Melville, *Confidence-Man*, XVI

I cherish the greatest respect towards everybody's religious obligations, never mind how comical. Melville, *Moby Dick*, XVII

By a toleration of what is detested we expose ourselves to the keenness of an adverse mind. Meredith, *Beauchamp's Career*, XXVIII

What is the meaning of that dread of one example of tolerance?
Meredith, *Diana of the Crossways*, XVIII

TONE

One learns a great deal from a mere tone. Kipling, *Captains Courageous*, III

TRADE: *see also* MONEY

There is profit and loss in all trades. The good pay for the bad.
Anonymous, *Maria Brown*, II

My education had ill suited me to trade, and the trader's first maxim I reversed, in lavishing when I ought to have accumulated. Burney, *Cecilia*, III

There's nothing methodizes a man but business. *Ibid.*

Business is to money what fine words are to a lady, a sure road to success. *Ibid.*

Nobody trades for the sake of trading; much less do men rob for the sake of thieving.
Defoe, *Captain Singleton*, 292

Trade is below a philosopher.   Fielding, H., *Joseph Andrews*, 155

Of what use would learning be in a country without trade?   *Ibid.*, 156

It is no unusual thing for both parties in a bargain to be overreached, though one must be the greater loser; as was he who sold a blind horse and received a bad note in payment.   Fielding, H., *Tom Jones*, 689

Trade will ever follow the best market.   Gentleman, *A Trip to the Moon*, II

Suffer not rich men to buy up all and, with their monopoly, to keep the market alone as please them.   More, *Utopia*, I

TRADITION: *see* CONVENTIONALITY

TRAVEL

Each man travels for himself.   Atherton, *Doomswoman*, XIX

To the lover of history travel is like food without salt: imagination has painted an historical city with the panorama of a great time; it has been to us a stage for great events. We find it a stage with familiar paraphernalia, and actors as commonplace as ourselves.   *Ibid.*

What are men to rocks and mountains? When we return [from our travels], it shall not be like other travellers, without being able to give one accurate idea of anything. Let *our* first effusions be less insupportable than those of the generality of travellers.   Austen, *Pride and Prejudice*, Volume II, IV

Travelling is the ruin of all happiness. There's no looking at a building here after seeing Italy.   Burney, *Cecilia*, I

The sin of a traveller is to spin longer yarns abroad than at home.   Caruthers, *Kentuckian in New-York*, Volume II, VIII

The art of traveling is far more practiced than understood.   Cooper, *Heidenmauer*, VI

A lazy traveller makes a long journey.   Cooper, *The Prairie*, VIII

One of the chief delights and benefits of travel is that one is perpetually meeting men of great abilities, of original mind, and rare acquirements, who will converse without reserve.   Disraeli, *Coningsby*, Book VII, II

Our first scrape generally leads to our first travel. Disappointment requires change of air; desperation change of scene.   Disraeli, *Sybil*, Book I, V

To the untravelled, territory other than their own familiar heath is invariably fascinating. Next to love, it is the one thing which solaces and delights.   Dreiser, *Sister Carrie*, XXIX

He who goes abroad will always have opportunities enough of knowing the world without troubling his head with Socrates, or any such fellows.   Fielding, H., *Joseph Andrews*, 155

If a man should sail round the world, and anchor in every harbor of it, without learning, he would return home as ignorant as he went out.   *Ibid.*

Not seldom long wandering unfits us for further travel.   Hardy, *Tess*, XV

Railroads give us wings; they annihilate the toil and dust of pilgrimage; they spiritualize travel. Transition being so facile, what can be any man's inducement to tarry in one spot?   Hawthorne, *The House of the Seven Gables*, XVII

Stay-at-homes say travelers lie. Yet a voyage to Ethiopia would cure them of that; for few skeptics are travelers; fewer travelers liars, though the proverb respecting them lies.   Melville, *Mardi*, XCVIII

Like the travail wherein smiths put wild horses when they show them, travel is good for nothing but to tame and bring men under.   Nashe, *The Unfortunate Traveller*, 119

He that is a traveller must have the back of an ass to bear all, a tongue like the tail of a dog to flatter all, the mouth of a hog to eat what is set before him, the ear of a merchant to hear all and say nothing: and if this be not the highest step of thraldom, there is no liberty or freedom.   *Ibid.*, 120

The only precept that a traveller hath most use of, and shall find most ease in, is: Believe nothing, trust no man; yet seem thou as thou swallowed'st all, suspected'st none, but wert easy to be gulled by everyone.   *Ibid.*, 120-121

No air, no bread, no fire, no water doth a man any good out of his own country.
                                                                                                                                                         Ibid., 124

The end of travel is improvement.   Richardson, *Clarissa Harlowe*, IV

The greatest advantage acquired in travelling and perusing mankind in the original, is that of dispelling those shameful clouds that darken the faculties of the mind, preventing it from judging with candor and precision.   Smollett, *Humphry Clinker*, 330

A man would act wisely if he could prevail upon himself to live contented without foreign knowledge or foreign improvements.   Sterne, *A Sentimental Journey*, 13

Pity the man who can travel from Dan to Beersheba and cry, 'Tis all barren.   *Ibid.*, 30

All the world is barren to him who will not cultivate the fruits it offers.   *Ibid.*

Was I in a desert, I would find out wherewith in it to call forth my affections.   *Ibid.*

The learned Smelfungus travelled from Boulogne to Paris, from Paris to Rome, and so on, but he set out with the spleen and jaundice, and every object he passed by was discolored or distorted. He wrote an account of them, but 'twas nothing but the account of his miserable feelings.   *Ibid.*

Mundungus had travelled straight on, looking neither to his right hand or his left, lest Love or Pity should seduce him out of his road.   *Ibid.*, 31

The advantage of travel is by seeing a great deal both of men and manners; it teaches us mutual toleration; and mutual toleration teaches us mutual love.   *Ibid.*, 67

Go but to the end of a street, I have a mortal aversion for returning back no wiser than I set out.   *Ibid.*, 72

I think there is a fatality in it: I seldom go to the place I set out for.   *Ibid.*, 82

TREACHERY; TREASON: *see also* TRUST; TRUTH

Love the treason, hate the traitor.   Anonymous, *The Wanderer*, I

He told them that mutiny on board a ship was the same thing as treason in a king's palace.   Defoe, *Captain Singleton*, 18

Treachery is nearly related to cowardice.   Donaldson, *Sir Bartholomew Sapskull*

A mind capable of treachery is most times very pusillanimous.
                                                                                 Fielding, S., *David Simple*, I

When the fox preacheth the geese perish. The crocodile shroudeth greatest treason under most pitiful tears: in a kissing mouth there lieth a galling mind.
                                                                                                 Lyly, *Euphues*, 129

Treason begins in the heart before it appears in overt acts.
                                                                     Swift, *Gulliver's Travels*, Lilliput

TREATMENT: *see also* GENEROSITY; KINDNESS; MEDICINE; etc.

Good treatment may never spoil people who are old enough to know its rarity and value.
                                                                   Allen, J. L., *Kentucky Cardinal*, VI

TRIAL: *see also* JUDGMENT; JUSTICE; LAW; MISERY; etc.

The fruit that will fall without shaking is ten times too mellow for me.
Anonymous, *The Modern Fine Gentleman*, I

Feathers sink to the bottom when the torrent is too violent.
August, *Horrid Mysteries*, III

A good man must suffer trouble.　　　　　Bunyan, *Pilgrim's Progress*, 290

Calm and unruffled we should meet our several trials, and think all that is ordained is
right.　　　　　Harley, *Priory of St. Bernard*, I

Gold is purified by fiery trials.　　　　　Johnstone, *The Reverie*, II

Actual trial generally results in demonstrating how much we are prone to exaggerate in
advance the difficulties of any undertaking.
Kennedy, J. P., *Horse Shoe Robinson*, XXXIX

Believe no man till thou hast tried him.　　　　　Kimber, *David Ranger*, I

What examples can be afforded by the patience of those who have never suffered, or the
chastity of those who were never solicited?　　　Lennox, *The Female Quixote*, II

The camel first troubleth the water before he drink, the frankincense is burned before it
smell, friends are tried before they are to be trusted.
Lyly, *Euphues and His England*, 378

We know not till put to the test what very severe trials nature can sustain. Death is not
so ready to relieve the wretched.　　　Parsons, *The Mysterious Warning*, I

A long succession of trials had reduced her to a state of horrid tranquillity.
Radcliffe, *The Castles of Athlin and Dunbayne*, 224

What woman can be said to be virtuous till she has been tried?
Richardson, *Clarissa Harlowe*, II

One effort, one trial, on a woman's virtue is not sufficient.　　　　　*Ibid.*

I should dread to make further trial of a woman virtuous at heart, for fear of succeeding.
Ibid.

Can a girl be degraded by trials, who is not overcome?　　　　　*Ibid.*

If there was nothing to try us on this earth, we should have no business here.
Ridley, *James Lovegrove*, II

TRIUMPH: *see also* SUCCESS; WAR AND PEACE; etc.

You only triumph over the misfortunes of your enemies.　　Reade, *Griffith Gaunt*, IX

To strike an adversary dumb is the tongue's triumph.　　　　　*Ibid.*, XX

TRUST: *see also* CONFIDENCE; HONESTY

It is not good to suspect a steward without a cause; but it is against prudence to trust
him too far.　　　Anonymous, *The History of Tom Jones in His Married State*, 271

What is a man's bond who is not worth a guinea?　　　　　Burney, *Cecilia*, I

The man who fills the post of trust never is the right sort of man.
Dickens, *Great Expectations*, XXX

It is a good maxim to trust a person entirely or not at all; for a secret is often innocently
blabbed out by those who know but half of it.　　　Fielding, H., *Amelia*, II

I cannot stand much romance; I always distrust it.　　　　　Gaskell, *Ruth*, XI

It is difficult to negotiate where neither will trust.　　　Johnson, *Rasselas*, 139

If, next to mistrusting Providence, there be aught that man should pray against, it is against mistrusting his fellow man.   Melville, *Confidence-Man*, IV

We should shut our ears to distrust, and keep them open only for its opposite.
Ibid., VI

How can that be trustworthy that teaches distrust?   *Ibid.*, XLV

To distrust the creature is a kind of distrusting of the Creator.   *Ibid.*

The proper defense for a man is his readiness to abide by his word.
Meredith, *Harry Richmond*, XXVIII

We distrust each other in this world too much.
Meredith, *Ordeal of Richard Feverel*, XXIX

Princes are not the only people in whom you must not put your trust.
Mitchell, *The Autobiography of a Quack*, 31

Causeless distrust is able to drive deceit into a simple woman's head.
Nashe, *The Unfortunate Traveller*, 85

Gentlemen of fortune usually trust little among themselves.
Stevenson, *Treasure Island*, XI

TRUTH: *see also* FALSEHOOD; HONESTY; TRUST

Truth is not to be spoken at all times.   Anonymous, *Ephraim Tristram Bates*, 170

We have a right to know the truth, no right to ask anything else from God, but the right to ask that.   Barrie, *Tommy and Grizel*, XXXV

The truth is always incredible, because the blind eyes of humanity can see only half-truths except by great effort.   Bates, *Puritans*, VI

Great is the force of truth, and it will prevail. It requires great courage to bear testimony against an error in the judgment of the multitude; as it is attended with present disreputation.   Brackenridge, *Modern Chivalry*, Part II, I

There are grains of truth in the wildest fable.   Bronte, C., *Jane Eyre*, XV

All systems make against, instead of leading to, the discovery of truth.
Brooke, *Emily Montague*, III

Suspect him of insincerity and treachery who sacrifices truth to complaisance and advises you to the pursuit of an object which would tend to his advantage.
Brown, W. H., *The Power of Sympathy*, 90

Truth is truth, whether one speaks it or not.   Burney, *Cecilia*, III

Truth is here presented naked and undisguised by the least garment borrowed from the plenteous wardrobe of fiction.   Burton, *Ascanius*, 4

Truth is not afraid to appeal to future and further discoveries for a sanction to the present.   *Ibid.*

Truth bears its own impress.   Butler, *Erewhon*, I

Truth is irresistible. The vivacity of its coloring has quite a different effect from the daub of falsity or invention.   Cleland, *Memoirs of a Coxcomb*, 53

Truth is powerful, and it is not always that we do not believe what we eagerly wish.
Cleland, *Memoirs of a Woman of Pleasure*, 48

Truth, which, like Beauty itself, floats elusive, obscure, half submerged, in the silent still waters of mystery.   Conrad, *Lord Jim*, XX

Vanity plays lurid tricks with our memory, and the truth of every passion wants some pretence to make it live.   *Ibid.*, XLI

It is a hard thing to fear truth.   Cooper, *The Deerslayer*, XVIII

Truth is a comparative and local property, being much influenced by circumstances; particularly by climate and by different public opinions.
                                        Cooper, *The Monikins*, Conclusion

Occultations of truth are just as certain as the aurora borealis, and quite as easily accounted for.   *Ibid.*

Truth is always bold.   Dickens, *Barnaby Rudge*, XXXV

That light is the ray of rays, the sun of suns, the moon of moons, the star of stars. It is the light of Terewth.   Dickens, *Bleak House*, XXV

It is a melancholy truth that even great men have their poor relations.   *Ibid.*, XXVIII

What will be, will be. It's the only truth going.   Dickens, *Hard Times*, Book II, II

A very sublime and grand thing is Truth, in its way, though like other sublime and grand things, such as thunderstorms and that, we're not always over and above glad to see it.   Dickens, *Old Curiosity Shop*, LXVI

There are yet great truths to tell, if we had either the courage to announce or the temper to receive them.   Disraeli, *Coningsby*, Book IV, I

"Nothing in the newspapers is ever true." "And that is why they are so popular; the taste of the age being so decidedly for fiction."   Disraeli, *Lothair*, LXXIII

Telling the truth often means no more than taking a liberty.   Eliot, *Felix Holt*, X

We don't mind how hard the truth is for the neighbors outside our walls.
                                        Eliot, *Middlemarch*, Book IV, XXXIX

That hard rind of truth which is discerned by unimaginative, unsympathetic minds.
                                        Eliot, *The Mill on the Floss*, Book VI, IV

Truth, the most powerful of all things, is the strongest friend of innocence.
                                        Fielding, H., *Amelia*, I

Out of love to yourself, you should confine yourself to truth, for by doing otherwise, you injure the noblest part of yourself, your immortal soul.
                                        Fielding, H., *Joseph Andrews*, 81

Truth is to be found only in the works of those who celebrate the lives of great men.
                                          Ibid., 157

What everybody says, there must be some truth in.   Fielding, H., *Tom Jones*, 437

As the brother never foresaw anything at a distance, but was most sagacious in immediately seeing everything the moment it happened; so the sister eternally foresaw at a distance, but was not so quick-sighted to objects before her eyes. As the sister often foresaw what never came to pass, so the brother often saw much more than was actually the truth.   *Ibid.*, 477

A man may speak truth with a smiling countenance.   *Ibid.*, 489

Wisdom and virtue will never injure truth, no more than she can injure them.
                                        Gentleman, *A Trip to the Moon*, II

Dexterity will avail little against the stubbornness of truth.
                                        Godwin, *Caleb Williams*, II

Truth is veiled, because we could no more look upon her glory than we can upon the sun.
                                        Haggard, *She*, X

Just enough truth to make the remark unbearable.   Hardy, *Desperate Remedies*, III

Truth is truth between man and woman, as between man and man.
                                        Hardy, *Tess*, XXVIII

The professor of humbug must have a head full of imagination, and a heart empty of every trace of candor or humanity. The first sacrifice he must make to it is truth, the next is friendship.   Hill, *Mr. George Edwards*, 101

I never knew anyone who was not ashamed of the truth. Did you ever notice that a railroad company numbers its cars from 1,000, instead of from 1?
Howe, The Story of a Country Town, XXX

Few men love the truth for its own sake.
Howells, A Modern Instance, VII

Two inconsistencies cannot both be right, but, imputed to man, they may both be true.
Johnson, Rasselas, 40

Truth, such as is necessary to the regulation of life, is always found where it is honestly sought.
Ibid., 53

That luminous truth which is the life of the world, that it is given to all men to see fitfully, and some to know permanently.
Keenan, The Money-Makers, XXIII

Truth is nothing but a bugbear, to keep children in awe.
Kidgell, The Card, II

Truth is not always injured by fiction.
Lennox, The Female Quixote, II

Nothing but truth can stand against subtlety of reasoning.
Lennox, Henrietta, I

Truth is too weak to combat prejudice.
Ibid., II

Truth, the most amiable, as well as the most natural of virtues.
Mackenzie, The Man of Feeling, 39

The nature of truth may be changed by the garb it wears.
Ibid., 43

With some minds, truth is, in effect, not so cruel a thing after all, seeing that, like a loaded pistol found by poor devils of savages, it raises more wonder than terror—its peculiar virtue being unguessed, unless, indeed, by indiscreet handling, it should happen to go off by itself.
Melville, Confidence-Man, XXI

Truth is like a threshing-machine; tender sensibilities must keep out of the way.
Ibid., XXII

The voice of the people is the voice of truth.
Ibid., XXIX

If Truth doesn't speak through the people, it never speaks at all.
Ibid.

Truth is in things, and not in words: truth is voiceless.
Melville, Mardi, XCIII

"What is truth?" "That question is more final than any answer."
Ibid.

Whate'er it be, an honest thought must have some germ of truth.
Ibid., CIX

To preach the truth to the face of Falsehood!
Melville, Moby Dick, IX

In landlessness alone resides the highest truth.
Ibid., XXIII

Truth hath no confines.
Ibid., XXXVI

[It is] vain to popularize profundities, and all truth is profound.
Ibid., XLI

Unless you own the whale, you are but a provincial and sentimentalist in Truth. But clear Truth is a thing for salamander giants only to encounter; how small the chances for the provincials then?
Ibid., LXXVI

There is no China Wall that man can build in his soul, which shall permanently stay the irruptions of those barbarous hordes which Truth ever nourishes in the loins of her frozen, yet teeming North; so that the Empire of Human Knowledge can never be lasting in any one dynasty, since Truth still gives new Emperors to the earth.
Melville, Pierre, Book IX, I

The everlasting elusiveness of Truth; the universal lurking insincerity of even the greatest and purest written thoughts.
Ibid., Book XXV, III

Truth loves to be centrally located.
Melville, Typee, XXVII

The true word spoken has its chance of somewhere alighting and striking root. Look not to that. Seeds perish in nature; good men fail. Look to the truth in you, and deliver it, with no afterthought of hope, for hope is dogged by dread; we give our courage as hostage for the fulfillment of what we hope. Hope is for boys and girls, to whom nature is kind. For men to hope is to tremble.   Meredith, *Beauchamp's Career*, XXIX

He spoke as if he saw the truth, and persisting in it so long, he was accredited by those who did not understand him, and silenced them that did.
    Meredith, *Ordeal of Richard Feverel*, XV

Sober truth is but dull matter to the reading rabble.   Peacock, *Crotchet Castle*, IX

Where there is no man there is no truth.   Peacock, *Headlong Hall*, VII

The Truth against the World.   Peacock, *The Misfortunes of Elphin*, VI

Truth is often perverted by education.   Radcliffe, *The Romance of the Forest*, 479

Truth is truth.   Richardson, *Clarissa Harlowe*, II

What everyone says, must be true.   *Ibid.*

No truth is immodest that is uttered in the vindicated cause of innocence and chastity.
    Ibid., IV

"I never lied to man, and hardly ever said truth to woman." The first is what all free-livers cannot say: the second, what every one can.   *Ibid.*

There is merit in owning a truth when it makes against us.
    Richardson, *Sir Charles Grandison*, Three, VI

Nothing but Truth can hold Truth.
    Schreiner, *The Story of an African Farm*, Part II, II

All things on earth have their price; and for truth we pay the dearest. We barter it for love and sympathy. The road to honor is paved with thorns; but on the path to truth, at every step you set your foot down on your own heart.   *Ibid.*, Part II, V

The words of truth in the mouth of folly.   Scott, *The Talisman*, XII

Few there be that can discern between truth and truth likeness between shows and substance.   Sidney, *Arcadia*, III

Truth doth truth deserve.   *Ibid.*

Truth is my best eloquence.   *Ibid.*, V

It is the first policy in a time of difficulty or danger always to know the worst—never to hide the truth from yourself—never to persuade yourself that the evil is unreal, and that things are better than they really are.   Simms, *Woodcraft*, XIX

Truth is mighty, and will prevail.   Smollett, *Peregrine Pickle*, 107

Endless is the search of truth.   Sterne, *Tristram Shandy*, II

The truth is the kindest thing we can give folks in the end.
    Stowe, *Orr's Island*, XXXVI

The devil often builds the ladder by which truth climbs up.
    Tourgee, *Pactolus Prime*, XI

No experience of what goes on in the world, no reading of history, no observation of life, has any effect in teaching the truth.   Trollope, *Barchester Towers*, XXXVII

It takes an age to ascertain the truth of any question.   Trollope, *The Warden*, XV

He told the truth, mainly. There was things which he stretched, but mainly he told the truth.   Twain, *Huckleberry Finn*, I

Tell the truth or trump—but get the trick.   Twain, *Pudd'nhead Wilson*, I

My veracity is dearer to me than my life; nor would I purchase the one by forfeiting the other.   Walpole, *The Castle of Otranto*, 24

Anything that is true must be true to local conditions.   Warner, *A Little Journey*, VIII

Nothing is ever quite true.   Wilde, *The Picture of Dorian Gray*, VI

It is perfectly monstrous, the way people go about nowadays saying things against one behind one's back that are absolutely and entirely true.   *Ibid.*, XV

The language of truth is too simple for inexperienced ears.
         Wright, *A Few Days in Athens*, XV

Truth is but approved facts.   *Ibid.*

TWINS

All twins are prodigies; and still I hardly know why this should be; for all of us in our own persons furnish numerous examples of the same phenomenon. Are not our thumbs twins? A regular Castor and Pollux? And all of our fingers? Are not our arms, hands, legs, feet, eyes, ears, all twins; born at one birth, and as much alike as they possibly can be? Can it be that the Greek grammarians invented their dual number for the particular benefit of twins?   Melville, *Redburn*, LIII

Allies are of the description of twins joined by a membrane, and supposing that one of them determines to sit down, the other will act wisely in bending his knees at once, and doing the same: he cannot but be extremely uncomfortable left standing.
         Meredith, *Beauchamp's Career*, IV

TYPE; TYPICALNESS: *see also* KIND

You are of the class, mammalia; order, primate; genus, homo; species, Kentucky.
         Cooper, *The Prairie*

An Oyster of the old school, whom nobody can open.   Dickens, *Bleak House*, X

Our people are sheep. Where two or three marked ones go, all the rest follow. Keep those two or three in your eye, and you have the flock.   *Ibid.*, LVIII

It is the variation, not the ordinary specimen, that is most typical, for the variation contains the rule in essence, and the deviation elucidates the rule.
         Moore, *Evelyn Innes*, II

I don't know in all this miserable world a more miserable spectacle than that of a young fellow of five or six and forty.   Thackeray, *Catherine*, IX

TYRANNY: *see also* FREEDOM; GOVERNMENT; etc.

There is such a thing as tyranny in judges. But let the power paramount, the people, take care that they exercise not tyranny themselves.
         Brackenridge, *Modern Chivalry*, Part II, I

The few are always tyrants.   *Ibid.*

We talk about the tyranny of words, but we like to tyrannize over them too; we are fond of having a large superfluous establishment of words to wait upon us on great occasions; we think it looks important, and sounds well.   Dickens, *David Copperfield*, LII

The darker tyrant he has been, the more ferocious is his doctrine.   *Ibid.*, LIX

Tyranny is ever hostile to every species of mental development, for its great object is to keep its victims in a state of ignorance and degradation, and therefore of helplessness.
         Hildreth, *Slave*, Volume I, XVI

What other tyrants [than slaveholders] are recorded in all the world's history, who have openly and publicly confessed, that they prefer to expose their victims to the imminent danger of eternal misery, rather than impart a degree of instruction, which might endanger their own unjust and usurped authority?   *Ibid.*, Volume I, XIX

Tyranny is not omnipotent.   *Ibid.*, Volume II, IX

Nature never intended man to be a tyrant. *Ibid.*, Volume II, XIII

Who may withstand the people? The times tell terrible tales to tyrants!
Melville, *Mardi*, CLXI

Paternal and maternal tyrants are the worst of all tyrants.
Richardson, *Clarissa Harlowe*, II

Your greatness licenses tyranny. Scott, *The Talisman*, XVII

Some men only live for great occasions. They sleep in the calm—but awake to double life, and unlooked for activity, in the tempest. They are the zephyr in peace, the storm in war. They smile until you think it impossible they should ever do otherwise, and you are paralyzed when you behold the change which an hour brings about in them. Their whole life in public would seem a splendid deception; and as their minds and feelings are generally beyond those of the great mass which gathers about, and in the end depends upon them, so they continually dazzle the vision and distract the judgment of those who passingly observe them. Such men become the tyrants of all the rest, and, as there are two kinds of tyranny in the world, they either enslave to cherish or to destroy.
Simms, *Yemassee*, XXVI

His spouse, by the force of pride, religion, and Cognac, had erected a most terrible tyranny in the house. Smollett, *Peregrine Pickle*, 126

UBIQUITOUSNESS: *see also* GOD

Time and place cannot bind Mr. Bucket. Like man in the abstract, he is here today and gone tomorrow—but, very unlike man indeed, he is here again the next day.
Dickens, *Bleak House*, LIII

UNCERTAINTY: *see also* DOUBT

Uncertainty doubles affliction. Kimber, *Maria*, I

UNDERSTANDING

I like people who understand what one says to them, and also what one doesn't say.
James, H., *Princess Casamassima*, XVII

UNITY: *see also* UNIVERSALITY

I cannot tear my soul out of my body. You must take both or neither.
Atherton, *Doomswoman*, XXIII

Virtue is one all over the world, and there is only one faith, one conceivable conduct of life, one manner of dying. Conrad, *Lord Jim*, XXXVI

He had grown to regard himself merely as a part of a vast blue demonstration.
Crane, *Red Badge of Courage*, I

The unities are a completeness—a kind of a universal dovetailedness with regard to place and time—a sort of a general oneness, if I may be allowed to use so strong an expression. Dickens, *Nicholas Nickleby*, XXIV

No man can understand and estimate the entire structure or its parts—what are its frailties and what its repairs, without knowing the nature of the materials.
Eliot, *Middlemarch*, Book II, XV

Scenes which make vital changes in our neighbors' lot are but the background of our own, yet, like a particular aspect of the fields and trees, they become associated for us with the epochs of our own history, and make a part of that unity which lies in the selection of our keenest consciousness. *Ibid.*, Book IV, XXXIV

In every machine the smallest parts conduce as much to the keeping it together, and to regulate its motions, as the greatest. Fielding, S., *David Simple*, II

UNITY (*continued*)

Each bright star is overhead somewhere.   Hardy, *Pair of Blue Eyes*, XIX

Where all unite, there is no excess. We praise God in the dances; it is a hymn written without our feet.   Judd, *Margaret*, Volume III

They will see the links of things as they pass, and wonder not, as foolish people do, that this great matter came out of that small one.
         Meredith, *Ordeal of Richard Feverel*, XXIX

A lady and her maid, when heartily of one party, will be too hard for half a score devils.
         Richardson, *Clarissa Harlowe*, II

As frothy a heart as a head.   *Ibid.*, III

Kindred souls are always near.   Richardson, *Sir Charles Grandison*, Three, VII

UNIVERSALITY; SPECIFICITY: *see also* UNITY

We love to feel within us the bond which unites the most distant eras—men, nations, customs, perish; the affections are immortal. They are the sympathies which unite the ceaseless generations. The past lives again, when we look upon its emotions—it lives in our own. That which was, ever is.   Bulwer, *Pompeii*, Book Three, II

The language of commiseration is universal.   Cooper, *Wish-ton-Wish*, V

In our general descriptions, we mean not universals, but would be understood with many exceptions.   Fielding, H., *Joseph Andrews*, 160

All things form but one whole; the universe a Judea, and God Jehovah its head.
         Melville, *Mardi*, III

Off masks, mankind, that I may know what warranty of fellowship with others, my own thoughts possess.   *Ibid.*, CIX

The universal thump is passed round, and all hands should rub each other's shoulder-blades, and be content.   Melville, *Moby Dick*, I

We are all somehow dreadfully cracked about the head, and sadly need mending.
         Ibid., XVII

You can not spill a drop of American blood without spilling the blood of the whole world.
         Melville, *Redburn*, XXXIII

The whole world is the patrimony of the whole world; there is no telling who does not own a stone in the Great Wall of China.   *Ibid.*, LVIII

We sailors sail not in vain. We expatriate ourselves to nationalize with the universe; and in all our voyages round the world we are still accompanied by those old circumnavigators, the stars, who are shipmates and fellow sailors of ours—sailing in heaven's blue, as we on the azure main.   Melville, *White Jacket*, XIX

UNNATURALNESS: *see also* NATURE

Cats that go ratting don't wear gloves.   Adams, H., *Democracy*, VIII

UTILITY: *see also* ART; BEAUTY; etc.

The man who washes his donkey's head loses time and soap.
         Adams, H., *Democracy*, VIII

Never sweep a room out of use; it only wears out brooms for nothing.
         Burney, *Cecilia*, II

Things unserviceable in one way may with advantage be applied in another.
         Melville, *Typee*, XIX

Hawks have their uses in destroying vermin; and though we cannot rely upon the taming of hawks, one tied by the leg in a garden preserves the fruit.

Meredith, *Beauchamp's Career*, XXIV

He is useless on top of the ground; he ought to be under it, inspiring cabbages.

Twain, *Pudd'nhead Wilson*, XXI

VACUITY

If Nature could but understand that vacuity is sometimes better than superfluity!

Glasgow, *The Descendant*, Book II, VII

VALUE: *see also* WORTH

Every man has the right to set a price on his own labor, and to refuse to work for less; the wisdom of it is another matter. He puts himself in the wrong only when he menaces the person or the property of the man who has an equal right not to employ him.

Aldrich, *Stillwater*, XIV

If you can't get the very best in this world, take nothing.

Atherton, *The Californians*, Book I, XI

Every qualification is raised at times by the circumstances of the moment to more than its real value.

Austen, *Sense and Sensibility*, Volume II, X

All men who do their best, do the same. A man's endowments, however godlike, merely fix the measure of his duty.

Bellamy, *Looking Backward*, IX

The value of a man's services to society fixes his rank in it.

Ibid.

I don't think that the things best worth having can be bought at all.

Bulwer, *The Caxtons*, Book IV, V

Physical qualities are always prized in proportion to the value that is attached to those that are purely intellectual.

Cooper, *Heidenmauer*, VII

Whether bread be cheap or dear don't much signify, if we have nothing to buy it with.

Disraeli, *Sybil*, Book VI, III

A bridge is a good thing—worth helping to make, though half the men who worked at it were rogues.

Eliot, *Felix Holt*, XVI

A guinea is as valuable in a leather as in an embroidered purse; and a codshead is a codshead, whether in a pewter or a silver dish.

Fielding, H., *Jonathan Wild*, 26

By low conversation, we contract a greater awe for high things than they deserve.

Ibid.

Consider that hat as the best, which will contain the largest booty.

Ibid., 95

The value of a man is in his intrinsic qualities; in that of which power cannot strip him, and which adverse fortune cannot take away.

Godwin, *St. Leon*, 93

How cheaply we prize a gift which we imagine to be already in our power!

Ibid., 136

What does this world afford which is really worth wishing for, but woman?

Johnstone, *The Pilgrim*, I

The foul toad hath a fair stone in his head, the fine gold is found in the filthy earth, the sweet kernel lieth in the hard shell.

Lyly, *Euphues*, 110

The sense of unworthiness is a guarantee of worthiness ensuing.

Meredith, *The Egoist*, XI

Here you could be drunk for five cents, and be lodged for three.

Mitchell, *Autobiography of a Quack*, 17

The world is not always worthy of good actions.

Reade, *Griffith Gaunt*, XIII

Worth is best known by want.

Richardson, *Clarissa Harlowe*, II

VALUE (*continued*)

Inborn worth must be always as much above conceit as annoyance.   *Ibid.,* IV

What can be misbestowed by a man on his person, who values it more than his mind?
Richardson, *Sir Charles Grandison,* One, I

Everything is good for something.   Sterne, *Tristram Shandy,* VII

The greatest mistake any man ever made is to suppose that the good things of the world
are not worth the winning.   Trollope, *Barchester Towers,* XXXVIII

A thing's worth what it fetches.   Trollope, *Can You Forgive Her?,* XIII

We all value what we have not got.   Trollope, *He Knew He Was Right,* LVI

A highwayman is a worthy character, when put in the balance with a seducer of virgins,
or, in other words, a maker of the prostitutes which fill our streets.
Woodfin, *The Auction,* I

VANGUARD

We are the pioneers of the world; the advance guard, sent on through the wilderness of
untried things, to break a new path in the New World that is ours. In our youth is our
strength; in our inexperience, our wisdom.   Melville, *White Jacket,* XXXVI

VANITY: *see also* PRIDE

Vanity is natural to the whole race of scribblers.
Anonymous, *The Adventures of Oxymel Classic,* II

When vanity throws a mist before the intellectual eye, the corporeal one is equally
bedimmed, and sees everything through a false medium.
Anonymous, *Memoirs of a Coquet,* 99

To the vain, every motion of the eye is a look of love, every smile a mark of affection, and
every polite compliment a proof of sincerity.   *Ibid.*

The vanity of men is greater than their desire for gain.   August, *Horrid Mysteries,* III

Vanity was the beginning and the end of Sir Walter Elliot's character; vanity of person
and of situation.   Austen, *Persuasion,* I

Vanity, not love, has been my folly.   Austen, *Pride and Prejudice,* Volume II, XIII

Half our preferences are due to the vanity they flatter.
Bulwer, *What Will He Do With It?,* Book II, X

The general opinion which ranks vanity among the lighter failings of humanity commits a serious mistake.   Collins, *Heart and Science,* XXXVI

The ruling passion of civilized humanity is conceit.   Collins, *I Say No,* IV

Smart talk is my form of conceit.   *Ibid.*

An educated criminal is almost invariably an inveterate egotist. We are all interesting
to ourselves—but the more vile we are, the more intensely we are absorbed in ourselves.
Collins, *Jezebel's Daughter,* Book III, VIII

I had a most unbounded stock of vanity and pride, and but a very little stock of virtue.
Defoe, *Moll Flanders,* 20

Vanity is the perfection of a fop.   *Ibid.,* 58

It may be that words are vain to save us; but feeble deeds are vainer far than words.
Disraeli, *Sybil,* Book V, III

I am not so vain as to think myself without vanity.   Edgeworth, *The Absentee,* VI

Our vanities differ as our noses do: all conceit is not the same conceit, but varies in correspondence with the minutiae of mental make in which one of us differs from another.   Eliot, *Middlemarch*, Book II, XV

The touchstone by which men try us is most often their own vanity.
                                                       Eliot, *Romola*, Book II, XXVI

Vanity is the pursuit of most men through their lives.
                                                       Fielding, H., *Joseph Andrews*, 57

All our passions are the slaves of Vanity.   *Ibid.*

However possible it may be to support disappointed love with patience, it is one of the characteristical marks of disappointed vanity, to throw the mind into perturbation and impatience.   Fielding, S., *The Countess of Dellwyn*, I

Poets never gave more eyes to Argus, or more hands to Briareus, than nature hath given fears, and consequently desires, to vanity, whose commands are as numerous as they are contradictory.   *Ibid.*, II

Those who have affirmed that love will conquer all things should have considered that there is no rule without an exception; for vanity is not to be so baffled, and still claims the honor of being unconquerable.   *Ibid.*

I live by vanity, and laugh at it.   Goldsmith, *The Vicar of Wakefield*, 110

People are generally quite as vain, or even more so, of their deficiencies, as of their available gifts.   Hawthorne, *The House of the Seven Gables*, V

The more insignificant an art or science is, the more vain the professors of it are of their knowledge.   Jenner, *The Placid Man*, I

Vanity cheats many a woman out of her honor.   Lennox, *Henrietta*, I

You were virtuous from vanity, not principle.   Lewis, *The Monk*, 354

Vanity of our knowledge is generally found in the first stages of its acquirement, because we are then looking back to that rank we have left, of such as know nothing at all.   Mackenzie, *The Man of the World*, I

He who is frank will often appear vain.   Melville, *Mardi*, CLXX

Reserve alone is vanity. But all mankind are egotists.   *Ibid.*

The world revolves upon an I; and we upon ourselves; for we are our own worlds.   *Ibid.*

Man has only to be but a little circumspect, and away flies the last rag of his vanity.
                                                       Melville, *Pierre*, Book XVIII, I

Vanity often produces unreasonable alarm.   Radcliffe, *A Sicilian Romance*, I

Nothing is so penetrating as the eye of a lover who has vanity.
                                                       Richardson, *Clarissa Harlowe*, I

Vanity is not excusable even in a woman.   *Ibid.*

If men of parts may not be allowed to be vain, who should?   *Ibid.*, II

Men of parts have the least occasion to be vain.   *Ibid.*

Without vanity a man may know those things of himself which everybody seeth and saith of him.   *Ibid.*, IV

Vanity is natural to the youthful mind.   Roche, *Nocturnal Visit*, II

Vanity makes a fool of the wisest.   Scott, *Kenilworth*, XXX

Ah! *Vanitas Vanitatum*! Which of us is happy in this world? Which of us has his desire? or, having it, is satisfied?   Thackeray, *Vanity Fair*, end

VARIETY; SAMENESS: *see also* COMPARISON/CONTRAST; DIFFERENCE

Things are so little different one from another, that there is no making pleasure out of anything.
Burney, *Cecilia*, II

Mrs. Karnegie being—as we all are in our various degrees—a compound of many opposite qualities, possessed a character with more than one side to it.
Collins, *Man and Wife*, XXX

It is impossible to gaze always upon a lovely countenance with equal admiration, for the senses becoming saturated, the heart requires something more—something to interest, to delight, to fix beyond the moment.
Dacre, *The Libertine*, XV

Men are so different at different times.
Dickens, *Nicholas Nickleby*, XVI

A multitude is to me as it were a strain of music, which, with an irresistible and magical influence, calls up from the unknown abyss of the feelings new combinations of fancy, which, though vague and obscure, as those nebulae of light that astronomers have supposed to be the rudiments of unformed stars, afterwards become distinct and brilliant acquisitions.
Galt, *Ayrshire*, V

Men are so much alike in their nature, that they grow intolerable unless varied by their circumstances.
Hawthorne, *The Blithedale Romance*, XVII

Variety is so necessary to contentedness that even the recurrence of luxuries disgusts.
Johnson, *Rasselas*, 179

Nothing is satisfactory that is one-sided.
Murfree, *The Story of Old Fort Loudon*, X

It is a long lane that has no turning.
Richardson, *Clarissa Harlowe*, II

What a variety there is in goodness.
Richardson, *Sir Charles Grandison*, Two, V

That boundless love of variety, which is inseparable from youth and inexperience.
Sleath, *The Orphan of the Rhine*, III

VEGETARIANISM

The only worthy thing she could think of doing was abjure meat.
Meredith, *Beauchamp's Career*, XLVIII

VENGEANCE; REVENGE

Custom has ennobled revenge, and some may say they put it in practice that we had better be out of the world, than out of the fashion.
Anonymous, *The History of Tom Jones in His Married State*, 76

Revenge is sweeter than religion.
Atherton, *Doomswoman*, XXVI

The last resource of the mean and downtrodden is revenge.
Ibid., XXXI

It is a strange thing that we cannot submit with equanimity to evils in the moral world, as we do in the natural. We expect a fair day, and there comes a foul. Is it any gratification to us, to beat the air, or stamp upon the puddle? Who would think of giving the cowskin to a hurricane?
Brackenridge, *Modern Chivalry*, Part II, I

It is not violence that best overcomes hate—nor vengeance that most certainly heals injury.
Bronte, C., *Jane Eyre*, VI

What does vengeance desire but to inflict misery?
Brown, C. B., *Edgar Huntley*, 24

Vengeance and retribution require a long time; it is the rule.
Dickens, *A Tale of Two Cities*, Book II, XVI

To see an enemy humiliated gives a certain contentment, but this is jejune compared with the highly blent satisfaction of seeing him humiliated by your benevolent action or concession on his behalf. That is a sort of revenge which falls into the scale of virtue.
Eliot, *Mill on the Floss*, Book III, VII

In taking revenge upon our enemies, we are only even with them; in passing over their malice we are superior. Lennox, *Sophia*, II

There is nothing so nearly allied to the Deity as the desire of revenging injuries. Manley, *Memoirs of Europe*, II

He was intent on an audacious, immitigable, and supernatural revenge. Melville, *Moby Dick*, XLI

Retribution, swift vengeance, eternal malice were in his whole aspect, and spite of all that mortal man could do, the solid white buttress of his forehead smote the ship's starboard bow, till men and timbers reeled. *Ibid.*, CXXXV

Oh, the refreshment there is in dealing with characters either contemptibly beneath us or supernaturally above! Meredith, *Beauchamp's Career*, XLVIII

Revenge in our tragedies continually is raised from hell: of hell do I esteem better than heaven, if it afford me revenge. Nashe, *The Unfortunate Traveller*, 146

There is no heaven but revenge. *Ibid.*

Revenge is the glory of arms, and the highest performance of valor: revenge is whatsoever we call law or justice. *Ibid.*, 148

The farther we wade in revenge, the nearer come we to the throne of the Almighty. *Ibid.*

Vengeance, though it comes with leaden feet, strikes with iron hands. Richardson, *Clarissa Harlowe*, II

Where vice goes before, vengeance will follow. *Ibid.*

No one knows what revenge for slighted love will make one do. *Ibid.*, III

What will vengeance do, after an insult committed? *Ibid.*

'Tis the guilty heart, not the guilty hand, which merits the vengeance of heaven. Roche, *Clermont*, IV

Revenge is a feast for the gods. If they have reserved it to themselves, it is because they hold it an enjoyment too precious for the possession of mere mortals. Scott, *Ivanhoe*, XXIV

For little more than the pleasure of revenge and the lust of bloodshed, our hostile clans do the work of executioners on each other. Scott, *Quentin Durward*, XXIII

Revenge may be wicked, but it's natural. Thackeray, *Vanity Fair*, II

There's plenty of boys that will come hankering and groveling around you when you've got an apple and beg the core off of you; but when they've got one, and you beg for the core and remind them how you give them a core one time, they say thank you 'most to death, but there ain't a-going to be no core. But I notice they always git come up with; all you got to do is wait. Twain, *Tom Sawyer Abroad*, I

VICARIOUSNESS: *see also* PLEASURE

My sister having so much to do, was going to church vicariously; that is to say, Joe and I were going. Dickens, *Great Expectations*, IV

VICE: *see also* GOOD AND EVIL; VIRTUE; etc.

Interest is the *primum mobile* of all human actions, at whose shrine are constantly sacrificed every tender virtue, every social perfection. Vice there puts on the appearance of virtue. Anonymous, *The Birmingham Counterfeit*, II

Grandeur and magnificence may change the very nature of vice, and render criminality innocent. Anonymous, *Genuine Memoirs of Maria Brown*, II

If a master scatters his vices among the family, they are soon picked up and worn as robes of honor.　　Anonymous, *The History of Tom Jones in His Married State*, 283

The devil corrects vice.　　Bunyan, *The Life and Death of Mr. Badman*, 194

Vices are the harpies that infect and foul the feast.
　　Cleland, *Memoirs of a Woman of Pleasure*, 214

Vice is nothing else but a misapplication and abuse of some right and laudable affections.
　　Collyer, *Felicia to Charlotte*, I

Gradual and terrible are the approaches of vice!　　Dacre, *Zofloya*, IV

The vice came in always at the door of necessity, not at the door of inclination.
　　Defoe, *Moll Flanders*, 128

Vices are sometimes only virtues carried to excess.　　Dickens, *Dombey and Son*, LVIII

There is something so outrageously suspicious in the nature of all vice, especially when joined with any great degree of pride, that the eyes of those whom we imagine privy to our failings are intolerable to us, and we are apt to aggravate their opinions to our disadvantage far beyond the reality.　　Fielding, H., *Amelia*, I

Many women have become abandoned, and have sunk to the last degree of vice, by being unable to retrieve their first slip.　　Fielding, H., *Tom Jones*, 26

The man, as well as the player, may condemn what he himself acts; nay, it is common to see vice sit as awkwardly on some men, as the character of Iago would on an honest face.
　　Ibid., 268

The good old theory of our forefathers that vice was in the naming of it.
　　Glasgow, *The Descendant*, Book II, V

He who in any manner participates in the vices of a nation, or a body of men, is reproached as if loaded with the whole guilt.　　Holcroft, *Hugh Trevor*, V

A series of crimes and follies may give an insight into vice, which the moral drawn from them may never be able to prevent being put in practice.　　Jenner, *The Placid Man*, II

I am sometimes ashamed to think that I could not secure myself from vice, but by retiring from the exercise of virtue.　　Johnson, *Rasselas*, 87

Vices take the deepest root in weakest minds.　　Johnstone, *The Reverie*, I

I am happy when I know my neighbor's vice.　　Meredith, *Ordeal of Richard Feverel*, I

Let him see vice in its nakedness. While he has yet some innocence, nauseate him. Vice, taken little by little, usurps gradually the whole creature.　　*Ibid.*, XX

Vice, to be hated, needs but to be seen.　　Parsons, *The Mysterious Warning*, IV

There can be no degradation where there is no vice.　　Radcliffe, *The Italian*, I

Vice ne'er yet stood still.　　Reade, *The Cloister and the Hearth*, LXXX

His vices are so much his masters that he attempts not to conquer them.
　　Richardson, *Clarissa Harlowe*, I

Vice was a coward, and would hide its head, when opposed by such a virtue as had presence of mind, and a full persuasion of its own rectitude, to support.　　*Ibid.*

His vices all ugly him over.　　Richardson, *Pamela*, 206

Vice is the greatest coward in the world, when it knows it will be resolutely opposed.
　　Richardson, *Sir Charles Grandison*, One, I

He seemed confident, that instead of reason, we were only possessed of some quality fitted to increase our natural vices; as the reflection from a troubled stream returns the image of an ill-shapen body, not only larger, but more distorted.
　　Swift, *Gulliver's Travels*, Houyhnhnms, V

He was the victim of a benefaction. Crane, *Active Service*, XIX

When a woman is left desolate and void of counsel, she is like a bag of money or a jewel dropped on the highway, which is a prey to the next comer. Defoe, *Moll Flanders*, 128

It is not the truth which you Inquisitors seek; it is not the guilty whom you punish; the innocent, having no crimes to confess, are the victims of your cruelty, or, to escape from it, become criminal, and proclaim a lie. Radcliffe, *The Italian*, II

One victim is enough at once. Scott, *Kenilworth*, XXXVIII

VILLAINY; KNAVERY; ROGUERY: *see also* GOOD AND EVIL; LIBERTINISM; etc.

A single bad act no more constitutes a villain in life than a single bad part on the stage. Fielding, H., *Tom Jones*, 268

The worst of men generally have the words rogue and villain most in their mouths. *Ibid.*

Knaves will no more endeavor to persuade us of the baseness of mankind than a highwayman will inform you that there are thieves on the road. *Ibid.*, 411-412

Honor, justice, virtue are all the juggle of knaves. Godwin, *Caleb Williams*, II

To be a knave, it is not necessary to be an infidel. Godwin, *St. Leon*, 334

What villain is not skilled in fair words? Lathom, *The Midnight Bell*, II

He who will act villainously in the transactions of private life cannot lay aside his nature when he acts for the public. *Ibid.*

He who can attest a villainy is best qualified to punish it. Meredith, *Beauchamp's Career*, II

Providence often defeats the deep laid schemes of villainy, and unmasks the contriver to the world. Parsons, *The Mysterious Warning*, III

There never was a rogue who had not a salvo to himself for being so. Richardson, *Clarissa Harlowe*, I

A witty villain deserves hanging at once, without ceremony, but a half-witted one deserves broken bones first, and hanging afterwards. *Ibid.*, II

I had not been a villain had she not been so much an angel. *Ibid.*

To have money, and will, and head, to be a villain, is too much for the rest of the world, when they meet in one man. *Ibid.*, III

VIOLENCE: *see also* WAR AND PEACE

Nothing bears so many stains of blood as gold. Dickens, *Barnaby Rudge*, XLV

He will never do violence to the sunshine any more. Dickens, *Bleak House*, XV

Some females are of a more bloody inclination than the males. Fielding, H., *Tom Jones*, 132

The more violent emotions ever tend to cure themselves. If the patient survive the first paroxysm, his mind speedily begins to verge towards its natural equilibrium. Hildreth, *Slave*, Volume II, V

Don Desperado/ Walked on the Prado,/ And there he met his enemy./ He pulled out a knife,a,/ And let out his life, a,/ And fled for his own across the sea. Kingsley, C., *Westward Ho!*, XII

When Christ said, "The kingdom of heaven must suffer violence," he meant not the violence of long babbling prayers, nor the violence of tedious invective sermons without wit. Nashe, *The Unfortunate Traveller*, 57

VIOLENCE (*continued*)

A single deed of violence and cruelty affects our nerves more than when these are exercised on a more extended scale. Scott, *Rob Roy*, XXXII

VIRGINITY: *see also* VIRTUE

Chastity cannot make amends for the want of all other perfections.
Anonymous, *The Modern Fine Gentleman*, II

Whoever is unchaste cannot reverence himself. Bacon, *The New Atlantis*, 209

Such a one as cannot keep her maidenhead will never keep a secret.
Deloney,*The Gentle Craft*, 144

Chastity is as great a virtue in a man as in a woman. Fielding, H., *Joseph Andrews*, 37

Last week I went with mistress to the Tower, to see the crowns and wild beastis; and there was a monstracious lion, with teeth half a quarter long; and a gentleman bid me not go near him, if I wasn't a maid; being as how he would roar, and tear, and play the dickens. Now I had no mind to go near him; for I cannot abide such dangerous honeymils, not I—but, mistress would go; and the beast kept such a roaring and bouncing, that I tho't he would have broke his cage and devoured us all; and the gentleman tittered forsooth; but I'll go to death upon it, I will, that my lady is as good a firchin, as the child unborn; and, therefore, either the gentleman told a fib, or the lion oft to be set in the stocks for bearing false witness against his neighbour.
Smollett, *Humphry Clinker*, 115

Her body is defiled, and that is too much to say of a woman and marry her after.
Woodfin, *The Auction*, II

VIRTUE: *see also* GOOD AND EVIL

For a week the amount of virtue in the old house would have supplied the neighborhood.
Alcott, *Little Women*, XVII

Virtue alone is true honor, true freedom, and solid, durable happiness.
Amory, *John Buncle*, I

Virtue is the only nobility. Anonymous, *The Adventures of a Kidnapped Orphan*, 73

Every man that is destitute of virtue is at heart a coward.
Anonymous, *The Birmingham Counterfeit*, I

The greatest personal advantages, if not strengthened by virtue, are the most fatal gifts that nature can dispense. *Ibid.*, II

Is not chastity the grand ornament of the female world?
Anonymous, *The Fruitless Repentance*, I

The unnatural, the infernal practice of breach of chastity can be traced to no other source than the absolute fiend. *Ibid.*

They lie under a mistake who fancy that virtue is an enemy to good breeding; that a man must turn off civility to commence a saint; and disband from the society of men to keep a correspondence with God.
Anonymous, *The History of Tom Jones in His Married State*, 269

All virtues are defective which are not tinctured with charity. *Ibid.*, 301–302

She lost her character, but she preserved her virtue.
Anonymous, *Memoirs of a Coquet*, 195

Virtue is its own reward, and vice its own punishment.
Anonymous, *The Modern Fine Gentleman*, I

Virtue, soon or late, meets the good it merits. *Ibid.*, II

The basis of republican virtue, humility and self-denial.

Brackenridge, *Modern Chivalry*, Part II, I

What is it that constitutes virtue? Is it the circumstance of being able and willing to resist temptation; or that of having no temptations to resist?

Bronte, A., *The Tenant of Wildfell Hall*, III

His virtue is the mere absence of vice; his good qualities are all of the negative kind.

Brooke, *Emily Montague*, I

It is a dangerous and too common mistake, that vice is natural to the human heart, and virtuous characters the creatures of fancy.

Ibid., II

Virtue is too lovely to be hid in cells. The world is her scene of action.

Ibid.

Let virtue be dressed in smiles.

Ibid.

Outward ceremonies will not compensate for the want of virtue.

Ibid., III

Those virtues which command esteem do not often inspire passion.

Ibid.

Those who never have been guilty of any indiscretion are generally people who have very little active virtue.

Ibid., IV

The impulses of love are so subtle, and the influence of false reasoning, when enforced by eloquence and passion, so unbounded, that no human virtue is secure from degeneracy.

Brown, C. B., *Wieland*, 260

There is a dignity in conscious virtue.   Brown, W. H., *The Power of Sympathy*, 17

There are a great many things done and said in company which a woman of virtue will neither see nor hear.

Ibid., 91

Virtue is God's empire.

Bulwer, *The Disowned*, LVII

Is virtue as inconsistent as vice?

Burney, *Cecilia*, III

Weak as virtues, frail as guilty natures.

Ibid.

The Erewhonians hold that unalloyed virtue is not a thing to be immoderately indulged in. The most that can be truly said for virtue is that there is a considerable balance in its favor, and that it is on the whole a good deal better to be on its side than against it; but there is much pseudo-virtue going about, which is apt to let people in very badly before they find it out. Those men are best who are not remarkable for vice or virtue.

Butler, *Erewhon*, X

There is no casting of swine's meat before men worse than that which would flatter virtue as though her true origin were not good enough for her, but she must have a lineage, deduced as it were by spiritual heralds, from some stock with which she has nothing to do. Virtue's true lineage is older and more respectable than any that can be invented for her.   Butler, *The Way of All Flesh*, XIX

There is no wonder that a virtue no better guarded than by a vice should not be a match for an attack on a corrupt sentinel.   Cleland, *Memoirs of a Coxcomb*, 106

As there are virtues which are their own reward, so there are vices which are amply their own punishment.

Ibid., 324

The rarest virtue that a single lady can possess—the virtue of putting wine on the table.

Collins, *I Say No*, IX

Virtue is the music of the soul, the harmony of the passions.

Collyer, *Felicia to Charlotte*, I

Virtue can slumber, even in the midst of misfortune.   Dacre, *The Libertine*, VIII

Gabrielle was still virtuous, though no longer innocent.

Ibid.

Such is the power of virtue over the heart, that even a long course of vice will not render us wholly invulnerable to its divine influence.

Ibid., XXIV

In what does virtue consist? Is it not in resisting?   Dacre, *Passions*, Letter LX

The cause of virtue is not desperate while it retains a single friend.
Day, *The History of Sandford and Merton*, 246

Every virtue may be learned and practiced at home; and it is only because we do not choose to have either virtue or religion among us, that so many adventurers are yearly sent out to smuggle foreign graces.
Ibid., 283

He that would excel others in virtue or knowledge must first excel them in temperance and application.
Ibid., 352

Virtue alone is an estate.
Defoe, *Moll Flanders*, 76

Her virtue could support itself with its own intrinsic worth, without borrowing any assistance from the vices of other women.
Fielding, H., *Amelia*, I

The woman who gives up the least outwork of her virtue doth, in that very moment, betray the citadel.
Ibid., II

Did ever mortal hear of a man's virtue!
Fielding, H., *Joseph Andrews*, 33

I once thought of making a little fortune by my person. I now intend to make a great one by my vartue.
Fielding, H., *Shamela*, 325

Mr. Square regarded all virtue as matter of theory only.
Fielding, H., *Tom Jones*, 82-83

One's virtue is a dear thing, especially to us poor servants; for it is our livelihood.
Ibid., 290

The virtue of a young lady is in the same situation with a poor hare, which is certain, whenever it ventures abroad, to meet its enemies; for it can hardly meet any other.
Ibid., 534

One fancied virtue is more dangerous than many acknowledged vices.
Fielding, S., *The Countess of Dellwyn*, I

Virtue consists in actions, and not in words.
Godwin, *Caleb Williams*, III

The good man and the bad are characters precisely opposite, not characters distinguished from each other by imperceptible shades.
Ibid.

That virtue which requires to be ever guarded is scarce worth the sentinel.
Goldsmith, *The Vicar of Wakefield*, 23

That single effort by which we stop short in the downhill path to perdition is a greater exertion of virtue than an hundred acts of justice.
Ibid., 135

The best virtue is never tiresome.
James, H., *Confidence*, VI

The virtue of prosperity is temperance, the virtue of adversity fortitude.
Lennox, *Sophia*, II

Our virtues are pigmies, that daren't grow for fear of the sty.
Meredith, *Ordeal of Richard Feverel*, IV

Virtue is so dear to the human heart, that when her form forsakes us, we pursue her shadow.
Radcliffe, *The Castles of Athlin and Dunbayne*, 96

What must that mind be which, though not virtuous itself, admires not virtue in another?
Richardson, *Clarissa Harlowe*, I

He always loved virtue, although he had not followed its rules as he thought.
Ibid.

Is even virtue itself the paragon of virtue?
Ibid., II

What must that virtue be which will not stand a trial?—What that woman who would wish to shun it?
Ibid.

A tragedy could hardly be justly called a tragedy, if virtue did not temporarily suffer, and vice for a while triumph.
Ibid., IV

A vixen in her virtue.   *Ibid.*

Those who want to be thought above hypocrisy and flattery fall into rusticity, if not ill manners: a common fault with such who, not caring to correct constitutional failings, seek to gloss them over by some nominal virtue.   Richardson, *Clarissa Harlowe*, IV

The man who loves virtue for virtue's sake loves it wherever he finds it.
Richardson, *Sir Charles Grandison*, Two, IV

Were all men virtuous, the institutes of religion and laws would be unnecessary.
Shebbeare, *The Sumatrans*, I

The seeds of virtue are seldom destroyed at once.
Smollett, *Ferdinand, Count Fathom*, XXXIV

His virtues were always ready to operate when his passions did not obscure his reason.
Walpole, *The Castle of Otranto*, 26

The virtue of man is false as his faith. What folly invented, knavery supports. Let us arise in our strength, examine, judge, and be free.
Wright, *A Few Days in Athens*, XVI

VISITATION

A wisitation is the lot of mortality. Mortality itself is a wisitation. The world is chock full of wisitations.   Dickens, *Nicholas Nickleby*, LVI

VOLUPTUOUSNESS: *see also* BEAUTY

Voluptuousness is an epidemical madness, which infects most who approach it.
Donaldson, *Sir Bartholomew Sapskull*, II

A judicious and limited voluptuousness is necessary to the cultivation of the mind, to the polishing of the manners, to the refining of sentiment and the development of understanding.   Godwin, *St. Leon*, 31

VULGARITY

The vulgar are apish; they live on imitation, and are carried away by the example of the great ones, as the inferior orbs by the motion of the superior.
Anonymous, *The History of Tom Jones in His Married State*, 283

A pun or a ludicrous expression frequently has more weight with the vulgar than the most solid argument.   Graves, *The Spiritual Quixote*, I

WANDERLUST: *see also* TRAVEL

It is so natural for mankind to be nomadic, that a very little taste of that primitive mode of existence subverts the settled habits of many preceding years.
Hawthorne, *The Marble Faun*, XXXII

WAR AND PEACE: *see also* FIGHTING; VIOLENCE; etc.

War is an evil which all the good it procures cannot compensate.
Anonymous, *The Birmingham Counterfeit*, I

War is the daughter of ferocity and violence; cruelty and murder are her offspring.
Ibid.

By war our manners are depraved, genius extinguished, and brutality, ignorance and barbarism, established upon the ruins of social virtue, literature and science.   *Ibid.*

In ordinary conditions politics are barely mentioned when Washington, the most political city in the world, is in evening dress, but war is a microbe.
Atherton, *Senator North*, Book III, IV

I am for war, if only to give you a chance to find out who your friends are.   *Ibid.*

There is nothing in the history of human nature or of nations to disprove that our friends of today may be our enemies of tomorrow.   *Ibid.*

An officer may resign when an unjust war is declared; and ought to resign, and refuse to be accessary to the homicide which it occasions.
Brackenridge, *Modern Chivalry*, Part II, II

Like the rainbow, Peace rests upon the earth, but its arch is lost in heaven.
Bulwer, *Pompeii*, Book Three, I

War, the court of last resort.   Chesnutt, *The House Behind the Cedars*, XI

A certain readiness to perish is not so very rare, but it is seldom that you meet men whose souls, steeled in the impenetrable armor of resolution, are ready to fight a losing battle to the last.   Conrad, *Lord Jim*, VII

It was a great peace, as if the earth had been one grave.   *Ibid.*, XXXIV

Battles become weariness. Carnage bores at last; death becomes the normal condition of things, and ceases to interest.   Cooke, *Surry of Eagle's-Nest*, LXVI

What can't be done by main courage, in war, must be done by circumvention.
Cooper, *The Last of the Mohicans*, XXVI

The warrior whose eye is open can see his enemy.   *Ibid.*, XXVIII

We come to fight, and not to musickate. Until the general whoop is given, nothing speaks but the rifle.   *Ibid.*, XXXII

Prejudice or not, confidence is not a bad thing when a conflict is unavoidable.
Cooper, *Miles Wallingford*, XVI

If fighting is to be done it is always wise to enter on it on equal terms.
Cooper, *The Prairie*, XVII

It is amazing what war will do for commerce, as well as what it does against it!
Cooper, *Satanstoe*, Volume I, XI

War, the red animal—war, the blood-swollen god.
Crane, *The Red Badge of Courage*, III

The guns squatted in a row like savage chiefs. They argued with abrupt violence. It was a grim pow-wow. Their busy servants ran hither and thither.   *Ibid.*, V

The guns, standing, six good comrades, in a bold row.   *Ibid.*, VI

He had rid himself of the red sickness of battle.   *Ibid.*, XXIV

It is doubtful whether our soldiers would be maintained if there were not pacific people at home who like to fancy themselves soldiers. War, like other dramatic spectacles, might possibly cease for want of a "public."   Eliot, *The Mill on the Floss*, Book II, IV

War on paper and war on the field are as different as darkness from light, fire from water, or heaven from earth.   Falkner, *Little Brick Church*, XXII

Might not a battle be as well decided by the greater number of broken heads, bloody noses, and black eyes, as by the greater heaps of mangled and murdered human bodies?
Fielding, H., *Tom Jones*, 212

I have often thought I could better understand how a man of honor could reconcile himself to the accursed and murderous trade of war, than to the system of the gaming table.   Godwin, *St. Leon*, 29

The violence of war admits no distinctions; the lance that is lifted at guilt and power will sometimes fall on innocence and gentleness.   Johnson, *Rasselas*, 144

Success alone is honor in war. Johnstone, *The Reverie*, II

A rich man's war and a poor man's fight.
Kirkland, *The Captain of Company K*, XXVI

On the whole, the fighters, dead and alive, ought to be very thankful that things turned out so well. *Ibid.*, XXVII

That bloody spendthrift, War. Melville, *Confidence-Man*, VII

To be effectual, war should be carried on like a monsoon, one changeless determination of every particle towards the one unalterable aim. Melville, *Israel Potter*, X

Peace is War against all kings. Melville, *Mardi*, CLXIV

War is pain, and hate is woe. Melville, *Moby Dick*, CXIX

The fiend-like skill we display in the invention of all manner of death-dealing engines, the vindictiveness with which we carry on our wars, and the misery and desolation that follow in their train, are enough of themselves to distinguish the white civilized man as the most ferocious animal on the face of the earth. Melville, *Typee*, XVII

War, the purifier and the pestilence. Meredith, *Beauchamp's Career*, III

Nations at war are wild beasts. The passions of these hordes of men are not an example for a living soul. Our souls grow up to the light: we must keep eye on the light, and look no lower. Nations have no worse than a soiled mirror of themselves in mobs.
Meredith, *Harry Richmond*, XXXIII

War or battle as a thing very beastly, and yet to no kind of beasts in so much use as to man, they do detest and abhor in Utopia. And contrary to the custom almost of all other nations, they count nothing so much against glory as glory gotten in war.
More, *Utopia*, II

War is the most terrible of all disasters, except dishonor. Page, *Red Rock*, II

Short intervals of peace, if peace that could be called which was only the delay of evils.
Radcliffe, *The Mysteries of Udolpho*, II

Gunpowder has spoiled war. War was always detrimental to the solid interests of mankind; but in old times it was good for something; it painted well, sang divinely, furnished Iliads. Reade, *The Cloister and the Hearth*, XLVI

I leave war to them that live by it. Scott, *St. Ronan's Well*, XXXIV

How can our wealth be spent and blood be lavished in a cause more glorious than in that of the Almighty? Shebbeare, *The Sumatrans*, II

Alas for humanity, the glory and the glare of warfare, under false notions of renown, are too often sufficient not only to conceal the bloodshed and the horror, but to stimulate to undue vengeance, and to make resistance premature, and turn the desire of justice into a passion for revenge. Simms, *The Partisan*, Volume II, V

For the wrong done by one captain, all the captains conspire to do greater wrongs; and the blazing dwelling by midnight, the poor woman and her naked children escaping from the flames to perish of hunger; the gibbeted soldier on the nighest tree; and the wanton murder of the shrieking babe, quieted in its screams upon the bayonet of the yelling soldiers—these are the means by which, repairing one wrong, war does a thousand greater. *Ibid.*

The conquest of new countries, at whatever expense of blood and treasure, is scarcely criminal in the eyes of civilized and Christian men. *Ibid.*, Volume II, XVI

Peace is only a name for civil war. Life itself is civil war; and our enemies are more or less strong and numerous, according to circumstances. Simms, *Woodcraft*, XIX

A poor prince who is weak in cavalry, and whose whole infantry does not exceed a single man, had best quit the field. Sterne, *A Sentimental Journey*, 51

The military, a profession which makes bad men worse. *Ibid.*, 60

What is war but the getting together of quiet and harmless people, with the swords in their hands, to keep the ambitious and turbulent within bounds?
Sterne, *Tristram Shandy*, VI

No wars are so furious and bloody, or of so long continuance, as those occasioned by difference in opinion, especially if it be in things indifferent.
Swift, *Gulliver's Travels*, Houyhnhnms, V

War is not altogether an evil; and ordained of Heaven, as our illnesses and fevers doubtless are, for our good. It teaches obedience and contentment under privations; it fortifies courage; it tests loyalty; it gives occasion for showing mercifulness of heart; moderation in victory; endurance and cheerfulness under defeat. The brave who do battle victoriously in their country's cause leave a legacy of honor to their children.
Thackeray, *Denis Duval*, VIII

Wars about trifles are always bitter, especially among neighbors.
Trollope, *Barchester Towers*, XXI

A battle is only truly great or small according to its results.
Twain, *Joan of Arc*, Book II, XXXI

They held it no sin to take military advantage of the enemy—in a small way; in a small way, but not in a large one. Twain, *Pudd'nhead Wilson*, II

WEAKNESS: *see also* STRENGTH

Nothing more awful than to watch a man who has been found out, not in a crime but in a more than criminal weakness. Conrad, *Lord Jim*, V

The commonest sort of fortitude prevents us from becoming criminals in a legal sense; it is from weakness unknown, but perhaps suspected, as in some parts of the world you suspect a deadly snake in every bush—from weakness that may lie hidden, watched, or unwatched, prayed against or manfully scorned, repressed or maybe ignored more than half a lifetime, not one of us is safe. *Ibid.*

Like a man bound treacherously while he sleeps, he woke up fettered by the long chain of disregarded years. He had to take up at once the burden of all his existence, and found it almost too heavy for his strength. Conrad, *Nigger of the Narcissus*, IV

The sun shorn of its beams may be gazed on with impunity. Dacre, *Passions*, XLIII

Of all human weaknesses, the one to which our common nature is the least disposed to confess is the weakness of having gone to sleep in a coach.
Dickens, *David Copperfield*, V

Weakness and want are the parents of vice. Godwin, *St. Leon*, 163

This weakness of character suggested that he was the sort of man who was born to ache a good deal before the fall of the curtain upon his unnecessary life should signify that all was well with him again. Hardy, *Jude the Obscure*, Part I, II

Weakness is not itself a sin. Holmes, *Elsie Venner*, XVIII

Nothing teaches a strong arm its impotence so much as knocking at empty air.
Meredith, *Ordeal of Richard Feverel*, XLII

It is weakness too much to remember what should have been done. Sidney, *Arcadia*, I

Stronger in longing, and weaker in hoping. *Ibid.*, II

WEALTH: *see also* MONEY; POVERTY; etc.

Many a man that wears buttons has been hung.
Brackenridge, *Modern Chivalry*, Part II, I

Wealth has ever been capriciously distributed. The mere physical relation of birth is all that entitles us to manors and thrones.   Brown, C. B., *Arthur Mervyn*, I

For the rich, the whole world is a safe asylum.   Brown, C. B., *Ormond*, 30

There is a no less honest and truth-revealing intoxication in prosperity, than in wine. The varnish of power brings forth at once the defects and the beauties of the human portrait.   Bulwer, *Rienzi*, Book IV, III

Riches are but a charge, and if we don't use them well, we may envy the poor beggar that has so much less to answer for.   Burney, *Camilla*, Two, IV

The blameless use of riches is difficult, though all who want them think nothing so easy as their disposal.   Burney, *Cecilia*, II

The most ludicrous of all moneyed whims is a desire to make others suppose that you think yourself poor.   Caruthers, *Kentuckian in New-York*, Volume I, XVIII

If all were poor, all would be rich.   Collens, *Eden of Labor*, XI

If none were allowed to get richer than his brethren, all would be rich.   *Ibid.*

Rich men who leave money behind them are the farmers who raise the crop of human wickedness.   Collins, *The Dead Secret*, Book III, I

Every man may be rich if he will.   Collyer, *Felicia to Charlotte*, II

Wealth has its peculiar woes.   Cooper, *The Headsman*, V

The custom of mankind in calculating the wealth that other people ought to have saved.
                    Dickens, *Barnaby Rudge*, Chapter the Last

A large fortune is a troublesome thing. Nobody is satisfied with what you do with it; very often not yourself.   Disraeli, *Coningsby*, Book IX, II

Two nations; between whom there is no intercourse and no sympathy; who are as ignorant of each other's habits, thoughts, and feelings, as if they were dwellers in different zones, or inhabitants of different planets; who are formed by a different breeding, are fed by a different food, are ordered by different manners, and are not governed by the same laws: [the nations of] THE RICH AND THE POOR.
                    Disraeli, *Sybil*, Book II, V

I was told that an impassable gulf divided the Rich from the Poor; I was told that the Privileged and the People formed Two Nations.   *Ibid.*, Book IV, VIII

Some people talk of morality, and some of religion, but give me a little snug property.
                    Edgeworth, *The Absentee*, II

Can riches adorn the mind more than the body?   Fielding, H., *Joseph Andrews*, 214

Wealth is never so much enjoyed as by one who has known what it is to be poor.
                    Fielding, S., *David Simple*, II

We wealthy are the tired people; the load is never lifted from our backs.
                    Frederic, *The Market-Place*, XXVII

Wealth serves no other purpose than to deprave the soul, and adulterate the fountains of genuine delight.   Godwin, *St. Leon*, 101

No man despises wealth who fully understands the advantages it confers.
                    Ibid., 138

The ordinary wealth of the world is something real and substantial, and can neither be created nor dissipated with a breath.   *Ibid.*, 208

Prosperity and ease have often been found the parents of wishes and inclinations unfelt before.   *Ibid.*, 262

No man is rich.   James, H., *The American*, VII

Wealth is nothing but as it is bestowed.   Johnson, *Rasselas*, 133

WEALTH (*continued*)

One small fortune is more plague than ten old husbands.　　　Kidgell, *The Card*, II

Do not be as puffed up in prosperity as you are cast down in adversity.
Marishall, *Miss Clarinda Cathcart*, II

Poor people make a very poor business of it when they try to seem rich.
Melville, *Redburn*, III

Though no man in Utopia have anything, yet every man is rich.　　　More, *Utopia*, II

It is wonderful how the possession of wealth brings out the virtues of a man; or, at any rate, acts as a varnish or a lustre to them, and brings out their brilliancy and color in a manner never known when the individual stood in the cold grey atmosphere of poverty.
Thackeray, *Barry Lyndon*, XVII

The man of great wealth is rarely one from whom humanity derives good, never the one from whom it derives the greatest.　　　Tourgee, *Murvale Eastman*, XXI

I love riches, whether it is wicked or not.　　　Trollope, *Ayala's Angel*, X

Diamonds are very nice. Nothing is so nice.　　Trollope, *The Eustace Diamonds*, XLIII

Among the obligations of wealth is the obligation of display. People of small means do not allow for the expansion of mind that goes along with the accumulation of property.
Warner, *A Little Journey*, XX

Wall Street does not celebrate the holiday time with gaily dressed shop windows. You may search as you will about this great city, but you will hardly find a spot more dismal, more chilling, more to be shunned on jolly Christmas Eve.
Webster, *The Banker and the Bear*, III

Nothing will bear a stronger proof than the instability of riches.
Young, *The Adventures of Emmera*, II

WEAPONRY: *see also* VIOLENCE; WAR AND PEACE

I mortally hate firearms; for so many accidents happen by them.
Fielding, H., *Tom Jones*, 290

WELFARE: *see also* POVERTY; WEALTH; etc.

We often choose what is not consonant to the welfare of our nature, and strive to avoid those incidents which are fated in the order of incontrollable events for our good.
Amory, *John Buncle*, I

WHIMSICALNESS

Never depend upon a whimsical man.　　　Bulwer, *The Caxtons*, Book IV, I

WHISPERING: *see also* TALK

Whisperings in conversation are censurable, to a proverb: "Where there is whispering, there is lying."　　　Richardson, *Sir Charles Grandison*, Two, III

WICKEDNESS: *see also* GOOD AND EVIL; etc.

Am I so wicked as to conceive a wickedness others cannot imagine?
Dickens, *The Mystery of Edwin Drood*, XX

In the seesaw of life it takes more than one person to toss up the weight of the world's wickedness.　　　Dunbar, *The Uncalled*, IV

Taking advantage of another person's good opinion of us, to injure that other, is the most ungenerous wickedness that can be committed.　　　Richardson, *Clarissa Harlowe*, IV

The height of wickedness or of shame is not arrived at all at once. *Ibid.*

Even wicked men soon grow weary of wickedness with the same person, and love variety. Richardson, *Pamela*, 36

WILL

The best thing a man can have, is work with a purpose in it, and the will to do it heartily. Alcott, *Old-Fashioned Girl*, XIX

The will is the tool of the understanding, which must fashion its conclusions on the notices of sense. Brown, C. B., *Wieland*, 55

The power to serve is as seldom joined with the will, as the will is with the power. Dickens, *Nicholas Nickleby*, XX

The beauty or ugliness of a character lay not only in its achievements, but in its aims and impulses; its true history lay, not among things done, but among things willed. Hardy, *Tess*, XLIX

What I've dared, I've willed; and what I've willed, I'll do. Melville, *Moby Dick*, XXXVII

It may seem strange that of all men sailors should be tinkering at their last wills and testaments, but there are no people in the world more fond of that diversion. *Ibid.*, XLIX

They do not feel that everything they hope for in human life is dependent upon one human will—the will of a mortal weather-vane. Meredith, *Sandra Belloni*, XXXVI

Limbs so supple; will so stubborn! Richardson, *Clarissa Harlowe*, I

Wills are sacred things. *Ibid.*

How prompt a thing is will! *Ibid.*

What a torment it is to have a will without a power! *Ibid.*, II

Who that makes a will should be afraid of a coffin? *Ibid.*, IV

Poor in everything but will. Richardson, *Pamela*, 400

His will is the mountain stream, which may indeed be turned for a little space aside by the rock, but fails not to find its course to the ocean. Scott, *Ivanhoe*, XXXIX

There is this trouble about special providences—namely, there is so often a doubt as to which party was intended to be the beneficiary. In the case of the children, the bears, and the prophet, the bears got more real satisfaction out of the episode than the prophet did, because they got the children. Twain, *Pudd'nhead Wilson*, IV

WIND: *see also* NATURE

'Tis a noble and heroic thing, the wind! Who ever conquered it? In every fight it has the last and bitterest blow. Run tilting at it, and you but run through it. Melville, *Moby Dick*, CXXXV

WISDOM: *see also* FOLLY; GENIUS; KNOWLEDGE AND LEARNING; etc.

"Will you read the New Testament wisely?" "I will if I am wise." Allen, J. L., *The Choir Invisible*, XIII

An ounce of luck is better than a pound of wisdom. Anonymous, *The Egg*, 11

There is no wisdom so good as that which is bought. *Ibid.*, 35

The first step to wisdom is not to love; the second is so to love as not to discover it. Anonymous, *The History of Tom Jones in His Married State*, 213

One wise man is of more account than ten thousand fools. Atherton, *Senator North*, Book III, IX

The wisest and the best of men, nay, the wisest and best of their actions, may be rendered ridiculous by a person whose first object in life is a joke.

Austen, *Pride and Prejudice*, Volume I, XI

So long as craft can master force, so long as religion has a cave from which oracles can dupe mankind, the wise hold an empire over earth.   Bulwer, *Pompeii*, Book One, IV

Our wisdom is eternal, but our life is short: make the most of it while it lasts.

Ibid., Book One, VIII

There is no wisdom like that which says "enjoy."   *Ibid.*, Book IV, III

Wisdom, taken lightly or easily, seemed but another shape of poetry.

Bulwer, *Pausanias*, Book I, IV

The wisdom of experience is necessary to youth and thoughtlessness.

Burney, *Camilla*, Three, VI

Wisdom should wear the crown, since beauty is but its outward form.

Child, *Philothea*, III

Mrs. Pontellier was beginning to realize her position in the universe as a human being, and to recognize her relations as an individual to the world within and about her. This may seem like a ponderous weight of wisdom to descend upon the soul of a young woman of twenty-eight—perhaps more wisdom than the Holy Ghost is usually pleased to vouchsafe to any woman.   Chopin, *The Awakening*, VI

Truly wise men are truly good men.

Collins, *The Woman in White*, Part I, Second Epoch

All our wisdom is insufficient to protect us from frauds, one outwitting us by gyrations and flapjacks, and another by adding new joints to the *cauda*.

Cooper, *The Monikins*, Conclusion

Perfection is always found in maturity, whether it be in the animal or in the intellectual world. Reflection is the mother of wisdom, and wisdom the parent of success.

Cooper, *The Prairie*, XIV

The wisdom of Love, the highest wisdom ever known upon this earth.

Dickens, *The Mystery of Edwin Drood*, X

There is no wisdom like frankness.   Disraeli, *Sybil*, Book IV, IX

A man can never do anything at variance with his own nature. He carries within him the germ of his most exceptional action; and if we wise people make eminent fools of ourselves on any particular occasion, we must endure the legitimate conclusion that we carry a few grains of folly to our ounce of wisdom.   Eliot, *Adam Bede*, XVI

No man can be wise on an empty stomach.   *Ibid.*, XXI

While still outside of us, wisdom often looks terrible, and wears strange forms, wrapped in the changing conditions of a struggling world.

Eliot, *Felix Holt*, Address to Working Men

Wisdom lies more in affection and sincerity than people are apt to imagine.

Eliot, *Middlemarch*, Book V, LII

There is nothing more widely misleading than sagacity if it happens to get on a wrong scent; and sagacity, persuaded that men usually act and speak from distinct motives, with a consciously proposed end in view, is certain to waste its energies on imaginary game.   Eliot, *The Mill on the Floss*, Book I, III

To retrieve the ill consequences of a foolish conduct, and by struggling manfully with distress to subdue it, is one of the noblest efforts of wisdom and virtue.

Fielding, H., *Amelia*, I

Wisdom and beauty do not always go together.   *Ibid.*

It is the common failing of old men to attribute all wisdom to themselves.   *Ibid.*, II

No man is wise at all hours; it is therefore no wonder that a boy is not so.
Fielding, H., *Tom Jones*, 86

True wisdom consists not in the contempt of either riches or pleasures.   *Ibid.*, 226

The wise man gratifies every appetite and every passion, while the fool sacrifices all the rest to pall and satiate one.   *Ibid.*

Wisdom teaches us not to buy at too dear a price.   *Ibid.*

Wisdom makes but a slow defense against trouble though at last a sure one.
Goldsmith, *The Vicar of Wakefield*, 127

Wisdom is a defense, and money is a defense; but the excellency of knowledge is that wisdom giveth life to them that have it.   Hardy, *Jude the Obscure*, Part Two, II

The profoundest wisdom must be mingled with nine-tenths of nonsense, else it is not worth the breath that utters it.   Hawthorne, *The Blithedale Romance*, XV

No sagacious man will long retain his sagacity, if he live exclusively among reformers and progressive people, without periodically returning into the settled system of things, to correct himself by a new observation from that old standpoint.   *Ibid.*, XVI

There is a wisdom that looks grave, and sneers at merriment; and again a deeper wisdom, that stoops to be gay as often as occasion serves, and oftenest avails itself of shallow and trifling grounds of mirth; because, if we wait for more substantial ones, we seldom can be gay at all.   Hawthorne, *The Marble Faun*, XLVIII

Wise with the wisdom of the ages and the taste of a thousand fountains.
James, H., *Roderick Hudson*, V

He that never thinks never can be wise.   Johnson, *Rasselas*, 75

Has wisdom no strength to arm the heart against calamity? External things are naturally variable, but truth and reason are always the same.   *Ibid.*, 78–79

A wise man is never dejected at a disappointment, and often turns a misfortune to his advantage in the end.   Johnstone, *The Reverie*, I

True wisdom consists in doing that which is most agreeable to ourselves.   *Ibid.*, II

Let fools laugh and stay at home. Wise men dare and win.
Kingsley, C., *Westward Ho!*, XXI

Could we learn wisdom without experience, mankind would be too happy.
Lee, *The Recess*, I

Is not he accounted most wise, whom other men's harms do make most wary?
Lyly, *Euphues*, 96

Fortune guideth men in the rough sea, but wisdom ruleth them in a strange land.
Lyly, *Euphues and His England*, 226

To be rich is the gift of fortune, to be wise the grace of God.   *Ibid.*, 228

Wisdom is great wealth.   *Ibid.*, 229

Wisdom hath no mint, counsel is no coiner.   *Ibid.*, 231

The greatest clerks are not the wisest men, who dig still at the root while others gather the fruit.   *Ibid.*, 237

Common consistency implies unchangeableness; but much of the wisdom here below lives in a state of transition.   Melville, *Mardi*, CXLIII

The wisest make the most consummate fools.   *Ibid.*

In action, wisdom goes by majorities.   Meredith, *Ordeal of Richard Feverel*, IV

All wisdom is mournful. It is therefore that the wise love the Comic Muse. Their own high food would kill them.   *Ibid.*, IX

Expediency is man's wisdom; doing right is God's. *Ibid.*, XIII

There is for the mind but one grasp of happiness: from that uppermost pinnacle of wisdom, whence we see that this world is well designed. *Ibid.*

The hag, Wisdom. *Ibid.*, XXXI

When one has attained that felicitous point of wisdom from which one sees all mankind to be fools, the diminutive objects may make what new moves they please, one does not marvel at them: their sedateness is as comical as their frolic, and their frenzies more comical still. *Ibid.*, XXXVI

The world is wise in not seeking to be too wise. *Ibid.*, XXXVII

Wisdom was not invented yesterday. Moore, G., *Evelyn Innes*, XXXV

Wisdom can boast no higher attainment than happiness.
Radcliffe, *The Mysteries of Udolpho*, I

We may make the world allow for and respect us as we please, if we can but be sturdy in our wills, and set out accordingly. Richardson, *Clarissa Harlowe*, I

We were wise by other people's experience. *Ibid.*

Wit and wisdom are two different things, and are very rarely seen together.
Richardson, *Sir Charles Grandison*, One, I

Over-wisdom is as foolish a thing as moderate folly. *Ibid.*

Wisdom out of its place is a prude. *Ibid.*, One, II

Wisdom itself, and the truest wisdom, goodness, is sometimes thought to sit ungracefully, when it is uncharacteristic, not to the man, but to the times. *Ibid.*, Two, IV

There may be some wisdom in much folly. *Ibid.*

None are wise but they who determine to be wiser. *Ibid.*, Three, VII

There is nothing helps in this world but to be very wise, and to know everything—to be clever. Schreiner, *The Story of an African Farm*, Part I, II

We don't give babies credit for half wisdom enough. Schreiner, *Undine*, XIII

Wisdom is arrayed in panoply of proof. Scott, *Kenilworth*, XXXV

The mind grows wise by watching, but her sister the body, of coarser materials, needs the support of repose. Scott, *The Talisman*, XXII

No destiny nor influence can bring man's wit to a higher point than wisdom and goodness. Sidney, *Arcadia*, I

What doth better become wisdom than to discern what is worthy the loving?
Ibid., II

Be wise, and that wisdom shall be a God unto thee; be contented, and that is thy heaven.
Ibid., III

Wisdom itself requires to go through a certain probation of folly, in order to acquire the degree of knowledge which shall teach what folly is—what shape it takes, and how it will affect us. Simms, *Woodcraft*, XIX

It ain't reasonable to think that a man kin find new wisdom about everything; and them sort of people who talk so fine, and strange, and sensible, in a new way, about the business that has been practiced ever since the world begun, they're always overdoing the business, and working agin nater. They're quite too knowing to give themselves a chance. *Ibid.*, XXX

Some folks are wise, and some are otherwise. Smollett, *Roderick Random*, 43

Sciences may be learned by rote, but wisdom not. Sterne, *Tristram Shandy*, V

A sound creed and a bad morality, that's the root of wisdom.
Stevenson, *Prince Otto*, Book III, II

It takes years and maturity to make the discovery that the power of faith is nobler than the power of doubt; and that there is a celestial wisdom in the ingenuous propensity to trust, which belongs to honest and noble natures.　　　　Stowe, *Orr's Island*, XXIV

Wisdom is a fox, who after long hunting, will at last cost you the pains to dig out; 'tis a cheese, which by how much the richer, has the thicker, the homelier, and the coarser coat; 'tis a sack-posset, wherein the deeper you go, you will find it the sweeter.
Swift, *A Tale of a Tub*, I

Wisdom is a hen, whose cackling we must value and consider, because it is attended with an egg; but then, lastly, 'tis a nut, which unless you choose with judgment, may cost you a tooth, and pay you with nothing but a worm.　　　　　　　　　　*Ibid.*

No mortal is wise at all times.　　　　　　　　　　　Thackeray, *Catherine*, I

Dorian is far too wise not to do foolish things now and then.
Wilde, *The Picture of Dorian Gray*, VI

We are not wise in the contempt of others, but in calm approbation of ourselves.
Wright, *A Few Days in Athens*, XI

WISH: *see also* DESIRE

What is magnetism but a wish?　　　　　　Bulwer, *The Caxtons*, Book II, V

What is a wish, but the acknowledged want of power to oblige, and a demonstration of one's poverty in every thing but will?　　　　　　　Richardson, *Pamela*, 354

WIT: *see also* EXPRESSION; GENIUS; LOGIC; KNOWLEDGE AND LEARNING; WISDOM; etc.

Shortness of memory [about debts], the prerogative of all great wits.
Anonymous, *The Adventures of an Author*, I

Wit is not a staple commodity.　　　　　　　　　　　　　*Ibid.*, II

It is the custom to consider that wit lies in obscurity.　　Bulwer, *Pompeii*, Book One, VI

What a wicked sort of sprite is a female wit, breathing only in mischief, a very will-o'-the-wisp, personified and petticoated, shining but to lead astray, dangerous past all fathom.　　　　　　　　　　　　　　　　Burney, *Camilla*, Three, V

Never judge the heart of a wit by the tongue.　　　　　　*Ibid.*, Five, IX

Wits have a pleasure in their own rattle that cruelly runs away with their discretion.
Ibid.

Active wit, however despicable when compared with intellectual, is yet surely better than the insignificant click-clack of modish conversation or even the pensive dullness of affected silence.　　　　　　　　　　　　　　　　Burney, *Cecilia*, I

Learn wit by my folly.　　　　　　　　Defoe, *Captain Singleton*, 255

Wit is generally observed to love to reside in empty pockets.
Fielding, H., *Joseph Andrews*, 44

He could not bear the thought that anybody's wit and parts should have power enough to make the world forget they were villains.　　　　Fielding, S., *David Simple*, I

Borrowed wit becomes the mouth as ill as borrowed clothes the body.　　　*Ibid.*

The woman who is possessed of wit, unless she can be so peculiarly happy as to live with people void of envy, had better be without it.　　　　　　　　　　　*Ibid.*

Wit is not one of the royal prerogatives.

Lawrence, H., *The Contemplative Man*, II

Wit is the better if it be the dearer bought. Lyly, *Euphues*, 92

A fine wit, a sharp sense, a quick understanding, is able to attain to more in a moment or a very little space, then a dull and blockish head in a month. *Ibid.*, 103

He that lendeth to all that will borrow sheweth great good will, but little wit. Lend not a penny without a pawn, for that will be a good gauge to borrow.

Lyly, *Euphues and His England*, 229

What is gotten with wit will be kept with wariness and increased with wisdom.

Ibid., 230

It is wit that flourisheth when beauty fadeth; that waxeth young when age approacheth, and resembleth the ivy leaf, who although it be dead, continueth green. *Ibid.*, 281

That is not wit which needs explaining. Melville, *Redburn*, IX

Modern wit has the reek of stable straw. It slouches, it sprawls.

Meredith, *Harry Richmond*, LI

It is almost impossible that any woman should be excellently witty and not make the utmost penny of her beauty. Nashe, *The Unfortunate Traveller*, 83

True wit is of the mind. Reade, *The Cloister and the Hearth*, LIII

He is always satisfied with wit at second-hand; wit upon memory; other men's wit.

Richardson, *Clarissa Harlowe*, II

Wit is a quality much talked of, but very little understood. *Ibid.*

There is not so much wit in wickedness. *Ibid.*

The wit of rakes and libertines consists mostly in saying bold and shocking things with such courage as shall make the modest blush, the impudent laugh, and the ignorant stare. *Ibid.*

Wit, that wicked misleader. *Ibid.*, IV

Wit is a dangerous weapon; but that species of it which cannot shine without a foil is not a wit to be proud of. Richardson, *Sir Charles Grandison*, Two, III

Sterling wit requires not a foil to set it off. *Ibid.*

No one so dull as a wit, when he does not hit off the scent at once.

Scott, *The Fair Maid of Perth*, XXXI

One wit, like a knuckle of ham in soup, gives a zest and flavor to the dish; but more than one serves only to spoil the pottage. Smollett, *Humphry Clinker*, 123

An ounce of a man's own wit is worth a ton of other people's.

Sterne, *Tristram Shandy*, II

Every man's wit must come from every man's own soul—and no other body's. *Ibid.*

Great wits jump. *Ibid.*, III

Wit is the outward mental casing of the man and has no more to do with the inner mind of thoughts and feelings than have the rich brocaded garments of the priest at the altar with the asceticism of the anchorite below them, whose skin is tormented with sackcloth and whose body is half-flayed with rods. Trollope, *Barchester Towers*, XX

Sir Abraham was a man of wit, and sparkled among the brightest at the dinner-tables of political grandees: indeed, he always sparkled; whether in society, in the House of Commons, or the courts of law, coruscations flew from him; glittering sparkles, as from hot steel, but no heat; no cold heart was ever cheered by warmth from him, no unhappy soul ever dropped a portion of its burden at his door.   Trollope, *The Warden*, XVII

WITNESS: *see also* LAW

Spoken words leave no traces; they pass as breath, mingle with air, and may be explained with latitude. But the pen is a witness on record.
Richardson, *Clarissa Harlowe*, II

WONDER: *see also* AWE

There is nothing so interesting to the juvenile mind as the wonderful; there is no power that it so eagerly covets as that of astonishing spectators by its miraculous exertions.
Godwin, *Caleb Williams*, II

Women love wonder and the wonderful.   Richardson, *Sir Charles Grandison*, Two, IV

Wonders are no wonders in a wonderful subject.   Sidney, *Arcadia*, II

WORD(S): *see also* EXPRESSION; LITERATURE; MEANING; etc.

I like good strong words, that mean something.   Alcott, *Little Women*, IV

Nice is a very nice word; it does for everything.   Austen, *Northanger Abbey*, XIV

To *torment* and to *instruct* might sometimes be used as synonymous words.   *Ibid.*

Speech is not made from dictionaries; but dictionaries from speech.
Brackenridge, *Modern Chivalry*, Part II, II

Definition: phrase substituted in lieu of [the word defined].   *Ibid.*

They've a temper, some words—particularly verbs: they're the proudest—adjectives you can do anything with, but not verbs.   Carroll, *Through the Looking Glass*, VI

Our words are giants when they do us an injury, and dwarfs when they do us a service.
Collins, *The Woman in White*, Part I, First Epoch

Chicken-hearted: an absurd simile drawn from an ignorance of the formation of the biped. The heart of a chicken has a just proportion to its other organs, and the domestic fowl is, in a state of nature, a gallant bird.   Cooper, *The Prairie*, VI

"Isn't there something that speaks louder than words?" "Yes, but let us hear the words, too."   Cowan, *Daybreak*, I

As we are not particular about the meaning of our liveries on state occasions, if they but be fine and numerous enough, so, the meaning or necessity of our words is a secondary consideration, if there be but a great parade of them.
Dickens, *David Copperfield*, LII

As individuals get into trouble by making too great a show of liveries, a nation has got into many great difficulties from maintaining too large a retinue of words.   *Ibid.*

"Papa is a preferable mode of address," observed Mrs. General. "Father is rather vulgar. The word Papa, besides, gives a pretty form to the lips. Papa, potatoes, poultry, prunes, and prism are all very good words for the lips; especially prunes and prism. You will find it serviceable, in the formation of a demeanor, if you sometimes say to yourself in company—on entering a room, for instance—Papa, potatoes, poultry, prunes and prism, prunes and prism." "Pray, my child, attend to the—hum—precepts of Mrs. General."   Dickens, *Little Dorrit*, Book II, V

I go, consequentementally.   *Ibid.*, Book II, XXVIII

A soldier with white hair who lives retired secrettementally.   *Ibid.*

I wait, patientissamentally.   *Ibid.*

Though home is a name, a word, it is a strong one; stronger than magician ever spoke, or spirit answered to, in strongest conjuration.   Dickens, *Martin Chuzzlewit*, XXXV

"If he's a gentleman's son at all, he's a fondling, that's my opinion." Mrs. Squeers intended to say "foundling," but, as she frequently remarked when she made any such mistake, it would be all the same a hundred years hence.

Dickens, *Nicholas Nickleby*, IX

Words are but the vague shadows of the volumes we mean. Little audible links, they are, chaining together great inaudible feelings and purposes.   Dreiser, *Sister Carrie*, I

People in general attach too much importance to words. They are under the illusion that talking effects great results. As a matter of fact, words are, as a rule, the shallowest portion of all the argument. They but dimly represent the great surging feelings and desires which lie behind. When the distraction of the tongue is removed, the heart listens.   *Ibid.*, XII

Might, could, would—they are contemptible auxiliaries.

Eliot, *Middlemarch*, Book II, XIV

If we use common words on a great occasion, they are the more striking, because they are felt at once to have a particular meaning, like old banners, or everyday clothes, hung up in a sacred place.   Eliot, *The Mill on the Floss*, Book VI, II

Dialect words—those terrible marks of the beast to the truly genteel.

Hardy, *The Mayor of Casterbridge*, XX

Nothing is more unaccountable than the spell that often lurks in a spoken word.

Hawthorne, *The Marble Faun*, XXV

Never was a word fitter for a quack's mouth than "humanity." Two syllables more, and the parsons would be riding it to sawdust. Humanity! Humanitomtity! It's the best word of the two for half the things done in the name of it.

Meredith, *Beauchamp's Career*, IV

Words once spoken cannot be recalled: but they may be contradicted by other words.

Richardson, *Clarissa Harlowe*, IV

I hate *but*. I know no form of expression in which he can appear, that is amiable, excepting as a *butt* of sack. *But* is a more detestable combination of letters than *no* itself. *No* is a surly, honest fellow, speaks his mind rough and round at once. *But* is a sneaking, evasive, half-bred, exceptious sort of a conjunction, which comes to pull away the cup just when it is at your lips.   Scott, *The Antiquary*, XI

Pax vobiscum will answer all queries.   Scott, *Ivanhoe*, XXVI

I blushed at many a word the first month which I found inconsequent and perfectly innocent the second.   Sterne, *A Sentimental Journey*, 67

As for the Bastile the terror is in the word. The Bastile is but another word for a tower, and a tower is but another word for a house you can't get out of.   *Ibid.*, 75

Their style is clear, masculine, and smooth, but not florid; for they avoid nothing more than multiplying unnecessary words, or using various expressions.

Swift, *Gulliver's Travels*, Brobdingnag

"I say orgies, not because it's the common term, because it ain't—obsequies bein' the common term—but because orgies is the right term. Obsequies ain't used in English no more, now—it's gone out. We say orgies now, in England. Orgies is better, because it means the thing you're after, more exact. It's a word that's made up out'n the Greek *orgo*, outside, open, abroad; and the Hebrew *jeesum*, to plant, cover up; hence in*ter*. So, you see, funeral orgies is an open er public funeral."   Twain, *Huckleberry Finn*, XXV

As to the Adjective: when in doubt, strike it out.   Twain, *Pudd'nhead Wilson*, XI

Always is a dreadful word. Women are so fond of using it. They spoil every romance by trying to make it last forever. It is a meaningless word, too. The only difference between a caprice and a lifelong passion is that the caprice lasts a little longer.
Wilde, *The Picture of Dorian Gray*, II

"I didn't say I like the book. I said it fascinated me. There is a great difference." "Ah, you have discovered that?"
Ibid., X

As though words could alter things.
Ibid., XIV

I never quarrel with actions. My one quarrel is with words.
Ibid., XVII

To define is to limit.
Ibid.

WORK: *see also* PROFESSION

If a man can live without working, he will not work.
Brackenridge, *Modern Chivalry*, Part II, II

So seldom do they ever exert themselves, that when they do work they seem determined that so meritorious an action shall not escape the observation of those around.
Melville, *Typee*, XXII

The secret of good work: to plod on and still keep the passion fresh.
Meredith, *The Egoist*, XII

Intellectual "work" is misnamed; it is a pleasure, a dissipation, and is its own highest reward.
Twain, *Connecticut Yankee*, XXVIII

WORLD: *see also* NATURE; UNIVERSALITY; WORLDLINESS; etc.

The microcosm of a public school.
Disraeli, *Vivian Grey*, Book I, II

The world is such a wheel-carriage, that it might very properly be called the whirl'd.
Galt, *Annals*, XXVI

The world is a great mart, where all things are for sale to him who bids the highest in the currency of our desires.
Haggard, *She*, XVIII

The world, that gray-bearded and wrinkled profligate, decrepit, without being venerable.
Hawthorne, *The House of the Seven Gables*, XII

Coarsely does the world translate all finer griefs that meet its eye. It is more a coarse world than an unkind one.
Hawthorne, *The Marble Faun*, XXXVI

The world is ever tyrannical; it warps our sorrows to edge them with keener affliction.
Mackenzie, *The Man of Feeling*, 73

Worlds pass worlds in space, as men, men, in thoroughfares; and after periods of thousand years, cry, "Well met, my friend, again!"
Melville, *Mardi*, CLXXXIV

The universe is finished; the copestone is on, and the chips were carted off a million years ago.
Melville, *Moby Dick*, II

The pulpit is ever this earth's foremost part; all the rest comes in its rear; the pulpit leads the world.
Ibid., VIII

The whole world's a ball, as scholars have it; and so 'tis right to make one ballroom of it.
Ibid., XL

This world is a lie.
Melville, *Pierre*, Book XIV, II

This world is a moving world; its Riddough's Hotels are forever being pulled down; it never stands still; and its sands are forever shifting.
Melville, *Redburn*, XXXI

In itself, each ship is an island, a floating colony of the tribe to which it belongs.
Ibid., XXXIII

As a man-of-war that sails through the sea, so this earth that sails through the air. We mortals are all on board a fast-sailing, never-sinking, world-frigate, of which God was the shipwright; and she is but one craft in a Milky-Way fleet, of which God is the Lord High Admiral. The port we sail from is forever astern. And though far out of sight of land, for ages and ages we continue to sail with sealed orders, and our last destination remains a secret to ourselves and our officers; yet our final haven was predestinated ere we slipped from the stocks at Creation.   Melville, *White Jacket*, The End

The world does not stone men.   Meredith, *Beauchamp's Career*, XL

The world has faults; glaciers have crevasses, mountains have chasms; but is not the effect of the whole sublime?   Meredith, *The Egoist*, VII

We weaken ourselves if we do not love the real world.   *Ibid.*

"Is the world agreeable to holiness?" "Are you in favor of monasteries?"   *Ibid.*

The system of the world is barter varied by robbery.
          Meredith, *Harry Richmond*, XXII

The great truth, that this world is well designed.
          Meredith, *Ordeal of Richard Feverel*, XV

The world is a variable monster; it rends the weak whether sincere or false; but those who weld strength with sincerity may practice their rites of religion publicly, and it fawns to them, and bellows to imitate.   Meredith, *The Tragic Comedians*, VI

The world is a university.   Richardson, *Sir Charles Grandison*, One, I

The world is ashamed of being virtuous.   Sterne, *Tristram Shandy*, VIII

The world grows more worldly every day.   Trollope, *Barchester Towers*, XLVIII

We live in an age that reads too much to be wise, and that thinks too much to be beautiful.   Wilde, *The Picture of Dorian Gray*, VIII

It can only be the next world [that says I am extremely wicked]. This world and I are on excellent terms.   *Ibid.*, XV

The world goes to the altar of its own accord.   *Ibid.*, XVIII

WORLDLINESS: *see also* WORLD

Those who are not of this world can do little else to arrest the errors of the obstinately worldly.   Eliot, *Middlemarch*, Book IV, XXXVI

WORSHIP: *see also* GOD; RELIGION; etc.

Veneration is a half-witted, obsequious brother to superstition. The man who is afflicted with the venerating habit goes through life in a graveyard, poking around among the tombs, hunting for antique monuments erected to the memory of the dead.
          Adams, F. U., *President John Smith*, X

This is not my idea of a chapel. There is nothing awful here, nothing melancholy, nothing grand. Here are no aisles, no arches, no inscriptions, no banners. No banners to be "blown by the night wind of Heaven." No signs that a "Scottish monarch sleeps below."   Austen, *Mansfield Park*, Volume One, IX

Devout worshippers never allow inconveniences to prevent them from performing their religious rites.   Eliot, *Adam Bede*, XV

Men are strongly inclined to worship what they do not understand. A grand secret, upon which imposers on mankind have totally relied for the success of their frauds.
          Fielding, H., *Tom Jones*, 496

What is worship?—to do the will of God—*that* is worship. And what is the will of God?—to do to my fellowman what I would have my fellowman to do to me—*that* is the will of God.   Melville, *Moby Dick*, X

Worship is usually a matter of theory rather than of practice.
                                          Eliot, *Middlemarch*, Book V, XLIII

Our own hearts are our best prayer-rooms, and the chaplains who can most help us are ourselves.   Melville, *White Jacket*, XXXVIII

Women who have nothing to do, and who cannot be made to understand that they should have duties, cannot live without some kind of idolatry.
                                          Trollope, *Phineas Finn*, XLIV

One should never put one's worship into words.
                                          Wilde, *The Picture of Dorian Gray*, IX

WORTH; WORTHINESS: *see* VALUE

ZEAL

There is no zeal blinder than that which is inspired with the love of justice against offenders.   Fielding, H., *Tom Jones*, 104

Where your own laudable zeal is concerned, you have ever seemed more ready to fly from the rebuke than from the fault.   Richardson, *Clarissa Harlowe*, IV

THE BRITISH AND AMERICAN NOVEL
1470-1900

Adams, Francis (1862-1893).
A Child of the Age (1894).
Adams, Frederick Upham (1859-1921).
President John Smith (1897).
Adams, Henry (1838-1918).
Democracy (1880).
Esther (1884).
Ainsworth, William Harrison (1805-1882).
Boscobel (1872).
Cardinal Pole (1863).
The Constable De Bourbon (1866).
Constable of the Tower (1861).
Crichton (1837).
The Goldsmith's Wife (1874).
Guy Fawkes (1841).
Jack Sheppard (1839).
John Law (1864).
The Lord Mayor of London (1862).
The Manchester Rebels (1873).
Old Saint Paul's (1841).
Rookwood (1834).
Saint James's (1844).
The Star-Chamber (1854).
Talbot Harland (1870).
The Tower of London (1840).
Windsor Castle (1843).
Alcott, Louisa May (1832-1888).
Little Men (1871).
Little Women (1868-1869).
Old-Fashioned Girl (1884).
Aldrich, Thomas Bailey (1836-1907).
Prudence Palfrey (1873).
The Queen of Sheba (1897).
The Stillwater Tragedy (1880).
The Story of a Bad Boy (1870).
Allen, Grant (1848-1899).
An African Millionaire (1897).
The British Barbarians (1895).
Allen, James Lane (1849-1925).
The Choir Invisible (1897).
A Kentucky Cardinal (1895).
Amory, Thomas (1691?-1788).
The Life of John Buncle (1756).
Annesley, James (1715-1760).
Memoirs of an Unfortunate Young Nobleman (1743).
Anonymous, *The Adventures of an Author* (1767).
——, *The Adventures of a Corkscrew* (1775).
——, *The Adventures of Jack Wander* (1766).
——, *The Adventures of a Jesuit* (1771).

——, *Adventures of a Kidnapped Orphan* (1747).
——, *The Adventures of Oxymel Classic, Esquire* (1768).
——, *The Adventures of Sylvia Hughes* (1761).
——, *The Birmingham Counterfeit* (1772).
——, *Continuation of Yorick's Sentimental Journey* (1788).
——, *A Court Intrigue* (1741).
——, *The Egg* (1772?).
——, *Fatal Friendship* (1770).
——, *Father Oswald* (1841).
——, *The Fruitless Repentance* (1769).
——, *Genuine Memoirs of the Celebrated Miss Maria Brown* (1766).
——, *The History of Betty Barnes* (1753).
——, *The History of the Human Heart* (1749).
——, *The History of Tom Jones in His Married State* (1750).
——, *The Ladies Advocate* (1749).
——, *The Lady's Drawing Room* (1744).
——, *The Letters of Maria* (1790).
——, *The Life of Jemmy Twitcher* (1770).
——, *The Life and Memoirs of Ephraim Tristram Bates* (1756).
——, *The Life and Opinions of Bertram Montfichet* (1761).
——, *The Life and Opinions of Miss Sukey Shandy* (1760).
——, *The Life of Sir Richard Perrott* (1770).
——, *The Life, Travels and Adventures of Christopher Wagstaff* (1762).
——, *Memoirs of a Coquet* (1765).
——, *Memoirs of the Court of H——* (1754).
——, *Memoirs of the Life of Tsonnonthouan* (1763).
——, *Memoirs of an Oxford Scholar* (1756).
——, *The Modern Fine Gentleman* (1774).
——, *A New Journey to the World in the Moon* (1741).
——, *The Peregrinations of Jeremiah Grant, Esquire* (1763).
——, *Philamour and Philamena* (1746).
——, *Private Letters from an American in England* (1769).
——, *Sophronia* (1761).
——, *A Supplement to the Life and Opinions of Tristram Shandy* (1760).
——, *The Temple-beau* (1754).
——, *The Theatre of Love* (1759).

Anonymous (*continued*)
———, *Travels into Several Remote Nations of the World* (1727).
———, *Unfortunate Sensibility* (1784).
———, *The Wanderer* (1766).
———, *Yorick's Meditations* (1760).
———, *Yorick Turned Trimmer* (1770).
Anstey, F. (1856-1934).
Jabberjee (1897).
Tourmalin's Time Cheques (1900).
Vice Versa (1882).
Arbuthnot, Archibald.
Memoirs of Miss Jenny Cameron (1746).
Arkwright, Richard.
The Queen Anne's Gate Mystery (1889).
Arthur, Timothy Shay (1809-1885).
Ten Nights in a Bar-Room (1854).
Atherton, Gertrude (1857-1948).
The Californians (1898).
The Doomswoman (1892).
Los Cerritos (1890).
Senator North (1900).
August, Karl Friedrich (1768-1847).
Horrid Mysteries (1797).
Austen, Jane (1775-1817).
Emma (1815).
Mansfield Park (1814).
Northanger Abbey (1818).
Persuasion (1818).
Pride and Prejudice (1813).
Sense and Sensibility (1811).
The Watsons (1871).
Bacon, Francis (1561-1626).
New Atlantis (1627).
Barr, Amelia Edith (1831-1919).
The Maid of Maiden Lane (1900).
The Squire of Sandal-Side (1886).
Barrie, Sir James (1860-1937).
The Little Minister (1891).
Sentimental Tommy (1896).
Tommy and Grizel (1900).
Barry, William Francis (1849-1930).
The New Antigone (1887).
The Two Standards (1898).
Bates, Arlo (1850-1918).
The Puritans (1898).
Beard, Oliver Thomas.
Bristling With Thorns (1884).
Beardsley, Aubrey (1872-1898).
Under the Hill (1896).
Beckford, William (1759-1844).
Azemia (1797).
The Elegant Enthusiast (1796).
Vathek (1786).
Beecher, Henry Ward (1813-1887).
Norwood (1868).
Bellamy, Edward (1850-1898).
Dr. Heidenhoff's Process (1890).
The Duke of Stockbridge (1900).

Equality (1897).
Looking Backward (1888).
Miss Ludington's Sister (1885).
Bennett, Emerson.
The Prairie Flower (1849).
Besant, Walter (1836-1901).
All Sorts and Conditions of Men (1882).
In Deacon's Orders (1895).
Bird, Robert Montgomery (1806-1854).
Nick of the Woods (1837).
Blackmore, R. D. (1825-1900).
Dariel (1898).
Lorna Doone (1869).
Borrow, George (1803-1881).
Lavengro (1851).
The Romany Rye (1857).
Boswell, James (1740-1795).
Dorando (1767).
Boyesen, Hjalmar Hjorth (1848-1895).
Falconberg (1889).
Social Strugglers (1893).
Brackenridge, Hugh Henry (1748-1816).
Modern Chivalry (1792-1815).
Braddon, Mary Elizabeth (1837-1915).
Lady Audley's Secret (1862).
Bridges, Thomas (*fl.* 1759-1775).
The Adventures of a Bank-Note (1770-1771).
Bronte, Anne (1820-1849).
Agnes Grey (1847).
The Tenant of Wildfell Hall (1848).
Bronte, Charlotte (1816-1855).
Jane Eyre (1847).
The Professor (1859).
Shirley (1849).
Villette (1853).
Bronte, Emily (1818-1848).
Wuthering Heights (1847).
Brooke, Frances Moore (1724-1789).
The History of Emily Montague (1769).
Brown, Charles Brockden (1771-1810).
Alcuin (1798).
Arthur Mervyn (1799-1800).
Edgar Huntley (1799).
Ormond (1799).
Wieland (1798).
Brown, William Hill (1765-1793).
The Power of Sympathy (1789).
Brunt, Samuel.
A Voyage to Cacklogallinia (1727).
Bulwer-Lytton, Edward George Earle (1803-1873).
Alice (1838).
The Caxtons (1849).
The Coming Race (1871).
Devereux (1829).
The Disowned (1852).
Ernest Maltravers (1837).
Eugene Aram (1832).

Falkland (1827).
Godolphin (1833).
Harold, the Last of the Saxon Kings (1848).
Kenelm Chillingly (1873).
The Last Days of Pompeii (1834).
The Last of the Barons (1843).
Leila (n.d.).
Lucretia (1846).
My Novel (1853).
Night and Morning (1841).
The Parisians (1872).
Paul Clifford (1830).
Pausanias (1859).
Pelham (1828).
The Pilgrims of the Rhine (1840).
Rienzi (1835).
A Strange Story (1862).
What Will He Do With It? (1859).
Zanoni (1842).
Zicci (n.d.).
Bunyan, John (1628-1688).
The Life and Death of Mr. Badman (1680).
Pilgrim's Progress (1678; 1684).
Burnett, Frances Hodgson (1849-1924).
Little Lord Fauntleroy (1886).
Through One Administration (1881).
Burney, Fanny (1752-1840).
Camilla (1796).
Cecilia (1782).
Evelina (1778).
Burton, John
Ascanius (1746).
Butler, Samuel (1835-1902).
Erewhon (1872).
The Way of All Flesh (1873-1883;
published 1903).
Cable, George Washington (1844-1925).
Bonaventure (1887).
Dr. Sevier (1884).
The Grandissimes (1880).
Madame Delphine (1881).
Caine, Hall (1853-1931).
The Bondman (1898).
The Christian (1897).
The Deemster (1887).
The Manxman (1894).
Carroll, Lewis: *see* Charles Dodgson.
Carteret, John Dunloe.
A Fortune Hunter (1886).
Caruthers, William Alexander (1802-1846).
The Cavaliers of Virginia (1834).
The Kentuckian in New-York (1834).
Caryl, Charles W.
New Era (1897).
Charles, Elizabeth Rundle (1828-1896).
Chronicles of the Schönberg-Cotta Family
(1864).
Chavannes, Albert.
The Future Commonwealth (1892).

Chesnutt, Charles Waddell (1858-1932).
The House Behind the Cedars (1900).
Child, Lydia Maria (1802-1880).
Philothea (1836).
Child, William Stanley.
The Legal Revolution of 1902 (1898).
Cholmondeley, Mary (1859-1925).
Red Pottage (1899).
Chopin, Kate (1851-1904).
The Awakening (1899).
Churchill, Winston (1871-1947).
Richard Carvel (1899).
Cleland, John (1709-1789).
Memoirs of a Coxcomb (1751).
*Memoirs of a Woman of Pleasure [Fanny
Hill]* (1749).
Collens, T. Wharton.
Eden of Labor (1876).
Collins, Wilkie (1824-1889).
Antonina (1850).
Armadale (1866).
Basil (1852).
The Black Robe (1881).
Blind Love (1890).
The Dead Secret (1857).
The Evil Genius (1886).
The Fallen Leaves (1879).
The Frozen Deep (n.d.).
The Haunted Hotel (1879).
Heart and Science (1883).
Hide-and-Seek (1854).
I Say No (1884).
Jezebel's Daughter (1880).
The Law and the Lady (1875).
The Legacy of Cain (1889).
Man and Wife (1870).
The Moonstone (1868).
My Lady's Money (1879).
The New Magdalen (1873).
No Name (1862).
Poor Miss Finch (1872).
The Queen of Hearts (1859).
A Rogue's Life (1879).
The Two Destinies (1876).
The Woman in White (1860).
Collyer, Mary (d. 1763).
Felicia to Charlotte (1744).
Conrad, Joseph (1857-1924).
Almayer's Folly (1895).
Lord Jim (1900).
The Nigger of the Narcissus (1897).
An Outcast of the Islands (1896).
Cooke, John Esten (1830-1886).
Mohun (1869).
Surry of Eagle's-Nest (1866).
The Virginia Comedians (1854).
Cooper, James Fenimore (1789-1851).
Afloat and Ashore (1844).
The Bravo (1831).

Cooper, James Fenimore (1789-1851)
(*continued*)
The Chainbearers (1845).
The Deerslayer (1841).
The Headsman (1833).
The Heidenmauer (1832).
Home as Found (1838).
Homeward Bound (1838).
Jack Tier (1848).
The Last of the Mohicans (1826).
Mercedes of Castile (1840).
Miles Wallingford (1844).
The Monikins (1835).
Ned Myers (1843).
Oak Openings (1848).
The Pathfinder (1840).
The Pilot (1823).
The Pioneers (1823).
The Prairie (1827).
Precaution (1820).
Red Rover (1828).
Redskins (1846).
Satanstoe (1845).
The Sea Lions (1849).
The Spy (1821).
Two Admirals (1842).
Water-Witch (1830).
The Ways of the Hour (1850).
Wing-and-Wing (n.d.).
Wish-ton-Wish (1829).
Corelli, Marie (1864-1924), *pseudonym* of
Mary MacKay.
A Romance of Two Worlds (1896).
The Sorrows of Satan (1895).
Vendetta (1886).
Wormwood (1890).
Coventry, Francis (d. 1759).
The History of Pompey the Little (1751).
Cowan, James.
Daybreak (1896).
Craddock, Charles Egbert: *see* Mary
Noailles Murfree.
Craig, Alexander.
Ionia (1898).
Craigie, Pearl (1867-1906).
The School for Saints (1897).
Craik, Dinah (1826-1887).
John Halifax (1897).
Olive (1850).
Crane, Stephen (1871-1900).
Active Service (1897).
The O'Ruddy (1900).
The Red Badge of Courage (1895).
Crawford, Frances Marion (1854-1909).
Casa Braccio (1895).
The Cigarette-Maker's Romance (1890).
Corleone (1896).
Don Orsino (1892).
Greifenstein (1889).
Khaled (1891).

Marzio's Crucifix (1889).
Mr. Isaacs (1899).
A Roman Singer (1898).
A Rose of Yesterday (1897).
Sant' Ilario (1889).
Saracinesca (1887).
Zoroaster (1885).
Crockett, S. R.
The Lilac Sunbonnet (1898).
Cummins, Maria S. (1827-1866).
The Lamplighter (1854).
Dacre, Charlotte (b. 1782).
The Libertine (1807).
The Passions (1811).
Zofloya (1806).
Dana, Richard Henry (1815-1882).
Two Years Before the Mast (1840).
Daniel, Charles S.
Ai: A Social Vision (1892).
Davies, Charles Maurice (1828-1910).
Broad Church (1875).
Philip Paternoster (1858).
'Verts; or, The Three Creeds (1876).
Davis, Mrs. Rebecca Harding (1831-1910).
Waiting for the Verdict (1868).
Davis, Richard Harding (1864-1916).
The King's Jackal (1898).
Day, Thomas (1748-1789).
The History of Sandford and Merton
(1789).
Defoe, Daniel (1661-1731).
Captain Singleton.
Colonel Jack.
Moll Flanders (1722).
Robinson Crusoe (1719).
Roxana (1724).
De Forest, John W. (1826-1906).
*Miss Ravenel's Conversion from Secession
to Loyalty* (1867).
Deland, Margaret (1857-1945).
John Ward, Preacher (1888).
Deloney, Thomas (1543-1600).
The Gentle Craft (1648).
Jack of Newbury (1597).
Thomas of Reading (1623).
Dering, Edward Heneage (1827-1892).
Sherborne (1875).
Dickens, Charles (1812-1870).
Barnaby Rudge (1841).
Bleak House (1852-1853).
The Cricket on the Hearth (1845).
David Copperfield (1849-1850).
Dombey and Son (1846-1848).
Edwin Drood (1870).
Great Expectations (1860-1861).
Hard Times (1854).
Little Dorrit (1855-1857).
Martin Chuzzlewit (1843-1844).
Nicholas Nickleby (1838-1839).
The Old Curiosity Shop (1840-1841).

Oliver Twist (1837-1838).
Our Mutual Friend (1864-1865).
Pickwick Papers (1836-1837).
A Tale of Two Cities (1859).
Disraeli, Benjamin (1804-1881).
Alroy (1833).
Coningsby (1844).
Contarini Fleming (1832).
Endymion (1880).
Henrietta Temple (1837).
Lothair (1870).
Sybil (1845).
Tancred (1847).
Venetia (1837).
Vivian Grey (1826-1827).
The Young Duke (1831).
Dodgson, Charles [*pseudonym*, Lewis
     Carroll] (1832-1898).
Alice's Adventure in Wonderland (1865).
Through the Looking Glass (1872).
Donaldson, William.
*The Life and Adventures of Sir Bartholo-
     mew Sapskull* (1768).
Donnelly, Ignatius (1831-1901).
The Golden Bottle (1892).
Douglas, Lady Gertrude.
Linked Lives (1876).
Doyle, Sir Arthur Conan (1859-1930).
Micah Clarke (1888).
A Study in Scarlet (1888).
Dreiser, Theodore (1871-1945).
Sister Carrie (1900).
DuBois, Edward (1774-1850).
St. Godwin (1800).
Duff, William (1732-1815).
The History of Rhedi (1773).
Du Maurier, George Louis Palmella Busson
     (1834-1896).
The Martian (1897).
Peter Ibbotson (1892).
Trilby (1894).
Dunbar, Paul Laurence (1872-1906).
The Uncalled (1898).
Eastman, Mrs. Mary H. (1818-1890).
Aunt Phillis's Cabin (1852).
Edgar, A. H.
John Bull and the Papists (1846).
Edgeworth, Maria (1767-1849).
The Absentee (1812).
Belinda (1833).
Castle Rackrent (1800).
Harrington (1833).
Leonora (1833).
Patronage (1833).
Vivian (1832).
Edson, Milan.
Solaris Farm (1900).
Edwards, M. Betham.
The Lord of the Harvest (1899).
Eggleston, Edward (1837-1902).

The Circuit Rider (1878).
The Faith Doctor (1891).
The Graysons (1887).
The Hoosier Schoolmaster (1871).
Roxy (1878).
Eliot, George [Marian Evans] (1819-1880).
Adam Bede (1859).
Daniel Deronda (1876).
Felix Holt the Radical (1866).
Middlemarch (1872).
The Mill on the Floss (1860).
Romola (1863).
Silas Marner (1861).
Falkner, William C. (1826-1889).
The Little Brick Church (1882).
The White Rose of Memphis (1881).
Farrar, Frederic W.
Eric (1858).
Ferriar, John (1764-1815).
Illustrations of Sterne (1798).
Fielding, Henry (1707-1754).
Amelia (1751).
Jonathan Wild (1743).
Joseph Andrews (1742).
Shamela (1741).
Tom Jones (1749).
Fielding, Sarah (1710-1768).
The Adventures of David Simple (1744).
The History of the Countess of Dellwyn
     (1759).
The History of Ophelia (1760).
The Lives of Cleopatra and Octavia (1757).
Foote, Mary Hallock (1847-1938).
The Led-Horse Claim (1882).
Ford, Emanuel (fl. 1607).
*The Most Pleasant History of Ornatus and
     Artesia* (1598).
Ford, Paul Leicester (1865-1902).
The Great K. & A. Train-Robbery (1897).
The Honorable Peter Stirling (1894).
Janice Meredith (1899).
Foster, Hannah (1759-1840).
The Coquette (1802).
Frederic, Harold (1856-1898).
The Damnation of Theron Ware (1896).
Gloria Mundi (1898).
The Market Place (1899).
The Return of the O'Mahony (1899).
Seth's Brother's Wife (1886).
Freeman, Mary E. Wilkins (1852-1930).
Pembroke (1894).
Froude, James Anthony (1818-1894).
The Nemesis of Faith (1849).
The Spirit's Trials (1847).
Fuller, Alvarado M. (1851-1924).
A.D. 2000 (1890).
Fuller, Henry Blake (1857-1929).
The Cliff-Dwellers (1893).
Fullerton, Georgiana Lady (1812-1885).
Ellen Middleton (1844).

Fullerton, Georgiana Lady (1812-1885)
(*continued*)
Grantley Manor (1847).
Mrs. Gerald's Niece (1869).
Galt, John (1779-1839).
Annals of the Parish (1821).
Ayrshire Legatees (1821).
The Last of the Lairds (1826).
Garland, Hamlin (1860-1940).
A Member of the Third House (1892).
Rose of Dutcher's Cooly (1895).
Gascoigne, George (1539-1577).
Master F. J. (1576).
Gaskell, Elizabeth Cleghorn (1810-1865).
Cousin Phillis (1865).
Cranford (1853).
Mary Barton (1848).
My Lady Ludlow (1858).
North and South (1855).
Ruth (1853).
Sylvia's Lovers (1863).
Wives and Daughters (1866).
Geissler, Ludwig A.
Looking Beyond (1891).
Gentleman, Francis (1728-1784).
A Trip to the Moon (1764-1765).
Gibbes, Phoebe.
*The Life and Adventures of Mr. Frances
Clive* (1764).
Gilman, Samuel C.
The Story of a Western Claim (1893).
Gissing, George (1857-1903).
The Emancipated (1890).
A Life's Morning (1888).
The Nether World (1889).
New Grub Street (1891).
Thyrza (1887).
The Town Traveller (1898).
The Whirlpool (1897).
Workers in the Dawn (1880).
Glasgow, Ellen (1874-1945).
The Descendant (1897).
The Voice of the People (1900).
Godwin, Francis (1562-1633).
The Man in the Moon (1638).
Godwin, William (1756-1836).
Caleb Williams (1794).
St. Leon (1799).
Goldsmith, Oliver (1728-1774).
The Vicar of Wakefield (1766).
Gould, Frederick James (1855-1938).
The Agnostic Island (1891).
Grant, Robert (1852-1940).
Unleavened Bread (1900).
Graves, Richard (1715-1804).
The Spiritual Quixote (1773).
Greeley, William (1801-1876).
Portrait of an English Churchman (1838).
Green, William Child.
The Abbot of Montserrat (1826).

Greer, Tom.
A Modern Daedalus (1887).
Greg, Percy (1836-1889).
Across the Zodiac (1880).
Gresley, W.
Charles Lever (1841).
Church-Clavering (1843).
Griffin, Gerald.
The Duke of Monmouth (1842).
Griffith, George Chetwynd.
The Angel of the Revolution (1894).
Olga Romanoff (1894).
Grousset (1844-1909).
The Conquest of the Moon (1894).
Guthrie, Thomas Anstey: *see* F. Anstey.
Guyton, Emma (1825-1887).
Husbands and Wives (1874).
Married Life (1863).
The Wife's Trials (1858).
Haggard, H. Rider (1856-1925).
Cleopatra (1889).
Eric Brighteyes (1891).
King Solomon's Mines (1885).
Mr. Meeson's Will (1888).
The People of the Mist (1894).
She (1887).
Hale, Edward Everett (1822-1909).
How They Lived in Hampton (1888).
In His Name (1900).
Hale, Mrs. Sarah J. (1788-1879).
Liberia (1853).
Hamilton, Elizabeth (1758-1816).
The Cottagers of Glenburnie (1808).
Memoirs of Modern Philosophers (1800).
Hardy, Thomas (1840-1928).
Desperate Remedies (1871).
Far From the Madding Crowd (1874).
The Hand of Ethelberta (1876).
An Indiscretion in the Life of an Heiress
(1868).
Jude the Obscure (1896).
A Laodicean (1881).
The Mayor of Casterbridge (1886).
A Pair of Blue Eyes (1873).
The Return of the Native (1878).
The Romantic Adventures of a Milkmaid
(1883).
Tess of the D'Urbervilles (1891).
The Trumpet-Major (1880).
Two on a Tower (1882).
Under the Greenwood Tree (1872).
The Well-Beloved (1897).
The Woodlanders (1887).
Harland, Henry (1861-1905).
The Cardinal's Snuff Box (1900).
Mea Culpa (1891).
Harley, Mrs. M.
Priory of St. Bernard (1786).
Harraden, Beatrice (1864-1936).
Ships That Pass in the Night (1889).

Harris, Elizabeth (1822-1852).
From Oxford to Rome (1847).
Rest in the Church (1848).
Harrison, Constance Cary (1843-1920).
The Anglomaniacs (1890).
Sweet Bells Out of Tune (1893).
Harte, Bret (1839-1902).
Clarence (1895).
Cressy (1889).
A First Family of Tasajara (1891).
Gabriel Conroy (1876).
In a Hollow of the Hills (1895).
Susy (1892).
The Three Partners (1897).
A Ward of the Golden Gate (1890).
Hawthorne, Nathaniel (1804-1864).
The Blithedale Romance (1852).
Fanshawe (1828).
The House of the Seven Gables (1851).
The Marble Faun (1860).
The Scarlet Letter (1850).
Hay, John (1838-1905).
The Bread-Winners (1883).
Helme, Elizabeth (d. 1816).
St. Margaret's Cave [The Nun's Story]
(1801).
Hewlett, Maurice (1861-1923).
The Death of Richard Yea-and-Nay (1900).
The Forest Lovers (1898).
Hildreth, Richard (1807-1865).
The Slave (1836).
Hill, John (1716?-1775).
The Adventures of Mr. George Edwards
(1751).
Hogg, James (1770-1835).
The Confessions of a Justified Sinner
(1824).
Holcroft, Thomas (1745-1816).
The Adventures of Hugh Trevor (1794).
Holland, Josiah Gilbert (1819-1881).
Arthur Bonnicastle (1873).
Sevenoaks (1875).
Holley, Marietta (1836-1926).
Samantha on the Race Problem (1892).
Holmes, Oliver Wendell (1809-1894).
Elsie Venner (1861).
The Guardian Angel (1867).
A Mortal Antipathy (1892).
Hooper, Johnson Jones (1815?-1863).
Some Adventures of Captain Simon Suggs
(1848).
Hope, Anthony (1863-1933).
The Prisoner of Zenda (1894).
Howe, E. W. (1853-1937).
The Story of a Country Town (1883).
Howells, William Dean (1837-1920).
The Lady of the Aroostook (1879).
Letters of an Altrurian Traveller (1896).
A Modern Instance (1882).
The Rise of Silas Lapham (1885).

A Traveller from Altruria (1894).
The Undiscovered Country (1880).
Howitt, William (1792-1879).
Woodburn Grange (1867).
Howland, Marie.
Papa's Own Girl [The Familistere] (1874).
Hudson, William Henry (1841-1922).
A Crystal Age (1887).
The Purple Land (1885).
Hughes, Thomas (1822-1896).
Tom Brown at Oxford (1891).
Tom Brown's Schooldays (1857).
Hume, Fergus (1859-1932).
The Mystery of a Hansom Cab (n. d.).
Humphreys, Mrs. Eliza.
Sheba (1889).
Ingelow, Jean (1820-1897).
Allerton and Dreux (1851).
Ireland, William Henry (1777-1835).
The Abbess (1799).
Jackson, Helen Hunt (1831-1885).
Ramona (1884).
James, G. P. R.
Richelieu (1895).
James, Henry (1843-1916).
The American (1877).
The Awkward Age (1899).
The Bostonians (1886).
Confidence (1880).
The Europeans (1878).
The Portrait of a Lady (1881).
The Princess Casamassima (1886).
Roderick Hudson (1876).
The Spoils of Poynton (1897).
The Tragic Muse (1890).
Washington Square (1890).
What Maisie Knew (1892).
Jefferies, Richard (1848-1887).
After London (1885).
Jenner, Charles (1736-1774).
The Placid Man (1770).
Jerome, Jerome K. (1859-1927).
Three Men in a Boat (1889).
Three Men on Wheels (1900).
Jewett, Sarah Orne (1849-1909).
Betty Leicester (1900).
The Country of the Pointed Firs (1896).
Deephaven (1877).
Jewsbury, Geraldine (1812-1880).
Zoe (1845).
Johnson, Samuel (1709-1784).
Rasselas (1759).
Johnston, Mary (1870-1936).
Prisoners of Hope (1898).
To Have and to Hold (1899).
Johnstone, Charles (1719-1800).
The History of Arsaces (1774).
The Pilgrim (1775).
The Reverie (1763).
Judd, Sylvester (1813-1853).

Judd, Sylvester (1813-1853) (*continued*)
Margaret (1845, 1851).
Kahlert, Karl Friedrich (1765-1813).
The Necromancer (1794).
Keate, George (1729-1797).
Journey to Margate (1779).
Keenan, Henry Francis.
The Money-Makers (1884).
Kelly, Hugh (1739-1777).
Memoirs of a Magdalen (1767).
Kelly, Isabella (c. 1770-c. 1820).
The Abbey of St. Asaph (1795).
Kennedy, Grace (1782-1825).
Father Clement (1842).
Kennedy, John Pendleton (1795-1870).
Horse-Shoe Robinson (1835).
Kidgell, John (fl. 1766).
The Card (1755).
Kimber, Edward (1719-1769).
The Juvenile Adventures of David Ranger (1757).
The Life and Adventures of Joe Thompson (1750).
Maria (1765).
King, Charles (1844-1933).
Sunset Pass (1890).
King, Edward (1848-1896).
Joseph Zalmonah (1893).
Kingsley, Charles (1819-1875).
Alton Locke (1850).
Hereward the Wake (1866).
Hypatia (1853).
Two Years Ago (1857).
Westward Ho! (1855).
Yeast (1857).
Kingsley, Henry (1830-1876).
Austin Elliott (1863).
Ravenshoe (1861).
Kingsley, Mary [*pseudonym*: Lucas Malet] (1852-1931).
A Counsel of Perfection (1888).
Kipling, Rudyard (1865-1936).
Captains Courageous (1897).
The Light That Failed (1890).
Kim (1900).
Kirkby, John (1705-1754).
The Capacity of Human Understanding (1745).
Kirkland, Joseph (1830-1894).
The Captain of Company K (1891).
Lathom, Francis (1777-1832).
The Midnight Bell (1798).
Lawrence, George Alfred (1827-1876).
Guy Livingstone (1857).
Lawrence, Herbert.
The Contemplative Man (1771).
The Life and Adventures of Common Sense (1769).
Lee, Sophia (1750-1824).
The Recess (1783-1785).

Leland, Thomas (1722-1785).
Longsword (1762).
Lennox, Charlotte (1720-1804).
The Female Quixote (1752).
Henrietta (1758).
Sophia (1762).
Lever, Charles (1806-1872).
Charles O'Malley (1841).
Harry Lorrequer (1839).
Tom Burke of "Ours" (1844).
Lewis, Matthew Gregory (1775-1818).
The Monk (1795).
Lloyd, E.
Varney the Vampyre (1847).
Locke, D. R. [*pseudonym*, Petroleum V. Nasby] (1833-1888).
A Paper City (1868).
Lyall, Edna (1857-1903).
Donovan (1882).
Lyly, John (1554-1606).
Euphues (1579).
Euphues and His England (1580).
Lyttleton, George (1709-1773).
The Court Secret (1741).
McCarthy, Charlotte (fl. 1745-1768).
The Fair Moralist (1745).
MacDonald, George (1824-1905).
Annals of a Quiet Neighbourhood (1867).
Salted With Fire (1897).
Seaboard Parish (n. d.).
MacKay, Mary: *see* Marie Corelli.
Mackenzie, Henry (1745-1831).
Julia De Roubigné.
The Man of Feeling (1771).
The Man of the World (1773).
Macnie, John [*pseudonym*, Ismar Thiusen].
The Diothas (1883).
Malet, Lucas: *pseudonym* of Mary Kingsley.
Mallock, W. H.
The Individualist (1899).
Malory, Sir Thomas (d. 1471).
Le Morte DArthur (c. 1470).
Manley, Mary Delariviere.
The Adventures of Rivella (1714).
Henry.
Memoirs of Europe (1710).
The New Atalantis (1709).
The Secret History of Queen Zarah (1705).
Marishall, Jean (fl. 1765-1788).
The History of Miss Clarinda Cathcart (1766).
Marryat, Frederick (1792-1848).
Jacob Faithful (1834).
Japhet in Search of a Father (1836).
Masterman Ready (1841-1842).
Monsieur Violet (1843).
Mr. Midshipman Easy (1836).
Peter Simple (1834).
Martineau, Harriet (1802-1876).
Illustrations of Political Economy (1833).

Marvel, Ik: *pseudonym* of Donald Grant
  Mitchell.
Maturin, Charles Robert (1780-1824).
  The Albigenses (1824).
  The Fatal Revenge (1807).
  Melmoth the Wanderer (1820).
  The Wild Irish Boy (1808).
Meeke, Mary (d. 1818).
  Count St. Blanchard (1795).
Melville, Herman (1819-1891).
  The Confidence Man (1857).
  Israel Potter (1855).
  Mardi (1849).
  Moby Dick (1851).
  Omoo (1847).
  Pierre (1852).
  Redburn (1849).
  Typee (1846).
  White Jacket (1850).
Mendes, H. Pereira (1852-1937).
  Looking Ahead (1899).
Meredith, George (1828-1909).
  The Adventures of Harry Richmond
    (1871).
  The Amazing Marriage (1895).
  Beauchamp's Career (1876).
  Diana of the Crossways (1885).
  The Egoist (1879).
  Evan Harrington (1861).
  Lord Ormont and His Aminta (1894).
  One of Our Conquerors (1891).
  The Ordeal of Richard Feverel (1859).
  Sandra Belloni (1864).
  The Tragic Comedians (1880).
  Vittoria (1867).
Merriman, Henry Seton (1862-1903).
  In Kedar's Tents (1897).
Michaelis, Richard (1839-1909).
  Looking Further Forward (1890).
Mitchell, Donald Grant (1822-1908).
  Doctor Johns (1895).
Mitchell, S. Weir (1829-1914).
  The Adventures of Francois (1898).
  The Autobiography of a Quack (1900).
  George Dedlow (1880).
  Hugh Wynne: Free Quaker (1896).
Moore, David A.
  The Age of Progress (1856).
Moore, George (fl. 1797-1811).
  Grasville Abbey (1797).
Moore, George (1852-1933).
  Esther Waters (1894).
  Evelyn Innes (1898).
  A Mummer's Wife (1885).
  Muslin (1886).
More, Sir Thomas (1478-1535).
  Utopia (1516).
Morier, James Justinian (1780-1849).
  The Adventures of Hajji Baba of Ispahan
    (1824).

Morris, Ralph.
  The Life and Astonishing Adventures of
    John Daniel (1751).
Morris, William (1834-1896).
  News from Nowhere (1890).
Mozeen, Thomas (d. 1768).
  Young Scarron (1752).
Murfree, Mary Noailles [*pseudonym:*
    Charles Egbert Craddock] (1850-
    1922).
  The Prophet of the Great Smoky Mountains
    (1885).
  The Story of Old Ford Loudon (1898).
Nashe, Thomas (1567-1601).
  The Unfortunate Traveller, or The Life of
    Jack Wilton (1594).
Norris, Frank (1870-1902).
  McTeague (1899).
  Moran of the Lady Letty (1898).
  Vandover and the Brute (1895).
Olerich, Henry.
  A Cityless and Countryless World (1893).
Oliphant, Margaret (1828-1897).
  A Beleaguered City (1880).
  The Doctor's Family (1863).
  Miss Marjoribanks (1866).
  The Perpetual Curate (1864).
  Phoebe Junior (1876).
  The Rector (1863).
  Salem Chapel (1863).
Paddock, Cornelia.
  The Fate of Madame La Tour (1881).
Page, Thomas Nelson (1853-1922).
  Red Rock (1898).
Paltock, Robert (1697-1767).
  The Life and Adventures of Peter Wilkins
    (1751).
Parsons, Eliza (1748-1811).
  Castle of Wolfenbach (1793).
  The Mysterious Warning (1796).
Payson, George (1824-1893).
  Golden Dreams of Leaden Realities (1853).
Peacock, Thomas Love (1785-1866).
  Crotchet Castle (1831).
  Gryll Grange (1861).
  Headlong Hall (1816).
  Maid Marian (1822).
  Melincourt (1817).
  The Misfortunes of Elphin (1829).
  Nightmare Abbey (1818).
Peck, Bradford.
  The World a Department Store (1900).
Peck, George W. (1840-1916).
  How Private George W. Peck Put Down the
    Rebellion (1887).
Phillpotts, Eden (1862-1960).
  Children of the Mist (1898).
Poe, Edgar Allan (1809-1849).
  The Narrative of Arthur Gordon Pym
    (1838).

Porter, Jane (1776-1850).
The Scottish Chiefs (1810).
Thaddeus of Warsaw (1803).
Radcliffe, Ann (1764-1823).
The Castles of Athlin and Dunbayne
(1796).
The Italian (1796).
The Mysteries of Udolpho (1794).
The Romance of the Forest (1791).
A Sicilian Romance (1790).
Read, Opie (1852-1939).
Balanyo (1897).
The Carpetbagger (1899).
In the Alamo (1900).
Judge Elbridge (1899).
A Yankee from the West (1898).
Reade, Charles (1814-1884).
Christie Johnstone (1853).
The Cloister and the Hearth (1861).
Griffith Gaunt (1866).
Hard Cash (1863).
It Is Never Too Late to Mend (1856).
Love Me Little, Love Me Long (1859).
Peg Woffington (1853).
Put Yourself in His Place (1870).
Singleheart and Double Face (n. d.).
A Terrible Temptation (n. d.).
The Wandering Heir (1875).
White Lies (n. d.).
Reid, Mayne (1818-1883).
The White Chief (1860).
Richardson, Samuel (1689-1761).
Clarissa (1747-1748).
Pamela (1740-1744).
Sir Charles Grandison (1749?).
Ridge, John Rollin (1827-1867).
*The Life and Adventures of Joaquín
Murieta* (1854).
Ridley, James (1736-1765).
The History of James Lovegrove (1761).
Roberts, J. W. (fl. 1893-1895).
Looking Within (1893).
Roche, Regina Maria (1764-1845).
Clermont (1798).
Nocturnal Visit (1800).
Roe, Edward Payson (1838-1888).
Barriers Burned Away (1872).
Opening a Chestnut Burr (1874).
Rosewater, Frank.
'96: A Romance of Utopia (1894).
Schindler, Solomon (1842-1915).
Young West (1894).
Schreiner, Olive (1855-1920).
Story of an African Farm (1883).
Undine (1876; published 1928).
Scott, Sarah (1723-1795).
A Description of Millenium Hall (1762).
The History of Cornelia (1750).
Scott, Sir Walter (1771-1832).
The Abbot (1820).

Anne of Geierstein (1829).
The Antiquary (1816).
The Betrothed (1825).
The Black Dwarf (1816).
The Bride of Lammermoor (1819).
Castle Dangerous (1832).
Count Robert of Paris (1832).
The Fair Maid of Perth (1828).
The Fortunes of Nigel (1822).
Guy Mannering (1815).
The Heart of Midlothian (1818).
The Highland Widow (1827).
Ivanhoe (1819).
Kenilworth (1821).
A Legend of Montrose (1819).
The Monastery (1820).
Old Mortality (1816).
Peveril of the Peak (1822).
The Pirate (1822).
Quentin Durward (1823).
Redgauntlet (1824).
Rob Roy (1817).
St. Ronan's Well (1824).
The Surgeon's Daughter (1827).
The Talisman (1825).
Waverley (1814).
Woodstock (1826).
Severance, Mark Sibley.
Hammersmith: His Harvard Days (1898).
Shaw, George Bernard (1856-1950).
Cashel Byron's Profession (1882).
The Irrational Knot (1880).
The Unsocial Socialist (1883).
Shebbeare, John (1709-1788).
*The History of the Excellence and Decline
of the Sumatrans* (1763).
Lydia (1755).
The Marriage Act (1754).
Sheehan, Patrick Augustine (1852-1913).
The Triumph of Failure (1899).
Sheldon, Charles M. (1857-1946).
In His Steps (1896).
Shelley, Mary (1797-1851).
Frankenstein (1816).
Sheridan, Frances (1724-1766).
The History of Nourjahad (1767).
Shorthouse, J. H. (1834-1903).
John Inglesant (1880).
Sidney, Sir Philip (1554-1586).
Arcadia (1584).
Simms, William Gilmore (1806-1870).
The Partisan (1835).
The Scout (1854).
Vasconselos (1856).
Woodcraft (1856).
The Yemassee (1835).
Sleath, Eleanor (1763-1815).
The Orphan of the Rhine (1798).
Smith, Titus K.
Altruria (1895).

Smollett, Tobias (1721).
Ferdinand, Count Fathom (1753).
Humphry Clinker (1771).
Peregrine Pickle (1751).
Roderick Random (1748).
Sir Launcelot Greaves (1760-1761).
Somerville, Edith Oenone (c. 1860-1949).
An Irish Cousin (1889).
Steel, Flora Annie (1847-1929).
The Hosts of the Lord (1900).
On the Face of the Waters (1897).
Sterne, Laurence (1713-1768).
A Sentimental Journey (1768).
Tristram Shandy (1760-1767).
Stevenson, Robert Louis (1850-1894).
The Beach of Falesá (1892).
The Black Arrow (1888).
David Balfour, or Catriona (1893).
The Ebb-Tide (1894).
John Nicholson (1887).
Kidnapped (1886).
The Master of Ballantrae (1889).
Prince Otto (1885).
St. Ives (1896-1897).
Treasure Island (1883).
The Wrecker (1892).
The Wrong Box (1889).
Stockton, Frank R. (1834-1908).
Bicycle of Cathay (1900).
The Late Mrs. Null (1886).
Mrs. Cliff's Yacht (1896).
Rudder Grange (1879).
Stoker, Bram (1847-1912).
Dracula (1897).
Stowe, Harriet Beecher (1811-1896).
The Minister's Wooing (1859).
The Pearl of Orr's Island (1862).
Uncle Tom's Cabin (1852).
Surtees, Robert Smith (1805-1864).
Ask Mamma (1858).
Handley Cross (1843).
Hawbuck Grange (1847).
Hillingdon Hall (1845).
Jarrock's Jaunts and Jollities (1838).
Mr. Facey Romford's Hounds (1865).
Mr. Sponge's Sporting Tour (1853).
Plain or Ringlets? (1860).
Swift, Jonathan (1667-1745).
Gulliver's Travels (1726).
A Tale of a Tub (1704).
Tarkington, Booth (1869-1946).
The Gentleman from Indiana (1899).
Taylor, Bayard (1825-1878).
Hannah Thurston (1864).
Thackeray, William Makepeace (1811-1863).
Barry Lyndon (1844).
Catherine: A Story (1839-1840).
Denis Duval (n. d.).
Henry Esmond, Esq. (1852).

The History of Samuel Titmarsh and the Great Hoggarty Diamond (1841).
Lovel the Widower (n. d.).
The Newcomes (1855).
Pendennis (1850).
Philip (1862).
Vanity Fair (1847-1848).
The Virginians (1859).
Thompson, Maurice (1844-1901).
Alice of Old Vincennes (1900).
Tourgee, Albion W. (1838-1905).
Bricks Without Straw (1880).
Murvale Eastman (1889).
Pactolus Prime (1890).
A Royal Gentleman (1874).
Trollope, Anthony (1815-1882).
The American Senator (1877).
Ayala's Angel (1881).
Barchester Towers (1857).
The Belton Estate (1866).
Can You Forgive Her? (1864).
Dr. Thorne (1858).
Dr. Wortle's School (1881).
The Duke's Children (1880).
The Eustace Diamonds (1873).
Framley Parsonage (1861).
The Golden Lion of Granpère (1872).
He Knew He Was Right (1869).
Is He Popenjoy? (1878).
Lady Anna (1874).
The Last Chronicles of Barset (1867).
Linda Tressel (1868).
Nina Balatka (1867).
Orley Farm (1862).
Phineas Finn (1869).
Phineas Redux (1874).
The Prime Minister (1876).
Rachel Ray (1862).
Ralph the Heir (1871).
The Small House at Allington (1864).
The Three Clerks (1858).
The Vicar of Bullhampton (1870).
The Warden (1855).
The Way We Live Now (1875).
Trowbridge, John Townsend (1827-1916).
Neighbor Jackwood (1856).
Tucker, George (1775-1861).
A Century Hence (1841?).
Tucker, Nathaniel Beverley (1784-1851).
The Partisan Leader (1836).
Twain, Mark (1835-1910).
A Connecticut Yankee in King Arthur's Court (1889).
The Gilded Age (1889), with Charles Dudley Warner.
The Great Dark (1898).
Huckleberry Finn (1885).
Joan of Arc (1896, 1899).
The Prince and the Pauper (1882).
Pudd'nhead Wilson (1894).

Twain, Mark (1835-1910). (*continued*)
Tom Sawyer (1876).
Tom Sawyer Abroad (1878).
Vinton, Arthur Dudley (1852-1906).
Looking Further Backward (1890).
Voynich, Ethel Lilian.
The Gadfly (1897).
Walcot, James.
The New Pilgrim's Progress (1748).
Wallace, Lew (1827-1905).
Ben Hur (1880).
The Fair God (1873).
The Prince of India (1893).
Walpole, Horace (1717-1797).
The Castle of Otranto (1764).
Ward, Elizabeth Stuart Phelps (1844-1911).
The Silent Partner (1871).
The Story of Avis (1879).
Ward, Mrs. Humphrey (1851-1920).
Helbeck of Bannisdale (1898).
The History of David Grieve (1892).
Miss Bretherton (1882).
Robert Elsmere (1888).
Ware, William
Zenobia (1837).
Warner, Charles Dudley (1829-1900).
A Little Journey in the World (1899).
[Also co-authored *The Gilded Age* with
Mark Twain.]
Warren, Samuel (1807-1877).
Ten Thousand a Year (1841).
Webber, Charles W. (1819-1856).
Old Hicks the Guide (1848).
Webster, Henry Kitchell (1875-1932).
The Banker and the Bear (1900).
Wells, H. G. (1866-1946).
The Invisible Man (1897).
The Island of Dr. Moreau (1896).
Love and Mr. Lewisham (1900).
The Time Machine (1895).
The War of the Worlds (1898).

The Wheels of Chance (1896).
When the Sleeper Wakes (1899).
The Wonderful Visit (1895).
Whitman, Walt (1819-1892).
Franklin Evans; or, The Inebriate (1846).
Whyte-Melville, George James (1821-1878).
The Gladiators (1863).
Wilde, Oscar (1854-1900).
The Picture of Dorian Gray (1891).
Wilson, Augusta Jane Evans (1835-1909).
Inez (1864).
Infelice (1875).
St. Elmo (1867).
Wister, Owen (1860-1938).
Lin Mc Lean (1898).
Wood, Mrs. Henry (1814-1887).
East Lynne (1861).
Woodfin, Mrs. A.
The Auction (1770).
Woods, Margaret Louisa (1856-1945).
The Vagabonds (1894).
Woolson, Constance Fenimore (1840-1894).
Anne (1882).
Wright, Frances (1795-1852).
A Few Days in Athens (1822, 1835).
Yonge, Charlotte M. (1823-1901).
Abbey Church (1844).
The Caged Lion (1870).
The Clever Woman of the Family (1865).
The Daisy Chain (1856).
The Dove in the Eagle's Nest (1866).
Dynevor Terrace (1857).
Heartsease (1854).
The Heir of Redclyffe (1853).
The Trial (1864).
Unknown to History (1882).
Young, Arthur (1741-1820).
The Adventures of Emmera (1767).
Zangwill, Israel (1864-1926).
Children of the Ghetto (1892).

INDEX TO QUOTATIONS
BY AUTHOR AND NOVEL

Cowan, James
   Daybreak, 148, 523, 601
Crane, Stephen
   Active Service, 52, 329, 585   *The O'Ruddy*, 52,
   83, 153, 186, 211, 270, 280, 302, 329, 349, 350,
   455, 510   *The Red Badge of Courage*, 50, 119,
   148, 427, 487, 577, 590   *The Third Violet*, 309,
   468
Crawford, Frances Marion
   Corleone, 503   *Don Orsino*, 177, 418, 453, 481
   Khaled, 329, 350   *Mr. Isaacs*, 83, 380   *A
   Roman Singer*, 544, 563   *A Rose of Yesterday*,
   10, 29, 74, 242, 309, 350, 380, 541, 550   *Sant'
   Illario*, 350
Dacre, Charlotte
   The Libertine, 5, 52, 100, 104, 231, 252, 256,
   260, 315, 350, 380, 407, 522, 541, 543, 582, 587
   The Passions, 1, 16, 52, 64, 83, 94, 106, 112, 119,
   135, 194, 196, 203, 218, 236, 244, 260, 272, 274,
   290, 318, 329, 350, 438, 440, 446, 453, 456, 458,
   513, 524, 559, 587, 592   *Zofloya*, 10, 53, 94, 218,
   248, 260, 278, 427, 481, 523, 584
Dana, Richard Henry
   Two Years Before the Mast, 53, 156, 350
Daniel, Charles S.
   Ai: A Social Vision, 309, 350, 501
Davis, Mrs. Rebecca Harding
   Waiting for the Verdict, 213, 266, 287, 350, 462,
   463, 546
Day, Thomas
   The History of Sandford and Merton, 22, 53,
   62, 70, 79, 83, 142, 156, 260, 277, 299, 407, 479,
   481, 588
Defoe, Daniel
   Captain Singleton, 44, 109, 119, 130, 218, 240,
   244, 289, 302, 432, 503, 568, 570, 599   *Colonel
   Jack*, 44, 109, 135, 169, 188, 218, 226, 260, 266,
   291, 350, 412, 432, 492, 506, 533   *Moll Flanders*,
   8, 36, 40, 53, 68, 92, 94, 112, 119, 130, 135, 145,
   150, 165, 173, 188, 218, 234, 251, 329, 350, 380,
   407, 412, 415, 441, 470, 497, 506, 515, 554, 555,
   559, 563, 580, 584, 585, 588   *Robinson Crusoe*,
   5, 6, 83, 130, 140, 169, 213, 218, 424, 497, 503, 524
   Roxana, 46, 196, 201, 213, 232, 251, 282, 350,
   380, 381, 476, 524, 559
De Forest, John W.
   *Miss Ravenel's Conversion from Secession to
   Loyalty*, 350, 381
Deloney, Thomas
   The Gentle Craft, 24, 108, 109, 132, 195, 329,
   350, 351, 411, 450, 470, 536, 563, 586   *Jack of
   Newbury*, 10, 24, 94, 108, 132, 146, 150, 211, 218,
   266, 291, 329, 351, 381, 398, 405, 407, 415
   Thomas of Reading, 5, 8, 78, 92, 213, 224, 351,
   398, 412, 461, 532, 551
Dickens, Charles
   Barnaby Rudge, 3, 7, 24, 27, 34, 40, 49, 53, 83,
   119, 142, 144, 161, 218, 228, 241, 242, 247, 251,
   252, 260, 266, 277, 351, 406, 410, 413, 423, 427,
   452, 456, 470, 500, 546, 558, 563, 566, 573, 585,
   593   *Bleak House*, 10, 15, 17, 27, 53, 78, 80, 100,
   119, 120, 135, 141, 163, 183, 201, 211, 224, 228,
   242, 270, 272, 309, 310, 351, 381, 407, 415, 425,
   428, 442, 443, 455, 478, 481, 510, 511, 516, 556,
   557, 566, 573, 576, 577, 585   *David Copperfield*,
   6, 7, 20, 37, 53, 62, 93, 95, 129, 142, 148, 153, 161,
   169, 173, 185, 222, 236, 242, 264, 266, 320, 329,

330, 351, 381, 403, 404, 422, 428, 452, 481, 498,
501, 525, 541, 543, 558, 576, 592, 601   *Dombey
and Son*, 14, 23, 36, 37, 64, 92, 96, 116, 153, 156,
157, 161, 185, 203, 214, 229, 242, 260, 268, 288,
306, 330, 351, 398, 415, 425, 428, 434, 438, 440,
446, 481, 493, 519, 526, 539, 544, 555, 563, 566,
568, 584   *Edwin Drood*, see *The Mystery of
Edwin Drood* *Great Expectations*, 7, 14, 27,
53, 68, 76, 96, 98, 157, 179, 188, 211, 212, 224,
285, 318, 330, 381, 463, 495, 533, 558, 571,
583   *Hard Times*, 10, 48, 49, 53, 83, 177, 203,
251, 279, 470, 488, 493, 556, 566, 573   *Little
Dorrit*, 14, 21, 53, 62, 135, 150, 173, 211, 224,
234, 251, 266, 382, 405, 411, 418, 440, 487,
496, 513, 523, 601   *Martin Chuzzlewit*, 29, 47,
62, 78, 83, 96, 120, 127, 131, 150, 161, 173,
210, 256, 260, 270, 274, 382, 418, 428, 446,
463, 514, 526, 602   *The Mystery of Edwin
Drood*, 17, 24, 73, 78, 112, 151, 232, 244, 289,
297, 310, 330, 425, 438, 455, 565, 594,
596   *Nicholas Nickleby*, 3, 24, 28, 47, 53, 60,
62, 77, 83, 92, 132, 142, 148, 151, 157, 237,
242, 254, 256, 267, 292, 293, 297, 307, 318,
330, 404, 425, 428, 445, 452, 456, 459, 462,
481, 531, 557, 558, 577, 582, 589, 595,
602   *The Old Curiosity Shop*, 53, 61, 62, 96,
112, 120, 135, 148, 151, 160, 173, 203, 229,
251, 264, 297, 310, 318, 351, 404, 451, 489,
522, 556, 558, 566, 573   *Oliver Twist*, 8, 40,
47, 53, 71, 112, 203, 237, 266, 310, 323, 330,
407, 424, 456, 470, 561   *Our Mutual Friend*,
2, 53, 83, 183, 218, 285, 330, 439, 470, 495,
527   *Pickwick Papers*, 4, 14, 29, 53, 83, 100,
102, 116, 120, 142, 145, 151, 176, 181, 203,
210, 224, 228, 237, 270, 279, 310, 318, 330,
351, 382, 413, 428, 444, 445, 455, 457, 463,
470, 485, 523, 525, 532, 535, 558, 559   *A Tale
of Two Cities*, 54, 120, 175, 214, 222, 248, 256,
270, 276, 318, 351, 428, 440, 448, 457, 463,
512, 517, 566, 582
Disraeli, Benjamin
   Coningsby, 10, 17, 33, 45, 54, 65, 72, 74, 76, 83,
   84, 100, 101, 104, 105, 111, 131, 135, 142, 154,
   157, 169, 178, 181, 203, 210, 224, 228, 242, 245,
   279, 281, 282, 291, 343, 351, 352, 403, 424, 428,
   433, 441, 451, 454, 467, 468, 472, 473, 493, 498,
   503, 507, 512, 514, 517, 519, 526, 531, 541, 546,
   553, 569, 573, 593   *Contarini Fleming*, 248,
   352   *Endymion*, 71, 503, 566   *Lothair*, 14,
   113, 382, 459, 558, 573   *Sybil*, 10, 24, 27, 28,
   54, 62, 71, 80, 90, 103, 141, 151, 160, 167, 173,
   211, 241, 242, 269, 272, 279, 318, 330, 352,
   403, 408, 443, 470, 484, 494, 517, 541, 563,
   566, 569, 579, 580, 593, 596   *Tancred*, 54, 224,
   282, 418   *Vivian Grey*, 170, 413, 472,
   603   *The Young Duke*, 62, 84, 476
Dodgson, Charles: *see* Carroll, Lewis
Donaldson, William
   *The Life and Adventures of Sir Bartholomew
   Sapskull*, 35, 54, 113, 157, 207, 227, 237, 260,
   266, 318, 412, 414, 457, 479, 481, 539, 570, 589
Doyle, Sir Arthur Conan
   Micah Clarke, 10, 24, 154, 188, 237, 248, 256,
   307, 408, 476, 492, 503, 543, 546
Dreiser, Theodore
   Sister Carrie, 31, 54, 65, 68, 79, 96, 132, 135,
   146, 148, 196, 200, 218, 231, 254, 269, 278, 291,

QUOTATION INDEX

QUOTATION INDEX

419, 429, 432, 452, 467, 479, 504, 552, 592   *The Guardian Angel*, 35, 60, 111, 122, 229, 257, 334, 357, 386, 400, 464, 499, 504, 546, 563   *A Mortal Antipathy*, 41, 191, 319, 334, 423

Hope, Anthony
The Prisoner of Zenda, 184, 214, 244, 253, 334, 515

Howe, E. W.
The Story of a Country Town, 23, 238, 257, 357, 386, 442, 504, 574

Howells, William Dean
The Lady of the Aroostook, 357   *A Modern Instance*, 1, 56, 92, 238, 312, 334, 357, 386, 489, 558, 574   *The Rise of Silas Lapham*, 3, 5, 11, 17, 33, 41, 45, 48, 50, 56, 65, 73, 74, 109, 144, 168, 170, 184, 191, 211, 214, 246, 262, 283, 289, 290, 334, 335, 357, 386, 387, 419, 420, 424, 444, 451, 482, 498, 517, 520, 521, 534, 541, 551, 556

Howland, Marie
Papa's Own Girl (also known as *The Familistere*), 196, 546

Hudson, William Henry
The Purple Land, 179, 238, 312, 319, 357

Jackson, Helen Hunt
Ramona, 524

James, Henry
The American, 2, 11, 20, 41, 42, 56, 63, 142, 204, 238, 267, 307, 312, 387, 453, 489, 515, 593   *The Awkward Age*, 246, 482   *The Bostonians*, 28, 97, 358, 387, 554   *Confidence*, 69, 104, 196, 204, 335, 358, 387, 432, 451, 547, 555, 588   *The Europeans*, 5, 20, 164, 207, 219, 251, 358, 471   *The Portrait of a Lady*, 65, 170, 358, 387, 441, 530, 531   *The Princess Casamassima*, 154, 163, 358, 461, 577   *Roderick Hudson*, 11, 268, 335, 387, 504, 597   *The Spoils of Poynton*, 25   *Washington Square*, 20, 358, 387, 399, 401, 412, 459

Jenner, Charles
The Placid Man, 59, 63, 65, 73, 80, 81, 85, 88, 115, 129, 143, 147, 158, 200, 207, 210, 230, 232, 238, 257, 265, 267, 276, 278, 279, 280, 288, 294, 303, 319, 335, 387, 408, 415, 434, 450, 476, 508, 509, 541, 553, 556, 558, 559, 581, 584

Jerome, Jerome K.
Three Men in a Boat, 151, 180, 262, 358, 401, 444, 486, 488, 507, 538

Jewett, Sarah Orne
The Country of the Pointed Firs, 74, 204, 290   *Deephaven*, 424

Johnson, Samuel
Rasselas, 2, 8, 11, 23, 31, 32, 33, 36, 38, 56, 61, 63, 85, 89, 97, 99, 122, 128, 131, 132, 145, 146, 163, 165, 170, 173, 174, 184, 189, 223, 225, 238, 249, 255, 268, 273, 275, 276, 278, 285, 287, 288, 294, 297, 300, 303, 304, 312, 315, 319, 387, 388, 403, 405, 406, 408, 412, 419, 429, 436, 441, 450, 453, 461, 464, 471, 473, 476, 479, 482, 492, 498, 500, 501, 508, 513, 516, 527, 533, 535, 541, 543, 549, 550, 563, 564, 567, 571, 574, 582, 584, 590, 593, 597

Johnston, Mary
To Have and to Hold, 436, 547

Johnstone, Charles
The History of Arsaces, 42, 90, 114, 131, 133, 154, 189, 204, 208, 214, 225, 238, 262, 273, 297, 335, 422, 433, 435, 461, 471, 473, 479, 488, 498,

504, 511, 516, 551   *The Pilgrim*, 35, 38, 67, 133, 160, 189, 201, 214, 238, 297, 312, 358, 388, 408, 488, 492, 518, 528, 579   *The Reverie*, 17, 38, 72, 91, 115, 151, 152, 195, 204, 225, 232, 234, 265, 276, 312, 342, 358, 414, 436, 451, 464, 488, 501, 508, 518, 536, 553, 571, 584, 591, 597

Judd, Sylvester
Margaret, 37, 42, 48, 57, 63, 69, 71, 106, 111, 193, 208, 214, 215, 229, 257, 307, 312, 335, 388, 406, 547, 578

Kahlert, Karl Friedrich
The Necromancer, 128, 215, 275, 312

Keenan, Henry Francis
The Money-Makers, 21, 415, 445, 574

Kelly, Hugh
Memoirs of a Magdalen, 388, 441, 531

Kelly, Isabella
The Abbey of St. Asaph, 8, 15, 282, 405

Kennedy, John Pendleton
Horse-Shoe Robinson, 299, 335, 358, 571

Kidgell, John
The Card, 35, 57, 129, 137, 204, 207, 239, 284, 288, 412, 414, 482, 486, 499, 558, 574, 594

Kimber, Edward
The Juvenile Adventures of David Ranger, 6, 25, 28, 102, 207, 239, 240, 323, 388, 484, 512, 564, 571   *The Life and Adventures of Joe Thompson*, 102, 106, 230, 534   *Maria*, 57, 504, 577

King, Edward
Joseph Zalmonah, 166, 388, 486

Kingsley, Charles
Alton Locke, 4, 133, 137, 166, 176, 215, 219, 249, 297, 312, 410, 415, 429, 493, 549   *Hereward the Wake*, 57, 85, 158, 219, 229, 249, 358, 417, 498, 545   *Westward Ho!*, 110, 154, 194, 204, 262, 285, 335, 358, 543, 564, 585, 597

Kipling, Rudyard
Captains Courageous, 99, 143, 486, 515, 539, 568   *The Light That Failed*, 30, 137, 358, 359, 547, 551   *Kim*, 108, 143, 401, 480

Kirkby, John
The Capacity of Human Understanding, 168, 215, 498, 522, 541

Kirkland, Joseph
The Captain of Company K, 359, 591

Lathom, Francis
The Midnight Bell, 219, 232, 297, 359, 501, 556, 585

Lawrence, George Alfred
Guy Livingstone, 28, 30, 57, 71, 110, 122, 140, 158, 176, 249, 335, 359, 388, 404, 476, 542

Lawrence, Herbert
The Contemplative Man, 106, 176, 219, 230, 255, 262, 401, 412, 436, 490, 540, 550, 600   *The Life and Adventures of Common Sense*, 42, 111, 152, 210, 262, 285, 304, 359, 408, 435, 508

Lee, Sophia
The Recess, 12, 36, 47, 94, 102, 137, 164, 230, 234, 255, 270, 273, 275, 410, 412, 461, 474, 504, 542, 597

Leland, Thomas
Longsword, 359, 473

Lennox, Charlotte
The Female Quixote, 28, 63, 105, 128, 166, 180, 191, 220, 246, 249, 275, 281, 408, 535, 547, 571, 574   *Henrietta*, 25, 104, 128, 137, 189, 195, 199, 204, 215, 231, 267, 297, 324, 335, 359, 388, 482,

Lennox, Charlotte (*continued*)
508, 510, 536, 537, 574, 581 *Sophia*, 6, 122,
208, 232, 233, 240, 315, 359, 421, 583, 588
Lewis, Matthew Gregory
The Monk, 35, 110, 233, 267, 284, 324, 388, 405,
458, 464, 468, 469, 492, 581
Locke, D. R.
A Paper City, 77, 388, 429, 486
Lyly, John
Euphues, 12, 17, 25, 32, 38, 42, 45, 57, 78, 85, 94,
99, 101, 106, 110, 116, 128, 132, 140, 145, 158,
159, 174, 178, 193, 196, 197, 198, 200, 204, 211,
244, 251, 275, 281, 304, 312, 335, 359, 388, 429,
435, 453, 498, 532, 550, 552, 555, 564, 570,
579, 597, 600 *Euphues and His England*, 6,
12, 17, 18, 32, 45, 57, 89, 106, 108, 111, 152,
167, 176, 184, 189, 204, 207, 215, 255, 270,
291, 335, 359, 388, 408, 413, 414, 429, 469,
521, 522, 533, 535, 539, 560, 565, 571, 597,
600
Lyttleton, George
The Court Secret, 6, 225, 233
McCarthy, Charlotte
The Fair Moralist, 18, 63, 93, 181, 204, 205,
233, 319, 335, 409, 522, 560
MacDonald, George
Seaboard Parish, 12
Mackenzie, Henry
Julia De Roubigné, 6, 8, 32, 89, 122, 131, 145,
197, 205, 239, 251, 265, 319, 343, 359, 388, 389,
409, 412, 482, 547 *The Man of Feeling*, 160,
197, 253, 257, 262, 264, 282, 285, 323, 415, 464,
533, 538, 574, 603 *The Man of the World* 4, 7,
25, 32, 89, 97, 106, 208, 244, 304, 405, 409, 410,
412, 414, 437, 447, 457, 461, 471, 482, 492, 494,
518, 536, 537, 547, 556, 581
Macnie, John
The Diothas, 270, 312
Malory, Sir Thomas
Le Morte DArthur, 25, 106, 137, 220, 336, 359,
405, 521
Manley, Mary Delariviere
The Adventures of Rivella, 137, 186 *Henry*,
336 *Memoirs of Europe*, 583 *The New
Atalantis*, 430 *The Secret History of Queen
Zarah*, 304, 359
Marishall, Jean
The History of Miss Clarinda Cathcart, 28, 93,
147, 189, 336, 359, 389, 498, 544, 594
Marryat, Frederick
Monsieur Violet, 122, 149, 290, 517, 542 *Mr.
Midshipman Easy*, 42, 163, 359, 456, 457, 542
Peter Simple, 7, 30, 109, 152, 312
Maturin, Charles Robert
Melmoth the Wanderer, 133, 336
Meeke, Mary
Count St. Blanchard, 205, 284, 389, 436
Melville, Herman
The Confidence-Man, 2, 12, 14, 18, 21, 25, 45,
65, 67, 69, 71, 85, 93, 99, 122, 129, 138, 140,
144, 147, 149, 152, 162, 163, 170, 191, 197,
205, 220, 223, 225, 227, 241, 243, 251, 255,
257, 262, 265, 284, 287, 294, 304, 319, 342,
405, 409, 430, 433, 447, 456, 457, 464, 478,
482, 495, 516, 527, 532, 538, 544, 547, 556,
557, 559, 561, 568, 572, 574, 591 *Israel
Potter*, 57, 65, 66, 74, 78, 106, 117, 143, 152,

164, 211, 227, 243, 249, 251, 257, 265, 270,
304, 430, 461, 501, 519, 523, 552, 556,
591 *Mardi*, 5, 12, 18, 25, 32, 35, 37, 44, 45,
48, 57, 60, 69, 71, 80, 85, 97, 106, 111, 113,
122, 123, 133, 138, 143, 147, 149, 152, 163,
164, 165, 166, 178, 181, 186, 197, 201, 210,
215, 220, 225, 231, 241, 243, 244, 246, 249,
265, 270, 275, 280, 281, 285, 287, 289, 294,
295, 304, 307, 319, 336, 359, 389, 399, 404,
406, 421, 424, 426, 430, 439, 442, 444, 449,
450, 454, 457, 464, 469, 473, 474, 499, 504,
512, 529, 530, 533, 537, 540, 547, 549, 551,
564, 567, 569, 574, 577, 578, 581, 591, 597,
603 *Moby Dick*, 1, 2, 7, 12, 18, 20, 21, 22, 30,
33, 37, 42, 45, 46, 48, 50, 66, 69, 77, 78, 85, 90,
97, 105, 107, 111, 117, 123, 124, 138, 140, 142,
143, 149, 152, 158, 159, 166, 170, 176, 180,
186, 189, 194, 197, 200, 205, 215, 220, 229,
231, 234, 239, 250, 251, 255, 257, 262, 265,
267, 271, 273, 280, 286, 290, 312, 319, 324,
389, 402, 409, 421, 430, 433, 435, 436, 439,
454, 457, 458, 459, 469, 474, 478, 484, 494,
516, 517, 519, 521, 523, 524, 534, 536, 538,
540, 544, 545, 547, 551, 554, 555, 556, 561,
564, 567, 574, 578, 583, 591, 595, 603,
605 *Omoo*, 57, 85, 101, 205 *Pierre*, 12, 15,
18, 19, 42, 57, 79, 85, 93, 124, 128, 138, 149,
154, 160, 184, 191, 205, 215, 220, 230, 239,
243, 244, 246, 251, 257, 275, 298, 305, 319,
320, 336, 389, 412, 423, 435, 444, 454, 474,
482, 512, 533, 535, 547, 574, 581,
603 *Redburn*, 5, 12, 19, 22, 37, 48, 71, 124,
138, 143, 164, 165, 184, 220, 229, 290, 312,
359, 410, 422, 424, 436, 439, 449, 476, 486,
504, 525, 542, 544, 557, 576, 578, 594, 600,
603 *Typee*, 25, 26, 42, 71, 74, 75, 101, 113,
176, 205, 249, 307, 320, 359, 389, 406, 426,
449, 507, 508, 514, 556, 574, 578, 591,
603 *White Jacket*, 12, 49, 57, 117, 131, 134,
138, 143, 164, 269, 299, 313, 320, 343, 389,
417, 420, 423, 430, 436, 449, 456, 526, 528,
544, 578, 580, 604, 605
Meredith, George
The Adventures of Harry Richmond, 4, 5, 12,
15, 21, 57, 86, 89, 97, 101, 115, 124, 143, 158,
191, 192, 207, 233, 239, 243, 249, 306, 320, 337,
399, 404, 412, 416, 449, 453, 459, 465, 482, 483,
515, 536, 559, 572, 591, 600, 604 *The Amazing
Marriage*, 3, 42, 59, 69, 105, 152, 205, 234,
246, 262, 268, 298, 305, 307, 360, 464, 499, 515
Beauchamp's Career, 12, 19, 42, 46, 48, 57,
75, 77, 78, 86, 91, 97, 110, 124, 138, 154, 162,
166, 168, 174, 180, 185, 189, 194, 197, 201, 205,
215, 225, 241, 243, 249, 265, 271, 275, 286, 290,
291, 295, 299, 315, 336, 337, 360, 361, 389, 399,
415, 416, 419, 422, 425, 434, 438, 443, 445, 447,
449, 451, 466, 467, 469, 474, 476, 477, 482, 484,
487, 490, 504, 505, 512, 514, 517, 528, 530, 536,
539, 542, 547, 549, 550, 551, 557, 562, 564, 567,
568, 575, 576, 579, 582, 583, 585, 591, 602, 604
Diana of the Crossways, 57, 75, 77, 86, 99, 110,
113, 146, 162, 166, 191, 199, 239, 258, 262, 284,
299, 361, 409, 425, 430, 449, 457, 465, 467, 471,
477, 499, 522, 523, 527, 530, 532, 542, 544, 549,
554, 568 *The Egoist*, 42, 63, 86, 116, 170,
190, 205, 210, 264, 281, 307, 337, 361, 389, 390,
437, 482, 515, 528, 554, 556, 561, 564, 579, 603,

229, 255, 265, 276, 289, 295, 305, 321, 340, 369, 409, 424, 431, 462, 514, 523, 529, 530, 531, 532, 538, 549, 560, 570, 591, 592, 602 *Tristram Shandy*, 8, 28, 35, 38, 47, 48, 70, 79, 89, 98, 104, 127, 139, 141, 142, 161, 165, 175, 176, 206, 207, 216, 223, 227, 234, 240, 245, 250, 263, 264, 265, 267, 276, 285, 289, 295, 298, 305, 321, 324, 340, 369, 394, 402, 410, 419, 421, 424, 431, 438, 447, 458, 461, 477, 479, 484, 493, 505, 521, 527, 539, 548, 559, 565, 575, 580, 592, 600, 604

Stevenson, Robert Louis
The Black Arrow, 32, 107 *Kidnapped*, 72, 190, 198, 285, 404 *The Master of Ballantrae*, 565 *Prince Otto*, 13, 63, 87, 98, 100, 108, 110, 186, 199, 201, 223, 240, 258, 264, 291, 340, 369, 394, 431, 473, 514, 519, 532, 536, 561, 599 *St. Ives*, 139, 517 *Treasure Island*, 28, 116, 572 *The Wrecker*, 27, 30, 252, 459, 499 *The Wrong Box*, 91, 139, 159, 233, 240, 315, 321, 433

Stoker, Bram
Dracula, 216, 250, 499

Stowe, Harriet Beecher
The Minister's Wooing, 245, 263, 324, 340, 420, 545 *The Pearl of Orr's Island*, 20, 46, 69, 79, 100, 127, 159, 192, 216, 229, 230, 231, 233, 246, 253, 263, 269, 276, 283, 321, 340, 341, 369, 370, 402, 410, 424, 431, 441, 484, 490, 505, 548, 575, 599 *Uncle Tom's Cabin*, 216, 243, 321, 437, 538

Surtees, Robert Smith
Mr. Facey Romford's Hounds, 70, 460

Swift, Jonathan
Gulliver's Travels, 46, 87, 91, 94, 180, 190, 227, 314, 370, 405, 406, 431, 433, 438, 485, 499, 543, 568, 570, 584, 592, 602 *A Tale of a Tub*, 63, 113, 175, 306, 505, 599

Tarkington, Booth
The Gentleman from Indiana, 468

Taylor, Bayard
Hannah Thurston, 87, 306, 370, 394, 441, 469, 517

Thackeray, William Makepeace
Barry Lyndon, 117, 139, 141, 155, 206, 370, 395, 416, 442, 488, 594 *Catherine: A Story*, 13, 266, 576, 599 *Denis Duval*, 192, 592 *Henry Esmond, Esq.*, 6, 13, 44, 150, 178, 231, 250, 341, 370, 553 *The History of Samuel Titmarsh and the Great Hoggarty Diamond*, 395 *Lovel the Widower*, 26, 133, 185, 370 *Pendennis*, 139, 192, 341, 447, 530 *Philip*, 20, 26, 282 *Vanity Fair*, 8, 22, 28, 43, 59, 67, 69, 81, 87, 90, 91, 100, 104, 108, 127, 139, 142, 152, 153, 159, 171, 185, 192, 195, 206, 209, 246, 267, 321, 341, 370, 395, 406, 416, 420, 465, 484, 515, 528, 549, 581, 583

Tourgee, Albion W.
Bricks Without Straw, 178, 250, 449 *Murvale Eastman*, 72, 76, 87, 98, 100, 216, 229, 241, 243, 250, 314, 341, 370, 431, 450, 487, 505, 544, 548, 565, 594 *Pactolus Prime*, 21, 298, 505, 538, 554, 575 *A Royal Gentleman*, 450, 539

Trollope, Anthony
The American Senator, 108 *Ayala's Angel*, 26, 30, 59, 143, 185, 192, 198, 221, 240, 341, 370, 371, 395, 416, 417, 477, 486, 565, 594 *Barchester Towers*, 26, 35, 36, 59, 77, 87, 94, 102, 113, 141, 146, 162, 192, 198, 199, 217, 258, 298, 306, 341, 371, 395, 445, 477, 514, 521, 575, 580, 592, 600, 604 *Can You Forgive Her?*, 580 *Dr. Wortle's*

School, 60, 221, 521 *The Eustace Diamonds*, 20, 23, 59, 155, 171, 175, 180, 221, 243, 246, 252, 255, 299, 306, 321, 341, 371, 395, 396, 410, 416, 425, 431, 496, 506, 513, 522, 594 *He Knew He Was Right*, 13, 49, 108, 153, 164, 199, 206, 221, 226, 246, 264, 267, 280, 286, 287, 291, 295, 314, 341, 371, 372, 396, 410, 455, 472, 484, 489, 522, 540, 580 *The Last Chronicles of Barset*, 59, 553 *Phineas Finn*, 16, 20, 33, 43, 88, 108, 111, 117, 129, 143, 155, 164, 165, 180, 193, 211, 221, 226, 231, 252, 266, 272, 291, 306, 321, 322, 341, 372, 396, 397, 414, 416, 421, 424, 433, 441, 466, 468, 510, 516, 519, 551, 605 *Phineas Redux*, 286 *The Small House at Allington*, 372 *The Three Clerks*, 59, 372 *The Warden*, 64, 67, 98, 192, 221, 286, 341, 468, 478, 519, 525, 531, 561, 575, 601 *The Way We Live Now*, 36, 46, 59, 60, 70, 100, 114, 153, 164, 171, 180, 283, 299, 341, 372, 397, 410, 416, 473, 486, 507, 511, 551, 552

Trowbridge, John Townsend
Neighbor Jackwood, 506

Tucker, George
A Century Hence, 436

Twain, Mark
A Connecticut Yankee in King Arthur's Court, 33, 78, 114, 149, 175, 193, 226, 245, 258, 271, 314, 436, 438, 511, 550, 603 *The Gilded Age*, 44, 67, 111, 139, 181, 187, 221, 250, 322, 342, 372, 373, 402, 416, 432, 433, 460, 468, 542, 548, 561 *Huckleberry Finn*, 36, 98, 100, 110, 113, 114, 141, 175, 194, 250, 271, 342, 343, 413, 432, 475, 478, 494, 514, 515, 552, 557, 562, 575, 602 *Joan of Arc*, 64, 111, 175, 192, 258, 263, 271, 434, 451, 452, 466, 473, 475, 550, 553, 592 *Pudd'nhead Wilson*, 4, 22, 36, 37, 70, 87, 92, 108, 127, 143, 153, 159, 167, 175, 177, 180, 181, 187, 206, 212, 234, 245, 271, 290, 416, 421, 441, 452, 468, 478, 486, 487, 513, 520, 575, 579, 592, 595, 602 *Tom Sawyer*, 127, 161, 193, 478, 562 *Tom Sawyer Abroad*, 4, 271, 287, 454, 494, 583

Vinton, Arthur Dudley
Looking Further Backward, 111

Walcot, James
The New Pilgrim's Progress, 397

Wallace, Lew
The Fair God, 153 *The Prince of India*, 322, 522

Walpole, Horace
The Castle of Otranto, 16, 21, 26, 233, 245, 280, 342, 438, 452, 486, 493, 505, 517, 575, 589

Ward, Elizabeth Stuart Phelps
The Silent Partner, 289, 373, 397, 423, 495

Ward, Mrs. Humphrey
Robert Elsmere, 72, 171, 193, 533, 542

Warner, Charles Dudley
The Gilded Age, 44, 67, 111, 139, 181, 187, 221, 250, 322, 342, 372, 373, 402, 416, 432, 433, 460, 468, 542, 548, 561 *A Little Journey in the World*, 3, 13, 104, 185, 198, 245, 322, 342, 373, 397, 441, 461, 494, 514, 531, 575, 594

Webber, Charles W.
Old Hicks the Guide, 210, 405, 432

Webster, Henry Kitchell
The Banker and the Bear, 60, 64, 78, 487, 531, 594

Wells, H. G.
The Time Machine, 450, 568

KEYWORD INDEX

actor (actors, actress), 2, 14, 267, 276, 536, 561, 569
acute (acuteness), 25, 28, 120, 209, 408, 444, 566
Adam (Adam and Eve: *see also* Eve), 4, 123, 127,
   163, 184, 197, 220, 257, 284, 370, 383, 384, 465,
   487, 493, 527, 534
adapt (adaptability, adapted, adapting), 3, 4, 96,
   177, 227, 294, 367, 389, 408, 476
add (added, adding, addition, additional,
   additions), 62, 165, 179, 189, 204, 231, 235,
   276, 290, 304, 324, 325, 368, 379, 382, 397, 405,
   412, 422, 469, 497, 499, 513, 542, 596
addicted, 151
address (addresses), 34, 109, 222, 351, 367, 386,
   392, 464, 601
adduce, 308
adhere (adhered, adherent, adhesion), 66, 286,
   420, 439, 542
adjective, 601, 602
adjunct, 187
adjure, 173
adjust, 498
administer (administered, administering,
   administration), 195, 225, 272
admiration (admirable, admire, admired,
   admirer), 4, 36, 47, 89, 104, 108, 113, 128,
   182, 204, 209, 291, 292, 324, 330, 335, 338, 346,
   354, 356, 360, 368, 373, 376, 379, 415, 427, 440,
   443, 450, 451, 452, 454, 481, 504, 518, 582, 588
admit (admits, admitting), 70, 132, 177, 221, 229,
   246, 308, 311, 329, 349, 386, 414, 455, 498, 564,
   590
admonish (admonishing, admonition, admonitory),
   151, 204, 310, 363, 427, 443, 552
adolescence, 69
adopt (adoption), 55, 136, 180, 455
adore (adorable, adoration), 111, 256, 337, 338,
   341, 345, 360, 373, 395, 397
adorn (adorned), 40, 345, 470, 593
adrift, 187, 214
adulation, 388, 410
adult, 69, 184
adulterate, 593
advance (advanced, advancement, advances), 10,
   37, 74, 126, 137, 190, 213, 262, 281, 304, 305,
   311, 314, 361, 374, 379, 383, 399, 405, 407, 459,
   486, 499, 500, 528, 539, 563, 571, 580
advantage (advantageous, advantages), 4, 13, 16,
   43, 54, 73, 75, 103, 127, 131, 161, 179, 187, 192,
   196, 202, 208, 251, 255, 264, 265, 276, 278, 279,
   313, 314, 334, 341, 347, 353, 357, 360, 364, 367,
   374, 390, 423, 436, 438, 464, 473, 482, 490, 510,
   523, 528, 533, 540, 550, 553, 556, 561, 570, 572,
   578, 586, 592, 593, 594, 597
adventure (adventurer, adventures, adventuress,
   adventurous), 4, 73, 119, 124, 187, 224, 259,
   368, 370, 385, 429, 530, 532, 553, 588
adversary, 84, 192, 442, 476, 550, 560, 571
adversity (adverse), 4, 5, 58, 106, 134, 208, 213,
   238, 244, 292, 300, 335, 351, 410, 435, 489, 501,
   568, 579, 588, 594
advertise (advertisement), 401, 465, 468, 486
advice (advisable, advise, adviser), 5, 6, 98, 104,
   369, 374, 385, 400, 412, 472, 572
advocacy (advocate, advocates), 6, 200, 337, 512
a-dying (*see also* death), 119
Aeolus, 68
Aesculapian, 400

aesthetic (*see also* beauty), 56
affable, 515
affair, 9, 19, 29, 52, 63, 78, 79, 130, 171, 181, 182,
   186, 204, 241, 259, 261, 276, 305, 330, 332, 334,
   341, 376, 384, 415, 457, 469, 502, 532, 544
affect (affectation, affected, affecting), 6, 7, 9, 11,
   13, 29, 39, 42, 54, 55, 64, 125, 150, 157, 200,
   214, 228, 267, 268, 293, 321, 323, 327, 340, 359,
   367, 375, 393, 407, 413, 414, 435, 456, 504, 511,
   530, 533, 545, 586, 598, 599
affection (affectionate, affections), 3, 7, 8, 21, 24,
   26, 33, 50, 71, 79, 83, 97, 117, 155, 165, 172,
   174, 176, 182, 183, 189, 194, 202, 203, 205, 208,
   264, 270, 291, 297, 324, 325, 326, 327, 328, 329,
   330, 332, 334, 340, 347, 349, 351, 356, 359, 366,
   377, 378, 380, 381, 384, 385, 396, 408, 420, 422,
   425, 429, 438, 446, 466, 468, 469, 470, 493, 497,
   498, 515, 526, 529, 543, 558, 560, 563, 570, 578,
   580, 584, 596
affianced, 393
affidavit, 310
affinity, 114, 203, 347, 350, 424
affirm (affirmative, affirmatives, affirmatize,
   affirms), 86, 209, 265, 354, 399, 581
afflict (afflicting, affliction, afflictions), 8, 49, 88,
   96, 130, 145, 153, 158, 208, 229, 254, 282, 298,
   320, 330, 407, 544, 566, 577, 603, 604
affluence (affluent), 8, 47, 226, 231
afford, 84, 101, 155, 207, 222, 223, 229, 244, 305,
   358, 361, 416, 462, 468, 470, 472, 571, 579, 583
affright, 189
affront, 8, 71, 253, 482
afraid, 59, 108, 110, 126, 139, 187, 188, 189, 194,
   246, 365, 366, 367, 441, 442, 550, 553, 572, 595
afterbirth, 529
afterlife, 118, 203, 404
after-pretenses, 93
after-reflection, 239
after-thought, 575
after-time, 183
age (aged *see also* ages), 8, 9, 10, 11, 12, 13, 21, 36,
   48, 57, 62, 69, 72, 83, 97, 149, 154, 156, 159,
   165, 170, 185, 191, 192, 194, 200, 246, 248, 256,
   271, 280, 281, 284, 289, 290, 292, 298, 303, 322,
   324, 325, 328, 329, 331, 337, 341, 347, 349, 354,
   355, 362, 366, 372, 373, 383, 404, 407, 419, 421,
   436, 438, 441, 448, 449, 456, 462, 472, 478, 490,
   512, 538, 543, 552, 557, 565, 566, 573, 575, 597,
   600, 604
agent (agencies, agents), 8, 25, 29, 105, 135, 141,
   159, 199, 213, 224, 236, 265, 288, 317, 426
ages (*see also* age), 34, 62, 94, 212, 224, 226, 242,
   320
aggravate (aggravates, aggravating, aggravation),
   105, 207, 223, 297, 406, 478, 584
aggregate (aggregation, aggregations), 80, 104,
   290, 407
aggression (aggressors), 13
aggrieves (*see also* grief), 89
agitate (agitated, agitation, agitations), 10, 14, 21,
   55, 69, 85, 117, 159, 339, 420, 427, 491, 545
agnostic (agnosticism), 379, 502
agony, 64, 112, 134, 229, 264, 333, 411, 459, 503,
   523, 525, 546
agree (agreeable, agreeableness, agreeablenesses,
   agreed, agreeing, agreement, agrees), 3,
   14, 15, 24, 81, 91, 101, 112, 144, 153, 187,

203, 211, 223, 227, 228, 234, 238, 249, 251, 286,
    312, 343, 345, 346, 366, 375, 377, 381, 383, 400,
    408, 423, 438, 477, 597, 604
aid, 210, 244, 280, 360, 363, 396, 482, 555
ailment, 401, 527, 549
aim (aiming, aims), 32, 79, 100, 130, 137, 150, 203,
    244, 252, 269, 270, 278, 314, 331, 356, 420, 447,
    461, 465, 497, 507, 519, 525, 526, 547, 591, 595
air, 1, 12, 45, 85, 101, 124, 127, 159, 174, 175, 181,
    186, 209, 219, 229, 279, 286, 287, 299, 303, 320,
    399, 423, 428, 430, 443, 447, 466, 468, 470, 478,
    484, 491, 520, 523, 526, 543, 546, 555, 569, 570,
    582, 592, 601, 604
air-built, 121, 148
airline, 541
airs, 99, 352
airy, 335, 422
alarm (alarmed), 119, 188, 232, 235, 250, 376, 414,
    449, 497, 508, 541, 546, 581
Alexander, 46, 465
algebra, 157
alibi, 310
alien (alienation), 14, 220, 331, 430
alive, 22, 168, 184, 228, 238, 309, 311, 316, 322,
    326, 376, 389, 413, 415, 427, 444, 452, 500, 519,
    537, 561, 591
allay, 332, 509
all-comprehending, 275
alleged, 240
Allen, Ethan, 251
all-erasing, 568
alleviation, 146
alleys, 31, 33
all-healing, 567
alliance (allied, allies, ally), 32, 61, 132, 176, 200,
    202, 254, 292, 331, 381, 394, 437, 483, 497, 576,
    583
alligator, 463
all-mastering, 188
All-merciful, 214
allot (allotment, allots, allotted), 139, 219, 261,
    319, 367
allow (allowable, allowance, allowed, allows), 94,
    159, 163, 180, 206, 208, 211, 219, 233, 252, 272,
    275, 294, 313, 315, 338, 339, 342, 357, 360, 374,
    377, 386, 389, 392, 393, 395, 406, 407, 421, 429,
    432, 438, 447, 453, 456, 463, 465, 485, 510, 563,
    564, 577, 581, 593, 594, 598, 604
alloy, 222, 235
all-potent, 23
all-subduing, 331, 464
allure (allured, allurement, allures, alluring), 55,
    108, 111, 217, 218, 239, 310, 533, 560
All-wise, 197
alma mater, 428
almanac, 565
almighty/Almighty, 196, 213, 214, 216, 255, 374,
    475, 583, 591
alms (alms-giving), 67, 456
alphabet, 132, 155, 157, 249, 289, 382
altar, 327, 379, 436, 503, 528, 600, 604
alter, 61, 127, 148, 208, 219, 222, 272, 311, 325,
    326, 342, 378, 397, 403, 430, 502, 532, 603
altercation, 388
alternative, 285, 294, 429, 433, 437
amateur, 173
amaze (amazing), 172, 256, 270, 426, 590

Amazon, 361
ambassadors, 12
ambiguities, 18
ambition (ambitious), 5, 14, 15, 16, 36, 46, 58, 64,
    156, 209, 229, 246, 255, 261, 314, 326, 340, 349,
    395, 422, 467, 480, 511, 524, 553, 592
ambivalence, 16, 17, 18, 19, 20
ambush, 7
amenable, 396
amend (amended, amending, amendment,
    amends), 2, 62, 92, 104, 105, 106, 167, 174,
    186, 218, 366, 380, 411, 448, 508, 586
Amens, 319
America (American, Americans), 3, 11, 37, 42,
    44, 50, 68, 105, 127, 159, 164, 167, 193, 241,
    270, 271, 287, 418, 449, 456, 460, 466, 468, 473,
    537, 540, 541, 554, 578
amiable (amiability, amicable, amity), 18, 39, 66,
    87, 119, 121, 122, 167, 202, 205, 277, 291, 299,
    332, 345, 358, 376, 382, 385, 393, 438, 483, 497,
    522, 536, 538, 574, 602
amorous, 67, 151
amount, 5, 195, 290, 310, 327, 399, 416, 456, 501,
    586
amphibious, 256
amphitheatre, 467
amplification, 475
amuse (amused, amusement, amusements,
    amuses, amusing), 16, 20, 26, 88, 117, 159,
    181, 182, 191, 194, 196, 238, 253, 264, 271, 275,
    367, 374, 407, 432, 441, 442, 460, 496, 502
analogy, 2, 140, 250, 257, 430
analysis (analytical, analyze, analyzed), 68, 95,
    160, 229, 418, 440
anathematizes, 17
anatomist, 548
ancestor, 63, 103, 139, 168, 184, 358
anchor (anchorage, anchored), 70, 197, 242, 569
anchorite, 524, 600
ancient, 15, 21, 30, 36, 63, 119, 136, 180, 249, 250,
    300, 340, 388, 395, 450, 479, 498, 513, 519, 566
anecdote, 191
angel (angelic, angelical, angels), 8, 15, 20, 21, 55,
    87, 95, 131, 183, 209, 214, 221, 243, 244, 263,
    298, 301, 307, 314, 351, 362, 370, 402, 419, 436,
    439, 444, 458, 463, 465, 500, 533, 585
anger (angry), 11, 21, 22, 83, 99, 107, 120, 154,
    199, 233, 240, 265, 281, 286, 338, 352, 366, 395,
    446, 447, 455, 527, 537, 566
angle (anglers, angling), 159, 179, 180, 540
anguish, 19, 107, 260, 261, 275, 331, 343, 382, 528,
    562
animal (animalcule, animalism, animals), 5, 20,
    22, 28, 34, 81, 111, 147, 150, 183, 224, 231,
    247, 252, 256, 258, 259, 261, 262, 268, 270, 272,
    281, 304, 311, 354, 356, 361, 362, 367, 369, 384,
    417, 419, 443, 448, 452, 467, 479, 481, 513, 524,
    539, 542, 545, 554, 568, 586, 590, 591, 596
animate (animated, animating), 11, 56, 248, 281,
    301, 377, 426, 437, 546
animosity, 21
annals, 260
annex, 429, 554
annihilate (annihilated, annihilating, annihila-
    tion), 277, 313, 347, 392, 420, 486, 513, 569
anniversary, 404
announce, 482, 539, 573

annoyance (annoyances, annoyed), 35, 100, 167, 201, 274, 288, 373, 580

annual (annuity, annum), 53, 157, 390, 414

anodyne, 95

anomalous (anomalously), 69, 220

anonymous, 93, 518, 555

answer (answerable, answered, answering, answers), 21, 28, 100, 127, 148, 168, 169, 179, 203, 211, 212, 219, 227, 265, 270, 290, 299, 300, 304, 308, 312, 354, 372, 384, 413, 424, 427, 454, 470, 471, 472, 474, 476, 478, 494, 516, 549, 563, 564, 574, 593, 602

ant, 520

antagonism (antagonist, antagonistic), 23, 327, 550

Antarctic, 521

antechamber, 544

antediluvian, 531

anti-Christian, 193

anticipate (anticipated, anticipation), 5, 63, 86, 236, 274, 347, 390, 449, 567

antidote, 525

antipathy (antipathetic, antipathies), 22, 23, 61, 217, 240, 326, 347

antiphony, 19

antique (antiquated, antiquity), 41, 100, 123, 250, 391, 507, 604

antisocial, 50

antithesis (antithetical), 490, 540

anxiety (anxieties, anxious, anxiously), 23, 48, 104, 108, 134, 165, 188, 244, 291, 322, 400, 411, 434, 477, 528

apartment, 3, 18, 73, 173

apathy (apathetic), 2, 23, 74

ape (aping, apish), 349, 448, 483, 589

apex, 76

aphorism (aphorist), 54, 490

apology (apologetic, apologies), 23, 27, 385

apoplexy, 121, 400, 401

apostle (apostolic), 57, 65, 163

apothecary, 25

appall (appal, appalling), 244, 257, 541

apparatus, 273

apparel, 352, 409

apparent, 188, 319, 367, 429, 487, 529

appeal (appeals, appellant), 10, 28, 171, 188, 228, 287, 294, 297, 312, 360, 420, 455, 483, 572

appear (appearance, appearances, appeared, appeareth, appears), 17, 22, 23, 24, 25, 26, 41, 75, 82, 88, 106, 115, 132, 187, 190, 197, 212, 220, 228, 230, 232, 242, 253, 254, 259, 260, 262, 263, 269, 292, 311, 318, 322, 344, 347, 349, 374, 375, 380, 385, 386, 395, 401, 427, 459, 462, 464, 466, 471, 475, 481, 482, 528, 530, 552, 570, 581, 583, 602

appeased, 241

appetite, 26, 102, 142, 272, 342, 383, 422, 428, 446, 458, 488, 597

applaud (applauding, applause), 15, 60, 97, 408, 464, 468, 473, 480, 502, 518, 550

apple, 12, 24, 289, 487, 583

apple-disease, 220

apply (applicable, application, applied, applying), 75, 179, 195, 252, 293, 311, 314, 326, 344, 352, 375, 400, 425, 451, 473, 492, 518, 521, 578, 588

appoint (appointed, appointment, appointments), 125, 154, 171, 214, 232, 285, 289, 364

appreciate (appreciated, appreciation, appreciative), 26, 68, 141, 167, 228, 260, 262, 297, 334, 358, 371, 373, 530

apprehend (apprehension, apprehensions, apprehensive, apprehensiveness), 5, 11, 22, 52, 81, 107, 189, 205, 271, 273, 357, 372, 487, 492, 514, 554

April (April Fools' Day), 13, 520

approach (approached, approaches), 87, 118, 127, 136, 187, 207, 225, 437, 461, 526, 584, 589, 600

approbation (see also approve), 18, 26, 27, 195, 296, 439, 599

appropriate, 104, 143, 367, 370, 458, 549

approve (approval, approved, approves: see also approbation), 1, 27, 192, 250, 331, 385, 387, 388, 405, 461, 539, 551, 564, 576

aptitude, 163, 372, 394

Arabia, 266

arbiter, 138

arbitrary, 74, 96, 209, 268, 308, 440, 487, 514

arch, 85, 215, 590, 604

archangel (see also angel), 211

archer, 269, 270

architecture (architect, architects, architectural), 26, 27, 174, 229, 313, 426, 485, 513

arch-mediocrity, 224

arctic, 18

ardor (ardent, ardently), 231, 255, 260, 289, 337, 353, 364, 387, 388, 391, 405, 451, 467, 508, 511, 553

arena, 399, 466

argument (argue, argued, arguer, argueth, argumentation, argumentative, arguments), 6, 21, 27, 28, 62, 63, 65, 182, 196, 217, 226, 254, 265, 288, 308, 331, 335, 339, 341, 368, 393, 439, 477, 497, 513, 518, 526, 532, 589, 590, 602

argumentum ad faeminam, 28

argumentum ad hominem, 28

Argus, 581

arise (arisen, arises, arising), 145, 148, 204, 210, 217, 248, 255, 257, 268, 294, 311, 325, 326, 329, 335, 429, 446, 471, 480, 495, 501, 535, 540, 589

aristocracy (aristocratic), 28, 266, 305, 468, 517

Aristotle, 10, 22, 151, 458

arithmetic (arithmetician), 156, 405

arm (arms: see also armor and army), 2, 42, 75, 78, 82, 119, 121, 126, 242, 271, 273, 303, 309, 310, 320, 328, 340, 456, 467, 487, 518, 545, 561, 576, 583, 592, 597

Armageddon, 274

armor (armed: see also arm and army), 97, 128, 285, 481, 489, 534, 590

army (armies: see also arm, armor, military, etc.), 49, 59, 110, 225, 246, 406, 413, 542

arraign (arraignment), 272, 294, 512

arrange (arranged, arrangement, arrangements, arranging), 137, 146, 177, 179, 180, 268, 319, 387, 395, 466

array (arrayed, arrayment), 25, 100, 256, 447, 528, 598

arrest (arrested), 231, 604

arrive, 112, 136, 262, 304, 305, 345, 385, 449, 565, 595

arrogance (arrogant), 58, 59, 272, 370

arrogate, 212

arrow, 8, 136, 269, 270, 352, 449, 480

arsenic, 117

August, 387, 520
auld-lang-syne, 529
aunt, 184
aurora borealis, 573
Austen, Jane, 181
austerity (austere), 161, 207, 411, 518
Australia, 271
author (authors, authorship), 33, 34, 35, 36, 59, 64,
   65, 71, 114, 124, 128, 161, 174, 175, 192, 203,
   273, 345, 350, 392, 426, 448, 450, 468, 495, 496,
   524, 544, 566
authority, 33, 54, 110, 113, 119, 169, 197, 248, 275,
   314, 369, 370, 391, 393, 395, 396, 530, 546, 576
authorize (authorized, authorizes), 201, 214, 253
autobiography, 30, 249
automatic, 138, 271
autumn, 9, 10
auxiliary, 330, 602
avail (availing, avails), 164, 200, 245, 286, 398,
   451, 469, 476, 573, 597
available, 555, 581
avalanche, 281
avarice (avaricious), 15, 36, 46, 185, 207, 259, 261,
   363, 376, 390, 445, 465, 538
avenge (*see also* revenge *and* vengeance), 479
average, 110, 112, 288, 418, 466
averments, 103
aversion, 57, 113, 240, 325, 347, 365, 421, 427, 482,
   570
averted, 203
avidity, 518
avoid (avoidable, avoidance, avoiding, avoids), 2,
   36, 104, 108, 122, 140, 157, 166, 221, 229, 236,
   247, 272, 322, 350, 360, 372, 385, 387, 388, 390,
   392, 400, 412, 471, 477, 502, 508, 513, 515, 518,
   521, 535, 536, 541, 554, 594, 602
avow (avowing), 250, 266, 350, 424
awake (awaken, awakened), 10, 43, 53, 58, 95,
   132, 139, 148, 149, 172, 255, 301, 316, 325, 330,
   335, 404, 448, 461, 474, 539, 577
award (awarder), 97, 297
aware, 205, 236, 264, 274, 383, 397, 405
awe (awed, awes), 22, 36, 37, 47, 90, 174, 189, 225,
   364, 405, 574, 579
awestruck, 495
awful (awfulness), 37, 118, 214, 283, 324, 347, 392,
   448, 488, 504, 539, 549, 562, 592, 604
awkward (awkwardest, awkwardness), 37, 142,
   186, 289, 451, 453, 481, 550, 584
ax (axe, axe-edge), 168, 255, 294
axiom, 60, 284, 295, 521, 530
azure, 123, 431, 578

babble (babbler, babbling), 103, 270, 444, 516,
   565, 585
baby (babe, babies, babyhood), 40, 47, 182, 205,
   391, 393, 545, 591, 598
Babylon, 303
bachelor (bachelordom, bachelors), 75, 184, 275,
   303, 310, 374, 380, 382, 391, 393, 397, 500, 540
backbone, 66
back-door, 268
background, 81, 466, 577
backwardness, 357
bad, 6, 14, 21, 31, 35, 37, 38, 46, 54, 56, 58, 61, 64,
   65, 66, 85, 86, 93, 96, 99, 103, 108, 110, 113,
   114, 125, 136, 141, 145, 151, 152, 155, 159, 166,

167, 190, 192, 193, 195, 207, 213, 217, 218, 219,
   220, 221, 222, 223, 234, 243, 252, 254, 257, 258,
   261, 274, 276, 277, 284, 299, 300, 312, 313, 323,
   324, 329, 340, 341, 343, 347, 348, 350, 353, 357,
   361, 374, 380, 384, 387, 389, 390, 394, 398, 401,
   408, 411, 413, 416, 432, 434, 437, 440, 460, 465,
   474, 476, 481, 488, 491, 505, 507, 508, 524, 527,
   537, 541, 543, 556, 557, 561, 563, 564, 568, 569,
   585, 588, 590, 592, 599
Badeker, 56
baffle (baffled, baffles), 175, 403, 485, 491, 581
bailiff, 170, 180, 311
bait, 18, 55
balance (balanced), 24, 37, 38, 96, 139, 142, 160,
   221, 224, 360, 427, 466, 580, 587
bald (baldness), 43, 111, 174
balefully, 538
ball, 116, 603
ballad, 382
balloon, 143, 291
ballot box, 167, 441
ballroom, 542, 603
balm, 120, 202, 206, 299, 384, 501
balsam, 195
Baltic Ocean, 152
bandit, 46
bane (baneful), 71, 359, 403, 432, 505, 534, 562
banish (banished, banishment), 153, 254, 434,
   478, 494, 500, 562, 563
bank (banker, banks), 77, 78, 96, 132, 142, 215,
   229, 260, 339, 455, 474, 486, 499, 556
bankbook, 183
bankrupt, 361, 457, 466
banners, 499, 602, 604
banns, 391
banquet, 276, 462
baptize (baptism, baptizing), 140, 449, 554
bar (barred), 149, 170, 185, 239, 411
barb, 43, 111
barbarian (barbarians, barbarism, barbarity,
   barbarous), 60, 63, 71, 74, 75, 76, 90, 104, 164,
   363, 389, 419, 484, 519, 574, 589
bargain, 38, 78, 101, 214, 390, 466, 523, 569
barleycorn, 532
barnacle, 57
barometer, 50
barren, 100, 116, 268, 421, 449, 451, 535, 570
barrier, 10, 45, 70, 439
barter (bartered), 390, 548, 575, 604
base (baseness), 38, 54, 91, 107, 114, 135, 188, 194,
   212, 218, 229, 267, 281, 316, 351, 422, 479, 483,
   503, 524, 538, 541, 544, 555, 585
bashful, 550, 553
bastard, 273, 384, 517, 545
Bastile, 602
bat, 133, 257, 274
Bath, 39
battalion, 499
batter (batteries, battery), 399, 551
battering-ram, 513
battle, 19, 57, 72, 98, 109, 110, 117, 140, 156, 159,
   169, 194, 227, 229, 246, 268, 274, 280, 295, 318,
   361, 363, 406, 430, 467, 502, 527, 541, 543, 549,
   590, 591, 592
battlefield, 356, 430
battleground, 126
bauble, 181
bayonet, 591

KEYWORD INDEX

170, 173, 182, 190, 213, 222, 223, 229, 248, 249,
267, 275, 282, 300, 303, 306, 310, 316, 323, 324,
360, 381, 401, 409, 417, 418, 427, 431, 444, 447,
453, 454, 461, 468, 469, 481, 485, 490, 495, 496,
527, 532, 545, 555, 558, 561, 603
bookish, 106, 302
bookseller, 34
bookworm, 34
boomer, 505
boon, 143, 220, 356, 357, 500
boot (boots), 313, 372, 406
bootjacks, 370
bootless, 509
booty, 579
bore (bored, bores), 62, 151, 173, 402, 546, 590
born, 3, 5, 9, 14, 47, 66, 68, 71, 87, 117, 118, 120,
124, 125, 134, 135, 136, 137, 154, 163, 172, 183,
201, 205, 218, 228, 231, 234, 256, 257, 261, 272,
283, 310, 311, 317, 328, 330, 347, 348, 360, 361,
362, 368, 369, 370, 378, 380, 388, 401, 404, 413,
418, 435, 436, 449, 473, 493, 514, 524, 538, 541,
546, 554, 564, 576, 592
borne, 3, 55, 172, 227, 316, 444, 452
borrow (borrowed, borrower, borrowing,
borrows), 102, 121, 170, 194, 195, 212, 213, 230,
413, 510, 526, 537, 561, 562, 572, 588, 599, 600
bosom, 6, 14, 15, 58, 83, 94, 164, 212, 213, 295, 330,
351, 361, 395, 416, 455, 539, 554, 564
Boston (Bostonian), 168, 534
bottle, 150, 151, 152, 203, 230, 325, 531
Bottle Conjuror, 152
bottle-deep, 206
bottom (bottomed, bottomless), 110, 128, 151, 304,
310, 324, 352, 370, 399, 481, 497, 505, 521, 571
bough, 315, 408, 423
Boulogne, 570
bound (bounded, bounding, bounds), 131, 161,
180, 201, 254, 272, 288, 306, 316, 324, 339, 349,
396, 407, 445, 498, 541, 592
boundary (boundaries), 429, 446, 448
boundless, 141, 165, 270, 300, 451, 551, 582
bounty (bounteous, bountiful), 201, 271, 280, 294,
431
bow (bows), 153, 158, 222, 261, 288, 334, 349, 352,
479, 583
Bowditch, 402
bowels, 105, 185, 474
bow-wow, 92
boy (boyhood, boys), 9, 10, 11, 12, 53, 55, 69, 83,
92, 99, 123, 156, 157, 161, 166, 209, 212, 247,
262, 270, 272, 291, 313, 328, 330, 343, 352, 357,
360, 362, 369, 382, 390, 409, 410, 439, 445, 483,
546, 575, 583, 597
brag (see also boast), 287, 306
brain (brains), 3, 27, 31, 43, 73, 77, 100, 105, 111,
138, 148, 153, 175, 178, 183, 186, 230, 238, 257,
268, 274, 278, 281, 300, 302, 307, 311, 333, 338,
340, 343, 346, 347, 354, 361, 382, 386, 409, 410,
438, 455, 458, 466, 467, 476, 534, 558, 564
brain-fed, 111
brain-racking, 478
branch (branches), 4, 11, 231, 305, 321, 486
brand, 296, 298, 324, 529, 549
brandy, 393
brass, 85
brat, 75
bravadoes, 533
bravos, 473

brave (bravery), 19, 42, 59, 66, 82, 105, 106, 107,
108, 117, 135, 139, 182, 219, 250, 273, 309, 344,
353, 362, 363, 385, 389, 489, 518, 540, 592
bray, 55
breach, 166, 201, 207, 232, 308, 327, 536, 586
bread, 17, 94, 143, 184, 239, 443, 570, 579
breadth (see also broad), 95, 562
break (breaker, breakers, breaking, breaks,
broken), 36, 46, 55, 85, 100, 108, 141, 143, 151,
165, 201, 204, 220, 238, 242, 243, 266, 267, 274,
281, 288, 293, 297, 308, 310, 314, 316, 321, 349,
364, 366, 383, 384, 402, 410, 414, 416, 431, 436,
445, 447, 457, 486, 492, 496, 541, 580, 585, 590
breakfast, 45, 143, 539
breast (breasts), 20, 38, 107, 188, 192, 213, 226,
259, 266, 278, 283, 298, 329, 332, 337, 351, 361,
404, 437, 444, 445, 447, 465, 482, 500, 521, 525,
545, 546
breastplate, 356
breath (breathe, breathes, breathing, breathings,
breaths), 40, 84, 118, 186, 193, 219, 269, 271,
320, 331, 334, 343, 390, 391, 399, 418, 421, 430,
434, 439, 440, 453, 474, 484, 500, 516, 519, 520,
534, 552, 568, 593, 597, 599, 601
breathless, 212
breech (breech-clout, breeches), 210, 239, 492
breed (bred, breedeth, breeding, breeds), 6, 25,
63, 64, 100, 106, 116, 117, 242, 269, 272, 291,
314, 345, 347, 350, 373, 389, 399, 408, 417, 440,
480, 484, 486, 504, 523, 524, 538, 539, 544, 556,
557, 586, 593
breeze (breezes), 124, 173, 200, 439, 520
brethren (see also brother and brotherhood), 33,
67, 541, 593
brevity, 49, 475
brew (brewed), 99, 352
bribe (bribed, bribery), 95, 96, 228, 446, 489, 559
bric-a-brac shop, 410
brick (brickmaker, brickyard), 122, 257
bride, 94, 379, 382, 386, 388, 389, 449
bridegroom, 142
bridesmaid, 91, 389
Bridewell, 469, 492
bridge, 274, 283, 336, 485, 579
bridle (bridle-bit), 102, 217, 276, 422, 522
bright (brighten, brighter, brightest, brightness),
102, 148, 176, 196, 214, 242, 247, 270, 277, 318,
321, 333, 337, 347, 431, 435, 440, 448, 450, 498,
500, 540, 546, 566, 578, 600
Bright's disease, 401
brilliant (brilliancies, brilliancy), 25, 31, 82, 490,
501, 540, 562, 582, 594
brim (brimful, brimmed, brims), 186, 363, 444,
501
bring (bringeth, bringing, brings, brought), 142,
169, 176, 199, 213, 223, 225, 228, 231, 269, 273,
303, 324, 328, 334, 335, 343, 345, 351, 375, 377,
381, 383, 385, 389, 398, 415, 417, 419, 421, 422,
434, 435, 436, 437, 438, 446, 453, 458, 461, 462,
471, 483, 486, 492, 495, 503, 511, 542, 559, 565,
569, 577, 598
British (Briton), 28, 31, 98, 115, 157
British Museum, 401
broad (broader, broadest: see also breadth), 213,
214, 229, 270, 288, 429, 444, 468, 490, 503, 535
broad-backed, 315
brokenhearted, 124
Bronte, Emily, 181

brood, 54, 183, 274, 275, 285
brook (brooks), 143, 235, 535
brooms, 578
brother, 49, 164, 184, 185, 194, 202, 206, 257, 280,
    347, 377, 391, 405, 468, 539, 573, 604
brotherhood, 49, 215
brother-in-law, 184
brother-wearers, 87
brow, 106, 180, 284, 307, 402, 454, 546
bruise (bruised, bruises), 260
brutality (brutal), 56, 226, 317, 363, 387, 589
brute (brutes), 15, 22, 58, 151, 162, 185, 201, 252,
    258, 262, 301, 302, 306, 386, 465, 529, 547, 551
brute force, 499
bubble (bubbling), 66, 139, 429
bucolic, 182
bucketful, 412
bud, 12, 99, 231
Buddha (Buddhist), 319, 505
buffalo, 270
buffet, 5, 362
buffoon, 51
bugbear, 125, 188, 347, 574
build (building, buildings, builds, built), 121, 165,
    199, 201, 226, 249, 251, 255, 292, 293, 297, 298,
    327, 328, 336, 359, 439, 485, 515, 521, 537, 542,
    544, 569, 574, 575
bull, 157, 367, 466
bullet, 173, 268, 270
bully, 49, 87, 464, 518, 542
bulwarks, 361, 364
bumpkins, 423
bungle (bungler), 41, 348, 394
burden (burdened, burdens, burthen, burthens),
    3, 35, 38, 44, 49, 55, 133, 139, 156, 188, 201, 234,
    308, 319, 343, 404, 490, 495, 521, 543, 592, 601
bureaucracy, 49
burgundy, 442
burlesque, 54, 299
burn (burned, burnest, burneth, burning, burns),
    59, 67, 78, 189, 285, 298, 302, 319, 330, 371, 425,
    451, 481, 517, 555, 571
burst, 109, 139, 175, 307, 310, 329, 532, 534
bury (buried), 91, 120, 123, 228, 249, 303, 322,
    382, 391, 449, 460, 521, 523
bush, 32, 153, 197, 562, 592
business, 8, 16, 67, 77, 78, 142, 145, 155, 177, 190,
    191, 202, 218, 228, 236, 265, 288, 289, 299, 304,
    310, 311, 320, 325, 327, 328, 335, 343, 352, 353,
    371, 375, 381, 394, 397, 402, 414, 447, 456, 460,
    464, 467, 480, 486, 495, 504, 510, 514, 531, 549,
    553, 555, 558, 563, 568, 571, 594, 598
businesslike, 96, 175
bust, 132, 137
bustle, 301, 312
busy, 3, 9, 11, 149, 159, 171, 259, 269, 318, 337,
    365, 412, 500, 506, 516, 546, 563, 590
butcher (butchery), 35, 429
butterflies, 10, 123, 201, 250, 415, 431
buy (bought), 50, 51, 74, 169, 170, 258, 260, 284,
    296, 386, 396, 530, 539, 569, 579, 595, 597
bystander, 452, 509

cabbage, 159, 579
cabin boy, 134
cabinet, 224, 521
cackle (cackling), 362, 599

Caesar, 127, 140, 143, 192, 208, 422
cage (caged, cages), 254, 279, 395, 459, 586
Cain, 544
cajoled (cajolery), 195, 474, 530
calamity (calamities), 5, 23, 49, 50, 71, 94, 97, 100,
    107, 122, 165, 169, 185, 189, 254, 259, 343, 362,
    409, 450, 486, 488, 532, 533, 537, 538, 552, 597
calculate (calculated, calculating, calculation,
    calculations), 83, 137, 160, 206, 217, 319, 328,
    342, 386, 389, 424, 427, 443, 475, 484, 528, 593
calendar, 123, 396, 567
call (called, calleth, calling, calls), 37, 126, 137,
    213, 217, 244, 267, 271, 276, 280, 286, 288, 293,
    298, 299, 313, 316, 319, 342, 344, 364, 370, 375,
    379, 382, 390, 401, 403, 404, 408, 413, 423, 424,
    449, 453, 459, 463, 464, 475, 495, 496, 502, 505,
    508, 509, 510, 513, 521, 524, 526, 532, 541, 544,
    546, 554, 559, 568, 570, 582, 583, 588, 603
callous, 8, 55, 186, 298, 355, 390, 412, 458, 529
calm (calmness, calms), 50, 57, 83, 99, 106, 137,
    210, 249, 277, 284, 286, 315, 316, 319, 324, 335,
    347, 383, 407, 409, 410, 412, 496, 519, 540, 548,
    571, 577, 599
calumny, 350
Calvin, John, 71
camel-driver, 87
camp-meeting, 502
canaille, 419
candid (candor), 25, 64, 67, 200, 423, 474, 528,
    570, 573
candle (candles), 31, 94, 192, 211, 255, 368, 517
cannibal (cannibalism, cannibalistically), 50, 71,
    85, 271
cannon (cannonade, cannonball), 176, 188, 280,
    430, 473
cant (canted, canting, cants), 97, 173, 267
canvas (canvassing), 124, 453, 489
capable, 117, 170, 173, 174, 196, 206, 211, 237,
    248, 253, 267, 275, 278, 292, 294, 297, 299, 326,
    332, 345, 378, 384, 418, 484, 493, 500, 504, 531,
    548, 570
capacity (capacities), 3, 50, 65, 103, 132, 198, 268,
    275, 305, 359, 367, 452, 473, 479, 541, 563
Cape Horn, 85, 457
capital, 51, 83, 140, 206, 227, 249, 382, 392, 415,
    416, 490, 568
capitalism, 50
caprice (caprices, capricious, capriciously), 69,
    106, 200, 257, 275, 276, 325, 347, 405, 427, 429,
    538, 593, 603
captain, 85, 134, 312, 313, 539, 542, 591
captivate (captivity), 216, 422
card, 53, 136, 207
care (cared, cares, caring), 29, 66, 78, 103, 125,
    137, 139, 148, 156, 184, 185, 189, 225, 237, 249,
    271, 280, 284, 300, 303, 318, 319, 327, 341, 344,
    346, 349, 352, 357, 360, 362, 375, 378, 380, 391,
    393, 394, 396, 398, 415, 429, 437, 444, 445, 448,
    450, 459, 462, 463, 469, 471, 475, 483, 488, 496,
    523, 532, 540, 566, 576
career, 44, 95, 135, 269, 355, 387, 468
careful (carefulness), 60, 144, 203, 207, 225, 232,
    377, 382, 392, 457, 463, 497
careless (carelessness), 95, 109, 155, 222, 240, 263,
    318
caress (caressed, caresses), 184, 258, 413
caricature (caricatured, caricatures,
    caricaturist), 299

chastise (chastening, chastisements), 336, 492, 559
chastity (chaste), 16, 68, 82, 283, 284, 357, 370,
    408, 436, 465, 493, 571, 575, 586
cheap (cheapening, cheaper, cheaply), 7, 17, 120,
    198, 271, 274, 345, 379, 561, 579
cheat (cheating, cheats), 58, 67, 68, 163, 192, 253,
    257, 331, 377, 401, 415, 462, 581
check (checked, checking, checks, cheque), 47, 54,
    220, 225, 258, 278, 333, 473, 483, 499, 511
checkmate, 84
cheek, 126, 154, 197, 347, 567
cheer (cheered, cheerful, cheerfully, cheerfulness,
    cheering, cheers, cheery), 10, 11, 40, 60, 67, 77,
    80, 84, 122, 134, 146, 150, 152, 161, 173, 203, 237,
    238, 283, 292, 318, 331, 384, 407, 431, 443, 471,
    498, 524, 526, 592, 601
chemistry (chemists), 135, 203, 519
cherish (cherished), 242, 245, 258, 327, 430, 435,
    450, 495, 568, 577
chess (chessmen, chess-pieces), 51, 84, 136, 257,
    318, 389
chicanery, 390
chicken-hearted, 187, 601
chide (chides, chiding), 204, 334, 409
chief (chiefest, chiefly, chiefs), 104, 164, 181, 201,
    224, 255, 276, 297, 338, 345, 397, 463, 522, 538,
    569, 590
child (childhood, childish, childishness, child-life,
    children), 1, 7, 11, 16, 30, 47, 52, 55, 58, 59, 68,
    69, 70, 84, 93, 102, 111, 114, 125, 126, 136, 144,
    149, 154, 155, 156, 162, 170, 182, 183, 184, 185,
    188, 189, 192, 202, 207, 217, 226, 232, 233, 235,
    238, 261, 267, 270, 273, 278, 293, 303, 306, 308,
    317, 321, 328, 331, 332, 344, 347, 352, 362, 367,
    380, 381, 382, 385, 387, 388, 392, 394, 396, 412,
    414, 418, 420, 422, 425, 427, 428, 431, 437, 438,
    449, 452, 468, 470, 475, 476, 481, 483, 484, 510,
    513, 516, 526, 532, 538, 546, 550, 574, 586, 591,
    592, 595, 601
child-wife, 381
chill (chilled, chilling, chills, chilly), 278, 447,
    470, 521, 526, 594
chimera, 244, 413, 519
chimney (chimney-piece, chimneys, chimney-
    sweep), 150, 250, 313, 321, 540
china/China (Chinamen, China Wall), 56, 74, 438,
    439, 574
chivalry (chivalric, chivalrous), 45, 62, 89, 162,
    225, 247, 313, 348, 357, 368, 462, 494, 526
choice (choicest, choose, chooses, choosing,
    chosen), 24, 65, 68, 70, 109, 112, 119, 135, 136,
    137, 144, 147, 154, 163, 173, 174, 181, 191, 197,
    200, 201, 207, 217, 228, 229, 235, 236, 238, 239,
    257, 278, 293, 319, 324, 325, 328, 340, 347, 348,
    353, 354, 357, 367, 374, 375, 376, 377, 378, 381,
    383, 384, 385, 387, 388, 390, 420, 430, 439, 453,
    461, 464, 465, 467, 474, 485, 490, 511, 513, 514,
    520, 522, 532, 538, 552, 561, 588, 594, 599
cholera, 401, 430
chord (chords), 53, 407, 463, 542
Christ (christen, Christendom, Christian,
    Christianity, Christianized, Christians), 8, 41,
    58, 60, 67, 70, 71, 72, 85, 95, 97, 100, 154, 178,
    198, 199, 205, 212, 213, 214, 215, 216, 255, 257,
    263, 269, 297, 298, 301, 398, 405, 415, 425, 505,
    585, 591
chronic, 220, 255, 401

chronicle (chroniclers), 34, 124, 156, 203
chronology, 213, 565
chrysalid (chrysalis), 20, 250
church (church-door, churches, churchwarden,
    churchyard), 3, 15, 20, 47, 71, 76, 77, 124, 126,
    137, 183, 193, 240, 313, 315, 336, 364, 380, 390,
    391, 392, 395, 434, 436, 502, 503, 504, 517, 547,
    583
cigars, cigarettes, 540
Circe, 218
circle (circles), 83, 168, 179, 223, 305, 329, 356,
    448, 451, 561
circulate (circulates, circulation, circulations),
    231, 313, 378, 520
circumscribe (circumscribed), 250, 313, 503
circumspect (circumspection), 102, 133, 581
circumstance (circumstances, circumstantial), 3,
    11, 16, 28, 33, 51, 52, 53, 60, 61, 72, 73, 80, 82,
    96, 101, 104, 106, 108, 122, 132, 137, 145, 154,
    161, 170, 176, 180, 191, 208, 218, 232, 233, 237,
    238, 248, 256, 259, 262, 268, 286, 291, 309, 334,
    347, 355, 394, 417, 427, 436, 441, 452, 470, 478,
    479, 481, 509, 526, 531, 535, 543, 555, 573, 579,
    582, 587, 591
circumvent (circumvented, circumvention,
    circumventions), 15, 115, 438, 590
citizen (citizens, citizenship), 73, 128, 225, 234,
    282, 303, 448, 457, 467, 486
city (cities), 31, 54, 73, 74, 75, 76, 81, 123, 298,
    319, 413, 415, 417, 429, 459, 460, 471, 478, 507,
    538, 540, 544, 560, 569, 589, 594
civil (civilities, civility), 7, 35, 73, 156, 304, 347,
    374, 466, 485, 528, 586, 591
civilization (civilize, civilized), 57, 60, 70, 71, 72,
    73, 74, 75, 76, 79, 113, 130, 135, 149, 162, 163,
    247, 256, 265, 267, 274, 281, 313, 341, 361, 373,
    380, 415, 421, 432, 459, 462, 477, 529, 542, 561,
    580, 591
claim (claimed, claims), 10, 47, 184, 185, 211, 226,
    246, 266, 285, 324, 404, 405, 425, 437, 438, 464,
    467, 483, 499, 526, 539, 563, 581
clairvoyance, 548
clamor (clamoring), 434, 466, 522
clash, 150, 524
class (classed, classes), 76, 104, 123, 154, 158, 163,
    226, 256, 258, 263, 287, 290, 297, 299, 318, 379,
    383, 385, 386, 397, 405, 410, 418, 445, 461, 469,
    481, 517, 531, 541, 542, 576
classic (classical), 157, 324
clay (clayey), 18, 216, 257, 374
clean (cleaned, cleanliness), 51, 59, 76, 358, 373,
    439, 484, 536
clear (clarity, clearer, clearest, clearing, clearly,
    clearness, clears), 33, 76, 95, 97, 115, 141, 164,
    172, 174, 185, 186, 212, 279, 297, 341, 352, 360,
    415, 423, 439, 448, 449, 452, 456, 496, 530, 536,
    539, 548, 574, 602
clergy (clergyman, clergymen), 76, 77, 263, 292,
    390, 475, 476, 477, 478, 481, 521
clerk (clerical, clerks), 34, 113, 336, 597
clever (cleverer, cleverest, cleverness), 77, 80, 81,
    82, 100, 102, 112, 156, 164, 181, 209, 274, 282,
    296, 319, 348, 356, 358, 364, 372, 374, 445, 518,
    536, 551, 598
client, 6, 446
climate (climates), 288, 509, 545, 573
climax, 77, 230, 383, 515

climb (climbed, climbing, climbs), 274, 280, 324, 368, 575

cling (clings), 185, 268, 321, 516, 528, 533, 545

cloak (cloaks), 204, 218, 227, 266, 267, 392, 462, 466, 504, 534, 538, 539

clock (clockwork), 63, 82, 258, 488

cloister (cloisters), 158, 274

close (closed, closeness, closing), 134, 139, 149, 213, 215, 221, 268, 282, 284, 316, 403, 407, 408, 454, 455, 478, 480, 496, 531, 541, 548, 555

closet (closets), 15, 321, 386, 497, 518

clothes (cloth, clothe, clothed, clothing), 3, 24, 157, 160, 221, 261, 269, 376, 396, 409, 413, 435, 436, 439, 453, 470, 471, 599, 602

cloud (clouded, cloud-pictures, clouds, cloudy), 4, 44, 135, 137, 213, 225, 239, 280, 291, 370, 431, 463, 548

clown, 91, 130, 224

cloys, 469

club, 147, 365, 451, 519

clue, 318, 353

clutches (clutching), 309, 545

coach (coaches, coachman), 28, 108, 316, 384, 542, 553, 592

coal (coals), 143, 187, 416, 446, 448

coarse (coarsely, coarse-minded, coarser), 90, 191, 200, 352, 356, 385, 449, 453, 465, 598, 599, 603

coast (coasts), 90, 166, 244, 439

coat (coats), 34, 164, 284, 489, 543, 599

cock (cock-fight), 109, 311

code (codes), 71, 270, 313, 514

co-existence, 218, 427

coffin, 18, 90, 126, 159, 595

cogitation (*see also* thought), 278

Cognac, 577

cohesion, 78, 152, 204, 467

coin (coinage, coined, coiner), 3, 23, 175, 211, 212, 241, 332, 378, 425, 480, 500, 505, 597

coincidence (coincide, coincidences, coincides), 13, 58, 137, 274, 313

cold (coldest, coldness), 5, 17, 18, 51, 59, 83, 142, 145, 148, 153, 165, 200, 203, 206, 219, 242, 243, 281, 293, 298, 316, 345, 390, 391, 413, 429, 446, 451, 467, 470, 476, 477, 481, 482, 496, 512, 538, 539, 543, 601

cold blood (cold-blooded), 21, 154, 543

cold-hearted (coldest-hearted), 410

cold-looking, 108

cold-water, 316

collar (collared), 154, 270

collateral, 501, 532

collect (collected, collecting, collection, collector), 27, 34, 56, 156, 248, 268, 370, 468, 490, 516

collective (collectively), 184, 215, 476

college (colleges), 129, 155, 156, 158, 159, 283

collision (collisions), 94, 481, 524, 541

colony (colonies, colonization), 77, 418, 603

color (colored, coloring, colors), 7, 11, 18, 30, 35, 43, 86, 90, 97, 133, 148, 153, 213, 221, 255, 269, 271, 289, 322, 328, 373, 417, 453, 468, 479, 507, 536, 563, 565, 572, 594

colorless, 397

colossal, 186, 261, 427, 541

column (columns), 159, 473

Comanches, 517

combat (combatant, combated, combating, combats), 36, 57, 169, 185, 192, 322, 399, 497,

534, 560, 574

combination (combinations, combine, combined, combines), 18, 51, 199, 218, 236, 256, 287, 312, 363, 408, 471, 472, 479, 513, 533, 558, 582, 602

come (came, comer, comers, comes, cometh, coming), 17, 32, 37, 42, 47, 49, 51, 62, 63, 74, 82, 106, 108, 127, 198, 213, 219, 221, 225, 233, 240, 244, 245, 248, 264, 268, 269, 272, 274, 275, 276, 286, 289, 294, 295, 299, 314, 316, 320, 323, 327, 332, 339, 349, 350, 361, 371, 385, 402, 404, 405, 408, 409, 411, 412, 413, 414, 416, 418, 419, 434, 437, 443, 444, 445, 446, 449, 457, 462, 465, 466, 468, 475, 476, 477, 478, 479, 482, 488, 492, 500, 501, 504, 507, 514, 520, 527, 529, 530, 531, 532, 536, 540, 545, 546, 547, 550, 555, 557, 561, 568, 578, 583, 585, 600, 602, 603

comedy (comedies: *see also* comic), 70, 124, 138, 142, 389, 394, 561

comely (comeliest, comeliness: *see also* beauty), 16, 38, 43

comet (comets), 494, 545

comfort (comfortable, comfortably, comforted, comforter, comfortless, comforts), 5, 54, 55, 73, 77, 85, 91, 96, 97, 100, 123, 146, 150, 171, 216, 219, 221, 223, 235, 237, 250, 254, 266, 273, 284, 297, 305, 370, 376, 382, 393, 427, 445, 492, 493, 505, 507, 531, 559, 564, 566

comic (comic Muse, comical), 16, 94, 153, 192, 568, 597, 598

comma, 183

command (commanded, commandment, commands), 67, 77, 87, 140, 173, 207, 248, 260, 275, 276, 280, 298, 369, 381, 390, 392, 414, 422, 426, 436, 437, 447, 449, 455, 493, 499, 520, 528, 538, 547, 581, 587

commemoration, 403

commence (commencement, commences), 44, 126, 157, 586

commendation (commend, commendable, commended, commending), 14, 71, 89, 223, 363, 376, 418, 442

comment (commentary, commentator), 113, 173, 399

commerce (commercial), 66, 77, 78, 390, 446, 530, 590

commiseration, 9, 145, 578

commit (commission, commissioned, commissioners, commitment, commits, committed, committing), 25, 50, 78, 96, 97, 102, 112, 113, 164, 177, 196, 218, 220, 221, 242, 259, 261, 272, 280, 284, 296, 297, 319, 349, 357, 395, 403, 415, 420, 439, 451, 464, 470, 492, 494, 507, 509, 513, 554, 564, 580, 583, 594

committee, 349

commodity, 6, 457, 599

common (commoner, commonest, commonly), 10, 79, 80, 85, 102, 103, 105, 125, 142, 143, 148, 149, 157, 159, 160, 161, 163, 172, 175, 180, 189, 201, 204, 209, 210, 223, 227, 229, 230, 233, 238, 240, 241, 248, 250, 251, 254, 262, 263, 271, 274, 290, 294, 297, 301, 302, 306, 307, 317, 319, 320, 343, 352, 356, 359, 367, 371, 376, 383, 384, 388, 394, 399, 408, 415, 424, 440, 441, 446, 451, 452, 454, 459, 463, 475, 477, 497, 500, 515, 516, 518, 522, 533, 534, 538, 544, 551, 552, 554, 584, 587, 589, 592, 597, 602

commonality (commonalty), 79, 230

KEYWORD INDEX

confess (confessed, confessing, confession, confessional, confessions), 93, 167, 168, 193, 196, 304,
361, 399, 479, 502, 506, 510, 561, 576, 585, 592
confidant (confidantes, confidants), 91, 550
confide (confided, confidence, confidences,
confident, confidential, confidentiality,
confiding, confidingly), 12, 18, 25, 89, 91, 93, 94,
115, 139, 147, 160, 162, 164, 205, 208, 222, 235,
242, 253, 259, 264, 278, 285, 350, 353, 357, 476,
497, 521, 526, 584, 590
confine (confined, confinement, confines), 15, 149,
183, 208, 209, 311, 339, 347, 358, 365, 408, 409,
451, 544, 548, 573, 574
confirm (confirmed, confirming, confirms), 164,
206, 273, 437, 479
conflict (conflicts), 65, 93, 94, 107, 163, 177, 356,
420, 499, 552, 590
conform (conformity, conforms), 16, 103, 209, 287,
332, 388
confound (confounded, confounding, confounds),
58, 178, 181, 189, 223, 231, 284, 314, 367, 383,
450, 513, 523
confuse (confusing, confusion), 151, 312, 332, 357,
427, 443, 448, 449, 482, 524, 548, 567
congees, 250
congenial, 18, 26, 79, 104, 202, 204
congenital, 320
congregation, 362, 475
congress/Congress (congressional, congressmen),
312, 466, 468
congruity, 235
conjecture (conjectures), 94, 275, 305, 424, 498, 568
conjugal, 373, 376, 380, 387
conjunction, 337, 474, 602
conjure (conjuration, conjurer), 15, 289, 343, 394,
602
connect (connected, connecting, connection,
connections), 35, 56, 69, 187, 202, 256, 307, 325,
348, 349, 407, 467, 470, 489, 491, 497, 504, 552
connubiality, 282
conquer (conquered, conquering, conqueror/
Conqueror, conquerors, conquers, conquest), 3,
18, 35, 94, 98, 104, 137, 142, 154, 183, 204, 206,
221, 259, 263, 282, 296, 320, 344, 363, 369, 383,
395, 404, 429, 483, 507, 523, 527, 535, 560, 581,
584, 591, 595
consanguinity, 149
conscience (consciences), 55, 59, 94, 95, 96, 97, 98,
100, 118, 149, 151, 154, 171, 179, 181, 185, 197,
226, 297, 303, 315, 329, 333, 338, 339, 361, 371,
414, 489, 493, 502, 503, 505, 517, 519
conscientious (conscientiously, conscientiousness),
16, 98, 179, 401
conscious (consciously, consciousness), 7, 33, 54,
84, 95, 97, 120, 122, 125, 132, 147, 150, 153, 182,
209, 210, 231, 232, 233, 267, 285, 291, 298, 331,
352, 353, 358, 359, 385, 389, 405, 407, 409, 437,
440, 442, 447, 457, 463, 467, 478, 479, 480, 498,
499, 508, 511, 519, 523, 525, 529, 562, 563, 565,
568, 577, 587, 596
consecrate (consecrated, consecrates, consecration), 98, 169, 284, 535
consent (consented), 19, 33, 38, 204, 223, 317, 354,
378, 397, 437, 443, 476, 535, 552
consequence (consequences, consequently), 3, 17,
29, 40, 54, 56, 58, 61, 91, 93, 98, 99, 100, 104, 110,
114, 116, 158, 182, 203, 272, 282, 304, 305, 309,
315, 354, 359, 362, 372, 375, 378, 415, 419, 454,

457, 466, 471, 477, 482, 485, 513, 537, 552, 596,
601
consequentementally, 601
conservatism, 100
conservative (conservatives), 226, 361
consider (considerable, considerate, consideration,
considerations, considered, considering,
considers), 10, 93, 117, 129, 153, 163, 203, 218,
220, 236, 248, 256, 257, 265, 267, 270, 277, 278,
280, 296, 301, 311, 312, 340, 344, 346, 347, 354,
358, 360, 366, 367, 370, 371, 374, 375, 376, 379,
380, 384, 385, 386, 389, 392, 398, 411, 417, 422,
438, 462, 467, 468, 473, 479, 497, 503, 507, 508,
509, 510, 514, 526, 542, 544, 562, 564, 579, 581,
587, 599 601
consist (consisted, consisteth, consists), 200, 223,
232, 239, 253, 254, 284, 322, 385, 388, 436, 475,
491, 534, 565, 587, 588, 597, 600
consistent (consistency, consistently), 22, 100, 193,
218, 263, 278, 304, 315, 417, 418, 426, 597
console (consolation, consoled, consoler, consoles,
consoling), 6, 8, 10, 86, 89, 100, 101, 112, 135, 182,
229, 254, 270, 305, 312, 324, 346, 373, 375, 408,
456, 527, 538, 557, 566
conspicuous (conspicuously), 83, 335, 383, 478
conspire (conspiracy), 91, 263, 280, 365, 476, 591
constancy, 7, 27, 193, 332, 370, 380, 408
constant (constantly), 45, 64, 210, 212, 249, 254,
297, 321, 340, 342, 432, 436, 452, 459, 481, 498,
502, 525, 531, 540, 541, 583
constellation (constellations), 62, 549
consternation, 73
constituent (constituents), 35, 466
constitute (constituted, constitutes, constituting),
86, 96, 122, 141, 145, 226, 227, 256, 261, 297, 350,
411, 441, 443, 546, 585, 587
constitution/Constitution (constitutional,
constitutions), 226, 241, 270, 280, 303, 320, 331,
367, 403, 418, 498, 544, 589
constrain (constrained, constraint), 39, 161, 224,
347
construct (constructed, construction, constructions, constructive), 26, 97, 138, 173, 284, 299,
317, 320, 513, 545
construe (construed), 227, 289
consul, 404
consult (consulted, consulting, consults), 98, 155,
160, 264, 312, 396, 466, 467, 566, 568
consume (consumed, consumes, consuming,
consumption), 21, 90, 94, 154, 155, 183, 271, 319,
345, 532, 562, 565, 566
consummate (consummated, consummately,
consummation), 30, 126, 149, 373, 412, 455, 597
contact, 54, 74, 127, 204, 356, 501
contagion (contagious), 59, 162, 188, 409, 412, 418,
501, 543
contain (containing, contains), 160, 241, 247, 399,
489, 490, 500, 541, 576, 579
contaminating, 74
contemplate (contemplating, contemplation,
contemplations, contemplative), 83, 122, 126,
143, 176, 182, 238, 307, 314, 319, 360, 382, 407,
478, 518, 522, 540, 562, 564, 565
contempt (contemptible, contemptibly), 4, 6, 11,
25, 41, 49, 53, 84, 101, 122, 133, 145, 156, 170,
182, 227, 303, 322, 350, 351, 354, 357, 363, 393,
408, 458, 459, 480, 481, 503, 525, 527, 528, 558,
583, 597, 599, 602

contend (contended, contending, contention),
11, 28, 94, 164, 221, 361, 435, 468
content (contented, contentedness, contentment),
15, 32, 40, 78, 91, 101, 133, 148, 149, 167, 202,
210, 236, 237, 247, 248, 258, 306, 319, 332, 334,
354, 368, 442, 457, 459, 461, 464, 469, 490, 494,
496, 498, 505, 509, 528, 536, 570, 578, 582, 592,
598
contents, 24, 310, 423
contest, 27, 101, 519
context, 502
contiguity, 80
continents, 567
contingency, 62, 456
continue (continual, continually, continuance,
continuation, continued, continues, continueth,
continuous), 88, 101, 104, 140, 151, 188, 239, 244,
265, 284, 301, 320, 354, 355, 360, 361, 373, 385,
399, 461, 463, 498, 500, 505, 507, 524, 577, 583,
592, 600, 604
contortions, 336
contract (contracted, contracts), 79, 101, 110, 117,
327, 354, 385, 498, 544, 579
contraction, 302, 559
contradict (contradiction, contradictory), 24, 66,
69, 101, 102, 206, 263, 298, 353, 363, 379, 382,
439, 441, 469, 479, 503, 591, 602
contrary (contraries, contrarieties, contrariety,
contrarily, contrariness), 58, 69, 83, 84, 94, 103,
174, 223, 228, 278, 293, 331, 336, 353, 374, 386,
430, 461, 464, 465, 483, 514, 528, 554, 558, 562,
591
contrast (contrasts), 17, 18, 44, 81, 82, 83, 84, 85,
86, 87, 88, 94, 259, 262, 265, 466, 496
contribute (contributed, contributes), 141, 235,
407, 489, 494
contrition, 8, 507
contrive (contrivance, contrivances, contrived,
contriver, contriving), 58, 77, 263, 282, 365, 411,
429, 461, 471, 485, 504, 511, 585
control (controlled/controled, controlling,
controls), 5, 35, 66, 72, 102, 139, 250, 309, 331,
342, 364, 391, 430, 447, 466, 473, 479, 482, 523,
564
controversies, 207
contumacy, 542
convenient (conveniences, conveniency, con-
veniently), 15, 16, 26, 46, 102, 126, 137, 157, 179,
213, 273, 308, 321, 370, 384, 385, 393, 452, 478,
509
convent, 91
convention (conventional, conventionalities,
conventionality, conventions), 22, 30, 73, 97, 103,
145, 242, 256, 270, 310, 373
converse (conversable, conversant, conversation,
conversational), 28, 62, 80, 103, 104, 122, 170,
172, 175, 182, 188, 196, 266, 303, 365, 367, 399,
465, 486, 495, 536, 539, 543, 548, 557, 569, 579,
594, 599
convert (converted, convertible, converting,
converts), 70, 201, 305, 338, 342, 352, 378, 416,
417, 419
convey (conveyed, conveying, conveys), 96, 113,
149, 172, 179, 190, 238, 282, 290, 293, 305, 378,
461, 477, 523
convict (convicted, conviction, convictions), 16, 36,
51, 102, 104, 111, 112, 136, 138, 164, 169, 228,

298, 350, 360, 376, 402, 405, 466, 495, 502, 518,
544
convince (convinced, convincing), 28, 53, 77, 213,
215, 228, 238, 244, 349, 378, 405, 441, 462, 477,
487, 488, 561
convivial (conviviality), 150, 152, 203
coo (cooing), 47, 357
cook (cookery, cookery-book, cooks), 23, 27, 100,
108, 142, 143, 343, 368, 388, 488
cool (cooler, cooling, coolness), 84, 105, 206, 207,
308, 327, 329, 336, 386, 401, 421, 434, 447, 485,
507
co-operate (co-operation), 54, 421
co-ordinate (co-ordinates), 93, 449
cope, 348, 513
copestone, 229, 449, 603
Coptic, 155
copy (copies), 166, 299, 323, 390, 399
coquet (coquetry, coquette), 104, 335, 371, 422, 536
cord (cords), 7, 359, 383, 506
cordial (cordiality, cordially), 108, 163, 255, 299,
350, 438, 458
core, 134, 304, 583
cork (corks, corkscrew), 151, 152, 355
corn (cornfields), 51, 58, 91, 274, 406, 443, 564
corner (corners, cornerstone), 173, 210, 242, 268,
289, 298, 300, 449, 544
coronation, 42
coroner, 401
coronet, 382
corporal (corporeal), 344, 407, 492, 546, 554, 580
corpse (corpses), 19, 118, 120, 124, 400, 446, 552
corpulent, 497
correct (correcting, correction, corrections,
correctness, corrector, correctors, corrects), 35,
65, 105, 173, 196, 206, 225, 233, 320, 353, 355,
434, 440, 484, 509, 518, 525, 561, 584, 589, 597
correspondence (corresponding), 154, 356, 427,
487, 552, 555, 581, 586
corrupt (corrupted, corrupter, corruptible,
corrupting, corruption, corruptions, corrupts),
74, 76, 104, 105, 106, 180, 215, 251, 255, 256, 263,
310, 322, 430, 469, 472, 479, 505, 541, 587
coruscations, 600
cosmopolitan, 398
cosmos, 148
cost (costly, costs), 38, 99, 150, 244, 398, 463, 487,
599
costume, 319
cottage (cottages), 284, 470, 545
cough (coughing, coughs), 182
council (see also counsel), 6
counsel (counselor, counsels), 5, 6, 110, 121, 245,
281, 314, 374, 382, 412, 434, 449, 543, 567, 585,
597
count (counted, counting, countless, counts), 36,
97, 117, 180, 183, 205, 216, 298, 300, 327, 343,
351, 401, 440, 454, 472, 500, 523, 536, 555,
591
countenance (countenanced, countenances,
countenancing), 24, 25, 26, 27, 55, 77, 91, 93, 106,
119, 133, 136, 147, 203, 205, 230, 252, 285, 295,
390, 393, 417, 427, 428, 512, 533, 550, 568, 573,
582
counter (counteracted, counteracting, counteracts), 133, 157, 304, 512
counterbalanced, 225

counterfeit (counterfeited, counterfeits), 3, 14, 23, 78, 105, 324, 527
counter-irritant, 116
counterpart (counterpoint), 81, 82, 83, 84, 85, 86, 87, 88
countervail, 492
country (countries), 15, 25, 73, 74, 76, 83, 86, 95, 119, 154, 164, 166, 176, 193, 201, 208, 239, 242, 270, 289, 300, 306, 311, 313, 314, 315, 316, 317, 323, 337, 344, 360, 389, 390, 398, 406, 408, 409, 418, 423, 426, 440, 449, 450, 451, 455, 460, 462, 466, 469, 471, 477, 478, 479, 514, 517, 520, 540, 562, 569, 570, 591, 592
country-dance, 375
countrymen, 451
couple (coupled, couples), 87, 136, 288, 330, 384, 385, 412, 481, 553
couplet, 463
courage (courageous), 16, 29, 51, 59, 86, 99, 105, 106, 107, 108, 109, 110, 133, 135, 169, 188, 189, 190, 233, 245, 247, 273, 280, 322, 325, 341, 344, 358, 363, 367, 368, 372, 413, 422, 433, 450, 526, 553, 572, 573, 575, 590, 592, 600
courier, 193
course (courses), 53, 61, 98, 125, 156, 159, 166, 203, 206, 209, 212, 213, 249, 255, 258, 270, 314, 319, 328, 329, 340, 341, 350, 361, 377, 379, 399, 417, 419, 420, 430, 433, 467, 473, 497, 499, 587, 595
court (courted, courting, courts), 15, 108, 109, 119, 151, 225, 258, 285, 287, 298, 308, 309, 310, 313, 335, 355, 466, 524, 538, 590, 600
court-chamberlain, 250
court circular, 2, 175
Court of Chancery, 309
courtesy (courteous, courteously, courtesies), 91, 108, 134, 142, 205, 329, 349, 526
courtier (courtiers), 108, 500
courtly, 106
courtship, 108, 109, 385, 388, 390, 393
cousin (cousins), 23, 184, 194, 335, 393
covenants, 205
cover (covered, covering, covers), 124, 217, 227, 266, 274, 323, 367, 444, 509, 524, 538, 539, 556, 602
covert, 287, 570
covet (coveted, coveteth, coveting, covetous, covetously, covetousness, covets), 109, 158, 207, 261, 280, 408, 467, 473, 503, 567, 601
coward (cowardice, cowardly, cowards), 19, 87, 96, 98, 106, 107, 108, 109, 110, 134, 163, 188, 190, 219, 244, 246, 310, 358, 362, 365, 405, 433, 448, 479, 481, 521, 570, 584, 586
coxcomb (coxcombry), 110, 116, 268
coy (coyness), 110
cozen (cozened), 197, 465
cradle (cradles), 39, 59, 69, 99, 125, 134, 135, 235, 388
craft (craftiness, craftsman, crafty), 42, 110, 177, 188, 197, 464, 596, 604
crammed (cramming), 191, 418
crater, 482, 561
craving (cravings), 90, 124, 269, 330, 336, 337, 484
crazy, 534, 542
create (created, creates, creating, creation/Creation, creations: *see also* creative *and* creator/Creator), 22, 24, 30, 35, 38, 110, 111, 117, 138, 159, 182, 185, 196, 203, 215, 216, 222, 224,

229, 256, 258, 278, 280, 302, 309, 310, 311, 324, 340, 342, 347, 358, 360, 365, 366, 380, 388, 390, 412, 432, 437, 439, 452, 475, 479, 524, 529, 538, 541, 545, 566, 593, 604
creative (creativity), 110, 111, 324, 474
creator/Creator, 214, 226, 253, 336, 432, 434, 567, 572
creature (creatures), 1, 2, 18, 69, 81, 84, 89, 108, 109, 110, 111, 112, 115, 117, 123, 129, 135, 136, 137, 138, 148, 149, 169, 185, 186, 188, 190, 196, 197, 213, 216, 219, 220, 234, 237, 238, 253, 256, 258, 261, 262, 280, 303, 311, 315, 330, 332, 339, 344, 347, 349, 351, 353, 357, 358, 359, 360, 363, 367, 392, 394, 401, 411, 413, 430, 438, 439, 440, 441, 478, 491, 499, 500, 516, 522, 531, 545, 549, 564, 572, 584, 587
credible (*see also* credulous), 111, 455, 457, 463
credit (creditor, credits), 25, 89, 110, 111, 142, 179, 184, 203, 211, 222, 233, 238, 251, 262, 280, 334, 350, 357, 358, 360, 416, 474, 476, 496, 508, 598
credit cards, 111
credulity, 16, 111, 112, 178, 344, 359, 423
credulous (*see also* credible), 57, 111, 328, 360, 476
creed (creeds: *see also* belief), 45, 46, 64, 97, 163, 235, 359, 408, 410, 467, 470, 505, 557, 599
creep (creeps, crept), 110, 165, 339, 351, 391, 490, 548
crew, 12, 265, 542
cricket (cricketer, cricketers), 12, 467
crime (crimes, criminal, criminality, criminals), 5, 14, 36, 51, 54, 96, 112, 113, 129, 151, 167, 188, 195, 199, 218, 219, 226, 227, 232, 239, 245, 254, 259, 260, 267, 273, 292, 294, 298, 308, 311, 312, 329, 341, 381, 388, 397, 420, 421, 437, 441, 442, 456, 457, 458, 469, 479, 491, 492, 505, 507, 528, 541, 546, 556, 580, 583, 584, 585, 591, 592
cringe (cringed, cringes), 110, 250, 280
cripple (crippled, cripples), 184, 219, 478
crisis, 10, 49, 388, 433
criterion, 181
critic (critical, criticism, criticize, criticized, critics), 35, 71, 113, 114, 154, 192, 267, 317, 352, 382, 452, 510, 530, 557, 558, 559
croak (croaked), 467
crocodile, 570
crop, 54, 343, 593
cross/Cross (crossed, crosses, crossing), 75, 136, 264, 289, 307, 319, 326, 439, 458, 540, 568
crossbreed, 100
cross-lights, 404
cross-purposes, 220, 320
crowd (crowded, crowding, crowds), 29, 75, 111, 125, 177, 274, 284, 307, 423, 477, 542, 543, 544, 564
crown (crowned, crowns), 5, 9, 43, 82, 99, 297, 328, 336, 395, 446, 488, 545, 586, 596
crucible, 519
crucified, 408, 505
cruel (cruelest, cruelly, cruelties, cruelty), 4, 15, 51, 66, 69, 75, 94, 109, 112, 114, 120, 139, 199, 204, 219, 225, 246, 260, 302, 303, 317, 333, 345, 363, 364, 370, 373, 378, 388, 395, 429, 447, 454, 455, 492, 497, 512, 523, 528, 537, 562, 574, 585, 586, 589, 599
Crusades (Crusaders), 54, 383, 494
crush (crushed, crushing), 114, 139, 164, 203, 220, 226, 274, 447, 454, 538

Crusoe's Island, 484
cry (cried, cries, crying), 47, 53, 69, 120, 160, 166,
    174, 200, 217, 249, 264, 265, 266, 270, 282, 306,
    336, 345, 356, 391, 421, 425, 431, 440, 449, 467,
    469, 484, 517, 530, 559, 563, 570
crystal (crystallized), 18, 240, 449
culpable, 1, 55, 161, 232, 295
culprit, 533
cultivate (cultivated, cultivating, cultivation),
    16, 26, 40, 67, 158, 169, 172, 225, 235, 344, 406,
    455, 470, 497, 510, 517, 546, 570, 589
culture (cultured), 76, 114, 182, 345, 352, 368, 402,
    419, 560
cunning (cunninger, cunningly), 61, 67, 84, 99,
    114, 115, 130, 147, 270, 286, 310, 313, 337, 356,
    357, 364, 430, 469, 475, 536, 538, 546, 560
cup (cups), 151, 152, 153, 170, 236, 255, 352, 429,
    431, 602
Cupid (cupidons), 328, 335, 336, 341, 342, 379
cure (cured, cures, cureth, curing), 52, 95, 133,
    240, 269, 281, 286, 291, 306, 329, 334, 389, 400,
    402, 437, 446, 450, 463, 506, 526, 542, 548, 557,
    562, 565, 569, 585
curfew, 322
curious (curiosity, curiouser), 78, 93, 115, 116, 154,
    218, 224, 238, 254, 284, 286, 289, 306, 317, 318,
    334, 336, 368, 387, 388, 397, 401, 407, 429, 500,
    502, 526, 564
currency, 155, 603
current, 139, 186, 206, 212, 316, 319, 480
curse (cursed, curses, cursing), 116, 117, 133, 158,
    215, 216, 274, 364, 372, 386, 415, 454, 489
curtain, 124, 135, 373, 488, 565, 567, 592
custom (customs), 5, 29, 61, 63, 74, 94, 103, 104,
    163, 185, 193, 194, 219, 261, 328, 347, 441, 497,
    498, 534, 547, 578, 582, 591, 593, 599
customary, 384, 476
customers, 78, 536
cut (cuts, cutteth), 100, 257, 260, 265, 271, 313, 357,
    361, 463, 504, 506, 517, 525, 531, 543, 544
cycle (cycles, cyclical), 247, 407
cynic (cynical, cynicism, cynics), 116, 174, 341,
    456, 530
cyphered, 405
Czar of Russia, 312

dabble, 519
daft, 286
dagger, 518
daily bread, 266
dainty, 86, 133, 274, 352
dam, 185, 339, 555
Dame Nature, 328, 430
damn (damnation, damnatory, damned,
    damnedest, damning), 135, 199, 214, 215, 236,
    338, 339, 352, 354, 475, 492, 503
damn-my-eyes, 299
damp (damper), 90, 291, 316
dance (dancers, dances, dancing), 104, 116, 175,
    250, 312, 320, 326, 375, 420, 423, 443, 457, 538,
    540, 563, 578
dandy (dandiacal, dandyism), 44, 110, 116
danger (dangerous, dangers), 6, 9, 13, 21, 48, 52,
    59, 60, 62, 90, 99, 105, 106, 107, 108, 109, 110,
    111, 112, 113, 114, 115, 116, 117, 126, 142, 151,
    153, 187, 188, 189, 196, 199, 202, 203, 206, 228,

239, 240, 247, 251, 254, 265, 267, 273, 276, 277,
    280, 288, 303, 310, 311, 337, 339, 344, 348, 366,
    374, 376, 377, 381, 384, 388, 398, 407, 409, 414,
    421, 423, 432, 435, 436, 438, 442, 447, 448, 449,
    458, 461, 466, 473, 475, 481, 487, 491, 496, 501,
    511, 512, 517, 518, 520, 527, 553, 555, 565, 575,
    576, 586, 587, 588, 599, 600
dare (dared, daring, daringness), 29, 110, 117, 126,
    162, 213, 224, 249, 307, 348, 360, 362, 427, 588,
    595, 597
daredevil, 71
dark (darken, darker, darkest, darkling, darkly,
    darkness), 3, 17, 18, 20, 44, 51, 58, 59, 71, 87, 88,
    90, 106, 112, 120, 138, 146, 187, 188, 211, 215,
    217, 219, 230, 232, 242, 248, 254, 256, 259, 260,
    271, 273, 291, 303, 306, 321, 322, 362, 403, 409,
    434, 444, 447, 452, 454, 474, 479, 487, 488, 505,
    518, 527, 543, 545, 546, 555, 559, 570, 576, 590
dastard, 188
date, 5, 123, 129, 355, 358, 399, 403, 417, 484
daughter (daughters), 8, 11, 23, 39, 46, 103, 118,
    182, 184, 185, 199, 323, 332, 345, 368, 374, 376,
    377, 379, 381, 386, 390, 391, 393, 535, 543, 589
David, 417, 550
dawg (see also dog), 185
dawn (dawned), 87, 106, 157, 340, 452, 464, 546
day (daily, days), 1, 2, 3, 5, 10, 11, 17, 23, 31, 44,
    49, 59, 63, 71, 74, 79, 84, 85, 87, 95, 97, 102, 104,
    118, 120, 121, 126, 139, 141, 142, 143, 148, 149,
    154, 164, 167, 174, 178, 183, 192, 196, 197, 201,
    203, 211, 214, 221, 230, 236, 238, 243, 246, 247,
    248, 249, 250, 255, 256, 258, 267, 268, 281, 288,
    292, 293, 305, 306, 309, 316, 317, 318, 319, 321,
    332, 334, 356, 376, 377, 384, 386, 388, 389, 393,
    396, 399, 403, 404, 418, 421, 428, 429, 430, 431,
    434, 445, 454, 460, 461, 463, 466, 468, 470, 471,
    486, 490, 493, 498, 504, 515, 516, 520, 522, 539,
    545, 546, 547, 551, 554, 558, 567, 568, 577, 582,
    604
Day of Judgment, 293
daydream, 149, 150, 236
daylight, 87, 431, 467
dazzle (dazzling), 171, 499, 577
deaf (deaf mute, deafness), 35, 71, 190, 311
deal (dealer, dealing, dealings, deals), 86, 139, 251,
    294, 477, 485, 486, 492, 511, 518, 525, 583
dear (dearer, dearest), 57, 170, 195, 206, 242, 258,
    299, 300, 341, 431, 480, 575, 579, 588, 597, 600
death (dead, deadly, deaths, die, died, dies, dying),
    3, 4, 7, 9, 11, 12, 13, 14, 18, 19, 29, 32, 43, 46, 49,
    52, 53, 55, 61, 62, 66, 69, 70, 71, 73, 75, 83, 87,
    91, 95, 96, 97, 99, 100, 101, 105, 106, 107, 109,
    113, 117, 118, 119, 120, 121, 122, 123, 124, 125,
    126, 127, 131, 133, 135, 136, 139, 140, 147, 149,
    152, 153, 156, 157, 159, 161, 162, 164, 165, 166,
    175, 176, 178, 179, 181, 185, 187, 189, 190, 209,
    214, 215, 216, 218, 219, 220, 223, 226, 228, 229,
    232, 237, 242, 243, 246, 249, 251, 253, 254, 259,
    266, 268, 270, 274, 281, 283, 286, 289, 291, 295,
    305, 306, 307, 313, 316, 317, 319, 320, 321, 322,
    323, 329, 333, 334, 337, 339, 340, 343, 345, 351,
    355, 356, 358, 359, 374, 376, 378, 385, 386, 389,
    390, 394, 400, 401, 404, 414, 415, 419, 420, 421,
    425, 426, 429, 430, 431, 435, 445, 446, 448, 449,
    451, 454, 457, 458, 460, 466, 468, 470, 471, 472,
    478, 481, 486, 492, 502, 507, 512, 516, 517, 524,
    528, 529, 530, 532, 539, 542, 543, 546, 547, 548,

648 KEYWORD INDEX

dialect, 233, 546, 602
dialogue, 35, 255, 561
dialstone, 568
diamond (diamonds), 67, 355, 395, 440, 594
diary, 97, 133, 316
dice (dice-box), 53, 135, 207
dictate, 54, 57, 95, 226, 371, 383, 429, 498, 524
dictator (dictators), 371, 504
diction, 475
dictionary (dictionaries), 33, 35, 601
diet, 71, 157, 190, 408, 413
difference (differ, different, differently, differing, differs), 57, 73, 84, 85, 86, 87, 89, 98, 107, 123, 125, 140, 141, 142, 160, 164, 170, 172, 173, 175, 180, 182, 204, 209, 211, 218, 233, 236, 242, 244, 245, 250, 252, 253, 256, 258, 263, 264, 268, 269, 270, 284, 294, 307, 311, 312, 313, 314, 318, 321, 327, 339, 340, 343, 344, 345, 347, 352, 355, 360, 367, 371, 375, 376, 390, 393, 394, 395, 400, 407, 415, 417, 419, 420, 426, 427, 440, 441, 446, 448, 463, 464, 465, 466, 471, 481, 486, 496, 502, 504, 505, 508, 515, 532, 534, 535, 541, 547, 551, 554, 568, 572, 573, 581, 582, 590, 592, 593, 598, 603
difficulty (difficult, difficulties), 5, 6, 28, 29, 32, 51, 53, 72, 78, 79, 125, 129, 133, 140, 141, 178, 179, 182, 188, 202, 217, 222, 224, 228, 237, 247, 249, 252, 259, 274, 276, 277, 303, 306, 307, 330, 331, 341, 345, 371, 392, 408, 416, 418, 441, 453, 457, 463, 466, 482, 488, 489, 491, 499, 504, 507, 514, 527, 530, 531, 535, 552, 571, 575, 593, 601
diffidence, 149, 507
diffuse (diffused, diffusive), 140, 146, 289, 299, 300, 435
dig (digging), 306, 317, 416, 502, 597, 599
digestion (digest, digested, digester, digestion, digestive), 7, 8, 143, 176, 195, 314, 401, 457, 460, 496, 510, 563
dignify (dignified), 66, 142, 151, 169, 174, 175, 393, 554
dignity, 5, 37, 83, 92, 141, 142, 151, 199, 220, 225, 338, 393, 409, 445, 587
digression, 142
dilapidation, 85, 174
dilate, 166
dilemma, 137
diligence (diligent), 33, 66, 297, 305
dim (dimly, dimness), 11, 203, 273, 275, 457, 499, 511, 548, 563, 602
dimension (dimensions), 37, 227, 449, 568
diminish (diminishing), 189, 280, 336, 338
diminutive, 598
dimples, 197, 546
dine (dining: see also dinner), 142, 143, 246, 376, 539, 550
dinner (see also dine), 23, 26, 27, 33, 143, 222, 250, 302, 315, 343, 368, 600
dinnerless, 143
diphtheria, 401
diplomacy (diplomatist), 65, 357
dipsomaniac, 152
dire (direful, direst), 85, 284, 547
direction (direct, directed, directs), 99, 115, 137, 143, 161, 175, 176, 201, 204, 218, 232, 238, 240, 253, 260, 276, 310, 313, 319, 325, 328, 339, 350, 360, 365, 404, 418, 427, 438, 439, 467, 477, 491, 498
director (directors), 176, 260, 446, 504
dirt (dirty), 57, 76, 211, 266, 514, 519

disadvantage (disadvantageous), 53, 72, 179, 262, 358, 388, 390, 427, 471, 495, 508, 555
disagreeableness (disagreeable), 14, 66, 115, 188, 202, 208, 224, 238, 245, 340, 377, 390, 412, 445, 467, 469, 521
disagreement (disagree), 307, 309, 383, 477
disappearance (disappear, disappears), 117, 133, 150, 460
disappointment (disappoint, disappointed, disappointing, disappointments), 111, 118, 125, 137, 143, 144, 171, 202, 206, 208, 226, 234, 239, 255, 257, 259, 281, 296, 300, 317, 330, 341, 387, 391, 397, 410, 411, 445, 450, 454, 456, 458, 485, 501, 555, 567, 569, 581, 597
disapprobation (disapproval, disapprove), 27, 356, 525, 538
disaster (disastrous), 57, 64, 124, 230, 264, 591
disbelief (disbelieve, disbeliever, disbelieves), 45, 93, 178, 331, 442
discard, 144, 177
discernment (discern, discerned, discerning, discerns), 121, 169, 197, 260, 296, 358, 369, 405, 457, 463, 464, 490, 536, 573, 575, 598
discharge (discharges), 191, 308, 313, 316, 400, 437, 442, 467, 559
disciple, 156
discipline, 344
disclaims, 479
disclosure (disclose, disclosures), 329, 521
discomfiture, 144
discomfort (discomforts), 18, 144, 386, 471
discomposure, 90
discontent (discontented), 2, 73, 78, 79, 101, 270, 446, 469, 523, 544
discord (discordance, discordant), 19, 94, 144, 149, 184, 204, 223, 282, 336
discount, 21
discouragement (discourage, discouraged), 196, 222, 242, 301, 313, 393, 412, 453
discourse (discourses), 152, 173, 174, 419, 476, 477, 490, 541
discoverer, 61, 370
discovery (discover, discoverable, discovered, discoveries), 29, 59, 66, 75, 141, 156, 174, 177, 188, 196, 201, 204, 208, 210, 217, 225, 232, 243, 293, 301, 302, 304, 326, 327, 328, 332, 353, 359, 361, 372, 373, 380, 386, 388, 446, 460, 462, 476, 479, 481, 490, 496, 499, 502, 517, 520, 521, 525, 542, 546, 559, 572, 595, 599, 603
discredit, 267
discrepancy, 423
discretion (discreet), 13, 144, 182, 231, 293, 308, 329, 339, 376, 447, 472, 521, 535, 599
discrimination (discriminate), 80, 100, 194, 272
discussion (discuss), 175, 234, 383, 393, 401, 432
disdain (disdainful, disdaining), 296, 436, 446, 481, 487, 513, 518, 544
disease (diseased, diseases), 50, 65, 75, 152, 209, 219, 229, 241, 242, 254, 274, 285, 286, 322, 331, 332, 337, 394, 400, 401, 402, 405, 407, 410, 418, 446, 549
disembarrassed, 533
disembodiment, 82, 148
disengage (disengaged, disengages), 375, 506, 533
disesteem, 222
disfavor, 66, 295, 479
disfigurement (disfigure), 291, 361, 542
disgrace (disgraced, disgraceful), 7, 25, 82, 89,

disgrace (*continued*)
114, 115, 144, 199, 219, 261, 344, 365, 366, 376, 380, 391, 412, 414, 421, 442, 469, 498, 529, 530

disguise (disguised, disguises), 7, 91, 141, 152, 156, 225, 252, 264, 290, 291, 303, 431, 473, 480, 482, 543

disgust (disgusting, disgusts), 26, 204, 264, 564, 582

dish, 276, 354, 384, 488, 579, 600

dishabille, 262

dishonesty (dishonest), 25, 250, 251, 252, 477, 523

dishonor (dishonorable, dishonored), 112, 175, 252, 253, 348, 405, 483, 591

disillusion, 273

disinclination, 375

disingenuous, 167

disinterestedness (disinterested), 93, 203, 256, 336, 427

dislike (disliked, dislikes, disliking), 22, 23, 101, 142, 144, 171, 241, 296, 323, 372, 378, 385, 497, 511, 513, 525, 540, 543, 558

dismal, 158, 275, 422, 522, 594

dismay, 106

dismissed, 448

disobedience (disobey, disobeyed, disobeying), 145, 298, 436, 437, 447, 499

disoblige (disobliged, disobliging), 89, 438

disorder (disordered), 48, 57, 78, 110, 112, 115, 174, 249, 258, 401, 408, 504

disparage, 415

disparity, 381, 384

dispassionateness (dispassionate), 82, 311

dispatch (despatch), 120, 127

dispel (dispelling), 273, 403, 570

dispensation (dispense, dispensed), 46, 73, 126, 173, 364, 426, 460, 487, 492, 510, 586

displacement, 333

display (displayed, displaying), 117, 190, 247, 423, 452, 591, 594

displeasure (displease, displeased), 27, 50, 60, 164, 237, 281, 375, 398, 524, 552

disposition (disposal, dispose, disposed, disposer, disposing, disposition, dispositions), 21, 39, 41, 60, 64, 67, 89, 102, 114, 122, 128, 139, 140, 143, 145, 169, 172, 187, 207, 216, 244, 283, 292, 294, 328, 340, 348, 349, 353, 355, 389, 450, 457, 469, 479, 497, 507, 518, 555, 556, 592, 593

dispraise, 323, 533

disproportion, 204, 335, 377

disprove, 590

disputation, (disputable, dispute, disputes), 27, 174, 203, 309, 319, 367, 400, 408, 490, 502, 527

disregard (disregarded), 179, 203, 269, 425, 592

disreputation, 572

disrespect, 147

dissatisfy (dissatisfied), 53, 179

dissect, 352

dissemble, 216, 225, 275, 335

dissension (dissent, dissenter), 45, 178, 190, 311, 390, 541

dissertation, 293

disseverment, 168

dissimulation, 127, 160, 390

dissipation (dissipate, dissipated), 88, 263, 346, 461, 593, 603

dissociate, 80

dissolution (dissolute, dissolve, dissolves), 199, 201, 458, 480, 548

dissonance (dissonant), 57, 403

dissuade, 28, 330

distaff, 367

distance (distanced, distances, distant), 34, 51, 73, 109, 121, 123, 193, 222, 243, 244, 269, 274, 318, 331, 340, 423, 449, 458, 471, 480, 496, 500, 526, 531, 542, 548, 573, 578

distaste, 479, 484

distemper (distempered), 110, 345, 400, 401, 408

distills, 567

distinction (distinct, distinctions, distinctive), 84, 87, 89, 145, 150, 151, 179, 215, 223, 268, 269, 283, 297, 325, 326, 340, 347, 360, 362, 367, 369, 379, 387, 389, 397, 405, 418, 419, 421, 424, 435, 453, 456, 484, 512, 519, 523, 530, 532, 550, 557, 582, 590, 596

distinguish (distinguishable, distinguished, distinguishing), 33, 156, 181, 183, 208, 213, 246, 259, 272, 275, 294, 328, 357, 366, 368, 376, 381, 389, 400, 407, 423, 427, 448, 450, 456, 457, 471, 496, 504, 505, 532, 534, 543, 588, 591

distortion (distort, distorted, distortions), 190, 425, 514, 570, 584

distraction (distract, distracted, distractions), 148, 156, 384, 389, 550, 577, 602

distress (distressed, distressful, distressing), 5, 47, 67, 86, 118, 145, 146, 180, 182, 204, 208, 238, 280, 315, 323, 351, 361, 403, 406, 458, 472, 501, 529, 533, 539, 549, 596

distribution (distribute, distributed), 235, 257, 389, 405, 593

distrust (distrustful, distrusting, distrusts), 52, 169, 257, 272, 308, 324, 429, 500, 526, 537, 557, 571, 572

disturbance (disturb, disturbances, disturber), 14, 15, 36, 44, 149, 159, 182, 187, 237, 314, 386, 466, 498, 531, 546, 548

dive, 85, 229

diverse (diversify, diversity), 51, 146, 256, 304

diversion (divert), 20, 51, 57, 146, 275, 346, 409, 483, 595

divination, 488

divine right, 44

divinity (divine, divinely, divineness, divines, divinities), 10, 22, 40, 48, 57, 119, 138, 146, 161, 182, 197, 212, 213, 214, 215, 216, 219, 225, 245, 250, 258, 261, 262, 265, 269, 270, 271, 287, 295, 300, 327, 336, 345, 371, 374, 400, 418, 430, 437, 438, 439, 441, 475, 477, 489, 490, 492, 521, 545, 549, 587, 591

division (divide, divided, divides), 29, 49, 104, 163, 183, 213, 230, 243, 256, 257, 277, 281, 286, 302, 343, 352, 361, 385, 386, 391, 421, 515, 565, 593

divorce (divorced), 332, 380, 386, 548

dizzy, 402

doctor (doctors), 25, 47, 121, 329, 357, 362, 400, 401, 421, 423, 491, 514

doctrine (doctrinal, doctrinally, doctrines), 28, 46, 135, 146, 175, 199, 217, 237, 374, 405, 418, 419, 502, 576

dodge (dodger, dodges, dodging), 5, 83, 527

doer (doers), 2, 218, 370

dog (dogged, dogs), 27, 32, 77, 87, 98, 113, 151, 164, 173, 184, 185, 193, 240, 262, 274, 286, 291, 332, 333, 352, 363, 386, 421, 505, 538, 570, 575

dog-in-the-manger, 291

dog-kennel, 47

dogma (dogmatism, dogmatist), 64, 65, 215, 218,

295, 305, 363, 401, 506, 519
dole, 173
doleful, 388
doll (dolls), 42, 202, 271, 543
dollar (dollars), 290, 415
domesticity (domestic), 105, 146, 149, 157, 163, 182, 353, 354, 365, 367, 369, 376, 382, 384, 392, 395, 498, 601
dominance (domination), 146, 147
dominion (domain), 34, 201, 225, 235, 336, 339, 345, 434, 523
donation, 212
donkey (donkey race), 317, 382, 578
Don Quixote, 196, 435
doom (doomed), 51, 90, 91, 97, 219, 245, 332, 498, 528
door (door-latch, doors, doorsill), 1, 3, 11, 30, 60, 73, 117, 124, 126, 130, 158, 176, 306, 315, 321, 339, 365, 383, 400, 404, 422, 429, 489, 490, 492, 522, 584, 601
dotage, 13
double (doubled, doubles, doublings), 40, 151, 179, 189, 313, 391, 416, 430, 431, 443, 465, 577
doubloon, 290
doubt (doubted, doubter, doubtful, doubting, doubts), 3, 10, 18, 43, 46, 48, 120, 140, 147, 153, 174, 178, 193, 208, 211, 220, 221, 236, 246, 272, 276, 291, 305, 315, 317, 329, 338, 339, 351, 366, 367, 393, 412, 414, 438, 449, 457, 465, 481, 484, 488, 492, 496, 497, 502, 513, 522, 543, 552, 590, 595, 599
doubt-provoking, 479
Doubting Thomas, 178
dove, 31, 32, 65, 340, 357, 443, 489
dovetail (dovetailedness), 335, 577
dowdy, 472
downfall, 151
downtrodden, 582
doxology, 544
doze, 417, 548
dozen, 293, 299, 355, 371, 392, 395, 418, 423, 517
dragon, 36, 41, 62, 438, 523
drama (dramatic, dramatis personae, dramatist), 135, 136, 137, 149, 183, 188, 237, 278, 317, 552, 561, 590
draught, 97, 168, 181, 229, 258, 293
draughty, 321
draw (drawn, draws), 40, 169, 200, 216, 227, 248, 274, 280, 299, 308, 310, 316, 317, 339, 424, 434, 436, 438, 455, 469, 474, 488, 492, 497, 518, 545, 584, 601
drawback (drawbacks), 83, 349, 397, 501, 507
drawing-room, 15, 131, 348, 561
drawlings, 477
dread (dreadful, dreadfully, dreads), 55, 57, 96, 117, 119, 123, 125, 130, 145, 159, 171, 187, 189, 192, 201, 210, 224, 250, 259, 262, 264, 267, 288, 316, 321, 350, 383, 392, 410, 421, 440, 447, 500, 504, 543, 544, 566, 568, 571, 575, 578, 603
dream (dreamed, dreamer, dreamers, dreaming, dreams), 10, 15, 30, 31, 45, 79, 147, 148, 149, 150, 159, 160, 183, 185, 197, 241, 244, 247, 257, 260, 269, 274, 275, 283, 317, 319, 326, 328, 341, 389, 407, 408, 449, 464, 465, 474, 478, 516, 541
dream-house, 149
dreamless, 319
dreary, 53, 309, 429, 449, 464
dregs, 51

dress (dressed, dressing), 24, 35, 38, 41, 42, 121, 150, 274, 295, 345, 352, 365, 368, 370, 382, 392, 409, 413, 428, 433, 441, 446, 472, 525, 536, 540, 564, 587, 589, 594
drift (drifting), 317, 547
drink (drank, drinking, drunk, drunken: see also drunkard), 32, 43, 85, 143, 150, 151, 152, 153, 158, 170, 194, 196, 258, 287, 302, 328, 341, 352, 383, 393, 406, 413, 433, 439, 450, 492, 496, 529, 538, 571, 579
drive (driven, driver, drives, driving), 133, 136, 174, 216, 260, 261, 263, 264, 288, 308, 319, 343, 370, 379, 382, 384, 459, 462, 470, 492, 524, 544, 565, 572
drivel, 156
drizzly, 90, 239
drollery (droll), 224, 438
droop (drooping, droops), 446, 459, 518
drop (dropped, drops), 13, 120, 149, 152, 191, 336, 355, 358, 371, 397, 431, 449, 484, 501, 502, 517, 565, 578, 585, 601
drown (drowned, drowning), 47, 134, 176, 217, 286, 351, 492, 496, 533, 562
drowsy, 277, 407, 459
drudge (drudgery), 137, 206, 532
drug, 52, 72, 504
drum, 53, 170, 320, 535
drunkard (drunkenness: see also drink), 150, 151, 162
dry (dries), 168, 198, 230, 257, 306, 313, 343, 400, 413, 534, 559
dry-goods, 193
dual, 16, 20
dual number, 576
dubious (see also doubt), 140
ducal, 382
duchess, 170
duck, 426, 459
ductile (ductilely), 409
duel, 153, 166, 197, 233
Duke of Wellington, 72
duke (dukes), 562
dull (dullard, dullness), 78, 79, 102, 104, 116, 141, 148, 153, 155, 162, 270, 298, 301, 334, 362, 374, 377, 382, 436, 467, 473, 513, 566, 575, 599, 600
dumbness (dumb), 22, 96, 123, 534, 535, 571
dunce, 17, 497
dungeon, 83, 126
dunghill, 271, 481
dupe (duped), 25, 47, 119, 128, 202, 273, 287, 537, 596
duplicate, 430, 431, 564
duplicity, 200, 283
durable, 182, 202, 500, 547
duration, 43, 165, 170, 184, 213, 301, 396, 432, 472
dust, 22, 145, 330, 339, 373, 399, 410, 422, 430, 464, 505, 558, 561, 569
Dutchman, 194
duty (duties), 8, 18, 38, 41, 46, 47, 67, 73, 76, 79, 93, 96, 98, 100, 101, 120, 148, 153, 154, 155, 156, 157, 165, 167, 182, 186, 198, 206, 229, 247, 255, 256, 282, 307, 308, 318, 343, 345, 366, 367, 370, 371, 375, 390, 393, 413, 414, 425, 442, 447, 448, 457, 461, 467, 469, 476, 481, 491, 497, 503, 504, 507, 514, 579, 605
dwarf (dwarfs), 276, 328, 601
dwell (dweller, dwellers, dwelling, dwellings, dwells, dwelt), 7, 40, 52, 79, 114, 233, 294, 402,

dwell (*continued*)
428, 438, 448, 493, 507, 535, 547, 566, 591,
593
dwindle (dwindles), 101, 320
dynasty, 61, 574
dyspepsia (dyspeptic), 142, 273, 457

eagerness (eager, eagerly), 9, 74, 115, 142, 171,
195, 207, 223, 238, 337, 449, 499, 525, 572, 601
eagle (eagles), 31, 32, 85, 141, 323, 398, 400, 409,
449, 459
early (earlier, earliest), 143, 149, 157, 182, 192,
222, 233, 236, 239, 274, 337, 340, 345, 447, 461,
466, 479
earn (earned), 201, 280, 373, 444
earnestness (earnest, earnestly), 18, 63, 99, 155,
262, 267, 280, 305, 362, 368, 394, 405, 438, 467,
561, 562
earrings, 87
ears (ear), 7, 27, 41, 47, 106, 109, 111, 158, 174,
176, 178, 181, 276, 290, 311, 316, 323, 332, 336,
340, 342, 369, 386, 406, 408, 412, 422, 431, 438,
441, 478, 512, 516, 521, 530, 561, 568, 570, 572,
576
earth (earthly, earthy), 1, 3, 11, 14, 15, 17, 18, 23,
29, 40, 41, 43, 47, 58, 68, 72, 77, 79, 82, 85, 103,
111, 118, 123, 127, 146, 148, 149, 156, 159, 163,
165, 168, 186, 202, 210, 215, 220, 227, 237, 243,
244, 245, 246, 248, 251, 258, 260, 264, 268, 269,
271, 274, 276, 277, 279, 280, 284, 287, 290, 292,
294, 296, 297, 303, 311, 317, 320, 323, 324, 333,
334, 336, 337, 341, 342, 360, 364, 375, 378, 379,
384, 298, 405, 407, 409, 416, 420, 423, 428, 429,
439, 440, 443, 448, 456, 465, 495, 503, 505, 511,
520, 522, 527, 528, 531, 545, 548, 558, 561, 562,
571, 574, 575, 579, 590, 591, 596, 603, 604
earthquake (earthquakes), 10, 448, 512, 520, 535
earthquake-shock, 95
easiness (ease, easier, easiest, easily, easy), 2, 28,
52, 55, 68, 77, 87, 94, 95, 96, 139, 140, 170, 171,
172, 173, 177, 179, 187, 188, 190, 210, 212, 222,
224, 234, 236, 238, 241, 246, 250, 251, 253, 265,
266, 268, 270, 272, 274, 278, 282, 290, 292, 294,
297, 300, 307, 312, 315, 319, 324, 341, 349, 361,
377, 382, 390, 401, 408, 409, 412, 414, 444, 452,
453, 457, 469, 487, 494, 502, 507, 508, 510, 515,
516, 518, 524, 526, 527, 531, 539, 540, 570, 593,
596
east/East, 33, 70, 478, 520
eat (ate, eaten, eating, eats), 21, 53, 58, 79, 82, 142,
143, 150, 151, 166, 180, 229, 271, 289, 309, 315,
316, 406, 418, 438, 441, 453, 456, 483, 487, 489,
529, 538, 570
ebb (ebb and flow, ebbs), 63, 265, 269, 420
ebony (ebon), 25, 279
ebullition, 207
eccentricity (eccentric, eccentricities), 3, 18, 210
Ecclesiastes, 545
ecclesiastic (ecclesiastical), 71, 556
echo (echoes), 18, 399, 443
eclat, 172
eclectic, 74
eclipse (eclipsed), 190, 500, 530
economics (economical, economist, economists,
economy), 155, 347, 365, 367, 379, 470, 488, 517
ecstacy/ecstasy (ecstatic), 43, 150, 201, 207, 446
Eden, 19, 213, 257, 325, 383, 464, 566

edification (edifies, edify), 43, 468, 478
edifice, 14, 513
edition, 36, 431
editor (editorials, editors), 34, 159, 543
education (educated, educating), 64, 82, 110, 143,
155, 156, 157, 158, 159, 163, 174, 197, 219, 234,
261, 293, 305, 346, 360, 361, 362, 364, 367, 373,
409, 415, 455, 470, 478, 479, 493, 547, 568, 575,
580
efface, 157, 183
effect (effecting, effects), 11, 35, 43, 50, 52, 54, 56,
57, 58, 59, 61, 90, 131, 148, 151, 191, 203, 204,
240, 241, 244, 248, 260, 274, 282, 290, 303, 309,
311, 314, 331, 357, 363, 364, 372, 376, 400, 423,
427, 468, 481, 491, 497, 508, 529, 536, 565, 568,
572, 575, 602, 605
effectiveness (effective), 159, 161, 178, 191, 219,
560
effectual (effectually), 59, 157, 372, 441, 506, 591
effeminate, 367
effervescence, 563
efficacy (efficacious), 122, 164, 316, 364, 462, 473
efficiency (efficient), 59, 308
effluence, 474
effort (efforts), 31, 82, 108, 135, 159, 175, 228, 249,
279, 280, 288, 303, 347, 353, 372, 427, 457, 478,
493, 523, 559, 571, 572, 588, 596
effrontery, 48
effusions, 190, 569
egg (eggs), 30, 46, 83, 92, 140, 191, 418, 443, 502,
599
ego (egoism, egos, egotism, egotist, egotistical,
egotists), 98, 159, 187, 229, 249, 291, 397, 458,
523, 543, 580, 581
egregious (egregiously), 59, 183, 490
Egyptian, 191
elaborated, 477
elapse (elapsed), 187, 231, 320
elasticity (elastic), 43, 64, 67, 96, 103, 161, 191,
403, 499
elation (elated, elates, elating), 94, 461, 473
elbow (elbowed, elbows), 222, 289, 369, 423, 541
elder (elderly, elders), 10, 12, 46, 57, 144, 303, 377,
384, 456, 539
election (elect, elected), 134, 280, 467, 497, 542
electric, 288
elegance (elegant, elegantly), 145, 181, 248, 347,
373, 376, 392, 416, 533, 558
elegiasts, 230
element (elements), 18, 54, 220, 269, 285, 304, 348,
358, 363, 415, 423, 427, 449, 464, 474, 493
elevation (elevate, elevated), 15, 33, 94, 103, 132,
169, 302, 327, 383, 408, 418, 464, 480, 496, 512,
528, 563
eligible, 217, 527
elixir, 519
elocution, 475
eloping, 376
eloquence (eloquent, eloquently), 6, 10, 39, 97,
104, 129, 145, 172, 173, 174, 175, 230, 270, 286,
356, 427, 439, 475, 476, 477, 483, 535, 541, 575,
587
elucidate (elucidates), 490, 576
elude (eluded, eluding, elusive, elusiveness), 27,
189, 314, 502, 548, 572, 574
emancipate, 38
embark (embarked, embarking), 117, 300, 383
embarrassment (embarrassing, embarrass-

enslave (enslaved, enslaves), 164, 361, 559, 577
entails, 333
entangle (entangled), 387, 390
enterprise (enterprising), 79, 316, 370, 427, 467
entertainment (entertain, entertained, entertaining), 20, 35, 77, 84, 85, 104, 139, 162, 239, 262, 301, 346, 350, 374, 385, 441, 496, 505, 525, 529, 539
enthusiasm (enthuse, enthusiast, enthusiastic, enthusiasts), 40, 70, 145, 154, 162, 173, 175, 236, 326, 383, 403, 423, 446, 465, 493, 546
enticed, 552
entitle (entitled, entitles), 89, 184, 327, 366, 392, 593
entrance (enter, entered, entering, enters, entrances), 118, 135, 140, 156, 184, 202, 203, 215, 246, 247, 268, 274, 284, 306, 323, 350, 352, 359, 364, 367, 393, 400, 403, 433, 436, 448, 458, 466, 467, 473, 507, 544, 590, 601
entrapped, 552
entreaty (entreat), 77, 90, 104
entrenchment (entrenching, entrenchments), 176, 555
entrust (entrusted), 212, 249, 466, 524
enunciate, 282
envelop (enveloped), 41, 117, 423
environment, 99
envy (enviable, envied, envies, envious), 25, 31, 36, 91, 127, 162, 163, 202, 204, 251, 255, 359, 379, 421, 453, 471, 484, 500, 510, 521, 530, 555, 593, 599
ephemeral (ephemerides), 552, 558, 567
Ephesus, 57
epic, 270, 337, 383, 463, 465, 495
Epicurus, 27
epidemic (epidemical), 374, 394, 589
epigram, 490
epilepsy, 400
epilogue, 539
episode, 54, 237, 595
epistle, 57
epitaph, 37, 84, 293
epithet, 543
epitome, 542
epoch (epochs), 235, 248, 577
equality (equable, equal, equally, equals, equivalent), 73, 94, 103, 119, 122, 125, 130, 158, 163, 164, 200, 202, 215, 220, 225, 231, 262, 302, 304, 323, 328, 341, 344, 361, 367, 368, 375, 378, 379, 385, 387, 394, 426, 434, 445, 457, 461, 465, 481, 492, 497, 528, 548, 551, 556, 557, 562, 579, 580, 582, 590
equanimity, 4, 348, 488, 582
equation, 56
equator, 18
equidistant, 13
equilibrium, 585
equipage (equip, equipment, equipped, equips), 24, 260, 261, 383
equity, 24, 38, 224, 307
equivalent (equivalents: see also equality), 205, 416, 497, 518
equivocation (equivocal), 96, 129, 467
era, 578
eradicate (eradicated), 61, 303, 479
erasures, 399
erection (erect, erected, erections), 2, 213, 229,

257, 518, 577, 604
errand (errand-boy, errands), 138, 274, 558
erratic (see also error), 464, 525
error (err, erred, erring, erroneous, errors, errs: see also erratic), 2, 13, 23, 38, 44, 53, 54, 55, 60, 61, 63, 71, 93, 105, 114, 115, 139, 140, 147, 164, 165, 206, 216, 217, 218, 224, 226, 232, 241, 247, 263, 272, 294, 295, 315, 317, 331, 334, 345, 350, 394, 418, 429, 430, 441, 442, 456, 473, 475, 476, 479, 483, 505, 507, 508, 513, 545, 562, 566, 572, 604
erudition, 402, 435, 490
erysipelas, 112
escape (escaped, escapes, escaping), 4, 118, 121, 144, 165, 218, 237, 255, 267, 270, 272, 291, 309, 310, 389, 390, 401, 409, 425, 429, 463, 477, 493, 515, 521, 524, 527, 529, 543, 585, 603
espieth, 223
espouse, 138, 203
essay (essaying, essays), 210, 248, 431, 558
essence (essences), 18, 52, 90, 109, 133, 154, 220, 224, 248, 254, 271, 275, 289, 291, 326, 339, 340, 436, 440, 576
essential (essentially, essentials), 165, 199, 265, 281, 315, 322, 347, 385, 398, 406, 493, 519, 549, 552
establishment (establish, established, establishing), 49, 70, 146, 206, 208, 278, 375, 379, 418, 457, 538, 541, 547, 562, 589
estate (estates), 26, 83, 103, 105, 150, 155, 206, 340, 350, 365, 515, 588
esteem (esteemed, estimable), 4, 126, 165, 183, 204, 220, 225, 235, 258, 319, 332, 340, 361, 366, 368, 413, 483, 510, 541, 542, 583, 587
estimation (estimate), 107, 129, 238, 381, 395, 436, 505, 525, 535, 577
estrangement, 187
eternity (eternal, eternality, eternally), 19, 49, 59, 62, 118, 121, 123, 127, 138, 141, 142, 143, 161, 165, 166, 176, 189, 192, 209, 213, 214, 215, 226, 231, 248, 250, 275, 311, 320, 321, 323, 324, 364, 370, 394, 398, 410, 438, 439, 448, 486, 492, 503, 513, 516, 523, 537, 539, 545, 546, 566, 573, 576, 583, 596
ethereals, 365
ethical, 171, 502
Ethiopia, 569
etiquette, 5, 73, 126, 166, 466
etymology, 502
Euclid, 476
eulogy (eulogistic), 87, 173, 473
Europe (European), 5, 11, 72, 75, 96, 289
evanescent, 29, 172, 544
evangelized, 75
evaporate (evaporates), 88, 393
evasion (evade, evaded, evading, evasive), 5, 166, 179, 432, 512, 602
Eve (see also Adam), 220, 355, 362, 460
evening (evenings), 9, 33, 137, 336, 429, 434, 456, 464, 477, 589
event (events, eventuality), 29, 51, 54, 55, 56, 57, 60, 69, 72, 73, 78, 79, 81, 85, 88, 90, 99, 122, 124, 134, 135, 136, 137, 138, 140, 148, 166, 168, 171, 181, 191, 201, 228, 230, 236, 247, 248, 250, 256, 274, 278, 279, 295, 303, 304, 317, 324, 356, 378, 399, 403, 410, 433, 442, 448, 488, 490, 569, 594
ever-gaping, 121

ever-increasing, 232
everlasting (everlastingly), 86, 118, 120, 165, 175, 191, 214, 335, 465, 574
Everlasting Book, 161
ever-present, 117
ever-variable, 426
everyday, 29, 177, 405, 407, 462, 544, 602
evidence (evidences, evident), 3, 23, 45, 89, 98, 208, 213, 217, 220, 232, 287, 298, 311, 357, 386, 393, 432, 441, 452, 492, 551
evil (evils), 1, 15, 17, 20, 44, 52, 56, 58, 63, 64, 65, 67, 75, 81, 82, 83, 84, 88, 94, 95, 96, 97, 99, 106, 119, 122, 123, 125, 126, 130, 131, 134, 136, 145, 158, 164, 167, 168, 188, 189, 201, 204, 217, 218, 219, 220, 221, 222, 225, 236, 238, 248, 257, 261, 272, 273, 275, 276, 277, 284, 285, 290, 294, 296, 311, 314, 316, 319, 322, 323, 329, 350, 370, 375, 385, 388, 392, 406, 411, 412, 414, 419, 427, 437, 442, 450, 454, 470, 471, 483, 485, 489, 492, 493, 498, 501, 504, 505, 508, 509, 510, 512, 513, 519, 524, 526, 529, 530, 534, 542, 549, 554, 556, 558, 560, 583, 589, 591, 592
evil-doers, 190, 219
evil-dreaders, 190
evince (evinces), 262, 299, 456, 488
exact (exacted, exacting, exactness, exacts), 37, 190, 195, 242, 318, 333, 366, 377, 396, 408, 427, 602
exaggeration (exaggerate, exaggerated, exaggerations), 53, 130, 166, 179, 191, 274, 288, 347, 352, 359, 476, 478, 533, 571
exaltation (exalt, exalted, exalts), 66, 89, 94, 155, 162, 181, 202, 228, 245, 277, 295, 331, 333, 385, 405, 408, 463, 465, 529
examination (examinations, examine, examined, examining), 33, 88, 159, 254, 294, 360, 376, 421, 464, 504, 527, 589
example (ensample, examples), 69, 114, 121, 166, 167, 185, 186, 195, 212, 249, 316, 322, 359, 445, 472, 497, 518, 542, 543, 544, 568, 571, 576, 589, 591
exasperation (exasperate, exasperated, exasperating), 75, 92, 186, 351, 379, 383
excellence (excel, excellencies, excellency, excellent, excellently), 16, 21, 23, 29, 35, 36, 39, 80, 84, 89, 128, 141, 167, 180, 211, 226, 246, 270, 300, 303, 314, 340, 359, 362, 402, 475, 483, 495, 521, 523, 525, 530, 558, 588, 597, 600, 604
exception (excepting, exceptional, exceptions), 80, 89, 109, 140, 167, 261, 382, 540, 578, 581, 596, 602
exceptious, 602
excess (exceed, exceeding, exceeds, excesses, excessive, excessively), 19, 60, 148, 150, 167, 214, 222, 225, 260, 275, 315, 347, 363, 377, 400, 408, 413, 437, 447, 449, 460, 497, 500, 504, 529, 563, 578, 584, 591
exchange (exchanged), 7, 167, 205, 273, 387, 416, 515
exchequer, 431
excise, 441
excitement (excitable, excitation, excite, excited, excitedly, excites, exciting), 12, 55, 86, 145, 160, 167, 202, 232, 266, 268, 288, 308, 343, 422, 450, 458, 461, 475, 477, 502, 518, 528, 551, 559
exclamation (exclaim, exclaimed), 42, 173, 384, 412

exclamation point, 249
exclude (excluded, excluding, exclusion), 49, 109, 163, 204, 346, 347, 471, 561
exclusiveness (exclusive, exclusively), 201, 251, 361, 455, 477, 523, 597
excursion, 250
excuse (excusable, excused, excuses, excusing), 60, 126, 128, 151, 154, 167, 168, 186, 260, 298, 329, 332, 338, 369, 370, 477, 498, 538, 552, 581
execration (execrable), 87, 218, 472, 505
execution (execute, executed, executing, executioner, executions), 58, 137, 147, 158, 162, 168, 176, 197, 216, 228, 310, 311, 386, 411, 518, 528, 558, 583
exemplary, 492
exemplification (exemplified), 256, 284
exemption (exempt), 296, 486, 500, 528, 559
exercise (exercised, exercises, exercising), 8, 13, 28, 46, 56, 104, 106, 110, 115, 156, 216, 223, 241, 254, 274, 275, 276, 306, 315, 330, 344, 347, 356, 360, 395, 408, 418, 440, 450, 472, 474, 504, 519, 568, 576, 584, 586
exertion (exert, exerted, exertions, exerts), 22, 161, 207, 222, 302, 373, 375, 389, 393, 409, 433, 438, 447, 473, 479, 482, 497, 498, 554, 601, 603
exhalations, 186, 336
exhaustion (exhaust, exhausted, exhaustive, exhausts), 34, 175, 320, 427, 436, 475, 486, 519, 548
exhibition (exhibit, exhibited, exhibitions, exhibits), 74, 119, 162, 190, 258, 334, 353, 379, 435, 452, 526, 527, 529
exhilarating, 150, 509
exhortations, 455, 483
exigency, 357
exile (exiled, exiles), 168, 254, 538
existence (exist, existed, existing, exists), 16, 18, 23, 50, 53, 54, 68, 75, 83, 119, 126, 135, 137, 139, 144, 145, 150, 151, 163, 169, 179, 182, 200, 202, 205, 209, 215, 221, 236, 253, 260, 277, 278, 288, 289, 293, 296, 297, 298, 301, 303, 311, 316, 318, 319, 321, 328, 330, 337, 338, 339, 340, 341, 347, 350, 355, 359, 366, 378, 390, 396, 403, 409, 411, 413, 426, 436, 439, 440, 449, 466, 470, 471, 472, 487, 489, 493, 494, 529, 530, 531, 541, 545, 562, 563, 564, 589, 592
exorcise (exorcises), 119, 370
expansion (expand, expansive), 156, 175, 244, 327, 479, 541, 561, 594
expatiate, 268, 387
expatriate (expatriated), 530, 578
expectation (expect, expectant, expectations, expected, expecting, expects), 15, 100, 122, 133, 142, 168, 170, 172, 177, 183, 197, 208, 221, 226, 233, 237, 243, 254, 262, 295, 296, 297, 302, 309, 315, 317, 323, 344, 353, 355, 357, 361, 362, 365, 369, 372, 375, 383, 387, 396, 406, 419, 422, 449, 461, 462, 469, 509, 513, 527, 528, 529, 546, 559, 566, 582
expedience (expediency, expedient, expedients), 3, 59, 130, 261, 302, 319, 342, 369, 417, 467, 471, 484, 541, 598
expel (expelled, expels), 79, 242, 268, 413
expenditure (expend, expense, expenses, expensive), 26, 53, 62, 122, 128, 141, 167, 173, 181, 196, 206, 227, 264, 291, 306, 341, 346, 353, 385, 397, 416, 446, 457, 471, 507, 517, 535, 591

experience (experienced, experiences, experiencing, *experientia*), 5, 9, 11, 12, 13, 16, 17, 44, 45, 47, 62, 64, 68, 74, 82, 84, 90, 110, 111, 127, 129, 145, 168, 169, 170, 171, 204, 206, 228, 234, 258, 260, 274, 284, 290, 310, 315, 326, 329, 334, 342, 349, 362, 369, 378, 379, 381, 395, 397, 399, 402, 417, 418, 448, 461, 482, 489, 497, 509, 529, 532, 541, 555, 565, 575, 596, 597, 598
experiment, 93, 99, 175, 511, 516, 539
expert (expertness), 287, 344, 550
expiation (expiations), 294, 506, 542
explanation (explain, explained, explainers, explaining, explains, explanations), 44, 98, 127, 171, 176, 234, 268, 314, 353, 387, 415, 424, 434, 475, 487, 498, 502, 600, 601
exploit, 55
exploration (exploring), 171, 383
explosive (exploded, explosives), 156, 274, 380
exponent, 153, 468
exposure (espose, exposed, exposes, exposing, expositor), 30, 105, 124, 129, 172, 184, 349, 390, 391, 430, 515, 518, 519, 525, 538, 556, 560, 568, 576
expound (expounded, expounds), 313, 415
expression (express, expressed, expresses, expressible, expressions), 5, 30, 40, 44, 53, 60, 62, 73, 74, 93, 171, 172, 173, 174, 175, 176, 225, 276, 290, 297, 300, 307, 310, 326, 327, 329, 349, 351, 352, 371, 383, 385, 421, 427, 442, 462, 487, 489, 496, 509, 530, 536, 537, 538, 541, 551, 556, 560, 563, 577, 589, 602
expunged, 378
exquisite, 41, 42, 76, 147, 172, 348, 422, 461, 513, 540
extend (extended, extends, extensive, extent), 8, 96, 115, 150, 183, 215, 301, 342, 408, 477, 498, 523, 586
extenuate (extenuator), 295, 447
exterior, 169, 267, 278
extermination, 175
external (externals), 56, 149, 162, 237, 251, 259, 275, 276, 344, 345, 426, 441, 555, 597
extinction (extinct), 333, 550
extinguish (extinguished), 16, 255, 298, 454, 538, 589
extolled, 298, 413
extorting, 378
extract, 428, 458, 496
extraordinary (extraordinaries), 22, 72, 113, 143, 152, 165, 197, 229, 250, 259, 270, 318, 359, 360, 389, 401, 435, 455, 552, 562
extravagance (extravagances, extravagant), 100, 234, 292, 451, 471, 496, 509
extremity (extreme, extremes, extremest, extremities), 26, 58, 71, 159, 174, 175, 215, 222, 230, 262, 284, 294, 333, 336, 350, 402, 408, 410, 433, 452, 475, 492, 524, 531
extrovertedness, 175
exultation (exulting, exults), 121, 182, 280, 370, 530
eyes (eye), 7, 11, 13, 18, 24, 25, 30, 33, 40, 41, 42, 43, 44, 48, 56, 63, 78, 79, 83, 84, 87, 99, 100, 111, 119, 120, 124, 131, 134, 137, 140, 148, 164, 166, 171, 174, 176, 179, 181, 183, 184, 188, 194, 203, 210, 219, 223, 226, 232, 233, 244, 248, 260, 274, 276, 279, 284, 290, 292, 294, 295, 300, 307, 310, 313, 316, 317, 323, 328, 332, 336, 337, 338, 340,

342, 343, 347, 349, 360, 363, 364, 365, 369, 371, 374, 386, 388, 389, 400, 402, 404, 407, 408, 414, 415, 419, 421, 422, 428, 431, 437, 438, 447, 448, 449, 451, 452, 453, 454, 458, 462, 468, 476, 477, 483, 491, 499, 500, 513, 515, 518, 519, 525, 528, 539, 541, 545, 546, 547, 559, 560, 572, 573, 576, 580, 581, 584, 590, 591, 603
eyesight, 369, 416
eyewitness, 250, 421
eyries, 163

fable (fables, fabulous), 135, 270, 567, 572
fabric (fabrics), 7, 121, 221, 231, 303, 454, 513
face (faces), 3, 5, 12, 17, 24, 25, 26, 40, 41, 43, 44, 45, 48, 50, 57, 63, 66, 70, 82, 86, 89, 90, 91, 113, 119, 120, 132, 135, 152, 169, 176, 177, 180, 187, 188, 198, 203, 210, 214, 222, 232, 248, 250, 251, 255, 266, 276, 277, 280, 285, 288, 299, 303, 306, 317, 337, 344, 360, 361, 369, 384, 397, 402, 406, 424, 431, 436, 446, 470, 484, 485, 488, 500, 502, 512, 516, 525, 532, 533, 543, 546, 558, 559, 562, 567, 574, 584, 591
facetious, 153
facility (facile, facilitated), 9, 145, 152, 452, 569
fact (facts), 11, 16, 25, 28, 41, 44, 46, 54, 122, 127, 130, 136, 149, 175, 176, 177, 180, 183, 193, 205, 224, 247, 248, 274, 297, 299, 303, 313, 330, 348, 359, 361, 371, 387, 389, 390, 401, 415, 418, 426, 441, 447, 450, 458, 459, 463, 466, 470, 476, 478, 516, 519, 530, 546, 552, 565, 576, 602
factions, 15, 184
factious, 282
faculty (faculties), 12, 20, 29, 48, 56, 109, 161, 182, 207, 209, 231, 246, 260, 268, 276, 318, 340, 344, 347, 402, 403, 425, 460, 519, 548, 570
fade (faded, fades, fadeth), 230, 269, 446, 453, 600
fads, 466
failure (fail, failed, faileth, failing, failings, fails), 3, 44, 53, 55, 67, 101, 110, 112, 113, 128, 149, 151, 152, 177, 182, 193, 194, 200, 204, 223, 226, 242, 243, 254, 262, 278, 297, 298, 318, 336, 372, 379, 434, 460, 461, 463, 490, 504, 507, 510, 524, 527, 530, 534, 550, 553, 554, 574, 580, 584, 589, 595, 597
fain (fained), 359, 409, 492
faintness (faint, fainting), 50, 82, 120, 177, 178, 352, 504, 561
fairness (fair, fairer, fairest, fairly), 9, 26, 38, 40, 44, 45, 80, 86, 87, 89, 107, 126, 132, 142, 158, 167, 173, 186, 206, 253, 254, 257, 289, 297, 299, 307, 313, 315, 316, 332, 359, 365, 369, 374, 385, 402, 411, 418, 428, 444, 447, 454, 483, 489, 508, 521, 533, 538, 549, 579, 582, 585
fair play, 74, 280
fairy, 69
fairy tales, 275
fait, 171
fait accompli, 96
faith (faithful, faithless), 46, 55, 70, 79, 80, 85, 112, 113, 114, 131, 174, 178, 182, 189, 190, 191, 193, 194, 202, 205, 206, 248, 254, 255, 270, 275, 286, 287, 290, 301, 386, 402, 418, 420, 426, 468, 481, 502, 503, 507, 539, 547, 549, 560, 566, 577, 589, 599
falcon, 216
fall (fallen, falling, falls, fell), 55, 105, 107, 119,

KEYWORD INDEX

139, 164, 174, 187, 197, 204, 214, 218, 241, 259, 270, 274, 281, 282, 284, 288, 291, 295, 314, 315, 326, 334, 340, 341, 348, 349, 354, 373, 374, 381, 388, 396, 400, 411, 420, 434, 437, 439, 446, 449, 455, 472, 476, 483, 484, 486, 493, 508, 509, 517, 529, 535, 537, 550, 551, 553, 555, 565, 571, 590
Fall [from grace], 355
fallacy (fallacies, fallacious), 69, 128, 178, 332, 334, 441, 465
fallibility (fallible), 212, 294
falsity (falsehood, falsehoods, falsest), 15, 17, 24, 25, 27, 41, 47, 55, 89, 96, 97, 100, 107, 128, 134, 164, 178, 179, 180, 181, 184, 192, 202, 204, 205, 217, 220, 233, 236, 247, 254, 260, 266, 267, 272, 275, 279, 280, 288, 297, 313, 320, 329, 335, 341, 351, 355, 356, 367, 372, 392, 414, 418, 423, 424, 463, 465, 466, 475, 477, 482, 486, 506, 507, 517, 518, 526, 527, 532, 533, 534, 555, 572, 574, 586, 587, 589, 591, 604
falter (faltered, faltering), 50, 100, 386, 454
fame (famous), 74, 84, 126, 127, 143, 181, 228, 273, 305, 402, 404, 406, 421, 489, 495, 519, 567
familiarity (familiar, familiarities, familiarize, familiarized, familiarly), 12, 37, 43, 62, 74, 84, 104, 117, 120, 172, 174, 181, 182, 197, 203, 250, 275, 278, 291, 315, 364, 401, 460, 538, 565, 569
family (families), 39, 49, 57, 120, 144, 152, 181, 182, 183, 184, 185, 186, 219, 231, 245, 285, 307, 308, 344, 345, 353, 376, 380, 381, 385, 396, 401, 415, 425, 455, 503, 521, 532, 584
famine, 198, 435
fan, 151
fanaticism (fanatic, fanatics), 95, 185, 254, 258, 502, 506
fancy (fancied, fancies, fancying), 4, 13, 25, 31, 37, 46, 86, 88, 104, 108, 111, 120, 132, 137, 148, 156, 177, 205, 239, 243, 247, 260, 262, 269, 274, 275, 276, 285, 318, 346, 347, 380, 385, 390, 456, 467, 470, 498, 499, 524, 540, 543, 558, 582, 586, 587, 588, 590
fancy-work, 485
fantasy (fantastic), 45, 185, 355
far (far-reaching, far-seeing, farther), 95, 176, 191, 242, 304, 447, 583, 604
farce, 124, 265, 271, 288
fare (fares), 143, 391, 436, 530
farewell, 57, 142, 447
farm (farmer, farmer-folk, farmers, farming, farms), 49, 57, 100, 382, 438, 476, 593
farthing, 67, 207, 394
fascination (fascinate, fascinated, fascinates, fascinating), 51, 76, 117, 164, 221, 253, 290, 306, 347, 348, 355, 373, 484, 486, 560, 569, 603
fashion (fashionable, fashioned, fashions), 12, 81, 94, 125, 138, 185, 197, 213, 249, 260, 281, 302, 325, 354, 379, 384, 393, 412, 435, 475, 478, 504, 505, 534, 546, 547, 582, 595
fast (fasting), 63, 100, 149, 194, 316, 317, 396, 434, 554, 604
fasten (fastened, fastens), 220, 268, 275, 506, 547
fastidious, 73, 386
fat (fatness, fatted, fatten, fatter, fattest), 58, 186, 299, 393, 415, 484, 497, 530, 547, 562
fatality (fatal), 31, 58, 68, 75, 87, 90, 112, 126, 136, 139, 141, 152, 178, 181, 224, 246, 254, 308, 331, 349, 394, 413, 481, 496, 510, 570, 580
fate/Fate (fated, fates/Fates), 5, 51, 115, 119, 134,

135, 136, 137, 138, 139, 203, 257, 265, 329, 332, 335, 337, 354, 371, 388, 415, 427, 431, 516, 544, 560, 594
father/Father (fatherhood, fathers), 7, 11, 47, 55, 105, 116, 118, 123, 126, 127, 149, 154, 156, 157, 163, 169, 170, 179, 180, 182, 183, 184, 185, 211, 212, 214, 216, 220, 234, 277, 280, 326, 332, 335, 337, 341, 344, 353, 418, 421, 438, 462, 468, 504, 538, 540, 601
father confessor, 78
father of lies, 218
fathom (fathomless), 213, 219, 241, 599
fatigue (fatigued, fatigues, fatiguing), 59, 125, 323, 367, 385, 420, 450, 538, 542
fault (faultiness, faultless, faults, faulty), 2, 9, 13, 23, 24, 25, 32, 53, 60, 62, 93, 96, 102, 130, 132, 139, 152, 169, 186, 187, 190, 195, 204, 206, 230, 232, 273, 295, 300, 304, 338, 339, 341, 348, 356, 363, 364, 367, 391, 401, 406, 414, 419, 422, 452, 475, 493, 514, 518, 519, 525, 532, 534, 589, 604, 605
favor (favorable, favorably, favored, favorite, favorites, favoritism, favors), 19, 27, 28, 49, 54, 58, 61, 66, 67, 72, 73, 99, 105, 109, 135, 136, 151, 158, 174, 187, 192, 195, 200, 205, 207, 225, 244, 261, 262, 268, 274, 278, 286, 294, 295, 298, 317, 323, 326, 329, 331, 350, 365, 389, 393, 400, 438, 439, 471, 476, 479, 482, 497, 506, 512, 520, 526, 533, 542, 587, 604
fawn (fawning, fawns), 4, 255, 604
fear (feared, feareth, fearful, fearfully, fearless, fear-nothing, fears), 1, 3, 4, 9, 19, 21, 22, 49, 57, 58, 59, 67, 69, 83, 90, 99, 104, 106, 107, 108, 116, 117, 118, 121, 122, 124, 125, 128, 133, 140, 163, 174, 180, 187, 188, 189, 190, 193, 194, 200, 202, 204, 211, 213, 216, 217, 222, 223, 224, 225, 233, 238, 240, 244, 251, 273, 274, 278, 283, 284, 304, 310, 317, 325, 332, 334, 336, 338, 341, 344, 351, 358, 385, 387, 391, 401, 415, 424, 425, 427, 432, 436, 461, 474, 485, 492, 493, 497, 498, 503, 505, 513, 516, 519, 521, 524, 530, 538, 539, 542, 543, 547, 550, 553, 571, 573, 581, 588
feast (feasts), 101, 113, 384, 411, 413, 443, 457, 461, 551, 583, 584
feat (feats), 225, 565
feather (feathered, feathers), 42, 58, 59, 116, 173, 189, 203, 257, 367, 371, 433, 483, 571
feature (featured, features, featuring), 14, 43, 63, 78, 86, 115, 119, 159, 229, 307, 354, 433, 472, 478, 488, 510
February, 466, 520
fee (fees), 253, 312, 400, 401
feebleness (feeble, feebler), 55, 57, 105, 172, 209, 255, 363, 395, 399, 435, 440, 543, 547, 563, 580
feed (feeds, fed), 67, 111, 143, 201, 254, 266, 291, 299, 369, 371, 418, 421, 446, 473, 524, 593
feelings (feel, feeling, feels, felt), 2, 3, 7, 12, 13, 28, 29, 30, 40, 45, 46, 47, 50, 55, 56, 58, 59, 60, 68, 71, 87, 89, 90, 91, 94, 99, 100, 102, 117, 120, 122, 138, 145, 146, 148, 150, 159, 160, 163, 170, 172, 182, 187, 190, 191, 195, 197, 198, 200, 204, 208, 214, 218, 220, 225, 229, 230, 231, 232, 233, 235, 241, 247, 251, 254, 259, 261, 262, 263, 265, 269, 271, 275, 278, 280, 281, 284, 286, 289, 290, 291, 293, 295, 296, 297, 301, 302, 304, 310, 317, 323, 325, 326, 327, 329, 330, 334, 336, 340, 341, 343, 347, 349, 351, 352, 353, 355, 357, 360, 363, 370,

feelings (*continued*)
371, 375, 377, 380, 382, 383, 387, 395, 396, 400,
401, 403, 407, 408, 409, 411, 412, 415, 417, 422,
425, 426, 427, 431, 432, 445, 449, 455, 462, 463,
464, 469, 470, 471, 474, 475, 478, 482, 483, 493,
494, 497, 499, 502, 505, 509, 513, 514, 523, 524,
525, 526, 527, 529, 530, 534, 536, 543, 549, 551,
552, 554, 556, 557, 560, 563, 564, 568, 570, 577,
578, 582, 593, 595, 600, 602
feign, 266, 485
felicitous, 598
felicity (felicitate, felicities), 75, 99, 104, 116, 118,
134, 135, 136, 208, 234, 236, 239, 333, 373, 376,
409, 437, 453, 461, 505, 543
fellow (fellows), 5, 6, 14, 26, 77, 87, 104, 138, 153,
172, 179, 186, 197, 203, 211, 213, 219, 227, 237,
240, 256, 257, 262, 265, 282, 290, 300, 301, 303,
316, 319, 333, 348, 349, 353, 360, 362, 386, 387,
405, 412, 418, 441, 442, 449, 450, 463, 491, 498,
514, 516, 552, 569, 576, 578, 602
fellow-countryman, 270
fellow-creature (fellow-creatures), 210, 235, 288,
308, 311, 347, 455, 500
fellow-feeling, 88, 418, 538
fellow-gossip, 516
fellow man (fellow men), 19, 22, 88, 153, 418, 572,
605
fellowship, 203, 205, 429, 578
fellow-sufferer, 385
fellow-voyagers, 257
felony (felon, felons), 112, 144, 187, 532
female (females, feminine), 13, 29, 34, 40, 43, 48,
82, 105, 107, 146, 155, 192, 195, 202, 224, 277,
343, 344, 345, 346, 347, 348, 349, 350, 351, 352,
353, 354, 355, 356, 357, 358, 359, 360, 361, 362,
363, 364, 365, 367, 370, 371, 376, 385, 395, 396,
422, 428, 445, 458, 492, 493, 518, 521, 559, 585,
586, 599
fence (fenced, fencing), 30, 51, 78, 486, 557
fermentation (ferment), 51, 529
ferocity (ferocious, fierce, fiercely), 18, 112, 168,
190, 291, 330, 446, 468, 497, 576, 589, 591
ferret, 24
fertility (fertile), 276, 543
fervor (fervent), 9, 162, 205, 336, 352, 446
fester (festering), 410, 555
festivals (festive), 42, 380
fetch (fetches), 118, 580
fetters (fettered), 149, 210, 323, 328, 471, 592
feud (feuding), 194
feudalism (feudal), 190, 318
fever (feverish, fevers), 62, 132, 148, 241, 301, 447,
592
fiat, 322
fib, 179, 586
fibres, 404, 422
fickleness (fickle), 7, 10, 134, 135, 139, 190, 346,
351
fiction (fictions), 48, 51, 105, 111, 190, 191, 192,
193, 247, 275, 462, 463, 465, 532, 572, 573, 574
fiddle (fiddler), 126, 152, 169, 496, 530
fiddlesticks, 296
fiddle-strings, 173
fidelity, 90, 193, 194, 333, 341, 375, 378, 562
fidgeting (fidgets, fidgety), 85, 167, 235
field (fields), 15, 83, 159, 164, 303, 306, 347, 399,
430, 431, 433, 524, 577, 590, 591
fiend (fiend-like, fiends), 114, 131, 138, 152, 215,

219, 264, 390, 430, 434, 440, 586, 591
fiery, 37, 86, 284, 399, 494, 571
fiffles, 462
fig (fig-leafed), 157, 392, 441, 499
fight (fighters, fighting, fights, fought), 29, 35,
38, 45, 46, 49, 87, 135, 140, 156, 185, 194, 196,
200, 220, 246, 280, 295, 329, 372, 390, 413, 430,
467, 474, 489, 494, 524, 543, 549, 590, 591, 595
figure (figured, figures), 25, 81, 84, 85, 147, 158,
177, 210, 238, 270, 275, 300, 302, 443, 469, 502,
516, 544, 559
Fiji, 520
filial (filial-hearted), 154, 182, 183, 330, 419, 437
fill (filled, filling, fills), 126, 141, 142, 143, 181,
402, 423, 434, 437, 496, 503, 534, 546, 567, 571,
580
filth (filthy), 291, 518, 579
finality (final, finalities), 54, 56, 120, 188, 204,
220, 247, 454, 476, 504, 549, 604
finance (financial), 350, 557
find (findeth, finding, finds, found), 2, 97, 156,
165, 168, 187, 193, 200, 203, 204, 207, 208, 217,
232, 233, 235, 236, 238, 239, 243, 247, 248, 249,
251, 254, 263, 265, 266, 271, 274, 276, 278, 282,
284, 290, 291, 293, 294, 306, 315, 319, 332, 333,
345, 349, 356, 357, 359, 362, 365, 367, 368, 372,
373, 374, 380, 384, 385, 394, 401, 402, 405, 406,
407, 408, 422, 424, 425, 435, 436, 437, 438, 440,
449, 451, 452, 453, 457, 458, 460, 461, 464, 467,
474, 476, 478, 479, 480, 484, 489, 493, 494, 496,
497, 505, 508, 509, 513, 521, 523, 525, 526, 527,
528, 532, 534, 535, 537, 543, 546, 549, 550, 555,
560, 561, 562, 567, 569, 570, 573, 574, 579, 581,
589, 590, 592, 593, 594, 595, 596, 599, 601, 602
fine (fined, fineness, finer, finery, fines, finest,
fining), 2, 6, 7, 25, 58, 88, 104, 111, 131, 150,
152, 163, 195, 199, 201, 204, 208, 209, 210, 214,
216, 221, 226, 231, 292, 299, 311, 321, 330, 331,
333, 346, 352, 362, 364, 382, 384, 385, 388, 406,
420, 428, 436, 453, 457, 458, 462, 463, 465, 476,
478, 483, 488, 492, 499, 513, 517, 529, 530, 539,
550, 553, 558, 568, 579, 598, 600, 601, 603
fine arts, 72
fine-hammered, 545
finger (fingered, fingers), 1, 45, 50, 78, 100, 120,
176, 213, 290, 297, 315, 335, 373, 458, 533, 547,
576
finish (finished, finishes, finishing), 95, 123, 125,
158, 229, 357, 603
finishing school, 158
finite, 286, 547
fire (fired, fires, firing), 13, 14, 17, 18, 22, 32, 45,
46, 48, 51, 56, 57, 59, 79, 83, 85, 95, 101, 110,
132, 143, 154, 175, 194, 203, 204, 216, 225, 257,
269, 271, 291, 302, 303, 306, 317, 322, 329, 331,
336, 339, 345, 347, 351, 360, 374, 376, 442, 444,
446, 454, 465, 481, 486, 493, 498, 503, 511, 552,
555, 570, 590
firearms, 594
fire-boys, 486
firebrand, 425
fireless, 470
fireside, 103, 239, 307, 385, 516
firm (firmer, firmly, firmness), 66, 67, 94, 98,
106, 110, 134, 174, 194, 231, 267, 279, 283, 344,
348, 350, 367, 435, 496, 542
firmament (firmaments), 111, 185, 225, 331
First Cause, 56

first impressions, 479
first sight, 204, 205
fish (fisheries, fishes), 31, 55, 71, 79, 108, 159, 179,
    258, 280, 281, 306, 314, 328, 402, 421
fist (fisticuffs), 194, 469
fit (fitful, fitfully, fitness, fits, fitted, fitter,
    fittest, fitting), 6, 47, 102, 194, 199, 213, 218,
    231, 241, 265, 279, 280, 281, 299, 306, 307, 324,
    325, 328, 334, 335, 344, 345, 350, 362, 367, 368,
    376, 395, 402, 409, 436, 446, 451, 457, 463, 467,
    493, 503, 504, 507, 521, 546, 557, 574, 584, 602
fix (fixed, fixes, fixing), 101, 135, 139, 157, 176,
    237, 274, 325, 360, 384, 388, 405, 420, 457, 506,
    531, 552, 557, 579, 582
flag, 435
flagititious, 378
flagrant, 533
flame (flames, flaming), 13, 14, 42, 57, 78, 94, 132,
    138, 151, 175, 189, 202, 291, 320, 329, 337, 345,
    446, 503, 591
flapjacks, 596
flare, 87, 331
flash (flashes, flashing), 198, 449, 463, 490
flat (flattened, flattest), 279, 478, 530
flattery (flatter, flattered, flatterer, flatterers,
    flatteries, flattering, flatters), 45, 69, 73, 86,
    102, 130, 194, 195, 196, 209, 228, 235, 325, 327,
    329, 369, 372, 379, 410, 417, 453, 461, 480, 481,
    490, 498, 532, 570, 580, 587, 589
flatulency, 473
flavor, 142, 236, 302, 600
flawless, 336
flea (fleas), 108, 445, 561
fleckless, 336
flee (fled, fleet, fleeting), 50, 149, 177, 187, 237,
    286, 585, 604
flesh (fleshless), 21, 87, 181, 207, 328, 381, 451,
    497, 511, 543, 548, 549
flexible, 96, 481
flight (flights), 27, 73, 166, 189, 247, 350, 403, 548
flighty, 349
fling (flings, flung), 112, 234, 404, 435
flinty, 481
flippancy (flippant), 367, 502
flirtation (flirt, flirting, flirts), 341, 373, 374, 396,
    491
flit (flits, flitting), 448, 516
float (floated, floating, floats), 162, 268, 316, 334,
    403, 463, 485, 572, 603
flock (flocks), 436, 484, 576
flog (flogged, flogging), 410, 492
flood (flooded), 217, 225, 316, 429, 486, 559, 563
floor (flooring), 53, 375, 542, 546
flourish (flourished, flourishes, flourisheth,
    flourishing), 231, 266, 311, 402, 505, 525, 600
flow (flowed, floweth, flowing, flows), 160, 195,
    201, 215, 226, 265, 269, 270, 281, 316, 330, 347,
    369, 420, 444, 481, 516, 518, 567
flower (flowers, flowery), 5, 9, 54, 85, 91, 123, 126,
    132, 150, 156, 168, 172, 178, 197, 251, 271, 283,
    322, 324, 328, 333, 345, 356, 368, 373, 431, 439,
    566
fluctuation (fluctuates, fluctuations, flux), 63, 64,
    77, 146, 254, 378
fluent (fluently), 527, 535
fluid (fluids), 152, 602
fly (flew, flies, flying), 30, 31, 58, 108, 132, 142,
    149, 152, 165, 173, 174, 231, 257, 270, 286, 291,

294, 295, 298, 316, 322, 368, 389, 421, 431, 436,
    439, 443, 467, 468, 475, 478, 490, 501, 502, 516,
    531, 539, 540, 557, 560, 581, 600, 605
fly-fisher (fly-fishing), 55, 179
foe (foes: *see also* enemy), 23, 37, 91, 127, 128, 135,
    152, 163, 178, 205, 236, 242, 268, 354, 403, 430,
    449, 492, 516
foible (foibles), 195, 292, 363, 364, 527
foil, 377, 600
folk (folks), 11, 21, 58, 65, 88, 125, 197, 211, 244,
    278, 321, 323, 331, 393, 401, 411, 429, 441, 471,
    472, 487, 500, 516, 575, 598
follow (followed, follower, followers, following,
    follows), 139, 148, 149, 150, 160, 179, 187, 208,
    210, 212, 269, 285, 287, 293, 302, 313, 314, 320,
    342, 348, 349, 350, 354, 357, 361, 363, 370, 374,
    411, 418, 422, 427, 429, 443, 471, 484, 486, 499,
    503, 507, 508, 521, 522, 533, 539, 569, 583, 588,
    591
folly (follies, fool, fooling, foolish, foolishest,
    foolishly, foolishness, fools), 1, 4, 6, 13, 19, 24,
    40, 41, 47, 53, 54, 55, 58, 63, 67, 69, 73, 81, 84,
    88, 91, 92, 94, 97, 98, 99, 104, 112, 114, 118, 128,
    136, 145, 147, 153, 161, 163, 164, 166, 167, 169,
    170, 177, 181, 186, 188, 191, 192, 193, 195, 196,
    197, 198, 209, 210, 213, 215, 216, 222, 225, 227,
    230, 233, 239, 241, 246, 248, 249, 253, 254, 258,
    259, 261, 262, 263, 264, 271, 272, 274, 275, 276,
    288, 294, 302, 304, 309, 320, 327, 335, 336, 337,
    338, 345, 350, 354, 356, 357, 359, 363, 364, 366,
    367, 368, 369, 371, 377, 379, 380, 382, 384, 385,
    388, 389, 391, 392, 396, 401, 403, 409, 410, 442,
    449, 457, 458, 461, 475, 479, 480, 481, 487, 497,
    501, 505, 507, 513, 520, 527, 533, 534, 535, 547,
    550, 553, 556, 559, 565, 575, 578, 580, 581, 584,
    589, 595, 596, 597, 598, 599
fondness (fond, fonder), 89, 92, 117, 132, 146, 162,
    168, 182, 198, 209, 238, 247, 259, 286, 315, 325,
    326, 328, 332, 350, 357, 358, 373, 374, 391, 401,
    403, 413, 414, 436, 444, 477, 493, 521, 532, 544,
    576, 595, 603
food, 21, 45, 59, 87, 99, 143, 161, 195, 260, 274,
    287, 334, 362, 408, 411, 418, 462, 470, 479, 540,
    547, 558, 569, 593, 597
fool's cap, 95, 142
fool's paradise/Fool's Paradise, 243, 274
foolish-wise, 254
foot (feet), 41, 43, 88, 90, 92, 116, 119, 148, 153,
    189, 214, 263, 276, 296, 308, 347, 365, 368, 374,
    384, 402, 411, 454, 476, 503, 516, 538, 556, 562,
    566, 575, 576, 578, 583
football, 135
footnotes, 399
foppery (fop), 536, 580
forbearance (forbear, forbearing), 89, 130, 179,
    198, 265, 330
forbid (forbidden, forbidding, forbids), 51, 90,
    109, 142, 207, 221, 328, 391, 401, 487, 533, 559
force (forced, forces, forceth, forcible, forcibly,
    forcing), 5, 27, 40, 54, 56, 78, 90, 107, 133, 135,
    136, 138, 152, 153, 156, 169, 177, 183, 198, 200,
    208, 209, 223, 243, 255, 266, 273, 278, 279, 304,
    307, 335, 342, 353, 355, 356, 357, 364, 370, 372,
    374, 381, 386, 395, 397, 400, 412, 417, 427, 436,
    440, 448, 463, 466, 492, 499, 504, 511, 518, 522,
    530, 538, 547, 551, 555, 560, 561, 572, 577, 596
foreboding (forboding, forebodings), 68, 236, 286,
    488

glass (glasses), 17, 20, 30, 40, 89, 98, 150, 151, 152, 293, 354, 363, 518
gleam (gleaming, gleamings), 11, 260, 284, 317, 464, 560
gleaned, 293
glibness (glib), 173, 336
glide (glides, gliding), 7, 134, 149, 273, 322, 407
glimmer (glimmering, glimmery), 148, 237, 254, 333, 407, 462
glimpse (glimpses), 56, 99, 123, 280, 306, 422, 436, 548
glitter (glittering, glitters), 477, 500, 600
globe (globes), 3, 157, 227, 430, 439
gloom (gloomiest, gloomy), 87, 124, 161, 225, 259, 275, 284, 291, 305, 320, 336, 412, 434, 552
glory (gloried, glories, glorified, glorify, glorifying, glorious), 41, 79, 87, 92, 94, 106, 107, 118, 122, 127, 137, 148, 149, 190, 206, 212, 214, 216, 222, 235, 266, 270, 273, 278, 281, 301, 325, 328, 329, 336, 366, 369, 376, 383, 413, 415, 421, 439, 451, 454, 465, 467, 489, 511, 528, 549, 573, 583, 591
gloss (glosses, glossing, glossy), 192, 275, 385, 436, 507, 567, 589
glove (gloves), 47, 253, 578
glow (glowing, glows), 11, 13, 55, 131, 187, 209, 240, 297, 537
glowworm, 107
glut (gluttony), 37, 212
goad (goaded), 97, 296
goal, 15, 361
goblins, 211
god/God (goddess, goddesses, gods/Gods), 4, 8, 32, 37, 43, 47, 53, 61, 70, 72, 83, 87, 95, 98, 108, 109, 110, 111, 124, 134, 135, 137, 138, 139, 140, 169, 171, 187, 197, 201, 206, 211, 212, 213, 214, 215, 216, 217, 219, 220, 227, 229, 245, 257, 263, 264, 271, 279, 281, 286, 287, 293, 294, 301, 302, 306, 310, 314, 322, 323, 324, 325, 326, 328, 330, 331, 336, 338, 339, 342, 343, 351, 356, 357, 359, 361, 367, 368, 370, 371, 373, 374, 382, 386, 391, 396, 404, 410, 414, 416, 420, 421, 427, 431, 432, 436, 437, 440, 441, 444, 446, 447, 453, 457, 459, 465, 474, 475, 484, 492, 494, 502, 503, 504, 505, 511, 512, 514, 517, 521, 523, 532, 535, 538, 539, 541, 547, 548, 549, 551, 553, 560, 564, 568, 572, 578, 583, 586, 587, 590, 597, 598, 604, 605
God Buonaparte, 214
God-forgive-me, 151
godliness/Godliness (godliest, godlike, godly), 19, 76, 212, 216, 217, 271, 281, 486, 579
Godwin, 230
gold (golden), 12, 18, 24, 64, 70, 78, 85, 104, 137, 159, 185, 216, 236, 317, 327, 336, 373, 374, 401, 415, 416, 422, 427, 430, 431, 442, 447, 534, 565, 571, 579, 585
golden age, 111
Goliath, 383, 550
good (goodness), 1, 3, 10, 12, 14, 20, 21, 24, 25, 27, 30, 31, 32, 37, 38, 39, 40, 43, 44, 45, 46, 49, 51, 52, 54, 55, 56, 59, 62, 63, 64, 65, 66, 67, 68, 70, 73, 74, 75, 76, 80, 81, 82, 83, 85, 86, 91, 94, 96, 97, 98, 99, 104, 105, 111, 112, 118, 122, 126, 131, 134, 135, 136, 137, 141, 144, 145, 147, 151, 152, 153, 154, 155, 157, 158, 163, 164, 166, 167, 168, 169, 170, 172, 174, 175, 177, 179, 180, 181, 182, 183, 184, 187, 189, 190, 192, 199, 200, 201,

204, 206, 207, 208, 209, 213, 214, 215, 216, 217, 218, 219, 220, 221, 222, 223, 224, 225, 231, 236, 240, 241, 242, 243, 248, 252, 254, 257, 263, 264, 265, 268, 269, 271, 272, 276, 277, 278, 282, 283, 284, 286, 292, 293, 294, 297, 301, 303, 307, 308, 310, 311, 312, 313, 315, 319, 320, 322, 323, 325, 327, 331, 334, 336, 337, 341, 342, 343, 345, 348, 351, 352, 353, 356, 359, 362, 363, 364, 365, 368, 369, 370, 373, 375, 376, 378, 379, 380, 382, 383, 385, 386, 387, 389, 390, 391, 393, 394, 395, 396, 397, 398, 399, 400, 402, 403, 404, 405, 406, 408, 411, 412, 413, 414, 417, 418, 427, 431, 434, 435, 436, 440, 441, 442, 443, 449, 450, 454, 456, 458, 459, 460, 461, 462, 463, 466, 467, 469, 472, 473, 474, 476, 477, 480, 481, 483, 484, 485, 486, 488, 489, 490, 491, 492, 493, 496, 497, 498, 501, 502, 503, 504, 505, 506, 508, 509, 510, 511, 512, 513, 514, 522, 523, 524, 525, 527, 528, 529, 530, 533, 534, 536, 537, 539, 540, 542, 543, 544, 549, 551, 553, 554, 556, 557, 558, 559, 560, 561, 568, 569, 570, 571, 574, 577, 579, 580, 582, 584, 586, 587, 588, 589, 590, 591, 592, 594, 596, 598, 600, 601, 603
good-breeding, 208
good-bye, 118, 445
good fortune, 207
good-heartedness, 222
good humor, 64, 158, 186, 264, 315, 323, 468, 489, 497, 542
good-looking, 347, 360, 373, 557
good luck, 61, 207, 342, 513
good-natured, 25, 222, 370, 516, 518
Good Samaritan, 488
good sense, 84, 98, 192, 357, 541
good taste, 551
good will, 82, 117, 174, 175, 205, 402, 419, 532
goose (geese), 58, 197, 371, 552, 570
Gordian knot, 16, 388
gormed, 173
gospel/Gospel, 180, 313, 336, 477, 503, 547
gossamer, 331
gossip, 352, 382, 484
gout, 183, 400
government (govern, governed, governing, government, governments, governs), 4, 15, 20, 26, 46, 73, 87, 107, 113, 116, 130, 150, 154, 164, 177, 194, 200, 223, 224, 225, 226, 250, 253, 256, 273, 280, 286, 304, 305, 306, 314, 316, 322, 323, 350, 379, 388, 391, 408, 414, 417, 429, 432, 440, 447, 449, 475, 478, 494, 497, 502, 513, 546, 565, 593
governors, 200, 224, 364
grace (graces), 24, 39, 42, 43, 64, 66, 108, 146, 174, 180, 187, 194, 199, 216, 217, 219, 226, 296, 300, 301, 316, 352, 356, 360, 364, 367, 414, 470, 475, 496, 528, 536, 565, 588, 597
graceful (gracefully, gracefulness), 65, 67, 187, 370, 440, 483, 486, 516, 544
gracious (graciously), 215, 336, 358, 364
grain (grains), 53, 109, 110, 158, 372, 426, 483, 564, 572, 596
grammar (grammarians, grammars), 42, 67, 156, 157, 186, 465, 576
grandam, 335
grandchildren, 270
grandee, 163, 600
grandeur (grand, grander, grandest, grandness),

8, 10, 18, 26, 37, 45, 71, 105, 126, 140, 153, 160,
177, 183, 212, 227, 228, 229, 256, 262, 268, 271,
281, 331, 341, 389, 404, 460, 484, 508, 514, 523,
535, 542, 545, 573, 583, 586, 604
grandfather, 12, 184, 330
grandmothers, 356
granite, 11, 134, 429
grant (granted, granting, grants), 9, 121, 185,
292, 300, 325, 350, 421, 476, 499, 538, 552
grape, 152, 529
grapple (grapples), 99, 120, 214, 259, 366, 512
grasp (grasping, grasps), 138, 177, 179, 197, 198,
318, 409, 449, 466, 513, 598
grass, 17, 25, 118, 290, 406
grasshopper (grasshoppers), 275, 486
gratification (gratifications, gratified, gratifies,
gratify, gratifying), 3, 31, 115, 116, 163, 165,
203, 206, 221, 234, 266, 291, 327, 332, 350, 388,
393, 428, 438, 447, 450, 474, 482, 519, 582, 597
gratitude (grateful), 21, 48, 67, 100, 127, 163, 173,
175, 209, 222, 226, 227, 326, 332, 368, 394
gratuitous, 357, 478
grave (gravely, graver, graves, gravest), 37, 41,
76, 83, 106, 119, 121, 123, 124, 125, 126, 131,
134, 135, 142, 155, 168, 187, 229, 230, 235, 247,
265, 283, 306, 318, 319, 330, 340, 380, 392, 441,
443, 486, 499, 517, 521, 590, 597
gravestone, 124, 183
graveyard, 604
gravitation, 260, 335
gravity, 227, 400, 532, 552
Great Britain (*see also* England), 142, 224
great-grandchildren, 184
greatheart, 449
greatness (great, greater, greatest), 3, 5, 8, 10, 15,
16, 18, 29, 43, 51, 55, 56, 69, 72, 73, 78, 81, 87,
89, 92, 93, 103, 105, 106, 112, 113, 114, 115, 118,
119, 124, 127, 132, 133, 137, 139, 143, 145, 148,
149, 154, 156, 159, 161, 164, 169, 171, 175, 177,
178, 184, 190, 192, 193, 197, 201, 202, 207, 208,
209, 210, 211, 212, 213, 214, 215, 216, 217, 218,
219, 220, 221, 223, 226, 227, 228, 229, 230, 231,
232, 236, 239, 243, 245, 246, 247, 248, 249, 251,
252, 254, 255, 256, 257, 258, 259, 260, 261, 262,
264, 266, 270, 271, 273, 275, 276, 278, 279, 280,
281, 282, 284, 286, 287, 294, 296, 297, 299, 301,
302, 303, 305, 306, 308, 309, 310, 311, 312, 316,
317, 318, 319, 320, 323, 324, 327, 329, 331, 333,
335, 338, 339, 340, 341, 343, 344, 345, 346, 348,
349, 350, 351, 353, 368, 383, 390, 391, 392, 398,
406, 410, 412, 413, 416, 417, 418, 419, 420, 421,
422, 423, 426, 427, 428, 434, 435, 437, 438, 439,
441, 443, 444, 448, 452, 453, 456, 458, 461, 463,
466, 467, 469, 470, 471, 476, 477, 479, 481, 485,
487, 488, 489, 490, 492, 493, 495, 496, 498, 500,
501, 502, 503, 504, 507, 509, 510, 512, 515, 517,
522, 524, 525, 526, 527, 529, 530, 531, 533, 534,
535, 536, 542, 544, 545, 548, 549, 555, 557, 558,
559, 561, 562, 563, 565, 566, 567, 568, 569, 570,
572, 573, 574, 576, 577, 578, 579, 580, 584, 586,
589, 592, 594, 597, 599, 600, 601, 602, 603, 604
Great Wall of China, 578
Greece (Greek, Greeks), 10, 138, 155, 166, 267,
305, 360, 421, 576, 602
greed (greedy), 58, 234, 266
greenhand, 12, 199
greet (greeted), 163, 215, 462, 548

grief (griefs, grieve, grieved, grieves), 10, 17, 19,
55, 68, 71, 89, 100, 124, 125, 150, 175, 214, 229,
230, 261, 277, 288, 290, 292, 304, 305, 307, 317,
385, 403, 435, 501, 507, 520, 532, 603
grievance, 86, 93, 312
grievous, 160, 168, 455, 458, 556
grim, 90, 148, 309, 450, 470, 522, 527, 590
grin (grinning, grins), 87, 269, 307, 468, 552
groove (grooves), 266, 320, 322, 335, 348
grossness (gross, grosser, grossest, grossly), 38,
149, 199, 257, 268, 298, 313, 345, 363, 365, 399,
419, 434, 497, 530
grotesque, 16, 264, 298, 532
ground, 82, 101, 116, 119, 120, 121, 205, 234, 245,
273, 303, 383, 404, 406, 416, 420, 443, 464, 478,
497, 507, 529, 532, 579, 597
groundwork, 23, 165, 171, 263
group psychology, 230
grovel (grovelled, grovelling), 28, 524, 583
growth (grew, grow, growing, grown, grows,
growths), 11, 45, 54, 68, 100, 165, 183, 185, 193,
202, 204, 220, 223, 228, 230, 231, 240, 248, 255,
260, 264, 268, 271, 275, 284, 285, 288, 296, 301,
303, 306, 324, 330, 332, 339, 362, 364, 365, 385,
399, 406, 428, 431, 444, 445, 447, 451, 470, 490,
494, 502, 515, 520, 530, 531, 540, 544, 548, 557,
562, 577, 582, 588, 591, 595, 598, 604
grudges, 292
guanoed, 282
guarantee, 3, 487, 579
guard (guarded, guards), 5, 40, 102, 115, 117, 129,
139, 155, 251, 267, 287, 340, 345, 359, 365, 372,
397, 413, 446, 536, 580, 587, 588
guardian (guardians), 156, 309, 312, 394, 441
guess (guesser, guesswork), 68, 79, 362, 388, 394,
401, 448, 449, 516, 527
guest (guests), 113, 226, 335, 405, 430, 434, 437,
517, 537
guidance (guide, guided, guides, guideth,
guiding), 9, 23, 94, 95, 98, 103, 134, 135, 155,
176, 210, 214, 231, 243, 250, 259, 276, 292, 301,
308, 340, 352, 370, 448, 461, 473, 488, 490, 497,
505, 555, 597
guidebook, 48
guile (guileful, guileless), 283, 293, 345, 435, 466
guilt (guiltiness, guiltless, guilty), 1, 5, 17, 44, 47,
51, 60, 88, 96, 112, 124, 133, 134, 135, 149, 184,
189, 219, 221, 223, 226, 231, 232, 233, 245, 251,
252, 267, 283, 284, 285, 294, 295, 296, 298, 310,
338, 339, 349, 386, 401, 436, 438, 446, 461, 488,
492, 493, 531, 547, 556, 583, 584, 585, 587, 590
guinea (guineas), 157, 315, 571, 579
gulf (gulfs), 82, 392, 412, 454, 566, 593
gull (gulled, gulling), 220, 570
gun (gunners, gunpowder, guns), 153, 302, 590,
591
gusto, 28
gypsy, 422
gyrations, 596

habeas corpus, 310
haberdasher, 220
habit (habits, habitual, habitually), 4, 15, 52, 57,
79, 95, 96, 103, 104, 106, 110, 141, 168, 170, 173,
201, 217, 220, 233, 234, 239, 240, 260, 261, 281,
293, 374, 375, 378, 389, 397, 398, 418, 441, 449,

habit (*continued*)
457, 468, 520, 522, 525, 527, 546, 547, 560, 563, 589, 593, 604
habitation, 3, 406, 550
habitudes, 234
hackney-coach, 382
Hades, 477
hag, 26, 598
haggard, 203, 274, 411
haggling, 342
hail, 257
hair (hairs), 6, 12, 20, 26, 36, 42, 45, 150, 159, 318, 363, 444, 445, 522, 529, 601
hale (haler), 302, 417
half (halves: *see also* half-____), 136, 212, 244, 251, 255, 258, 282, 286, 298, 347, 421, 598, 602
half-civilized, 313
half-confidence, 93
half-conscious, 69
half-feathered, 389
half-flayed, 600
half-fledged, 69
half-known, 257
half-penny, 565
half-perceptions, 154
half-truths, 572
half-waking, 548
halfway (halfway house), 114, 490
half-witted, 585, 604
half-worthy, 4
hall (halls), 30, 298, 376, 486
halo, 22, 41
halt, 140
halter (halters), 117, 187, 294
ham, 443, 600
hamlets, 109
hammer, 184, 422
hammock, 501
hamper, 163, 449, 505
hand (hands), 2, 31, 38, 45, 47, 50, 63, 67, 74, 75, 83, 90, 91, 111, 120, 123, 130, 141, 155, 157, 161, 163, 176, 199, 202, 204, 207, 208, 213, 214, 215, 225, 226, 230, 245, 249, 250, 256, 257, 279, 280, 281, 287, 296, 299, 306, 308, 309, 310, 332, 356, 359, 362, 367, 370, 379, 381, 388, 394, 399, 400, 429, 434, 443, 444, 449, 452, 463, 467, 473, 477, 485, 486, 489, 492, 493, 495, 496, 507, 519, 521, 539, 545, 550, 557, 566, 570, 576, 578, 581, 583, 592
handbill, 93
handcuff, 45
handful, 243, 320
handgun, 32
handicraftsman, 464
handiwork, 356
handkerchief, 455
handle (handles, handling), 204, 313, 317, 550, 574
handsome, 9, 14, 19, 40, 64, 140, 162, 173, 197, 234, 349, 354, 360, 376, 378, 384, 391, 553
handspike, 138
handwriting, 310
hang (hanged, hanging, hangings, hangman, hangs, hung), 23, 53, 70, 132, 134, 168, 170, 233, 266, 268, 286, 288, 291, 302, 308, 311, 351, 364, 386, 398, 421, 424, 488, 492, 511, 532, 533, 540, 554, 577, 585, 592, 602

hang-dog, 252
hank, 359, 371
hankering, 583
hap, 184
happen (happened, happeneth, happening, happens), 111, 136, 168, 189, 191, 214, 245, 246, 257, 258, 274, 298, 345, 346, 352, 371, 395, 403, 407, 408, 428, 432, 441, 457, 467, 482, 488, 489, 496, 497, 541, 520, 527, 540, 556, 573, 574, 594, 596
happiness (happier, happiest, happily, happinesses, happy), 12, 15, 17, 19, 20, 24, 28, 32, 50, 53, 62, 63, 69, 70, 73, 74, 75, 77, 82, 89, 95, 96, 97, 103, 104, 116, 118, 121, 125, 128, 136, 137, 146, 148, 154, 157, 163, 164, 165, 172, 182, 183, 185, 191, 192, 202, 208, 212, 223, 225, 234, 235, 236, 237, 238, 239, 240, 247, 248, 250, 251, 254, 255, 258, 280, 282, 283, 290, 291, 292, 293, 303, 304, 306, 312, 314, 316, 317, 321, 323, 328, 331, 333, 334, 339, 346, 348, 352, 353, 358, 359, 360, 361, 363, 365, 371, 373, 374, 375, 376, 377, 378, 380, 384, 388, 391, 392, 393, 394, 395, 396, 397, 398, 404, 408, 417, 420, 429, 431, 445, 464, 465, 474, 488, 492, 500, 505, 510, 527, 528, 529, 531, 538, 540, 556, 560, 562, 564, 569, 581, 584, 586, 597, 598, 599
harangue (harangues, haranguing), 152, 225, 475, 477, 490
harass (harassed), 58, 501
harbor (harbors), 85, 126, 203, 316, 338, 543, 569
hard-heartedness (hard-hearted), 112, 315
hardiness (hardy), 25, 70, 188
hard-learnt, 422
hardship (hardships), 19, 411, 477, 537
hardworking, 53
hare, 588
hare-bells, 118
harem, 389
harm (harmful, harms), 25, 52, 69, 78, 114, 153, 183, 196, 240, 400, 410, 439, 471, 472, 503, 525, 562, 597
harmless, 111, 220, 237, 283, 297, 357, 427, 592
harmony (harmonics, harmonies, harmonious, harmonize), 19, 43, 104, 134, 158, 223, 237, 288, 303, 321, 325, 422, 423, 483, 487, 530, 551, 587
harness, 511
harp (harps), 56, 68, 269, 358
harpies, 584
harpooneers, 458
harshness (harsh, harshly), 5, 49, 56, 140, 295, 391
Harvard, 158
harvest, 58, 159, 213, 343, 383, 547
haste (hasty), 57, 119, 120, 160, 163, 175, 200, 237, 306, 344, 388, 428, 434
hat (hats), 16, 145, 367, 485, 508, 553, 579
hatchet, 463
hatred (hate, hated, hatedst, hateful, hater, haters, hates, hating, hatreds), 19, 22, 23, 58, 59, 62, 74, 81, 90, 91, 109, 111, 139, 164, 166, 170, 180, 189, 197, 202, 214, 216, 220, 221, 223, 225, 240, 241, 261, 272, 281, 291, 292, 293, 297, 319, 321, 329, 332, 334, 339, 340, 350, 359, 360, 370, 372, 374, 375, 378, 392, 410, 411, 416, 431, 442, 452, 457, 461, 463, 471, 492, 507, 524, 534, 543, 555, 570, 582, 584, 591, 602
haughtiness (haughty), 66, 437, 481, 510, 538
haul (hauled, hauls), 179, 359

haunt (haunted, haunting, haunts), 82, 118, 119, 188, 309, 321, 435, 524, 534
haven, 604
havoc, 566
hawk (hawks), 126, 331, 443, 579
hazard (hazards), 116, 220, 474
head (heads), 6, 11, 16, 28, 29, 33, 42, 55, 58, 65, 66, 73, 77, 81, 83, 94, 95, 100, 106, 129, 138, 144, 150, 152, 156, 160, 164, 167, 168, 209, 211, 225, 241, 242, 250, 260, 267, 276, 288, 291, 297, 298, 302, 307, 318, 329, 339, 340, 366, 367, 368, 402, 409, 419, 426, 432, 442, 445, 454, 457, 465, 473, 476, 481, 490, 491, 493, 500, 505, 506, 509, 511, 513, 515, 518, 529, 535, 539, 554, 556, 569, 572, 573, 578, 579, 584, 585, 590, 600
headache (headaches), 56, 371, 401
headful, 302
headpiece, 356, 482
headstone, 84
headstrong, 9, 199, 447, 515
heal (healer, healing, heals), 163, 195, 216, 263, 402, 416, 566, 582
health (healthful, healthy), 8, 19, 25, 30, 83, 97, 107, 122, 125, 141, 151, 206, 209, 223, 241, 263, 279, 299, 312, 319, 375, 418, 462, 471, 489, 492, 507, 538
heap (heaped, heaps), 154, 186, 404, 590
hear (heard, hearer, hearers, heareth, hearing, hears), 17, 70, 90, 104, 140, 152, 191, 192, 195, 223, 232, 244, 259, 266, 275, 284, 287, 293, 304, 308, 316, 323, 337, 340, 357, 360, 372, 376, 382, 388, 400, 402, 412, 421, 422, 425, 431, 432, 436, 441, 457, 458, 470, 475, 476, 477, 482, 494, 503, 508, 516, 519, 523, 526, 527, 539, 544, 547, 560, 564, 570, 587, 601
hearken, 31
hearsay, 469
hearse (hearse-drivers), 122, 486
heart (hearts), 5, 6, 8, 10, 11, 12, 19, 24, 26, 28, 31, 32, 33, 34, 36, 39, 41, 42, 45, 47, 48, 49, 52, 53, 54, 55, 57, 58, 59, 61, 64, 65, 66, 67, 70, 71, 74, 77, 78, 79, 83, 87, 88, 90, 91, 94, 96, 97, 99, 100, 102, 103, 105, 106, 107, 108, 109, 111, 120, 121, 124, 125, 126, 138, 140, 143, 144, 145, 148, 150, 152, 153, 154, 157, 158, 160, 161, 167, 169, 170, 172, 173, 174, 175, 176, 178, 181, 183, 188, 189, 192, 193, 194, 195, 197, 201, 203, 204, 205, 207, 208, 211, 214, 219, 221, 222, 223, 226, 227, 230, 233, 238, 239, 241, 242, 243, 247, 248, 251, 252, 254, 255, 256, 259, 261, 262, 263, 266, 267, 273, 274, 283, 285, 286, 288, 291, 292, 293, 294, 295, 296, 297, 298, 300, 301, 304, 307, 309, 321, 324, 325, 326, 327, 328, 329, 330, 331, 332, 334, 335, 336, 337, 338, 339, 340, 341, 342, 348, 351, 353, 355, 356, 359, 362, 363, 364, 365, 366, 368, 369, 371, 372, 375, 376, 379, 384, 392, 395, 396, 400, 407, 409, 410, 411, 412, 416, 422, 426, 427, 428, 431, 434, 435, 436, 437, 438, 439, 440, 444, 446, 447, 451, 452, 454, 455, 456, 458, 461, 463, 464, 465, 469, 473, 474, 477, 479, 480, 483, 486, 489, 493, 500, 503, 505, 508, 509, 510, 512, 513, 514, 515, 518, 521, 522, 524, 526, 527, 528, 529, 530, 531, 532, 533, 534, 535, 537, 539, 541, 543, 548, 551, 553, 556, 558, 559, 560, 565, 570, 571, 573, 578, 582, 583, 586, 587, 588, 592, 597, 599, 601, 602, 605
heartaches, 148

heart-beat, 548
heartbreak, 327
heart-dilating, 237
heart-felt, 145
heart-knowledge, 334
heartless, 6, 138, 243, 324, 361, 429
heart on the sleeve, 54
heart-sickness, 329
heartstrings, 183, 387
heart-swelling, 235
hearth (hearthstone), 37, 83, 85, 546
hearty (heartily), 187, 272, 320, 487, 520, 539, 578, 595
heat (heated, heatedness), 21, 28, 150, 279, 291, 311, 465, 601
heath, 17, 118, 569
heathen (heathenish, heathenism, heathens), 75, 135, 218, 352, 405, 430, 476
heaven/Heaven (heavenly, heavens, heavenwards), 3, 8, 15, 17, 18, 32, 37, 38, 51, 56, 58, 67, 71, 79, 114, 127, 130, 134, 135, 138, 149, 163, 184, 209, 210, 214, 215, 220, 226, 229, 233, 235, 243, 244, 245, 248, 253, 254, 274, 280, 286, 290, 293, 297, 307, 335, 337, 340, 342, 357, 362, 364, 368, 374, 379, 384, 387, 389, 390, 396, 405, 406, 412, 421, 434, 437, 440, 442, 444, 447, 464, 465, 467, 492, 500, 502, 505, 520, 528, 542, 545, 551, 558, 563, 578, 583, 585, 590, 592, 598, 604
heaven-begotten, 154
heaven-insulting, 494
heavy (heavier, heaviest, heavily), 102, 201, 230, 239, 240, 242, 259, 277, 301, 319, 380, 404, 466, 477, 548, 592
Hebrew, 431, 502, 602
hecatomb, 54
heed (heedless, heeds), 117, 217, 433, 448, 562
height (heighten, heightened, heightens, heights), 9, 32, 84, 106, 119, 145, 197, 215, 241, 276, 318, 346, 368, 454, 465, 490, 497, 551, 562, 567, 595
heir (heiress, heiresses, heirs), 29, 83, 101, 183, 360, 397, 400, 414
hell/Hell (hells), 14, 16, 32, 130, 165, 180, 220, 234, 243, 244, 245, 291, 307, 316, 342, 374, 453, 491, 502, 504, 534, 563, 583
hell-glimpses, 244
hell-makers, 274
helm, 45, 257
help (helped, helper, helps), 51, 52, 129, 139, 153, 184, 191, 208, 256, 263, 290, 302, 307, 317, 326, 336, 343, 354, 358, 368, 379, 381, 389, 392, 401, 405, 411, 412, 453, 481, 482, 512, 531, 559, 579, 598, 605
helpless (helplessness), 72, 83, 140, 308, 331, 460, 563, 576
helpmeet, 394
hemisphere (hemispheres), 270, 335
hen, 52, 109, 532, 599
henpecked, 394
Henry the Eighth, 497
herald (heralds), 75, 139, 245, 587
hereafters, 138
hereditary, 184, 221, 253, 356
heresy (heretic, heretics), 69, 71, 152, 244, 285, 390, 408, 503
heritage, 14, 245
hermit (hermitage, hermitages), 1, 71, 243, 290, 501, 524

heroism (hero, heroes, heroic, heroically, heroics, heroine, heroines, heroisms), 5, 10, 17, 18, 19, 24, 42, 66, 84, 107, 110, 174, 188, 190, 191, 192, 245, 246, 247, 248, 249, 250, 305, 328, 344, 355, 361, 422, 462, 517, 532, 534, 544, 564, 595

herons, 568

hesitation (hesitate, hesitating), 50, 174, 197, 384

heterodox, 336

heterogeneous, 316

hew (hewers, hews), 22, 255

hide (hid, hidden, hides, hiding), 22, 24, 51, 53, 90, 91, 112, 148, 150, 151, 186, 188, 222, 259, 266, 267, 269, 274, 284, 289, 317, 328, 329, 338, 370, 386, 413, 416, 423, 472, 481, 520, 522, 529, 533, 539, 547, 575, 584, 587, 592

hide-and-seek, 123, 137, 331

hideousness (hideous), 19, 123, 247, 299, 542, 553

hieroglyphics, 449, 563

higgling, 342

high (higher, highest, highly), 54, 93, 158, 216, 235, 240, 244, 246, 252, 260, 267, 269, 274, 279, 290, 297, 298, 305, 325, 331, 338, 339, 344, 345, 435, 561, 574, 583, 596, 597, 598, 603

high-fed, 132, 361

high-flown, 104

high-hearted, 472

high-jinks, 450

high-lifted, 494

highroad, 399, 459

high-souled, 205

high-stomached, 458

high-toned, 562

highwater, 397

highway, 45, 53, 85, 239, 585

highwayman, 388, 474, 487, 549, 580, 585

hilarity, 151

hill (hills, hilly), 118, 243, 428, 478, 481, 534

hindrance (hinder, hinders), 250, 272, 480

hint (hinted, hinting, hints), 61, 73, 138, 197, 266, 293, 305, 320, 372, 385, 448, 529

Hippocrates, 401

hire (hired), 71, 125, 436, 497, 543

history (historian, historians, historical, histories), 10, 48, 64, 65, 84, 96, 103, 113, 139, 156, 180, 182, 191, 192, 193, 234, 242, 247, 248, 249, 250, 259, 290, 303, 313, 318, 321, 344, 352, 353, 358, 370, 373, 387, 410, 440, 456, 464, 470, 483, 524, 526, 530, 532, 547, 569, 575, 576, 577, 590, 595

hoards, 104, 564

hoarse, 109

hoary, 12

hobby, 438

hobby horse, 438, 447

hobnob, 503

hodman, 189

hog (hogs), 64, 143, 430, 570

hold (held, holden, holding, holds), 171, 206, 225, 230, 255, 260, 270, 290, 294, 300, 312, 313, 340, 342, 351, 365, 405, 413, 427, 431, 434, 441, 461, 473, 476, 482, 492, 496, 504, 509, 511, 518, 526, 534, 552, 561, 566, 575, 592, 596

hole (holes), 56, 165, 211, 385, 416, 453, 454, 521, 535

holiday (holidays), 74, 123, 205, 394, 406, 561, 594

hollow, 3, 205, 235, 266, 271, 307, 368, 402, 542

holy (holiest, holiness), 18, 22, 38, 111, 183, 206,

238, 250, 293, 298, 380, 405, 422, 494, 503, 517, 525, 545, 547, 563, 604

Holy Ghost, 596

Holy Guide-Book, 48

holy of holies, 36

Holy Scriptures, 520

homage, 7, 156, 266, 318, 347, 377, 449, 550

home (homes), 1, 4, 19, 24, 71, 76, 84, 86, 87, 131, 146, 151, 152, 157, 162, 169, 172, 175, 184, 191, 206, 230, 232, 236, 250, 266, 270, 287, 322, 324, 336, 375, 377, 383, 395, 415, 431, 443, 451, 457, 462, 476, 482, 494, 520, 525, 533, 550, 569, 588, 590, 597, 602

homeless, 333

homely (homelier), 192, 200, 281, 420, 478, 599

Homer, 191, 370, 465

homestead (homesteads), 85, 315, 406

homicide, 402, 590

homo, 576

honesty (honest, honester, honestly), 26, 29, 32, 70, 86, 87, 91, 96, 114, 131, 136, 145, 150, 153, 181, 184, 193, 218, 241, 244, 250, 251, 252, 253, 258, 264, 281, 293, 307, 310, 311, 313, 325, 334, 337, 355, 358, 367, 373, 375, 381, 385, 402, 435, 444, 446, 447, 455, 472, 487, 489, 497, 510, 521, 522, 540, 551, 556, 574, 584, 593, 599, 602

honey (honeycomb), 26, 57, 66, 99, 132, 299, 368

honeymoon, 383, 384, 390

honor (honorable, honorably, honored, honors), 34, 40, 63, 71, 82, 89, 96, 97, 105, 123, 131, 138, 157, 158, 165, 181, 207, 208, 209, 220, 235, 251, 252, 253, 261, 279, 300, 308, 311, 313, 314, 324, 325, 342, 357, 359, 376, 391, 409, 414, 415, 421, 455, 465, 466, 480, 486, 499, 500, 511, 514, 517, 521, 526, 532, 533, 547, 562, 575, 581, 584, 585, 586, 590, 591, 592

hood, 24

hoodwinked, 446

Hoosier, 468

hope (hoped, hopeful, hopes, hoping), 1, 6, 10, 28, 31, 35, 43, 45, 53, 99, 103, 125, 130, 133, 134, 140, 146, 148, 168, 183, 187, 189, 220, 237, 238, 242, 243, 248, 253, 254, 255, 269, 286, 289, 290, 295, 304, 312, 314, 317, 321, 328, 339, 340, 374, 377, 383, 391, 401, 405, 411, 412, 421, 429, 434, 439, 448, 449, 450, 455, 474, 481, 484, 489, 498, 501, 505, 506, 507, 515, 521, 526, 529, 538, 542, 547, 550, 575, 592, 595

hopelessness (hopeless, hopelessly), 2, 133, 255, 309, 326, 329, 447, 539

Horace, 121, 439

hordes, 274, 574, 591

horror (horrible, horrid, horrors), 9, 73, 74, 75, 84, 88, 107, 109, 112, 122, 187, 220, 252, 254, 257, 288, 303, 307, 361, 422, 471, 571, 591

horse (horses), 22, 81, 114, 147, 157, 159, 175, 185, 213, 224, 261, 264, 316, 382, 396, 401, 420, 422, 433, 437, 454, 472, 496, 508, 511, 569

horseback, 39, 255

horsefly, 382

horsemanship, 419

horsemen, 122

horsepower, 566

horse-races, 441

horse-riding, 192

horseshoe, 463

horsewhip, 511

idea (*continued*)
104, 113, 119, 122, 126, 148, 157, 160, 166, 168,
172, 174, 180, 184, 189, 191, 201, 209, 223, 228,
235, 252, 268, 269, 270, 272, 275, 278, 289, 293,
297, 298, 303, 304, 310, 312, 320, 324, 330, 357,
360, 378, 409, 410, 427, 434, 435, 438, 452, 460,
470, 486, 490, 492, 496, 497, 499, 504, 507, 515,
522, 530, 537, 538, 541, 547, 551, 562, 563, 564,
565, 569, 604
ideal/Ideal (idealism, ideality, idealize, ideals),
29, 30, 31, 54, 119, 226, 238, 246, 268, 269, 325,
353, 360, 362, 464, 489, 490, 502, 517, 550
identical, 296, 307
identify (identifying), 112, 278
identity, 18, 269, 270, 271, 444, 543
idiomatical, 340
idiosyncrasy (idiosyncrasies), 270, 348
idiot (idiotic, idiots), 69, 161, 195, 196, 237, 244,
262, 298, 301, 310, 354, 440
idleness (idle)—2, 59, 115, 131, 176, 182, 203, 206,
226, 238, 272, 303, 306, 314, 367, 439, 441, 472,
498, 506, 550, 563, 566
idol (idolaters, idolatry, idolize, idolized, idols),
75, 129, 134, 183, 267, 345, 438, 468, 474, 605
ifs, 147
ignis-fatuus-like, 327
ignited, 540
ignoble, 29, 143, 208, 315
ignominy, 41
ignorance (ignorant, ignorantly), 5, 6, 7, 20, 51,
56, 67, 91, 101, 108, 159, 170, 186, 189, 221, 235,
267, 272, 273, 278, 301, 302, 303, 304, 305, 314,
319, 345, 346, 349, 359, 365, 367, 370, 391, 400,
401, 402, 412, 440, 448, 449, 450, 457, 458, 465,
475, 502, 503, 505, 506, 514, 518, 519, 524, 527,
532, 550, 562, 569, 576, 589, 593, 600, 601
ignore (ignored), 65, 455, 592
Iliad (Iliads, Ilium), 42, 386, 591
ill (illness, illnesses, ills), 1, 6, 18, 75, 108, 109,
131, 136, 167, 168, 172, 182, 218, 220, 221, 227,
237, 241, 243, 271, 282, 293, 320, 326, 344, 346,
374, 376, 378, 382, 400, 401, 402, 404, 406, 407,
412, 424, 449, 461, 471, 487, 499, 516, 528, 563,
568, 589, 592, 596, 599
ill-assortedness (ill-assorted), 388, 390
ill-boding, 136
illbreeding, 492
ill-drawn, 190
ill-fated, 180
ill-favored, 363
ill-gotten, 102, 473
ill-guided, 294
ill humor, 264
ill-judged (ill-judging), 137, 181, 206
ill luck, 10, 136, 308
ill-natured, 237, 470
ill-shapen, 584
ill-temper, 91
ill treatment, 308
ill-usage (ill-used), 137, 296, 463
ill will, 447
illegibility, 35
illiberality (illiberal), 260, 315, 409
illimitable, 289
illiterate, 391
illumination (illuminate, illuminated), 43, 176,
192, 488

illusion (illusions), 17, 55, 148, 149, 273, 337, 342,
434, 462, 463, 531, 561, 602
illustration (illustrate, illustrated, illustrates,
illustrator), 273, 370, 450, 502
illustrious, 67, 181, 273, 344
image (images), 75, 119, 148, 169, 193, 212, 216,
263, 274, 275, 308, 374, 409, 417, 441, 465, 476,
500, 507, 531, 534, 542, 543, 584
imagination/Imagination (imaginable,
imaginary, imaginations, imaginative,
imagine, imagined, imagines, imagining), 4, 13,
25, 29, 31, 48, 63, 84, 111, 116, 118, 121, 145, 147,
148, 167, 178, 181, 183, 187, 193, 200, 203, 210,
214, 219, 221, 224, 228, 230, 234, 236, 237, 238,
246, 247, 255, 259, 261, 269, 273, 274, 275, 276,
277, 278, 284, 289, 290, 293, 295, 310, 327, 329,
330, 331, 344, 346, 347, 376, 389, 391, 399, 413,
423, 430, 431, 435, 440, 453, 454, 463, 464, 465,
479, 495, 499, 500, 504, 517, 522, 527, 528, 532,
569, 573, 579, 584, 594, 596
imbecility (imbecile), 110, 158, 272, 309, 333, 346,
365, 513
imbruted, 512
imitation (imitate, imitated, imitates, imitative),
2, 22, 42, 156, 180, 215, 259, 276, 281, 295, 354,
418, 463, 483, 589, 604
immaculate, 107, 430, 540
Immaculate Conception, 504
immaterial, 418, 564
immaturity, 387
immeasurable, 215, 337, 451
immediate (immediately), 274, 277, 356, 493
immemorial (immemorially), 457, 464, 514
immensity (immense), 124, 165, 171, 214, 274, 290,
317, 321, 324, 362, 415, 423, 437, 501, 530
immersed, 382
imminent, 407, 576
immitigable, 583
immoderately, 89, 587
immodesty (immodest), 414, 575
immolated, 104, 481
immorality (immoral, immoralities, immorally),
60, 157, 207, 214, 283, 297, 310, 374, 417, 418,
419, 517, 519
immortality (immortal, immortalities, immortals),
22, 35, 105, 123, 124, 125, 143, 160, 184, 231,
257, 268, 273, 277, 296, 320, 336, 401, 406, 449,
474, 483, 545, 548, 573, 578
immovable, 277, 400
immunity (immunities), 53, 220
immutable, 259, 315
imp (impish), 338, 443, 553
impair (impaired, impairs), 510, 551
impalpable, 179, 284
impart (imparted, imparting), 299, 353, 410, 520,
576
impartiality (impartial), 138, 248, 277, 420, 429,
454, 456, 519
impassable, 593
impassible, 534
impassioned, 448
impatience (impatient), 219, 254, 259, 361, 391,
422, 444, 445, 450, 493, 499, 546, 581
impeccables, 453
impediment (impede, impeded, impediments),
187, 301, 310, 332, 334, 527
impel (impelled), 98, 349, 401, 432, 494

KEYWORD INDEX

impending, 168
impenetrableness (impenetrable), 277, 308, 348, 590
imperative (imperatively), 78, 515, 521
imperceptible (imperceptibly), 112, 156, 204, 248, 348, 380, 588
imperfection (imperfect, imperfections), 31, 116, 194, 281, 290, 296, 304, 306, 311, 453, 477, 518, 519
imperial, 498
imperilled, 466
imperious, 115, 154, 275, 318, 319, 378
imperishable, 172, 552
impermeable, 492
impersonal, 271
impersonation (impersonate, impersonations), 249, 337
impertinence (impertinent), 277, 360, 366
imperturbability (imperturbable), 119, 430
impervious, 326
impetuosity (impetuously), 17, 160
impiety, 501
impious, 378, 505
implacable, 64, 227, 357
implant (implanted, implants), 117, 213, 218, 226, 263, 266, 421, 425, 510
implication (implicitly, implied, implies, imply), 54, 91, 92, 127, 164, 203, 320, 340, 387, 391, 399, 402, 418, 436, 480, 521, 535, 540, 568, 597
implore, 405
impolitic, 128
imponderable, 564
importance (important), 52, 53, 64, 81, 105, 159, 160, 172, 173, 224, 226, 248, 256, 261, 277, 278, 279, 280, 281, 325, 333, 335, 352, 371, 376, 389, 395, 457, 472, 503, 506, 576, 602
importunity (importunities), 355, 393
imposition (impose, imposed, imposers, imposing), 106, 167, 251, 274, 278, 378, 476, 487, 509, 543, 604
impossibility (impossibilities, impossible), 21, 32, 33, 45, 65, 102, 122, 133, 135, 141, 163, 167, 172, 177, 178, 206, 213, 226, 228, 250, 254, 257, 265, 274, 278, 297, 327, 331, 340, 361, 374, 410, 420, 432, 437, 441, 469, 480, 487, 491, 502, 552, 577, 582, 600
imposture (impostor), 96, 128, 278, 423, 532
impotence (impotent), 9, 319, 592
impoverished, 223
impracticable, 378
impregnable, 64
impression (impress, impressed, impresses, impressionable, impressions, impressive, impressively), 55, 83, 84, 124, 132, 148, 149, 152, 155, 160, 165, 171, 208, 221, 230, 242, 251, 260, 273, 276, 278, 279, 282, 296, 300, 318, 339, 349, 351, 408, 409, 422, 436, 452, 453, 477, 509, 513, 539, 565, 572
imprint, 278, 428
imprisonment (imprison, imprisoned, imprisoning, imprisonments, imprisons), 279, 311, 395, 492
improbability (improbabilities), 178, 179, 180, 485
impropriety (improper), 102, 326, 372, 524
improvement (improvable, improve, improved, improvements, improver, improving), 53, 74, 106, 173, 252, 279, 294, 305, 327, 345, 349, 406,

407, 431, 453, 486, 570
imprudence (imprudent, imprudently), 353, 393, 395, 491
impudence (impudent), 27, 265, 279, 301, 391, 430, 472, 600
impulse (impulses, impulsive), 15, 16, 20, 54, 67, 74, 95, 115, 136, 146, 157, 173, 185, 242, 254, 259, 271, 276, 279, 286, 356, 370, 425, 427, 452, 455, 497, 587, 595
impunity, 274, 313, 379, 387, 592
imputation (impute, imputed), 67, 223, 368, 405, 508, 541, 574
inability, 272, 314
inaccessibility, 477
inaccurate, 69
inaction, 99
inactivity (inactive), 20, 301
inadequate, 520
inanimate, 307, 427, 446, 472
inappreciable, 541
inappropriate, 397
inarticulate, 174, 422
inattention, 108, 186, 478
inaudible, 474, 602
inborn, 549, 580
incalculable, 274
incantations, 512
incapacity (incapable), 50, 71, 121, 171, 219, 272, 278, 301, 311, 315, 369, 389, 399, 449, 457, 518, 532, 539
incarnate, 95, 347, 558
incense, 195, 571
incentive, 12, 162, 464
incessant, 115, 295, 438
incident (incidents), 35, 58, 99, 137, 191, 248, 279, 318, 335, 471, 486, 545, 561, 594
incisive, 86
incitement (incite, incited, incitements), 57, 408, 523
incivility, 326
inclemency, 368
inclination (inclinations, incline, inclined, inclining), 5, 12, 88, 108, 109, 134, 140, 150, 154, 157, 186, 235, 259, 278, 289, 295, 297, 311, 322, 332, 335, 351, 356, 357, 382, 397, 430, 437, 440, 462, 464, 515, 516, 537, 568, 584, 585, 593, 604
income, 53, 146, 155, 235, 333, 377, 415, 511, 522
incommodities, 14, 387
incompatible, 90, 94, 108, 183, 233, 341
incompetence (incompetent), 49
incompleteness (incomplete), 89, 292, 356, 445
incomprehensible, 165, 259, 350, 390, 551
inconceivable, 82
incongruous, 72, 491
inconsequent (inconsequential), 259, 602
inconsiderableness (inconsiderable), 256, 277, 400
inconsiderate (inconsiderately), 227, 392, 457
inconsistence (inconsistencies, inconsistency, inconsistent), 9, 24, 64, 100, 131, 146, 149, 199, 236, 262, 279, 430, 450, 574, 587
inconstancy (inconstant), 9, 38, 128, 216, 341, 496
incontestable, 441
incontinency, 151
incontrollable, 594
inconvenience (inconveniences, inconvenient, inconveniently), 47, 81, 82, 224, 251, 311, 318, 383, 471, 484, 489, 505, 604

ingredient (ingredients), 237, 314, 330
ingress, 322
inhabitant (inhabit, inhabitants, inhabits), 10, 23, 75, 220, 234, 249, 300, 431, 593
inherent, 55, 183, 200, 514
inheritance (inherit, inherited), 137, 183, 243, 244, 245, 258, 273, 385, 499, 534
inhumanity (inhuman, inhumanities, inhumanly), 166, 214, 215, 220, 345, 518
inimical, 25
iniquity (iniquities, iniquitous), 58, 103, 131, 217, 378, 415, 475
initiation, 358, 554
initiative, 360
injudicious, 248
injunctions, 477
injury (injure, injured, injures, injuries, injurious), 14, 89, 100, 116, 125, 131, 139, 187, 192, 199, 203, 205, 240, 250, 261, 265, 275, 283, 297, 298, 301, 308, 311, 329, 347, 365, 482, 484, 489, 508, 513, 528, 530, 537, 541, 573, 574, 582, 583, 594, 601
injustice, 59, 68, 88, 119, 131, 134, 136, 209, 295, 296, 297, 298, 309, 312, 327, 345, 347, 350, 357, 447, 487
ink, 191, 332, 464
ink-black, 221
inkstand, 561
inlander, 33
inlawed, 158
inmate (inmates) 19, 205
inn (inns), 81, 323
innateness (innate), 283, 519, 552
inner, 451, 491, 600
inner-consciousness, 99
innocence (innocent, innocently), 7, 17, 44, 46, 47, 52, 59, 67, 95, 112, 116, 120, 125, 126, 136, 174, 203, 218, 232, 233, 240, 245, 263, 270, 279, 282, 283, 284, 285, 295, 299, 310, 314, 338, 361, 365, 378, 404, 429, 443, 483, 488, 489, 511, 513, 524, 536, 539, 552, 556, 559, 571, 573, 575, 583, 584, 585, 587, 602
innuendoes, 523
innumerable, 112, 256, 399, 482, 522, 566
inoculated, 379
inoffensive, 111
inopportunity, 122
inordinate, 332
inquests, 401
inquiry (inquire, inquirers, inquires, inquiries), 134, 238, 285, 304, 334, 345, 361, 375, 388, 401, 425, 498, 546
inquisition/Inquisition, 126, 241, 285, 370, 440
inquisitive, 116, 419
inquisitor/Inquisitor, 284, 389, 585
insanity (insane), 33, 285, 286, 312, 419
insatiability (insatiable, insatiate), 26, 116, 228, 266, 286, 433, 538
insect (insects), 18, 22, 82, 329, 424, 485
inscription (inscribe, inscriptions), 390, 604
inscrutableness (inscrutable), 203, 215, 216, 220, 239
insecurity, 51, 233
insensibility (insensible, insensibly), 294, 298, 415, 419, 501, 529, 556
inseparable, 81, 178, 226, 281, 324, 470, 497, 507, 582

insidious, 401
insight (insights), 69, 160, 282, 286, 306, 346, 358, 454, 464, 490, 556, 584
insignificance (insignificant), 17, 42, 56, 258, 270, 277, 581, 599
insincerity (insincere), 199, 478, 537, 572, 574
insinuates, 195, 482
insipid, 39, 275, 326, 374, 443
insist (insisted, insisting), 191, 248, 279, 484, 562
insolence (insolent), 1, 10, 95, 154, 364, 412, 473, 489, 514, 538
inspection (inspect), 161, 252, 294, 379, 401, 418, 543, 564
inspiration (inspirations, inspire, inspired, inspirer, inspires, inspiring), 53, 118, 133, 201, 208, 228, 246, 276, 286, 289, 320, 348, 362, 370, 373, 377, 438, 447, 475, 490, 493, 546, 579, 587, 605
instability, 260, 594
installment, 17
instances, 208, 392, 414, 480
instant (instantaneous, instantaneously, instants), 135, 141, 150, 210, 244, 261, 303, 435, 463, 478, 492, 513, 550, 552
instigation, 387
instinct (instinctive, instinctively, instincts), 58, 61, 88, 97, 135, 164, 234, 242, 246, 262, 266, 274, 276, 287, 295, 309, 322, 335, 336, 347, 356, 362, 370, 373, 420, 427, 429, 447, 457, 484, 490, 502, 527, 528, 529, 545
institution (institutes, institutions), 77, 131, 193, 217, 218, 219, 272, 287, 309, 322, 347, 387, 393, 455, 500, 589
instruction (instruct, instructed, instructing, instructions, instructive, instructress, instructs), 19, 83, 155, 157, 158, 247, 248, 250, 257, 267, 287, 295, 302, 303, 305, 345, 358, 408, 413, 427, 480, 558, 576, 601
instrument (instruments), 50, 128, 131, 160, 171, 212, 214, 216, 219, 241, 264, 320, 326, 331, 337, 363, 365, 378, 399, 422, 449, 496, 517, 542, 546, 560
insufferable, 297
insufficiency (insufficient), 2, 56, 477, 497, 541, 596
insular (insulate), 257, 492
insult (insulted, insulters, insulting, insults), 4, 110, 146, 197, 218, 280, 345, 379, 381, 385, 386, 458, 459, 473, 530, 583
insuperable, 348
insupportable, 97, 569
insure (insurable, insured), 134, 302, 324, 331, 385, 474, 486, 542
insurrection, 54, 437
integrity, 89, 164, 287, 288, 418, 483
intellect (intellects, intellectual), 11, 20, 28, 37, 44, 57, 59, 75, 84, 87, 94, 104, 112, 116, 120, 141, 193, 194, 219, 220, 222, 239, 242, 263, 268, 276, 288, 301, 327, 334, 347, 349, 356, 366, 368, 373, 383, 400, 407, 408, 410, 419, 425, 452, 479, 499, 502, 519, 533, 543, 548, 555, 579, 580, 596, 599, 603
intelligence (intelligences, intelligent), 33, 43, 51, 74, 81, 83, 101, 130, 137, 148, 178, 209, 239, 288, 303, 309, 345, 348, 420, 434, 440, 473, 563
intelligible, 214, 365
intemperance, 56, 440, 559

intensity (intense, intensely, intenseness, intensest), 34, 68, 69, 117, 170, 187, 240, 288, 291, 321, 324, 335, 380, 399, 405, 427, 546, 580
intention (intend, intended, intending, intends, intent, intentional, intentions), 3, 31, 99, 104, 186, 200, 202, 204, 208, 221, 250, 284, 301, 309, 312, 322, 323, 327, 329, 353, 366, 377, 392, 393, 396, 404, 413, 427, 428, 438, 439, 444, 447, 463, 509, 561, 567, 577, 583, 588, 595, 602
interchange (interchanged, interchanging), 104, 256, 289
intercourse, 7, 202, 233, 367, 407, 464, 593
interdependence, 288, 289
interdict, 328
interest (interested, interesting, interestingness, interests), 28, 29, 34, 46, 54, 55, 74, 83, 85, 96, 104, 114, 128, 141, 143, 155, 182, 184, 191, 192, 198, 203, 223, 224, 230, 234, 237, 242, 247, 248, 259, 260, 262, 266, 276, 289, 301, 304, 311, 314, 316, 318, 330, 335, 346, 374, 397, 412, 418, 423, 427, 436, 451, 453, 454, 460, 462, 472, 478, 482, 488, 503, 509, 515, 516, 522, 524, 531, 540, 543, 558, 580, 582, 590, 601
interference (interfere, interfered), 310, 345, 384, 510
interindebtedness, 1
interior, 182, 417, 423, 545
interlinked, 215
intermeddle, 160
intermediate, 378
interminable, 163, 192
intermit (intermitted, intermittent), 317, 429
internal, 95, 296, 301
interposition (interpose), 244, 477
interpretation (interpret, interpreted, interpreter, interpreters, interpreting, interprets), 30, 54, 62, 64, 144, 149, 154, 223, 256, 287, 289, 290, 303, 312, 314, 353, 357, 503, 545
interruption (interrupt, interrupted, interruptions), 104, 191, 274, 320
interspaces, 36
interspersed, 196
intervention (intervenes, intervening), 157, 249, 482
intestate, 122
intimacy (intimacies), 202, 206, 324, 334, 501, 521
intimate (intimated, intimately, intimates, intimations), 26, 93, 149, 259, 266, 330, 372, 401, 424, 530, 535
intimidate (intimidated), 51, 125
intolerable (intolerableness, intolerably, intolerant), 10, 67, 159, 210, 264, 280, 324, 344, 348, 399, 412, 478, 582, 584
intoxication (intoxicate, intoxicated, intoxicates, intoxicating), 151, 153, 236, 312, 388, 473, 593
intractable, 438
intrepidity (intrepid), 22, 107, 280
intricacy (intricacies, intricate), 259, 305, 428, 469
intrigue (intrigues), 29, 232, 235, 371
intrinsic, 236, 530, 579, 588
introduction (introduce, introduced), 191, 219, 346, 400, 406, 490, 533
introspectiveness, 434
introvertedness, 175
intrusive, 545
intuition (intuitions, intuitive, intuitively), 18, 294, 313, 346, 348, 356, 386, 473, 546
inures, 234

invade, 243, 447, 556
invalidate (invalidated), 379, 542
invalidism, 105
invariable (invariably), 122, 151, 230, 355, 373, 456
invective, 585
invention (invent, invented, inventing, inventions, inventive, invents), 65, 77, 97, 130, 138, 139, 202, 210, 219, 263, 274, 340, 341, 384, 390, 410, 431, 432, 436, 450, 483, 513, 523, 539, 556, 572, 576, 587, 591, 598
inventory, 261
inversions, 174
invest (invested), 336, 423, 466, 568
investigation (investigating, investigator), 112, 259, 285, 322, 521
inveterate, 93, 264, 478, 580
invigorate (invigorates, invigorator), 82, 407, 555
invincible, 230, 233, 315, 363
inviolate, 308
invisible, 31, 39, 85, 138, 187, 227, 248, 275, 359, 424, 429, 520
invitation (invite, invited, invites, inviting), 130, 327, 443, 522
involuntary (involuntarily), 97, 135, 265, 276, 306, 321, 325, 341
involution, 362
involvement, (involve, involved, involves), 139, 186, 201, 290, 310, 419, 441, 467, 469, 556
invulnerable, 587
inward, 94, 136, 206, 233, 287, 478, 497, 522
Ireland (Irish, Irishman, Irishmen), 151, 268, 270, 299, 310, 329, 455, 459
irksome, 208, 433, 555
iron, 78, 106, 227, 254, 296, 493, 538, 583
iron hand, 469
iron-nerved, 112
irony (ironical), 72, 362, 517, 524
irrationality (irrational), 111, 324
irreconcilableness, 186
irregular (irregularity), 258, 498
irregular verb, 327
irrelevant, 311
irreligious, 556
irremediable, 186, 383
irresistible (irresistibly), 42, 90, 195, 228, 278, 388, 423, 572, 582
irrespective, 420
irresponsible, 315
irreverence (irreverences, irreverent, irreverential), 154, 201, 459
irrevocable, 206, 388
irritation (irritate, irritated, irritating), 75, 235, 262, 334, 378, 426, 455
irruptions, 574
Isaac, 517
Ishmael, 271
island (islanded, islanders, islands, isle), 42, 74, 75, 185, 242, 257, 290, 322, 359, 389, 520, 603
Isles of the Sea, 71
Isms, 71
isolation (isolate, isolated), 5, 10, 54, 64, 80, 219, 233, 290, 331, 337, 383
Israel, 417
issue (issued), 87, 284, 429, 440, 531, 559
Italy (Italian, Italians), 41, 110, 177, 305, 379, 412, 504, 569
itch, 90, 560

iteration, 4
Ivanhoe, 193
ivory, 64
ivy, 600

Jack's beanstalk, 8
jack of all trades, 66
jacket, 257, 466
jackknife, 185
Jacob, 65, 331
Jacobin, 45
jade, 134, 139, 251, 264, 433, 438
jail (jails), 62, 225, 249
jam, 422, 448
January, 520
japonica, 42
jar (jars), 183, 240
jargon, 270, 428
jaundice, 570
jaws, 121, 123
jays, 483
jealousy (jealous, jealousies, jealously), 10, 21, 34,
    99, 104, 128, 203, 240, 280, 290, 291, 334, 380,
    389, 391, 539
Jehovah, 578
jejune, 582
jeopardy, 85, 202, 436
Jerusalem, 507
jest (jestee, jester, jests), 25, 28, 127, 141, 169, 202,
    265, 338, 385
Jesus Christ, 216
Jew's-harp, 332
jewel (jewels), 42, 181, 204, 319, 364, 585
jilt (jilted, jilting, jilts), 139, 203, 389
Joan of Arc, 175, 451
Job, 165
jockey, 65
jog (jogs), 142, 379
jog-trot, 337
John the Baptist, 507
joie de vivre, 161, 162, 292
join (joined, joining), 197, 315, 324, 378, 382, 395,
    413, 448, 463, 474, 492, 576, 584, 595
joke (jokes, joking), 264, 265, 292, 398, 457, 471,
    531, 596
jollity (jolly), 11, 186, 315, 320, 382, 387, 594
Jones, John Paul, 270
journey (journeying, journeys), 44, 59, 108, 134,
    140, 192, 306, 317, 383, 399, 404, 566, 569
Jove, 191, 341, 395, 409
joy (joyful, joyless, joyous, joys), 8, 19, 25, 31, 35,
    37, 42, 48, 71, 87, 99, 122, 124, 138, 149, 150,
    151, 165, 183, 204, 212, 222, 225, 230, 238, 240,
    244, 255, 257, 260, 290, 292, 293, 303, 319, 322,
    327, 328, 334, 336, 341, 351, 361, 362, 377, 405,
    422, 427, 428, 437, 442, 507, 517, 531, 535, 545,
    546
Judah, 216
Judea, 578
judgment (judge, judged, judges, judging, judg-
    ments), 3, 22, 27, 41, 46, 51, 58, 65, 66, 67, 71, 80,
    82, 86, 92, 98, 99, 111, 113, 121, 128, 131, 140,
    158, 169, 176, 181, 182, 185, 187, 193, 206, 207,
    213, 215, 227, 237, 256, 259, 281, 292, 293, 294,
    295, 308, 309, 311, 313, 325, 327, 336, 344, 349,
    350, 361, 370, 375, 382, 386, 387, 388, 393, 414,
    419, 424, 430, 432, 440, 444, 452, 456, 465, 472,

485, 488, 497, 500, 507, 513, 516, 525, 527, 570,
    572, 576, 577, 589, 599
judicature, 399
judicial, 312, 405
judicious (judiciously), 11, 13, 35, 83, 153, 169,
    224, 296, 315, 486, 490, 589
juggle (juggler), 257, 290, 585
juice (juicy), 152, 212, 335, 467
July, 520
jumble, 270, 321
jump (jumping, jumps), 279, 376, 486, 600
June, 520
Junebug, 87
jungle, 430
Jupiter, 457
jury (juries), 41, 294, 308, 309
justice (just, justices, justly, justness), 1, 53, 66, 75,
    96, 120, 129, 145, 151, 154, 158, 171, 205, 208,
    213, 215, 216, 223, 224, 244, 248, 249, 260, 262,
    278, 294, 295, 296, 297, 298, 299, 301, 308, 309,
    311, 312, 313, 318, 341, 374, 378, 383, 384, 401,
    405, 407, 411, 418, 427, 464, 469, 474, 475, 476,
    492, 507, 524, 526, 527, 529, 538, 566, 583, 585,
    588, 591, 605
justification (justifiable, justified, justifies,
    justify), 3, 28, 103, 113, 170, 212, 290, 295, 299,
    326, 346, 391, 397, 456, 458, 485, 508, 524, 540,
    557, 558
juvenile (juveniles), 193, 601
juxtaposition, 389

kaleidoscope, 515
keel, 18
keenness (keen, keener, keenest, keenly), 17, 203,
    230, 246, 287, 408, 409, 453, 459, 528, 536, 537,
    568, 577, 603
keep (keeper, keeping, keeps, kept), 88, 131, 150,
    151, 193, 200, 221, 238, 243, 244, 251, 253, 266,
    286, 290, 295, 301, 304, 309, 315, 322, 329, 336,
    337, 353, 375, 379, 380, 383, 391, 393, 404, 413,
    414, 415, 421, 422, 423, 431, 438, 443, 444, 451,
    453, 454, 458, 464, 469, 472, 475, 480, 485, 486,
    487, 490, 491, 500, 508, 514, 516, 518, 519, 521,
    523, 534, 536, 542, 547, 558, 565, 567, 572, 574,
    576, 577, 586, 591, 600, 603
Kentucky, 576
kernel, 579
kettle, 142
key, 134, 161, 176, 421, 434, 534, 547
keyhole, 34, 339, 521, 567
kick (kicked, kickee, kicker, kicks), 70, 109, 117,
    251, 335, 372, 438, 556
kill (killed, killing, kills), 70, 107, 116, 128, 152,
    162, 188, 194, 300, 309, 349, 351, 362, 400, 404,
    421, 442, 471, 543, 545, 554, 597
killibeate, 142
kin (kindred, kinship), 40, 54, 307, 507, 560, 578
kind (kinder, kindest, kindliest, kindly, kindness,
    kindnesses, kinds), 1, 46, 70, 76, 93, 97, 100, 108,
    117, 127, 134, 162, 181, 189, 201, 205, 209, 212,
    214, 217, 222, 226, 233, 237, 238, 242, 251, 253,
    257, 263, 283, 290, 291, 295, 297, 299, 300, 305,
    306, 307, 310, 326, 327, 329, 339, 340, 342, 343,
    351, 352, 364, 367, 369, 396, 410, 415, 420, 429,
    444, 447, 459, 470, 475, 481, 495, 508, 524, 530,
    534, 537, 540, 543, 549, 568, 572, 575, 577, 587

kindle (kindled, kindles), 138, 203, 291, 327, 342, 345, 446
king (kingdom, kingdoms, kings), 5, 16, 34, 57, 58, 61, 68, 81, 82, 122, 123, 163, 164, 175, 184, 189, 210, 224, 225, 244, 255, 267, 271, 338, 340, 369, 370, 407, 408, 416, 417, 449, 456, 485, 515, 550, 551, 552, 567, 570, 585, 591
Kingdom of God, 297
kiss (kissed, kissing), 87, 143, 152, 217, 300, 321, 377, 503, 561, 570
kitchen, 23, 143, 343, 388
kite, 146, 489
kitten (kittlings), 40, 47, 107
knack, 48, 56
knavery (knave, knaves, knavish), 63, 81, 112, 213, 251, 311, 342, 446, 458, 556, 585, 589
knee (knees), 77, 199, 242, 250, 351, 362, 382, 443, 462, 511, 557, 576
kneel (kneeling), 250, 365, 372, 442, 475, 504
knife, 67, 452, 585
knight (knighthood), 25, 84, 91, 300, 336, 405, 444, 486, 537
knit (knits, knitted, knitting), 183, 205, 331, 347, 386, 546
knock (knocking, knocks), 123, 126, 135, 158, 228, 268, 271, 341, 399, 481, 512, 514, 565, 592
knot (knots, knotty), 152, 506, 565
knout, 159
know (knew, knoweth, knowing, known, knows), 5, 38, 106, 142, 148, 149, 154, 156, 157, 159, 160, 162, 164, 169, 170, 187, 188, 191, 192, 193, 197, 200, 201, 211, 213, 214, 218, 219, 221, 223, 225, 228, 236, 237, 239, 240, 241, 243, 244, 246, 248, 249, 250, 252, 254, 262, 263, 265, 269, 270, 271, 272, 275, 277, 279, 281, 284, 285, 287, 288, 289, 291, 292, 293, 294, 295, 301, 302, 303, 304, 305, 306, 308, 309, 310, 312, 314, 315, 321, 325, 326, 327, 332, 333, 334, 335, 336, 339, 340, 341, 343, 346, 347, 349, 350, 351, 353, 354, 356, 357, 359, 360, 361, 362, 363, 364, 365, 366, 370, 373, 376, 378, 379, 381, 382, 383, 385, 386, 387, 390, 391, 392, 393, 394, 396, 397, 401, 402, 405, 407, 410, 411, 417, 421, 424, 427, 428, 432, 433, 437, 440, 443, 444, 448, 449, 450, 451, 452, 454, 455, 460, 461, 462, 463, 465, 466, 473, 474, 476, 477, 482, 485, 488, 491, 492, 493, 495, 496, 498, 503, 510, 514, 515, 516, 517, 518, 519, 520, 521, 523, 527, 528, 529, 532, 533, 534, 537, 538, 543, 545, 546, 547, 549, 550, 555, 557, 558, 559, 560, 562, 563, 564, 565, 569, 571, 572, 574, 575, 576, 577, 578, 579, 581, 583, 584, 593, 594, 596, 598
know-nothing, 553
knowledge, 7, 11, 20, 22, 25, 28, 35, 40, 44, 45, 53, 65, 70, 87, 94, 98, 102, 115, 118, 131, 132, 147, 155, 157, 158, 159, 169, 170, 190, 215, 220, 237, 247, 248, 250, 263, 269, 274, 281, 287, 288, 293, 296, 297, 300, 301, 302, 303, 304, 305, 306, 313, 324, 334, 342, 344, 345, 354, 365, 367, 368, 393, 402, 408, 413, 414, 419, 440, 446, 447, 456, 457, 463, 465, 476, 479, 480, 482, 488, 493, 495, 502, 506, 518, 519, 520, 536, 538, 545, 556, 570, 581, 588, 597, 598
knuckle, 600
knucklebone, 552
Koran, 271
Krishna, 505

labor (labored, laborer, laboring, laborious, labors), 14, 27, 53, 58, 71, 78, 79, 133, 158, 161, 174, 193, 201, 229, 236, 247, 297, 306, 310, 319, 325, 344, 358, 367, 368, 382, 418, 428, 432, 470, 482, 537, 538, 539, 541, 579
labyrinth, 129
lace, 344, 490
lad (lads), 2, 11, 280, 372, 402
ladder, 118, 243, 321, 368, 575
lady (ladies), 6, 8, 14, 34, 42, 50, 66, 86, 91, 99, 108, 109, 141, 142, 144, 145, 150, 154, 158, 162, 166, 191, 230, 245, 253, 294, 295, 300, 324, 326, 332, 335, 344, 345, 346, 347, 348, 349, 351, 352, 358, 359, 360, 364, 365, 371, 374, 375, 376, 377, 378, 379, 380, 382, 384, 389, 390, 393, 394, 395, 396, 400, 412, 427, 445, 459, 462, 478, 500, 509, 521, 525, 530, 550, 564, 568, 578, 586, 587, 588
lady-ship, 365
lady-state, 365
lake, 237
Lake of Sin, 361
lamb (lambkin, lambs), 32, 82, 173, 267, 270, 300, 309, 431, 484, 489, 508, 539
lame, 140, 516
lament (lamentable, lamentation, lamenting, laments), 120, 121, 207, 374, 379, 400, 420, 431, 451, 552
lamps, 517
lance (lances) 37, 300, 590
land (landed, landing, lands), 18, 57, 66, 85, 90, 94, 98, 116, 124, 146, 212, 213, 257, 267, 278, 296, 309, 313, 314, 317, 336, 385, 401, 408, 413, 417, 432, 434, 449, 478, 485, 494, 505, 597, 604
landlady, 170
landlessness, 574
landlubber, 85
landmark (landmarks), 290, 498, 501
landscape, 30, 42, 66, 81, 85, 148
landsman, 12
lane, 582
language (languages), 4, 29, 105, 113, 132, 157, 172, 174, 177, 190, 194, 195, 217, 223, 244, 268, 275, 289, 301, 306, 307, 327, 329, 340, 349, 367, 427, 428, 444, 447, 465, 473, 478, 480, 495, 500, 502, 526, 536, 541, 563, 576, 578
languid, 145, 443
languish (languishes, languishing), 263, 325
languor, 84, 272, 429
lantern, 333
lantern-jawed, 532
lap-dog, 230
lapidary, 469
Laplander, 155
lapse (lapses), 61, 134, 316, 450
lark, 431, 539
lash (lashes), 232, 272, 518
lass (lassies), 38, 423
lassitudes, 437
Last Supper, 214
latent, 508, 554
Latin, 156, 157, 223
latitude, 37, 236, 601
latitudinarian, 418
laudable, 46, 162, 447, 584, 605
laughter (laugh, laughable, laughed, laughing, laughs), 17, 25, 53, 61, 71, 85, 95, 101, 116, 138, 139, 142, 178, 196, 197, 200, 205, 235, 236, 244,

257, 264, 265, 271, 285, 291, 296, 307, 321, 342, 347, 362, 380, 382, 399, 408, 418, 421, 422, 430, 449, 499, 503, 518, 525, 532, 581, 597, 600
laughter-loving, 210
launching, 124
laurel (laurels), 444, 454
lavish (lavished, lavishing), 327, 432, 568, 591
law (laws), 4, 31, 51, 52, 59, 61, 64, 65, 75, 96, 98, 113, 114, 118, 124, 130, 138, 151, 164, 171, 173, 189, 194, 197, 200, 201, 203, 215, 217, 225, 226, 228, 239, 241, 246, 250, 252, 256, 260, 262, 279, 283, 287, 296, 297, 298, 303, 307, 308, 309, 310, 311, 312, 313, 314, 325, 328, 335, 345, 347, 370, 374, 378, 380, 381, 390, 392, 396, 399, 410, 417, 426, 428, 429, 430, 432, 440, 441, 458, 469, 474, 487, 494, 510, 513, 514, 517, 528, 542, 545, 552, 554, 562, 583, 589, 593, 600
Law of God, 513
law-breakers, 313
lawful, 187, 312, 342, 358
lawgiver, 311
lawing, 309
law-keepers, 313
lawless, 96, 429
lawmaker (lawmakers, lawmaking), 164, 415, 425
lawsuit, 311, 312
lawyer (lawyers), 91, 96, 141, 191, 250, 308, 309, 310, 311, 312, 313, 314, 478, 500
laxity (lax), 234, 249
laziness (lazy), 54, 272, 372, 569
lead (leader, leaders, leading, leads, led), 115, 126, 127, 134, 135, 137, 153, 155, 161, 170, 201, 204, 215, 242, 250, 252, 272, 276, 279, 281, 291, 314, 317, 325, 327, 329, 348, 350, 356, 379, 417, 431, 438, 443, 452, 480, 484, 489, 493, 497, 505, 527, 530, 559, 569, 572, 599, 603
leaden, 296, 338, 583
leadership, 360
leading-strings, 420
leaf, 53, 182, 383, 426, 431, 490, 600
league (leagued), 205, 409
leak, 134, 140
lean (leanest, leaning, leanness, leans), 86, 133, 255, 264, 402, 439, 497
leap (leaping, leaps), 121, 123, 138, 249, 260, 282, 339, 381
learn (learned, learning, learns, learnt), 6, 51, 66, 67, 99, 106, 121, 123, 152, 156, 157, 158, 162, 169, 170, 179, 187, 209, 210, 219, 222, 235, 238, 244, 247, 248, 249, 257, 273, 275, 279, 283, 299, 300, 301, 302, 303, 304, 305, 306, 307, 319, 320, 321, 324, 326, 328, 333, 335, 341, 343, 344, 347, 349, 350, 352, 354, 356, 361, 363, 365, 367, 378, 379, 382, 400, 404, 412, 416, 423, 440, 457, 462, 469, 477, 478, 492, 495, 501, 503, 514, 527, 540, 546, 552, 556, 568, 569, 570, 588, 597, 599
least-instructed, 331
leave-takings, 445
lecture (lecturer, lectures, lecturing), 155, 157, 287, 398, 433, 476, 477
leech-like, 280
legacy, 592
legal (legality, legalizing, legally), 119, 130, 297, 308, 309, 310, 419, 492, 592
legend, 148
legibly, 144
legion, 338

legislation (legislate, legislator, legislators), 96, 113, 314, 361, 464, 503
legitimate (legitimated, legitimately), 63, 191, 263, 309, 415, 596
leisure (leisurely), 2, 5, 236, 238, 266, 314, 315, 318, 434
lend (lendeth), 46, 206, 299, 437, 600
length (lengths), 141, 161, 244, 309, 321, 395, 399, 475, 536
lenient (leniently), 349, 393
lent, 460, 484
leopard, 346, 430
leprosies, 221
lesion, 386
lessen (lessened, lessens), 391, 483, 499, 515
lesson (lessoning, lessons), 5, 15, 156, 161, 169, 171, 178, 223, 248, 284, 287, 295, 301, 306, 307, 320, 335, 352, 422, 448, 499
lethargy, 193
letter (letters), 25, 52, 63, 113, 172, 181, 200, 222, 289, 330, 335, 336, 346, 401, 424, 602
letter-writing, 29, 186
lettre de cachet, 440
levee, 170
leveller, 150, 269
levelling, 164, 541
lever, 74
Leviathan, 561
levity, 11, 56, 173, 226, 315
lewdness (lewd), 102, 351, 413
liable, 88, 217, 278, 327, 329, 424
liar (liars: *see also* lie), 97, 180, 446, 569
libeller, 518
liberal/Liberal (liberalism, liberality, Liberals), 94, 97, 315, 418, 426, 467, 509, 528, 561
liberate (liberated), 409, 511
libertinism (libertine, libertines), 252, 315, 316, 600
liberty (liberties), 15, 29, 80, 86, 98, 196, 197, 200, 201, 208, 209, 245, 263, 272, 274, 296, 299, 314, 321, 348, 351, 368, 377, 381, 385, 399, 440, 449, 465, 511, 538, 551, 570, 573
library (libraries), 170, 404, 418
license (licensed, licenses), 159, 274, 312, 348, 365, 399, 521, 577
lichen, 305
lickpenny, 314
lie (lies, lieth, lying), 18, 22, 29, 83, 95, 122, 163, 178, 179, 180, 183, 184, 215, 224, 229, 250, 251, 253, 257, 264, 265, 274, 277, 293, 297, 311, 312, 314, 318, 320, 327, 350, 356, 381, 396, 414, 430, 434, 437, 444, 448, 463, 471, 483, 504, 505, 514, 516, 519, 535, 546, 548, 551, 552, 563, 569, 570, 575, 579, 585, 586, 594, 599, 602, 603
lieu, 601
lieutenant (lieutenants), 77, 138
life (lifelong, lifetime, live, lived, lives, living), 3, 4, 7, 9, 10, 11, 12, 13, 15, 16, 17, 18, 19, 21, 22, 23, 29, 30, 31, 32, 34, 35, 38, 39, 40, 44, 49, 50, 52, 53, 54, 55, 56, 60, 61, 62, 64, 65, 68, 72, 74, 75, 77, 78, 79, 81, 83, 84, 85, 86, 87, 88, 90, 91, 92, 94, 95, 96, 99, 100, 102, 103, 104, 105, 106, 108, 109, 110, 113, 115, 117, 118, 119, 120, 121, 122, 123, 124, 125, 126, 127, 129, 130, 132, 133, 134, 135, 136, 137, 139, 140, 142, 143, 144, 146, 147, 148, 149, 150, 151, 152, 153, 154, 156, 157, 158, 159, 160, 161, 162, 163, 164, 165, 166, 169, 170, 171, 177, 178,

magistrate (magisterial, magistrates), 22, 96, 102, 284, 492

magnanimity (magnanimous), 85, 88, 305, 329, 344, 368, 405

magnetism (magnet, magnetic), 33, 40, 150, 223, 241, 324, 337, 599

magnificence (magnificent), 42, 150, 217, 248, 264, 413, 466, 476, 583

magnify (magnified, magnifying), 370, 409, 412, 459, 561

magnitude, 37, 160, 290, 442

Mahomet (Mahometan), 215, 503

maid (maiden, maidens, maids), 10, 13, 42, 54, 75, 108, 191, 291, 335, 363, 366, 385, 388, 393, 442, 465, 516, 568, 578, 586

maidenhead (maidenheads), 392, 586

maidservants, 549

mail, 489

mailboat, 274

mainspring, 74

maintain (maintained, maintaining, maintains, maintenance), 224, 299, 304, 335, 344, 353, 415, 426, 461, 479, 497, 512, 541, 590, 601

majesty (majestic, majestically), 19, 22, 72, 122, 214, 225, 310, 311, 409, 446, 464

majority (majorities), 54, 478, 490, 518, 597

Maker, 213, 231, 285, 303, 490, 551, 580

making-up, 393

malady, 31, 147, 165, 220, 337, 401, 500, 562

male (males), 146, 206, 226, 343–374, 385, 387, 401, 406, 467, 585

malefactor (malefactors), 492

malevolence, 522, 556

malice (malicious), 25, 37, 43, 97, 114, 197, 256, 259, 291, 297, 400, 534, 552, 583

malignity (malign, malignant, maligned), 55, 175, 308, 427, 488

malpractice, 402

maltreat, 100

mama (mamas, mammas), 183, 378, 395

mammalia, 576

mammon/Mammon, 209, 414

man (men), 1–41; 43; 45–96; 98–114; 116–119; 121–164; 166–326; 328–331; 333–334; 336–411; 413–442; 444–519; 521–575; 577–598; 600; 603–605

Man Friday, 424

man in the moon, 178

man of fashion, 25

man of flesh, 21

man of letters, 34

man of sense, 375

Man of Sorrows, 545

man of straw, 21

man-of-war, 164, 299, 320, 604

man of the world, 360

man-woman, 364

management (manage, managed, manager, managers, manages, managing), 52, 102, 143, 175, 182, 185, 250, 264, 358, 362, 365, 379, 396, 407, 446, 491, 513, 550

Mandarins, 226

maneuvering (manoeuvring), 375

mangle (mangled), 517, 590

manhood, 22, 25, 69, 94, 226, 357, 538, 559

mania (manias), 21, 35, 195, 268, 285

maniac, 285

manifestation (manifest, manifestations, manifestly, manifests), 52, 214, 227, 296, 339, 345, 396, 463, 477, 549

manipulation, 486

mankind, 14, 16, 26, 30, 36, 45, 46, 49, 60, 66, 80, 88, 94, 105, 111, 112, 114, 123, 145, 153, 164, 183, 195, 197, 201, 206, 215, 223, 227, 230, 234, 236, 238, 240, 248, 249, 250, 251, 252, 253, 256, 257, 258, 260, 262, 267, 273, 279, 292, 293, 294, 295, 312, 314, 333, 336, 351, 375, 379, 380, 387, 406, 407, 410, 411, 414, 415, 418, 429, 435, 436, 449, 450, 451, 454, 456, 460, 464, 471, 472, 477, 479, 485, 496, 503, 504, 506, 513, 518, 524, 528, 541, 544, 554, 555, 556, 567, 570, 578, 581, 585, 591, 593, 596, 597, 598, 604

manliness (manfully, manliest, manly), 84, 107, 108, 199, 269, 295, 343, 345, 349, 350, 352, 363, 364, 403, 433, 560, 596

manner (manners), 5, 14, 41, 63, 64, 72, 73, 74, 79, 83, 92, 103, 106, 132, 141, 166, 168, 170, 171, 174, 209, 211, 221, 222, 223, 228, 231, 242, 253, 266, 282, 289, 293, 304, 345, 349, 350, 388, 400, 407, 415, 436, 440, 441, 442, 451, 466, 470, 475, 477, 486, 492, 495, 508, 510, 513, 521, 531, 540, 570, 577, 584, 589, 591, 594

manors, 593

manrope, 420

mansion (mansions), 243, 277, 443

mantle, 538

mantua-maker, 394

manual, 224

manufactured, 544

manuscript, 36

many-compounded, 223

many-sided, 65, 368

mar (marred), 410, 478

Marathon, 451

marble, 42, 58, 65, 137, 202, 319, 429, 436

march (marches), 320, 389, 407, 422

March, 246, 434, 520

mare, 13, 416

mareslaughter, 401

margin, 148, 302, 443, 454

marigold, 416

mariners, 285

maritime, 516

mark (marked, marks), 22, 32, 34, 85, 130, 135, 167, 192, 196, 197, 219, 228, 249, 295, 317, 339, 363, 380, 397, 403, 428, 478, 479, 497, 502, 510, 558, 567, 576, 580, 581, 602

market (marketable), 78, 260, 270, 289, 342, 350, 360, 485, 569

marksmanship, 352

marplot, 205

marriage (marital, marriageable, marriages, married, marries, marry, marrying), 41, 86, 91, 94, 103, 109, 114, 124, 125, 152, 182, 191, 193, 225, 240, 259, 291, 315, 316, 326, 327, 330, 335, 341, 345, 353, 367, 374, 375, 376, 377, 378, 379, 380, 381, 382, 383, 384, 385, 386, 387, 388, 389, 390, 391, 392, 393, 394, 395, 396, 397, 398, 416, 439, 455, 456, 481, 520, 540, 558, 586

marrow, 158, 257

Mars, 256

mart, 603

martial, 246

martyrdom (martyr, martyrdoms, martyrs), 54,

minstrels, 25
mint, 224, 500, 597
mint-juleps, 143
minute (minutes, minutest, minutiae), 10, 134,
    177, 194, 246, 248, 265, 268, 309, 323, 344, 347,
    407, 409, 448, 466, 498, 564, 565, 566, 567, 581
miracle (miracles, miraculous), 15, 29, 31, 244,
    300, 315, 342, 410, 504, 520, 601
mirage, 222
mire (miry), 327, 430, 561
mirror, 151, 152, 166, 176, 191, 204, 275, 292, 337,
    377, 496, 591
mirth, 11, 51, 142, 265, 307, 403, 408, 597
misanthropy (misanthrope, misanthropes,
    misanthropic), 93, 156, 349, 410, 485, 493, 501
misapplication, 108, 584
misapprehension, 110, 200, 265
misbegotten, 390
misbestowed, 580
miscarriage, 312
mischance, 57, 117
mischief (mischievous), 13, 36, 40, 55, 69, 82, 136,
    157, 163, 184, 198, 202, 204, 208, 212, 218, 223,
    258, 276, 362, 370, 410, 411, 415, 442, 506, 556,
    599
misconduct, 286, 556
misconstruction, 349, 455, 522
miscreant (miscreants), 233, 455
misdeed, 63
misdemeanor, 164
misdoing, 186, 443
miser (miserliness, misers), 260, 411
misery (miserable, miserably, miseries), 5, 8, 17,
    19, 46, 53, 56, 76, 82, 87, 91, 95, 104, 105, 119,
    136, 163, 203, 218, 219, 232, 234, 236, 237, 238,
    239, 243, 250, 272, 275, 318, 323, 324, 333, 336,
    339, 379, 386, 387, 388, 407, 411, 412, 418, 425,
    438, 445, 465, 476, 488, 493, 497, 505, 511, 516,
    522, 531, 533, 538, 554, 556, 570, 576, 582, 591
misfortune (misfortunate, misfortunes), 14, 17, 41,
    46, 49, 53, 81, 89, 97, 139, 168, 190, 230, 244,
    249, 260, 261, 269, 272, 308, 309, 317, 329, 335,
    371, 374, 380, 412, 413, 435, 444, 486, 506, 524,
    555, 571, 597
misgiving, 9
misguiders, 364
mishap, 208, 510
misinformation, 110
misinterpret, 350
mislead (misleader, misleading, misleads,
    misled), 103, 129, 305, 458, 488, 490, 500, 523,
    596, 600
mismanagement, 82
misnamed, 603
misplaced, 193, 194, 272
misread, 112
misrepresentation (misrepresentations,
    misrepresented, misrepresenters), 275, 400, 447
miss (missed, misses), 37, 201, 217, 290, 475, 510
misshaped, 362
mission, 95, 343, 358, 462
missionary (missionaries), 71, 75, 77, 352, 362
mist (mistiness, mists, misty), 9, 91, 118, 259, 290,
    317, 413, 423, 424, 533, 548, 562
mistake (mistaken, mistakes, mistook), 28, 34, 69,
    72, 80, 93, 122, 146, 153, 164, 171, 180, 206, 221,
    239, 242, 247, 251, 252, 270, 284, 287, 300, 305,

331, 335, 340, 348, 352, 372, 411, 420, 427, 434,
    441, 450, 455, 468, 478, 479, 481, 485, 487, 503,
    514, 518, 519, 533, 555, 556, 562, 563, 580, 586,
    587, 602
mistress (mistresses), 38, 168, 200, 216, 334, 350,
    378, 379, 380, 381, 388, 394, 415, 471, 484, 532,
    538, 552, 586
mistrust (mistrusted, mistrusting), 26, 57, 91,
    176, 232, 251, 332, 356, 510, 572
misunderstood, 393, 477
misuse (misuses), 127, 199
mitigate (mitigating), 260, 508
mixture (mix, mixed, mixing), 31, 55, 102, 111,
    164, 213, 219, 249, 327, 420, 457, 459, 462, 463,
    483, 497, 530
moan, 335, 444
mob (mobs), 73, 200, 413, 558, 591
mock-life, 457
mock turtle, 398
mockery (mock, mocking, mocks), 7, 85, 235, 245,
    265, 417, 443, 457, 478, 520
mode (modes, modish), 33, 44, 58, 59, 103, 123,
    155, 224, 243, 253, 287, 288, 296, 452, 589, 599,
    601
model (modeling, models), 43, 79, 250, 270, 295,
    394, 436, 550
moderation (moderate), 4, 179, 210, 218, 276, 305,
    319, 342, 364, 401, 413, 502, 511, 553, 592
modernity (modern), 44, 71, 74, 78, 111, 175, 190,
    221, 322, 348, 418, 427, 456, 490, 519, 522, 542,
    544, 550, 600
modesty (modest, modestly), 7, 30, 38, 43, 48, 75,
    161, 202, 209, 210, 222, 227, 233, 250, 264, 294,
    346, 348, 350, 355, 366, 367, 369, 400, 406, 408,
    413, 414, 480, 491, 600
modification (modified, modifies, modify), 139,
    228, 262, 401, 433, 451, 548
mold, 281, 367, 465
mole (moles), 3, 133, 347
molehill, 332, 454
molest, 430
Moliere, 398
mollusca, 164
moment (moments), 9, 23, 46, 50, 104, 117, 120,
    126, 145, 165, 210, 214, 227, 230, 232, 233, 241,
    254, 259, 265, 274, 278, 282, 288, 290, 296, 308,
    319, 339, 342, 360, 369, 372, 382, 392, 397, 401,
    407, 418, 422, 431, 438, 444, 448, 454, 458, 461,
    462, 463, 466, 468, 476, 477, 493, 498, 499, 500,
    515, 521, 531, 537, 543, 548, 553, 557, 562, 564,
    565, 567, 573, 579, 582, 588, 600
momentous, 518, 563
monarchy (monarch, monarchical, monarchs), 2,
    34, 81, 226, 538, 604
monastery (monasteries), 279, 543, 604
Monday, 175, 489
money (moneyed, monied), 17, 21, 28, 30, 39, 40,
    52, 54, 55, 58, 74, 82, 92, 103, 113, 120, 161, 202,
    205, 206, 220, 224, 235, 251, 253, 260, 270, 298,
    300, 309, 311, 313, 316, 341, 348, 350, 353, 355,
    372, 376, 380, 385, 388, 395, 398, 399, 402, 414,
    415, 416, 424, 443, 444, 460, 463, 468, 469, 471,
    487, 492, 494, 540, 542, 566, 568, 585, 593, 597
money-getting, 61
money-hoarder, 500
mongrel, 456
monitor, 8, 95

negotiate (negotiators), 369, 571
Negro (Negroes), 25, 271, 455, 548
neigh (neighing, neighs), 439, 499
neighbor (neighborhood, neighborly, neighbors),
40, 51, 54, 67, 71, 81, 84, 96, 106, 109, 120, 128,
186, 195, 207, 237, 282, 292, 293, 298, 310, 317,
324, 342, 375, 391, 412, 421, 433, 459, 474, 497,
499, 500, 505, 524, 525, 527, 541, 555, 573, 577,
584, 586, 592
Nemesis, 54, 96, 341
nephews, 51
nepotism, 49
Nero, 114
nerve (nerves, nervous, nervousness), 7, 69, 85,
173, 182, 260, 307, 339, 358, 376, 425, 433, 438,
500, 534, 586
nervous system, 450
nest, 191, 432, 535
nestled, 163
net, 274
nettle (nettles), 22, 78
neuter, 445
neutral, 117
never-sinking, 604
new, 9, 63, 125, 126, 150, 171, 204, 228, 243, 250,
268, 279, 305, 313, 318, 332, 392, 408, 428, 434,
436, 449, 466, 476, 477, 478, 486, 502, 519, 520,
554, 558, 562, 564, 574, 580, 591, 597, 598
newborn, 545
new-created, 23
New England, 406, 418, 490
new-fashioned, 249
New South Wales, 138
New Testament, 595
New World, 63, 580
New York, 459
Newgate Prison, 492
news, 49, 111, 176, 214, 358, 398, 412, 433, 434,
460, 516
newspaper (newspapers), 34, 103, 111, 159, 191,
274, 314, 399, 441, 473, 496, 534, 543, 573
Niagara, 33
nicety (nice, nicest), 95, 165, 173, 220, 301, 315,
324, 434, 497, 530, 594, 601
niche, 449
niece, 382
Niger, 455
niggard (niggards), 85, 89
nighest, 591
night (nights), 8, 17, 23, 84, 107, 111, 112, 121,
133, 143, 148, 149, 153, 154, 192, 205, 213, 257,
282, 318, 319, 335, 403, 406, 407, 429, 432, 434,
444, 460, 478, 495, 539, 547, 566, 568, 604
nightfall, 434
night-hawk, 165
night-shirt, 106
night-sky, 212
Nile, 429
nimble (nimbler, nimblest, nimbly), 191, 423,
475, 516, 557
nimble-witted, 360
ninny, 272
nobility (noble, noble-minded, nobleness, nobler,
noblest), 15, 26, 44, 48, 55, 64, 83, 93, 94, 100,
121, 127, 137, 147, 164, 171, 197, 199, 200, 205,
206, 208, 212, 217, 240, 245, 246, 251, 260, 264,
286, 289, 298, 318, 327, 328, 329, 333, 336, 339,

342, 348, 350, 351, 354, 368, 395, 416, 418, 435,
449, 451, 452, 453, 455, 459, 461, 462, 475, 479,
485, 496, 523, 538, 546, 548, 556, 562, 565, 573,
586, 595, 596, 599
Nobody, 234
nod, 54, 294 454
noddle, 444
nodes, 524
noise (noises, noisy), 69, 87, 172, 181, 189, 217,
225, 301, 316, 531, 560, 568
nomadic, 589
no-man's-land, 20
nominal, 589
non-conformity (non-conformist), 435
non-dancing, 362
non-existent, 523
nonsense, 177, 264, 282, 313, 333, 359, 369, 398,
435, 441, 457, 485, 597
noodle, 53
noon, 112, 315
noose, 308, 383
normal, 228, 241, 256, 590
North, 33, 142, 574
Northwest passage, 108, 410
nose (noses), 38, 82, 98, 146, 150, 216, 270, 285,
288, 314, 450, 475, 488, 581, 590
nostalgia, 435
nostrils, 296
notable, 114, 378, 391
note (noted, notes), 155, 203, 274, 320, 452, 481,
533, 569
notice (noticeable, notices), 148, 196, 277, 317,
348, 351, 356, 418, 478, 488, 494, 547, 574, 583,
595
notice-takers, 363
notion (notions), 97, 122, 142, 160, 196, 268, 280,
290, 326, 335, 352, 367, 380, 382, 392, 420, 446,
497, 513, 562, 591
notorious, 266
noun, 223
nourishment (nourish, nourished, nourishes,
nourishing), 4, 266, 322, 337, 352, 431, 439, 462,
530, 574
novel (novelist, novelists, novels), 34, 35, 48, 64,
65, 100, 104, 190, 191, 192, 193, 246, 249, 282,
283, 290, 321, 330, 335, 341, 349, 372, 380, 399,
445, 517, 566
novel-reading, 100
novelty (novelties), 14, 116, 232, 370, 435, 436,
519, 520
novices, 158
noxious, 191, 458
nudity (nude), 436
nugatory, 205, 514
nuisance, 171, 182, 301, 373
number (numbers), 78, 142, 157, 167, 181, 202,
225, 245, 268, 270, 278, 302, 355, 364, 402, 464,
520, 530, 540, 542, 553, 574
number one/Number One, 270, 525
numerical, 329
numerous, 83, 459, 576, 581, 591, 601
nun (nunnery), 32, 274
nuptial (nuptials), 376, 379
nurse (nursed, nurselings, nurseries, nurses,
nursing), 134, 157, 226, 272, 328, 343, 346, 349,
377, 401, 478, 497, 544
nurture, 303, 426, 526

KEYWORD INDEX

nut, 599
nutritious, 408
nutshell, 155
nymph/Nymph, 42, 359

oak, 3
oar (oars), 278, 319
oath (oaths), 6, 177, 298, 310, 338, 385, 487
oats, 22, 496
obdurate, 325, 455
obedience (obedient, obey, obeyed, obeying), 45,
    51, 115, 154, 184, 201, 246, 287, 298, 314, 345,
    358, 374, 378, 381, 392, 396, 429, 436, 437, 438,
    447, 538, 592
obituary, 124
object (objected, objecting, objection, objection-
    able, objections, objective, objectless, objects),
    21, 22, 32, 40, 46, 54, 56, 57, 67, 68, 85, 87, 90,
    101, 121, 122, 133, 160, 181, 188, 190, 199, 225,
    237, 238, 256, 260, 266, 267, 275, 276, 278, 279,
    280, 281, 288, 297, 299, 310, 311, 326, 329, 330,
    331, 332, 334, 335, 336, 337, 339, 340, 342, 345,
    360, 366, 368, 376, 383, 384, 392, 404, 408, 409,
    417, 424, 427, 429, 437, 438, 442, 449, 452, 461,
    474, 481, 482, 486, 493, 494, 509, 524, 535, 537,
    543, 550, 559, 570, 572, 573, 576, 596, 598
oblation, 212
obligation (obligations, oblige, obliged, obligers,
    obliges, obliging, obligingly), 7, 38, 58, 89, 93,
    131, 147, 175, 182, 186, 187, 189, 198, 207, 209,
    212, 222, 224, 227, 254, 297, 306, 307, 308, 354,
    435, 437, 438, 441, 478, 481, 482, 487, 534, 594,
    599
obliquity, 455
obliterate (obliterated, obliterating), 213, 408,
    443, 565
oblivion (oblivious), 35, 56, 83, 124, 153, 226, 228,
    409
obloquy, 60, 281
obscenity (obscene), 13, 385
obscurity (obscure, obscured), 109, 181, 214, 399,
    419, 438, 448, 475, 529, 572, 582, 589, 599
obsequiousness (obsequies, obsequious), 123, 556,
    602
observation (observance, observances, observant,
    observed, observer, observers, observes,
    observing), 3, 9, 113, 120, 121, 137, 145, 209,
    218, 222, 226, 249, 259, 284, 288, 292, 294, 303,
    309, 334, 351, 372, 382, 409, 419, 442, 443, 452,
    455, 459, 461, 513, 566, 568, 575, 577, 597, 599,
    601, 603
obsession, 438
obsolete, 308, 328
obstacle (obstacles), 2, 34, 36, 41, 54, 205, 246,
    302, 318, 328, 439, 509
obstinacy (obstinate, obstinately), 11, 14, 45, 54,
    88, 102, 321, 351, 365, 391, 428, 439, 604
obtain (obtained, obtaining, obtains), 141, 238,
    260, 280, 296, 306, 329, 332, 385, 396, 400, 471,
    472, 483, 508, 522, 549, 550, 552, 553
obtrude (obtruded), 157, 530
obvious, 115, 178, 435, 489
occasion (occasional, occasionally, occasioned,
    occasions), 21, 23, 73, 95, 106, 107, 160, 182, 189,
    191, 196, 212, 218, 237, 246, 247, 288, 289, 315,
    319, 329, 331, 335, 348, 356, 359, 383, 389, 400,

413, 440, 451, 453, 457, 465, 473, 475, 476, 489,
    491, 492, 493, 494, 498, 521, 523, 530, 558, 576,
    577, 581, 590, 592, 596, 597, 601, 602
occultations, 573
occupancy (occupied, occupy), 249, 361, 370, 407,
    424, 439, 563
occupation (occupations), 83, 182, 232, 313, 353,
    361, 416, 439, 486, 543
occurrence (occur, occurred, occurrences, occurs),
    57, 105, 184, 238, 268, 278, 330, 337, 412, 413,
    490
ocean (oceans), 63, 74, 85, 124, 138, 170, 257, 290,
    304, 324, 403, 407, 412, 420, 422, 427, 430, 439,
    501, 509, 519, 521, 546, 595
October, 520
ocular, 456, 499
odd (oddest), 78, 86, 278, 397, 462, 559
odds, 47, 203
ode, 93
odious (odiously), 291, 348, 367, 379, 432, 468, 493,
    508, 510, 523, 537
odor (odors), 19, 120, 399
offend (offended, offender, offenders, offends),
    187, 203, 204, 208, 242, 252, 297, 313, 365, 390,
    435, 445, 492, 519, 543, 605
offense (offenses), 13, 23, 82, 118, 129, 172, 173,
    187, 199, 204, 249, 296, 308, 309, 333, 356, 389,
    398, 408, 441, 492, 506
offensive, 114, 256, 473
offer (offered, offering, offers), 97, 167, 211, 230,
    244, 317, 360, 366, 367, 369, 376, 402, 406, 435,
    448, 458, 468, 520, 570
office (offices), 113, 208, 263, 266, 311, 314, 344,
    347, 367, 377, 389, 391, 406, 467, 468
office-holders, 193
officer (officers), 159, 314, 413, 441, 472, 555, 590,
    604
official (officially), 49, 171, 540, 556
officious (officiously), 227, 556
offspring, 8, 10, 111, 136, 185, 226, 232, 255, 274,
    378, 410, 430, 556, 589
ogre, 79, 214
oil, 465
old (older, oldest), 3, 9, 10, 11, 12, 13, 26, 43, 47,
    52, 54, 63, 87, 89, 93, 102, 120, 125, 142, 156,
    157, 160, 163, 165, 169, 170, 185, 192, 193, 204,
    205, 240, 242, 247, 262, 279, 309, 316, 322, 325,
    332, 360, 363, 366, 368, 369, 377, 379, 382, 391,
    392, 393, 396, 427, 428, 429, 431, 434, 445, 457,
    460, 464, 466, 468, 478, 490, 491, 494, 496, 500,
    523, 538, 540, 548, 553, 557, 564, 565, 567, 576,
    578, 584, 586, 587, 597, 602
old-fashioned, 503
old maid, 32, 387, 389, 396, 516
Old World, 63
olive-wood, 339
Olympus, 467
omen (omens), 139, 461, 534
ominous, 434
omission (omitted, omitting), 156, 192, 248, 439
omnipotence (omnipotent), 30, 212, 336, 542, 576
omnipresence (omnipresent), 212, 215, 464
omniscience, 440
omnivorous, 74
One (oneness), 281, 321, 577
one-eyed, 81
one-sided, 202, 582

parson (parsons), 102, 130, 140, 264, 341, 381, 391, 402, 475, 477, 490, 514, 604
part (parted, parting, partings, parts), 4, 10, 99, 112, 117, 120, 139, 146, 166, 184, 188, 192, 214, 215, 219, 254, 256, 267, 271, 282, 288, 299, 311, 317, 323, 331, 332, 340, 344, 346, 350, 375, 381, 382, 398, 406, 414, 415, 421, 425, 445, 457, 462, 463, 471, 499, 501, 502, 505, 518, 530, 531, 535, 541, 549, 557, 561, 565, 573, 577, 581, 585, 599
partake (partakes), 196, 215, 225, 240, 263, 305, 412, 443, 471
partial, 257, 343, 409, 453, 563
partiality, 405, 419, 426
participation (participate, participates), 51, 182, 391, 584
particle, 271, 591
particular, 104, 237, 261, 264, 361, 364, 408, 456, 508, 561
partner (partners, partnership), 223, 375, 388, 392, 396, 423
party (parties), 15, 97, 128, 146, 165, 181, 192, 194, 203, 296, 309, 312, 314, 339, 341, 362, 379, 384, 385, 397, 413, 451, 466, 467, 473, 493, 530, 552, 569, 578, 595
passable, 465
passage (passages), 174, 362, 502, 555, 566
passion (passionate, passionately, passions), 2, 7, 9, 15, 16, 17, 22, 28, 30, 36, 46, 54, 57, 61, 66, 70, 83, 84, 88, 94, 103, 107, 108, 115, 116, 142, 151, 163, 167, 176, 202, 203, 205, 206, 212, 214, 216, 221, 222, 224, 228, 230, 237, 240, 241, 242, 253, 254, 261, 266, 269, 286, 291, 292, 293, 301, 307, 308, 311, 325, 327, 328, 330, 331, 332, 333, 334, 335, 338, 339, 342, 343, 344, 346, 355, 356, 359, 362, 381, 387, 389, 402, 422, 431, 435, 438, 445, 446, 447, 448, 450, 451, 455, 458, 465, 472, 475, 476, 481, 483, 494, 496, 497, 498, 499, 501, 502, 505, 507, 511, 523, 524, 526, 529, 530, 534, 535, 543, 572, 580, 581, 587, 589, 591, 597, 603
passiveness (passive, passively), 48, 107, 357, 362, 485, 509
passport, 220
past, 7, 165, 166, 169, 170, 187, 191, 196, 239, 245, 247, 248, 249, 250, 255, 273, 277, 294, 296, 322, 326, 336, 351, 373, 379, 380, 386, 403, 407, 411, 422, 424, 428, 434, 435, 441, 448, 449, 450, 464, 484, 488, 508, 517, 533, 561, 562, 564, 565, 567, 578, 599
pasteboard, 78, 91
pastime (pastimes), 394, 413, 450, 561
pastor (pastors), 77, 476
pastry, 143
patch (patched, patches, patching, patching-up), 141, 217, 344, 564
paternity (paternal), 290, 577
path (paths), 16, 34, 72, 106, 126, 155, 260, 269, 279, 318, 325, 350, 358, 411, 455, 483, 500, 575, 580, 588
pathetic, 323, 398, 466, 531, 550
pathos, 35, 44, 142, 264, 477
patience, 84, 97, 137, 209, 229, 253, 254, 281, 311, 349, 383, 391, 392, 446, 450, 475, 542, 571, 581
patient (patients), 52, 165, 298, 302, 327, 334, 361, 400, 401, 402, 450, 546, 585
patientissamentally, 601
patriarch, 65, 462
patrician, 142

patrimony (patrimonial), 184, 578
patriotism (patriot, patriot-yeoman, patriots), 83, 152, 214, 423, 451, 467, 494
patronage (patron), 45, 158, 342
patterns, 250
pauper (paupers), 220, 470, 552
pause (pauses), 254, 422, 437, 451, 535
pausing-places, 317
paved, 575
pavement, 434
pawn (pawns), 84, 600
pax vobiscum, 602
payment (paid, pay, paying, pays), 12, 41, 57, 102, 115, 139, 155, 156, 157, 173, 186, 193, 195, 198, 220, 224, 252, 266, 298, 302, 305, 314, 321, 351, 362, 375, 376, 378, 402, 414, 416, 429, 437, 438, 449, 467, 471, 480, 485, 487, 492, 523, 526, 562, 568, 569, 575, 599
peace, 95, 118, 126, 130, 134, 164, 168, 213, 225, 233, 255, 257, 258, 284, 285, 314, 317, 319, 345, 374, 384, 417, 419, 438, 442, 443, 451, 480, 492, 504, 529, 531, 567, 577, 590, 591
peace-loving, 430
peacemaker, 214
peach, 159
peacock (peacocks), 173, 401, 452, 483
peal, 320
pearl (pearls), 17, 27, 42, 99, 336
pears, 315
peasant (peasantry, peasants), 258, 270, 273, 496, 530
pebbles, 128
peccadillo, 419
pecking, 537
peculiar (peculiarities, peculiarity, peculiarly), 117, 122, 151, 210, 242, 276, 281, 282, 299, 333, 343, 346, 349, 357, 367, 368, 372, 411, 421, 438, 462, 478, 480, 484, 485, 505, 530, 546, 557, 574, 593, 599
pecuniary, 53, 208, 471, 533
pedantry (pedant, pedantic), 80, 247, 458
peddlers, 486
pedigree (pedigrees), 228, 451, 532
peeled, 552
peep, 274
peer (peerless), 117, 430
peevish, 86
pen (penned, penning, pens), 34, 141, 155, 175, 249, 300, 356, 390, 467, 478, 493, 518, 561, 601
penalty (penal, penalties), 8, 13, 267, 312, 313, 328, 396, 419, 477, 492
pencil, 452
penetration (penetrate, penetrated, penetrates, penetrating), 65, 66, 134, 171, 224, 248, 280, 300, 328, 361, 414, 422, 448, 520, 542, 564, 581
penitence (penitent, penitents), 8, 70, 390, 492, 506, 507
penman, 307
penny (penniless), 390, 431, 536, 541, 564, 600
pensive, 77, 599
penury, 406
people, 1, 4, 5, 9, 11, 17, 19, 21, 22, 23, 24, 26, 28, 32, 33, 34, 35, 42, 46, 49, 50, 51, 53, 55, 57, 59, 61, 62, 67, 69, 70, 73, 76, 77, 80, 81, 83, 91, 94, 96, 98, 99, 100, 102, 103, 105, 106, 109, 112, 115, 116, 120, 122, 125, 127, 128, 130, 131, 132, 137, 140, 141, 142, 144, 145, 146, 147, 149, 151, 152,

153, 154, 158, 159, 160, 162, 163, 165, 168, 173, 175, 177, 179, 180, 182, 185, 186, 188, 191, 192, 193, 196, 197, 200, 201, 202, 203, 204, 205, 208, 209, 211, 217, 221, 223, 224, 225, 228, 229, 232, 233, 234, 236, 239, 240, 242, 245, 251, 252, 256, 257, 258, 262, 263, 264, 266, 268, 269, 270, 271, 272, 274, 275, 276, 277, 278, 280, 281, 289, 290, 292, 294, 296, 298, 299, 300, 302, 303, 304, 305, 306, 309, 312, 314, 316, 317, 318, 319, 321, 325, 333, 334, 335, 336, 339, 340, 341, 352, 353, 374, 375, 377, 378, 379, 380, 381, 383, 385, 386, 389, 390, 391, 393, 394, 395, 398, 401, 407, 412, 414, 415, 416, 417, 418, 419, 421, 423, 425, 431, 432, 434, 436, 437, 441, 443, 444, 445, 450, 452, 454, 456, 457, 458, 459, 462, 463, 464, 466, 467, 468, 470, 479, 480, 481, 482, 483, 485, 490, 491, 494, 496, 497, 498, 499, 500, 501, 502, 504, 506, 508, 514, 515, 521, 523, 525, 527, 529, 530, 537, 539, 540, 541, 550, 551, 552, 557, 558, 559, 560, 562, 564, 570, 572, 574, 576, 577, 578, 581, 587, 590, 592, 593, 594, 595, 596, 597, 598, 599, 600, 602

people-pleaser, 467

peopled, 324, 387

pepper, 17

percentage, 75, 179, 559

perception (perceive, perceived, perceives, perceptions), 110, 164, 212, 216, 218, 259, 270, 296, 298, 314, 320, 325, 359, 372, 380, 408, 418, 420, 451, 452, 481, 527, 547, 550, 568

perch, 459

perdition, 129, 220, 361, 524, 588

peremptory, 266

perennially, 309

perfection (perfect, perfected, perfectest, perfections, perfectly), 29, 37, 40, 41, 53, 70, 78, 79, 89, 118, 133, 147, 174, 186, 210, 212, 223, 226, 246, 253, 258, 263, 267, 272, 277, 278, 281, 287, 290, 300, 306, 321, 325, 331, 333, 337, 344, 346, 353, 364, 368, 374, 386, 387, 407, 419, 427, 438, 439, 440, 452, 453, 457, 461, 463, 465, 466, 513, 525, 540, 542, 543, 545, 548, 551, 559, 563, 580, 583, 586, 596

perfidy, 208

performance (perform, performed, performer, performing, performs), 38, 59, 112, 146, 154, 155, 174, 192, 216, 249, 250, 264, 271, 289, 300, 301, 307, 311, 344, 393, 395, 422, 452, 453, 487, 497, 504, 520, 539, 565, 583, 604

perfume, 19, 251, 299

perfunctory, 274

pericranium, 444

peril (perilous, perils), 106, 107, 110, 116, 117, 166, 200, 220, 313, 357, 436, 443, 455, 477

period (periods), 5, 11, 13, 17, 69, 87, 117, 126, 135, 156, 173, 183, 213, 248, 249, 260, 280, 294, 375, 395, 434, 449, 450, 476, 499, 549, 565, 566, 567, 603

periodical (periodically), 286, 399, 476, 597

periodicity, 314

perish (perished), 25, 35, 78, 126, 154, 398, 406, 439, 465, 468, 531, 548, 570, 574, 578, 590, 591

periwig, 34

perjury (perjuries, perjuring), 311, 341, 351, 385

permanence (permanent, permanently), 34, 63, 74, 202, 238, 409, 484, 544, 574

permeated, 330

permission (permit, permits, permitted, permitting), 208, 214, 219, 251, 297, 329, 330, 379, 387, 470, 499, 513, 518, 523, 540, 554, 568

pernicious, 131, 340, 491

perpendicular, 114

perpetration (perpetrate, perpetrated, perpetrates, perpetrating), 87, 218, 253, 254, 284, 455

perpetual (perpetually), 142, 147, 168, 201, 210, 225, 302, 319, 403, 415, 426, 444, 484, 504, 566, 569

perpetual motion, 310

perplexity (perplexed, perplexing), 145, 147, 184, 233, 272, 445, 454

perquisites, 494

persecution (persecuting), 97, 453, 554

perseverance (persevere), 1, 169, 177, 232, 263, 379, 453, 454, 547

Persian, 430

persistence (persist, persistent, persistently, persisting, persists), 217, 303, 342, 354, 405, 431, 443, 453, 454, 511, 516, 536, 575

person (persons), 3, 4, 6, 7, 13, 14, 15, 22, 25, 27, 29, 36, 38, 44, 47, 60, 63, 66, 72, 79, 81, 86, 87, 98, 103, 104, 109, 110, 112, 116, 119, 122, 125, 130, 132, 141, 146, 147, 151, 153, 155, 164, 171, 174, 177, 182, 186, 190, 191, 194, 198, 199, 204, 205, 206, 208, 213, 214, 216, 219, 221, 222, 227, 232, 233, 238, 240, 247, 250, 259, 262, 264, 265, 269, 270, 271, 272, 275, 277, 280, 283, 290, 292, 295, 296, 299, 305, 309, 311, 315, 316, 323, 324, 332, 333, 334, 335, 339, 341, 342, 347, 348, 354, 364, 367, 368, 374, 375, 385, 390, 392, 395, 399, 400, 406, 410, 413, 415, 416, 419, 421, 429, 437, 438, 439, 440, 442, 446, 447, 480, 483, 484, 494, 495, 497, 498, 499, 500, 509, 510, 518, 519, 521, 528, 530, 536, 539, 549, 550, 552, 554, 556, 557, 561, 562, 563, 565, 571, 576, 579, 580, 588, 594, 595, 596

personage, 108, 314, 423, 457

personal (personally, personalness), 14, 157, 160, 169, 203, 204, 281, 314, 346, 364, 378, 383, 385, 418, 454, 466, 473, 488, 503, 518, 519, 528, 544, 551, 586

personality (personalities), 199, 271, 398, 434, 563

personating, 267

personification (personified), 271, 277, 534, 599

perspective (perspectives), 404, 454

perspicuity, 463, 536

persuasion (persuade, persuaded, persuades, persuading, persuasive), 5, 28, 35, 67, 131, 224, 232, 244, 278, 282, 330, 348, 358, 369, 391, 452, 455, 504, 560, 575, 584, 585, 596

pertain (pertains), 356, 540

pertinacity (pertinacious), 28, 441

perturbation (perturbations), 190, 482, 581

Peru (Peruvian), 10, 166

perusal (perusing), 113, 527, 570

pervade (pervades, pervading), 114, 193, 254, 505, 546

perversity (perverse, perverseness, perversion), 69, 134, 160, 167, 245, 335, 391, 455, 507, 537, 559

pervert (perverted, perverter, perverting, perverts), 131, 218, 289, 314, 417, 455, 505, 518, 525, 575

pessimism, 11

pest, 562

pestilence, 198, 591
pet (petted), 478, 540
petition (petitioned, petitioner), 115, 212, 455
petticoat (petticoated, petticoats), 349, 467, 599
petty, 55, 272, 274, 288, 448
petulance, 483
pew, 382
pewter, 579
Phaedon, 402
phantasies, 546
phantom (phantoms), 150, 253, 271, 272, 274, 336, 404, 405, 429, 461
Pharisee, 71
Pharoah, 122
phase (phases), 69, 74, 368, 397
phenomenon (phenomena), 111, 378, 576
philanthropy (philanthropist, philanthropists), 67, 75, 138, 162, 208, 296, 455, 456, 464, 541, 567
Philistine (Philistia, philistinish), 398
philoprogenitiveness, 324
philosophy (philosopher, philosophers, philosophic, philosophical, philosophically, philosophize, philosophizes, philosophizings), 2, 3, 12, 46, 48, 58, 71, 72, 80, 85, 120, 121, 177, 191, 197, 207, 224, 231, 236, 238, 261, 265, 273, 279, 281, 292, 326, 328, 332, 345, 348, 359, 361, 383, 386, 402, 408, 418, 420, 456, 457, 458, 475, 478, 483, 484, 501, 519, 526, 555, 559, 569
phiz, 85
phlegmatic, 498
Phoebus Apollo, 63
phonograph, 173
phosphorescence (phosphorescent), 11, 274
photography, 30
phrase (phrases), 18, 33, 45, 144, 150, 172, 173, 242, 256, 267, 434, 464, 477, 478, 490, 601
phraseology, 173
phrenzy, 327
physic (physick), 229, 400, 402, 416, 437, 494
physical (physically), 13, 37, 48, 49, 54, 87, 100, 106, 110, 148, 242, 251, 260, 279, 308, 347, 418, 419, 450, 529, 551, 579, 593
physician (physicians), 163, 204, 250, 400, 401, 402, 412, 521, 527, 559, 566, 567
physiognomist, 428
physiology, 193
physique, 458
piano, 347, 422
pick (picked, picking), 194, 397, 481, 494, 562, 584
pickaxe, 121
pickle, 12
pickpocket, 34, 35, 200, 401, 544
picnic, 319
picquet, 380
picture (pictured, pictures), 29, 41, 56, 83, 86, 146, 183, 190, 234, 248, 252, 260, 273, 290, 321, 376, 417, 449, 495, 534, 536
picturesque, 25, 81, 274, 387, 478, 488
pie-crusts, 487
piece (pieces), 84, 182, 248, 282, 293, 313, 318, 373, 411, 414, 492, 495, 506, 512, 522
pierce (pierced, pierces, piercing), 83, 174, 210, 226, 292, 300, 338, 342, 422, 452, 463, 468, 518
piety (pious), 55, 87, 173, 364, 374, 404, 458, 478, 494, 504, 505, 514, 530, 542

pig (pigs), 160, 212, 435, 439, 440, 496, 500
pigeon, 323
pigmy (pigmies, pygmies), 401, 449, 588
pike (pike-keepers, pike-keeping), 485
pile (piled, piling), 443, 449, 534
pilgrimage (pilgrim, pilgrims), 105, 148, 187, 258, 430, 434, 503, 569
pill (pills), 189, 204
pillaged, 308
pillars, 303
pillory, 59
pilot, 469, 498
pilot fish, 85
pin, 395, 529
pin-money, 381
pinch, 421, 525
Pindar, 276
pine, 266
pine-stem, 430
pinions, 163
pinnacle, 88, 598
pint, 531
pioneers, 580
pip, 434
pipe (pipes), 151, 259, 420, 421, 540
piquant, 85
pique (piqued, piques), 452, 482
piracy (pirate), 542, 562
pistol (pistols), 176, 185, 442, 574
pit (pitting), 88, 392, 447
pitched, 274
pitchfork, 252, 429
pitfalls, 312
pity (pitied, pities, pitiful, pitifulest, pitiless, pitying), 18, 35, 64, 85, 88, 91, 102, 114, 120, 125, 127, 129, 136, 138, 139, 177, 178, 182, 188, 193, 209, 230, 236, 257, 261, 284, 297, 310, 313, 335, 338, 347, 356, 357, 361, 382, 413, 420, 432, 444, 450, 458, 459, 467, 512, 542, 570
placards, 274
place (placed, places, placing), 3, 7, 17, 34, 48, 52, 59, 73, 119, 145, 148, 165, 170, 178, 181, 182, 201, 205, 211, 215, 219, 220, 227, 238, 244, 249, 250, 254, 261, 262, 264, 278, 290, 294, 301, 303, 305, 309, 319, 323, 331, 340, 344, 347, 351, 352, 353, 356, 357, 377, 381, 390, 399, 407, 420, 432, 437, 439, 441, 443, 449, 455, 459, 460, 463, 464, 469, 473, 475, 478, 481, 482, 484, 490, 493, 502, 507, 509, 512, 514, 520, 521, 540, 543, 544, 545, 546, 549, 550, 554, 557, 559, 561, 563, 570, 577, 590, 598, 602
placid, 96, 176, 240, 277
placid-minded, 52
plagiarist, 29
plague/Plague (plagued), 94, 378, 418, 486, 594
plaguy, 398, 401
plain (plainer, plainest, plainness, plains), 4, 14, 38, 39, 40, 44, 53, 84, 85, 103, 106, 143, 152, 163, 191, 192, 213, 220, 301, 313, 320, 329, 372, 376, 439, 448, 451, 476, 527, 530
plain-dealing, 201, 264
plain-speaking, 27
plaintive, 547
plan (planned, planning, plans), 63, 99, 137, 180, 205, 228, 245, 322, 385, 475, 498, 511
planet (planets), 65, 134, 213, 248, 314, 457, 547, 548, 593

popularity (popular, popularize, popularly), 36, 48, 127, 230, 330, 362, 415, 423, 436, 468, 497, 502, 516, 566, 573, 574
population, 54, 257, 334, 380, 385, 389, 395, 468
populous, 439, 468, 478
porcelain, 86, 229, 374
pore, 519
pork, 212
porridge, 421
port, 85, 187, 319, 364, 496, 547, 604
port wine, 315
portable, 191, 490
portals, 85
portents, 478
porter (porters), 196, 261
portion, 40, 71, 102, 219, 320, 346, 376, 430, 477, 601, 602
portmanteau, 46
portraiture (portrait, portraits), 30, 31, 172, 274, 299, 428, 445, 485, 593
portray, 171
Portuguese, 240
pose, 426
position (positions), 119, 137, 154, 173, 177, 242, 270, 295, 311, 333, 368, 370, 509, 514, 525, 538, 540, 557, 596
positive, 3, 25, 29, 205, 217, 236, 479
possession (possess, possessed, possesses, possessing, possessor, possessors), 33, 104, 105, 107, 122, 132, 150, 162, 163, 168, 180, 183, 184, 198, 200, 206, 227, 228, 233, 237, 238, 242, 243, 245, 246, 254, 255, 260, 261, 265, 268, 276, 278, 281, 282, 288, 294, 296, 306, 310, 313, 342, 356, 370, 376, 383, 384, 385, 386, 388, 389, 405, 411, 415, 427, 437, 438, 443, 446, 448, 453, 458, 460, 465, 466, 468, 469, 474, 482, 484, 510, 511, 527, 528, 531, 537, 541, 555, 563, 578, 582, 583, 584, 587, 594, 599
possibility (possibilities, possible, possibly), 13, 17, 74, 92, 116, 124, 128, 137, 140, 142, 168, 179, 182, 198, 214, 220, 239, 276, 299, 303, 313, 320, 323, 327, 339, 343, 354, 376, 384, 385, 386, 400, 404, 418, 420, 432, 438, 450, 456, 459, 469, 491, 498, 511, 558, 560, 565, 576, 581
post, 571
post-time, 314
posterity (posterities), 10, 172, 229, 336, 464, 469
posthumous, 181
postulate (postulates), 295
posture, 250, 267, 457
pot (pots), 139, 189, 291
potato (potatoes), 54, 231, 601
potato-disease, 54
potent, 25, 46, 104, 105, 119, 188, 234, 331, 415, 513
pottage, 600
poultry, 601
pound (pounds), 172, 184, 207, 290, 314, 486, 497, 541, 595
pour (poured, pours), 181, 465, 559
poverty, 33, 34, 36, 70, 145, 146, 162, 184, 265, 272, 280, 317, 340, 377, 469, 470, 471, 472, 481, 483, 490, 549, 561, 594, 599
power (powerful, powerfully, powerless, powers), 1, 4, 6, 7, 10, 12, 15, 16, 27, 29, 31, 32, 35, 36, 37, 39, 40, 41, 42, 49, 50, 56, 61, 65, 76, 80, 83, 89, 96, 99, 102, 103, 109, 111, 114, 127, 128, 134, 138, 140, 142, 143, 146, 147, 149, 158, 161, 162, 163, 164, 167, 171, 173, 176, 181, 182, 185, 190, 199, 201, 208, 209, 210, 212, 213, 214, 217, 219, 220, 224, 225, 226, 228, 230, 233, 235, 236, 238, 246, 252, 253, 254, 256, 260, 263, 278, 280, 281, 282, 283, 285, 290, 296, 300, 302, 303, 310, 311, 312, 316, 319, 320, 330, 337, 339, 340, 345, 350, 351, 352, 353, 355, 356, 357, 359, 361, 363, 364, 365, 367, 375, 380, 381, 383, 384, 385, 394, 407, 408, 410, 411, 412, 414, 415, 423, 424, 425, 428, 430, 445, 447, 453, 459, 460, 465, 466, 472, 473, 475, 477, 479, 480, 483, 488, 491, 496, 497, 503, 508, 510, 511, 512, 513, 520, 521, 522, 524, 528, 530, 535, 537, 538, 539, 541, 552, 553, 559, 560, 563, 566, 572, 573, 576, 579, 587, 590, 593, 595, 599, 601
power-strength, 472
pow-wow, 590
practic, 502
practicable, 467
practicality (practical), 80, 156, 348, 361, 362, 386, 400, 451, 457, 473, 555, 556, 563
practice (practiced, practicers, practices, practicing), 9, 16, 24, 46, 66, 71, 86, 103, 114, 115, 116, 117, 128, 153, 161, 179, 204, 211, 219, 224, 308, 312, 322, 324, 331, 362, 364, 376, 389, 396, 418, 450, 451, 456, 457, 473, 477, 478, 484, 485, 498, 502, 505, 510, 520, 530, 542, 549, 569, 582, 584, 586, 588, 598, 604
practitioner (practitioners), 173, 264
Prado, 585
pragmatical, 258, 305
prairie, 18, 270, 290
praise (praised, praises, praiseworthiness, praiseworthy, praising), 82, 89, 90, 190, 191, 195, 204, 208, 212, 223, 240, 261, 273, 274, 291, 308, 316, 328, 333, 338, 363, 369, 374, 376, 384, 392, 414, 425, 431, 434, 437, 473, 474, 479, 533, 535, 537, 578
prate, 291
prattle, 68
prayer (pray, prayed, prayers, praying), 8, 70, 103, 143, 315, 320, 357, 474, 475, 503, 504, 511, 572, 585, 592, 601
prayer-book, 477
prayer-meeting, 478
prayer-rooms, 605
preachment (preached, preacher, preachers, preaches, preacheth, preaching, preachments), 23, 71, 76, 86, 102, 122, 146, 152, 163, 243, 267, 292, 362, 436, 450, 475, 476, 477, 478, 484, 497, 502, 547, 570, 574
precarious, 93, 125, 236
precaution (precautions), 59, 310
precedence (precede, precedency, precedent, precedents, precedes, preceding), 103, 158, 310, 340, 449, 499, 535, 537, 589
precept (precepts), 70, 71, 78, 476, 570, 601
precinct (precincts), 196
precious (preciousness), 62, 91, 132, 183, 205, 206, 253, 281, 317, 374, 477, 565, 583
precious metals, 224
precipice, 91
precipitates, 380
precision (preciseness), 237, 408, 570
precluded, 236

predecessor (predecessors), 51, 473
predestination (predestinated, predestined), 135, 351, 604
predicament, 96, 135
prediction (predict), 65, 247, 478
predilections, 429
predisposition (predispose), 54, 476
predominance (predominant, predominate), 187, 275, 296, 304, 311, 447, 522, 526
pre-eminence (pre-eminent), 37, 507
pre-engaged, 309
preference (preferable, preferences, preferment, preferred, preferring, prefers), 131, 157, 168, 239, 272, 288, 291, 294, 304, 315, 368, 372, 391, 399, 405, 421, 425, 449, 450, 456, 478, 543, 576, 580, 601
pregnant, 73
prehistoric, 187
prejudice (prejudiced, prejudices), 24, 27, 52, 57, 103, 111, 129, 163, 221, 228, 230, 273, 295, 298, 312, 344, 409, 421, 458, 478, 479, 480, 483, 574, 590
premature, 70, 101, 258, 317, 591
premeditated (premeditatedly), 167, 174
premises, 129, 309
premium, 163
preoccupied, 29, 519
pre-ordaining, 135
preparation (preparations, prepare, prepared, preparedness, prepares), 55, 100, 105, 108, 117, 121, 125, 156, 175, 283, 295, 314, 316, 339, 365, 379, 380, 394, 395, 397, 461, 466, 479, 480, 512, 524, 550
preponderance (preponderate), 94, 254
prepossession, 38, 364
prerogative (prerogatives), 196, 224, 262, 559, 599, 600
presages, 257
Presbyterian, 271
prescription (prescribe, prescribed, prescribes, prescribing, prescriptive), 100, 103, 201, 292, 322, 382, 388, 400, 401, 433, 445, 527
presence, 55, 93, 98, 106, 120, 137, 203, 209, 212, 226, 235, 250, 327, 352, 353, 358, 432, 444, 509, 549, 584
present (presented, presently, presents), 1, 6, 16, 47, 56, 72, 83, 100, 120, 126, 131, 133, 166, 168, 169, 189, 191, 211, 213, 230, 247, 248, 249, 254, 259, 272, 273, 277, 287, 294, 296, 306, 317, 383, 405, 407, 422, 436, 441, 448, 449, 452, 464, 469, 477, 478, 493, 498, 510, 511, 513, 559, 561, 564, 567, 572
presentiment (presentiments), 134, 140, 369, 428, 478, 534
presentment, 278
preservation (preservative, preserve, preserved, preserver, preserves, preserving), 12, 40, 51, 66, 182, 224, 311, 322, 332, 345, 366, 376, 381, 411, 436, 440, 457, 474, 488, 489, 493, 510, 514, 515, 540, 579, 586
preside (presided, presiding), 224, 280, 365
president, 68
press (pressed, pressing), 112, 116, 201, 286, 350, 399, 426, 476, 528
pressure, 44, 53, 64, 229, 282, 399, 466, 559
presumption (presume, presumed, presumest, presumptuous, presumptuously), 50, 105, 116,

134, 221, 229, 244, 391, 418
pretend (pretence, pretended, pretenders, pretends, pretense, pretenses, pretension, pretensions), 3, 24, 25, 110, 119, 197, 198, 204, 229, 267, 269, 271, 276, 305, 332, 345, 347, 360, 365, 399, 418, 444, 469, 477, 481, 488, 515, 519, 537, 555, 572
pretty (prettier, prettiest, prettinesses), 31, 42, 43, 50, 70, 164, 172, 176, 182, 194, 198, 202, 273, 316, 344, 348, 352, 356, 360, 364, 371, 372, 392, 393, 394, 601
prevail (prevails), 135, 163, 183, 225, 275, 287, 502, 533, 570, 572, 575
prevalence (prevalent), 209, 234, 478
prevarication, 179
prevention (prevent, prevented, preventing, prevents), 87, 96, 104, 137, 139, 163, 187, 188, 225, 227, 231, 245, 273, 285, 298, 309, 311, 315, 373, 384, 391, 412, 422, 437, 471, 479, 480, 492, 493, 509, 535, 553, 570, 584, 592, 604
previous, 215, 243, 249, 462, 468
prey (preying, preys), 2, 16, 20, 33, 88, 97, 272, 314, 372, 378, 532, 585
price (priced, prices), 17, 58, 74, 139, 245, 353, 355, 358, 410, 451, 523, 530, 541, 552, 575, 579, 597
pricked, 285
prickles, 351
pride (prided, priding, proud, proudest, proudlier, proudly), 8, 9, 11, 20, 42, 45, 46, 57, 67, 83, 94, 116, 122, 123, 124, 133, 157, 164, 171, 187, 208, 209, 210, 221, 231, 246, 251, 261, 262, 264, 267, 288, 299, 306, 311, 336, 341, 350, 359, 360, 364, 365, 366, 371, 382, 385, 400, 405, 435, 458, 459, 463, 470, 471, 479, 480, 481, 482, 483, 484, 501, 538, 577, 580, 584, 600, 601
priest (priestess, priestesses, priests), 187, 244, 351, 384, 408, 423, 428, 459, 482, 600
priestcraft, 503
prig, 441
primate, 576
prime, 12, 201, 203
prime minister, 111
primitive, 3, 49, 331, 373, 450, 589
primum mobile, 583
prince (princely, princes), 36, 44, 46, 87, 133, 189, 190, 225, 278, 320, 446, 456, 500, 519, 536, 541, 572, 591
Prince of Darkness, 214, 351
principal, 4, 87, 104, 105, 190, 317, 345, 364, 453, 509, 528
principle (principles), 16, 37, 41, 51, 54, 55, 59, 75, 78, 80, 83, 90, 93, 100, 103, 105, 115, 125, 154, 155, 164, 167, 183, 188, 211, 245, 248, 251, 252, 253, 254, 258, 259, 260, 276, 289, 295, 302, 308, 310, 330, 351, 403, 418, 437, 447, 456, 461, 467, 479, 481, 484, 486, 487, 488, 495, 497, 502, 514, 522, 526, 528, 533, 541, 581
print (printers, prints), 48, 323, 399, 401, 402, 486, 503
priority (priorities), 383, 484
prison (prisoner, prisoners), 77, 78, 113, 142, 201, 279, 321, 448, 484, 601
pristine, 548
privacy (private, privy), 82, 87, 95, 104, 113, 129, 154, 155, 177, 178, 183, 190, 222, 232, 245, 292, 308, 343, 393, 418, 431, 440, 445, 472, 478, 479, 486, 490, 501, 518, 521, 552, 565, 584, 585

KEYWORD INDEX

prostration, 433, 489, 501
protection (protect, protecting, protectiveness, protector, protects), 130, 183, 208, 290, 354, 367, 369, 399, 489, 542, 596
protest, 118, 477
Protestant, 503
protestations, 177
prototype, 518
proverb (proverbs), 55, 123, 172, 203, 346, 469, 489, 490, 513, 539, 569, 594
proverbially, 497
provide (provided, providing), 157, 190, 304, 322, 344, 384, 455, 456, 457, 488, 505, 557
providence/Providence (providences), 3, 38, 49, 74, 75, 134, 135, 136, 137, 154, 161, 215, 216, 219, 235, 284, 296, 319, 337, 356, 367, 400, 572, 585, 595
province, 57, 258, 293, 346, 362, 367, 371, 488
provincial (provincials), 81, 262, 542, 574
provision (provisions), 64, 376, 377, 405, 446, 469, 479
provocation (provoke, provoked, provoking), 106, 140, 184, 267, 296, 300, 386, 433, 511, 531, 549
prowess, 262, 336, 433
prowling, 316
proximately, 1
proxy, 280, 426
prude, 598
prudence (prudent, prudently), 49, 106, 117, 133, 139, 145, 185, 187, 189, 210, 225, 242, 249, 297, 323, 339, 341, 344, 358, 365, 376, 384, 388, 393, 395, 396, 413, 417, 448, 485, 491, 549, 571
prune (pruned, pruner), 463, 601
prurience, 196
Prussians, 270
pry (prying), 116, 242, 414, 521
pseudo-virtue, 587
psychical, 517
psychology (psychologist, psychologists), 242, 348, 491
public (publicly), 48, 49, 50, 67, 82, 95, 116, 129, 130, 132, 136, 151, 153, 155, 157, 158, 159, 183, 192, 280, 297, 304, 324, 342, 355, 366, 375, 385, 402, 418, 431, 434, 437, 440, 441, 463, 466, 467, 468, 472, 485, 490, 491, 504, 518, 524, 540, 544, 551, 558, 559, 573, 576, 577, 585, 590, 602, 603, 604
publication, 36
publish (published, publishing), 34, 91, 112, 259, 299, 307, 399
puckers, 516
pudding (puddings), 143, 293, 347
puddle, 582
puff (puffed), 486, 525, 540, 555, 564, 594
pull (pulled, pulling, pulls), 314, 383, 545, 602, 603
pulpit, 266, 399, 475, 476, 603
pulsation (pulse), 320, 400, 401, 541
pulverize, 22
pumpkin, 368
pun, 589
punch, 152
punctual, 532
pungency, 230
punishment (punish, punished, punishes, punishing, punishments), 56, 88, 119, 133, 151, 219, 271, 296, 298, 301, 308, 312, 324, 392, 396, 419,

445, 469, 491, 492, 493, 503, 507, 511, 540, 585, 586, 587
pupil (pupils), 146, 158, 305
puppet (puppets), 390, 515
puppy, 98
purblind, 84
purchase (purchased, purchases, purchasing), 198, 227, 244, 245, 299, 318, 385, 415, 416, 458, 516, 575
purgatorial, 503
purge (purged), 167, 494
purification (purified, purifier, purifies, purify, purifying), 102, 223, 415, 430, 474, 493, 503, 518, 542, 571, 591
Puritan (Puritan-morals, Puritanism), 418, 502, 504
purity (pure, purely, pureness, purer, purest), 30, 43, 45, 97, 145, 156, 166, 179, 186, 214, 219, 220, 221, 232, 236, 237, 260, 267, 269, 274, 280, 300, 330, 337, 370, 386, 388, 398, 404, 418, 423, 427, 436, 447, 451, 489, 493, 510, 514, 527, 547, 551, 552, 574, 579
purlieu, 49
purple, 220
purpose (purposed, purposes), 6, 29, 59, 80, 112, 125, 131, 136, 158, 190, 191, 208, 214, 218, 219, 224, 225, 228, 244, 247, 256, 263, 276, 288, 301, 303, 309, 314, 315, 320, 331, 345, 367, 381, 395, 425, 428, 455, 457, 472, 473, 479, 492, 493, 494, 501, 522, 524, 541, 563, 593, 595, 602
purposeless, 173
purse (purser, purses), 24, 111, 141, 207, 271, 302, 309, 313, 314, 343, 413, 544, 579
purse proud, 538
pursuit (pursue, pursued, pursues, pursuing, pursuits), 2, 4, 15, 29, 83, 108, 133, 135, 141, 145, 150, 202, 235, 238, 246, 261, 272, 281, 283, 296, 305, 306, 312, 315, 316, 333, 356, 363, 376, 384, 394, 418, 429, 461, 485, 487, 494, 497, 498, 502, 512, 554, 565, 572, 581, 588
push (pushed, pushes), 210, 244, 252, 429, 449, 494, 529
pushiness, 494
pusillanimous, 570
put (puts, putting), 280, 283, 305, 359, 365, 381, 394, 413, 452, 476, 477, 486, 500, 505, 523, 530, 532, 540, 547, 551, 552, 565, 579, 580, 584
putrescent, 361
puzzle (puzzled, puzzles, puzzling), 269, 307, 334, 419
pyramid/Pyramid (pyramidical), 48, 56, 210, 229, 564
Pythagoras, 166

quackery (quack, quacks), 494, 602
quadrille, 317, 434
quadruped, 157, 281
quaff (quaffed, quaffing), 236, 413
quagmire, 372, 388
quaint, 86
Quaker, 444
quakes, 187
qualification (qualifications, qualified, qualifier, qualifies, qualify, qualifying), 113, 154, 157, 180, 190, 259, 314, 323, 344, 345, 346, 352, 354, 367, 368, 376, 400, 542, 549, 567, 579, 585

513, 517, 526, 538, 539, 556, 571, 572, 589, 590, 605

reading (read, reader, readers, reads), 34, 35, 36, 49, 51, 64, 76, 83, 142, 155, 156, 158, 161, 182, 191, 192, 212, 213, 247, 248, 249, 251, 267, 281, 282, 283, 289, 290, 300, 302, 303, 304, 308, 311, 314, 324, 349, 360, 361, 363, 364, 377, 401, 409, 417, 424, 428, 429, 431, 433, 440, 451, 452, 454, 461, 463, 465, 468, 469, 473, 475, 476, 477, 481, 485, 490, 495, 496, 512, 518, 527, 528, 551, 556, 561, 563, 566, 575, 595, 604

real estate, 184

reality (real, realism, realities), 7, 11, 20, 23, 24, 49, 55, 56, 81, 86, 110, 122, 125, 132, 147, 148, 149, 163, 165, 183, 197, 203, 211, 212, 219, 221, 225, 230, 236, 253, 271, 273, 274, 275, 287, 296, 306, 319, 320, 321, 326, 329, 330, 339, 341, 346, 347, 351, 358, 412, 428, 429, 444, 445, 449, 452, 463, 469, 470, 472, 480, 495, 496, 506, 507, 509, 512, 515, 516, 529, 530, 543, 548, 550, 551, 558, 561, 563, 564, 579, 584, 593, 604

realization (realize, realized, realizes), 31, 71, 168, 213, 254, 441, 469, 502, 525, 596

realm (realms), 51, 208, 224, 313, 317, 348

reap (reaped, reaping), 99, 170, 213

reappear, 142, 214, 403

rear (reared, rearing), 130, 134, 309, 314, 481, 495, 603

reason (reasonable, reasonableness, reasonably, reasoned, reasoners, reasoning, reasons), 1, 13, 15, 24, 28, 33, 38, 53, 55, 56, 79, 84, 85, 90, 95, 97, 98, 99, 103, 106, 110, 115, 116, 125, 135, 149, 150, 151, 156, 157, 159, 168, 169, 174, 177, 179, 180, 193, 195, 196, 205, 215, 218, 220, 235, 236, 237, 240, 245, 248, 249, 253, 257, 262, 263, 265, 272, 274, 275, 276, 279, 285, 286, 287, 290, 296, 297, 301, 309, 312, 314, 315, 316, 324, 326, 335, 338, 339, 340, 342, 344, 345, 346, 348, 349, 350, 354, 357, 360, 366, 367, 369, 372, 374, 383, 384, 394, 404, 408, 417, 418, 419, 422, 426, 428, 430, 432, 442, 446, 447, 448, 454, 460, 461, 462, 470, 475, 479, 483, 488, 489, 495, 496, 497, 498, 499, 502, 504, 505, 507, 508, 509, 511, 513, 525, 532, 534, 539, 543, 551, 559, 574, 584, 587, 589, 597, 598

reason-fit, 162

reasserts, 512

rebellion (rebel, rebellious, rebelliousness), 322, 361, 428, 437, 438, 512

rebirth, 47, 48

rebound, 103

rebuke (rebukes), 95, 356, 499, 605

recall (recalled), 6, 82, 196, 211, 318, 443, 602

recede (receded, receding), 337, 407, 449, 499

receipts, 95

receive (received, receives, receiving), 126, 135, 207, 211, 212, 226, 227, 248, 253, 254, 262, 267, 278, 282, 294, 332, 343, 350, 351, 379, 409, 410, 412, 437, 443, 452, 478, 481, 497, 499, 504, 508, 532, 537, 555, 564, 569, 573

receptacles, 76

receptiveness, 499

recesses, 520

recipe, 59, 235

recipient, 119, 380

reciprocity (reciprocal), 51, 57, 163, 205, 499, 527

recital, 471

recite (recited), 191, 463

reckless (recklessly), 106, 346, 377, 387

reckon (reckoned, reckoning, reckons), 82, 193, 250, 271, 314, 371, 404, 475

reclaimed, 139, 164

recluse, 290

recognition (recognize, recognized, recognizes, recognizing), 164, 167, 210, 212, 215, 261, 262, 268, 279, 331, 354, 356, 394, 404, 419, 474, 546, 596

recoil (recoils), 200, 219, 491, 524

recollection (recollect, recollecting, recollections), 85, 127, 146, 275, 330, 397, 403, 562, 567

recomfort, 254

recommendation (recommend, recommendations, recommends), 24, 25, 191, 222, 348, 350, 381, 383, 392, 436, 452

recompense (recompensed), 312, 484, 515

reconciliation (reconcile, reconciled, reconciles), 3, 49, 86, 95, 103, 112, 122, 135, 136, 179, 234, 307, 420, 458, 499, 500, 523, 543, 590

record (recorded, recording, records), 85, 97, 171, 198, 247, 250, 296, 302, 381, 404, 485, 576, 601

recounting, 186

recourse, 19, 28, 440

recovery (recover, recovered), 133, 265, 271, 284, 364, 366, 379, 400, 402

recreant, 345

recreation, 20

rectify (rectified), 360, 450

rectitude, 219, 267, 295, 388, 409, 411, 418, 479, 513, 514, 539, 584

rector, 67

recurrence (recur, recurrent), 188, 322, 407, 582

red coat, 542

redeem (redeems), 164, 265, 277

Redeemer, 164, 393

redistribution, 541

red-man, 513

redness (red, reddened), 45, 123, 126, 189, 298, 385, 430, 590

redoubles, 511

redoubtable, 423

redress (redressed), 100, 196, 284

redskin, 163, 296

reduce (reduced, reduces, reducing), 146, 164, 228, 244, 259, 272, 309, 322, 333, 361, 409, 432, 449, 457, 484, 503, 518, 541, 546, 571

reek, 466, 600

reel (reeled, reeling), 156, 583

re-election, 466

re-established, 204

reference (refer, refers), 286, 487, 526

refilled, 544

refined-looking, 557

refinement (refine, refined, refinements, refiner, refining), 8, 20, 38, 39, 75, 177, 179, 203, 236, 302, 340, 349, 363, 425, 456, 466, 497, 500, 536, 540, 544, 589

reflection (reflect, reflected, reflecting, reflections, reflects), 5, 44, 61, 88, 100, 106, 109, 112, 120, 125, 149, 151, 164, 196, 214, 229, 245, 260, 262, 269, 274, 275, 280, 297, 345, 360, 376, 389, 405, 406, 444, 449, 457, 461, 462, 467, 474, 475, 482, 489, 500, 508, 514, 527, 546, 560, 561, 563, 584, 596

reflex, 563

reflux, 77
reformation (reform, reformed, reformer, reformers, reforming), 61, 63, 70, 152, 234, 288, 315, 350, 356, 391, 392, 434, 446, 500, 501, 506, 507, 530, 597
refrain (refrained), 474, 492
refreshment (refresh, refreshed, refreshing), 68, 116, 135, 168, 407, 443, 583
refuge, 91, 163, 216, 229, 303, 384, 501, 539, 549, 562
refusal (refused, refuses, refusing), 109, 121, 189, 273, 311, 330, 343, 371, 374, 381, 387, 390, 395, 443, 477, 482, 499, 504, 517, 526, 565, 579, 590
refutation, 102, 115
regain (regained), 268, 355
regard (regarded, regardeth, regarding, regards), 88, 143, 149, 181, 184, 215, 221, 225, 243, 261, 295, 324, 335, 372, 375, 401, 403, 405, 411, 413, 415, 421, 431, 437, 441, 501, 525, 526, 528, 529, 556, 577, 588
regeneration (regenerate), 501, 554
re-gilding, 416
regiment, 369
region (regions), 124, 257, 324, 408, 420, 448, 451, 563
register (registered, registers), 231, 404
regret (regrets, regretted, regretting), 10, 66, 80, 148, 228, 270, 290, 317, 320, 322, 340, 389, 398, 462, 468, 501, 530
regularity (regular, regularly), 11, 51, 71, 102, 151, 155, 156, 199, 265, 320, 327, 343, 477, 576
regulation (regulate, regulated, regulations), 103, 177, 260, 375, 380, 478, 480, 541, 550, 551, 574, 577
rehearsal (rehearsals, rehearse, rehearsed), 86, 138
reign (reigning, reigns), 46, 88, 130, 142, 225, 283, 336, 545
rein (reined, reins), 102, 204, 225, 276, 303, 367, 511
reiteration (reiterate, reiterated), 27, 564
rejection (reject, rejected, rejecting, rejections, rejects), 6, 178, 212, 279, 307, 334, 376, 443, 461, 482, 524
rejoice (rejoices, rejoicing), 239, 242, 261, 262, 290, 304, 370, 405, 435, 443, 454, 501, 553
relapsed, 505
relation (relate, related, relates, relations), 33, 47, 67, 172, 191, 202, 239, 240, 249, 253, 277, 288, 308, 326, 331, 335, 356, 386, 437, 460, 462, 467, 476, 480, 532, 542, 570, 573, 593, 596
relative (relatives), 185, 236, 272, 295, 296, 324, 333
relaxation (relax, relaxes), 148, 278, 553
releases, 249
relent (relentlessly), 201, 478
reliance (reliable, relied, relies, rely, relying), 93, 107, 111, 244, 293, 350, 360, 514, 579, 604
relief (relieve, relieved, relieves, relieving), 41, 67, 77, 123, 145, 260, 272, 347, 385, 401, 407, 411, 417, 428, 462, 491, 492, 501, 543, 559, 564, 571
religion (religions, religious, religiously), 25, 47, 58, 64, 66, 70, 71, 72, 74, 76, 80, 93, 102, 103, 111, 159, 169, 172, 178, 189, 191, 201, 205, 215, 217, 218, 237, 250, 253, 264, 266, 267, 268, 286,

311, 314, 320, 324, 325, 336, 352, 355, 373, 385, 400, 408, 419, 432, 440, 456, 465, 476, 478, 479, 494, 497, 502, 503, 504, 505, 506, 522, 525, 530, 537, 539, 543, 568, 577, 582, 588, 589, 593, 596, 604
religionist, 46
religious-good, 223
relish, 6, 141, 241, 343, 501, 532
reliving, 155
reluctance (reluctant), 19, 119, 296, 340, 350, 511
remain (remains), 126, 163, 213, 226, 246, 254, 305, 311, 328, 329, 346, 357, 360, 371, 372, 373, 378, 415, 424, 448, 503, 505, 524, 528, 555, 604
remark (remarked, remarking, remarks), 160, 323, 381, 428, 464, 480, 573, 602
remarkable, 4, 109, 118, 170, 181, 183, 221, 293, 344, 347, 470, 493, 520, 544, 587
remedy (remedial, remedies), 52, 110, 120, 164, 251, 281, 303, 311, 400, 442, 506, 559
remembrance (remember, remembered, remembering, remembers, remembrancer, remembrances), 5, 8, 101, 117, 125, 151, 172, 181, 183, 192, 196, 216, 221, 237, 248, 264, 304, 322, 332, 353, 366, 384, 397, 401, 403, 404, 429, 435, 443, 459, 460, 463, 484, 485, 489, 559, 565, 592
remind (reminded), 40, 223, 431, 520, 583
reminiscence (reminiscences), 19, 120, 254, 285
remission, 204
remnant, 182
remonstrance (remonstrances, remonstrate, remonstrating), 412, 455, 511
remorse (remorseless), 95, 148, 217, 252, 315, 333, 373, 405, 411, 459, 506, 522, 544, 566
remoteness (remote, remotest), 30, 37, 90, 123, 124, 190, 273, 275, 290, 320, 331, 355, 427, 437, 461, 462, 478, 529, 543
remove (removed, removes, removing), 223, 230, 319, 454, 459, 478, 479, 602
remunerates, 461
Remus, 157
rend (rending, rends), 154, 270, 425, 428, 604
render (rendered, rendering, renders), 1, 111, 129, 167, 170, 195, 227, 236, 237, 263, 282, 290, 297, 322, 331, 334, 345, 389, 409, 419, 449, 468, 477, 484, 486, 492, 497, 502, 504, 507, 529, 532, 583, 587, 596
renewal (renew, renewed), 112, 229, 241, 392, 544
renovators, 434
renown (renowned), 11, 104, 230, 335, 591
rent (rentals), 155, 228
renunciation (renounce), 137, 363, 506
repair (repaired, repairing, repairs), 164, 232, 240, 333, 414, 428, 501, 543, 577, 591
reparation, 506, 507
repartee, 54
repay (repaying), 182, 215, 343, 561
repentance (repent, repentant, repented, repenteth, repents), 119, 125, 187, 196, 199, 233, 244, 277, 293, 304, 350, 387, 404, 405, 421, 506, 507, 513
repercussion, 507
repetition (repeat, repeated, repeating, repeats, repetitions), 23, 104, 192, 247, 250, 254, 264, 304, 324, 329, 342, 434, 477, 488, 492, 503, 507, 531
repining (repine, repinings), 134, 163, 247, 374

replace (replaced), 213, 274
replanted, 231
replete, 261
reply (replied, replies), 355, 433, 449, 468, 541
report (reported, reporting, reports), 52, 66, 145, 165, 175, 262, 272, 274, 284, 295, 350, 410, 516
repose (reposes), 2, 165, 235, 243, 257, 288, 384, 407, 521, 539, 540, 548, 598
repositories, 159, 423
reprehensible, 462
represent (representation, representative, represented, representing, represents), 31, 35, 165, 171, 190, 223, 224, 260, 262, 267, 373, 388, 390, 418, 466, 474, 494, 504, 507, 508, 561, 602
repression (repress, repressed), 457, 490, 592
reprieve (reprieved), 121, 296
reprimand, 508
reprisals, 13
reproach (reproached, reproaches, reproaching), 93, 96, 109, 174, 197, 262, 386, 440, 493, 508, 584
reproduction (reproduce), 148, 171, 465
reproof, 5, 508
reprove (reproved, reprover, reproves, reproving), 204, 232, 499, 513
reptile (reptiles), 79, 257, 512
republic, 12, 113, 296, 399, 524
republican (republicanism), 429, 467, 587
repudiate, 387, 405
repugnance (repugnant), 92, 319, 490, 540
repulse (repulsed, repulses), 93, 455, 458, 533
repulsion, 54, 183
repulsive, 353, 509
reputation (reputable, reputations, repute, reputed), 36, 41, 113, 114, 181, 259, 260, 322, 352, 355, 399, 402, 421, 444, 459, 468, 473, 478, 479, 508
request, 187, 189
requirement (require, required, requirements, requires, requisite, requisition), 84, 155, 159, 185, 207, 211, 213, 218, 224, 228, 277, 294, 301, 306, 314, 316, 334, 335, 336, 344, 345, 348, 359, 364, 374, 383, 391, 402, 408, 416, 437, 438, 442, 457, 465, 485, 488, 493, 497, 502, 517, 521, 528, 530, 531, 536, 543, 544, 551, 569, 572, 582, 588, 598, 600
requited, 345
rescue (rescues), 59, 181, 435, 508
research, 457
resemblance (resemble, resembles, resembleth), 17, 25, 180, 255, 259, 323, 356, 458, 546, 600
resentment (resent, resenting), 64, 100, 172, 199, 297, 302, 309, 338, 450, 494, 508, 509
reservation (reservations, reserve, reserved, reserves), 33, 175, 209, 251, 296, 381, 405, 509, 510, 569, 581, 583
reside (residence, resides), 25, 432, 574, 599
resignation (resign, resigned), 55, 247, 364, 398, 422, 445, 458, 474, 509, 516, 590
resistance (resist, resistant, resisted, resisteth, resisting, resistless), 10, 27, 94, 100, 108, 136, 154, 167, 169, 194, 218, 234, 246, 291, 293, 322, 340, 348, 365, 370, 386, 429, 432, 434, 437, 455, 464, 466, 481, 509, 511, 533, 559, 560, 563, 587, 591
resolution (resolutely), 106, 206, 225, 363, 445, 584

resolution (resolutions), 66, 106, 159, 169, 255, 344, 349, 363, 391, 404, 493, 497, 509, 510, 521, 590
resolve (resolvable, resolved, resolves), 10, 15, 126, 147, 197, 222, 229, 249, 254, 285, 290, 331, 377, 391, 392, 472, 497, 546
resort (resorting), 468, 590
resource (resources), 25, 35, 151, 265, 399, 423, 474, 510, 582
resourcefulness, 510
respect (respectability, respectable, respectably, respected, respectful, respectfully, respecting, respects), 12, 13, 20, 36, 39, 72, 76, 83, 106, 125, 126, 164, 169, 174, 176, 178, 182, 197, 227, 233, 252, 261, 269, 295, 297, 330, 340, 344, 349, 353, 376, 377, 379, 405, 411, 415, 461, 466, 470, 476, 492, 509, 510, 511, 528, 545, 555, 568, 569, 587, 598
respire, 439
respite, 8
respond (responded, responding), 269, 327, 423
response (responses, responsive), 160, 297, 356, 434, 474, 541
responsibility (responsibilities, responsible), 113, 119, 224, 265, 296, 303, 430, 440, 502, 511
rest (resteth, resting, rests), 115, 121, 148, 184, 223, 230, 301, 321, 323, 337, 382, 384, 392, 410, 419, 420, 421, 436, 479, 490, 516, 517, 548, 597
resting-place, 2, 213, 323
restless, 5, 115, 332, 431, 566
restoration (restore, restored), 102, 142, 237, 459, 491, 493, 501, 563
restraint (restrain, restrained, restrains), 73, 201, 258, 351, 407, 408, 433, 461, 492, 511, 512, 528, 543
restriction (restrict), 29, 64, 76, 511
result (resulted, resulting, results), 3, 51, 52, 53, 54, 56, 59, 69, 75, 84, 95, 113, 178, 201, 256, 303, 317, 324, 348, 349, 356, 379, 405, 410, 452, 471, 480, 481, 488, 496, 502, 514, 524, 529, 536, 545, 553, 566, 571, 592, 602
resume, 404, 523
resurrection, 293, 446, 449
retain (retained, retainer, retains), 181, 210, 307, 355, 360, 397, 398, 509, 513, 521, 543, 548, 588, 597
retaliation, 511
reticence (reticent), 357, 371
retinue (retinues), 5, 601
retirement (retire, retired, retiring), 7, 36, 88, 222, 239, 263, 322, 335, 413, 485, 543, 584, 601
retrace, 129
retract, 197
retreat (retreats), 125, 137, 372, 438, 543
retrench, 104
retribution (retributive), 96, 215, 296, 390, 504, 511, 512, 582, 583
retrieval (retrieve, retrieving), 112, 207, 350, 508, 584, 596
retroact, 277
retrograde, 507
retrospection (retrospective), 21, 529
return (returned, returning, returns), 166, 187, 220, 227, 231, 247, 252, 257, 318, 350, 355, 381, 385, 395, 404, 409, 414, 422, 429, 437, 460, 497, 499, 505, 526, 561, 569, 570, 584, 597

reunite, 548
reveal (revealed, reveals), 31, 126, 191, 209, 229,
   247, 271, 294, 295, 325, 328, 414, 454, 520, 529
revelation/Revelation (revelations), 34, 111, 124,
   251, 304, 339, 499, 505, 512, 541
revelry (revel), 403, 431
revenge (revengeful, revenges, revenging), 53,
   66, 90, 118, 126, 133, 198, 309, 338, 365, 421,
   485, 538, 582, 583, 591
reverberation, 289
reverence (revere, revered, reverenced), 10, 40,
   65, 105, 181, 284, 334, 336, 347, 408, 422, 502,
   506, 510, 511, 522, 549, 567, 586
reverends, 510
reverie (reveries), 148, 500
reverse (reversed, reverses), 84, 151, 166, 214,
   249, 285, 309, 359, 417, 449, 566, 568
reversionary, 505
revert (reverting), 83, 183, 248, 278
review (reviewing, reviews), 34, 35, 113, 114, 375,
   453, 476, 491, 525
revile, 453
revivalist, 419
revivals, 249
revive (revived, reviving), 255, 292, 333, 336, 400,
   405
revolt, 240, 370, 512, 566
revolution (revolutions), 50, 61, 63, 70, 163, 184,
   281, 368, 385, 389, 456, 512, 535
revolve (revolves, revolving), 138, 247, 281, 561,
   581
reward (rewarded, rewards), 56, 67, 70, 89, 108,
   115, 154, 158, 192, 200, 228, 236, 293, 299, 312,
   327, 384, 460, 462, 492, 504, 512, 513, 526, 586,
   587, 603
rewriting, 490
rhapsodize, 113
rhetoric (rhetorical), 28, 75, 173, 283, 476, 559
rheumatism (rheumatics), 53, 478
rhyme (rhymes, rhyming), 303, 463, 464, 530
rib, 353
ribbons, 373
rich (richer, richest, richly), 6, 18, 32, 46, 52, 55,
   76, 94, 174, 195, 204, 207, 225, 228, 239, 246,
   260, 263, 265, 280, 284, 289, 299, 306, 317, 333,
   334, 345, 364, 365, 377, 378, 379, 403, 409, 414,
   415, 416, 431, 443, 449, 465, 469, 470, 471, 472,
   487, 510, 569, 591, 593, 594, 597, 599, 600
rid, 126, 307, 414, 437, 486, 560, 590
riddle (riddles), 290, 394, 424
ride (ridden, rider, riderless, riders, rides,
   riding, rode), 77, 81, 139, 147, 148, 175, 204,
   224, 266, 316, 317, 324, 384, 430, 433, 438, 602
ridicule (ridiculed, ridiculing), 63, 73, 128, 362,
   366, 513, 517, 518, 519, 555
ridiculous, 31, 51, 73, 112, 150, 161, 217, 227, 256,
   269, 276, 380, 418, 423, 435, 454, 481, 596
riding-coat, 437
rifle (rifling), 185, 299, 590
right (rightly, rightness), 10, 21, 26, 27, 54, 55, 56,
   63, 67, 77, 89, 92, 97, 98, 105, 122, 125, 129, 136,
   139, 152, 153, 155, 160, 183, 187, 192, 197, 200,
   201, 206, 207, 212, 217, 218, 219, 223, 225, 227,
   229, 236, 244, 250, 262, 265, 268, 272, 277, 278,
   280, 283, 291, 294, 297, 298, 299, 303, 305, 306,
   309, 310, 312, 314, 319, 322, 323, 342, 347, 355,

357, 365, 371, 373, 375, 386, 387, 390, 399, 400,
   407, 416, 433, 440, 441, 453, 455, 456, 457, 459,
   461, 462, 468, 473, 475, 479, 481, 484, 485, 492,
   493, 495, 496, 497, 500, 502, 511, 513, 514, 516,
   518, 521, 523, 540, 541, 544, 545, 550, 562, 564,
   568, 570, 571, 572, 574, 579, 584, 598, 603
right-about, 507
righteousness (righteous), 72, 98, 120, 215, 246,
   269, 310, 512, 513, 514
rights, 69, 125, 196, 257, 265, 328, 347, 350, 356,
   387, 397, 472
rigid (rigidly), 347, 456, 536
rigmarole, 69
rigor (rigorous, rigorously), 204, 295, 308, 492
rim, 98, 215
rind, 101, 573
ring (ringing, rings), 92, 180, 390, 476, 534
riotous, 416
ripeness (ripe, ripen, ripening, riper), 7, 12, 13,
   183, 223, 279, 299, 304, 337
ripples, 546
rise (risen, riser, rises, rising), 2, 120, 122, 123,
   162, 166, 228, 236, 250, 257, 268, 281, 295, 301,
   308, 318, 321, 336, 340, 357, 377, 411, 442, 445,
   451, 459, 474, 493, 507, 539, 553, 568
risible, 265
risk (risked, risks), 203, 221, 254, 397, 433, 480,
   515
rite (rites), 75, 240, 541, 604
ritual, 178
rivalry (rival, rivalries, rivals), 104, 114, 139, 156,
   176, 196, 272, 291, 350, 354, 370, 377, 415
river (rivers), 40, 152, 201, 276, 281, 301, 546, 566
road (roads), 81, 108, 134, 141, 142, 147, 168, 175,
   237, 244, 251, 280, 306, 312, 325, 379, 411, 451,
   453, 481, 501, 549, 568, 570, 575, 585
roam (roams), 148, 208
roar (roaring), 66, 270, 493, 586
robbery (rob, robbed, robber, robs), 53, 96, 255,
   298, 457, 482, 492, 561, 562, 568, 604
robe (robes), 33, 42, 141, 584
Robinson Crusoe, 543
robustness (robust), 241, 271, 344, 346
rock (rocked, rocking, rocks), 62, 86, 125, 126,
   305, 316, 330, 363, 403, 430, 431, 439, 509, 546,
   569, 595
rocking-chair, 148
rods, 600
roguery (rogue, rogues), 64, 86, 251, 253, 263, 264,
   283, 305, 364, 391, 579, 585
roll (rolled, rolling), 404, 439, 566
romance/Romance (romances, romancing,
   romantic), 4, 11, 30, 64, 99, 109, 111, 190, 191,
   199, 246, 247, 248, 249, 261, 274, 318, 319, 342,
   355, 389, 395, 434, 463, 465, 470, 475, 483, 496,
   515, 531, 567, 571, 603
Rome (Roman, Romans), 101, 134, 324, 404, 421,
   449, 459, 468, 507, 570
Romulus, 157
roof (roofing), 284, 434, 485, 542
room (rooms), 11, 21, 48, 62, 98, 120, 125, 133, 203,
   226, 229, 233, 242, 268, 277, 287, 321, 339, 372,
   375, 401, 412, 433, 470, 488, 491, 578, 601
roost, 459
rooster, 532
root (rooted, rootedly, roots), 12, 15, 18, 52, 93,

KEYWORD INDEX

KEYWORD INDEX

satiety (satiate, satiated), 26, 384, 429, 562, 597
satire (satirist, satirists), 139, 263, 293, 508, 513, 517, 518, 519
satisfaction (satisfied, satisfy, satisfying), 21, 129, 150, 212, 238, 286, 321, 331, 338, 365, 370, 378, 384, 402, 405, 428, 431, 437, 450, 452, 461, 466, 467, 486, 518, 545, 553, 581, 582, 593, 595, 600
satisfactory, 41, 177, 181, 445, 509, 549, 582
saturated, 582
Saturday (Saturdays), 175, 399, 486
sauce (sauces), 26, 76, 195
saucy, 108, 174
Saul, 97, 417
saunter (sauntering), 277, 315
sausage, 443
sausage-makers, 464
savagery (savage, savages), 8, 12, 15, 42, 73, 74, 75, 101, 105, 112, 153, 175, 210, 249, 262, 265, 325, 426, 428, 430, 503, 508, 519, 540, 574, 590
save (saved, saves, saving, savings), 3, 52, 75, 126, 134, 135, 152, 211, 215, 254, 260, 277, 294, 295, 298, 310, 313, 356, 367, 384, 406, 412, 420, 432, 467, 471, 484, 504, 508, 517, 528, 530, 546, 547, 553, 565, 580, 593
savior/Saviour, 312, 336, 372, 528
savor (savoreth), 143, 186, 204, 371, 502
sawdust, 602
saws, 490
Saxon, 168
say (said, saith, saying, sayings, says), 92, 102, 104, 117, 172, 201, 213, 219, 220, 223, 225, 229, 242, 246, 252, 265, 270, 287, 293, 302, 305, 308, 311, 312, 313, 315, 321, 323, 330, 334, 336, 338, 340, 343, 347, 350, 351, 355, 359, 361, 366, 371, 372, 373, 375, 379, 381, 382, 389, 393, 397, 402, 408, 416, 447, 458, 463, 475, 476, 484, 487, 489, 490, 499, 501, 519, 527, 532, 534, 560, 564, 566, 569, 570, 573, 575, 576, 577, 581, 582, 600, 601
scaffold, 168, 265
scale, 2, 32, 100, 141, 212, 331, 399, 421, 431, 582, 586
scan, 567
scandal (scandalous), 118, 141, 362, 368, 405, 412, 470, 480, 519
scandalmonger, 52
scanty, 418, 470
scapegrace, 161
scar (scars), 169, 194, 428, 444
scarcity (scarce), 215, 238, 260, 266, 341, 588
scarecrow, 39, 309
scarlet fever, 112
scatter (scattered, scattering, scatters), 78, 92, 283, 316, 422, 429, 445, 546, 584
scene (scenes), 19, 44, 49, 53, 68, 99, 118, 137, 144, 157, 168, 192, 204, 236, 248, 276, 277, 320, 323, 365, 394, 403, 488, 436, 561, 569, 577, 587
scenery, 54, 192, 404
scent (scenting), 315, 596, 600
sceptre, 538
scheme (schemes, scheming), 15, 58, 60, 193, 194, 275, 276, 286, 335, 353, 440, 505, 519, 585
scholar (scholarly, scholars, scholarship), 113, 155, 156, 157, 158, 168, 169, 247, 304, 305, 362, 511, 603
school (schooling, schools), 30, 61, 156, 157, 158, 159, 203, 207, 236, 303, 320, 326, 364, 387, 402, 456, 467, 473, 478, 576, 603

schoolboy (schoolboys), 156, 181
schoolmaster (schoolmasters), 156, 300, 465, 470
science (sciences, scientific), 113, 158, 161, 162, 188, 196, 250, 283, 288, 301, 305, 306, 308, 319, 331, 345, 402, 419, 447, 457, 469, 486, 488, 490, 502, 503, 510, 519, 520, 530, 561, 581, 589, 599
scoff (scoffers), 305, 510
scold (scolding, scolds), 262, 498
sconce, 517
scope, 262, 331, 499
scorch (scorched, scorching), 90, 194
score, 578
scorn (scorned, scornful, scornfully, scorning, scorns), 12, 88, 139, 233, 238, 244, 251, 263, 281, 298, 370, 414, 418, 468, 481, 538, 592
Scotch (Scottish), 28, 241, 604
scoundrel (scoundrels), 196, 559
scourge, 432, 484
scramble, 237, 442
scrape, 569
scratch (scratches), 155, 497, 529
scream (screamed, screams), 190, 591
screen, 17
scribe (scribbler, scribblers, scribbling), 34, 534, 567, 580
scripture/Scripture (scriptures/Scriptures), 45, 67, 71, 289, 420, 502, 520, 528
scroll (scrolls), 183, 185
scruff, 455
scrupulosity (scruple, scruples, scrupulous), 11, 16, 97, 102, 208, 264, 274, 303, 347, 365, 371, 489, 511, 519
scrutiny (scrutinize), 35, 256, 301, 528
sculpture (sculptor), 27, 29, 30, 199, 436, 464
scurviest, 308
sea (seas), 7, 21, 57, 63, 79, 85, 90, 107, 116, 124, 126, 138, 148, 228, 257, 272, 280, 281, 286, 290, 296, 299, 307, 312, 317, 323, 324, 336, 383, 389, 401, 404, 419, 430, 434, 439, 519, 522, 566, 585, 597, 604
sea-demon, 241
seafaring, 350, 489
seal (sealed, seals), 70, 127, 256, 339, 423, 424, 484, 507, 604
sealion, 256
seaman, 37, 83
sear (searing), 368, 529
search (searched, searching), 58, 69, 115, 146, 196, 240, 276, 286, 345, 422, 471, 479, 548, 575, 594
seasickness (seasick), 241, 401
season (seasoned, seasons), 5, 10, 11, 12, 18, 26, 57, 117, 148, 170, 221, 248, 322, 333, 334, 368, 409, 427, 429, 459, 466, 520, 547, 567
seasonable, 402, 423
seasoning, 206
seat (seated, seats), 163, 224, 291, 295, 315, 360, 403, 541, 548
seaweed, 547
seclusion, 115, 228, 539, 543
second class, 167
second-hand, 195, 600
second-rate, 466
secondary, 601
secrecy (secret, secretly, secrets), 12, 13, 26, 29, 40, 44, 56, 78, 86, 88, 89, 92, 115, 116, 117, 123, 148, 157, 158, 171, 186, 188, 192, 196, 206, 225,

KEYWORD INDEX

227, 232, 236, 241, 247, 252, 256, 277, 290, 307,
318, 319, 327, 328, 329, 330, 336, 340, 348, 351,
353, 374, 385, 394, 403, 407, 410, 414, 423, 434,
437, 443, 450, 464, 475, 478, 492, 498, 505, 510,
521, 522, 525, 526, 528, 530, 532, 547, 551, 553,
555, 561, 563, 566, 571, 586, 604
secretion, 418, 558
secrettementally, 601
sect, 45, 295
sectarian (sectarians, sectaries), 178, 513
security (secure, securely, secures, securing,
securities), 36, 58, 74, 77, 117, 137, 160, 181, 200,
201, 216, 224, 259, 261, 285, 309, 333, 351, 377,
387, 391, 409, 440, 461, 521, 522, 534, 537, 560,
584, 587
sedan-chair, 14
sedateness, 598
seduction (seduce, seduced, seducer, seduces,
seducing, seductive), 129, 274, 276, 305, 351,
369, 421, 522, 570, 580
see (saw, seeing, seen, sees, seest, seeth), 51, 84,
94, 111, 121, 137, 140, 142, 149, 165, 169, 170,
176, 187, 189, 194, 198, 212, 215, 216, 219, 221,
235, 244, 260, 262, 265, 269, 270, 271, 273, 274,
276, 280, 287, 290, 291, 293, 294, 295, 303, 311,
313, 318, 321, 331, 332, 338, 340, 341, 348, 353,
354, 357, 359, 364, 368, 375, 376, 377, 386, 388,
391, 394, 396, 405, 407, 409, 410, 411, 424, 427,
430, 431, 432, 435, 436, 438, 439, 440, 444, 446,
448, 449, 452, 454, 456, 457, 459, 464, 465, 468,
470, 471, 475, 478, 485, 488, 493, 495, 496, 497,
498, 499, 503, 504, 509, 512, 514, 527, 528, 530,
532, 539, 540, 543, 547, 557, 558, 559, 562, 567,
568, 569, 570, 573, 574, 575, 578, 580, 581, 582,
584, 587, 590, 598
seed (seeds), 12, 52, 102, 150, 170, 218, 223, 249,
288, 299, 306, 411, 547, 553, 574, 589
seek (seeker, seekers, seeking, seeks, sought), 3,
57, 72, 74, 109, 123, 130, 154, 215, 229, 238, 239,
243, 295, 304, 310, 336, 345, 347, 356, 361, 369,
390, 411, 423, 428, 464, 501, 512, 515, 524, 532,
537, 539, 546, 574, 585, 589, 598
seem (seemed, seeming, seems), 24, 168, 236, 269,
271, 274, 282, 284, 288, 290, 293, 294, 296, 301,
303, 307, 308, 310, 312, 317, 318, 320, 321, 329,
333, 336, 339, 340, 342, 348, 360, 362, 365, 404,
410, 418, 419, 428, 429, 430, 439, 446, 449, 461,
462, 470, 476, 486, 487, 488, 502, 504, 513, 519,
529, 531, 545, 547, 560, 570, 584, 594, 595, 596,
605
seemly, 188
seership, 286
seesaw, 103, 594
seize (seized, seizes, seizing), 180, 239, 303, 305,
324, 346, 348, 390, 407, 442, 455
selection (selected), 27, 102, 390, 555, 577
self (selves), 3, 12, 23, 155, 203, 223, 240, 246, 247,
260, 270, 277, 282, 311, 324, 337, 342, 418, 427,
443, 466, 511, 517, 522, 523, 524, 525, 526, 527,
528, 529
self-accusing, 239
self-acting, 361
self-admiration, 4
self-applause, 528
self-approbation, 235
self-assurance, 162
self-besotted, 507

self-caused, 221
self-collectedness, 519
self-command, 523
self-complacency (self-complacent), 54, 75
self-conceit, 154
self-condemnation, 233
self-confidence (self-confiding), 46, 117
self-conquest, 80
self-consciousness (self-conscious), 209, 429, 523
self-consequence, 472
self-contained, 463
self-contradiction, 524
self-control, 105, 479, 523
self-created, 285
self-criticism, 519
self-deception, 524
self-defense, 128, 220, 264
self-degradation, 267
self-denial (self-denying, self-denyingly), 64, 227,
267, 353, 371, 379, 380, 390, 470, 472, 503, 524,
587
self-dependence, 349
self-destruction (self-destroyer), 524, 554
self-determination, 201
self-development, 525
self-devotion, 361
self-displeasure, 524
self-distrust, 434
self-esteem, 336, 525
self-evident, 488
self-exaltation, 477
self-examination, 525
self-exposure, 525
self-flattery, 195
self-forgetfulness, 349
self-glorification (self-glorifying), 4, 214
self-guidance, 361
self-humiliation, 330
self-importance (self-important), 257, 537
self-improvement, 525
self-indulgence, 504, 525, 530
self-infliction, 526
self-interest (self-interested), 107, 131, 158, 230,
289, 312, 445
self-knowledge, 495, 527
self-love, 82, 159, 194, 242, 293, 325, 328, 350, 472,
481, 526, 528
self-made (self-making), 135, 482
self-mastery, 546
self-pity, 459
self-possession, 133, 523
self-preservation, 475, 528, 554
self-questioning, 563
self-realization, 525
self-reliant, 10
self-renouncing, 422
self-reproach, 411, 528
self-respect (self-respecting), 327, 482, 503, 525,
528
self-restraint, 523
self-revelation, 525
self-risking, 31
self-sacrifice, 48, 484, 507, 517
self-same, 539
self-satisfaction, 45
self-seekers, 467
self-support, 529

self-swindler, 250
self-taught, 156
self-torture, 97, 524, 528
self-worship, 528
selfishness (selfish), 17, 29, 50, 57, 76, 88, 130, 134,
    148, 167, 199, 200, 203, 204, 209, 213, 233, 259,
    260, 262, 311, 328, 330, 334, 339, 340, 379, 385,
    420, 427, 437, 456, 458, 483, 484, 504, 526, 528
semblance, 511
semi-pagan, 70
senate/Senate (senator/Senator), 438, 444, 466
send (sending, sends, sent), 206, 216, 245, 358,
    363, 393, 400, 421, 424, 449, 469, 478, 539, 543,
    547, 558, 580, 588
senile, 291
sensation (senations), 110, 113, 182, 187, 207, 216,
    290, 314, 324, 384, 403, 413, 427, 478, 529, 530,
    543, 562, 563, 566
sense (senses), 10, 11, 20, 37, 49, 51, 60, 68, 69, 76,
    79, 90, 97, 98, 107, 133, 141, 146, 148, 152, 153,
    158, 163, 166, 172, 173, 189, 196, 198, 201, 203,
    207, 209, 213, 215, 218, 222, 230, 231, 233, 239,
    242, 250, 253, 254, 262, 265, 270, 278, 282, 284,
    286, 287, 288, 293, 298, 301, 302, 303, 307, 314,
    340, 350, 352, 353, 356, 360, 367, 369, 370, 371,
    378, 385, 398, 400, 401, 405, 407, 413, 420, 422,
    426, 429, 432, 438, 439, 441, 442, 444, 448, 455,
    456, 458, 460, 462, 471, 482, 488, 489, 490, 497,
    501, 503, 504, 507, 510, 511, 514, 515, 519, 522,
    529, 530, 533, 534, 539, 542, 545, 548, 549, 551,
    556, 557, 579, 582, 592, 595, 600
sensibility (sensibilities), 23, 31, 49, 139, 263, 303,
    356, 408, 422, 444, 482, 483, 508, 529, 563, 574
sensibleness (sensible, sensibly), 27, 41, 62, 64, 73,
    157, 169, 197, 209, 216, 230, 267, 272, 317, 326,
    335, 365, 369, 384, 394, 405, 420, 429, 459, 497,
    503, 529, 566, 598
sensitiveness (sensitive, sensitivity), 7, 52, 95, 100,
    209, 213, 233, 348, 355, 447, 529
Sensorium, 529
sensualism (sensual, sensuality), 86, 258, 325, 363,
    437, 449, 481, 496, 530, 547
sensuous, 87
sentence (sentences), 59, 121, 124, 173, 174, 183,
    254, 302, 309, 311, 360, 398, 477, 511
sentient, 530
sentimentalism (sentiment, sentimental,
    sentimentalist, sentimentalists, sentimentality,
    sentiments), 3, 7, 47, 56, 57, 67, 69, 71, 104, 109,
    115, 126, 130, 141, 143, 156, 157, 160, 164, 172,
    174, 175, 178, 192, 208, 223, 225, 226, 239, 259,
    291, 328, 330, 333, 350, 363, 373, 388, 402, 409,
    411, 422, 434, 451, 456, 458, 466, 476, 481, 497,
    503, 505, 526, 529, 530, 531, 558, 561, 574, 589
sentinel, 587, 588
sentry-box, 176
separation (separate, separated, separates,
    separating), 127, 244, 302, 324, 338, 343, 346,
    349, 364, 366, 378, 391, 418, 530, 531, 541, 545,
    548
September, 520
Septimus Severus, 127
sepulchre, 494
sequence, 182
sequestered, 75
seraglio, 389

seraph, 111
sere, 490
serenade, 544
serenity (serene), 17, 77, 288, 442, 457, 531
sergeant, 406
series, 299, 345, 584
seriousness (serious, seriously), 16, 51, 79, 94, 203,
    208, 227, 282, 298, 318, 349, 376, 385, 393, 409,
    414, 445, 447, 467, 510, 512, 518, 531, 532, 580
sermon (sermonizing, sermons), 76, 152, 166, 248,
    315, 381, 460, 475, 476, 477, 478, 498, 585
serpent (serpents), 25, 59, 65, 83, 91, 220, 357, 363,
    487
servant (servants), 119, 163, 165, 193, 211, 213,
    218, 288, 307, 309, 345, 377, 381, 396, 447, 464,
    473, 521, 532, 565, 588, 590
serve (served, serves, serving), 1, 5, 89, 154, 166,
    195, 203, 221, 226, 227, 267, 306, 334, 348, 405,
    416, 435, 437, 451, 467, 486, 532, 563, 593, 595,
    597, 600
service, 54, 60, 177, 210, 214, 215, 219, 226, 315,
    385, 406, 419, 472, 481, 492, 507, 532, 561, 579
serviceable, 156, 159, 265, 558, 601
servility (servile), 224, 281, 345, 538
servitude, 57, 126, 146, 200, 532
set (sets), 315, 331, 339, 351, 360, 379, 408, 429,
    449, 458, 461, 479, 490, 498, 500, 503, 509, 513,
    521, 524, 530, 536, 540, 547, 567, 570, 575, 579,
    598
setting, 212, 281, 438, 496, 567
settle (settled, settling), 139, 236, 250, 283, 342,
    346, 382, 388, 417, 456, 557, 589, 597
settlement (settlements), 302, 309
severity (severe, severely, severer, severest,
    severities), 79, 168, 194, 232, 298, 308, 312, 401,
    405, 406, 429, 479, 518, 535, 571
sew, 506
sewer, 221
sex (sexes, sexuality), 29, 58, 107, 204, 206, 253,
    284, 294, 326, 330, 338, 343, 344, 345, 346, 347,
    349, 350, 351, 352, 353, 354, 355, 356, 357, 358,
    359, 361, 362, 363, 364, 365, 366, 367, 368, 369,
    370, 372, 373, 374, 392, 467, 493, 521, 532, 540,
    542, 547, 549
sexless, 40
sexton (sextons), 402, 486
shabby, 211, 443
shackle (shackled, shackles), 187, 379, 382
shade (shades), 1, 7, 23, 64, 81, 83, 85, 86, 141, 149,
    157, 190, 257, 463, 464, 467, 489, 530, 539, 588
shadow (shadowed, shadows, shadowy), 9, 23, 40,
    54, 58, 98, 116, 119, 121, 122, 123, 138, 149, 168,
    179, 212, 216, 233, 235, 237, 248, 257, 266, 277,
    319, 321, 337, 350, 363, 414, 418, 434, 438, 440,
    462, 500, 520, 527, 532, 533, 547, 548, 552, 568,
    588, 602
shadowings-forth, 275
shadowless, 165
shaft (shafts), 231, 519
Shah of Persia, 422
shake (shaken, shakes, shaking), 53, 55, 133, 135,
    138, 147, 178, 204, 243, 267, 307, 448, 495, 515,
    571
Shakespeare, 62, 68, 174, 305, 417, 560, 561
shallowness (shallow, shallowest), 13, 26, 66, 154,
    160, 161, 193, 219, 278, 288, 307, 347, 363, 423,

KEYWORD INDEX

435, 533, 535, 537, 543, 544, 556, 597, 602
shallows, 361, 430
sham (shams), 97
shame (shameful, shamefully, shames); 60, 106,
  110, 112, 123, 125, 132, 133, 137, 213, 219, 238,
  245, 255, 261, 265, 272, 285, 316, 344, 345, 362,
  371, 376, 378, 405, 413, 472, 510, 518, 521, 527,
  533, 534, 547, 570, 595
shamefacedness, 344
shameless, 545
shanty, 552
shape (shapes), 11, 22, 36, 37, 62, 120, 131, 140,
  146, 161, 214, 259, 268, 280, 289, 299, 325, 339,
  347, 377, 379, 405, 441, 444, 453, 596, 598
share (shared, sharing), 69, 137, 156, 158, 259,
  292, 351, 377, 529, 563
shark (sharks), 20, 111, 215, 314
sharp (sharpen, sharpened, sharpeneth, sharpens,
  sharper, sharpest), 81, 83, 111, 131, 142, 204,
  232, 263, 294, 359, 433, 452, 499, 525, 530, 545,
  600
shatter (shattered, shattering), 126, 360
shaving, 290, 463
shed (shedding, sheds), 82, 169, 299, 426, 559
sheep, 222, 353, 562, 576
sheep-stealer, 541
sheepishness (sheepish), 10, 40
sheer, 442
sheet (sheets), 81, 257, 421
sheet-anchor, 255
sheiks, 458
shelf (shelves), 35, 360, 419, 495, 545, 579
shelter (sheltered, sheltering), 163, 315, 471, 489
shepherd (shepherds), 65, 239
shield (shielded), 308, 330, 342, 414, 489, 538, 542
shift (shifting, shifts), 118, 239, 321, 343, 404, 559,
  603
shilling (shillings), 70, 180, 280, 310, 565
shimmery, 321
shin, 293
shine (shines, shining), 83, 85, 86, 161, 210, 225,
  248, 269, 305, 318, 366, 367, 372, 391, 410, 435,
  439, 440, 483, 500, 502, 514, 525, 599, 600
shingle, 82
shining-place, 393
shining-time, 5
ship (shipped, ships), 18, 33, 85, 124, 130, 140, 158,
  205, 328, 333, 336, 350, 402, 420, 424, 430, 453,
  454, 469, 547, 570, 583, 603
shipmate (shipmates), 320, 424, 578
ships of war, 71
shipwrecked, 285
shipwright, 604
shirk, 201, 432
shirt (shirts), 34, 291
shirt-sleeves, 262
shiver (shivered, shivering), 189, 217, 511
shoals, 310, 322, 355
shock (shocked, shocking), 10, 55, 107, 116, 124,
  208, 211, 316, 372, 409, 469, 482, 495, 496, 508,
  516, 554, 600
shoe (shod, shoemaker, shoes), 41, 289, 351, 422,
  503
shoot (shooting, shoots, shot), 32, 82, 88, 153, 242,
  312, 449, 494
shop (shops), 87, 388, 594

shore (shores), 37, 75, 79, 123, 280, 359, 403
shorn, 489, 592
shortcoming (shortcomings), 56, 112
short cut, 306
shorthand, 155
short-lived, 543
shortness (short, shortest), 21, 56, 134, 148, 166,
  174, 315, 318, 321, 322, 352, 402, 475, 477, 483,
  488, 490, 507, 540, 563, 564, 566, 588, 596, 599
short-sighted, 134, 135, 245
shoulder (shoulders), 35, 42, 139, 147, 186, 197,
  249, 366, 444, 467, 490, 513
shoulder blades, 119, 578
shout (shouting, shouts), 307, 413, 462, 466
shovelfuls, 257
show (shew, sheweth, shewing, showed, showing,
  shown, shows), 50, 87, 107, 150, 153, 155, 184,
  193, 204, 215, 230, 243, 244, 249, 262, 267, 281,
  301, 305, 320, 321, 323, 326, 335, 339, 343, 344,
  350, 351, 353, 357, 365, 367, 372, 379, 396, 402,
  405, 408, 410, 429, 441, 442, 444, 460, 470, 472,
  475, 477, 480, 483, 486, 488, 490, 493, 499, 504,
  510, 511, 512, 520, 528, 532, 533, 538, 550, 556,
  557, 560, 561, 569, 575, 600, 601
shower (showers), 134, 334
shrewdness (shrewd, shrewdest, shrewdly), 120,
  333, 348, 394
shriek (shrieking, shrieks), 384, 591
shrimps, 183
shrine, 104, 129, 430, 481, 583
shrink (shrinking, shrinks, shrunk), 100, 124,
  134, 179, 209, 227, 280, 360, 403, 499, 543, 547
shrivelled, 152
shroud (shroudeth, shrouds), 125, 427, 439, 539,
  570
shrubberies, 217
shuffling, 179, 250
shun (shunned, shunning), 130, 261, 301, 314, 337,
  347, 535, 588, 594
shut (shuts), 158, 243, 378, 416, 476, 485, 489,
  528, 563, 572
shuttle, 423, 433
shyness (shy), 91, 102, 181, 209, 282, 431, 568
sick-bed, 157, 506
sickness (sick, sickened, sickening, sickly), 13, 55,
  67, 87, 97, 124, 182, 195, 197, 241, 254, 255, 259,
  290, 303, 329, 374, 393, 400, 401, 402, 457, 549,
  590
sick-room, 402
sickle, 170
sieve, 257
sifted, 313
sigh (sighed, sighs), 77, 267, 268, 327, 438
sight (sights), 21, 68, 70, 71, 101, 108, 120, 125,
  160, 178, 181, 184, 232, 238, 243, 259, 275, 291,
  336, 337, 339, 383, 389, 425, 438, 454, 463, 498,
  500, 562, 604
sign (signed, signs), 35, 69, 82, 133, 210, 231, 233,
  255, 271, 282, 289, 330, 331, 349, 366, 385, 425,
  461, 476, 490, 500, 523, 529, 534, 537, 539, 554,
  555, 604
signal, 177, 431
significance (significant, signification), 112, 123,
  173, 278, 290, 317, 322, 448, 468, 482, 534
signify (signifies, signifieth), 142, 152, 154, 214,
  226, 256, 341, 354, 416, 438, 473, 492, 579, 592

sly, 364, 365, 371, 486
small change, 535
smallness (small, smaller, smallest), 99, 100, 149,
    155, 171, 204, 211, 219, 220, 225, 238, 252, 257,
    321, 324, 329, 343, 352, 363, 368, 398, 430, 453,
    484, 485, 490, 528, 545, 560, 574, 577, 578, 592,
    594
smallpox, 41, 136, 331
small talk, 91
smallware, 245
smart (smarting, smartly, smartness), 51, 187,
    225, 364, 395, 550, 580
smatterers, 305
smattering, 307
smell (smelling, smells, smelt), 175, 332, 371, 540,
    571
smile (smiled, smiles, smiling), 13, 18, 61, 71, 85,
    91, 128, 134, 146, 168, 209, 214, 235, 240, 259,
    261, 265, 277, 282, 283, 292, 307, 309, 329, 341,
    360, 364, 385, 388, 428, 431, 439, 450, 485, 538,
    539, 546, 567, 573, 577, 580, 587
smirk, 445
smite (smiter, smitten, smote), 56, 119, 244, 330,
    475, 583
smith (smiths), 57, 569
smock, 291
smoke (smoking, smoky), 55, 274, 313, 321, 362,
    417, 540, 554
smooth (smooths), 25, 78, 108, 180, 182, 328, 338,
    361, 369, 379, 546, 567, 602
smother (smothered, smothery), 85, 88, 132, 250
smoulder (smouldering), 448, 481
smuggle (smuggled), 457, 588
snail, 216, 499
snake (snakes), 19, 220, 592
snap, 100, 383
snare, 482
snarl (snarling), 113
sneaking, 602
sneer (sneered, sneers), 59, 132, 293, 385, 412,
    520, 597
sneeze, 72
snore (snorer, snoring), 53, 494, 566
snort (snorting, snorts), 430, 439
snow (snowy), 16, 107, 538
snowball, 167
snuff (snuffs), 114, 287
snuffbox, 234
snug, 593
soap, 429, 578
soar (soaring, soarings, soars), 34, 85, 103, 213,
    317, 370, 459, 464, 473, 516, 526
sob, 17, 307
sober, 20, 38, 85, 132, 151, 152, 153, 162, 312, 327,
    499, 575
sobriquet, 424
socialness (social, sociality, socially), 14, 49, 55,
    75, 119, 131, 156, 163, 181, 206, 208, 217, 235,
    256, 286, 297, 305, 350, 407, 471, 538, 540, 541,
    542, 543, 545, 553, 561, 583, 589
social system, 541
society (societies), 7, 64, 71, 75, 80, 81, 98, 103,
    104, 111, 112, 114, 145, 155, 156, 163, 165, 195,
    196, 199, 202, 203, 218, 223, 289, 308, 309, 311,
    313, 314, 322, 349, 350, 351, 353, 356, 360, 361,
    372, 374, 379, 380, 385, 386, 406, 437, 438, 455,
    460, 461, 492, 497, 500, 501, 504, 512, 528, 529,

535, 537, 540, 541, 542, 544, 579, 586, 600
Socrates (Socratic), 255, 519, 569
Sodom, 265
sofa, 239
soften (softened, softener, softeners, softening,
    softens), 58, 77, 169, 214, 237, 282, 325, 339,
    385, 419, 443, 455, 474, 545, 566, 567
softness (soft, softer, softest, softly), 17, 94, 164,
    243, 291, 295, 338, 342, 344, 357, 367, 370, 371,
    403, 422, 434, 441, 455, 487, 530, 560, 562, 563
soil (soiled), 15, 52, 77, 121, 138, 158, 197, 208,
    231, 324, 426, 496, 530, 591
sojourn, 519
solace (solaces), 543, 569
solar system, 79, 486
soldiery (soldier, soldiers), 16, 24, 53, 54, 68, 71,
    72, 130, 139, 250, 254, 406, 481, 528, 542, 543,
    590, 591, 601
sole, 191, 220, 249, 280, 320, 337, 338
solemnity (solemn, solemnize, solemnized), 37, 38,
    83, 269, 282, 309, 333, 374, 388, 390, 392, 454,
    462, 517
solicitation (solicit, solicitations, solicited,
    soliciting, solicits), 9, 131, 301, 325, 369, 471,
    533, 571
solicitude (solicitous), 109, 150
solidarity, 49
solidity (solid), 65, 238, 407, 463, 543, 583, 586,
    589, 591
solitariness (solitary), 21, 106, 228, 275, 285, 324,
    331, 335, 389, 438, 450, 485, 543, 544
solitude, 274, 290, 304, 377, 500, 522, 543, 544
Solomon, 101, 197, 203, 545
solution (solve, solves, solving), 147, 265, 345, 469,
    565
solvency, 20
sombre, 238
Somnus, 320
son (sons), 7, 10, 11, 24, 62, 103, 123, 180, 182,
    183, 184, 185, 215, 220, 257, 279, 282, 300, 416,
    449, 451, 517, 527, 562, 602
son-in-law, 184
Son of God, 556
song (songs), 53, 162, 270, 346, 357, 388, 421, 462,
    495, 538, 544, 547
sonnet, 31, 462
soothe (soothed, soothes, soothing), 97, 101, 195,
    201, 229, 403, 417, 455, 462
sooty, 313
sophisticated, 121
sophistry, 544
sorcery (sorcerer), 191, 227
sordidness (sordid), 29, 207, 209, 385, 390, 464,
    541, 544
sore (sorer, sores), 322, 329, 523, 555
sorrow (sorriest, sorrowful, sorrow-laden,
    sorrows, sorry), 2, 5, 8, 9, 19, 23, 44, 47, 49, 55,
    57, 64, 68, 70, 87, 88, 99, 100, 101, 107, 120, 127,
    146, 161, 167, 172, 177, 183, 185, 192, 203, 214,
    222, 229, 242, 243, 246, 257, 260, 264, 265, 284,
    292, 294, 303, 305, 307, 310, 317, 320, 321, 331,
    351, 359, 366, 372, 373, 382, 403, 405, 417, 422,
    431, 433, 444, 449, 461, 462, 472, 480, 483, 486,
    493, 498, 507, 516, 520, 523, 538, 539, 544, 545,
    554, 603
sot (sots, sottish), 152, 245, 351
soul (souls), 1, 3, 5, 10, 12, 19, 20, 26, 29, 30, 31, 34,

soul (*continued*)
40, 41, 43, 45, 47, 48, 51, 52, 65, 68, 71, 81, 82,
85, 89, 90, 91, 93, 94, 97, 98, 99, 102, 107, 110,
115, 118, 123, 125, 130, 132, 133, 134, 135, 139,
140, 142, 148, 150, 158, 160, 163, 165, 166, 169,
172, 175, 176, 187, 189, 192, 200, 202, 203, 205,
208, 209, 211, 215, 216, 217, 219, 220, 226, 227,
229, 231, 232, 235, 242, 246, 257, 263, 268, 269,
270, 272, 273, 275, 277, 280, 283, 285, 286, 291,
296, 297, 302, 308, 315, 316, 322, 324, 325, 327,
328, 330, 331, 333, 337, 340, 346, 348, 354, 355,
360, 365, 367, 368, 382, 390, 391, 396, 397, 407,
409, 410, 412, 421, 422, 424, 425, 430, 431, 435,
438, 445, 449, 452, 459, 463, 465, 467, 470, 471,
474, 475, 482, 487, 491, 498, 499, 500, 502, 504,
511, 512, 518, 521, 522, 523, 529, 538, 539, 541,
544, 545, 546, 547, 548, 554, 561, 562, 564, 567,
573, 574, 577, 578, 587, 590, 591, 593, 596, 600,
601
soulfulness (soulful), 545, 546, 548, 560
soul—suicide, 547
soul-wasting, 288
soundness (sound, sounded, sounding, sounds), 4,
12, 31, 56, 77, 89, 120, 165, 173, 174, 181, 183,
185, 189, 192, 205, 209, 244, 270, 286, 290, 294,
295, 304, 313, 322, 332, 336, 398, 404, 416, 418,
420, 421, 422, 446, 456, 470, 496, 539, 544, 560,
576, 599
soup, 398, 600
sour (souring, sours), 362, 409
sour grapes, 52, 55
source (sources), 74, 78, 164, 175, 214, 242, 249,
251, 294, 301, 353, 358, 429, 444, 474, 538, 556,
586
south/South (southern/Southern), 33, 142, 143,
227, 387, 418
sovereignty (sovereign, sovereigns), 2, 44, 76, 98,
154, 160, 223, 224, 225, 250, 252, 290, 296, 308,
313, 328, 331, 338, 381, 500, 551
sow (sowing, sown), 52, 99, 111, 213, 218, 258, 299,
343, 547
space (spaces), 35, 36, 58, 85, 173, 191, 215, 216,
260, 268, 300, 303, 323, 327, 407, 470, 516, 544,
547, 563, 564, 568, 595, 600, 603
spaceless, 448
spade, 121, 126, 496
Spanish (Spaniard), 194, 241
spar, 42
spare (spared, spares, sparing), 26, 66, 89, 122,
182, 205, 211, 214, 356, 413, 418, 430, 432, 474,
493, 506, 525
spark (sparks), 18, 149, 298, 465, 473
sparkle (sparkled, sparkles), 22, 175, 600
sparrow, 565
spawn, 430
spear, 489
special, 308, 343, 371, 493, 595
species, 3, 14, 22, 47, 101, 117, 132, 180, 203, 220,
256, 261, 262, 265, 339, 344, 345, 347, 360, 402,
406, 464, 487, 516, 528, 543, 546, 576, 600
specificity, 578
specimen, 576
speck (speckless), 336, 454
speckled, 432
spectacle (spectacles), 103, 107, 340, 379, 442, 454,
511, 515, 517, 528, 576, 590
spectator (spectators), 29, 276, 290, 431, 601

spectre, 320, 534
speculation (speculate, speculations, speculative),
43, 137, 234, 279, 301, 361, 383, 520, 539
speech (speak, speaker, speaketh, speaking,
speaks, speeches, spoke, spoken), 7, 12, 25, 33,
45, 54, 57, 78, 80, 84, 89, 90, 97, 98, 108, 109,
126, 138, 141, 143, 160, 164, 171, 172, 173, 174,
175, 179, 203, 214, 233, 246, 267, 268, 276, 289,
294, 297, 307, 317, 320, 329, 335, 340, 350, 356,
359, 369, 371, 384, 385, 387, 389, 395, 397, 398,
412, 437, 443, 448, 457, 458, 472, 474, 475, 478,
484, 503, 504, 505, 518, 526, 532, 534, 535, 536,
537, 538, 539, 540, 557, 561, 565, 572, 573, 574,
575, 590, 596, 601, 602
speed (speedily), 57, 101, 430, 511, 585
spell (speller, spells, spelt), 157, 181, 522, 527,
539, 549, 558, 602
spelling-book, 35
Spencer, 418
spend (spending, spendings, spends, spent), 3,
150, 161, 226, 279, 280, 293, 298, 399, 415, 443,
450, 532, 562, 591
spendthrift, 591
sphere (spheres), 21, 31, 103, 122, 141, 146, 155,
214, 241, 271, 274, 275, 356, 358, 393, 430, 434,
459, 464, 500, 534, 542, 545
Sphinx/Sphynx (Sphinxes), 374, 423, 450
spice, 91, 477
spider, 132, 485, 494
spill (spilled, spilling, spills), 109, 517, 578
spin (spun), 110, 327, 569
spindle, 359
spine, 435
spinning-jennies, 456
spinster (spinsters), 75, 380, 387, 445
spirit (spirits), 4, 5, 8, 15, 31, 35, 56, 59, 64, 68, 82,
86, 90, 92, 104, 106, 110, 111, 120, 137, 140, 147,
148, 149, 156, 158, 168, 186, 199, 202, 210, 211,
221, 230, 233, 257, 260, 263, 276, 278, 316, 320,
323, 333, 345, 351, 366, 381, 389, 415, 416, 437,
439, 448, 449, 451, 462, 464, 465, 466, 470, 471,
472, 489, 495, 500, 507, 508, 513, 523, 545, 546,
548, 549, 556, 560, 565, 602
spirit-touching, 86
spiritless, 147
spirituality (spiritual), 20, 40, 107, 124, 173, 216,
258, 282, 327, 334, 341, 418, 476, 502, 504, 529,
546, 548, 549, 563, 587
spiritualize, 569
spite (spiteful), 4, 46, 232, 262, 267, 313, 326, 337,
347, 351, 366, 407, 465, 547, 549, 562
spleen, 6, 97, 519, 570
splendid (splendidly), 89, 200, 260, 411, 577
splendor, 14, 102, 318, 416, 471, 550, 567
splice, 166
split, 440
spoil (spoiled, spoiler, spoiling, spoils, spoilt), 146,
155, 219, 223, 250, 263, 282, 316, 343, 360, 391,
432, 570, 591, 600, 603
sponge, 63
spontaneous (spontaneously), 45, 155, 209, 241,
322, 360, 378, 388, 498, 564
spontaneous combustion, 154
spool, 321
spoons, 462
sport, 139, 148, 196, 215, 303, 316, 394, 430, 454,
504

sportive, 175, 275, 328
sportsmen, 266
spot (spots, spotted), 134, 213, 221, 312, 332, 356, 375, 406, 493, 538, 550, 565, 569
spotless, 418, 493
spouse (spouses), 154, 392, 577
sprawls, 600
spread (spreadeth, spreads), 4, 212, 219, 232, 418, 443, 448, 557
sprightly, 391
spring (springs, sprung), 11, 54, 55, 107, 137, 140, 188, 217, 225, 248, 271, 320, 328, 346, 368, 374, 403, 408, 441, 467, 472, 485, 490, 505, 520, 526, 528, 565
spring-carriage, 324
springtime, 44
sprinkle (sprinkled, sprinkling), 170, 291
sprite, 599
sprout, 150, 197
spruce-looking, 85
spur (spurs), 204, 225, 296, 311, 334, 432, 484
spurious, 97
spurn (spurned, spurning, spurns), 85, 154, 407
spy (spies, spying), 71, 206, 232, 294, 369, 549
squander (squanders), 89, 416
square (squares, squaring), 5, 179, 222, 497
squat (squatted, squatter, squatters), 408, 590
squeak, 431
squeamish, 90, 315
squeezed, 309
squint, 495
squirm, 478
squirrel-headed, 352
stab, 351
stability (stable), 158, 225, 266, 278, 281, 472, 484, 600
staff, 250, 435
stage (stages, staging), 93, 135, 138, 146, 151, 244, 245, 277, 311, 321, 330, 428, 463, 483, 561, 569, 581, 585
stage managers, 137
stagger, 170
stagnation (stagnant), 79, 240, 263, 347, 434
staid, 12
stain (stained, stains), 90, 149, 221, 232, 416, 453, 585
stained-glass windows, 183
stair-head, 557
stairs, 443, 549
stake (staked, stakes, staking), 74, 138, 207, 271, 310, 315, 336, 525
stale, 86, 192, 394
stalk (stalking, stalks), 213, 229, 443
stammerers, 454
stamp (stamped, stamps), 107, 202, 207, 408, 476, 500, 582
stand (standeth, standing, stands, stood), 83, 99, 187, 211, 213, 215, 223, 228, 229, 249, 251, 271, 288, 289, 312, 324, 338, 344, 366, 375, 380, 385, 390, 394, 400, 403, 411, 416, 430, 444, 445, 447, 449, 454, 457, 472, 476, 478, 481, 483, 486, 499, 500, 502, 510, 511, 512, 528, 557, 562, 566, 571, 574, 576, 584, 588, 594, 603
standard (standards), 86, 166, 217, 224, 295, 418, 419, 422, 453, 489, 540
stander-by (standers by), 217, 452
standpoint, 597

standstill, 293
staple, 283, 540, 599
star (stars), 3, 31, 36, 51, 55, 82, 92, 138, 176, 212, 217, 244, 259, 289, 335, 406, 431, 432, 434, 444, 454, 469, 477, 500, 545, 549, 573, 578, 582
star-strewn, 563
starboard, 583
stare (starers, staring), 24, 172, 177, 188, 274, 485, 552, 600
start (starting, starts), 136, 213, 272, 360, 440, 477, 507, 547
startling, 230, 477, 561
starvation (starve, starved, starves, starving), 17, 24, 33, 87, 89, 137, 201, 251, 266, 306, 345, 354, 432, 456, 459, 462, 547
state (states, stating), 35, 45, 48, 55, 69, 76, 97, 132, 139, 148, 193, 219, 224, 225, 226, 232, 247, 259, 274, 280, 287, 288, 289, 290, 309, 311, 319, 321, 327, 339, 341, 349, 353, 367, 368, 371, 374, 375, 382, 385, 388, 389, 391, 395, 407, 410, 420, 428, 451, 461, 470, 475, 477, 493, 497, 502, 503, 504, 512, 537, 546, 549, 552, 553, 554, 563, 571, 576, 597, 601
stately, 422
statement (statements), 141, 180, 228, 309, 530
statesmanship (statesman, statesmen), 68, 272, 345, 408, 473, 549
station (stations), 110, 120, 145, 154, 164, 237, 262, 361, 413, 459, 481, 550, 559
stationary, 101, 296
statistics (statistical), 180, 488, 520
statuary, 119
statue (statues), 46, 180, 290, 318
stature, 154, 185, 213, 231, 290
status, 549, 550
statute (statute-book), 75, 347
staunchest, 361
stay (stayed, stays), 148, 174, 254, 339, 383, 429, 430, 432, 460, 500, 503, 531, 550, 574, 597
stay-at-homes, 569
steadiness (steadiest, steadily, steady), 53, 55, 64, 97, 105, 155, 206, 211, 224, 319, 338, 383, 399, 420, 482, 485, 494, 545, 554, 563
steal (stealing, steals, stolen), 58, 113, 158, 237, 307, 313, 348, 390, 436, 508, 513, 562, 566
stealthy, 566
steam engine, 2
steamer, 246
steamforce, 438
steed, 17, 158, 227, 430
steel (steeled), 17, 356, 371, 505, 590, 601
steering, 249
stellar, 37
stem, 385
stench, 249, 296
step (stepping, steps), 129, 133, 142, 147, 149, 164, 201, 218, 234, 276, 295, 341, 377, 381, 402, 440, 448, 449, 452, 466, 487, 501, 518, 541, 570, 575, 595
stereotype (stereotyped), 151, 426
sterile, 60
sterling, 306, 332, 442, 500, 600
sternness (stern, sternest), 140, 148, 291, 298, 330, 456
stick (sticketh, sticks), 143, 280, 310, 398, 480, 536
stiffness (stiff, stiff-rumped), 42, 431, 444
stifle (stifled, stifling), 51, 94, 97, 546, 548

stupidity (stupid), 3, 43, 46, 59, 84, 87, 113, 132, 178, 206, 272, 358, 372, 381, 399, 417, 418, 434, 450, 458, 514, 550, 551
stupor, 11
sturdy, 419, 598
sturdy-tempered, 4
stutterers, 454
sty, 467, 588
style (styles), 29, 40, 84, 173, 174, 186, 312, 320, 443, 445, 483, 551, 602
subdue (subdued, subduer, subdues, subduing), 2, 142, 147, 216, 266, 327, 331, 364, 395, 427, 472, 485, 494, 501, 523, 528, 556, 557, 560, 567, 596
subject (subjected, subjecting, subjects), 4, 13, 34, 35, 36, 55, 80, 98, 104, 118, 175, 186, 190, 203, 223, 225, 227, 246, 257, 258, 265, 267, 268, 289, 308, 325, 333, 334, 348, 353, 360, 375, 386, 397, 441, 447, 452, 464, 468, 475, 478, 493, 516, 526, 530, 532, 541, 547, 552, 555, 559, 601
subjection, 200, 241, 353, 378, 473
subjective (subjectivity), 55, 434
subjugation (subjugators), 552
sublimates, 567
sublimity (sublime, sublimer, sublimest), 133, 175, 201, 212, 229, 262, 279, 285, 344, 349, 409, 439, 440, 460, 475, 504, 509, 552, 557, 573, 604
sublunary, 479
submerge (submerged, submergence), 563, 572
submission (submissive, submissiveness, submit, submits, submitting), 58, 59, 118, 120, 134, 135, 229, 254, 266, 269, 299, 304, 311, 328, 330, 367, 374, 377, 383, 391, 427, 480, 485, 511, 539, 546, 552, 566, 582
subordination (subordinate), 73, 225, 354, 473, 516, 538
suborn, 421
subscription (subscribe), 382, 455
subsequent, 324, 362, 380
subservient, 167, 358, 461, 538
subside (subsided, subsides), 21, 255, 378, 482
subsist (subsists), 224, 340, 564
substance (substantial), 3, 11, 30, 58, 123, 143, 146, 165, 196, 215, 236, 268, 275, 337, 439, 446, 486, 497, 530, 532, 533, 548, 552, 575, 593, 597
substantives, 156
substitution (substitute, substituted, substituting), 45, 140, 154, 255, 483, 505, 513, 601
subtlety/subtility (subtile, subtilize, subtle, subtler, subtlest, subtleties), 19, 108, 110, 117, 128, 159, 218, 236, 254, 275, 284, 286, 339, 345, 348, 352, 399, 422, 452, 466, 468, 477, 483, 499, 504, 518, 534, 546, 549, 552, 556, 574, 587
subtraction, 62, 405
suburb, 561
subvert (subversive, subverts), 228, 283, 340, 440, 589
success (succeed, succeeded, succeeding, succeeds, successes, successful, successfully), 16, 29, 33, 36, 60, 68, 78, 80, 89, 92, 114, 115, 139, 146, 148, 149, 152, 156, 179, 180, 181, 195, 249, 250, 258, 263, 265, 282, 318, 327, 329, 335, 338, 341, 342, 346, 348, 352, 353, 405, 414, 417, 442, 446, 453, 456, 460, 462, 499, 515, 526, 533, 541, 553, 558, 563, 568, 571, 591, 596, 604
succession (successive), 310, 453, 550, 565, 568, 571

succor, 47, 85, 232, 254, 337, 474
succumb, 117, 362, 447
suck (sucked, sucking), 132, 467, 545
suddenness (sudden, suddenly), 131, 165, 189, 249, 324, 339, 373, 407, 408, 504, 523, 535, 548, 554
sue (sues), 389, 455
suffer (suffered, sufferer, sufferers, suffering, sufferings, suffers), 1, 9, 10, 14, 19, 38, 52, 70, 83, 85, 89, 91, 96, 100, 109, 116, 125, 132, 134, 137, 139, 154, 160, 184, 187, 217, 221, 233, 246, 261, 273, 292, 297, 309, 310, 330, 333, 343, 349, 351, 358, 361, 363, 377, 381, 401, 405, 409, 417, 420, 428, 435, 444, 445, 450, 454, 459, 487, 488, 498, 506, 507, 509, 513, 515, 518, 522, 525, 538, 554, 562, 566, 569, 571, 585, 588
sufficient (suffices), 162, 172, 468, 478, 488, 530, 591
suffrages, 167
sugar (sugared), 69, 117, 189, 204
sugar-plum (sugar-plums), 192, 228
suggestion (suggest, suggested, suggesting, suggestions, suggestiveness, suggests), 25, 167, 218, 274, 288, 290, 354, 427, 443, 498, 505, 510, 564, 592
suicide (suicidal), 68, 124, 135, 285, 360, 389, 508, 509, 517, 529, 554
suit (suited, suits), 254, 309, 327, 344, 345, 373, 396, 408, 540, 568
suitable, 155, 345, 374, 381, 434
suitor, 108
sulky, 14
sullen, 14, 431, 451
sullied, 403
sultry, 387
sum (sum-total, summed, sums), 17, 220, 288, 290, 302, 378, 382, 399, 405, 415, 424, 435, 526, 534, 536
summer (summer-like, summers), 42, 82, 84, 86, 89, 183, 249, 315, 381, 434, 490, 520, 531
summit, 304, 324, 481
sun (suns), 16, 18, 26, 28, 32, 37, 41, 50, 57, 59, 63, 82, 84, 87, 118, 124, 138, 148, 158, 165, 166, 171, 173, 190, 212, 225, 227, 233, 244, 248, 257, 259, 265, 270, 280, 281, 314, 318, 319, 337, 356, 364, 368, 399, 416, 425, 426, 427, 430, 431, 444, 483, 498, 502, 532, 543, 567, 573, 592
sunbeam (sunbeams), 237, 255, 546
Sunday, 76, 159, 175, 315, 503
Sunday best, 25
sunlight, 40, 44, 336, 539
sunny, 11, 38, 85, 214, 303
sunset (sunsets), 118, 336
sunshine, 5, 11, 39, 41, 89, 142, 148, 239, 253, 315, 328, 428, 585
superabundant, 161
superannuated, 431
superciliousness (supercilious), 146, 253
superficial (superficialities, superficially), 3, 11, 135, 277, 303, 355, 468
superfluity (superfluities, superfluous), 137, 377, 416, 469, 535, 576, 579
superhuman, 560
superimposed, 71
super-induce, 367
superintendence (superintend, superintendent), 378, 554

superiority (superiorness, superiors), 4, 13, 22, 25, 28, 39, 74, 93, 106, 120, 138, 147, 154, 162, 166, 173, 175, 180, 189, 201, 205, 250, 276, 290, 297, 301, 305, 322, 327, 336, 344, 345, 348, 349, 350, 351, 354, 360, 366, 367, 370, 372, 393, 394, 407, 409, 412, 418, 423, 456, 457, 461, 473, 479, 480, 483, 497, 526, 529, 535, 539, 541, 549, 555, 557, 583, 589
superlative, 247, 248
supernatural (supernaturally), 90, 124, 199, 294, 343, 532, 583
super-refinements, 500
superscription, 424
supersedes, 159
superstition (superstitious), 55, 57, 64, 102, 136, 156, 272, 344, 470, 474, 498, 555, 604
superstructure, 44, 249, 255
supineness, 224
supper, 85
supple, 595
supplicate (supplicants), 472, 474
supply (supplied, supplies, supplying), 109, 132, 267, 305, 306, 388, 411, 433, 436, 550, 558, 559, 586
support (supportable, supported, supporters, supporting, supports), 4, 50, 57, 65, 119, 168, 218, 226, 254, 275, 278, 280, 287, 297, 336, 344, 384, 389, 431, 471, 482, 486, 504, 528, 529, 531, 534, 537, 542, 581, 584, 588, 589, 598
supposition (suppose, supposed, supposes, supposing, suppositions), 214, 218, 263, 275, 285, 300, 301, 309, 310, 322, 329, 334, 335, 343, 347, 362, 366, 376, 377, 402, 410, 413, 419, 456, 473, 474, 475, 480, 498, 505, 553, 554, 555, 576, 580, 593
suppression (suppress, suppressed), 89, 117, 380, 421, 444, 555
supremacy (supreme, supremely), 147, 212, 247, 279, 288, 295, 307, 357, 361, 418, 422, 429, 492, 504, 545, 555
sure (surely, surer, surest), 190, 243, 269, 271, 283, 296, 358, 369, 404, 448, 452, 453, 472, 478, 484, 497, 523, 530, 566, 568, 597
surface, 3, 11, 182, 278, 385, 408, 496, 546, 551
surfeit (surfeiting), 148, 150, 384
surgeon, 400
surging, 602
surly, 367, 602
surmise (surmises, surmisings), 134, 423
surmount (surmounted), 318, 444
surpass, 275, 427
surprise (surprised, surprises, surprising), 9, 47, 51, 53, 90, 114, 121, 122, 125, 150, 173, 204, 340, 345, 348, 353, 364, 382, 416, 424, 463, 476, 519, 555, 566
surrender (surrendered, surrendering, surren-ders), 27, 29, 82, 369, 373, 425, 447, 462, 482, 504, 524, 555
surroundings (surround, surrounded, surround-ing, surrounds), 3, 53, 61, 69, 82, 85, 148, 149, 181, 213, 233, 245, 247, 257, 261, 320, 359, 373, 423, 470, 546
survey (surveyed), 88, 174, 409, 417, 557
survival (survive, survived, survives), 126, 127, 183, 205, 253, 323, 324, 337, 494, 585
susceptibility (susceptibilities, susceptible), 203, 253, 524, 529

suspect (suspectable, suspected, suspected'st, suspecteth, suspecting, suspects), 24, 128, 129, 195, 199, 206, 227, 232, 233, 240, 260, 284, 290, 304, 332, 378, 381, 386, 392, 423, 435, 457, 505, 519, 525, 527, 551, 556, 570, 571, 572, 592
suspend (suspended, suspends), 3, 120, 190
suspense, 168, 192, 376, 411, 555
suspension, 50
suspicion (suspicions, suspicious, suspiciously), 9, 23, 99, 103, 128, 196, 234, 236, 247, 283, 284, 290, 299, 304, 308, 325, 372, 375, 505, 521, 525, 526, 555, 556, 584
sustain (sustained, sustaining, sustains), 55, 117, 190, 230, 297, 311, 399, 488, 509, 571
sustenance, 479
swagger (swaggerer, swaggering), 109, 252
swain, 538
swallow (swallowed, swallowed'st, swallows), 67, 121, 147, 381, 403, 439, 512, 570
swamp (swamps), 52, 79
swan (swans), 270, 371
swarm, 74, 224
swarthy, 261
sway (swayed), 5, 103, 135, 160, 167, 335, 523
swear (swearing, swears, swore, sworn), 108, 193, 247, 268, 310, 357, 364, 371, 396, 401, 474
sweat (sweated, sweating, sweats), 58, 211, 449, 494
sweep (sweeping), 135, 213, 273, 318, 546, 561, 578
sweet-briar, 299
sweet-faced, 360
sweethearts, 386
sweetmeats, 192, 441
sweetness (sweet, sweetening, sweetens, sweeter, sweetest, sweetly), 4, 10, 19, 28, 43, 47, 81, 82, 117, 118, 121, 147, 158, 187, 201, 206, 252, 253, 255, 289, 299, 316, 318, 321, 329, 334, 335, 336, 339, 342, 348, 355, 357, 363, 383, 388, 390, 392, 423, 445, 446, 451, 462, 465, 475, 476, 480, 486, 487, 492, 513, 530, 531, 539, 560, 562, 579, 582, 599
sweet tooth, 441
swell (swelled, swelling, swells, swoln), 21, 198, 201, 297, 421, 472, 566
swerve (swerved, swerves), 356, 433
swiftness (swift, swiftest, swiftly), 50, 84, 139, 181, 204, 255, 260, 274, 411
swimming (swim, swimmer, swims, swum), 12, 31, 170, 280, 324, 426, 468, 496
swindle (swindler, swindling), 181, 415, 417
swine (swinish), 27, 212, 218, 587
swing, 416, 493
Swiss, 438
swoop, 85
sword (swords), 5, 6, 18, 34, 46, 63, 73, 96, 147, 190, 257, 284, 308, 363, 517, 529, 537, 550, 592
sword of Damocles, 9
swordsman, 82, 197, 550
sycophant, 86
syllable (syllables), 172, 215, 264, 602
sylph, 557
sylvan, 148
symbol (symbolically, symbols), 111, 255, 257, 289, 414, 429, 534
symmetry, 367, 426
sympathy (sympathetic, sympathetically,

sympathies, sympathize, sympathized, sympathizes), 5, 6, 17, 40, 57, 64, 69, 70, 71, 76, 88, 90, 104, 165, 171, 202, 214, 231, 235, 251, 278, 280, 290, 322, 325, 330, 335, 347, 348, 350, 351, 353, 356, 359, 368, 372, 373, 375, 395, 396, 398, 403, 410, 422, 426, 427, 429, 441, 466, 490, 500, 528, 534, 545, 553, 556, 557, 575, 578, 593
symptom (symptoms), 97, 162, 283, 549
synod, 265
synonymous, 10, 46, 223, 315, 394, 470, 509, 601
syntax, 428, 465
system (systematic, systematized, systems), 24, 45, 74, 77, 79, 84, 141, 156, 157, 163, 180, 258, 281, 327, 345, 355, 361, 374, 379, 389, 390, 401, 407, 430, 433, 457, 479, 504, 507, 512, 522, 529, 541, 546, 557, 572, 590, 592, 604

tabernacle, 220
table (tables), 67, 142, 156, 185, 191, 239, 299, 442, 443, 445, 446, 458, 541, 587, 590
table-talk, 557
taboo, 359
taches, 25
tacit (tacitly), 93, 168, 350, 365, 436
taciturnity (taciturn), 172, 544
tackled, 382
tact (tactful), 65, 486, 541, 557
tags, 305
Tahiti, 257
tail, 4, 109, 306, 309, 363, 478, 570
tail-end, 198
taint (tainted), 287, 418, 518
take (taken, takes, taking, takings, took), 6, 9, 13, 15, 27, 37, 54, 56, 88, 108, 124, 129, 140, 155, 216, 238, 245, 263, 266, 268, 272, 283, 291, 294, 295, 296, 297, 299, 310, 316, 321, 325, 327, 338, 342, 344, 348, 350, 352, 356, 360, 362, 379, 381, 382, 383, 385, 388, 390, 392, 393, 396, 399, 401, 402, 405, 409, 424, 437, 441, 443, 444, 449, 453, 455, 456, 457, 459, 461, 465, 468, 471, 476, 477, 482, 483, 485, 488, 489, 502, 507, 508, 509, 510, 512, 515, 518, 527, 529, 536, 539, 540, 541, 552, 553, 557, 561, 573, 575, 576, 579, 584, 598, 599
tale (tales), 62, 123, 169, 179, 183, 192, 255, 313, 337, 359, 388, 400, 515, 552, 579
talent (talents), 1, 26, 29, 81, 86, 107, 156, 161, 209, 211, 228, 243, 345, 346, 355, 377, 386, 477, 483, 519, 522, 525, 557
talisman, 15
talk (talkative, talked, talkers, talking, talks), 13, 18, 33, 52, 53, 84, 99, 103, 104, 148, 152, 153, 172, 173, 174, 177, 180, 192, 199, 200, 205, 213, 215, 222, 244, 258, 267, 271, 274, 280, 282, 290, 294, 301, 304, 309, 325, 346, 352, 357, 359, 367, 368, 372, 377, 380, 385, 393, 394, 398, 402, 419, 423, 425, 432, 457, 462, 463, 468, 496, 505, 508, 516, 534, 535, 543, 546, 554, 557, 566, 576, 580, 593, 598, 600, 602
tally, 149, 396
tambourine, 557
tame (tamed, taming), 48, 261, 278, 355, 395, 459, 569, 579
tamper, 56, 313
tangible, 542
tangle (tangled), 44, 489
tantalize (tantalized, tantalizing), 137, 254

tap, 545
taper, 203
tappa, 42
tardiness (tardy), 436, 497
tares, 343
target, 5, 317
tarnish (tarnished), 275, 360
tarry (tarries), 256, 569
task (tasks), 72, 129, 192, 223, 315, 409, 449, 516, 526
taskmaster, 355
taste (tastes), 17, 42, 43, 50, 64, 79, 83, 92, 142, 143, 153, 168, 177, 212, 264, 305, 317, 325, 357, 358, 371, 379, 382, 441, 462, 470, 475, 495, 502, 516, 532, 557, 558, 573, 589, 597
tasteless, 165, 347
Taurus, 157
tax (taxed, taxes, taxing), 32, 55, 195, 361, 371, 376, 385, 419, 457, 537, 558
tax-gatherer, 80
taxpayers, 120
tea (teacup, tea-drinking, tea-parties), 19, 56, 142, 352, 368
teach (taught, teachable, teachableness, teacher, teachers, teaches, teacheth, teaching), 2, 54, 58, 76, 77, 78, 125, 145, 146, 155, 156, 157, 158, 161, 166, 169, 170, 171, 179, 190, 214, 216, 221, 228, 237, 253, 254, 261, 267, 269, 279, 284, 287, 298, 300, 302, 303, 304, 305, 313, 325, 327, 329, 330, 342, 354, 355, 360, 366, 372, 377, 378, 381, 385, 389, 401, 402, 411, 413, 418, 419, 421, 452, 457, 458, 484, 496, 497, 499, 502, 505, 511, 516, 522, 532, 557, 558, 561, 570, 572, 575, 592, 597, 598
tear (tearing, tears, torn), 8, 12, 14, 19, 56, 62, 166, 173, 182, 184, 203, 230, 264, 267, 279, 307, 323, 343, 347, 354, 382, 387, 403, 422, 424, 471, 475, 506, 530, 558, 559, 570, 577, 586
tease (teaser, teasing), 97, 291, 363, 383
technical (technically), 7, 334
tediousness (tedious, tedium), 223, 320, 356, 402, 475, 490, 566, 585
teeming, 574
teens, 385
teething, 4
teetotaler, 153
telegraph, 274
tell (teller, telling, tells, told), 82, 149, 162, 173, 176, 179, 180, 181, 191, 192, 195, 198, 200, 206, 213, 214, 233, 235, 247, 248, 249, 252, 261, 262, 275, 277, 313, 316, 321, 324, 326, 334, 351, 353, 357, 360, 361, 372, 386, 387, 390, 399, 400, 413, 416, 425, 433, 442, 449, 460, 464, 466, 495, 496, 503, 519, 521, 526, 528, 538, 542, 548, 565, 570, 573, 575, 577, 578, 593
temerity, 11, 350
temper (tempered, tempering, tempers), 2, 5, 8, 17, 21, 32, 66, 86, 113, 131, 136, 141, 142, 144, 154, 208, 218, 226, 243, 246, 281, 294, 299, 301, 343, 348, 351, 354, 378, 380, 389, 395, 404, 426, 429, 438, 455, 465, 477, 484, 500, 509, 522, 523, 525, 526, 559, 573, 601
temperament (temperaments), 64, 69, 254, 367, 397, 486
temperance, 408, 559, 588
temperate zone, 149
temperature, 18
tempest, 24, 204, 445, 453, 577

tempestuous, 90, 126, 134
temple (temples), 14, 40, 75, 232, 337, 528, 542
temporal, 143
temporary (temporarily), 127, 230, 250, 367, 471, 588
temporizers, 467
temptation (tempt, temptations, tempted, tempter, tempting, tempts), 15, 41, 112, 115, 130, 139, 145, 178, 220, 251, 287, 308, 322, 325, 366, 375, 415, 421, 432, 442, 466, 500, 502, 549, 552, 559, 560, 565, 587
Tempus fugit, 566
tenacity (tenacious), 264, 311, 428, 447
tend (tended, tending, tends), 187, 233, 237, 282, 303, 309, 329, 389, 417, 433, 444, 485, 503, 511, 541, 551, 572, 585
tendency (tendencies), 114, 159, 164, 171, 223, 242, 251, 260, 330, 417, 418, 453, 478, 479
tenderness (tender, tenderest), 7, 15, 17, 32, 33, 64, 65, 67, 71, 120, 136, 139, 160, 182, 185, 187, 208, 216, 232, 242, 252, 291, 315, 329, 333, 335, 339, 349, 351, 355, 356, 371, 383, 387, 402, 419, 422, 428, 435, 499, 547, 560, 574, 583
tenet (tenets), 502, 503, 566
tennis-ball, 150
Tennyson, 474
tenor, 551
tense (tenses), 291, 448
tent, 65, 425, 431
tenure, 154, 318
tepid, 447
term (termed, terms), 90, 102, 113, 157, 172, 197, 201, 205, 253, 290, 315, 317, 381, 388, 416, 467, 492, 543, 590, 602, 604
term-day, 313
termination (terminate), 204, 322
terra firma, 516
terrestrial, 429, 458
terrible, 16, 26, 37, 41, 43, 55, 121, 125, 126, 168, 176, 188, 189, 199, 233, 262, 349, 363, 439, 447, 500, 502, 523, 524, 526, 535, 546, 548, 551, 577, 584, 591, 596, 602
terrific, 107
terrify (terrified, terrifies, terrifying), 129, 188, 228, 272, 318, 409
territory, 569
terror (terrors), 37, 90, 107, 116, 124, 127, 164, 188, 189, 215, 216, 233, 281, 284, 285, 294, 304, 429, 442, 477, 492, 501, 504, 506, 529, 535, 560, 574, 602
test (tested, tests), 246, 325, 328, 457, 460, 461, 484, 499, 530, 543, 545, 571, 592
testaments, 595
testator, 495
testification, 547
testimony, 311, 386, 572
tetanus, 307
tether, 55
tetrameter, 465
text (texts), 289, 290, 315, 331, 476, 477, 502, 507
textbook, 449
texture, 386
thank (thankful, thankfulness, thanks), 173, 192, 368, 433, 474, 520, 522, 591
thankless, 241, 482
Thanksgiving Day, 520
thaw (thawed, thaws), 152, 189, 201, 532

theater/theatre (theatres, theatrical), 35, 74, 146, 446, 459, 558, 560, 561
theft (thief, thievery, thieves, thieving), 44, 59, 180, 181, 232, 260, 261, 312, 359, 409, 492, 506, 561, 562, 568, 585
theme (themes), 72, 267, 522, 552, 561
theocracy, 122
theology (theologian, theological), 57, 67, 419, 420, 502, 503
theory (theoretic, theoretical, theories), 3, 16, 24, 45, 102, 159, 211, 248, 281, 284, 305, 312, 347, 371, 395, 401, 440, 454, 456, 457, 461, 486, 559, 561, 584, 588, 604
thick (thickening, thicker), 26, 121, 153, 274, 446, 466, 473, 599
thighbones, 540
thimbleful, 289
thin (thinned, thinnest, thinning), 124, 239, 362, 374, 393, 424, 435, 462
thin-lipped, 448
think (thinker, thinkest, thinketh, thinking, thinks: *see also* thought), 46, 59, 74, 77, 99, 104, 111, 118, 119, 124, 138, 143, 150, 159, 160, 165, 167, 169, 171, 174, 181, 211, 212, 215, 219, 221, 228, 229, 237, 242, 245, 246, 250, 251, 266, 268, 271, 272, 273, 278, 280, 281, 282, 283, 288, 289, 293, 297, 302, 304, 305, 307, 309, 316, 317, 322, 324, 326, 329, 333, 337, 338, 345, 347, 349, 350, 351, 353, 356, 359, 360, 362, 363, 364, 366, 368, 369, 370, 371, 372, 375, 376, 377, 381, 383, 386, 389, 391, 393, 394, 395, 396, 397, 401, 403, 406, 407, 409, 411, 412, 415, 419, 421, 422, 438, 441, 442, 447, 448, 451, 452, 454, 457, 463, 464, 467, 469, 470, 471, 473, 474, 475, 476, 479, 480, 483, 485, 487, 489, 494, 497, 502, 503, 505, 508, 510, 512, 514, 522, 525, 530, 531, 535, 540, 541, 542, 547, 550, 551, 553, 556, 558, 560, 562, 563, 564, 565, 566, 570, 571, 576, 577, 580, 582, 584, 597, 604
thirst (thirsts), 12, 151, 336, 415, 433, 474, 477, 562
thistles, 383
thorn (thorns), 19, 57, 88, 383, 545, 575
thoroughbred, 472
thoroughfares, 603
thought (thoughts: *see also* think), 2, 6, 12, 13, 15, 18, 27, 31, 33, 56, 57, 68, 79, 80, 83, 91, 102, 103, 104, 113, 116, 124, 138, 141, 145, 149, 150, 152, 155, 159, 170, 171, 176, 186, 198, 201, 208, 209, 212, 216, 217, 220, 225, 229, 239, 243, 246, 251, 253, 260, 261, 265, 267, 268, 275, 286, 287, 288, 302, 303, 304, 305, 307, 312, 315, 317, 320, 321, 324, 333, 336, 346, 353, 354, 355, 357, 358, 361, 366, 374, 377, 378, 381, 389, 396, 399, 404, 407, 408, 412, 427, 434, 438, 440, 441, 444, 454, 464, 465, 474, 475, 489, 491, 492, 494, 498, 500, 501, 511, 513, 515, 529, 534, 536, 546, 549, 561, 562, 563, 564, 565, 567, 574, 588, 589, 590, 593, 598, 599, 600
thoughtfulness (thoughtful), 486, 563
thoughtlessness (thoughtless), 347, 411, 596
thraldom, 110, 570
thread (threads), 110, 215, 319, 321, 356, 359, 423, 433, 474
threadbare, 561
threat (threaten, threatened, threatens, threats), 99, 117, 176, 179, 183, 286, 420, 454, 477, 496,

506, 565
threshing-machine, 574
threshold, 36, 362
thrift (thrifty), 469, 490, 565
thrill (thrilled, thrills), 404, 405, 437, 564
thrive, 47, 486
throat (throats), 17, 158, 181, 242, 260, 313, 356
throb (throbbing), 187, 425, 504
throne (throned, thrones), 133, 163, 224, 331, 350,
    377, 381, 545, 583, 593
throng (thronging), 499, 552
throttles, 356
throw (throwing, thrown, throws), 162, 194, 208,
    212, 225, 245, 278, 288, 293, 327, 380, 384, 386,
    389, 409, 420, 428, 438, 456, 466, 470, 471, 482,
    502, 561, 580, 581
thrust (thrusting, thrusts), 78, 119, 189, 252, 272,
    288, 356
thumbs, 576
thumbscrews, 241
thump, 184, 422, 578
thunder (thunders), 55, 58, 92, 520
thunderbolt, 198
thunder-glooms, 249
thunderstorm (thunderstorms), 8, 573
Thursday, 175
thwarting, 12, 136
Tiberius, 127
ticket, 390
tickle (tickled, tickleth, ticklish), 184, 369, 455,
    532
tide (tides), 59, 138, 143, 265, 268, 399, 420, 428,
    443, 485, 567
tide-beating, 439
tidings, 406, 516
tidy, 418
tie (tied, ties), 32, 49, 131, 183, 185, 191, 248, 298,
    308, 336, 352, 380, 383, 386, 393, 425, 538, 541,
    579
tiger (tigress, tyger), 430, 489
tight (tightens), 152, 221
tight-lacing, 371
tightrope, 20
tiller, 45
tilting, 595
timber (timbers), 544, 583
time (times), 6, 9, 11, 13, 20, 23, 34, 35, 52, 53, 58,
    61, 62, 63, 65, 74, 78, 94, 95, 103, 117, 122, 126,
    136, 137, 138, 140, 141, 145, 146, 153, 157, 159,
    162, 165, 166, 168, 169, 170, 171, 173, 174, 177,
    178, 181, 182, 184, 196, 202, 204, 206, 209, 213,
    214, 217, 229, 230, 232, 236, 243, 244, 245, 247,
    248, 249, 250, 256, 258, 259, 274, 275, 277, 278,
    289, 292, 295, 296, 299, 302, 306, 308, 309, 315,
    316, 317, 320, 322, 325, 327, 328, 329, 331, 332,
    333, 339, 342, 343, 345, 355, 357, 365, 366, 372,
    373, 377, 379, 381, 382, 392, 393, 394, 395, 396,
    398, 403, 404, 407, 408, 409, 412, 415, 418, 421,
    422, 423, 424, 425, 428, 429, 431, 433, 436, 438,
    439, 443, 444, 448, 449, 450, 452, 456, 457, 458,
    459, 463, 464, 467, 470, 477, 483, 486, 488, 489,
    494, 496, 497, 500, 505, 507, 510, 512, 518, 520,
    523, 526, 527, 529, 532, 540, 544, 545, 548, 556,
    558, 561, 563, 564, 565, 566, 567, 568, 569, 570,
    571, 575, 577, 578, 579, 582, 591, 598, 599
time-honored, 477
timely, 124, 315

time-servers, 225
timidity (timid), 9, 47, 100, 156, 206, 283, 329,
    353, 442, 450, 511, 568
timorous, 59, 109
tin kettle, 224
tincture (tinctured, tinctures), 160, 291, 586
tindering, 421
tinge (tinged), 90, 242
tingling, 405, 564
tinkering, 595
tinkle, 148
tinsel (tinselled), 477, 561
tint (tints), 328, 538
tiny, 454
tipped, 365
tirade, 174, 329
tire (tired, tires, tiring), 162, 175, 303, 312, 323,
    396, 397, 419, 485, 593
tiresome, 249, 588
tissue, 191, 230
Titans, 467
title (titles), 23, 24, 29, 52, 99, 165, 206, 245, 267,
    306, 409, 469, 495, 517
title-page, 249
tittered, 586
toad (toads), 25, 187, 579
toadstool (toadstools), 164, 271
tobacco, 55, 343, 540
today, 104, 172, 250, 281, 298, 448, 449, 450, 458,
    468, 549, 551, 577, 590
toe (toes), 229, 518
toil (toiling, toils), 8, 22, 154, 244, 280, 303, 319,
    334, 415, 461, 485, 486, 569
toilsome, 318, 422
token (tokens), 182, 281, 335, 506, 510
tolerable (tolerably), 39, 90, 234, 276, 316, 319,
    354, 392, 418, 493, 558
toleration (tolerance, tolerate), 130, 217, 277, 305,
    314, 431, 450, 503, 568, 570
toll, 485
tomb (tombs), 123, 159, 319, 385, 501, 547, 604
tomb-makers, 486
tombstone, 463
tomorrow, 4, 62, 104, 164, 365, 396, 436, 448, 449,
    450, 458, 549, 551, 567, 577, 590
ton, 600
tone (tones), 182, 265, 267, 282, 358, 375, 404, 421,
    443, 477, 541, 568
tongue (tongues), 1, 36, 80, 82, 93, 96, 102, 111,
    139, 152, 172, 173, 174, 176, 179, 194, 232, 266,
    270, 284, 290, 294, 308, 336, 347, 348, 349, 351,
    352, 363, 365, 399, 401, 422, 439, 443, 454, 474,
    499, 516, 535, 537, 565, 570, 571, 599, 602
tongue in the cheek, 54
tool (tools), 3, 155, 208, 263, 301, 555, 595
tooth (teeth), 55, 83, 148, 382, 452, 458, 506, 522,
    586, 599
toothache, 97
top (topped), 110, 146, 220, 336
toper, 151
topic (topics), 305, 354, 506
topmost, 124
torment (tormented, tormenting, torments), 10,
    23, 90, 184, 189, 241, 247, 262, 267, 291, 325,
    340, 366, 374, 378, 461, 534, 555, 595, 600, 601
tornadoes, 249
torpedo, 419

torpid, 273
torrent, 240, 446, 571
torture (tortured, tortures, torturing), 125, 147,
 159, 232, 233, 245, 297, 324, 390, 405, 408, 448,
 538, 545
toss (tossed), 430, 552, 594
total (totally), 218, 309, 349, 405
tottles, 229
touch (touched, touches, toucheth, touching), 54,
 78, 83, 119, 146, 179, 191, 209, 214, 220, 262,
 264, 265, 290, 299, 328, 350, 357, 365, 376, 397,
 404, 413, 429, 432, 435, 451, 457, 464, 465, 476,
 482, 528, 538, 546, 560, 566
touchstone, 60, 81, 336, 581
touchy, 253
tough, 141
tower/Tower (towers), 9, 22, 229, 430, 507, 513,
 586, 602
town (towns), 25, 73, 74, 84, 85, 142, 157, 190, 287,
 308, 343, 398, 402, 403, 430, 468, 471, 493, 512,
 516
toy (toying, toys), 16, 156, 551, 559
trace (traceable, traced, traces), 134, 213, 214,
 220, 261, 359, 419, 489, 530, 573, 586, 601
track (tracks), 79, 314, 420, 497
tractable, 36
trade (trader, trades, trading), 126, 138, 220, 289,
 299, 364, 416, 486, 541, 550, 568, 569, 590
trade-name, 98
tradition (traditionally, traditionary, traditions),
 103, 249, 262, 355, 418
traduced, 508
tragedy (tragedies, tragic, tragical, tragically),
 13, 17, 65, 70, 124, 183, 193, 229, 322, 341, 427,
 443, 446, 472, 501, 559, 583, 588
trail, 169, 249, 320
train (trained, training, trainings), 34, 157, 159,
 171, 207, 246, 283, 370, 406, 430, 457, 522, 591
trait (traits), 60, 114, 234, 356, 512, 515
traitor, 118, 176, 255, 291, 338, 570
tramp (tramped, tramps), 268, 271, 512
trample (trampled, trampling), 153, 363, 538
trance (tranced, trancelike), 123, 148, 255, 340
tranquility/tranquillity (tranquil), 91, 117, 196,
 202, 237, 427, 466, 484, 571
tranquillize (tranquillizer), 434, 494
transaction (transactions), 265, 300, 375, 585
transcendental, 456
transcribe, 113
transfer (transferred), 47, 183, 372, 399, 419
transfigured, 286
transformation (transform, transformed,
 transforms), 44, 61, 62, 64, 120, 179, 188, 214,
 218, 302, 334, 340, 511, 548
transgression (transgress, transgresses, transgressions), 38, 102, 226, 232, 260, 308, 507
transient, 43, 55, 230
transition (transitions), 204, 407, 561, 569, 597
transitory, 367, 392, 418, 498, 507
translation (translate, translating, translator),
 127, 307, 493, 603
translucent, 20
transmutation (transmute, transmuted), 196, 519
transparent, 128, 519
transplantation (transplanting), 11, 54
transport (transporting, transports), 159, 311,
 358, 426, 460

transverse, 521
trap, 270, 283
trash, 210
travailing, 478
travel (traveler/traveller, travelers/travellers,
 traveling/travelling, travelled, travels), 31, 46,
 52, 53, 75, 137, 175, 213, 220, 240, 282, 287, 290,
 388, 404, 407, 434, 442, 495, 550, 560, 569, 570
traverse (traversed, traverses), 193, 197, 494
treachery (treacherous, treacherously), 91, 128,
 175, 203, 219, 280, 310, 538, 570, 572, 592
tread (treads), 170, 269, 448, 464, 566
treason (treasons), 128, 313, 416, 570
treasure (treasures), 7, 70, 71, 138, 212, 317, 392,
 409, 415, 591
treasury, 245
treatises, 159
treatment (treat, treated, treating, treats), 5, 135,
 226, 252, 261, 280, 312, 332, 333, 341, 367, 372,
 373, 374, 379, 381, 391, 401, 406, 410, 471, 556,
 570
tree (trees), 11, 12, 18, 39, 62, 82, 141, 158, 258,
 280, 290, 317, 320, 420, 426, 428, 429, 567, 577,
 591
tremble (trembles, trembling, tremblings), 87,
 96, 109, 131, 187, 189, 233, 236, 253, 422, 492,
 505, 575
tremendous, 118, 529
tremulous, 339, 546
trenchant, 269
trespass (trespassed, trespasser, trespasses), 274,
 329, 364
trial (trials), 5, 29, 67, 86, 112, 204, 233, 259, 297,
 408, 421, 541, 548, 551, 560, 571, 588
triangle, 129
tribe (tribes), 163, 175, 430, 508, 603
tribunal, 35, 94, 294, 322
tribute, 127, 326, 458
trick (tricks), 110, 130, 251, 390, 417, 424, 426,
 567, 572, 575
trifle (trifled, trifles, trifling), 9, 27, 142, 145, 172,
 211, 232, 238, 245, 261, 275, 278, 287, 321, 346,
 368, 389, 407, 409, 460, 476, 509, 563, 592, 597
trigonometry, 157
trimeter, 465
trimmings, 179, 471
tripped, 337
triumph (triumphal, triumphant, triumphantly,
 triumphed, triumphing, triumphs), 15, 17, 18,
 24, 29, 62, 88, 94, 105, 123, 178, 199, 209, 215,
 219, 220, 221, 264, 345, 355, 370, 373, 395, 462,
 470, 510, 512, 526, 553, 560, 571, 588
trivial, 72, 193, 273, 434
trodden, 507, 550
troops, 467, 499
tropes, 476
trophies, 435
tropic (tropics), 17, 85
trot, 255
trouble (troubled, troubles, troublesome,
 troubleth, troubling), 8, 31, 50, 54, 55, 58, 74,
 83, 96, 110, 117, 125, 141, 162, 170, 185, 209,
 238, 239, 243, 251, 261, 268, 272, 280, 321, 333,
 346, 347, 348, 353, 367, 380, 381, 393, 395, 412,
 427, 431, 448, 456, 468, 469, 483, 500, 514, 522,
 546, 548, 569, 571, 584, 593, 595, 597, 601
trousers, 540

718

trout-stream, 469
trowel, 557
troy-weight, 157
truant, 409
truce-making, 72
truck-horses, 22
truckle, 414
true-born, 270
true-hearted, 329
truffles, 271
trump, 575
trumpet, 332, 421, 516, 519
trunk (trunks), 11, 12, 223
trust (trusted, trustees, trusting, trusts,
  trustworthy), 10, 39, 68, 89, 111, 127, 135, 153,
  160, 181, 208, 228, 232, 236, 240, 246, 250, 252,
  253, 255, 273, 280, 281, 282, 283, 289, 293, 301,
  324, 330, 351, 357, 373, 384, 396, 467, 472, 473,
  488, 521, 570, 571, 572, 599
truth (true, truer, truest, truly, truthful, truthfulest, truthfulness, truths), 9, 16, 17, 18, 20, 24,
  25, 28, 29, 30, 39, 40, 42, 45, 46, 47, 48, 58, 63,
  67, 68, 69, 70, 71, 73, 75, 81, 83, 88, 91, 95, 97,
  103, 105, 107, 108, 109, 112, 113, 120, 121, 122,
  123, 125, 127, 128, 129, 133, 135, 143, 145, 146,
  147, 148, 149, 150, 151, 153, 155, 157, 160, 162,
  163, 164, 169, 170, 173, 174, 176, 177, 178, 179,
  180, 182, 184, 189, 191, 192, 194, 198, 200, 202,
  203, 204, 205, 206, 208, 210, 211, 213, 220, 227,
  228, 229, 232, 235, 237, 242, 244, 246, 247, 248,
  254, 257, 260, 264, 268, 269, 273, 274, 278, 280,
  284, 289, 291, 292, 294, 300, 302, 303, 306, 310,
  313, 320, 321, 326, 327, 328, 329, 330, 335, 337,
  338, 340, 341, 342, 346, 347, 355, 356, 360, 362,
  364, 376, 379, 381, 384, 389, 390, 394, 400, 408,
  413, 414, 415, 417, 418, 419, 420, 423, 426, 428,
  429, 434, 435, 441, 442, 446, 449, 450, 451, 455,
  456, 457, 458, 460, 462, 463, 466, 467, 474, 478,
  479, 482, 485, 488, 489, 490, 492, 496, 502, 503,
  504, 505, 507, 509, 512, 518, 522, 528, 530, 532,
  533, 534, 537, 539, 541, 545, 548, 550, 551, 552,
  555, 557, 558, 560, 562, 564, 565, 567, 572, 573,
  574, 575, 576, 585, 586, 587, 597, 598, 600, 604
truth-revealing, 593
try (tried, tries, trying), 67, 95, 169, 176, 178, 228,
  233, 266, 269, 294, 305, 310, 312, 322, 335, 355,
  366, 371, 381, 391, 394, 396, 397, 416, 442, 497,
  539, 561, 571, 594, 603
tub, 514
Tuesday, 175
tuft-hunting, 2
tug, 319
tulip, 464
tumble (tumbler, tumblers, tumbling), 87, 151,
  457
tumbleabout, 318
tumbledown, 85
tumult, 132, 316, 427
tune (tunes), 101, 169, 204, 326, 371, 422, 423
tunic, 514
tunnel, 165
turbulence (turbulent), 15, 402, 507, 592
turkey (turkey-cock, turkeys), 4, 520
Turkey (Turk, Turkish, Turks), 70, 71, 100, 389
turn (turned, turneth, turning, turns), 214, 245,
  250, 280, 285, 292, 306, 314, 331, 335, 337, 341,
  348, 350, 354, 383, 401, 411, 428, 432, 433, 443,

453, 457, 467, 475, 500, 504, 508, 509, 512, 518,
  538, 549, 551, 552, 563, 582, 591, 595, 597
turnkey, 112, 162
turnpike, 85
turpitude, 218
turtledove, 398
tutor (tutors), 158, 171, 567
twaddle, 435
twain, 107
tweezers, 352
twelvemonth, 11, 156
twentieth century, 212
twig (twigs), 158, 223, 255, 532
twilight, 512
twin (twins), 93, 468, 576
twined, 359
twinges, 120
twinkling, 284, 434
twirl, 495
twist, 495
two-edged, 517
two-edged sword, 193
tyger, 489
type (typical, typicalness), 31, 66, 110, 228, 257,
  299, 431, 507, 508, 521, 540, 576
tyranny (tyrannical, tyrannically, tyrannize,
  tyrant, tyrants), 1, 5, 100, 101, 103, 114, 115,
  118, 146, 158, 164, 188, 224, 270, 311, 312, 315,
  325, 328, 331, 340, 361, 375, 395, 408, 415, 438,
  439, 449, 472, 487, 500, 538, 542, 547, 552, 554,
  576, 577, 603

ubiquitousness (ubiquitous), 564, 577
udder, 418
ugliness (uglier, ugliest, uglification, ugly), 4, 9,
  19, 25, 38, 39, 40, 42, 43, 44, 53, 70, 84, 91, 114,
  122, 156, 172, 181, 188, 222, 243, 257, 261, 274,
  277, 346, 368, 384, 390, 450, 496, 584, 595
ultimate, 287, 379, 433, 553
umpire, 95
unabashed, 222
unable, 275, 301, 386, 389, 457, 481, 568, 584
unacceptable, 76
unaccommodating, 177
unaccountable, 149, 220, 240, 365, 602
unaccustomed, 50, 238, 528
unacquainted, 210, 303
unadoring, 391
unadorned, 40
unaffectedness (unaffected, unaffectedly), 6, 14,
  65, 88, 339
unaided, 301
unalloyed, 103
unalterable (unalterably), 65, 138, 222, 382, 436,
  591
unamiable, 542
unanimous, 294, 417
unanointed, 491
unappreciated, 410
unapprehensiveness, 564
unarmed, 514, 518
unassisted, 520
unassuming, 202, 540
unattainable (unattained), 43, 273, 356, 399, 482
unauthorized, 243, 269
unavailing, 139, 147, 229, 238, 459

KEYWORD INDEX

unfriendly, 5
ungenerous, 194, 199, 260, 350, 518, 594
ungenial, 52
ungenteelly, 211
ungentle, 528
ungodliness (ungodly), 271, 539
ungraceful (ungracefully), 420, 598
ungracious, 436
ungrateful, 227, 339
unguarded, 165
unguessed, 247, 574
unhackneyed, 533
unhappiness (unhappy), 8, 67, 76, 100, 102, 118,
  153, 223, 225, 232, 236, 238, 239, 254, 342, 369,
  379, 385, 394, 412, 601
unheard-of, 51
unhinge, 315, 374
unhistoric, 248
unhonest, 416, 539
unhumanizing, 242
unical, 275
unicorn, 241
uniform (uniformly), 36, 154, 167, 263, 312, 351,
  426, 460, 498, 499
unimaginative, 573
unimproved, 413
uninfluenced, 329, 420
uninformed, 304, 480
uninitiated, 171
uninspired, 511
uninstructed (uninstructive), 294, 305, 427
unintellectual, 57
unintelligible, 72, 171
uninterested, 260
uninteresting, 39, 64, 326, 466, 469
uninterrupted, 173, 345, 461
uninvented, 163
union (unions), 65, 182, 232, 374, 378, 381, 383,
  384, 390, 392, 409, 422, 426, 488, 542, 548
unique, 312
unison, 107
unit, 294, 517, 553
united (unite, unites, uniting), 79, 80, 86, 185, 202,
  262, 292, 320, 340, 409, 451, 460, 528, 578
United States, 142, 196
Unitrinitarian, 505
unity (unities), 164, 577, 578
universality (universal, universally, universals),
  31, 67, 73, 123, 145, 185, 191, 221, 254, 256, 281,
  282, 303, 307, 313, 338, 376, 389, 393, 405, 415,
  426, 427, 447, 474, 492, 498, 503, 518, 574, 577,
  578
universe, 14, 37, 93, 135, 153, 179, 183, 191, 215,
  220, 232, 244, 258, 270, 295, 300, 306, 356, 399,
  403, 407, 409, 426, 429, 444, 457, 481, 487, 492,
  500, 501, 535, 545, 547, 561, 578, 596, 603
university, 444, 496, 604
unjust (unjustly), 51, 53, 59, 88, 167, 212, 245, 248,
  253, 295, 297, 298, 308, 315, 316, 345, 347, 400,
  511, 528, 576, 590
unkindness (unkind, unkindly), 134, 198, 300,
  330, 459, 518, 603
unknown, 55, 118, 149, 163, 212, 228, 270, 272,
  287, 304, 327, 416, 423, 424, 448, 449, 452, 498,
  521, 555, 568, 582, 592
unlawful, 133, 163, 534
unlearned, 307

unlike, 12, 141, 268, 270, 321, 326, 533
unlikely (unlikeliest), 73, 415
unlimited, 213, 226, 358, 520, 541
unlock, 161, 521, 526
unlooked, 577
unloose (unloosed), 485, 506
unloved (unlovely), 82, 219
unlucky, 342, 513
unman (unmans), 338, 339, 550
unmanlike, 114
unmarried, 387, 389, 396
unmasks, 585
unmeaning, 186, 261, 423
unmentionable, 37
unmeritorious, 406
unmindful, 428
unmistakable, 551
unmixed, 160
unmodified, 88
unmoral, 417
unmuscular, 363
unnaturalness (unnatural), 94, 194, 216, 319, 326,
  363, 368, 401, 425, 463, 513, 578, 586
unnecessary, 262, 345, 423, 495, 502, 535, 589, 602
unnoticed (unnoticeable), 221, 258, 289
unobservant, 262
unopened, 495
unpalatable, 478
unpardonable, 403
unpenetrated (unpenetrating), 247, 459
unperfect, 429
unpitying, 99
unpleasantness (unpleasant), 122, 135, 153, 477
unpledged, 220
unpolishes, 22
unpopular, 472
unpracticed, 275
unprepared, 187, 306, 509
unprincipled, 67, 356, 484
unpropitious, 326
unproven, 331
unpunished, 283
unquestioning, 330
unquiet, 118, 159, 539
unravel (unravelable, unravelling), 78, 215, 359
unread, 35
unreal, 575
unreality (unrealities), 187, 199
unrealized, 269, 531
unreason, 78
unreasonable, 100, 188, 306, 338, 581
unreasoning, 78
unrecognizable, 492
unredressed, 320
unrefutable, 421
unregenerate, 241
unrelenting, 240
unreliable, 250
unrequited, 17
unreserved, 350, 366
unrespected, 258
unrest, 7, 296
unrestrained, 104
unretracing, 319
unreturned, 327
unrighteously, 249
unripe, 13

valet (valet de chambre, valets), 130, 544
valetudinarian, 241
valley (vale), 42, 533, 562
valor (valiant), 38, 87, 106, 107, 108, 123, 133, 134,
    241, 363, 583
valor-ruined, 107
valuation, 425
value (valuable, valued, values), 11, 27, 56, 80, 83,
    86, 133, 155, 156, 161, 169, 171, 174, 181, 190,
    202, 212, 235, 245, 275, 290, 304, 306, 319, 322,
    341, 345, 351, 358, 367, 378, 397, 410, 413, 434,
    437, 451, 473, 477, 481, 500, 530, 536, 537, 541,
    548, 558, 567, 570, 579, 580, 599
valueless, 272
vanguard, 580
vanish (vanished, vanishes), 93, 126, 146, 319,
    450, 482, 509, 567
Vanitas Vanitatum, 581
vanity/Vanity (vain, vainer, vanities), 9, 11, 15,
    98, 100, 103, 111, 121, 130, 133, 134, 148, 162,
    164, 187, 196, 208, 210, 240, 244, 245, 262, 266,
    267, 272, 304, 305, 315, 319, 326, 330, 331, 346,
    350, 351, 355, 356, 359, 366, 375, 410, 416, 422,
    428, 429, 430, 459, 464, 465, 471, 473, 476, 477,
    480, 481, 484, 498, 500, 510, 528, 532, 535, 562,
    572, 574, 578, 580, 581
vanquish (vanquished, vanquisher), 18, 233, 251
vanward, 181
vapor (vapors), 149, 410, 434, 543
variable, 19, 213, 415, 597, 604
variance, 94, 426, 429, 497, 596
variation, 547, 576
variety (varied, varies, varieties, various,
    varying), 85, 96, 142, 171, 175, 252, 264, 291,
    307, 312, 324, 354, 408, 413, 422, 426, 427, 440,
    443, 457, 460, 463, 501, 546, 549, 581, 582, 595,
    602, 604
varnish (varnished), 26, 53, 90, 313, 593, 594
vassal (vassals), 5
vastness (vast), 2, 5, 37, 56, 88, 213, 241, 272, 288,
    289, 296, 297, 327, 408, 427, 431, 450, 457, 485,
    552, 577
Vatican, 404
vault (vaults), 189, 434, 454
vegetable (vegetarianism), 362, 443, 582
vegetation, 17
vehemence (vehement), 28, 447, 537
vehicle (vehicles), 18, 217, 459
veil (veiled, veiling), 33, 91, 423, 424, 434, 438,
    539, 573
vein (veins), 78, 168, 291, 497
velocity, 136, 529
velvet, 442
venal (venial), 9, 524
veneer, 368
venerable, 41, 302, 342, 603
veneration (venerating), 221, 247, 603
vengeance, 492, 517, 550, 582, 583, 591
venom (venomous), 268, 382
vent (vented), 88, 207, 313, 332, 467, 523, 555
venture (ventures, venturing, venturous), 38, 51,
    241, 313, 353, 369, 394, 443, 445, 550, 588
Venus, 463
Venus de' Medici, 42
veracity, 128, 162, 366, 428, 575
verb (verbs), 157, 305, 601
verbiage, 312

verbosity (verbose), 398, 443
verdant, 257, 270
verdict, 294, 309, 386, 399
verdure, 464
verge (verges), 36, 536, 585
veriest, 538
verify, 230
verities, 20
vermin, 219, 537, 579
versatility (versatile), 239, 553
verse (verses, versifiers), 77, 191, 330, 464, 465,
    490
Vespasian, 127
vessel (vessels), 162, 174, 242, 369, 542
Vestal, 444
vested, 33
vestment, 536
vestry, 15
vesture, 49, 428
Vesuvius, 9, 561
veteran, 567
vexation (vex, vexed), 8, 235, 247, 321, 455, 456,
    460, 546
vibration (vibrate, vibrated, vibrates, vibrating,
    vibrations), 242, 328, 331, 422, 423, 433, 529,
    546
vicarious (vicariously), 363, 583
vice (vices), 16, 23, 25, 27, 36, 38, 41, 52, 59, 64, 67,
    72, 75, 82, 93, 106, 107, 112, 157, 166, 179, 195,
    207, 218, 219, 220, 222, 233, 237, 251, 258, 261,
    266, 272, 284, 291, 292, 314, 322, 344, 345, 347,
    378, 394, 396, 409, 412, 414, 417, 432, 440, 456,
    470, 482, 491, 497, 501, 506, 507, 508, 518, 522,
    537, 541, 559, 583, 584, 587, 588, 592
vicious (viciously), 16, 46, 52, 114, 115, 167, 220,
    251, 259, 267, 315, 345, 497, 512
vicissitude (vicissitudes), 63, 122, 190, 257, 389,
    456
victim (victims), 26, 33, 56, 119, 154, 219, 242,
    297, 314, 348, 349, 362, 382, 427, 481, 538, 576,
    585
victory (victories, victoriously), 14, 18, 20, 27, 57,
    62, 87, 119, 122, 135, 162, 241, 329, 400, 435,
    516, 523, 553, 592
victuals (vittles), 142, 143, 492
vies, 199
view (viewing, views), 53, 100, 111, 173, 178, 183,
    189, 192, 203, 215, 245, 260, 316, 320, 322, 323,
    324, 326, 355, 356, 376, 392, 400, 405, 408, 416,
    442, 456, 468, 485, 488, 496, 498, 564, 596
vigilance (vigilant), 139, 330, 402, 408, 441
vigor (vigorous), 16, 55, 64, 70, 100, 241, 294, 548
vileness (vile, vilely, viler, vilest), 79, 93, 107, 257,
    263, 293, 315, 390, 416, 436, 439, 455, 504, 519,
    580
vilify (vilified), 217, 299
village (villagers, villages), 74, 81, 157, 182, 257,
    270, 423, 486, 540
villain (villainies, villainously, villains, villainy),
    8, 218, 243, 256, 258, 265, 299, 431, 492, 585, 599
vindication (vindicate, vindicated), 95, 135, 295,
    310, 384, 575
vindictiveness (vindictive, vindictively), 67, 350,
    370, 380, 591
vine (vines), 45, 57, 152, 317, 463
vinegar, 17, 67, 382
vineyard, 486

violation (violate, violated, violates, violating), 218, 242, 435, 466, 493, 540
violence (violences, violent, violently), 21, 22, 54, 80, 92, 99, 102, 159, 174, 188, 202, 229, 230, 235, 326, 328, 337, 342, 365, 380, 381, 391, 395, 427, 442, 446, 447, 455, 465, 499, 507, 516, 546, 547, 561, 571, 582, 585, 586, 589, 590
violet, 328, 332, 431
violin, 332
viper, 537
virginity (virgins/Virgins), 268, 325, 351, 430, 493, 520, 580, 586
virtue (virtues, virtuous, virtuously), 1, 3, 8, 11, 18, 19, 33, 38, 42, 43, 44, 59, 63, 66, 67, 72, 74, 77, 82, 87, 95, 97, 100, 106, 107, 115, 120, 122, 126, 128, 131, 136, 139, 142, 145, 152, 155, 160, 163, 164, 166, 181, 185, 186, 188, 192, 199, 201, 204, 206, 207, 209, 211, 212, 214, 217, 218, 220, 223, 224, 233, 235, 236, 237, 238, 240, 247, 248, 251, 252, 253, 254, 259, 260, 261, 263, 265, 266, 267, 277, 284, 292, 297, 298, 306, 314, 315, 325, 327, 331, 343, 344, 345, 348, 349, 350, 355, 356, 357, 359, 364, 366, 376, 391, 392, 393, 395, 396, 402, 405, 406, 408, 409, 411, 412, 413, 414, 415, 417, 418, 421, 422, 425, 433, 436, 437, 440, 441, 442, 445, 447, 450, 452, 456, 460, 461, 462, 466, 471, 474, 480, 481, 482, 483, 488, 491, 493, 497, 498, 501, 504, 505, 508, 513, 514, 520, 524, 525, 526, 528, 533, 536, 546, 558, 560, 561, 568, 571, 573, 574, 580, 581, 583, 584, 585, 586, 587, 588, 589, 594, 596, 604
virulence (virulent), 225, 401
visibility (visible, visibly), 9, 25, 78, 210, 221, 238, 248, 268, 271, 284, 451, 454, 529, 534
vision (visions), 15, 31, 54, 79, 89, 99, 149, 163, 176, 177, 191, 222, 260, 273, 274, 275, 288, 368, 399, 454, 504, 577
visionary, 275, 423
visit (visitation, visited, visits), 137, 163, 245, 268, 327, 328, 336, 357, 401, 418, 471, 589
vista, 95
vitality (vital, vitalities, vitalized, vitals), 30, 49, 164, 233, 243, 316, 361, 404, 467, 468, 500, 577
vivacity, 25, 30, 42, 277, 345, 394, 572
vividness (vivid, vividly), 7, 111, 148, 274, 314, 379, 440, 511, 549, 563
vivisecting, 322
vocabulary, 392
vocation, 112, 244, 330, 486, 527, 557
vogue, 185, 540
voice (voices, voicing), 2, 5, 7, 10, 41, 55, 71, 94, 95, 130, 136, 142, 153, 160, 174, 179, 212, 230, 269, 287, 307, 329, 343, 356, 375, 382, 399, 404, 422, 426, 440, 457, 470, 475, 477, 491, 498, 512, 522, 535, 539, 544, 560, 574
voiceless, 387, 574
void, 37, 40, 67, 301, 329, 521, 585, 599
volcano (volcanoes, volcano-peak), 448, 482
volume (volumes), 54, 165, 174, 191, 192, 316, 323, 389, 465, 538, 561, 602
voluminous, 317, 490
voluntary (voluntarily), 156, 229, 273, 388, 390, 411, 509, 512
volunteers, 225
voluptuousness (voluptuous), 75, 403, 589
vortex, 274
votary (votaries), 29, 72, 115, 223, 339

vote, 73, 133, 252, 466, 467
voucher, 251
vouchsafe (vouchsafed), 69, 548, 596
vow (vowed, vows), 151, 177, 193, 284, 316, 332, 396, 487, 537
voyage (voyager, voyagers, voyages), 12, 75, 90, 116, 166, 312, 320, 328, 334, 359, 383, 445, 458, 547, 569, 578
vulgarity (vulgar), 4, 43, 45, 83, 113, 127, 172, 174, 190, 202, 322, 331, 400, 405, 458, 468, 471, 477, 479, 489, 496, 503, 558, 589, 601
vulture, 111, 395

wade, 583
wafer, 427
wag (wagged, wagging), 1, 265, 478
wager, 384
wages, 17, 135, 155, 167, 485, 514
wagon wheel, 557
wailing, 120, 507
waistcoat, 83, 112, 455
wait (waited, waiting), 210, 277, 294, 306, 349, 355, 371, 393, 428, 448, 487, 545, 546, 566, 576, 583, 597, 601
waiting-women, 544
waived, 383
wake (wakeful, wakefulness, wakes), 12, 90, 120, 148, 149, 273, 398, 407, 409, 446, 465, 486, 539, 592
walk (walked, walking, walks), 72, 87, 120, 137, 142, 172, 175, 252, 256, 258, 263, 279, 283, 299, 322, 324, 356, 371, 384, 409, 430, 443, 471, 502, 514, 533, 556, 585
wall (walls), 11, 20, 78, 156, 257, 274, 315, 340, 440, 564, 573
Wall Street, 594
wallet, 152
wallowing, 258
wand, 15, 337
wander (wandered, wanderer, wandering, wanderings, wanders), 34, 79, 182, 286, 288, 304, 325, 350, 452, 454, 495, 522, 563, 569
wanderlust, 589
wane (waning), 42, 290, 480
want (wanted, wanting, wants), 19, 51, 54, 80, 83, 100, 107, 129, 132, 133, 145, 146, 169, 171, 178, 181, 196, 208, 211, 214, 216, 234, 236, 239, 240, 242, 250, 266, 267, 268, 273, 284, 289, 296, 300, 301, 302, 304, 306, 309, 316, 318, 320, 327, 344, 350, 354, 361, 365, 373, 375, 376, 379, 383, 384, 387, 388, 389, 392, 393, 394, 403, 407, 412, 414, 415, 416, 419, 423, 432, 433, 434, 445, 452, 457, 458, 459, 463, 470, 471, 472, 473, 475, 480, 482, 487, 488, 490, 501, 502, 506, 526, 537, 539, 540, 542, 546, 553, 557, 565, 572, 579, 586, 587, 589, 592, 593, 599
wantonness (wanton), 176, 274, 388, 465, 563, 591
war (wars), 37, 72, 94, 95, 117, 123, 135, 153, 168, 198, 247, 249, 308, 312, 317, 329, 337, 349, 359, 374, 415, 416, 442, 443, 446, 451, 467, 486, 523, 525, 526, 549, 568, 577, 589, 590, 591, 592
warder, 9
wardrobe, 446, 572
ware (wares), 360, 536
warfare, 35, 321, 479, 591
wariness (wary), 597, 600

warlike, 225
warming pans, 77
warmth (warm, warmed, warmer, warmest, warmly, warms), 18, 21, 27, 33, 41, 45, 84, 85, 152, 187, 202, 203, 206, 236, 242, 243, 259, 262, 266, 294, 298, 300, 315, 397, 410, 413, 425, 434, 451, 477, 528, 530, 599, 601
warn (warned, warning, warnings, warns), 243, 293, 301, 310, 326, 419, 428, 429, 478, 513, 520
warp (warps), 319, 433, 466, 473, 603
warrant, 155, 186, 304, 382
warranty, 327, 578
warrior (warriors), 47, 175, 430, 590
wash (washed, washes, washing), 26, 70, 113, 262, 293, 332, 453, 540, 567, 578
Washington, 73, 460, 466, 538, 540, 589
Washington, George, 271, 314
waste (wasted, wasteful, wastes, wasting), 37, 94, 100, 161, 169, 271, 302, 391, 398, 473, 477, 478, 482, 488, 525, 566, 596
waste paper, 48
watch (watched, watchers, watches, watchful, watchfulness, watching), 7, 10, 12, 76, 87, 92, 118, 151, 157, 165, 191, 194, 234, 240, 258, 272, 289, 295, 311, 339, 426, 432, 438, 504, 511, 526, 539, 548, 550, 566, 592, 598
watchman, 330
water (watering, waters, watery), 22, 25, 31, 37, 42, 44, 57, 66, 75, 78, 79, 82, 85, 95, 123, 124, 132, 134, 148, 150, 152, 197, 198, 201, 204, 243, 270, 278, 279, 301, 307, 317, 337, 339, 359, 401, 402, 429, 430, 432, 439, 442, 486, 498, 501, 532, 570, 571, 572, 590
watermelon, 143
water mill, 568
waters of Babylon, 56
wave (waves), 37, 63, 290, 355, 547
waver (wavered, wavering), 96, 259, 388, 479
wax (waxes, waxeth), 42, 57, 138, 303, 320, 351, 560, 600
way (ways), 52, 134, 135, 137, 139, 146, 147, 165, 183, 201, 205, 211, 220, 223, 224, 225, 236, 243, 244, 265, 273, 291, 327, 355, 362, 365, 476, 507, 522, 535, 541, 549, 553, 559, 578, 598
wayfarer, 318
waywardness, 294
weaklings, 103
weak-minded, 435
weakness (weak, weaken, weakened, weakens, weaker, weakest, weakly, weaknesses), 13, 19, 35, 39, 50, 64, 65, 79, 83, 94, 101, 102, 129, 135, 139, 149, 154, 158, 163, 164, 173, 174, 195, 199, 206, 216, 243, 259, 263, 264, 276, 278, 281, 282, 286, 288, 292, 294, 295, 298, 309, 311, 315, 319, 327, 329, 330, 332, 345, 350, 351, 353, 356, 357, 363, 366, 367, 368, 369, 371, 374, 378, 382, 385, 389, 395, 410, 422, 425, 439, 441, 444, 446, 447, 456, 466, 468, 471, 472, 477, 479, 480, 487, 488, 498, 504, 506, 514, 517, 523, 524, 533, 542, 550, 551, 553, 555, 557, 559, 574, 584, 587, 591, 592, 604
weal, 286, 430
wealth (wealthiest, wealthily, wealthy), 111, 122, 146, 154, 162, 202, 225, 235, 251, 306, 312, 352, 370, 400, 402, 411, 422, 457, 465, 466, 470, 471, 473, 522, 535, 591, 592, 593, 594, 597
wealth-producing, 466

wean, 57, 359
weapon (weaponry, weapons), 96, 172, 176, 204, 224, 284, 349, 352, 416, 423, 479, 513, 517, 518, 536, 537, 594, 600
wear (weareth, wearing, wears, worn), 151, 169, 175, 227, 243, 269, 281, 307, 311, 355, 356, 373, 385, 388, 395, 403, 448, 466, 478, 489, 499, 530, 555, 574, 578, 584, 592, 596
weariness (wearies, wearisome, weary), 31, 49, 59, 94, 148, 190, 192, 214, 247, 318, 324, 384, 403, 434, 449, 457, 462, 473, 475, 486, 561, 590, 595
weather (weathers), 50, 77, 141, 213, 324, 328, 333, 488, 534, 539, 542, 545
weather-beaten, 429
weather-vane, 595
weave (weaver, weaving, woven), 7, 110, 138, 274, 303, 319, 423
web, 78, 110, 132, 183, 331, 494, 508
Webster, 280
wed (wedded, wedding, weddings, wedlock, weds), 108, 181, 307, 320, 374, 375, 378, 379, 380, 383, 384, 385, 386, 387, 388, 389, 390, 391, 392, 393, 394, 397, 398, 402, 540
wedding-bells, 320
wedding day, 380, 384, 392
wedding-gown, 385
wedding night, 392
wedge, 494
Wednesday, 175
weed (weeding, weeds), 43, 138, 157, 197, 307, 431
week (weekly, weeks), 120, 127, 156, 193, 341, 355, 378, 399, 403, 431, 475, 477, 545, 546
weekday (weekdays), 315, 476
weep (wept), 13, 73, 209, 225, 253, 259, 307, 404, 428, 559
weight (weighed, weights), 24, 44, 50, 66, 94, 100, 157, 160, 170, 240, 260, 307, 322, 339, 399, 411, 417, 420, 434, 437, 444, 467, 473, 498, 555, 589, 594, 596
weighty, 344, 368
weird, 472
welcome, 122, 537
weld, 55, 604
welfare, 260, 594
well, 454, 512, 591
well-adjusted, 483
well-armed, 551
well-being, 48
well-bred, 59, 144, 550
well-built, 543
well-constructed, 86
well-disciplined, 499
well-distinguished, 199
well-doing, 1
well-educated, 376
well-established, 93
well-fleshed, 331
well-furnished, 445
well-greased, 419
well-informed, 80, 272, 346, 409, 410
well-judged, 137
well-looking, 234
well-made, 316
well-marked, 371
well-ordered, 314

well-proportioned, 408
well-protected, 52
well-regulated, 311
well-spread, 561
well-spring, 351
well-tested, 414
well-timed, 25
well-to-do, 52
well-wishers, 205
Wesley, John, 71
west/West (Western), 33, 143, 74
West Indies, 455
West Point, 159
Westminster Abbey, 42
whack, 475
whale (whales), 2, 18, 37, 79, 107, 158, 180, 189,
  430, 439, 454, 534, 561, 574
whale-lines, 117
whaleman, 37
wheel (wheels), 212, 248, 266, 281, 440, 512, 529,
  542
wheelbarrow, 136, 371
wheel-carriage, 603
wheeze, 540
whim (whims), 101, 104, 470, 593
whimpering, 382
whimsical, 134, 151, 236, 276, 348, 594
whip (whipping, whips), 99, 204, 311, 511, 538
whirl (whirl'd, whirls), 298, 316, 603
whirlpools, 86
whirlwind, 365
whiskers (whiskerandoes), 369, 430
whiskey, 151
whisper (whispered, whisperers, whispering,
  whisperings, whispers), 24, 74, 97, 116, 120,
  217, 269, 270, 431, 440, 464, 522, 561, 594
whist, 50, 380
whistle, 538
white-haired, 163
white heat, 262
white lies, 179
white man (white men), 21, 143
whited sepulchre, 466, 542
whiteness (white, whitens), 6, 74, 154, 163, 189,
  221, 252, 269, 271, 298, 314, 346, 431, 434, 474,
  502, 534, 601
whitewash (whitewashed, whitewashing), 26, 504
whole-hearted, 121
wholeness (whole, wholly), 126, 243, 244, 253, 258,
  452, 559, 584, 587
wholesome, 8, 31, 225, 237, 408
whoop, 590
whore, 381, 489
whoresons, 486
wickedness (wicked), 5, 8, 46, 51, 70, 75, 95, 118,
  130, 131, 150, 152, 157, 176, 198, 209, 214, 217,
  219, 220, 223, 228, 240, 257, 258, 262, 265, 298,
  332, 342, 344, 347 410, 426, 432, 504, 514, 521,
  524, 533, 583, 593, 594, 595, 599, 600, 604
wide-mouthed, 421, 523
wideness (wide, widely, widen, widened,
  widening, widens, wider, widest), 160, 169, 185,
  196. 219, 260, 273, 276, 284, 300, 304, 327, 368,
  474, 500, 567
widow (widows), 32, 109, 378, 381, 382, 384, 389,
  394, 396, 475, 540, 562
wife (wives), 30, 51, 86, 119, 127, 138, 184, 185,

202, 205, 220, 239, 243, 291, 310, 311, 344, 345,
  347, 374, 375, 376, 377, 378, 379, 380, 381, 382,
  383, 384, 385, 386, 388, 389, 390, 391, 392, 393,
  394, 395, 396, 397, 398, 462, 481, 521, 538, 540
wig, 73, 318
wight (wights), 125, 435
wild boar, 116
wild oats, 343, 419
wilderness, 333, 383, 580
wildness (wild, wilder, wildest, wildish, wildly,
  wilds), 66, 74, 90, 103, 105, 124, 148, 149, 152,
  161, 163, 175, 204, 213, 270, 275, 280, 285, 286,
  291, 322, 323, 327, 349, 362, 422, 446, 451, 463,
  511, 516, 524, 556, 569, 572, 591
wiles (wily), 7, 106, 392, 560
will (willed, wills), 37, 53, 93, 102, 122, 123, 125,
  135, 138, 139, 148, 155, 161, 184, 193, 208, 212,
  213, 215, 234, 235, 243, 246, 267, 270, 275, 276,
  280, 281, 295, 308, 322, 326, 327, 337, 338, 345,
  359, 364, 374, 378, 379, 380, 391, 405, 432, 436,
  467, 472, 474, 479, 504, 507, 511, 513, 521, 559,
  564, 566, 585, 595, 598, 599, 600, 605
willful (willfully), 50, 237, 267, 379, 447, 492, 524,
  536
willing (willingly), 74, 135, 156, 162, 163, 187,
  198, 204, 211, 212, 217, 273, 294, 299, 310, 339,
  346, 365, 381, 416, 448, 509, 524, 587
will-o'-the-wisp, 254, 305, 599
willow, 3
wilt, 388
win (winner, winning, wins, won), 29, 30, 46, 57,
  84, 101, 134, 163, 225, 244, 264, 285, 293, 307,
  314, 317, 327, 329, 332, 334, 337, 338, 357, 359,
  366, 370, 406, 408, 413, 429, 454, 502, 553, 580,
  597
winch, 251
wind (wind-shifted, windings, winds), 5, 16, 34,
  59, 66, 78, 95, 107, 118, 135, 149, 198, 212, 213,
  257, 268, 269, 272, 280, 368, 420, 422, 453, 478,
  485, 498, 520, 546, 563, 595, 604
windlass, 138
windmill, 196, 420
window (windows), 3, 19, 41, 48, 71, 148, 176, 183,
  234, 274, 365, 368, 386, 404, 490, 594
wine (wines), 32, 38, 43, 50, 67, 81, 100, 148, 150,
  151, 152, 153, 204, 230, 240, 313, 402, 405, 413,
  415, 443, 567, 587, 593
wine-press, 170
wing (winged, wings), 20, 31, 45, 103, 127, 149,
  151, 163, 165, 183, 189, 203, 257, 263, 274, 287,
  323, 328, 332, 371, 398, 415, 444, 464, 468, 502,
  516, 566, 567, 569
wink, 54, 294, 365, 454
winter (wintry), 11, 62, 82, 86, 107, 142, 213, 248,
  322, 434, 490
wipe (wiping), 120, 373
wire (wire-drawn, wire-woven), 350, 365, 431
wisdom (wisdoms, wise, wisely, wiser, wisest), 4,
  5, 10, 19, 21, 22, 46, 51, 58, 59, 60, 65, 73, 74, 92,
  93, 94, 102, 104, 111, 112, 115, 117, 122, 123,
  126, 128, 134, 138, 139, 140, 142, 149, 154, 155,
  158, 160, 163, 164, 166, 168, 169, 170, 171, 196,
  197, 204, 206, 209, 213, 215, 216, 219, 224, 225,
  229, 235, 237, 238, 239, 241, 246, 248, 250, 253,
  259, 264, 265, 266, 276, 278, 279, 281, 292, 295,
  302, 304, 307, 309, 310, 311, 316, 317, 319, 322,
  325, 335, 337, 339, 344, 345, 354, 356, 358, 359,

KEYWORD INDEX

363, 364, 367, 380, 382, 384, 391, 394, 400, 401,
407, 408, 414, 415, 425, 429, 431, 434, 436, 438,
445, 446, 447, 448, 449, 450, 452, 456, 457, 458,
467, 469, 470, 474, 475, 480, 484, 490, 494, 496,
504, 509, 511, 514, 519, 525, 528, 535, 537, 538,
539, 543, 545, 550, 556, 557, 560, 564, 567, 570,
573, 576, 579, 580, 581, 590, 595, 596, 597, 598,
599, 600, 604
wish (wished, wishes, wishing), 4, 47, 55, 68, 72,
111, 122, 127, 136, 169, 191, 198, 228, 231, 232,
234, 238, 239, 244, 248, 252, 262, 263, 265, 268,
272, 275, 280, 302, 310, 318, 323, 333, 335, 337,
338, 351, 376, 378, 381, 387, 403, 421, 442, 445,
452, 459, 460, 473, 476, 488, 491, 501, 505, 514,
515, 516, 517, 521, 523, 524, 557, 559, 560, 572,
579, 588, 593, 599
wisp, 135
wit (witling, wits, wittiest, witty), 6, 7, 19, 34, 35,
38, 41, 81, 86, 99, 100, 104, 117, 158, 175, 190,
194, 197, 199, 207, 251, 263, 265, 267, 276, 277,
287, 294, 295, 296, 301, 309, 310, 318, 335, 338,
340, 343, 345, 350, 359, 360, 363, 364, 369, 371,
391, 404, 408, 442, 450, 457, 465, 470, 477, 481,
483, 490, 518, 520, 553, 585, 598, 599, 600, 601
witch (witchcraft, witcheries, witches), 15, 80,
192, 364
withdraw (withdraweth, withdraws), 306, 509
withdrawal, 334
wither (withered, withering, withers), 11, 26, 75,
172, 270, 274, 466, 532
withstand (withstood), 241, 245, 420, 440, 577
witless, 363, 513
witness (witnessed, witnesses), 65, 177, 244, 308,
421, 430, 452, 507, 586, 601
wizard, 219
wizened, 445
woe (woe-begone, woeful, woefully, woes), 19, 32,
41, 88, 110, 118, 124, 138, 177, 184, 286, 307,
359, 386, 412, 430, 458, 503, 538, 545, 567, 591,
593
wolf (wolfish), 32, 123, 260, 267, 431, 470
woman (womanly, women), 10, 16, 19, 28, 30, 39,
40, 41, 42, 43, 46, 47, 50, 54, 63, 64, 65, 66, 68,
69, 72, 73, 75, 76, 82, 97, 98, 100, 102, 106, 107,
108, 109, 113, 114, 115, 116, 117, 120, 125, 130,
131, 134, 143, 146, 150, 152, 153, 154, 162, 164,
167, 169, 173, 174, 176, 180, 182, 183, 184, 186,
188, 189, 191, 193, 194, 195, 199, 200, 202, 203,
206, 207, 209, 210, 211, 217, 220, 221, 223, 225,
242, 243, 244, 246, 253, 264, 267, 268, 271, 272,
273, 276, 280, 283, 284, 290, 291, 294, 295, 298,
300, 301, 305, 307, 308, 309, 310, 313, 316, 325,
326, 327, 328, 329, 330, 331, 332, 333, 334, 335,
336, 337, 338, 339, 340, 341, 342, 343, 344, 345,
346, 347, 348, 349, 350, 351, 352, 353, 354, 355,
356, 357, 358, 359, 360, 361, 362, 363, 364, 365,
366, 367, 368, 369, 370, 372, 373, 374, 375, 376,
377, 378, 379, 380, 381, 386, 387, 388, 389, 391,
392, 393, 395, 396, 397, 404, 406, 410, 413, 414,
420, 423, 427, 431, 432, 435, 442, 445, 446, 447,
452, 453, 454, 456, 457, 458, 460, 461, 463, 464,
469, 470, 471, 472, 477, 481, 483, 490, 491, 493,
496, 497, 511, 512, 515, 521, 522, 529, 530, 531,
532, 540, 542, 548, 549, 552, 553, 559, 560, 561,
571, 572, 573, 575, 581, 584, 585, 586, 587, 588,
591, 596, 599, 600, 601, 603, 605
womanhood, 353, 356

womanite (womenites), 347
womanized, 358
womankind, 477
womb, 215
wonder (wondered, wonderful, wonderfully,
wondering, wonders, wondrous), 3, 7, 12, 13, 17,
18, 29, 36, 37, 43, 46, 51, 111, 112, 115, 118, 124,
146, 148, 149, 152, 153, 162, 166, 168, 185, 197,
203, 205, 207, 211, 215, 218, 247, 254, 256, 258,
266, 269, 275, 279, 287, 289, 301, 312, 313, 319,
330, 332, 336, 339, 340, 342, 365, 370, 388, 405,
406, 422, 423, 424, 427, 444, 452, 453, 457, 462,
510, 521, 524, 526, 535, 549, 552, 562, 563, 567,
574, 578, 587, 594, 597, 601
Wonderland, 183
wonder-worker, 37
wont (wonted), 331, 357, 477
woodcock, 227
woodpecker, 453
woods (wood, wooden, woodland), 11, 42, 53, 74,
82, 169, 313, 322, 348, 395, 476, 487, 512, 531,
543
woof, 319, 423
wooing (woo, wooed, wooer, wooers, wooeth,
woos), 108, 125, 134, 364, 381, 388, 471, 560
woolen, 541
word/Word (worded, wording, words), 21, 26, 36,
39, 45, 49, 52, 53, 57, 65, 66, 68, 78, 79, 91, 102,
105, 108, 109, 111, 119, 123, 124, 127, 152, 156,
172, 173, 174, 175, 177, 178, 179, 185, 186, 191,
195, 196, 197, 200, 203, 205, 206, 212, 213, 222,
223, 226, 228, 229, 245, 246, 252, 253, 266, 268,
273, 276, 278, 282, 293, 300, 302, 303, 305, 307,
310, 314, 340, 347, 354, 356, 357, 362, 368, 369,
371, 372, 382, 384, 390, 392, 393, 395, 397, 398,
399, 404, 411, 413, 416, 420, 422, 428, 431, 432,
440, 445, 448, 454, 455, 457, 459, 462, 468, 470,
472, 476, 477, 478, 488, 497, 499, 503, 518, 521,
522, 526, 530, 535, 537, 538, 539, 541, 544, 553,
556, 557, 564, 566, 568, 572, 574, 575, 576, 580,
585, 588, 598, 601, 602, 603, 605
Word of God, 213
work (worked, worker, working, workings,
works), 2, 3, 4, 12, 13, 16, 29, 31, 34, 35, 40, 42,
52, 59, 61, 63, 64, 67, 74, 82, 83, 92, 95, 99, 111,
114, 116, 120, 126, 134, 137, 143, 149, 152, 163,
167, 178, 179, 190, 192, 201, 212, 214, 215, 216,
217, 219, 223, 226, 239, 241, 242, 252, 254, 274,
275, 288, 297, 300, 302, 306, 309, 312, 313, 316,
317, 319, 331, 339, 340, 341, 343, 347, 351, 357,
358, 359, 366, 368, 383, 394, 400, 403, 405, 407,
410, 416, 423, 425, 427, 432, 443, 453, 454, 470,
475, 476, 477, 478, 485, 486, 489, 501, 503, 506,
507, 520, 531, 532, 540, 541, 542, 545, 547, 558,
566, 567, 573, 579, 583, 595, 603
workhouse, 47, 435
workman, 3, 301, 485
world (worlds), 1, 3, 5, 7, 8, 10, 11, 12, 13, 14, 15,
17, 20, 22, 24, 25, 26, 29, 31, 32, 33, 35, 37, 38,
40, 42, 43, 44, 46, 47, 48, 49, 51, 54, 56, 57, 58,
59, 60, 61, 62, 63, 64, 65, 66, 68, 70, 71, 73, 75,
76, 78, 79, 83, 85, 87, 88, 91, 94, 96, 99, 100, 102,
103, 107, 109, 110, 111, 113, 115, 116, 117, 118,
119, 120, 121, 122, 123, 124, 125, 126, 127, 128,
135, 138, 140, 141, 143, 146, 148, 153, 156, 158,
159, 160, 161, 163, 164, 166, 167, 169, 170, 171,
174, 176, 177, 180, 181, 182, 184, 185, 186, 187,

232, 245, 253, 259, 262, 273, 280, 283, 290, 302, 316, 324, 325, 326, 328, 334, 335, 337, 339, 341, 342, 343, 346, 347, 348, 349, 350, 351, 352, 353, 355, 361, 364, 366, 371, 372, 374, 375, 376, 377, 378, 379, 381, 385, 389, 393, 395, 396, 399, 401, 412, 414, 416, 417, 418, 419, 439, 442, 452, 457, 464, 467, 477, 478, 483, 484, 490, 491, 499, 500, 511, 513, 529, 537, 540, 550, 554, 557, 559, 560, 576, 588, 596, 600

youngster (youngsters), 75, 420

youth (youthful, youthfulness, youths), 8, 9, 10, 11, 12, 13, 21, 36, 40, 57, 60, 69, 111, 115, 117, 123, 133, 155, 157, 159, 161, 170, 187, 196, 197, 210, 223, 233, 237, 239, 268, 274, 314, 316, 332, 358,

372, 385, 387, 416, 420, 423, 429, 446, 464, 474, 480, 499, 507, 510, 512, 516, 520, 532, 580, 581, 582

zeal (zealot, zealots, zealous), 67, 70, 80, 397, 557, 605

zephyrs, 577

zest, 281, 600

zigzag (zigzagging, zigzags), 136, 192, 361, 467

Zodiac, 281

zone (zones), 439, 593

zoological gardens, 459